Managing Human Resources

Fifth Canadian Edition

Monica Belcourt
Professor of Human Resources Management,
York University

George Bohlander
Professor of Management,
Arizona State University

Scott Snell
Professor and Director of Executive Education,
Cornell University

NELSON / E D U C A T I O N

NELSON / EDUCATION

**Managing Human Resources,
Fifth Canadian Edition**

by Monica Belcourt, George Bohlander,
and Scott Snell

**Associate Vice President,
Editorial Director:**
Evelyn Veitch

Publisher:
Veronica Visentin

Acquisitions Editor:
Shannon White

Senior Developmental Editor:
Karina Hope

Photo Researcher:
Cindy Howard

Permissions Coordinator:
Cindy Howard

Content Production Manager:
Carrie McGregor

Copy Editor:
Erin Moore

Proofreader:
Kelli Howey

Indexer:
Belle Wong

Production Coordinator:
Ferial Suleman

Design Director:
Ken Phipps

Interior Design Modifications:
Jack Steiner

Cover Design:
Johanna Liburd

Cover Images:
© Stockbyte. All rights Reserved.

Compositor:
Integra

Printer:
R.R. Donnelley

**Library and Archives Canada
Cataloguing in Publication Data**

Belcourt, Monica
  Managing human resources / Monica Belcourt, George Bohlander, Scott Snell.
— 5th Canadian ed.

First-3rd Canadian eds. written by Monica Belcourt . . . [et al.].
Includes bibliographical references and index.
ISBN-13: 978-0-17-640729-2
ISBN-10: 0-17-640729-4

  1. Personnel management—Textbooks. I. Bohlander, George W. II. Snell, Scott, 1958- III. Title.

HF5549.B333 2007   658.3
C2006-904321-3

To my son Brooker Belcourt, for his intelligent and insightful observations on the complexities of human behaviour

To my wife, Ronnie Bohlander, and to our children, Ryan and Kathryn

To my wife, Marybeth Snell, and to our children, Sara, Jack, and Emily

THE INTEGRATED LEARNING SYSTEM

The Integrated Learning System (ILS) anchors chapter concepts, provides a framework for study, and links all of the instructor resources.

Icons that identify the learning objectives appear throughout the text and end-of-chapter materials. The ILS provides structure for instructors preparing lectures and exams and helps students learn quickly and study efficiently.

HIGHLIGHTS IN HRM

This popular boxed feature provides real-world examples of how organizations perform HR functions. The Highlights are introduced in the text discussion and include topics such as small businesses and international issues.

REALITY CHECK

Reality Check presents an interview with a Canadian expert in the field, illustrating how the material in the chapter is used in the real world.

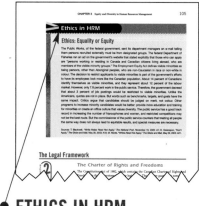

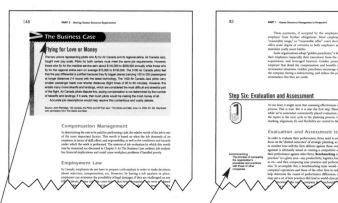

ETHICS IN HRM

Ethics in HRM provokes debate and discussion among students around the often gray areas of human resources management, including drug testing of employees and electronic surveillance of employees at work.

THE BUSINESS CASE

The Business Case features the business or financial implications of the adoption of HR practices. It also helps students build the skills necessary to recommend practices and projects, based on the projected costs and benefits, to senior management.

KEY TERMS IN MARGIN

Key terms appear in boldface and are defined in margin notes next to the text discussion. The key terms are also listed at the end of each chapter and in the glossary.

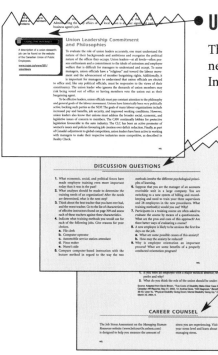

USING THE INTERNET

The Internet is referenced in all chapters, with new government, research, and business Internet links and addresses.

DISCUSSION QUESTIONS

Discussion questions following the chapter summary offer an opportunity to focus on each of the learning objectives in the chapter and to stimulate critical thinking. Many of these questions allow for group analysis and class discussion.

CAREER COUNSEL

Career Counsel on the Managing Human Resources website (www.belcourt5e.nelson.com) provides a dynamic link to the Internet, enabling students to relate chapter content to job searching and career development. The Career Counsel exercises allow students to develop a career plan.

INTERNET EXERCISE

Internet exercise requires the use of the content available on the Internet in order to develop a solution.

HRM EXPERIENCE EXERCISES

These skill-building exercises help students gain practical experience when dealing with employee/management concerns. Students can work through the exercises on either an individual or team basis.

BIZFLIX EXERCISES

Short film clips taken from popular movies provide real-world examples of HR in action. BizFlix Exercises encourage students to see and consider the HR issues and content in the world around them.

CASES

Two or more case studies per chapter present current HRM issues in real-life settings that encourage consideration and critical analysis. The end of the text features six real cases used in Excalibur, the Canadian University Tournament in Human Resources.

brief contents

contents

part 1

HUMAN RESOURCES MANAGEMENT IN PERSPECTIVE

chapter 1

chapter 2

Strategy and Human Resources Planning, 46

MEETING HUMAN RESOURCES REQUIREMENTS

chapter 4 — Job Analysis, Employee Involvement, and Flexible Work Schedules, 144

DEVELOPING EFFECTIVENESS IN HUMAN RESOURCES

chapter 8

IMPLEMENTING COMPENSATION AND SECURITY

chapter 9

chapter 10

chapter 12

Safety and Health, 512

ENHANCING EMPLOYEE–MANAGEMENT RELATIONS

part 6
EXPANDING HUMAN RESOURCES MANAGEMENT HORIZONS

chapter 15

International Human Resources Management, 636

chapter 16

Creating High-Performance Work Systems

(see the Managing Human Resources website, www.belcourt5e.nelson.com)

preface

The fifth Canadian edition of *Managing Human Resources* will place your students at the forefront in understanding how organizations can gain sustainable competitive advantage through people. The role of HR managers is no longer limited to service functions such as recruiting and selecting employees. Today, HR managers assume an active role in the strategic planning and decision making at their organizations. Using human resources effectively is critical to the success of any work organization.

In the first chapter, we begin by explaining the key challenges to HRM in developing the flexible and skilled workforce needed to compete effectively. Side by side with the competitive challenges, HRM must also address important employee concerns such as managing a diverse workforce, recognizing employee rights, and adjusting to new work attitudes. This chapter also discusses the important partnership with line managers and the competencies required of HR management. Then the textbook continues with the introduction, explanation, and discussion of the individual practices and policies that make up HRM. We recognize the manager's changing role and emphasize current issues and real-world problems and the policies and practices of HRM used to meet them.

Although we focus on the HR role of managers, we do not exclude the impact and importance of the HR department's strategic role in developing, coordinating, and enforcing policies and procedures relating to HR functions. Whether the reader becomes a manager, a supervisor, or an HR specialist, or is employed in other areas of the organization, *Managing Human Resources* provides a functional and practical understanding of HR programs to enable readers to see how HR affects all employees, the organization, the community, and the larger society.

Issues of strategy and talent have become such central concerns of HR today that we have reorganized and reemphasized the topics in this edition of the book. The second chapter of the book specifically addresses the issues of HR strategy and planning. Chapter 5 focuses on expanding and managing the talent pool in organizations. The detailed coverage of these topics solidifies *Managing Human Resources* as perhaps the premier text for thought leadership.

Organizations in today's competitive world are discovering that it is *how* the individual HR functions are combined that makes all the difference. Managers typically don't focus on HR issues such as staffing, training, and compensation in isolation from one another. Each of these HR practices is combined into an overall system to enhance employee involvement and productivity. *Managing Human Resources* ends with a final online chapter that focuses on development of high-performance work systems. We outline the various components of the system, including work-flow design, HR practices, management processes, and supporting technologies. We also discuss the strategic processes used to implement high-performance work systems and the outcomes that benefit both the employee and the organization as a whole.

What's Dynamic in the Fifth Canadian Edition

Many new features and much new information are provided in this revision. We introduce overall text improvements that more accurately reflect HRM in today's business world and help the reader understand HRM issues more effectively.

- The fifth Canadian edition reflects the body of knowledge required by students to pass the national knowledge exam, given by the Canadian Council of Human Resource Associations, as one of the steps toward the granting of the HR designation, the CHRP (Certified Human Resources Professional). The lead author, Dr. Monica Belcourt, participated in the development of the standards for the new national certification process. This text covers more than 90 percent of the material being tested on the national knowledge exam. As a CHRP herself, Dr. Belcourt is very familiar with the competencies required for the profession and has written the text with these required professional competencies (RPCs) as the foundation for learning about HR.

- HRM Experience: We build upon a popular addition to the previous edition of *Managing Human Resources* by including many new experiential exercises to explore significant issues in HR. These skill-building exercises will help students gain practical experience when dealing with employee/management concerns such as pay-for-performance; effective team building; employee benefits; reducing employee stress; employee rights; balancing competitive challenges and employee concerns; customizing HR for different types of human capital; designing selection criteria and methods; and assessing the strategic fit of high-performance work systems (HPWS). Students can work through the new exercises on either an individual or a team basis.

- Human Resources Information Systems (HRIS): Throughout the text, we have specifically highlighted the use of HRIS to facilitate the managing of employees and the efficient performance of HR functions. For example, the impact of information technology on HR and the role of HRIS in such areas as compensation, recruitment and selection, training, job analysis, and safety are discussed.

- Diversity: Because we believe that diversity issues are an integral part of every HRM activity, updated and expanded coverage is included throughout the text.

- HRM Strategy: The increasingly important role HRM plays in strategic planning is covered in Chapter 2. However, elsewhere we also discuss the role of human capital and Six Sigma; HR benchmarking; Balanced Scorecard and performance diagnosis; global HR strategy; as well as strategic alignment and implementing high-performance work systems.

- Contemporary employment issues such as global sourcing, offshoring, alternative work arrangements, temporary workers and the like are covered throughout the book.

- Global and international concerns are covered in more detail in this edition. This includes issues such as the World Trade Organization, China and the impact of globalization of HR; multinationals, joint ventures and the like, and global rights issues such as data protection, rights, and intellectual property. Although these issues have perhaps been peripheral to HRM in the past, they are increasingly seen as front and centre to many organizations.

- Comprehensive Cases: Six comprehensive cases are found at the end of the book. This exciting development features real cases used in Excalibur, the Canadian University Tournament in Human Resources, in which university students from across Canada are asked to demonstrate their knowledge of HR to a jury. After students have developed solutions to the problems faced by dynamic companies such as Cirque du Soleil and TELUS, the instructor can compare their responses to the one generated by the winning university team, and the answer prepared by an HR professor.

- The Business Case is a feature in every chapter on the business or financial implications of the adoption of HR practices. This feature was included to address the concerns that employers have with the inability of HR professionals to make the business case for recommended HR practices. We analyze, for example, the financial benefits of interest-based bargaining over traditional bargaining.

- We have readdressed the important role of compensation in HRM by heightening our discussion of pay-for-performance, healthcare cost savings, strategic pension planning, and effective employee awards.

- Expanded discussions cover major issues, including

Balanced Scorecard	performance diagnosis
child and elder care	person–organization fit
competency assessment for training	privacy legislation
conflict resolution techniques	role of human capital
cumulative trauma disorders	safety issues for youth
interest-based bargaining	strategic compensation planning
offshoring and outsourcing	violence and terrorism in the workplace

- Many new Highlights in HRM boxes and new Reality Checks present the reader with up-to-date real-world examples. Dr. Monica Belcourt, as a former president of the Human Resources Professionals Association of Ontario, is very involved in the HR profession, with access to some of the leaders in HR in Canada. The Reality Checks and Highlights in HRM reflect this access.

- Ethics in HRM: After the Enron scandal and scandals closer to home, Canadians are preoccupied with the ethics of those working in organizations. The popular Ethics in HRM provides new examples of the ethical dilemmas faced by HR practitioners.

- Internet: The ever-growing role of the Internet in HR activities is evident throughout the text. A few examples include online recruiting in Chapter 5 and online staffing in Chapter 6; Web-based training and e-learning in Chapter 7; and online 360-degree performance appraisal in Chapter 8.

- Most chapters have at least one new end-of-chapter case study highlighting chapter content. These cases have been selected to provide students with both current and practical HR problems and issues.

- Ancillaries: There are online ancillaries for instructors and students. A completely revised instructor's manual and test bank play a strategic role in the Integrated Learning System. A new set of PowerPoint presentation slides makes teaching and preparation easier and more convenient.

Features of the Book

Use of the Integrated Learning System continues for the fifth edition and ancillaries. This integrated structure creates a comprehensive teaching and testing system. Designed to facilitate understanding and retention of the material presented, each chapter contains the following pedagogical features:

- **Learning objectives** listed at the beginning of each chapter provide the basis for the Integrated Learning System. Icons that identify the learning objectives appear throughout the text and all ancillaries.

- **Highlights in HRM** is a popular boxed feature that provides real-world examples of how organizations perform HR functions. These popular boxed features are introduced in the text discussion and include topics such as small businesses and international issues.

- **Reality Check** presents an interview with a Canadian expert in the field, illustrating how the material in the chapter is used in the real world.

- **Ethics in HRM** provokes debate and discussion among students, as they struggle with the often grey areas of human resources management, such as drug testing of employees and electronic surveillance of employees at work.

- **The Business Case** features the business or financial implications of the adoption of HR practices. The Business Case will help students build the skills necessary to recommend HR practices and projects, based on the projected costs and benefits, to senior management.

- **Career Counsel** on the *Managing Human Resources* website (www.belcourt5e .nelson.com) provides a dynamic link to the Internet, enabling students to relate chapter content to job searching and career development. The Career Counsel exercises allow students to develop a career plan.

- **The Internet** is referenced in all chapters, with new government, research, and business Internet links and addresses.

- **Key terms** appear in boldface and are defined in margin notes next to the text discussion. The key terms are also listed at the end of the chapter and appear in the glossary at the end of the text.

- **Figures**, with an abundance of graphic materials and flowcharts, provide a visual, dynamic presentation of concepts and HR activities. All figures are systematically referenced in the text discussion.

- **Summary** includes a paragraph or two for each learning objective, providing a brief and focused review of the chapter.

- **Discussion questions** following the chapter summary offer an opportunity to focus on each of the learning objectives in the chapter and to stimulate critical thinking. Many of these questions allow for group analysis and class discussion.

- **Internet exercise,** new to this edition, requires the use of the content available on the Internet in order to develop a solution.

- **HRM Experience,** an experiential activity (described earlier), is included in each chapter.

- **BizFlix** is a new feature that encourages students to see the HR issues and content in the world around them. BizFlix are short film clips taken from popular movies that provide real-world examples of HR in action.

- **Two or more case studies** per chapter present current HRM issues in real-life settings that allow for student consideration and critical analysis.

- **Chapter 16, Creating High-Performance Work Systems,** and the chapter feature Career Counsel, appear on the Internet at the *Managing Human Resources* website (www.belcourt5e.nelson.com). The Career Counsel sections help students with job search strategies and value assessment and salary negotiation tactics.

Ancillary Teaching and Learning Materials

For Students

- Online Study Guide to Accompany Managing Human Resources. In partnership with Captus Press, Nelson is pleased to offer a free online study guide prepared by Dr. Monica Belcourt (to access, visit www.belcourt5e.nelson.com). Complete with chapter summaries, multiple-choice questions, short-answer questions, and progress checks, this supplement will enhance your learning experience. Equally important, the study guide provides the opportunity to practise taking multiple-choice tests in preparation for the National Knowledge Examination, given by the Canadian Council of Human Resource Associations (CCHRA), a first step in becoming a CHRP (Certified Human Resource Professional).

- **Internet Course.** For students seeking extra help, a full online HRM course is available from Captus Press. Supplement classroom teaching by accessing the Internet server and listening to lectures given by Dr. Monica Belcourt. You can then scroll to areas of interest and access necessary information. Please contact Captus Press directly for information on the cost of these options (www.captus.com).

- **InfoTrac® College Edition.** With InfoTrac, students can receive anytime, anywhere online access to a database of full-text articles from hundreds of popular and scholarly periodicals, such as *Canadian Business, Canadian Business Review, Business Week, Canadian Labour, HR Magazine,* and *HR Professional,* among others. Students can use its fast and easy search tools to find relevant news and analytical information among the tens of thousands of articles in the database—updated daily and going back as far as four years—all at a single website. InfoTrac is a great way to expose students to online research techniques, with the security that the content is academically based and reliable. An InfoTrac College Edition subscription card is packaged free with all new copies of *Managing Human Resources.*

- **Website.** A comprehensive website includes practice quizzes, chapter Web links, study tips, and information on degrees and careers in human resource management (www.belcourt5e.nelson.com).

- **Online exam prep for National Knowledge Exam.** The Canadian Council of Human Resources Associations (CCHRA) offers an online preparation course for the National Knowledge Exam, the first exam leading to the designation of CHRP (Certified Human Resource Professional). The course includes a diagnostic test that assesses knowledge of the Required Professional Capabilities (RPCs) and links to appropriate content in this text and others. There are also three practice exams, online multimedia lectures, and quizzes. For more information, contact your provincial HR association, the CCHRA website (www.cchra-ccarh.ca), or Captus Press (http://webclients.captus.com/cchra/).

For Instructors

The following instructor support materials are available to adopters from your sales representative.

- **Instructor's Resource Guide.** For each chapter in the textbook, the *Instructor's Resource Guide* contains a chapter synopsis and learning objectives, a very detailed lecture outline, and answers to the end-of-chapter discussion questions.

- **Test Bank.** The new test bank provides more than 100 questions for each text chapter. There are true/false, multiple-choice, and essay items for each chapter, arranged by learning objective. Page references from the text are included. Each objective question is coded to indicate whether it covers knowledge of key terms, understanding of concepts and principles, or application of principles.

- **Computerized Test Bank.** The computerized testing software contains all the questions from the test bank and allows the instructor to edit, add, delete, or randomly mix questions for customized tests.

- **PowerPoint™ Presentation Slides.** Created specifically for the new edition by Dr. Monica Belcourt, these presentation slides will add colour and interest to lectures.
- **Instructor's Resource CD.** (ISBN 0-17-644183-2) The Instructor's Manual, Test Bank, Computerized Test Bank, and PowerPoint slides are provided on a single CD-ROM.
- **BizFlix.** These short film clips from popular and current movies show HR in action. End-of-chapter BizFlix exercises in the text stimulate students to see how the filmed scenarios apply to chapter topics.
- **Video.** (ISBN 0-17-644175-1) An introductory video featuring CBC news programming is available for instructors. Use these video clips to introduce a topic or stimulate discussion.
- *JoinIn*™ **on TurningPoint®.** Transform any lecture into a truly interactive student experience with *JoinIn*. Combined with your choice of several leading keypad systems, *JoinIn* turns your ordinary PowerPoint® application into powerful audience response software. With just a click on a handheld device, your students can respond to multiple-choice questions, short polls, interactive exercises, and peer review questions. You can take attendance, check student comprehension of difficult concepts, collect student demographics to better assess student needs, and even administer quizzes without collecting papers or grading. In addition, we provide interactive text-specific slide sets that you can modify and merge with any existing PowerPoint lecture slides for a seamless classroom presentation. This interactive tool is available to qualified college and university adopters. For more information, contact your Thomson representative or visit http://turningpoint.thomsonlearningconnections.com.
- **Website.** A comprehensive website includes practice quizzes, chapter web links, study tips, and information on degrees and careers in human resource management. We have also included a link for instructors that contains downloadable ancillaries and supplementary cases and solutions. The website can be found at www.belcourt5e.nelson.com.
- **Nelson ePacks.** Online content in WebCT and Blackboard is available for this title. Visit the Instructor's Resource area at www.belcourt5e.nelson.com for details.

Acknowledgments for the Fifth Canadian Edition

In preparing the manuscript for this edition, we have drawn not only on the current literature but also on the current practices of organizations that furnished information relating to their HR programs. We are indebted to the leaders in the field who have influenced us through their writings and personal associations. We have also been aided by our present and former students, by our colleagues at the Human Resources Professionals Association of Ontario with whom we have been associated, by HR managers, and by our academic colleagues.

We would like to express our appreciation to the following reviewers who have helped shape the text:

Gordon Barnard, Durham College
Stéphane Brutus, Concordia University
Julie Bulmash, George Brown College

Joan Condie, Sheridan College
Tim DeGroot, McMaster University
Julie Aitken Harris, University of Western Ontario
Robert Isaac, University of Calgary
Don MacCormac, University of PEI
Colleen Marshall, Confederation College
Jessica Nicholson, McMaster University
Robert Oppenheimer, Concordia University
Carolin Rekar-Munro, Durham College
Maria Rotundo, University of Toronto
Sudhir Saha, Memorial University
Aaron Schat, McMaster University
Pat Sniderman, Ryerson Polytechnic University
Indira Somwaru, Seneca College
Krista Uggerslev, University of Manitoba
Diane White, Seneca College
Deborah Zinni, Brock University

Additionally, we would like to thank the graduate HR students who provided research assistance in the preparation of the fifth edition: Christine Thrussell and Mary Ho, both candidates in the Masters of Human Resources Management at York University.

We appreciate the efforts of the team at Thomson Nelson who helped to develop and produce this text. They include Jackie Wood, Acquisitions Editor, Shannon White, Acquisitions Editor, Veronica Visentin, Publisher, and Charmaine Sherlock, Marketing Manager; as well as the wonderful sales representatives who have enthusiastically supported the book. Special appreciation is extended to Karina Hope, Senior Developmental Editor, who has managed the process very professionally, and through her suggestions, has improved the product.

Our greatest indebtedness is to our spouses—Michael Belcourt, Ronnie Bohlander, and Marybeth Snell—who have contributed in so many ways to this book. They are always sources of invaluable guidance and assistance. Furthermore, by their continued enthusiasm and support, they have made the process a more pleasant and rewarding experience. We are most grateful to them for their many contributions to this publication, to our lives, and to our families.

about the authors

Monica Belcourt

Monica Belcourt is a full Professor, Human Resources Management, and founding Director of the Graduate Program in HRM at the Atkinson Faculty of Liberal and Professional Studies, York University. She has an extensive and varied background in human resources management. After receiving a B.A. in psychology from the University of Manitoba, she joined the Public Service Commission as a recruitment and selection specialist. During her tenure with the federal government, she worked in training, HRM research, job analysis, and HR planning.

Dr. Belcourt alternated working in HRM with graduate school, obtaining an M.A. in psychology from York University, an M.Ed. in adult education from the University of Ottawa, and a Ph.D. in management from York University. She also holds the designation of Certified Human Resource Professional (CHRP). Her research is grounded in the experience she gained as Director of Personnel for the 63 000 employees at CP Rail; Director of Employee Development, National Film Board; and as a functional HR specialist for the federal government. She has taught HRM at Concordia University, Université du Québec à Montréal, McGill University, and York University, where she founded and managed the largest undergraduate program in HRM in Canada. She created Canada's first degrees in human resources management: B.HRM, B.HRM (honours), and a Master's in HRM. A full description of these degrees can be found at www.atkinson.yorku.ca/mhrm/.

Dr. Belcourt is Director of the International Alliance for HR Research (IAHRR), which is a catalyst for the discovery, dissemination, and application of new knowledge about HRM. The IAHRR programs are described at www.yorku.ca/hrresall. Her research interests focus on strategic HRM, and she has published more than 100 articles, several of which received best paper awards. A practitioner publication is *Making Government the Best Place to Work: Building Commitment,* published by the Institute of Public Administration of Canada, which can be downloaded at IPAC's website, www.ipac-iapc.ca.

Dr. Belcourt is Series Editor for the Nelson Series in Human Resources Management: *Performance Management through Training and Development; Occupational Health and Safety; Human Resources Management Systems; Recruitment and Selection in Canada; Compensation in Canada; Strategic Human Resources Planning; Research, Measurement and Evaluation in HRM; The Canadian Labour Market;* and a forthcoming text on labour relations.

Active in many professional associations and not-for-profit organizations, Dr. Belcourt was the President of the Human Resources Professionals Association of Ontario, served on the national committee for HR certification, and was a board member of CIBC Insurance and the Toronto French School. She is a frequent commentator on HRM issues for Workopolis, CTV, *Canada AM*, CBC, *The Globe and Mail, The Canadian HR Reporter,* and other media. She has been recognized as a champion of HR by *The Canadian HR Reporter.*

George Bohlander

George Bohlander is Professor of Management at Arizona State University. He received his M.B.A. from the University of Southern California and his Ph.D. from the University of California at Los Angeles. His areas of expertise include employment law, training and development, work teams, public policy, and labour relations. He has received the Outstanding Undergraduate Teaching Excellence Award presented by the College of Business at ASU and also received the prestigious ASU Parents Association Professorship for his contributions to students and teaching.

Dr. Bohlander is an active researcher and author. He has published over 50 articles and monographs in professional and practitioner journals such as *National Productivity Review*, *HR Magazine*, *Labor Law Journal*, *The Journal of Collective Bargaining in the Public Sector*, and others. Dr. Bohlander continues to be a consultant to public and private organizations including the U.S. Postal Service, American Productivity & Quality Center, BFGoodrich, McDonnell Douglas, Rural/Metro Corporation, and Del Webb. He is also an active labour arbitrator.

Scott Snell

Scott Snell is Professor of Human Resource Studies and Director of Executive Education in the School of Industrial and Labor Relations at Cornell University. He received a B.A. in Psychology from Miami University as well as M.B.A. and Ph.D. degrees in Business Administration from Michigan State University. Prior to joining the faculty at Cornell, Dr. Snell was on the faculty of business at Penn State University. During his career, he has taught courses in human resource management and strategic management to undergraduates, graduates, and executives.

Professor Snell has worked with companies such as AT&T, GE, IBM, Merck, and Shell to address the alignment of human resource systems with strategic initiatives such as globalization, technological change, and knowledge management. His research and teaching interests focus on the development and deployment of intellectual capital as a foundation of an organization's core competencies. He has published a number of articles in professional journals and is the author of two textbooks. In addition, Dr. Snell has served on the editorial boards of *Journal of Managerial Issues*, *Digest of Management Research*, *Human Resource Management Review*, *Human Resource Planning*, and *Academy of Management Journal*.

The World of Human Resources Management

After studying this chapter, you should be able to

objective 1 Identify how firms gain sustainable competitive advantage through people.

objective 2 Explain how globalization is influencing human resources management.

objective 3 Describe the impact of information technology on managing people.

objective 4 Identify the importance of change management.

objective 5 State HR's role in developing intellectual capital.

objective 6 Differentiate how TQM and reengineering influence HR systems.

objective 7 Discuss the impact of cost pressures on HR policies.

objective 8 Discuss the primary demographic and employee concerns pertaining to HRM.

objective 9 Provide examples of the roles and competencies of today's HR managers.

There's an old joke that goes . . . The organization of the future will be so technologically advanced that it will be run by just one person and a dog. The person will be there to feed the dog, and the dog will be there to make sure that the person doesn't touch anything.

In the past, observers feared that machines might one day eliminate the need for people at work. In reality, just the opposite has been occurring. People are more important in today's organizations than ever before. As Ed Gubman, author of *The Talent Solution,* points out, "In many fast-growing economies, it may be easier to access money and technology than good people." Competitive advantage belongs to companies that know how to attract, select, deploy, and develop talent.[1]

We use a lot of words to describe the importance of people to organizations. The term *human resources* implies that people have capabilities, i.e., the knowledge and skills that drive organizational performance (along with other resources such as money, materials, and information). Other terms such as *human capital* and *intellectual assets* all have in common the idea that people make the difference in how an organization performs. Successful organizations are particularly adept at bringing together different kinds of people to achieve a common purpose. This is the essence of **human resources management** (**HRM**).

human resources management (HRM)
The process of managing human talent to achieve an organization's objectives

If you have ever held a job, you have experienced some aspect of HRM. How were you hired? The application form and the interview format were designed by HR specialists. The amount of money you were paid and the benefits that you received were determined first by employment regulations issued by governments, and secondly by an analysis of your job done by HR professionals. Any training you received, or bonuses given as a result of a positive performance appraisal, were all carefully thought through by someone in the HR department. Your work conditions, including instructions about the hazards on your job, were the result of work done by HR. As you read this text, and you apply the content to any jobs that you have had, you will realize why employees live in the world of HRM.

Why Study Human Resources Management?

objective 1

As you embark on this course, you may be wondering how the topic of human resources management relates to your interests and career aspirations. The answer to the question "Why study HRM?" is pretty much the same regardless of whether you plan on working in an HR department or not. Staffing the organization, designing jobs and teams, developing skillful employees, identifying approaches for improving their performance, and rewarding employee successes—all typically labelled HRM issues— are as relevant to line managers as they are to managers in the HR department. The HR professional supports managers as they manage their employees to achieve organizational goals. See Highlights in HRM 1.1 for a day in the life of an HR generalist and see Figure 1.1 on page 6 for a snapshot of pay rates for HR jobs.

To work with people effectively, we have to understand human behaviour, and we have to be knowledgeable about the various systems and practices available to help us build a skilled and motivated workforce. At the same time, we have to be aware of economic, technological, social, and legal issues that either facilitate or constrain our efforts to achieve organizational goals.[2] Because employee skills, knowledge, and

Highlights in HRM 1.1

A Day in the Life of an HR Generalist

Deena Durack is an HR generalist. Responsible for 15 manager groups and 1200 employees at a local hospital, Deena's days are filled with recruitment, new hire documentation, benefits administration, collective agreement interpretation, payroll changes, educational loans, redeployment, management, employee and retirement counselling, job fairs, and special projects. Beginning with recruitment, Deena develops job postings for available positions that are based on the job descriptions and are posted internally or externally on the hospital's website, sent to professional associations, and sometimes, but not often, sent to various newspapers. Around 25 résumés arrive every day that must be screened for qualifications, knowledge, skills and abilities (KSAs), and work history. The résumés that pass are sent to the hiring manager and she arranges interviews. Half of her day is then spent on developing interview questions about the job and creating a scoring guide in which to evaluate the candidates. A salary range will be given beforehand to the hiring manager that is based on either market data from a salary survey or on the recommendation of the compensation analyst. If the candidate is successful, references will be checked and she will write up a letter of offer that includes benefits information.

Deena also advises employees about their benefits. As part of her labour relations duties, Deena will give advice on the interpretation of the collective agreement with respect to the rights and duties of employees and managers. Here, she will handle general questions on scheduling hours of work and attendance issues. Scheduling issues can be anything from whether an employee should be paid premiums for working shifts or if the manager has to pay premiums on certain weekends. Attendance support questions are varied. Deena may run a report for a manager on number of absences. Patterns of absences are analyzed to determine if the absenteeism is to be considered punitive or if there are valid reasons for absenteeism. If an employee is missing many hours the manager will speak with that individual to determine if there is a way she/he can help through scheduling changes or, if necessary, a way for the individual to contact the Employee Assistance Program (EAP) if there are problems outside of work. This is all done with the coordination of the HR manager and the departmental manager.

As another part of her job as a generalist, Deena will go to job fairs to promote the organization and market positions that are currently available. She sits on the Corporate Events Committee where she organizes and chairs the staff and children's holiday parties as well as the company picnic. She is also a member of the Staff Recognition Committee where discussions and decisions are made on yearly service awards and on the types of gifts to be purchased for employees who are retiring. Special projects can also come up as a generalist. She developed a new manager's manual to assist them in the orientation to HR processes and sat on the bargaining committee for a new collective agreement. Her busy day may also include creating voluntary exit packages when the hospital is in a redeployment process and she will meet with employees to advise them on their rights concerning their severance packages. And then there is the human side of being a generalist. Daily, a manager or an employee will come to her office just to talk. As a generalist she will sit and listen and may offer advice.

Figure 1.1	Average Pay Rates for HR Professionals
HR Assistant	$36,100 to $41,800
HR Generalist	$50,000 to $54,900
HR Specialist	$54,900 to $62,900
HR Manager	$75,800 to $78,000
HR Director	$107,000 to $111,600
HR Top Executive	$136,900 to $140,800

Adapted from: Watson Wyatt Annual Compensation Series 2005/6; Toronto Board of Trade Compensation and Benefits Survey 2005.

abilities are among the most distinctive and renewable resources on which a company can draw, their strategic management is more important than ever. As Thomas J. Watson, the founder of IBM, said, "You can get capital and erect buildings, but it takes people to build a business."[3]

While "competing through people" may be a theme for human resources management, the idea remains only a framework for action. On a day-to-day basis, managers focus on specific challenges and issues that pertain to human resources. Figure 1.2 provides an overall framework for human resources management. From this figure, we can see that HRM has to help blend many aspects of management; at this point we will simply classify them as either "competitive challenges" or "employee concerns." By balancing sometimes competing demands, HRM plays an important role in getting the most from employees and providing a work environment that meets their short-term and long-term needs. We will use this framework as a basis for our discussion throughout the rest of this chapter.

Figure 1.2   Overall Framework for Human Resources Management

COMPETITIVE CHALLENGES
- Globalization
- Technology
- Managing change
- Human capital
- Responsiveness
- Cost containment

HUMAN RESOURCES
- Planning
- Recruitment
- Staffing
- Job design
- Training/development
- Appraisal
- Communications
- Compensation
- Benefits
- Labour relations

EMPLOYEE CONCERNS
- Background diversity
- Age distribution
- Gender issues
- Job security
- Educational levels
- Employee rights
- Privacy issues
- Work attitudes
- Family concerns

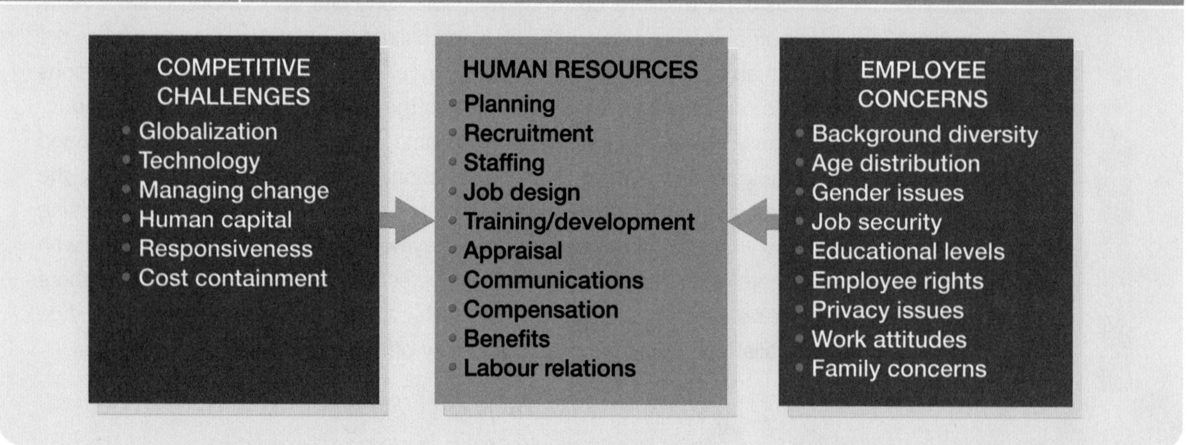

Competitive Challenges and Human Resources Management

Professional organizations such as the Human Resources Professionals of each province and the Conference Board of Canada conduct ongoing studies of the most pressing competitive issues facing firms. By seeking the input of chief executives and HR managers, these organizations keep a finger on the pulse of major trends. For the past decade or so, there has been a constant theme around the following issues:

- Going global
- Embracing new technology
- Managing change
- Managing talent, or human capital
- Responding to the market
- Containing costs

These trends extend beyond "people issues" per se, but they all focus on the need to develop a skilled and flexible workforce in order to compete in the 21st century.

Challenge 1: Going Global

In order to grow and prosper, many companies are seeking business opportunities in global markets. Competition—and cooperation—with foreign companies has become an important focal point for business. China could surpass the United States to become the largest economy in the world by 2041, and India could be the third largest. These countries can produce goods and provide services at a fraction of the cost of Canadian workers. As the vice-president and chief economist of the Conference Board of Canada stated, "There are billions of people in Asia who want to get to where we are, and they're prepared to work longer and harder. So we have to work smarter."[4]

The Impact of Globalization

By partnering with firms in other regions of the world and using information technologies to coordinate distant parts of their businesses, companies such as Motorola, General Electric, and Toyota have shown that their vision for the future is to offer customers "anything, anytime, anywhere" around the world. The manufacturing of cars in Canada provides a good example of the impact of **globalization**. There is no such thing as a Canadian car. Most parts—up to 85 percent—of cars manufactured in Canada come from other countries. On the other hand, Canadian content represents about 10 percent for cars assembled outside of Canada.[5] A recent study suggests that about 37 percent of Canada's workforce will be impacted by globalization, with knowledge workers and manufacturing jobs taking the brunt of the impact of the competition by lower-wage countries.[6]

Numerous free-trade agreements forged between nations in the last half-century have helped quicken the pace of globalization. The first major trade agreement of the 20th century was made in 1948, following World War II. Called the General Agreement on Tariffs and Trade (GATT), it established rules and guidelines for global commerce between nations and groups of nations. Since GATT began, world trade has increased more than sixfold. GATT paved the way for the formation of the European Union in 1986; the North American Free Trade Agreement (NAFTA), encompassing Canada, the United States, and Mexico, in 1994; and the Asia-Pacific Economic Cooperation (APEC) in 1989, which loosened trade restrictions among Pacific Rim countries.

globalization
The trend toward opening up foreign markets to international trade and investment

USING THE INTERNET

To learn more about NAFTA, go to:

www.nafta-sec-alena.org

The World Trade Organization (WTO), headquartered in Lausanne, Switzerland, now has more than 148 member countries, accounting for more than 97 percent of world trade.[7]

Globalization and Corporate Social Responsibility. Even though globalization has led to a great improvement in people's living standards in the last half-century, free-trade agreements still stir fierce debate. When NAFTA talks were first underway, U.S. and Canadian citizens worried that the agreement would lead to a loss of jobs to Mexico, where labour costs are cheaper. Other people worry that free trade is creating a "have/have not" world economy, in which the people in developing economies and the world's environment are being exploited by companies in richer, more developed countries. This has sparked anti-free-trade protests in many nations.

Concerns such as these, coupled with numerous scandals plaguing corporations in recent years, have led to a new focus on **corporate social responsibility**, or good citizenship. Companies are discovering that being socially responsible helps the bottom line. Moreover, workers applying for jobs are saying corporate responsibility is now more important to their job selection. One of HR's leadership roles is to spearhead the development and implementation of corporate citizenship throughout the organization.[8]

corporate social responsibility
The responsibility of the firm to act in the best interests of the people and communities affected by its activities

USING THE INTERNET

Sources of information about companies and their programs to promote corporate social responsibility can be found on this news service at:

www.csrwire.com

Effect of Globalization on HRM

For all of the opportunities afforded by international business, when managers talk about "going global," they have to balance a complicated set of issues related to different geographies, cultures, employment laws, and business practices. Human resources issues underlie each of these concerns and include such things as gauging the knowledge and skill base of foreign workforces and figuring out how best to hire and train them, sometimes with materials that must be translated into a number of different languages. Relocating managers and other workers to direct the efforts of a foreign workforce is a challenge as well. HR personnel are frequently responsible for implementing training programs and development opportunities to enhance managers' understanding of foreign cultures and practices. In many cases, HR managers must adjust the compensation plans of employees working abroad to ensure that they receive fair and equitable pay in parts of the world where living costs differ. Perhaps the most difficult task is retaining these employees in the face of the culture shock they and their families are likely to experience.

So while managing across borders provides new and broader opportunities for organizations, it also represents a quantum leap in the complexity of human resources management. In fact, the international arena for HRM is so involved that we have devoted an entire chapter (Chapter 15) to discussing its competitive, cultural, and practical implications.

Challenge 2: Embracing New Technology

Advancements in information technology have enabled organizations to take advantage of the information explosion. With computer networks, unlimited amounts of data can be stored, retrieved, and used in a wide variety of ways, from simple record keeping to controlling complex equipment. The effect is so dramatic that at a broader level, organizations are changing the way they do business. Use of the Internet to transact business has become so pervasive for both large and small companies that e-commerce is rapidly becoming the organizational challenge of the new millennium. Even following the "dot-com bust," in which many promising new Internet companies failed rapidly, the Web is transforming the way traditional bricks-and-mortar companies do business. Organizations are connected via computer-mediated relationships, and they are giving rise to a new generation of "virtual" workers who work from home, in hotels, in their cars, or wherever their work takes them. The implications for HRM are at times mind boggling.

From Touch Labour to Knowledge Workers

The introduction of advanced technology tends to reduce the number of jobs that require little skill and to increase the number of jobs that require considerable skill. In general, this transformation has been referred to as a shift from "touch labour" to **"knowledge workers,"** in which employee responsibilities expand to include a richer array of activities such as planning, decision making, and problem solving.[9] In many cases, current employees are being retrained to assume new roles and responsibilities. Even when employees are displaced, they also require retraining.

knowledge workers
Workers whose responsibilities extend beyond the physical execution of work to include planning, decision making, and problem solving

Technology, transportation, communications, and utilities industries tend to spend the most on training. Knowledge-based training has become so important that Microsoft Canada Co. has contributed nearly $5 million to offer grants to provide access to the latest computer technology and training to Canadian community organizations and schools. Working with Partners in Learning, Unlimited Potential, and Ministries of Education, the program supports schools by offering training and support to teachers, providing free upgrades, and donating used computers.[10]

Influence of Technology in HRM

Information technology has, of course, changed the face of HRM in Canada and abroad. Perhaps the most central use of technology in HRM is an organization's **human resources information system (HRIS).** Organizations determined to improve productivity and lower costs are finding HR a good place to start. Because HR affects the entire workforce—everyone who works for the company must be hired, trained, and paid, usually through HR—the impact of HRIS can be dramatic. It can be a potent weapon for lowering administrative costs, increasing productivity, speeding up response times, and improving decision making and customer service.

human resources information system (HRIS)
A computerized system that provides current and accurate data for purposes of control and decision making

The most obvious impact has been operational—that is, automating routine activities, alleviating administrative burdens, reducing costs, and improving productivity internal to the HR function itself. As shown in Highlights in HRM 1.2 on page 10, the most frequent uses include automating payroll processing, maintaining employee records, and administering benefits programs. One of the big trends in recent years has been toward HRIS "self-service"—setting up systems, usually on an intranet, to allow managers to access employee records themselves for administrative purposes, and to allow employees to access and change their own benefits and other personal information. Merck's HR system was redesigned to enable line managers and employees to enter, retrieve, and edit data in order to make better decisions faster. This has helped alleviate many of the paper burdens Merck's HR group previously faced and offers greater convenience to both managers and their employees.

Today, however, software applications are available to automate far more HR activities than just payroll, records, and benefits information. All sorts of routine HR activities, from front to back, have seen some sort of automation. Companies are now using software to recruit, screen, and pretest applicants online before hiring them as well as to train and promote employees once they've been hired. For example, Merck's

Highlights in HRM 1.2

Most Common HR Information Systems Applications

Payroll	76.7%
Benefits administration	57.1
Benefits enrollment	41.4
Recruiting—applicant tracking	39.1
Personnel administration	39.1
Training and development	31.6
Employee self-service	24.8
Manager self-service	18.0
Other	3.8

Source: "How HR Managers Use Technology Applications to Control HR Department Costs," *Human Resource Department Management Report,* no. 4–5 (May 2004). This text is republished with the express written consent of IOMA © 2006; any further use requires publisher's permission. Please contact IOMA directly at: content@ioma.com or by phone, 212-576-8744; www.ioma.com.

staffing management system supports the hiring process by tracking applicants' information, scanning résumés, and making the information immediately accessible to line managers so they can search systematically for the people whose skills they want. Managers can search online for internal and external talent by running searches of candidates who have been categorized by skill set. An outside vendor that specializes in Web-based recruiting administers the system and acts as a conduit between Merck and broader databases such as Monster.com and Hotjobs.com.[11]

Corning, Inc. uses HR software, among other things, to set the developmental goals of its employees once they've been hired and gauge how well they are meeting them. Employees can look online to see their own goals and mark their progress as well as see everyone else's goals in the command chain, from the CEO down to their immediate supervisors. This "cascading" of goals has helped Corning's employees align their personal goals with the organization's overall objectives in order to reach higher levels. "Like any large company, we tended to get 'silo-ed' and fragmented the more we grew," said one vice-president at a company using a system similar to Corning's. "We needed a better way to pull our global team together and get people focused on what the priorities are for our business."

According to a survey by Cedar Group, a technology consulting firm, prepackaged, or "canned," HR Web-based solutions are as commonly used as custom-designed systems. Generally, companies also have the choice of hosting the applications on their own servers or having a vendor do it for them. Most companies have outside vendors such as Oracle-PeopleSoft (sometimes called *ASPs*, which stands for *application service providers*) support the applications, instead of the IT groups within their own organizations.

So what sort of system should HR professionals choose from among the many options available to them? Experts say the first step in choosing an HRIS is for HR personnel to evaluate the biggest "headaches" they experience, or the most time-consuming tasks, and then choose the applications that can have the strongest impact on the firm's financial measures—that is, the ones that get the "biggest bang for the buck." These applications are more likely to get "buy-in" from the firm's top managers. HR managers should then calculate the costs based on average salaries, or HR hours, that could be saved by using an HRIS, along with the hours of increased productivity that would occur as a result.

Other factors that need to be evaluated include the following:

- *Fit of the application to the firm's employee base.* If many of the firm's employees work on a factory floor, is the system appropriate, or does HR need to install kiosks in employee areas? How will the information be secured? Will employees need to be assigned passwords? Can they access the information from offsite, say, from their homes?
- *Ability to upgrade or customize the software.* What sorts of costs will be involved to upgrade the software in the coming years?
- *Compatibility with current systems.* Does the HRIS link into existing, or planned, information systems easily and inexpensively?
- *User friendliness.* Does the software provide additional features such as links to learning resources or help for managers who might need it?
- *Availability of technical support.* Should the HRIS system be supported internally or should the vendor host it? What are the vendor's technical support capabilities?
- *Time required to implement and train staff members to use the HRIS, including HR and payroll personnel, managers, and employees.* Who is responsible for training employees and how will it be done?
- *Initial costs and annual maintenance costs.* Is a "suite" of applications needed or just a few key applications? Experts advise HR managers to price each application separately and then ask vendors for a "bundled" price.[12]

When an effective HRIS is implemented, perhaps the biggest advantage gained is that HR personnel can concentrate more effectively on the firm's strategic direction instead of on routine tasks. This can include forecasting personnel needs (especially for firms planning to expand, contract, or merge), planning for career and employee promotions, and evaluating the impact of the firm's policies—both those related to HR functions and other functions—to help improve the firm's earnings and strategic direction. "We wanted our HR teams to focus on people issues instead of data problems," explains Sandra Hoffman, CIO of MAPICS, an HR applications provider.

The initial drive to adopt human resources information systems was related to cutting HR costs. But HR managers have since discovered that the systems have allowed them to share information with line managers, who, by having access to it, have been able to come up with better production practices and cost-control solutions. As a result, HR managers are now asking their application providers to develop additional software to meet certain goals, such as lowering a company's total spending on employee health care and improving customer service.[13]

Challenge 3: Managing Change

Technology and globalization are only two of the forces driving change in organizations and HRM. Today, being able to manage change has become paramount to the firm's success. As one pundit put it, "No change means no chance." Successful companies, says Harvard Business School professor Rosabeth Moss Kanter, develop a culture that just keeps moving all the time.[14] Given the pace of today's commerce, organizations can rarely stand still for long. In highly competitive environments, where competition is global and innovation is continuous, change has become a core competency of organizations.

Types of Change

Programs focused on total quality, continuous improvement, downsizing, reengineering, outsourcing, and the like are all examples of the means organizations are using to modify the way they operate in order to be more successful. Some of these changes are **reactive change**, resulting when external forces have already affected an organization's performance. Other changes are **proactive change**, initiated by managers to take advantage of targeted opportunities, particularly in fast-changing industries in which followers are not successful.

reactive change
Change that occurs after external forces have already affected performance

proactive change
Change initiated to take advantage of targeted opportunities

Managing Change through HR

In a survey by the American Management Association (AMA), 84 percent of executives polled said that they have at least one change initiative going on in their organizations. Yet surprisingly, only about two-thirds said that their companies have any sort of formal change-management program to support these initiatives![15] This is unfortunate because successful change rarely occurs naturally or easily. Most of the major reasons why change efforts can fail come down to HR issues. Some of the top reasons are as follows:[16]

1. Not establishing a sense of urgency
2. Not creating a powerful coalition to guide the effort
3. Lacking leaders who have a vision
4. Lacking leaders who communicate the vision
5. Not removing obstacles to the new vision
6. Not systematically planning for and creating short-term "wins"
7. Declaring victory too soon
8. Not anchoring changes in the corporate culture

© STOCKBYTE GOLD/GETTY IMAGES

Formal change management programs help to keep employees focused on the success of the business.

Most employees—regardless of occupation—understand that the way things were done five or ten years ago is very different from how they are done today (or will be done five or ten years from now). Responsibilities change, job assignments change, and work processes change. And this change is continuous—a part of the job—rather than temporary. Nevertheless, people often resist change because it requires them to modify or abandon ways of working that have been successful or at least familiar to them. As the president of the Human Resource Planning Society put it: "Non-technical, unattended human factors are, in fact, most often the problem in failed change projects." To manage change, executives and managers, including those in HR, have to envision the future, communicate this vision to employees, set clear expectations for performance, and develop the capability to execute by reorganizing people and reallocating assets. Organizations that have been successful in engineering change typically build into their change-management planning these key elements:

- They link the change to the business strategy.
- They create quantifiable benefits.

- They engage key employees, customers, and their suppliers, early.
- They integrate required behaviour changes.
- They lead clearly, unequivocally, and consistently.
- They invest to implement and sustain change.
- They communicate continuously and personally.
- They sell commitment to the change, not communication about the change.[17]

Challenge 4: Managing Talent, or Human Capital

objective **5**

human capital
The knowledge, skills, and capabilities of individuals that have economic value to an organization

The idea that organizations "compete through people" highlights the fact that success increasingly depends on an organization's ability to manage talent, or **human capital.** The term *human capital* describes the economic value of employees' knowledge, skills, and capabilities. Although the value of these assets may not show up directly on a company's balance sheet, it nevertheless has tremendous impact on an organization's performance. The following quotations from notable CEOs illustrate this point:[18]

- "If you look at our semiconductors and melt them down for silicon, that's a tiny fraction of the costs. The rest is intellect and mistakes." (Gordon Moore, Intel)
- "An organization's ability to learn, and translate that learning into action rapidly, is the ultimate competitive business advantage." (Jack Welch, General Electric)
- "Successful companies of the 21st century will be those who do the best jobs of capturing, storing and leveraging what their employees know." (Lew Platt, Hewlett-Packard)

Human Capital and HRM

Human capital is intangible and elusive and cannot be managed the way organizations manage jobs, products, and technologies. One of the reasons for this is that the employees, *not* the organization, own their own human capital. If valued employees leave a company, they take their human capital with them, and any investment the company has made in training and developing those people is lost.

To build human capital in organizations, managers must continue to develop superior knowledge, skills, and experience within their workforce. Even governments understand the value of human capital investments. Staffing programs focus on identifying, recruiting, and hiring the best and the brightest talent available. Training programs complement these staffing practices to provide skill enhancement, particularly in areas that cannot be transferred to another company if an employee leaves.[19] In addition, employees need opportunities for development on the job. The most highly valued intelligence tends to be associated with competencies and capabilities that are learned from experience and are not easily taught.[20] Consequently, managers have to do a good job of providing developmental assignments to employees and ensuring their job duties and requirements are flexible enough to allow for growth and learning.

Beyond the need to invest in employee development, organizations have to find ways of using the knowledge that currently exists. Too often, employees have skills that go unused. As the CEO of Buckman Laboratories noted, "If the greatest database in the company is housed in the individual minds of the associates of the organization, then that is where the power of the organization resides. These individual knowledge bases are continually changing and adapting to the real world in front of them. We have to connect these individual knowledge bases together so that they do whatever they do best in the shortest possible time."[21] Efforts to empower employees and encourage their participation and involvement more fully utilize the human capital available. (Employee empowerment is discussed fully in later chapters.)

In companies such as Bell Canada and Toys "R" Us, managers are evaluated on their progress toward meeting developmental goals. These goals focus on skill development and gaining new competencies and capabilities. In a growing number of instances, pay is attached to this knowledge and skill acquisition. Skill-based pay, for example, rewards employees for each new class of jobs they are capable of performing. We will discuss skill-based pay (or pay-for-knowledge) more in Chapter 9.

Developmental assignments, particularly those involving teamwork, can also be a valuable way of facilitating knowledge exchange and mutual learning. Effective communication (whether face to face or through information technology) is instrumental in sharing knowledge and making it widely available throughout the organization. As Dave Ulrich, professor of business at the University of Michigan, noted: "Learning capability is *g* times *g*—a business's ability to *generate* new ideas multiplied by its adeptness at *generalizing* them throughout the company."[22]

HR programs and assignments are often the conduit through which knowledge is transferred among employees. A recent survey by the Human Resource Planning Society revealed that 65 percent of responding companies believed that their HR group plays a key role in developing human capital. Boeing Satellite Systems, for example, has created a "lessons learned" site on its intranet where all areas of the company can store the knowledge they have learned. As information and intellectual capital are posted to the company's electronic newsgroups, they can be analyzed and consolidated by editorial teams. Employees can access and use this new codified knowledge directly from the Internet. Executives at Boeing estimate that this form of intellectual capital has reduced the cost of developing a satellite by as much as $25 million.[23]

HR managers and line managers each play an important role in creating an organization that understands the value of knowledge, documents the skills and capabilities available to the organization, and identifies ways of utilizing that knowledge to benefit the firm. We will address these issues throughout the text, but particularly in Chapters 5 and 7 on career development and training.

Challenge 5: Responding to the Market

objective **6**

Meeting customer expectations is essential for any organization. In addition to focusing on internal management issues, managers must also meet customer requirements of quality, innovation, variety, and responsiveness. These standards often separate the winners from the losers in today's competitive world. How well does a company understand its customers' needs? How fast can it develop and get a new product to market? How effectively has it responded to special concerns? "Better, faster, cheaper"—these standards require organizations to constantly align their processes with customer needs. Management innovations such as total quality management (TQM) and process reengineering are but two of the comprehensive approaches to responding to customers. Each has direct implications for HR.

Total Quality Management, Six Sigma, and HRM

total quality management (TQM)
A set of principles and practices whose core ideas include understanding customer needs, doing things right the first time, and striving for continuous improvement

Total quality management (TQM) is a set of principles and practices whose core ideas include understanding customer needs, doing things right the first time, and striving for continuous improvement. Total quality management techniques were developed in the mid-1940s by Dr. W. Edwards Deming after studying Japanese companies rebuilding following World War II. The TQM revolution began in the mid-1980s, led by companies such as Motorola, Xerox, and Ford. But since that time, criteria spelled out in the Malcolm Baldrige National Quality Award have provided the impetus for both large and small companies to rethink their approach to HRM. Currently, the Baldrige Award is given annually in each of five categories: manufacturing, service, small business, education, and healthcare.[24]

Unfortunately, early TQM programs were no panacea for responding to customer needs and improving productivity. In many cases, managers viewed quality as a quick fix and became disillusioned when results did not come easily. When TQM initiatives do work, it is usually because managers have made major changes in their philosophies and HR programs. More recently, companies such as Maple Leaf Foods, Honda of Canada Manufacturing, and Home Depot have adopted a more systematic approach to quality, called **Six Sigma,** which includes major changes in management philosophy and HR programs. Six Sigma is a statistical method of translating a customer's needs into separate tasks and defining the best way to perform each task in concert with the others. By examining the optimal process, Six Sigma can have a powerful effect on the quality of products, the performance of customer service, and the professional development of employees. What makes Six Sigma different from other quality efforts is that it catches mistakes before they happen. In a true Six Sigma environment, variation from standard is reduced to only 3.4 defects per million.[25]

Six Sigma
A process used to translate customer needs into a set of optimal tasks that are performed in concert with one another

The importance of HR to Six Sigma begins with the formation of teams, and extends to training, performance management, communication, culture, and even rewards. As individuals progress through Six Sigma training, they can move up from "green belt" to eventually achieve "black belt" status. Many of Dow's key HR slots require black-belt certification, for example. If this all sounds a bit hokey, take note of the successful companies that have made cultural—and performance—transformation as a result: Motorola credits Six Sigma with $16 billion in savings over the past 12 years; Ford reports that it saved more than $4 billion in one year alone; Motorola is so committed to Six Sigma that it now conducts Six Sigma training for employees of other firms who attend its Motorola University.[26] The most important quality-improvement techniques stress employee motivation, change in corporate culture, and employee education. Organizations known for product and service quality strongly believe that employees are the key to that quality, as illustrated in the Reality Check on page 16 for Goodyear Canada in Medicine Hat, Alberta.

One of the reasons that HR programs are so essential to programs such as Six Sigma is that they help balance two opposing forces. According to Laurie Broedling, an organizational psychologist and human resources expert, "One set of forces (the need for order and control) pulls every business toward stagnation, while another set of forces (the need for growth and creativity) drives it toward disintegration." Six Sigma's focus on continuous improvement drives the system toward disequilibrium, while Six Sigma's focus on customers, management systems, and the like provides the restraining forces that keep the system together. HR practices help managers balance these two forces. Like human resources information systems, TQM has helped HR departments progress

Many Canadian companies use business process reengineering to improve productivity at their plants.

Reality Check

Six Sigma

Nine months after conducting a pilot class for Six Sigma Black Belts in October 2002, Goodyear Canada is in the midst of a major business transformation. Already there are 19 Black Belts (full-time project leaders) and seven Green Belts (part-time project leaders) working in offices, warehouses, and the eight Canadian tire and rubber products manufacturing plants. Projects currently under way are projected to yield $10 million in waste reduction, capital equipment purchase avoidance, and increased sales through elimination of production bottlenecks.

Goodyear's tire manufacturing facility in Medicine Hat, Alberta, needed to produce more rubber from its Banbury rubber mixer in order to meet its daily quota and lessen its dependence on rubber produced by outside sources. In buying material, the factory was paying freight charges to get the rubber to the factory. By optimizing the Banbury uptime and increasing the Banbury output, the factory could reduce the amount of rubber it needed to purchase. Using the tools of Six Sigma, the factory determined that it could stagger shift rotations so that an operator was always available to keep the Banbury mixer running. They also were able to increase the batch weight sizes of some of the compounds by 4 percent to 11 percent. In addition, staging batches at the top of the conveyor and reducing the gate delay realized gains of two to three seconds per batch. Although three seconds does not sound like a great amount, over the course of a week, it adds about 150 minutes of productivity. After six months, the factory has increased its Banbury mixer output by more than 5 percent, generating savings of over $110,000. The Medicine Hat plant estimates that it can save $250,000 to $400,000 annually by implementing the new procedures.

Gary Blake, Goodyear Canada Six Sigma champion, and a Black Belt, says that it is a problem-solving model that applies rigorous statistical thinking to reduce defects, improve cycle time, and increase customer satisfaction. The methodology is being applied not only to traditional manufacturing processes, but also to transactional processes—supply chain, purchasing, invoicing, sales, and marketing. A Six Sigma team follows five major steps known as DMAIC to clearly Define the scope of the project, Measure customer requirements and process outputs, Analyze the current situation and set clear goals, Improve the process through planned experimentation, and finally Control to validate and lock in the improvement—then sustaining it so that there is no backslide. The model moves the organization to whatever goals are required by the customer. Six Sigma derives its name from the Greek letter *sigma*, which is sometimes used to denote variation from a standard, and the statistical concept that if you measure the defects in a process, you can figure out how to get rid of them and get ever closer to perfection. A Six Sigma company cannot produce more than 3.4 defects per million opportunities. For a process with only one specification limit, this results in six process standard deviations between the mean of the process and the customer's specification limit.

from a focus on functional activities to strategic planning. Better business thinking builds more strategic HR thinking.[27]

Reengineering and HRM

reengineering
Fundamental rethinking and radical redesign of business processes to achieve dramatic improvements in cost, quality, service, and speed

In addition to TQM and Six Sigma programs, some companies take a more radical approach to process redesign called reengineering. **Reengineering** has been described as "the fundamental rethinking and radical redesign of business processes to achieve dramatic improvements in cost, quality, service and speed."[28] Reengineering often requires that managers start over from scratch in rethinking how work should be done, how technology and people should interact, and how entire organizations should be structured. HR issues are central to these decisions. First, reengineering requires that managers create an environment for change, and, as we mentioned previously, HR issues drive change. Second, reengineering efforts depend on effective leadership and communication processes, two other areas related to HRM. Third, reengineering requires that administrative systems be reviewed and modified. Selection, job descriptions, training, career planning, performance appraisal, compensation, and labour relations are all candidates for change to complement and support reengineering efforts. We will return to these issues, and speak more directly to the organizational development tools necessary for reengineering, in later chapters.

Challenge 6: Containing Costs

Investments in reengineering, TQM, human capital, technology, globalization, and the like are all very important for organizational competitiveness. Yet at the same time, there are increasing pressures on companies to lower costs and improve productivity to maximize efficiency. Like other functional department managers, human resources managers are now under pressure to show top managers the "bottom line" financial results their departments are achieving. Labour costs are one of the largest expenditures of any organization, particularly in service- and knowledge-intensive companies. Organizations are taking many approaches to lowering labour-related costs. Firms are also downsizing, outsourcing, offshoring, and engaging in employee leasing in an attempt to enhance productivity. Each of these efforts has a big impact on HR policies and practices.

Downsizing

downsizing
Planned elimination of jobs

Downsizing is the planned elimination of jobs. For example, when L. L. Bean saw that sales had fallen, the company undertook a number of efforts to identify what it called "smart cost reductions." Bean's TQM activities helped the company target quality problems and saved an estimated $30 million. But the cuts were not enough, and ultimately Leon Gorman, president of the firm, and Bob Peixotto, vice-president of HR and quality, realized the company needed to eliminate some jobs. Instead of simply laying off people, however, the company started early retirement and "sweetened" voluntary separation programs. Then the company offered employee sabbaticals for continuing education.[29]

The pain of downsizing has been widespread throughout Canada. Virtually every major corporation within the country has undergone some cycle of downsizing. Around 40 percent of organizations are permanently reducing their workforces, with cuts as much as 15 percent. Of these reductions, about one-third was accomplished through attrition, about one-quarter through voluntary severance or early retirement, and the rest by layoffs.[30] Historically, layoffs tended to affect manufacturing firms and line workers in particular, but in the 1990s the layoffs began to encompass white-collar workers in greater numbers. One of the hardest-hit industries has been information technology.[31]

But downsizing is no longer being regarded as a short-term fix when times are tough. It's now become a tool continually used by companies to adjust to changes in technology, globalization, and the firm's business direction. For example, in a study that surveyed 450 senior HR executives at companies that had downsized in the past three years, only 21 percent said that financial difficulties had spurred the cutbacks, compared to 78 percent in a similar study in 1994. In fact, 34 percent of the executives said that the downsizing was done to strengthen their companies' future positions; 21 percent said it was done to achieve fundamental staff realignment; 17 percent said it was due to a merger or acquisition.

Whatever the reason, while some firms improve efficiency (and lower costs) with layoffs, many others do not obtain such benefits. These kinds of trade-offs have led some firms to establish a policy of "no layoffs." For example, in an industry that has seen layoffs in the tens of thousands, Southwest Airlines hasn't laid off a single employee. In fact, the company hasn't had layoffs in 30 years. These practices are admittedly an exception, but some firms are taking such an approach because of downsizing's toll on retention and recruitment. A study by Watson Wyatt of 750 companies showed that companies with excellent recruiting and retention policies provide a nearly 8-percent higher return to shareholders compared to those that don't. Those with a strong commitment to job security earned an additional 1.4 percent for shareholders.

Advocates of a no-layoff policy often note that layoffs may backfire after taking into account such hidden costs as the following:

- Severance and rehiring costs
- Accrued vacation and sick-day payouts
- Pension and benefit payoffs
- Potential lawsuits from aggrieved workers
- Loss of institutional memory and trust in management
- Lack of staffers when the economy rebounds
- Survivors who are risk averse, paranoid, and political

In contrast, companies that avoid downsizing say they get some important benefits from such policies:

- A fiercely loyal, more productive workforce
- Higher customer satisfaction
- Readiness to snap back with the economy
- A recruiting edge
- Workers who aren't afraid to innovate, knowing their jobs are safe[32]

More than one executive has concluded that you don't get dedicated and productive employees if at the first sign of trouble you show them that you think they are expendable.

To approach downsizing more intelligently, companies have made special efforts to reassign and retrain employees for new positions when their jobs are eliminated. This is consistent with a philosophy of employees as assets, as intellectual capital.

Outsourcing, Offshoring, and Employee Leasing

Over the past 25 years, the employment relationship between companies and employees has shifted from relationship-based to transaction-based. Fewer people are working for one employer over the course of their lifetimes, and the Internet has created a workforce that is constantly scanning for new opportunities. More people are choosing to work on a freelance or contract basis, or to work part-time, especially women. Outsourcing is evidence of this trend.[33] **Outsourcing** simply means hiring someone outside the company to perform tasks that could be done internally. Companies often hire the services of accounting firms, for example, to take care of financial services. They may hire advertising firms to handle promotions, software firms to develop data-processing systems, or law firms to handle legal issues. Maintenance, security, catering, and payroll are being outsourced in order to increase the organization's flexibility and lower its overhead costs. Interest in outsourcing has been spurred by executives who want to focus their organization's activities on what they do best versus peripheral activities. Increasingly, outsourcing is changing the way HR departments operate as well. Indeed, outsourcing has been one of the most prominent HR trends of the last ten years, and will continue to be until the last dollar of excess costs has been wrung out. Telus Sourcing Solutions, a Vancouver-based communications giant, has made deals with the Calgary Board of Education, the Calgary Health Region, and the Government of British Columbia to manage some HR functions such as payroll.[34]

outsourcing
Contracting outside the organization to have work done that formerly was done by internal employees

Offshoring, also referred to as "global sourcing," is the controversial practice of moving jobs overseas. Nonetheless, almost half of 500 senior finance and HR leaders surveyed said their firms are either offshoring or are considering offshoring in the next three years, according to a study by Hewitt Associates.[35] Cost reduction is the overwhelming motivator for doing so—companies estimate that they can save 40–60 percent on labour costs by offshoring work to countries such as India, where highly educated workers can perform the same jobs as Canadian workers at half the price. For example, a scripted call centre worker earns about US$2 an hour, while the same worker in Canada earns about $15. A New Delhi chartered accountant earns about US$15,000 per year, while a chartered accountant in Canada would earn about five times that figure. Other markets include the Philippines, Russia, China, Mexico, Brazil, and Hungary. Tiger Brand Knitting Co., which has been operating for more than a century in Cambridge, Ontario, moved 175 jobs to China. But hidden costs can chew up most, if not all, of the profits gained from offshoring, including those associated with finding foreign vendors, productivity lost during the transition, domestic layoff costs, language difficulties, foreign regulatory challenges, and political and economic instability that can threaten operations.

offshoring
The business practice of sending jobs to other countries

In Chapter 2, you will learn about the other ways firms can get a competitive edge besides just cutting labour costs. But offshoring is going to continue to be a fact of life as the global economy shifts and the lure of low labour costs continues to entice corporations. Too often, however, the decision to offshore is made by top managers and finance, without HR's initial input: "Companies can minimize hidden costs and maximize their returns by enabling HR to have a seat at the table early so they can carefully address issues such as skill and language requirements, labour costs by market, alternative talent pools, workforce training, retraining and change management," says Mark Arian, a corporate restructuring and change practice leader for Hewitt. To minimize problems, line and HR managers have to work together with the firm's other functional groups to define and communicate transition plans, minimize the number of unknowns, and help employees identify their employment options.[36]

As an alternative to downsizing, outsourcing, and offshoring, many companies, especially small ones, have decided to sign **employee leasing** agreements with professional employer organizations (PEOs). A PEO—typically a larger company—takes over the management of a smaller company's HR tasks and becomes a co-employer to its employees. The PEO performs all the HR duties of an employer—hiring, payroll, and performance appraisal. Because PEOs can co-employ a large number of people

employee leasing
The process of dismissing employees who are then hired by a leasing company (which handles all HR-related activities) and contracting with that company to lease back the employees

working at many different companies, they can provide employees with benefits such as health plans that small companies can't afford. The value of employee leasing lies in the fact that an organization can essentially maintain its working relationships with its employees but shift some employment costs to the PEO, in return for a fee. Full-service PEOs sell an even broader range of services, including high-end benefits such as adoption assistance, usually found only at the largest corporations. More details on employee leasing will be discussed in Chapter 5.[37]

Productivity Enhancements

Pure cost-cutting efforts such as downsizing, outsourcing, and leasing may prove to be disappointing interventions if managers use them as simple solutions to complex performance problems. Overemphasis on labour costs perhaps misses the broader issue of productivity enhancement.

Employee productivity is the result of a combination of employees' abilities, motivation, and work environment, and the technology they have to work with. Since productivity can be defined as "the output gained from a fixed amount of inputs," organizations can increase productivity either by reducing the inputs (the cost approach) or by increasing the amount that employees produce, by adding more human and/or physical capital to the process. Nonetheless, it is quite possible for managers to cut costs only to find that productivity falls even more rapidly. Conversely, managers may find that increasing investment in employees (raising labour costs) may lead to even greater returns in enhanced productivity.

In absolute terms, Canada lags most western nations including the United States, which remains the world's most productive nation. That said, the growth in output per worker is now climbing faster in less-developed countries such as China and India that have lacked expertise and technology in the past but are making strides to close the gap. However, even in the wake of the last recession, new investments in technology kept the productivity of workers climbing upward. The problem is that this rapid investment in faster computers and more-efficient machine tools is beginning to level off. This will limit how much assistance technology can offer employees in terms of their productivity in the years to come. And employees are already working more hours than they have at any time since 1973. This means that any additional productivity will have to come from the enhanced ability of employees, their motivation, and their work environment—which makes the job of the HR manager in the coming years all the more crucial.[38] Figure 1.3 shows some of the topics that we cover in this textbook that help managers increase productivity in their organizations.

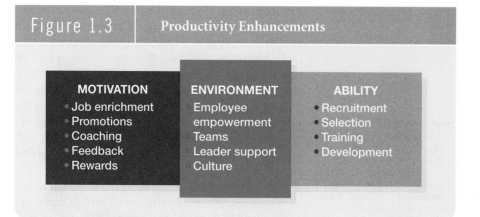

Figure 1.3   Productivity Enhancements

MOTIVATION
- Job enrichment
- Promotions
- Coaching
- Feedback
- Rewards

ENVIRONMENT
- Employee empowerment
- Teams
- Leader support
- Culture

ABILITY
- Recruitment
- Selection
- Training
- Development

Demographic and Employee Concerns

objective

8 ▷

In addition to the competitive challenges facing organizations, managers in general—and HR managers in particular—need to be concerned about changes in the makeup and the expectations of their employees. As we noted at the beginning of this chapter, HRM involves being an advocate for employees, being aware of their concerns, and making sure that the exchange between the organization and its employees is *mutually* beneficial. Highlights in HRM 1.3 shows a summary of social concerns in HRM. We will discuss some of these issues here and address all of them in greater detail throughout the book.

Highlights in HRM 1.3

Social Issues in HRM

Changing Demographics: The coming decades will bring a more diverse and aging workforce. This has major implications for all aspects of HRM as it alters traditional experience and expectations regarding the labour pool. Among the issues in this area are:

- Shrinking pool of skilled entry-level workers
- Globalization
- Diversity strategies
- Retirement issues
- Continual skills development
- Outsourcing, offshoring, and the use of temporary and part-time employees

Employer/Employee Rights: This area reflects the shift toward organizations and individuals attempting to define rights, obligations, and responsibilities. Among the issues here are:

- Relationship employment versus transactional-based employment
- Equal pay for work of equal value
- Concern for privacy
- Ethics
- Legal compliance
- Whistle-blowing
- Mandated benefits

Attitudes toward Work and Family: Because of the increase of working women as well as employee mobility and a growing concern about family issues, there is demand for recognizing and supporting family-related concerns. Among the issues are:

- Day care and elder care
- Flextime
- Job sharing
- Alternative work schedules
- Job rotation
- Telecommuting
- Parental leave

Because the Canadian population is becoming more diverse, companies that don't hire minorities reflecting the change are likely to find themselves at a competitive disadvantage.

Demographic Changes

Among the most significant challenges to managers are the demographic changes occurring in Canada. Because they affect the workforce of an employer, these changes—in employee background, age, gender, and education—are important topics for discussion.

The Diversity Challenge

Canada has always been a country of immigrants, with the exception of the Aboriginals. The majority of Canadians are immigrants or descendants of early generations of immigrants. Between 1991 and 2001, nearly 1.5 million immigrants arrived in Canada. Immigrants account for up to 70 percent of labour force growth. Prior to 1960, most immigrants came from Europe. Since 1988, the largest proportion of immigrants have come from Asia. Roughly one in every five Canadians will be a visible minority by 2017, when Canada celebrates its 150th anniversary.[39] In cities such as Toronto and Vancouver, minorities represent nearly half the population.

To accommodate the shift in demographics, many organizations have increased their efforts to recruit and train a more diverse workforce. RBC Financial Group is a leader in the recruitment and integration of visible minorities. Their CEO, Gordon Nixon, chairs the Diversity Leadership Council, which is made up of senior leaders from across their businesses. The Council sets goals of diversity and employment equity to ensure that the talent pipeline is filled with qualified candidates from diverse groups.[40]

Age Distribution of Employees

In Canada, nearly 18 million people (or about two-thirds of the population) are part of the labour force, which can be defined as those over 15 years of age who are employed or looking for work. Of these, about one-fifth are between 15 and 30 and one-third are over 45 years of age. By 2015, 48 percent of the workforce will be aged 45–64.[41] Imbalance in the age distribution of the labour force has significant implications for employers. Companies such as Hydro Quebec are finding that large portions of their workforces are nearing retirement. Beyond the sheer number of employees they will have to replace, managers are concerned that the expertise of these employees is likely to be drained too rapidly from the company. However, older workers now are choosing to work longer, reversing several decades of declining participation, as described in Highlights in HRM 1.4. Good health and longer life expectancies play the biggest role in extended work lives. But some retirees have returned to the workforce because of economic needs.

Home Depot is one company that is making an effort to attract older workers. Bob Nardelli, Home Depot's CEO, said he intends to hire older employees in direct proportion to their increase as a share of the population.

The other problem that accompanies age imbalances in the workforce might be referred to as the "echo boom" effect. The echo boom or Generation Y (those born in the 1980s and 1990s) account for 19 percent of Canada's workforce and are highly educated, techno-savvy, team oriented, and adaptable. Similar to the trends with baby boomers, those who constitute the new population bulge are experiencing greater competition for advancement from others of approximately the same age. This situation challenges the ingenuity of managers to develop career patterns for employees to

Highlights in HRM 1.4

Old, But Not Out

The number of Canadians 55 and older is about 27 percent of the workforce, compared to 29 percent under 35, and 44 percent between 35 and 55. The average age of retirement is declining, from 65 in the early 1970s to about 61 in 2003. Those who are laid off just before retirement are often unable to find work again. Most of these workers are concentrated in traditional sectors, such as manufacturing, which have seen no growth. The combination of low literacy and education rates, coupled with high salary expectations and their unwillingness to move to where the jobs are located, makes this group fairly unemployable.

However, after 2010, older workers will have higher education levels, more training, and more transferable skills, all of which will make them more employable. Many older workers want to continue to work after they retire, mostly because they enjoy work. Indeed the labour force participation rate of those 55–69 years of age rose to a record 47 percent. Their ability to learn and adapt to new technologies does not differ from that of younger workers. However, they do want flexible arrangements such as reduced hours, special assignments, temporary work, job sharing, telecommuting, and consulting work.

As employers face labour shortages in specific occupations such as health care workers, there will be more attempts to provide innovative HR programs to retain older workers. For example, the average age of retirement for a registered nurse is 57, so in an attempt to retain these experienced nurses, the Province of New Brunswick is introducing a phased-in retirement program. Nurses can reduce their work hours by about 50 percent and access their pension plans to supplement their incomes. The Older Worker Pilot Project of Human Resources and Social Development Canada seeks to test innovative approaches to help older workers remain employed. This collaborative project between the federal government and the provinces and territories attempts to reintegrate displaced older workers into the labour market. A survey by CARP (Canada's Association for the Fifty Plus) found that the most important HR practices to retain older workers are to show appreciation and respect, while recognizing the older workers' skills and experiences.

Sources: Adapted from Susan Singh, "Globalization Puts Focus on HR," *Canadian HR Reporter*, 18, 11 page 1, 2005; P. Cross, "Recent Changes in the Labour Market," *Canadian Economic Observer,* Statistics Canada 11-010, March 2005; Jennifer Thomas and Marianne Chilco, "Coming of Age," *Benefits Canada,* 25, no. 3, March 2001: 36–38; Nicole Wassink, "Your Workforce Is Ageing. . .Are You Ready?" The Conference Board of Canada, May 2001; "Retention Strategies for Older Nurses Could Ease Shortages," *Canadian HR Reporter*, August 1, 2003, 1.

smooth out gaps in the numbers and kinds of workers.[42] Managers will have to develop procedures to ensure that work groups composed of different age groups learn to work together, as illustrated in Highlights in HRM 1.5 on page 24.

Gender Distribution of the Workforce

Women represent 50.8 percent of Canada's population, and the percentage of women in the labour force is 46.69 percent. Educational attainment of women is increasing relative to men. More women than men complete high school and the majority of

Highlights in HRM 1.5

Intergenerational Issues

When Jason Traynor was a junior human resources administrator at Peregrine Incorporated, he faced serious challenges with a workforce of different ages. The reason for many of the issues was that General Motors had recently sold off the fabrication plant as part of their new business strategy to get out of auto parts manufacturing and focus solely on assembling vehicles. With the sale of the plant came the condition that any GM employee would be allowed to return to the main GM autoplex as positions came open through employee attrition. Once a GM employee left, he had to be replaced. More times than not, GM would "call out" (recruit) 30 to 40 employees with only two or three days' notice to Peregrine. With no pool of candidates available to them Peregrine had to react quickly as not to disrupt production at General Motors.

Due to time constraints, prescreening was minimal. There were often no interviews, reference checks, or selection instruments. On several occasions, people would be selected on Friday night for a Monday morning start. The majority of the new hires were young and right out of high school. These new employees, with limited post secondary education and little, if any, factory experience were earning $28 an hour, plus benefits, which equalled approximately $85,000 per year. The job was so lucrative that many opted out of pursuing further education. The biggest challenge came when the 18 to 19-year-olds were thrown into a working environment of pre-retirement 60-year-old factory workers. There was conflict and complaints about everything from the type of music choice on the shop floor to clothing tastes and inappropriate sexual comments.

One of the greatest challenges began when the senior employees began interacting with the junior employees and the new employees would attempt to "use" the system in the same way that a 25-year employee did. The junior employees learned very quickly how to manipulate the collective agreement to their advantage. Activities such as punch card fraud, not badging in or out, and leaving the facility unauthorized while still on the clock were quickly becoming the norm. According to Jason Traynor, "This is not the kind of behaviour you want in your new hires." Having new employees acting as though they had put in 20 years of service often created conflict between the two generations as many of the senior employees felt that these "kids" had not paid their dues and were simply riding the coattails of the senior membership. Addiction problems were rampant among the new employees—many having never been exposed to the readily available supply of drugs and alcohol. Linked to this were the increasing levels of casual absenteeism. Many new hires were terminated and a great deal of time and energy was spent with the union who fought to reinstate these employees.

An independent third party consulting company was asked to help manage these issues. Self-directed workshops were initiated to teach the workers about teamwork and quality. Employee assistance programs were created to help struggling employees. A labour council was started to deal with conflict on the factory floor. The company adopted aptitude testing and joint interviewing with the union in an attempt to select employees that were more qualified.

In the end, Peregrine eventually failed and went out of business.

university students are now women. Employers who want to attract the talent that women have to offer are taking measures to ensure that women are treated equally in the workplace in terms of advancement opportunities and compensation. They also need to accommodate working parents through parental leaves, part-time employment, flexible work schedules, job sharing, telecommuting, and child and elder care assistance.

Rising Levels of Education

Over the years, the educational attainment of the Canadian labour force has risen. School attendance rates for those aged 15–25 have risen to 73 percent in 2001 (from 41 percent 20 years earlier). Not coincidentally, some of the fastest-growing sectors of employment over the past few decades have been in areas requiring higher levels of education.[43] Figure 1.4 shows the average payoff in annual earnings from education. Experts estimate that the value of a college or university degree is $1 million over the course of a career, according to the Association of Universities and Colleges of Canada. The unemployment rates of those with only high school education average 12–20 percent higher than degree holders of the same age.[44] It is important to note, however, that while the complexity of jobs is increasing significantly, the skills gap is huge and widening. More than 3 million Canadians (aged 16–65) have problems dealing with printed material. The BHP Ekati Diamond Mine in the Northwest Territories realized that a large number of candidates had not completed high school, and so the company hired educators to deliver training in basic maths and literacy, using actual workplace

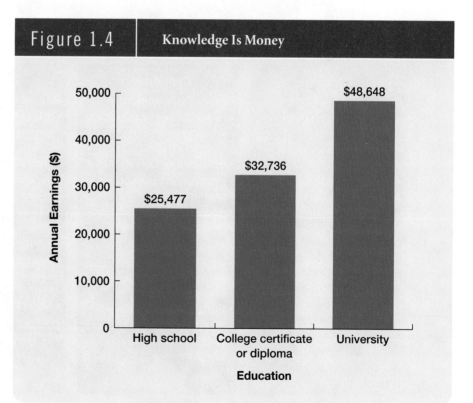

Figure 1.4 | **Knowledge Is Money**

Source: "Knowledge is Money" is adapted from Statistics Canada website, "Average Earnings of Population 15 Years and Over by Highest Level of Schooling by Province and Territory," (2001 Census), http://www.40.statcan.ca/101cst01/labor50a.htm; Last modified 2004-09-01.

documents and manuals as teaching tools. Many employers are using a tool, The Test of Workplace Essential Skills (TOWES), developed at the Bow Valley College in Calgary, Alberta, to assess employee competence in three essential skills: reading text, document use, and numeracy. The test results provide managers with information about the gaps in existing skills sets in employees; managers can then turn to educators or institutions for remedial training. As a result, businesses now spend millions of dollars on basic skills training for their employees.[45]

And it's not just workers with four-year degrees that are in great demand. Companies are having trouble finding trained and certified workers such as pipe fitters, motorcycle mechanics, and air traffic controllers. As the baby boomer generation retires, the problem will likely worsen. HR departments will have to offer higher compensation packages to attract qualified candidates, and recruiting and selection systems will have to function much more competitively in order to identify talent.

Figure 1.5 Model of Diversity Management

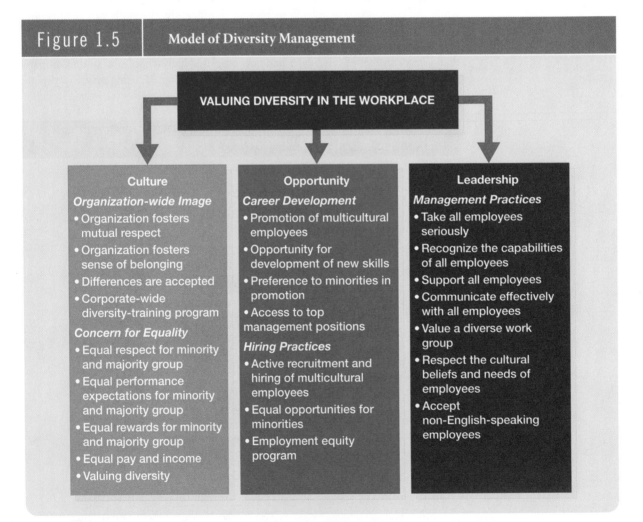

Source: Reprinted by permission of Sage Publications from "Managing for Effective Workforce Diversity" by Kathleen Iverson from *The Cornell Hotel and Restaurant Administration Quarterly* 41, no. 2 (April 2000): 31–38.

HR managers are interested in these trends because the economy and job market are critical to HR's operations. For example, given that minorities and women have increased their share of the labour force, HR managers frequently analyze how each group is represented in both fast-growing and slow-growing occupations. Women, for example, are fairly well represented in fast-growing occupations such as health services but are also represented in some slow-growth occupations such as secretarial, computer processing, and financial records processing.

But these are only the initial efforts to provide an overall environment that values and utilizes a diverse workforce. **Managing diversity** means being acutely aware of characteristics common to employees, while also managing these employees as individuals. It means not just tolerating or accommodating all sorts of differences but supporting, nurturing, and utilizing these differences to the organization's advantage.[46] Figure 1.5 summarizes a model for developing a diversity strategy in organizations. While there are important social reasons for including a broader spectrum of workers, there are some essential business reasons as well. Highlights in HRM 1.6 shows the primary business reasons for diversity management.

managing diversity
Being aware of characteristics common to employees, while also managing employees as individuals

Cultural Changes

The attitudes, beliefs, values, and customs of people in a society are an integral part of their culture. Naturally, their culture affects their behaviour on the job and the environment within the organization, influencing their reactions to work assignments, leadership styles, and reward systems. Like the external and internal environments of which it is a part, culture is undergoing continual change. HR policies and procedures therefore must be adjusted to cope with this change.

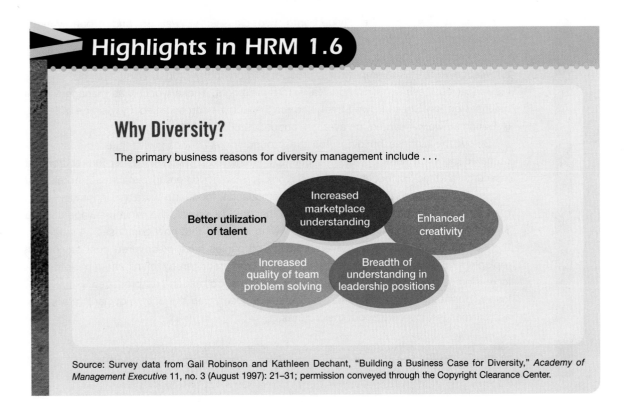

Highlights in HRM 1.6

Why Diversity?

The primary business reasons for diversity management include . . .

- Better utilization of talent
- Increased marketplace understanding
- Enhanced creativity
- Increased quality of team problem solving
- Breadth of understanding in leadership positions

Source: Survey data from Gail Robinson and Kathleen Dechant, "Building a Business Case for Diversity," *Academy of Management Executive* 11, no. 3 (August 1997): 21–31; permission conveyed through the Copyright Clearance Center.

The Changing Nature of the Job

The era of the full-time permanent job seems to have disappeared. The number of self-employed is also increasing, accounting for 18 percent of employment and 75 percent of new job growth in the 1990s. Nearly half of all the jobs created in the last two decades have been nonstandard—that is, part-time, temporary, or contract work. As job security erodes, so do pension plans and health care benefits, especially for part-timers. Nonstandard jobs represent about 30 percent of all employment now. As shown in Ethics in HRM, labour force participants have become increasingly polarized into haves and have-nots. We return to the subject of changing employment options in Chapter 4.[47]

Employee Rights

Over the past few decades, federal legislation has radically changed the rules for management of employees by granting them many specific rights. Among these are laws granting the right to equal employment opportunity (Chapter 3), union representation if desired (Chapter 14), a safe and healthful work environment (Chapter 12), pension plans regulated by the government (Chapter 11), equal pay for men and women performing essentially the same job (Chapter 9), and privacy in the workplace.

Ethics in HRM

Skywalkers and Groundworkers

Canadian workers can be divided into two classes: skywalkers and groundworkers. Skywalkers, those working in white-collar jobs in highrise buildings, are well educated and well trained and earn good incomes. Their jobs are secure and they receive full benefits. For these knowledge workers, the employment prospects in computer programming, financial analysis, insurance, business services, and real estate are bright. Those working as managers in the highrises on Bay Street, Howe Street, and rue St-Jacques earned an hourly average of $30.70. (A Canadian worker earned, on average, about $19.66 in 2006.)

Below the highrise buildings toil the groundworkers. Those with little education and outdated skills are suffering massive unemployment. Groundworkers suffer further from job insecurity and lack of benefit programs. Look for these workers in restaurants, hotels, and shops. The "McJobs" they hold in the accommodation, food, and beverage industries paid a mere $12 per hour, and many earned far less than this, being paid the minimum wage of about $7 an hour. Those working part-time—a growing segment that now comprises 34 percent of the Canadian workforce—fare even worse. Companies have discovered cost savings by replacing full-time employees with part-time workers, thereby eliminating benefits and increasing staffing flexibility. This restructuring of the job market has produced winners and losers, but many would argue that all Canadians lose when the unemployment rate is high and citizens feel insecure about their futures.

Sources: Heather Scoffiled, "Hold the McJobs: Canada's High End Employment Boom," *The Globe and Mail*, February 17, 2006, B1 and B4; Statistics Canada, *Statistics Canada Measures of Weekly Earnings*, Cat. No. 72-0002-XPB, 1997, 2002.

An expanded discussion of the specific areas in which rights and responsibilities are of concern to employers and employees will be presented in Chapter 13.

Concern for Privacy

HR managers and their staffs, as well as line managers in positions of responsibility, generally recognize the importance of discretion in handling all types of information about employees. The Personal Information Protection and Electronic Documents Act (PIPEDA) is a federal law that deals with the collection, use, and disclosure of personal information (note that Quebec is the only province with similar laws, although Ontario, British Columbia, and others have draft legislation in place). This law requires federally regulated organizations holding personal information on customers or employees to obtain their consent before it uses, collects, or discloses this information. Employer responses to the issue of information privacy vary widely. IBM was one of the first companies to show concern for how personal information about employees was handled. It began restricting the release of information as early as 1965 and in 1971 developed a comprehensive privacy policy. The Royal Bank, the Hudson's Bay Company, and Zero Knowledge Systems in Montreal are among other employers that have developed privacy programs.[48] We will discuss the content of such programs and present some recommended privacy guidelines in Chapter 13. Globalization has added another twist to privacy compliance. For example, EU countries prohibit the transfer of personal data to countries with inadequate data protection laws, such as China. In Chapter 13, we will discuss the content of privacy programs, along with the privacy employees can expect while on the job, and present some recommended privacy guidelines.

USING THE INTERNET

The Canadian Policy Research Network is a great site for information on workplace trends and job issues:

www.jobquality.ca

Changing Attitudes toward Work

Employees today are less likely to define their personal success only in terms of financial gains. Personal fulfillment and self-expression—as well as a balance between work and family—are key factors in a complex array of job attitudes. Many people view life satisfaction as more likely to result from balancing the challenges and rewards of work with those in their personal lives. Though most people still enjoy work, and want to excel at it, they tend to be focused on finding interesting work and may pursue multiple careers rather than being satisfied with just "having a job." In fact, in a survey of more than 1000 Canadians, career success was defined as achieving work–life balance by 30 percent. People also appear to be seeking ways of living that are less complicated but more meaningful. These new lifestyles cannot help having an impact on the way employees must be motivated and managed. Consequently, HRM has become more complex than it was when employees were concerned primarily with economic survival. Research conducted by the Canadian Policy Research Network outlines the types of job attributes desired by employees, as shown in Figure 1.6 on page 30. What matters most to Canadians is the soft stuff—relationships with others and the intrinsic aspects of a job.

Balancing Work and Family

Work and the family are connected in many subtle and not-so-subtle social, economic, and psychological ways. Because of the new forms that the family has taken—such as

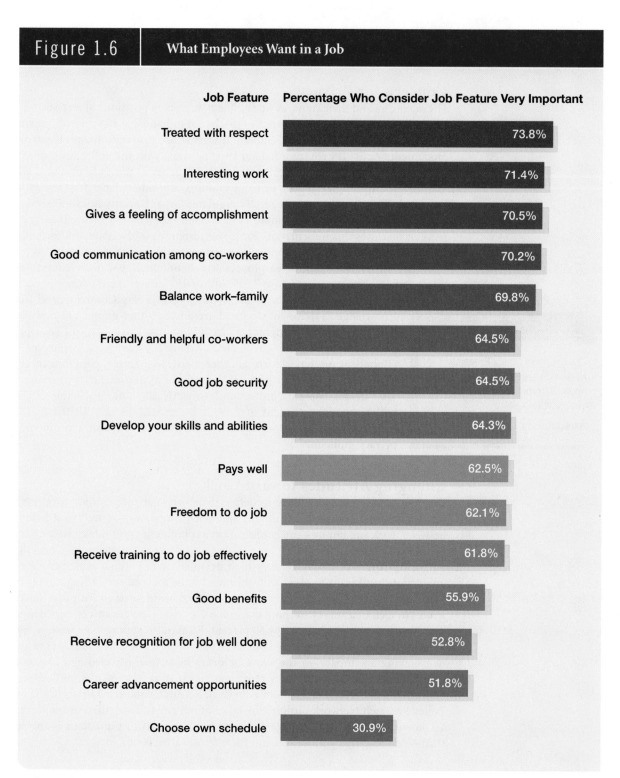

Figure 1.6   **What Employees Want in a Job**

Job Feature   Percentage Who Consider Job Feature Very Important

Job Feature	Percentage
Treated with respect	73.8%
Interesting work	71.4%
Gives a feeling of accomplishment	70.5%
Good communication among co-workers	70.2%
Balance work–family	69.8%
Friendly and helpful co-workers	64.5%
Good job security	64.5%
Develop your skills and abilities	64.3%
Pays well	62.5%
Freedom to do job	62.1%
Receive training to do job effectively	61.8%
Good benefits	55.9%
Receive recognition for job well done	52.8%
Career advancement opportunities	51.8%
Choose own schedule	30.9%

Source: Graham S. Lowe and Grant Schellenberg "Employee Basic Value Proposition: Strong HR Strategies Must Address Work Values." *Canadian HR Reporter* 15, No. 12: 18; www.jobquality.ca. Reprinted with permission.

Parents today face real challenges in balancing work and home life.

the two-wage-earner and the single-parent family—work organizations find it necessary to provide employees with more family-friendly options. "Family friendly" is a broad term that may include unconventional hours, daycare, part-time work, job sharing, pregnancy leave, parental leave, executive transfers, spousal involvement in career planning, assistance with family problems, and telecommuting. Nora Spinks, an expert in work–life harmony, is profiled in Highlights in HRM 1.7. Still, there are acknowledged costs. In professional firms such as law, career paths and promotions are programmed in a lockstep manner. Time away from work can slow down—and in some cases derail—an individual's career advancement.[49]

Furthermore, family-friendly companies have to balance the benefits they provide to families versus their single employees. A majority of employees have no children under 18. A Conference Board survey of companies with family-friendly programs found that companies acknowledge that childless employees harbour resentment against employees with children who are able to take advantage of these programs.[50] However, the demand from employees for balance and the resulting benefits for both employees and employers lead to more employers adopting HR practices to reduce stress from imbalance, as outlined in The Business Case on page 32.

Highlights in HRM 1.7

Work–Life Harmony

Nora Spinks, president and CEO of Work–Life Harmony, a consulting company specializing in work–life balance issues, comments on the demographic issues affecting employee behaviour: "Women are in the workplace to stay; they have fewer and shorter career breaks and have more opportunities to make or influence organizational decisions. There is a high proportion of the aging 'boomer' workforce that are asking, 'What is my legacy?' They are rethinking priorities and lifestyles and reducing the number of hours they are working. At the same time, the nexus generation [i.e., the generation born in the 1980s] is entering the workforce and managerial positions with a fresh perspective and different outlook on the work experience. They see work as a means to having a life, not as life in and of itself. The boomers tend to live to work, the nexus generation work to live. Growing up, they witnessed people give up a life for the sake of a job, only to see them ultimately lose employment in periods of downsizing and restructuring. They don't want the same experience.

"A recent international study of students found that young people about to enter the workforce wanted to have a challenging career with plenty of opportunity to grow personally and professionally, and they wanted to be able to take advantage of those opportunities while achieving work–life balance. It is up to organizations, executives, and managers to create the kinds of environments to make that possible. It is the only way for them to meet increasing customer/client demands, meet the challenges of global competition, and reach their organizational objectives."

The Business Case

Work–Life Balance

Health Canada estimates the annual financial loss from the challenge of employees balancing work and family obligations at $2.7 billion due to lost time relating to stress, medical leaves, dealing with dependants, and other family responsibilities. The Conference Board of Canada reports that nearly half of Canadians surveyed reported stress due to trying to balance their work and home lives. Those with high levels of stress miss an average of 7.2 days of work, compared to a national average of 5.7 days. Employees suffering from imbalance are more likely to be absent and are more likely to quit, or be less productive.

Organizations are addressing the issue by offering flextime (88 percent), providing opportunities for telework (50 percent), and providing family responsibility leave (63 percent). Organizations that have adopted these policies report that the benefits are increased employee commitment, reduced absenteeism, and reduced number of short-term disability claims. Those that offer flexible schedules state that they are better able to meet client needs through increased service coverage.

Sources: "The Business Case for Work–Life Balance," HRSDC, Government of Canada, www.hrsdc.gc.ca, retrieved February 6, 2006; Wendy Creelman and Jane Boyd, "What Do Employees Need and Want," *Canadian HR Reporter*, 13, no. 21, December 4, 2000, G4; K.L. Johnson and J.A Rooney, *Work Life Compendium 2001:150 Canadian Statistics on Work, Family and Well-being*, Centre for Families, Work and Well-being, Guelph Ontario, 2001.

The Partnership of Line Managers and HR Departments

objective **9**

We have taken a good deal of time up front in this book to outline today's competitive and social challenges to reinforce the idea that managing people is not something that occurs in a back room called the HR department. Managing people is every manager's business, and successful organizations combine the experience of line managers with the expertise of HR specialists to develop and utilize the talents of employees to their greatest potential. Addressing HR issues is rarely the exclusive responsibility of HR departments acting alone. Instead, HR managers work side by side with line managers to address people-related issues of the organization. And while this relationship has not always achieved its ideal, the situation is rapidly improving. HR managers are assuming a greater role in top-management planning and decision making, a trend that reflects the growing awareness among executives that HRM can make important contributions to the success of an organization.

Responsibilities of the Human Resources Manager

Although line managers and HR managers need to work together, their responsibilities are different, as are their competencies and expertise. The major activities for which an HR manager is typically responsible are as follows:

1. *Advice and counsel.* The HR manager often serves as an in-house consultant to supervisors, managers, and executives. Given their knowledge of internal employment issues (policies, collective agreements, past practices, ethics and corporate governance, and the needs of employees) as well as their awareness of external trends (economic and employment data, new legal and regulatory issues, and the like), HR managers can be an invaluable resource for making decisions. For example, larger companies have begun appointing "chief ethics officers" to help their employees wade through grey areas when it comes to right and wrong. The firm's top HR manager is in a good position for this job. In smaller companies, however, this task frequently falls on the shoulders of individual HR managers. HR managers are also being relied on more heavily to advise compensation committees, which are more closely scrutinizing executives' pay than they have in years past.

2. *Service.* HR managers also perform a host of service activities such as recruiting, selecting, testing, planning and conducting training programs, and hearing employee concerns and complaints. Technical expertise in these areas is essential for HR managers and forms the basis of HR program design and implementation. Moreover, managers must be convinced that the HR staff is there to help them increase their productivity rather than to impose obstacles to their goals. This requires not only the ability on the part of the HR executive to consider problems from the viewpoint of line managers and supervisors but also skill in communicating with the managers and supervisors.

3. *Policy formulation and implementation.* HR managers generally propose and draft new policies or policy revisions to cover recurring problems or to prevent anticipated problems. Ordinarily, these are proposed to the senior executives of the organization, who actually issue the policies. HR managers may monitor performance of line departments and other staff departments to ensure conformity with established HR policies, procedures, and practices. Perhaps more important, they are a resource to whom managers can turn for policy interpretation.

4. *Employee advocacy.* One of the enduring roles of HR managers is to serve as an employee advocate—listening to employees' concerns and representing their needs to managers. Effective employee relations provide a support structure when disruptive changes interfere with normal daily activities.

Throughout this book we will not only emphasize the importance of the contributions that HRM makes to the organization but also give serious consideration to its effects on the individual and on society.

Increasingly, employees and the public at large are demanding that employers demonstrate greater social responsibility in managing their human resources. Complaints that job stress is devitalizing the lives and injuring the health of employees are not uncommon. Charges of discrimination against women, minorities, the physically and mentally disabled, and the elderly with respect to hiring, training, advancement, and compensation are being levelled against some employers. Issues such as equal pay for work of equal value, daycare for the children of employees, elder care for their parents, and alternative work schedules are concerns that many employers must address as the workforce grows more diverse. All employers are finding that privacy and confidentiality of information about employees are serious matters and deserve the greatest protection that can be provided.

Top management generally recognizes the contributions that the HR program can make to the organization and thus expects HR managers to assume a broader role in the overall organizational strategy. Thus HR managers must remember the bottom line if they are to fulfill their role.

Competencies of the Human Resources Manager

As top executives expect HR managers to assume a broader role in overall organizational strategy, many of these managers will need to acquire a complementary set of competencies.

1. *Business mastery.* HR professionals need to know the business of their organization thoroughly. This requires an understanding of its economic and financial capabilities so that they can "join the team" of business managers in order to develop the firm's strategic direction. It also requires that HR professionals develop skills at external relations focused on their customers.

2. *HR mastery.* HR professionals are the organization's behavioural science experts. In areas such as staffing, development, appraisal, rewards, team building, and communication, HR professionals should develop competencies that keep them abreast of changes.

3. *Change mastery.* HR professionals have to be able to manage change processes so that HR activities are effectively merged with the business needs of the organization. This involves interpersonal and problem-solving skills, as well as innovativeness and creativity.

4. *Personal credibility.* HR professionals must establish personal credibility in the eyes of their internal and external customers. Credibility and trust are earned by developing personal relationships with customers, by demonstrating the values of the firm, by standing up for one's own beliefs, and by being fair-minded in dealing with others. Highlights in HRM 1.8 outlines the code of ethics HR professionals should follow.

The ability to integrate business, HR, and change competencies is essential. By helping their organizations build a sustained competitive advantage and by learning to manage many activities well, HR professionals are becoming full business partners. The competencies required for obtaining the HR professional designation (CHRP—Certified Human Resources Professional) are outlined in Figure 1.7 on page 36. Those working in HR positions who hold a CHRP are compensated at better rates than those without a CHRP. In 2003, about 14 000 people held the CHRP designation. In this field, which has been growing at about 10 percent a year, the employment rate is higher than the national average.[51]

Role of the Line Manager

As much as we might say about the role of the HR department, in the final analysis managing people depends on effective supervisors and line managers. As one executive at Merck put it, "Human resources are far too important to be left to the personnel

USING THE INTERNET

Compensation rates and the job outlook for HR professionals can be found on the HRDC website at:

www.jobfutures.ca

USING THE INTERNET

The Canadian Council of Human Resources Associations' website links to all the provincial HR associations at:

www.cchra-ccrarh.ca

Highlights in HRM 1.8

Code of Ethics for HR Professionals

As Human Resources practitioners and members of the Human Resources Professionals Association of Ontario, including but not limited to the following categories, Certified Human Resources Professionals, CHRP Candidates or CHRP Exam Registrants, we commit to abide by the Code of Ethics of the Canadian Council of Human Resources Associations (CCHRA).

Principles:

1. Competence

HR practitioners must maintain competence in carrying out professional responsibilities and provide services in an honest and diligent manner.

They must ensure that activities engaged in are within the limits of their knowledge, experience and skill. When providing services outside one's level of competence, or the profession, the necessary assistance must be sought so as not to compromise professional responsibility.

2. Legal Requirements

HR practitioners must adhere to any statutory acts, regulations or by-laws which relate to the field of Human Resources Management, as well as all civil and criminal laws, regulations and statutes that apply in their jurisdiction.

They must not knowingly or otherwise engage in or condone any activity or attempt to circumvent the clear intention of the law.

3. Dignity in the Workplace

HR practitioners support, promote and apply the principles of human rights, equity, dignity and respect in the workplace, within the profession and in society as a whole.

4. Balancing Interests

HR practitioners must strive to balance organizational and employee needs and interests in the practice of their profession.

5. Confidentiality

HR practitioners must hold in strict confidence all confidential information acquired in the course of the performance of their duties and not divulge confidential information unless required by law and/or where serious harm is imminent.

6. Conflict of Interest

HR practitioners must either avoid or disclose a potential conflict of interest that might influence or might be perceived to influence personal actions or judgments.

7. Professional Growth and Support of Other Professionals

HR practitioners must maintain personal and professional growth in Human Resources Management by engaging in activities that enhance the credibility and value of the profession.

8. Enforcement

The Canadian Council of Human Resources Associations works collaboratively with its Member Associations to develop and enforce high standards of ethical practice.

Source: Reprinted with the permission of the Canadian Council of Human Resources Associations (CCHRA).

| Figure 1.7 | Human Resource Competency Model |

The Canadian Council of Human Resources Associations (www.cchra-ccarh.ca) has delineated the body of knowledge that a Certified Human Resources Professional (CHRP) in Canada must acquire. The Required Professional Competencies (RPCs) were grouped into the following eight functions:

FUNCTION	EXAMPLE
Professional practice in HR	Understands and adheres to the HR association code of ethics
	Stays current in professional development
Organizational effectiveness	Maintains an inventory of talent for the use of the organization
	Gathers and analyzes employee feedback to assist decision making
Staffing	Identifies potential sources of qualified applicants
	Evaluates recruitment effectiveness
Employee and labour relations	Interprets the collective agreement
	Collects and develops information required for decision making in bargaining
Total compensation	Ensures compliance with legally required programs
	Monitors the competitiveness of the compensation program relative to comparable organizations
Organizational learning and development	Conducts an evaluation of the program
	Monitors, documents, and reports on career development activities
Workplace health and safety	Responds to any refusals to perform work that is considered to be unsafe
	Establishes effective programs for accident prevention, incident investigation, inspections, fire and emergency response, and required training
Human resources information management	Assesses requests for HR information in light of corporate policy, freedom of information legislation, evidentiary privileges, and contractual or other releases
	Contributes to the development of information security measures

All RPCs are listed and described on the CCHRA website—www.cchra-ccrarh.ca, then go to PARC (Professional Assessment Resource Centre). Information about becoming a CHRP is also provided on this site.

department." Although HR managers have the responsibility for coordinating programs and policies pertaining to people-related issues, managers and employees themselves are ultimately responsible for performing these functions.

We understand that most readers of this book will be line managers and supervisors, rather than HR specialists. The text is, therefore, oriented to helping people manage people more effectively, whether they become first-line supervisors or chief executive officers. Students now preparing for careers in organizations will find that the study of HRM provides a background that will be valuable in managerial and supervisory positions. Discussions concerning the role of the HR department can provide a better understanding of the functions performed by this department. A familiarity with the role of HR should help facilitate closer cooperation with the department's staff and fuller utilization of the assistance and services available from this resource.

SUMMARY

 People have always been central to organizations, but their strategic importance is growing in today's knowledge-based industries. An organization's success increasingly depends on the knowledge, skills, and abilities of its employees.

 Globalization influences the majority of the Canadian economy and affects the free flow of trade among countries. This influences the number and kinds of jobs that are available and requires that organizations balance a complicated set of issues related to managing people in different geographies, cultures, legal environments, and business conditions. HR functions such as staffing, training, compensation, and the like have to be adjusted to take into account the differences in global management.

 Advanced technology has tended to reduce the number of jobs that require little skill and to increase the number of jobs that require considerable skill, a shift we refer to as moving from touch labour to knowledge work. This displaces some employees and requires that others be retrained. In addition, information technology has influenced HRM through human resources information systems (HRIS) that streamline HR processes, make information more readily available to managers and employees, and enable HR departments to focus on the firm's strategies.

 Both proactive and reactive change initiatives require HR managers to work with line managers and executives to create a vision for the future, establish an architecture that enables change, and communicate with employees about the processes of change.

 In order to "compete through people," organizations have to do a good job of managing human capital: the knowledge, skills, and capabilities that have value to organizations. Managers must develop strategies for identifying, recruiting, and hiring the best talent available; for developing these employees in ways that are firm-specific; for helping them to generate new ideas and generalize them through the company; for encouraging information sharing; and for rewarding collaboration and teamwork.

 In order to respond to customer needs better, faster, and more cheaply, organizations have instituted total quality management (TQM) and reengineering programs. Each of these programs requires that HR be involved in changing work processes, training, job design, compensation, and the like. HR issues also arise when communicating with employees about the new work systems, just as with any change initiative. Better business thinking builds more strategic HR thinking.

In order to contain costs, organizations have been downsizing, outsourcing, offshoring, and leasing employees, and enhancing productivity. HR's role is to maintain the relationship between a company and its employees while implementing the changes.

The workforce is becoming increasingly diverse, and organizations are doing more to address employee concerns and to maximize the benefit of different kinds of employees. Demographic changes, social and cultural differences, and changing attitudes toward work can provide a rich source of variety for organizations. But to benefit from diversity, managers need to recognize the potential con-

cerns of employees and make certain that the exchange between the organization and employees is mutually beneficial.

In working with line managers to address the organization's challenges, HR managers play a number of important roles; they are called on for advice and ethics counsel, for various service activities, for policy formulation and implementation, and for employee advocacy. To perform these roles effectively, HR managers must contribute business competencies, state-of-the-art HR competencies, and change-management competencies. Ultimately, managing people is rarely the exclusive responsibility of the HR function. Every manager's job is managing people, and successful companies combine the expertise of HR specialists with the experience of line managers to develop and utilize the talents of employees to their greatest potential.

KEY TERMS

corporate social responsibility, 8
downsizing, 17
employee leasing, 19
globalization, 7
human capital, 13
human resources information
  system (HRIS), 9

human resources
  management (HRM), 4
knowledge workers, 9
managing diversity, 27
offshoring, 19
outsourcing, 19
proactive change, 12

reactive change, 12
reengineering, 17
Six Sigma, 15
total quality management
  (TQM), 14

DISCUSSION QUESTIONS

1. Are people always an organization's most valuable asset? Why or why not? Name other strategic or valuable assets of organizations.

2. Suppose your boss asked you to summarize the major people-related concerns in opening an office in Tokyo. What issues would be on your list?

3. Will technology eliminate the need for human resources managers?

4. What are the pros and cons of change? Does it help or hurt organizational performance? Do you like change? Why or why not?

5. Can you think of a situation in which, if a particular person left an organization, the organization's expertise would drop rapidly?

6. In groups, debate the proposition: *Employees are an expense and their numbers should be reduced.*

7. Do pressures on cost containment work against effective management of people? Why or why not?

8. What are the pros and cons of having a more diverse workforce? Is Canada in a better position to compete globally because of its diverse population? Can you find examples from the media sources?

9. In your opinion, what is the most important role of HR managers? Should HR professionals be the "voice" for employees? Why or why not?

INTERNET EXERCISE

Go to a job board such as careerbuilder.ca or monster.ca, and find three HR generalist jobs. Make a list of the tasks that the successful candidates would be expected to do. Go to Highlights in HRM 1.1, and compare these tasks to the description of "A Day in the Life of an HR Generalist." What are the similarities and differences? Also make a list of the education, experience, and skill requirements for these jobs. Are they identical across all jobs? What might account for the differences? If the salary is mentioned as part of the ad, does it correspond to the salary rates given in Figure 1.1?

HRM Experience

Balancing Competitive Challenges and Employee Concerns

Today, human resources management is not just the responsibility of the personnel department. If people are a competitive resource, then line managers play an increasingly important role in managing the workforce. But this is not an either/or situation. Rather than seeing line managers take over responsibility from HR managers, we see both groups working together to handle workforce issues. But how do they work together?

Assignment

1. Working in teams of four to six individuals, identify what role the HR department would play and what role line managers would play in the following activities. Where would overlaps occur, and would there be any likely problems?
   a. Recruiting and selection
   b. Training and development
   c. Compensation
   d. Performance evaluation
   e. Labour relations
2. How would potential problems be resolved?
3. Write the groups' findings on flip charts and post for all to see. One member from each team should explain his or her group's findings to all class members.
4. Point out the similarities and differences across the teams. Save these points and revisit them—possibly revising them—as you study subsequent chapters in this textbook.

BIZFLIX EXERCISES

Babe: Herding Sheep, Babe's Way

This chapter's introduction to human resources management emphasized its role in helping managers bring together different types of people to reach a common purpose. An earlier chapter section, "Demographic and Employee Concerns," highlighted those differences. Watch this scene from *Babe* while recalling those discussions.

Babe is a charming Australian film featuring eccentric, quiet Farmer Hoggett (James Cromwell), who trains a pig he won at the fair to herd his sheep. His eccentricity turns to determination when he enters the pig in the Australian National Sheepdog Championships. The Academy Award–winning visual effects include a seamless mixture of animatronic doubles, computer images, and live animals.

This scene comes from the "a pig that thinks it's a dog" segment that appears about 40 minutes into the film. Farmer Hoggett's sheepdogs, Rex (voiced by Hugo

Weaving) and Fly (voiced by Miriam Margolyes), along with Babe (voiced by Christine Cavanaugh) the pig, accompany him to his sheep herd. Hoggett needs to gather the sheep into a pen so he can shear their wool. Before leaving for the pasture, Farmer Hoggett saw Babe carefully divide some chickens into two groups based on their colour. Hoggett suspects that perhaps Babe has some herding skills.

What to Watch for and Ask Yourself

• Are Babe's methods of herding sheep different from those used by the sheepdogs? If yes, what are the differences?

• Does Babe discover that he cannot successfully herd sheep as a sheepdog herds them? What does he do?

• Does Farmer Hoggett accept Babe for what he is—a pig, not a sheepdog?

case study 1

Outsourcing HR at BMO

In 2003, the Bank of Montreal outsourced all the HR processing work to Exult Inc., a human resources outsourcer. Exult will take over BMO's HR systems and administrative functions in a deal worth $75 million over ten years. Exult will handle all payroll, HR call centre management and information systems and support, employee data, staffing, and records management for BMO's 34 000 employees. BMO is Exult's first Canadian client. Rose Patten, executive vice-president of HR for BMO, sees the arrangement as a partnership, not a handoff. According to Patten, the outsourcing arrangement will allow BMO to concentrate its HR strategy on four key areas: "talent management, performance alignment and compensation, equity and employment, and learning and development."

Exult chairman and CEO Jim Madden is very pleased with the 100 BMO employees who have accepted offers to manage the HR outsourced functions and to expand the number of Canadian clients. A BMO former manager of Information Management says, "The one thing that is exciting is being able to see outside the box that we are in today, being able to see different businesses." The majority of the 250 employees affected by the outsourcing arrangement have been offered positions with Exult or other BMO departments.

More companies are turning to self-service applications by which clients or employees can do such things as change their home address online as a way to empower customers and employees and cut down on administrative costs. If Exult performs as promised, BMO will save 20 percent over what it would cost to do the same functions inhouse. "It's no surprise that companies are outsourcing functions as a way to save money and focus on core business," says David Rhodes, a principal at management-consulting firm Towers Perrin. He says businesses are "buying expertise and the ability to work very effectively" when they decide to outsource.

Sources: George Tischelle and Elisabeth Goodridge, "Prudential Financial Expects Savings by Outsourcing HR," *InformationWeek* (January 28, 2002): 873–81; Virginia Galt, "Take Our Business; Take Our People," *The Globe and Mail,* May 19, 2003: B1.

QUESTIONS

1. What are the pros and cons of outsourcing the HR function?
2. What do you think BMO should worry about most?
3. How can Exult make certain that BMO is happy with its service?

case study 2

Organizational Change at Honeywell

Honeywell Limited is Canada's leading heating control company. It offers technology that enhances comfort, saves energy, protects the environment, and increases security and safety. Honeywell, which has operated in Canada since 1930, currently employs 2800 people at more than 50 locations across the country. Its annual sales are $500 million.

In 1991 the main Honeywell Canada operation in Scarborough, Ontario, faced a tough challenge: it was no longer competitive, and if it did not change how it did business, every employee's job would be at risk. The traditional manufacturing operations were to be set aside and replaced by empowered teams of skilled and motivated workers. This did not look easy at the time. The average unionized employee was 48 years old and had worked at his routine factory job for 18 years. Among the plant's workers, more than 50 ethnic groups were represented.

Relations with the union were strained. However, both the Canadian Auto Workers (CAW) and management had one goal in common: to improve worker skills. This could be done by implementing work teams, which could also result in saving jobs.

Throughout the change process, the union was treated as a partner. It collaborated with management in establishing a Learning for Life program that encouraged workers to take courses in computer technology, total quality management, English as a second language, and diversity management. Today, more than 70 percent of the company's employees are taking courses. As their chairman stated: "At Honeywell, learning isn't an option; it's required. Everyone is expected to complete at least 40 hours of learning each year." There is a $10-million state-of-the-art learning centre that each year provides an average of 31 000 student days of learning and more than 1400 classes.

The Honeywell plant is now organized into 43 teams, which produce six types of heating control products. The empowered and trained workers order their own supplies, set up the machines according to established production schedules, and are responsible for quality. Employees rotate between positions and learn all aspects of production. Barriers between managers and employees have been eliminated—in other words, there are no suits, ties, or reserved parking spaces.

The results to date? Cycle times have been reduced to 1.2 hours from 80 hours; inventory has been decreased from $13.5 million to $3 million; and factory throughput per person has been increased from $85,000 to $155,000. The rotating of jobs has meant a reduction in repetitive strain injuries. Because their jobs have become more technologically advanced and require more skills, the workers are earning higher wages. The Scarborough factory now employs 400 people and is a Honeywell Centre of Excellence for producing valves and actuators, which are exported all over the globe.

Source: Adapted from K. Dorrell, "Breaking Down the Barriers," *Plant* 56, no. 17 (Nov. 24, 1997), 12–13. honeywell.ca. Reprinted by permission.

QUESTIONS

1. Identify the trends affecting the management of people that Honeywell Canada faced in 1991.
2. Discuss what role the HR department played, and how its results should be measured.

CAREER COUNSEL

Most students are legitimately worried about jobs and career prospects. Career Counsel is a feature at the end of each chapter designed to help students manage their working lives and to prepare for a career. The assessment exercises are designed to encourage introspection and self-discovery. We encourage you to complete these exercises on the *Managing Human Resources* website and compile them into a separate career planning workbook. Start by accessing www.belcourt5e.nelson.com.

NOTES AND REFERENCES

1. Edward L. Gubman, *The Talent Solution: Aligning Strategy and People to Achieve Extraordinary Results* (New York: McGraw-Hill Professional Publishing, 1998).
2. "Retiring Workforce, Widening Skills Gap, Exodus of 'Critical Talent' Threaten Companies: Deloitte Survey," *Canadian Corporate News* (February 15, 2005); "The Importance of HR," *HRFocus* 73, no. 3 (March 1996): 14.
3. T. J. Watson, Jr., *A Business and Its Beliefs: The Ideas That Helped Build IBM* (New York: McGraw-Hill, 1963).
4. Jennifer Rivkin, "The New Rules of Growth" *Profit*, vol. 24, Issue 5, page 58, 2005.
5. Helmar Drost and Richard Hird, *An Introduction to the Canadian Labour Market*, 2nd edition, Thomson Nelson, 2006.
6. HRPAO, "Globalization of Knowledge Work Threatens

2.4 Million Canadian Jobs," retrieved December 19, 2005, from www.hrpao.org/hrpao/knowldedgecentre
7. "FTAA Progress Report," *The New American* 18, no. 12 (June 17, 2002): 7. For more information, see the website for the World Trade Organization at www.wto.org/english/thewto_e/whatis_e/10ben_e/10b07_e.htm; Christian Doeringer, "Going Global? Let HR Pave the Way," *China Staff* 10, no. 8 (July–August 2004): 36–42.
8. Nancy R. Lockwood, "Corporate Social Responsibility: HR's Leadership Role," *HRMagazine* 49, no. 2 (December 2004): S1–11.
9. Peter F. Drucker, "Knowledge-Worker Productivity: The Biggest Challenge," *California Management Review* 41, no. 2 (Winter 1999): 79–94; A. D. Amar, *Managing Knowledge*

Workers (Westport, CT: Quorum, 2002); Cynthia C. Froggat, *Work Naked: Eight Essential Principles for Peak Performance in the Virtual Workplace* (New York: John Wiley and Sons, 2002); Mary Ann Roe, "Cultivating the Gold-Collar Worker," *Harvard Business Review* 79, no. 5 (May 2001): 32–33. See also D. P. Lepak and S. A. Snell, "The Human Resource Architecture: Toward a Theory of Human Capital Development and Allocation," *Academy of Management Review* 24, no. 1 (1999): 31–48; "China Engineers Next Great Leap with Wave of 'Knowledge Workers,'" *Milwaukee Journal Sentinel* (via Knight-Ridder/Tribune News Service), December 31, 2003; "Edward Yourdon's New Book Helps 'Knowledge Workers' Put Emotion Aside to Look at the Facts of the New Economic Reality," *PR Newswire* (October 4, 2004).

10. Anonymous, "Microsoft Commits $4.5 Million to Create Better Access to Technology, Training and Skills Development in Canada," *Canada News Wire*, December 6, 2006, page 1.

11. Scott A. Snell, Donna Stueber, and David P. Lepak, "Virtual HR Departments: Getting Out of the Middle," in R. L. Heneman and D. B. Greenberger (eds.), *Human Resource Management in Virtual Organizations* (Columbus, OH: Information Age Publishing, forthcoming); Samuel Greengard, "How to Fulfill Technology's Promise," *Workforce* (February 1999): HR Software Insights supplement, 10–18.

12. Robb, "Building a Better Workforce," 86–92; "How to Implement an Effective Process for a New HR Management System," *HRFocus* (January 2005): 3–4.

13. Bruce Shutan, "HRMS Flexibility Unlocks Secret to Success," *Employee Benefits* (August 1, 2004).

14. John P. Kotter, "Ten Observations," *Executive Excellence* 16, no. 8 (1999): 15–16.

15. Jennifer J. Laabs, "Change," *Personnel Journal* (July 1996): 54–63.

16. John P. Kotter, "Leading Change: Why Transformation Efforts Fail," *Harvard Business Review* (March–April 1995): 59–67; Kotter, "Ten Observations," 15–16; Edward E. Lawler III, Alec Levenson, and John W. Boudreau, "HR Metrics and Analytics: Use and Impact," *Human Resource Planning* 27, no. 4 (December 2004): 27–36.

17. Lee G. Bolman and Terry E. Deal, "Four Steps to Keeping Change Efforts Heading in the Right Direction," *Journal of Quality and Participation* 22, no. 3 (May/June 1999): 6–11; "Coaching Employees through the Six Stages of Change," *HRFocus* 79, no. 5 (May 2002): 9; Stefan Stern, "Forever Changing," *Management Today* (February 7, 2005): 40; Dennis Smillie, "Managing Change, Maximizing Technology," *Multi-Housing News* 40, no. 1 (January 2005): 4.

18. For information on a company that does measure its intellectual capital, see the Skandia AFS website and look at the company's Business Navigator at http://www.skandia.com/en/index; Donald C. Busi, "Assignment Reviews (ARs): Moving toward Measuring Your Most Valuable Asset," *Supervision* 66, no. 1 (January 2005): 3–7.

19. David Lepak and Scott Snell, "Knowledge Management and the HR Architecture," in S. Jackson, M. Hitt, and A. DeNisi (eds.), *Managing Knowledge for Sustained Competitive Advantage: Designing Strategies for Effective Human Resource Management* (SIOP Scientific Frontiers Series, forthcoming); David Lepak and Scott Snell, "Examining the Human Resource Architecture: The Relationship among Human Capital, Employment, and Human Resource Configurations," *Journal of Management,* forthcoming; Steve Bates, "Study Links HR Practices with the Bottom Line," *HRMagazine* 46, no. 12 (December 2001): 14; Ann Pomeroy, "Cooking Up Innovation: When It Comes to Helping Employees Create New Products and Services, HR's Efforts Are a Key Ingredient," *HRMagazine* 49, no. 11 (November 2004): 46–54.

20. Gary S. Becker, *Human Capital* (New York: Columbia University Press, 1964); Charles A. O'Reilly III and Jeffrey Pfeffer, "Cisco Systems: Acquiring and Retaining Talent in Hypercompetitive Markets," *Human Resource Planning* 23, no. 3 (2000): 38–52.

21. For more on Buckman Labs and their approach to managing human capital, visit their website at www.buckman.com. The company is also well known for its knowledge management initiatives, called Knowledge Nurture, as well as its knowledge management system, called K'Netix; see http://www.knowledge-nurture.com.

22. Dave Ulrich, Steve Kerr, and Ron Ashkenas, *The GE Work-Out: How to Implement GE's Revolutionary Method for Busting Bureaucracy & Attacking Organizational Problems* (New York: McGraw-Hill Professional Publishing, 2002).

23. Joseph E. McCann, *Managing Intellectual Capital: Setting the Agenda for Human Resource Professionals* (New York: Human Resource Planning Society, 1999); Benoit Guay, "Knowledge Management Is a Team Sport," *Computing Canada* 27, no. 3 (July 13, 2001): 23; Pimm Fox, "Making Support Pay," *Computerworld* 36, no. 11 (March 11, 2002): 28.

24. C. W. Russ Russo, "Ten Steps to a Baldrige Award Application," *Quality Progress* 34, no. 8 (August 2001): 49–56; "Nonprofits Aim to Apply for Baldrige Award," *Quality* 43, no. 11 (November 2004): 11–13.

25. The term Six Sigma is a registered trademark of Motorola. It is based on the Greek letter sigma, used as a symbol of variation in a process (the standard deviation). For more information see Peter S. Pande, Robert P. Neuman, and Roland R. Cavanagh, *The Six Sigma Way: How GE, Motorola, and Other Top Companies Are Honing Their Performance* (New York: McGraw-Hill, 2000).

26. Joseph A. Defeo, "Six Sigma: Road Map for Survival," *HRFocus* 76, no. 7 (July 1999): 11–12; Michele V. Gee and Paul C. Nystrom, "Strategic Fit between Skills Training and Levels of Quality Management: An Empirical Study of American Manufacturing Plants," *Human Resource Planning* 22, no. 2 (1999): 12–23; Linda Heruing, "Six Sigma in Sight," *HRMagazine* 49, no. 3 (March 2004): 76–81.

27. Ed Gubman, "HR Strategy and Planning: From Birth to Business Results," *Human Resource Planning* 27, no. 1 (March 2004): 13–21.

28. M. Hammer and J. Champy, *Reengineering the Corporation* (New York: HarperCollins, 1994). See also Michael Hammer, *Beyond Reengineering: How the Process-Centered Organization Is Changing Our Work and Our Lives* (New York: HarperBusiness, 1996); William M. James, "Best HR Practices for Today's Innovation Management," *Research-Technology Management* 45, no. 1 (January–February 2002): 57–61.

29. "Up to Speed: L. L. Bean Moves Employees as Workloads Shift," *Chief Executive* (July–August 1996): 15; Darrell Rigby, "Look before You Lay Off," *Harvard Business Review* 80, no. 4 (April 2002): 20–21.

30. Monica Belcourt and Ken McBey, *Strategic Human Resources Planning,* 3rd edition, Thomson Nelson, 2006.

31. "World atWork Finds One-Third of Companies Downsized after 9/11," *Report on Salary Surveys* (December 2002): 2.

32. Stephanie Armour, "Some Companies Choose No-Layoff Policy," *USA Today*, December 17, 2001, B-1; Gene Koretz, "Hire Math: Fire 3, Add 5," *Business Week Online* (March 13, 2000); Michelle Conlin, "Where Layoffs Are a Last Resort," *Business Week Online* (October 8, 2001); Lynn Miller, "Downsizing Trend Brings New Change to HR Directors," *HRMagazine* 45, no. 1 (January 2001); Norman E. Amundson, William A. Borgen, Sharalyn Jordan, and Anne C. Erlebach, "Survivors of Downsizing: Helpful and Hindering Experiences," *Career Development Quarterly* 52, no. 3 (March 2004): 256–72.

33. Gubman, "HR Strategy and Planning," 13–21.

34. Gubman, "HR Strategy and Planning," 13–21; Thomas W. Gainey, Brian S. Klaas, and Darla Moore, "Outsourcing the Training Function: Results from the Field," *Human Resource Planning* 25, no. 1 (2002): 16–23; Helen G. Drinan, "Outsourcing: Opportunity or Threat?" *HRMagazine* 47, no. 2 (February 2002): 8–9; George Tischelle and Elisabeth Goodridge, "Prudential Financial Expects Savings by Outsourcing HR," *InformationWeek* (January 28, 2002): 873, 881; Denise Pelham, "Is It Time to Outsource HR?" *Training* 39, no. 4 (April 2002): 50–52; Tom Anderson, "HR Outsourcing Expected to Surge this Year," *Employee Benefit News* (February 1, 2005); Catherine McLean "Telus Enters New Arena with HR Service Subsidiary: Signs Up a Dozen Public Sector Companies," *The Globe and Mail,* October 31, 2005.

35. Karyn Siobhan Robinson, "HR Needs Large Role in Offshoring," *HRMagazine* 590, no. 45 (May 2004): 30–32.

36. Gainey, Klaas, and Moore, "Outsourcing the Training Function," 16–23; Drinan, "Outsourcing: Opportunity or Threat?" 8–9; Tischelle and Goodridge, "Prudential Financial Expects Savings by Outsourcing HR," 873, 881; Pelham, "Is It Time to Outsource HR?" 50–52; Pam Babcock, "America's Newest Export: White-Collar Jobs," *HRMagazine* 49, no. 4 (April 2004): 50–54.

37. Elliot Spagat, "Procter & Gamble to Outsource about 80% of Back-Office Work," *The Wall Street Journal Online* (June 14, 2002); "Outsourcing HR," *Industry Week* 249, no. 10 (May 15, 2000): 71; Carolyn Hirschman, "For PEOs, Business Is Booming," *HRMagazine* 45, no. 2 (February 2000): 42–47; Brian Klaas, "Trust and the Role of Professional Employer Organizations: Managing HR in Small and Medium Enterprises," *Journal of Managerial Issues* 14, no. 1 (Spring 2002): 31–49; Chris Pentilla, "Got It Covered: If You Can't Afford to Offer Employee Benefits on Your Own, Why Not Join Forces with a PEO?" *Entrepreneur* 32, no. 2 (February 2004): 66–68.

38. Patrick Barta and Andrew Caffrey, "Productivity Leap Shows Potential of U.S. Economy—Rise at 8.6 Percent Pace, Positive for Profits, Doesn't Bode Very Well for Employment," *The Wall Street Journal*, May 8, 2002, A1; Jon E. Hilsenrath, "The Economy: Big U.S. Service Sectors Boosted Late 1990s Surge in Productivity," *The Wall Street Journal*, April 22, 2002, A2; Karen Lowry Miller, "Economy: Out of Steam—A Dip in U.S. Productivity Provokes Anxious Questions," *Newsweek International* (February 21, 2005): 34.

39. Helmar Drost and Richard Hird, *An Introduction to the Canadian Labour Market*, 2nd edition, Thomson Nelson, 2006.

40. Anonymous, "Unleashing Canada's People Power," *The National Post,* June 21, 2005, A16.

41. P. Cross, "Changes in the Labour Market," *Canadian Economic Observer*, Statistics Canada no. 11-010, March 2005; M. Armstrong-Stassen and A. Templer, "Adapting Training for Older Employees: The Canadian Response to an Aging Workforce," *Journal of Management Development*, vol. 24, no. 1, 2005: pp. 57–67.

42. Peter Francese, "My, You've Grown: The Teen Economy Is Like Totally Awesome," *The Wall Street Journal*, June 28, 2000, S3. Jennifer Rivkin, "The New Rules of Growth," *Profit* 24, 5, 58, 2005.

43. The U.S. Department of Labor's Bureau of Labor Statistics keeps up-to-date projections and percentages on educational requirements for different kinds of jobs. Interested readers can access this information at www.bls.gov; Louis Uchitelle, "College Degree Still Pays, but It's Leveling Off," *The New York Times,* January 13, 2005: C1.

44. Wallace Imen, "The Value of A Degree: A Million Bucks," *The Globe and Mail,* May 24, 2005: C1.

45. Uyen Yu, "Northern Mine Develops Essential Skills in its Workforce," *Canadian HR Reporter,* July 18, 2005: 8; David Hayes, "Canadian Organizations Move to Develop Workplace Literacy and Numerical Skills," *Canadian HR Reporter,* July 18, 2005: 7; Conrad Murphy, "Assessing Essential Skills to Recruit and Train," *Canadian HR Reporter,* July 18, 2005: 11.

46. Kathleen Iverson, "Managing for Effective Workforce Diversity," *Cornell Hotel and Restaurant Administration Quarterly* 41, no. 2 (April 2000): 31–38; Gail Johnson, "Time to Broaden Diversity Training," *Training* 41, no. 9 (September 2004): 16.

47.   Industry Canada Key Small Business Statistics, May 2003.

48.   Chris Conrath, "Complying with PIPEDA" *Computer World Canada,* 18, no.1 January 2002.

49.   Todd Raphael, "The Drive to Downshifting," *Workforce* 80, no. 10 (October 2001): 23; Jim Olsztynski, "Flexible Work Schedules May Make More Sense: One in Six Americans Qualifies as a Caregiver Who May Benefit from Flextime," *National Driller* 26, no. 2 (February 2005): 16–19.

50.   Leah Carlson, "Flextime Elevated to National Issue," *Employee Benefit News* (September 15, 2004).

51.   Monica Belcourt and Andrew Templer, "The CHRP Edge: Part 2" *HR Professional,* December 2002–January 2003, 36–39.

chapter 2

Strategy and Human Resources Planning

After studying this chapter, you should be able to

objective **1**
Identify the advantages of integrating human resources planning and strategic planning.

objective **2**
Understand how an organization's competitive environment influences strategic planning.

objective **3**
Recognize the importance of internal resource analysis.

objective **4**
Describe the basic tools for human resources forecasting.

objective **5**
Explain the linkages between competitive strategies and HR.

objective **6**
Understand the requirements of strategy implementation.

objective **7**
Recognize the methods for assessing and measuring the effectiveness of strategy.

O ne of the clichés about company annual reports is that they often claim that "people are our most important asset." Although we might believe this to be true, the fact is that historically managers often have not acted as though they themselves really believed it. In the past, executives often tried to remove human resources from the strategy equation, by substituting capital for labour where possible, or by creating hierarchical structures that separated those who think from those who actually do the work. But much is changing today.

In a recent survey, nearly 80 percent of corporate executives said the importance of HRM in their firms has grown substantially over the past ten years, and two-thirds said that HR expenditures are now viewed as a strategic investment rather than simply a cost to be minimized.[1]

Strategic Planning and Human Resources

objective 1

strategic planning
Procedures for making decisions about the organization's long-term goals and strategies

human resources planning (HRP)
The process of anticipating and providing for the movement of people into, within, and out of an organization

strategic human resources management (SHRM)
The pattern of human resources deployments and activities that enable an organization to achieve its strategic goals

As we explained in Chapter 1, "competing through people" is the theme for this book. To quote a former minister of finance for the federal government, Ralph Goodale: "In today's world, the greatest point of differentiation—the real basis of competitive advantage—is brain power. An idea can create whole new industries. Knowledge and creativity have become the true measures of economic potential."[2] But the idea remains only a premise for action until we put it into practice. To deliver on this promise, we need to understand some of the systems and processes in organizations that link human resources management and strategic management. A few definitions may be helpful up front.

First of all, **strategic planning** involves a set of procedures for making decisions about the organization's long-term goals and strategies. In this chapter, we discuss strategic plans as having a strong external orientation that covers major portions of the organization. They especially focus on how the organization will position itself relative to competitors in order to achieve long-term survival, value, and growth. **Human resources planning (HRP),** by comparison, is the process of anticipating and making provision for the movement of people into, within, and out of an organization. Overall, its purpose is to help managers deploy human resources as effectively as possible, where and when they are needed, in order to accomplish the organization's goals. **Strategic human resources management (SHRM),** then, combines strategic planning and HR planning. It can be thought of as the pattern of human resources deployments and activities that enable an organization to achieve its strategic goals.

Although planning has always been an essential process of management, increased emphasis on HR issues becomes especially critical when organizations consider global strategies, mergers, relocation of plants, innovation, downsizing, outsourcing, offshoring, or the closing of operating facilities. Dramatic shifts in the composition of the labour force require that managers become more involved in planning, since such changes affect the full range of HR practices (such as employee recruitment, selection, training, compensation, and motivation).

Strategic Planning and HR Planning: Linking the Processes

As organizations plan for their future, HR managers must be concerned with meshing HRP and strategic planning for the organization as a whole.[3] Through strategic planning, organizations set major objectives and develop comprehensive plans to achieve those objectives. Human resources planning relates to strategic planning in several ways, but at a fundamental level we can focus on two issues: strategy formulation and strategy implementation. Human resources planning provides a set of inputs into the strategic *formulation* process in terms of what is possible; that is, whether the types and numbers of people are available to pursue a given strategy. For example, when Indigo executives contemplated the move into Web-based commerce to compete with Amazon.com, one of the issues they had to address was whether they had the talent needed to succeed in that arena.

In addition to strategy formulation, HRP is important in terms of strategy *implementation* as well. Once the strategy is devised, executives must make primary resource allocation decisions, including those pertaining to structure, processes, and human resources.[4] Companies such as GE, IBM, and CIGNA have taken strides to combine these two aspects of strategic management.[5]

All the available evidence suggests that the integration of HRP and strategic planning tends to be most effective when there is a reciprocal relationship between the two processes. In this relationship, the top management team recognizes that strategic-planning decisions affect—and are affected by—HR concerns. Figure 2.1

Figure 2.1 Linking Strategic Planning and Human Resources

	BUSINESS/CORPORATE	HUMAN RESOURCES
Mission, Vision, and Values	• Identify purpose and scope • Clarify long-term direction • Establish enduring beliefs and principles	• Capture underlying philosophy • Establish foundation of culture • Guide ethical codes of conduct
SWOT Analysis: External Analysis	• Opportunities and threats (OT) • Environmental scanning (legal, etc.) • Industry/competitor analysis	• Demographic trends • External supply of labour • Competitor benchmarking
SWOT Analysis: Internal Analysis	• Strengths and weaknesses (SW) • Core competencies • Resources: People, process, systems	• Culture, competencies, composition • Forecast demand for employees • Forecast supply of employees
Strategy Formulation	• Corporate strategy • Business strategy • Functional strategy: Alignment	• Productivity and efficiency • Quality, service, speed, innovation • External fit/alignment and internal fit
Strategy Implementation	• Design structure, systems, etc. • Allocate resources • Leadership, communication, and change	• Reconcile supply and demand • Downsizing, layoffs, etc. • HR practice: Staffing, training, rewards, etc.
Evaluation	• Assessment and benchmarking • Ensuring alignment • Agility and flexibility	• Human capital metrics • Balanced Scorecard

illustrates the basic outline of how companies have begun aligning HRP and strategic planning in this way. While this figure begins to address this issue of strategic alignment, we will raise the issue at several points throughout the chapter.

As we look at trends in the best of companies, there is virtually no distinction between strategic planning and HRP; the planning cycles are the same and HR issues are seen as inherent in the management of the business. As James Walker, a noted HRP expert, put it, "Today, virtually *all* business issues have people implications; *all* human resource issues have business implications."[6] HR managers are important facilitators of the planning process and are viewed as credible and important contributors to creating the organization's future. This positive linkage occurs when the HR manager becomes a member of the organization's management steering committee or strategic-planning group. Once this interactive and dynamic structure exists, HR managers are recognized as contributing strategic planners alongside other top managers.[7]

This is an important element for the rest of our discussion in this chapter. Traditionally, authors—and too many HR managers—have treated HR planning and strategic planning as separate activities. Instead, we provide a step-by-step process to show how the two aspects of planning can be integrated.

Step One: Mission, Vision, and Values

mission
The basic purpose of the organization as well as its scope of operations

The first step in strategic planning is establishing a mission, vision, and values for the organization. The **mission** is the basic purpose of the organization, as well as its scope of operations. It is a statement of the organization's reason for existing. The mission often is written in terms of general clients it services. Depending on the scope of the organization, the mission may be broad or narrow. For example, the mission of Tim Hortons is as follows:

> Our guiding mission is to deliver superior quality products and services for our customers and communities through leadership, innovation and partnerships. Our vision is to be the quality leader in everything we do.

strategic vision
A statement about where the company is going and what it can become in the future; clarifies the long-term direction of the company and its strategic intent

core values
The strong and enduring beliefs and principles that the company uses as a foundation for its decisions

The **strategic vision** of the organization moves beyond the mission statement to provide a perspective on where the company is headed and what the organization can become in the future. Although the terms *mission* and *vision* often are used interchangeably, the vision statement ideally clarifies the long-term direction of the company and its strategic intent. Organizational **core values** are the strong enduring beliefs and principles that the company uses as a foundation for its decisions.

These are the underlying parameters for how the company will act toward customers, employees, and the public in general. In many cases, the values capture the underlying philosophy of the company culture and give direction to its employees. The values also place limits on what behaviour is seen as ethical and acceptable. Highlights in HRM 2.1 shows the mission, vision, and values of WestJet.

Highlights in HRM 2.1

WestJet: Mission, Vision, and Values

WestJet:

Our mission:

To enrich the lives of everyone in WestJet's world by providing safe, friendly, affordable air travel.

Our vision:

WestJet will be the leading low-fare airline that:

People want to work with . . .

Customers want to fly with . . .

and Shareholders want to invest with.

At WestJet we have legendary values:

- We are positive and passionate about everything we do.
- We take our jobs seriously, but not ourselves.
- We embrace change and innovation.
- We are friendly and caring toward our People and our Customers, and we treat everyone with respect.
- We provide our People with the training and tools they need to do their jobs.
- We celebrate our successes.
- We personify the hard-working "can-do" attitude.
- We are honest, open, and keep our commitments.
- We are team WestJet!

At WestJet we keep the spirit alive by:

- Being successful in the air.
- Being successful on the ground.
- Celebrating new markets.
- Providing legendary service.
- Experiencing legendary growth.
- Creating internal "magic" and external "wow."

Source: www.westjet.com. Reprinted with permission.

Step Two: Environmental Analysis

The mission, vision, and values drive the second component of the strategic management process: analysis of external opportunities and threats. Changes in the external environment have a direct impact on the way organizations are run and people are managed. Some of these changes represent opportunities, and some of them represent real threats to the organization. Because of this, successful strategic management depends on an accurate and thorough evaluation of the environment. **Environmental scanning** is the systematic monitoring of the major external forces influencing the

environmental scanning
Systematic monitoring of the major external forces influencing the organization

organization.[8] Managers attend to a variety of external issues; however, the following six are monitored most frequently:

1. Economic factors, including general, regional, and global conditions
2. Industry and competitive trends, including new processes, services, and innovations
3. Technological changes, including information technology, innovations, and automation
4. Government and legislative issues, including laws and administrative rulings
5. Social concerns, including child care, elder care, the environment, and educational priorities
6. Demographic and labour market trends, including age, composition, and literacy

By scanning the environment for changes that will likely affect an organization, managers can anticipate their impact and make adjustments early.

USING THE INTERNET

For the latest information about legislation and other factors that affect the practice of HR, do your own environmental scanning at:

www.hrmguide.net/canada

Competitive Environment

While many factors in the general environment may influence strategic decisions, analysis of the firm's competitive environment is central to strategic planning. The competitive environment includes the specific organizations with which the firm interacts. As shown in Figure 2.2, the competitive environment includes customers, rival firms, new entrants, substitutes, and suppliers. In strategic planning, firms analyze the competitive environment in order to adapt to or influence the nature of competition. A general rule of thumb about this analysis is: The more power each of these forces has, the less profitable (and therefore attractive) the industry will be. Let's look at each of the five forces.

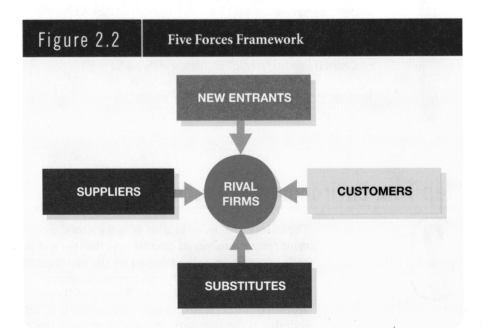

Figure 2.2   Five Forces Framework

Customers

One of the most important assessments a firm can make is identifying the needs of its customers. At a fundamental level, strategy focuses on creating customer value—and different customers often want different things. For example, in the hotel industry, business travellers may want convenient locations with meeting facilities. Vacationers may want resort locations with swimming pools, golf courses, and luxury spas. Other travellers may just want an inexpensive room next to the highway. The point is that, increasingly, "one size does not fit all" and organizations need to know how they are going to provide value to customers. That is the foundation for strategy, and it influences the kind of skills and behaviour that will be needed from employees. For example, actions and attitudes that lead to excellent customer service can include the following:

- Speed of delivering normal orders
- Willingness to meet extraordinary needs
- Merchandise delivered in good condition
- Readiness to take back defective goods and resupply new goods quickly
- Availability of installation and repair services and parts

Rival Firms

In addition to customer analysis, perhaps the most obvious element of industry analysis is examining the nature of competition. The first question to consider is: Who is the competition? Often the answer is clear to everyone, but sometimes it is not. For example, for many years, Toys "R" Us viewed its main competitors to be other toy stores. However, other retailers such as Zellers and Wal-Mart soon moved into this space very successfully. This had a direct effect on human resources planning for Toys "R" Us. While in the past, Toys "R" Us had been successful with a volume-based approach (that is, "stack it high, and let it fly"), bigger retailers soon gained an advantage—who can beat Wal-Mart's volume and cost advantage? As a consequence, Toys "R" Us had to modify its strategy to compete more on customer service and the expertise of its employees. But did Toys "R" Us have the number and kind of employees required to compete in this way? Were its staffing, training, performance management, and compensation practices aligned with this strategy?

New Entrants

As suggested previously, new companies can sometimes enter an industry to compete with established firms. And sometimes they can't. To protect their position, companies often try to establish entry barriers to keep new firms out of the industry. However, when new firms do enter an industry it is often because they have a different—and perhaps better—way to provide value to customers. For example, when WestJet entered the airline business, it distinguished itself by providing excellent service and low prices in regions where customers did not have many options. The HR implications of this are clear. When we look at the challenges faced by traditional airlines because of the threat of low-cost carriers such as WestJet, we can clearly see that new entrants can change the "rules of the game" in an industry. The impact on labour costs, productivity, skills required, and work design are important considerations in both strategic planning and human resources planning.

Substitutes

At times, the biggest opportunity or threat in an industry is not with direct competition, but from substitution. In the telephone industry, for example, cellular

CP PHOTO/JIM FOX

Via Rail is trying to position itself as a substitute for airplanes for short distances.

technology is rapidly substituting for land-line phone systems. Similarly, some firms are using new technology to offer telephone service over the Internet (VOIP). These substitutes offer the same service or function as traditional firms, but through a different method. That implies that firms may need to adjust their skill base in order to support different technologies. Or they may need to think about how they will compete in different ways. As an example, think about how the travel business has changed over the years. Travel agents used to be the key resource for flights, hotels, rental cars, and the like. The focus was almost exclusively on transactions. However, with the advent of online reservation systems, travel agents have had to adapt their approach. Today, they are as likely to compete based on the service they provide and the expertise they have about particular locations.

Suppliers

Organizations rarely create everything on their own, but instead have suppliers that provide them with key inputs. These inputs can include raw materials for production, money (from banks and shareholders), information, and people. This last factor—people, or labour as it is historically called—has direct implications for strategic planning and human resources planning. Because of its central role in both strategic planning and HRP, we explore it next in much more detail.

External Supply of Labour

Many factors influence the labour supply, including demographic changes in the population, national and regional economics, education level of the workforce, demand for specific employee skills, population mobility, and governmental policies. National and regional unemployment rates are often considered a general barometer of labour supply. Consider these facts about Canadian workers:

- Labour force growth is expected to slow and then decline to about 2015, finally falling to zero growth between 2016 and 2040. About one-half of Canadian employers say they cannot find qualified staff, with Alberta reporting the most difficulty, at 73 percent of employers searching for qualified employees. Recently, about one-third of Canadian firms reported that they were unable to pursue new growth opportunities because of shortages of workers.

- Nearly 40 percent of the owners of small to medium sized Canadian businesses plan to retire in the next five years, and only one-third have succession plans.

- Immigrants make up nearly 70 percent of the total growth of the labour force, and it is possible that immigration could account for virtually all labour force growth by 2011. The fastest-growing segment of the workforce in terms of race will be Asian Canadians (an increase primarily affected through immigration).

- In 2005, older workers (55 years of age and older) represented 26.68 percent of the population and 13.46 percent of the labour force. Generation Y (or Nexters) workers (those born in the 1980s and 1990s) represented 16.59 percent of the population and 19 percent of the labour force.

- Women made up approximately 50.8 percent of the population of Canada and 46.69 percent of the workforce in 2005. Today, three of every five college graduates are women.

- Nearly 34 percent of the workforce is composed of part-timers, temps, and self-employed and the number has been steadily rising.

- The greatest numbers of bilingual people are found in Quebec (41 percent), followed by New Brunswick (34 percent), Prince Edward Island, and Ontario (both at 12 percent).

- A great deal of churning occurs every year in the labour market. The number of permanent separations of people from their jobs averaged about 20 percent of all employees every year. One-third were laid off, one-third quit, and one-third left for other reasons (e.g., retire, raise kids, go back to school).

- The demand for workers will be highest in these sectors: health, natural and applied sciences and social science, education, and government service. Interestingly, forecasters are predicting strong demand for human resources managers and specialists in human resources.

- The percentage of Canadians (over 15 years of age) who have secondary school education is 14 percent, with university 25.83 percent, and those with graduate degrees 3.22 percent. On average nationwide, high school graduates can expect to earn about $25,477 annually. Those with university degrees can expect to earn, on average, nearly double that amount.[9]

USING THE INTERNET

See if there are labour shortages or surpluses for the job that you want at:

http://lmi-imt.hrdc-drhc.gc.ca/standard.asp?pcode=lmiv_main_q4&lcode=E

These labour force trends illustrate the importance of monitoring demographic changes as a part of environmental scanning. Fortunately, labour market analysis is aided by various published documents. Statistics Canada and HRSDC publish many studies on the labour force, as do various provincial governments. In addition, local chambers of commerce and city planning departments may assist both large organizations and new business ventures with labour market analysis.

These sources of information are invaluable. In a rapidly changing environment, it is extremely risky to be caught off guard. Such changes are important for many reasons, some related to operational issues and some to strategic issues. HRP has to focus on both. At an operational level, the change in labour supply directly influences hiring plans that must take into account the demographic composition of the population in the area where the organization is located. Similarly, with a "maturing" workforce, HRP must consider the implications for recruitment and replacement policies.

From a strategic standpoint, changes in the labour supply can limit the strategies available to firms. For example, WestJet wishes to add Quebec City to its network, but their CEO stated: "Our limitation on going to Quebec City is simply the number of French speaking flight attendants we have within our organization. But hiring people in Calgary who are bilingual is a bit of a challenge."[10] High-growth companies in particular may find it difficult to find the talent they need to expand their businesses. While unemployment rates vary by sector, the shortage of talent in high-skill jobs continues to create real challenges for firms.

In Highlights in HRM 2.2 on page 56, David Foot, a demographer at the University of Toronto, explains why HR professionals must become aware of the need to scan.

Highlights in HRM 2.2

Spotting Trends in the Global Economy

Every human resource professional recognizes that anticipating trends is an important part of the job. Furthermore, senior HR professionals want to influence strategy, not just respond to strategies determined by the "real players" at the boardroom table.

David Foot, a famous Canadian economist and demographer at the University of Toronto, says that HR professionals are often ill-equipped to contribute to their organization's strategy. He contends that HR people are experienced in dealing with micro issues, but often lack the big picture or macro perspective that is necessary to deal with corporate or strategic issues.

Having worked with executives and boards of directors, he is very familiar with the issues facing them and with the inability of HR managers to advance the HR view of the implications of strategic decisions. He offers this example: A company is thinking about going global—say, by expanding into Mexico. The HR person has very little knowledge about the labour market of that country (where there are many young people but relatively few seniors). Furthermore, he or she is likely to be preoccupied with important micro issues, such as how to hire employees and what the local health and safety rules are, when he or she ought to be considering, for example, Mexico's regional unemployment and education rates by region to determine plant location.

Other executives can think strategically when faced with changes in the environment. Foot asks: "How many HR professionals could answer the question 'How does the exchange rate impact HR planning?' Those with a macro perspective would immediately determine: 1. How much business is internal/external? 2. Have the financial people bought insurance against exchange rate fluctuations? 3. If the Canadian dollar depreciates, and there will be more demand for our products, what are the opportunities to access labour in external markets such as Poland or Mexico? How can we recruit these people faster than other companies? This mindset is crucial to being at the boardroom table.

"Let me give you another example of reactionary micro thinking. Low unemployment rates traditionally result in demands from business for higher immigration levels to ease labour shortages. But this traditional HR response will become increasingly inappropriate in the new millennium because more immigrants will only compete with the children of boomers who will be entering the labour force. A proactionary macro-thinking HR person will, therefore, be able to advise the CEO that this is likely to be a short-term, not a long-term labour shortage and to think internally rather than externally for new workers. This information could be crucial in influencing the company's strategic planning for the next five years."

Step Three: Internal Analysis

As organizations conduct external analyses of environmental opportunities and threats, they also analyze their internal strengths and weaknesses. Internal analysis provides strategic decision makers with an inventory of organizational skills and resources as well as their performance levels.

To be sure, many resources combine to give organizations a competitive advantage. But in contrast to the past, the advantages due to physical assets are being supplanted by intangible assets, including people. As James Brian Quinn noted, "With rare exceptions, the economic and producing power of firms lies more in its intellectual and service capabilities than in its hard assets—land, plant, and equipment."[11]

The Three Cs: Culture, Competencies, and Composition

In the context of human resource planning, internal analysis focuses especially on "the three Cs": culture, competencies, and composition.

Culture: Auditing Values, Beliefs, and Attitudes

Think about our initial discussion (in Step One) of mission, vision, and values. Because managers increasingly understand that employee-oriented cultures are critical to success, they often conduct **cultural audits** to examine the attitudes and beliefs of the workforce as well as the activities they engage in. At one level, this analysis focuses on whether critical values are embraced and demonstrated by employees throughout the organization. Employee surveys, for example, can measure how employees feel on a number of critical issues, and can be very useful for upward assessment and feedback of (and for) management.

However, these audits can go much deeper. Sears, for example, found that positive employee attitudes on ten essential factors—including workload and treatment by bosses—are directly linked to customer satisfaction and revenue increases.[12]

Cultural audits essentially involve discussions among top-level managers of how the organization's culture reveals itself to employees and how it can be influenced or improved. The cultural audit may include such questions as the following:

- How do employees spend their time?
- How do they interact with each other?
- Are employees empowered?
- What is the predominant leadership style of managers?
- How do employees advance within the organization?

By conducting in-depth interviews and making observations over a period of time, managers are able to learn about the culture of their organization and the attitudes of its employees. With the increased diversity of the workplace, cultural audits can be used to determine whether there are different groups, or subcultures, within the organization that have distinctly different views about the nature of work, the quality of managers, and so on. Before any HR planning can take place, managers have to gain a clear idea of how employees view their organization.

Competencies: People as a Strategic Resource

A growing number of experts now argue that the key to a firm's success is based on establishing a set of **core competencies**—integrated skills and knowledge sets within an organization that distinguish it from its competitors and deliver value to customers. McDonald's, for example, has developed core competencies in management efficiency and training. Federal Express has core competencies in package routing, delivery, and employee relations. Royal Dutch Shell has core competencies in oil exploration and production.[13] Core competencies tend to be limited in number,

cultural audits
Audits of the culture and quality of work life in an organization

core competencies
Integrated knowledge sets within an organization that distinguish it from its competitors and deliver value to customers

but they provide a long-term basis for technology innovation, product development, and service delivery.

In many cases, people are a key resource that underlies a firm's core competencies. Particularly in knowledge-based industries such as software and information services, success increasingly depends on "people-embodied know-how." This includes the knowledge, skills, and abilities of employees. Organizations can achieve a sustained competitive advantage through people if they are able to meet the following criteria:[14]

1. *The resources must be valuable.* People are a source of competitive advantage when they improve the efficiency or effectiveness of the company. Value is increased when employees find ways to decrease costs, provide something unique to customers, or some combination of the two. Empowerment programs, total-quality initiatives, and continuous improvement efforts at companies such as UPS are intentionally designed to increase the value that employees represent on the bottom line.

2. *The resources must be rare.* People are a source of competitive advantage when their knowledge, skills, and abilities are not equally available to competitors. Companies such as Microsoft and Four Seasons Hotels invest a great deal to hire and train the best and the brightest employees in order to gain an advantage over their competitors.

3. *The resources must be difficult to imitate.* People are a source of competitive advantage when employee capabilities and contributions cannot be copied by others. Disney, Southwest Airlines, and Starbucks are each known for creating unique cultures that get the most from employees (through teamwork) and are difficult to imitate.

4. *The resources must be organized.* People are a source of competitive advantage when their talents can be combined and deployed to work on new assignments at a moment's notice. Companies such as IBM and GE have invested in information technology to help allocate and track employee assignments to temporary projects. Teamwork and cooperation are two other pervasive methods for ensuring an organized workforce.

These four criteria highlight the importance of people and show the closeness of HRM to strategic management.

Composition: The Human Capital Architecture

A related element of internal analysis for organizations that compete on competencies is determining the composition of the workforce. That is, managers need to determine whether people are available, internally or externally, to execute an organization's strategy. In some respects, this has traditionally been the focal point of human resources planning. Managers have to make tough decisions about whom to employ internally, whom to contract externally, and how to manage different types of employees with different skills who contribute in different ways to the organization. The Province of British Columbia recognizes the value of human capital, as described in Highlights in HRM 2.3.

Figure 2.3 on page 60 shows that different skill groups in any given organization can be classified according to the degree to which they create strategic value and are unique to the organization. As a general rule, managers often consider contracting externally (or outsourcing) skill areas that are not central to the firm's core competence. HRP plays an important role in helping managers weigh the costs and benefits of using one approach to employment versus another.

Highlights in HRM 2.3

The Measurement of Human Capital

The Office of the Auditor General of British Columbia recognized that human capital is critically important to the delivery of high-quality service to the province's citizens. So it set out to measure whether training and development (T&D) were being used to increase human capital in the B.C. public service. As a first step, it defined human capital as the collective brainpower in an organization. This brainpower consists of

- *facts* acquired through informal and formal education;
- *skills* gained through training and practice;
- *experience* gained through reflection on past successes and mistakes;
- *value judgments* based on individual perceptions; and
- *social networks* developed through relationships with co-workers, colleagues, and customers.

The audit took several measures, including a large-scale survey of a random sample of full-time employees and an in-depth audit of three ministries. Some of the data generated by this audit are the following:

- Thirty-six percent of government employees had received no formal training.
- The average B.C. government employee received 17 hours of training (compared to a Canadian benchmark of 29 hours).
- Less than 1 percent of payroll was spent on training (compared to the 4 percent that the best employers spend).
- Forty percent of employees had had their jobs redefined.
- Forty-three percent of senior managers would reach age 55 in the next five years and be eligible to retire.
- Thirty-three percent of employees with less than one year of employment did not feel they had been trained properly to carry out their duties.

The audit revealed that most T&D decisions were based on requests made from individual employees, and that most programs they attended consisted of one- and two-day courses outside the organization. It had never been ascertained whether these courses increased employees' skills or helped the organization achieve its goals. There was no way of knowing how effective this training was; nor was there any accounting for T&D expenditures.

Government employees generally believed that training was of great value to them and their organizations. Paradoxically, they also believed that they weren't being supported in their work; and only half thought they had the tools and resources they needed to do their jobs. (A full copy of the report is available at www.bcauditor.com/auditorgeneral.htm.)

Sources: Adapted from J. McCannel and L. McAdams, "The Learning Culture in the Public Service," *Public Sector Management* 11, no. 1 (2000); www.ipac-iapc.ca.

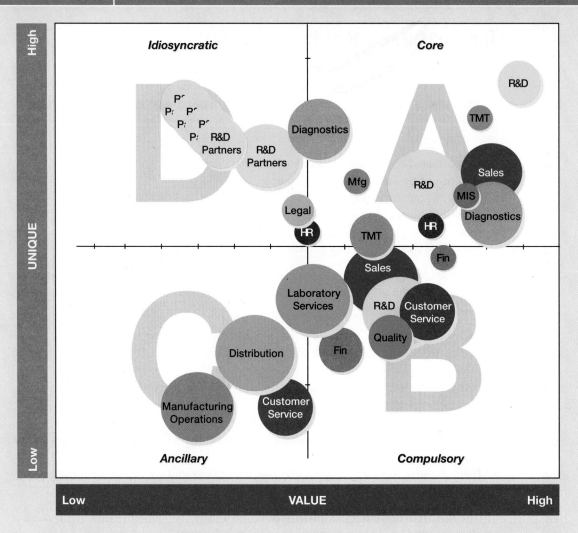

Figure 2.3 | Mapping Human Capital

Evidence from research suggests that employment relationships and HR practices for different employees vary according to which segment they occupy in this matrix. Here are some general trends:

Core Knowledge Workers. This group of employees tends to have firm-specific skills that are directly linked to the company's strategy (such as R&D scientists in a pharmaceuticals company or computer scientists in a software development company). These employees typically are engaged in knowledge work that involves considerable autonomy and discretion. Companies tend to make long-term commitments to these employees, investing in their continuous training and development and perhaps giving them an equity stake in the organization.

Traditional Job-Based Workers. This group of employees has skills that are quite valuable to a company, but not particularly unique (such as salespeople in a department store or truck drivers for a courier service). These employees tend to be employed to perform a predefined job. As it is quite possible that they could leave to go to another firm, managers frequently make less investment in training and development and tend to focus more on paying for short-term performance achievements.

USING THE INTERNET

The Canadian Policy Research Networks operates a great site for information on workplace trends and job issues:

www.jobquality.ca

Contract Labour. This group of employees typically has skills that are of less strategic value and generally available to all firms (such as clerical workers, maintenance workers, and staff workers in accounting and human resources). Individuals in these jobs are increasingly hired from external agencies on a contract basis, and the scope of their duties tends to be limited. Employment relationships tend to be transactional, focused on rules and procedures, with less investment in development. Ethics in HRM describes some issues associated with contract employees. The Business Case on page 62 outlines the advantages to the employer of hiring contract labour.

Alliance Partners. This group of individuals has skills that are unique, but frequently not directly related to a company's core strategy (such as lawyers, consultants, and research lab scientists). Although companies perhaps cannot justify their internal employment, given their tangential link to strategy, these individuals have skills that are specialized and not readily available to all firms. As a consequence, companies tend to establish longer-term alliances and partnerships with them and nurture an ongoing relationship focused on mutual learning. Considerable investment is made in the exchange of information and knowledge.[15]

Ethics in HRM

The Employment Contract

The number of organizations substituting part-time workers for full-time employees is growing. Employees—even those with excellent track records and many years of service—are considered expendable as organizations revise their strategies to become more competitive and more profitable. When yet another reorganization occurs, management reveals the new plan with excitement. However, while management thinks it is telling employees, "We will provide you with meaningful, challenging, and skill-building work that will be good for your résumé— you are responsible for your own employment," employees are hearing, "We will work you to the bone, pay you enough to prevent you from quitting, and fire you when we no longer need you. Oh, and by the way, you are our most valuable resource."

Some employment contracts are extremely one-sided, with employers determining when to hire and when to fire, without obligation or guilt. This kind of contract works when people need jobs more than organizations need employees. However, as some sectors continue to experience rapid growth, and as the labour market for certain skills becomes tighter, employees are making contractual demands that place them in the driver's seat. They are demanding signing bonuses, stock equity, retention bonuses, and sufficient notification with predetermined buyouts for termination. Furthermore, the courts are ruling that if an employee is retained for a series of uninterrupted contracts, then that contract worker is de facto an employee.

The Business Case

Hiring Contract Workers Pays

Contract workers (also called temporary workers or "temps") are defined as paid workers with a specified end date for their job or completion of a task or project. In 2003, 12.5 percent of all Canadian workers were contract workers.

Employers want to hire people on contract for several reasons, including

- The ability to terminate their contracts easily
- There is no requirement to pay benefits
- Reduced need for training and development investments
- Part-time workers earn less, because they rarely benefit from seniority provisions.
- Typically, contract workers are not entitled to paid sick leave or vacation pay.
- There is no obligation on the part of the employer to pay into a pension plan.
- Typically contract employees do not participate in company incentive compensation programs that award merit pay or bonuses.

As you can see, the employer can save a lot of money by hiring only contract employees. The use of contract workers has the additional benefits of functional flexibility (employers can hire the workers with the exact skills needed) and numerical flexibility (workers can be added or discharged as work demand fluctuates).

A growing organization must decide whether to hire full-time or part-time employees, and the chart below will assist in this decision.

The Advantages and Limitations of Part-Time Employment

ADVANTAGES FOR THE EMPLOYER	ADVANTAGES FOR THE EMPLOYEE
Work scheduling flexibility	Control over personal time
Reduced compensation costs	More variety in jobs
Increased ability to add/reduce programs	Consultant tax advantages

LIMITATIONS FOR THE EMPLOYER	LIMITATIONS FOR THE EMPLOYEE
No organizational loyalty	No job security
Costs of continuous replacement	Limited benefits
Costs of continual training	Stresses of continuous learning
Strategic competencies can quit	Lack of training and career progression

Sources: Adapted from Helmar Drost and H. Richard Hird, *An Introduction to the Canadian Labour Market,* 2nd edition, Thomson Nelson, 2006; Barbara Moses, "Loss of Loyalty Cuts Both Ways," *The Globe and Mail*, November 6, 1997: B17. Also, R.S. Echlin, "Courts Apply Smell Test in Judging Contract Workers as Long Term Employees," *The Globe and Mail*, November 22, 1999: B1.

objective 4

Forecasting: A Critical Element of Planning

While internal analysis of the three Cs (culture, competencies, and composition) may reveal a great deal about where the organization is today, things change. And in an important sense strategic planning is about managing that change. Managers must continually forecast both the needs and the capabilities of the firm for the future in order to do an effective job at strategic planning. As shown in Figure 2.4, managers focus on (at least) three key elements: (a) forecasting the demand for labour, (b) forecasting the supply of labour, and (c) balancing supply and demand considerations. Careful attention to each factor helps top managers meet their human resources requirements.

Consider for a moment the high costs of not forecasting—or forecasting poorly. If job vacancies are left unfilled, the resulting loss in efficiency can be very costly, particularly when lead time is required to train replacements. As ridiculous as it may sound, we have seen situations in which employees are laid off in one department while applicants are hired for similar jobs in another department. This kind of mistake can be frustrating, to say the least, and can be confounded when over-hiring results in having to lay off employees who were just recently hired. Poor forecasting also makes it difficult for employees to effectively assess their own careers and development. As a result, some of the more competent and ambitious workers may seek other employment where they feel they will have better career opportunities.[16]

| Figure 2.4 | Model of HR Forecasting |

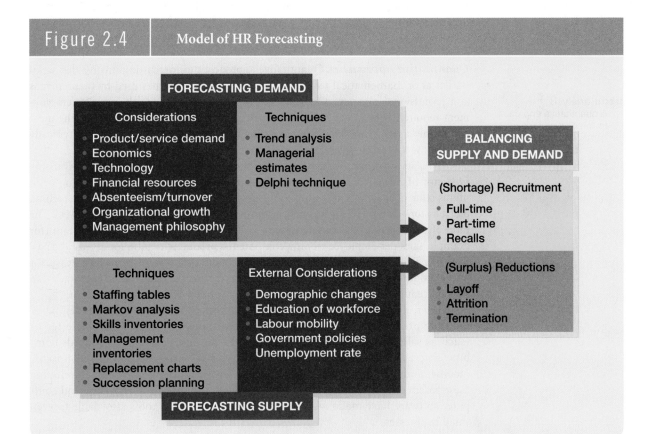

On the plus side, accurate forecasting provides the kind of information managers need to make sound decisions. It can help them ensure that they have the right number and right kind of people in the right places at the right times, doing things that provide value to both the organization and the employees.

Forecasting Demand for Employees

If a key component of forecasting is predicting the number and type of people needed to meet organizational objectives, the question remains: "How can this be done?" A variety of factors, including competitive strategy, technology, structure, and productivity, can influence the demand for labour. For example, as noted in Chapter 1, use of advanced technology is generally accompanied by less demand for low-skilled workers and more demand for knowledge workers. External factors such as business cycles—economic and seasonal trends—can also play a role. For example, retailers such as The Bay and Canadian Tire rely heavily on temporary employees between November and January, during the holiday season.

There are two approaches to HR forecasting: quantitative and qualitative. When concentrating on human resources needs, forecasting is primarily quantitative in nature and, in large organizations, is accomplished by highly trained specialists. Quantitative approaches to forecasting can employ sophisticated analytical models, although forecasting may be as informal as having one person who knows the organization anticipate future HR requirements. Organizational demands will ultimately determine which technique is used. Regardless of the method, however, forecasting should not be neglected, even in relatively small organizations.

trend analysis
A quantitative approach to forecasting labour demand based on an organizational index such as sales

Quantitative Approaches. Quantitative approaches to forecasting involve the use of statistical or mathematical techniques; they are the approaches used by theoreticians and professional planners. One example is **trend analysis,** which forecasts employment requirements on the basis of some organizational index and is one of the most commonly used approaches for projecting HR demand. Trend analysis is typically done in the following several stages:

First, select an appropriate business factor. This should be the best available predictor of human resources needs. Frequently, sales or value added (selling price minus costs of materials and supplies) is used as a predictor in trend analysis. Second, plot a historical trend of the business factor in relation to the number of employees. The ratio of employees to the business factor will provide a labour productivity ratio (for example, sales per employee). Third, compute the productivity ratio for at least the past five years. Fourth, calculate human resources demand by multiplying the business factor by the productivity ratio. Finally, project human resources demand out to the target year. This procedure is illustrated in Figure 2.5 for a hypothetical building contractor.

Other, more sophisticated statistical planning methods include modelling or multiple predictive techniques. Whereas trend analysis relies on a single factor (such as sales) to predict employment needs, the more advanced methods combine several factors, such as interest rates, gross national product, disposable income, and sales, to predict employment levels. While the costs of developing these forecasting methods used to be quite high, advances in technology and computer software have made rather sophisticated forecasting tools affordable to even small businesses.

Figure 2.5	Example of Trend Analysis of HR Demand

YEAR	BUSINESS FACTOR (SALES IN THOUSANDS)	÷	LABOUR PRODUCTIVITY (SALES/EMPLOYEE)	=	HUMAN RESOURCES DEMAND (NUMBER OF EMPLOYEES)
2000	$2,351		14.33		164
2001	$2,613		11.12		235
2002	$2,935		8.34		352
2003	$3,306		10.02		330
2004	$3,613		11.12		325
2005	$3,748		11.12		337
2006	$3,880		12.52		310
2007*	$4,095		12.52		327
2008*	$4,283		12.52		342
2009*	$4,446		12.52		355

*Projected figures

Qualitative Approaches. Admittedly, forecasting is frequently more an art than a science, providing inexact approximations rather than absolute results. The ever-changing environment in which an organization operates contributes to this situation. For example, estimating changes in product or service demand is a basic forecasting concern, as is anticipating changes in national or regional economics. A community hospital anticipating internal changes in technology, organization, or administration must consider these environmental factors in its forecasts of staffing needs. Also, the forecasted staffing needs must be in line with the organization's financial resources.

In contrast to quantitative approaches, qualitative approaches to forecasting are less statistical, attempting to reconcile the interests, abilities, and aspirations of individual employees with the current and future staffing needs of an organization. In both large and small organizations, HR planners may rely on experts who help prepare forecasts to anticipate staffing requirements. **Management forecasts** are the opinions (judgments) of supervisors, department managers, experts, or others knowledgeable about the organization's future employment needs. Another qualitative forecasting method, the Delphi technique, attempts to decrease the subjectivity of forecasts by soliciting and summarizing the judgments of a pre-selected group of individuals. The final forecast thus represents a composite group judgment. The Delphi technique requires a great deal of coordination and cooperation in order to ensure satisfactory forecasts. This method works best in organizations in which dynamic technological changes affect staffing levels.

Ideally, forecasting should include the use of both quantitative and qualitative approaches. In combination, the two approaches complement each other, providing a more complete forecast by bringing together the contributions of both theoreticians and practitioners.

management forecasts
The opinions (judgments) of supervisors, department managers, experts, or others knowledgeable about the organization's future employment needs

Forecasting Supply of Employees

Just as an organization must forecast its future requirements for employees, it must also determine whether sufficient numbers and types of employees are available to staff anticipated openings. As with demand forecasts, the process involves both tracking current levels and making future projections.

staffing tables
> Graphic representations of all organizational jobs, along with the numbers of employees currently occupying those jobs and future (monthly or yearly) employment requirements

Markov analysis
> A method for tracking the pattern of employee movements through various jobs

Staffing Tables and Markov Analysis. An internal supply analysis may begin with the preparation of staffing tables. **Staffing tables** are graphic representations of all organizational jobs, along with the numbers of employees currently occupying those jobs (and perhaps also future employment requirements derived from demand forecasts). Another technique, called **Markov analysis,** shows the percentage (and actual number) of employees who remain in each job from one year to the next, as well as the proportions of those who are promoted, demoted, or transferred, or who exit the organization. As shown in Figure 2.6, Markov analysis can be used to track the pattern of employee movements through various jobs and to develop a transition matrix for forecasting labour supply.

Forecasting the supply of human resources requires that managers have a good understanding of employee turnover and absenteeism. We have included formulas for computing turnover and absenteeism rates in an appendix to this chapter. The calculations are easily made and used by managers of both large and small organizations.

skill inventories
> Files of personnel education, experience, interests, skills, and so on that allow managers to quickly match job openings with employee backgrounds

Skill Inventories and Management Inventories. While staffing tables, Markov analysis, turnover rates, and the like tend to focus on the number of employees in particular jobs, other techniques are more oriented toward the types of employees and their skills, knowledge, and experiences. **Skill inventories** can also be prepared that list

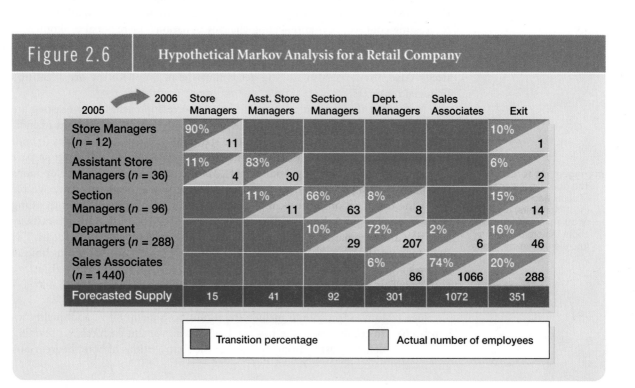

Figure 2.6	Hypothetical Markov Analysis for a Retail Company					
2005 → 2006	Store Managers	Asst. Store Managers	Section Managers	Dept. Managers	Sales Associates	Exit
Store Managers (*n* = 12)	90% 11					10% 1
Assistant Store Managers (*n* = 36)	11% 4	83% 30				6% 2
Section Managers (*n* = 96)		11% 11	66% 63	8% 8		15% 14
Department Managers (*n* = 288)			10% 29	72% 207	2% 6	16% 46
Sales Associates (*n* = 1440)				6% 86	74% 1066	20% 288
Forecasted Supply	15	41	92	301	1072	351

■ Transition percentage   ■ Actual number of employees

each employee's education, past work experience, vocational interests, specific abilities and skills, compensation history, and job tenure. Of course, confidentiality is a vital concern in setting up any such inventory. Nevertheless, well-prepared and up-to-date skill inventories allow an organization to quickly match forthcoming job openings with employee backgrounds. When data are gathered on managers, these inventories are called *management inventories*. And all of this analysis is made simpler these days through the use of HR information systems and enterprise systems provided by companies such as Oracle-PeopleSoft and SAP.

replacement charts
Listings of current jobholders and people who are potential replacements if an opening occurs

Replacement Charts and Succession Planning. Both skill and management inventories—broadly referred to as talent inventories—can be used to develop employee **replacement charts,** which list current jobholders and identify possible replacements should openings occur. Figure 2.7 shows an example of how an

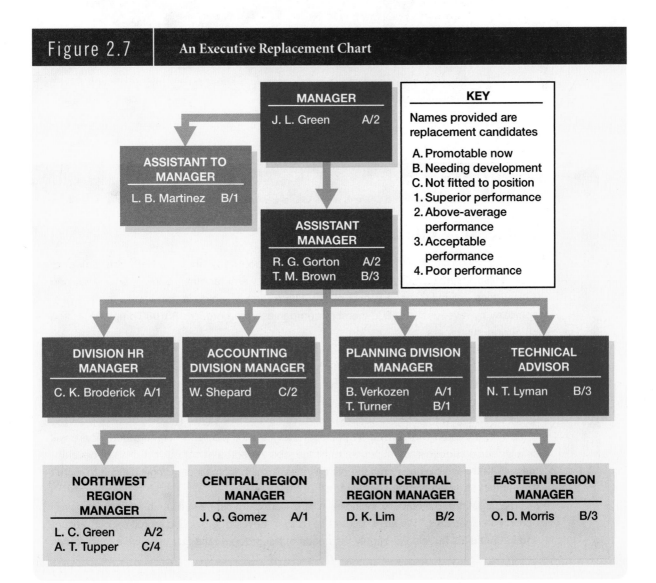

Figure 2.7   **An Executive Replacement Chart**

In addition to qualitative, or statistical, approaches, HR managers also rely on the opinions of managers in their organizations to help forecast the demand for future employees.

© PHOTODISC/GETTY IMAGES

Reality Check

Succession Planning

Allianz Canada is the 12th-largest insurance company in Canada, with sales of $850 million, and employs 850 direct employees and another 550 in wholly owned subsidiaries. Allianz Canada is part of the Allianz Group, which is the world's 12th-largest company by revenues with 500 member companies in the group, 180 000 employees, and 60 million customers.

The parent company initiated a survey of the group companies in 2002, asking, "Given your expansion strategies and retention and turnover rates, what are your projected needs for senior management for the next five years?" The statistics were compiled. When the executives of the company regained consciousness, they realized there was a problem with meeting the HR needs of the organization. Paul Juniper, vice-president of HR, says, "The corporate objective is to have one person available to fill [replace] every senior job in the organization. There will simply not be enough internal people to fill the jobs expected at our current rates of development. With the anticipated demographic changes, it will become increasingly difficult to recruit from outside to make up the shortfall."

The larger group members, including Allianz Canada, have been given a "quota" for development. Juniper says, "We are expected not only to develop, grow, and recruit for our present and future needs but also to supply the needs of the group. In the first year, we expect to see development plans for at least one president and two senior vice-presidents. This means an increasing number of Canadians will be offered international postings within the organization and an increasing number of foreign nationals will rotate through positions within Allianz Canada."

To meet this need, Allianz Canada has initiated a succession planning and leadership development project. Completed first steps have included an overall inventory of management resources, including database information on education, background, special skills, development areas, languages spoken, and willingness to travel for all existing managers. The "tombstone data" (unchangeable information such as date of birth) provides a picture of the strengths and weaknesses of the internal labour supply, which then helps managers make decisions about development and helps to rank projects such as leadership development schools or stretch assignments.

The senior leadership of the organization has been asked to identify individuals who may be potential replacements for them. One priority is to prepare the development plans for those identified as successors for the senior executive committee, which includes an open discussion about their futures. Senior managers' bonuses contain a component for management development within their staff.

The next step is to push the program down two levels in the organization. Paul Juniper continues, "As Allianz Canada consists of a main company and a wholly owned subsidiary, HR is working to entrench a belief that we are managing one overall talent pool for the benefit of both companies and for the worldwide group. The parent company and the HR department ensure that the issue of succession planning is on the agenda."

succession planning
The process of identifying, developing, and tracking key individuals for executive positions

organization might develop a replacement chart for the managers in one of its divisions. Note that this chart provides information on the current job performance and promotability of possible replacements. As such, it can be used side by side with other pieces of information for **succession planning**—the process of identifying, developing, and tracking key individuals so that they may eventually assume top-level positions. See Reality Check for a description of how one Canadian organization does it.

In today's fast-moving environment, succession planning may be more important—and more difficult to conduct—than ever before. Executives frequently lament that their firms are chronically short of talent. Yet in a recent survey of 150 executives with the nation's 1000 largest companies, while all agreed on the value of identifying successors, only 72 percent said they are currently preparing someone to take their place. According to William Byham, CEO of Development Dimensions International (DDI), the typical company expects 33-percent turnover in the executive ranks in the next five years and, among these companies, roughly one-third are worried that they will not be able to find suitable replacements. And the cost of replacing these managers is extremely high, says Byham. "The average one-year estimated replacement cost is $750,000. That includes finding the new [person], training and development costs and opportunity costs of getting the new hire up to speed." Highlights in HRM 2.4 on page 70 shows a checklist for evaluating the "success" of succession planning.[17]

Highlights in HRM 2.4

Succession-Planning Checklist

RATE THE SUCCESS OF YOUR SUCCESSION PLANNING

For each characteristic of a best-practice succession-planning and management program appearing in the left column below, enter a number to the right to indicate how well you believe your organization manages that characteristic. Ask other decision makers in your organization to complete this form individually. Then compile the scores and compare notes.

Characteristics of a Best-Practice Succession-Planning and Management Program	How Would You Rate Your Organization's Succession Planning and Management Program on the Characteristic?				
Your organization has successfully...	Very Poor (1)	Poor (2)	Neither Poor Nor Good (3)	Good (4)	Very Good (5)
1 Clarified the purpose and desired results of the succession-planning and management program.					
2 Determined what performance is required now for all job categories in the organization by establishing competency models.					
3 Established a means to measure individual performance that is aligned with the competencies currently demonstrated by successful performers.					
4 Determined what performance is needed in the future by establishing future competency models for all job categories.					
5 Created an ongoing means by which to assess individual potential against future competency models.					
6 Established a means by which to narrow gaps through the use of individual development plans (IDPs).					
7 Created a means to follow up and hold people accountable.					
8 Created a means by which to document competence and find organizational talent quickly when needed.					
9 Created and sustained rewards for developing people.					
10 Established a means by which to evaluate the results of the succession planning and management program.					

Total (add up the scores for items 1–10 and place in the box on the right)

SCORES

50–40 Congratulations. The succession-planning and management program in your organization conforms with best practices.

29–20 Okay. While your organization could make improvements, you appear to have some of the major pieces in place for a succession-planning and management program.

39–30 Pretty good. Your organization is on the way toward establishing a first-rate succession-planning and management program.

19–10 Not good at all. Your organization is probably filling positions on an as-needed basis.

9–0 Give yourself a failing grade. You need to take steps immediately to improve the succession-planning and management practices of your organization.

Source: From William J. Rothwell, "Putting Success into Your Succession Planning," *The Journal of Business Strategy* 23, no. 3 (May/June 2002): 32–37. Republished with permission—Thomson Media, One State Street, 26th Floor, New York, NY 10004.

Step Four: Formulating Strategy

The forecasting techniques discussed previously provide critical information for strategic planning. Recall that we noted at the beginning of the chapter that HR analysis is an input to strategy formulation. However, a word of caution is needed here. Because HR forecasting techniques take us deep into the specifics of labour supply and demand, we need to be careful not to lose sight of the larger strategic picture. One of the biggest concerns among executives is that (at times) HR managers cannot "see the forest for the trees" because they become mired in the administrative details of their planning models. SWOT analysis, discussed shortly, helps managers combine various sources of information into a broader framework for analysis.

After managers have analyzed the internal strengths and weaknesses of the firm, as well as external opportunities and threats, they have the information they need to formulate corporate, business, and HR strategies for the organization. A comparison of *strengths, weaknesses, opportunities,* and *threats* normally is referred to as a **SWOT analysis.** SWOT analysis helps executives summarize the major facts and forecasts derived from external and internal analyses. Strategy formulation builds on SWOT analysis to use the strengths of the organization to capitalize on opportunities, counteract threats, and alleviate internal weaknesses. In short, strategy formulation moves from simple analysis to devising a coherent course of action.

SWOT analysis
A comparison of strengths, weaknesses, opportunities, and threats for strategy formulation purposes

Corporate Strategy

In any industry, firms decide where and how they will compete. Corporate strategy focuses on domain selection; that is, where they will compete. Some firms choose a concentration strategy that focuses on only a limited portion of the industry. For example, Sleep Country Canada specializes in mattresses.

Growth and Diversification

As companies grow, their strategic choices tend to focus on geographic, volume, and product expansion. HR planning is a vital input to these decisions. Growth hinges on three related elements: (a) increased productivity, (b) a greater number of employees, and (c) developing or acquiring new skills. Concerns about staffing, training, motivation, performance, and the like can either enable growth or limit its potential. As companies diversify into new businesses, managers inevitably are faced with a "make or buy" decision. That is, should they develop the capabilities inhouse or contract externally? For example, when IBM entered the personal computer market in the early 1980s, it contracted with (startup companies) Intel and Microsoft to make the hardware and operating systems for its PC. The decision did not rest solely on human resources issues, but they were an important part of the equation.

Some companies diversify far beyond their core businesses. GE, for example, has diversified from its original base in electrical and home appliance products to such wide-ranging industries as health, finance, insurance, truck and air transportation, and even media, with its ownership of NBC. In order to manage such a diverse portfolio, GE has invested heavily in the development of general management skills and leadership ability. CEO Jeffrey Immelt has stated that GE's future depends on pursuing businesses that leverage human capital (in contrast to its traditional focus on manufacturing). This new strategy is strongly linked to human resources. In fact, the strategy is viable only because the company has done such an enviable job developing talent over the years.

Mergers and Acquisitions

In addition to strategies of growth and diversification, corporate Canada has seen a host of mergers and acquisitions in recent years. And while there are some important competitive reasons for mergers such as these, it is unfortunate to note that many of them have not gone well. Not surprisingly, perhaps, the failure rate among firms is very high. Some estimates suggest that only about 15 percent of all mergers achieve their objectives (measured by return on investment, shareholder value, and the like). Often the failure is due to cultural inconsistencies, as well as conflicts among the managers of each firm. Clearly, these concerns point directly to the importance of effective HR planning prior to—and during—the merger process. Highlights in HRM 2.5 shows key HR activities associated with different phases of a merger or acquisition.

Strategic Alliances and Joint Ventures

Sometimes firms do not acquire or merge with another firm, but instead pursue cooperative strategies such as a strategic alliance or joint venture. Especially when firms enter into international joint ventures, the issues of culture (both company culture and national culture) become paramount. On the front end, HR plays a vital role in assessing the compatibility of cultures and potential problems. As the alliance is formed, HR helps select key executives and develop teamwork across the respective workforces. In addition, HR is typically involved in the design of performance assessment and mutual incentives for the alliance. And, of course, one of the controversial issues related to such alliances is the inevitable issue of outsourcing or offshoring work to other locations.

Business Strategy

While we think about corporate strategy as domain selection, business strategy is viewed in terms of domain navigation. It is more focused on how the company will compete against rival firms in order to create value for customers. We can think of **value creation** in a cost/benefit scenario (that is, value = benefits − costs). Companies can increase customer value either by decreasing costs to customers or by increasing their benefits (or some combination of the two). And their business strategies reflect these choices.

value creation
What the firm adds to a product or service by virtue of making it; the amount of benefits provided by the product or service once the costs of making it are subtracted

Low-Cost Strategy: Compete on Productivity and Efficiency

A low-cost strategy means keeping your costs low enough so that you can offer an attractive price to customers (relative to competitors). Organizations such as McDonald's have been very successful at using a low-cost strategy. Critical success factors for this strategy focus on efficiency, productivity, and minimizing waste. These types of companies often are large and try to take advantage of economies of scale in production and distribution. In many cases, the large size allows them to sell their products and services at a lower price, which leads to higher market share, volume, and (hopefully) profits. However, even a low-cost leader must offer a product or service that customers find valuable. As Gordon Bethune, CEO of Continental Airlines, put it, "You can make a pizza so cheap that no one will buy it."[18] Ultimately organizations need to use a cost strategy to increase value to customers, rather than take it away.

Highlights in HRM 2.5

Key HR Activities Associated with Merger or Acquisition Phases

HR ISSUES	KEY HR ACTIVITIES
STAGE 1—PRECOMBINATION	
• Identifying reasons for the M&A • Forming M&A team/leader • Searching for potential partners • Selecting a partner • Planning for managing the process • Planning to learn from the process	• Participate in preselection assessment of target firm • Assist in conducting thorough due diligence assessment • Participate in planning for combination • Assist in developing HR practices that support rapid learning and knowledge transfer
STAGE 2—COMBINATION	
• Selecting the integration manager(s) • Designing/implementing transition teams • Creating the new structure/ strategies/leadership • Retaining key employees • Managing the change process • Communicating to and involving stakeholders • Developing new policies and practices	• Assist in recruiting and selecting integration manager(s) • Assist with transition team design and staffing • Develop retention strategies and communicate to top talent • Assist in deciding who goes • Facilitate establishment of a new culture • Provide assistance to ensure implementation of HR policies and practices
STAGE 3—SOLIDIFICATION AND ASSESSMENT	
• Solidifying leadership and staffing • Assessing the new strategies and structures • Assessing the new culture • Assessing the concerns of stakeholders • Revising as needed • Learning from the process	• Participate in establishing criteria and procedures for assessing staff effectiveness • Monitor the new culture and recommend approaches to strengthen it • Participate in stakeholder satisfaction • Assist in developing and implementing plans for continuous adjustment and learning

Source: From *Managing Human Resources Through Strategic Partnerships*, 9th ed. by JACKSON/SCHULER, 2006. Reprinted with permission of South-Western, a division of Thomson Learning: www.thomsonrights.com Fax 800-730-2215.

A low-cost strategy has several links to HR planning. The first has to do with productivity. A common misconception about low-cost strategies is that they inevitably require cutting labour costs. On the contrary, there are several good examples of companies that pay their employees "top dollar," but gain back cost advantages because of excellent productivity. That is, they get a terrific "bang for the buck." Either they produce more from the workforce they have, or they can produce the same amount with a smaller workforce. Starbucks is an often-recognized example of a company that pays its employees among the highest wages in its industry, yet still has the lowest overall costs among all competitors. This is because highly motivated employees can often work more efficiently, ensure better quality, eliminate waste, and provide better service.

The second way that low-cost strategies are linked to HR pertains to outsourcing. In some cases, companies seeking low cost may consider contracting with an external partner that can perform particular activities or services as well (or better) at a lower cost. This decision directly links strategic planning to human resources planning. Decisions such as these often result in layoffs, transfers, and the like. As noted before, organizations need to have a clear understanding of their core processes and skills in order to make these decisions. Too often, firms approach outsourcing decisions based on costs alone, but this can lead to detrimental effects in the long run if core skills and capabilities are eroded.

Differentiation Strategy: Compete on Value Added

While decreasing costs is one important way to enhance customer value, another involves providing something unique and distinctive to customers. A differentiation strategy is often based on high product quality, innovative features, speed to market, or superior service. Four Seasons's commitment to quality and luxury, FedEx's focus on speed and flexible delivery, Holt Renfrew's commitment to fashion and customer service, and Sony's emphasis on innovation and product development are all easily identifiable examples of differentiation strategies.

Each of these strategies is rooted in the management of human resources. Companies that focus on service, for example, need to identify and support ways to empower employees to serve customers better. In contrast to the company that

The use of part-time employees helps to contain labour costs at fast food restaurants.

© TONY FREEMAN/PHOTOEDIT

emphasizes low cost and efficiency, you may find that differentiating companies will bend the rules a bit more, allow more flexibility to let you "have it your way," and customize products and services around the customer's particular needs. In place of rigid rules, service-oriented companies often try to embed their values in the cultural values of the company. David Pace, executive vice-president of partner resources at Starbucks, noted that the key feature he looks for in new employees is "discernment," the ability to make good decisions on their own.

Functional Strategy: Ensuring Alignment

In addition to formulating corporate and business-level strategies, managers also need to "translate" strategic priorities into functional areas of the organization (such as marketing, manufacturing, human resources, and the like). This involves all aspects of the business, but in particular there needs to be a clear alignment between HR and the requirements of an organization's strategy. In this regard, HR policies and practices need to achieve two types of fit: external and internal.[19]

External Fit/Alignment

External fit (or *external alignment*) focuses on the connection between the business objectives and the major initiatives in HR. For example, as noted earlier, if a company's strategy focuses on achieving low cost, HR policies and practices need to reinforce this idea by reinforcing efficient and reliable behaviour, enhanced productivity, and the like. On the other hand, if the organization competes through innovation and new product development, then HR policies and practices would be more aligned with the notion of enabling creativity and flexibility. Highlights in HRM 2.6 on page 76 shows the external fit between major business objectives and HR imperatives at Inco.

Internal Fit/Alignment

In addition to external alignment or fit, managers need to ensure that HR practices are all aligned with one another internally to establish a configuration that is mutually reinforcing. Job design, staffing, training, performance appraisal, and compensation—the entire range of HR practices—need to focus on the same workforce objectives (such as efficiency, creativity, and loyalty). Unfortunately, often one HR practice, such as training, might be focused on teamwork and sharing, while another HR practice, such as appraisal and compensation programs, reinforces the ideas of individual achievement. Charles Schwab and Company, for example, faced this very situation. The company has a reputation in the financial services industry for developing a culture of teamwork that has been important to its strategy. However, when it changed its compensation strategy to provide more rewards to high-performing brokers, it ran into a potential problem of sending mixed signals to employees: Which is more important, teamwork or individual high flyers?[20]

While we raise the issue of alignment and fit here as an element of strategy formulation, it clearly links directly to strategy implementation as well. At the end of this chapter, we raise the issue again in the context of evaluating and assessing the success of strategic planning.

Highlights in HRM 2.6

Achieving Strategic Fit at Inco

Inco is a Canadian-based global company with operations and an extensive marketing network in over 40 countries and overall sales of about US$2.5 billion. Inco is one of the world's premier mining and metals companies and the world's second largest producer of nickel.

For over half of its first century of existence, Inco Limited had a quasi-monopoly in the nickel market, and by the early 1950s it was supplying about 85 percent of the western world's nickel. However, in the late 1970s nickel went on the London Metal Exchange. The world, not Inco, began to set prices. Over the next 25 years, Inco continued to produce about the same amount of nickel in a growing market, experiencing a significant drop in its market share. Realizing that the company would probably not survive in such a state—too big to be a niche player, too small to fend off predators—the board and senior management developed a new growth strategy for its core mining and metals business. The growth strategy included developing new low-cost ore bodies in New Caledonia and Labrador, as well as innovative new products and increased market presence and sales in Asia.

There was a need for a strong leadership team to execute the new strategies. Inco had been downsizing for 25 years, however (going from 50 000 employees in 1975 to 10 000 in 2002), and did not have all the managerial talent it required. Increased effort needed to be put into developmental programs to identify and develop high-potential employees, not only in Canada, but wherever Inco operated. Mark J. Daniel, vice-president of Human Resources at Inco, explains, "Our goal is to have leadership be a competitive advantage. We started in the future and worked back. What will the industry look like in 20 years? What part do we want to play in that? How will we get there and what talent will be required?"

The company's view of the future revealed that it needed international managers with technical and engineering training. In addition to all the usual issues associated with developing people with global experience, Inco also faced the reality that some developing countries, such as Indonesia (as well as many developed countries), want to maximize the employment of their own nationals. At the same time, Inco was losing some promising Indonesian engineers because of the lack of developmental opportunities at the management level. These engineers were using Inco as a training ground and then moving on to other companies to become managers. Inco's approach to solving this problem was to develop an arrangement with the Indonesian government whereby additional Canadians could be sent to Indonesia for development and Indonesians would be sent for developmental assignments in Canada.

All these efforts are part of a comprehensive HR strategy to support Inco's business strategies.

Step Five: Strategy Implementation

objective 6

As the old saying goes, "Well begun is half done." But only half. Like any plan, formulating the appropriate strategy is not enough. Managers must also ensure that the new plans are implemented effectively. Recently organizations have been paying more attention to implementation and execution. As Larry Bossidy, a former CEO of Honeywell, noted,

"My job these days is to restore the discipline of execution to a company that had lost it. Many people regard execution as detail work that's beneath the dignity of a business leader. That's wrong. To the contrary, it's the leader's most important job."[21]

Figure 2.8 shows the now classic 7-S framework and reveals that human resources management is instrumental to almost every aspect of strategy implementation, whether it pertains to structure, systems, style, skills, staff, or shared values. While *strategy* lays out the route that the organization will take in the future, organizational *structure* is the framework in which activities of the organization members are coordinated. If the strategy requires redeployment or reorganization of employees, HR will be intimately involved. Closely related to structure are *systems* and processes. These include formal and informal procedures that govern everyday activity. As organizations consider reengineering and process redesign to implement strategies, HR helps ensure that the best workflow models are in place and—importantly—that employees are involved in sharing their advice.

Shared values were discussed earlier in the chapter as a guiding parameter for strategic planning. They arise again as an important issue in implementation as well. Strategic change often requires employees and managers to modify, or abandon, their old ways of doing things. HR managers play a central role as guardians of the corporate culture, the principles on which the company is founded, the fundamental ideas around which the business is built. This is tightly connected to the issue of *style*, which refers not only to the leadership approach of top managers, but also the way in which employees present themselves to the outside world (to suppliers, customers, and so on).

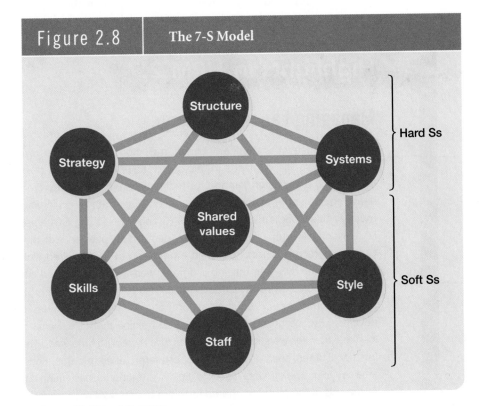

Figure 2.8	The 7-S Model

Source: McKinsey & Company

Skills and *staff* relate directly to the concerns of human resources management and point to the critical role that HR plays in strategy implementation. At a fundamental level, HR's role in strategy implementation focuses on reconciling (1) human resources demanded and (2) human resources available.

Taking Action: Reconciling Supply and Demand

Through HRP, organizations strive for a proper balance between demand considerations and supply considerations. Demand considerations are based on forecasted trends in business activity. Supply considerations involve determining where and how candidates with the required qualifications can be found to fill vacancies. Because of the difficulty in locating applicants for the increasing number of jobs that require advanced training, this aspect of planning has been receiving a great deal more attention. Greater planning effort is also needed in recruiting members of the designated groups for managerial jobs and technical jobs that require advanced levels of education.

In an effort to meet the demand for human resources, organizations have several staffing possibilities, including hiring full-time employees, having current employees work overtime, recalling laid-off workers, and using temporary employees. Read Highlights in HRM 2.7 to see how one Nova Scotia company deals with labour shortages. The 2010 Winter Olympics organizations are deeply concerned about labour shortages. A multi-stakeholder group consisting of representatives from the federal and provincial governments, Tourism BC, First Nations, and the 2010 bid community have joined forces to address the skills gap, and their report on HR Planning "Planning for Gold" can be found on the website of the Ministry of Economic Development (www.ecdev.gov.bc.ca/2010OlympicGames/default.htm).

Highlights in HRM 2.7

Managing Labour Shortages

Dexter, a construction company based in Bedford, Nova Scotia, was facing a skills gap in its labour market. The demands in this sector have changed and there is less need for manual labourers and a greater demand for technicians with computer literacy skills. For example, a heavy equipment operator or surveyor used to operate by observing and pen and paper; now much of this work is dictated by GPS (Global Positioning Systems) and integrated software. Ron Hyson, director of HR for Dexter, decided to partner with the Nova Scotia Community College to recruit, select, and train employees in the required skills. About 350 candidates applied for the two-year training program, were tested, and then interviewed. A final group of 30 was selected to receive training in all fields of construction. They were cross-trained in surveying and heavy equipment operations and were given courses in management development, job costing, and safety. The training methods were varied. About 40 percent of the time, trainees were in the classroom. The remaining time was spent in the field in six to eight functional areas, such as surveying. Work terms of six months, consisting of rotations in each area for four weeks, were used to help the students determine their interests and abilities. At the end of the program, the trainees are guaranteed employment.

However, when forecasts show a surplus of employees, organizations may restrict hiring; reduce work hours; institute work sharing; or consider layoffs, demotions, and/or terminations. Additionally, over time organizations may try to reduce their workforce by relying on attrition (a gradual reduction of employees through resignations, retirements, and deaths). Over the past two decades, early retirements have become a more and more common means for organizations to reduce excess labour supply. Organizations as diverse as community colleges, healthcare facilities, and travel companies encourage employees to accept early retirement by offering "sweetened" retirement benefits. The various types of benefits are discussed in Chapter 11.

Organizational Downsizing, Outsourcing, and Offshoring

As discussed in Chapter 1, organizations have undertaken the extremely painful task of downsizing and restructuring over the past decade to reduce "head count." Because of either economic or competitive pressures, organizations have found themselves with too many employees or with employees who have the wrong kinds of skills. In an effort to reconcile labour supply and demand considerations, companies such as Motorola, Corning, and Hewlett-Packard have eliminated thousands of jobs.[22] These job cuts are not simply restricted to hourly workers. Technical, professional, and managerial positions have been (and are still being) eliminated at an unprecedented rate. The federal government is planning to create a new agency, Shared Services Organization (a form of outsourcing), which will result in the reduction of about 41 000 employees.[23] In many cases, the move is part of a longer-term process of restructuring to take advantage of new technology, corporate partnerships, and cost minimization.

Making Layoff Decisions

Decisions about employee layoffs are usually based on seniority and/or performance. In some organizations, especially those with collective agreements, seniority may be the primary consideration. In other organizations, such factors as ability and fitness may take precedence over seniority in determining layoffs. There are several options available to employers when it comes to dealing with surplus employees: layoffs, attrition, and termination.

Layoff Strategies. Employee layoff decisions are usually based on seniority and/or ability. With unionized organizations, the criteria for determining an employee's eligibility for layoff are typically set forth in the collective agreement. As a rule, job seniority receives significant weight in determining which employees are laid off first. Similar provisions in the collective agreement provide for the right of employees to be recalled for jobs they are still qualified to perform. Organizational policy as well as provisions in the collective agreement should therefore establish and define clearly the employment rights of each individual and the basis on which layoff selections will be made and re-employment effected. The rights of employees during layoffs, the conditions concerning their eligibility for recall, and their obligations in accepting recall should also be clarified. It is common for collective agreements to preserve the re-employment rights of employees laid off for periods of up to two years, provided that they do not refuse to return to work if recalled sooner.

While it has become customary for employers to recognize seniority in unionized employees, nonunion employees are not always given the same consideration. Due to the demand for a technically skilled workforce, the ability of employees to change jobs and learn new skills, as well as their performance and competencies, is given a great deal of weight in layoff decisions. The most important reason for using seniority as a basis for layoffs is the objective nature of the decision: number of years of work, not perception of ability, is the basis for the decision. The system is fair, and employees themselves can calculate their own probability of being employed.

One of the major disadvantages of overemphasizing seniority is that less competent employees receive the same rewards and security as more competent ones. The seniority system ignores talent and effort. The payroll is also higher than under other systems, because more experienced workers tend to earn more money. Also, the practice of using seniority as the basis for deciding which workers to lay off may well have a disproportionate impact on women and minority workers, who often have less seniority than other groups.

Under the umbrella of layoff strategies are several work reduction options: reduced workweek, reduced shifts, transfers to related companies, and so on. Under the reduced workweek, employees work about 20 to 30 hours per week. This option allows the organization to retain a skilled workforce and lessens the financial and emotional impact of a full layoff, and at the same time reduces the costs of production. Some organizations have worked out arrangements so that employment insurance benefits make up most of the difference of the lost wages. However, it is sometimes difficult to predict how much work is available each week; also, overhead fixed costs such as rent and administration continue, independent of the number of hours worked.

Reduced shift work is based on a similar concept of reducing costs by reducing the number of hours worked. Some plants operate three shifts a day and may shut down the midnight to 8:00 a.m. shift to save money. In some rare cases, organizations can transfer laid-off employees to a sister company. Layoffs are the fastest way to achieve workforce reduction; attrition is the slowest.

Attrition Strategies. Some organizations have adopted a no-layoff policy. These firms view people as their most important asset and recognize that their competencies and attitudes are valuable and cannot be easily replaced. They prefer to reduce the workforce through attrition. **Attrition** refers to the "natural" departure of employees through quits, retirements, and deaths. The turnover rates of an organization vary greatly by industry and by occupation. For example, university professors rarely quit, while turnover among fast-food workers can reach 300 percent a year. Most organizations can easily estimate how many people will leave the organization and so can slowly reduce the workforce through natural means.

Attrition must be supplemented by other practices. Hiring freezes are usually implemented at the same time as the organization adopts a strategy of workforce reduction through attrition. A **hiring freeze** means that organizations will not hire new workers as planned, or will hire only in areas critical to the success of the organization. Sometimes the practice is to not replace the worker who has left or been fired.

These practices have several advantages. Organizations can control and predict compensation expenses. But the savings go beyond the salaries and benefits redeemed from departing employees. Take, for example, the costs of employing a manager earning $60,000 a year. Her benefits probably cost another $20,000. However, the costs of replacing her would include recruitment costs ($5,000), paperwork and time in hiring costs ($1,000), orientation and training expenses ($7,000), and office supplies and space ($10,000). Thus, the organization can save significantly by not replacing workers.

However, the disadvantages are significant. Current employees may be overburdened with the work of those who left; their skills may not match the skill sets of the departed workers; and, of course, no new skills or ideas are infiltrating the organization. The major disadvantage of reduction through attrition is that the organization cannot

attrition
A natural departure of employees from organizations through quits, retirements, and deaths

hiring freeze
A practice whereby new workers are not hired as planned, or workers who have left the organization are not replaced

control who leaves and who stays. Valuable employees may be retiring, while less needed ones are still on the job. And the process takes a very long time compared to layoffs, which can be accomplished in days.

Some organizations attempt to accelerate attrition by offering incentives to employees to leave. These incentives include cash bonuses for people to leave during a specified time, accelerated or early retirement benefits, and free outplacement services. However, the buyout process must be carefully managed. Employees with valuable skills who can easily find another job may be the first to cash in. People in key positions should not be targeted for this program. Another disadvantage is that buyouts require a great deal of money up front, which may work against the goal of cost reduction. For example, Ontario Hydro paid out millions in buyouts for a few thousand employees. Employers must be cautious when extending offers of early retirements. An older worker was awarded $250,000 plus benefits in a wrongful dismissal suit, on the grounds that he had been forced to accept the "voluntary" early-retirement option.

To sustain a no-layoffs policy, some organizations ask for volunteers to transfer into divisions where employee shortages are developing. This causes other problems. For example, highly competent employees who have years of experience, expertise, and contacts in one position may not be as productive in another division. Skill match is a recurrent problem. Mandatory transfers allow the employer to match employee skills with vacant positions more accurately. There may be associated morale problems as individuals move into jobs or divisions they do not like, or leave their team and its working style. In addition, union contracts may forbid or inhibit these types of transfers.

If the surplus of employees is deemed to be permanent, terminations may be the only option.

termination
Practice initiated by an employer to separate an employee from the organization permanently

***Termination Strategies.* Termination** is a practice initiated by an employer to separate an employee from the organization permanently. Termination is different from firing, in which an employee is released for such causes as poor performance, high absenteeism, or unethical behaviour. The purpose of termination is to reduce the size of the workforce and thereby save money.

A termination strategy begins with the identification of employees who are in positions that are no longer considered useful or critical to the company's effectiveness. The managers of these employees are contacted about redeployment or termination options. Next the employee is told the news, with varying degrees of advance notice. CIBC gives three months' notice, allows the employee and the manager to prepare a redeployment plan, and allows up to six months for retraining and repositioning. At CIBC, the emphasis is on retaining competent employees whose jobs have been eliminated; the title of the program, Employment Continuity, reflects this strategy.

severance pay
A lump-sum payment given to terminated employees

Employers cannot terminate without some form of compensation to the employee. **Severance pay,** a lump-sum payment given to terminated employees, is calculated on the basis of years of service and salary. Every province has legislation such as the Employment Standards Act, which establishes minimum standards for termination and severance pay. The legal minimum varies by province; for example, a clerk making $500 a week with eight years' service would receive about $4,000 in severance pay. A typical severance package would include

- a lump sum severance payment,
- an extension of group benefits such as medical and dental plans for a predetermined period,
- an option for the employee to convert group life insurance to a private policy,
- some pension plan options.

These payments, if accepted by the employee, immediately discharge the employer from further obligations. Most employers now refer to "ballpark," "reasonable range," or "reasonable offer" court decisions. The ballpark approach offers some degree of certainty to both employers and employees, and thus helps minimize costly court battles.

Some organizations adopt "golden parachutes," a form of severance pay, to protect their employees (especially their executives) from the downsizing effects of mergers, acquisitions, and leveraged buyouts. Golden parachutes are guarantees by the employer that detail the compensation and benefits that employees will receive in termination situations. Golden parachutes encourage managers to work actively with the company during a restructuring, and reduce the possibility of legal challenges on termination. But they are costly.

Step Six: Evaluation and Assessment

At one level, it might seem that assessing effectiveness is the final step in the planning process. That is true. But it is also the first step. Planning is cyclical, of course, and while we've somewhat conveniently placed evaluation at the end, it actually provides the inputs to the next cycle in the planning process. Issues of measurement, benchmarking, alignment, fit, and flexibility are central to the evaluation process.

Evaluation and Assessment Issues

In order to evaluate their performance, firms need to establish a set of parameters that focus on the "desired outcomes" of strategic planning, as well as the metrics they will use to monitor how well the firm delivers against those outcomes. Because strategic management is ultimately aimed at creating a competitive advantage, many firms evaluate their performance against other firms. **Benchmarking** is the process of identifying "best practices" in a given area—say, productivity, logistics, brand management, training, and so on—and then comparing your practices and performance to those of other companies. To accomplish this, a benchmarking team would collect information on its own company's operations and those of the other firm in order to determine gaps. The gaps help determine the causes of performance differences, and ultimately the team would map out a set of best practices that lead to world-class performance.

benchmarking
The process of comparing the organization's processes and practices with those of other companies

Interestingly, the target company for benchmarking does not need to be a competitor. For example, when Xerox wanted to learn about excellent customer service, it benchmarked L. L. Bean. By working with non-competing companies, Xerox was able to get access to information a competitor would not divulge.

In the context of HR strategy, metrics fall into two basic categories: human capital metrics and HR metrics. Human capital metrics assess aspects of the workforce, while HR metrics assess the performance of the HR function itself. The Saratoga Institute publishes the annual *Human Capital Benchmarking Report,* which includes benchmarking information from almost 900 companies (see Highlights in HRM 2.8). Clients can use the information from studies of such areas as pay structure, return on investment per employee, turnover rates, and cost-per-hire and time-to-fill for key employees. This kind of detailed information clarifies potential bases of competitive advantage and reveals a path for developing future HR strategies.[24]

USING THE INTERNET

Look at the sectors and studies being conducted by the Human Resources Benchmarking Association at:

www.hrba.org

Highlights in HRM 2.8

The Top Ten Measures of Human Capital

The top ten areas to measure, as recommended by Jac Fitz-enz, chair of the Saratoga Institute (now part of Spherion's Human Capital Consulting Group), in an issue of *Workforce* magazine (http://www.workforce.com), won't all apply to your company, but some will:

1. **Your most important issues.** These are the targets of all lower-level measures. Focus on them and ensure that your metrics lead in a direct line to them.
2. **Human capital value added.** How do your workers optimize themselves for the good of the company and for themselves? This is the primary measure of an individual's contribution to profitability.
3. **Human capital ROI.** This is the ratio of dollars spent on pay and benefits to an adjusted profit figure.
4. **Separation cost.** How many people are leaving? From which departments? What does it cost the company? The average cost of separation for an employee is at least six months' equivalent of revenue per employee.
5. **Voluntary separation rate.** Lost personnel equal potential lost opportunity, lost revenue, and the cost of workers having to fill the gaps under greater stress. Cutting the separation rate saves the cost of hiring and keeps customer service quality high.
6. **Total labour-cost/revenue percentage.** This is total benefits and compensation cost as a percentage of organizational revenue and shows how much of what you are taking in through revenue goes to support the company's total labour cost, including temporary, seasonal, and contract or contingent workers. This metric can help you track changes in your workforce. Best approach: Compare it to your revenue factor and compensation, benefits, and contingent off-payroll costs. If the metric is rising, determine whether compensation or benefits costs are up or revenue is down. This will help you decide what actions to take.
7. **Total compensation/revenue percentage.** This is the percentage of the company's revenues allocated to the direct costs of employees. Before creating strategies to address concerns, compare this metric to your revenue factor, compensation costs, and benefits costs to analyze what is happening with workers.
8. **Training investment factor.** Basic skills are crucial: Workers who cannot read, write, do simple calculations, or talk intelligently with customers need to have these skill deficiencies addressed.
9. **Time to start.** Recruitment will continue to be a challenge. The amount of the time it takes from approval of a job requisition until the person is on the job is a strategic indicator of revenue production.
10. **Revenue factor.** This is the basic measure understood by managers.

Source: "The Top 10 Measures of Human Capital Management," *HRFocus* 78, no. 5 (May 2001): 8. Copyright © 2001. Reprinted by permission of the publisher via Copyright Clearance Center.

Measuring Strategic Alignment

Earlier in the chapter, we discussed the importance of strategic alignment and fit as an element of strategy formulation and implementation. As an element of evaluation, some very useful techniques help managers assess the extent to which they have achieved these objectives.

Strategy Mapping and the Balanced Scorecard

Balanced Scorecard (BSC)
A measurement framework that helps managers translate strategic goals into operational objectives

One of the most enthusiastically adopted tools for mapping a firm's strategy in order to ensure strategic alignment is the **Balanced Scorecard (BSC).** Developed by Harvard professors Robert Kaplan and David Norton, the BSC is a framework that helps managers translate strategic goals into operational objectives. The model has four related cells: (1) financial, (2) customer, (3) processes, and (4) learning. The logic of the BSC is firmly rooted in human resources management. People management and learning help organizations improve their internal processes and provide excellent customer service. Internal processes—product development, service, and the like—are critical for creating customer satisfaction and loyalty, and they are also important for ensuring productivity to contain costs for better financial performance. Customer value creation, in turn, drives up revenues, which enhances profitability.

Figure 2.9 shows how this might work at Starbucks. In each cell, Starbucks would identify the key metrics that help translate strategic goals to operational imperatives. For example, under customer metrics, Starbucks might look at percentage of repeat

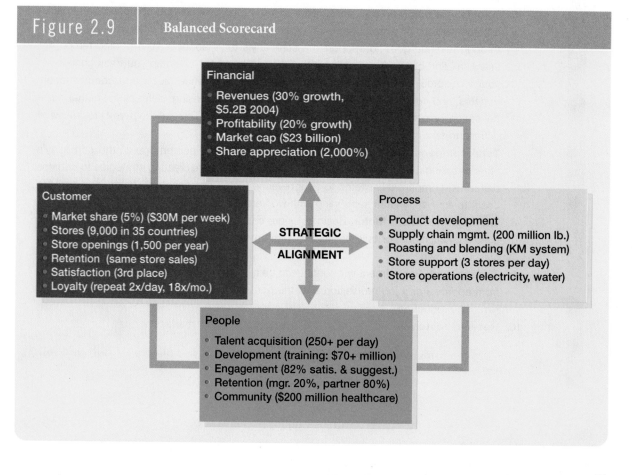

Figure 2.9   **Balanced Scorecard**

Financial
- Revenues (30% growth, $5.2B 2004)
- Profitability (20% growth)
- Market cap ($23 billion)
- Share appreciation (2,000%)

Customer
- Market share (5%) ($30M per week)
- Stores (9,000 in 35 countries)
- Store openings (1,500 per year)
- Retention (same store sales)
- Satisfaction (3rd place)
- Loyalty (repeat 2x/day, 18x/mo.)

STRATEGIC ALIGNMENT

Process
- Product development
- Supply chain mgmt. (200 million lb.)
- Roasting and blending (KM system)
- Store support (3 stores per day)
- Store operations (electricity, water)

People
- Talent acquisition (250+ per day)
- Development (training: $70+ million)
- Engagement (82% satis. & suggest.)
- Retention (mgr. 20%, partner 80%)
- Community ($200 million healthcare)

customers, number of new customers, growth rate, and the like. Under people metrics, managers might measure the numbers of suggestions provided by employees, participation in Starbucks' stock sharing program, employee turnover, training hours spent, and the like. Each of these cells links vertically. People management issues such as rewards, training, and suggestions can be linked to efficient processes (brewing the perfect cup, delivering top-notch customer service, and so forth). These processes then lead to better customer loyalty and growth. Growth and customer loyalty in turn lead to higher profitability and market value.

Measuring Internal Fit

Recall that internal fit means that HR practices are all aligned with one another to establish a configuration that is mutually reinforcing. Figure 2.10 shows an example of how organizations can assess the internal fit of their HR practices. There are essentially three steps. First, managers need to identify the key workforce objectives they hope to achieve. Often this information can come from the people/learning cell of the Balanced Scorecard, and might include loyalty, customer service, productivity, and creativity. Second, managers would identify each of the HR practices used to elicit or reinforce those workforce objectives (job design, staffing, training, appraisal, compensation, and so on). Third, managers

Figure 2.10 | Assessing Internal Fit

WORKFORCE OBJECTIVES

ORGANIZATION	SALES PRODUCTIVITY	CUSTOMER SERVICE	MERCHANDISE INFORMATION	STOCK MAINTENANCE	TOTAL
Structure/Workflow					
• Cross-functional teams	3	2	0	−1	4
• Rotation (depts.)	3	3	−1	−1	4
Staffing					
• Test battery	2	2	1	1	6
• Select for experience	5	3	2	2	12
Training					
• Retail selling skills	4	5	1	1	11
Rewards					
• Results appraisal	5	−4	−2	−5	−6
• Individual incentives	5	−5	−3	−5	−8
Leadership					
• Corporate	3	3	1	0	7
• Store manager	4	2	2	2	10
Technologies					
• Merchandise IS	5	2	5	1	13
• Daily postings	4	−3	4	−1	4
	43/55	10/55	10/55	26/55	57/220

FUNCTIONAL COHESION

5 = Strongly supports the priority
0 = Neutral
−5 = Strongly counterproductive

SYSTEM COHERENCE

would evaluate each HR practice on a scale of –5 (not supportive) to 5 (supportive). By tallying up the ratings across managers, organizations can get a very clear idea of which HR practices are working together to achieve the workforce objectives, and which are not.

An important caveat to this analysis is that internal fit is a necessary, but insufficient, cause of strategic alignment. A company could have nearly perfect alignment among its HR practices, and they still might not be aligned with the competitive strategy. For that reason, it is important for managers to assess both internal fit and external alignment.

Ensuring Strategic Flexibility for the Future

organizational capability
The capacity of the organization to act and change in pursuit of sustainable competitive advantage

Apart from the need to establish and measure fit between HR and strategy, HR is also focused on ensuring flexibility and agility when the environment changes. Ultimately, successful HRP helps increase **organizational capability**—the capacity of the organization to continuously act and change in pursuit of sustainable competitive advantage.[25]

Flexibility can be achieved in two primary ways: coordination flexibility and resource flexibility. *Coordination flexibility* occurs through rapid reallocation of resources to new or changing needs. Through HRP, managers can anticipate upcoming events, keep abreast of changes in legal regulations, forecast economic trends, recognize competitor moves, and the like. With advance notice, managers can move people into and out of jobs, retrain them for new skill requirements, and modify the kinds of incentives they use. Use of a contingency workforce composed of part-timers, temporary employees, and external partners also helps achieve coordination flexibility.[26] *Resource flexibility,* on the other hand, results from having people who can do many different things in different ways. Cross-training, job rotations, team-based work modes, and the like are all focused on establishing a flexible workforce.

We will draw on these ideas throughout the text. But at this point we want to close the chapter by emphasizing that strategic planning is a process designed to ensure superior performance today, as well as establishing the capability and agility to respond tomorrow. As the great hockey player Wayne Gretzky used to say, "I don't skate to where the puck is. I skate to where the puck is going to be."

SUMMARY

Strategic human resources management (SHRM) integrates strategic planning and HR planning. It can be thought of as the pattern of human resources deployments and activities that enables an organization to achieve its strategic goals. HR planning and strategies becomes especially critical when organizations consider global strategies, mergers, relocation of plants, innovation, and downsizing, or when dramatic shifts in the composition of the labour force are occurring.

Analyzing the firm's competitive environment is central to strategic planning. The competitive environment includes the specific organizations with which the firm interacts. Firms analyze the competitive environment in order to adapt to or influence the nature of competition.

Conducting an internal analysis to gauge the firm's strengths and weaknesses involves looking at a firm's "three Cs"—its culture, competencies, and composition. An internal analysis enables strategic decision makers to inventory the organization's skills and resources as well as their performance levels.

An organization's success increasingly depends on the knowledge, skills, and abilities of employees, particularly as they help establish a set of core competencies that distinguish an organization from its competitors. When employees' talents are valuable, rare, difficult to imitate, and organized, an organization can achieve a sustained competitive advantage through its people.

HRP is a systematic process that involves forecasting demand for labour, performing supply analysis, and balancing supply and demand considerations. Forecasting demand requires using either quantitative or qualitative methods to identify the number and type of people needed to meet organizational objectives. Supply analysis involves determining whether sufficient employees are available within the organization to meet demand and also whether potential employees are available on the job market. Reconciling supply and demand requires a host of activities, including internal and external recruitment.

As organizations plan for their future, top management and strategic planners must recognize that strategic-planning decisions affect—and are affected by—HR functions. On one hand, HRP plays a reactive role in ensuring that the right number and type of employees are available to implement a chosen business plan. On the other hand,

HRP can proactively identify and initiate programs needed to develop organizational capabilities on which future strategies can be built. HRP and strategic planning tend to be most effective when there is a reciprocal relationship between the two processes.

Formulating an HR strategy is only half of the HR battle: The strategy must also be implemented. Employment forecasts must be reconciled against the internal and the external supplies of labour the firm faces. This can include hiring, downsizing, outsourcing, and offshoring. If there is a labour shortage, the firm might have to reformulate its long- and short-term strategic plans.

Firms need to establish a set of parameters that focus on the "desired outcomes" of strategic planning, as well as the metrics they will use to monitor how well the firm delivers against those outcomes. Issues of measurement, benchmarking, alignment, fit, and flexibility are central to the evaluation process. Firms use benchmarking, strategy mapping, and the Balanced Scorecard (BSC) as tools to gauge their outcomes.

KEY TERMS

attrition, 80
Balanced Scorecard (BSC), 84
benchmarking, 82
core competencies, 57
core values, 50
cultural audits, 57
environmental scanning, 52
hiring freeze, 80
human resources
   planning (HRP), 48

management forecasts, 65
Markov analysis, 66
mission, 50
organizational capability, 86
replacement charts, 67
severance pay, 81
skill inventories, 66
staffing tables, 66
strategic human resources
   management (SHRM), 48

strategic planning, 48
strategic vision, 50
succession planning, 69
SWOT analysis, 71
termination, 81
trend analysis, 64
value creation, 72

DISCUSSION QUESTIONS

1. Identify the three key elements of the human resources planning model and discuss the relationships among them.
2. What environmental forces influence the future of community colleges and universities? List these

and discuss the implications for programming and the demand for faculty.
3. What criteria must be met if firms are to achieve a competitive advantage through their employees?

4. Which approach do you think should be relied on more heavily for strategy formulation—the quantitative or qualitative approach?

5. Explain the difference between a firm's corporate strategy and business strategy. Why do firms need to look at both aspects?

6. Nortel, when faced with declining demand for its products, eliminated over 50 000 jobs in the late 1990s. What downsizing options were used, and why?

7. Most students have had some experience with part-time employment. In groups, prepare a report for management that would lessen some of the limitations of part-time employment described in Figure 4.7.

8. Why is organizational capability important to firms and how can HR managers enhance it?

INTERNET EXERCISE

The number one issue for some employers is finding and keeping good employees. Replacing employees costs money, but exactly how much? Go to www .uwex.edu/ces/cced/publicat/turn.html and use this online employee turnover calculator to determine the cost to your employer if you (or a member of your student group who has a job) quit your job.

HRM Experience

Customizing HR for Different Types of Human Capital

Part of strategic planning in HR is mapping an organization's human capital. When we look at the strategic value of a person's skills as well as their uniqueness, we soon discover that organizations comprise different kinds of workers who have very different kinds of skills. Some are core knowledge workers; some are more traditional job-based employees; some are contract workers; and some are external partners. In this context, it is unlikely that we would manage all of these employees the same way (as much as we might want to for fairness). There are differences in HR practices for different groups. That's not bad, but it makes the job of HR managers more difficult.

Assignment

The following are descriptions of three different employees. How would you characterize each worker? What role does each play when it comes to the organization's strategy?

Andrea Bascomb is a highly talented computer programmer for MiniFluff, Inc. She is among the elite set of engineers in the computer industry that is doing leading-edge work on advanced computer modelling. In truth, CEO Bill Ding believes that the future of the company rests on the innovative work that Andrea and her team are doing. He worries that someone might lure Andrea away to work for them. So he wants to give her all the room she needs to grow and stay committed to MiniFluff.

Calvin Duff is a salesperson on the retail side of MiniFluff. He has daily contact with customers and is responsible for making sales and communicating with service personnel. Make no mistake: To many customers, Calvin and his co-workers are the "face" of MiniFluff. Always on the lookout for a better situation, Calvin has thought about working for PeachTree Computing, MiniFluff's main competitor. In truth, other salespeople have found that they can leave MiniFluff and get "up to speed" easily at other firms. Their skills are very transferable and the transition is not difficult. Bill Ding and other managers at MiniFluff recognize this fact, so they try to keep salespeople loyal and productive, recognizing that many of them do eventually leave.

Evelyn Frank is a part-time secretary for MiniFluff. She handles routine typing and filing work for the company, particularly in peak periods in the summer and around the holidays. She usually works for a few weeks at a time and then takes time off. The executives at MiniFluff have considered either outsourcing the job to an agency or automating it through a new computer system. But for now things are steady.

BIZFLIX EXERCISES

U-571: Setting Strategy

Watch the scene from *U-571*. It shows several aspects of strategic planning described earlier in this chapter.

This action-packed World War II thriller shows a U.S. submarine crew's efforts to retrieve an Enigma encryption device from a disabled German submarine. After the crew gets the device, a German vessel torpedoes and sinks the U.S. submarine. The survivors must now use the disabled German submarine to escape from the enemy with their prize. The film's almost nonstop action and extraordinary special effects look and sound best with a home theatre system.

The scene comes from the "160 metres" segment toward the film's end. Lt. Andrew Tyler (Matthew McConaughey) is now the submarine's commander following the drowning death of Lt. Commander Mike

Dahlgren (Bill Paxton), the original commander. Lt. Tyler says, "Chief." Chief Petty Officer Henry Klough (Harvey Keitel) approaches the map table. The film continues to its dramatic end with the execution of the strategy Tyler describes.

What to Watch for and Ask Yourself
- Does Lt. Tyler analyze the submarine's external environment? Does he engage in environmental scanning as described earlier in this chapter?
- What is Lt. Tyler's assessment of the submarine's strengths and weaknesses?
- Does Lt. Tyler consider threats and opportunities in forming his strategic plan? Has he done a SWOT analysis as described earlier in this chapter?

case study 1

The Federal Government

In the mid-1990s the federal government undertook the largest mass layoff in Canadian history. Roughly 20 000 employees were affected. Some of the departments announcing cuts were Transport, Natural Resources, Public Works, and Human Resources.

Everyone was scrambling. Most workers did not know who would be affected. Even the president of the Public Service Alliance of Canada (PSAC) did not know which of his 165 000 members were to be terminated. (The Treasury Board, which was responsible for downsizing the civil service, had refused to release names for fear of violating the Privacy Act.) The president of the PSAC complained to reporters, "We are in a hell of a position trying to find these people so we can provide them assistance or even guidance and advice. At the same time, because of that fear mentality that's out there, some of the individuals are saying, 'If I go to the union that might hurt my chances of keeping my job.' It's absolutely ridiculous what's going on out there, and it's another reason why we need more time."

PSAC faced the difficult task of protecting its employees from the effects of a proposed bill (C-76) that would override the key job security provisions of the union's labour contracts. Under the old legislation, government employees had the right to another job in the public service if their positions were eliminated. The new legislation gives public employees whose jobs are terminated 60 days to choose between a generous buyout, a chance at another job, and early retirement.

The government expected about 15 000 workers to take the buyout and another 4000 (over age 50) to accept early retirement programs. The buyouts cost $1 billion. In a novel twist, PSAC wanted to open up the incentive package so that affected workers who did not want to leave the government could swap their packages with employees who wanted to leave but whose positions were not terminated. Many workers in the Ministry of Transport were transferred to the soon-to-be privatized airports and ports.

Government workers had good reason to worry. According to psychologists, people who work in huge organizations do not develop networks of external contacts that may lead to new jobs. Their skills are very narrow because of the volumes of work. For example, a clerk in the government might spend his or her entire year processing a form unique to the government. Many of these individuals have worked for only one employer and have no job search skills. Public perceptions about the easy working life of civil servants may work against their employability. And while government workers in the 1990s were waiting for the axe to fall, they were expected to continue to work.

Source: This case was developed from information in newspapers, including *The Globe and Mail*, May 2, 1995: A13, and May 26, 1995: A1.

QUESTIONS

1. What downsizing strategies did the federal government adopt? What were the limitations of these strategies?
2. What should the government have done to help laid-off workers find new jobs?
3. What should the government have done to manage survivor sickness?
4. If you were a federal employee about to be laid off, what would you do to optimize your chances of re-employment?

case study 2

Filling the Shoes

Bata Ltd. is a multinational shoe company headquartered in Canada that has more than 55 000 employees worldwide, located in 67 subsidiaries. Every single subsidiary has a succession plan in place. Each senior position has three possible successors: a person who could fill the job immediately; a second who could be ready in two years; and a third who could be considered in five years. There are developmental plans for each employee on the chart; these plans are contained in a master file that lists such things as the highest position the employee can be expected to attain, the training programs completed, and areas that need improvement.

The methods for developing these senior managers are varied. For example, Bata has four levels of management training: (1) for high-potential middle managers; (2) for potential company managers; (3) for executive managers who are ready to lead the company now; and (4) for existing company managers. Employees know who is on the chart.

For those not currently part of the management succession plan, there are annual opportunities to earn a place. Formal appraisal programs identify those who are doing well and make recommendations for further training. Another method for developing managers is to offer them temporary "testing" assignments. Managers can replace people on vacation for trial periods to test and upgrade their skills. A system like this one runs the risk of simply repeating the managerial styles and thinking of the previous generation. So Bata, very conscious of the need to look for new blood (i.e., new ways of thinking and acting), also identifies people who have suggested new business opportunities and who are open to divergent perspectives.

Source: Adapted from D. Brown, "You Have to Become Deputy Before You Become Sheriff," *Canadian HR Reporter*, February 14, 2000: 9.

QUESTIONS

1. Bata Ltd. has a plan for replacing senior managers. Should this plan be extended to lower levels? Would the plan be similar, or does the training of supervisors and middle managers require different selection criteria and developmental methods?
2. What are the advantages and disadvantages of making employees aware who is part of the succession chart?

CAREER COUNSEL

To learn about job search strategies, visit the *Managing Human Resources* website (www.belcourt5e.nelson.com).

NOTES AND REFERENCES

1. "The Importance of HR," *HRFocus* 73, no. 3 (March 1996): 14; "Retiring Workforce, Widening Skills Gap, Exodus of 'Critical Talent' Threaten Companies: Deloitte Survey," *Canadian Corporate News* (February 15, 2005).

2. Daniel Leblanc, "Billions Set Aside for Schooling Skills," *The Globe and Mail*, November 15, 2005: A7.

3. Scott A. Snell, Mark Shadur, and Patrick M. Wright, "Human Resources Strategy: The Era of Our Ways," in M. A. Hitt, R. E. Freeman, and J. S. Harrison (eds.), *Handbook of Strategic Management* (Oxford, UK: Blackwell, 2002), 627–49; Patrick M. Wright, Benjamin Dunford, and Scott A. Snell, "Human Resources and the Resource-Based View of the Firm," *Journal of Management* 27, no. 6 (2002): 701–21.

4. "The Importance of HR," 14. For data from a similar survey conducted in Canada, see David Brown, "HR's Role in Business Strategy: Still a Lot of Work to Be Done," *Canadian HR Reporter* 14, no. 19 (November 5, 2001): 1–20; "How Should the HR Dept. of 2004 Be Structured?" *Human Resource Department Management Report*, no. 3 (November 2003): 1.

5. T. J. Watson, Jr., *A Business and Its Beliefs: The Ideas That Helped Build IBM* (New York: McGraw-Hill, 1963).

6. James W. Walker, "Integrating the Human Resource Function with the Business," *Human Resource Planning* 14, no. 2 (1996): 59–77; James W. Walker, "Perspectives," *Human Resource Planning* 25, no. 1 (2002): 12–14.

7. Patrick Wright, Gary McMahan, Scott Snell, and Barry Gerhart, "Comparing Line and HR Executives' Perceptions of HR Effectiveness: Services, Roles, and Contributions," *Human Resource Management* 40, no. 2 (2001): 111–23; Ryan Langlois, "Fairmont Hotels: Business Strategy Starts with People," *Canadian HR Reporter* 14, no. 19 (November 5, 2001): 19–25.

8. Eileen Abels, "Hot Topics: Environmental Scanning," *Bulletin of the American Society for Information Science* 28, no. 3 (February/March 2002): 16–17; William M. James, "Best HR Practices for Today's Innovation Management," *Research-Technology Management* 45, no. 1 (January/February 2002): 57–60; Jay J. Jamrog and Miles H. Overholt, "Building a Strategic HR Function: Continuing the Evolution," *Human Resource Planning* 27, no. 1 (March 2004): 51.

9. Statistics Canada, *The Daily*, February 2003; Statistics Canada, CANSIM, table 282-0002, retrieved March 16, 2006; Statistics Canada, 2001 Census of Population, retrieved March 16, 2006; Canadian Federation of Independent Businesses as reported in *The Globe and Mail* , "No Help at the Inn," March 17, 2006, B1; HRSDC, *Looking Ahead: A Ten Year Outlook for the Canadian Labour Market*," retrieved February 13, 2006 from www.hrsdc.gc.ca; Gabriel Bouchard, "As Labour Pool Shrinks, Top Talent Will Become High-Priced Free Agents," *Canadian HR Reporter*, May 23, 2005: R10; Bruce Little, "Hiring Not Layoffs Is the Trend to Watch," *The Globe and Mail*, March 29, 2004: B2, www.psc-cfp.gc.ca/centres/annual-annuel/2004, retrieved January 16, 2006.

10. Brent Jang, "Revenue May Rise One-Fifth This Year: WestJet," *The Globe and Mail*, March 22, 2006: B6.

11. J. B. Quinn, "The Intelligent Enterprise: A New Paradigm," *Academy of Management Executive* 6, no. 4 (2002): 48–63.

12. Jennifer Laabs, "The HR Side of Sears' Comeback," *Workforce* 78, no. 3 (March 1999): 24–29; Anthony Early, Jr., "A Passion for Personal Success," *Vital Speeches of the Day* 65, no. 6 (January 1, 1999): 184–87.

13. For more information on methods to identify a firm's core competencies, see Khalid Hafeez, YanBing Zhang, and Naila Malak, "Core Competence for Sustainable Competitive Advantage: A Structured Methodology for Identifying Core Competence," *IEEE Transactions on Engineering Management* 49, no. 1 (February 2002): 28–35. See also Geert Duysters and John Hagedoorn, "Core Competences and Company Performance in the World-Wide Computer Industry," *Journal of High Technology Management Research* 11, no. 1 (Spring 2000): 75–91; Quinn, "The Intelligent Enterprise," 48–63; Jane Wollman Rusoff, "Outsourced Solutions: Brokerage Firms Looking to Focus on Their Core Competencies Find the Most Value in a Resource-Rich Clearing Partner," *Research* 27, no. 11 (November 2004): 37–40.

14. Snell, Shadur, and Wright, "Human Resources Strategy," 627–49; Wright, Dunford, and Snell, "Human Resources and the Resource-Based View of the Firm," 701–21.

15. D. P. Lepak and S. A. Snell, "The Human Resource Architecture: Toward a Theory of Human Capital Development and Allocation," *Academy of Management Review* 24, no. 1 (1999): 31–48; David Lepak and Scott Snell, "Examining the Human Resource Architecture: The Relationship among Human Capital, Employment, and Human Resource Configurations," *Journal of Management* 24, no. 1 (January 1999): 31; Mike Berry, "HR Must Push for Change to Drive Human Capital Strategy," *Personnel Today* (April 6, 2004): 4.

16. Stephenie Overman, "Gearing Up for Tomorrow's Workforce," *HRFocus* 76, no. 2 (February 1999): 1, 15; Kathryn Tyler, "Evaluate Your Next Move," *HRMagazine* 46, no. 11 (November 2001): 66–71; Bill Leonard, "Turnover at the Top," *HRMagazine* 46, no. 5 (May 2001): 46–52.

17. Robert Grossman, "Heirs Unapparent," *HRMagazine* 44, no. 2 (February 1999): 36–44; "Succession Planning Is the Top Issue for Executives," *HRFocus* 79, no. 6 (June 2002): 9; Sarah Fister Gale, "Bringing Good Leaders to Light," *Training* 38, no. 6 (June 2001): 38–42; William J. Rothwell, "Putting Success into Your Succession Planning," *Journal of Business Strategy* 23, no. 3 (May/June 2002): 32–37; Mary Maxwell, "Putting Success into Succession Planning," *Nursing Economics* 22, no. 5 (September–October 2004): 285–87.

18. John Huey, "Outlaw Flyboy CEOs," *Fortune*, 142, no. 11 (November 13, 2000): 237–50.

19. Brian Becker, Mark Huselid, and Dave Ulrich, *The HR Scorecard: Linking People, Strategy, and Performance* (Cambridge, MA: Harvard Business School Press, 2001). See also Shari Caudron, "How HR Drives Profits," *Workforce* 80, no. 12 (December 2001): 26–31.

20. "A Singular Sensation for Schwab Brokers," *Business Week Online* (January 24, 2002).

21. Larry Bossidy, Ram Charan, and Charles Burck, *Execution: The Art of Getting Things Done* (New York: Crown Business, 2002).

22. Jesse Drucker, "Motorola to Cut 7,000 More Jobs and Take $3.5 Billion in Charges," *The Wall Street Journal*, June 28, 2002, B6; Dennis K. Berman, "Corning Sets a $1 Billion Charge to Cut 4,000 More Employees," *The Wall Street Journal*, October 4, 2001, B2; Jaikumar Vijayan, "HP/Compaq Brace Workers for Integration, Layoffs," *Computerworld* 36, no. 14 (April 1, 2002): 6; "Planning to Outsource," *HRFocus* 81, no. 5 (May 2004): 1.

23. "Shakeup of Federal Workforce Could Scrap Thousands of Jobs, Save $4B a Year," *Canadian Press Newswire*, August 10, 2005.

24. Ray Brillinger, "Best Practices: Human Resources Benchmarking," *Canadian HR Reporter* 14, no. 12 (June 18, 2001): 12; Chris Mahoney, "Benchmarking Your Way to Smarter Decisions," *Workforce* 79, no. 10 (October 2000): 100–103.

25. P. M. Wright and S. A. Snell, "Toward a Unifying Framework for Exploring Fit and Flexibility in Strategic Human Resource Management," *Academy of Management Review* 22, no. 4 (1998): 756–72; Snell, Shadur, and Wright, "Human Resources Strategy," 627–49; Wright, Dunford, and Snell, "Human Resources and the Resource-Based View of the Firm," 701–21.

26. R. Sanchez, "Strategic Flexibility in Product Competition," *Strategic Management Journal* 16 (1995): 135–59; Wright and Snell, "Toward a Unifying Framework."

Calculating Turnover and Absenteeism

Throughout this chapter we have emphasized that HRP depends on having an accurate picture of both the supply of and the demand for employees. Two factors, employee turnover and absenteeism, have a direct impact on HR planning strategy and recruitment processes. In this appendix, we provide a detailed discussion of turnover and absenteeism, methods for measuring them, and suggestions for managing their impact.

Employee Turnover Rates

Employee turnover refers simply to the movement of employees out of an organization. The average annual turnover rate in Canada is 14.8 percent, putting pressure on employers, ranging from a low of 6.7 percent in the transportation sector to a high of 35.9 percent in the retail sector. It is one of the chief determinants of labour supply. Even if everything else about an organization stays the same, as employees turn over, its supply of labour goes down. This involves both direct and indirect costs to the organization.

Computing the Turnover Rate

The following formula for computing turnover rates is often used:

$$\frac{\text{Number of separations during the month}}{\text{Total number of employees at midmonth}} \times 100$$

Thus, if there were 25 separations during a month and the total number of employees at midmonth was 500, the turnover rate would be:

$$\frac{25}{500} \times 100 = 5 \text{ percent}$$

Turnover rates are computed on a regular basis to compare specific units such as departments, divisions, and work groups. Another method of computing the turnover rate is one that reflects only the avoidable separations (S). This rate is computed by subtracting unavoidable separations (US)—for example, due to pregnancy, return to school, death, or marriage—from all separations. The formula for this method is as follows:

$$\frac{S - US}{M \times 100} = T \text{ (turnover rate)}$$

where M represents the total number of employees at midmonth. For example, if there were 25 separations during a month, 5 of which were US, and the total number of employees at midmonth (M) was 500, the turnover rate would be:

$$\frac{25 - 5}{500} \times 100 = 4 \text{ percent}$$

In looking at the impact of turnover on HR planning and recruitment, it is vitally important to recognize that quantitative rates of turnover are not the only factor to be considered. The *quality* of employees who leave an organization is equally important. If poor employees leave, what experts refer to as "functional turnover," this can prove to be beneficial to the organization. The costs of keeping unproductive workers may be far more than the costs to recruit and train a new, more effective performer.

Determining the Costs of Turnover

Replacing an employee is time-consuming and expensive. Costs can generally be broken down into three categories: separation costs for the departing employee, replacement costs, and training costs for the new employee. These costs are conservatively estimated at two to three times the monthly salary of the departing employee, and they do not include indirect costs such as low productivity prior to quitting and lower morale and overtime for other employees because of the vacated job. Consequently, reducing turnover could result in significant savings to an organization. Highlights in HRM 2.A1 details one organization's costs associated with the turnover of a single computer programmer. Note that the major expense is the cost involved in training a replacement.

> **USING THE INTERNET**
>
> Calculate employee turnover at:
> www.uwex.edu/ces/cced/
> publicat/turn.html

Employee Absenteeism Rates

How frequently employees are absent from their work—the absenteeism rate—is also directly related to HR planning and recruitment. When employees miss work, the organization incurs direct costs of lost wages and decreased productivity. It is not uncommon for organizations to hire extra workers just to make up for the number of absences totalled across all employees. In addition to these direct costs, indirect costs may underlie excessive absenteeism. A certain amount of absenteeism is, of course, unavoidable. There will always be some who must be absent from work because of sickness, accidents, serious family problems, or other legitimate reasons. However, chronic absenteeism may signal deeper problems in the work environment.

Computing Absenteeism Rates

Managers should determine the extent of the absenteeism problem, if any, by maintaining individual and departmental attendance records and by computing absenteeism rates. Although there is no universally accepted definition of "absence" or a standard formula for computing absenteeism rates, the method most frequently used is the following:

$$\frac{\text{Number of worker-days lost through job absence during period}}{\text{Average number of employees} \times \text{number of workdays}} \times 100$$

Highlights in HRM 2.A1

Costs Associated with the Turnover of One Computer Programmer

Turnover costs = Separation costs + Replacement costs + Training costs

Separation costs

1. Exit interview = cost for salary and benefits of both interviewer and departing employee during the exit interview = $30 + $30 = $60
2. Administrative and recordkeeping action = $30

Separation costs = $60 + $30 = $90

Replacement costs

1. Advertising for job opening = $2,500
2. Preemployment administrative functions and recordkeeping action = $100
3. Selection interview = $250
4. Employment tests = $40
5. Meetings to discuss candidates (salary and benefits of managers while participating in meetings) = $250

Replacement costs = $2,500 + $100 + $250 + $40 + $250 = $3,140

Training costs

1. Booklets, manuals, and reports = $50
2. Education = $240/day for new employee's salary and benefits × 10 days of workshops, seminars, or courses = $2,400
3. One-to-one coaching = ($240/day per new employee + $240/day per staff coach or job expert) × 20 days of one-to-one coaching = $9,600
4. Salary and benefits of new employee until he or she gets "up to par" = $240/day for salary and benefits × 20 days = $4,800

Training costs = $50 + $2,400 + $9,600 + $4,800 = $16,850

Total turnover costs = $90 + $3,140 + $16,850 = $20,080

Source: Adapted from the book *Turning Your Human Resources Department into a Profit Center*™ by Michael Mercer, Ph.D. (Castlegate Publishers, Inc., Barrington, Illinois). Copyright 2002 Michael Mercer. Reproduced with permission from Michael Mercer, Ph.D., www.DrMercer.com.

If 300 worker-days are lost through job absence during a month having 25 scheduled working days at an organization that employs 500 workers, the absenteeism rate for that month is:

$$\frac{300}{500 \times 25} \times 100 = 2.4 \text{ percent}$$

Job absence is defined as the failure of employees to report to work when their schedules require it, whether or not such failure to report is excused. Scheduled vacations, holidays, and prearranged leaves of absence are not counted as job absence. However, many employees feel that they have a right to use their negotiated "sick days," as described in Highlights in HRM 2.A2.

Costs of Absenteeism

Traditional accounting and information systems often do not generate data that reflect the costs of absenteeism. Consequently, their usefulness in HR planning is often limited. To accentuate the impact of absenteeism on organizational performance, managers should translate the data into dollar costs. A system for computing absenteeism costs for an individual organization is available. Organizations with computerized absence-reporting systems should find this additional information easy and inexpensive to generate. The cost of each person-hour lost to absenteeism is based on the hourly weighted-average salary, costs of employee benefits, supervisory costs, and incidental costs.

For example, XYZ Company, with 1200 employees, has 78 000 person-hours lost to absenteeism; the total absence cost is $560,886. When this figure is divided by 1200 employees, the cost per employee is $467.41. (In this example, we are assuming the absent workers are paid. If absent workers are not paid, their salary figures are omitted from the computation.)

Highlights in HRM 2.A2

"My Right to Be Sick!"

Canadian employees are absent, on average, seven days a year. The rate of absenteeism is even higher for public-sector employees. These levels of short-term absenteeism are rising, due both to the increased stresses felt by the survivors of downsizing and to the sense of entitlement felt by many employees ("My contract says I can have ten days of sick leave a year; therefore I will take ten days"). The chart below illustrates the rising costs of absenteeism:

Factor	1997	2000	2003
Average days absent	5.7	6.1	6.7
Direct cost per employee	$2,843	$3,550	$4,100
Percentage of payroll	5.6%	7.1%	7.4%
Indirect costs (overtime/training)	5.8%	7.3%	7.6%

Most employers do not track absenteeism rates, and yet controlling absenteeism could alleviate labour shortages in certain sectors. Take, for example, the continuing shortage of health care workers. Canada's health care workers are absent 11.7 days a year compared to the average of 6.7. If the absenteeism rate in this sector were reduced to the national average, there would be 5500 fewer nursing jobs to fill.

Sources: David Brown, "Short Term Absences Double," *Canadian HR Reporter* 13, no. 18 (October 23, 2000): 1; Barbara Sibald, "Could Reducing Absenteeism Help Solve Health Care Worker Shortage?" *E-Canadian Medical Association Journal*, November 27, 2001.

Absenteeism and HR Planning

While an employer may find that the overall absenteeism rate and costs are within an acceptable range, it is still advisable to study the statistics to determine whether there are patterns in the data. Rarely does absenteeism spread itself evenly across an organization. It is very likely that employees in one area (or occupational group) may have nearly perfect attendance records, while others in a different area may be absent frequently. Think of absenteeism as the canary in the mine shaft, warning of problems in the unit. By monitoring these differential attendance records, managers can assess where problems might exist and, more important, begin planning ways to resolve or improve the underlying causes. For example, incentives could be provided for perfect attendance. Alternatively, progressive discipline procedures might be used with employees having a record of recurring absenteeism.

By establishing a comprehensive absenteeism policy, Allen-Bradley cut absenteeism 83.5 percent in a 25-month period. This reduced the strain on labour costs and increased productivity. Part of the company's attendance policy reads:

> It is important to the successful operation of the Motion Control Division that employees be at work each scheduled workday. Each employee is performing an important set of tasks or activities. Excessive and/or avoidable absenteeism places unfair burdens on co-workers and increases the company's cost of doing business by disruption of work schedules, [creating] inefficiency and waste, delays, costly overtime, job pressures and customer complaints.[1]

NOTES AND REFERENCES

1. Allen-Bradley Employee Handbook.

NEL

Equity and Diversity in Human Resources Management

After studying this chapter, you should be able to

objective **1**
Explain the reasons for employment equity legislation.

objective **5**
Describe how employment equity is implemented in organizations.

objective **2**
Identify and describe the major laws affecting employment equity, and explain how they are enforced.

objective **6**
Discuss sexual harassment as an employment equity issue.

objective **3**
Describe pay equity and strategies for implementing it.

objective **7**
Explain and give examples of diversity management.

objective **4**
Discuss the Employment Equity Act with respect to its origins, its purpose, and its continued enforcement.

Managers and human resource professionals are expected to manage employees in ways that comply with and respect the laws and regulations of Canada. These rules have been written to protect employees and employers. In some cases, the laws have been created because of previous situations where employees were not treated fairly. In other cases, the laws simply reflect the values of society. Human rights legislation and employment equity legislation, introduced in this chapter, arose because of both of these cases. But they are not the only laws that govern the employment relationship. In other chapters you will become familiar with other legislation, always introduced in the context of the functions, such as the regulations governing the handling of hazardous material in the occupational health and safety chapter (Chapter 12). It is important to know that managers (and employees) cannot do whatever they want at work, without suffering consequences. The consequences range from criminal charges, costly and time-consuming litigation, negative publicity for the organization, and a decrease in organizational morale and commitment. Therefore, following the laws and regulations is just good business, as you will see in the discussion of equity and diversity.

Canada is one of the most diverse countries in the world—a kaleidoscope of cultures, languages, and nationalities consisting of more than 200 different ethnic groups. Nearly 20 percent of our citizens were born outside Canada, with more than nine out of ten of these immigrants making their homes in urban centres. By 2016, about one in every five citizens will be a visible minority. The workplace not only must reflect this reality but also must accommodate this diversity. In the field of HRM, perhaps no topic has received more attention in recent decades than employment equity. **Employment equity**, or the treatment of employed individuals in a fair and nonbiased manner, has attracted the attention of the media, the courts, practitioners, and legislators. Employment equity legislation affects all aspects of the employment relationship. When managers ignore the legal aspects of HRM, they risk incurring costly and time-consuming litigation, negative public attitudes, and damage to organization morale.

employment equity
The employment of individuals in a fair and nonbiased manner

Employment equity is not only a legal topic; it is also an emotional issue. It concerns all individuals regardless of their sex, religion, age, national origin, colour, or position in an organization. Supervisors should be aware of their personal biases and how these attitudes can influence their dealings with subordinates. It should be emphasized that covert as well as blatantly intentional discrimination in employment is illegal.

In this chapter we emphasize the legislation governing employment equity, and describe the organizational response to this legislation. Today, compliance with employment equity involves managing diversity with the goal of utilizing fully the organization's human capital.

Employment Equity

objective **1**

Central to Canada's economic growth and prosperity in a highly competitive global marketplace will be a barrier-free environment in which all Canadians can fully explore and develop their career potential. Labour force statistics (see Chapter 1) indicated changing patterns of immigration, rising labour force participation rates for women, and an aging population with a proportionally higher incidence of disabilities. Women, visible minorities, and people with disabilities make up over 60 percent of Canada's labour force, and their numbers continue to rise.[1] Members of designated groups entering Canada's labour pool constitute a vital resource, and their full participation in the workplace will be fundamental to an organization's ability to understand and respond to the needs of a rapidly changing marketplace. As a society, we have moved beyond principle to imperative in ensuring equal access to employment opportunities.

By definition, equity means fairness and impartiality. In a legal sense, it means justice based on the concepts of ethics and fairness and a system of jurisprudence administered by courts and designed mainly to mitigate the rigours of common law. The implementation of employment equity—or "affirmative action" as it is termed in the United States—has involved establishing policies and practices designed to ensure equitable representation in the workforce and to redress past discriminations. There are four **designated groups** in Canada that have not received equitable treatment in employment.

designated groups
Women, visible minorities, Aboriginal peoples, and persons with disabilities who have been disadvantaged in employment

Status of Designated Groups

Women, Aboriginal peoples, visible minorities, and people with disabilities face significant (albeit different) disadvantages in employment, even though they make up about 60 percent of Canada's workforce. Some of these disadvantages include high unemployment, occupational segregation, pay inequities, and limited opportunities for career progress.

Women tend to be concentrated in occupations that are accorded lower status and pay. In 2002, the percentage of women in the population was 50.8 percent and they constituted 46.7 percent of the total workforce but were not equally represented in all occupations. Women are underrepresented as semi-professionals and technicians; as supervisors in crafts and trades; in skilled crafts and trades; and as other sales and service personnel.[2] Women are also underrepresented in management positions and as members of boards. Women cite the top barriers to women's advancement in Highlights in HRM 3.1.

Highlights in HRM 3.1

Barriers to the Advancement of Women

1. Commitment to personal and family responsibilities
2. Lack of mentoring opportunities
3. Lack of female role models
4. Stereotyping and preconceptions of women's roles and abilities
5. Exclusion from informal networks of communication
6. Failure of senior leaders to assume accountability for women's advancement

Source: A. Tomlinson, "Wall Street Rougher than Bay Street," *Canadian HR Reporter* 15, no. 5 (March 11, 2002): 1 and 14.

First Nations people constitute roughly 4.4 percent of the population, but constitute only 1.6 percent of the workforce. Their unemployment rate is more than twice the national average. The median income for the Canadian population is $25,000 while the median for Aboriginals is $16,000.[3] In western Canada they will account for a substantial portion of labour market growth. However, many Aboriginal people face major barriers to employment, which are often compounded by low educational achievement and lack of job experience, as well as by language and cultural barriers. In urban centres, many Aboriginal workers are concentrated in low-paying, unstable employment. Economic self-sufficiency and participation in the economy are seen as essential to Aboriginal development. Interestingly, Native values such as cooperation and consensus decision making have become more closely aligned with management approaches.[4] A study in one Canadian company showed that the creation of an Aboriginal networking group, based on cultural concepts such as talking circles and collective decision making, resulted in Aboriginals with strong feelings of belonging and a sense of professional purpose, and this in turn made them willing to help recruit other Aboriginals.[5] Highlights in HRM 3.2 describes how Manitoba Hydro and SaskTel reach out to the Aboriginal population.

People with disabilities represent 12.4 percent of Canada's population, but again, their workforce representation is low at 1.6 percent. The unemployment rate for employable people with disabilities is much higher than the national unemployment rate, which was 7.5 percent in 2003. About one-third of those with disabilities became disabled as adults, resulting in 70 percent of them forced to make career changes. People with disabilities face attitudinal barriers, physical demands that are unrelated to actual job requirements, and inadequate access to the technical and human support systems that would make productive employment possible. Seventy percent of those with disabilities need some kind of workplace accommodation, and in 80 percent of the cases the cost is less than $500.[6] Employers seek to redress attitudinal barriers by focusing on abilities, not disabilities.

The visible minority population in Canada experienced a growth rate of 25 percent since the 1996 Census, compared to an overall population growth of 4 percent. Visible minority groups vary in their labour force profiles and in their regional distributions. Studies have shown that Latin Americans and Southeast Asians experience lower-than-average incomes, higher rates of unemployment, and reduced access to job interviews, even when they have the same qualifications as other candidates. Systemic barriers that negatively affect employment for visible minorities include culturally biased aptitude tests, lack of recognition of foreign credentials, and excessively high language requirements. Recent statistics indicate that although visible minorities—73 percent of whom are immigrants—tend to be better educated, they also have the highest unemployment rates.[7] The unemployment rate of recent immigrants (12.1 percent) was still nearly twice that of the Canadian-born population (6.4 percent).[8] As such, there are targeted efforts to recruit them to ensure representation.

Figure 3.1 on page 104 shows the workforce representation of the designated groups in the Canadian labour force. Ethics in HRM on page 105 describes some of the issues in employment equity.

USING THE INTERNET

You'll find a good first stop for any information on diversity at the website of Diversity Inc.:

www.diversityinc.com

WorkAble Solutions provides job seekers and employers with information on the benefits of hiring persons with disabilities:

www.workablesolutionsbc.ca

The Government of Ontario presents extensive resources and information on workplace diversity and creating accessibility for people with disabilities:

www.equalopportunity.ca

Highlights in HRM 3.2

Outreach Efforts

Human Resources Development Canada awarded Manitoba Hydro the Vision award for creativity and innovation in its employment equity programs. Currently, Aboriginal people make up 8.3 percent of Manitoba Hydro's workforce. In northern Manitoba, where there is a greater concentration of Aboriginal people, 27.4 percent of the corporation's workforce is Aboriginal. The goal is to get the overall corporate representation of Aboriginal people up to 10 percent, and up to 33 percent in the north. The creative ways in which these goals are being reached include the following:

- A zero tolerance policy of workplace harassment and discrimination.
- An outreach and partnership program with Aboriginal organizations to provide information about employment and training opportunities.
- Partnerships with postsecondary institutions to provide educational programs and career information and to brand Manitoba Hydro as an employer of choice.
- A review of training programs to ensure that there are no systemic barriers.
- Systematic recruitment efforts to introduce Aboriginals by means of internships, co-op placements, summer employment, and part-time work.

The most successful program is the pre-employment training designed to facilitate the entry of Aboriginals into Manitoba Hydro's training programs, which are more like apprentice-ship programs. The pre-employment training provides academic upgrading, a rotation through three trades to familiarize candidates with these jobs, and workshops to deal with the concerns and issues about being away from home.

SaskTel is a Crown corporation providing cellular, phone, Internet, and multimedia services to 13 cities and more than 500 remote communities in Saskatchewan, many of them inhabited by First Nations and Métis people. SaskTel cares about the Aboriginal population both as customers and employees (8 percent of SaskTel's workforce is Aboriginal and the company has a target of 13.5 percent, the provincial rate). The company's call centre can offer service in three different First Nations languages.

Sources: Laura Bogomolny, Peter Evans, Andy Holloway, Zena Olijnyk, Erin Pooley, and Andrew Wahl, "The Best Workplaces in Canada" *Canadian Business*, April 10–23, 2006; Cheryl Petten, "Manitoba Hydro Recognized for Employment Equity Efforts," *Windspeaker* 20, no. 4 (August 2002): 31.

Benefits of Employment Equity

Employment equity makes good business sense. It contributes to the bottom line by broadening the base of qualified individuals for employment, training, and promotions, and by helping employers avoid costly human rights complaints. Employment equity enhances an organization's ability to attract and keep the best-

Workplace accommodation for persons with disabilities is usually inexpensive.

When looking for employees, employers need to assess abilities.

qualified employees, which results in greater access to a broader base of skills. It also enhances employee morale by offering special measures such as flexible work schedules and work sharing. Finally, it improves the organization's image in the community.[9]

The Charter of Rights and Freedoms, the federal Canadian Human Rights Act, and pay equity and employment equity acts are the governing pieces of legislation dealing with employment equity.

Figure 3.1	Representation of Designated Groups in the Labour Force	
	REPRESENTATION IN THE CANADIAN POPULATION	**REPRESENTATION IN THE WORKFORCE**
Women	50.8%	46.7%
Aboriginal people	4.4	1.6
People with disabilities	12.4	2.3
Members of visible minorities	13.4	11.7

Source: Statistics Canada website: www.statcan.ca/english/Pgdb/labor20a.htm, table 282-0002.

Ethics in HRM

Ethics: Equality or Equity

The Public Works, of the federal government, sent its department managers an e-mail telling them persons recruited externally must be from designated groups. The federal Department of Fisheries ran an ad on the government's website that stated explicitly that those who can apply are "persons working or residing in Canada and Canadian citizens living abroad, who are members of the visible minority groups." The Employment Equity Act defines visible minorities as being persons, other than Aboriginal peoples, who are non-Caucasian in race or non-white in colour. The decision to restrict applicants to visible minorities is part of the government's efforts to have its employees look more like the Canadian population. About 14 percent of Canadians identify themselves as visible minorities, and they represent about 12 percent of the labour market. However, only 7.8 percent work in the public service. Therefore, the government decreed that about 3 percent of job postings would be restricted to visible minorities. Unlike the Americans, quotas are not in place. But words such as benchmarks, targets, and goals have the same impact. Critics argue that candidates should be judged on merit, not colour. Other programs to increase minority candidates would be better: provide more education and training for minorities or create an office culture that values diversity. The public service has a good track record in increasing the number of francophones and women, and restricted competitions may not be the best route. But the commissioner of the public service counters that treating all people the same way does not always lead to equitable results, and special measures are necessary.

Sources: T. Blackwell, "White Males Need Not Apply," *The National Post*, November 19, 2005: A1; E. Greenspon, "Don't Apply," *The Globe and Mail*, May 30, 2003: A16; M. Wente, "Whites Need Not Apply," *The Globe and Mail*, May 29, 2003: A21.

The Legal Framework

objective 2

The Charter of Rights and Freedoms

The Constitution Act of 1982, which contains the Canadian Charter of Rights and Freedoms, is the cornerstone of equity legislation. The Charter guarantees some fundamental rights to every Canadian, including:

- Fundamental freedoms (s. 2) that comprise the standard rights of freedom of speech, press, assembly, association, and religion.
- Democratic rights (ss. 3 to 5), covering franchise rights.
- Mobility rights (s. 6), concerning the right to move freely from province to province for the purposes of residence and/or employment.
- Legal rights (ss. 7 to 14), conferring standard procedural rights in criminal proceedings.
- Equality rights (s. 15), guaranteeing no discrimination by law on grounds of race, ethnic origin, colour, religion, sex, age, or mental and physical ability.
- Language rights (ss. 16 to 23).[10]

Although the Charter has offered many Canadians opportunities with regard to their own individual rights and responsibilities, it has also been a source of disappointment. The enactment of the Charter created high expectations on the part of various groups, especially unions, which believed that under Section 2 all employees would have a fundamental right to associate, to bargain collectively, and to strike. However, in 1987 the Supreme Court of Canada, in ruling on a challenge to federal public-sector laws relating to compulsory arbitration, back-to-work legislation, and wage restraint legislation, declared that Section 2 of the Charter does not include the right to bargain collectively and to strike. In the Court's view, these were not fundamental freedoms, but rather statutory rights created and regulated by legislation. As a result of this ruling, governments can weaken the collective bargaining process by limiting salary increases, legislating strikers back to work, and imposing compulsory arbitration.

Canadian Human Rights Act (CHRA)

The Canadian Human Rights Act was passed by Parliament on July 14, 1977, and became effective in March 1978. This act proclaims that

> every individual should have an equal opportunity with other individuals to make for himself or herself the life that he or she is able and wishes to have, consistent with his or her duties and obligations as a member of society, without being hindered in or prevented from doing so by discriminatory practices based on race, national or ethnic origin, colour, religion, age, sex or marital status, or convictions for an offence for which a pardon has been granted or by discriminatory employment practices based on physical handicap.[11]

The act applies to all federal government departments and agencies, to Crown corporations, and to other businesses and industries under federal jurisdiction, such as banks, airlines, railway companies, and insurance and communications companies.

For those areas not under federal jurisdiction, protection is available under provincial human rights laws. Provincial laws, although very similar to federal ones, do differ from province to province. Every province and territory has a human rights act (or code), and each has jurisdiction prohibiting discrimination in the workplace.

The prohibited grounds of discrimination in employment include race, religion, sex, age, national or ethnic origin, physical handicap, and marital status (see Figure 3.2 for a complete listing). Employers are permitted to discriminate if employment preferences are based on a **bona fide occupational qualification** (BFOQ) or BFOR (bona fide occupational requirement). A BFOQ is justified if the employer can establish necessity for business operations. In other words, differential treatment is not discrimination if there is a justifiable reason. For example, adherence to the tenets of the Roman Catholic Church was deemed a BFOQ for employment as a teacher in a Roman Catholic school.[12] Business necessity also relates to the safe and efficient operation of an organization. There is an ongoing debate as to whether male guards should be allowed to work in women's prisons.

bona fide occupational qualification (BFOQ)
A justifiable reason for discrimination based on business reasons of safety or effectiveness

Enforcement of the Canadian Human Rights Act

The Canadian Human Rights Commission (CHRC) deals with complaints concerning discriminatory practices covered by the Canadian Human Rights Act. The CHRC may choose to act on its own if it feels that sufficient grounds exist for a finding of discrimination. It also has the power to issue guidelines interpreting the act.

| Figure 3.2 | Prohibited Grounds of Discrimination in Canada |

This document provides comparative information on the grounds of discrimination covered by federal, provincial and territorial human rights legislation in Canada. In some instances, prohibited grounds for employment differ from those for the provision of services.

PROHIBITED GROUND	JURISDICTION	COMMENTS
Race or colour		
Employment	all jurisdictions	
Provision of Service	all jurisdictions	
Religion		
Employment	all jurisdictions	Yukon's Act reads "religion or creed, or religious belief, religious association or religious activity"
Provision of Service	all jurisdictions	Yukon's Act reads "religion or creed, or religious belief, religious association or religious activity"
Physical or mental disability		
Employment	all jurisdictions	Quebec uses the phrase "handicap or use of any means to palliate a handicap"
Provision of Service	all jurisdictions	Quebec uses the phrase "handicap or use of any means to palliate a handicap"
Dependence on alcohol or drugs		
Employment	all except Yukon and Northwest Territories	Policy to accept complaints in British Columbia, Alberta, Saskatchewan, Manitoba, Ontario, New Brunswick and Prince Edward Island Included in "handicap" ground in Quebec Previous dependence only in New Brunswick and Nova Scotia
Provision of Service	all except Yukon, Northwest Territories and Quebec	Previous dependence only in New Brunswick and Nova Scotia Included in "handicap" ground in Quebec

(continued on next page)

Age

Employment	all jurisdictions	British Columbia: 19–65 Alberta: 18+ Saskatchewan: 18–64 Ontario: 18–65 Newfoundland: 19–65 Quebec: except as provided for by law
Provision of Service	all except British Columbia, Alberta and Newfoundland	For tenancy only in British Columbia Saskatchewan does not include accommodation In Ontario, applies to those 18 years and older, although 16- and 17-year-olds who have left the care of parents or guardians are protected regarding accommodation In Quebec, except as provided for by law

Sex (includes pregnancy and childbirth)

Employment	all jurisdictions	British Columbia includes breast feeding Alberta uses the term "gender" Manitoba includes gender-determined characteristics Ontario recognizes the protection of transgendered persons and accepts complaints related to "gender identity"; Ontario accepts complaints related to female genital mutilation In Quebec, pregnancy as such is considered a ground of discrimination
Provision of Service	all jurisdictions	Alberta uses the term "gender" Manitoba includes gender-determined characteristics Ontario recognizes the protection of transgendered persons and accepts complaints related to "gender identity"; Ontario accepts complaints related to female genital mutilation In Quebec, pregnancy as such is considered a ground of discrimination

Marital status

Employment	all jurisdictions	Quebec uses the term "civil status"
Provision of Service	all jurisdictions	Quebec uses the term "civil status"

Family status

Employment	all except New Brunswick as and Newfoundland	Saskatchewan defines being in a parent-child relationship Quebec uses the term "civil status"
Provision of Service	all except New Brunswick and Newfoundland	Saskatchewan defines as being in a parent-child relationship Quebec uses the term "civil status"

Sexual orientation

Employment	all jurisdictions	The Supreme Court of Canada read sexual orientation into the *Alberta Human Rights, Citizenship and Multiculturalism Act* in 1998
Provision of Service	all jurisdictions	The Supreme Court of Canada read sexual orientation into the *Alberta Human Rights, Citizenship and Multiculturalism Act* in 1998

National or ethnic origin (including linguistic background)

Employment	all except British Columbia and Alberta	Saskatchewan and Northwest Territories use the term "nationality" Ontario's Code includes both "ethnic origin" and "citizenship"
Provision of Service	all except British Columbia and Alberta	Saskatchewan and Northwest Territories use the term "nationality" Ontario's Code includes both "ethnic origin" and "citizenship"

Ancestry or place of origin

Employment	Yukon, British Columbia, Alberta, Saskatchewan, Manitoba, Northwest Territories, Ontario and New Brunswick	
Provision of Service	Yukon, British Columbia, Alberta, Saskatchewan, Manitoba, Northwest Territories, Ontario and New Brunswick	

(continued on next page)

Language

Employment	Yukon, Ontario and Quebec	Ontario accepts complaints on the grounds of ancestry, ethnic origin, place of origin and race New Brunswick will accept language-related complaints filed on the basis of ancestry, although not an enumerated ground
Provision of Service	Yukon, Ontario and Quebec	Ontario accepts complaints on the grounds of ancestry, ethnic origin, place of origin and race New Brunswick will accept language-related complaints filed on the basis of ancestry, although not an enumerated ground

Social condition or origin

Employment	Quebec, Northwest Territories, New Brunswick and Newfoundland	
Provision of Service	Quebec, Northwest Territories, New Brunswick and Newfoundland	

Source of income

Employment	Alberta, Saskatchewan, Manitoba, Quebec, Prince Edward Island and Nova Scotia	Defined as "receipt of public assistance" in Saskatchewan Included under social condition in Quebec
Provision of Service	British Columbia, Alberta, Saskatchewan, Manitoba, Ontario, Prince Edward Island and Nova Scotia	Applies to tenancy only (not public services or facilities) in British Columbia Defined as "receipt of social assistance" in Saskatchewan Ontario bans discrimination in accommodation on the grounds of receipt of public assistance Included under social condition in Quebec Applies to occupancy or accommodation only in Nova Scotia

Assignment, attachment or seizure of pay

Employment	Newfoundland	Included under social condition in Quebec
Provision of Service	Newfoundland	Included under social condition in Quebec

Based on association

Employment	Yukon, Manitoba, Ontario, New Brunswick, Nova Scotia, Northwest Territories and Prince Edward Island	Northwest Territories has prohibition on basis of "political association"
Provision of Service	Yukon, Manitoba, Ontario, New Brunswick, Nova Scotia, Northwest Territories and Prince Edward Island	Northwest Territories has prohibition on basis of "political association"

Political belief

Employment	Yukon, British Columbia, Manitoba, Quebec, Nova Scotia, Prince Edward Island, New Brunswick and Newfoundland	Newfoundland has prohibition on basis of "political opinion"
Provision of Service	Yukon, Manitoba, Quebec, Nova Scotia, Prince Edward Island, New Brunswick and Newfoundland	Yukon includes political activity and political association Newfoundland has prohibition on basis of "political opinion"

Record of criminal conviction

Employment	Yukon and Quebec	Yukon's Act reads "criminal charges or criminal record"
Provision of Service	Yukon, British Columbia, Quebec and Prince Edward Island	Yukon's Act reads "criminal charges or criminal record"

Pardoned conviction

Employment	Federal, Yukon and Northwest Territories	
Provision of Service	Federal, Yukon and Northwest Territories	

Source: Canadian Human Rights Commission "Prohibited Ground of Employment Discrimination by Jurisdiction." http://www.chrc-cdp.ca/publications/prohibitedgrounds-en.asp. Reproduced with the permission of the Minister of Public Works and Government Services, 2006.

Individuals have a right to file a complaint if they feel they have been discriminated against. (The CHRC may refuse to accept a complaint if it has not been filed within a prescribed period of time, if it is deemed trivial, or if it was filed in bad faith.) The complainant must first complete a written report describing the discriminatory

USING THE INTERNET

The Canadian Human Rights Commission deals with complaints concerning discriminatory practices covered by legislation. This site includes a summary of the duty to accommodate:

www.chrc-ccdp.ca/preventing_
discrimination/toc_tdm-en.asp

action. A CHRC representative reviews the facts and determines whether the claim is legitimate. Once a complaint has been accepted by the CHRC, an investigator is assigned the task of gathering more facts from both the complainant and the accused. The investigator then submits a report to the CHRC recommending a finding of either substantiation or nonsubstantiation of the allegation. If the allegation is substantiated, a settlement may be arranged in the course of the investigation. If the parties are unable to reach agreement, a human rights tribunal consisting of up to three members may be appointed to further investigate the complaint. If the tribunal finds that a discriminatory practice did take place, or that the victim's feelings or self-respect have suffered as a result of the practice, it may order the person or organization responsible to compensate the victim. Former employees of Majestic Electronics received $300 000 in compensation because they were harassed after they refused to obey the racist and sexist orders of the company president.[13]

Any person who obstructs an investigation or a tribunal, or who fails to comply with the terms of a settlement, can be found guilty of an offence, which may be punishable by a fine and/or jail sentence. If the guilty party is an employer or an employee organization, the fine can be as high as $50,000 (up to $5,000 for individuals).[14]

The Enforcement of Provincial Human Rights Laws

Provincial human rights laws are enforced in a manner very similar to that of the federal system. At the provincial level, the employers tend to be small and medium-sized businesses, many of which lack an HR professional who is knowledgeable about human rights legislation. Employers and employees alike may have little experience in matters of discrimination.

The majority of cases are resolved at the investigation stage. If no agreement can be reached, the case is presented to the province's human rights commission. The members of the commission study the evidence and then submit a report to the minister in charge of administering human rights legislation. The minister may appoint an independent board of inquiry, which has powers similar to those of a tribunal at the federal level. Failure to comply with the remedies prescribed by the board of inquiry may result in prosecution in provincial court. Individuals may be fined between $500 and $1,000, and organizations or groups between $1,000 and $10,000. These levies vary from province to province.

Pay Equity

objective **3**

As a result of a 1978 amendment to the Canadian Human Rights Act, pay equity became enacted as law. Pay equity law makes it illegal for employers to discriminate against individuals on the basis of job content. The goal of pay equity is to eliminate the historical wage gap between men and women and to ensure that salary ranges reflect the value of the work performed. In 2002, women aged 15 and over who had employment income made 79.3 cents for every $1 earned by their male counterparts (the gap was smaller for younger women).[15]

By definition, pay equity means equal pay for work of equal value. It is based on two principles. The *first* is equal pay for equal work.[16] Male and female workers must be paid the same wage rate for doing identical work. The *second* is equal pay for similar or substantially similar work (equal pay for work of comparable worth). This means that male and female workers must be paid the same wage rate for jobs of a similar nature that may have different titles (e.g., "nurse's aide" and "orderly").

Implementation of pay equity is based on comparing the work of female-dominated job classes to the value of work performed by males. Comparisons require the use of a gender-neutral, unbiased comparison system to evaluate the jobs in an establishment.[17] Comparisons must be based on the amount and type of skill, effort, and responsibility needed to perform the job and on the working conditions where it is performed. The comparison must be done in such a way that the characteristics of "male" jobs, such as heavy lifting and "dirty" working conditions, are valued fairly in comparison to the characteristics of "female" jobs, such as manual dexterity and caring for others.[18]

The federal pay equity legislation applies to that section of the workforce under its jurisdiction and covers all organizations regardless of number of employees. The federal pay equity system is complaint-based, meaning that complaints can be raised by an employee, a group of employees, or a bargaining agent.[19] Some recent decisions included compensating high school secretaries at rates similar to the male job class of audio-visual technicians and comparing a female job class of law clerk with that of the male job class of investigator.[20] However, at the time of publication, there are plans to replace this system with a proactive model where employers take the initiative to ensure jobs of equal value receive equal pay. A more comprehensive review of pay equity is provided in Chapter 9.

The Employment Equity Act (1995)

objective **4**

Employers and Crown corporations that have 100 employees or more and that are regulated under the Canada Labour Code must implement employment equity and report on their results. Under the act, the employer is required to

- provide its employees with a questionnaire that allows them to indicate whether they belong to one of the four designated groups;
- identify jobs in which the percentage of members of designated groups falls below their availability in the labour market;
- communicate information on employment equity to its employees, and consult and collaborate with employee representatives;
- identify possible barriers in existing employment systems that may be limiting the employment opportunities of members of designated groups;
- develop an employment equity plan aimed at promoting an equitable workplace;
- make all reasonable efforts to implement its plan;
- monitor, review, and revise its plan from time to time; *and*
- prepare an annual report on its employment equity data and activities.[21]

The concept of employment equity is rooted in the wording of federal and provincial employment standards legislation, human rights codes, and the Canadian Charter of Rights and Freedoms. Employment equity involves identifying and removing systemic barriers to employment opportunities that adversely affect women, visible minorities, Aboriginal peoples, and people with disabilities. Employment equity also involves implementing special measures and making reasonable accommodation.[22]

Under the Federal Contractors Program (FCP), contractors who bid for goods and services contracts with the federal government valued at $200 000 or more, and who employ 100 persons or more, are required to implement an employment equity program. (For a list of this program's implementation criteria, see Highlights in HRM 3.3.) To assist in the process, the federal government provides professional consulting services to employers throughout Canada regarding how to implement

Highlights in HRM 3.3

Implementation Criteria for Federal Contractors Program

1. Communication by the organization's CEO to employees, unions, and/or employee associations of the commitment to achieve equality in employment through the design and implementation of an employment equity plan.

2. Assignment of senior personnel with responsibility for employment equity.

3. Collection and maintenance of information on the employment status of designated-group employees by occupation and salary levels and with regard to hiring, promotion, and termination in relation to all other employees.

4. Analysis of designated-group representation within the organization in relation to their representation in the supply of qualified workers from which the contractor may reasonably be expected to recruit employees.

5. Elimination or modification of those human resource policies, practices, and systems, whether formal or informal, shown to have or likely to have an unfavourable effect on the employment status of designated-group employees.

6. Establishment of goals for the hiring, training, and promotion of designated-group employees. Such goals will consider projections for hiring, promotions, terminations, layoffs, recalls, retirements, and, where possible, the projected availability of qualified designated-group members.

7. Establishment of a work plan for reaching each of the goals in 6 above.

8. Adoption of special measures where necessary to ensure that goals are achieved, including the provision of reasonable accommodation as required.

9. Establishment of a climate favourable to the successful integration of designated-group members within the organization.

10. Adoption of procedures to monitor the progress and results achieved in implementing employment equity.

11. Authorization to allow representatives of the CHRC access to the business premises and to the records noted in 3 above in order to conduct on-site compliance reviews for the purpose of measuring the progress achieved in implementing employment equity.

Source: Human Resources and Skills Development Canada, *Federal Contractors Program: Information for Suppliers and Organizations,* 1991. Reproduced with the permission of Her Majesty the Queen in Right of Canada 2006.

employment equity. Federally regulated employers must conduct a workforce analysis to identify underrepresentation of members of designated groups; review their employment systems, policies, and practices to identify employment barriers; and prepare a plan outlining the steps they will take to remove any identified barriers. Most provinces have similar legislation governing employment equity.

Winners of merit awards for initiatives in employment equity include the Bank of Nova Scotia, for increasing the number of visible minorities in its workforce to 19 percent, and the Saskatchewan Wheat Pool, for its partnerships with the Aboriginal community—particularly its investment in an MBA program in Aboriginal Business. In the face of threats to employment equity legislation, employers are showing willingness to keep the practice alive. As Robert Rochon, director of employment equity for National Grocer Co., puts it: "Regardless of any legislative requirement, [employment equity] is a good business decision for us. When you consider the changing face of Canada, it just makes good business sense to reflect the customers that you serve."[23]

Administration and Enforcement of the Employment Equity Act

Human Resources Development Canada is responsible for administering the Federal Contractors Program. The Canadian Human Rights Commission is mandated under the Canadian Human Rights Act[24] to prohibit discrimination in the establishments of federally regulated businesses.[25]

The CHRC is authorized to conduct on-site compliance reviews. Failure to comply may result in fines ranging from $10,000 for first offenders to $50,000 for repeat offenders.

The Implementation of Employment Equity in Organizations

objective **5**

The implementation of employment equity in an organization follows the precepts of any change management program. Thus, successful implementation must employ strategic planning, which must be incorporated into an overall business strategy. The Federal Contractors Program outlined in Highlights in HRM 3.3 provides a good overview of what a plan should incorporate. The process involves six main steps: senior management commitment; data collection and analysis; employment systems review; establishment of a workplan; implementation; and a follow-up process that includes evaluation, monitoring, and revision.

Step 1: Senior Management Commitment

Commitment to an employment equity plan necessitates a top-down strategy. A more supportive culture is created when the CEO or owner–operator publicly introduces written policy describing the organization's commitment to employment equity. This policy must be strategically posted throughout the organization and sent to each employee. The CEO, all members of the board of directors, as well as the staff at the Law Society of Upper Canada are fully committed and all have received equity and human rights training. As an example, the world's largest food service company, Compass Group, has employment equity as a top priority, by making it a topic at every board meeting, where workforce data are reviewed and built into the performance scorecard of all managers.[26]

An employment equity policy statement may raise many questions, so it is important to be thorough in this process in order to keep concerns to a minimum. The policy statement should be supplemented with a communiqué explaining what employment equity is, the rationale for the program, and its implications for current and future employees. Assurances must be given at this time that all information provided will be treated confidentially and will not be used to identify individuals other than for the purpose of employment equity program activities. The communiqué should also list the names of persons responsible for administering the program and outline any planned activities the employer may deem necessary to establish the program (e.g., analysis of the workforce or of policies and procedures).

This commitment to employees and candidates for employment applies to all aspects of the employment relationship, including recruitment, work assignment, training opportunities, compensation, promotions, transfers, and terminations.

Communication tools may include periodic information sessions, workplace posters, departmental or small group meetings conducted by line management, orientation and training programs, newsletters, and vehicles such as videos, brochures, employee handbooks, and memos from the union. An innovative approach to communications was taken at the Centre de recherche industrielle du Québec (CRIQ), where employees decided to create a video to demonstrate that seemingly harmless comments and attitudes can have devastating consequences for members of designated groups. Their goal was to sensitize people without lecturing or pointing fingers. The employees acted in the video, selected its music, and directed and produced it. Its title was *Moi . . . des préjugés? (Me . . . prejudiced?)*. The video depicts the experiences of a Black man, a person who is deaf, and a woman, all of whom are seeking employment with a company, and who are confronted with opinions and attitudes that have everything to do with prejudice and nothing to do with the requirements of the job.[27]

Assignment of Accountable Senior Staff

Senior management must place the responsibility for employment equity in the hands of a senior manager, a joint labour–management committee, and an employment equity advisory committee with mechanisms for union consultation (or, in nonunionized settings, for consultation with designated employee representatives). They must designate line management responsibility and accountability. Anyone given responsibility for employment equity must be knowledgeable about the problems and concerns of designated groups; have the status and ability needed to gain the cooperation of employees at all levels in the organization; have access to financial and human resources required to conduct planning and implementation functions; have sufficient time to devote to employment equity issues; monitor and be in a position to report to the CEO on the results of employment equity measures; and be prepared to serve as the employment equity contact person with federal and provincial government agencies.

Among the employment areas committee members may be required to review are employment practices, advertising and recruitment policies, company-sponsored training, the organization of work schedules and facilities, and systems for promotion to management positions. While committees are usually given responsibility for making recommendations and reporting on issues, ultimate authority generally rests with senior management.

Employers covered by the Employment Equity Act are legally obligated to consult with designated employee representatives or, in unionized settings, with bargaining agents. Consultation means that the employer must supply sufficient information and opportunity to employee representatives or bargaining agents to enable them to ask questions and submit advice on the implementation of employment equity.

The labour movement in Canada generally supports the concept of employment equity, so long as unions are fully informed and involved from the beginning with respect to an employer's planning process. This makes sense considering that unions are the legitimate representatives of employee interests in unionized settings. Supportive mechanisms for achieving employment equity have been reported by Human Resources Development Canada.[28] Many employers and unions have successfully negotiated family-friendly policies such as parental leave, child care provisions, and flexible hours.

Step 2: Data Collection and Analysis

stock data
Data showing the status of designated groups in occupational categories and compensation level

flow data
Data that provide a profile of the employment decisions affecting designated groups

The development of an internal workforce profile is an important tool in employment equity planning. Without this information an organization would not be able to determine where it stands relative to the internal and external workforce. Profiles must be based on both stock data and flow data. **Stock data** provide a snapshot of the organization. They show where members of designated groups are employed in the organization, at what salaries and status, and in what occupations on a particular date. **Flow data** refer to the distribution of designated groups in applications, interviews, hiring decisions, training and promotion opportunities, and terminations. They provide information on the movement of employees into and through the organization. Computerized reporting systems and tracking software are available from Human Resources Development Canada to assist employers in gathering, reporting, and analyzing their internal workforce data.

Most of the information necessary for equity planning (e.g., salary, sex, access to benefits, seniority status, occupational and career history within the organization) is contained in existing personnel files. Information pertaining to the distribution of members of designated groups in the employer's organization must be accumulated by the employer through a self-identification process. Under the Employment Equity Act, employers may gather data on members of designated groups as long as employees voluntarily agree to be identified or identify themselves as members of designated groups, and as long as the data are used only for employment equity planning or reporting purposes.

Creating a climate of trust in the management of the program is a major challenge. Employers can encourage participation and confidence in the program by providing focused employment equity training to managers and by providing opportunities for managers to be recognized for their contributions to the development and administration of effective employment equity strategies. Companies such as Pratt & Whitney have introduced equity and diversity training for their supervisors. Cameco Corporation in northern Saskatchewan has committed to improving the job prospects of Aboriginals as part of its long-term employment strategy, based on economics, not just a keen sense of social responsibility. Mentoring, basic training, educational support, and family assistance programs mean a lot to those employees who may be the first in their families to have full-time paid employment.[29]

If an employer administers a self-identification questionnaire, confidentiality and a clear commitment at senior levels to the concept of employment equity should be

COURTESY OF FIRST NATIONS UNIVERSITY OF CANADA

First Nations University is a unique university in Canada that caters to the advanced education needs of Aboriginals.

communicated. Having employees self-identify is crucial to the success of the program, but problems may arise with self-identification. Under some provincial employment equity acts, terms such as "Aboriginal" and "racial minority" are not defined. Some employees, who have "hidden" disabilities such as epilepsy or partial deafness, may not wish to label themselves for fear of future discriminatory treatment. Some minorities, such as Aboriginals, have never disclosed their ethnic origins for similar reasons.

If too many employees with nonvisible disabilities do not identify themselves as disabled, the program could end up being designed to recruit more employees with disabilities, leaving another segment of the employee population underrepresented. Thus, because inaccurate data were accumulated on one group, the other group will not benefit from the employment equity efforts. An additional concern is that individuals with disabilities may need some form of accommodation to help them perform their jobs better. If they do not self-identify, they have denied themselves certain basic rights. Highlights in HRM 3.4 outlines words and actions which are appropriate in dealing with persons with disabilities. A self-identification form should contain the following:

- An explanation of the employer's employment equity policy, the purpose of the employment equity program, and the need for the information requested.
- An indication that the information supplied will be confidential and will be used only for employment equity purposes by those persons identified as responsible for the program.
- The categories for self-identification, with brief explanations and examples.
- An indication that the form has been reviewed by the relevant human rights agency.
- Space for comments and suggestions.
- The name of the contact person for information and suggestions.[30]

Once the personal information forms have been completed, all occupations within the organization must be cross-referenced to the National Occupational Classification (NOC). This manual was created by Statistics Canada for use in statistical surveys and for other purposes. Personal data are organized under the four-digit NOC classifications. When building a workforce profile, employers should first refer to the four-digit unit groups and then determine which one each job belongs in. For example, secretaries and stenographers are classified in unit group 4111, which in turn can be assigned to the "clerical workers" group.

A full workforce analysis can be generated once all the information has been loaded and the reports are complete. This utilization analysis will include a distribution of members of designated groups according to occupations and salary levels throughout the organization. Comparisons will show which designated groups exhibit **underutilization** and which groups exhibit **concentration** in specific occupations or levels, in proportion to their numbers in the labour market.[31]

Step 3: Employment Systems Review

"Employment systems" or "employment practices" are the means by which employers carry out such personnel activities as recruitment, hiring, training and development, promotion, job classification, discipline, and termination. Some of these practices are found in personnel manuals and collective agreements, while others remain more informal and based on traditional practices.

An important legal principle is that employers are accountable even when discrimination is the unintended result of employment systems that block the progress of

underutilization
Term applied to designated groups that are not utilized or represented in the employer's workforce proportional to their numbers in the labour market

concentration
Term applied to designated groups whose numbers in a particular occupation or level are high relative to their numbers in the labour market

Highlights in HRM 3.4

Suggestions for Inclusion

Person who is blind, or person with a visual impairment
Identify yourself and anyone with you; if you have met before, explain the context of the meeting; speak in a normal tone of voice and indicate to whom you are speaking if in a group; remove obstacles; describe the surroundings ("There is a door on your right"); if offering to guide, ask the person to take your arm above the elbow and walk about a half-step ahead; plan ahead to obtain material in audio cassettes or Braille

Person with a physical disability or person with a mobility impairment
Rearrange furniture or objects to accommodate a wheelchair or other mobility aids; avoid leaning on a mobility aid; push someone in a wheelchair only when asked; give directions that include distance and physical objects such as curbs.

Person who is deaf, deafened, or person with a hearing impairment
Speak clearly and at a pace that allows the sign language interpreter to interpret and to allow for questions; write notes or use gestures for one-on-one discussions; face the person to facilitate lip-reading; speak clearly, slowly, and directly to the person, not the interpreter; reduce or eliminate background noise

Person who is unable to speak, or person with a speech impairment; person with a learning, developmental, or psychiatric disability
When needed, offer assistance and provide guidance, repeat information when necessary, speak directly to the person and listen actively

Sources: Treasury Board of Canada Secretariat, *Creating a Welcoming Workplace for Employees with Disabilities*; David Brown, "Focus on Ability not Disability," *Canadian HR Reporter* 13, no. 22 (December 18, 2000): 12.

particular groups of employees or potential employees for reasons unrelated to qualifications, merit, or business requirements. This unintentional discrimination is referred to as systemic discrimination.

Systemic Barriers in Employment Practices

systemic discrimination
The exclusion of members of certain groups through the application of employment policies or practices based on criteria that are not job-related

Systemic discrimination refers to the exclusion of members of certain groups through the application of employment policies or practices based on criteria that are neither job-related nor required for the safe and efficient operation of the business. Systemic discrimination can create legal concerns for an organization. Many employment barriers are hidden, unintentionally, in the rules and the procedures and even the facilities that employers provide to manage their human resources. (See Figure 3.3 on page 120 for examples of systemic barriers, along with possible solutions.) Inequity can result if these barriers encourage or discourage individuals based on their membership in certain groups rather than on their ability to do a job that the employer needs done. In one case, the Supreme Court of Canada ruled that a physical fitness test discriminated against women and required the employer to reinstate the woman as a firefighter.[32]

Figure 3.3	Employment Practices

EXAMPLES OF SYSTEMIC BARRIERS

1. Recruitment practices that limit applications from designated groups, e.g., word of mouth, internal hiring policies.
2. Physical access that restricts those who are mobility impaired, e.g., no ramps, heavy doors, narrow passageways.
3. Job descriptions and job evaluation systems that undervalue the work of positions traditionally held by women.
4. A workplace environment that does not expressly discourage sexual or racial harassment.

EXAMPLES OF POSSIBLE SOLUTIONS

1. Word of mouth could be supplemented by calls to community organizations representing designated groups or to the local Canada Employment Centre.
2. Facility upgrading.
3. Rewrite job descriptions, rationalize evaluation systems, provide special training for supervisors.
4. Issue a company policy against these practices, with guidelines and follow-up through appraisal and discipline procedures, and develop complaint and problem-solving mechanisms for an employee to use.

Source: Human Resources and Skills Development Canada. *Employment Equity: A Guide for Employers,* Employment and Immigration Canada, Cat. No. 143-5-91, May 1991, p. 19. Reproduced with permission of Her Majesty the Queen in Right of Canada 2006.

Another example of systemic discrimination occurs when an employer's workforce represents one group in our society and the company recruits new employees by posting job vacancies within the company or by word of mouth among the employees. This recruitment strategy is likely to generate candidates similar to those in the current workforce, thereby unintentionally discriminating against other groups of workers in the labour market. A better approach might be to vary recruitment methods by contacting outside agencies and organizations. The Toronto Police Force has established an eight-member recruitment task force to boost its community representation, in part by educating visible minority groups about career opportunities in the force.[33]

The following employment practices and issues may need to be reviewed: job classifications and descriptions, recruitment processes, training and development, performance evaluation systems, promotions and upward mobility, levels of compensation, access to benefits, termination processes, discipline procedures, facilities (i.e., building design, barrier-free access), and access to assistance.

The usual test for identifying systemic barriers involves using the following criteria to assess the policy:

- Is it job-related?
- Is it valid? (i.e., does it, or the required qualification, have a direct relationship to job performance?)
- Is it consistently applied?
- Does it have an adverse impact? (i.e., does it affect members of designated groups more than those of dominant groups?)
- Is it a business necessity?
- Does it conform to human rights and employment standards legislation?[34]

If the employee profiles indicate that certain types of people are underrepresented, then special measures may be undertaken to correct this imbalance.

Special Measures and Reasonable Accommodation

Special measures are initiatives designed to accelerate the entry, development, and promotion of members of designated groups from among the interested and qualified workforce. For example, some special measures may include targeted recruitment or special training initiatives aimed mainly at correcting, over a specified period of time, employment inequities stemming from past discrimination. These measures are intended to hasten the achievement of fair representation of the four designated groups in an employer's workforce. Highlights in HRM 3.5 describes the special measures used by the federal government.

Highlights in HRM 3.5

Participation in the Federal Public Service

The goals of the Employment Equity program in the federal government are to

- establish a workforce of qualified employees that reflects the diversity of the Canadian population which they serve,
- ensure equal access to job opportunities,
- correct conditions that have historically impeded the full participation of designated groups.

Discussions with Aloma Lawrence, Chief Employment Equity Advisor of the Public Service Commission, indicated that although visible minorities represented 8.7 percent of the labour force, they represented only 6.8 percent of the federal employee population in 2002. To accomplish the EE goals, the Public Service Commission has established a number of special measures, which include the following:

- Outreach: The recruiting teams of the federal government have established a visible presence within the visible minority communities. Through contacts with visible minority associations, such as the Association of Black Law Enforcers, recruiters make presentations and hold information sessions about the recruitment processes used by the federal government to fill jobs. Recruiters talk about the structured interviews and tests, procedures that may be unfamiliar to visible minority candidates.
- Creation of specific tools: The brochure "So You're Thinking of Working for the Federal Government" was developed specifically for the visible minority communities. Workshops that explain the types of tests used, such as the managerial in-basket or the written communications test, are held within these communities. The Public Service Commission has also introduced tools for use by managers and human resources professionals in developing and implementing employment equity strategies and approaches. New tools include "Improving Employment Equity Representation: Tips and Tools," "Guidelines for Assessing Persons with Disabilities," and "Guidelines for Fair Assessment in a Diverse Workplace."

(continued on next page)

- Composition of recruitment teams: An effort was made to place visible minorities on the recruitment teams, particularly because selection decisions could be made on perceptions of "fit," and culture plays a large role in this. In 2002, the PSC established an inventory of 100 visible minorities, trained in interviewing processes, who were invited by managers to sit on selection boards. The federal government, like other public-sector employers, has been finding it difficult to recruit visible minorities in areas of law enforcement, such as correctional officers. However, building relationships with visible minority communities is beginning to result in greater interest in federal government jobs.

Is the process working? Yes; the number of visible minorities working in the federal public service has increased from 5.9 percent in 2001 to 6.8 percent in 2002. Career development is vital to the retention of good employees, and in 2001 the PSC launched a career assignment program for visible minorities. Because visible minorities represent only 4.1 percent of the executive group, for example, the Career Assignment Program develops participants for executive-level positions. The ultimate goal is to match participation rates in the labour market. However, with the special measures adopted by the PSC, progress is slow but certain.

reasonable accommodation
Attempt by employers to adjust the working conditions or schedules of employees with disabilities or religious preferences

Reasonable accommodation involves adjusting employment policies and practices so that no individual is denied benefits, disadvantaged with respect to employment opportunities, or blocked from carrying out the essential components of a job because of race, colour, sex, or disability. Human rights tribunals across Canada have placed employers under a duty to demonstrate a degree of flexibility in meeting the reasonable needs of employees. It is no longer acceptable for employers to simply assume that all employees will "fit in" no matter what their special needs. Employers must find the means to alter systems to meet the needs of their employees as long as this does not cause "undue hardship to the employer." Reasonable accommodation may include redesigning job duties, adjusting work schedules, providing technical, financial, and human support services, and upgrading facilities. The City of Toronto developed award-winning facilities in its Barrier Free Access program, which was designed to allow people with disabilities accessible passage throughout city facilities. The Canadian military has adopted a policy that allows Native service men to wear their hair in traditional braids.

Highlights in HRM 3.6 recounts two court cases on accommodation.

Reasonable accommodation benefits all employees. When a company provides compensation for child care expenses for employees taking company-sponsored courses it does more than remove a barrier to women; it also assists any employee with sole-parenting responsibilities. The flexible work schedules adopted by some companies in northern Canada benefit Aboriginal employees, who are prepared to work atypical hours in exchange for significant breaks away from the work site to take part in traditional hunting and fishing activities. Many other employees also benefit from these flexible work schedules.

Special arrangements should be made to accommodate people who are visually impaired, illiterate, or unfamiliar with the English language by using tools such as Braille forms, confidential interviews, or translation. Leah Levy, the founder of the Gulf Islands Dog Biscuit Company, found it easy to accommodate deaf employees by installing a white board for messages, and a light indicating when the doorbell rang.[35] Suggestions for an accessible workplace are found in Figure 3.4.

Highlights in HRM 3.6

The Duty to Accommodate

- Two employees of the Ford Motor Company of Oakville, Ontario, became members of a religious group that observed its Sabbath from Friday sunset to Saturday sunset. Both employees were required to work two Friday nights out of four, which they refused to do. They tried, but failed, to make alternative arrangements with other workers. They were disciplined and ultimately terminated for unauthorized absenteeism. After a 71-day hearing, the Human Rights Commission decided it would constitute undue hardship on Ford to accommodate the religious absences of these employees.
- The Ontario Human Rights Commission found that the City of Ancaster, Ontario, had discriminated against a part-time firefighter when they turned him down for a full-time job because he had partial vision in one eye. As such he was unable to obtain a class F driver's licence, a job requirement for driving ambulances that are driven by firefighters. The tribunal felt that the city should have accommodated him by assigning him to firefighter duties exclusively.

Source: Laura Cassiani, "Law Takes Tough Stand on Accommodation," *Canadian HR Reporter*, Feb. 26, 2001 issue, pages 1 and 5.

Figure 3.4	Suggestions for an Accessible Workplace

- Install easy-to-reach switches.
- Provide sloping sidewalks and entrances.
- Install wheelchair ramps.
- Reposition shelves so materials are easy to reach.
- Rearrange tables, chairs, vending machines, dispensers, and other furniture and fixtures.
- Widen doors and hallways.
- Add raised markings on control buttons.
- Provide designated accessible parking spaces.
- Install hand controls or manipulation devices.
- Provide flashing alarm lights.
- Remove turnstiles and revolving doors or provide alternative accessible paths.
- Install holding bars in toilet areas.
- Redesign toilet partitions to increase access space.
- Add paper cup dispensers at water fountains.
- Replace high-pile, low-density carpeting.
- Reposition telephones, water fountains, and other needed equipment.
- Add raised toilet seats.
- Provide a full-length bathroom mirror.

Source: Statistics Canada website: www.statcan.ca/english/Pgdb/labor20a.htm, table 282-0002.

Step 4: Establishment of a Workplan

The workforce analysis and the review of employment systems will provide the employer with a useful base from which to develop a workplan with realistic goals and timetables. A narrative statement or summary of the conclusions drawn from the examination of the workforce analysis forms part of the employment equity workplan. The summary should include any restrictions faced in hiring due to collective agreements, staff movements, or the need for specialized skills in a particular profession. The identification of restrictions helps form an overall employment equity strategy.

The plan should be considered a working tool designed to achieve results. It is a document that describes how proposed actions are to be achieved. The plan should be an integral part of the organization's overall operational plans, and must include

- numerical goals with time frames (numerical goals can be expressed in numbers—for example, 42 percent of our personnel should be women);
- explanations about the proposed improvement in the hiring, training, and promotion of the four designated groups to increase their representation and improve their distribution throughout the organization;
- descriptions of specific activities to achieve the numerical goals; and
- an outline of monitoring and evaluation procedures to follow program implementation.

Numerical goals must be realistic numbers related to the workforce analysis. The goals must catalogue opportunities for hiring, training, and promotion, and must demonstrate a valid effort to correct underrepresentation or concentration of all designated groups in specific occupations or occupational categories. Non-numerical goals include activities such as implementation of barrier-free design, targeted recruitment and advertising, modification of employment policies or practices, and provision of developmental training.

The overall goal for an organization is to achieve a representative workforce. An organization's workforce is representative when it reflects the demographic composition of the external workforce. A nonrepresentative workforce is an indicator of the need for evaluation and action to remove the barriers that block or discourage certain groups from employment and advancement. Workplan initiatives in conjunction with special measures and reasonable accommodation should contribute to the overall success of this goal.

Step 5: Implementation

The implementation of employment equity is idiosyncratic in that no two plans will be the same. Each strategy should be designed to meet the needs of the particular organization. The success of plan implementation depends on senior management's commitment to the process, how the roles and responsibilities are defined, what resources are available, the effectiveness of the communications strategy, the acceptance of plan initiatives and objectives, and the availability of training. The plan, in essence a living document, will be affected by the changes in the internal and external environment throughout the implementation period. Therefore, its strategies may be modified or eliminated when results are not achieved or if resource restraints or economic conditions necessitate a different strategy. The implementation is guided and monitored by those responsible and accountable for its outcome.

Step 6: Evaluation, Monitoring, and Revision

By monitoring progress, the employer will be able to evaluate the overall success of the equity initiatives used to achieve a representative workforce, as well as respond to organizational and environmental changes. Annual progress reports provided to all employees communicate initiatives and achievements. Interim reports on special projects heighten program visibility and acceptance; they also promote management commitment and accountability. Research suggests that the wage gaps between white men and the designated groups are closing more rapidly in organizations with formal employment equity programs than in organizations without such programs.[36]

The monitoring activity is an essential component in the planning cycle. Only through monitoring can an employer determine whether goals are being attained and problems resolved, whether new programs are succeeding, and whether strategies have been effective. If the employer finds, upon review of the program, that there are negative results, alterations to the existing plan will have to be made with new goals. In this regard, the planning process is evolutionary, in that the achievement of employment equity involves organizational changes and builds on experience.

Sexual Harassment

objective **6**

sexual harassment
Unwelcome advances, requests for sexual favours, and other verbal or physical conduct of a sexual nature in the working environment

Sexual situations in the work environment are not new to organizational life. Sexual feelings are a part of group dynamics, and people who work together may come to develop these kinds of feelings for one another. Unfortunately, however, often these encounters are unpleasant and unwelcome, as witnessed by the many reported instances of sexual harassment.[37]

According to one study, only four of every ten Canadian women who suffer **sexual harassment** at work take any formal action, and only one out of every two women believes that a complaint would be taken seriously in her workplace.[38] This belief is reinforced by cases such as the one involving a female Sears employee who was shot to death by her manager. Fifteen months earlier, she had complained to her employer that she was being sexually harassed by her manager. The company maintained that his behaviour did not constitute sexual harassment and that he was merely a "persistent pursuer." In keeping with this position, they made no effort to stop the manager's behaviour.[39] The City of Richmond has only four women among the more than 200 firefighters and none of them are on active duty. At least one has complained of harassment, saying that she found obscenities on her locker, and feces in her boots, and that her water pressure was not turned on during a fire inside a building.[40] Sexual harassment costs, as Highlights in HRM 3.7 on page 126 shows.

Many organizations are developing policies to deal with sexual harassment in the workplace. Such policies are intended as preventive measures not only against damage to reputation and employee morale, but also against the kind of litigation that Magna International faced when it was sued on the grounds that Magna employees had attempted to win contracts from purchasing officers for the Big Three automakers by wooing them with gifts and entertainment, including trips to topless bars.[41] Some organizations have put policies in place to attempt to deal with the issue. For example, the sexual harassment policy at B.C. Hydro focuses on avoidance and resolution rather than punishment after the fact. In another organization, the Canadian

USING THE INTERNET

The Canada Labour Code defines sexual harassment and outlines the employer's responsibilities. Go to the following website and search for sexual harassment:

www.hrsdc.gc.ca/

Highlights in HRM 3.7

The Cost of Sexual Harassment

In 2002, sexual harassment complaints topped the list of complaints heard by provincial human rights commissions; 64 percent of working women say they have experienced some form of sexual harassment throughout their careers (up from 48 percent in the previous year). Harassment affects productivity, retention, morale, turnover, and absenteeism rates. It also affects an employee's self-esteem, home life, and stress levels. Some 48 percent of women executives say they left a job because of inhospitable organizational culture and harassment.

An employee at the Victoria Tea Company in Ontario was found guilty of sexual harassment and ordered to pay the victim $50,600. A supervisor at SkyCable in Brandon, Manitoba, was ordered to pay $100,000 in damages for creating a poisoned work atmosphere. The four women employees testified that the supervisor had made inappropriate remarks, sexual advances, and derogatory comments on an ongoing basis. The poisoned work environment generated by his conduct took a toll on their psychological and physical health and caused them significant pain and suffering. The supervisor's remarks were clearly persistent, repetitious, and serious enough to create a hostile work environment for all the complainants. The Canadian Human Rights Tribunal ruled that the supervisor must compensate the four women for lost wages, hurt feelings, and legal costs. But what exactly is sexual harassment? According to Canadian legal cases, the following behaviours define sexual harassment:

- Sexually degrading words or remarks used to describe an individual or group;
- Inquiries or comments about an individual's sex life;
- Sexual flirtations, advances, and propositions;
- Demands for sexual favours;
- Verbal threats or abuse;
- Leering;
- Unwanted gestures;
- Display of sexually offensive material; and
- Sexual assault.

Sources: "Sexual Harassment Endangered Health," *Tribunal OH & S Canada* 18, no. 6 (September 2002): 10; Laura Cassiani, "Sexual Harassment Persists Despite Workplace Fallout," *Canadian HR Reporter* 14, no. 7 (April 9, 2001): 1.

Armed Forces, 90 000 members have been trained to recognize and avoid harassment of all kinds.

Highlights in HRM 3.8 on page 128 provides a sample of questions that can be used during a sexual harassment audit. An instrument like this one, which is essentially a test, is a valuable tool for determining what employees know and do not know about sexual harassment.

The Ontario Human Rights Code identifies three kinds of sexual harassment:

1. When someone says or does things to you of a sexual nature and you do not want or welcome it. This includes behaviour that a person should know you do not want or welcome. For example, your supervisor makes you feel

Sexual harassment encounters are unpleasant, causing personal and organizational hardships.

uncomfortable by talking about sex all the time. The Human Rights Code says that when you show that you do not welcome or want the remarks or actions, the person must stop doing those things right away.

2. A person who has authority or power to deny you something such as a promotion or a raise makes sexual suggestions or requests that you do not want or welcome. For example, your teacher says you must have sex with him or her or you will not pass the course. Even if you do not complain about a sexual suggestion or request, it can still be sexual harassment unless it is clear that you welcome or want it.

3. A person with authority or the power to deny you something important punishes you or threatens to do something to you for refusing a sexual request. For example, your employer fires you, or threatens to fire you, because you refuse to go on a date.

York University has developed a comprehensive program to deal with sexual harassment issues. To augment its program, it has published a booklet titled *Sexual Assault and Harassment on Campus,* which is intended for students and employees. This booklet provides safety tips for women and men as well as definitions of sexual harassment and other forms of harassment.[42] A pamphlet titled *Sexual Harassment and You: What Every Student Should Know* is made available to any interested person. York's policy states:

York University strives to provide an environment wherein all students, faculty and staff are able to learn, study, teach and work, free from sexual harassment.

Sexual harassment is:

1. Unwanted sexual attention of a persistent or abusive nature, made by a person who knows or ought reasonably to know that such attention is unwanted;
2. The making of an implied or express promise of reward for complying with a sexually oriented request;
3. The making of an implied or express threat or reprisal, in the form of actual reprisal or in the denial of opportunity, for refusal to comply with a sexually oriented request;
4. Sexually oriented remarks and behaviour which may reasonably be perceived to create a negative psychological and emotional environment [sometimes labelled a hostile environment] for work and study.

Incidents of sexual harassment shall be investigated and dealt with by the University in accordance with guidelines and procedures put in place for that purpose from time to time.

Highlights in HRM 3.8

Questions Asked in Auditing Sexual Harassment

Activity	Is This Sexual Harassment?		Are You Aware of This Behaviour in the Organization?		
• Employees post cartoons on bulletin boards containing sexually related material.	Yes	No	Uncertain	Yes	No
• A male employee says to a female employee that she has beautiful eyes and hair.	Yes	No	Uncertain	Yes	No
• A male manager habitually calls all female employees "sweetie" or "darling."	Yes	No	Uncertain	Yes	No
• A manager fails to promote a female employee when she will not grant sexual favours.	Yes	No	Uncertain	Yes	No
• Male employees use vulgar language and tell sexual jokes that are overheard by, but not directed at, female employees.	Yes	No	Uncertain	Yes	No
• A male employee leans and peers over the back of a female employee when she wears a low-cut dress.	Yes	No	Uncertain	Yes	No
• A supervisor gives a female (male) subordinate a nice gift on her (his) birthday.	Yes	No	Uncertain	Yes	No
• Two male employees share a sexually explicit magazine while observed by a female employee.	Yes	No	Uncertain	Yes	No

Students, faculty and staff who, it is determined, have sexually harassed another member(s) of the University community will be subject to discipline and sanctions as are appropriate in the circumstances, including but not limited to discipline and sanctions provided for in Presidential Regulations (in the case of students), and relevant collective agreements.[43]

For sexual harassment policies to succeed, confidentiality is necessary, and so is a method for filing complaints. Highlights in HRM 3.9 describes a company whose method for filing complaints became a problem. Without organizational commitment to zero tolerance with respect to harassment, any such policy will be meaningless. Highlights in HRM 3.10 on page 130 presents some suggestions for an effective sexual harassment policy.[44]

Highlights in HRM 3.9

The Aftermath of Sexual Harassment

Sexual harassment has been making headlines for decades and companies have invested vigorously in programs for its prevention in the workplace. Due to its continued sensitivity and the need to protect individuals and companies, "ABC Manufacturing" (a real organization which preferred not to be identified) will be profiled in order to depict how sexual harassment is still a prevalent and problematic issue in today's workplace.

ABC Manufacturing is a reputable company with business history built around strong business ethics and core values. As part of its corporate mandate on how ABC Manufacturing does business, it invested in diversity training for all employees. The program goes beyond training on the human rights codes. It stressed mutual respect in the workplace and the business case for diversity. In fact, ABC had previously won awards for its progressive diversity programs. The key to the success of their program is the open door policy. Employees were comfortable going to the human resources department with their concerns, including reporting allegations of sexual harassment. In 99 percent of cases, the complainants were satisfied with the resolutions of their cases. Resolutions included punishments ranging from agreed misunderstandings to terminations.

ABC Manufacturing first devised its policy on sexual harassment from the understanding of "here's the law." The policy then developed into a comprehensive diversity plan to respect all individuals regardless of race, gender, religion, age, sexual orientation, culture, or nationality. It also included the linkage to the business strategy. This integrated approach and training seemed effective. All complaints were resolved within the organization avoiding potential outside legal cost and time. Then, two years ago, ABC Manufacturing got a call from the Human Rights Commission with a complaint of sexual harassment. Management was confused. Apparently, a temporary student worker had filed a report about a permanent employee who had called her frequently at home. Checking their records, there had been no report made at ABC or at the temp agency that had placed her. The accused employee was called in and questioned about the incident in which he denied having done anything wrong. To get him to back up his story, the permanent employee was asked to provide records of phone calls from his home. He promptly went on stress-mitigated sick leave and retained legal counsel that prevented ABC from investigating the matter further. The complainant also refused to discuss the matter directly with ABC Manufacturing.

With no other alternatives to investigate the alleged harassment, ABC was forced to speak through the lawyer of the accused employee and the Human Rights Commission. The alleged victim asked for an extraordinary amount of money that ABC would not pay without any facts. The permanent employee now on sick leave refused to speak of the matter for it was not in his best interests. As ABC learned more of the facts of her complaint, corporate lawyers recommended to pay off the temporary worker but asserted that they were to accept no responsibility since they could not validate the story. Further complicating matters, without the facts the permanent employee could not be disciplined while on sick leave or terminated. After one and a half years of legal quagmire, the Human Rights Commission proposed that ABC pay a nominal sum with an apology to the victim. Although the Commission did not find fault with ABC's handling of the situation, they believed that the incident took place. They also believe that there was potential for future incidents due to the imbalance of power between the permanent and temporary employees.

(continued on next page)

ABC paid the sum of money requested but instead of an apology, they put out an assurance that this would rectify the situation in their policy. The worker is still on sick leave collecting benefits and will not return without a full restitution of his reputation. Given the circumstances, this cannot happen since the facts were never divulged and the matter with the temporary worker has been settled. Resolving this situation with the permanent worker will require more legal maneuvering.

ABC thought that it had a world-class diversity program firmly embedded within the corporation. As pointed out by the Human Rights Commission, ABC management found that there was a flaw in the execution of its policy. They had made sure that every permanent employee underwent its best in class diversity training program. Due to co-employment liabilities, ABC did not give the temporary worker the diversity training. Legally, temporary employees work for the agency that assigned them to the company. The agency did not provide the worker with diversity training either. As such, the temporary workers did not know their rights, procedures, or open door policy in human resources. Without knowledge of an effective course of action, the temporary worker went to the Human Rights Commission for resolution of her complaint. Upon further investigation, however, ABC learned that this was not an isolated incident. There were other incidents, involving temporary student workers, which were not reported. ABC reacted quickly to this finding and while they do not take on the responsibility of training temporary workers in diversity, they make sure that all employees, permanent or temporary, are fully aware of their rights and ability to contact human resources. This mandatory training became part of the new employee orientation program for both permanent and temporary employees.

Highlights in HRM 3.10

Basic Components of an Effective Sexual Harassment Policy

1. Develop a comprehensive organization-wide policy on sexual harassment and present it to all current and new employees. Stress that sexual harassment will not be tolerated under any circumstances. Emphasis is best achieved when the policy is publicized and supported by top management.
2. Hold training sessions with supervisors to explain their role in providing an environment free of sexual harassment, and proper investigative procedures when charges occur.
3. Establish a formal complaint procedure whereby employees can discuss problems without fear of retaliation. The complaint procedure should spell out how charges will be investigated and resolved.
4. Act immediately when employees complain of sexual harassment. Communicate widely that investigations will be conducted objectively and with appreciation for the sensitivity of the issue.
5. When an investigation supports employee charges, discipline the offender at once. For extremely serious offences, discipline should include penalties up to and including discharge. Discipline should be applied consistently across similar cases and among managers and hourly employees alike.
6. Follow up on all cases to ensure a satisfactory resolution of the problem.

The concepts of harassment in the workplace are being broadened to include psychological harassment, such as bullying. A law in Quebec bans psychological harassment, which is defined as any repeated, hostile or unwanted conduct, verbal comments, actions, or gestures that affect an employee's dignity or psychological or physical integrity. This protection, the first of its kind in Canada, requires employers to create policies to prevent this type of harassment.[45]

Managing Diversity

objective 1

diversity management
The optimization of an organization's multicultural workforce in order to reach business objectives

Managing diversity goes beyond Canadian employment equity legislation's four designated groups in addressing the need to create a fair work environment. The terms "diversity management" and "employment equity" are often used interchangeably, but there are differences. **Diversity management** is voluntary; employment equity is not. Managing diversity is a broader, more inclusive concept encompassing such factors as religion, personality, lifestyle, and education. By managing diversity, organizations hope to gain a strategic and competitive advantage by helping all employees perform to their full potential.[46]

The City of Toronto led by example when it recognized "non-Christian City of Toronto staff" by giving them two days of paid time off for religious holidays if they agreed to work Christmas Day and Good Friday (Christian holidays) at straight time.[47] Also, McDonald's Restaurants of Canada used multi-age teams and found the diversity of ages led to a remarkable synergy.[48]

Organizations such as CN, the Bank of Montreal, and Warner-Lambert are pioneers in the diversity movement. According to Marie Tellier, Canadian National's assistant vice-president of employment equity, the hiring and development and good management of a diverse workforce whose values and expectations are different from their managers is no longer an option—it is an economic necessity. In the context of an increasingly diverse labour force, diversity management is not only a legal obligation, but also a necessity imposed by market laws, by competition, and by the need to be the best to survive.[49]

Statistics show that the ethnocultural profile of Canada has been changing since the 1960s and will continue to change dramatically over the next 20 years. European immigrants who led the first wave of immigrants in the early years of the 20th century have been surpassed by immigrants from Asia, including the Middle East.[50]

According to the 2001 Census, the number of Canadians who were born outside of Canada reached its highest level in 70 years, representing 18.4 percent of the population. The flow of immigrants to Canada has averaged about 1 percent of the population for decades, except during the 1990s when it averaged 0.6 percent to 0.9 percent. Of the 1.8 million immigrants who came to Canada between 1991 and 2001, 58 percent came from Asia, including the Middle East; 20 percent from Europe; 11 percent from the Caribbean and Central and South America; 8 percent from Africa; and 3 percent from the United States.[51] The goal of diversity management is to have the workforce at all levels resemble the population.

CEOs in Canada recognize that ethnic groups possess expertise such as language skills, knowledge of foreign cultures and business practices, and natural trade links with overseas markets that can be used to capture market share in emerging economies and new Canadian markets.[52] Ebco, a manufacturing company in Richmond, British Columbia, which has won awards for excellence in race relations, is doing business in

Germany and Taiwan because it was able to tap the networks and skills of its employees, who trace their origins to 48 different countries. The spending power of these groups is another motivating factor to incorporate them into all levels of the workforce.[53] According to Edgar Ware, ethnocultural business manager at Digital Equipment of Canada, "We have an obligation to the cultural fabric. We want to look like the people we sell to."[54] Digital's goal is to balance a diversity strategy with the organization's business plan.

Besides the moral issues surrounding diversity, there is a critical economic need for Canada to increase its share of world trade and expand its trade portfolio (see The Business Case). Our export market is dominated by the United States, Japan, and the United Kingdom. If Canadian business continues to rely heavily on these markets, our export growth and standard of living may not keep pace with other international markets.[55] Third World countries in emerging markets are going to require new

The Business Case

The Economic Values of Diversity

Although employment equity and its partner, employment diversity, were launched on moral grounds, increasingly, these initiatives are sustained on business grounds. The first principle to understand is that members of the designated groups are consumers, and not just potential employees. For example, the purchasing power of persons with disabilities is estimated to be $120 billion. Racial minorities control more than $76 billion of combined purchasing power. Women control 80 percent of the consumer dollars spent in North America.

The second business fundamental is that employees who are members of the designated groups represent an organizational resource that facilitates the understanding and linkages to these markets by helping various departments to understand the lifestyles, consumption needs and wants, purchasing preferences, media usage habits, and brand loyalty of these groups.

A study of nearly a thousand companies operating in the European Economic Union reported that a diverse workforce brings these benefits to business: (in rank order)

- Access to new labour pool
- Benefits related to a company's reputation
- Commitment to equality and diversity as company values
- Innovation and creativity
- Compliance with laws
- Competitive advantage
- Economic effectiveness
- Marketing opportunities
- Enhanced customer satisfaction.

Sources: European Commission, "Business Case for Diversity," Directorate-General for Employment, Social Affairs, and Equal Opportunity, Luxembourg, 2005; Aparita Bhandari, "Ethnic Marketing—It's More Than Skin Deep," *The Globe and Mail*, September 7, 2005; B. Siu, "Beyond Quotas: The Business Case for Employment Equity," *Canadian HR Reporter*, June 4, 2001.

investments in infrastructure, public systems, and productive capital. Given the multicultural background of many of its workers, Canada is in an excellent position to provide these services.[56] Canadian companies such as Nortel and SNC-Lavalin have already begun to tap the potential of these emerging markets.

Creating an Environment for Success

Transforming an organizational culture into a culture that embraces diversity can be a complex and lengthy process. Diversity initiatives should be taken slowly so that everyone can understand that this change is an evolutionary process and that expectations should be realistic. Individuals must fully understand the time, effort, commitment, and risk involved and the need for a systematic approach.[57]

Leadership is one of the most important variables in an organization's ability to successfully incorporate diversity into its business strategy. In a recent Conference Board of Canada survey, 86 percent of respondents indicated that responsibility rested with human resources.[58] The initiative should not be perceived as a human resources program or policy, but rather as a business imperative. In the words of Prem Benimadhu, vice-president of human resources research for the Conference Board, "Building a racially and culturally diverse workforce has been perceived as a human resources issue. But as long as it is, it's not going to be in the mission statement of organizations."[59] Only 6 percent of firms surveyed by the Conference Board study mentioned ethnic and cultural diversity in their mission statements.

Diversity initiatives should be linked directly to the business objectives and goals of the most senior levels of management. (See Figure 3.5 on page 134.) Reality Check on page 135 demonstrates how the BMO Financial Group has woven its program into its organizational fabric.

Organizations seeking to incorporate the value of diversity into their corporate philosophy must make use of appropriate internally and externally focused communications. For example, the National Bank of Canada participates annually in Montreal's La semaine des communautés culturelles, a week dedicated to the celebration of Montreal's multiculturalism. The bank believes that its visible demonstrations of commitment to ethnocultural diversity in the community it serves help raise the bank's profile.[60]

Cross-functional teams established to promote the diversity initiative are used successfully as communication vehicles by many leading-edge organizations. Toronto's Sunnybrook Health Sciences Centre has implemented the Patient Diversity Task Force to examine and report on the barriers faced by its patients, residents, and families.[61] Other organizations seek to raise the awareness of ethnocultural diversity.

Training is essential to the success of diversity implementation. A number of companies, including Imperial Oil and Connaught Laboratories, have incorporated diversity training. Cultural etiquette is an important aspect of diversity training that aims to explain the differences, or diversity, in people.

The Department of National Defence includes diversity training in its basic officer training course.[62] A consortium of European and North American businesses is attempting to develop a global diversity standard, by which companies will be able to use software to rate the success of their diversity programs.[63]

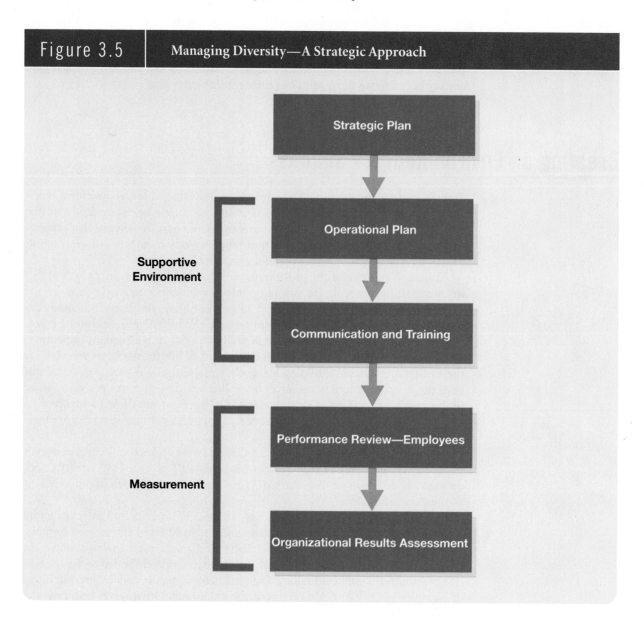

Figure 3.5   Managing Diversity—A Strategic Approach

Of even greater importance than training is the need to incorporate elements of diversity into all core training programs and to tailor those elements to meet the needs of specific business units or groups of employees.[64]

An added advantage of implementing a diversity initiative relates to its impact on employee retention. Retention of well-qualified and skilled employees is an important goal, considering the amount of resources—in both time and money—spent on recruiting and hiring new employees. Canadian organizations spend an average of 28 hours recruiting a new management or professional employee, 42 hours recruiting a new executive, and 20 hours recruiting a new technical/supervisory employee.[65] Maintaining a balanced and diversified workforce during periods of downsizing continues to be a major challenge.

Much the same as is required under employment equity, an overall review of policies and employment practices must be considered. In this regard, the use of an employee attitude survey may prove beneficial in finding areas of systemic or perceived discrimination. The evaluation criteria used most often by Canadian organizations are staff attitudes, increases in promotions for minority employees, reduction in turnover of minority employees, reduction in number of harassment suits, recruitment statistics for minorities, and improvements in productivity.[66]

Reality Check

BMO Financial Group

BMO Financial Group, well known throughout the Canadian marketplace as an exemplary leader in diversity and workplace equity issues, won the Catalyst Award for promoting women's careers. It was the first time a Canadian organization had won the award. (Catalyst recognizes organizations in North America for outstanding achievements in employment equity.) In 2002 and 2003, BMO was the only major Canadian bank to be cited by *Maclean's* magazine as one of Canada's top 100 employers and has twice won the Vision Award from Human Resources Development Canada. Rose M. Patten, senior executive vice-president, Human Resources, and head of the Office of Strategic Management, oversees the equity campaign from her Toronto office.

"One of BMO's keys to success is the ability to integrate our programs into the fabric of the organization. At BMO Financial Group, our commitment to fostering a diverse and equitable workplace is reflected not only in our corporate values and part of our cultural fabric; it is how we do business. We don't just talk about values; we live them. BMO's people strategies focus on the importance of talented, engaged, and high-performing employees. An important element of this is maintaining an equitable and supportive workplace, which reflects the diversity of the communities in which we do business. These objectives are explicitly aligned with strategic initiatives from the top, and, subsequently, are carefully measured and connected to performance. As part of this, diversity is seen as a strategic imperative at BMO.

"In 1992, BMO put its commitment into action by establishing a National Advisory Council on the Equitable Workplace to oversee enterprise-wide implementation of all workplace equality initiatives. Chaired by Tony Comper, then president of BMO, and comprised of the bank's most senior business line and corporate executives, the council set the strategic direction for quantitative and qualitative diversity goals, and measured performance against those goals on a quarterly basis. Today, the council is known as the Chairman's Council on the Equitable Workplace, and is still chaired by Tony Comper, now chairman and chief executive officer of BMO Financial Group.

"More recently, the council produced a unique diversity model linking diversity and workplace equity to the enterprise's strategic objectives. In the model, diversity and workplace equity are placed at the centre of six key business initiatives: corporate values and strategies, competition for talent acquisition and retention of people, managerial competency, customer and community business interface, corporate image and brand equity, and legislative compliance. Corporations in Canada, the U.S., and Europe have since adopted this framework to understand diversity's influence on business strategy—breaking traditional paradigms.

(continued on next page)

"When our efforts toward advancement of women began in 1990, we only had 6 percent of women in executive positions; today we have 35 percent. This was achieved in part as a result of a task force on the advancement of women sponsored by our then president, Tony Comper, in 1990. Discussions with employees revealed several widely held beliefs about why women were so underrepresented at senior levels at the company. To study whether these beliefs were supported by facts, the task force developed a statistical profile study on men and women at BMO. The results told a compelling story, and the company resolved to address the situation.

"In addition, BMO's Annual Employee Survey was redesigned to include a comprehensive Diversity Index, a compilation of questions enabling BMO to measure how well employees think their employer is doing in living up to its commitment to creating a diverse workforce and an equitable workplace. The index enables BMO to use fact-based information about our employee base in prioritizing diversity action plans and strategies. The most recent survey indicated that, more than ever, employees believe that men and women have an equal opportunity for promotion.

"Today, BMO's commitment to diversity and workplace equity continues to be supported by a comprehensive system of goal setting, monitoring and evaluation processes using clear metrics and benchmarks. As our progress towards the goal of a diverse workforce and an equitable and supportive workplace continues to be recognized, we at BMO will continue to be trailblazers pushing ourselves to new heights."

A final element in achieving success is monitoring progress and providing qualitative and quantitative evidence of change. For example, during their performance appraisals, all salaried employees at Levi Strauss & Co. (Canada) are evaluated on their ability to meet both business and aspirational goals. Aspirational goals are based on the company's core values, which include valuing diversity, following ethical management practices, and encouraging new behaviours, recognition, communications, and empowerment. These aspirations are the shared values and behaviours that will drive the company toward its mission of "sustained responsible commercial success."[67] When management measures performance as a function of diversity initiatives, values are instilled in the minds of all employees, and it is demonstrated that change and diversity are part of day-to-day business. To achieve success in diversity, it is vital to set an example and to create an atmosphere that respects and values differences. Canadian organizations have recognized the competitive advantage of embracing diversity in their business strategies.

SUMMARY

objective 1
Employment equity refers to the employment of individuals in a fair and nonbiased manner. Four groups in Canada—women, visible minorities, Aboriginals, and persons with disabilities—tend to be concentrated in a few occupations that are accorded lower status and pay.

objective 2
The Canadian Human Rights Act applies to all federally governed departments and agencies, and all organizations incorporated under federal jurisdiction. The act prohibits discrimination on the basis of grounds such as race, religion, sex, age, national or ethnic origin, physical

handicap, and marital status. The Canadian Human Rights Commission enforces the act through a formal complaint procedure.

 Pay equity is an amendment to the Canadian Human Rights Act that makes it illegal for employers to discriminate against individuals on the basis of job content. By definition, pay equity means equal pay for work of equal value.

 The Employment Equity Act requires all federally regulated employers to prepare an employment equity plan. The Canadian Human Rights Commission is mandated under the Canadian Human Rights Act to prohibit discrimination in the establishments of federally regulated businesses.

 The implementation of employment equity involves six steps: senior management support, data collection and analysis, an employment system review, establishment of a workplan, implementation, strategy, and a follow-up process that includes monitoring, reviewing, and revision.

 Sexual harassment is an employment equity issue undergoing continued debate.

 Managing diversity does more than incorporate employment equity. The goal of diversity management is to optimize the utilization of an organization's multicultural workforce with the goal of realizing strategic advantage.

KEY TERMS

bona fide occupational
  qualification (BFOQ), 106
concentration, 118
designated groups, 101

diversity management, 131
employment equity, 100
flow data, 117
reasonable accommodation, 122

sexual harassment, 125
stock data, 117
systemic discrimination, 119
underutilization, 118

DISCUSSION QUESTIONS

1. Here are some myths about employment equity:
   - It leads to hiring unqualified workers.
   - It causes an overnight change in the workforce makeup.
   - It's a plan that would make Calgary's workforce look like Toronto's.
   - This program lays off white males to make room for designated group members.
   - It's a program mainly for racial minorities.
   - Employers who implement the plan can destroy hard-won seniority provisions that protect all workers.
   - It's the end of hiring for white males.

   In groups, determine if group members share these beliefs. As human resource professionals, how would you work with employees who held these beliefs?

   Go to the website of the Alliance for Employment Equity (www.web.net/~allforee/empeqity .htm), and compare your answers.

2. While the process for filing a complaint of discrimination appears clear, many would choose not to do so. List the reasons why alleged "victims" of discrimination in employment would not file a complaint.

3. Find a male class job (i.e., a job in which the majority of workers are male) and a female class job that seem to require similar educational background and technical skills. (For example, compare female dominated police dispatchers with male dominated radio

technical supervisors, or female dominated health technicians to male dominated transportation workers.) Then, using an Internet salary compensation index, calculate the pay rates. Are there differences? How would you account for these differences?

4. List as many jobs as you can where you could hire male only applicants, based on a BFOQ.

5. "Discrimination against older persons does not generate the same degree of moral outrage as other forms of discrimination." Do you agree? If you find this quote offensive, read the full text of the Human Rights Commission's discussion paper on human rights for the aging (www.ohrc.on.ca).

6. After receiving several complaints of sexual harassment, the HR department of a city library decides to establish a sexual harassment policy. What should be included in the policy? How should it be implemented?

7. Describe how an organization can make best use of a multicultural workforce.

INTERNET EXERCISE

Although women represent over half the population and nearly 47 percent of the workforce, only about 37 percent of them hold managerial positions. Using the Public Service Human Resources Management Agency website www.hrma-agrh.gc.ca/ee, develop a list of actions that managers can do to create a work environment that will lead to the advancement of women. Would you recommend this same list for the advancement of other designated groups?

HRM Experience

Preventing Sexual Harassment

Over the past decade the problem of sexual harassment has captured the attention of all managers and employees. While it is widely known that sexual harassment is both unethical and illegal, the incidents of sexual harassment continue to plague business. Unfortunately, when these cases arise, they cause morale problems among employees, embarrassment to the organization, and costly legal damages. Consequently, all managers and supervisors play a central role in preventing sexual harassment complaints. It is important that managers understand the definition of sexual harassment, who is covered by sexual harassment guidelines, and how to prevent its occurrence. This skill-building exercise will provide you with knowledge in each of these areas.

Assignment

1. Working in teams of female and male members, develop a list of behaviours that could be classified as quid pro quo harassment or hostile environment. Explore the possibility that some sexual harassing behaviours might be viewed differently by female and male employees. Give examples.

2. Many sexual harassment incidents go unreported. Fully discuss why this can occur and what might be done to reduce this problem.

3. The cornerstone to addressing sexual harassment is achieving organizational awareness through training. Develop a sexual harassment training program for a company of 250 employees that covers, at a minimum, the following: (1) who should attend the training sessions, (2) the content outline for the training program (the list of materials your team

wants to teach), (3) specific examples to illustrate the training materials, and (4) how to investigate sexual harassment complaints.

4. This chapter will assist you with this assignment. You can obtain additional materials from employment equity publications and websites of the federal government and from various HR magazines.

5. Be prepared to present your training outline to other class members.

BIZFLIX EXERCISES

Legally Blonde: Sexual Harassment

Review the earlier section "Sexual Harassment" before watching this scene from *Legally Blonde*. Several aspects of that discussion appear in the scene.

Elle Woods' (Reese Witherspoon) boyfriend, Warner Huntington III (Matthew Davis), wants to go to Harvard Law School instead of keeping their relationship alive. Elle pursues him vigorously by applying to and getting accepted to Harvard Law School. This is a charming comedy, dedicated to blonde women everywhere in the world. It is filled with stereotyping, giving many delightful twists to its surprise conclusion.

This scene comes from the "Poor Judgment" segment near the end of the film. It follows the successful use of Elle's hunch about key witness Enrique Salvatore (Greg Serano) in Brooke Windam's (Ali Larter) trial. The film continues after she leaves Professor Callahan's (Victor Garber) office. Elle sees Emmett (Luke Wilson) in the building lobby and tells him she is quitting the internship.

What to Watch for and Ask Yourself
- Does Professor Callahan sexually harass Elle? If yes, what is the evidence in these scenes?
- Did Elle behave appropriately or inappropriately in Professor Callahan's office?

case study 1

Hiring People with Disabilities: Determining Attitudes

In Canada, 40.3 percent of people with disabilities of working age have jobs. To accommodate 75 percent of these individuals would cost organizations less than $1,000 each. A pool of talented and motivated people is available, and the accommodation costs are reasonable. Why won't more organizations hire them?

Norma Daggett, HR director for Denton Plastics, would like to introduce more diversity into the company's workforce by hiring qualified people with disabilities. Before proceeding to the hiring phase, she would like to get a sense of how the current workforce will respond to her diversity plan. To that end, she has developed the following test consisting of true/false statements that will help her determine employee attitudes toward people with disabilities.

1. Most people with disabilities do not require special work arrangements.
2. The real problem for the people with disabilities is holding a job, not getting one.

3. Employees with disabilities tend to have more accidents than other employees.
4. These employees are less likely to have a record of absenteeism.
5. People with the most severe impairments are likely to be at the top in job performance.
6. Turnover tends to be higher among employees with disabilities than among other employees.
7. Other employees tend to respond negatively when accommodations (e.g., wheelchair ramps) are made for employees with disabilities.

The Canadian Council on Rehabilitation and Work shares knowledge and attempts to influence attitudes for equitable employment for people with disabilities; visit their website at www.ccrw.org.

QUESTIONS

1. Give a true or false response to each of the above statements.
2. Refer to the correct answers (based on statistical evidence) given at the end of the chapter. For each item you answered incorrectly, ask yourself, "Where did I get that idea?" See if you can detect any personal bias toward people with disabilities.
3. Why are people with disabilities still underemployed?

case study 2

Fighting Fires

In British Columbia, the competition for firefighting jobs is fierce, with more than 1600 people applying for about 60 jobs. At one time, the provincial Ministry of Forests required all job applicants to pass this physical fitness test:

- Lift a 23-kilogram bar in an upright rowing motion 18 times.
- Carry pumps and hoses, weighting as much as 50 kilograms, over a timed distance.
- Perform a shuttle run, which involves darting back and forth at an increasingly faster pace between cones situated 20 metres apart.

The B.C. Government and Service Employees Union argued that the average man, with training, could easily pass the test, whereas the average woman, even with training, could not. Only 35 percent of women who applied for the firefighter's job passed the test; about 70 percent of the men did.

The University of Victoria scientists who designed the tests argued that most women could reach the standard, although they would have to work harder than most men to do so. Female firefighters said they had to train year round to pass the test, but they took this as a personal responsibility and as the cost of qualifying for the job. Their safety, as well as that of their colleagues and the public, depends on their strength and endurance. The B.C. Ministry of Forests spokeswoman suggested that lowering the standards would be a mistake: "Already male firefighters are asking if blazes will be designated as 'guy' fires and 'girl' fires. We want the fittest people."

QUESTIONS

1. Did the standards result in safer and more effective firefighting crews, or were they inadvertently keeping women out of a traditionally male job?
2. Was this a BFOQ? The ministry was challenged on the basis of sex discrimination. What did the Supreme Court rule, and what was its reasoning?
3. Female applicants had the chance to train and try the test at B.C. university campuses. Was this special preparation discriminatory?
4. Did the changes made fix the underlying problems? Explain.
5. What other advice would you give their managers?

case study 3

What Went Wrong?

Early in her appointment as a member of the executive team in a large institution, Debra became aware of hostility between several subordinates and herself. Those who had been unsuccessful applicants for her job said publicly that her experience was inappropriate for the position. Shortly after that, she heard rumours suggesting that her appointment was predicated on a sexual relationship with her boss.

Rumours proliferated through e-mail chat and comments were made at national meetings. When Debra confronted her superior about the situation, he suggested that the rumours reflected professional jealousy and were not worthy of a response. While she made numerous attempts to squelch the insinuations, at no time did her boss address the rumours or condemn those who made remarks. Over the course of several months, Debra sensed that he enjoyed hearing the insinuations. As time passed, she began to feel that her authority was being undermined.

Six months into the appointment, her boss's marriage ended. The event refueled the rumour mill. Shortly afterwards, Debra's superior was replaced. Upon his arrival, her new boss requested Debra's resignation. While performance was not an issue, he stated that she did not fit in well with the new executive team. When Debra brought in her lawyer to discuss concerns about sexual harassment, the organization settled quickly to avoid public trial or publicity. Now on leave, Debra is reluctant to return to the organization, and she is aware that prospective employers know of her experience and that rumours will make it difficult to secure a similar position.

Source: *Sexual Harassment Is Still A Management Issue,* The Conference Board of Canada, Ottawa 2001. Used by permission.

QUESTIONS

1. What went wrong?
2. What should have been done?

CAREER COUNSEL

Find out how to handle prohibited questions during a job interview by visiting the *Managing Human Resources* website (www.belcourt5e.nelson.com).

NOTES AND REFERENCES

1. Human Resources Development Canada, "Annual Report, Analysis of Employers' Reports," www.hrdc-drhc.gc.ca/LEEP/Annual_Reports/03.

2. Human Resources Development Canada, *Annual Report, Employment Equity Act, 2003*, Labour Standards and Workplace Equity, Cat. No. MP31-5/2002; Human Resources Development Canada, "Workplace Equity," http://info.load-otea.hrdc-drhc.gc.ca/workplace_equity/leep/annual/2002/.

3. Shannon Kie, "Feds Pledge Big Money But No Plan to Tackle Aboriginal Unemployment," *Canadian HR Reporter*, January 30, 2006: 3.

4. L. Redpath and M.O. Nielsen, "A Comparison of Native Culture, Non-Native Culture and New Management Ideology," *Canadian Journal of Administrative Studies* 14, no. 3 (1996): 327–39.

5. Deborah Zinni, Barry Wright, and Mark Julien, "Want to Retain Aboriginal Employees?" *HR Professional*, August/September 2005.

6. Alar Prost and David Redmond, "Employers Need Help with Integration," *Canadian HR Reporter*, December 19, 2005: 7.

7. Statistics Canada website, "Designated Minority Representation," www.statcan.ca/english/IPS/Data/96F0030XIE2001008.htm.

8. Human Resources Development Canada, "Workplace Equity," www.statcan.ca/Daily/English/030311/d030311a.htm; http://info.load-otea.hrdc-drhc.gc.ca/workplace_equity/leep/annual/2002/2002annualrep08.shtml.

9. *Employment Equity: A Guide for Employers*, Employment and Immigration Canada, Cat. No. LM-143-5-91, May 1991: 9.

10. Victor S. Mackinnon, "The Canadian Charter of Rights and Freedoms," *Public Administration: Canadian Materials* (North York: Captus Press, 1993): 179–80.

11. Canadian Human Rights Act, Canadian Human Rights Commission, 1978, Paragraph 2, Subsection (a).

12. A.P. Aggarwal, *Sex Discrimination: Employment Law and Practices* (Toronto: Butterworths Canada, 1994).

13. "Firm Pays $300,000 in Racial Harassment Settlements," *Human Resources Management in Canada*, Report Bulletin No. 72 (February 1989) (Scarborough, ON: Prentice-Hall Canada): 1–2.

14. Canadian Human Rights Act, Paragraph 46, Section 2(a), (b).

15. Human Resources Development Canada, *Annual Report, Employment Equity Act, 2001*, Labour Standards and Workplace Equity, Cat. No. LT-020-12-01.

16. Russel J.G. Juriansz, *Equal Pay Legislation and Ontario's New Pay Equity Act* (Toronto: Blake, Cassels & Graydon, 1995): 3–5.

17. Susan Riggs, "Comparing Apples and Oranges: Job Evaluations," *Worklife* 8, no. 1 (1991): 7–10.

18. "Achieving Pay Equity First Goal, But through Co-operation: Commissioner," *Pay Equity Commission Report* 1, no. 1 (March 1988): 6.

19. Morley Gunderson and Roberta Edgecombe Robb, "Equal Pay for Work of Equal Value: Canada's Experience," *Advances in Industrial and Labour Relations* 5 (1991): 151–68. See also John

G. Kelly, *Pay Equity Management* (Toronto: CCH Canadian, 1988): 45–54.

20. David Brown, "New Rules Proposed for Pay Equity," *Canadian HR Reporter*, May 31, 2004, 1 and 2.

21. *Introduction to Employment Equity* (Ottawa: Human Resources Development Canada, 1996).

22. http://laws.justice.gc.ca/en/E-5.401/48928.html.

23. Kelly Toughill, "Firms Back Equity: To Some It's 'Good Business' Despite Harris's Vow to Scrap It," *Toronto Star*, June 21, 1995: A2.

24. Canadian Human Rights Act, S.C. 1976–77, as amended.

25. R.G.L. Fairweather, Canadian Human Rights Commission, *The Standing Committee on Legal and Constitutional Affairs*, May 29, 1986: 10.

26. Shenaz Mode, "Employment Equity: An Important Piece in the Human Rights Puzzle," *HR Professional*, April/May 2005: 26.

27. *Towards Equity: 1993 Merit Awards*, Employment Equity Branch, Human Resources Development Canada, June 1994: 17–18.

28. *Workplace Innovations Overview—1996*, Bureau of Labour Information, Human Resources Development Canada: 1–84.

29. *Towards Equity: 1993 Merit Awards:* 11–12; Laura Cassiani, "Canada's Quiet Labour Crisis," *Canadian HR Reporter* 14, no. 3 (February 12, 2001): 1 and 8.

30. L. Young, "Employers Need to Scrutinize All Job Testing for Human Rights Violations, Supreme Court Rules," *Canadian HR Reporter*, October 4, 1999: 3.

31. Ibid., 18.

32. Aggarwal, *Sex Discrimination*.

33. Nicholas Keung, "Police Recruit Ethnic Officers to Boost Force," *Toronto Star*, July 25, 1997: A7.

34. *Employment Equity: A Guide for Employers*: 19.

35. Wendy Stueck, "Business Taps Talents of Disabled Workers," *The Globe and Mail*, May 18, 2004: B4.

36. Joanne Leck, Sylvie St. Onge, and Isabelle La Lancettee, "Wage Gap Changes among Organizations Subject to the Employment Equity Act," *Canadian Public Policy* 21, no. 44 (December 1995): 387–400.

37. Seymour Moskowitz, "Adolescent Workers and Sexual Harassment," *Labor Law Journal* 51, no. 3 (Fall 2000): 78–84. For an excellent reference guide on sexual harassment, see William Petrocelli and Barbara Kate Repa, *Sexual Harassment on the Job: What It Is and How to Stop It* (Berkeley, CA: Nolo Press, 1998).

38. "Sexual Harassment," *CACSW Fact Sheet*, Canadian Advisory Council on the Status of Women, March 1993.

39. "Inquest Probes Murder-Suicide Involving Harassment Victim," *Sexual Harassment, Workplace Diversity Update* 5, no. 3 (March 1997): 4.

40. Shannon Kari, "B.C. Fire Chief Vows Policy to Combat Sexual Harassment," *The Globe and Mail*, May 31, 2005: A1.

41. Malcolm McKillop, "A Manager's Guide to Sexual Impropriety," *The Globe and Mail*, October 7, 1997: B23.

42. Dale Hall and Siobhan McEwan, *Sexual Assault and Harassment on Campus*, York University Sexual Harassment Education and Complaint Centre, York University, 1995.

43. *Sexual Harassment and You: What Every Student Should Know*, Sexual Harassment Education and Complaint Centre, York University, 1986.

44. For a good review of sexual harassment policy, see Dana S. Connell, "Effective Sexual Harassment Policies: Unexpected Lessons from Jacksonville Shipyards," *Employee Relations Law Journal* 17, no. 2 (Autumn 1991): 191–205.

45. Katherine Harding, "Taking Aim at Bullies," *The Globe and Mail*, March 19, 2003: C1.

46. Christine L. Taylor, "Dimensions of Diversity in Canadian Business: Building a Business Case for Valuing Ethnocultural Diversity," *Conference Board of Canada Report 143-95*, April 1995: 1.

47. Paul Moloney, "Toronto Okays Non-Christian Holidays for Staffers," *Toronto Star*, May 17, 1995: A6.

48. S. Hood, "Generational Diversity," *HR Professional*, June–July 2000: 19.

49. Jennie Constantinides, "Diversity Management: At CN, the 'Token' Will Be Broken," *Human Resources Professional* 7, no. 4 (April 1991): 29–30.

50. Lindsay Scotton, "We Are the World: The Many Faces of Canada Come Together on Winning Images in a Contest to Depict Racial Harmony," May 19, 1995: B3. See also "Logo & Poster Design Exhibition," *Voices of Harmony* 1, no. 1 (Summer 1995): 1–7.

51. Statistics Canada, *Canada's Ethnocultural Portrait*; Anderson, "Immigration Shifts Population Kaleidoscope."

52. Ibid.

53. Jana Schilder, "The Rainbow Connection: Employers Who Promote Diversity May Discover a Pot of Gold," *Human Resources Professional* 11, no. 3 (April 1994): 13–15.

54. Ibid.

55. Doug Nevison, "Profiting in the Pacific Rim: Can Canada Capture Its Share?" *Conference Board of Canada Report*, 1994: 117-94.

56. World Bank, 1993.

57. R. Roosevelt Thomas, Jr., "Beyond Race and Gender," *AMACOM*, 1991: 34.

58. Taylor, "Dimensions of Diversity in Canadian Business": 13.

59. John Spears, "The Many Colours of Money: Diversity Boosts Profit, Firms Told," *Toronto Star*, May 9, 1995.

60. Taylor, "Dimensions of Diversity in Canadian Business": 15.

61. *Continuing In-Patient Focused Care Excellence*, Sunnybrook Community and Public Affairs, Sunnybrook Health Science Centre, Toronto, April 1995.

62. P. Lungen, "Military Addresses Racism Issue," *Canadian Jewish News* 30, no. 7 (February 17, 2000): 6.

63. L. Young, "Global Diversity Standard in Works," *Canadian HR Reporter*, April 5, 1999: 1.

64. Claudine Kapel, "Variation Is the Theme: Organizations That Value Diversity Glimpse Profits in Improved Productivity," *Human Resources Professional* 1, no. 3 (April 1994): 9–12.

65. *Compensation Planning Outlook*, Conference Board of Canada, 1992.

66. Taylor, "Dimensions of Diversity in Canadian Business."

67. Ibid., 18.

ANSWERS TO CASE STUDY 1

1. T

2. F

3. F

4. T

5. T

6. F

7. F

Job Analysis, Employee Involvement, and Flexible Work Schedules

After studying this chapter, you should be able to

objective 1

Discuss the relationship between job requirements and the performance of HRM functions.

objective 2

Indicate the methods by which job analysis typically is completed.

objective 3

Identify and explain the various sections of job descriptions.

objective 4

Provide examples illustrating the various factors that must be taken into account in designing a job.

objective 5

Discuss the various job characteristics that motivate employees.

objective 6

Describe the different group techniques used to maximize employee contributions.

objective 7

Differentiate and explain the different adjustments in work schedules.

O rganizations are "reengineering" themselves in an attempt to become more effective. Companies such as Canadian Pacific and Ducks Unlimited Canada are breaking into smaller units and getting flatter. There is emphasis on smaller scale, less hierarchy, fewer layers, and more decentralized work units. As organizational reshaping takes place, managers want employees to operate more independently and flexibly to meet customer demands. To do this, they require that decisions be made by the people who are closest to the information and who are directly involved in the product or service delivered. The objective is to develop jobs and basic work units that are adaptable enough to thrive in a world of high-velocity change.

In this chapter, we will discuss how jobs can be designed so as to best contribute to the objectives of the organization and at the same time satisfy the needs of the employees who are to perform them. Clearly, the duties and responsibilities present in jobs greatly influence employee productivity, job satisfaction, and employment retention.[1] Therefore, the value of job analysis, which defines clearly and precisely the requirements of each job, will be stressed. We will emphasize that these job requirements provide the foundation for making objective and legally defensible decisions in managing human resources. The chapter concludes by reviewing several innovative job design and employee contribution techniques that increase job satisfaction while improving organizational performance. Teamwork and the characteristics of successful teams are highlighted. Stacy Sullivan, director of HR at Google, notes that "the work environment and the sense of team spirit have become a critical job element."[2]

Relationship of Job Requirements and HRM Functions

objective **1**

job
A group of related activities and duties

position
The different duties and responsibilities performed by only one employee

job family
A group of individual jobs with similar characteristics

job specification
A statement of the needed knowledge, skills, and abilities of the person who is to perform the job

A **job** consists of a group of related activities and duties. Ideally, the duties of a job should consist of natural units of work that are similar and related. They should be clear and distinct from those of other jobs to minimize misunderstanding and conflict among employees and to enable employees to recognize what is expected of them. For some jobs, several employees may be required, each of whom will occupy a separate position. A **position** consists of different duties and responsibilities performed by only one employee. In a city library, for example, four employees (four positions) may be involved in reference work, but all of them have only one job (reference librarian). Where different jobs have similar duties and responsibilities, they may be grouped into a **job family** for purposes of recruitment, training, compensation, or advancement opportunities.

Recruitment

Before they can find capable employees for an organization, recruiters need to know the job specifications for the positions they are to fill.[3] A **job specification** is a statement of the knowledge, skills, and abilities required of the person performing the job. In the HR department for the City of Calgary, Alberta, the job specification for a senior personnel analyst includes the following:

1. Appropriate university degree, preferably at the master's level.
2. Four to five years of corporate management experience.

3. Working knowledge of employment equity, human rights legislation, statistical analysis, investigative procedures, and organizational development[4]

Because job specifications establish the qualifications required of applicants for a job opening, they serve an essential role in the recruiting function. These qualifications typically are contained in the notices of job openings. Whether posted on organizational bulletin boards or HRIS Internet sites or included in help-wanted advertisements or employment agency listings, job specifications provide a basis for attracting qualified applicants and discourage unqualified ones.

Selection

In addition to job specifications, managers and supervisors use job descriptions to select employees and orient them to jobs. A **job description** is a statement of the tasks, duties, and responsibilities of a job. (See "Job Descriptions" later in this chapter.)

job description
A statement of the tasks, duties, and responsibilities of a job to be performed

In the past, job specifications used as a basis for selection sometimes bore little relation to the duties to be performed under the job description. Examples of such non-job-related specifications abounded. Applicants for the job of labourer were required to have a high school diploma. Firefighters were required to be at least six feet tall. And applicants for skilled craft positions—plumbers, electricians, machinists—were required to be male. These kinds of job specifications discriminated against members of certain designated groups, many of whom were excluded from these jobs.

In 1984, charges of discrimination were brought against the Vancouver Fire Department because it required that candidates for a firefighter's job be at least five feet nine. The Human Rights Board that heard the case could not find any correlation between the height of a firefighter and injuries or efficiencies or capacity to perform the job. The Vancouver Fire Department was found in violation of the Human Rights Act. An organization must be careful to ensure that managers with job openings do not hire employees on the basis of "individualized" job requirements that satisfy personal whims but bear little relation to successful job performance. In one case known to the authors, a company desired to hire only tall salespeople—male or female—on the assumption that tall individuals presented a more authoritative stature.[5]

Training and Development

Any discrepancies between the knowledge, skills, and abilities (often referred to as KSAs) demonstrated by a jobholder and the requirements contained in the description and specification for that job provide clues to training needs. Also, career development as a part of the training function is concerned with preparing employees for advancement to jobs where their capacities can be utilized to the fullest extent possible. The formal qualification requirements set forth in high-level jobs indicate how much more training and development are needed for employees to advance to those jobs.

Performance Appraisal

The requirements contained in the description of a job provide the criteria for evaluating the performance of the holder of that job. The results of performance appraisal may reveal, however, that certain requirements established for a job are not completely valid. As we have already stressed, these criteria must be specific and job-related. If the criteria used to evaluate employee performance are vague and not job-related, employers may find themselves being charged with unfair discrimination.

The Business Case

Flying for Love or Money

The two unions representing pilots who fly for Air Canada and its regional airline, Air Canada Jazz, fought over pay scale. Pilots for both carriers must meet the same job requirements. However, those who fly for the mainline service earn about $140,000 to $200,000 annually while those who fly for the regional airline earn on average $75,000 to $100,000. The 3100 Air Canada pilots feel that the pay differential is justified because they fly bigger planes (carrying 150 to 250 passengers) at longer distances (14 hours) with the latest technology. The 1400 Air Canada Jazz pilots carry smaller passenger loads over shorter distances (flight times of 60 to 90 minutes). However, this entails many more takeoffs and landings, which are considered the most difficult and stressful part of the flight. Air Canada pilots dispute this, saying compensation is not determined by the number of takeoffs and landings; if it were, then bush pilots would be making the most money of all.

Accurate job descriptions would help resolve this contentious and costly debate.

Source: John Partridge, "Air Canada, the Pilots and All That Jazz," *The Globe and Mail*, June 14, 2003: B1, B4. Reprinted with permission from The Globe and Mail.

Compensation Management

In determining the rate to be paid for performing a job, the relative worth of the job is one of the most important factors. This worth is based on what the job demands of an employee in terms of skill, effort, and responsibility, as well as the conditions and hazards under which the work is performed. The systems of job evaluation by which this worth may be measured are discussed in Chapter 9. As The Business Case outlines, job analysis has financial implications and could cause workplace problems if handled poorly.

Employment Law

In Canada, employers do not have to prepare a job analysis in order to make decisions about selection, compensation, etc. However, by having a job analysis in place, employers can minimize the possibility of legal damages, if they are challenged on any HR decisions. In one case, the court found that new job requirements were not based on job-related information, and the job analysis was seriously flawed, resulting in the potential of discriminating against members of the designated groups.

Job Analysis

objective **2**

Job analysis is sometimes called the cornerstone of HRM because the information it collects serves so many HRM functions. **Job analysis** is the process of obtaining information about jobs by determining the duties, tasks, or activities of those jobs.[6] The procedure involves systematically investigating jobs by following a number of predetermined steps specified in advance of the study.[7] When completed, job analysis results

job analysis
The process of obtaining information about jobs by determining the duties, tasks, or activities of jobs

in a written report summarizing the information obtained from the analysis of 20 or 30 individual job tasks or activities.[8] HR managers use these data to develop job descriptions and job specifications. These documents, in turn, are used to perform and enhance the different HR functions such as the development of performance appraisal criteria or the content of training classes. Reality Check on page 150 describes the three reasons that EDS Canada Inc. undertakes job analyses. But employees and managers can also use them to plan careers. Best Buy Canada Ltd, a national retailer of consumer electronic products based in Burnaby, B.C. (which also operates Future Shop) is introducing new and more consistent job classification and titling, so that employees can use this information to plan their career ladders.[9] The ultimate purpose of job analysis is to improve organizational performance and productivity. Figure 4.1 illustrates how job analysis is performed, including the functions for which it is used.

As contrasted with job design, which reflects subjective opinions about the ideal requirements of a job, job analysis is concerned with objective and verifiable information about the actual requirements of a job. The job descriptions and job specifications developed through job analysis should be as accurate as possible if they are to be of

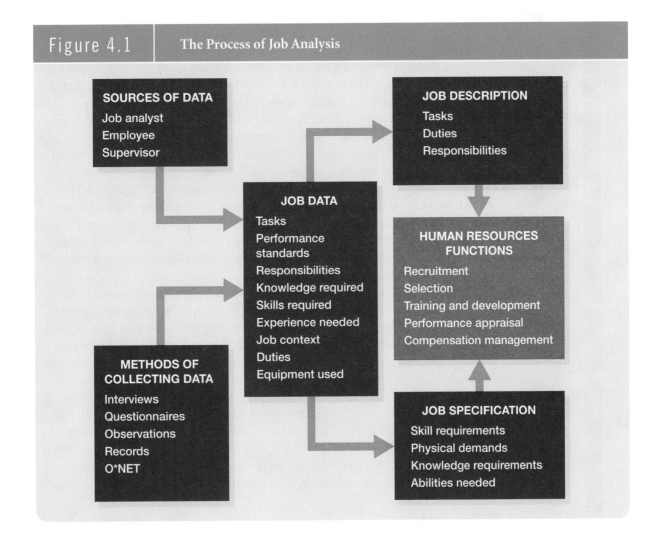

Figure 4.1 The Process of Job Analysis

value to those who make HRM decisions. These decisions may involve any of the HR functions—from recruitment to termination of employees.

Gathering Job Information

Job data may be obtained in several ways. The more common methods of analyzing jobs are through interviews, questionnaires, observations, and diaries.

- *Interviews.* The job analyst may question individual employees and managers about the job under review.
- *Questionnaires.* The job analyst may circulate carefully prepared questionnaires to be filled out individually by jobholders and managers. These forms will be used to obtain data in the areas of job duties and tasks performed, purpose of

Reality Check

Job Analysis at EDS Canada Inc.

As the senior human resources specialist at EDS Canada Inc., Don Weatherbee is responsible for conducting job analyses. While new job codes and classifications are normally developed by head office in Texas, there are three cases that warrant job analysis in Canada. The first is to comply with pay equity legislation that states that men and women should be paid equally for performing work of equal value. In order to comply with pay equity, jobs are analyzed and weighted for *Specialized Knowledge, Effort, Responsibility,* and the *Working Environment.* Salary survey companies are often retained to do this type of analysis since they are the experts in making sure that the pay grades are in compliance with the act.

The second occasion is when new jobs are created, which need to be classified and their compensation rates assessed. In one example, EDS Canada Inc. did not have an entry-level position in HR and so the task force developed an HR administrator position. On another occasion, a business services consultant position needed to be developed at the top end of the business analyst family. Because these positions were new to EDS Canada Inc., the full range of duties needed to be assessed and coded.

The third occasion occurs when, through acquisitions and transitioning people to EDS Canada Inc., job analysis is needed to verify what the employees do since job titles are frequently poor indicators of what a person actually does. For example, when EDS Canada Inc. won a contract bid to do IT outsourcing for a land registry company, a job analysis was needed in order to create new job codes for the employees that were transitioning to the company.

Information for both the employees and their supervisors is gathered on a job summary questionnaire (JSQ). This is done to ensure that there is no artificial inflation of job duties. There is one form for management and another form for professional, technical, clerical, trades, and services. The management questionnaire is more detailed as it includes areas of responsibilities, supervision given to direct reports, and previous work history that explains how it relates to the present job. Each questionnaire is designed to determine the percentage of time spent on each task, what that task is, for whom the task is done, how it is accomplished, and why it is done.

the job, physical setting, requirements for performing the job (skill, education, experience, physical and mental demands), equipment and materials used, and special health and safety concerns.

- *Observations.* The job analyst may learn about the jobs by observing and recording on a standardized form the activities of jobholders. Videotaping jobs for later study is an approach used by some organizations.
- *Diaries.* Jobholders themselves may be asked to keep a diary of their work activities during an entire work cycle. Diaries are normally filled out at specific times of the work shift (such as every half hour or hour) and maintained for a two- to four-week period.

USING THE INTERNET

For a general information site on job analysis, consult HR-Guide at:

www.hr-guide.com/jobanalysis.htm

Although HR specialists, called job analysts, are the personnel primarily responsible for the job analysis program, they usually enlist the cooperation of the employees and managers in the departments where jobs are being analyzed. These managers and employees are the sources of much of the information about the jobs, and they may be asked to prepare rough drafts of the job descriptions and specifications the job analysts need.

Controlling the Accuracy of Job Information

If job analysis is to accomplish its intended purpose, the job data collected must be accurate. Care must be taken to ensure that all important facts are included. A job analyst should be alert for employees who tend to exaggerate the difficulty of their jobs in order to inflate their egos and their paycheques. Ethics in HRM describes this more fully. When interviewing employees or reviewing their questionnaires, the job analyst must look for any responses that do not agree with other facts or impressions the analyst has received. Furthermore, when job information is collected from employees, a representative group of individuals should be surveyed. For example, the results of one study indicated that the information obtained from job analysis was related to race. In another study, the experience level of job incumbents influenced job analysis outcomes.

Ethics in HRM

Inflation

At some point in your working life, you will be asked to describe your job, perhaps when being interviewed by a job analyst or by answering questions on a form. Most employees have a reasonable expectation that their answers will affect their lives in significant ways. The information obtained may be used to reclassify the job to either a higher or lower pay level. Most employees believe that standards of performance may change—and the employer will expect them to work faster or to do more—although that is not the goal of job analysis.

As a result of these beliefs and expectations, employees have a vested interest in "inflating" their job descriptions, by making the job sound very important and very difficult. Thus night clerks in hotels become auditors and receptionists become administrators. Making a job sound more important than it is may reflect an employee's sincere belief in the significance of his or her contribution, or an attempt to lobby for higher pay.

A job analyst who doubts the accuracy of information provided by employees should obtain additional information from them, from their managers, or from other individuals who are familiar with or perform the same job. It is common practice to have the descriptions for each job reviewed by the jobholders and their managers. The job description summaries contained in the National Occupational Classification can also serve as a basis for the job analyst's review.

The NOC and Job Analysis

Commonly referred to as the NOC, the National Occupational Classification is compiled by the federal government. The purpose of the NOC is to compile, analyze, and communicate information about occupations. This information can be used for employment equity, human resource planning, and occupational supply and demand forecasts and analyses.

The NOC is a composite of the Canadian labour market and has helped bring about a greater degree of uniformity in the job titles and descriptions used by employers in different parts of the country. This uniformity has facilitated the movement of workers from regions that may be experiencing widespread unemployment to areas where employment opportunities are greater. Also, the NOC code numbers facilitate the exchange of statistical information about jobs and are useful in reporting research in the HR area, in vocational counselling, and in charting career paths through job transfers and/or advancements. Some professional associations provide a job classification system that is intended to be more current than the NOC.[10]

USING THE INTERNET

The NOC contains standardized and comprehensive descriptions of about 25 000 occupations at:

www23.hrdc-drhc.gc.ca/2001

Approaches to Job Analysis

The systematic and quantitative definition of job content that job analysis provides is the foundation of many HRM practices. Specifically, the job analysis serves to justify job descriptions and other HRM selection procedures. Several different job analysis approaches are used to gather data, each with specific advantages and disadvantages.[11] Five of the more popular methods are functional job analysis, the position analysis questionnaire system, the critical incident method, task inventory analysis, and computerized HRIS and job analysis.

Functional Job Analysis

functional job analysis (FJA)
A quantitative approach to job analysis that utilizes a compiled inventory of the various functions or work activities that can make up any job and that assumes that each job involves three broad worker functions: (1) data, (2) people, and (3) things

The **functional job analysis (FJA)** approach utilizes an inventory of the various types of functions or work activities that can constitute any job. FJA thus assumes that each job involves performing certain functions. Specifically, three broad worker functions form the bases of this system: (1) data, (2) people, and (3) things. These three categories are subdivided to form a hierarchy of worker-function scales, as shown in Figure 4.2. The job analyst, when studying the job under review, indicates the functional level for each of the three categories (for example, "copying" under DATA) and then reflects the relative involvement of the worker in the function by assigning a percentage figure to each function (such as 50 percent to "copying"). This is done for each of the three areas, and the three functional levels must equal 100 percent. The result is a quantitatively evaluated job. FJA can easily be used to describe the content of jobs and to assist in writing job descriptions and specifications.

Figure 4.2	Difficulty Levels of Worker Functions	
DATA (4TH DIGIT)	**PEOPLE (5TH DIGIT)**	**THINGS (6TH DIGIT)**
0 Synthesizing	0 Mentoring	0 Setting up
1 Coordinating	1 Negotiating	1 Precision working
2 Analyzing	2 Instructing	2 Operating-controlling*
3 Compiling	3 Supervising	3 Driving-operating*
4 Computing	4 Diverting	4 Manipulating
5 Copying	5 Persuading	5 Tending
6 Comparing	6 Speaking-signalling*	6 Feeding-offbearing*
	7 Serving	7 Handling
	8 Taking instructions—helping*	

*Hyphenated factors are single factors.

Source: U.S. Department of Labor, Employment and Training Administration, *Revised Handbook for Analyzing Jobs* (Washington, DC: U.S. Government Printing Office, 1991), 5.

The Position Analysis Questionnaire System

**position analysis
questionnaire (PAQ)**
A questionnaire covering
194 different tasks that,
by means of a five-point
scale, seeks to determine
the degree to which dif-
ferent tasks are involved
in performing a partic-
ular job

The **position analysis questionnaire (PAQ)** is a quantifiable data collection method covering 194 different worker-oriented tasks. Using a five-point scale, the PAQ seeks to determine the degree, if any, to which the different tasks, or job elements, are involved in performing a particular job.

A sample page from the PAQ covering 11 elements of the Information Input Division is shown in Figure 4.3 on page 154. The person conducting an analysis with this questionnaire would rate each of the elements using the five-point scale shown in the upper-righthand corner of the sample page. The results obtained with the PAQ are quantitative and can be subjected to statistical analysis. The PAQ also permits dimensions of behaviour to be compared across a number of jobs and permits jobs to be grouped on the basis of common characteristics.

The Critical Incident Method

critical incident method
A job analysis method
by which important job
tasks are identified for
job success

The objective of the **critical incident method** is to identify critical job tasks. Critical job tasks are those important duties and job responsibilities performed by the jobholder that lead to job success. Information about critical job tasks can be collected through interviews with employees or managers or through self-report statements written by employees.

Suppose, for example, that the job analyst is studying the job of reference librarian. The interviewer will ask the employee to describe the job on the basis of what is done, how the job is performed, and what tools and equipment are used. The reference librarian may describe the job as follows:

> I assist patrons by answering their questions related to finding books, periodicals, or other library materials. I also give them directions to help them find materials within the building. To perform my job I may have to look up

Figure 4.3	A Sample Page from the PAQ

INFORMATION INPUT

1   INFORMATION INPUT

1.1   Sources of Job Information

Rate each of the following items in terms of the extent to which it is used by the worker as a source of information in performing his job.

1.1.1   Visual Sources of Job Information

	Extent of Use (U)
NA	Does not apply
1	Nominal/very infrequent
2	Occasional
3	Moderate
4	Considerable
5	Very substantial

01 U   Written materials (books, reports, office notes, articles, job instructions, signs, etc.)

02 U   Quantitative materials (materials which deal with quantities or amounts, such as graphs, accounts, specifications, tables of numbers, etc.)

03 U   Pictorial materials (pictures or picturelike materials used as *sources* of information, for example, drawings, blueprints, diagrams, maps, tracings, photographic films, x-ray films, TV pictures, etc.)

04 U   Patterns/related devices (templates, stencils, patterns, etc., used as *sources* of information when *observed* during use; do *not* include here materials described in item 3 above)

05 U   Visual displays (dials, gauges, signal lights, radarscopes, speedometers, clocks, etc.)

06 U   Measuring devices (rulers, calipers, tire pressure gauges, scales, thickness gauges, pipettes, thermometers, protractors, etc., used to obtain visual information about physical measurements; do *not* include here devices described in item 5 above)

07 U   Mechanical devices (tools, equipment, machinery, and other mechanical devices which are *sources* of information when *observed* during use or operation)

08 U   Materials in process (parts, materials, objects, etc., which are *sources* of information when being modified, worked on, or otherwise processed, such as bread dough being mixed, workpiece being turned in a lathe, fabric being cut, shoe being resoled, etc.)

09 U   Materials *not* in process (parts, materials, objects, etc., not in the process of being changed or modified, which are *sources* of information when being inspected, handled, packaged, distributed, or selected, etc., such as items or materials in inventory, storage, or distribution channels, items being inspected, etc.)

10 U   Features of nature (landscapes, fields, geological samples, vegetation, cloud formations, and other features of nature which are observed or inspected to provide information)

11 U   Man-made features of environment (structures, buildings, dams, highways, bridges, docks, railroads, and other "man-made" or altered aspects of the indoor or outdoor environment which are *observed or inspected* to provide job information; do *not* consider equipment, machines, etc., that an individual uses in his work, as covered by item 7)

Source: *Position Analysis Questionnaire,* copyright 1969, 1989 by Purdue Research Foundation, West Lafayette, IN 47907. Reprinted with permission.

materials myself or refer patrons to someone who can directly assist them. Some individuals may need training in how to use reference materials or special library facilities. I also give library tours to new patrons. I use computers and a variety of reference books to carry out my job.

After the job data are collected, the analyst then writes separate task statements that represent important job activities. For the reference librarian one task statement might be, "Listens to patrons and answers their questions related to locating library materials." Typically the job analyst writes five to ten important task statements for each job under study. The final product is written task statements that are clear, complete, and easily understood by those unfamiliar with the job. The critical incident method is an important job analysis method because it teaches the analyst to focus on employee behaviours critical to job success.

Task Inventory Analysis

task inventory analysis
An organization-specific list of tasks and their descriptions used as a basis to identify components of jobs

The **task inventory analysis** method can be considered a job-oriented type of job analysis. Unlike the PAQ, which uses a standardized form to analyze jobs in different organizations, a task inventory questionnaire can be tailor-made to a specific organization.

The technique is developed by identifying—with the help of employees and managers—a list of tasks and their descriptions that are components of different jobs. The goal is to produce a comprehensive list of task statements that are applicable to all jobs. Task statements then are listed on a task inventory survey form to be completed by the person analyzing the job under review. A task statement might be, "Inventories current supplies to maintain stock levels." The job analysis would also note the importance and frequency of use of the task to the successful completion of the job.

HRIS and Job Analysis

Human resource information systems have greatly facilitated the job analysis process. Available today are various software programs designed specifically to analyze jobs and to write job descriptions and job specifications based on those analyses. These programs normally contain generalized task statements that can apply to many different jobs. Managers and employees select those statements that best describe the job under review, indicating the importance of the task to the total job where appropriate. Advanced computer applications of job analysis combine job analysis with job evaluation (see Chapter 9) and the pricing of organizational jobs. Computerized job analysis systems can be expensive to initiate, but where the organization has many jobs to analyze the cost per job may be low. HR publications such as the *Canadian HR Reporter* contain advertisements from numerous software companies offering HRIS job analysis packages.

USING THE INTERNET

More information on PAQ can be found at:

www.paq.com

Job Analysis in a Changing Environment

The traditional approach to job analysis assumes a static job environment where jobs remain relatively stable apart from incumbents who might hold these jobs. Here, jobs can be meaningfully defined in terms of tasks, duties, processes, and behaviours necessary for job success. This assumption, unfortunately, discounts technological advances that are often so accelerated that jobs, as they are defined today, may be obsolete tomorrow. The following statement by two HR professionals highlights this concern: "Typically, job analysis looks at how a job is currently done. But the ever-changing business market makes it difficult to keep a job analysis up-to-date. Also, companies are asking employees to do more, so there is a question of whether "jobs" as we know them are obsolete. This means we must do an analysis of work as quickly as possible, leading to more emphasis on technology-related options, such as Web-based job analysis."[12]

Furthermore, downsizing, the demands of small organizations, and the need to respond to global change can alter the nature of jobs and the requirements of individuals needed to successfully perform them. For organizations using "virtual jobs" and "virtual teams" there is a shift away from narrow job specifications and descriptions to a world where work is "dejobbed" and emphasis is placed on the distribution of work. In a dynamic environment where job demands rapidly change, obsolete job analysis information can hinder an organization's ability to adapt to change.

When organizations operate in a fast-moving environment, several novel approaches to job analysis may accommodate needed change. First, managers might adopt a future-oriented approach to job analysis. This "strategic" analysis of jobs requires that managers have a clear view of how jobs should be restructured in terms of duties and tasks in order to meet future organizational requirements. Second, organizations might adopt a competency-based approach to job analysis, in which emphasis is placed on characteristics of successful performers rather than on standard job duties, tasks, and so on. These competencies would match the organization's culture and strategy and might include such things as interpersonal communication skills, decision-making ability, conflict resolution skills, adaptability, and self-motivation.[13] This technique of job analysis serves to enhance a culture of TQM and continuous improvement, because organizational improvement is the constant aim. Either of these two approaches is not without concerns, including the ability of managers to accurately predict future job needs, the necessity of job analysis to comply with employment equity guidelines, and the possibility of role ambiguity created by generically written job descriptions.

Job Descriptions

As previously noted, a job description is a written description of a job and the types of duties it includes. Since there is no standard format for job descriptions, they tend to vary in appearance and content from one organization to another. However, most job descriptions will contain at least three parts: the job title, a job identification section, and a job duties section. If the job specifications are not prepared as a separate document, they are usually stated in the concluding section of the job description. Highlights in HRM 4.1 shows a job description for an HR generalist. This sample job description includes both job duties and job specifications and should satisfy most of the job information needs of managers who must recruit, interview, and orient a new employee.

Job descriptions are of value to both the employees and the employer. From the employees' standpoint, job descriptions can be used to help them learn their job duties and to remind them of the results they are expected to achieve.[14] From the employer's standpoint, written job descriptions can serve as a basis for minimizing the misunderstandings that occur between managers and their subordinates concerning job requirements. They also establish management's right to take corrective action when the duties covered by the job description are not performed as required.

Job Title

Selection of a job title is important for several reasons. First, the job title is of psychological importance, providing status to the employee. For instance, "sanitation engineer" is a more appealing title than "garbage collector." Second, if possible, the title should provide some indication of what the duties of the job entail. Titles such as *meat inspector, electronics assembler, salesperson,* and *engineer* obviously hint at the nature of the duties of these jobs. The job title also should indicate the relative level occupied by its holder in the organizational hierarchy. For example, the title *junior engineer* implies that this job occupies a lower level than that of *senior engineer.* Other titles that indicate the relative level in the organizational hierarchy are *welder's helper* and *laboratory assistant.*

Highlights in HRM 4.1

Job Description for a Human Resources Generalist

HUMAN RESOURCE GENERALIST

Position Summary

Reporting to the Director of Human Resources, the generalist position will provide assistance and support to the development and implementation of HR initiatives and processes. Supporting employee relations, performance management, compensation and benefits, training and development, as well as recruiting are key aspects of the role.

Specific Responsibilities:
- Assist HR Director with Employee Relations responsibilities such as performing exit interviews and updating company policies and job descriptions
- Providing support to internal clients regarding employee relations and performance management issues.
- Coordinate all aspects of the annual performance management process including gathering feedback and facilitating its successful implementation.
- Partner with the HR Director to manage all aspects of the annual compensation process. Ensure that issues of internal and external equity and competitiveness are identified and addressed.
- Conduct recruitment activities for all hourly and non-management salaried employees including performing the interview, administering testing, checking references, and creating/delivering job offers.
- Coordinate training and development activities including the scheduling, administration, and tracking of internal and external training, and evaluating training effectiveness.
- Participate in training and make presentations (employee meetings, etc.) as required.
- Coordinate and conduct the formal company orientation of new employees
- Participate in the continuous improvement and development of HR programs, policies, and procedures.
- Support the implementation of HR change initiatives.
- Other projects as assigned.

Knowledge, Skills, and Abilities Required

Knowledge and/or training of:

- HR policies and procedures
- Employment legislation
- Recruitment and staffing practices
- Multiple HR disciplines
- Proven knowledge of compensation, performance management, HRIS, research, and training and development
- Organizational development experience including leadership development strategies

(continued on next page)

Skills:

- Excellent written and oral communication skills
- Strong interpersonal skills
- Possess well-developed negotiation/facilitation skills
- Innovative thinker with proven problem-solving skills
- Proficient in Microsoft Office

Ability to:

- Change priorities quickly
- Confront issues directly
- Organize and prioritize work

Other:

- Works well under pressure
- Team player who inspires confidence
- Possesses excellent judgment, tact, and diplomacy
- Hands-on approach
- Enthusiasm for change and ability to work in a demanding and dynamic environment
- Assertive, flexible, and aligns with our strong core values
- Self-starter

Minimum Qualifications:

- Bachelor's degree in HR or related field **and** working towards HR designation
- One to two years of experience in human resources preferably in a generalist capacity

Job Identification Section

The job identification section of a job description usually follows the job title. It includes such items as the departmental location of the job, the person to whom the jobholder reports, and the date the job description was last revised. Sometimes it also contains a payroll or code number, the number of employees performing the job, the number of employees in the department where the job is located, and the NOC code number. "Statement of the Job" usually appears at the bottom of this section and distinguishes the job from other jobs—something the job title may fail to do.

Job Duties, or Essential Functions, Section

Statements covering job duties are typically arranged in order of importance. These statements should indicate the weight, or value, of each duty. Usually, but not always, the weight of a duty can be gauged by the percentage of time devoted to it. The statements should stress the responsibilities all the duties entail and the results they are to accomplish. It is also general practice to indicate the tools and equipment used by the employee in performing the job. Remember, the job duties section must comply with law by listing only the essential functions of the job to be performed (see "Job Analysis" earlier in this chapter).[15]

Job Specifications Section

As stated earlier, the personal qualifications an individual must possess in order to perform the duties and responsibilities contained in a job description are compiled in the job specification. Typically the job specification covers two areas: (1) the skill required to perform the job and (2) the physical demands the job places on the employee performing it.

Skills relevant to a job include education or experience, specialized training, personal traits or abilities, and manual dexterities. The physical demands of a job refer to how much walking, standing, reaching, lifting, or talking must be done on the job. The condition of the physical work environment and the hazards employees may encounter are also among the physical demands of a job.

Job specifications should also include interpersonal skills or specific behavioural attributes necessary for job success. For example, behavioural competencies might include the ability to make decisions on imperfect information, decisiveness, the ability to handle multiple tasks, and conflict-resolution skills. Behavioural attributes can be assessed by asking applicants situational interview questions (see Chapter 6). For example, a manager could ask an applicant about a time he or she had to make a critical decision quickly.

Problems with Job Descriptions

Managers consider job descriptions a valuable tool for performing HRM functions. Nevertheless, several problems are frequently associated with these documents, including the following:

1. If they are poorly written, using vague rather than specific terms, they provide little guidance to the jobholder.
2. They are sometimes not updated as job duties or specifications change.
3. They may violate the law by containing specifications not related to job success.
4. They can limit the scope of activities of the jobholder, reducing organizational flexibility.

Writing Clear and Specific Job Descriptions

When writing a job description, it is essential to use statements that are terse, direct, and simply worded.[16] Unnecessary words or phrases should be eliminated. Typically, the sentences that describe job duties begin with a present-tense verb, with the implied subject of the sentence being the employee performing the job. The term "occasionally" is used to describe duties that are performed once in a while. The term "may" is used in connection with duties performed only by some workers on the job.

Even when set forth in writing, job descriptions and specifications can still be vague. To the consternation of many employers, however, today's legal environment has created what might be called an "age of specifics." Human rights legislation requires that the specific performance requirements of a job be based on valid job-related criteria.[17] Personnel decisions that involve either job applicants or employees and are based on criteria that are vague or not job-related are increasingly successfully challenged. Managers of small businesses, in which employees may perform many different job tasks, must be particularly concerned about writing specific job descriptions.

Managers may find that writing job descriptions is a tedious process that distracts from other supervisory responsibilities. Fortunately, software packages are available to simplify this time-consuming yet necessary task. One program provides an initial library of more than 2500 prewritten job descriptions. Since the program works much like a word processor, text can be easily deleted, inserted, or modified to user demands.

Job Design

job design
An outgrowth of job analysis that improves jobs through technological and human considerations in order to enhance organization efficiency and employee job satisfaction

It is not uncommon for managers and supervisors to confuse the processes of job analysis and job design. Job analysis is the study of jobs as currently performed by employees. It identifies job duties and the requirements needed to perform the work successfully. **Job design,** which is an outgrowth of job analysis, is concerned with structuring jobs in order to improve organization efficiency and employee job satisfaction. Job design is concerned with changing, modifying, and enriching jobs in order to capture the talents of employees while improving organization performance.[18] For example, companies such as Harley-Davidson and Lucent Technologies, which are engaged in continuous improvement, or process reengineering, may revamp their jobs in order to eliminate unnecessary job tasks or find better ways of performing work. Job design should facilitate the achievement of organizational objectives.[19] At the same time, the design should recognize the capabilities and needs of those who are to perform the job.

As Figure 4.4 illustrates, job design is a combination of four basic considerations: (1) the organizational objectives the job was created to fulfill; (2) behavioural concerns that influence an employee's job satisfaction; (3) industrial engineering considerations, including ways to make the job technologically efficient; and (4) ergonomic concerns, including workers' physical and mental capabilities.

Behavioural Concerns

Two job design methods seek to incorporate the behavioural needs of employees as they perform their individual jobs. Both methods strive to satisfy the intrinsic needs of

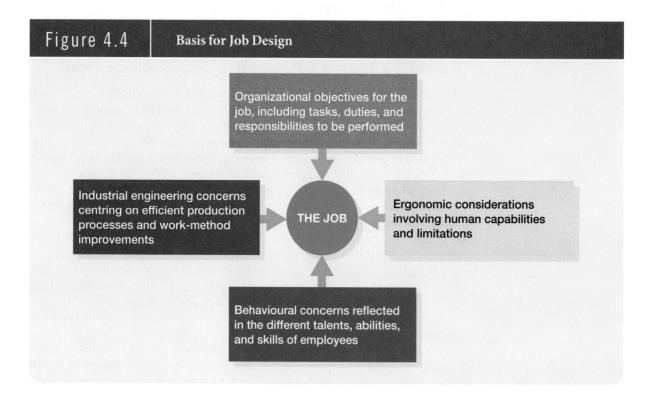

| Figure 4.4 | **Basis for Job Design** |

Organizational objectives for the job, including tasks, duties, and responsibilities to be performed

Industrial engineering concerns centring on efficient production processes and work-method improvements

THE JOB

Ergonomic considerations involving human capabilities and limitations

Behavioural concerns reflected in the different talents, abilities, and skills of employees

employees. The job enrichment model and the job characteristics model have long been popular with researchers and practitioners as ways to increase the job satisfaction of employees.

Job Enrichment

job enrichment
Enhancing a job by adding more meaningful tasks and duties to make the work more rewarding or satisfying

Any effort that makes work more rewarding or satisfying by adding more meaningful tasks to an employee's job is called **job enrichment.** Originally popularized by Frederick Herzberg, job enrichment is touted as fulfilling the high motivational needs of employees, such as self-fulfillment and self-esteem, while achieving long-term job satisfaction and performance goals.[20] Job enrichment, or the *vertical expansion* of jobs, may be accomplished by increasing the autonomy and responsibility of employees. Herzberg discusses five factors for enriching jobs and thereby motivating employees: achievement, recognition, growth, responsibility, and performance of the whole job versus only parts of the job. For example, managers can use these five factors to enrich the jobs of employees by

- Increasing the level of difficulty and responsibility of the job
- Allowing employees to retain more authority and control over work outcomes
- Providing unit or individual job performance reports directly to employees
- Adding new tasks to the job that require training and growth
- Assigning individuals specific tasks, thus enabling them to become experts

These factors allow employees to assume a greater role in the decision-making process and become more involved in planning, organizing, directing, and controlling their own work. Vertical job enrichment can also be accomplished by organizing workers into teams and giving these teams greater authority for self-management.

In spite of the benefits to be achieved through job enrichment, it must not be considered a panacea for overcoming production problems and employee discontent. Job enrichment programs are more likely to succeed in some jobs and work situations than in others. They are not the solution to such problems as dissatisfaction with pay, with employee benefits, or with employment security. Moreover, not all employees object to the mechanical pacing of an assembly line, nor do all employees seek additional responsibility or challenge. Some prefer routine jobs because they can let their minds wander while performing their work.

objective **5**

job characteristics model
A job design theory that purports that three psychological states (experiencing meaningfulness of the work performed, responsibility for work outcomes, and knowledge of the results of the work performed) of a jobholder result in improved work performance, internal motivation, and lower absenteeism and turnover

Job Characteristics

Job design studies explored a new field when behavioural scientists focused on identifying various job dimensions that would improve simultaneously the efficiency of organizations and the job satisfaction of employees. Perhaps the theory that best exemplifies this research is the one advanced by Richard Hackman and Greg Oldham.[21] Their **job characteristics model** proposes that three psychological states of a jobholder result in improved work performance, internal motivation, and lower absenteeism and turnover. A motivated, satisfied, and productive employee (1) experiences meaningfulness of the work performed, (2) experiences responsibility for work outcomes, and (3) has knowledge of the results of the work performed. Hackman and Oldham believe that five core job dimensions produce the three psychological states. The five job characteristics are as follows:

1. *Skill variety:* The degree to which a job entails a variety of different activities, which demand the use of a number of different skills and talents by the jobholder

2. *Task identity:* The degree to which the job requires completion of a whole and identifiable piece of work, that is, doing a job from beginning to end with a visible outcome

3. *Task significance:* The degree to which the job has a substantial impact on the lives or work of other people, whether in the immediate organization or in the external environment

4. *Autonomy:* The degree to which the job provides substantial freedom, independence, and discretion to the individual in scheduling the work and in determining the procedures to be used in carrying it out

5. *Feedback:* The degree to which carrying out the work activities required by the job results in the individual being given direct and clear information about the effectiveness of his or her performance

The job characteristics model appears to work best when certain conditions are met. One of these conditions is that employees must have the psychological desire for the autonomy, variety, responsibility, and challenge of enriched jobs. When this personal characteristic is absent, employees may resist the job redesign effort. In addition, job redesign efforts almost always fail when employees lack the physical or mental skills, abilities, or education needed to perform the job. Forcing enriched jobs on individuals lacking these traits can result in frustrated employees.

Employee Empowerment

Job enrichment and job characteristics are specific programs by which managers or supervisors can formally change the jobs of employees. A less structured method is to allow employees to initiate their own job changes through the concept of empowerment. **Employee empowerment** is a technique of involving employees in their work through the process of inclusion. Empowerment encourages employees to become innovators and managers of their own work, and it involves them in their jobs in ways that give them more control and autonomous decision-making capabilities (see Highlights in HRM 4.2). As described by one manager, employee empowerment involves "pushing down decision-making responsibility to those close to internal and external customers."

While defining empowerment can become the first step to achieving it, in order for empowerment to grow and thrive, organizations must encourage these conditions:

> **employee empowerment**
> Granting employees power to initiate change, thereby encouraging them to take charge of what they do

- *Participation.* Employees must be encouraged to take control of their work tasks. Employees, in turn, must care about improving their work process and interpersonal work relationships.

- *Innovation.* The environment must be receptive to people with innovative ideas and encourage people to explore new paths and to take reasonable risks at reasonable costs. An empowered environment is created when curiosity is as highly regarded as is technical expertise.

- *Access to information.* Employees must have access to a wide range of information. Involved individuals decide what kind of information they need for performing their jobs.

- *Accountability.* Empowerment does not involve being able to do whatever you want. Empowered employees should be held accountable for their behaviour toward others, producing agreed-on results, achieving credibility, and operating with a positive approach.

Additionally, employee empowerment succeeds when the culture of the organization is open and receptive to change. An organization's culture is largely created

Highlights in HRM 4.2

Organizations Empower Their Employees

In today's highly competitive and dynamic business environment, employers as diverse as Home Depot, Wal-Mart, Cigna Health Care, Costco, Auto Zone, Disney, and Applebee's have turned to their employees to improve organizational performance. Empowered employees have made improvements in product or service quality, have reduced costs, and have modified or, in some cases, designed products.

- At Kraft Foods, employees at the company's food plant participated in work-redesign changes and team building that increased productivity, reduced overhead, and cut assembly time.
- Avon Products empowered its minority managers to improve sales and service in inner-city markets. Grounded in the belief that minority managers better understand the culture of inner-city residents, Avon turned an unprofitable market into a highly productive sales area.
- At Ford's factory, one group of employees made a suggestion saving $115,000 a year on the purchase of gloves used to protect workers who handle sheet metal and glass. The group figured out how to have the gloves washed so they could be used more than once.
- Home Depot's Special Project Support Teams (SPST) work to improve the organization's business and information services. Employees with a wide range of backgrounds and skills collaborate to address a great variety of strategic and tactical business needs.
- Herman Miller, Inc., a manufacturer of office equipment, expects its employees to participate with managers in decisions involving product quality and service. Herman Miller prides itself on having a corporate culture regarded as highly egalitarian.
- At Zero Knowledge Systems, a Montreal company that produces privacy software for Internet users, employees choose their own job titles. A top developer chose the title International Man of Mystery.

through the philosophies of senior managers and their leadership traits and behaviours. Effective leadership in an empowered organization is highlighted by managers who are honest, caring, and receptive to new ideas and who exhibit dignity and respect for employees as partners in organizational success.

Industrial Engineering Considerations

industrial engineering
A field of study concerned with analyzing work methods and establishing time standards

The study of work is an important contribution of the scientific management movement. **Industrial engineering,** which evolved with this movement, is concerned with analyzing work methods and establishing time standards. Specifically, it involves the study of work cycles to determine which, if any, elements can be modified, combined, rearranged, or eliminated to reduce the time needed to complete the cycle. Next, time standards are established by recording the time required to complete each element in the work cycle, using a stopwatch or work-sampling technique. By combining the times for each element, observers can determine the total time required. This time is subsequently adjusted to allow for the skill and effort demonstrated by the observed worker and for interruptions that may occur in performing the work. The adjusted time becomes the time standard for that particular work cycle.

Industrial engineering constitutes a disciplined and objective approach to job design. Unfortunately, the concern of industrial engineering for improving efficiency and simplifying work methods may cause the behavioural considerations in job design to be neglected. What may be improvements in job design and efficiency from an engineering standpoint can sometimes prove psychologically unsound. For example, the assembly line with its simplified and repetitive tasks embodies sound principles of industrial engineering, but these tasks are often not psychologically rewarding for those who must perform them. Thus, to be effective, job design must also provide for the satisfaction of behavioural needs.

Ergonomic Considerations

ergonomics
An interdisciplinary approach to designing equipment and systems that can be easily and efficiently used by human beings

Ergonomics attempts to accommodate the human capabilities and limitations of those who are to perform a job. It is concerned with adapting the entire job system—the work, the work environment, the machine and equipment, and the processes—to

Figure 4.5	Computer Workstation Ergonomics Checklist

Use the following list to identify potential problem areas that should receive further investigation. Any "no" response may point to a problem.

1. Does the workstation ensure proper worker posture, such as
   - Thighs in the horizontal position?
   - Lower legs in the vertical position?
   - Feet flat on the floor or on a footrest?
   - Wrists straight and relaxed?

2. Does the chair
   - Adjust easily?
   - Have a padded seat with a rounded front?
   - Have an adjustable backrest?
   - Provide lumbar support?
   - Have casters?

3. Are the height and tilt of the work surface on which the keyboard is located adjustable?

4. Is the keyboard detachable?

5. Do keying actions require minimal force?

6. Is there an adjustable document holder?

7. Are armrests provided where needed?

8. Are glare and reflections minimized?

9. Does the monitor have brightness and contrast controls?

10. Is there sufficient space for knees and feet?

11. Can the workstation be used for either right or lefthanded activity?

Source: The National Institute for Occupational Safety and Health (NIOSH), *Elements of Ergonomics Programs: A Primer Based on Workplace Evaluations of Musculoskeletal Disorders* (Washington, DC: U.S. Government Printing Office, March 1997).

© GARY O'CONNOR/PHOTOEDIT

Employees may experience fewer repetitive strain injuries by working in ergonomically designed work stations.

match human characteristics. In short, it seeks to fit the job to the person rather than the person to the job.[22] Ergonomics attempts to minimize the harmful effects of carelessness, negligence, and other human fallibilities that otherwise may cause product defects, damage to equipment, or even the injury or death of employees. In 2003, overexertion and ergonomic problems were responsible for 40 percent of workplace lost-time injuries.[23]

Equipment design must consider the physical ability of operators to use the equipment and to react through vision, hearing, and touch to the information the equipment conveys. Designing equipment controls to be compatible with both the physical characteristics and the reaction capabilities of the people who must operate them and the environment in which they work is increasingly important. Ergonomics also considers the requirements of a diverse workforce, accommodating, for example, women who may lack the strength to operate equipment requiring intense physical force or short people who may lack the stature to reach equipment controls. Managers must adapt the workplace to the labour force or risk sacrificing quality and productivity.

Ergonomics improves productivity and morale and yields positive return on investment (ROI). The new Autotrans automotive plant in Ingersoll, Ontario, uses a hand-controlled crane, ensuring that the operator need never bend or lift. GDX, a producer of automotive sealing systems in Welland, Ontario, made ergonomic changes in all departments, but particularly in those where employees were required to do heavy repetitive work for six to eight hours. As a result of the ergonomics program, injuries have declined markedly and productivity has improved.[24]

Ergonomics has proven cost-effective at organizations such as Compaq Computer, 3M, and Pratt & Whitney. Unfortunately, many thousands of workplace injuries occur yearly resulting from motions such as lifting, bending, and typing. Therefore, ergonomics has recently focused on elimination, or at least reduction, of many repetitive-motion injuries, particularly those related to the back and wrist. For example, with the increased use of computers, ergonomics has particular application at employee workstations. Figure 4.5 provides a checklist of potential repetitive-motion problem areas for employees using computers.

Designing Work for Group/Team Contributions

objective **6**

Although a variety of group techniques have been developed to involve employees more fully in their organizations, all of these techniques have two characteristics in common—enhancing collaboration and increasing synergy. In increasing the degree of collaboration in the work environment, these techniques can improve work processes and organizational decision making. In increasing group synergy, the techniques underline the adage that the contributions of two or more employees are greater than the sum of their individual efforts. Furthermore, research has shown that working in a group setting strengthens employee commitment to the organization's goals, increases employee acceptance of decisions, and encourages a cooperative

employee involvement groups (EIs)
Groups of employees who meet to resolve problems or offer suggestions for organizational improvement

approach to workplace tasks.[25] Two collaborative techniques are discussed here: employee involvement groups and employee teams.

Employee Involvement Groups

Groups of five to ten employees doing similar or related work who meet regularly to identify, analyze, and suggest solutions to shared problems are often referred to as **employee involvement groups (EIs)**. Also widely known as quality circles (QCs), EIs are used principally as a means of involving employees in the larger goals of the organization through their suggestions for improving product or service quality and cutting costs.[26] Generally, EIs recommend their solutions to management, which decides whether to implement them.

The employee involvement group process, illustrated in Figure 4.6, begins with EI members brainstorming job-related problems or concerns and gathering data about these issues. The process continues through the generation of solutions and recommendations that are then communicated to management. If the solutions are implemented, results are measured, and the EI and its members are usually recognized for the contributions they have made. EIs typically meet four or more hours per month, and the meetings are chaired by a group leader chosen from the group. The leader does not hold an authority position but instead serves as a discussion facilitator.

Although EIs have become an important employee contribution system, they are not without their problems and their critics. First, in order to achieve the results desired, those participating in EIs must receive comprehensive training in problem identification, problem analysis, and various decision-making tools such as statistical analysis

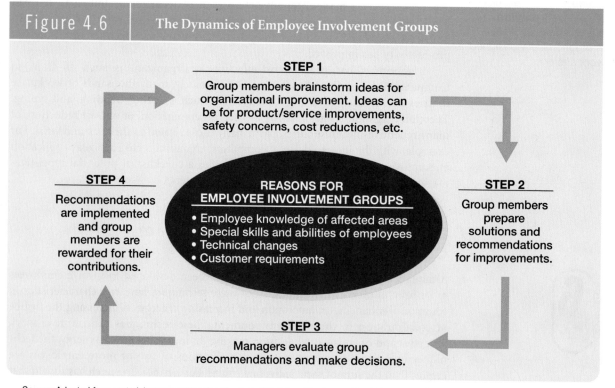

Figure 4.6   The Dynamics of Employee Involvement Groups

STEP 1
Group members brainstorm ideas for organizational improvement. Ideas can be for product/service improvements, safety concerns, cost reductions, etc.

STEP 2
Group members prepare solutions and recommendations for improvements.

STEP 3
Managers evaluate group recommendations and make decisions.

STEP 4
Recommendations are implemented and group members are rewarded for their contributions.

REASONS FOR EMPLOYEE INVOLVEMENT GROUPS
- Employee knowledge of affected areas
- Special skills and abilities of employees
- Technical changes
- Customer requirements

Source: Adapted from materials prepared by The Family and Relationship Center, 7946 Ivanhoe Avenue, La Jolla, CA 92037.

and cause-and-effect diagrams. Comprehensive training for EIs is often cited as the most important factor leading to their success. Second, managers should recognize the group when a recommendation is made, regardless of whether the recommendation is adopted. This approach encourages the group to continue coming up with ideas even when they are not all implemented by management. Third, some organizations have found that EIs run out of ideas, and management must feed them ideas to keep the process going. Finally, and most important, managers and supervisors must exhibit a participative/democratic leadership style in which employees are encouraged to work collaboratively with management to improve organizational performance.

Employee Teams

During the past decade perhaps one of the more radical changes to how work is done is the introduction of organizational teams. Jim Barksdale, president and CEO of Netscape Communications, states, "These days it seems as if every time a task needs to be accomplished within an organization, a team is formed to do it." This statement simply emphasizes the increasing importance of teams to organizational success in an ever-dynamic business climate. At such diverse organizations as Federal Express, Hewlett-Packard, Calvin Klein, and Lockheed Martin Aeronautics, the benefits of employee teams have included more integration of individual skills, better performance in terms of quality and quantity, solutions to unique and complex problems, reduced delivery time, reduced turnover and absenteeism, and accomplishments among team members.[27]

employee teams
An employee contributions technique whereby work functions are structured for groups rather than for individuals and team members are given discretion in matters traditionally considered management prerogatives, such as process improvements, product or service development, and individual work assignments

Employee teams are a logical outgrowth of employee involvement and the philosophy of empowerment. Although many definitions of teams exist, we define a work team as a group of individuals working together toward a common purpose, in which members have complementary skills, members' work is mutually dependent, and the group has discretion over tasks performed. Furthermore, teams seek to make members of the work group share responsibility and accountability for their group's performance. Inherent in the concept of employee teams is that employees, not managers, are in the best position to contribute to workplace performance. With work teams, managers accept the notion that the group is the logical work unit to apply resources to resolve organizational problems and concerns.[28]

Teamwork also embraces the concept of *synergy*. Synergy occurs when the interaction and outcome of team members is greater than the sum of their individual efforts.[29] Unfortunately, synergy may not automatically happen, but rather, it must be nurtured within the team environment.[30] Figure 4.7 on page 168 lists the factors contributing to a synergistic team setting.

Teams can operate in a variety of structures, each with different strategic purposes or functional activities. Figure 4.8 on page 168 describes common team forms. One form, self-directed teams, is often championed as being the highest form of team structure. Self-directed teams, also called *autonomous work groups, self-managed teams,* or *high-performance teams,* are groups of employees who are accountable for a "whole" work process or segment that delivers a product or service to an internal or external customer. Team members acquire multiple skills enabling them to perform a variety of job tasks. To varying degrees, team members work together to improve their operations, handle day-to-day concerns, and plan and control their work. Typical team functions include setting work schedules, dealing directly with external customers, training team members, setting performance targets, budgeting, and purchasing equipment or services.

Self-directed teams are designed to give the team "ownership" of a product or service. In a manufacturing environment, a team might be responsible for a whole product or a clearly defined segment of the production process. Similarly, in a service

Figure 4.7	Synergistic Team Characteristics

Team synergy is heightened when team members engage in these positive behaviours.

- *Support.* The team exhibits an atmosphere of inclusion. All team members speak up and feel free to offer constructive comments.

- *Listening and Clarification.* Active listening is practised. Members honestly listen to others and seek clarification on discussion points. Team members summarize discussions held.

- *Disagreement.* Disagreement is seen as natural and is expected. Member comments are nonjudgmental and focus on factual issues rather than personality conflicts.

- *Consensus.* Team members reach agreements through consensus decision making. Consensus decisions require finding a proposal that is acceptable to all team members, even if not the first choice of individual members. Common ground among ideas is sought.

- *Acceptance.* Team members are valued as individuals, recognizing that each person brings a valuable mix of skills and abilities to team operations.

- *Quality.* Each team member is committed to excellent performance. There is emphasis on continuous improvement and attention to detail.

environment, a team is usually responsible for entire groupings of products and services, often serving clients in a designated geographic area. Providing employees this type of ownership usually requires broader job categories and the sharing of work assignments. Work teams at the Lauralco aluminum smelter in Deschambault, Quebec, were given responsibility for health and safety, and in the first year, reduced accident frequency rates by half, and after seven years by 80 percent. "When we need

Figure 4.8	Forms of Employee Teams

Cross-Functional Teams. A group staffed with a mix of specialists (e.g., marketing, production, engineering) and formed to accomplish a specific objective. Cross-functional teams are based on assigned rather than voluntary membership.

Project Teams. A group formed specifically to design a new product or service. Members are assigned by management on the basis of their ability to contribute to success. The group normally disbands after task completion.

Self-Directed Teams. Groups of highly trained individuals performing a set of interdependent job tasks within a natural work unit. Team members use consensus decision making to perform work duties, solve problems, or deal with internal or external customers.

Task Force Teams. A task force is formed by management to immediately resolve a major problem. The group is responsible for developing a long-term plan for problem resolution that may include a charge for implementing the solution proposed.

Process-Improvement Teams. A group made up of experienced people from different departments or functions and charged with improving quality, decreasing waste, or enhancing productivity in processes that affect all departments or functions involved. Team members are normally appointed by management.

new ideas for protective clothing, we send employees to trade shows, not managers. If an accident occurs, the team member responsible for safety calls the team into a huddle, and the manager gets involved only if there is an injury," says Lynda Macguire, the plant's OH&S administrator.

To compete in today's national and international markets, managers have formed virtual teams.[31] **Virtual teams** use advanced computer and telecommunications technology to link team members who are geographically dispersed—often worldwide.[32] Management may form a cross-functional team (see Figure 4.8) to develop a new pharmaceutical drug and have the team operate in a virtual environment to achieve its goal. Virtual teams provide new opportunities for training, product development, and product market analysis. Importantly, virtual teams provide access to previously unavailable expertise and enhance cross-functional interactions.[33] However, although virtual teams have many benefits, they are not without their problems. Paulette Tichenor, president of Organizational Renaissance, a team training organization, notes these concerns with virtual teams: language and cultural barriers, unclear objectives, time conflicts due to diverse geographical locations, selecting people who are self-starters and have technological skills, and behavioural problems caused by a lack of close interpersonal contact.[34]

Regardless of the structure or purpose of the team, the following characteristics have been identified with successful teams:

- Commitment to shared goals and objectives
- Motivated and energetic team members
- Open and honest communication
- Shared leadership
- Clear role assignments
- Climate of cooperation, collaboration, trust, and accountability
- Recognition of conflict and its positive resolution

virtual team
A team with widely dispersed members linked together through computer and telecommunications technology

© TAXI/GETTY IMAGES

Team members brainstorm, support, and challenge each other, and interact as they work together for a common goal.

Unfortunately, not all teams succeed or operate to their full potential. Therefore, in adopting the work-team concept, organizations must address several issues that could present obstacles to effective team function, including overly high expectations, group compensation, training, career movement, and power.[35] For example, new team members must be retrained to work outside their primary functional areas, and compensation systems must be constructed to reward individuals for team accomplishments. Since team membership demands more general skills and since it moves an employee out of the historical career path, new career paths to general management must be created from the team experience. Finally, as the team members become capable of carrying out functions, such as strategic planning, which were previously restricted to higher levels of management, managers must be prepared to utilize their newfound expertise.

Another difficulty with work teams is that they alter the traditional manager–employee relationship.[36] Managers often find it hard to adapt to the role of leader rather than supervisor and sometimes feel threatened by the growing power of the team and the reduced power of management. Furthermore, some employees may also have difficulty adapting to a role that includes traditional supervisory responsibilities. Therefore, from our experience in working with teams, extensive attention must be given to training team members as they move through the four stages of team development—forming, storming, norming, and performing.[37] Complete training would cover the importance of skills in (1) team leadership, (2) mission/goal setting, (3) conduct of meetings, (4) team decision making, (5) conflict resolution, (6) effective communication, and (7) diversity awareness.[38]

Flexible Work Schedules

Flexible work schedules are not a true part of job design because job tasks and responsibilities are not changed. Nevertheless, we discuss adjustments in work schedules here because they alter the normal workweek of five 8-hour days in which all employees begin and end their workday at the same time. Employers may depart from the traditional workday or workweek in their attempt to improve organizational productivity and morale by giving employees increased control over the hours they work.

Speaking on the importance of flexible work schedules, Lois Brakon, codirector of the Families and Work Institute, notes, "Flexible schedules are going to be the way good, competitive businesses work."[39] Flexible work schedules may be assigned by the organization or requested by individual employees. The more common flexible work schedules are the compressed workweek, flextime, job sharing, and telecommuting. Highlights in HRM 4.3 explains why students value flexible scheduling.

The Compressed Workweek

Under the compressed workweek, the number of days in the workweek is shortened by lengthening the number of hours worked per day. This schedule is best illustrated by the four-day, 40-hour week, generally referred to as 4/10 or 4/40. Employees working a four-day workweek might work ten hours a day, Monday through Thursday. Although the 4/10 schedule is probably the best known, other compressed arrangements include reducing weekly hours to 38 or 36 hours or scheduling 80 hours over nine days (9/80), taking one day off every other week.

Managers cite the following reasons for implementing compressed workweek schedules:

- Recruitment and retention of employees[40]
- Coordinating employee work schedules with production schedules
- Accommodating the leisure-time activities of employees while facilitating employee personal appointments—medical, dental, financial[41]
- Improvements in employee job satisfaction and morale

The major disadvantage of the compressed workweek involves employee standards legislation governing the payment of overtime to non-supervisory employees working more than a specified number of hours a week (see Chapter 9). Another disadvantage of the compressed workweek is that it increases the amount of stress on managers and employees, and long workdays can be exhausting.

Flextime

flextime
Flexible working hours that permit employees the option of choosing daily starting and quitting times, provided that they work a set number of hours per day or week

Flextime, or flexible working hours, permits employees the option of choosing daily starting and quitting times, provided that they work a certain number of hours per day or week.[42] With flextime, employees are given considerable latitude in scheduling their

Highlights in HRM 4.3

Why Students Value Flexible Scheduling

When students choose an employer they consider work-life balance to be the fourth most important factor in their selection decision. The first three considerations are opportunities for advancement, good people to work with, and good people to report to. Students do want to be challenged, but are not interested in committing to an 80-hour workweek. Flexible work arrangements, such as flextime, job sharing, a compressed workweek, and telecommuting, offer the following advantages:

- Reduces the time and cost of traveling to work. Students with high debt loads would be attracted to these cost savings.
- Enables the student to complete their degree part-time. Through job sharing or the compressed workweek, students can attend classes and earn money to help pay for their educations, while at the same time acquiring work experience and contacts that may prove helpful in obtaining that first job after graduation.
- Provides the option for work-life balance. Students have a broad range of interests from volunteering with disadvantaged youth to extreme skiing, and flexible work arrangements allow them the time to enjoy these activities.

One size fits all does not apply to a diverse workforce. To attract employees of various ages and lifestyles, the key is flexibility. By 2009, 90 percent of employers will offer flex hours and 71 percent will offer employees the option to work from home on a part-time basis.

Source: Adapted from Graham Donald, "What Students Want," Canadian HR Reporter, December 9, 2006: 15 and 21. Manny Campione and Laura Williams, "Diverse Labour Force Demands Diverse Options," Canadian HR Reporter, October 23, 2006: 14.

work. However, there is a "core period" during the morning and afternoon when all employees are required to be on the job. Flexible working hours are most common in service-type organizations—financial institutions, government agencies, and other organizations with large clerical operations.

Flextime provides both employees and employers with several advantages. By allowing employees greater flexibility in work scheduling, employers can reduce some of the traditional causes of tardiness and absenteeism. Employees can adjust their work to accommodate their particular lifestyles and, in doing so, gain greater job satisfaction. Employees can also schedule their working hours for the time of day when they are most productive. In addition, variations in arrival and departure times can help reduce traffic congestion at the peak commuting hours. In some cases, employees require less time to commute, and the pressures of meeting a rigid schedule are reduced.

From the employer's standpoint, flextime can be most helpful in recruiting and retaining personnel, particularly among younger candidates, as shown in Highlights in HRM 4.4 on page 172. It has proved invaluable to organizations wishing to improve service to customers or clients by extending operating hours. Qwest, a

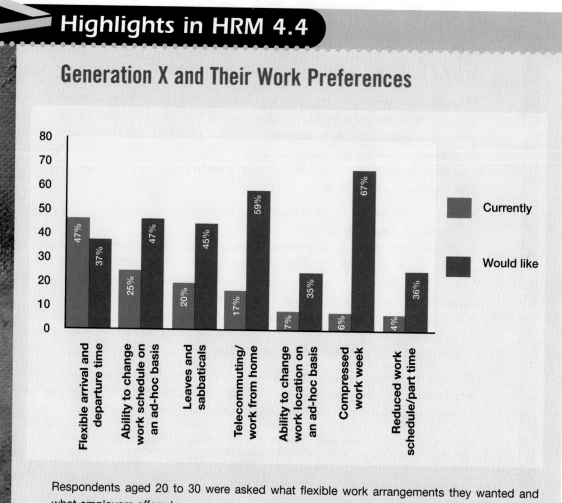

Highlights in HRM 4.4

Generation X and Their Work Preferences

Currently

Would like

Flexible arrival and departure time: 47% / 37%

Ability to change work schedule on an ad-hoc basis: 25% / 47%

Leaves and sabbaticals: 20% / 45%

Telecommuting/work from home: 17% / 59%

Ability to change work location on an ad-hoc basis: 7% / 35%

Compressed work week: 6% / 67%

Reduced work schedule/part time: 4% / 36%

Respondents aged 20 to 30 were asked what flexible work arrangements they wanted and what employers offered.

Source: A. Thomlinson, "Younger Workers Not So Different after All," *Canadian HR Reporter* 15, no. 2 (January 28, 2002): 2.

telecommunications company, uses flextime to keep its business offices open for customers who cannot get there during the day. Research demonstrates that flextime can have a positive impact on the performance measures of reliability, quality, and quantity of employee work.

There are, of course, several disadvantages to flextime. First, it is not suited to some jobs. It is not feasible, for example, where specific workstations must be staffed at all times. Second, it can create problems for managers in communicating with and instructing employees. Flextime schedules may also force these managers to extend their workweek if they are to exercise control over their subordinates.

Job Sharing

The arrangement whereby two part-time employees perform a job that otherwise would be held by one full-time employee is called job sharing. Job sharers usually work three days a week, "creating an overlap day for extended face-to-face conferencing." Their pay is three-fifths of a regular salary; however, job sharers usually take on additional responsibilities beyond what the original job would require. Employers note that without job sharing two good employees might otherwise be lost.

Job sharing is suited to the needs of families in which one or both spouses desire to work only part-time.[43] It is suited also to the needs of older workers who want to phase into retirement by shortening their workweek. For the employer, the work of part-time employees can be scheduled to conform to peaks in the daily workload. Job sharing can also limit layoffs in hard economic times. A final benefit is that employees engaged in job sharing have time off during the week to accommodate personal needs, so they are less likely to be absent. About 8 percent of Canada's workforce work from home.

Job sharing does have several problems, however. Employers may not want to employ two people to do the work of one because the time required to orient and train a second employee constitutes an added burden. They may also want to avoid prorating employee benefits between two part-time employees. This problem may be reduced, however, by permitting the employees to contribute the difference between the health insurance (or life insurance) premiums for a full-time employee and the pro rata amount the employer would otherwise contribute for a part-time employee. The key to making job sharing work is good communications between partners, who can use a number of ways to stay in contact—phone calls, written updates, e-mail, and voice mail.[44]

telecommuting
Use of personal computers, networks, and other communications technology such as fax machines to do work in the home that is traditionally done in the workplace

Telecommuting

One of the more dynamic changes and potentially the most far reaching is telecommuting. **Telecommuting** is the use of personal computers, networks, and other communications technology such as fax machines to do work in the home that is traditionally done in the workplace.

A variant of telecommunicating is the virtual office, where employees are in the field helping customers or are stationed at other remote locations working as if they were in the home office.[45]

Both managers and HR professionals note the following advantages of telecommuting:[46]

- Increased flexibility for employees
- Ability to attract workers who might not otherwise be available
- Lessened burden on working parents
- Less time and money wasted on physical commuting
- Increased productivity
- Reduced absenteeism

© BOB DAEMMERICH/PHOTOEDIT

Telecommuting allows employees to balance both work and family responsibilities.

Perhaps the strongest economic reason in favour of telecommuting is its power to retain valued employees. Retention is a top priority for employers largely because the costs of replacing employees are far higher than those involved in installing a telecommunicating arrangement. Figure 4.9 presents suggestions for establishing a successful telecommuting program.

While telecommuting offers significant benefits to employers, it also presents potential drawbacks. These include the loss of creativity as employees are not interacting with one another on a regular basis, the difficulty of developing appropriate performance standards and evaluation systems for telecommuters, and the need to formulate an appropriate technology strategy for allocating the necessary equipment.[47] Additionally, managers may believe that telecommuting negatively affects employee–supervisor relationships through loss of knowledge or information, trust, and a sense of connectedness.[48] Employers wishing to have their employees telecommute must also comply with employment standards regulations and equipment purchase or rental agreements with employees (see Chapter 3). Employees who are denied the opportunity to work from home may feel discriminated against and elect to pursue legal action or simply become disgruntled employees. Overall, however, these flexible job arrangements have significant advantages to employers and employees as discussed in Highlights in HRM 4.5.

Figure 4.9 | Keys for Successful Telecommuting

- *Identify jobs best suited to distance work.* Those involving sales, customer service, and auditing are logical choices.

- *Select responsible employees.* Employees who are self-starters, motivated, and trustworthy and who can work independently are ideal candidates. Establish employee feedback procedures and performance review methods for employee evaluation.

- *Establish formalized telecommuting procedures.* Telecommuting guidelines could cover hours of availability, office reporting periods, performance expectations, and weekly progress reports or e-mail updates.

- *Begin a formal training program.* Training for both telecommuters and managers should include the technical aspects of equipment usage and relationship factors such as how and when to contact the office or availability and location of support facilities.

- *Keep telecommuters informed.* Physical separation can make telecommuters feel isolated and invisible. Department and staff updates, inclusion of telecommuters on project teams, required attendance at meetings, and "chat room" discussions all keep telecommuters "in the loop."

- *Recognize when telecommuting isn't working.* State in telecommunicating policies that the arrangement may be terminated when it no longer serves company needs or if the employee's performance declines.

Source: Adapted from Barbara Hemphill, "Telecommuting Productivity," *Occupational Health and Safety* 73, no. 3 (March 2004): 16.

Highlights in HRM 4.5

Flextime and Work–Life Balance

Nora Spinks, president and CEO of Work–Life Harmony Enterprises, works with employers to create organizational cultures that enable employees to achieve work–life balance. The firm's goal is to develop successful work environments where individuals and organizations have the ability to reach their full potential and where employees have full and satisfying lives outside their work.

Spinks asserts that employers benefit from these family-friendly policies: "The most effective and productive employees are those who do work they enjoy, are challenged, have access to the necessary resources to meet that challenge, have control over how they work, receive recognition, rewards, and compensation based on the effort they put forth, and feel their life outside of work is respected and valued. These employees are highly resilient. In today's world of work, individual and organizational resiliency is critical for success. People in resilient, adaptable, responsive environments have the ability to change, the capacity to adapt to change, the energy to drive change and the flexibility to react positively to change, regardless of the intensity or the factors outside of their immediate control such as market forces, economic pressures, and social or political circumstances."

Today's most popular employee-support initiative is workplace flexibility: flextime with core hours and flexible start and end times, compressed workweeks (full workload completed in less than five days per week), and/or permanent part-time hours with equal status, pro-rated benefits, and the same development opportunities as full-time employees. Gaining in popularity are creative alternatives such as extended workweeks (full workload completed in six days) and self-funded or radical sabbaticals (setting aside a portion of pay for a period of time and taking an extended leave while collecting the banked salary—e.g., 2.5 years working at 85-percent pay and six months away from the workplace on a self-funded sabbatical).

Employees are using the time gained from workplace flexibility to fulfill family responsibilities, create a balanced lifestyle, continue their education, make a contribution to their community, or volunteer in developing countries.

Spinks argues strongly for these policies: "Establishing control over hours of work has very specific, well-documented results: reduction in illness, injury, absenteeism, presenteeism (physically present, but mentally and emotionally absent), turnover, conflict, and unhealthy lifestyles and behaviours such as smoking, drinking, and drugs.

"When you work too hard or too long, you tend to rely on substances such as nicotine, caffeine, or sugar boosters to get you through the day. When you are tired all the time, your ability to solve problems and resolve conflicts is decreased significantly. When you are run down, you become uninterested and disengaged. Employees who have control over their working hours have more energy, more time, and are more engaged at home, at work, and in the community. Employers, customers, and co-workers benefit during the day, and employees, their family, friends, and community benefit at the end of the day.

(continued on next page)

"When I started in this field many years ago, employers had no understanding of the issues. I received several letters from companies saying, 'Thank you for your interest, but all our charitable dollars have been allocated for this year.' So we began to build the business case for supportive work environments. In the '80s and '90s, progressive HR departments began to implement programs and policies to address the issues. Now, employers across all sectors, from all industries, are beginning to see the strategic advantages of a family-friendly, employee-supportive work environment. I now work with CEOs in boardrooms, integrating these concepts into corporate strategy.

"I think there are many reasons why employers are embracing these policies now: labour force demographics, tight labour markets, and an increasing body of evidence documenting the costs and benefits of supportive work environments and the high costs of work–life imbalance and stress in the workplace."

SUMMARY

Job requirements reflect the different duties, tasks, and responsibilities contained in jobs. Job requirements, in turn, influence HR functions performed by managers, including recruitment, selection, training and development, performance appraisal, compensation, and various labour relations activities.

Job analysis data may be gathered using several collection methods—interviews, questionnaires, observations, and diaries. Other more quantitative approaches include use of the functional job analysis, the position analysis questionnaire system, the critical incident method, task inventory analysis, and computerized job analysis. It is the prevailing opinion of the courts that HRM decisions on employment, performance appraisal, and promotions must be based on specific criteria that are job-related. These criteria can be determined objectively only by analyzing the requirements of each job.

3 The format of job descriptions varies widely, often reflecting the needs of the organization and the expertise of the writer. As a minimum, job descriptions should contain a job title, a job identification section, and an essential functions section. A job specification section also may be included. Job descriptions should be written in clear

and specific terms with consideration given to their legal implications.

4 Job design is a combination of four basic considerations: organizational objectives; industrial engineering concerns of analyzing work methods and establishing time standards; ergonomic considerations, which accommodate human capabilities and limitations to job tasks; and employee contributions.

5 In the job characteristics model, five job factors contribute to increased job performance and satisfaction—skill variety, task identity, task significance, autonomy, and feedback. All factors should be built into jobs, since each factor influences different employee psychological states. When jobs are enriched through the job characteristics model, employees experience more meaningfulness in their jobs, acquire more job responsibility, and receive direct feedback from the tasks they perform.

To improve the internal process of organizations and increase productivity, greater efforts are being made by organizations to involve groups of employees in work operations. Employee involvement groups are composed of employees in work units charged with offering suggestions for improving product or service quality or fostering workplace effectiveness. Employee teams stress employee collaboration over individual accomplishment. Teams rely on the expertise and different abilities of members to achieve a specific goal or objective. Self-directed teams are characterized by their willingness to perform traditional managerial tasks.

 Changes in work schedules—which include the compressed workweek, flextime, job sharing, and telecommuting—permit employees to adjust their work periods to accommodate their particular lifestyles. Employees can select from among these HR techniques to accommodate diverse employee needs while fostering organizational effectiveness.

KEY TERMS

critical incident method, 153
employee empowerment, 162
employee involvement groups
   (EIs), 166
employee teams, 167
ergonomics, 164
flextime, 170
functional job analysis (FJA), 152

industrial engineering, 163
job, 146
job analysis, 149
job characteristics model, 161
job description, 147
job design, 160
job enrichment, 161
job family, 146

job specification, 146
position, 146
position analysis questionnaire
   (PAQ), 153
task inventory analysis, 155
telecommuting, 173
virtual team, 169

DISCUSSION QUESTIONS

1. In Chapter 1, an HR generalist was interviewed about her job, and she described some typical tasks (page 5). Compare these tasks to the job description of the HR generalist on page 157. How are they the same? Why would there be differences?

2. Discuss the various methods by which job analysis can be completed. Compare and contrast these methods, noting the pros and cons of each.

3. Working with a group of three or four students, develop different job descriptions, based on your personal knowledge of a job. Use the Job Analysis Questionnaire from the University of Guelph www.uoguelph.ca/hr/download/ to help you prepare the job description. Compare the descriptions, highlighting similarities and differences.

4. Explain how industrial engineering and ergonomics can both clash with and complement each other in the design of jobs.

5. The job characteristics model has five components that enhance employee jobs—skill variety, task identity, task significance, autonomy, and feedback. Give an example illustrating how each component can be used to improve the organization and the job of the employee. (Suggestion: Consider your present or a recent job to answer this question.)

6. Figure 4.8 shows the different forms of employee teams. Provide an example of where each type of team can be used. How do teams create synergy?

7. As a small-business employer, explain how nontraditional work schedules might make it easier for you to recruit employees.

INTERNET EXERCISE

The Centre for Collaborative Organization (www .workteams.unt.edu/tfs.html), based at the University of North Texas, publishes a list of competencies that can be used to assess the effectiveness of your work groups. Place these seven competencies on a rating form, anchored by numerical ratings ranging from (1) strongly disagree to (5) strongly agree. Then after you have completed a group project (in any class) evaluate the team member's performance against these competencies.

HRM Experience

Establishing Ground Rules for Team Success

Professional trainers understand that setting ground rules for teams is a cornerstone for continued team success. Ground rules—or team norms—are agreed-on formal rules that guide group member behaviour. Norms established prior to the team's task regulate the behaviour of group members. Ground rules simply state how members want to be treated and how members agree to treat others. When team members follow the established norms, then norms help maintain order, promote positive behaviour, and can be used to correct undesirable actions. Remember, because teams operate in different settings, different norms may be appropriate in different arrangements.

Assignment

1. Working within your team, select what you believe are the ten most important norms for team behaviour.
2. From the following Behaviour List, have each team member *silently* select two lists of ten items each of the behaviours they believe most critical for team success. The first list of ten items (your A list) is considered the most important for group conduct. The second list (the B list) is desired items but those not of major importance.
3. In a group discussion, have all team members select a final list of ten items from both lists. These become your team's final norms. Select no more than ten items. During your discussion, items can be modified or combined to meet your team's specific needs.
4. Prepare a written document of chosen behaviours and have all team members sign the form. You have now established a written contract for positive team conduct.

Behaviour List

While working in our team, individuals should . . .

1. Do their fair share of the work.
2. Check to ensure that everyone clearly understands what is to be done.
3. Encourage planning, including short-range agendas as well as long-range goals.
4. Encourage open and candid opinions about issues.
5. Listen willingly and carefully to other people's ideas, even if those people have a different viewpoint.
6. Prepare thoroughly before meetings.
7. Make team members feel at ease in discussions.
8. Ask questions when they do not clearly understand tasks or procedures.
9. Propose specific analyses of the pros and cons of decisions faced by the team.
10. Follow through on task assignments.
11. Help other members when assistance is requested.
12. Treat all team members as equals.
13. Paraphrase or restate what someone else says in order to check meaning.
14. Openly voice opinions and share ideas.
15. Be flexible in arranging meeting schedules.
16. Compliment others for things they have said or done.

17. Be willing to meet whenever it is necessary to discuss a problem.
18. Deal with conflict directly, bringing it to the attention of the team.
19. Express enthusiasm about what the team is doing.
20. Encourage budgeting of the team's time.
21. At the end of a meeting, restate their own responsibilities to check for agreement.
22. Be serious about the team's work.
23. Arrive on time for regularly scheduled meetings.
24. Be willing to listen to other team members' ideas.
25. Get the team's approval on important matters before proceeding.

BIZFLIX EXERCISES

Intolerable Cruelty: Just Doing My Job

This chapter discussed several aspects of job analysis and job design. Try to apply much of that discussion to this scene from the film *Intolerable Cruelty.* Use the questions below as guides to your viewing.

Ruthless, beautiful Marilyn Rexroth (Catherine Zeta-Jones) matches the brilliance of divorce attorney Miles Massey (George Clooney). Conflict rises and falls as the two try to outwit each other in this charming romantic comedy. The film twists and turns in typical Coen brothers (Ethan Coen, co-screenwriter with Joel Coen, director) fashion as it reaches its predictable end.

This scene comes from "The War Room" segment that occurs about 20 minutes into the film. It follows Rex Rexroth's (George Herrmann) escapade with a young woman (Kristen Dattilo). His wife, Marilyn Rexroth, hired private detective Gus Petch (Cedric the Entertainer) to videotape the event. He now needs some legal help. Miles Massey meets his new client and discusses the case. The film continues with some women sitting by The Waters swimming pool talking about their ex- and present husbands.

What to Watch for and Ask Yourself

- What knowledge, skills, and abilities (KSAs) are required for the successful performance of Miles Massey's job?
- Recall the earlier chapter section "Job Analysis." Apply some observations from that section to this scene. What duties, tasks, and activities do you infer from the scene for Massey's job?
- Job design views certain job characteristics as important for a person's motivation and satisfaction (see the earlier section "Job Design"). Which of the five core job dimensions appear(s) in Miles Massey's job?

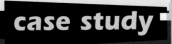

case study 1

Ducks Unlimited Canada

Ducks Unlimited Canada, a not-for-profit environmental agency, has as its goal the protection of wetland habitats in Canada. Relying on its 100 000 members, 7000 volunteers, and 330 employees, this charitable organization has saved more than 7.29 million hectares (18 million acres in Canada). Ducks Unlimited has no problem attracting biologists, scientists, and accountants, because their recruits are committed to a conservation ethic and are dedicated to protecting the environment. It has also helped recruitment that Ducks Unlimited has reorganized itself to flatten its management structure. The goal was to empower the employees and facilitate decision making. People working in the field no longer have to go up and down the power ladder to obtain approvals at every step. Field employees feel more in control of what they are doing.

The human resources administrator cites many advantages to an empowered workforce: increased retention, increased motivation, and decreased absenteeism and sick days.

Source: Adapted from "Taking Care of the People," *Canadian Health Care Manager* 6, no. 3 (April–May 1999): 5–9.

QUESTIONS

1. What arguments could be advanced both for and against the use of employee empowerment?
2. Empowerment is mainly a motivational tool, but at Ducks Unlimited the employees arrive dedicated and committed to the environmental cause. Does Ducks Unlimited need to implement empowerment?
3. How might a manager at a traditional organization react to the implementation of empowerment?

case study 2

But My Job Has Changed

Job descriptions are a critical tool used for job orientation and training and, importantly, in annual employee performance evaluations. When the duties and responsibilities listed in the job description do not reflect current job content employee/management disagreements can arise, as this case illustrates.

Both employees and managers agree that Brenda Batten has been an exceptional employee. As a senior technical representative (STR) for Blackhawk Aironics, she is valued for her knowledge in airplane instrumentation. One manager described her as "simply an expert in the complex technology of satellite weather systems."

In May 2004, Blackhawk Aironics implemented a new work reorganization plan. STRs such as Brenda now work largely by telecommuting with managers and engineers at company headquarters, and with customers scattered throughout the country. Additionally, under the new work plan, STRs were given more freedom to deal directly with customers and engineers without supervisory intervention. This freedom greatly facilitated customer service needs and demands in an aviation market everyone considers highly dynamic.

Brenda's current job description reflects the technical dimensions of her position but not the telecommuting requirements now performed. Personal competencies such as decision-making, self-motivation, problem-solving, and communication skills are not covered.

In May 2005, Brenda met with her manager, Martin Eaton, for her annual performance review. Unfortunately, unlike past meetings, which were highly satisfactory, this meeting quickly developed into a disagreement. At the centre of the controversy were the factors to be used to measure Brenda's new job demands. Martin wanted to place major emphasis on the tasks and duties listed in her current job description. As he explained to Brenda, "I hardly see you anymore, and I have no objective criteria or performance data by which to measure those behaviours you now use." Brenda, in response, acknowledged that some things in the current job description were still important aspects of her job, but overall the current job description did not capture the full scope of her new duties and responsibilities. Brenda concluded that she was satisfied with Martin's evaluation of the technical aspects of her job, but she was clearly not pleased with the overall evaluation of her performance. As she told Martin, "It's simply not fair, you just don't know what I do now."

QUESTIONS

1. Given the facts of this case, is it possible for Brenda and Martin to reach a satisfactory result? Explain.
2. How could an organization go about identifying and measuring the personal competencies of employees?
3. How could the company prevent this problem from occurring in the future? Explain.

Source: Based on an actual case known to the authors. All names are fictitious.

CAREER COUNSEL

Complete the exercise on the Managing Human Resources website to find your dream job (www.belcourt5e .nelson.com)

NOTES AND REFERENCES

1. Arnold B. Bakker, Evangelia Demeroob, and Willem Verbeke, "Using the Job Demands Resources Model to Predict Burnout and Performance," *Human Resources Management* 43, no. 1 (Spring 2004): 83.

2. Pam Withers, "Retention Strategies That Respond to Worker Values," *Workforce* 80, no. 7 (July 2001): 37–41.

3. Thiagarajan Srinivasan and Brian H. Kleiner, "How to Hire Employees Effectively," *Management Research News* 25, no. 5 (2002): 65–75.

4. Personal correspondence with the City of Calgary Personnel Services Department.

5. L.E. Babillard, *Canadian Human Rights Reporter/Canadien des Droits de la Personne*, 1985.

6. Donald M. Truxillo, Matthew E. Paronto, Michelle Collins, and Jefferson L. Sulzer, "Effects of Subject Matter Expert Viewpoint on Job Analysis Results," *Public Personnel Management* 33, no. 1 (Spring 2004): 33–44.

7. George T. Milkovich and Jerry M. Newman, *Compensation*, 8th ed. (Boston: McGraw-Hill Irwin, 2005).

8. Richard Henderson, *Compensation Management in a Knowledged-Based World*, 9th ed. (Englewood Cliffs, NJ: Prentice Hall, 2003).

9. Claudine Kapel and Catherine Shepard, "Career Ladders Create Common Language for Defining Jobs," *Canadian HR Reporter*, June 14, 2004: 15.

10. The *NOC* contains standardized and comprehensive descriptions of about 25 000 occupational titles: www23.hrdc-drhc.gc.ca/2001/e/groups/index.shtml

11. A detailed description of different job analysis techniques is beyond the scope of this text. For those interested in more comprehensive information or job analysis tools, see Michael T. Bannick and Edward Levine, *Job Analysis: Methods, Research, and Applications for Human Resource Management in the New Millennium* (Thousand Oaks, CA: Sage, 2002).

12. Helen Palmer and Will Valet, "Job Analysis: Targeting Needed Skills," *Employment Relations Today* 28, no. 3 (Autumn 2001): 85–92.

13. Erich P. Prien, Kristin O. Prien, and Louis G. Gamble, "Perspectives on Nonconventional Job Analysis Methodologies," *Journal of Business and Psychology* 18, no. 3 (Spring 2004): 337.

14. Chris Burand, "Good Job Descriptions Can Boost Productivity," *American Agent and Broker* 74, no. 10 (October 2002): 8.

15. Chi Ming Chow and Brian H. Kleiner, "How to Differentiate Essential Job Duties from Marginal Job Duties," *Managerial Law* 44, no. 1/2 (2002): 121–26.

16. Jamie Swedberg, "Put It in Writing," *Credit Union Management* 26, no. 12 (December 2003): 50–53.

17. Catano, V., Wiesner, W., Hackett, R. and Methot, L., *Recruitment and Selection in Canada*, 3rd edition, Nelson Series in Human Resources Management, Toronto, 2005.

18. Sharon K. Parker, Toby D. Wall, and John L. Cordery, "Future Work Design Research and Practice: Toward an Elaborated Model of Work," *Journal of Occupational and Organizational Psychology* 74 (November 2001): 413–40.

19. A. S. Evangelista and Lisa A. Burke, "Work Redesign and Performance Management in Times of Downsizing," *Business Horizons* 46, no. 2 (March/April 2003): 71.

20. For Herzberg's important article on job enrichment, see Frederick Herzberg, "One More Time: How Do You Motivate Employees?" *Harvard Business Review* 46, no. 2 (January–February 1968): 53–62.

21. For the original article on the job characteristics model, see J. Richard Hackman and Greg R. Oldham, "Motivation through the Design of Work: Test of a Theory," *Organizational Behavior and Human Performance* 16, no. 2 (August 1976): 250–79.

22. Scott Smith, "Ergonomics and Manufacturing Excellence," *Occupational Hazards* 64, no. 9 (September 2002): 47–48.

23. Anonymous, "Push On to Reduce Workplace Injuries," *The Hamilton Spectator,* March 2, 2005: 1.

24. Muriel Draaisma, "Auto Plant Finds Ergonomics Makes Good Business Sense," *Workplace News* 4, no. 2 (June 2001): 11.

25. Bernie Knill, "Practical Ergonomics for Plant People," *Material Handling Management* 57, no. 2 (September 2002): 5323; Andrew J. DuBrin, *Fundamentals of Organizational Behavior*, 3rd ed. (Cincinnati, OH: South-Western, 2005): Chapter 10.

26. Ann Pomeroy, "Great Places, Inspired Employees," *HRMagazine* 49, no. 7 (July 2004): 46.

27. Debbie D. Dufrene and Carol M. Lehman, *Building High Performance Teams*, 2nd ed. (Cincinnati, OH: South-Western, 2005).

28. Debra J. Housel, *Team Dynamics* (Mason, OH: South-Western, 2002).

29. Alden M. Hayashi, "Building Better Teams," *Sloan Management Review* 45, no. 2 (Winter 2004): 5.

30. Jon R. Katzenbach and Douglas Smith, "The Discipline of Teams," *Harvard Business Review* 83, no. 7 (July–August 2005): 162. See also Leigh Thompson, "Improving the Creativity of Organizational Work Groups," *The Academy of Management Executive* 17, no. 1 (February 2003): 96.

31. Michael Hansen, "Virtual Teams That Work: Creating Conditions for Virtual Team Effectiveness," *Personal Psychology* 57, no. 1 (Spring 2004): 243.

32. Ruth Wageman, "Multinational Work Teams: A New Perspective," *Administrative Science Quarterly* 48, no. 2 (June 2003): 332.

33. Stacie A. Furst, Martha Reeves, Benson Rosen, and Richard S. Blackburn, "Managing the Life Cycle of Virtual Teams," *Academy of Management Executive* 18, no. 2 (May 2004): 6.

34. Interview with Paulette Tichenor, Arizona State University, Tempe, Arizona, January 18, 2004. See also Bradley L. Kirkman, Benson Rosen, Paul E. Tesluk, and Cristina B. Gibson, "The Impact of Team Empowerment on Virtual Team Performance: The Moderating Role of Face-to-Face Interaction," *Academy of Management Journal* 47, no. 2 (April 2004): 175.

35. David Clutterbuck, "Teams and Learning: The Agenda Has Changed," *Training Strategies for Tomorrow* 17, no. 2 (2003): 10.

36. Glenn Parker, "Leading a Team of Strangers," *Training and Development* 57, no. 2 (February 2003): 21.

37. For a discussion of the stages of team development, see Don Hellriegel and John W. Slocum, Jr., *Organizational Behavior*, 10th ed. (Cincinnati, OH: South-Western, 2004): 203–206.

38. Charles E. Naguin and Renee O. Tynan, "The Team Halo Effect: Why Teams Are Not Blamed for Their Failures," *Journal of Applied Psychology* 88, no. 2 (April 2003): 332.

39. Vicki Powers, "Keeping Work and Life in Balance," *Training and Development* 58, no. 7 (July 2004): 32.

40. Rosalind Chait Barnett and Douglas T. Hall, "How to Use Reduced Hours to Win the War for Talent," *Organizational Dynamics* 29, no. 3 (Winter 2001): 101.

41. Michael White, Stephen Hill, Patrick McGovern, and Colin Mills, "'High Performance' Management Practices: Working Hours and Work-Life Balance," *British Journal of Industrial Relations* 41, no. 2 (June 2003): 175. See also Virginia Smith Major, Katherine J. Klein, and Mark G. Ehrhart, "Work Time, Work Interference with Family, and Psychological Distress," *Journal of Applied Psychology* 87, no. 3 (June 2002): 427.

42. Sara Fisher Gale, "Formalized Flextime: The Perk That Brings Productivity," *Workforce* 80, no. 2 (February 2001): 39–42.

43. Sherry E. Sullivan, David F. Martin, William A. Carden, and Lisa A. Mainiero, "The Road Less Traveled: How to Manage the

Recycling Career Stage," *Journal of Leadership and Organizational Studies* 10, no. 2 (Fall 2003): 34.

44. Kenneth L. Schultz, John O. McClain, and L. Joseph Thomas, "Overcoming the Dark Side of Worker Flexibility," *Journal of Operations Management* 21, no. 1 (January 2003): 81.

45. Anne-Mette Jhalager, "Virtual Working: Traditional and Emerging Institutional Framework for the Contingent Workforce," *International Journal of Manpower* 24, no. 2 (2003): 422–39.

46. "Time to Take Another Look at Telecommuting," *HRFocus* 79, no. 5 (May 2002): 6.

47. Gus Manchehri and Theresa Pinkerton, "Managing Telecommuters: Opportunities and Challenges," *American Business Review* 21, no. 1 (January 2003): 9.

48. Jathan W. Janove, "Managing by Remote Control," *HRMagazine* 49, no. 3 (April 2004): 119–24.

Expanding the Talent Pool: Recruitment and Careers

After studying this chapter, you should be able to

objective **1**
Explain the advantages and disadvantages of external recruitment.

objective **5**
Describe the conditions that help make a career management program successful.

objective **2**
Explain the advantages and disadvantages of recruiting from within the organization.

objective **6**
Explain why diverse recruitment and career development activities are important to companies.

objective **3**
Discuss how job opportunities can be inventoried and employee potential assessed.

objective **4**
Explain how a career management program integrates individual and organizational needs.

n earlier chapters we stressed that many HR challenges centre on the idea that organizations increasingly compete on the basis of their employee talents and capabilities. Even though workers seemed to be in plentiful supply following the recession of 2001, that began changing as the economy recovered. Moreover, as the baby boomers begin retiring, the demand for labour is expected to grow.

Increased competition for talent means that recruiting has acquired new importance for managers. Today, many jobs require higher skill levels, and no longer can managers rely solely on unsolicited applications to fill these positions. To stay apace of their competitors and expand their operations around the world, companies are also having to look globally for workers. It is therefore essential that organizations do a good job of broadening their pools of talent—the number and kinds of people able to contribute to the success of the organization, and the variety of ways in which they recruit and retain them.

Of course, unlike physical assets, human assets (employees) can decide to leave the firm of their own accord as well as join it. And in the war for talent, rival firms are likely to lure valued employees away. Employees may find that their options and opportunities are more attractive across firms rather than within only one firm. Flatter organization structures mean that there are fewer positions for promotion, so individuals must look for advancement opportunities outside the firm. At the same time, as economic cycles lead organizations first to hire—and then to lay off—and then to hire again, employment security can be assured only when individuals take control of their own careers. The upshot is that individuals are less likely to work in the same job for extended periods and, in fact, most are unlikely to spend their entire careers with only one firm. In other words, today's labour market—for both employees and employers—has become more "free agent" oriented.[1]

In this chapter we will discuss various sources and approaches to expanding the talent pool in organizations. Specifically, we will discuss both external sources of recruitment and internal sources (such as promotion, transfers, and the like). But beyond recruiting itself, we will also discuss the approaches that organizations take toward career management over time. As organizations consider the long-term implications for managing talent, career progressions are taking on new importance. Finally, at the end of the chapter, we devote special attention to the recruitment and career development of minorities and women.

Recruiting Talent Externally

objective 1

Recruitment is the process of locating potential individuals who might join an organization and encouraging them to apply for existing or anticipated job openings. During this process, efforts are made to inform the applicants fully about the qualifications required to perform the job and the career opportunities the organization can offer its employees. Whether a particular job vacancy will be filled by someone from within the organization or from outside will, of course, depend on the availability of personnel, the organization's HR policies, and the requirements of the job to be staffed.

Unless managers intend to reduce the size of the workforce, any job vacancy is a cue that a replacement from outside must be found to replace a departing employee.

An old adage goes something like this: "When the president or CEO of the organization retires, a chain reaction of promotions occurs. Everyone moves up a slot, and someone new is hired into a starting position in the mailroom." Of course this almost never occurs, but the story provides a framework for how some companies approach their recruiting philosophy. More realistically, when there is an opening, managers must make careful decisions about whom to bring into the position, and how best to approach the decision. The question therefore is not whether to bring people into the organization, but rather at which level they are to be brought in.

In the past few years, an astonishing number of the nation's largest companies, including CN, have brought in outsiders to be their new CEOs. Stock prices rose and fell based on a CEO's appointment. Hiring someone from the outside was seen as essential for revitalizing organizations.[2]

Outside Sources for Recruitment

The outside sources from which employers recruit will vary with the type of position to be filled. A computer programmer, for example, is not likely to be recruited from the same source as a machine operator. Trade schools can provide applicants for entry-level positions, though these recruitment sources are not as useful when highly skilled employees are needed. Some firms keep detailed statistics by job type on the sources from which their employees are hired. This helps human resources managers make better decisions about the places to begin recruiting when different job openings arise.

The condition of the labour market may also help determine which recruiting sources an organization will use. During periods of high unemployment, organizations may be able to maintain an adequate supply of qualified applicants from unsolicited résumés alone. A tight labour market, one with low unemployment, may force the employer to advertise heavily and/or seek assistance from local employment agencies. How successful an organization has been in reaching its employment equity goals may be still another factor in determining the sources from which to recruit. Typically, an employer at any given time will find it necessary to use several recruitment sources.

Several other studies have suggested that an employee's recruitment source can affect that employee's subsequent tenure and job performance in both large and small organizations.[3] In general, applicants who find employment through referral by a current employee tend to remain with the organization longer and give higher-quality performance than employees recruited through the formal recruitment sources of advertisements and employment agencies. Informal recruiting sources may also yield higher selection rates than formal sources. Employers are cautioned, however, that relying on only one or two recruitment sources to secure job applicants could have an adverse effect on designated groups.

USING THE INTERNET

The Electronic Recruiting Exchange is a source of networking and information for recruiters and HR professionals at:

www.erexchange.com

Advertisements

One of the most common methods of attracting applicants is through advertisements. Although websites, newspapers, and trade journals are the media used most often, radio, television, billboards, posters, and e-mail are also used. Advertising has the advantage of reaching a large audience of possible applicants. Some degree of selectivity can be achieved by using newspapers and journals directed toward a particular group of readers. Professional journals, trade journals, and publications of unions and various fraternal or nonprofit organizations fall into this category.

The preparation of recruiting advertisements not only is time-consuming, but also requires creativity in developing design and message content. Well-written advertisements highlight the major assets of the position while showing the responsiveness of the organization to the job and career needs of the applicants. Fairmont Hotels and Resorts use different job advertisements to create a value proposition that appeals to different types of candidates. Also, there appears to be a correlation between the accuracy and completeness of information provided in advertisements and the recruitment success of the organization. Among the information typically included in advertisements is that the recruiting organization is an equal opportunity employer.

Advertising can sometimes place a severe burden on an organization's employment office. Even though the specifications for the openings are described thoroughly in the advertisement, many applicants who know they do not meet the job requirements may still be attracted. They may apply with the hope that the employer will not be able to find applicants who do meet the specifications.

Unsolicited Applications and Résumés

Many employers receive unsolicited applications and résumés from individuals who may or may not be good prospects for employment. Even though the percentage of acceptable applicants from this source may not be high, it is a source that cannot be ignored. In fact, it is often believed that individuals who contact the employer on their own initiative will be better employees than those recruited through university or college placement services or newspaper advertisements.

Good public relations dictates that any person contacting an organization for a job be treated with courtesy and respect. If there is no possibility of employment in the organization at present or in the future, the applicant should be tactfully and frankly informed of this fact. Telling an applicant to "fill out an application, and we will keep it on file" when there is no hope for his or her employment is not fair to the applicant. Research has shown that a candidate who has been treated well by a potential employer will, on average, tell one other person. On the other hand, a candidate who has been treated poorly—perhaps receiving a tardy rejection letter or no letter all—will, on average, tell 11 other people.[4]

Internet Recruiting

The Internet is the most commonly used search tactic by job seekers; 60 percent of Canadians with Internet access have gone online in search of a job. Both companies and applicants find the approach cheaper, faster, and potentially more effective. The most popular job sites are Monster and Workopolis, followed by Hot Jobs, Careerclick, and Campus Worklink.[5] Applicant tracking systems can match the job requirements with the experiences and skills of applicants. Companies with high turnover who are in a constant job search mode use the Internet to screen walk-in candidates. We have all seen students walk into retail stores and hand in their résumés. Now these candidates are given a business card with a Web address and a password, and they complete an online assessment, which allows the company to evaluate the suitability and track candidates more effectively. But companies are still reporting problems with Internet recruiting. The most frequent complaint is that up to 80 percent of the candidates who respond are appropriate for the position. Most companies (up to 65 percent) do not use screening tools to manage these applications.[6] Highlights in HRM 5.1 provides guidelines for setting up an online job posting system.

Highlights in HRM 5.1

Guidelines for Setting Up an Online Job Posting System

Below is a list of best practices for online recruitment:

- Links to careers from the home page
- About the company: benefits
- About the company: culture
- A university recruiting section
- Job search by job category
- Job search by key word
- Urgent-needs jobs highlighted
- Complete job description
- One click to apply
- Pre-assessment tool customized for each position
- Choice of cut-and-paste form or résumé builder
- Attachment of formatted résumé
- Application automatically connected to a job
- Anonymous application
- E-mail to a friend
- Profiling
- Reuse of candidate information for multiple applications
- Online user feedback

To begin building an electronic job posting system, organizations need an e-mail software program with the capability to display job postings and accept recruiting requests for available openings.

Designing and Administering the System

To design and administer the system, organizations need

- An automated process to enter job postings into the system and to delete listings once they are filled
- The capability to automatically calculate each listing's expiration date
- A system that automatically assigns numbers to job postings
- The capability to preschedule job positions for future postings
- A way for coordinators to revise and delete postings after they are on the system
- Security measures that allow access to authorized users only

Sources: "Canadian Employers Lagging behind in Use of Corporate Websites for Recruitment," *Canadian HR Reporter*, November 19, 2001. Condensed from Sharon M. Tarrant, "Setting Up an Electronic Job-Posting System," *Training and Development*, January 1994, 39–42.

Employee Referrals

The recruitment efforts of an organization can be greatly aided by employee referrals, or recommendations from the firm's current employees about potential candidates. In fact, word-of-mouth recommendations are the way most job positions are filled. (Apparently there is truth to the phrase, "It's not what you know, but who you know.") Employee referrals account for about one-third of new hires.[7] Sierra Wireless Inc. employees are paid up to $3,000 a head for each referral who lands a job. Managers have found that the quality of employee-referred applicants is normally quite high, since employees are generally hesitant to recommend individuals who might not perform well.

There are several suggested ways to increase the effectiveness of employee referral programs:

- *Up the ante.* Companies pay high commissions to employment agencies and search firms, so why not do the same thing with employees when they provide a good referral? Other recruitment incentives used by organizations include complimentary dinners, discounts on merchandise, all-expenses-paid trips, and free insurance. When employers pay higher bonuses for "hot" skills, employees are more likely to focus on people they know in that area.

- *Pay for performance.* Some firms save part of the referral bonus until the new hire has stayed for six months. This encourages referring employees to help the new hires succeed.

- *Tailor the program.* Companies typically need more of certain types of skills than others, but the referral programs do not always reflect this. Part of a good referral program is educating employees about the kinds of people the organization wants to hire. This includes some communication of the skills required, but also a reaffirmation of the values and ethics sought in applicants.

- *Increase visibility.* One of the best ways to publicize a referral program is to celebrate successes. Some companies use novel approaches such as "job of the month" or "celebrity endorsements" from managers. The idea is to keep everyone thinking about bringing in good people.

- *Keep the data.* Even if a referral does not get the job, it might be a good idea to keep the résumé on file just in case another vacancy arises.

- *Rethink your taboos.* Some companies are reluctant to take on certain potential hires, such as former employees, relatives, and the like. In a tight labour market, it is a good idea to broaden the search.

- *Widen the program.* Just as it may make sense to consider hiring former employees, it may make sense to ask them for referrals even if they are not candidates for the jobs themselves. A number of companies have mailing lists of "corporate friends" that can be used to seek out potential candidates.

- *Measure results.* No surprise here. After the program is implemented, managers need to take a hard look at the volume of referrals, the qualifications of candidates, and the success of new hires on the job. These results are then fed back to fine-tune the program.[8]

nepotism
A preference for hiring relatives of current employees

Some potential negative factors are associated with employee referrals. They include the possibility of inbreeding and the adverse impact on designated groups. Since employees and their referrals tend to have similar backgrounds, employers who rely heavily on employee referrals to fill job openings may intentionally or unintentionally screen out, and thereby discriminate against, members of designated groups. Furthermore, organizations may choose not to employ relatives of current employees. The practice of hiring relatives, referred to as **nepotism,** can invite charges of favouritism, especially in appointments to desirable positions. The High School of Montreal was accused of nepotism when the director hired three relatives and four family friends to work as teachers and office staff, with fewer qualifications than other employees.[9] Nepotism, however, gets mixed reviews, in part because family members are in an ideal position to pass job knowledge and skills on to one another. Many corporate dynasties (Ford Motor Company and the Rockefeller Foundation among them) have been built on nepotism. Labour unions would not have flourished without it. In recent years, a number of law firms and universities have dropped restrictions against hiring spouses on the basis that they are prejudicial.[10]

Executive Search Firms

In contrast to public and private employment agencies, which help job seekers find the right job, executive search firms (often called "headhunters") help employers find the right person for a job. Firms such as Korn/Ferry International and the Caldwell Partners seek out candidates with qualifications that match the requirements of the positions their client firm is seeking to fill. Executive search firms do not advertise in the media for job candidates, nor do they accept a fee from the individual being placed.

The fees charged by search firms may range from 30 to 40 percent of the annual salary for the position to be filled. For the recruitment of senior executives, this fee is paid by the client firm, whether or not the recruiting effort results in a hire. It is for this practice that search firms receive the greatest criticism.

Nevertheless, as noted earlier, hiring new chief executive officers (CEOs) from outside the organization has become commonplace. A large number of these new CEOs are placed in those positions through the services of an executive search firm. Because high-calibre executives are in short supply, a significant number of the nation's largest organizations, including Ryerson University, have used search firms to fill their top positions. Figure 5.1 shows the results of a study that investigated the key

Figure 5.1	Factors That Motivate Executive Talent

Working for a great company and having a great job are more important to most executives than compensation.*

Great company (brand)

Values and culture	58%
Well managed	50%
Exciting challenges	38%
Strong performance	29%
Industry leader	21%
Many talented people	20%
Good at development	17%
Inspiring mission	16%
Fun with colleagues	11%
Job security	8%

Great jobs (products)

Freedom and autonomy	56%
Exciting challenges	51%
Career advancement and growth	39%
Fit with boss I admire	29%

Compensation and lifestyle (price)

Differentiated compensation	29%
High total compensation	23%
Geographic location	19%
Respect for lifestyle	14%
Acceptable pace and stress	1%

*Each number represents the percentage of the top 200 executives who agreed each factor was important.

Source: Adapted from E.G. Chambers, H. Hanafield-Jones, S.M. Hankin, and E.G. Michaels, III, "Win the War for Top Talent," *Workforce* 77, no.12 (December 1998): 50–56. Used with permission of McKinsey & Co.

factors that are important to an executive involved in a job search. However, newer data suggest that CEOs who are promoted from within their organizations actually outperform those hired from the outside. In light of the numerous CEO-related scandals that have occurred in recent times, human resources personnel are increasingly being called on to demand more from executive search firms and to assist boards of directors in the careful selection of top executives.[11]

Educational Institutions

Educational institutions typically are a source of young applicants with formal training but relatively little full-time work experience. High schools are usually a source of employees for clerical and blue-collar jobs. Community colleges, with their various types of specialized training, can provide candidates for technical jobs. These institutions can also be a source of applicants for a variety of white-collar jobs, including those in the sales and retail fields. Some management-trainee jobs are also staffed from this source. For technical and managerial positions, colleges and universities are generally the primary source.

Some employers fail to take full advantage of college and university resources because of a poor recruitment program.[12] Consequently, their recruitment efforts fail to attract many potentially good applicants. Another common weakness is the failure to maintain a planned and continuing effort on a long-term basis. Furthermore, some recruiters sent to campuses are not sufficiently trained or prepared to talk to interested candidates about career opportunities or the requirements of specific openings. Attempts to visit too many campuses instead of concentrating on selected institutions and the inability to use the campus placement office effectively are other recruiting weaknesses. Mismanagement of applicant visits to the organization's headquarters and the failure to follow up on individual prospects or to obtain hiring commitments from higher management are among other mistakes that have caused employers to lose well-qualified prospects. Recruiters should be aware of what attracts students to employers. A survey was commissioned by nine large employers that asked about 20 000 students from nearly every Canadian university and college about the factors they considered in choosing full-time employment. Read about their rankings in Figure 5.2.

Some students fail to take advantage of their institutions' career management programs, which provide assessment tools and offer workshops in job search, résumé writing, cover letter writing, and interview skills. Recruiters are impressed by students who have used these services, and as one on-campus recruiter from Hydro One said: "Those who have gone through a career management program are much better prepared from the outset of the campus recruitment process. They come to the career fairs ready to ask pertinent questions and you get the sense that they have done their research. They are persistent and follow through without being pushy or aggressive. In general, they are organized and completely ready for the school-to-work transition. They get it."[13]

Professional Associations

Many professional associations and societies offer a placement service to members as one of their benefits. Listings of members seeking employment may be advertised in their journals or publicized at their national meetings. A placement centre is usually established at national meetings for the mutual benefit of employers and job seekers. The Human Resource Professionals Association of Ontario (HRPAO), for example, helps employers and prospective HR employees come together.

Figure 5.2	Taking the Student Pulse

Opportunities for advancement	86.7%
Good people to work with	82.2%
Good training opportunities/developing new skills	82.1%
Good people to report to	79.6%
Challenging work	71.8%
Work–life balance	70.2%
Good initial salary level	70.1%
Job security	69.1%
Opportunities to have a personal impact	68.8%
Good health and benefits plan	63.2%
Strong commitment to employee diversity	49.5%
Commitment to social responsibility	48.6%
Organization is a leader in its field	47.1%
Opportunity to travel	36.1%

Source: Graham Donald, "People and Opportunities the Biggest Draw for Students," *Canadian HR Reporter*, April 25, 2005: page 9.

Labour Unions

Labour unions can be a principal source of applicants for blue-collar and some professional jobs. Some unions, such as those in the maritime, printing, and construction industries, maintain hiring halls that can provide a supply of applicants, particularly for short-term needs. Employers wishing to use this recruitment source should contact the local union under consideration for employer-eligibility requirements and applicant availability.

Public Employment Agencies

Each province maintains an employment agency that is responsible for administering its employment insurance program. The agency is called the Department of Human Resources Development, or similar, and maintains local public employment offices in most communities of any size. Individuals who become unemployed must register at one of these offices and be available for "suitable employment" before they can receive their weekly unemployment cheques. This requirement means that public employment agencies are able to refer those applicants with the required skills who are available for employment to employers with job openings.

HRSDC has developed a nationwide computerized job bank that lists job openings, and provincial employment offices are connected to this job bank. The computerized job bank helps facilitate the movement of job applicants to different geographic areas. Most of these offices now have a local job bank book that is published as a daily computer printout. Job openings are listed along with other pertinent information, such as number of openings, pay rates, and job specifications. The local job bank makes it possible for the agency's employment interviewers to keep a list of all the job openings in the geographic area for which the applicants assigned to them might qualify. Also, applicants looking for a specific job can review the computer printout and apply directly to the organization that has the opening. HRSDC provides all kinds of labour market information including occupational profiles, industry profiles, and job outlooks.

In addition to matching unemployed applicants with job openings, public employment agencies may assist employers with employment testing, job analysis, evaluation programs, and community wage surveys.

Private Employment and Temporary Agencies

Charging a fee enables private employment agencies to tailor their services to the specific needs of their clients. However, it is common for agencies to specialize in serving a specific occupational area or professional field. Depending on who is receiving the most service, the fee may be paid by the employer, the job seeker, or both. It is not uncommon for private employment agencies to charge an employer a 25–30-percent fee, based on the position's annual salary, if the employer hires an applicant found by the agency.

Private employment agencies differ in the services they offer, their professionalism, and the calibre of their counsellors. If counsellors are paid on a commission basis, their desire to do a professional job may be offset by their desire to earn a commission. Thus they may encourage job seekers to accept jobs for which they are not suited. Because of this, job seekers would be wise to take the time to find a recruiter who is knowledgeable, experienced, and professional. When talking with potential recruiters, individuals should discuss openly their philosophies and practices with regard to recruiting strategies, including advertising, in-house recruiting, screening procedures, and costs for these efforts. They should try to find a recruiter who is flexible and who will consider their needs and wants.

A large-scale Statistics Canada survey of over 25 000 employees found that the most frequent source of employee leads was family and friends, followed by personal initiative. (See Figure 5.3.) Obviously the use of the Internet has increased since the 1999 study; another study found that 12 percent of Canadians who found jobs in 2003 found them on the Internet, a higher rate than any other country and much higher than the global average of 3 percent.[14]

Improving the Effectiveness of External Recruitment

With all of the uncertainties inherent in external recruiting, it is sometimes difficult to determine whether an organization's efforts to locate promising talent are effective and/or cost-efficient. However, managers can do several things to maximize the probability of success. These include calculating yield ratios on recruiting sources, calculating costs of recruitment, training organizational recruiters, and conducting realistic job previews.

Yield Ratios

yield ratio
The percentage of applicants from a recruitment source that make it to the next stage of the selection process

Yield ratios help indicate which recruitment sources are most effective at producing qualified job candidates. Quite simply, a **yield ratio** is the percentage of applicants from a particular source that make it to the next stage in the selection process. For example, if 100 résumés were obtained from an employment agency, and 17 of the applicants submitting those résumés were invited for an on-site

Figure 5.3	Sources of Information Leading to Employees' Current Employment

TYPE OF SOURCE	% OF THOSE WHO USED SOURCE TO FIND CURRENT EMPLOYMENT N = 24 983
Family/friends	37.7
Personal initiative	21.6
Help wanted ads	17.7
Directly recruited by employer	10.7
Other	8.7
Used more than one	4.0
Canada Employment Centre HRSDC	3.0
Recruitment agency	2.2
On-campus recruitment	2.0
Union posting	0.5
News story	0.2
Job fair	0.2
Internet	0.2
Did not respond	8.0

Source: A. Bissonnette and V.M. Catano, "Revisiting the Efficacy of Recruitment Methods," Poster presented at the 11th European Workshop on Organizational Psychology Congress, Lisbon, Portugal, May 2003.

interview, the yield ratio for that agency would be 17 percent (17/100). This yield ratio could then be recalculated for each subsequent stage in the selection process (for example, after the interview and again after the final offer), which would result in a cumulative yield ratio. By calculating and comparing yield ratios for each recruitment source, it is possible to find out which sources produce qualified applicants.

Costs of Recruitment

The cost of various recruiting procedures can be computed using a fairly simple set of calculations. For example, the average source cost per hire (SC/H) can be determined by the following formula:

$$\frac{SC}{H} = \frac{AC + AF + RB + NC}{H}$$

where AC = advertising costs, total monthly expenditure (example: $28,000)

AF = agency fees, total for the month (example: $19,000)

RB = referral bonuses, total paid (example: $2,300)

NC = no-cost hires, walk-ins, nonprofit agencies, etc. (example: $0)

H = total hires (example: 119)

Substituting the example numbers into the formula gives

$$\frac{SC}{H} = \frac{\$28{,}000 + \$19{,}000 + \$2{,}300 + \$0}{119}$$

$$= \frac{\$49{,}300}{119}$$

$$= \$414 \text{ (source cost of recruits per hire)}$$

When combined with information about yield ratios, these calculations can provide invaluable information to managers about the utility of different approaches to and sources of recruitment. In that way, they can make more informed decisions about both controlling the costs of recruitment and increasing its effectiveness. For example, although advertisements and employee referrals may both yield qualified applicants, managers may find that referral bonuses are a more economical alternative.

Organizational Recruiters

The size of an organization influences who performs the recruitment function. For large employers, professional HR recruiters are hired and trained to find new employees. In smaller organizations, recruitment may be done by an HR generalist; if the organization has no HR position, recruitment may be carried out by managers and/or supervisors. Regardless of who does the recruiting, it is imperative that these individuals have a good understanding of the knowledge, skills, abilities, experiences, and other characteristics required for the job. All too often, a new person in the HR department or a line manager may be given a recruitment assignment even before that person has been given interview training, before he or she fully understands the job, and before he or she fully comprehends the values and goals of the organization.

It is important to remember that recruiters have an influence on an applicant's job decision. Because recruiters can often enhance the perceived attractiveness of a job and an organization, they are often a main reason why applicants select one organization over another. On this basis we can conclude that personable, enthusiastic, and competent recruiters have an impact on the success of an organization's recruitment program.

Realistic Job Previews

realistic job preview (RJP)
Informing applicants about all aspects of the job, including both its desirable and undesirable facets

Another way organizations may be able to increase the effectiveness of their recruitment efforts is to provide job applicants with a **realistic job preview (RJP).** An RJP informs applicants about all aspects of the job, including both its desirable and undesirable facets. In contrast, a typical job preview presents the job in only positive terms. The RJP may also include a tour of the working area, combined with a discussion of any negative health or safety considerations. Proponents of the RJP believe that applicants who are given realistic information regarding a position are more likely to remain on the job and be successful, because there will be fewer unpleasant surprises. In fact, a number of research studies on RJP report these positive results:

- Improved employee job satisfaction
- Reduced voluntary turnover
- Enhanced communication through honesty and openness
- Realistic job expectations

Like other HR techniques, however, RJPs must be tailored to the needs of the organization and should include a balanced presentation of positive and negative information. But the RJP can also be a source of "employer branding." Organizations can use the unique values and work environments to create an employer brand that will attract candidates. For example, the North Shore Health Region, in British Columbia, realized that it had unique attributes that could give a competitive advantage in recruiting nurses. Recruitment materials were prepared that captured the main appeal of this employer: a small, friendly full-service hospital. This message was reinforced in all recruitment efforts and was credible (realistic) because it was based on research with existing employees.[15]

Recruiting Talent Internally

objective 2

While we typically think about recruiting being focused on attracting potential employees from outside the organization, most organizations try to follow a policy of filling job vacancies above the entry-level position through promotions and transfers. By filling vacancies in this way, an organization can capitalize on the investment it has made in recruiting, selecting, training, and developing its current employees, who might look for jobs elsewhere if they lack promotion opportunities. Procter & Gamble is one organization that recruits its top managers exclusively from within the company. Companies are also more likely to promote from within than they have been in the past, one survey of executives found.[16]

Advantages and Limitations of Recruiting from Within

Promotion rewards employees for past performance and is intended to encourage them to continue their efforts. It also gives other employees reason to anticipate that similar efforts by them will lead to promotion, thus improving morale within the organization. This is particularly true for members of designated groups who have encountered difficulties in finding employment and have often faced even greater difficulty in advancing within an organization. Most organizations have integrated promotion policies as an essential part of their employment equity programs.

If an organization's promotion policy is to have maximum motivational value, employees must be made aware of that policy. The following is an example of a policy statement that an organization might prepare:

> "Promotion from within" is generally recognized as a foundation of good employment practice, and it is the policy of our organization to promote from within whenever possible when filling a vacancy. The job vacancy will be posted for five calendar days to give all qualified full- and part-time personnel an equal opportunity to apply.

While a transfer lacks the motivational value of a promotion, it sometimes can serve to protect employees from layoff or to broaden their job experiences. Furthermore, the transferred employee's familiarity with the organization and its operations can eliminate the orientation and training costs that recruitment from the outside would entail. Most important, the transferee's performance record is likely to be a more accurate predictor of the candidate's success than the data gained about outside applicants.

Side by side with the potential advantages of internal recruitment, managers need to be aware of potential limitations as well. For example, certain jobs at the middle and upper levels that require specialized training and experience cannot be easily filled from within the organization and may need to be filled from the outside. This is especially common in small organizations. Also, for certain openings it may be necessary to hire individuals from the outside who have gained from another employer the knowledge and expertise required for these jobs.

Even though HR policy encourages job openings to be filled from within the organization, potential candidates from the outside should be considered in order to prevent the inbreeding of ideas and attitudes. Applicants hired from the outside, particularly for certain technical and managerial positions, can be a source of new ideas and may bring with them the latest knowledge acquired from their previous employers. Indeed, excessive reliance on internal sources can create the risk of "employee cloning." Furthermore, it is not uncommon for firms to attempt to gain secrets from their competitors by hiring away their employees: Procter & Gamble sued a rival papermaker when it hired former employees who had a great deal of knowledge about the making of Charmin toilet paper and Bounty paper towels—both P&G products. Amazon.com was sued by Wal-Mart, which accused it of hiring away employees who had in-depth knowledge about Wal-Mart's sophisticated inventory systems.[17]

Methods for Identifying Qualified Candidates

The effective use of internal sources requires a system for locating qualified job candidates and for enabling those who consider themselves qualified to apply for the opening. Qualified job candidates within the organization can be located in a number of ways, which we discuss next.

Human Resources Information Systems

As discussed in Chapter 2, information technology has made it possible for organizations to create databases that contain the complete records and qualifications of each employee within an organization. Combined with increasingly user-friendly search engines, managers can access this information and identify potential candidates for available jobs. Companies such as PeopleSoft and SAP are leaders in developing automated staffing and skills management software. Similar to the skills inventories mentioned earlier, these information systems allow an organization to rapidly screen its entire workforce to locate suitable candidates to fill an internal opening. These data can also be used to predict the career paths of employees and to anticipate when and where promotion opportunities may arise. Since the value of the data depends on its being kept up-to-date, the systems typically include provisions for recording changes in employee qualifications and job placements as they occur.[18]

Job Posting and Bidding

job posting and bidding
Posting vacancy notices and maintaining lists of employees looking for upgraded positions

Organizations may communicate information about job openings through a process referred to as **job posting and bidding.** The jobs are frequently posted on electronic bulletin boards or on regular bulletin boards where employees congregate. Job openings can also be announced in employee publications, special handouts, direct mail, and public-address messages. Many companies have developed online job posting systems whereby employees looking for upgraded positions can post their names, résumés, and the positions they are interested in applying for. (Refer to Highlights in HRM 5.1 for some guidelines for setting up an online job posting system.) As a position becomes available, the list of employees seeking that position is retrieved, and the records of these employees reviewed to select possible candidates for interviews. The employees can be electronically notified about interview schedules and track their progress electronically through the various hiring stages.[19]

The system of job posting and bidding can provide many benefits to an organization. However, these benefits may not be realized unless employees believe the system is being administered fairly. Furthermore, job bidding is more effective when it is part of a career development program in which employees are made aware of opportunities available to them within the organization. For example, HR departments may provide new employees with information on job progression that describes the lines of job advancement, training requirements for each job, and skills and abilities needed as they move up the job progression ladder.

Identifying Talent through Performance Appraisals

Performance appraisals are discussed more fully in Chapter 8. For our purposes here, we want to note that managers measure and evaluate an employee's performance for several reasons, none more important than for making developmental and career decisions. Successful performers are often good candidates for a promotion. In contrast, poorly performing employees may need—and benefit from—a transfer to another area or even a demotion.

Identifying and developing talent in individuals is a role that all managers should take seriously. As they conduct formal appraisals, they should be concerned with their subordinates' potential for managerial or advanced technical jobs and encourage their growth in that direction. In addition to immediate managers, others in the organization should have the power to evaluate, nominate, and sponsor employees with promise.

Inventorying Management Talent

As we discussed in Chapter 2, skill inventories are an important tool for succession planning. These inventories provide an indication of the skills employees have as well as their interests and experiences. In this way, they help managers pay better attention to the developmental needs of employees, both in their present jobs and in managerial jobs to which they may be promoted. An equally important part of this process is identifying high-potential employees who may be groomed as replacements for managers who are reassigned, retire, or otherwise vacate a position. At GE, for every position at or above a director level, two or three people are usually identified who can easily step in when the current jobholder moves on.

Unfortunately, many companies do a poor job of managing their talent. In a study conducted by McKinsey and Company, three-quarters of corporate officers said their companies were chronically short of talent. At the same time, half of the respondents to a similar survey acknowledged that they were not doing effective succession planning and were unprepared to replace key executives.[20] Some signs that the firm needs to work harder at grooming internal talent are shown in Figure 5.4 on page 200.

assessment centre
A process by which individuals are evaluated as they participate in a series of situations that resemble what they might be called on to handle on the job

Using Assessment Centres

There are other very effective ways to assess a person's career potential. Pioneered in the mid-1950s by Douglas Bray and his associates at AT&T, assessment centres are considered one of the most valuable methods for evaluating personnel. An **assessment centre** is a

Figure 5.4	Warning Signs of a Weak Talent "Bench"

1. It takes a long time to fill key positions
2. Key positions can be filled only by hiring from the outside.
3. Vacancies in key positions cannot be filled with confidence in the abilities of those chosen for them.
4. Replacements for positions often are unsuccessful in performing their new duties.
5. Promotions are made on the basis of whim, favouritism, or nepotism.

Source: Adapted from William Rothwell, *Effective Succession Planning* (New York: AMACOM, 2000).

process (not a place) by which individuals are evaluated as they participate in a series of situations that resemble what they might be called on to handle on the job. The popularity of the assessment centre can be attributed to its capacity for increasing an organization's ability to select employees who will perform successfully in management positions or to assist and promote the development of skills for their current position. These centres may use in-basket exercises, leaderless group discussions, and other approaches:

- *In-basket exercises.* This method is used to simulate a problem situation. The participants are given several documents, each describing some problem or situation requiring an immediate response. They are thus forced to make decisions under the pressure of time and also to determine what priority to give each problem.
- *Leaderless group discussions.* With this activity, trainees are gathered in a conference setting to discuss an assigned topic, either with or without designated group roles. The participants are given little or no instruction in how to approach the topic, nor are they told what decision to reach. Leaderless group trainees are evaluated on their initiative, leadership skills, and ability to work effectively in a group setting.
- *Role playing.* The exercise might involve preparing for and engaging in a customer meeting or a team-leader meeting with one's subordinates. A trained assessor then assesses the participant using a structured rating scale.
- *Behavioural interviews.* The interviewer asks the participant a series of questions about what he or she would do in particular work circumstances. Sometimes behavioural interviews are combined with videos showing work simulations, and participants are asked at intervals to make choices about what they would do in the situations shown.

The various activities of the Public Service Commission assessment centre are described in Highlights in HRM 5.2. Participation in these activities provides samples of behaviour that are representative of what is required for advancement. At the end of the assessment centre period, the assessors' observations are combined and integrated to develop an overall picture of the strengths and needs of the participants. A report is normally submitted to senior management, and feedback is given to the participants.

Increasing attention is being given to the validity of assessment centre procedures. Before the assessment centre is run, the characteristics or dimensions to be studied should be determined through job analyses. The exercises used in the centre should reflect the job for which the person is being evaluated; that is, the exercises should have content validity. While the assessment centre methodology lends itself readily to content validation, predictive validity has also been observed in many instances. A strong positive relationship is found between assessments and future performance on the job.[21]

Highlights in HRM 5.2

The Assessment Centre Program of the Public Service Commission

The first step in the use of an assessment centre is to work with managers, who are asked by psychologists to keep a diary of their daily activities and problems. They are then questioned about their work in order to identify the major problems that a manager might face. The focus is on identifying the abilities needed to resolve these problems. This information is used to develop the simulation exercises.

Candidates for managerial positions, playing the role of a manager, are asked to respond to a series of letters, memos, and variance reports (reports detailing how the results varied from the planned results). They then present, in oral and written forms, the approach they would use to resolve the problem. These approaches include the establishment of priorities, plans, solutions, and decisions.

The selection board, composed of the hiring manager, at least one outside manager, and a staffing officer, is trained to understand the simulation and the various effective approaches. The candidates are evaluated on how well they got their ideas across and on how well they plan, monitor, and control programs.

Everyone involved strongly identifies with the realistic nature of the simulation. Candidates get so involved in the simulation that they forget it is a test, and managers feel they can actually visualize these people at work. Even unsuccessful candidates claim they learn about themselves in the process.

Source: The Personal Psychology Centre, Public Service Commission, Government of Canada, Ottawa.

While assessment centres have proved quite valuable in identifying managerial talent and in helping with the development of individuals, it should be noted that the method tends to favour those who are strong in interpersonal skills and have the ability to influence others. Some individuals find it difficult to perform at their best in a situation that for them is as threatening as taking a test. The manner in which assessment centre personnel conduct the exercises and provide feedback to the participants will play a major role in determining how individuals react to the experience.

Career Management: Developing Talent over Time

While we can think of recruitment as a stand-alone activity, limited to a single job at a single point in time, often this is not the case. Inevitably decisions about talent—regardless of whether they pertain to recruiting, transferring, promoting, developing, or deploying people—need to be considered within the context of long-term priorities of the business and the employees. Increasingly, managers are not making these decisions on a "one-off" basis, but rather as part of a comprehensive approach to career management.

Integrating career development with other HR programs creates synergies in which all aspects of HR reinforce one another. Figure 5.5 illustrates how HR structures relate to some of the essential aspects of the career management process. For example, in planning careers, employees need organizational information—information that strategic planning, forecasting, succession planning, and skills inventories can provide. Similarly, as they obtain information about themselves and use it in career planning, employees need to know the career paths within the organization and how management views their performance.[22]

The Goal: Matching Individual and Organizational Needs

In the final analysis, a career development program should be viewed as a dynamic process that matches the needs of the organization with the needs of employees.

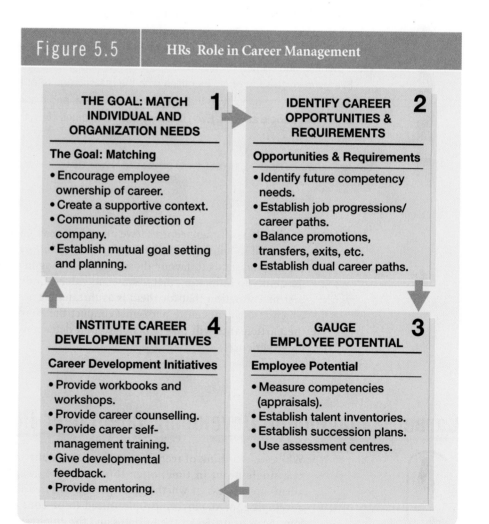

Figure 5.5   HRs Role in Career Management

THE GOAL: MATCH INDIVIDUAL AND ORGANIZATION NEEDS   1

The Goal: Matching

- Encourage employee ownership of career.
- Create a supportive context.
- Communicate direction of company.
- Establish mutual goal setting and planning.

IDENTIFY CAREER OPPORTUNITIES & REQUIREMENTS   2

Opportunities & Requirements

- Identify future competency needs.
- Establish job progressions/ career paths.
- Balance promotions, transfers, exits, etc.
- Establish dual career paths.

INSTITUTE CAREER DEVELOPMENT INITIATIVES   4

Career Development Initiatives

- Provide workbooks and workshops.
- Provide career counselling.
- Provide career self-management training.
- Give developmental feedback.
- Provide mentoring.

GAUGE EMPLOYEE POTENTIAL   3

Employee Potential

- Measure competencies (appraisals).
- Establish talent inventories.
- Establish succession plans.
- Use assessment centres.

The Employee's Role

Although some firms play a role in the planning of their employees' careers, ultimately employees are responsible for initiating and managing their own career planning. Because having a successful career involves creating your own career path—not just following a path that has been established by the organization—it is up to each individual to identify his or her own knowledge, skills, abilities, interests, and values and seek out information about career options in order to set goals and develop career plans. Managers should encourage employees to take responsibility for their own careers, offering continuing assistance in the form of feedback on individual performance and making available information about the organization, the job, and career opportunities that might be of interest.

The organization is responsible for supplying information about its mission, policies, and plans and for providing support for employee self-assessment, training, and development. Significant career growth can occur when individual initiative combines with organizational opportunity. Career development programs benefit managers by giving them increased skill in managing their own careers, greater retention of valued employees, increased understanding of the organization, and enhanced reputations as people developers. As with other HR programs, the inauguration of a career development program should be based on the organization's needs as well.

Assessment of needs should take a variety of approaches (surveys, informal group discussions, interviews, and so on) and should involve personnel from different groups, such as new employees, managers, long-time employees, minority employees, and technical and professional employees. Identifying the needs and problems of these groups provides the starting point for the organization's career development efforts. As shown in Figure 5.6, organizational needs should be linked with individual

USING THE INTERNET

Career Services at the University of Waterloo provides a Career Development e-manual that allows for self assessment and feedback at:

www.cdm.uwaterloo.ca/getting started.asp

Figure 5.6   Balancing Individual and Organizational Needs

ORGANIZATION'S NEEDS

Strategic	Operational
• Current competencies	• Employee turnover
• Future competencies	• Absenteeism
• Market changes	• Talent pool
• Mergers, etc.	• Outsourcing
• Joint ventures	• Productivity
• Innovation	
• Growth	
• Downsizing	
• Restructuring	

INDIVIDUAL'S NEEDS

Personal	Professional
• Age/tenure	• Career stage
• Family concerns	• Education & training
• Spouse employment	• Promotion aspirations
• Mobility	• Performance
• Outside interests	• Potential
	• Current career path

CAREER MANAGEMENT

career needs in a way that joins personal effectiveness and satisfaction of employees with the achievement of the organization's strategic objectives.

The Organization's Role: Establishing a Favourable Context

If career development is to succeed, it must receive the complete support of top management. Ideally, senior line managers and HR department managers should work together to design and implement a career development system. The system should reflect the goals and culture of the organization, and the HR philosophy should be woven throughout. An HR philosophy can provide employees with a clear set of expectations and directions for their own career development. For a program to be effective, managerial personnel at all levels must be trained in the fundamentals of job design, performance appraisal, career planning, and counselling.

One of the most important indicators of management support comes in the form of mentoring. This is true regardless of whether it is done formally as part of an ongoing program or informally as merely a kind gesture to a less experienced employee. Dealing with uncertainty is one of the biggest challenges any individual faces in his or her career. Receiving advice and counsel from someone who has gone through similar experiences can prove to be invaluable to employees. We devote an entire section to mentoring later in this chapter.

Blending Individual and Organizational Goals

Before individuals can engage in meaningful career planning, not only must they have an awareness of the organization's philosophy, but they must also have a good understanding of the organization's more immediate goals. Otherwise, they may plan for personal change and growth without knowing whether or how their own goals match those of the organization. For example, if the technology of a business is changing and new skills are needed, will the organization retrain to meet this need or hire new talent? Is there growth, stability, or decline in the number of employees needed? How will turnover affect this need? Clearly, an organizational plan that answers these kinds of questions is essential to support individual career planning.

At the same time, it would be unrealistic to expect that individuals can establish their career goals with *perfect* understanding of where they are going or—for that matter—where the organization is going. Individuals change over time, and because of that, their needs and interests change. Similarly, organizations also change their directions and adjust their strategies to cope with change. So while goal setting is critical, building in some flexibility is probably a good idea.

Identifying Career Opportunities and Requirements

While talent management integrates a number of related HR activities, those who direct the process have to keep a steady watch on the needs and requirements of the organization. This involves an analysis of the competencies required for jobs, the progression among related jobs, and the supply of ready (and potential) talent available to fill those jobs.

Begin with Competency Analysis

It is important for an organization to study its jobs carefully in order to identify and assign weights to the knowledge and skills that each one requires. This can be achieved with job analysis and evaluation systems such as those used in compensation programs. The system used at Sears measures three basic competencies for each job: know-how, problem solving, and accountability. Know-how is broken down into three types of job knowledge: technical, managerial, and human relations. Problem solving and accountability also have several dimensions. Scores for each of these three major competencies are assigned to each job, and a total value is computed for each job. For any planned job transfer, the amount of increase (or decrease) the next job represents in each of the skill areas, as well as in the total point values, can be computed. This information is then used to make certain that a transfer to a different job is a move that requires growth on the part of the employee.

Sears designs career development paths to provide the following experiences: (1) an increase in at least one skill area on each new assignment, (2) an increase of at least 10 percent in total points on each new assignment, and (3) assignments in several different functional areas.[23]

Identify Job Progressions

job progressions
The hierarchy of jobs a new employee might experience, ranging from a starting job to jobs that successively require more knowledge and/or skill

career paths
Lines of advancement in an occupational field within an organization

Once the skill demands of jobs are identified and weighted according to their importance, it is then possible to plan **job progressions.** A new employee with no experience is typically assigned to a "starting job." After a period of time in that job, the employee can be promoted to one that requires more knowledge and/or skill. While most organizations concentrate on developing job progressions for managerial, professional, and technical jobs, progressions can be developed for all categories of jobs. These job progressions then can serve as a basis for developing **career paths**—the lines of advancement within an organization—for individuals.

Figure 5.7 illustrates a typical line of advancement in the human resources area of a large multinational corporation. It is apparent that one must be prepared to move geographically in order to advance very far in the human resources department of this firm. This would also be true of other career fields within the organization.

Figure 5.7	Typical Line of Advancement in HR Management

				Vice president, HR
			Corporate HR director	
		Corporate HR manager	Division HR director	
		Asst. division HR director		
	Regional HR manager	Plant HR manager		
	Asst. plant HR manager			
Regional HR associate	HR supervisor			
HR associate				

Many organizations prepare interesting and attractive brochures to describe the career paths that are available to employees. General Motors has prepared a career development guide that groups jobs by fields of work such as engineering, manufacturing, communications, data processing, financial, HR, and scientific. These categories give employees an understanding of the career possibilities in the various fields.

Although these analyses can be quite helpful to employees—and are perhaps essential for organizations—a word of caution is appropriate here for readers. Many successful careers are not this methodical, nor do they proceed in a lockstep manner. In today's working world, career progressions often occur as much through creating and capitalizing on arising opportunities as they do through rational planning. So while it is a good idea for organizations to map out a career path, and individuals would do well to establish a strategy for advancement, many successful individuals readily admit that their career paths are quite idiosyncratic to their circumstances. These people often note that they have been fortunate to be "in the right place at the right time." Of course, others describe them as being extremely career savvy.

Recognize Lots of Possibilities

Career development and planning systems were once primarily focused on promotions and hierarchical advancement. However, in today's flatter organizations and more dynamic work environment, an individual's career advancement can occur along several different paths: transfers, demotions—even exits—and promotions. HR policies have to be flexible enough to adapt as well as helpful enough to support the career change.

promotion
A change of assignment to a job at a higher level in the organization

A **promotion** is a change of assignment to a job at a higher level in the organization. The new job normally provides an increase in pay and status and demands more skill or carries more responsibility. Promotions enable an organization to utilize the skills and abilities of its personnel more effectively, and the opportunity to gain a promotion serves as an incentive for good performance. The three principal criteria for determining promotions are merit, seniority, and potential. Often the problem is to determine how much consideration to give to each factor. A common problem in organizations that promote primarily on past performance and seniority is called the Peter Principle. This refers to the situation in which individuals are promoted as long as they have done a good job in their previous job. The trouble is this continues until someone does poorly in his or her new job. Then he or she is no longer promoted. This results in people being promoted to their level of incompetence. There are other intrafirm challenges related to promotions. Sometimes extremely good employees are prevented from being promoted to other departments because their current managers are reluctant to lose them. At other firms, an employee who tries, but fails, to advance to a position in another department is earmarked for the next round of layoffs.[24]

transfer
Placement of an individual in another job for which the duties, responsibilities, status, and remuneration are approximately equal to those of the previous job

In flatter organizations, there are fewer promotional opportunities; so many individuals find career advancement through lateral moves. A **transfer** is the placement of an employee in another job for which the duties, responsibilities, status, and remuneration are approximately equal to those of the previous job (although as an incentive, organizations may offer a salary adjustment). Individuals who look forward to change or want a chance to learn more may seek out transfers. In addition, transfers frequently provide a broader foundation for individuals to prepare them for an eventual promotion. A transfer may require the employee to change work group, workplace, work shift, or organizational unit; it may even necessitate moving to another geographic area. Transfers make it possible for an organization to place its employees in jobs where there is a greater need for their services and where they can acquire new knowledge and skills.

A downward transfer, or *demotion*, moves an individual into a lower-level job that can provide developmental opportunities. Although such a move is ordinarily considered unfavourable, some individuals actually may request it in order to return to their "technical roots." It is not uncommon, for example, for organizations to appoint temporary leaders (especially in team environments) with the proviso that they will eventually step down from this position to resume their former position.

Transfers, promotions, and demotions require individuals to adjust to new job demands and usually to a different work environment. A transfer that involves moving to a new location within Canada or abroad places greater demands on an employee because it requires that employee to adapt not only to a new work environment but also to new living conditions. The employee with a family has the added responsibility of helping family members adjust to the new living arrangements. Even though some employers provide all types of **relocation services**—including covering moving expenses, helping to sell a home, and providing cultural orientation and language training—there is always some loss of productive time. Pre-transfer training, whether related to job skills or to lifestyle, has been suggested as one of the most effective ways to reduce lost productivity.

When one considers the numerous changes that may accompany a career move within an organization, it should come as no surprise that many individuals are opting to accept career changes that involve *organizational exit*. Given limited career opportunities within firms, coupled with the need for talent in other companies, many individuals are discovering that their best career options may involve switching companies.

While some employees leave voluntarily, other employees are forced to leave. Even so, many organizations now provide **outplacement services** to help terminated employees find a job elsewhere. These services can be used to enhance a productive employee's career as well as to terminate an employee who is unproductive. If an organization cannot meet its career development responsibilities to its productive workers, HR policy should provide for assistance to be given them in finding more suitable career opportunities elsewhere. Jack Welch, chairman of General Electric, was one of the first executives to make a commitment to employees that while the company could no longer guarantee lifetime employment, it would try to ensure *employability*. That is, GE has committed to providing employees with the skills and support they would need to find a job in another organization.[25]

relocation services
Services provided to an employee who is transferred to a new location, which might include help in moving, selling a home, orienting to a new culture, and/or learning a new language

outplacement services
Services provided by organizations to help terminated employees find a new job

Consider Dual Career Paths for Employees

One of the most obvious places where career paths have been changing is in technical and professional areas. One of the ironies of organizations in the past has been that the most successful engineers, scientists, and professionals were often promoted right out of their area of specialization into management. Instead of doing what they were good at, they were promoted into a job they often didn't understand and often didn't enjoy. It has become apparent that there must be another way to compensate such individuals without elevating them to a management position. The solution has been to develop dual career paths, or tracks, that provide for progression in special areas such as information technology, finance, marketing, and engineering, with compensation that is comparable to that received by managers at different levels.

Many organizations have found that this is the solution to keeping employees with valuable knowledge and skills performing tasks that are as important to the organization as those performed by managers. Highlights in HRM 5.3 on page 208 shows the dual career path devised by Xenova Group, a biopharmaceuticals company, to recognize both the scientific and the managerial paths of employees.

Highlights in HRM 5.3

Dual Career Tracks: Xenova System

Scientist
Plans and undertakes laboratory work to achieve agreed-on project goals, using inputs from colleagues, the external scientific community, literature, and suppliers.

Senior Scientist
Plans and undertakes experimental programs and laboratory work to achieve agreed-on project or scientific goals, uses inputs from and provides outputs to colleagues, community, and suppliers.

Section Leader
Leads and manages a team of scientists from both science and operational management standpoint; makes significant contribution to management of groups of scientists and the general management of the department.

Research Associate
Provides expertise and direction to programs and projects through in-depth understanding of a scientific specialism; leads or forms part of a scientific team with the main purpose of providing expertise in a scientific discipline.

Department Head
Leads and manages a department of scientists to provide Xenova with a well-managed and motivated scientific resource; makes a significant contribution to the general management of the company or division of the company.

Principal Scientist
Provides scientific expertise and understanding of the highest level to ensure scientific leadership and direction; maintains a personal standing as a world-recognized and highly respected scientist and uses this to further the aims of the company through science.

Source: Adapted from Alan Garmonsway and Michael Wellin, "Creating the Right Natural Chemistry," *People Management* 1, no. 19 (September 21, 1995): 36–39.

Pursue the Boundaryless Career

A generation ago, the "organization man" served as a popular career icon. Career success was synonymous with ascending a corporate hierarchy over the course of a lifetime spent in a single firm. Today, however, individuals pursuing *boundaryless careers* may prefer to see themselves as self-directed "free agents" who develop a portfolio of employment opportunities by proactively moving from employer to employer, simultaneously developing and utilizing their marketable skills. As shown in Figure 5.8, it is possible to map the different career profiles. Employees

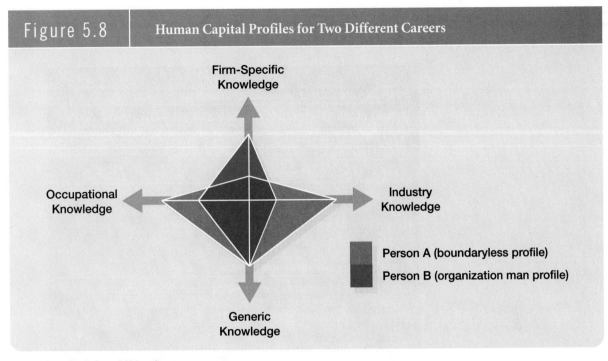

Figure 5.8 | **Human Capital Profiles for Two Different Careers**

Firm-Specific Knowledge

Occupational Knowledge

Industry Knowledge

Person A (boundaryless profile)
Person B (organization man profile)

Generic Knowledge

Source: Scott Snell, Cornell University.

pursuing boundaryless careers develop their human capital along dimensions of industry and occupational knowledge. That is, they may be experts in computer programming or have great insights into trends in the banking industry. In contrast, individuals pursuing more traditional careers develop their knowledge in ways specific to a given firm.

Both approaches can be beneficial, but they are not the same. Under the boundaryless career model, success depends on continually learning new skills, developing new relationships, and capitalizing on existing skills and relationships. These individuals place a premium on flexibility and the capacity to do several different types of tasks, to learn new jobs, to adjust quickly to different group settings and organizational cultures, and to move from one firm, occupation, or industry to another. Their employment security depends on their marketable skills rather than their dedication to one organization over time. A number of studies have shown that people with boundaryless careers find them very satisfying. Organizations can also benefit from boundaryless careers because it allows them to attract top talent from all over the world on a project-by-project basis.[26]

Track Career Stages

Knowledge, skills, abilities, and attitudes as well as career aspirations change as one matures. While the work that individuals in different occupations perform can vary significantly, the challenges and frustrations that they face at the same stage in their careers are remarkably similar. A model describing these stages is shown in Figure 5.9 on page 210. The stages are (1) preparation for work, (2) organizational entry, (3) early career, (4) midcareer, and (5) late career. The typical age range and the major tasks of each stage are also presented in the figure.

Figure 5.9	Stages of Career Development

Stage 5: Late Career (ages 55–retirement):

Remain productive in work, maintain self-esteem, prepare for effective retirement.

Stage 4: Midcareer (ages 40–55):

Reappraise early career and early adulthood goals, reaffirm or modify goals, make choices appropriate to middle adult years, remain productive.

Stage 3: Early Career (ages 25–40):

Learn job, learn organizational rules and norms, fit into chosen occupation and organization, increase competence, pursue goals.

Stage 2: Organizational Entry (ages 18–25):

Obtain job offer(s) from desired organization(s), select appropriate job based on complete and accurate information.

Stage 1: Preparation for Work (ages 0–25):

Develop occupational self-image, assess alternative occupations, develop initial occupational choice, pursue necessary education.

The first stage—preparation for work—encompasses the period prior to entering an organization, often extending until age 25. It is a period in which individuals must acquire the knowledge, abilities, and skills they will need to compete in the marketplace. It is a time when careful planning, based on sound information, should be the focus. The second stage, typically from ages 18 to 25, is devoted to soliciting job offers and selecting an appropriate job. During this period one may also be involved in preparing for work. Reality Check outlines how one organization, Career Edge, solves the problem of finding that first job when employers ask for experience. The next three stages entail fitting into a chosen occupation and organization, modifying goals, making choices, remaining productive, and, finally, preparing for retirement. In the remainder of the chapter we will examine some of the activities of primary concern to the student, who is likely to be in the early stages. Retirement planning will be discussed in Chapter 11.

career plateau
A situation in which for either organizational or personal reasons the probability of moving up the career ladder is low

Avoid the Plateau Trap

Author Judith Bardwick was the first to label the "plateauing" phenomenon.[27] A **career plateau** is a situation in which for either organizational or personal reasons the probability of moving up the career ladder is low. According to Bardwick, only 1 percent of

Reality Check

Career Edge Making a Difference

Career Edge is Canada's youth internship program that helps university, college, and high school graduates launch their careers as full-time paid interns. For recent graduates with no work experience, obtaining that first job can be difficult. They are caught in the cycle of "no experience, no job; no job, no experience." Career Edge helps graduates obtain that first job, which then leads, in most cases, to a permanent job. Career Edge also operates Ability Edge, a national internship program for graduates with disabilities. Career Edge contacts host organizations, who agree to provide an internship combining four elements: employment experience, learning, coaching, and networking. Because the interns are employed by Career Edge, employers do not have to fight for additional positions (a very difficult task in any organization), but can employ the interns from contract budgets. The interns are paid a stipend of $1,500 per month.

All job posting is done electronically. Employers post internships on the Career Edge website (www.careeredge.org). Underemployed or unemployed graduates can sign on and search for internships by sector, company, educational discipline, recency, city, length of internship desired, and so on. When a fit is found, the full job description is made available. The site also offers information on job search skills such as résumé and interview preparation.

Frances Randle, the former president and CEO of Career Edge, says: "The contact is made directly between the candidate and the host organization, because these students have to learn how to market themselves, and companies have to commit to the intern directly. Interns are looking for practical experience, increased confidence in their abilities, learning about their fields, getting experience in that field, having challenging work, developing a network, and getting feedback on performance, in that order. Companies want recent university graduates who are enthusiastic, flexible, interested in learning, yet with some technical skills and the ability to communicate."

Since opening for business in October 1996, when the youth unemployment rate was nearly 18 percent, Career Edge has placed 5500 interns at 850 companies. About 50 percent of the interns find full-time work with their host organizations.

the labour force will not plateau in their working lives. There are three types of plateaus: structural, content, and life. A *structural plateau* marks the end of promotions; one will now have to leave the organization to find new opportunities and challenges. A *content plateau* occurs when a person has learned a job too well and is bored with day-to-day activities. A *life plateau* is more profound and may feel like a midlife crisis. People who experience life plateaus often have allowed work or some other major factor to become the most significant aspect of their lives, and they experience a loss of identity and self-esteem when there is no longer success in that area. Figure 5.10 on page 212 lists some probing questions employees can ask themselves if they find themselves in, or trying to overcome, a career plateau.

Organizations can help individuals cope with plateaus by providing opportunities for lateral growth when opportunities for advancement do not exist. Companies with international divisions can encourage employees to take assignments abroad to

Figure 5.10	**Career Plateau Questions**

1. Do I accept high-visibility assignments?
2. Do I continue to advance my education, both formal and vocational?
3. Am I recognized by other leaders in my organization?
4. Am I routinely promoted?
5. Am I known as a versatile employee?
6. Do I continue to get larger-than-normal raises?
7. Do I rate at the high end of the performance ratings?
8. Do I have a plan with measurable objectives, and have I updated it recently?

Source: John Rosche, "Who's Managing Your Career?" *Contract Management* 44, no. 2 (February 2004): 20–22.

expand their horizons. Career enrichment programs can help people learn more about what gives them satisfaction within a company, as well as what kinds of opportunities will make them happiest if they go elsewhere.

Career Development Initiatives

Although career management involves a good deal of analysis and planning, the reality is that it needs to provide a set of tools and techniques that help employees gauge their potential for success in the organization. Informal counselling by HR staff and supervisors is used widely. As we mentioned earlier in the chapter, many organizations give their employees information on educational assistance, employment equity programs and policies, salary administration, and job requirements. Career planning workbooks and workshops are also popular means of helping employees identify their potential and the strength of their interests.

In a recent study undertaken by Drake Beam Morin, the six most successful career-management practices used within organizations are as follows:

- Placing clear expectations on employees so that they know what is expected of them throughout their careers with the organization.
- Giving employees the opportunity to transfer to other office locations, both domestically and internationally.
- Providing a clear and thorough succession plan to employees.
- Encouraging performance through rewards and recognition.
- Giving employees the time and resources they need to consider short- and long-term career goals.
- Encouraging employees to continually assess their skills and career direction.

In contrast, organizations also need to be mindful of the internal barriers that inhibit employees' career advancement. Generally, these barriers can include such things as the following:

- Lack of time, budgets, and resources for employees to plan their careers and to undertake training and development.

- Rigid job specifications, lack of leadership support for career management, and a short-term focus.
- Lack of career opportunities and pathways within the organization for employees.[28]

Career-Planning Workbooks

Several organizations have prepared workbooks to guide their employees individually through systematic self-assessment of values, interests, abilities, goals, and personal development plans. General Motors' *Career Development Guide* contains a section called "What Do You Want Your Future to Be?" in which the employee makes a personal evaluation. General Electric has developed an extensive set of career development programs, including workbooks to help employees explore life issues that affect career decisions.

Some organizations prefer to use workbooks written for the general public. Popular ones include Richard N. Bolles's *What Color Is Your Parachute?,* Andrew H. Souerwine's *Career Strategies: Planning for Personal Growth,* John Holland's *Self-Directed Search,* and John W. Slocum and G. Scott King's *How to Pack Your Career Parachute.*[29] These same books are recommended to students for help in planning their careers.

Career-Planning Workshops

Workshops offer experiences similar to those provided by workbooks. However, they have the advantage of providing a chance to compare and discuss attitudes, concerns, and plans with others in similar situations. Some workshops focus on current job performance and development plans. Others deal with broader life and career plans and values.

As mentioned earlier, employees should be encouraged to assume responsibility for their own careers. A career workshop can help them do that. It can also help them learn how to make career decisions, set career goals, create career options, seek career-planning information, and at the same time build confidence and self-esteem.[30]

Career Counselling

career counselling
The process of discussing with employees their current job activities and performance, their personal and career interests and goals, their personal skills, and suitable career development objectives

Career counselling involves talking with employees about their current job activities and performance, their personal and career interests and goals, their personal skills, and suitable career development objectives. While some organizations make counselling a part of the annual performance appraisal, career counselling is usually voluntary. Career counselling may be provided by the HR staff, managers and supervisors, specialized staff counsellors, or outside consultants. Several techniques for career counselling are outlined at the end of this chapter. (See the chapter appendix titled "Personal Career Development.") The obligation of employees to return the organization's investments in their development are outlined in Ethics in HRM on page 214. As employees approach retirement, they may be encouraged to participate in pre-retirement programs, which often include counselling along with other helping activities. Pre-retirement programs will be discussed in Chapter 11. Supporting career development activities can help the organization achieve retention and productivity goals as outlined in The Business Case on page 214.

Determining Individual Development Needs

Because the requirements of each position and the qualifications of each person are different, no two individuals will have identical developmental needs. For one individual, self-development may consist of developing the ability to write reports,

Ethics in HRM

Individual Investment or Organizational Investment?

Organizations such as Procter & Gamble and IBM invest a great deal of time and money in developing their professional sales staff and management personnel. Similarly, the federal government offers new university recruits up to six months of language training and tuition-paid university courses, as well as several weeks of skills training, within the first two years on the job.

Other organizations refuse to invest in the long-term development of their employees. They cite statistics suggesting that over one-third of university recruits will quit within the first year. In addition, they argue that other corporations will raid these highly trained personnel.

Do employees who have received the benefit of extensive development programs at the employer's expense have an obligation to remain with the organization so that it can realize a return on its investment?

The Business Case

The Value of Career Development Programs

Career development programs may not appear to offer the obvious return on investments that absenteeism or safety management programs offer. However, employers should start to measure the following in order to make the business case for career development:

Attraction: Do organizations establish reputations as "academies" that develop talent through solid career development and mentoring programs?

Retention: Do units with strong career development programs have higher retention rates of top talent than those without?

Employability: If organizations cannot guarantee lifetime employment, do they have a moral responsibility to provide career development programs that ensure that employees are employable?

Commitment: In those organizations with career development programs, is there a correlation between employee commitment and productivity?

One company did measure retention and commitment changes that occurred as a result of a career development program and the ROI was 190 percent. A manufacturer of technical equipment was experiencing a 37-percent turnover among highly valuable engineers. As part of the solution, the company created a high-potential development program. The participants attended workshops, identified learning projects, were paired with an executive sponsor and an external mentor. Eighteen months later turnover was down from 27 percent to 1 percent, and participants were more productive, as measured by their superiors.

Sources: Jack Ito and Celeste Brotheridge, "Does Supporting Employees Career Adaptability Lead to Commitment, Turnover, or Both?" *Human Resource Management*, Spring 2005, 44, 1, 05–19; Catherine Mossop, "Mentoring Can Drive Business Goals," *Canadian HR Reporter*, July 12, 2004, 6.

give talks, and lead conferences. For another, it may require developing interpersonal skills in order to communicate and relate more effectively with a diverse workforce. Periodic performance appraisals can provide a basis for determining each employee's progress. Conferences in which these appraisals are discussed are an essential part of self-improvement efforts.

In helping individuals plan their careers, it is important for organizations to recognize that younger employees today seek meaningful training assignments that are interesting and involve challenge, responsibility, and a sense of empowerment. They also have a greater concern for the contribution that their work in the organization will make to society. Unfortunately, they are frequently given responsibilities they view as rudimentary, boring, and composed of too many "make-work" activities. Some organizations are attempting to retain young managers with high potential by offering a **fast-track program** that enables them to advance more rapidly than those with less potential. A fast-track program may provide for a relatively rapid progression—lateral transfers or promotions—through a number of managerial positions requiring exposure to different organizational functions; it may also provide opportunities to make meaningful decisions. The Accelerated Executive Development Program (AXEDP, run jointly by the Public Service Human Resources Management Agency and the Canada School of Public Service), identifies candidates who can be developed very quickly—over the course of four to five years—to fill positions at the assistant deputy minister level. The program uses a number of development techniques, including stretch assignments, access to a coach and learning adviser, group learning sessions, and small action learning projects led by a trained facilitator.[31]

fast-track program
A program that encourages young managers with high potential to remain with an organization by enabling them to advance more rapidly than those with less potential

Career Self-Management Training

In response to the growing view that employees should assume greater responsibility for their own career management, many organizations are establishing programs for employees on how they can engage in *career self-management*. The training focuses on two major objectives: (1) helping employees learn to continuously gather feedback and information about their careers and (2) encouraging them to prepare for mobility.

The training is not geared to skills and behaviours associated with a specific job, but rather toward long-term personal effectiveness. Employees typically undertake self-assessments to increase awareness of their own career attitudes and values. In addition, they are encouraged to widen their viewpoint beyond the next company promotion to broader opportunities in the marketplace. For many, these external opportunities have not been seen as viable options, much less something the company would acknowledge. Participants might be encouraged to engage in career networking or to identify other means to prepare for job mobility, such as hearing reports from employees who made transitions to new job opportunities both within and outside the organization.[32]

Mentoring

When one talks with men and women about their employment experiences, it is common to hear them mention individuals at work who influenced them. They frequently refer to immediate managers who were especially helpful as career developers. But they also mention others at higher levels in the organization that provided guidance and support to them in the development of their careers. These executives and managers who coach, advise, and encourage employees of lesser rank are called **mentors.**

At times, individuals can be overly restrictive in their definitions of who constitutes a mentor, or what that mentor can do. The top ten myths about mentors are shown in Figure 5.11 on page 216. In reality, informal mentoring goes on daily within

mentors
Executives who coach, advise, and encourage individuals of lesser rank

Figure 5.11	Top Ten Myths about Mentors

Myth 1: *Mentors exist only for career development.* Sometimes the mentor focuses on formal career development. Sometimes the mentor is teacher, counsellor, and friend. Some mentors assume all these roles. This enhances both personal and professional development.

Myth 2: *You need only one mentor.* We can have multiple mentors in our lives. Different mentors provide different things and tap different facets of our lives.

Myth 3: *Mentoring is a one-way process.* Learning flows both ways. The mentor often learns from the protégé, so the growth is reciprocal.

Myth 4: *A mentor has to be older than the protégé.* Age does not matter. Experience and wisdom matter. Don't deprive yourself of learning opportunities from others who have rich experiences.

Myth 5: *A mentor has to be the same gender and race as the protégé.* The purpose of mentoring is to learn. Don't deprive yourself. Seek mentors who are different from you.

Myth 6: *Mentor relationships just happen.* Being in the right place at the right time can help, but the key to selecting a good mentor is what (not whom) you need. Don't be afraid to actively seek a mentor.

Myth 7: *Highly profiled people make the best mentors.* Prestige and success can be good, but good advice, leadership styles, work ethics, and the like vary by individuals. Good mentors are people who challenge you according to your needs, readiness, and aspirations.

Myth 8: *Once a mentor, always a mentor.* Over time, the mentor should pull back and let the protégé go his or her own way. Although the two may maintain contact, the relationship changes over time.

Myth 9: *Mentoring is a complicated process.* The most complicated part is getting out of a bad mentor relationship. If the relationship is not productive, find a tactful way to disengage.

Myth 10: *Mentor–protégé expectations are the same for everyone.* Individuals seek mentors for the same reasons: resources, visibility, enhanced skills, and counsel. But each individual brings different expectations. The key is understanding where the protégé is now, not where he or she should be.

every type of organization. Generally, the mentor initiates the relationship, but sometimes an employee will approach a potential mentor for advice. Most mentoring relationships develop over time on an informal basis. They frequently end that way, too. However, proactive organizations emphasize formal mentoring plans that assign a mentor to employees considered for upward movement in the organization. GE, for example, selects the top 20 percent of its performers and allows these people to choose their own mentors from a list of top executives. Under a good mentor, learning focuses on goals, opportunities, expectations, standards, and assistance in fulfilling one's potential.[33]

Figure 5.12 shows a list of the most effective features of mentors as well as partners. In order to form an effective mentoring relationship, an employee seeking a mentor should follow a few general guidelines:

1. *Research the person's background.* Do your homework. The more you know about your potential mentor, the easier it will be to approach him or her and establish a relationship that will work for both of you.

2. *Make contact with the person.* Have a mutual friend or acquaintance introduce you, or get involved with your potential mentor in business settings. That will help the mentor see your skills in action.

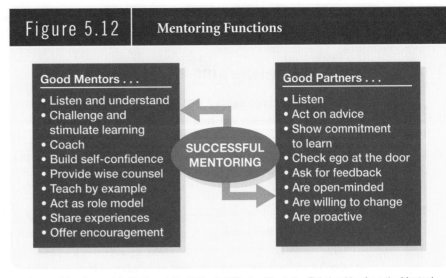

Figure 5.12 | **Mentoring Functions**

Good Mentors . . .
- Listen and understand
- Challenge and stimulate learning
- Coach
- Build self-confidence
- Provide wise counsel
- Teach by example
- Act as role model
- Share experiences
- Offer encouragement

SUCCESSFUL MENTORING

Good Partners . . .
- Listen
- Act on advice
- Show commitment to learn
- Check ego at the door
- Ask for feedback
- Are open-minded
- Are willing to change
- Are proactive

Source: Matt Starcevich, Ph.D. and Fred Friend, "Effective Mentoring Relationships from the Mentee's Perspective," *Workforce*, supplement (July 1999): 2–3. Used with permission of the Center for Coaching and Mentoring, Inc., http://coachingandmentoring.com.

3. *Request help on a particular matter.* Let the mentor know that you admire him or her, and ask for help in that arena. For example, you might say, "You're good at dealing with customers. Would it be OK if I came to you for advice on my customers?" Keep your request simple and specific.

4. *Consider what you can offer in exchange.* Mentoring is a two-way street. If you can do something for your potential mentor, then by all means, tell him or her.

5. *Arrange a meeting.* Once your specific request has been accepted, you're ready to meet with your potential mentor. Never go into this meeting cold. Set goals, identify your desired outcomes, and prepare a list of questions. Listen attentively. Then ask your prepared questions and request specific suggestions.

6. *Follow up.* After the meeting, try some of your potential mentor's suggestions and share the results. Express appreciation by identifying something in particular that was significant to you.

7. *Ask to meet on an ongoing basis.* After your potential mentor has had a chance not only to meet and interact with you, but also to see the value of what he or she can provide, you're in a good position to request an ongoing relationship. Suggest that you meet with him or her regularly, or ask permission to get help on an ad hoc basis.[34]

Highlights in HRM 5.4 on page 218 provides suggestions for the ground rules of mentoring. Organizations with formal mentoring programs include Shell International and the Bank of Montreal. Alternatively, given the importance of the issue, a number of mentoring organizations have begun to spring up. One such organization, Menttium Corporation, helps create and monitor mentoring partnerships so that the right people are matched with one another. When done well, the mentoring process is beneficial for both the pupil and the mentor. One survey found, for example, that 77 percent of companies with successful mentoring programs reported that they effectively increased employee retention.[35]

Highlights in HRM 5.4

Rules of Networking

Barbara Moses, president of BBM Human Resource Consultants and the author of *Career Intelligence: Mastering the New Work and Personal Realities*, states that networking is an increasingly important career skill. Networking is not about using someone to get ahead; rather, it is about expanding relationships and developing mutually supportive ones. Here are some do's and don'ts of networking:

Don'ts

- Don't call once a year, feigning friendship and concern, when it is obvious that the rest of the year you don't care if this person exists. Do keep in touch throughout the year, giving information about mergers and moves, or anything that might benefit the other person.
- Don't approach everyone you meet as a potential business lead. People you meet at parties or on planes should be appreciated for their characteristics, not for what they can do for you. Make new friends, not new contacts. Too often, people hang out in herds, actors with actors; bankers with bankers. Parties and planes offer the opportunity to add breadth to your world.
- Don't use information interviewing. Some guru suggested that calling someone and saying, "I am currently exploring careers. Can I meet with you to discuss your business?" is now seen as the transparent and tired job-search technique that it is. Volunteer work and internships will impress an employer more.

Successful mentoring is built on a common understanding of interests and "ground rules." Here are some to consider before establishing a mentor–protégé relationship:

Do's

1. Formalize the expectations with a written agreement that outlines the behaviours of each person.
2. Understand that either party can withdraw from the relationship at any time, and it is not necessary to provide an explanation.
3. All documents exchanged, such as company plans or résumés, will be treated as confidential.
4. The mentor cannot be solicited for a job. Doing so is grounds for breaking the relationship.
5. Respect each other's time. Arrive on time and prepared with a list of questions or topics to be discussed.
6. Provide feedback honestly. For example, the protégé could state, "This is not the kind of information I need at this stage" or the mentor might advise, "You should not skip meetings just because they are tedious; it is an important part of this company's culture to be visible at these meetings."

Source: Adapted from Barbara Moses, "The Right and Wrong Ways to Network," *The Globe and Mail*, September 4, 1997, B10. Reprinted with permission from The Globe and Mail.

The Mentoring Partnership matches skilled immigrants with established professionals who share the same occupation. This allows immigrants to tap into social and career networks that many Canadians take for granted, and has resulted in 70 percent of the protégés obtaining a job.[36]

Not surprisingly, mentoring is also being done over the Internet. E-mentoring brings experienced business professionals together with individuals needing counselling. Highlights in HRM 5.5 discusses the advantages of e-mail mentoring.

- *Society of Canadian Women in Science and Technology (SCWIST)* is an association that has assembled thousands of women in technology fields to act as online mentors to visitors to its website: www.harbour.sfu.ca/scwist/.
- *Peer Resources,* at www.mentors.ca, provides information about mentoring and coaching.

Even though participants in e-mentoring typically never meet in person, many form long-lasting e-mail connections that tend to be very beneficial. Still, most participants see these connections as supplements to—rather than substitutes for—in-company mentors.

Highlights in HRM 5.5

E-Mentoring

Virtual mentoring is often an excellent way for busy mentors (and equally busy protégés) to deal with time constraints. Those who are comfortable with e-mail and the Internet say that both have many advantages over real-time meetings. Because there are no geographic boundaries to e-mentoring (i.e., no need for the mentor and the protégé to be in the same city), a wider range of possible mentors is accessible. Scheduling is easier, since either party can log on at any time to ask questions or offer counsel. Because the mentor can take time to consider the answers to questions, the individual being mentored gets more reasoned responses. People seeking advice often maintain a log of their questions and the answers to them; these can be shared later with others in similar situations. Because e-mentoring is more efficient in many ways, mentors can advise more people. The technology can even help match mentors and protégés.

IBM Canada runs a pilot e-mentoring program in which 40 girls from grades seven and eight have been matched with computer programmers, sales personnel, and administrators, the goal being to stimulate their interest in technology careers.

The downside is that e-mentoring uses "flat" technology and so cannot convey emotions or facial expressions that in a face-to-face interaction often alert the mentor to underlying problems. That being said, the advantages of e-mentoring—quick feedback, well-considered responses, and more informal communication—make it one of the more popular ways for employees to build organizational know-how.

career networking
The process of establishing mutually beneficial relationships with other business people, including potential clients and customers

Networking

As the number of contacts grows, mentoring broadens into a process of **career networking.** As a complement to mentoring, in which relationships are more selective, networking relationships tend to be more varied and temporary. The networks can be internal to a particular organization or connected across many different organizations.

According to the Monster.com Career Center (http://content.monster.com/career/networking/), there are many ways to identify networking contacts. Some of the best places to consider are the following:

- Your university or college alumni association or career office networking lists
- Your own extended family
- Your friends' parents and other family members
- Your professors, advisers, coaches, tutors, and clergy
- Your former bosses and your friends' and family members' bosses
- Members of clubs, religious groups, and other organizations to which you belong
- All of the organizations near where you live or go to school

Through networking, individuals often find out about new jobs, professional trends, and other opportunities. In a survey of executives by the human resources firm Drake Beam Morin, 61 percent said that they had found new positions in the previous year through networking. Another study of 15 high-ranking executive women found that although many of them lacked formal mentors, they had successfully engaged in a kind of "360-degree" networking: The women made it a point to form and maintain relationships with people above, below, and at the same level as themselves, which helped advance their careers.[37]

Developing a Diverse Talent Pool

Today some organizations offer extensive career development programs that include programs geared to special groups, such as women, minorities, the older workforce, and dual-career couples. Let's examine some of these special programs more closely.

Recruitment and Development of Women

In Chapter 3 we discussed some of the current trends in the employment of women in jobs that until recently were held predominantly by men. Included among these jobs are management-level positions. Organizations are continually concerned, as a result of employment equity requirements and because of the need for strong leadership, about increasing the proportion of women they employ as managers.

A major employment obstacle for women, both skilled and unskilled, is the stereotyped thinking that persists within our society. Still another barrier has been that women in the past had fewer years of experience in the workforce and were not as likely as men to have professional training and preparation for entrance or advancement into management positions. This situation is changing, however. Today, there have been significant increases in the enrollment of women in programs leading to degrees in management and other professional fields. In addition, more women are enrolling in management seminars and certification programs that will further prepare them for higher managerial positions.

Eliminating Women's Barriers to Advancement

Despite some of the changes taking place, women in management traditionally have been at a disadvantage because they have not been part of the so-called "good old boys'" network, an informal network of interpersonal relationships that has traditionally provided a means for senior (male) members of the organization to pass along news of advancement opportunities and other career tips to junior (male) members. Women have typically been outside the network, lacking role models to serve as mentors.

To combat their difficulty in advancing to management positions, women in several organizations have developed their own women's networks. The Bank of Montreal has a women's network that any female employee can join in order to facilitate career development. Corporate officers are invited to regularly scheduled network meetings to discuss such matters as planning, development, and company performance. Network members view these sessions as an opportunity to let corporate officers know of women who are interested in and capable of furthering their careers. Employees who have had a senior manager take an interest in their careers have received more promotions and compensation than those who have not.[38]

As we mentioned previously, several online e-mentoring networks are available. Advancing Women is expressly devoted to working women (www.advancingwomen .com). In addition, an organization devoted to helping employers break down barriers to upward mobility for women is Catalyst, a not-for-profit organization. Catalyst (www.catalystwomen.org) not only courts corporate officers but also offers career

Artificial barriers or "glass ceilings" are being shattered by successful women executives and entrepreneurs.

© GETTY IMAGES

advice, job placement, continuing education, and related professional development for women of all ages. Catalyst is regarded as a leading resource for information on women and work.

There is substantial evidence that stereotyped attitudes toward women are changing. As women pursue career goals assertively and attitudes continue to change, the climate for women in management will be even more favourable. Research has shown that newer male managers tend to be more receptive to the advancement of women managers. That said, and despite the fact that more women hold managerial positions than they have in years past, the proportion of women in top echelons of management—board chair, CEO, president, executive VP—still remains extremely low, around 3 percent. Although these data suggest that there has been some progress, there is much left to do to break the "glass ceiling"—the invisible barrier of attitudes, prejudices, and "good old boys'" networks that blocks the progress of women who seek important positions in organizations.

Glass-Ceiling Audits

The glass ceiling can be defined as "those artificial barriers based on attitudinal or organizational bias that prevent qualified individuals from advancing upward in their organizations into management level positions."[39] A study commissioned by the Women's Executive Network in Canada revealed that the majority of women executives feel that they have hit the glass ceiling—that they face more barriers than similarly qualified men. Women hold only 14 percent of corporate officer positions in Canada's 500 largest corporations.[40] Glass ceiling audits are conducted to identify practices that appear to limit the access of upwardly mobile women to:

- Upper-level management and executive training
- Rotational assignments
- International assignments
- Opportunities for promotion
- Opportunities for executive development programs at universities
- Desirable compensation packages
- Opportunities to participate on high-profile project teams
- Upper-level special assignments

Organizations are increasingly conducting their own glass-ceiling audits prior to government review to avoid fines and externally imposed corrective action. These audits can document any ceilings and the reasons they exist. Self-audits are one step to tapping the potentials of a diversified workforce. Women are also breaking through the glass ceiling by starting their own businesses. As one entrepreneur put it, "It's not hard to break through the glass ceiling when you own it."

Preparing Women for Management

As noted earlier, opportunities for women to move into management positions are definitely improving. In addition to breaking down the barriers to advancement, the development of women managers demands a better understanding of women's needs and the requirements of the management world.

Many employers now offer special training to women who are on a management career path. They may use their own staff or outside firms to conduct this training. Opportunities are also available for women to participate in seminars and workshops that provide instruction and experiences in a wide variety of management topics.

In addition to formal training opportunities, women today are provided with a wealth of information and guidance in books and magazines. Business sections in bookstores are stocked with numerous books written especially for women who want a better idea of the career opportunities available to them. Many books are devoted to the pursuit of careers in specific fields.[41]

Popular magazines that contain many articles about women and jobs include *Working Woman, New Woman, Savvy, The Executive Female,* and *Enterprising Women.* These magazines are also recommended reading for men who want a better understanding of the problems that women face in the world of work.

Accommodating Families

One of the major problems women have faced is that of having both a managerial career and a family. Women managers whose children are at an age requiring close parental attention often experience conflict between their responsibility to the children and their duty to the employer. If the conflict becomes too painful, they may decide to forgo their careers, at least temporarily, and leave their jobs.

In recent years many employers, including CIBC, have inaugurated programs that are mutually advantageous to the career-oriented woman and the employer. These programs, which include alternative career paths, extended leave, flextime, job sharing, and telecommuting, provide new ways to balance career and family. These efforts are paying off. Both IBM and KPMG, for example, report that their programs have helped them retain and increase their numbers of women workers.

Nonetheless, maintaining a balance between work and family still appears difficult for employees. And it's now not just mothers who are feeling the tug-of-war between work and family. The number of stay-at-home dads has increased dramatically as well.[42]

Recruitment and Development of Minorities

Many organizations have specific career planning programs for minority employees. These programs are intended to equip employees with career planning skills and development opportunities that will help them compete effectively for advancement.

We observed in Chapter 4 that many employers make a special effort to recruit minorities. Once individuals from minority groups are on the job, it is important for employers to provide opportunities for them to move ahead in the organization as they improve their job skills and abilities. The province of Manitoba has a Career Gateway Program which recruits members of visible minorities for term placements in positions where there will be a future recruitment need, and then provides support for training and career development. The province also provides volunteer opportunities, which may then lead to placements. The federal government has a website (www.ncvm.gc.ca/) that offers tools for career planning for visible minorities through the National Council of Visible Minorities.

Advancement of Minorities to Management

The area of employment that has been the slowest to respond to employment equity appeals is the advancement of minorities to middle- and top-management positions.

HR has the primary responsibility to ensure that minorities have equal access to management positions.

While visible minorities tend to be better educated, they continue to have higher rates of unemployment and fewer executive positions.[43]

Visible minorities who aspire to higher levels in an organization are likely to find that their careers will start off like rockets but that as they reach the middle ranks a barrier makes it very difficult to move to the top. Visible minorities, including Aboriginals, tend to have reduced access to job interviews, higher rates of unemployment, and lower compensation.[44] Given the talent shortages existing in most industries, few organizations can afford to neglect the development of potential managers.

While minority managers do play a part in creating a better climate for groups that are discriminated against in advancement opportunities, top management and the HR department have the primary responsibility to create conditions in the organization that are favourable for recognizing and rewarding performance on the basis of objective, nondiscriminatory criteria.

Providing Internships

One approach to helping minority students prepare for management careers is to give them employment experiences while they are still in school. Most employers work with educational institutions to place and train interns, who are then frequently hired on a permanent basis after their schooling is finished. The Canadian Association for Internships was created to increase the number of internships available within Canadian organizations. [45]

Organizing Training Courses

As part of diversity management programs some organizations offer specialized programs to facilitate the promotion of visible minority employees. For example, the Department of Citizenship and Immigration has established a development program "for individuals in a visible minority whose potential to progress to senior (feeder groups) and executive levels would have been identified as early as possible in their career. The program features individual coaching, a career map, and a training and development path for each individual, with milestones and regular checkpoints. Developmental assignments, internship programs, and education leave are used to round up the development of these employees of high potential. Assessment of the program, by both the participating visible minorities and the implicated managers is mandatory."[46]

While minority managers do play a part in creating a better climate for groups that are discriminated against in advancement opportunities, top managers and the HR department have the primary responsibility for creating conditions within their organizations that are favourable for recognizing and rewarding performance on the basis of objective, nondiscriminatory criteria. Highlights in HRM 5.6 shows how to design a tailored approach to diversity planning.

Highlights in HRM 5.6

Diversity Recruitment That Works

Workforce diversity will help your organization reach new markets and develop greater intellectual capital. But to leverage diversity, you must first have it—at all levels.

Making It Real

To tap into and retain a diverse pool of top talent, HR professionals must:

- Understand demographic changes in the workforce.
- Ensure that majority groups aren't marginalized in the process.
- Educate staff that diversity is not synonymous with minority, and at the same time try to increase access and opportunities for people of colour and other minorities.
- Build long-term relationships with minority organizations, not look for quick fixes.
- Learn how to effectively interview diverse groups.
- Make sure that they're not just "grafting" minorities onto the organization without making appropriate internal culture changes that will enable them to thrive.
- Become the employer of choice for a diverse workforce.
- Ensure retention by developing a diversity-friendly culture.
- Foster a culturally sensitive work environment.
- Network for strategic alliances to enable long-term diversity recruitment.
- Measure the effectiveness of their recruitment efforts.

Putting Theory into Action

To maximize the effectiveness of diversity at all levels of an organization, the diversity has to first exist. Here are some methods an organization may want to try:

- Offer corporate internships and scholarships.
- Sponsor job fairs in minority communities. Develop partnerships with minority student professional organizations.
- Develop partnerships with minority organizations.
- Tap all known websites where résumés of diverse individuals can be found

Steps to Take Now

Consider implementing the following initiatives:

- Identify and begin building connections with national minority organizations, not only for access to university and college-age minority students, but for access to the organization's members who might be viable candidates for mid- and senior-level positions.
- Target recruitment advertising to minority publications.
- Use your internal employee resource groups. Ask minority employees to provide insight on effective places and ways to recruit diverse candidates. Obviously, this strategy depends on how your existing minority employees view the organization's commitment to diversity.
- Develop training for hiring leaders to ensure that diverse applicants aren't discounted in the interviewing process because they are different.

(continued on next page)

- Understand the "cultural norms" of diverse candidates.
- Partner with your marketing group to ensure that all marketing—not just recruitment advertising—features a diverse mix of individuals.

Source: Condensed from Patricia Digh, "Getting People in the Pool: Diversity Recruitment That Works," *HRMagazine* 44, no. 10 (October 1999): 94–98. Reprinted with the permission of *HRMagazine*, published by the Society for Human Resource Management, Alexandria, VA, via Copyright Clearance Center.

Other Important Talent Concerns

Employing the Older Workforce

Many of those working today will reach retirement age by 2010. This is estimated to create a worker shortfall. Even today, however, there is a definite trend by organizations to hire older people. The move has come both as a result of changing workforce demographics and as a change in the attitudes of employers and employees. Organizations realize that older workers have proven employment experience, have job "savvy," and are reliable employees. They are also an excellent recruitment source to staff part-time and full-time positions that are otherwise hard to fill. In addition, more older employees want to continue working, especially in light of financial concerns. There is a growing consensus that the labour force can be segmented by age, and divided into four groups: the traditionalists (born 1922–1945), the boomers (1946–1964), the Gen Xers (1965–1980), and the Gen Yers (born after 1981). Each of these groups may possess distinct values, and goals, and thus have different recruitment expectations. Highlights in HRM 5.7 captures some of the differences in recruitment strategies for each of these groups.

Retirees often return to the workforce at the behest of their employers, who can't afford to lose the knowledge accumulated by longtime employees or their reliable work habits that have a positive effect on the entire work group. To prevent an exodus of talent, employers will need to implement human resources strategies to help retain and attract the talent older workers have to offer. Moreover, as the workforce ages, employers will need to make workplace adaptations to help older workers cope with the physical problems they will experience, such as poorer vision, hearing, and mobility. For some firms, especially in jobs for which it's difficult to attract and retain skilled, reliable employees, older workers can be the permanent solution to an intractable problem. Many older workers gravitate to non-full-time forms of work, especially independent contracting or consulting, on-call work (such as substitute nursing or teaching), and temporary work in administrative or IT roles.[47]

Employing Dual-Career Couples

As discussed throughout this book, the employment of both members of a couple has become a way of life in North America. Economic necessity and social forces have encouraged this trend to the point that over 80 percent of all marriages are now

Highlights in HRM 5.7

The Four Generations

GENERATION	TRADITIONALISTS BORN 1922–1945	BABY BOOMERS BORN 1946–1964	GENERATION X BORN 1965–1980	GENERATION Y BORN AFTER 1981
Life-defining events	Great Depression, WWII, Korean War, rise of labour unions.	Civil rights movement, Cold war, Quebec crisis, Trudeau era.	Personal computers, AIDS, corporate downsizing, fall of Communism.	Digital age, reality TV, attacks of 9/11, corporate and government scandals.
Attitudes & values	Loyalty, dedication, sacrifice, honour, compliance, hard-working.	Personal growth, youthfulness, equality, ambition, collaboration.	Independence, pragmatism, results-driven, flexibility and adaptive.	Confident, optimistic, civic minded, innovative, diversity focused, techno-savvy.
Goal	To build a legacy.	To put their stamp on things.	To maintain independence in all areas of their lives.	To find work and create a life that has meaning.
Recruitment expectations	Formal, traditional methods of recruitment. Employer-driven negotiations.	In-person, relationship building, recruitment. Balanced negotiations.	On-site tours, meeting with current employees. Open employee-driven negotiation.	Review/evaluation of organization's reputation. Valued employee-driven negotiation.
Unique selling proposition	The organization's legacy, stability and strong loyalty to its employees.	The organization's market leadership and growth.	The organization's career growth, learning and development opportunities.	The organization's social responsibility, diversity, and creativity.
Key messages	Your experience will be valued here. You will be given the support to learn the organization's IT systems.	You can be a star here. Your personal growth is important to us.	You will work independently.	You will work with experts from across divisions. You will have a variety of experiences.

Source: Giselle Kovary and Adwoa Bauhene, n-gen People Performance Inc., "Recruiting the Four Generations," *Canadian HR Reporter,* May 23, 2005: R6.

dual-career partnerships
Couples in which both members follow their own careers and actively support each other's career development

dual-career partnerships in which both members follow their own careers and actively support each other's career development.

As with most lifestyles, the dual-career arrangement has its positive and negative sides. A significant number of organizations are concerned with the problems facing dual-career couples and offer assistance to them. Flexible working schedules are the most frequent organizational accommodation to these couples. Other arrangements include leave policies under which either parent may stay home with a newborn, policies that allow work to be performed at home, daycare on organization premises, and job sharing.

The difficulties that dual-career couples face include the need for quality child care, the time demands, and the emotional stress. However, the main problem these couples face is the threat of relocation. Many large organizations now offer some kind of job-finding assistance for spouses of employees who are relocated, including payment of fees charged by employment agencies, job counselling firms, and executive search firms. Organizations are also developing networking relationships with other employers to find jobs for the spouses of their relocating employees. These networks can provide a way to "share the wealth and talent" in a community while simultaneously assisting in the recruitment efforts of the participating organizations.[48]

Relocating dual-career couples to foreign facilities is a major issue that international employers face. Fewer employees are willing to relocate without assistance for their spouses. Many employers have developed effective approaches for integrating the various allowances typically paid for overseas assignments when husband and wife work for the same employer. Far more complex are the problems that arise when couples work for two different employers. The problems associated with overseas assignments of dual-career couples will be examined in greater detail in Chapter 15.

SUMMARY

1 In order to expand the talent pool of organizations—the number and kind of people available for employment—organizations must focus on multiple approaches to recruitment and career management. Outside sources for recruitment are especially useful for filling jobs with special qualifications and to acquire individuals with new skills, ideas, and perspectives. Which outside sources and methods are used in recruiting will depend on the recruitment goals of the organization, the conditions of the labour market, and the specifications of the jobs to be filled.

2 Employers usually find it advantageous to use internal promotion and transfer to fill as many openings as possible above the entry level. By recruiting from within, an organization can capitalize on previous investments made in recruiting, selecting, training, and developing its current employees. Further, internal promotions can reward employees for past performance and send a signal to other employees that their future efforts will pay off. However, potential candidates from the outside should occasionally be considered in order to prevent the inbreeding of ideas and attitudes.

The legal requirements governing employment equity make it mandatory that employers exert a positive effort to recruit and promote members of designated groups so that their representation at all levels within the organization will approximate their proportionate numbers in the labour market. These efforts include recruiting not only those members who are qualified but also those who can be made qualified with reasonable training and assistance.

Job opportunities may be identified by studying jobs and determining the knowledge and skills each one requires. Once that is accomplished, it is possible to plan job progressions. These progressions can then serve as a basis for developing career paths. Once career paths are developed and employees are identified on the career ladders, it is possible to inventory the jobs and determine where individuals with the required skills and knowledge are needed or will be needed.

Identifying and developing talent is a responsibility of all managers. In addition to immediate superiors, there should be others in the organization who can nominate and sponsor employees with promise. Many organizations use assessment centres to identify managerial talent and recommend developmental experiences in order that each individual may reach her or his full potential. Mentoring has been found to be valuable for providing guidance and support to potential managers.

Beyond recruiting per se, organizations also need to consider the progression of employees through a series of jobs. In this way, they can manage not only the immediate contribution of individuals to the organization, but also the long-term contribution throughout their careers. A career development program is a dynamic process that should integrate individual employee needs with those of the organization. It is the responsibility of the employee to identify his or her own KSAs as well as interests and values and to seek out information about career options. The organization should provide information about its mission, policies, and plans and what it will provide in the way of training and development for the employee.

In order to be successful, a career management program must receive the support of top management. The program should reflect the goals and the culture of the organization, and managerial personnel at all levels must be trained in the fundamentals of job design, performance appraisal, career planning, and counselling. Employees should be aware of the organization's philosophy and its goals; otherwise they will not know how their goals match those of the organization. HRM policies, especially those concerning rotation, transfers, and promotions, should be consistent with the goals. The objectives and opportunities of the career development program should be announced widely throughout the organization.

The first step in facilitating the career development of women is to eliminate barriers to advancement. Forming women's networks, providing special training for women, accepting women as valued members of the organization, providing mentors for women, and accommodating families have been found to be effective ways to facilitate a woman's career development.

While a diversified workforce is composed of many different groups, an important segment is minority groups. In addition to creating conditions that are favourable for recognizing and rewarding performance, many organizations have special programs such as internships that provide hands-on experience as well as special training opportunities. Other groups that require the attention of management are older workers and dual-career couples, who often need flexible working schedules.

KEY TERMS

assessment centre, 199
career counselling, 213
career networking, 220
career paths, 205
career plateau, 210
dual-career partnerships, 228

fast-track program, 215
job posting and bidding, 198
job progressions, 205
mentors, 215
nepotism, 190
outplacement services, 207

promotion, 206
realistic job preview (RJP), 196
relocation services, 207
transfer, 206
yield ratio, 194

DISCUSSION QUESTIONS

1. In what ways do executive search firms differ from the traditional employment agencies?

2. Explain how realistic job previews (RJPs) operate. Why do they appear to be an effective recruitment technique?

3. More than 50 percent of all MBAs leave their first employer within five years. While the change may mean career growth for the individuals, it represents a loss to the employers. What are some of the probable reasons an MBA would leave his or her first employer?

4. What are the advantages and disadvantages of filling openings from internal sources?

5. How might retired executives in any organization assist in the career management of current employees?

6. The chapter outlines the factors that attract executives (Figure 5.1) and those that attract students to employers (Figure 5.2). Compare and contrast the two lists. Why are there differences? How would you tailor your recruitment message to each group?

Is it stereotyping (and therefore potentially discriminatory) to develop different recruitment strategies for each group?

7. What contributions can a career management program make to an organization that is forced to downsize its operations?

8. What are some of the barriers to advancement opportunities for women in many organizations?

9. The Ottawa Police Services recognized that traditional recruiting practices may not work in a multicultural society. New immigrants may not view policing as an honourable profession, based on their previous experiences. Sitting in large groups hearing about opportunities in the police force is not effective, as many are reluctant to ask questions. Newcomers also do not know about the "ride along" program that most forces operate as a way to introduce potential recruits to the daily work of a police officer. Design a recruitment campaign for the police force that would be sensitive to the perceptions and needs of a multicultural candidate base.

INTERNET EXERCISE

Think about the job that you would like to obtain when you graduate. Use The Riley Guide (www.rileyguide.com/counsel.html) to find articles on exploring career options, how to research the labour market, etc. Prepare a paper based on your findings for your job.

HRM Experience

Career Management

We often think that successful people plan their careers out in advance and then work toward their goals in a very logical, sequential manner. Although some successes are designed and implemented this way, others are created through insight, preparedness, and taking advantage of opportunities as they arise.

Assignment

1. Form teams of four to six members. Identify three different people to interview about their careers. One person should be in the early stages of his or her career; one should be in midcareer; and one should be in the final stages of his or her career.

2. Ask each person to identify his or her career goals and how they have changed or are expected to change over time.

3. Ask each person to describe the sequence of events that led to where he or she is. How well does that story align with the traditional model of careers?

4. Ask each person what (if anything) he or she would do differently. Ask what advice he or she has for you about how to approach your career.

BIZFLIX EXERCISES

In Good Company: Carter Manages His Career

This chapter described many ways a company can recruit employees. The scenes from the film *In Good Company* show other ways a company can find new employees. Use the questions below as guides while viewing these scenes.

A corporate takeover brings star advertising executive Dan Foreman (Dennis Quaid) a new boss who is half his age. Carter Duryea (Topher Grace)—Dan's new boss—wants to prove his worth as the new marketing chief at *Sports America,* Waterman Publishing's flagship magazine. Carter applies his unique approaches while dating Dan's daughter, Alex (Scarlett Johansson).

These scenes come from the "Breaking News" segment that appears in about the first five minutes of the film. They follow Carter's presentation of his concepts for marketing cell phones to children under age five. Mark Steckle (Clark Greg) tells his staff that Teddy K. (Malcolm

McDowell) asked him to take over marketing at the magazine division of Waterman Publishing, Teddy K.'s recent acquisition. Carter Duryea discusses Mark's move to Waterman Publishing and the prospect of Carter following him to head advertising sales for *Sports America.* The film continues with Dan Foreman soon learning that Carter is his new boss.

What to Watch for and Ask Yourself

• Do these scenes show external or internal recruitment?

• Recall an earlier discussion in this chapter of the employee's role in career planning. What does Carter do to help his career?

• Review the earlier section "Career Development Initiatives." Which of those initiatives appear in these scenes? What is Mark Steckle's role in Carter's career development?

case study 1

UPS Delivers the Goods

When Jordan Colletta joined UPS in 1975, fresh out of school and newly married, he wasn't thinking about building a career. He just wanted some security. A former tracing clerk, Colletta managed to go a long way—to vice-president of the shipper's e-commerce sales team. His advancement in the company was steady, the result of careful planning through UPS's career development programs. By putting resources into such programs and helping reps set goals and develop skills, businesses can allow employees to grow within their organization and reduce turnover rates in the process, as UPS has found: its turnover rate among full-time workers is just 4 percent.

Developing salespeople starts with a clear mission. At UPS, employees meet annually with managers to identify their strengths and decide what skills they need for a new job within the company. "We lay the foundation for future development and map out immediate, midterm, and future goals," Colletta says. "When I was a tracing clerk, I told my supervisor that my goal was to become a district sales manager. I then became a driver, then a salesperson, and in 1986 I reached my goal."

UPS spends $300 million annually on classroom and online training for its employees. Career development entails implementing training programs and Internet career centres that can help companies grow their staffs. Employees take courses in order to acquire the pedigree that will make them candidates for management positions. But learning isn't just in the classroom. Mentoring programs in which managers coach lower-level employees are also valuable. "Mentors are especially important," Colletta says. "They help you understand the opportunities that are out there. They helped me see what I couldn't because I couldn't look that far ahead yet."

Progress must be routinely monitored. Employee reviews and 360-degree reports are good ways to track improvement. So is a manager's involvement. "Have an open door policy to keep the communication lines open," he says.

Finally, when it comes to encouraging participation in these programs, companies should highlight successes. Colletta announces promotions during weekly calls with UPS directors and immediately sends messages to his employees throughout the country. "It can't be about talk," Colletta says. "You can't say 'We have opportunities to develop you' and then look around and not see anyone getting ahead. You have to celebrate it."

Source: Adapted from Eduardo Javier Canto, "Rising through the Ranks," *Sales and Marketing Management* 153, no. 7 (July 2001): 66. Copyright © 2001. Reprinted by permission of Reprint Management Services; Lea N. Soupata, "Prepare for the Future," *Executive Excellence* 21, no. 11 (November 2004): 15–16.

QUESTIONS

1. What do you think are the main strengths of UPS's career development program?
2. What are the key outcomes that UPS wants to achieve?
3. What suggestions do you have for improving the program?

case study 2

Human Resources Career Progression

If you ask Andrea Taylor how she went from being a part-time clerk to the director of human resources at the White Pages in eight years, without hesitation she will tell you it was "networking." After graduating with a degree in sociology from Brock University, she did what many students do. She travelled in Europe for three months. When she came home, she completed her internship at Timothy's coffee shop and quickly left to join a photocopying service in a large downtown building where Bell Canada was a tenant. Eventually she made a contact in Bell who encouraged her to apply to Tele-Direct, which is commonly known as the Yellow Pages. Since there were no vacancies available, Andrea took a more stable job at Techno-Graph as a shipper and receiver. In the meantime, she persistently called Tele-Direct, once a week for a year, in order to see if there was a spot for her on the team.

Finally, a short-term contract position opened up in Ad Traffic, from 4 p.m. to midnight. Looking for another job before her contract expired, Andrea was encouraged by the same contact to apply to the human resources department because they were looking for a junior administration assistant. She was told not to apply since she was not a permanent employee. Regardless, she put her name in. On the very last day of her employment, she was called into the HR department and informed that she got the job. While conducting her various junior duties such as filing, posting job listings, and doing research, she discovered "that I just loved human resources." She checked out a local college offering certificate programs and began to take courses at night.

The contact who originally suggested that she apply was now leaving to become the national manager, and Andrea was selected to replace her as the new HR assistant manager. Moving up the ranks, Andrea became responsible for everything from new hires to collective agreements and the implementation of new human resources initiatives. When the company changed ownership and direction (and HR was outsourced), Andrea left the organization to seek employment where she could practise HR. Her networking served her well again when another contact turned down a job, but recommended Andrea—who became the HR director of a Web designing company. Three years later, another contact in the sales department from the Yellow Pages suggested she apply, and she became the HR director of the White Pages.

Today Andrea finds herself in a position where she is recommended for jobs. Unofficially, Andrea had created mentors out of contacts and the relationships have served both parties well. This happened because she treated every chance encounter with great respect that turned them into lifelong business relationships. "You never know who or where you will meet the next contact that changes your life."

QUESTIONS

1. How did Andrea become so successful in such a short period of time?
2. After reviewing the chapter, suggest all possible ways that Andrea prepared herself for career advancement.

CAREER COUNSEL

Visit the *Managing Human Resources* website (www.belcourt5e.nelson.com) for assistance in preparing a career plan.

NOTES AND REFERENCES

1. Sherry Sullivan, "The Changing Nature of Careers: A Review and Research Agenda," *Journal of Management* 25, no. 3 (1999): 457–84; Steve Prentice, "A Game Plan for Career Survival," *Canadian HR Reporter* 15, no. 11 (June 3, 2002): 27–28; Mark Tatge, "Prescription for Growth," *Forbes* 171, no. 4 (February 17, 2003): 64–67.

2. Jill Jusko, "CEO Turnover Slows in 2003," *Industry Week* 253, no. 7 (July 2004): 20; Yan Zhang and Nandini Rajagopalan, "When the Known Devil Is Better Than an Unknown God: An Empirical Study of the Antecedents and Consequences of Relay CEO Successions," *Academy of Management Journal* 47,

no. 4 (August 2004): 483–500; Nicholas Varchaver, "Glamour! Fame! Org Chart!" *Fortune* 150, no. 10 (November 15, 2004): 136–143.

3. Douglas P. Shuit, "Monster Board Games," *Workforce Management* 82, no. 2 (November 2003): 37–42.

4. Rob Yeung, "Finders Keepers," *Accountancy Magazine* 134, no. 1335 (November 2004): 42–44.

5. Canadian Interactive Reid Report, 2004.

6. David Brown, "Unwanted Online Job Seekers Swamp HR Staff," *Canadian HR Reporter*, April 5, 2004: 1.

7. Mike Martin, "Friends in Need," *The Globe and Mail*, April 13, 2005: C1.

8. Keith Swenson, "Maximizing Employee Referrals," *HRFocus* 76, no. 1 (January 1999): 9–10.

9. Allison Lampert and Kevin Dougherty, "Nepotism Charges Fly at School," *The Gazette*, December 6, 2005: A6.

10. "In Praise of Nepotism?" *Business Ethics Quarterly* 15, no. 1 (January 2005): 153–161; Richard Reeve and Gavin Sheridan, "Nepotism: Is It Back?" *New Statesman* 135 (September 29, 2003): 22–25.

11. Roger Kenny, "The Boardroom Role of Human Resources," *Corporate Board* 25, no. 150 (January–February 2005): 12–17.

12. Louis Uchitelle, "College Degree Still Pays, but It's Leveling Off," *The New York Times*, January 13, 2005: C1.

13. Jeremy O'Krafka, "HR Gains from Knowing How Schools Prepare Students for the Job Hunt," *Canadian HR Reporter*, April 25, 2005: 8.

14. A. Bissonette and V. Catano, 2003, *Revisiting the Efficacy of Recruiting Methods*, Paper presented at the 11th Congress of the European Association of Work and Organizational Psychology Lisbon Portugal.

15. Gail Pickard, "Vancouver Health Region Brands Its Advantages," *Canadian HR Reporter*, December 1, 2003: G3.

16. Max Messmer, "Recognizing Potential Stars by Promoting from Within," *Strategic Finance* 86, no. 5 (October 2004): 9–11.

17. Debbie Mack, "P&G Fights to Protect Its Bounty," *Corporate Legal Times* 13, no. 135 (February 2003): 64.

18. "How to Implement an Effective Process for a New HR Management System," *HRFocus* 82, no. 1 (January 2005): 3–4.

19. "The Pros and Cons of Online Recruiting," *HR Focus* 81 (April 2004 Supplement): S2.

20. Robert Rodriguez, "Filling the HR Pipeline," *HRMagazine* 49, no 9 (September 2004): 78–84; James W. Walker, "Perspectives," *Human Resource Planning* 25, no. 1 (2002): 12–14.

21. Paul W. B. Atkins and Robert E. Wood, "Self versus Others' Ratings as Predictors of Assessment Center Ratings: Validation Evidence for 360-Degree Feedback Programs," *Personnel Psychology* 55, no. 4 (Winter 2002): 871–905.

22. Ellen Ernst Kossek, Karen Roberts, Sandra Fisher, and Beverly Demarr, "Career Self-Management: A Quasi-Experimental Assessment of the Effects of a Training Intervention," *Personnel Psychology* 51, no. 4 (Winter 1998): 935–62; Shelly Green, "Attracting Top Talent Despite Business Challenges," *Journal of Career Planning and Employment* 62, no. 4 (Summer 2002): 24–28; Cynthia Jones, "Step by Step: Creating a Strategic

Management System for Career Services Delivery," *Journal of Career Planning and Employment* 62, no. 3 (Spring 2002): 21–27.

23. Peg O'Herron and Peggy Simonsen, "Career Development Gets a Charge at Sears Credit," *Personnel Journal* 74, no. 5 (May 1995): 103–106. See also Jules Abend, "Behind the Scenes at: Sears," *Bobbin* 39, no. 11 (June 1998): 22–26; Shari Caudron, "The De-Jobbing of America," *Industry Week* 243, no. 16 (September 5, 1994): 30–36; Edward E. Lawler III, "From Job-Based to Competency-Based Organizations," *Journal of Organizational Behavior* 15, no. 1 (January 1994): 3–15; Douglas T. Hall, "Accelerate Executive Development—At Your Peril!" *Career Development International* 4, no. 4 (1999): 237–39.

24. "How a Talent Management Plan Can Anchor Your Company's Future," *HR Focus* 81, no. 10 (October 2004): 7–10.

25. Elizabeth Craig, John Kimberly, and Hamid Bouchikhhi, "Can Loyalty Be Leased?" *Harvard Business Review* 80, no. 9 (September 2002): 24–34; Edward Potter, "Improving Skills and Employability in the 21st Century," *Industrial and Labor Relations Review* 55, no. 4 (July 2002): 739–45.

26. Suzanne C. de Janasz, Shery E. Sullivan, and Vicki Whiting, "Mentor Networks and Career Success: Lessons for Turbulent Times," *Academy of Management Executive* 17, no. 4 (November 2003): 78–92.

27. Judith Bardwick, *The Plateauing Trap* (New York: AMACOM, 1986). See also Judith Bardwick, *Danger in the Comfort Zone: From Boardroom to Mailroom—How to Break the Entitlement Habit That's Killing American Business* (New York: AMACOM Book Division, 1995); Max Messmer, "Moving beyond a Career Plateau," *National Public Accountant* 45, no. 7 (September 2000): 20–21; John Rosche, "Who's Managing Your Career?" *Contract Management* 44, no. 2 (February 2004): 20–22.

28. Larry Cambron, "Career Development Pays," *Far Eastern Economic Review* 164, no. 42 (October 25, 2001): 83.

29. For up-to-date career information and guidance as well as an opportunity for self-analysis, see Richard Bolles, *What Color Is Your Parachute 2005: A Practical Manual for Job-Hunters & Career-Changers* (Berkeley, CA: Ten Speed Press, 2004).

30. Susan Wells, "Smoothing the Way," *HRMagazine* 46, no. 6 (June 2001): 52–58; Heath Row, "Market Yourself," *Fast Company* 58 (May 2002): 24.

31. Uyen Vu, "Developing Public Service Leaders," *Canadian HR Reporter*, September 26, 2005: 11.

32. Thomas A. Stewart, "What's in It for Me?" *Harvard Business Review* 83, no. 1 (January 2005): 8.

33. de Janasz, Sullivan, and Whiting, "Mentor Networks and Career Success," 78–92.

34. Jeff Barbian, "The Road Best Traveled," *Training* 39, no. 5 (May 2002): 38–42; Kathleen Barton, "Will You Mentor Me?" *Training and Development* 56, no. 5 (May 2002): 90–92.

35. Elaine Biech, "Executive Commentary," *Academy of Management Executive* 17, no. 4 (November 2003): 92–94.

36. "Mentoring Program for Skilled Immigrants Receives Major Boost," *Market News Publishing*, November 2, 2005.

37. de Janasz, Sullivan, and Whiting, "Mentor Networks and Career Success," 78–92.

38. Audrey J. Merrell and Erika Hayes James, "Gender and Diversity in Organizations: Past, Present and Future Directions," *Sex Roles* 45, no. 5/6 (September 2001): 243.

39. Robert Schwab, "Dancing on the Glass Ceiling," *Colorado Biz* 31, no. 5 (May 2004): 18–23. A host of reports on glass ceiling issues can be found on the U.S. Department of Labor's website at www.dol.gov.

40. Asha Tomlinson, "Is There a War of the Sexes? It Depends on Who You Ask," *Canadian HR Reporter* 15, no. 18 (October 21, 2002): 3; David Brown, "Progress Slow, Incremental for Women," *Canadian HR Reporter* 16, no. 7 (April 7, 2003): 11.

41. The interested reader should find the following books very informative: Johanna Hunsaker and Phillip Hunsaker, *Strategies and Skills for Managerial Women* (Cincinnati, OH: South-Western, 1991); Marian Ruderman and Patricia Ohlott, *Standing at the Crossroads: Next Steps for High-Achieving Women* (New York: John Wiley and Sons, 2002).

42. "Mothers' Labor Force Participation," *Monthly Labor Review* 137, no. 5 (May 2004): 2.

43. Statistics Canada, "Census of Population: Earnings, Level of Schooling; Field of Study and School Attendance," www.statcan .ca/Daily/English/030311/d030311a.htm, www.statcan.ca/english/ Pgdb/labor20a.htm table 282-0002, Statistics Canada, CANSIM II, table 282-0002; Sharon Collins-Lowry, *Black Corporate Executives: The Making and Breaking of a Black Middle Class* (Philadelphia: Temple University Press, 1996).

44. Statistics Canada, "Census of Population."

45. University of Alberta, Canadian Association for Internship Programs, www.cs.ualberta.ca/~cafip/.

46. Treasury Board of Canada Secretariat, "Employment Equity," www.tbs-sct.gc.ca/ee/pmp/promo/cic-vm-mv2_e.asp.

47. Christopher Reynolds, "Boomers, Act II," *American Demographics* 27, no. 8 (October 2004): 10–12; Theresa Minton-Eversole, "Senate Forum Explores Ways to Keep Aging Workforce Working," *HR Magazine* 48, no. 10 (October 2003): 30.

48. Darin E. Hartley, "Tools for Talent," *Training and Development* 58, no. 4 (April 2004): 20–23.

Personal Career Development

We have observed that there are numerous ways for an employer to contribute to an individual employee's career development and at the same time meet the organization's HR needs. The organization can certainly be a positive force in the development process, but the primary responsibility for personal career growth still rests with the individual. One's career may begin before and often continue after a period of employment with an organization. To help you, as students and prospective employees, achieve your career objectives, this appendix is included to provide some background for your personal development and decisions. Also, complete the exercises at the end of each chapter in the Career Counsel section, and you will be able develop a personal career development plan.

Developing Personal Skills and Competencies

In planning a career, one should attend to more than simply acquiring specific job knowledge and skills. Job know-how is clearly essential, but one must develop other skills to be successful as an employee. To succeed as a manager, one must achieve a still higher level of proficiency in such major areas as communication, time management, self-motivation, interpersonal relationships, and the broad area of leadership.

Hundreds of self-help books have been written on these topics, and myriad opportunities to participate in workshops are available, often sponsored by one's employer.[1] One should not overlook sources of valuable information such as articles in general-interest magazines and professional journals. For example, the pointers on the basic skills of successful career management listed in Highlights in HRM 5.A1 are taken from a competency assessment conducted at Caterpillar.

Choosing a Career

Many years ago, when Peter Drucker was asked about career choice, he said, "The probability that the first job choice you make is the right one for you is roughly one in a million. If you decide your first choice is the right one, chances are that you are just plain lazy."[2] The implications of this statement are just as true today. One must often do a lot of searching and changing to find a career path that is psychologically and financially satisfying.

Highlights in HRM 5.A1

Career Competencies at Caterpillar

During the Caterpillar business unit's career development training process in Joliet, Illinois, the company compiled the following competencies as necessary for success within the reorganized, changing organization:

- *Interpersonal skills:* Possesses team-building and leadership skills; can effectively lead groups and facilitate group interaction
- *Problem-solving skills:* Can analyze and use problem-solving approaches
- *Communication skills:* Can verbalize articulately, make presentations, and write cogently
- *Leadership skills:* Is recognized by peers as a natural leader; accomplishes results without formal authority
- *Organization and planning skills:* Can manage time; sets and achieves goals
- *Technical skills:* Possesses education specific to assignments and job content; understands and uses appropriate level of technical skills
- *Responsibility:* Takes initiative; accepts accountability for own work and additional tasks for the good of the group
- *Assertiveness:* Able and comfortable with communicating openly and directly; demonstrates self-confidence and awareness of others' perceptions
- *Flexibility:* Can adapt to organizational changes and changing market needs; willingly considers new ideas and implements new ways of doing things
- *Judgment:* Can determine level of risk and appropriate action; accepts accountability for significant decisions

Source: Peggy Simonsen and Cathy Wells, "African Americans Take Control of Their Careers," *Personnel Journal* 73, no. 4 (April 1994): 99–108. See also David Dubois, "The Seven Stages of One's Career," *Training and Development* 54, no. 12 (December 2000): 45–50.

Use of Available Resources

A variety of resources are available to aid in the process of choosing a satisfying career. Counsellors at colleges and universities, as well as those in private practice, are equipped to assist individuals in evaluating their aptitudes, abilities, interests, and values as they relate to career selection. There is broad interest among business schools in a formal instructional program in career planning and development, and other units in the institutions, such as placement offices and continuing education centres, offer some type of career planning assistance.

Accuracy of Self-Evaluation

Successful career development depends in part on an individual's ability to conduct an accurate self-evaluation. In making a self-evaluation, one needs to consider factors that are personally significant. The most important internal factors are one's academic aptitude and achievement, occupational aptitudes and skills, social skills, communication skills, leadership abilities, and interests and values. The latter should include consideration of salary level, status, opportunities for advancement, and growth on the job. External factors that should be assessed include family values and expectations, economic conditions, employment trends, job market information, and perceived effect of physical or psychological disabilities on success.

Significance of Interest Inventories

Psychologists who specialize in career counselling typically administer a battery of tests. The *Strong Vocational Interest Blank* (SVIB), developed by E. K. Strong, Jr., was among the first of the interest tests.[3] Somewhat later, G. Frederic Kuder developed inventories to measure degree of interest in mechanical, clerical, scientific, and persuasive activities, among others. Both the Strong and the Kuder interest inventories have been used widely in vocational counselling.

Strong found substantial differences in interests that vary from occupation to occupation and that a person's interest pattern, especially after age 21, tends to become quite stable. By taking his test, now known as the *Strong Interest Inventory*, one can learn the degree to which his or her interests correspond with those of successful people in a wide range of occupations. Personality type can also be obtained by using a special scoring key on an individual's Strong Interest Inventory answer sheet. This key, developed by John Holland, provides scores on six personality types: (1) realistic, (2) investigative, (3) artistic, (4) social, (5) enterprising, and (6) conventional. These categories characterize not only a type of personality, but also the type of working environment that a person would find most satisfying. In the actual application of Holland's theory, combinations of the six types are examined. For example, a person may be classified as realistic-investigative-enterprising (RIE). Jobs in the RIE category include mechanical engineer, lineperson, and air-traffic controller. To facilitate searching for occupations that match one's category, such as RIE, Holland has devised a series of tables that correlate the Holland categories with jobs in the U.S. *Dictionary of Occupational Titles (DOT).*[4]

Another inventory that measures both interests and skills is the *Campbell Interest and Skill Survey (CISS).*[5] The CISS can be used not only to assist employees in exploring career paths and options but also to help organizations develop their employees or to reassign them because of major organizational changes. In completing the inventory, individuals report their levels of interest and skill using a six-point response scale on 200 interest items and 120 skill items. CISS item responses are translated into seven orientations—influencing, organizing, helping, creating, analyzing, producing, and adventuring—and further categorized into 29 basic scales such as leadership and supervision, to identify occupations that reflect today's workplace.

Highlights in HRM 5.A2 shows a sample profile for one individual. Note that at the top of the profile the range of scores is from 30 to 70, with 50 in the midrange. Corresponding verbal descriptions of scores range from very low to very high. Also note that on the profile two types of scores are profiled: interest (a solid diamond ◆) and skill (an open diamond ◊). The interest score ◆ shows how much the individual

Highlights in HRM 5.A2

Campbell Interest and Skill Survey: Individual Profile

SAMPLE　　　ORIENTATIONS AND BASIC SCALES　　　DATE SCORED 6/9/2005

ORIENTATIONS AND BASIC SCALES	INTEREST ◆	SKILL ◇	INTEREST/SKILL PATTERN
Influencing	39	47	
Leadership	42	49	
Law/Politics	42	46	
Public Speaking	36	40	Avoid
Sales	44	36	Avoid
Advertising/Marketing	52	42	
Organizing	47	58	Explore
Supervision	52	56	Explore
Financial Services	51	52	
Office Practices	58	65	Pursue
Helping	59	63	Pursue
Adult Development	48	56	Explore
Counseling	58	59	Pursue
Child Development	44	59	Explore
Religious Activities	42	49	
Medical Practice	68	61	Pursue
Creating	59	58	Pursue
Art/Design	66	64	Pursue
Performing Arts	54	52	
Writing	36	34	Avoid
International Activities	57	48	Develop
Fashion	69	70	Pursue
Culinary Arts	66	70	Pursue
Analyzing	32	36	Avoid
Mathematics	34	36	Avoid
Science	38	38	Avoid
Producing	57	62	Pursue
Mechanical Crafts	45	51	
Woodworking	63	58	Pursue
Farming/Forestry	54	60	Explore
Plants/Gardens	66	74	Pursue
Animal Care	62	71	Pursue
Adventuring	47	57	Explore
Athletics/Physical Fitness	56	56	Pursue
Military/Law Enforcement	52	54	
Risks/Adventure	59	58	Pursue

Profile scale ranges: VERY LOW 30　35, LOW 40　45, MID-RANGE 50, HIGH 55　60, VERY HIGH 65　70 likes the specified activities; the skill score ◊ shows how confident the individual feels about performing these activities.

There are four noteworthy patterns of combinations of the interest and skill scores as shown in Figure 5.A1: Pursue, Develop, Explore, and Avoid. For the individual whose scores are profiled in Highlights in HRM 5.A1, one would interpret the scores on the seven orientation scales (as shown in the left-hand column of the profile) as follows:

Influencing	Pursue
Organizing	Indeterminate
Helping	Pursue
Creating	Avoid
Analyzing	Avoid
Producing	Indeterminate
Adventuring	Develop

On the basis of such profiles, individuals can see how their interests and skills compare with those of a sample of people happily employed in a wide range of occupations. Completed answer sheets can be mailed to a scoring centre, or software is available and may be obtained for inhouse scoring.

Evaluating Long-Term Employment Opportunities

In making a career choice, one should attempt to determine the probable long-term opportunities in the occupational fields one is considering. While even the experts can err in their predictions, one should give at least some attention to the opinions that are available. Human Resources and Social Development Canada (HRSDC) publishes studies on career prospects. Many libraries have publications that provide details about jobs and career fields. In recent years, a considerable amount of computer software has been developed to facilitate access to information about career fields and to enable individuals to match their abilities, aptitudes, interests, and experiences with the requirements of occupational areas.

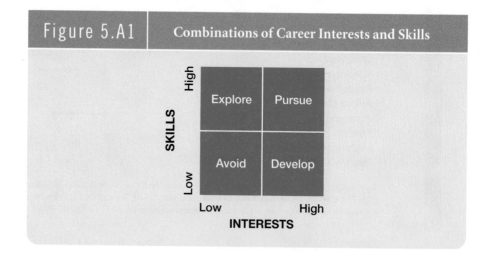

Figure 5.A1   **Combinations of Career Interests and Skills**

Choosing an Employer

Once an individual has made a career choice, even if only tentatively, the next major step is deciding where to work. The choice of employer may be based primarily on location, on immediate availability of a position, on starting salary, or on other basic considerations. However, the university or college graduate who has prepared for a professional or managerial career is likely to have more sophisticated concerns. Douglas Hall proposes that people frequently choose an organization on the basis of its climate and how it appears to fit their needs. According to Hall, people with high needs for achievement may choose aggressive, achievement-oriented organizations. Power-oriented people may choose influential, prestigious, power-oriented organizations. Affiliative people may choose warm, friendly, supportive organizations. We know that people whose needs fit with the climate of an organization are rewarded more and are more satisfied than those who fit in less well, so it is natural to reason that fit would also be a factor in one's choice of an organization. As noted at the outset of this chapter, it is increasingly unlikely that individuals will remain with only one organization for their entire career. The old model of "the organization man" who starts and stays with the same company is being replaced by a more flexible career model that Hall calls a "protean" career (based on the Greek god Proteus, who could change shape at will).[6]

entrepreneur
One who starts, organizes, manages, and assumes responsibility for a business or other enterprise

Becoming an Entrepreneur

USING THE INTERNET

To determine if you have what it takes to be an entrepreneur, go to:

www.wd.gc.ca/tools/xindex_e.asp of the Government of Canada.

At the opening of the century, no discussion of careers would be complete if entrepreneurship opportunities were not mentioned. Being an **entrepreneur**— one who starts, organizes, manages, and assumes responsibility for a business or other enterprise—offers a personal challenge that many individuals prefer over being an employee. Small businesses are typically run by entrepreneurs who accept the personal financial risks that go with owning a business but who also benefit directly from the success of the business.[7]

Since the details of organizing a business are beyond the scope of this book, Figure 5.A2 on page 242 is presented to provide an overview of the basic steps in starting a new business.[8]

Keeping a Career in Perspective

For most people, work is a primary factor in the overall quality of their lives. It provides a setting for satisfying practically the whole range of human needs and is thus of considerable value to the individual. Nevertheless, it is advisable to keep one's career in perspective so that other important areas of life are not neglected.

Developing Off-the-Job Interests

Satisfaction with one's life is a product of many forces. Some of the more important ingredients are physical health, emotional well-being, financial security, harmonious

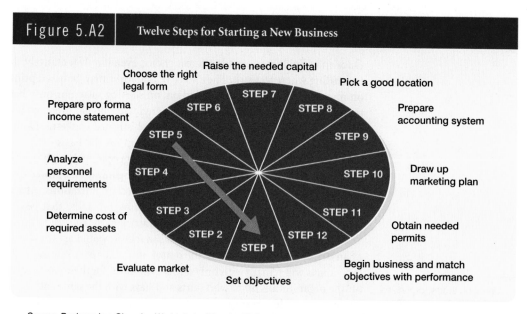

Figure 5.A2 | Twelve Steps for Starting a New Business

Raise the needed capital

Choose the right legal form

Pick a good location

Prepare pro forma income statement

Prepare accounting system

Analyze personnel requirements

Draw up marketing plan

Determine cost of required assets

Obtain needed permits

Evaluate market

Begin business and match objectives with performance

Set objectives

STEP 1, STEP 2, STEP 3, STEP 4, STEP 5, STEP 6, STEP 7, STEP 8, STEP 9, STEP 10, STEP 11, STEP 12

Source: *Business in a Changing World*, 3rd edition, by W. Cunningham, R. Aldag, and S. Block: 139 © 1993. Reprinted with permission of South-Western, a division of Thomson Learning: www.thomsonrights.com. Fax 800-730-2215.

interpersonal relationships, freedom from too much stress, and achievement of one's goals. While a career can provide some of the satisfaction that one needs, most people find it necessary to turn to interests and activities outside their career. Off-the-job activities not only provide a respite from daily work responsibilities but also offer satisfaction in areas unrelated to work.

Balancing Marital and/or Family Life

The career development plans of an individual as well as of an organization must take into account the needs of spouses and children. As we have said, the one event that often poses the greatest threat to family needs is relocation. Conflict between a desire to advance in one's career and a desire to stay in one place and put down family roots often borders on the disastrous. Many employers now provide assistance in this area, including relocation counselling, in an effort to reduce the severity of the pain that can accompany relocations.

While relocation may be the most serious threat to employees with families, there are also other sources of conflict between career and family. Some work-related sources of conflict are number of hours worked per week, frequency of overtime, and the presence and irregularity of shift work. In addition, ambiguity and/or conflict within the employee's work role, low level of leader support, and disappointments due to unfulfilled expectations affect one's life away from the job. Some family-related sources of conflict include the need to spend an unusually large amount of time with the family and its concerns, spouse employment patterns, and dissimilarity in a couple's career orientations. Those who are "married" to their jobs to the extent that they fail to provide the attention and caring essential to marriage and family relationships can be said to lack an appreciation for the balance needed for a satisfying life. One should always be aware that "to be a success in the business world takes hard work, long hours, persistent effort, and constant attention. To be a success in marriage takes hard work, long hours, persistent effort, and constant attention. The problem is giving each its due and not shortchanging the other."[9]

Planning for Retirement

While retirement appears to be a long way off for the individual who is still in the early stages of a career, it is never too early to plan for it. In order to enjoy retirement one should prepare for it by giving careful attention to health, finances, family, and interpersonal relationships throughout one's adult life. While most large organizations have pre-retirement programs, many participants in those programs are unfortunately already too close to actual retirement. Thus it is each individual's responsibility to plan early in order to have time to set the stage for a healthy and satisfying retirement as free as possible from worries—especially those that could have been avoided or minimized earlier in life. While employer-sponsored pre-retirement programs are usually considered very helpful by the participants, as we will see in Chapter 11, they are not a substitute for continual personal concern for oneself.

KEY TERMS

entrepreneur, 241

NOTES AND REFERENCES

1. A selection of self-help publications on a variety of topics may be found in any bookstore. College and university bookstores typically have a wide selection in their trade or general books department. Two particularly useful books might be Edward Crip and Richard Mansfield, *The Value-Added Employee: 31 Competencies to Make Yourself Irresistible to Any Company* (London: Butterworth-Heinemann, 2001); Daniel Goleman, *Emotional Intelligence* (New York: Bantam Books, 1995).

2. Mary Harrington Hall, "A Conversation with Peter Drucker," *Psychology Today* (March 1968): 22.

3. E. K. Strong, Jr., of Stanford University, was active in the measurement of interests from the early 1920s until his death in 1963. Since then his work has been carried on by the staff of the Measurement Research Centre, University of Minnesota. The Strong Interest Inventory is distributed by Consulting Psychologists Press, Inc., P.O. Box 60070, Palo Alto, CA 94306, to qualified people under an exclusive license from the publisher, Stanford University Press.

4. Gary D. Gottfredson and John L. Holland, *Dictionary of Holland Occupational Codes* (Lutz, FL: Psychological Assessment Resources, December 1996).

5. The *Campbell Interest and Skill Survey* (copyright 1992) is published and distributed by NCS Assessments, P.O. Box 1416, Minneapolis, MN 55440. For recent research in this area, see David Lubinski, Camilla P. Benbow, and Jennifer Ryan, "Stability of Vocational Interests among the Intellectually Gifted from Adolescence to Adulthood: A 15-Year Longitudinal Study," *Journal of Applied Psychology* 80, no. 1 (February 1995): 196–200.

6. Douglas T. Hall and Jonathan E. Moss, "The New Protean Career Contract: Helping Organizations and Employees Adapt," *Organizational Dynamics* 26, no. 3 (Winter 1998): 22–37. See also Douglas T. Hall, *The Career Is Dead, Long Live the Career: A Relational Approach to Careers* (San Francisco: Jossey-Bass,

1996); Douglas T. Hall, "Protean Careers of the 21st Century," *Academy of Management Executive* 10, no. 4 (1996): 8–16; Douglas T. Hall and Associates, *Career Development in Organizations* (San Francisco: Jossey-Bass, 1986); Yue-Wah Chay and Samuel Aryee, "The Moderating Influence of Career Growth Opportunities on Careerist Orientation and Work Attitudes: Evidence of the Protean Career Era in Singapore," *Journal of Organizational Behavior* 20, no. 5 (September 1999): 613–23.

7. Abraham Sagie and Dov Abraham, "Achievement Motive and Entrepreneurial Orientation: A Structural Analysis," *Journal of Organizational Behavior* 20, no. 3 (May 1999): 375–87; Eleni T. Stavrous, "Succession in Family Businesses: Exploring the Effects of Demographic Factors on Offspring Intentions to Join and Take Over the Business," *Journal of Small Business Management* 37, no. 3 (July 1999): 43–61; Julie Rose, "The New Risk Takers," *Fortune Small Business* 12, no. 2 (March 2002): 28–34.

8. For information on starting a business, the interested reader might look into Bob Adams, *Adams Streetwise Small Business Startup* (Holbrook, MA: Adams Media Corporation, 1996); Linda Pinson and Jerry Jinnett, *Anatomy of a Business Plan: Starting Smart, Building a Business and Securing Your Company's Future* (Chicago: Upstart, 1996); Kenneth Cook, *AMA Complete Guide to Strategic Planning for Small Business* (Lincolnwood, IL: NTC Business Books, 1995); Priscilla Y. Huff, *101 Best Small Businesses for Women* (Rocklin, CA: Prima, 1996); Constance Jones, *The 220 Best Franchises to Buy: The Sourcebook for Evaluating the Best Franchise Opportunities* (New York: Bantam Doubleday Dell, 1993).

9. Christopher Caggiano, "Married . . . with Companies," *Inc.* 17, no. 6 (May 1995): 68–76; Sue Shellenbarger, "Sustaining a Marriage When Job Demands Seem to Be Endless," *The Wall Street Journal*, December 8, 1999, B1.

chapter 6

Employee Selection

After studying this chapter, you should be able to

objective 1

Explain the objectives of the personnel selection process.

objective 2

Identify the various sources of information used for personnel selection.

objective 3

Compare the value of different types of employment tests.

objective 4

Illustrate the different approaches to conducting an employment interview.

objective 5

Describe the various decision strategies for selection.

There is perhaps no more important topic in HRM than employee selection. If it is true that organizations succeed or fail on the basis of talents of employees, then managers directly influence that success by the people they hire. Regardless of whether the company is large or small, hiring the best and the brightest employees lays a strong foundation for excellence. Alternatively, it is common to hear managers who don't recognize this point lament the inordinate amount of time they spend trying to fix bad selection decisions. In addition, employment equity legislation has also provided an impetus for making sure that the selection process is done well. The bottom line is, good selection decisions make a difference. So do bad ones.

Matching People and Jobs

selection
The process of choosing individuals who have relevant qualifications to fill existing or projected job openings

In conjunction with the recruiting process, which is designed to increase the number of applicants whose qualifications meet job requirements and the needs of the organization, **selection** is the process of reducing that number and choosing from among those individuals who have the relevant qualifications.

Figure 6.1 shows in broad terms that the overall goal of selection is to maximize "hits" and avoid "misses." Hits are accurate predictions and misses are inaccurate ones. The cost of one type of miss would be the direct and indirect expense of hiring an employee who turns out to be unsuccessful. The cost of the other type of miss is an opportunity cost—someone who could have been successful didn't get a chance.

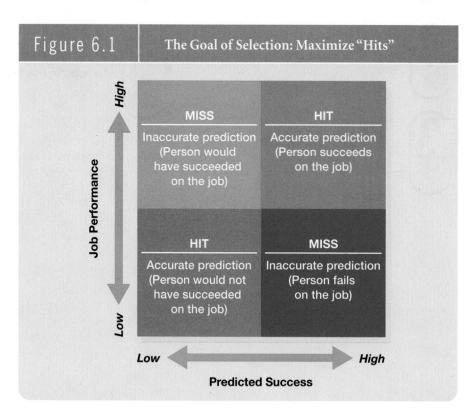

Figure 6.1   The Goal of Selection: Maximize "Hits"

Job Performance High	**MISS** Inaccurate prediction (Person would have succeeded on the job)	**HIT** Accurate prediction (Person succeeds on the job)
Low	**HIT** Accurate prediction (Person would not have succeeded on the job)	**MISS** Inaccurate prediction (Person fails on the job)
	Low Predicted Success High	

While the overall selection program is often the formal responsibility of the HR department, line managers typically make the final decision about hiring people in their unit. It is important therefore that managers understand the objectives, policies, and practices used for selection. In that way, they can be highly involved in the process from the very beginning. Those responsible for making selection decisions should have adequate information upon which to base their decisions. Information about the jobs to be filled, knowledge of the ratio of job openings to the number of applicants, and as much relevant information as possible about the applicants themselves are essential for making sound decisions.

Person-Job Fit: Beginning with Job Analysis

In Chapter 4 we discussed the process of analyzing jobs to develop job descriptions and specifications. Job specifications, in particular, help identify the *individual competencies* employees need for success—the knowledge, skills, abilities, and other factors (KSAOs) that lead to superior performance. By identifying competencies through job analysis, managers can then use selection methods such as interviews, references, psychological tests, and the like to measure applicant KSAOs against the competencies required for the job. This is often referred to as *person-job fit*. Research has demonstrated that complete and unambiguous specification of required competencies (via job analysis) reduces the influence of racial and gender stereotypes and helps the interviewer differentiate between qualified and unqualified applicants. Research also shows that applicants whose KSAOs are well matched to the jobs they are hired for perform better and are more satisfied.[1]

Person-Organization Fit

In addition to the requirements of the job, many organizations also place a priority on finding individuals that meet broader organizational requirements. Companies such as Edward Jones, a Toronto-based brokerage firm, and Intuit, an Edmonton-based financial software company, place a high priority on selecting individuals who match the values and culture of the organization. Although there are at times potential concerns that this may create an overly uniform workforce (and raises diversity concerns), the need for teamwork and flexibility has created a keen interest in this type of person-organization fit. In many instances, managers will pass up potential employees if they don't embrace the values of the organization—even if they have excellent technical skills for the job.[2]

Ordinarily, managers are well acquainted with the requirements pertaining to skill, physical demands, and other factors for jobs in their organizations. Interviewers and other members of the HR department who participate in selection should maintain a close liaison with the various departments so that they can become thoroughly familiar with the jobs and competencies needed to perform them.

The Selection Process

In most organizations, selection is an ongoing process. Turnover inevitably occurs, leaving vacancies to be filled by applicants from inside or outside the organization or by individuals whose qualifications have been assessed previously. It is common to have a waiting list of applicants who can be called when permanent or temporary positions become open.

objective 1

The number of steps in the selection process and their sequence will vary, not only with the organization but also with the type and level of jobs to be filled. Each step should be evaluated in terms of its contribution. The steps that typically make up the selection process are shown in Figure 6.2. Not all applicants will go through all of these steps. Some may be rejected after the preliminary interview, others after taking tests, and so on.

As shown in Figure 6.2, organizations use several different means to obtain information about applicants. These include application blanks, interviews, tests, and background investigations. Regardless of the method used, it is essential that it conform to accepted ethical standards, including privacy and confidentiality, as well as legal requirements. Above all, it is essential that the information obtained be sufficiently reliable and valid.

Obtaining Reliable and Valid Information

reliability
> The degree to which interviews, tests, and other selection procedures yield comparable data over time and alternative measures

The degree to which interviews, tests, and other selection procedures yield comparable data over a period of time is known as **reliability.** For example, unless interviewers judge the capabilities of a group of applicants to be the same today as they did yesterday, their judgments are unreliable (that is, unstable). Likewise, a test that gives widely different scores when it is administered to the same individual a few days apart is unreliable.

Reliability also refers to the extent to which two or more methods (interviews and tests, for example) yield similar results or are consistent. Inter-rater reliability—agreement between two or more raters—is one measure of a method's consistency. Unless the data on which selection decisions are based are reliable, in terms of both stability and consistency, they cannot be used as predictors.

validity
> The degree to which a test or selection procedure measures a person's attributes

In addition to having reliable information pertaining to a person's suitability for a job, the information must be as valid as possible. **Validity** refers to what a test or other selection procedure measures and how well it measures it. In the context of personnel selection, validity is essentially an indicator of the extent to which data from

USING THE INTERNET

The *Canadian Human Rights Reporter* is a useful source of information on human rights cases and legal guidelines for screening and assessment at:

www.cdn-hr-reporter.ca

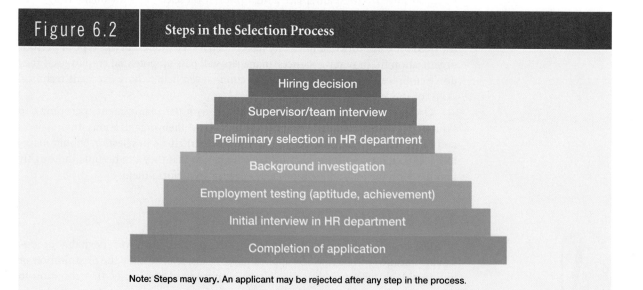

Figure 6.2	Steps in the Selection Process

Hiring decision

Supervisor/team interview

Preliminary selection in HR department

Background investigation

Employment testing (aptitude, achievement)

Initial interview in HR department

Completion of application

Note: Steps may vary. An applicant may be rejected after any step in the process.

a procedure (interview or test, for example) are predictive of job performance. Like a new medicine, a selection procedure must be validated before it is used. There are two reasons for validating a procedure. First, validity is directly related to increases in employee productivity, as we will demonstrate later. Second, employment equity regulations emphasize the importance of validity in selection procedures.[3] Although we commonly refer to "validating" a test or interview procedure, validity in the technical sense refers to the inferences made from the use of a procedure, not to the procedure itself.

Three recognized approaches to validation are: criterion-related validity, content validity, and construct validity.

Criterion-Related Validity

criterion-related validity
The extent to which a selection tool predicts, or significantly correlates with, important elements of work behaviour

The extent to which a selection tool predicts, or significantly correlates with, important elements of work behaviour is known as **criterion-related validity.** Performance on a test, for example, is compared with actual production records, supervisory ratings, training outcomes, and other measures of success that are appropriate to each type of job. In a sales job, for example, it is common to use sales figures as a basis for comparison. In production jobs, quantity and quality of output may provide the best criteria of job success.

concurrent validity
The extent to which test scores (or other predictor information) match criterion data obtained at about the same time from current employees

There are two types of criterion-related validity: concurrent and predictive. **Concurrent validity** involves obtaining criterion data from *current employees* at about the same time that test scores (or other predictor information) are obtained. For example, a supervisor is asked to rate a group of clerical employees on the quantity and quality of their performance. These employees are then given a clerical aptitude test, and the test scores are compared with the supervisory ratings to determine the degree of relationship between them. **Predictive validity,** on the other hand, involves testing *applicants* and obtaining criterion data *after* those applicants have been hired and have been on the job for some indefinite period. For example, applicants are given a clerical aptitude test, which is then filed away for later study. After the individuals have been on the job for several months, supervisors, who should not know the employees' test scores, are asked to rate them on the quality and quantity of their performance. Test scores are then compared with the supervisors' ratings.

predictive validity
The extent to which applicants' test scores match criterion data obtained from those applicants/ employees after they have been on the job for some indefinite period

Regardless of the method used, cross-validation is essential. **Cross-validation** is a process in which a test or battery of tests is administered to a different sample (drawn from the same population) for the purpose of verifying the results obtained from the original validation study.

cross-validation
Verifying the results obtained from a validation study by administering a test or test battery to a different sample (drawn from the same population)

Correlational methods are generally used to determine the relationship between predictor information such as test scores and criterion data. The correlation scatterplots in Figure 6.3 on page 250 illustrate the difference between a selection test of zero validity (A) and one of high validity (B). Each dot represents a person. Note that in scatterplot A there is no relationship between test scores and success on the job; in other words, the validity is zero. In scatterplot B, those who score low on the test tend to have low success on the job, whereas those who score high on the test tend to have high success on the job, indicating high validity. In actual practice we would apply a statistical formula to the data to obtain a coefficient of correlation referred to as a *validity coefficient.* Correlation coefficients range from 0.00, denoting a complete absence of relationship, to +1.00 and to −1.00, indicating a perfect positive and perfect negative relationship, respectively.

A thorough survey of the literature shows that the averages of the maximum validity coefficients are 0.45 where tests are validated against *training* criteria and 0.35 where tests are validated against job *proficiency* criteria. These figures represent the predictive power

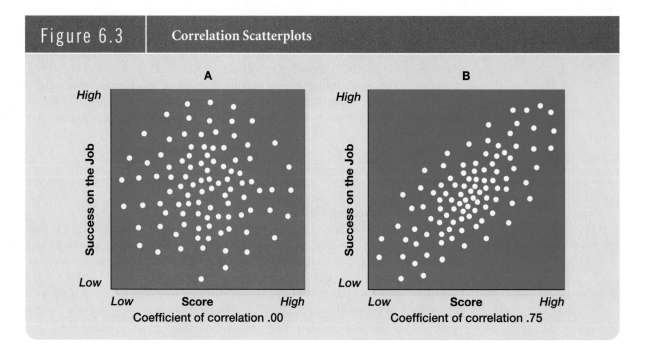

Figure 6.3 | **Correlation Scatterplots**

of single tests.[4] A higher validity may be obtained by combining two or more tests or other predictors (interview or biographical data, for instance), using the appropriate statistical formulas. The higher the overall validity, the greater the chances of hiring individuals who will be the better performers. The criterion-related method is generally preferred to other validation approaches because it is based on empirical data.

For several decades, personnel psychologists believed that validity coefficients had meaning only for the specific situation (job and organization). More recently, as a result of several research studies—many involving clerical jobs—it appears that validity coefficients can often be generalized across situations, hence the term **validity generalization.** When there are adequate data to support the existence of validity generalization, the development of selection procedures can become less costly and time-consuming. The process involves analyzing jobs and situations and, on the basis of these analyses, consulting tables of generalized validities from previous studies using various predictors in similar circumstances. It is advisable for organizations to employ the services of an industrial-organizational psychologist experienced in test validation to develop the selection procedures.[5]

validity generalization
The extent to which validity coefficients can be generalized across situations

Content Validity

When it is not feasible to use the criterion-related approach, often because of limited samples of individuals, the content method is used. **Content validity** is assumed to exist when a selection instrument, such as a test, adequately samples the knowledge and skills needed to perform a particular job.

The closer the content of the selection instrument is to actual work samples or behaviours, the greater its content validity. For example, a civil service examination for accountants has high content validity when it requires the solution of accounting problems representative of those found on the job. Asking an accountant to lift a 27-kilogram box, however, is a selection procedure that has content validity only if the job description indicates that accountants must be able to meet this requirement.

content validity
The extent to which a selection instrument, such as a test, adequately samples the knowledge and skills needed to perform a particular job

Content validity is the most direct and least complicated type of validity to assess. It is generally used to evaluate job knowledge and skill tests, to be described later. Unlike the criterion-related method, content validity is not expressed in correlational terms. Instead, an index is computed (from evaluations of an expert panel) that indicates the relationship between the content of the test items and performance on the job.[6] While content validity does have its limitations, it has made a positive contribution to job analysis procedures and to the role of expert judgment in sampling and scoring procedures.

Construct Validity

The extent to which a selection tool measures a theoretical construct, or trait, is known as **construct validity.** Typical constructs are intelligence, mechanical comprehension, and anxiety. They are in effect broad, general categories of human functions that are based on the measurement of many discrete behaviours. For example, the Bennett Mechanical Comprehension Test consists of a wide variety of tasks that measure the construct of mechanical comprehension.

Measuring construct validity requires showing that the psychological trait is related to satisfactory job performance and that the test accurately measures the psychological trait. There is a lack of literature covering this concept as it relates to employment practices, probably because it is difficult and expensive to validate a construct and to show how it is job-related.[7]

construct validity
The extent to which a selection tool measures a theoretical construct or trait

Sources of Information about Job Candidates

objective **2**

Many sources of information are used to provide as reliable and valid a picture as possible of an applicant's potential for success on the job. Figure 6.4 shows the results of a survey that asked HR executives to evaluate the effectiveness of various selection

| Figure 6.4 | The Effectiveness of Selection Methods |

In a survey of 201 HR executives, participants were asked which selection methods produce the best employees. The mean rating for nine methods on a 5-point scale (1 = not good, 3 = average, 5 = extremely good):

Work samples	3.68
References/recommendations	3.49
Unstructured interviews	3.49
Structured interviews	3.42
Assessment centres	3.42
Specific aptitude tests	3.08
Personality tests	2.93
General cognitive ability tests	2.89
Biographical information blanks	2.84

Source: Excerpted from IOMA's *HRFocus* publication and reprinted with the express written consent of IOMA © 2006; any further use requires the publisher's permission. Please contact IOMA directly at: content@ioma.com or by phone, 212-576-8744; www.ioma.com.

techniques. In this section, we will study the potential contributions of application forms; biographical information blanks; background investigations; polygraph, or lie detector, tests; honesty and integrity tests; and graphology. Because interviewing plays such a major role in selection and because testing presents unique challenges, there will be expanded discussions of these sources of information later in the chapter. Assessment centres, which are often used in managerial selection, were discussed in Chapter 5.

Application Forms

Most organizations require application forms to be completed because they provide a fairly quick and systematic means of obtaining a variety of information about the applicant. Application forms serve several purposes. They provide information for deciding whether an applicant meets the minimum requirements for experience, education, and so on. They provide a basis for questions the interviewer will ask about the applicant's background. They also offer sources for reference checks. For certain jobs, a short application form is appropriate. For example, McDonald's uses a form that is quite brief but asks for information that is highly relevant to job performance. It also provides information regarding the employer's conformity with various laws and regulations. For scientific, professional, and managerial jobs, a more extended form is likely to be used.

Even when applicants come armed with elaborate résumés, it is important that they complete an application form early in the process. Individuals frequently exaggerate or overstate their qualifications on a résumé. They also omit unflattering information. The consequences of falsifying information on applications and résumés are frequently high, as described in Ethics in HRM.

Other cases highlight the importance of integrity in job applications. Some staffing experts estimate that at least 30 percent of applicants "stretch" the truth on their résumés. Others estimate that the percentage is much higher. One technique for anticipating problems of misrepresentation is to ask applicants to transcribe specific résumé material onto a standardized application form. The applicant is then asked to sign a statement that the information contained on the form is true and that he or she accepts the employer's right to terminate the candidate's employment if any of the information is subsequently found to be false.[8]

Many managers remain unclear about the questions they can ask on an application form. While most know they should steer clear of issues such as age, race, marital status, and sexual orientation, other issues are less clear. The following are some suggestions for putting together an application form:

- *Application date.* The applicant should date the application. This helps managers know when the form was completed and gives them an idea of the time limit (for example, one year) that the form should be on file.
- *Educational background.* The applicant should provide grade school, high school, college, and university attendance—but not the dates attended, since that can be connected with age.
- *Experience.* Virtually any questions that focus on work experience related to the job are permissible.
- *Arrests and criminal convictions.* Questions about arrests, convictions, and criminal records are to be avoided. If bonding is a requirement, the candidate can be asked if she or he is eligible.
- *Country of citizenship.* Such questions are not permitted. It is allowable to ask whether the person is legally entitled to work in Canada.

Ethics in HRM

Writing It Wrong

Most candidates for white-collar jobs prepare a résumé and submit it to prospective employers. They also complete the application form, answering questions required by employers for comparison purposes. Some recruitment agencies noticed during the last recession that résumé padding increased. Applicants were "stretching" the dates of their employment, misleading employers about the nature of their duties, and misrepresenting their salaries. While you are writing a résumé, adding three months to your previous employment, saying you were a night auditor instead of clerk, and adding $950 to your last salary seem like relatively harmless lies.

What are the facts? Studies of "creative" résumé writing indicate that about 25 percent of résumés contain inaccuracies, including one-third that report incorrect dates, one-tenth misrepresent reasons for leaving, and the rest exaggerate education attainments or omit criminal records. The probability is that about two-thirds of employers check references. Some former employers give only dates of employment and previous salary ranges.

Most organizations require you to sign a statement saying that the information you supply is true, and that if it is not you will be dismissed. Some cases of résumé padding have been heavily publicized. A Toronto Stock Exchange manager was dismissed for lying about having a master's degree. A Member of Parliament listed an ILB on his résumé, which normally stands for International Baccalaureate of Law, but which he claimed stood for Incomplete Baccalaureate of Law. In one heart-wrenching case, a person who was ready to retire was found to have lied about his age decades earlier to get a job. On discovery, he was dismissed and lost his pension. In another case, a Canadian businessman was sentenced to eight months in jail in New Zealand for lying on his résumé, by listing false qualifications such as an MBA. Academic fraud happens 5 percent of the time. The president of Selection Protection Services, a background check firm, offers this advice to job seekers: "Don't lie." She describes one candidate who wrote honours degree on her résumé when she did not have one. She did not get the job, because dishonesty is a deal breaker.

In a labour market where there are too many people chasing too few jobs, candidates will also lie on their résumés, but do so by dropping experience and educational qualifications. This practice, called "stripping," is used because job seekers are ready to take any job in order to survive or to hold them over until the jobs they really want are available. Knowing that graduate degrees will act as barriers to jobs as labourers or administrative assistants, applicants simply don't list the degrees or previous professional jobs. Understandably, employers don't want to hire those who are overqualified and who would soon quit for better jobs.

Sources: Jason Chow, "Job Shadow," *Financial Post Business*, May 2006, 29; Rick Spence, "Should Executives Do Their Own Reference Checks?" *The Toronto* Star, May 13, 2004; E. Urquhart, "Should We Edit Our Job Skills?" *The Globe and Mail*, June 20, 2003: C1; P. Waldie, "Davy Sentenced to Eight Months in N.Z. Court," *The Globe and Mail*, May 30, 2002: B6; J. Schilder, "Trial by Hire," *Human Resource Professional* 11, no. 2 (March 1994): 21–23.

- *References.* It is both permissible and advisable that the names, addresses, and phone numbers of references be provided. (We will cover this in more detail later.)
- *Disabilities.* Employers should avoid asking about disabilities, hospitalization, and if candidates have received workers' compensation.

Many of these issues will be addressed again, particularly in the section on employment interviews.

Some organizations use what is referred to as a *weighted application blank (WAB)*. The WAB involves the use of a common standardized employment application form that is designed to distinguish between successful and unsuccessful employees. If managers can identify application items (such as where someone went to school) that have predicted employee success in the past, they may use that information to screen other applicants. Some evidence suggests that use of the WAB has been especially helpful for reducing turnover costs in the hospitality industry.

Online Applications

Perhaps the biggest change in the hiring process in recent years has been the proliferation of the online applications process. Today's systems enable employers to mine résumés, spot qualified applicants, and conduct screening tests online. However, most Canadian companies do not use recruitment software, either because their company is not large enough or they feel that it is not cost effective. However, those that do report savings. For example, the Federal Public Service created an e-recruitment prototype, the Public Service Resourcing System, and found that the number of referrals to hiring managers for posted jobs went from 237 to 34.[9]

Companies report that the downside of posting jobs and accepting online applications is that it can lead to a large volume of them being submitted—many of which fail to meet minimum qualifications. The upside, however, is that generating a larger number of applicants tends to promote greater employee diversity. Home Depot, for example, successfully implemented an online application system called the Job Preference Program to get a broader pool of applicants than it previously had been getting. It ultimately enabled the company to hire more women.[10]

Biographical Information Blanks

One of the oldest methods for predicting job success uses biographical information about job applicants. As early as 1917, the Life Insurance Agency Management Association constructed and validated a biographical information blank (BIB) for life insurance salespeople. BIBs cover such issues as family life, hobbies, club memberships, sales experience, and investments. Like application forms, BIBs reveal information about a person's history that may have shaped his or her behaviour. Sample questions from a BIB might include the following:

- At what age did you leave home?
- How large was the town/city in which you lived as a child?
- Did you ever build a model airplane that flew?
- Were sports a big part of your childhood?
- Do you play any musical instruments?

Both the BIB and the application form can be scored like tests. And because biographical questions rarely have obviously right or wrong answers, BIBs are difficult to fake. The development of a scoring system requires that the items that are valid predictors of job success (positively or negatively correlated) be identified and that weights be established for different responses to these items. By totalling the scores for each item, it is possible to obtain a composite score on the BIB as a whole for each applicant. Studies have shown that an objective scoring of BIB and application forms is one of the most potentially valid methods of predicting job success. This method has been useful in predicting all types of behaviour, including employee theft, turnover, and performance in jobs such as sales, nursing, and management.[11]

Background Investigations

When the interviewer is satisfied that the applicant is potentially qualified, information about previous employment as well as other information provided by the applicant is investigated. Following the terrorist attacks of 9/11 and a rash of corporate scandals at companies such as Enron, Tyco, and WorldCom, background investigations have become standard procedure for many companies to prevent a variety of problems ranging from embezzlement and theft of merchandise to workplace violence. The vast majority (over 90 percent) of Canadian companies surveyed by the *Canadian HR Reporter* indicated that they conduct background checks for previous employment history (92 percent), academic qualifications (53 percent), criminal record (50 percent), and credit rating (11 percent).[12]

Like the application process, many checks that were once done manually are now being done online using existing computer databases. However, this frequently requires checking many different databases on a county-by-county basis. Information on international applicants is even harder to come by. Additionally, delving into areas of an applicant's background irrelevant to the job requirements he or she is applying for can leave firms exposed to violation-of-privacy claims.

Checking References

Many organizations use both mail and the telephone to check references. But while references are commonly used to screen and select employees, they have not proved successful for predicting employee performance. Written letters of reference are notoriously inflated, and this limits their validity. Generally, telephone checks are preferable because they save time and provide for greater candour. But faxes and e-mail are also used. InfoTech first calls references to establish contact, then faxes or e-mails them a two-page questionnaire, asking them to numerically rank the applicant's various job-related attributes. There's room at the end of the questionnaire for comments and recommendations. The most reliable information usually comes from supervisors, who are in the best position to report on an applicant's work habits and performance. Written verification of information relating to job titles, duties, and pay levels from the former employer's HR office is also very helpful. Highlights in HRM 6.1 on page 256 includes a list of helpful questions to ask about applicants when checking their references.[13]

As a legal protection for all concerned, it is important to ask the applicant to fill out forms permitting information to be solicited from former employers and other reference sources. Even with these safeguards, many organizations are reluctant to put into writing an evaluation of a former employee, and some employers even hesitate to answer questions and/or verify information about former employees over the phone. Note that there is no legal obligation to provide a reference letter for an employee, unless you have promised to do so in writing. A survey by the SHRM found that although 75 percent of companies do provide references, many reported that the information consists only of

Highlights in HRM 6.1

Sample Reference-Checking Questions

Just the Facts

What were the candidate's dates of employment?

What was the candidate's title?

What were the candidate's general responsibilities?

What is your relationship to the candidate (peer, subordinate, superior)?

How long have you known the candidate?

On the Job

How would you describe the overall quality of the candidate's work? Can you give me some examples?

(For superiors) What areas of performance did you have to work on?

What would you say are the candidate's strengths?

What would you say are the candidate's weaknesses?

How would you compare the candidate's work to the work of others who performed the same job?

What kind of environment did the candidate work in?

How much of a contribution do you think the candidate made to your company or department?

How would you describe the candidate's ability to communicate?

How does the candidate handle pressure/deadlines?

How well does the candidate get along with co-workers?

How well does the candidate get along with managers?

How well does the candidate supervise others? Can you give me your impressions of his or her management style? Describe the candidate's success in motivating subordinates.

How does the candidate handle conflict situations?

Based on the candidate's performance with your company, do you think he or she would be good in the type of position we're considering him or her for?

What motivates the candidate? How ambitious is he or she?

The Bottom Line

Why did the candidate leave your company?

Would you rehire this person?

Would you recommend this candidate for this type of position?

What type of work is the candidate ideally suited for?

Were there any serious problems with the candidate that we need to be aware of before making a hiring decision?

Do you have any additional information to share with us about this candidate?

Source: Carolyn Hirschman, "The Whole Truth," *HRMagazine* 45, no. 6 (June 2000): 86–72. Copyright 2000 by Society for Human Resource Management, Alexandria, VA. Reproduced with permission of Society for Human Resource Management in the format Textbook via Copyright Clearance Center.

employment dates and position. This results in problems for the next employers. A survey of Canadian companies found that the majority had to terminate an employee for reasons that could have been discovered through a reference check. For example, the City of Waterloo fired its Chief Administrative Officer after it uncovered an employment history where the candidate broke rules and misled his previous employer, all well publicized but not checked either by the recruiting firm or the City.[14]

Using Credit Reports

The use of consumer credit reports by employers as a basis for establishing an applicant's eligibility for employment has become more restricted. For positions of trust, such as those involving financial instruments in banks, credit reports must be used. Applicants must agree in writing to a credit report and have the right to review its contents. More importantly, the reason for the credit report must be job-related.

Polygraph Tests

The polygraph, or lie detector, is a device that measures the changes in breathing, blood pressure, and pulse of a person who is being questioned. It consists of a rubber tube around the chest, a cuff around the arm, and sensors attached to the fingers that record the physiological changes in the examinee as the examiner asks questions that call for an answer of yes or no. Questions typically cover such items as whether a person uses drugs, has stolen from an employer, or has committed a serious undetected crime. The RCMP uses a polygraph test to identify candidates who meet their standards of honesty and suitability. However, the use of lie detector tests for employment purposes is prohibited under the Employment Standards Acts in both Ontario and New Brunswick. Check provincial legislation before considering the use of a polygraph.

Honesty and Integrity Tests

Many employers have dramatically increased their use of pencil-and-paper honesty and integrity tests. They are inexpensive. These tests have commonly been used in settings such as retail stores where employees have access to cash or merchandise. Common areas of inquiry include beliefs about frequency and extent of theft in our society, punishment for theft, and perceived ease of theft. For example, Payless ShoeSource has used a paper-and-pencil honesty test to reduce employee theft. When the company began its program, losses totalled nearly $21 million per year among its 4700 stores. Within only one year of implementing its screening program, inventory shrinkage fell by 20 percent to less than 1 percent of sales.

Potential items that might be used on an integrity test are shown in Figure 6.5 on page 258. A comprehensive analysis of honesty tests reveals that they are valid for predicting job performance as well as a wide range of disruptive behaviours such as theft, disciplinary problems, and absenteeism.[15] Nevertheless, honesty tests have come under fire, too. Sobeys, a chain food store based in Stellarton, Nova Scotia, used an integrity test and failed an applicant, even though she had worked for them previously for six years without any incident. The applicant filed a complaint with the Nova Scotia Human Rights Commission, and the outcome is still pending. Additionally some candidates find the questions, such as "I like to take chances," offensive. The British Columbia Civil Liberties Union has called for legislation banning integrity tests as an invasion of privacy. Given these events, HRM specialists should use the results from honesty tests very cautiously and most certainly in conjunction with other sources of information.[16]

Figure 6.5	Integrity Test Question Examples

TO TEST TENDENCY TO	DESCRIPTION
Protect	Contains items that require individuals to indicate whether they would protect friends or co-workers who had engaged in counterproductive behaviours. *Example:* I would turn in a fellow worker I saw stealing money.
Be lenient	Contains items in which test takers indicate whether they would be lenient with respect to the wrongdoings of others. *Example:* An employee should be fired if the employer finds out the employee lied on the application bank.
Admit thought	Includes items that require test takers to indicate the degree to which they would engage in counterproductive thoughts or behaviours. *Example:* I've thought about taking money from an employer without actually doing it.
Admit behaviour	Contains items in which individuals admit to directly participating in actual counterproductive behaviours. *Example:* Over the last three years, what's the total amount of money you've taken without permission from your employer?
Consider common	Includes items that require the individual to indicate whether there are excuses or justifications for stealing or performing other questionable behaviours. *Example:* Most people I've worked with have stolen something at one time or another.
Excuse	Contains items in which individuals indicate whether there are excuses or justifications for stealing or performing other questionable behaviours. *Example:* Someone who steals because his family is in need should not be treated the same as a common thief.
Lie	Contains items that measure the extent to which the test taker is responding in a socially desirable manner. *Example:* Never in my whole life have I wished for anything I was not entitled to.

Note: The number of items in each category was 2, 8, 13, 9, 17, 8, and 7 respectively.

Source: Stephen Dwight and George Alliger, "Reactions to Overt Integrity Test Items," *Educational and Psychological Measurement* 57, no. 6 (December 1977): 937–48, copyright © 1997 by Sage Publications, Inc. Reprinted with the permission of Sage Publications, Inc.

Graphology

Graphology, a term that refers to a variety of systems of handwriting analysis, is used by some employers to make employment decisions. Graphologists obtain a sample of handwriting and then examine such characteristics as the size and slant of letters, amount of pressure applied, and placement of the writing on the page. From their observations, graphologists draw inferences about such things as the writer's personality traits, intelligence, energy level, organizational abilities, creativity, integrity, emotional maturity, self-image, people skills, and entrepreneurial tendencies. Graphology is used extensively in France, Germany, Switzerland, Israel, and the United Kingdom in making employment decisions.[17]

Organizations using handwriting analysis say they prefer it to typical personality tests because it requires only that job candidates take a few minutes to jot down a short essay. By contrast, a battery of personality tests and interviews with psychologists can take several hours and can cost thousands of dollars. In addition, the available evidence shows graphology to be a reliable predictor of personality when compared with other psychological tests. However, its predictive validity for job performance and occupational success remains questionable. In the academic community, where formal and rigorous validity studies are customary, use of graphology for employment decisions has been viewed with considerable skepticism.[18]

Employment Tests

objective **3**

The formal introduction of psychological selection techniques into the Canadian Army in 1941 represented both a pragmatic response to the contingencies of war and an attempt to make selection decisions more democratic. Prior to 1941, entry into officer training was often based on social status or monetary favours (as opposed to proven ability). Since that time, employment tests have played an important part in the HR programs of both public and private organizations.

One of the drawbacks of pre-employment testing is that it creates the potential for legal challenges. Many companies have been taken to court by candidates claiming that the tests they took were discriminatory. In Canada, the fitness test required for firefighters was challenged as having an adverse impact on female applicants, because even with training, most could not meet the aerobic standard. There is also some evidence that the more tests that are required, the higher the likelihood of a lawsuit. The relative frequency of discrimination suits also appears to vary by industry and job type. Police, firefighting, and teaching areas—which generally require applicants to pass more tests—appear to be more prone to discrimination litigation.[19]

Nonetheless, tests have played a more important part in government HR programs in which hiring on the basis of merit is required by law. Government agencies experienced the same types of problems with their testing programs as did organizations in the private sector. However, their staffs were forced to improve their testing programs rather than to abandon them.

While it is often advisable to use consultants, especially if an organization is considering the use of personality tests, managers should have a basic understanding of the technical aspects of testing and the contributions that tests can make to the HR program. They should also do a thorough job analysis to determine the crucial job requirements and related skills that actually need to be tested for and eliminate any unnecessary or duplicate tests.

Nature of Employment Tests

An employment test is an objective and standardized measure of a sample of behaviour that is used to gauge a person's knowledge, skills, abilities, and other characteristics (KSAOs) in relation to other individuals.[20] The proper sampling of behaviour— whether verbal, manipulative, or some other type—is the responsibility of the test author. It is also the responsibility of the test author to develop tests that meet accepted standards of reliability.[21] Data concerning reliability are ordinarily presented in the manual for the test. While high reliability is essential, it offers no assurance that the test provides the basis for making valid judgments—that is, that the test actually measures the knowledge, skills, and abilities necessary to do a job successfully. It is the responsibility of the HR staff to conduct validation studies before a test is adopted for regular use. Again, this involves doing a thorough job analysis. One way to measure a test's validity is to test current employees and create a benchmark score to which applicants' scores can be compared. Other considerations are cost, time, ease of administration and scoring, and the apparent relevance of the test to the individuals being tested—commonly referred to as "face validity." While face validity is desirable, it is no substitute for technical validity, described earlier in this chapter. Adopting a test just because it appears relevant is bad practice; many a "good-looking" test has poor validity.

USING THE INTERNET

The Buros Center for Testing presents reviews of the reliability and validity of tests at:

www.unl.edu/buros/

Classification of Employment Tests

Employment tests may be classified in different ways. Generally, they are viewed as measuring either aptitude or achievement. **Aptitude tests** measure a person's capacity to learn or acquire skills. **Achievement tests** measure what a person knows or can do right now.

aptitude tests
Measures of a person's capacity to learn or acquire skills

achievement tests
Measures of what a person knows or can do right now

Cognitive Ability Tests

Cognitive ability tests measure mental capabilities such as general intelligence, verbal fluency, numerical ability, and reasoning ability. A host of paper-and-pencil tests measure cognitive abilities, including the General Aptitude Test Battery (GATB), the Scholastic Aptitude Test (SAT), the Graduate Management Aptitude Test (GMAT), and the Bennett Mechanical Comprehension Test. Figure 6.6 provides examples of questions from the General Competency Test administered by the Public Service Commission of Canada.

Although cognitive ability tests can be developed to measure very specialized areas such as reading comprehension and spatial relations, many experts believe that the validity of cognitive ability tests simply reflects their connection to general intelligence. However, measures of general intelligence (such as IQ) have been shown to be good predictors of performance across a wide variety of jobs.[22]

Personality and Interest Inventories

Whereas cognitive ability tests measure a person's mental capacity, personality tests measure disposition and temperament. Years of research show that five dimensions can summarize personality traits. The "Big Five" factors are the following:

1. *Extroversion*—the degree to which someone is talkative, sociable, active, aggressive, and excitable
2. *Agreeableness*—the degree to which someone is trusting, amiable, generous, tolerant, honest, cooperative, and flexible
3. *Conscientiousness*—the degree to which someone is dependable and organized and perseveres in tasks
4. *Neuroticism*—the degree to which someone is secure, calm, independent, and autonomous
5. *Openness to experience*—the degree to which someone is intellectual, philosophical, insightful, creative, artistic, and curious[23]

Figure 6.6	General Competency Test Level 1

The GCT was developed by the Personnel Psychology Centre, Assessment, Testing and Counselling Directorate, the Public Service Commission of Canada. The GCT 1 has 50 multiple-choice questions and the test takes 85 minutes. There are three types of questions, and an example from each is found below:

Understanding Written Material Example:
Government of Canada
Memorandum
To: All employees
From: Manager

We are pleased to announce that our Ministry's budget has been increased and consequently we will experience an increase in staff size. Because new positions will become available, we will be holding interviews within the next few weeks.
The main focus of this interview is a change concerning:

1. Better ministerial policy
2. Better budget publicity
3. More human resources
4. More office space.

Solving Numerical Questions:
You are in charge of financial services and must calculate overtime pay for employees in your division. Due to a heavy workload, an employee had to do 35 hours of overtime in two weeks. Seven of these hours are at "double time" (i.e., twice usual pay), the rest are at "time and a half." The employee's usual pay is $375 a week at $10 an hour. How much overtime money should the employee be paid for the two-week period?

- 1. $340
- 2. $420
- 3. $560
- 4. $760

Drawing Logical Conclusions:
One of your duties is the selection and disposal of boxes of obsolete files. According to regulations, ordinary files become obsolete after 24 months, confidential files after 36 months, and classified files after 48 months. Which of the following boxes of files can be disposed of?

A box containing ordinary files dated 26 months ago and classified files dated 34 months ago.

A box containing ordinary files dated 38 months ago and confidential files dated 28 months ago.

- 1. A only
- 2. B only
- 3. Both A and B
- 4. Neither A nor B

Answers can be found on page 293.

Source: General Competency Test: Level 1 – (GCT1) Practice Test: Information (http://www.psc-cfp.gc.ca/gct1_info_e.htm) September 7, 2006. Reproduced with the permission of the Personnel Psychology Centre, Public Service Commission of Canada 2006.

Figure 6.7 illustrates facets and sample items from the well-known California Psychological Inventory (CPI). Other personality tests include the Myers-Briggs Type Indicator (MBTI) and the 180-question Caliper test. The predictive validity of personality and interest inventories historically has been quite low. However, when used in combination with cognitive ability tests, measures of personality traits (such as

Figure 6.7	CPI Personality Facets and Sample Items

AGREEABLENESS

- Consideration—I like to do little things for people to make them feel good.
- Empathy—I take other people's circumstances and feelings into consideration before making a decision.
- Interdependence—I tend to put group goals first and individual goals second.
- Openness—I do not have to share a person's values to work well with that person.
- Thought agility—I think it is vital to consider other perspectives before coming to conclusions.
- Trust—I believe people are usually honest with me.

CONSCIENTIOUSNESS

- Attention to detail—I like to complete every detail of tasks according to the work plans.
- Dutifulness—I conduct my business according to a strict set of ethical principles.
- Responsibility—I can be relied on to do what is expected of me.
- Work focus—I prioritize my work effectively so the most important things get done first.

EXTROVERSION

- Adaptability—For me, change is exciting.
- Competitiveness—I like to win, even if the activity isn't very important.
- Desire for achievement—I prefer to set challenging goals, rather than aim for goals I am more likely to reach.
- Desire for advancement—I would like to attain the highest position in an organization some day.
- Energy level—When most people are exhausted from work, I still have energy to keep going.
- Influence—People come to me for inspiration and direction.
- Initiative—I am always looking for opportunities to start new projects.
- Risk-taking—I am willing to take big risks when there is potential for big returns.
- Sociability—I find it easy to start up a conversation with strangers.
- Taking charge—I actively take control of situations at work if no one is in charge.

NEUROTICISM

- Emotional control—Even when I am very upset, it is easy for me to control my emotions.
- Negative affectivity—I am easily displeased with things at work.
- Optimism—My enthusiasm for living life to its fullest is apparent to those with whom I work.
- Self-confidence—I am confident about my skills and abilities.
- Stress tolerance—I worry about things that I know I should not worry about.

OPENNESS TO EXPERIENCE

- Independence—I tend to work on projects alone, even if others volunteer to help me.
- Innovativeness/creativity—I work best in an environment that allows me to be creative and expressive.
- Social astuteness—I know what is expected of me in different social situations.
- Thought focus—I quickly make links between causes and effects.
- Vision—I can often foresee the outcome of a situation before it unfolds.

Source: Mark J. Schmit, Jenifer A. Kihm, and Chet Robie, "Development of a Global Measure of Personality," *Personnel Psychology* 53, no.1 (Spring 2000): 153–93. Reprinted by permission.

conscientiousness) can lead to a better prediction of job performance.[24] Read about testing at Steelcase in Highlights in HRM 6.2.

It is important to note that personality tests can be problematic if they inadvertently discriminate against individuals who would otherwise perform effectively. Demonstrating job-relatedness and validity of some personality characteristics is not always easy. The use of personality tests may also be seen as an invasion of privacy.[25]

Highlights in HRM 6.2

Testing at Steelcase

Founded in 1912, Steelcase is an office furniture manufacturing company with a mission of transforming the way that people work. Steelcase makes it their business to study the way that people work and create solutions that allow employees and teams to maximize their full potential and have a better work experience. With over 13 000 employees and 30 locations worldwide, Steelcase is able to achieve high standards of excellence in office environments by adhering to Seven Core Values that were displayed by their founders. These are to:

- Act with integrity
- Tell the truth
- Keep commitments
- Treat people with dignity and respect
- Promote positive relationships
- Protect the environment
- Excel

According to Gene Lai, vice-president of operations, Steelcase uses tests to ensure that candidates will enact these values. According to Lai, hiring managers can be a costly process. The wrong candidate can not only damage the company's reputation and undermine the credibility within the market but also selecting the wrong manager could do untold damage to the relationship Steelcase has carefully built with its employees over many years.

As part of the managerial selection process, candidates are given tests, conducted by a qualified industrial psychologist, which assess cognitive abilities, motivation, behaviours, and emotional stability. The use of professional psychologists is stressed because there are too many limitations of readily available selection tests that are "open" to interpretation, not properly proctored, and based on the assumptions of unqualified personnel. From experience, Gene Lai states that, "it's not the technical skills or normal behaviours that get a person into trouble; it is how people react when under stress." The psychological assessment uncovers these potential "de-railers" and also outlines a person's strengths.

Whether or not the candidate is chosen, he or she is given formal feedback from the industrial psychologist. If the candidate is chosen, the assessment data are integrated into a formal personal development plan. The industrial psychologist also works with the individual as a personal coach. From day one, the new employee has a personal development plan that is shared with the individual's manager. The new employee also has access to the coach for any problems that may arise and assistance in overcoming any barriers to success.

Organizations use a variety of tests to determine an applicant's abilities, knowledge, and skills.

Beyond the initial hiring decision, personality and interest inventories may be most useful for helping with occupational selection and career planning. Interest tests such as the Kuder Inventory measure an applicant's preferences for certain activities over others (such as sailing versus poker).

Physical Ability Tests

In addition to learning about a job candidate's mental capabilities, employers frequently need to assess a person's physical abilities. These types of tests are reportedly being used more widely today for selection than ever before. Particularly for demanding and potentially dangerous jobs such as those held by firefighters and police officers, physical abilities such as strength and endurance tend to be good predictors not only of performance, but also of accidents and injuries.[26]

Despite their potential value, physical ability tests tend to work to the disadvantage of women and disabled job applicants, a tendency that has led to several recent lawsuits. Evidence suggests that the average man is stronger, faster, and more powerful than the average woman, but women tend to have better balance, manual dexterity, flexibility, and coordination than men. For example, applicants who take the RCMP's Physical Fitness Abilities Requirement Evaluation (PARE) are required to run 350 metres, complete a standing broad jump of about 2 metres, and pick up and carry a heavy bag for 15 metres. According to one RCMP officer, "If you're a bigger person, the PARE test is easier, no doubt." The fact that women fail the test in greater numbers than men has resulted in a complaint before the Canadian Human Rights Commission. The RCMP is defending the PARE test on the grounds that it simulates common police activities such as chasing a suspect on foot, carrying an injured person, and forcing open a door. On the basis of these differences, it is clear that (as with other methods for screening potential employees) the use of physical ability tests should be carefully validated on the basis of the essential functions of the job.[27]

Job Knowledge Tests

Government agencies and licensing boards usually develop job knowledge tests, a type of achievement test designed to measure a person's level of understanding about a particular job. The uniform CPA examination used to licence certified public accountants is one such test. Most civil service examinations, for example, are used to determine whether an applicant possesses the information and understanding that will permit placement on the job without further training.[28]

Work Sample Tests

Work sample tests, or job sample tests, require the applicant to perform tasks that are actually a part of the work required on the job. Like job knowledge tests, work sample tests are constructed from a carefully developed outline that experts agree includes the major job functions; the tests are thus considered content-valid. Organizations that are interested in moving toward *competency-based selection*—that is, hiring based on observation of behaviours previously shown to distinguish successful employees—increasingly use work samples to see potential employees "in action."[29]

Work samples have been devised for many diverse jobs: a map-reading test for traffic control officers, a lathe test for machine operators, a complex coordination test for pilots, an in-basket test for managers, a group discussion test for supervisors, and a judgment and decision-making test for administrators, to name a few. The reports are that this type of test is cost-effective, reliable, valid, fair, and acceptable to applicants.[30] Related to the job sample test is the job simulation, used by nearly one-third of those surveyed in 2005. Prudential Grand Valley Reality, a real estate firm in Kitchener, Ontario, uses an online video-based assessment that simulates the job of a real estate agent. The candidate plays the role of an agent and interacts with virtual clients who are interested in buying or selling a property. The recruit is taken thorough the entire sales cycle, from building rapport to closing the deal, and must demonstrate the ability to handle objections, negotiate price, understand client needs, and handle periodic rejection.[31]

The Employment Interview

objective 4

Traditionally, the employment interview has a central role in the selection process—so much so that it is rare to find an instance in which an employee is hired without some sort of interview. Depending on the type of job, applicants may be interviewed by one person, members of a work team, or other individuals in the organization. While researchers have raised some doubts about its validity, the interview remains a mainstay of selection because (1) it is especially practical when there are only a small number of applicants; (2) it serves other purposes, such as public relations; and (3) interviewers maintain great faith and confidence in their judgments. Nevertheless, the interview can be plagued by problems of subjectivity and personal bias. In those instances, the judgments of different interviewers may vary dramatically and the quality of the hire can be called into serious question.

In this section, we review the characteristics, advantages, and disadvantages of various types of employment interviews. We highlight the fact that the structure of the interview and the training of interviewers strongly influence the success of the hiring process.[32]

Interviewing Methods

Interview methods differ in several ways, most significantly in terms of the amount of structure, or control, exercised by the interviewer. In highly structured interviews, the interviewer determines the course that the interview will follow as each question is asked. In the less structured interview, the applicant plays a larger role in determining the course the discussion will take. An examination of the different types of interviews from the least structured to the most structured reveals these differences.

nondirective interview
An interview in which the applicant is allowed the maximum amount of freedom in determining the course of the discussion, while the interviewer carefully refrains from influencing the applicant's remarks

The Nondirective Interview

In the **nondirective interview,** the interviewer carefully refrains from influencing the applicant's remarks. The applicant is allowed the maximum amount of freedom in determining the course of the discussion. The interviewer asks broad, open-ended questions—such as "Tell me more about your experiences on your last job"—and permits the applicant to talk freely with a minimum of interruption. Generally, the nondirective interviewer listens carefully and does not argue, interrupt, or change the subject abruptly. The interviewer also uses follow-up questions to allow the applicant to elaborate, makes only brief responses, and allows pauses in the conversation; the pausing technique is the most difficult for the beginning interviewer to master.

The greater freedom afforded to the applicant in the nondirective interview is particularly valuable in bringing to the interviewer's attention any information, attitudes, or feelings that may often be concealed by more structured questioning. However, because the applicant determines the course of the interview and no set procedure is followed, little information that comes from these interviews enables interviewers to cross-check agreement with other interviewers. Thus the reliability and validity of the nondirective interview may be expected to be minimal. This method is most likely to be used in interviewing candidates for high-level positions and in counselling, which we will discuss in Chapter 13.

The Structured Interview

More attention is being given to the structured interview as a result of employment equity requirements and a concern for maximizing validity of selection decisions.[33] Because a **structured interview** has a set of standardized questions (based on job analysis) and an established set of answers against which applicant responses can be rated, it provides a more consistent basis for evaluating job candidates. For example, staff members of Weyerhaeuser Company's HR department have developed a structured interviewing process with the following characteristics:

structured interview
An interview in which a set of standardized questions having an established set of answers is used

1. The interview process is based exclusively on job duties and requirements critical to job performance.
2. It uses four types of questions: situational questions, job knowledge questions, job sample/simulation questions, and worker requirements questions.
3. There are sample (benchmark) answers, determined in advance, to each question. Interviewee responses are rated on a five-point scale relative to those answers.
4. The process involves an interview committee so that interviewee responses are evaluated by several raters.
5. It consistently follows the same procedures in all instances to ensure that each applicant has exactly the same chance as every other applicant.
6. The interviewer takes notes and documents the interview for future reference and in case of a legal challenge.

A structured interview is more likely to provide the type of information needed for making sound decisions. According to one report, structured interviews are twice as likely as nondirective interviews to predict on-the-job performance. Structured interviews are also less likely than nondirective interviews to be attacked in court.[34]

Most employment interviewers will tend toward either a nondirected or a structured format. However, within the general category of structured interviews, there are more specific differences that relate to the format of questions. These include the situational interview and behavioural description interview, discussed next.

The Situational Interview

situational interview
An interview in which an applicant is given a hypothetical incident and asked how he or she would respond to it

One variation of the structured interview is called the **situational interview.** With this approach, an applicant is given a *hypothetical* incident and asked how he or she would respond to it. The applicant's response is then evaluated relative to pre-established benchmark standards. Interestingly, many organizations are using the situational interview to select new university or college graduates. Highlights in HRM 6.3 shows a sample question from a situational interview used to select systems analysts at a chemical plant. Highlights in HRM 6.4 on page 268 lists some of the funniest things heard in interviews.

The Behavioural Description Interview

behavioural description interview (BDI)
An interview in which an applicant is asked questions about what he or she actually did in a given situation

In contrast to a situational interview, which focuses on hypothetical situations, a **behavioural description interview (BDI)** focuses on *actual* work incidents in the interviewee's past. The BDI format asks the job applicant what he or she actually did in a given situation. For example, to assess a potential manager's ability to handle a problem employee, an interviewer might ask, "Tell me about the last time you disciplined an employee." Such an approach to interviewing, based on a critical-incidents job analysis, assumes that past performance is the best predictor of future performance. It also may be somewhat less susceptible to applicant faking. In addition, recent research indicates that the behavioural description interview is

Highlights in HRM 6.3

Sample Situational Interview Question

QUESTION:
It is the night before your scheduled vacation. You are all packed and ready to go. Just before you get into bed, you receive a phone call from the plant. A problem has arisen that only you can handle. You are asked to come in to take care of things. What would you do in this situation?

RECORD ANSWER:

_____

_____

_____

_____

SCORING GUIDE:
Good: "I would go in to work and make certain that everything is OK. Then I would go on vacation."
Good: "There are no problems that *only* I can handle. I would make certain that someone qualified was there to handle things."
Fair: "I would try to find someone else to deal with the problem."
Fair: "I would go on vacation."

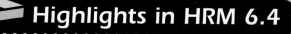

Highlights in HRM 6.4

Too Funny for Interviews

The *Canadian HR Reporter* asked its readers to reveal the funniest things they ever heard in an interview. Here is a sample of the responses:

- One candidate asked the president of a company how old she was
- An applicant applying for an accounting position said "I'm terrible in math"
- "I've been terminated from the last five companies I've worked for because they don't know what they are doing there"
- "No, I didn't come prepared to make a presentation. I thought you were joking"
- When asked to describe the company's main client group, the candidate said "Well, they're all idiots, aren't they"
- A candidate was asked how he prepared for the job interview and replied "I washed my jean jacket"
- A candidate was asked what quick decisions he's had to make and he replied "I asked my wife to leave and she did"

Adapted from: Todd Humber, "What's the Funniest Thing Heard in an Interview," *Canadian HR Reporter*, May 23, 2005. G2.

more effective than the situational interview for hiring higher-level positions such as general managers and executives.[35] Over 90 percent of Canadian employers surveyed use the behavioural interview. See Highlights in HRM 6.5 for behavioural questions posed by BMO Financial. The Business Case outlines the advantages of the behavioural interview.

Highlights in HRM 6.5

Behavioural Interviews at BMO

The BMO Financial Group has been using behavioural interviewing for almost every position it fills, and after several revisions feels that it is a solid predictive tool in the hiring process. Below is a list of competencies and the questions BMO uses to evaluate them:

Business acumen behaviours
- Tell me about a time when you had to accomplish something that had a tight deadline and when you had to accomplish many things at once.
- Tell me about a challenging assignment that you had in the past year and how you handled this challenge.
- Describe a time when you had to decide what to do about a business situation where no guidelines existed or no precedents had been set.

Analytical and systems thinking behaviours
- Tell me how you approached the most difficult or challenging project that you had to solve.
- Give me an example of a situation where you had to handle a project unlike anything you ever had to do.
- Tell me about a time when your team had to complete a challenging project.

Customer and client service behaviours
- Describe to me a time when you turned around a very angry client and how you did it.
- Give me an example of a particularly difficult situation involving an external client and how you handled it.
- Tell me about a time when you felt particularly effective in establishing or maintaining a business relationship with a client.

Source: Adapted from Todd Humber, "How BMO Financial Selects Employees," *Canadian HR Reporter*, December 6, 2004: G2.

The Business Case

Behavioural Interviews Bring Big Returns

Fairmont Hotels and Resorts Inc., formerly Canadian Pacific Hotels, with nearly 31 000 employees at 81 hotels in six countries, measures the effectiveness of selection tools. Using a Gallup selection tool, Fairmont has tracked the performance of sales personnel by selecting those who matched the characteristics of the best performers. Those superior employees produce two to three times more revenue than others. A financial organization decided to assess the ROI (return on investment) of competency-based behavioural interviewing. They focused first on the sales and marketing function, which employed about 100 people, with average annual salaries of $135,000 ($90,000 plus a variable bonus of 50 percent for on-target performance). Turnover was about 20 percent a year. Elementary statistics suggest that the output of a group of workers forms a bell-shaped distribution, resulting in a small portion (about 10 percent) of staff working at above or below acceptable performance, while the majority worked in the acceptable range. The recruiters decided to delineate the competencies that differentiated the superior performers from the average performers and to use these to improve the selection procedure.

Here is how the ROI was calculated:

Assume 20 new recruits a year.

Two recruits, on average, would be superior performers under the current recruiting system.

Under the new system, all 20 would be superior, for a net increase of 18 new superior employees.

Performing above average is worth about 48 percent of the average annual salary to the company.

Therefore: $18 \times (\$135,000 \times .48) = \$1,166,000$

(continued on next page)

But the recruitment process is not perfect, and so must be discounted by .545 (the consultants' estimate of how good they were at selecting superior candidates and rejecting inferior candidates).

Therefore: $545 \times \$1,166,000 = \$635,000$

The *cost* of the competency project for sales and marketing was $130,000.

The *benefit* was $635,000 for an ROI of 488 percent.

The long-term ROI may be higher, as superior recruits may have lower turnover, shorter learning curves, and increasingly effective performance.

Interviews must be as valid as tests, because they are so expensive. The average cost per hire of an executive is $43,000, a manager or professional $17,000, a technical person $13,000, and clerical and administrative support around $3,000.

Sources: Adapted from A. Davis, "What Is the Cost of Hiring?" *Canadian HR Reporter* 16, no. 11 (June 2, 2003): 12; T. Tritch, "Fairmont's Talent Strategy Delivers Results," *Gallup Management Journal*, www.gmj.gallup.com, May 13, 2003; Lionel LaRoche and Stephen Martin, "Demonstrating the Bottom-Line Impact of HR: A Competencies Case Study," *Canadian HR Reporter* 13, no. 22 (December 18, 2000): 29–31.

The Panel Interview

panel interview
An interview in which a board of interviewers questions and observes a single candidate

Another type of interview involves a panel of interviewers who question and observe a single candidate. In a typical **panel interview** the candidate meets with three to five interviewers who take turns asking questions. After the interview the interviewers pool their observations and their rating scores if the interview is structured to reach a consensus about the suitability of the candidate. HRM specialists using this method report that panel interviews provide several significant advantages over traditional one-to-one interviews, including higher reliability because of multiple inputs, greater acceptance of the decision, and shorter decision time. Studies also suggest that if the panels are composed of a diverse group of interviewers, hiring discrimination is minimized.[36]

In this panel interview, one of the participants is connecting by videoconference.

© DIGITAL VISION/GETTY IMAGES

The Computer Interview

With advances in information technology, more and more organizations are using computers and the Internet to help with the interviewing process.

Typically, a computer interview requires candidates to answer a series (75 to 125) of multiple-choice questions tailored to the job. These answers are compared either with an ideal profile or with profiles developed on the basis of other candidates' responses. The computer interview can also be used as a screening device to help filter out unqualified applicants applying online who don't merit a personal interview. Depending on the vendor and the software used, a computer interview conducted in conjunction with online tests can measure everything from contradictory responses and latent responses (time delays related to answering a question) to the applicant's typing speed and ability to use different kinds of software.

CareerBuilder.com, for example, offers a service called IntelligentHire that screens out the ten most qualified and interested applicants posting for a job on CareerBuilder's site. IntelligentHire then generates a report for the employer that includes the applicants' résumés, answers to questions, background check results, and their overall rankings against one another.[37]

A few years ago, Pic 'n Pay Shoe Stores created a computerized interview that could be conducted over the phone using an 800 number. The interview focused on honesty, work attitude, drug use, candour, dependability, and self-motivation. After implementing the system, the company cut turnover by 50 percent and reduced employee theft by almost 40 percent. In addition to the benefits of objectivity, some research evidence suggests that applicants may be less likely to engage in "impression management" in computerized interviews than in face-to-face interviews. So far, organizations have used the computer mainly as a complement to, rather than as a replacement for, conventional interviews.[38]

Video Interviews

Organizations such as Nike are using videoconference technologies to evaluate job candidates. While some use their own inhouse systems, others use outside service partners. Kinko's, for example, rents videoconferencing rooms at a quarter of its 900 stores for about $150 per hour.

Video interviews have several potential advantages related to flexibility, speed, and cost. Employers can make preliminary assessments about candidates' technical abilities, energy level, appearance, and the like before incurring the costs of a face-to-face meeting. The goal, of course, is to enable faster, higher-quality decisions at lower cost.

A number of companies allow recruiters to videotape job applicants and post video interviews to a website. Corporations log on to the sites and check out candidates free of charge or for a small fee, depending on the vendor. By recording and playing back the interviews to several companies' executives, firms can eliminate complications involved in setting up many more interviews.[39]

Simulations and Games

Some organizations are creating simulations that mimic the real world conditions of work. For example, Burnaby-based Re/Max Realty Company uses videos featuring actors posing as home buyers, and candidates must respond to their questions. L'Oreal SA, the French-based cosmetics company, developed a virtual business strategy game in which candidates became general managers of a fictitious cosmetics company, and made all decisions virtually. Since it started using the game six years ago, L'Oreal has hired 186 top players from 28 countries, including two each

BRIGITTE BOUVIER

Erica Chean plays a virtual business strategy game that gives winners a shot at working for L'Oreal.

year from Canada. These simulations tend to attract tech-savvy candidates, and allow them to "try out" the job and the industry to see if there is a fit.[40]

Guidelines for Employment Interviewers

Apart from the characteristics of the interviews themselves, there are several important tips for interviewers. Organizations should be cautious in selecting employment interviewers. Qualities that are desirable include humility, the ability to think objectively, maturity, and poise. Given the importance of diversity in the workforce, experience in associating with people from a variety of backgrounds is also desirable. Qualities to avoid in interviewers include overtalkativeness, extreme opinions, and biases.

A Review of the Best

There have been several reviews of research studies on the employment interview.[41] Each of these reviews discusses and evaluates numerous studies concerned with such questions as "What traits can be assessed in the interview?" and "How do interviewers reach their decisions?" Highlights in HRM 6.6 presents some of the major findings of these studies. It shows that information is available that can be used to increase the validity of interviews.

Figure 6.8 on page 274 summarizes the variables and processes involved in the employment interview. The figure shows that a number of applicant characteristics may influence the perception of the interviewer and thus the hiring decision. In addition, many interviewer and situational factors may also influence the perceptual and judgmental processes. For example, the race and sex of an applicant may shape the expectations, biases, and behaviours of an interviewer, which in turn may affect the interview outcome. Even a limited understanding of the variables shown in Figure 6.8 can help increase the interviewing effectiveness of managers and supervisors.

Interviewer Training

Training has been shown to dramatically improve the competence of interviewers. If not done on a continuing basis, training should at least be done periodically for managers, supervisors, and HR representatives who conduct interviews. Interviewer training programs should include practice interviews conducted under guidance. Practice interviews may be recorded on videotape and evaluated later in a group training session. Some variation in technique is only natural. However, the following list presents ten ground rules for employment interviews that are commonly accepted and supported by research findings. Their apparent simplicity should not lead one to underestimate their importance.

1. *Establish an interview plan.* Examine the purposes of the interview and determine the areas and specific questions to be covered. Review job requirements, application-form data, test scores, and other available information before seeing the applicant.

Highlights in HRM 6.6

Some Major Findings from Research Studies on the Interview

1. Structured interviews are more reliable than unstructured interviews.
2. Interviewers are influenced more by unfavourable than by favourable information.
3. Interrater reliability is increased when there is a greater amount of information about the job to be filled.
4. A bias is established early in the interview, and this tends to be followed by either a favourable or an unfavourable decision.
5. Intelligence is the trait most validly estimated by an interview, but the interview information adds nothing to test data.
6. Interviewers can explain why they feel an applicant is likely to be an unsatisfactory employee but not why the applicant may be satisfactory.
7. Factual written data seem to be more important than physical appearance in determining judgments. This increases with interviewing experience.
8. An interviewee is given a more extreme evaluation (positive/negative) when preceded by an interviewee of opposing value (position/negative).
9. Interpersonal skills and motivation are probably best evaluated by the interview.
10. Allowing the applicant time to talk makes rapid first impressions less likely and provides a larger behaviour sample.
11. Nonverbal as well as verbal interactions influence decisions.
12. Experienced interviewers rank applicants in the same order, although they differ in the proportion that they will accept. Experienced interviewers tend to be more selective than less experienced ones.

2. *Establish and maintain rapport.* This is accomplished by greeting the applicant pleasantly, by explaining the purpose of the interview, by displaying sincere interest in the applicant, and by listening carefully.

3. *Be an active listener.* Strive to understand, comprehend, and gain insight into what is only suggested or implied. A good listener's mind is alert, and face and posture usually reflect this fact.

4. *Pay attention to nonverbal cues.* An applicant's facial expressions, gestures, body position, and movements often provide clues to that person's attitudes and feelings. Interviewers should be aware of what they themselves are communicating nonverbally.

5. *Provide information as freely and honestly as possible.* Answer fully and frankly the applicant's questions. Present a realistic picture of the job.

6. *Use questions effectively.* To elicit a truthful answer, questions should be phrased as objectively as possible, giving no indication of what response is desired.

7. *Separate facts from inferences.* During the interview, record factual information. Later, record your inferences or interpretations of the facts. Compare your inferences with those of other interviewers.

Figure 6.8 | Variables in the Employment Interview

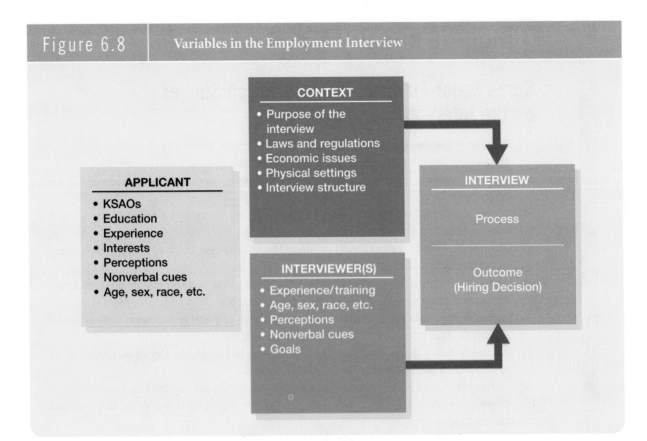

8. *Recognize biases and stereotypes.* One typical bias is for interviewers to consider strangers who have interests, experiences, and backgrounds similar to their own to be more acceptable. Stereotyping involves forming generalized opinions of how people of a given gender, race, or ethnic background appear, think, feel, and act. The influence of sex-role stereotyping is central to sex discrimination in employment. Avoid the influence of "beautyism." Discrimination against unattractive people is a persistent and pervasive form of employment discrimination. Also avoid "halo error," or judging an individual favourably or unfavourably overall on the basis of only one strong point (or weak point) on which you place high value.

9. *Control the course of the interview.* Establish an interview plan and stick to it. Provide the applicant with ample opportunity to talk, but maintain control of the situation in order to reach the interview objectives.

10. *Standardize the questions asked.* To increase reliability and avoid discrimination, ask the same questions of all applicants for a particular job. Keep careful notes; record facts, impressions, and any relevant information, including what was told to the applicant.

Employment Equity: Are Your Questions Legal?

The entire subject of pre-employment questioning is complex. Federal and provincial requirements sometimes vary in the types of questions that may be asked during the interview. However, all jurisdictions forbid direct questions about race, sex, colour, age, religion, and national origin, and most look with disapproval on indirect questions dealing with the same topics. Some of the questions that interviewers once felt free to ask can be potentially hazardous. Human rights commissions have severely limited the areas of questioning. In general, if the question is job-related, is asked of everyone, and does not discriminate against a certain class of applicants, it is likely to be acceptable to government authorities. Readers who are interested in a more comprehensive discussion should consult Catano et al., *Recruitment and Selection in Canada,* third edition (2005).

Particular care has to be given to questions asked of female applicants about their family responsibilities. It is inappropriate, for example, to ask, "Who will take care of your children while you are at work?" or "Do you plan to have children?" or "What is your husband's occupation?" or "Are you engaged?" It is, in fact, inappropriate to ask applicants of either gender questions about matters that have no relevance to job performance.

Employers have found it advisable to provide interviewers with instructions on how to avoid potentially discriminatory questions in their interviews. The examples of appropriate and inappropriate questions shown in Highlights in HRM 6.7 on page 276 may serve as guidelines for application forms as well as pre-employment interviews. Complete guidelines may be developed from current information available from provincial human rights commissions. Once an individual is hired, the information needed but not asked in the interview may be obtained if there is a valid need for it and if it does not lead to discrimination.

Medical Examination

A medical examination is generally given to ensure that the health and fitness of applicants is adequate to meet the job requirements. It also provides a baseline against which subsequent medical examinations can be compared and interpreted. The last objective is especially important for determining work-caused disabilities under workers' compensation law.

In the past, requirements for physical characteristics such as strength, agility, height, and weight were often determined by the employer's invalidated notions of what should be required. Many requirements that tend to discriminate against women have been questioned and modified so as to represent typical job demands.

Medical examinations and inquiries about a candidate directed to medical professionals can be conducted only after an offer (preferably written) of employment has been made. The offer can be made conditional on the applicant's ability to perform the essential duties of the job as determined by a job-related medical examination. Any medical inquiries must be directly related to assessing the candidate's abilities to perform the essential duties of the job. This allows the applicant with a disability the opportunity to be considered exclusively on merits during the selection process. Before human rights legislation was introduced, employers would screen out applicants with disabilities based on medical information requested on application forms or obtained through pre-employment medical examinations. These methods are now deemed discriminatory.

An employer may ask a candidate if she or he has any disability-related needs that would require accommodation to enable performance of the essential duties of the job. The interviewer should be cautioned about probing as to the nature of the disability. Later employment-related decisions may be perceived to be based on this information and thereby characterized as discriminatory. To ensure neutrality, and to avoid the possibility of a complaint to the Canadian Human Rights Commission, such

Highlights in HRM 6.7

Appropriate and Inappropriate Interview Questions

SUBJECT	AVOID ASKING	PREFERRED
Name	about name change; whether it was changed by court order, marriage, or other reason maiden name	
Address	for addresses outside Canada	ask place and duration of current or recent address
Age	for birth certificates, baptismal records, or about age in general	ask applicants if they are eligible to work under Canadian laws regarding age restrictions
Sex	males or females to fill in different applications	
	about pregnancy, child-bearing plans, or childcare arrangements	can ask applicant if the attendance requirements can be met
Marital Status	whether applicant is single, married, divorced, engaged, separated, widowed, or living common-law	if transfer or travel is part of the job, the applicant can be asked if he or she can meet these requirements
Family Status	number of children or dependants about childcare arrangements	can ask if the applicant would be able to work the required hours and, where applicable, overtime
National or Ethnic Origin	about birthplace, nationality of ancestors, spouse, or other relatives whether born in Canada for proof of citizenship	since those who are entitled to work in Canada must be citizens, permanent residents, or holders of eligible-valid work permits, applicants can be asked if they are legally entitled to work in Canada
Military Service	about military service in other countries	inquiry about Canadian military service where employment preference is given to veterans by law
Language	mother tongue where language skills obtained	ask if applicant understands, reads, writes, or speaks languages required for the job
Race or Colour	any question about race or colour, including colour of eyes, skin, or hair	

Photographs	for photo to be attached to applications or sent to interviewer before interview	
Religion	about religious affiliation, church membership, frequency of church attendance, if applicant will work a specific religious holiday, or for references from clergy or religious leader	explain the required work shift, asking if such a schedule poses problems for the applicant
Height and Weight	no inquiry unless there is evidence they are genuine occupational requirements	
Disability	for listing of all disabilities, limitations, or health problems whether applicant drinks or uses drugs whether applicant has ever received psychiatric care or been hospitalized for emotional problems whether applicant has received workers' compensation	ask if applicant has any condition that could affect ability to do the job ask if the applicant has any condition that should be considered in selection
Medical Information	if currently under physician's care, name of family doctor if receiving counselling or therapy	
Pardoned Conviction	whether an applicant has ever been convicted if an applicant has ever been arrested whether an applicant has a criminal record	if bonding is a job requirement ask if applicant is eligible
Sexual Orientation	about the applicant's sexual orientation	
References	The same restrictions that apply to questions asked of applicants also apply to questions asked of the applicant's references.	

Source: Excerpt from Guidelines to Screening and Selection in Employment from www.chrc-ccdp.ca/publications/screen-preselection.asp. Canadian Human Rights Commission. Reproduced with the permission of the Minister of Public Works and the Government Services Canada, 2004.

USING THE INTERNET

The Treasury Board Secretariat of the federal government publishes its policies on the accommodation of persons with disabilities at:

www.tbs-sct.gc.ca/pubs_pol/hrpubs/TB_852/ppaed_e.asp

information should remain exclusively with the examining physician, not in the personnel file.

If the employee has a disability, the employer has a duty to accommodate his or her needs. The accommodation can be accomplished either by changing some of the essential duties of the position or by providing the appropriate equipment. To determine whether an individual can do the essential duties of a particular position, the employer should conduct a physical demands analysis, checklists for which are available through most provincial ministries of labour.

As mentioned earlier, requirements for physical characteristics such as height were in the past often determined by an employer's notion of what should be required. Under human rights legislation, employers are prohibited from imposing their own standards where it has the effect of excluding members of the designated groups, unless it can be shown that the requirements are reasonable and bona fide. Such standards are often based on the vital statistics of the average white Anglo-Saxon male. There is little evidence to demonstrate that characteristics such as height and weight constitute bona fide occupational requirements.

Drug Testing

The Canadian Human Rights Commission and some of its provincial counterparts have issued policies on employment-related drug testing. Addiction to drugs or alcohol is considered a disability, and the employer is to be guided by legislation and by practices such as workplace accommodation. The medical examination cannot be conducted until a conditional offer of employment is made in writing, and the examination can determine only the individual's ability to perform the essential duties.

If the employer has established that drug testing is job-related—typically, this involves safety issues—the candidate must be informed that job offers are conditional on the successful passing of a drug test and that this test will be required during the course of employment. The employer then has the right to demand a medical examination. If an employee refuses, he or she can be dismissed.

The following types of testing are not allowed:

- Pre-employment drug testing
- Pre-employment alcohol testing
- Random drug testing, and
- Random alcohol testing of employees in non-safety-sensitive positions.

There is widespread opposition to drug testing in the workplace, which is why only about 2 percent of companies in Canada do it, compared to about 80 percent of American companies. Canadian companies which operate in both countries, such as those in cross-border trucking, may argue that testing is a bona fide occupational qualification for drivers, otherwise they would be banned from driving in the U.S. Syncor Canada, a world leader in mining and extracting crude oil, feels that drug testing of heavy equipment operators could be justified on safety grounds, but not for those in an office environment.[42]

The Canadian Civil Liberties Association takes the position that "no person should be required to share urine with a stranger" as a condition of employment. Employee Assistance Programs (EAPs) play an important role in helping employees with drug and alcohol problems. EAPs will be discussed in Chapter 12.

USING THE INTERNET

The CHRC policy on drug and alcohol testing can be found at:

www.chrc-ccdp.ca/legislation_policies/

Reaching a Selection Decision

While all of the steps in the selection process are important, the most critical step is the decision to accept or reject applicants. Because of the cost of placing new employees on the payroll, the short probationary period in many organizations, and employment equity considerations, the final decision must be as sound as possible. Thus it requires systematic consideration of all the relevant information about applicants. It is common to use summary forms and checklists to ensure that all of the pertinent information has been included in the evaluation of applicants. In the Reality Check, read about how The Bay reaches recruits and reaches selection decisions for its candidates.

Reality Check

Selection at The Bay

Canada's oldest corporation and largest department store retailer is the Hudson's Bay Company, which was established in 1670 and operates as The Bay and Zellers. Tina Peacock, human resources manager for Merchandise Services & Corporate Offices, has been with HBC for more than 20 years. She helps the company achieve its goals by carefully applying selection methods to identify key potential candidates for many different positions, such as merchandise buyer, financial manager, and systems manager.

"In addition to succession planning," states Peacock, "we follow established trends, such as growth in our business units, turnover, and performance results, to identify those positions that may become vacant during the year. Through a number of training programs provided inhouse, we are able to fill our positions internally. In fact, 80 percent are staffed from internal promotions. For the other 20 percent, we hire externally. As a proactive measure in anticipation of those openings, we run recruiting ads so that we always have a 'stable' of competent candidates.

"It is important that we work closely with the managers because they know what is needed to run their business. My role is to provide them with qualified candidates who possess the basic job knowledge with the right competencies to work in our fast-paced, changing environment. For instance, a number of managers are tapped into the marketplace, so they are able to get the ball rolling by identifying candidates in the industry before an ad is placed. Our role is to prescreen those candidates to ensure they have the attributes needed to successfully perform in our environment.

"We work very closely with an ad agency to assist us in preparing the ad and to provide advice on the marketing strategies of where and when to place the ad. They save you a lot of time, especially when they understand your business. Running our ads for a particular position yields us other qualified candidates for other positions we had not counted on.

"Many of our ads yield as many as 250 résumés. Based on the competencies required for a position, we prescreen the résumés. It is not uncommon for me to receive over fifty phone calls per day when an ad is running. If I can delegate some of those calls, I do; however, if they have asked me for something specific, I make an effort to call them back because they are our customers and they are important to us. Once I have determined a short list, I then conduct a

(continued on next page)

pretty thorough telephone interview before bringing in any candidates. Questions regarding salary expectations, any information that may be missing on the résumé, and some very job-specific questions are reviewed. We are always looking to improve our systems. Our next ad will incorporate a voice response system that has been developed internally by our Information Services Department. Candidates who wish to apply to an ad will be asked to call our system and respond to some basic job-related questions. At the end of the session, the candidate will be advised whether they possess the basic requirements of the job and whether they should apply to this position.

"The questions we ask during the face-to-face interview are open-ended questions that look for behavioural attributes specific to the competencies and key job requirements. For example, we want the candidates to demonstrate how they have gone about performing their job duties in the past. For those candidates who proceed to a final interview, we ask each of them to complete a communications survey. Using an outside consultant, we have developed a prediction performance program profile that has identified benchmark attributes for our buyers, merchandising trainees, and store managers. The results are graphed and compared against the benchmark. This profile is not used as a basis for determining whether we should hire a candidate or not. It provides us with another opportunity to fully assess the individual's capabilities by asking more focused questions. In this way, it ensures that we have fully investigated the individual's background and credentials. We provide each of our candidates with a written assessment of the report, whether they are hired or not, and ask them to comment on the accuracy of the results. Based on these responses, the report has been assessed at an accuracy of over 90 percent."

Peacock says in closing: "Systems in the workplace will continue to change, but the bottom line is that we need the best people to technically do the job and, most importantly, they must be customer focused."

Summarizing Information about Applicants

Fundamentally, an employer is interested in what an applicant can do and will do. An evaluation of candidates on the basis of assembled information should focus on these two factors, as shown in Figure 6.9. The "can-do" factors include knowledge and skills, as well as the aptitude (the potential) for acquiring new knowledge and skills. The "will-do" factors include motivation, interests, and other personality characteristics. Both factors are essential to successful performance on the job. The employee who has the ability (can do) but is not motivated to use it (will not do) is little better than the employee who lacks the necessary ability.

It is much easier to measure what individuals can do than what they will do. The can-do factors are readily evident from test scores and verified information. What the individual will do can only be inferred. Responses to interview and application-form questions may be used as a basis for obtaining information for making inferences about what an individual will do.

Decision Strategy

The strategy used for making personnel decisions for one category of jobs may differ from that used for another category. The strategy for selecting managerial and executive personnel, for example, will differ from that used in selecting clerical and technical

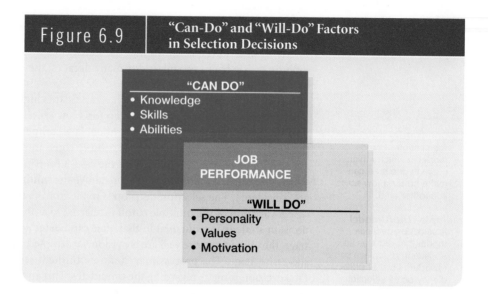

Figure 6.9 "Can-Do" and "Will-Do" Factors in Selection Decisions

personnel. While many factors are to be considered in hiring decisions, the following are some of the questions that managers must consider:

1. Should the individuals be hired according to their highest potential or according to the needs of the organization?

2. At what grade or wage level should the individual be started?

3. Should initial selection be concerned primarily with an ideal match of the employee to the job, or should potential for advancement in the organization be considered?

4. To what extent should those who are not qualified but are qualifiable be considered?

5. Should overqualified individuals be considered?

6. What effect will a decision have on meeting employment equity plans and diversity considerations?

In addition to these types of factors, managers must also consider which approach they will use in making hiring decisions. There are two basic approaches to selection: clinical (personal judgment) and statistical.

Clinical Approach

In the clinical approach to decision making, those making the selection decision review all the data on applicants. Then, on the basis of their understanding of the job and the individuals who have been successful in that job, they make a decision. Different individuals often arrive at different decisions about an applicant when they use this approach because each evaluator assigns different weights to the applicant's strengths and weaknesses. Furthermore, personal biases and stereotypes are frequently covered up by what appear to be rational bases for acceptance or rejection.

Statistical Approach

In contrast to the clinical approach, the statistical approach to decision making is more objective. It involves identifying the most valid predictors and weighting them through statistical methods such as multiple regression.[43] Quantified data such as scores or ratings from interviews, tests, and other procedures are then combined according to their weighted value. Individuals with the highest combined scores are selected. A comparison of the clinical approach with the statistical approach in a wide variety of situations has shown that the statistical approach is superior. Although this superiority has been recognized for many decades, the clinical approach continues to be the one most commonly used.

With a strictly statistical approach, a candidate's high score on one predictor (such as a cognitive ability test) will make up for a low score on another predictor (such as the interview). For this reason, this model is a **compensatory model.** However, it is frequently important that applicants achieve some minimum level of proficiency on all selection dimensions. When this is the case, a **multiple cutoff model** can be used in which only those candidates who score above the minimum cutoff on all dimensions are considered. The selection decision is made from that subset of candidates.[44]

A variation of the multiple cutoff is referred to as the **multiple hurdle model.** This decision strategy is sequential in that after candidates go through an initial evaluation stage, the ones who score well are provisionally accepted and are assessed further at each successive stage. The process may continue through several stages (hurdles) before a final decision is made regarding the candidates. This approach is especially useful when either the testing or training procedures are lengthy and expensive.

Each of the statistical approaches requires that a decision be made about where the cutoff lies—that point in the distribution of scores above which a person should be considered and below which the person should be rejected. The score that the applicant must achieve is the cutoff score. Depending on the labour supply and diversity and antidiscrimination considerations, it may be necessary to lower or raise the cutoff score.

The effects of raising and lowering the cutoff score are illustrated in Figure 6.10. Each dot in the centre of the figure represents the relationship between the test score (or a weighted combination of test scores) and the criterion of success for one individual. In this instance, the test has a fairly high validity, as represented by the elliptical pattern of dots. Note that the high-scoring individuals are concentrated in the satisfactory category on job success, whereas the low-scoring individuals are concentrated in the unsatisfactory category.

If the cutoff score is set at A, only the individuals represented by areas 1 and 2 will be accepted. Nearly all of them will be successful. If more employees are needed (that is, there is an increase in the selection ratio), the cutoff score may be lowered to point B. In this case, a larger number of potential failures will be accepted, as shown in quadrants 2 and 4. Even if the cutoff is lowered to C, the total number of satisfactory individuals selected (represented by the dots in areas 1, 3, and 5) exceeds the total number selected who are unsatisfactory (areas 2, 4, and 6). Thus the test serves to maximize the selection of probable successes and to minimize the selection of probable failures. This is all we can hope for in predicting job success: the probability of selecting a greater proportion of individuals who will be successful rather than unsuccessful.

While the most valid predictors should be used with any selection strategy, a related factor contributes to selecting the best-qualified people: selectivity, or having an adequate number of applicants or candidates from which to make a selection. Selectivity is typically expressed in terms of a **selection ratio,** which is the ratio of the number of applicants to be selected to the total number of applicants. A ratio of 0.10, for example, means that 10 percent of the applicants will be selected. A ratio of 0.90 means that 90 percent will be selected. If the selection ratio is low, only the most promising applicants will normally be hired. When the ratio is high, very little selectivity will be possible, because even applicants having mediocre ability will have to be hired if the vacancies are to be filled.

It should be noted that how much of a contribution any predictor will make to the improvement of a given selection process is a function not only of the validity of

compensatory model
A selection decision model in which a high score in one area can make up for a low score in another area

multiple cutoff model
A selection decision model that requires an applicant to achieve some minimum level of proficiency on all selection dimensions

multiple hurdle model
A sequential strategy in which only the applicants with the highest scores at an initial test stage go on to subsequent stages

selection ratio
The number of applicants compared with the number of people to be hired

| Figure 6.10 | Test Score Scatterplot with Hypothetical Cutoffs |

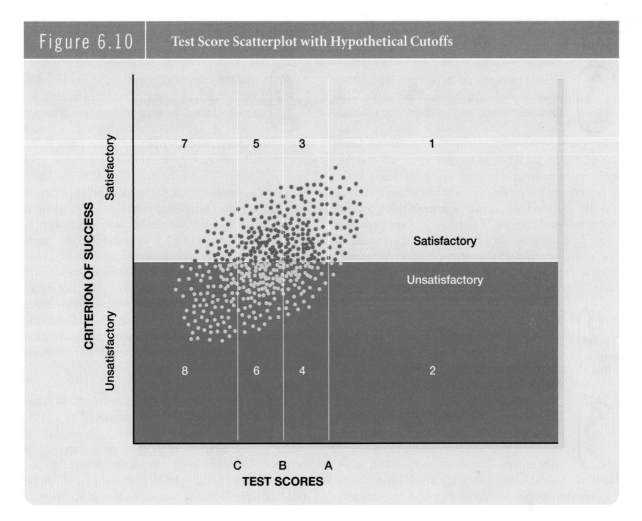

the predictor and the selection ratio, but also of the proportion of people who are judged successful using current selection procedures.

Final Decision

After a preliminary selection has been made in the employment department, the applicants who appear most promising are then referred to departments with vacancies. There they are interviewed by the managers or supervisors, who usually make the final decision and communicate it to the employment department. Because of the weight that is usually given to their choices, managers and supervisors should be trained so that their role in the selection process does not negate the more rigorous efforts of the HR department staff.

In large organizations, notifying applicants of the decision and making job offers is often the responsibility of the HR department. This department should confirm the details of the job, working arrangements, wages, and so on, and specify a deadline by which the applicant must reach a decision. If, at this point, findings from the medical examination are not yet available, an offer is often made contingent on the applicant's passing the examination.

SUMMARY

The selection process should provide as much reliable and valid information as possible about applicants so that their qualifications can be carefully matched with job specifications. The information that is obtained should be clearly job-related or predictive of success on the job and free from potential discrimination. Reliability refers to the consistency of test scores over time and across measures. Validity refers to the accuracy of measurement. Validity can be assessed in terms of whether the measurement is based on a job specification (content validity), whether test scores correlate with performance criteria (predictive validity), and whether the test accurately measures what it purports to measure (construct validity).

Interviews are customarily used in conjunction with application forms, biographical information blanks, references, background investigations, cognitive ability tests, job knowledge tests, and work sample tests.

The value of tests should not be overlooked because they are more objective than the interview and can provide a broader sampling of behaviour. Cognitive ability tests are especially valuable for assessing verbal, quantitative, and reasoning abilities. Personality and interest tests are perhaps best for placement. Physical ability tests are most useful for predicting job performance, accidents, and injuries, particularly for physically demanding work. Job knowledge and work sample tests are achievement tests that are useful for determining whether a candidate can perform the duties of the job without further training.

The interview is an important source of information about job applicants. It can be unstructured, wherein the interviewer is free to pursue whatever approach and sequence of topics might seem appropriate. Alternatively, an interview can be structured wherein each applicant receives the same set of questions, which have pre-established answers. Some interviews are situational and can focus on hypothetical situations or actual behavioural descriptions of previous work experiences. Interviews can be conducted by a single individual, by a panel, or via a computer or video interface. Regardless of the technique chosen, those who conduct interviews should receive special training to acquaint them with interviewing methods and employment equity considerations. The training should also make them more aware of the major findings from research studies on the interview and how they can apply these findings. Medical examinations and drug testing are generally not permitted under human rights legislation.

In the process of making decisions, all "can-do" and "will-do" factors should be assembled and weighted systematically so that the final decision can be based on a composite of the most reliable and valid information. While the clinical approach to decision making is used more than the statistical approach, the former lacks the accuracy of the latter. Compensatory models allow a candidate's high score on one predictor to make up for a low score on another. However, multiple cutoff and multiple hurdle approaches require minimal competency on each selection criterion. Whichever of these approaches is used, the goal is to select a greater proportion of individuals who will be successful on the job.

KEY TERMS

DISCUSSION QUESTIONS

1. What is meant by the term *criterion* as it is used in personnel selection? Give some examples of criteria used for jobs with which you are familiar.

2. What are some of the problems that arise in checking references furnished by job applicants? Are there any solutions to these problems?

3. What characteristics do job knowledge and job sample tests have that often make them more acceptable to the examinees than other types of tests?

4. Personality tests, like other tests used in employee selection, have been under attack for several decades. What are some of the reasons why applicants find personality tests objectionable? On what basis could their use for selection purposes be justified?

5. Compare briefly the major types of employment interviews described in this chapter. Which type would you prefer to conduct? Why?

6. Speed dating? Speed job interviewing? Speed interviewing is growing in popularity. It is a technique that gives candidates 10 or 15 minutes with a potential employer before moving on to another interview. The largest speed interviewing event happened in Montreal in October 2005, when Videotron Ltee, a division of Quebecor Media, held a job fair to hire 300 employees from sales reps to systems architects. They interviewed 2000 applicants in one day. All applicants who lined up had been pre-screened, and their interviews with recruiters and functional specialists lasted five to seven minutes. Those who were successful wrote a test, and then those who made the short list got second interviews lasting 15–30 minutes. At the end of the day, the company filled 200 of the 300 positions. Discuss the advantages and limitations of this process. Assess its reliability and validity.

INTERNET EXERCISE

Take an online personality test such as the leadership quiz offered on the Monster.ca website (http://content.monster.ca/tools/quizzes/leadership/). Is this test valid? How could an organization use this test?

HRM Experience

Designing Selection Criteria and Methods

Making hiring decisions is one of the most important—and difficult—decisions a manager makes. Without good information, managers have almost no chance of making the right choice. They might as well be using a Ouija board. The process begins with a sound understanding of the job: the tasks, duties, and responsibilities required and the knowledge, skills, and abilities needed to do it. Job analysis is very helpful in making certain that all the information is needed to ensure a person-job fit, but it may not be enough. Other information about company values, philosophy, and the like may be required to ensure person-organization fit.

Assignment

1. Working in teams of four to six individuals, choose a job with which you are familiar and identify the most important knowledge, skills, abilities, and other characteristics needed for someone to perform well.

2. Next, identify which methods you would use to tap these qualities. Would you use applications, interviews, psychological tests, work samples, or what? Explain why you would use these methods and justify the cost and time required.

3. After you have identified your selection criteria and methods, do a "reality check" in a real organization. Interview a manager who employs someone in that job. For example, if the job you selected is salesperson, go to a local business to learn how they select individuals for sales jobs. Compare what you thought would be a good selection approach with what you learned in the company you visited.

4. Identify the reasons for any discrepancies between your approach and theirs. Are the reasons justified and sound?

BIZFLIX EXERCISES

Bowfinger: The Lookalike

Some major learning objectives of this chapter include understanding the goals of an organization's selection process, using different types of information in employee selection, and using different employment interview approaches. Watch this humorous scene from *Bowfinger* with those learning objectives in mind.

This film, which brought Steve Martin and Eddie Murphy together for the first time, offers a funny look at Hollywood filmmaking. Bobby Bowfinger (Martin), perhaps the least successful director in films, wants to produce a low-budget film with top star Kit Ramsey (Murphy). Bowfinger's problem: Recruit a crew and cast with almost no budget and trick Kit into appearing in his film.

Bowfinger interviews several candidates for the Kit Ramsey lookalike role. He rejects everyone until Jifferson—Jiff—Ramsey (Murphy) auditions. This scene is an edited version of "The Lookalike" sequence early in the film. It includes Jiff's audition and interview, and a brief look at his first workday.

What to Watch for and Ask Yourself

- Which steps in the employee selection process shown earlier in Figure 6.2 appear in this scene? Which steps did Bobby Bowfinger skip?
- Does Bobby Bowfinger have valid selection criteria for filling the role of the Kit Ramsey lookalike? Do you predict Jiff Ramsey's success as a Kit Ramsey substitute?
- Which type of employment interview did Bowfinger use? See the earlier section "The Employment Interview" for a discussion of different employment interview approaches.

case study 1

Searching for Spies

The Canadian Security Intelligence Service (CSIS) is a civilian-run agency, formerly the Security Services of the RCMP. Its role is defensive—to protect Canada from terrorists and foreign spies. It does not send armed spies overseas. Selecting spies used to be a secret process. There was no public knowledge about how spies were recruited, what the job description was, and what the selection criteria and methods were.

Each year CSIS receives 3000 unsolicited applicants for about 100 openings. However, most of these applications are from unqualified James Bond wanna-be's. CSIS wants highly qualified, well-educated, multilingual, multiskilled employees. It recruits openly, and its selection criteria and processes are public.

If you want to apply, CSIS looks for Canadian citizens who are university graduates, preferably with advanced degrees. You must have a valid driver's licence and be able to relocate anywhere in Canada at any time. You will have lived or studied abroad, be proficient in English and French, and have a third or fourth language. CSIS looks for generalists—people who are knowledgeable about international and political issues and who have investigative and analytical skills. As a CSIS employee, you will not be able to discuss your work with outsiders at any time.

CSIS recruits at government job fairs. As an applicant, you must go through the following selection process:

- Submit a résumé
- Complete a 12-page application, which also involves writing a 500-word essay explaining why you want to become an intelligence officer
- Attend a group information session, where recruiters and intelligence officers answer questions
- Attend a suitability interview, where your motivation and verbal and people skills are judged
- Take a battery of psychological and aptitude tests
- Have your language skills tested
- Attend a national assessment panel—veterans will assess your motivation, knowledge of CSIS, and general awareness of public affairs
- Be submitted to security clearance procedures (including a polygraph test, fingerprints, lie detector test, credit check, criminal record check, and references back to teen years), which take three months and cost thousands of dollars
- Go to a final interview

This is a multiple-hurdle model of selection. As a candidate you will have to pass each hurdle before being allowed to continue to the next. If successful, you will be on probation for five years, undergo 12 weeks of classroom training and language training, and spend two or three years at an operations desk at headquarters, before being transferred to the field under the guidance of a mentor.

Source: Adapted from J. Sallot, "The Spy Masters' Talent Hunt Goes Public," *The Globe and Mail*, June 22, 1999: A1, A10. Reprinted by permission of *The Globe and Mail*.

QUESTIONS

1. Do you think the selection system used by CSIS is valid? Using your knowledge of validity, rate each step in this process.
2. One reason CSIS went public was to increase the representation of women from 10 percent to a target of 50 percent. Are there any possible problems with discrimination in this selection system? Discuss.

case study 2

Aptitude Tests at an Electronics Corporation

An electronics plant in Midland, Ontario, has begun using aptitude tests as part of its selection process. Before new candidates will be considered for new job openings and for promotions, they must pass eight different aptitude tests. One test for manual dexterity requires applicants to move small metal pegs from holes on one side of a board to holes on the other side as fast as they can. In another test, employees are shown pictures of two cows—one white and the other spotted—and asked, "Which cow would be easier to see from an airplane?"

The company's employees see no relationship between their jobs and the cow test; they also find it humiliating to have to move pegs on a board in order to qualify for jobs they have been doing for years. In one testing session, 80 percent of employees failed. The price of failure is exclusion from higher-paying and more desirable jobs. Even more shameful is the fact that people with less seniority and little plant experience are passing the aptitude tests.

The dispute is deeply rooted. The union feels that the tests are allowing management to replace experienced workers with new hires who work for less pay. The fact that test results are almost always confidential has led to suspicions that the results are being manipulated in some way. After seeing their colleagues fail the tests, some workers are so discouraged that they don't even try for new jobs or promotions. Other changes that have been introduced along with the tests include 12-hour rotating shifts, the "flexible" replacement of workers, and new computerized inspection systems.

Management defends the testing, claiming that new plants and new work methods require aptitudes such as problem solving and flexible thinking. These skills are not usually associated with the stereotype of the senior blue-collar worker. In the past, young people had no need to even graduate from high school if there was a plant in town offering big paycheques for manual labour. The tests that have been introduced discriminate against older workers with less formal education. In demand today are employees who can do many jobs, solve problems, make decisions, provide creative solutions, and function effectively as part of an empowered work team.

Source: Reprinted by permission of the author Megan Terepocki.

QUESTIONS

1. Do you see any problems with the way the company's testing program is being managed? Discuss.
2. Suggest how the program might be modified.
3. The union is fighting to eliminate the testing. On what grounds could the union base its arguments?
4. If an employee files a complaint with the Ontario Human Rights Commission on the grounds that the test discriminated against him as an older worker, what kinds of information will have to be gathered to determine the validity of his claim?

case study 3

Nike: Hiring Gets Off on the Right Foot

Technology is changing how companies recruit and select employees. Nike, the world's largest shoe manufacturer, is one example of a company using computer-assisted interviewing. The company has used an Aspen Tree product to hire some of its 24 000-plus employees, including employees for Niketowns, retail stores that showcase Nike products. At a single store opened in Las Vegas, for example, 6000 people responded to ads for workers needed to fill 250 positions. Nike used IVR (interactive voice response) technology to make the first cut. Applicants responded to eight questions over the telephone; 3500 applicants were screened out because they weren't available when needed or didn't have retail experience. The rest had a computer-assisted interview at the store, followed by a personal interview.

"We think it's important to give a personal interview to anyone who comes to the store," said Nike's manager of human resources for the retail division. "Applicants are customers as well as potential hires."

The computer interview identified candidates who had been in customer service environments, had a passion for sports, and would make good Nike customer service representatives. Interviews were done in batches. The computer interview (which includes a video showing three scenarios for helping a customer and asks the applicant to choose the best one) was given every 45 minutes to a group of applicants. As applicants completed the interview, a printer in the next room printed their responses. Areas that needed to be probed further were flagged, as were areas that indicated particular strengths.

While the applicant completed an application form online, the interviewer used the printout to prepare for the applicant's human interview. Some applicants would be given only a short interview; other, more likely candidates would be interviewed at greater length. The computer not only helped interviewers screen for people who lost their temper in work situations or who demonstrated other undesirable behaviours, but it also helped the interviewers determine what to ask to reconcile inconsistencies in the computer interview or to probe applicant strengths in desired areas. Because Nike uses behavioural-based interviewing, applicants must document their areas of strength with examples from their work. Some applicants were offered jobs on the spot. Others were called back for second interviews.

Using computer-assisted interviewing has helped Nike staff up fast as well as reduce turnover in the retail division. The company saved $2.4 million during a three-year period by reducing turnover from 87 to 51 percent, although other processes for coaching and leading within the stores have also played a part.

Other areas of the company are finding ways to use recruitment technology, too. When an international division found itself besieged with as many as 400 résumés a week, it hired a solutions provider to automate the process of responding to applicants and tracking them. (Nike has a policy of responding to each potential employee with an individual letter.) Susannah Sanchez Perez applied for a job with Nike in May 2004, and remembers being impressed by how quickly the company responded to her. "I received an e-mail straightaway telling me that it would respond to me within three weeks," she said. "In fact, it only took four days for Nike to call me and invite me in for an interview. It took a long time to fill out the online form and that could be streamlined, but I was impressed by how professional the company seemed."

Source: Linda Thornburg, "Computer-Assisted Interviewing Shortens Hiring Cycle," *HRMagazine* 43, no. 2 (February 1998): 73–79. Adapted with the permission of *HRMagazine,* published by the Society for Human Resource Management, Alexandria, VA, via Copyright Clearance Center. See also Alex Blyth, "Winning Recruitment Race," *Personnel Today,* May 2004, 26.

QUESTIONS

1. What do you think are the prime advantages and disadvantages of Nike's computer-based interviewing system?
2. Are there any employment equity concerns regarding this system?
3. If interviews serve a public relations role, what should Nike be concerned about?
4. How would you suggest that Nike might modify and improve its system?

CAREER COUNSEL

The résumé preparation exercises on the *Managing Human Resources* website (www.belcourt5e .nelson.com) will help you tailor your résumé to the position.

NOTES AND REFERENCES

1. Patrick D. Converse, Fredrick L. Oswald, Michael A. Gillespie, Kevin A. Field, and Elizabeth B. Bizot, "Matching Individual to Occupations Using Abilities and the O*NET," *Personnel Psychology* 57, no. 2 (Summer 2004): 451–488; George Callaghan and Paul Thompson, "'We Recruit Attitude': The Selection and Shaping of Routine Call Centre Labour," *Journal of Management Studies* 39, no. 2 (March 2002): 233–54; Terry Beehr, Lana Ivanitskaya, Curtiss Hansen, Dmitry Erofeev, and David Gudanoski, "Evaluation of 360-Degree Feedback Ratings: Relationships with Each Other and with Performance and Selection Predictors," *Journal of Organizational Behavior* 22, no. 7 (November 2001): 775–88.

2. Helena D. Cooper-Thomas, Annelies Van Vianen, and Neil Anderson, "Changes in Person-Organization Fit: The Impact of Socialization Tactics on Perceived and Actual P-O Fit," *European Journal of Work & Organizational Psychology* 13, no. 1 (March 2004): 52–79; Dan Cable and Charles Parsons, "Socialization Tactics and Person-Organization Fit," *Personnel Psychology* 54, no. 1 (Spring 2001): 1–23; Amy Kristof-Brown, "Perceived Applicant Fit: Distinguishing between Recruiters' Perceptions of Person-Job and Person-Organization Fit," *Personnel Psychology* 53, no. 3 (Autumn 2000): 643–71.

3. Mary-Kathryn Zachary, "Discrimination without Intent," *Supervision* 64, no. 5 (May 2003): 23–29; Neal Schmitt, William Rogers, David Chan, Lori Sheppard, and Danielle Jennings, "Adverse Impact and Predictive Efficiency of Various Predictor Combinations," *Journal of Applied Psychology* 82, no. 5 (October 1997): 719–30; Charlene Marmer Solomon, "Testing at Odds with Diversity Efforts?" *Personnel Journal* 75, no. 4 (April 1996): 131–40; Scott E. Maxwell and Richard D. Arvey, "The Search for Predictors with High Validity and Low Adverse Impact: Compatible or Incompatible Goals?" *Journal of Applied Psychology* 78, no. 3 (June 1993): 433–37.

4. Namok Choi, "A Psychometric Examination of the Personal Attributes Questionnaire," *Journal of Social Psychology* 144, no. 3 (June 2004): 348–52; Frank J. Landy, "Test Validity Yearbook," *Journal of Business Psychology* 7, no. 2 (1992): 111–257. See also Edwin E. Ghiselli, "The Validity of Aptitude Tests in Personnel Selection," *Personnel Psychology* 26, no. 4 (Winter 1973): 461–77; J. E. Hunter and R. H. Hunter, "Validity and Utility of Alternative Predictors of Job Performance," *Psychological Bulletin* 96 (1984): 72–98; Ivan Robertson and Mike Smith, "Personnel Selection," *Journal of Occupational and Organizational Psychology* 74, no. 4 (November 2001): 441–72.

5. Jesus F. Salgado and Neil Anderson, "Validity Generalization of GMA Tests across Countries in the European Community," *European Journal of Work & Organizational Psychology* 12, no. 1 (March 2003): 1–17; Calvin C. Hoffman and S. Morton McPhail, "Exploring Options for Supporting Test Use in Situations Precluding Local Validation," *Personnel Psychology* 51, no. 4 (Winter 1998): 987–1003; Leaetta Hough and Frederick Oswald, "Personnel Selection: Looking toward the Future—Remembering the Past," *Annual Review of Psychology* 51 (2000): 631–64.

6. Kobi Dayan, Ronen Kasten, and Shaul Fox, "Entry-Level Police Candidate Assessment Center: An Efficient Tool or a Hammer to Kill a Fly?" *Personnel Psychology* 55, no. 4 (Winter 2002): 827–50; S. Messick, "Foundations of Validity: Meaning and Consequences in Psychological Assessment," *European Journal of Psychological Assessment* 10 (1994): 1–9; Michael Lindell and Christina Brandt, "Assessing Interrater Agreement on the Job Relevance of a Test: A Comparison of the CVI, T, $r^{WG(J)}$, and $r^{*WG(J)}$ Indexes," *Journal of Applied Psychology* 84, no. 4 (August 1999): 640–47.

7. D. Brent Smith and Lill Ellingson, "Substance versus Style: A New Look at Social Desirability in Motivating Contexts," *Journal of Applied Psychology* 87, no. 2 (April 2002): 211–19; Ken Craik et al., "Explorations of Construct Validity in a Combined Managerial and Personality Assessment Programme," *Journal of Occupational and Organizational Psychology* 75, no. 2 (June 2002): 171–93.

8. Pamela Babock, "Spotting Lies," *HRMagazine* 48, no. 10 (October 2003): 46–51; Tammy Prater and Sara Bliss Kiser, "Lies, Lies, and More Lies," *A.A.M. Advance Management Journal* 67, no. 2 (Spring 2002): 9–14.

9. Todd Humber, "Recruitment Isn't Getting Any Easier," *Canadian HR Reporter*, May 23, 2005; www.psc-cfp.gc.ca/centres/annual-annuel/2004/chapter_3_e.htm, retrieved January 16, 2006.

10. "The Pros and Cons of Online Recruiting," *HRFocus* 81 (April 2004): S1; Rob Drew, "Career Portals Boost Online Recruiting," *HRMagazine* 49, no. 4 (April 2004): 111–114; Samuel Greengard, "Smarter Screening Takes Technology and HR Savvy," *Workforce* 81, no. 6 (June 2002): 56–62; Scott R. Kaak, Hubert S. Field, William F. Giles, and Dwight R. Norris, "The Weighted Application Blank," *Cornell Hotel and Restaurant Administration Quarterly* 39, no. 2 (April 1998):

18–24; Brad Bingham, Sherrie Ilg, and Neil Davidson, "Great Candidates Fast: On-Line Job Application and Electronic Processing: Washington State's New Internet Application System," *Public Personnel Management* 31, no. 1 (Spring 2002): 53–64; Sarah Fister Gale, "Internet Recruiting: Better, Cheaper, Faster," *Workforce* 80, no. 12 (December 2001): 74–77; Tim Armes, "Internet Recruiting," *Canadian Manager* 24, no. 1 (Spring 1999): 21–22; "Top Firms Recruit on Web," *USA Today,* September 22, 2000: A1; Cora Daniels, "To Hire a Lumber Expert, Click Here," *Fortune* 141, no. 7 (April 3, 2000): 267–70.

11. Margaret A. McManus and Mary L. Kelly, "Personality Measures and Biodata: Evidence Regarding Their Incremental Predictive Value in the Life Insurance Industry," *Personnel Psychology* 52, no. 1 (Spring 1999): 137–48; Andrew J. Vinchur, Jeffrey S. Schippmann, Fred S. Switzer III, and Philip L. Roth, "A Meta-Analytic Review of Predictors of Job Performance for Salespeople," *Journal of Applied Psychology* 83, no. 4 (August 1998): 586–97; Gary R. Kettlitz, Imad Zbib, and Jaideep Motwani, "Validity of Background Data as a Predictor of Employee Tenure among Nursing Aides in Long-Term Care Facilities," *Health Care Supervisor* 16, no. 3 (March 1998): 26–31; Yen Chung, "The Validity of Biographical Inventories for the Selection of Salespeople," *International Journal of Management* 18, no. 3 (September 2001): 322–29; Teri Elkins and James Phillips, "Job Context, Selection Decision Outcome, and the Perceived Fairness of Selection Tests: Biodata as an Illustrative Case," *Journal of Applied Psychology* 85, no. 3 (June 2000): 479–84; Herschel Chait, Shawn Carreher, and M. Ronald Buckley, "Measuring Service Orientation with Biodata," *Journal of Managerial Issues* 12, no. 1 (Spring 2000): 109–20.

12. Todd Humber, "Recruitment Isn't Getting Any Easier," *Canadian HR Reporter,* May 23, 2005.

13. Kathleen Samey, "A Not-So-Perfect Fit," *Adweek* 44, no. 47 (December 1, 2003): 34; Ann Fisher, "How Can We Be Sure We're Not Hiring a Bunch of Shady Liars?" *Fortune* 147, no. 10 (May 26, 2003); Diane Lacy, Saundra Jackson, and Anne St. Martin, "References, Cafeteria Changes, Smokers," *HRMagazine* 48, no. 4 (April 2003): 37–38; Carolyn Hirschman, "The Whole Truth," *HRMagazine* 45, no. 6 (June 2000): 86–92; Samuel Greengard, "Are You Well Armed to Screen Applicants?" *Personnel Journal* (December 1995): 84–95; "The Final Rung: References," *Across the Board* (March 1996): 40; Judith Howlings, "Staff Recruitment: Your Rights and Obligations," *People Management* (May 30, 1996): 47; "Read between the Lines," *Management Today* (February 1996): 14; Diane Domeyer, "Reference Checks Offer Valuable Insight," *Women in Business* 51, no. 4 (July/August 1999): 32.

14. Victor Catano, Willi Wiesner, Rick Hackett, and Laura Methot, *Recruitment and Selection in Canada,* 3rd edition, Thomson Nelson 2005.

15. Thomas J. Ryan, "Nerves of Steal," *SGB* 37, no. 6 (June 2004): 8–10; D. S. Ones, C. Viswesvaran, and F. L. Schmidt, "Comprehensive Meta-Analysis of Integrity Test Validities: Findings and Implications for Personnel Selection and Theories

of Job Performance," *Journal of Applied Psychology* 78 (August 1993): 679–703. See also Deniz S. Ones and Chockalingam Viswesvaran, "Gender, Age and Race Differences on Overt Integrity Tests: Results across Four Large-Scale Job Applicant Data Sets," *Journal of Applied Psychology* 83, no. 1 (February 1998): 35–42; McFarland and Ryan, "Variance in Faking across Noncognitive Measures."

16. "Honesty Tests Flawed," *People Management* 3, no. 2 (January 23, 1997): 15; Hays, "Tests Are Becoming Common in Hiring"; Stephen A. Dwight and George M. Alliger, "Reactions to Overt Integrity Test Items," *Educational and Psychological Measurement* 57, no. 6 (December 1997): 937–48. Catano, et al. ibid.

17. Klass Hogenesch, "A New Science for Finding the Right Employee?" *NZ Business* 18, no. 2 (March 2004): 10; Bill Leonard, "Reading Employees," *HRMagazine* 44, no. 4 (April 1999): 67–73; Steven Thomas and Steve Vaught, "The Write Stuff: What the Evidence Says about Using Handwriting Analysis in Hiring," *S.A.M. Advanced Management Journal* 66, no. 4 (Autumn 2001): 31–35.

18. Dirk D. Steiner and Stephen W. Gilliland, "Fairness Reactions to Personnel Selection Techniques in France and the United States," *Journal of Applied Psychology* 81, no. 2 (April 1996): 134–41.

19. Ely A. Leightling and Pamela M. Ploor, "When Applicants Apply through the Internet." *Employee Relations Law Journal* 30, no. 2 (Autumn 2004): 3–13; "EEOC Clarifies the Definition of Who Is an 'Applicant' in the Context of Internet Recruiting and Hiring," *Fair Employment Practices Guidelines,* no. 587 (April 1, 2004): 3–13; Kathryn Tyler, "Put Applicants' Skills to the Test," *HRMagazine* 45, no. 1 (January 2000): 74–80. For a counterargument, see Kevin R. Murphy and Ann Harris Shiarella, "Implications of the Multidimensional Nature of Job Performance for the Validity of Selection Tests: Multivariate Frameworks for Studying Test Validity," *Personnel Psychology* 50, no. 4 (Winter 1997): 823–54.

20. For books with comprehensive coverage of testing, including employment testing, see Anne Anastasi and Susana Urbina, *Psychological Testing,* 7th ed. (New York: Macmillan, 1997); Gary Groth-Marnat, *Handbook of Psychological Assessment* (New York: John Wiley and Sons, 1996); Lee J. Cronbach, *Essentials of Psychological Testing,* 5th ed. (New York: HarperCollins, 1990).

21. Standards that testing programs should meet are described in *Standards for Educational and Psychological Tests* (Washington, DC: American Psychological Association, 1986). HR managers who want to examine paper-and-pencil tests should obtain specimen sets that include a test manual, a copy of the test, an answer sheet, and a scoring key. The test manual provides the essential information about the construction of the test; its recommended use; and instructions for administering, scoring, and interpreting the test. Test users should not rely entirely on the material furnished by the test author and publisher. A major source of consumer information about commercially available tests—the *Mental Measurements Yearbook (MMY)*—is available in most libraries. Published periodically, the *MMY* contains descriptive information plus critical reviews by experts in the various types of tests. The reviews are useful in evaluating

a particular test for tryout in employment situations. Other sources of information about tests include *Test Critiques,* a set of volumes containing professional reviews of tests, and *Tests: A Comprehensive Reference for Assessments in Psychology, Education, and Business.* The latter describes more than 3100 tests published in the English language. Another source, *Principles for the Validation and Use of Personnel Selection Procedures,* published by the Society for Industrial and Organizational Psychology, is a valuable guide for employers who use tests. Other publications present detailed information on how to avoid discrimination and achieve fairness in testing.

22. Harold W. Goldstein, Kenneth P. Yusko, Eric P. Braverman, D. Brent Smith, and Beth Chung, "The Role of Cognitive Ability in the Subgroup Differences and Incremental Validity of Assessment Center Exercises," *Personnel Psychology* 51, no. 2 (Summer 1998): 357–74; Sara Rynes, Amy Colbert, and Kenneth Brown, "HR Professionals' Beliefs about Effective Human Resource Practices: Correspondence between Research and Practice," *Human Resource Management* 41, no. 2 (Summer 2002): 149–74; Mary Roznowski, David Dickter, Linda Sawin, Valerie Shute, and Sehee Hong, "The Validity of Measures of Cognitive Processes and Generalizability for Learning and Performance on Highly Complex Computerized Tutors: Is the g Factor of Intelligence Even More General?" *Journal of Applied Psychology* 85, no. 6 (December 2000): 940–55.

23. Kris Frieswick, "Casting to Type," *CFO* 20, no. 9 (July 2004): 71– 73; Timothy Judge and Joyce Bono, "Five-Factor Model of Personality and Transformational Leadership," *Journal of Applied Psychology* 85, no. 5 (October 2000): 751–65; J. Michael Crant and Thomas S. Bateman, "Charismatic Leadership Viewed from Above: The Impact of Proactive Personality," *Journal of Organizational Behavior* 21, no. 1 (February 2000): 63–75.

24. Arielle Emmett, "Snake Oil or Science? The Raging Debate on Personality Testing," *Workforce Management* 83, no. 10 (October 2004): 90–93; Gregory Hurtz and John Donovan, "Personality and Job Performance: The Big Five Revisited," *Journal of Applied Psychology* 85, no. 6 (December 2000): 869–79.

25. George B. Yancey, "The Predictive Power of Hiring Tools," *Credit Union Executive Journal* 40, no. 4 (July–August 2000): 12–18; In the case of *Soroka v Dayton Hudson Corporation* (1993), plaintiffs sued on the grounds that the selection test violated California's Fair Employment laws and that certain items, especially MMPI items, constituted an unlawful invasion of privacy. Although the case was settled out of court, the California state appellate court, in a preliminary injunction, found that certain questions violated the plaintiffs' rights to privacy and that Target Stores had not shown these questions to be job-related. See Dwight and Alliger, "Reactions to Overt Integrity Test Items"; Daniel P. O'Meara, "Personality Tests Raise Questions of Legality and Effectiveness," *HRMagazine* 39, no. 1 (January 1994): 97–100; Jeffrey A. Mello, "Personality Tests and Privacy Rights," *HRFocus* 73, no. 3 (March 1996): 22–23.

26. Walter C. Borman, Mary Ann Hanson, and Jerry W. Hedge, "Personnel Selection," *Annual Review of Psychology* 48 (1997): 299–337; Charles Sproule and Stephen Berkley, "The Selection of Entry-Level Corrections Officers: Pennsylvania Research," *Public Personnel Management* 30, no. 3 (Fall 2001): 377–418.

27. M. S. Sothmann, D. L. Gebhardt, T. A. Baker, G. M. Kastello, and V. A. Sheppard, "Performance Requirements of Physically Strenuous Occupations: Validating Minimum Standards for Muscular Strength," *Ergonomics* 47, no. 8 (June 22, 2004): 864–76; T. L. Stanley, "The Wisdom of Employment Testing," *Supervision* 65, no. 2 (February 2004): 11–14; M. Brewster, "RCMP Ease Fitness Rules for Women," *The Globe and Mail,* July 14, 1997: A4.

28. It may be interesting to note that the origins of the civil service system go back to 2200 B.C., when the Chinese emperor examined officials every three years to determine their fitness for continuing in office. In 1115 B.C. candidates for government posts were examined for their proficiency in music, archery, horsemanship, writing, arithmetic, and the rites and ceremonies of public and private life.

29. Rachel Suff, "Testing the Water: Using Work Sampling for Selection," *IRS Employment Review,* no. 802 (June 18, 2004): 44–49; Leonard D. Goodstein and Alan D. Davidson, "Hiring the Right Stuff: Using Competency-Based Selection," *Compensation & Benefits Management* 14, no. 3 (Summer 1998): 1–10.

30. Linda Marsh, "By Their Actions Shall Ye Know Them," *Works Management* 50, no. 11 (November 1997): 52–53; Florence Berger and Ajay Ghei, "Employment Tests: A Facet of Hospitality Hiring," *Cornell Hotel and Restaurant Administration Quarterly* 36, no. 6 (December 1995): 28–31; Malcolm James Ree, Thomas R. Carretta, and Mark S. Teachout, "Role of Ability and Prior Job Knowledge in Complex Training Performance," *Journal of Applied Psychology* 80, no. 6 (December 1995): 721–30.

31. Igor Kotlyar and Ravit Ableman, "Simulation Turns Recruitment Into a Two Way Street," *Canadian HR Reporter,* December 1, 2003: G6; Humber, ibid.: R2.

32. James Bassett, "Stop, Thief!" *Gifts & Decorative Accessories* 104, no. 1 (January 2003): 130–34; Cynthia Kay Stevens, "Antecedents of Interview Interactions, Interviewers' Ratings, and Applicants' Reactions," *Personnel Psychology* 51, no. 1 (Spring 1998): 55–85; Laura Gollub Williamson, James E. Campion, Stanley B. Malos, and Mark V. Roehling, "Employment Interview on Trial: Linking Interview Structure with Litigation Outcomes," *Journal of Applied Psychology* 82, no. 6 (December 1997): 900–12; Richard A. Posthuma, Frederick Morgeson, and Michael Campion, "Beyond Employment Interview Validity: A Comprehensive Narrative Review of Recent Research and Trends over Time," *Personnel Psychology* 55, no. 1 (Spring 2002): 1–8.

33. David E. Terpstra and Bryan R. Kethley, "Organizations' Relative Degree of Exposure to Selection Discrimination Litigation," *Public Personnel Management* 31, no. 3 (February 2002): 277–94; Schmidt and Rader, "Exploring the Boundary Conditions for Interview Validity"; Williamson, Campion, Malos, and Roehling, "Employment Interview on Trial."

34. "MSPB Calls for Use of Structured Interviews to Assess Candidates for Federal Jobs," *PA Times* 26, no. 5 (May 2003): 13; Robert J. Lavigna and Steven W. Hays, "Recruitment and

Selection of Public Workers: An International Compendium of Modern Management Trends and Practices," *Public Personnel Management* 33, no. 3 (Fall 2004): 237–54; For an excellent review of research on the structured interview, see Michael A. Campion, David K. Palmer, and James E. Campion, "A Review of Structure in the Selection Interview," *Personnel Psychology* 50, no. 3 (Autumn 1997): 655–702. See also Karen van der Zee, Arnold Bakker, and Paulien Bakker, "Why Are Structured Interviews So Rarely Used in Personnel Selection?" *Journal of Applied Psychology* 87, no. 1 (February 2002): 176–84.

35. Jesus F. Salgado and Silvia Moscoso, "Comprehensive Meta-Analysis of the Construct Validity of the Employment Interview," *European Journal of Work and Organizational Psychology* 11, no. 3 (September 2002): 299–325; Allen Huffcutt, Jeff Weekley, Willi Wiesner, Timothy Degroot, and Casey Jones, "Comparison of Situational and Behavior Description Interview Questions for Higher-Level Positions," *Personnel Psychology* 54, no. 3 (Autumn 2001): 619–44.

36. Peter Herriot, "Assessment by Groups: Can Value Be Added?" *European Journal of Work & Organizational Psychology* 12, no. 2 (June 2003): 131–46; Salgado and Moscoso, "Comprehensive Meta-Analysis"; Amelia J. Prewett-Livingston, John G. Veres III, Hubert S. Field, and Philip M. Lewis, "Effects of Race on Interview Ratings in a Situational Panel Interview," *Journal of Applied Psychology* 81, no. 2 (April 1996): 178–86. See also Damodar Y. Golhar and Satish P. Deshpande, "HRM Practices of Large and Small Canadian Manufacturing Firms," *Journal of Small Business Management* 35, no. 3 (July 1997): 30–38; Philip L. Roth and James E. Campion, "An Analysis of the Predictive Power of the Panel Interview and Pre-Employment Tests," *Journal of Occupational and Organizational Psychology* 65 (March 1992): 51–60.

37. Michele V. Rafter, "Candidates for Jobs in High Places Sit for Tests That Size Up Their Mettle," *Workforce Management* 83, no. 5 (May 2004): 70–73; Patricia Buhler, "Computer Interview:

Managing in the New Millennium," *Supervision* 63, no. 10 (October 2002): 20–23; For more information about Interactive Information Services, see their website at www.iiserve.com/about.html.

38. Victoria Reitz, "Interview without Leaving Home," *Machine Design* 76, no. 7 (April 1, 2004): 66; Linda Thornburg, "Computer-Assisted Interviewing Shortens Hiring Cycle," *HRMagazine* 43, no. 2 (February 1998): 73–79; Dan Hanover, "Hiring Gets Cheaper and Faster," *Sales and Marketing Management* 152, no. 3 (March 2000): 87; Jessica Clark Newman et al., "The Differential Effects of Face-to-Face and Computer Interview Modes," *American Journal of Public Health* 92, no. 2 (February 2002): 294; David Mitchell, "ijob.com Recruiting Online," *Strategic Finance* 80, no. 11 (May 1999): 48–51.

39. Hanover, "Hiring Gets Cheaper and Faster."

40. Marjo Johne, "Prize for Playing the Game: A Career," *The Globe and Mail,* April 26, 2006: C1.

41. Posthuma, Morgeson, Campion, "Beyond Employment Interview Validity"; Schmidt and Rader, "Exploring the Boundary Conditions for Interview Validity."

42. Catano et al., ibid; "Alberta's Suncor Says Its Reviewing Drug Testing After Human Rights Ruling," *Canadian Press Newswire*, January 12, 2002., www.chrc-ccdp.ca/legislation_policies/alcohol_drug_testing-en.asp.

43. Multiple regression is a statistical method for evaluating the magnitude of effects of more than one independent variable (e.g., selection predictors) on a dependent variable (e.g., job performance) using principles of correlation and regression.

44. David E. Bowen and Cheri Ostroff, "Understanding HRM—Firm Performance Linkages: The Role of the Strengths of the HRM System," *Academy of Management Review* 29, no. 2 (April 2004): 203–22; Ann Marie Ryan, Joshua Sacco, Lynn McFarland, and David Kriska, "Applicant Self-Selection: Correlates of Withdrawal from a Multiple Hurdle Process," *Journal of Applied Psychology* 85, no. 2 (April 2000): 163–79.

ANSWERS TO FIGURE 6.6

3, 3, 4

Training and Development

After studying this chapter, you should be able to

objective **1**

Discuss the systems approach to training and development.

objective **2**

Describe the components of training-needs assessment.

objective **3**

Identify the principles of learning and describe how they facilitate training.

objective **4**

Identify the types of training methods used for managers and non-managers.

objective **5**

Discuss the advantages and disadvantages of various evaluation criteria.

objective **6**

Describe the special training programs that are currently popular.

Training has become increasingly vital to the success of modern organizations. Recall that in Chapter 2 we noted that organizations often compete on competencies—the core sets of knowledge and expertise that give them an edge over their competitors. Training plays a central role in nurturing and strengthening these competencies, and in this way has become part of the backbone of strategy implementation. In addition, rapidly changing technologies require that employees continuously hone their knowledge, skills, and abilities (KSAs) to cope with new processes and systems. Jobs that require little skill are rapidly being replaced by jobs that require technical, interpersonal, and problem-solving skills. Other trends toward empowerment, total-quality management, teamwork, and international business make it necessary for managers, as well as employees, to develop the skills that will enable them to handle new and more demanding assignments.

The Scope of Training

Many new employees come equipped with most of the KSAs needed to start work. Others may require extensive training before they are ready to make much of a contribution to the organization. Almost any employee, however, needs some type of ongoing training to maintain effective performance or to adjust to new ways of work.

The term *training* is often used casually to describe almost any effort initiated by an organization to foster learning among its members. However, many experts distinguish between *training*, which tends to be more narrowly focused and oriented toward short-term performance concerns, and *development*, which tends to be oriented more toward broadening an individual's skills for future responsibilities. The two terms tend to be combined into a single phrase—*training and development*—to recognize the combination of activities organizations use to increase the skill base of employees.

The primary reason that organizations train new employees is to bring their KSAs up to the level required for satisfactory performance. As these employees continue on the job, additional training provides opportunities for them to acquire new knowledge and skills. As a result of this training, employees may be even more effective on the job and may be able to perform other jobs in other areas or at higher levels.

Investments in Training

Research shows that an organization's revenues and overall profitability are positively correlated to the amount of training it gives its employees. Overall, the average expenditure in Canada on training and development was 1.75 percent of payroll, and organizations annually provided about 30 hours of training per employee. Basically all large Canadian employers offer training, while about half of organizations with fewer than 20 employees offer training. The best employers in Canada reported an average of 44.2 training hours per employee versus an average of 26.5 hours for the rest.[1] The BMO Financial Group is one organization that does better than the average—it has an annual training budget of $71 million, which is 2.5 percent of payroll. Its employees receive on average 41 hours of annual training.[2] While a good deal of money is spent on executive development and management training, Figure 7.1 shows that by far the

USING THE INTERNET

The Canadian Society for Training and Development is the professional association for those working in training and development in Canada:

www.cstd.ca

Figure 7.1	Training Dollars Spent by Program Type
Professional skills	14.7% of all training spending
Managerial skills	12.7
Information technology	9.8
Technical processes	9.0
Occupational health and safety	7.5
Interpersonal communication	7.1
Orientation	6.9
Customer relations	6.8
Executive development	6.7
Product knowledge	6.3
Business practices	4.7
Sales	4.6
Basic skills	2.2

Source: R.O Patrick and J. Cooney, 2005 Learning and Development Outlook, 2005, The Conference Board of Canada, Ottawa. Used by permission.

greatest proportion of training is spent on rank-and-file employees and supervisors. Ethics in HRM on page 298 describes the debate about forcing employers to provide training and forcing employees to take training. The types of training given employees range from simple, on-the-job instruction to sophisticated skills training conducted on multimillion-dollar simulators. Other types of training include customer service, sales and management training, personal growth, and communication skills training.[3]

A Systems Approach to Training

From the broadest perspective, the goal of training is to contribute to the organization's overall goals. Training programs should be developed with this in mind. Managers should keep a close eye on organizational goals and strategies and orient training accordingly. Unfortunately, many organizations never make the connection between their strategic objectives and their training programs. Instead, fads, fashions, or "whatever the competition is doing" can sometimes be the main drivers of an organization's training agenda. As a result, much of an organization's investment can be wasted—training programs are often misdirected, poorly designed, and inadequately evaluated—and these problems directly affect organizational performance.

To ensure that investments in training and development have maximum impact on individual and organizational performance, a systems approach to training should be used. The systems approach involves four phases: (1) needs assessment, (2) program design, (3) implementation, and (4) evaluation. A model that is useful to designers of training programs is presented in Figure 7.2 on page 299. We will use this model as a framework for organizing the material throughout this chapter.

Ethics in HRM

Mandatory or Voluntary?

There is only one payroll training tax in North America. The Quebec government program that forces employers to spend 1 percent of payroll on training may not have the intended consequences of increasing training investments in employees. Using data from a Statistics Canada survey, Alan Saks of the University of Toronto and Robert Haccoun of the Université de Montréal matched Quebec employers with Ontario employers and found that there were no differences in amounts spent on training. The paperwork is so cumbersome that many employers prefer to pay the 1-percent tax rather than go through the thick guidebooks necessary to report the training.

If there is little effect gained by forcing employers to provide training, are there benefits by forcing employees to attend training? The answer is not clear: Some studies report some slight benefits in outcomes (such as improved job performance) when employees voluntarily attend courses; other studies see no differences.

There may be more serious problems than performance results created by forcing employees to attend courses. Half of the 24 employees of SaskTel who participated in a training program on process re-engineering required psychological counselling, or stress leave, or both in its aftermath. Trainees said they were subjected to a greenhouse environment: Windows were papered over, employees were not allowed to communicate with one another, and all were subjected to verbal abuse from the training consultants. As the president of the Ontario Society for Training and Development commented: "That's not training, that's assault."

Seagulls Pewter and Silversmiths of Pugwash, Nova Scotia, sent its employees to seminars based on the controversial Est therapy. Employees complained to their union that the seminars, in which participants were encouraged to delve into painful emotions, often drove participants to breakdowns. In another example, a large insurance company hired a consultant to conduct management training for hundreds of supervisors and managers. The company did not realize that the consultant was a member of L. Ron Hubbard's Church of Scientology and was teaching management principles developed by Scientologists. Critics contend that Scientology is a cult, not a religion. Employees resented being subjected to psychological concepts based on "tones" that catalogue emotions; to the ruthless devotion to ferreting out and firing problem employees; and to "religious scriptures."

The employees in these organizations were required to participate in programs that caused them undue stress and sometimes violated their moral or religious beliefs. Those who organized the programs believed that employees with the "right" attitudes would be more effective.

Sources: K. Harding, "A Taxing Way to Train Staff," *The Globe and Mail*, June 4, 2003: C1; D. Brown, "Legislated Training, Questionable Results," *Canadian HR Reporter* 15, no. 9, May 6, 2002: 1; A. Thomlinson, "Mandatory or Voluntary?" *Canadian HR Reporter* 15, no. 6, March 25, 2002: 1; Edward Kay, "Trauma in Real Life," *The Globe and Mail Report on Business Magazine*, November 1996: 82–92; J. Saunders, "How Scientology's Message Came to Allstate," *The Globe and Mail*, April 24, 1995: B1; R. Sharpe, "Agents of Intimidation," *The Globe and Mail*, March 28, 1995: B8.

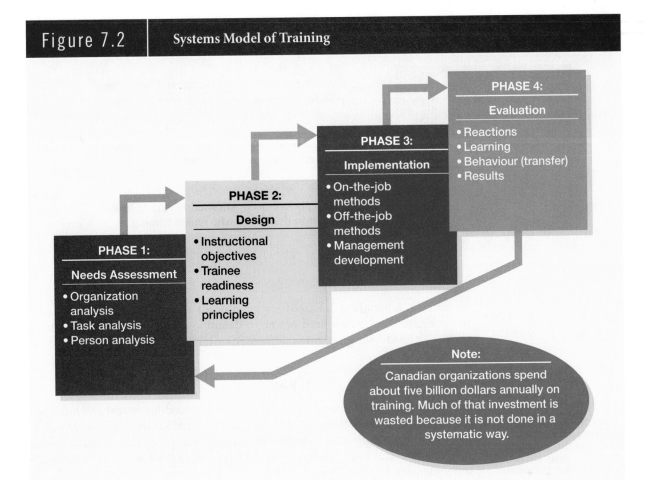

| Figure 7.2 | Systems Model of Training |

PHASE 4:

Evaluation

- Reactions
- Learning
- Behaviour (transfer)
- Results

PHASE 3:

Implementation

- On-the-job methods
- Off-the-job methods
- Management development

PHASE 2:

Design

- Instructional objectives
- Trainee readiness
- Learning principles

PHASE 1:

Needs Assessment

- Organization analysis
- Task analysis
- Person analysis

Note:

Canadian organizations spend about five billion dollars annually on training. Much of that investment is wasted because it is not done in a systematic way.

Phase 1: Conducting the Needs Assessment

Managers and HR staffs should stay alert to the kinds of training that are needed, where they are needed, who needs them, and which methods will best deliver needed KSAs to employees. If workers consistently fail to achieve productivity objectives, this might be a signal that training is needed. Likewise, if organizations receive an excessive number of customer complaints, this too might suggest inadequate training. To make certain that training is timely and focused on priority issues, managers should approach needs assessment systematically by utilizing the three different types of analysis shown in Figure 7.3 on page 300: organization analysis, task analysis, and person analysis. Each of these is discussed next.

To ensure that their firms' training dollars are spent wisely, about half of managers surveyed by the Institute of Management and Administration (IOMA) say their companies engage in needs assessment before initiating a training program. But much of the money spent on training still goes wasted. A separate study by the American Society for Training and Development (ASTD) found that, unfortunately, because of the costs, expertise, and time required, organizations conduct needs assessment less than 50 percent of the time. Ironically, as the speed of change increases, with time and

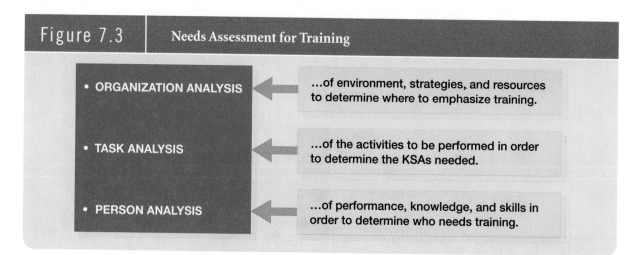

Figure 7.3   Needs Assessment for Training

- **ORGANIZATION ANALYSIS** ← ...of environment, strategies, and resources to determine where to emphasize training.

- **TASK ANALYSIS** ← ...of the activities to be performed in order to determine the KSAs needed.

- **PERSON ANALYSIS** ← ...of performance, knowledge, and skills in order to determine who needs training.

resources at a premium, the need for good needs assessment actually increases. In these cases, the process need not be so daunting and labourious. Highlights in HRM 7.1 provides some tips for rapidly assessing training needs.[4]

Organization Analysis

organization analysis
Examination of the environment, strategies, and resources of the organization to determine where training emphasis should be placed

The first step in needs assessment is identifying the broad forces that can influence training needs. **Organization analysis** is an examination of the environment, strategies, and resources of the organization to determine where training emphasis should be placed.

Economic and public policy issues influence training needs. For example, since the September 11 terrorist attacks, the training of airport security personnel has increased substantially. It has also increased for flight crews of airlines, employees in the transportation industry, workers in nuclear power plants, and even security staff at theme parks.

According to Chris Rogers, senior consultant for loss control in the Entertainment Practices Group of Aon Corporation (a risk management firm), there is an emphasis today on training theme park security in a tactic called "aggressive hospitality," which calls for staff to greet people and look them in the eye and offer to assist, rather than waiting to be approached by visitors. "This is one of the best and simplest security measures," he says. When staff members engage visitors, they become more aware of them. This heightened level of attention also discourages troublemakers from coming to the facility, because they generally go where they can remain anonymous.[5]

Other training issues tend to revolve around the strategic initiatives of an organization. Mergers and acquisitions, for example, frequently require that employees take on new roles and responsibilities and adjust to new cultures and ways of conducting business. Nowhere is this more prevalent than in grooming new leaders within organizations. Other issues such as technological change, globalization, reengineering, and total quality management all influence the way work is done and the types of skills needed to do it. Still other concerns may be more tactical, but no less important in their impact on training. Organizational restructuring, downsizing, empowerment, and teamwork, for example, have immediate training requirements. Finally, trends in the workforce itself have an impact on training needs. As older workers near retirement, younger workers need to focus on gaining the skills and knowledge needed to

Highlights in HRM 7.1

Notes on Rapid Needs Assessment

NOTE 1: Look at the problem scope. Common sense suggests that small, local matters may require less information gathering than big problems with a major impact on the organization. Ask managers a series of questions about the nature of the problem and its impact on the organization and gear your analysis accordingly.

NOTE 2: Do organizational scanning. Stay connected with what is going on in the organization in order to anticipate upcoming training needs. If a new technology is about to be launched, the need for training should take no one by surprise. In short, needs assessment isn't an event with a start-and-stop switch. It is the process of being engaged in your business.

NOTE 3: Play "give and take." Get the information you need, but don't drag your feet with excessive analysis before reporting back to managers. Show them that you are sensitive to their need for action by giving them updates on the information you have collected. If necessary, explain that better value may be gained by further analysis.

NOTE 4: Check "lost and found." Often, information gathered for a different purpose may bear on your training issue. Performance data (such as errors, sales, and customer complaints) and staffing data (such as proficiency testing, turnover, and absenteeism) can be very helpful as a starting point.

NOTE 5: Use plain talk. Instead of using clinical terms such as *analysis* or *assessment*, use straight talk with managers that tells them what you are doing: (1) Identify the problem, (2) identify alternative ways to get there, (3) implement a solution based on cost/benefit concerns, and (4) determine the effectiveness and efficiency of the solution.

NOTE 6: Use the Web. Information technology allows you to communicate with others, perhaps by setting up an electronic mailing list to post questions, synthesize responses, share resources, get feedback, gather information on trends, and the like.

NOTE 7: Use rapid prototyping. Often the most effective and efficient training is that which is "just-in-time, just enough, and just for me." Create a rapid prototype of a training program, evaluating and revising as you implement and learn more about the problems.

NOTE 8: Seek out exemplars. Find those in the organization that currently demonstrate the performance the organization wants. Bring others together with them to talk about the performance issues, and let the exemplars share their experiences and insights. This avoids the risk of packaging the wrong information, and people learn just what they need to know from each other.

Source: Condensed from Ron Zemke, "How to Do a Needs Assessment When You Think You Don't Have Time," *Training* 35, no. 3 (March 1998): 38–44. Reprinted with permission from the March 1998 issue of *Training Magazine*. Copyright 1998. Bill Communications, Inc., Minneapolis, MN. All rights reserved. Not for resale.

take their place. Organizations as diverse as Inco and Quebec Hydro are facing situations in which they need to prepare the next generations of employees as the current groups approach retirement.

Side by side with forces that influence training needs, organization analysis involves close examination of the resources—technological, financial, and

© RICHARD T. NOWITZ/CORBIS

A company must carefully analyze the job duties of its employees to determine their training needs.

human—that are available to meet training objectives. Organizations typically collect data to use in the analysis, data such as information on direct and indirect labour costs, quality of goods or services, absenteeism, turnover, and number of accidents. The availability of potential replacements and the time required to train them are other important factors in organization analysis.

In recent years, as organizations continue to keep a tight rein on costs, training budgets are often constrained—even while organizations recognize the need for more and better training. To cope with resource constraints while contributing to strategic imperatives, managers have to be more focused and efficient with their training budgets. Companies have found that by using information technology wisely, they cut their training budget by as much as 30 to 50 percent while keeping service levels high. In order to "do more with less," managers have to plan carefully where they will spend their training dollars, and this means doing rigorous organization analysis. Other companies have outsourced their training programs to external partners in order to cut costs. However, evidence suggests that while many companies find they can provide equal or better service to employees in this way, surprisingly few actually reduce their training costs as a result.[6]

Task Analysis

task analysis
The process of determining what the content of a training program should be on the basis of a study of the tasks and duties involved in the job

competency assessment
Analysis of the sets of skills and knowledge needed for decision-oriented and knowledge-intensive jobs

The second step in training-needs assessment is task analysis. **Task analysis** involves reviewing the job description and specifications to identify the activities performed in a particular job and the KSAs needed to perform them. Task analysis often becomes more detailed than job analysis, but the overall purpose is to determine the exact content of the training program.

The first step in task analysis is to list all the tasks or duties included in the job. The second step is to list the steps performed by the employee to complete each task. Once the job is understood thoroughly, the type of performance required (such as speech, recall, discrimination, and manipulation), along with the skills and knowledge necessary for performance, can be defined. For example, in the task of taking a chest x-ray, a radiologist correctly positions the patient (manipulation), gives special instructions (speech), and checks the proper distance of the x-ray tube from the patient (discrimination). The types of performance skills and knowledge that trainees need can be determined by observing and questioning skilled jobholders and/or by reviewing job descriptions. This information helps trainers select program content and choose the most effective training method.

However, like job analysis, task analysis appears to be shifting from an emphasis on a fixed sequence of tasks to the more flexible sets of competencies required for superior performance. Companies such as RBC Financial Group have found that as jobs change toward teamwork, flexibility requires that employees adjust their behaviour as needed. **Competency assessment** focuses on the sets of skills and knowledge employees need to be successful, particularly for decision-oriented and knowledge-intensive jobs. But competency assessment goes beyond simply describing the traits an employee must have to successfully perform the work. It also captures elements of how those traits should be used within an organization's context and culture. That might include an employee's motivation levels, personality traits, interpersonal skills, and so on. General Electric, for example, uses a formal competency assessment program based on 45 different employee behaviours. While training programs based on work-oriented task analysis can become dated as work undergoes dynamic change, training programs based on competency assessment are more flexible and perhaps have more durability. The practice has been adopted extensively in the healthcare industry. Highlights in HRM 7.2 shows an example of a competency assessment used for designing training programs for public health professionals. The American Public Human Services Association has adopted the model as an infrastructure for training universal skills.[7]

Highlights in HRM 7.2

Competency Assessment for Training Public Health Workers

- Analytic discipline
  - Determining appropriate use of data and statistical methods
  - Making relevant inferences from data
- Communication discipline
  - Communicating effectively both in writing and orally
  - Presenting accurately and effectively demographic, statistical, programmatic, and scientific information for professional and lay audiences
- Policy and program-planning discipline
  - Developing mechanisms to monitor and evaluate programs (effectiveness, quality)
- Culture discipline
  - Developing and adapting approaches that take into account cultural differences
- Basic science discipline
  - Understanding research methods in all basic public health sciences
  - Applying the basic public health sciences, including behavioural and social sciences, biostatistics, epidemiology, environmental public health, and prevention of chronic and infectious diseases and injuries
- Finance and management discipline
  - Monitoring program performance
- Orientation to public health
  - Public health process
  - Core functions and essential services
  - Ethics and values of public health
  - Legal basis of public health

Source: Margaret Potter, Christine Pistella, Carl Fertman, and Virginia Dato, "Needs Assessment and a Model Agenda for Training the Public Health Workforce," *American Journal of Public Health* 90, no. 8 (August 2000): 1294–96. Reprinted by permission of American Public Health Association.

Person Analysis

person analysis
Determination of the specific individuals who need training

Along with organization and task analyses, it is necessary to perform a person analysis. **Person analysis** involves determining which employees require training and, equally important, which do not. In this regard, person analysis is important for several reasons. First, thorough analysis helps organizations avoid the mistake of sending all employees into training when some do not need it. In addition, person analysis helps managers determine what prospective trainees are able to do when they enter training so that the programs can be designed to emphasize the areas in which they are deficient.

Companies such as Hewlett-Packard have used performance appraisal information as an input for person analysis. However, while performance appraisal may reveal who is not meeting expectations, it typically does not reveal why. If performance deficiencies are due to ability problems, training may likely be a good intervention. However, if performance deficiencies are due to poor motivation or factors outside an employee's control, training may not be the answer. Ultimately managers have to sit down with employees to talk about areas for improvement so that they can jointly determine the developmental approaches that will have maximum benefit.[8]

Phase 2: Designing the Training Program

Once the training needs have been determined, the next step is to design the type of learning environment necessary to enhance learning. The success of training programs depends on more than the organization's ability to identify training needs. Success hinges on taking the information gained from needs analysis and utilizing it to design first-rate training programs. Experts believe that training design should focus on at least four related issues: (1) instructional objectives, (2) trainee readiness and motivation, (3) principles of learning, and (4) characteristics of instructors.

Instructional Objectives

instructional objectives
Desired outcomes of a training program

As a result of conducting organization, task, and person analyses, managers will have a more complete picture of the training needs. On the basis of this information, they can more formally state the desired outcomes of training through written instructional objectives. Generally, **instructional objectives** describe the skills or knowledge to be acquired and/or the attitudes to be changed. One type of instructional objective, the performance-centred objective, is widely used because it lends itself to an unbiased evaluation of results. For example, the stated objective for one training program might be that "Employees trained in team methods will be able to perform these different jobs within six months." Performance-centred objectives typically include precise terms, such as "to calculate," "to repair," "to adjust," "to construct," "to assemble," and "to classify."

Robert Mager, an internationally known training expert, emphasizes the importance of instructional objectives by noting that "before you prepare for instruction, before you select instructional procedures or subject matter or material, it is important to be able to state clearly just what you intend the results of that instruction to be. A clear statement of instructional objectives will provide a sound basis for choosing methods and materials and for selecting the means for assessing whether the instruction will be successful."[9]

Trainee Readiness and Motivation

Two preconditions for learning affect the success of those who are to receive training: readiness and motivation. *Trainee readiness* refers to both maturity and experience factors in the trainee's background. Prospective trainees should be screened to determine that they have the background knowledge and the skills necessary to absorb what will be presented to them. Recognizing individual differences in readiness is as important in organizational training as it is in any other teaching situation. It is often desirable to group individuals according to their capacity to learn, as determined by test scores, and to provide an alternative type of instruction for those who need it.

The receptiveness and readiness of participants in training programs can be increased by having them complete questionnaires about why they are attending training and what they hope to accomplish. Participants may also be asked to give copies of their completed questionnaires to their managers.

The other precondition for learning is *trainee motivation*. Individuals who are conscientious, goal-oriented, self-disciplined, and persevering are more likely to perceive a link between effort they put into training and higher performance on the job. For optimum learning to take place, trainees must recognize the need for new knowledge or skills, and they must maintain a desire to learn as training progresses. By focusing on the trainees themselves rather than on the trainer or training topic, managers can create a training environment that is conducive to learning. Six strategies can be essential:

1. Use positive reinforcement.
2. Eliminate threats and punishment.
3. Be flexible.
4. Have participants set personal goals.
5. Design interesting instruction.
6. Break down physical and psychological obstacles to learning.

While most employees are motivated by certain common needs, they differ from one another in the relative importance of these needs at any given time. For example, new college or university graduates often have a high desire for advancement, and they have established specific goals for career progression. Training objectives should be clearly related to trainees' individual needs to succeed in training programs.[10]

Principles of Learning

As we move from needs assessment and instructional objectives to employee readiness and motivation, we shift from a focus on the organization to a focus on employees. Ultimately, training has to build a bridge between employees and the organization. One important step in this transition is giving full consideration to the psychological principles of learning—that is, the characteristics of training programs that help employees grasp new material, make sense of it in their own lives, and transfer it back to the job.

Because the success or failure of a training program is frequently related to certain principles of learning, managers as well as employees should understand that different training methods or techniques vary in the extent to which they utilize these principles. All things considered, training programs are likely to be more effective if they incorporate the principles of learning shown in Figure 7.4 on page 306.

Figure 7.4	Principles of Learning

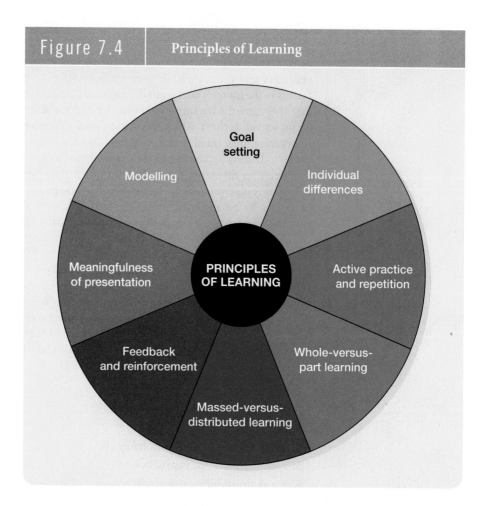

Goal Setting

The value of goal setting for focusing and motivating behaviour extends into training. When trainers take the time to explain the goals and objectives to trainees—or when trainees are encouraged to set goals on their own—the level of interest, understanding, and effort directed toward training is likely to increase. In some cases, goal setting can simply take the form of a "road map" of the course/program, its objectives, and its learning points.[11]

Meaningfulness of Presentation

One principle of learning is that the material to be learned should be presented in as meaningful a manner as possible. Quite simply, trainees are better able to learn new information (from training) if they can connect it with things that are already familiar to them. Trainers frequently use colourful examples to which trainees can relate. The examples make the material meaningful. In addition, material should be arranged so that each experience builds on preceding ones. In this way, trainees are able to integrate the experiences into a usable pattern of knowledge and skills.

Modelling

The old saying "A picture is worth a thousand words" applies to training. Just as examples increase the meaningfulness of factual material or new knowledge in a training environment, modelling increases the salience of behavioural training. Work by Albert Bandura and others on social learning theory underscores the point that we learn vicariously. Quite simply, we learn by watching. For example, if you were learning to ride a horse, it would be much easier to watch someone do it—and then try it yourself—than to read a book or listen to a lecture and hope you can do it right.[12]

Modelling can take many forms. For example, real-life demonstrations or videotapes are often helpful; even pictures and drawings can get the visual message across. The point is that modelling demonstrates the desired behaviour or method to be learned. In some cases, modelling the wrong behaviour can even be helpful if it shows trainees what not to do and then clarifies the appropriate behaviour.

Individual Differences

People learn at different rates and in different ways. For example, some individuals can remember new information after hearing it only once (echoic memory) or seeing it only once (iconic memory). Others may have to work longer or find other techniques for retrieving the information, but this may have nothing to do with their intelligence. Some students do horribly in large lecture settings but then excel in small discussion classes. Others may have the opposite ability. To the extent possible, training programs should try to account for and accommodate these individual differences in order to facilitate each person's style and rate of learning.[13]

Active Practice and Repetition

Those things we do daily become a part of our repertoire of skills. Trainees should be given frequent opportunity to practise their job tasks in the way that they will ultimately be expected to perform them. The individual who is being taught how to operate a machine should have an opportunity to practise on it. The manager who is being taught how to train should be given supervised practise in training.

In some cases, the value of practice is that it causes behaviours to become second nature. For example, when you first learned to drive a car, you focused a great deal on the mechanics: "Where are my hands, where are my feet, how fast am I going?" As you practised driving, you began to think less about the mechanics and more about the road, the weather, and the traffic. Other forms of learning are no different—by practising, a trainee can forget about distinct behaviours and concentrate on the subtleties of how they are used.

Whole-versus-Part Learning

Most jobs and tasks can be broken down into parts that lend themselves to further analysis. Determining the most effective manner for completing each part then provides a basis for giving specific instruction. Learning to sell a product, for example, is made up of several skills that are part of the total process. Although the process sounds daunting, it can essentially be broken down into a few discrete steps: finding customer opportunities; eliciting a prospective customer's needs by learning the proper questions to ask him or her; presenting the firm's product in a way that meets those needs; and finally, learning how and when to ask the customer to buy the product (closing the deal). In evaluating whole-versus-part learning, it is necessary to consider the nature of the task to be learned. If the task can be broken down successfully, it probably should be broken down to facilitate learning; otherwise, it should probably be taught as a unit.

Massed-versus-Distributed Learning

Another factor that determines the effectiveness of training is the amount of time devoted to practice in one session. Should trainees be given training in five 2-hour periods or in ten 1-hour periods? It has been found in most cases that spacing out the training will result in faster learning and longer retention. This is the principle of *distributed learning*. Since the efficiency of the distribution will vary with the type and complexity of the task, managers should refer to the rapidly growing body of research in this area when they require guidance in designing a specific training situation.

Feedback and Reinforcement

Can any learning occur without feedback? Some feedback comes from self-monitoring while other feedback comes from trainers, fellow trainees, and the like. As an employee's training progresses, feedback serves two related purposes: (1) knowledge of results and (2) motivation.

The informational aspects of feedback help individuals focus on what they are doing right and what they are doing wrong. In this way, feedback serves a "shaping" role in helping individuals approach the objectives of training. Think about when you first learned how to throw a baseball, ride a bicycle, or swim. Someone, perhaps a parent, told you what you were doing right and what things to correct. As you did, you perhaps got better.

In addition to its informational aspects, feedback also serves an important motivational role. At times, progress in training, measured in terms of either mistakes or successes, may be plotted on a chart commonly referred to as a "learning curve." Figure 7.5 presents an example of a learning curve common in the acquisition of many job skills. In many learning situations there are times when progress does not occur. Such periods show up on the curve as a fairly straight horizontal line called a *plateau*. A plateau may be the result of reduced motivation or of ineffective methods of task performance. It is a natural phenomenon of learning, and there is usually a spontaneous recovery, as Figure 7.5 shows.

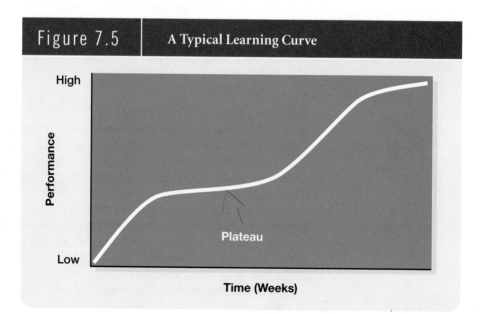

Figure 7.5	A Typical Learning Curve

Verbal encouragement or more extrinsic rewards may help reinforce desired behaviour over time. At times, reinforcement is simply the feeling of accomplishment that follows successful performance. (In some cases it may be impossible to distinguish between feedback and rewards.) Reinforcement is generally most effective when it occurs immediately after a task has been performed.

In recent years some work organizations have used **behaviour modification,** a technique that operates on the principle that behaviour that is rewarded—positively reinforced—will be exhibited more frequently in the future, whereas behaviour that is penalized or unrewarded will decrease in frequency. For example, in safety training it is possible to identify "safe" behavioural profiles—that is, actions that ensure fewer accidents—as well as unsafe profiles. As a follow-up to training, or as part of the training itself, managers can use relatively simple rewards to encourage and maintain desired behaviour. Companies have found that nothing more than words of encouragement and feedback are needed to strengthen the behaviours required and desired from training. Other more formal rewards such as awards and ceremonies may prove useful as well. However, the idea with behaviour modification is that behaviour can be motivated and gradually shaped toward the desired profile using reinforcement.[14]

behaviour modification
A technique that operates on the principle that behaviour that is rewarded, or positively reinforced, will be exhibited more frequently in the future, whereas behaviour that is penalized or unrewarded will decrease in frequency

Characteristics of Instructors

The success of any training effort will depend in large part on the teaching skills and personal characteristics of those responsible for conducting the training. What separates good trainers from mediocre ones? Often a good trainer is one who shows a little more effort or demonstrates more instructional preparation. However, training is also influenced by the trainer's personal manner and characteristics. Here is a short list of desirable traits:

1. *Knowledge of subject.* Employees expect trainers to know their job or subject thoroughly. Furthermore, they are expected to demonstrate that knowledge (what some experts call "active intelligence").

2. *Adaptability.* Some individuals learn faster or slower than others, and instruction should be matched to the trainee's learning ability.

3. *Sincerity.* Trainees appreciate sincerity in trainers. Along with this, trainers need to be patient with trainees and demonstrate tact in addressing their concerns.

4. *Sense of humour.* Learning can be fun; very often a point can be made with a story or anecdote.

5. *Interest.* Good trainers have a keen interest in the subject they are teaching; this interest is readily conveyed to trainees.

6. *Clear instructions.* Naturally, training is accomplished more quickly and retained longer when trainers give clear instructions.

7. *Individual assistance.* When training more than one employee, successful trainers always provide individual assistance.

8. *Enthusiasm.* A dynamic presentation and a vibrant personality show trainees that the trainer enjoys training; employees tend to respond positively to an enthusiastic climate.[15]

For training programs to be most successful, organizations should reward managers who prove to be excellent trainers. Too often managers are not recognized for their contributions to this important aspect of HRM. Likewise, training specialists in the HR function should be recognized for their role in the training program.

Phase 3: Implementing the Training Program

Despite the importance of needs assessment, instructional objectives, principles of learning, and the like, choices regarding instructional methods are where "the rubber meets the road" in implementing a training program. A major consideration in choosing among various training methods is determining which ones are appropriate for the KSAs to be learned. For example, if the material is mostly factual, methods such as lecture, classroom, or programmed instruction may be fine. However, if the training involves a large behavioural component, other methods such as on-the-job training, simulation, or computer-based training (CBT) might work better.[16]

In order to organize our discussion of various training methods, we will break them down into two primary groups: those used for non-managerial employees and those used for managers.

USING THE INTERNET

Training programs can be purchased and a list of these is available at:

www.trainingreport.ca/dir2000/direct.cfm

Training Methods for Non-managerial Employees

A wide variety of methods are available for training employees at all levels. Some methods have a long history of usage. Newer methods have emerged over the years out of a greater understanding of human behaviour, particularly in the areas of learning, motivation, and interpersonal relationships. More recently, technological advances, especially in computer hardware and software, have resulted in training devices that in many instances are more effective and economical than the traditional training methods.

On-the-Job Training

on-the-job training (OJT)
A method by which employees are given hands-on experience with instruction from their supervisor or other trainer

By far, the most common method used for training non-managerial employees is **on-the-job training (OJT)**. In fact, one estimate suggests that organizations spend three to six times as much on OJT as on classroom training. OJT has the advantage of providing hands-on experience under normal working conditions and an opportunity for the trainer—a manager or senior employee—to build good relationships with new employees. As time becomes a critical resource—and "just-in-time training" is needed most—OJT is viewed by some to be potentially the most effective means of facilitating learning in the workplace.[17]

Although it is used by all types of organizations, OJT is often one of the most poorly implemented training methods. Three common drawbacks are (1) the lack of a well-structured training environment, (2) poor training skills of managers, and (3) the absence of well-defined job performance criteria. To overcome these problems, training experts suggest the following:

1. Develop realistic goals and/or measures for each OJT area.
2. Plan a specific training schedule for each trainee, including set periods for evaluation and feedback.
3. Help managers establish a non-threatening atmosphere conducive to learning.
4. Conduct periodic evaluations, after training is completed, to prevent regression.[18]

Highlights in HRM 7.3 shows the basic steps of an OJT program. The method is used frequently in organizations to ensure that new employees have adequate guidance

Highlights in HRM 7.3

The PROPER Way to Do On-the-Job Training

P

Prepare. Decide what employees need to be taught. Identify the best sequence or steps of the training. Decide how best to demonstrate these steps. Have materials, resources, and equipment ready.

R

Reassure. Put each employee at ease. Learn about his or her prior experience, and adjust accordingly. Try to get the employee interested, relaxed, and motivated to learn.

O

Orient. Show the employee the correct way to do the job. Explain why it is done this way. Discuss how it relates to other jobs. Let him or her ask lots of questions.

P

Perform. When employees are ready, let them try the job themselves. Give them an opportunity to practice the job and guide them through rough spots. Provide help and assistance at first, then less as they continue.

E

Evaluate. Check the employees' performance, and question them on how, why, when, and where they should do something. Correct errors; repeat instructions.

R

Reinforce and Review. Provide praise and encouragement, and give feedback about how the employee is doing. Continue the conversation and express confidence in his or her doing the job.

Source: Scott Snell, Cornell University.

before taking on work responsibilities on their own. For example, KLM Royal Dutch Airlines uses on-the-job training to train its cabin attendants. The airline started a program that places cabin attendant trainees in the classroom for a certain period and then gives them additional training during an evaluation flight. On these flights, experienced cabin attendants provide the trainees with on-the-job training, based on a list of identified job tasks. Some tasks, such as serving meals and snacks, are demonstrated during the actual delivery of services to passengers. Other tasks are presented to trainees away from passengers between meal service.[19]

Apprenticeship Training

apprenticeship training
A system of training in which a worker entering the skilled trades is given thorough instruction and experience, both on and off the job, in the practical and theoretical aspects of the work

An extension of OJT is **apprenticeship training.** With this method, individuals entering industry, particularly in the skilled trades such as machinist, laboratory technician, and electrician, are given thorough instruction and experience, both on and off the job, in the practical and theoretical aspects of the work. Only 18 percent of Canadian employers train apprentices, and most do so to ensure a steady supply of workers and to shape apprentices to their own requirements. About 90 percent of apprenticeship training occurs in the workplace and is provided by employers to standards of skill and safety set by industry. For example, Bonneville Power Administration and General Physics Corporation developed an apprenticeship program for substation operators to give employees both a strong technical foundation in the fundamentals of electricity and a hands-on ability to operate equipment within the power substation. Ultimately, the program was also designed to help future electrical operators respond to emergencies. In Europe, organizations such as BAE Systems and Ford Motor Company use apprenticeship programs extensively for their engineers.[20]

Cooperative Training, Internships, and Governmental Training

cooperative training
A training program that combines practical on-the-job experience with formal educational classes

Similar to apprenticeships, **cooperative training** programs combine practical on-the-job experience with formal classes. However, the term *cooperative training* is typically used in connection with high school and college programs that incorporate part- or full-time experiences. In recent years there has been an increased effort to expand opportunities that combine on-the-job skill training with regular classroom training so that students can pursue either technical work or a college degree program.

internship programs
Programs jointly sponsored by colleges, universities, and other organizations that offer students the opportunity to gain real-life experience while allowing them to find out how they will perform in work organizations

Internship programs, jointly sponsored by colleges, universities, and a variety of organizations, offer students the chance to get real-world experience while finding out how they will perform in work organizations. Organizations benefit by getting student-employees with new ideas, energy, and eagerness to accomplish their assignments. EnCana, an oil and gas company based in Calgary, has developed the Oil and Gas Production Field Operator Career Pathway program, which offers high school students an opportunity to earn credits while learning about field production work, in alliance with Southern Alberta Institute of Technology. The courses are offered as an option and students graduate with a field operator certificate from SAIT, and have a chance of obtaining a paid internship in the summer.[21] The internship program of a community college is described in Highlights in HRM 7.4. Highlights in HRM 7.5 on page 314 shows how to make the most from internship opportunities.

Apprenticeships are a good way to train employees, especially in skilled trade sectors.

© PETER HVIZDAK/THE IMAGE WORKS

Highlights in HRM 7.4

Internship Program at Durham College

The work-study program in human resources at Durham College, Ontario, is designed to transition an HR student into an HR practitioner. According to the coordinator of the human resources program, Dr. Carolin Rekar-Munro, each project must allow for the transfer of theories learned in class to a project management format at the field placement location. Students are required to write objectives in a draft proposal, similar to management by objectives, in which the criteria used to measure the success of the placement must be both qualitative and quantitative in content.

For the three-year diploma program, students in their final year will work two days per week from October to April and gain 344 hours of field placement experience. For the one-year post-diploma certificate program, students will attain 200 hours of field placement experience over a five-week block following final exams. Cohorts are also put into teams during the experience and attend weekly seminars in which the students can share their experiences and get advice on issues they are facing at their respective placements. According to Dr. Rekar-Munro, this peer group process helps to establish a network of HR professionals.

By focusing on application-based projects, students will be in a position to decide if they wish to pursue careers in HR and will have acquired valuable experience in project management. Employers also benefit as they receive both a quality HR project and the chance to preview a potential new staff member. This work-study program gives employers a unique probationary period and 30 to 40 percent of students are hired at their field placements to continue their projects. For example, Dr. Rekar-Munro points to a student who created a health and safety manual for people with English as a Second Language (ESL), who was then hired by her field placement employer to complete the work.

The federal government and various provincial governments have begun working together with private employers to sponsor a multitude of training programs. For example, the federal government has invested money in the Information Technology program at the Nova Scotia Community College, Marconi campus, which installed a high tech infrastructure to support customized training for the petroleum industry.[22]

Classroom Instruction

When most people think about training, they think about classrooms. There is good reason for this. Beyond its pervasiveness in education, classroom training enables the maximum number of trainees to be handled by the minimum number of instructors. This method lends itself particularly well to what is called "blended" learning in which lectures and demonstrations are combined with films, DVDs, videotapes, or computer instruction. When it is not possible to obtain videotapes, audiotapes can be very valuable. For example, to instruct flight-crew trainees, airlines might play actual cockpit tapes recorded on airplanes involved in accidents. After listening to the tape, the trainees discuss the behaviour of the crew during the crisis. By listening to the recorded statements of others and observing their failure to operate as a team, pilot

Highlights in HRM 7.5

Making the Most of Internships

Today, many colleges and universities encourage students to apply for internships as part of the curriculum. Done well, internships provide advantages to students, universities, and potential employers.

Benefits for Students

Those who intern with organizations before graduation have higher starting salaries, more job offers, a shorter time in which they obtain their first position, faster movement into jobs with more prestige, greater challenges and financial rewards, and faster promotion. They are better prepared for the world of work.

Benefits for Colleges and Universities

Internships help colleges and universities get in touch with the marketplace. As students succeed in the workplace, student recruitment improves. Strong internship programs increase the retention of students and their placement after graduation.

Benefits for Potential Employers

Interns can provide your organization with competent assistance without a large financial outlay. Internships also let organizations evaluate a prospective employee nearly risk-free. At the end of the internship, there are no obligations to continue the relationship, but if it's a good match the organization has a leg up on hiring the person—it eliminates recruitment expenses and greatly reduces the cost per hire.

How to Increase the Value of Interns

To increase the internal value of your internship programs, take the following steps:

1. Assign the intern to projects that are accomplishable and provide training as required.
2. Involve the intern in the project-planning process.
3. Appoint a mentor or supervisor to guide the intern.
4. Invite project suggestions from other staff members.
5. Ask interns to keep a journal of their work activities.
6. Rotate interns throughout the organization.
7. Explain the rationale behind work assignments.
8. Hold interns accountable for projects and deadlines.
9. Treat interns as part of the organizational staff and invite them to staff meetings.
10. Establish a process for considering interns for permanent hire.

Source: Condensed from John Byrd and Rob Poole, "Highly Motivated Employees at No Cost? It's Not an Impossible Dream," *Nonprofit World* 19, no. 6 (November/December 2001): 312–32. Reprinted by permission of *Nonprofit World*, www.snpo.org, telephone: 734-451-3582.

trainees will develop an understanding of the need for balancing their sense of self-reliance with an ability to listen to subordinates. Despite the rise of many other types of learning—electronic and otherwise—classroom instruction is still the number one training method, as Figure 7.6 shows.[23]

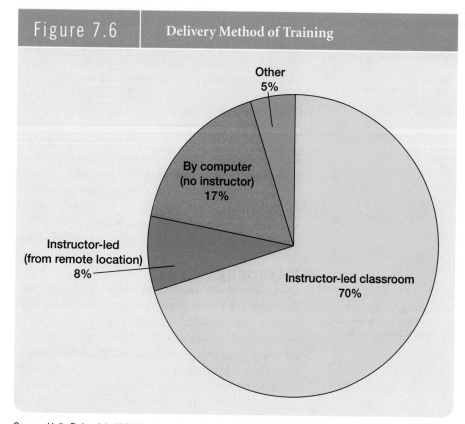

Figure 7.6   **Delivery Method of Training**

Other
5%

By computer
(no instructor)
17%

Instructor-led
(from remote location)
8%

Instructor-led classroom
70%

Source: Holly Dolezalek, "2004 Industry Report," *Training* (October 2004): 34.

Programmed Instruction

One method of instruction that is particularly good for allowing individuals to work at their own pace is programmed instruction. Programmed instruction—increasingly referred to as *self-directed learning*—involves the use of books, manuals, or computers to break down subject matter content into highly organized, logical sequences that demand continuous response on the part of the trainee. After being presented with a small segment of information, the trainee is required to answer a question, either by writing it in a response screen or by pushing a button. If the response is correct, the trainee is told so and is presented with the next step (screen) in the material. If the response is incorrect, further explanatory information is given and the trainee is told to try again.

A major advantage of programmed instruction is that it incorporates a number of the established learning principles discussed earlier in the chapter. With programmed instruction, training is individualized, trainees are actively involved in the instructional process, and feedback and reinforcement are immediate. While programmed instruction may not increase the amount an individual learns, it typically increases the speed at which he or she learns.

Audiovisual Methods

To teach skills and procedures for many production jobs, certain audiovisual devices can be used. At the simplest level, videotapes are often used to illustrate the steps in a procedure such as assembling electronic equipment or working with a problem employee. Using camcorders permits trainers and trainees to view an on-the-spot recording and to get immediate feedback about progress toward learning objectives.

Golf and tennis coaches frequently tape their students to let them see their mistakes. RBC Financial Group uses videoconferencing extensively, broadcasting about 40 hours of programming per month. All 1300 branches across Canada are hooked by satellite, and the employees can listen to the keynote speaker, see slides and video presentations, ask questions, and take multiple-choice tests.[24]

Other technologies, such as CDs and DVDs, allow trainees to access any segment of the instructional program, which is especially useful for individualized instruction when employees have different levels of knowledge and ability. Such technology is currently used to teach doctors to diagnose illness, to help dairy farmers increase their productivity, and to teach CPR trainees to revive victims of heart attacks. More recent applications tackle the difficult managerial skills of leadership, supervision, and interpersonal relations.

Extending these kinds of video technologies with a teleconferencing infrastructure allows an instructional program to be transmitted to many locations simultaneously and permits immediate interaction among trainees. These methods are becoming quite powerful as tools for bringing continuing- and distance-education to life.

E-Learning

The simpler, audiovisual, programmed, and computer-oriented training methods just discussed are evolving into what trainers today refer to as e-learning. **E-learning** covers a wide variety of applications such as Web and computer-based training (CBT) and virtual classrooms. It includes delivery of content via the Internet, intranets and extranets, audiotape, videotape, satellite and broadcast interactive TV, DVD, and CD-ROM. (An e-learning version of this course can be purchased at www.captus.com.) E-learning makes it possible to provide drill and practice, problem solving, simulation, gaming forms of instruction, and certain very sophisticated forms of individualized tutorial instruction in a way that's more engaging for learners than traditional classroom instruction. It is also cheaper for employers to administer because, in many instances, it can be delivered directly via employees' PCs. Companies are engaging in more e-learning than ever before and are reporting that they are saving anywhere from 30 to 70 percent on their training costs by doing so.[25]

E-learning transforms the learning process in several ways. First, as we have said, it allows the firm to bring the training to employees rather than vice versa, which is generally more efficient and cost-effective. The nuclear power plant industry is a case in point: Nuclear power plant training is frequent and time-consuming. For workers just to remove their protective gear and commute to a separate training venue can take anywhere from an hour or more. One nuclear power company that switched to e-learning reported that it saved nearly $1 million and 10 000 employee hours in just a year by doing so.

E-learning also allows employees to search through a virtual sea of information in order to customize their own learning in their own time and space. More companies are demanding access to individual training components for employees to use when and where they need them. This helps alleviate the boredom trainees experience during full-blown training courses, and employees are more likely to retain the information when they can immediately put it to use. Cisco has 3000 training VoDs (videos on demand) that employees can download off the company's intranet as needed. As new training VoDs are published by managers at Cisco, older, less requested VoDs are automatically removed and archived.[26]

Although e-learning systems can be very sophisticated, they need not be overly expensive. Many e-learning training programs use existing applications employees are familiar with such as PowerPoint, Word, and Adobe Acrobat and convert them into Flash programs so they can be easily viewed online with any Web browser. Web-based training can also be revised rapidly, thereby providing continuously updated training material.

This not only makes it easier and cheaper to revise training curricula, but also saves travel and classroom costs. When combined with other communications technology such as e-mail, teleconferencing, videoconferencing, and groupware, Web-based training can be even more effective. A summary of these advantages includes the following:

- Learning is self-paced.
- The training comes to the employee.
- The training is interactive.
- Employees do not have to wait for a scheduled training session.
- The training can focus on specific needs as revealed by built-in tests.
- Trainees can be referred to online help or written material.
- It is easier to change a website than to retype, photocopy, and distribute new classroom-training materials.
- Recordkeeping is facilitated.
- The training can be cost-effective if used for both large and small numbers of employees.

One catch to e-learning is that it requires some planning so that both employees inhouse connecting through a fast corporate Internet connection and employees off-site with wireless modems or slow dialup connections are able to access the training material. To cope with this limitation, companies frequently supply their offsite personnel with CDs and DVDs containing the same training material employees onsite are able to download. Highlights in HRM 7.6 shows the different types of media firms use to train their employees and the frequency with which they use the media.

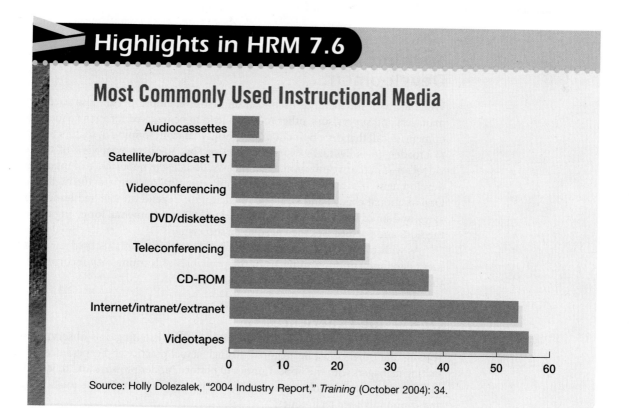

Highlights in HRM 7.6

Most Commonly Used Instructional Media

Source: Holly Dolezalek, "2004 Industry Report," *Training* (October 2004): 34.

Simulation Method

Sometimes it is either impractical or unwise to train employees on the actual equipment used on the job. An obvious example is training employees to operate aircraft, spacecraft, and other highly technical and expensive equipment. The simulation method emphasizes realism in equipment and its operation at minimum cost and maximum safety.

Southwest Airlines boasts perhaps the most technologically advanced flight simulator in the airline industry: a $10.8 million full-motion Boeing 737-700 unit housed in a 10 000-square-metre (110,000-square-foot) flight operations training centre. The facility can house up to six 737 simulators and can train up to 300 (of Southwest's 4100) pilots at one time. The centre has a staff of 110 employees. In addition to the simulators and their associated briefing and computer programming rooms, the training centre houses eight classrooms, each fully equipped with closed-circuit TV, computers, conventional audiovisual equipment, and telephone and Internet hookups. On an average day, the flight operations training centre will have 80 to 120 pilots in its classrooms and on its simulators.[27]

As with e-learning and computer-based training, the distinction between simulation and computer-based training has blurred. For example, a simulation developed by Wicat in partnership with Airbus and Singapore Airlines runs on a PC and replicates a cockpit with control displays and throttle/flap controls. Even though the PC-based simulation is relatively inexpensive, it is powerful. Pilots are taken through a self-paced program that simulates "taxi, takeoff, climb, cruise, descent, approach, landing, and go-around." These types of technologies are making it easier to offer training in new and different ways. Given advances in telecommunications, the possibilities seem limitless.[28]

Training Methods for Management Development

While many of the methods used to train first-level employees are also used to train managers and supervisors, other methods tend to be reserved for management development. Recall that development differs somewhat from training in that its purpose is to broaden an individual's experience and provide a longer-term view of that individual's role in the organization. Over the past decade, the importance of management development has grown as organizations attempt to compete through people. Organizational change and strategic revitalization depend on talented leaders, managers, and supervisors. Management development is instrumental for giving managers the skills and perspectives they need to be successful.[29]

As with training for non-managerial employees, the methods used for management development differ in terms of the principles of learning they incorporate and their appropriateness for delivering various KSAs.

On-the-Job Experiences

Some skills and knowledge can be acquired just by listening and observing or by reading. But others must be acquired through actual practice and experience. By presenting managers with the opportunities to perform under pressure and to learn from their mistakes, on-the-job development experiences are some of the most powerful and commonly used techniques.

However, just as on-the-job training for first-level employees can be problematic if not well planned, on-the-job management development should be well organized, supervised, and challenging to the participants. Methods of providing on-the-job experiences include the following:

1. *Coaching* involves a continuing flow of instructions, comments, and suggestions from the manager to the subordinate. (*Mentoring*, discussed in Chapter 5, is a similar approach to personal and informal management development.)

2. *Understudy assignments* groom an individual to take over a manager's job by gaining experience in handling important functions of the job.

3. *Job rotation* provides, through a variety of work experiences, the broadened knowledge and understanding required to manage more effectively.

4. *Lateral transfer* involves horizontal movement through different departments, along with upward movement in the organization.

5. *Special projects* and *junior boards* provide an opportunity for individuals to become involved in the study of current organizational problems and in planning and decision-making activities.

6. *Action learning* gives managers release time to work full-time on projects with others in the organization. In some cases, action learning is combined with classroom instruction, discussions, and conferences.

7. *Staff meetings* enable participants to become more familiar with problems and events occurring outside their immediate area by exposing them to the ideas and thinking of other managers.

8. *Planned career progressions* (discussed in Chapter 5) utilize all these different methods to provide employees with the training and development necessary to progress through a series of jobs requiring higher and higher levels of knowledge and/or skills.[30]

Although these methods are used most often to develop managers for higher-level positions, they also provide valuable experiences for those who are being groomed for other types of positions in the organization. And while on-the-job experiences constitute the core of management training and development, other off-the-job methods of development can be used to supplement these experiences.

Seminars and Conferences

Seminars and conferences, like classroom instruction, are useful for bringing groups of people together for training and development. In management development, seminars and conferences can be used to communicate ideas, policies, or procedures, but they are also good for raising points of debate or discussing issues (usually with the help of a qualified leader) that have no set answers or resolutions. In this regard, seminars and conferences are often used when attitude change is a goal.

Case Studies

A particularly useful method used in classroom learning situations is the case study. Using documented examples, participants learn how to analyze (take apart) and synthesize (put together) facts, to become conscious of the many variables on which management decisions are based, and, in general, to improve their decision-making skills. Experienced educators and trainers generally point out that the case study is most appropriate when:

1. Analytic, problem-solving, and critical-thinking skills are most important.
2. The KSAs are complex and participants need time to master them.
3. Active participation is desired.
4. The process of learning (questioning, interpreting, and so on) is as important as the content.
5. Team problem solving and interaction are possible.[31]

Even when case studies may be appropriate, they are often mismanaged. As with any other development technique, implementation is crucial for effectiveness.

Management Games

Training experiences have been brought to life and made more interesting through the development of management games, in which players are faced with the task of making a series of decisions affecting a hypothetical organization. The effects that every decision has on each area within the organization can be simulated with a computer programmed for the game. A major advantage of this technique is the high degree of participation it requires.

Games are now widely used as a management development method. Many of them have been designed for general use but more recently have been adapted for specific industries. It might be amusing to learn that the Marine Corps's basic warfare group has used the computer game *Doom* to help trainees learn how to develop strategies. Similarly, Bell Canada has its managers play *TeleSim*, a computer simulation for the telecommunications industry developed by Thinking Tools and Coopers & Lybrand to teach executives how to act in an increasingly open, competitive market.[32]

As the development of industry-specific games has increased, there are now simulations for a wide variety of organizations. For example, Lufthansa Airlines and Delta Air Lines have each developed management games designed to teach participants business issues related to today's stiff competition and low or no profits in their industry. Managers working in teams compete with one another running fictitious airline companies and have to balance issues of routing, schedules, costs, profits, and the like. Delta's game was so popular that after the company's managers were trained, the game was rolled out to front-line employees.[33]

Role-Playing

Role-playing consists of assuming the attitudes and behaviour—that is, playing the role—of others, often a supervisor and a subordinate who are involved in a particular problem. By acting out another's position, participants in the role-playing can improve their ability to understand and cope with others. Role-playing should also help them learn how to counsel others by helping them see situations from a different point of view. Role-playing is used widely in training healthcare professionals to be empathic and sensitive to the concerns of patients. It is also used widely in training managers to handle employee issues relating to absenteeism, performance appraisal, and conflict situations.

At times, participants may be hesitant to try role-playing. Successful role-play takes planning. Instructors should do the following:

1. Ensure that members of the group are comfortable with each other.
2. Select and prepare the role-players by introducing a specific situation.
3. To help participants prepare, ask them to describe potential characters.
4. Realize that volunteers make better role-players.
5. Prepare the observers by giving them specific tasks (such as evaluation or feedback).
6. Guide the role-play enactment through its bumps (because it is not scripted).
7. Keep it short.
8. Discuss the enactment and prepare bulleted points of what was learned.[34]

Role-play is a versatile teaching model, applicable to a variety of training experiences. Planned and implemented correctly, role-play can bring realism and insight into dilemmas and experiences that otherwise might not be shared. Computer programs that simulate role-playing have also been developed. *Virtual Leader*, a product by SimuLearn, is one such program: Management trainees interact with animated "employees"—some of whom are more cooperative than others. The trainees are then given feedback as to how well they applied their managerial skills to each situation.

Behaviour Modelling

One technique that combines several different training methods, and therefore multiple principles of learning, is the behaviour modelling technique. **Behaviour modelling** involves four basic components:

behaviour modelling
An approach that demonstrates desired behaviour and gives trainees the chance to practise and role-play those behaviours and receive feedback

1. *Learning points.* At the beginning of instruction, the essential goals and objectives of the program are enumerated. In some cases, the learning points are a sequence of behaviours that are to be taught. For example, the learning points might describe the recommended steps for giving employees feedback.
2. *Modelling.* Participants view films, DVDs, or videotapes in which a model manager is portrayed dealing with an employee in an effort to improve his or her performance. The model shows specifically how to deal with the situation and demonstrates the learning points.
3. *Practice and role-play.* Trainees participate in extensive rehearsal of the behaviours demonstrated by the models. The greatest percentage of training time is spent in these skill-practice sessions.
4. *Feedback and reinforcement.* As the trainee's behaviour increasingly resembles that of the model, the trainer and other trainees provide social reinforcers such as praise, approval, encouragement, and attention. Videotaping behaviour rehearsals provides feedback and reinforcement. Emphasis throughout the training period is placed on transferring the training to the job.

Does behaviour modelling work? Several controlled studies have demonstrated success in helping managers interact with employees, handle discipline, introduce change, and increase productivity. Military training is a classic example of how behaviour modelling can work. Drill sergeants model the behaviour expected of new recruits, who, in turn, by emulating them, develop discipline and confidence.[35]

Phase 4: Evaluating the Training Program

Training, like any other HRM function, should be evaluated to determine its effectiveness. A variety of methods are available to assess the extent to which training programs improve learning, affect behaviour on the job, and impact the bottom-line performance of an organization. Unfortunately, few organizations adequately evaluate their training programs. In many ways, this goes beyond poor management; it is poor business practice. Given the substantial monetary stake that organizations have in training, it would seem prudent that managers would want to maximize the return on that investment.

Figure 7.7 shows that four basic criteria are available to evaluate training: (1) reactions, (2) learning, (3) behaviour, and (4) results. Some of these criteria are easier to measure than others, but each is important in that it provides different information about the success of the programs. The combination of these criteria can give a total picture of the training program in order to help managers decide where problem areas lie, what to change about the program, and whether to continue with a program.[36] Reality Check shows how these four levels have been applied at CONEXUS, the largest credit union in Saskatchewan.

Criterion 1: Reactions

One of the simplest and most common approaches to training evaluation is assessing participant reactions. Happy trainees will be more likely to want to focus on training principles and to utilize the information on the job. Conversely, dissatisfaction with job training contributes to low employee job satisfaction. Trainees can do more than tell you whether they liked a training program, though. They can give insights into the content and techniques they found most useful. They can critique the instructors or make suggestions about participant interactions, feedback, and the like. Potential questions might include the following:

- What were your learning goals for this program?
- Did you achieve them?
- Did you like this program?

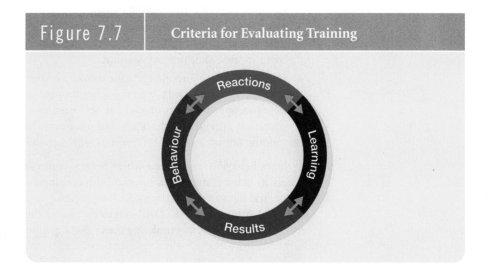

| Figure 7.7 | Criteria for Evaluating Training |

Reality Check

A Classic Four-Level Evaluation

CONEXUS is the largest credit union in Saskatchewan with assets of $1.1 billion. According to Gayle Johnson, CHRP, EVP human resources and corporate secretary, its training and development budget for its 465 employees is 6 percent of payroll. Three percent is spent on university education, and the other 3 percent is spent on training. Its largest training program is one that develops financial service representatives (their title is to be changed to "relationship managers"). The training consists of several steps and each is measured.

Inhouse and classroom-based modules teach content, such as computer literacy, cash duties, and introduction to CONEXUS's products and services, and progresses through to more advanced training, such as consumer lending practices, estates, and minimal mortgage lending. Each three- to five-day module is followed by a work period of three to 12 months, so that employees can apply their knowledge. The four levels of measurement of the effectiveness of training are the following:

1. Reaction: "Smile sheets" are completed by each participant at the end of the classroom training, asking questions such as "What did you get from this session?"
2. Comprehensive Review: Exams are given after each module and the results are fed back to the employees and managers.
3. Employee Performance Competencies: Every job family has a number of job-specific competencies, and managers are asked to rate the participants on these performance competencies.
   The changes in ratings are tracked.
4. Results: These vary by module. For example, after the cash-lending module, the performance tracked would be the number of call-outs to customers and the number of sales.

- Would you recommend it to others who have similar learning goals?
- What suggestions do you have for improving the program?
- Should the organization continue to offer it?

While evaluation methods based on reactions are improving, too many conclusions about training effectiveness are still based on broad satisfaction measures that lack specific feedback. Furthermore, it should be noted that positive reactions are no guarantee that the training has been successful. It may be easy to collect glowing comments from trainees, but gratifying as this information is to management, it may not be useful to the organization unless it somehow translates into improved behaviour and job performance that is measurable. In the final analysis, reaction measures should not stop with assessing the training's entertainment value.[37]

Criterion 2: Learning

Beyond what participants *think* about the training, it might be a good idea to see whether they actually learned anything. Testing knowledge and skills before beginning a training program gives a baseline standard on trainees that can be measured again after training to determine improvement. However, in addition to testing trainees before and after training, parallel standards can be measured for individuals in a control group to compare with those in training to ensure that improvements are due to training and not some other factor (such as changes in jobs or compensation). The control group should be made up of employees who have not received the training but who match the trainees in such areas as experience, past training, and job level. Federal Express took this approach by studying 20 van drivers who attended a weeklong new-hire training program. The company then compared the performance of these drivers with a control group of 20 drivers who had received only on-the-job training. FedEx found that the drivers who had been formally trained made fewer package processing errors, saving the company about $500 per trained driver.[38]

Criterion 3: Behaviour

You might be surprised to learn that much of what is learned in a training program never gets used back on the job. It's not that the training was necessarily ineffective. In fact, on measures of employee reactions and learning, the program might score quite high. But for several reasons, trainees may not demonstrate behaviour change back on the job. **Transfer of training** refers to the effective application of principles learned to what is required on the job. To maximize transfer, managers and trainers can take several approaches:

transfer of training
Effective application of principles learned to what is required on the job

1. *Feature identical elements.* Transfer of training to the job can be facilitated by having conditions in the training program come as close as possible to those on the job.

2. *Focus on general principles.* When jobs change or the work environment cannot be matched exactly, trainers often stress the general principles behind the training rather than focusing on rote behaviour. This approach helps trainees learn how to apply the main learning points to varying conditions on the job.

3. *Establish a climate for transfer.* In some cases, trained behaviour is not implemented because old approaches and routines are still reinforced by other managers, peers, and employees. To prevent this kind of problem, the manager should ensure that the work environment supports, reinforces, and rewards the trainee for applying the new skills or knowledge.

4. *Give employees transfer strategies.* Particularly in settings that are not conducive to transfer, managers should also provide trainees with strategies and tactics for dealing with their transfer environment. One approach, called *relapse prevention (RP)*, teaches individuals how to anticipate and cope with the inevitable setbacks they will encounter back on the job—that is, a relapse into former behaviours. By identifying high-risk situations that jeopardize transfer and developing coping strategies, relapse prevention can help employees gain better control over maintaining learned behaviours.[39]

There are several methods for assessing transfer of learned skills back to the job. At Xerox, for example, managers use multiple methods, including observations of trainees once they return to their regular positions, interviews with the trainees' managers, and examination of trainees' post-training performance appraisals. They combine these indices to ascertain whether training and development have influenced job behaviours.

Criterion 4: Results, or Return on Investment (ROI)

Training managers are under pressure to show that their programs produce "bottom-line" results.[40] Most organizations today measure their training in terms of its return on investment (ROI), which is also sometimes referred to as the *utility* the firm gets for its training dollars. A company's ROI refers to the benefits derived from training relative to the costs incurred. HR managers are responsible for calculating and presenting these benefits to the company's top managers. The benefits can include higher revenues generated, increased productivity, improved quality, lower costs, more satisfied customers, higher job satisfaction, and lower employee turnover. TD Bank Financial Group takes ROI very seriously. The job of six employees, working in a group called Learning Outcomes, is to measure the value of the bank's training investment, about $50 million a year.[41]

The following are the types of questions HR managers should try to answer as they calculate a training program's benefits:

- How much did quality improve because of the training program?
- How much has it contributed to profits?
- What reduction in turnover and wasted materials did the company get after training?
- How much has productivity increased and by how much have costs been reduced?

To answer these questions, HR managers use various types of data such as sales data, human resources and financial data, and employee-survey and control-group data gathered from various sources within the organization. Of course, the costs of the training program need to be measured, too. The costs of training include the various expenses incurred as a result of training, including the direct costs of the programs (materials, travel, meeting site, meals, equipment, trainer salary or fee, and so on) as well as the indirect costs of the programs (participants' salaries, lost productivity while attending the training, and so on). The ROI formula can then be calculated fairly simply:

$$ROI = Results/Training\ Costs$$

If the ROI ratio is >1, the benefits of the training exceed the cost of the program; if the ROI ratio is <1, the costs of the training exceed the benefits. ROI can also be measured in terms of how long it takes before the benefits of the training pay off. This payback analysis is done by adding the costs and dividing the benefits realized in a single month. The result will indicate the overall time required for the training to pay for itself. Highlights in HRM 7.7 on page 326 shows some simple examples of ROI calculations.[42] The Business Case on page 326 discusses the return on training investment.

Benchmarking

Closely related to calculating the firm's training ROI is the process of benchmarking developmental services and practices against those of recognized leaders in industry. While no single model for exact benchmarking exists, the simplest models are based on the late W. Edwards Deming's classic four-step process. The four-step process advocates that managers:

1. *Plan.* Conduct a self-audit to define internal processes and measurements; decide on areas to be benchmarked and choose the comparison organization.
2. *Do.* Collect data through surveys, interviews, site visits, and/or historical records.

Highlights in HRM 7.7

Calculating Training ROI: Examples

If the ROI ratio is >1, the benefits of the training exceed the cost of the program, and if the ratio is <1, the costs of the training program outweigh the benefits.

Example 1: A program to train new machine operators costs $15,000 to develop and implement. After completing the training program, the average number of parts produced each year increased by 3000, and the profit on each new part is $10, producing a net result of $30,000.

$$ROI = \$30,000/\$15,000 = 2$$

Example 2: A safety program costs the company $25,000 to develop and implement. One year later, there had been a small decrease in accidents, saving the company a total of $10,000.

$$ROI = \$10,000/\$25,000 = 0.4$$

In Example 1, the program resulted in a ROI of 2, indicating that the benefits of the program outweigh its cost. However, in Example 2, the ROI was only 0.4, indicating that the costs of the program outweigh the benefits.

Source: Richard J. Wagner and Robert J. Weigand, "Can the Value of Training Be Measured? A Simplified Approach to Evaluating Training," *The Health Care Manager* 23, no.1 (January–March 2004): 71–78. Reprinted by permission of Lippincott Williams & Wilkins.

The Business Case

Return on Training Investment

Organizations spend about 2 percent of payroll on training, an estimated $750 billion around the globe. Most organizations (four out of five) do not measure the ROI on their training dollars, citing barriers such as the difficulty of doing so, the cost, lack of training, and lack of experience. However, at TD Bank, which has 1500 branches, 45 000 employees, and 30 different businesses, a focus on measuring the ROI of training captures results such as revenues and profitability. TD has a front-end process—that is, the business units determine the business results expected, the job performance that will generate these results, and the role that training plays.

According to the Conference Board of Canada, a positive relationship exists between formal training expenditures and performance indicators, such as employee productivity and company profitability. H.J. Heinz Company Canada provided training for its staff in response to increased competition and the need for new technologies. The training costs of $869,000 were repaid within 20 months due to increased productivity, reduced absenteeism, and fewer damaged containers.

A useful tool for developing Return on Training Investment (ROTI) can be found at the website of FuturEd Inc.: www.futured.com/audited/returned.htm.

Sources: S. Carrigan, "Training: Investment in the Future," *Canadian HR Reporter* 14, no. 11 (June 4, 2001): G1; "What Should You Expect from Your Investment in Training?" *Strategis*, Industry Canada, "Canadian Training Solutions," www.strategis.gc.ca.

3. *Check.* Analyze data to discover performance gaps and communicate findings and suggested improvements to management.

4. *Act.* Establish goals, implement specific changes, monitor progress, and redefine benchmarks as a continuous improvement process.

To use benchmarking successfully, managers must clearly define the measures of competency and performance and must objectively assess the current situation and identify areas for improvement. To this end, experts in this area are attempting to work out ways of measuring what training departments do. Three broad areas that most HR training and developmental practitioners consider essential to measure are as follows:

1. *Training activity:* How much training is occurring?

2. *Training results:* Do training and development achieve their goals?

3. *Training efficiency:* Are resources utilized in the pursuit of this mission?

The ASTD and its Institute for Workplace Learning have established a project that allows organizations to measure and benchmark training and development activities against each other. This benchmarking forum, which shares findings from more than 800 companies, compares data on training costs, staffing, administration, design, development, and delivery of training programs. Not only do initiatives such as these help organizations evaluate their training programs, but the process serves as a feedback loop to reinitiate needs assessment and design of future training.[43] Highlights in HRM 7.8 shows several aspects of training that can be benchmarked against organizations considered superior in the training function, and how those aspects are calculated.

Highlights in HRM 7.8

Benchmarking HR Training

MEASUREMENT	HOW TO CALCULATE
Percentage of payroll spent on training	Total training expenditures ÷ total payroll
Training dollars spent per employee	Total training expenditures ÷ total employees served
Average training hours per employee	Total number of training hours (hours × participants) ÷ total employees served
Percentage of employees trained per year	Total number of employees receiving training ÷ total employee population
HRD staff per 1000 employees	Number of human resource development staff ÷ total employee population × 1000
Cost savings as a ratio of training expenses	Total savings in scrap or waste ÷ dollars invested in training
Profits per employee per year	Total yearly gross profits ÷ total number of employees
Training costs per student hour	Total costs of training ÷ total number of hours of training

Special Topics in Training and Development

While we have focused almost exclusively on the processes underlying a systems model of training—needs assessment, principles of learning, implementation methods, evaluation—it may be useful to discuss some of the more popular topics that are covered in these training programs. As we noted in the beginning of this chapter, there is a wide variety of training programs. In addition to training that addresses KSAs reflecting the demands of a particular job, many employers develop training programs to meet the needs of a broader base of employees. In this final section, we summarize some of these programs, including orientation training, basic skills training, team training, and diversity training. Global training will be covered in Chapter 15.

Orientation Training

To get new employees off to a good start, organizations generally offer a formal orientation program. **Orientation** is the formal process of familiarizing new employees with the organization, their jobs, and their work units. Most executives believe that formal orientation programs are effective in helping to retain and motivate employees. These and other reported benefits include the following:

orientation
The formal process of familiarizing new employees with the organization, their jobs, and their work units

1. Lower turnover
2. Increased productivity
3. Improved employee morale
4. Lower recruiting and training costs
5. Facilitation of learning
6. Reduction of the new employee's anxiety[44]

Intuit Canada is a leading example of effective orientation practices (see Highlights in HRM 7.9).

The more time and effort spent in helping new employees feel welcome, the more likely they are to identify with the organization and become valuable members of it. Unlike training, which emphasizes the *what* and the *how*, orientation often stresses the *why*. It is designed to influence employee attitudes about the work they will be doing and their role in the organization. It defines the philosophy behind the organization's rules and provides a framework for job-related tasks. And as plans, policies, and procedures change in organizations, even current employees need to be kept up to date and continually reoriented to changing conditions.

For a well-integrated orientation program, cooperation between line and staff is essential. The HR department ordinarily is responsible for coordinating orientation activities and for providing new employees with information about conditions of employment, pay, benefits, and other areas not directly under a supervisor's direction. However, the supervisor has the most important role in the orientation program. New employees are interested primarily in what the supervisor says and does and what their new co-workers are like. Before the arrival of a new employee, the supervisor should inform the work group that a new worker is joining the unit. It is also common practice for supervisors or other managerial personnel to recruit co-workers to serve as volunteer "sponsors," or mentors, for incoming employees. In addition to providing practical help to newcomers, experienced colleagues represent an important source of information about the norms and nuances of the work group, the culture of the organization, and what it expects from its employees. These relationships are vital to the

Highlights in HRM 7.9

Wowing the Candidate

Intuit Canada, headquartered in Edmonton, Alberta, is a leading developer of financial software, including personal finance management, small business accounting, and tax preparation, with products such as Quicken. Intuit, like other organizations profiled in this report, is a top employer; it was ranked number two in Canada by the *Globe and Mail* survey and 45th of the 100 Best Companies to Work for in America by *Fortune* magazine in 2002. What makes Intuit special is its success in a highly competitive industry. There are many factors, but evidence of its success is its low attrition rate of 3 percent, which is remarkable in a sector where the average turnover is 20 percent. Ninety-four percent of its employees report that Intuit is a "great place to work," according to their annual surveys.

Intuit is very careful about the first few days of a new employee's work life. There are too many stories about employees in other organizations showing up very excited about their new job, only to discover that no one remembers they are hired, supplies and offices are not ready, and the reporting manager is absent. Intuit is committed to wowing the candidate—now employee—on the first day. Upon arriving at work, new employees are greeted by name by the receptionist who gives them a stainless steel coffee mug engraved with their names. The hiring manager is called and arrives promptly. He knows the candidate and takes him to the work-station, showing him the computer, telephone, and office supplies. The next step is to introduce the new employee to colleagues and other team members and a "buddy" who has volunteered to guide the new employee and answer all questions for the next three weeks. New employees often struggle with simple questions such as: How does the photocopier work? Do most people bring their lunches to work? The IT person arrives next and helps set up voice mail, e-mail, Internet access, etc. Intuit considers it vital that when the new employee goes home that night, he should be able to answer the universal question "How was your first day on the job?" with "Wow, am I ever glad that I took this job!"

This informal orientation is completed by a formal orientation, in which information about the strategy, vision, plans, history—including war stories and all the successes—is shared. A key part of this orientation is a discussion of Intuit values. At the end of the first week, and again at the end of the first month, feedback about the new employee's experiences is solicited. What worked, what was frustrating, how can the orientation be improved?

Source: M. Belcourt and S. Taggar, "Making Government the Best Place to Work: Building Commitment," IPAC, New Directions Series, no. 8, 2002.

socialization of new employees and contribute significantly to their long-term success within the organization.

Given the immediate and lasting impact of orientation programs, careful planning—with emphasis on program goals, topics to be covered, and methods of organizing and presenting them—is essential. In many cases, organizations devise checklists for use by those responsible for conducting the orientation so that no item of importance to employees is overlooked. The checklist would include such things as (1) an introduction to other employees, (2) an outline of training, (3) expectations for attendance, conduct, and appearance, (4) the conditions of employment, such as hours and pay periods, (5) an explanation of job duties, standards, and appraisal criteria, (6) safety regulations, (7) a list of the chain of command, and (8) an explanation of the organization's purpose and strategic goals. Highlights in HRM 7.10 shows the types of materials new hires can be given and the various steps that can ease their transition into the workplace.[45]

Basic Skills Training

The National Literacy Secretariat and Human Resources Development Canada finds that 1 percent of Canadians have literacy skills below the level they need to succeed. Experts define an illiterate individual as one having a sixth-grade education or less. Working adults who improve their literacy skills gain better pay and more promotions and are employed for longer periods of time. Employers launch literacy training in order to improve productivity. Avon Foods in Nova Scotia and Palliser's Furniture in Manitoba created workplace education programs to give workers easy access to skills upgrading. Businesses report that they are already having a harder time finding workers with the basic skills they seek. Many businesses say it's their top problem.[46]

These figures have important implications for society at large and for organizations that must work around these skill deficiencies. Never has this been more true. Basic skills have become essential occupational qualifications, having profound

Highlights in HRM 7.10

Checklist for Orienting New Employees

Items in Orientation Packet
- Welcome letter with company background
- Map of facility, including parking information
- IDs, keys, and parking decals
- Current organization chart
- Telephone numbers, e-mail addresses, and locations of key personnel
- Copy of employee's specific job goals and descriptions
- List of unique terms in the industry, company, and job
- Training class schedules
- Safety and emergency procedures
- Copy of policy handbook, including office hours and telephone and e-mail rules
- List of employee benefits, including insurance plans
- Holiday schedule

Follow-Up Activities
- Ensure that employee has completed required paperwork, including benefit enrollment forms
- Revisit performance standards
- Schedule first performance appraisal meeting

implications for product quality, customer service, internal efficiency, and workplace and environmental safety. A list of typical basic skills includes the following:

- Reading
- Writing
- Computing
- Speaking
- Listening
- Problem solving
- Managing oneself
- Knowing how to learn
- Working as part of a team
- Leading others

Ford and AT&T are among the many companies who now offer remedial courses to their employees. Although there are different possible approaches to ensuring that employees have basic skills, the establishment of inhouse basic skills programs has come increasingly into favour.[47] To implement a successful program in basic and remedial skills, managers should do the following:

1. Explain to employees why and how the training will help them in their jobs.
2. Relate the training to the employees' goals.
3. Respect and consider participant experiences, and use these as a resource.
4. Use a task-centred or problem-centred approach so that participants "learn by doing."
5. Give feedback on progress toward meeting learning objectives.

A workplace education program in the City of Charlottetown won an award of excellence for Municipal Workplace Literacy Achievements in 2003 by following these principles. The key to developing a successful basic-skills program is *flexibility*, reinforcing the principle of individual differences while acknowledging the reality of work and family constraints.

Team Training and Cross-Training

As we discussed earlier in the book, organizations rely on teams to attain strategic and operational goals. Whether the team is an aircrew, a research team, or a manufacturing or service unit, the contributions of the individual members of the team are a function not only of the KSAs of each individual but also of the interaction of the team members. Teamwork behaviours that differentiate effective teams are shown in Figure 7.8 on page 332. They include both process dynamics and behavioural dynamics. The fact that these behaviours are observable and measurable provides a basis for training team members to function more effectively in the pursuit of their goals.[48]

Coca-Cola's Fountain Manufacturing Operation (which makes the syrup for Coke and Diet Coke) developed team training for its manufacturing employees. The program focused on three skill categories: (1) technical, (2) interpersonal, and (3) team action. The technical component, called Four-Deep Training, meant that each individual should learn four different jobs to allow for team flexibility. The interpersonal skills component, called Adventures in Attitudes, focused on listening,

Job-specific and general skills training are both essential for career success.

© GETTY IMAGES

conflict resolution, influence, and negotiation. Team-action training focused on team leadership, management of meetings, team roles, group dynamics, and problem solving—all skills needed to function effectively as a team. The training not only

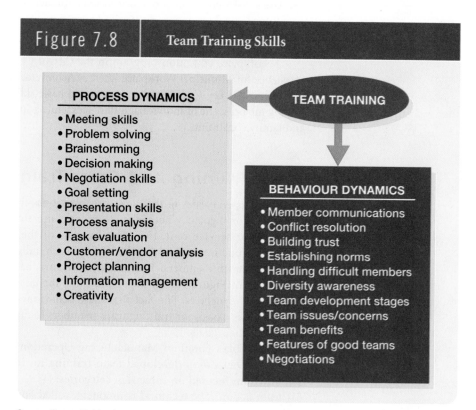

Figure 7.8   Team Training Skills

PROCESS DYNAMICS
- Meeting skills
- Problem solving
- Brainstorming
- Decision making
- Negotiation skills
- Goal setting
- Presentation skills
- Process analysis
- Task evaluation
- Customer/vendor analysis
- Project planning
- Information management
- Creativity

TEAM TRAINING

BEHAVIOUR DYNAMICS
- Member communications
- Conflict resolution
- Building trust
- Establishing norms
- Handling difficult members
- Diversity awareness
- Team development stages
- Team issues/concerns
- Team benefits
- Features of good teams
- Negotiations

Source: George Bohlander and Kathy McCarthy, "How to Get the Most from Team Training," *National Productivity Review* (Autumn 1996): 25–35.

increased quality and customer satisfaction, but also has helped decrease costs and set up a model for preparing employees for the future.[49] KPMG has found that accounting graduates are attracted to their corporate culture of team building, as well as its sponsorship of company activities like hockey and baseball, according to a managing partner based in Vancouver, B.C.[50]

In the last few years other organizations have developed exercises to generate enthusiasm and enhance team participation. Managers who want to design team training for their organization should keep the following points in mind:

1. Team building is a difficult and comprehensive process. Since many new teams are under pressure to produce, there is little time for training. You cannot cover everything in a twenty-24 blitz. Team training works best when it is provided over time and parallels team development.

2. Team development is not always a linear sequence of "forming, storming, norming, and performing." Training initiatives can help a team work through each of these stages, but managers must be aware that lapses can occur.

3. Additional training is required to assimilate new members. Large membership changes may result in teams reverting to a previous developmental stage.

4. Behavioural and process skills need to be acquired through participative exercises. Team members cannot internalize subjects such as conflict resolution through passive listening. Hands-on experiences are much better.[51]

cross-training
The process of training employees to do multiple jobs within an organization

Closely related to team training is **cross-training.** Cross-trained employees learn how to do different jobs within an organization as well as their own. Part of the motivation for cross-training is that it gives firms flexible capacity. Workers can be dynamically shifted when and where they are needed, unlike specialized workers and equipment, which cannot. Moreover, by keeping workers interested and motivated, cross-training can cut turnover, increase productivity, pare down labour costs, and lay the foundation for careers rather than dead-end jobs. In a sense, cross-training represents a shift from Henry Ford's assembly line production to flexible production. Some companies are using cross-training to keep their workers and plants in the country versus offshoring them. Pace, a company that sells soldering equipment, watched all of its competitors move offshore. To keep up with the productivity of its low-cost rivals abroad, Pace grouped workers into teams and trained each team to build an entire product as well as different products. "Some of the people could only do certain things and if they had no work, they would just sit and wait," said one Pace manager. "Now they have ownership of it all." Employees have an incentive to learn because their hourly wages get bumped up as they master more skills. Now Pace builds products to meet actual customer demand, rather than storing inventory, which is more costly, and it has been able to shorten its production times and move its operations into one building versus two. Other companies that have been able to successfully utilize cross-training include IBM, John Deere, and GE Financial Assurance. In addition to making them more productive, research shows that cross-training gives employees the "big picture," making them more creative and better problem solvers.[52]

Diversity Training

Many organizations offer some form of diversity training. This emphasis is sparked by an awareness of the varied demographics of the workforce, the challenges of employment equity, the dynamics of stereotyping, the changing values of the workforce, and the potential competitive payoffs from bringing different people together for a common purpose. There are basically two types of diversity training: (1) awareness building, which helps employees appreciate the benefits of diversity, and (2) skill building, which provides the KSAs necessary for working with people who are different. For example, a skill-building diversity program might teach managers how to conduct performance appraisals with people from different cultures or teach male supervisors how to coach female employees toward better career opportunities. All of the diverse dimensions—race, gender, age, disabilities, lifestyles, culture, education, ideas, and backgrounds—should be considered in the design of a diversity training program.[53]

Connaught Laboratories has won a host of awards for its diversity training program. About 800 employees participated in a three-hour program that covered topics such as government policies, trends in demographics, terminology, designated groups, and the benefits of a new work environment. In addition, managers attended a one-day workshop on learning to manage diversity. Highlights in HRM 7.11 shows some characteristics of effective diversity training programs. Increasingly, diversity training is being combined with other training programs, an occurrence that some believe represents the "mainstreaming" of diversity with other strategic issues facing organizations. Honeywell, for example, subsumes diversity training within a week-long advanced management program and as part of its sales training programs. General Electric trains mentors and protégés in a program that isn't explicitly a diversity initiative but nevertheless clearly helps women and ethnic minorities.

Organizations that have been successful with diversity training realize that it is a long-term process that requires the highest level of skill. Ineffective training in this area can be damaging and can create more problems than it solves. Unfortunately, many consulting firms have added diversity training to their list of programs without adequate personnel to handle the assignment. To avoid the pitfalls of substandard diversity training, managers will want to do the following:

1. *Forge a strategic link.* Begin by establishing the reasons for diversity training. Clarify the links between diversity and business goals in order to provide

Highlights in HRM 7.11

Characteristics of Effective Diversity Training Programs

- Steering committee represents all levels of the organization and a mix of races, ages, and genders.
- Workshops include the following:
  - Top executives demonstrate their commitment by early participation.
  - Each participant is given a workbook with support materials.
  - Participants are made aware of key topics and company policies.
  - Participants are asked to describe specific steps they would take to support diversity.
  - Participants create a list of diversity ground rules or behavioural norms.
  - Managers discuss and revise rules for their areas.
  - Participants link diversity training to other HR initiatives such as recruitment and selection, career management, and compensation.
- Managers are accountable for achieving goals of diversity training.

a context for training. Employment equity and valuing diversity are not the same thing. Ultimately diversity enhances differences and unites those differences toward a common goal.

2. *Check out consultant qualifications.* Recognize that there are no certification criteria for consultants, so ensure that they are qualified. Background and experience checks are essential.

3. *Not settle for "off the shelf" programs.* Each company has somewhat different goals, and the training should reflect this.

4. *Choose training methods carefully.* Most diversity training is really education (awareness building). Managers may hope they are developing skills, but this requires more in-depth training. Employees may benefit from either awareness or skill building, but they are not the same.

5. *Document individual and organizational benefits.* Diversity training, when done well, can enhance communications, improve responsiveness to social issues, reduce lawsuits, create a climate of fairness, improve productivity on complex tasks, and increase revenues and profits. These criteria extend beyond affirmative action goals and support the competitive capability of the organization.

SUMMARY

Today we find that organizational operations cover a broad range of subjects and involve personnel at all levels, from orientation through management development. In addition to providing the training needed for effective job performance, employers offer training in such areas as personal growth and wellness. In order to have effective training programs, the systems approach is recommended. This approach consists of four phases: (1) needs assessment, (2) program design, (3) implementation, and (4) evaluation.

Needs assessment begins with organization analysis. Managers must establish a context for training by deciding where training is needed, how it connects with strategic goals, and how organizational resources can best be used. Task analysis is used to identify the knowledge, skills, and abilities that are needed. Person analysis is used to identify which people need training.

In designing a training program, managers must consider the two fundamental preconditions for learning: readiness and motivation. In addition, principles of learning should be considered in order to create an environment that is conducive to learning. These principles include goal setting, meaningfulness of presentation, modelling, individual differences, active practice and repetition, whole-versus-part learning, massed-versus-distributed learning, and feedback and reinforcement.

In the training of non-managerial personnel a wide variety of methods are available. On-the-job training is one of the most commonly used methods because it provides the advantage of hands-on experience and an opportunity to build a relationship between supervisor and employee. Apprenticeship training and internships are especially effective because they provide both on- and off-the-job experiences. Other off-the-job methods include the conference or discussion method, classroom training, programmed instruction, computer-based training, simulation, closed-circuit TV, teletraining, and interactive e-learning. All of these methods can make a contribution to the training effort with relatively little cost per trainee.

The training and development of managers is a multibillion-dollar business. As with non-managerial personnel, a wide variety of training methods are used for developing managers. On-the-job experiences include coaching, understudy assignment, job rotation, lateral transfer, project and committee assignments, and staff meetings. Off-the-job experiences include analysis of case studies, management games, role playing, and behaviour modelling.

objective 5 Evaluation of a training program should focus on several criteria: participant reactions, learning, behaviour change on the job, and bottom-line results such as return on investment. Transfer of training is measured via examination of the degree to which trained skills are demonstrated back on the job. Benchmarking and utility analysis help evaluate the impact of training and provide the information for further needs assessment.

objective 6 Special issues in training involve programs that are important to a broad range of employees. Orientation training, for example, begins and continues throughout an employee's service with an organization. By participating in a formal orientation program, employees acquire the knowledge, skills, and attitudes that increase the probabilities of their success with the organization. To make an orientation effective there should be close cooperation between the HR department and other departments in all phases of the program, from initial planning through follow-up and evaluation. Basic skills training, team training, and diversity training are also critically important in today's organizations.

KEY TERMS

apprenticeship training, 311
behaviour modelling, 321
behaviour modification, 309
competency assessment, 302
cooperative training, 312

cross-training, 333
e-learning, 316
instructional objectives, 304
internship programs, 312
on-the-job training (OJT), 310

organization analysis, 300
orientation, 328
person analysis, 304
task analysis, 302
transfer of training, 324

DISCUSSION QUESTIONS

1. What economic, social, and political forces have made employee training even more important today than it was in the past?

2. What analyses should be made to determine the training needs of an organization? After the needs are determined, what is the next step?

3. Think about the best teacher that you have ever had, and the worst teacher. Go to the list of characteristics of effective instructors found on page 309 and assess each of these teachers against these characteristics.

4. Indicate what training methods you would use for each of the following jobs. Give reasons for your choices.
   a. File clerk
   b. Computer operator
   c. Automobile service station attendant
   d. Pizza maker
   e. Nurse's aide

5. Compare computer-based instruction with the lecture method in regard to the way the two methods involve the different psychological principles of learning.

6. Suppose that you are the manager of an accounts receivable unit in a large company. You are switching to a new system of billing and record-keeping and need to train your three supervisors and 28 employees in the new procedures. What training method(s) would you use? Why?

7. Participants in a training course are often asked to evaluate the course by means of a questionnaire. What are the pros and cons of this approach? Are there better ways of evaluating a course?

8. A new employee is likely to be anxious the first few days on the job.
   a. What are some possible causes of this anxiety?
   b. How may the anxiety be reduced?

9. Why is employee orientation an important process? What are some benefits of a properly conducted orientation program?

INTERNET EXERCISE

As you read, one of the principles of learning is to understand the motivation of learners. To assess your own motivational and learning style, go to www .learnativity.com, and click on the learning styles and motivation styles assessments. After you have completed these, and been provided with the results, determine the conditions under which you learn best.

HRM Experience

Training and Learning Principles

It is surprising how many training programs don't explicitly incorporate principles of learning into their design (such as goal setting, modelling, individual differences, and feedback). It is not that difficult to build learning principles into the training process, even for very simple instructional programs. To prove this point, do the following assignment for building a paper airplane.

Assignment

1. Form teams of four to six members. Identify someone on the team who knows how to make a paper airplane. That person will be the *trainer.*
2. Identify someone who will be the *observer/recorder.* That person will not participate in the training, but will write down how many (and how effectively) principles of learning are used in the instruction:
   a. Goal setting
   b. Modelling
   c. Meaningfulness
   d. Individual differences
   e. Whole-versus-part learning
   f. Distributed learning
   g. Active practice
   h. Feedback
3. Give the trainer ten to 15 minutes to train the group in making a paper airplane. The observer will keep notes of effective and ineffective training techniques (demonstrated learning principles).
4. Have someone from each team—not the trainer—volunteer to come before the class for a friendly competition. The instructor will give each team member two minutes to make a paper airplane. And then just for fun, they can compete by seeing which one flies the farthest. As always, no wagering, please.
5. To finish the exercise, the observers/recorders will lead a discussion of the learning principles that were demonstrated. Discuss also, if they were done in this setting, why they might not be done in other training settings.

BIZFLIX EXERCISES

Backdraft: Probie's Training Experiences

Watch the scenes from the film *Backdraft* to see examples of the training and development discussions in this chapter. Use the discussion questions below as guides to your viewing of the scenes.

Two brothers follow their late father, a legendary Chicago firefighter, and join the City of Chicago Fire Department. Stephen "Bull" McCaffrey (Kurt Russell) joins first and rises to the rank of lieutenant. Younger brother Brian (William Baldwin) joins later. After graduation from the fire academy, Brian becomes a member of Bull's Engine Company 17. Sibling rivalry tarnishes their work relationships, but they continue to fight Chicago fires successfully. Add a plot element about a mysterious arsonist, and you have the basis for an extraordinary film. The intense, unprecedented special effects give the viewer an unparalleled experience of what it is like to fight a fire. Chicago firefighters applauded the realism of the fire scenes.

These scenes are an edited composite built from two parts of the film. Part I: "On-the-Job Training:

Probie's First Day" appears early in *Backdraft* as part of "The First Day" sequence. This part shows Engine Company 17 preparing to fight a garment factory fire. Part II: "Back at Station 17: Probie Continues Training" comes from "The Probie's Life" segment that appears about 30 minutes later in the film. The term *probie* is jargon for a probationary firefighter—someone just starting with the department.

What to Watch for and Ask Yourself

- Which training methods described earlier in this chapter appear in these scenes? Link the training methods discussed to specific moments and examples in the scenes.
- Did Brian McCaffrey receive any classroom instruction?
- Review the earlier section "Phase 4: Evaluating the Training Program." Assess the training Brian received using the criteria discussed in that section.

case study 1

Service at the Chateau Whistler

The Chateau Whistler in Whistler, British Columbia, is one of the world's leading hotels and has been named the number one ski resort in North America for the past eight years. The 557-room hotel opened in 1989 and currently has 650 full-time employees.

The orientation program for new employees at the Chateau Whistler reflects the same standards that guests enjoy at the hotel. New recruits have raw talents such as energy and enthusiasm but have to be trained quickly in the art of excellent service.

On day one of the orientation program, an "Orientation Game" is played; then the employees are introduced to the hotel (the types of rooms, the amenities, etc.). Then the following are discussed:

- Salary and benefits, including health care, pension plan, discounted ski passes, staff meals, food discounts, discounted rates at other properties, and health club access
- Employment standards, human rights, and labour relations (although the hotel is not unionized)
- Health and safety, including WHMIS (Workplace Hazardous Materials Information System) and MSDS (Material Safety Data Sheets) and the environmental program

- Harassment policy
- The wellness program
- The incentive program

New employees also receive a tour of the town of Whistler, so that they can talk to guests about the key attractions and establish a network of friends.

Day two is devoted to the Service Plus Program. The Service Plus Code is spelled out this way:

S support
E empathy
R responsiveness
V valuing differences
I interdependence
C caring
E expectations

The day two program focuses on the guest–employee interaction and strives to teach employees how to provide excellent service, deal empathetically and effectively with problems reported by guests, and solve problems creatively. Training consists of role plays such as "handling the difficult guest." Specifically, the new recruits gain an understanding of the CP Hotel's mission statement and commitment to service, the changing service culture, and the high service expectations of the guests.

The third component of the orientation program is "Guest for a Night," during which employees who have been working at the hotel for three months eat at the restaurants, enjoy the facilities, and spend one night in the hotel as a guest. According to David Roberts, the hotel's general manager, the goal of the Guest for a Night program is to ensure that employees can talk knowledgeably about guest rooms, restaurants, and other facilities, and understand the level of quality that the hotel provides.

As part of this program, employees are asked to fill out a feedback survey, just like a guest. Also at this time, employees are invited to be part of a focus group to express concerns and provide feedback about their work experiences.

Through these orientation and training programs, employees develop knowledge and skills in service excellence. More importantly, they develop a commitment to the company. At a ten-year reunion party given for 600 people, 599 said it was the best working experience of their lives.

QUESTIONS

1. Compare the Chateau Whistler's orientation program to the list of activities presented in Highlights in HRM 6.1. Would you add anything?
2. The hospitality sector has high turnover rates among employees. Why does the Chateau Whistler invest so much time, money, and energy into its orientation program?
3. Describe the activities in the orientation and training programs that would ensure a high degree of transfer of training to the job.
4. How would you measure the success of this program? What results criteria would you try to measure?

People Development Strategies at Credit Union Central of Saskatchewan

There are 128 credit unions in Saskatchewan, with assets ranging from less than $1 million to more than a billion dollars. All of these are affiliated with Credit Union Central of Saskatchewan, which facilitates cooperation among credit unions and provides consulting services, trade association functions, and liquidity management.

Credit Union Central, together with the four largest Saskatchewan credit unions, developed a plan to implement a comprehensive human resources management system to produce, first, a better alignment of employee performance to organizational objectives and, second, more focused training to produce desired business results and an enhanced ability to retain employees through opportunities for professional development. Working with Hay Management Consultants, the first step was to develop a competency glossary, followed by performance management processes and tools, selection and staffing tools, and then succession planning.

Competencies can be defined as attitudes, skills, knowledge, or behaviours that are essential to perform at work and that differentiate superior performers. The competency glossary defines core competencies, which apply to all roles within the organization, and role-specific competencies. Competency target levels indicating superior performance are set for each role.

An example of a core competency, based on the key values and strategies of the organization, is "results orientation":

When your employee tried to improve his/her own performance he/she

1. identified areas of waste or inefficiency but didn't take any action.
2. made some changes to work methods in order to reach particular goals that had been set for him/her.
3. made specific changes in the system and his/her own work methods in order to improve performance beyond goals set.
4. set own challenging goals that were accomplished with a significant amount of planning, analysis, and effort.
5. set individual goals by thinking through the costs and benefits, and explicitly considered potential profits, risks, and return on investment, in order to make decisions that ended up having a positive organizational impact.
6. took a calculated entrepreneurial risk and committed significant organizational resources to act on an idea that ended up significantly improving performance.

A role-specific competency might be "concern for order, quality, and compliance" defined as follows:

When your employee demonstrated attention to detail in his/her work, he/she . . .

1. checked on the work to ensure it was accurate, complied with all relevant regulations, and followed all standard practices and procedures.
2. monitored the accuracy and quality of his/her own work and others' work consistently and systematically and kept a detailed record of work when it was necessary.
3. during the project, monitored the progress of the project against milestones and deliverables, took action to ensure the procedures put in place were effective, and quickly corrected any weaknesses or deficiencies.

4. established and utilized a procedure and/or system to facilitate work efficiency and ensure high-quality output; modified and improved the procedure and/or system when a weakness was identified, in order to ensure that high-quality work was being produced.

Managers work with employees to assess competency levels. The competency glossary and a competency assessment questionnaire enable managers and employees to discuss skills, abilities, and behaviours using a common framework. Training and development plans are based on gaps between target performance and actual performance. A developmental resource kit, which includes training courses, seminars, books, and work opportunities, all classified by competency, assists with building development plans.

This approach has resulted in clear direction on performance and development plans to move employees toward optimum performance levels.

QUESTIONS

1. Describe the advantages of the approach used to identify performance gaps.
2. Why would managers resist or support this approach?
3. Describe methods that you would use to evaluate the effectiveness of this approach at level 2 (learning), level 3 (behaviour), and level 4 (organizational results).

case study 3

Orientation at Bell Canada

On May 15th, 2006, Bell Canada began to roll out a new orientation program with a large e-based component for new hires. The website that introduces new employees to their orientation is an upbeat and interactive design where new employees can quickly find much of the information necessary to orient themselves to their new company. The orientation process allows for a consistent message to be delivered to all employees across Canada, in either French or English, and grants the new hire's immediate supervisor more tools that can be used to help welcome the employee over the first few days and months of his career at Bell.

It is only the starting point for a new career at Bell Canada. Bell's corporate culture promotes self-service, where much of the information relating to an individual's options regarding career growth and development is posted on the intranet. This provides each individual private access to only their information. This orientation process aligns with the culture of self-service and acquaints new employees with the knowledge of how things get done around Bell and provides links for where they can look for more information. It also encourages the new hires to ask for direction from their managers and to seek information on any items that may have been missed during their first few weeks.

While orientation is a necessary step in welcoming and guiding a new employee, it is a costly endeavour for organizations. Bell's decision to move to a large online orientation component was a conscious decision to find savings where possible. In a national company, the transportation costs of bringing all new hires to a central location may have benefits but other options such as intranet information, conference calls, and other forms of communication should be considered. The current program at Bell gives the same message and without the costs involved in a classroom-dependent process. The extra bonus in this method is that employees have access to information that aids in their education about their work environment, and permits them to begin contributing to their teams as soon as possible.

Given the high cost of hiring new employees, it is important that the employee is able to start being productive as soon as possible. As part of connecting the new employee to the organization, and allowing the transition to occur, Bell has leveraged an already established program using employees known to be Pride Builders. This program identifies employees across all levels and departments who take special pride in their work and display excellent organizational citizenship and desired behaviours. According to Randi Haimovitz, project designer of the orientation program, Pride Builders make it a priority to connect with the new hires within their first few weeks at work and when possible meet them for a coffee in order to provide valuable company information and make the new hire feel more welcomed. New hires are also introduced to other new employees outside of their immediate business units via semi-annual forums.

QUESTIONS

1. What are the advantages of the orientation program at Bell? Can you describe some of the limitations?
2. The goals of orientation programs are to explain to new employees the "whys," not just the "whats" and "hows" of their new jobs. What elements in Bell's orientation program would be conducive to meeting this objective? Do you think orientation should be a supplement to a live orientation and why or why not?

CAREER COUNSEL

Complete the training list on the *Managing Human Resources* website (www.belcourt5e.nelson.com).

NOTES AND REFERENCES

1. A. Thomlinson, "T & D Spending Up in US as Canada Lags Behind," *Canadian HR Reporter* 15, no. 6 (March 25, 2002): 1; Industry Canada, "Canadian Training Solutions," http://strategix.ic.gc.ca/epic/internet; Uyen Vu, "$824 to Train Isn't Enough," *Canadian HR Reporter*, July 18, 2005, p. 2; Jayne Jackson, "Needs Assesssment Put Training Department Budget on Course," *Canadian HR Reporter*, November 17, 2003, G3.
2. Chris Howe, "Canada's Best Employers: Making the List: Special Report to the International Foundation Gives Canadian Perspective," *Employee Benefits Journal*, 29, no. 2 (June 2004), 52–55.
3. "Spending on Training Remains Steady in 2004 According to ASTD," *Lifelong Learning Market Report* 10, no. 1 (January 7, 2005): 3–4; "What to Do Now That Training Is Becoming a Major HR Force," *HR Focus* (February 2005): 5–6.

4. David Dubois and William Rothwell, "Competency-Based or a Traditional Approach to Training?" *Training and Development* 58, no. 4 (April 2004): 46–59; Bob Rosner, "Training Is the Answer . . . But What Was the Question?" *Workforce* 78, no. 5 (May 1999): 42–52. See also Irwin L. Goldstein and J. Kevin Ford, *Training in Organizations: Needs Assessment, Development and Evaluation*, 4th ed. (Belmont, CA: Wadsworth, 2002). For the classic citation on needs assessment, see William McGehee and Paul W. Thayer, *Training in Business and Industry* (New York: John Wiley and Sons, 1961).
5. Laurie Bassi and Daniel McMurrer, "How's Your Return on People?" *Harvard Business Review* 8, no. 3 (March 2004): 18; Tracy Mauro, "Helping Organizations Build Community," *Training and Development* 56, no. 2 (February 2002): 25–29;

Liam Lahey, "RFIDs Touted as Standard for Airport Security," *Computing Canada* 28, no. 13 (June 21, 2002): 21; Caroline Wilson, "Ensuring a Smooth Ride," *Security Management* 46, no. 8 (August 2002): 92.

6. "E-Learning and Teleconferencing Join Needs Assessment to Control Training Costs," *Managing Training & Development*, no. 3 (December 2003): 1; Thomas Gainey, Brian Klaas, and Darla Moore, "Outsourcing the Training Function: Results from the Field," *Human Resource Planning* 25, no. 1 (2002): 16; Sarah Fister Gale, "Creative Training: Doing More with Less," *Workforce* 80, no. 10 (October 2001): 82–88.

7. Patty Davis, Jennifer Naughton, and William Rothwell, "New Roles and New Competencies for the Profession: Are You Ready for the Next Generation," *Training and Development* 58, no. 4 (April 2004): 26–38; David Dubois and William Rothwell, "Competency-Based or a Traditional Approach to Training?" *Training and Development* 58, no. 4 (April 2004): 46-59; Catherine Robbins, Elizabeth Bradely, Maryanne Spicer, and Gary Mecklenburge, "Developing Leadership in Healthcare Administration: A Competency Assessment Tool/Practitioner Application," *Journal of Healthcare Management* 46, no. 3 (May/June 2001): 188–202; Margaret Potter, Christine Pistella, Carl Fertman, and Virginia Dato, "Needs Assessment and a Model Agenda for Training the Public Health Workforce," *American Journal of Public Health* 90, no. 8 (August 2000): 1294–96.

8. Thomas Hoffman, "Motivation: These IT Leaders Keep Staffers Upbeat during Lean Times by Targeting What Drives Them: Technology and Training," *Computerworld* 38, no. 1 (January 5, 2004): 39; Elwood Holton, Reid Bates, and Sharon Naquin, "Large-Scale Performance-Driven Training Needs Assessment: A Case Study," *Public Personnel Management* 29, no. 2 (Summer 2000): 249–67.

9. Gail Johnson, "The Development Framework: Booz Allen Hamilton's Holistic Method of Employee Development Gives Its Employee a Roadmap to Success—Both Professionally and Personally," *Training* 40, no. 2 (February 2003): 32–34; Robert Mager, "Contract Training Tips," *Security Management* 45, no. 6 (June 2001): 30; Robert Mager, *What Every Manager Should Know about Training: An Insider's Guide to Getting Your Money's Worth from Training* (Atlanta, GA: Center for Effective Performance, 1999).

10. Debbie Schachter, "How to Set Performance Goals: Employee Reviews Are More Than Annual Critiques," *Information Outlook* 8, no. 9 (September 2004): 26–30; "Burger Olympics," *Training* 41, no. 7 (July 2004): 20; Jason A. Colquitt and Marcia J. Simmering, "Conscientiousness, Goal Orientation, and Motivation to Learn during the Learning Process: A Longitudinal Study," *Journal of Applied Psychology* 83, no. 4 (August 1998): 654–65; Sherry Ryan, "A Model of the Motivation for IT Retraining," *Information Resources Management Journal* 12, no. 4 (October–December 1999): 24–32; Kimberly A. Smith-Jentsch, Florian G. Jentsch, Stephanie C. Payne, and Eduardo Salas, "Can Pretraining Experiences Explain Individual Differences in Learning?" *Journal of Applied Psychology* 81, no. 1 (February 1996): 110–16.

11. J. Kevin Ford, Eleanor M. Smith, Daniel A. Weissbein, Stanley M. Gully, and Eduardo Salas, "Relationships of Goal Orientation, Metacognitive Activity, and Practice Strategies with Learning Outcomes and Transfer," *Journal of Applied Psychology* 83, no. 2 (April 1998): 218–33; Annette Towler and Robert Dipboye, "Effects of Trainer Expressiveness, Organization, and Trainee Goal Orientation on Training Outcomes," *Journal of Applied Psychology* 86, no. 4 (August 2001): 664–73; Steve Kozlowski, Stanley Gully, Kenneth Brown, and Eduardo Salas, "Effects of Training Goals and Goal Orientation Traits on Multidimensional Training Outcomes and Performance Adaptability," *Organizational Behaviour and Human Decision Processes* 85, no. 1 (May 2001): 1–31.

12. The classics by Albert Bandura here include *Social Foundations of Thought and Action: A Social Cognitive Theory* (Englewood Cliffs, NJ: Prentice Hall, 1986) and *A Social Learning Theory* (Englewood Cliffs, NJ: Prentice Hall, 1977). See also Melesa Altizer Bolt, Larry Killough, and Hian Chye Koh, "Testing the Interaction Effects of Task Complexity in Computer Training Using the Social Cognitive Model," *Decision Sciences* 32, no. 1 (Winter 2001): 1–20; Susan Pedersen and Min Liu, "The Transfer of Problem-Solving Skills from a Problem-Based Learning Environment: The Effect of Modelling an Expert's Cognitive Processes," *Journal of Research on Technology in Education* 35, no. 2 (Winter 2002): 303–21.

13. M. K. Kacmar, P. W. Wright, and G. C. McMahan, "The Effect of Individual Differences on Technological Training," *Journal of Managerial Issues* 9, no. 1 (Spring 1997): 104–20; Stanley Gully, Stephanie Payn, K. Lee Kiechel Koles, and John-Andrew Whiteman, "The Impact of Error Training and Individual Differences on Training Outcomes: An Attribute-Treatment Interaction Perspective," *Journal of Applied Psychology* 87, no. 1 (February 2002): 143–55; Steven John Simon, "The Relationship of Learning Style and Training Method to End-User Computer Satisfaction and Computer Use: A Structural Equation Model," *Information Technology, Learning, and Performance Journal* 18, no. 1 (Spring 2000): 41–59.

14. "Can Technology Actually Boost Behaviour Change?" *Managing Training & Development* no. 3 (November 2003): 3; Don Hartshorn, "Reinforcing the Unsafe Worker," *Occupational Hazards* 62, no. 10 (October 2000): 125–28; Fred Luthan and Alexander Stajkovic, "Reinforce for Performance: The Need to Go beyond Pay and Even Rewards," *Academy of Management Executive* 13, no. 2 (May 1999): 49–57.

15. Greg Hopkins, "How to Design an Instructor Evaluation," *Training and Development* 53, no. 3 (March 1999): 51–52; Beth Thomas, "How to Hire Instructors Who Love Training," *Training and Development* 53, no. 3 (March 1999): 14–15; John L. Bennett, "Trainers as Leaders of Learning," *Training and Development* 55, no. 3 (March 2001): 42–45; Ruth Palombo Weiss, "Deconstructing Trainers' Self-Image," *Training and Development* 55, no. 12 (December 2001): 34–39.

16. Eduardo Salas and Janis Cannon-Bowers, "The Science of Training: A Decade of Progress," *Annual Review of Psychology* 52 (2001): 471–99.

17. Diane Walter, *Training on the Job* (Alexandria, VA: American Society for Training and Development, 2001); Toni Hodges, *Linking Learning and Performance: A Practical Guide to Measuring Learning and On-the-Job Application* (Burlington, MA: Butterworth-Heinemann, 2001); Gary Sisson, *Hands-On Training: A Simple and Effective Method for On-the-Job Training* (San Francisco: Barrett-Koehler, 2001).

18. Teresa M. McAleavy, "U.S. Schools Fail to Provide Job Training," *Knight-Ridder/Tribune Business News* (June 9, 2004); "Eight Steps to Better On-the-Job Training," *HRFocus* 80, no. 7 (July 2003): 11; Alison Booth, Yu-Fu Chen, and Gylfi Zoega, "Hiring and Firing: A Tale of Two Thresholds," *Journal of Labor Economics* 20, no. 2 (April 2002): 217–48.

19. Ronald L. Jacobs and Michael J. Jones, "Teaching Tools: When to Use On-the-Job Training," *Security Management* 41, no. 9 (September 1997): 35–39.

20. Information found on the Apprenticeship page, Spokane Community College website, February 9, 2005, www.scc .spokane.edu/tech/apprent/; Virginia Galt, "Few Employers Taking on Apprentices," *The Globe and Mail*, March 22, 2006, C2.

21. John Byrd and Rob Poole, "Highly Motivated Employees at No Cost? It's Not an Impossible Dream," *Nonprofit World* 19, no. 6 (November/December 2001): 312–32; Uyen Vu, "EnCana Builds Talent Pipeline into High School Classrooms," *Canadian HR Reporter*, April 11, 2005, 3.

22. "Major Investment in Training Programs at NSCC, Marconi Campus," News Release *Entreprise Cape Breton Corporation*, May 17, 2002.

23. Phil Britt, "E-Learning on the Rise in the Classroom: Companies Move Content Online: Cisco Systems' Employees and Partners Routinely Watch Videos on the Internet," *EContent* 27, no. 11 (November 2004): 36–41; Heather Johnson, "The Whole Picture: When It Comes to Finding Out How Employees Feel about Training, Many Companies Fail to Get a Clear Picture," *Training* 47, no. 7 (July 2004): 30–35.

24. S. Wintroe, "Satellites Present Cost Savings," *Financial Post*, June 16, 2003, FE 6.

25. "What to Do Now That Training Is Becoming a Major HR Force," *HRFocus* (February 2005): 5–6; Britt, "E-Learning on the Rise in the Classroom," 36–41; "Employers, Employees Embrace e-learning," *The Globe and* Mail, May 25, 2001, E2; Tammy Galvin, "The Delivery," *Training* 38, no. 10 (October 2001): 66–72; Kenneth G. Brown, "Using Computers to Deliver Training: Which Employees Learn and Why?" *Personnel Psychology* 54, no. 2 (Summer 2001): 271–96; Bill Roberts, "E-Learning New Twist on CBT," *HRMagazine* 46, no. 4 (April 2001): 99–106.

26. Scott A. Snell, Donna Stueber, and David P. Lepak, "Virtual HR Departments: Getting Out of the Middle," in R. L. Heneman and D. B. Greenberger (eds.), *Human Resource Management in Virtual Organizations* (Greenwich, CT: Information Age Publishing, 2002).

27. "Soup to Nuts: Simulator Manufacturing Is a Lucrative but Risky Business, Which Is Why Market Leader CAE Has Tapped into the More Stable World of Flight Training," *Air Transport World* 40, no. 5 (May 2003): 69–71; "SimsSir: Modelling and Simulation Are Leading the Assault on New Learning Technologies That Are Winning Favor with the U.S. Military," *Training and Development* 57, no. 10 (October 2003): 46–52.

28. For other applications of simulation in training used at Boeing and Eastman Kodak, see George Tischelle, "E-Learning Gets a Dose of Reality," *InformationWeek* 895 (July 1, 2002): 57. For applications of simulation training used in the U.S. Navy, see John Flink, "This Is Really Neat Stuff," *United States Naval Institute Proceedings* 128, no. 7 (July 2002): 68–69. For applications of simulation training used in medical schools, see David Noonan, "Is the Cadaver Dead?" *Newsweek* 139, no. 25 (June 24, 2002): 62. For applications of simulation training used in the police force, see Jim Weiss and Mickey Davis, "Deadly Force Decision-Making," *Law and Order* 50, no. 6 (June 2002): 58–62.

29. Martin Delahoussaye, Kristine Ellis, and Matt Bolch, "Measuring Corporate Smarts," *Training* 39, no. 8 (August 2002): 20–35; Daniel Crepin, "From Design to Action: Developing a Corporate Strategy," *Quality Progress* 35, no. 2 (February 2002): 49–56; Brad Miller, "Making Managers More Effective Agents of Change," *Quality Progress* 34, no. 5 (May 2001): 53–57.

30. Joseph Alutto, "Just-in-Time Management Education in the 21st Century," *HRMagazine* 44, no. 11 (1999): 56–57; Gordon Dehler, M. Ann Welsh, and Marianne W. Lewis, "Critical Pedagogy in the 'New Paradigm,'" *Management Learning* 493, no. 4 (December 2001): 493–511.

31. Chris Whitcomb, "Scenario-Based Training to the F.B.I.," *Training and Development* 53, no. 6 (June 1999): 42–46; Anne Hoag, Dale Brickley, and Joanne Cawley, "Media Management Education and the Case Method," *Journalism and Mass Communication Educator* 55, no. 4 (Winter 2001): 49–59.

32. Jenny C. McCune, "The Game of Business," *Management Review* 87, no. 2 (February 1998): 56–58; Phaedra Brotherton, "Let the Games Begin," *American Gas* 81, no. 3 (April 1999): 19–20; A. J. Faria, "The Changing Nature of Business Simulation/Gaming Research: A Brief History," *Simulation and Gaming* 32, no. 1 (March 2001): 97–110.

33. Matt Bolch, "Games Employees Play: Delta Air Lines Uses a Blended e-Learning Program to Teach Employees the Economic Realities of the Airline Industry," *Training* 40, no. 4 (April 2003): 44–48; Leonard Hill, "Games People Play," *Air Transport World* 37, no. 3 (March 2000): 97–98.

34. Christopher Hosford, "Serious Fun: Computer Training Finds a Niche," *Meeting News* 28, no. 7 (December 2004): 16; Rick Sullivan, "Lessons in Smallness," *Training and Development* 56, no. 3 (March 2002): 21–23; James W. Walker, "Perspectives," *Human Resource Planning* 23, no. 3 (2000): 5–7.

35. T. L. Stanley, "Be a Good Role Model for Your Employees," *Supervision* 65, no. 5 (January 2004): 5–8; Gary May and William Kahnweiler, "The Effect of a Mastery Practice Design on Learning and Transfer in Behaviour Modelling Training," *Personnel Psychology* 53, no. 2 (Summer 2000): 353–73.

36. Wendy Larlee, "Training Programs: Key to Collections: Companies in the Collections Business Face Significant

Challenges: Putting Solid Training Program in Place Can Help," *Collections & Credit Risk* 9, no. 2 (December 2004): 42–44; Heather Johnson, "The Whole Picture: When It Comes to Finding Out How Employees Feel about Training, Many Companies Fail to Get a Clear Picture," *Training* 47, no. 7 (July 2004): 30–35; Martin Delahoussaye, "Show Me the Results," *Training* 39, no. 3 (March 2002): 28–29; Reinout van Brakel, "Why ROI Isn't Enough," *Training and Development* 56, no. 6 (June 2002): 72–74.

37. "Dissatisfaction with Job Training Contributes to Low Job Satisfaction," *Managing Training & Development* (November 2003): 8; James Pershing and Jana Pershing, "Ineffective Reaction Evaluation," *Human Resource Development Quarterly* 12, no. 1 (Spring 2001): 73–90.

38. Andreas Putra, "Evaluating Training Programs: An Exploratory Study of Transfer of Learning onto the Job at Hotel A and Hotel B, Sydney, Australia," *Journal of Hospitality and Tourism Management* 11, no. 1 (April 2004): 77–78; Thomas Hoffman, "Simulations Revitalize e-Learning," *Computerworld* 37, no. 31 (August 4, 2003): 26–28; Donna Abernathy, "Thinking outside the Evaluation Box," *Training and Development* 53, no. 2 (February 1999): 18–23.

39. Jathan Janove, "Use It or Lose It," *HRMagazine* 47, no. 4 (April 2002): 99–104; Max Montesino, "Strategic Alignment of Training, Transfer-Enhancing Behaviours, and Training Usage: A Posttraining Study," *Human Resource Development Quarterly* 13, no. 1 (Spring 2002): 89–108; Siriporn Yamnill and Gary McLean, "Theories Supporting Transfer of Training," *Human Resource Development Quarterly* 12, no. 2 (Summer 2001): 195–208.

40. Delahoussaye, "Show Me the Results," 28–29; van Brakel, "Why ROI Isn't Enough," 72–74.

41. Uyen Vu, "Numbers-Cruncher Makes Impact on Training Culture at TD," *Canadian HR Reporter*, July 12, 2004, 1.

42. Richard J. Wagner and Robert J. Weigand, "Can the Value of Training Be Measured? A Simplified Approach to Evaluating Training," *The Health Care Manager* 23, no. 1 (January–March 2004): 71–79; van Brakel, "Why ROI Isn't Enough," 72–74; Sarah Fister Gale, "Measuring the ROI of E-Learning," *Workforce* 81, no. 8 (August 2002): 74–77; Earl Honeycutt, Kiran Karande, Ashraf Attia, and Steven Maurer, "A Utility-Based Framework for Evaluating the Financial Impact of Sales Force Training Programs," *Journal of Personal Selling and Sales Management* 21, no. 3 (Summer 2001): 229–38.

43. "Three Quick and Easy Ways to Gauge Your Training Outcomes," *IOMA's Report on Managing Training & Development* (January 2005): 4–5; "Use This Eight-Step Process to Predict the ROI of Your Training Programs," *IOMA's Human Resource Department Management Report* (December 2004): 4–5; Ellen Drost, Colette Frayne, Keven Lowe, and J. Michael Geringer, "Benchmarking Training and Development Practices: A Multi-Country Comparative Analysis," *Human Resource Management* 41, no. 1 (Spring 2002): 67–86; Daniel McMurrer,

Mark Van Buren, and William Woodwell, "Making the Commitment," *Training and Development* 54, no. 1 (January 2000): 41–48.

44. Lisa Bertagnoli, "Basic Training: Orientation Is Proving to Be an Important First Step in Establishing Employee Bonds That Last," *WWD* (September 30, 2004): 40S; Jonathan Thom, "Creating Effective Orientation Programs," *San Diego Business Journal* 25, no. 33 (August 16, 2004): A6; Howard Klein and Natasha Weaver, "The Effectiveness of an Organizational-Level Orientation Training Program in the Socialization of New Hires," *Personnel Psychology* 53, no. 1 (Spring 2000): 47–66.

45. Ellen Drost, Colette Frayne, Keven Lowe, and J. Michael Geringer, "Benchmarking Training and Development Practices: A Multi-Country Comparative Analysis," *Human Resource Management* 41, no. 1 (Spring 2002): 67–86; Daniel McMurrer, Mark Van Buren, and William Woodwell, "Making the Commitment," *Training and Development* 54, no. 1 (January 2000): 41–48; Mike Frost, "Creative New Employee Orientation Programs," *HRMagazine* 47, no. 8 (August 2002): 120–21; Marilyn Moats Kennedy, "Setting the Right Tone, Right Away," *Across the Board* 36, no. 4 (April 1999): 51–52.

46. "How to Prepare for Training's Critical Role in the Labor Force of the Future," *IOMA's Report on Managing Training & Development* (September 2004): 2–3; Steve Hook, "Basic Skills Training on Target," *Times Educational Supplement* 4444 (August 31, 2001): 39.

47. "Corporate America Can't Write," *Work & Family Newsbrief* (January 2005): 4; Matt Bolch, "School at Work," *Training* 39, no. 2 (February 2002); Slav Kanyba, "Community Colleges React to Job-Training Request," *San Fernando Valley Business Journal* 9, no. 2 (June 7, 2004): 1–2.

48. "What Makes Teams Work?" *HRFocus* 79, no. 4 (April 2002): S1–S3; John Annett, David Cunningham, and Peter Mathias-Jones, "A Method for Measuring Team Skills," *Ergonomics* 43, no. 8 (August 2000): 1076–94; Alan Auerbach, "Making Decisions under Stress: Implications for Individual and Team Training," *Personnel Psychology* 52, no. 4 (Winter 1999): 1050–53.

49. "Behaviour-Based Sales Team Training Produces a 56 percent Increase in Revenues," *Managing Training & Development* (April 2004): 1; Sandra N. Phillips, "Team Training Puts Fizz in Coke Plant's Future," *Personnel Journal* 75, no. 1 (January 1996): 87–92.

50. Pam Withers, "The 25 Best Companies to Work for in BC: 10 KPMG," *BC Business*, 31, no. 1, January 2003, 52.

51. Gail Johnson, "Time to Broaden Diversity," *Training* 41, no. 9 (September 2004): 16; George W. Bohlander and Kathy McCarthy, "How to Get the Most from Team Training," *National Productivity Review* (Autumn 1996): 25–35.

52. Lorraine Mirabella, "Productivity Gains in Maryland Mean Less Hiring But More Job Cross-Training," *The Baltimore Sun (via Knight-Ridder/Tribune Business News)* (April 17, 2004).

53. Gary Stern, "Small Slights Bring Big Problems," *Workforce* 81, no. 8 (August 2002): 17; Bill Leonard, "Ways to Tell If a Diversity Program Is Measuring Up," *HRMagazine* 47, no. 7 (July 2002): 21.

Appraising and Improving Performance

After studying this chapter, you should be able to

Explain the purposes of performance appraisals and the reasons
they can sometimes fail.

Explain the various methods
used for performance evaluation.

Identify the characteristics of an
effective appraisal program.

Outline the characteristics of an
effective performance appraisal
interview.

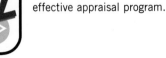

Describe the different sources of
appraisal information.

n the preceding chapters, we have discussed some of the most effective methods available to managers for acquiring and developing top-notch employees. But talented employees are not enough—successful organizations are particularly adept at engaging their workforce to achieve goals that benefit the organization as well as the individuals.

In this chapter we turn to performance appraisal programs, which are among the most helpful tools an organization can use to maintain and enhance productivity and facilitate progress toward strategic goals. While we will focus mainly on formal performance appraisal procedures, the processes of managing and evaluating performance can be informal as well. All managers monitor the way employees work and assess how this matches organizational needs. They form impressions about the relative value of employees to the organization and seek to maximize the contribution of every individual. Yet while these ongoing informal processes are vitally important, most organizations also have a formal performance appraisal once or twice a year. In fact, in a survey of employees conducted by Mercer Human Resources Consulting, only a third of the 2600 respondents had received a formal performance appraisal in the past year, and only 26 percent receive regular coaching from their manager on improving performance. Of those who said they'd had a formal performance appraisal in the past 12 months, 62 percent expressed a strong sense of commitment to their organization, compared to 49 percent of employees who hadn't.[1]

The success or failure of a performance appraisal program depends on the philosophy underlying it, its connection with business goals, and the attitudes and skills of those responsible for its administration. Many different methods can be used to gather information about employee performance. However, gathering information is only one step in the appraisal process. The information must be evaluated in the context of organizational needs and communicated to employees so that it will result in high levels of performance.

Performance Appraisal Programs

performance appraisal
A process, typically performed annually by a supervisor for a subordinate, designed to help employees understand their roles, objectives, expectations, and performance success

performance management
The process of creating a work environment in which people can perform to the best of their abilities

The **performance appraisal** can be defined as a process, typically delivered annually by a supervisor to a subordinate, designed to help employees understand their roles, objectives, expectations and performance success. Nearly nine out of ten companies use some form of performance appraisal rating system.[2] **Performance management** is the process of creating a work environment in which people can perform to the best of their abilities. Advocates see these HR programs as among the most logical means to appraise, develop, and effectively utilize the knowledge and abilities of employees. However, a growing number of observers point out that performance appraisals frequently fall short of their potential. In an ongoing survey of employee attitudes by the HR consulting firm Watson Wyatt, only 30 percent of employees said they thought their company's performance management process actually improved employee performance; only one in five thought it helped poorly performing employees do better.[3]

The push toward teamwork, continuous improvement, learning, and the like has caused numerous organizations to rethink their approach to appraisal. Some argue that performance appraisal discourages teamwork because it frequently focuses on individual achievement and produces a self-focus rather than a team focus. Others contend that appraisals are useful only at the extremes—highly effective or highly ineffective employees—and are not as useful for the majority of employees in the middle. Others point out that appraisals may focus on short-term achievements rather than long-term improvement and learning. They are sometimes too subjective or inconsistent or autocratic in that they create a distance between manager and employee rather than creating a team environment. Companies such as Xerox, Motorola, and Procter & Gamble have modified their performance appraisals to better acknowledge the importance of teamwork, continuous improvement, and quality. Each of these issues is discussed at greater length throughout the chapter.[4]

Purposes of Performance Appraisal

It might seem at first glance that performance appraisals are used for a rather narrow purpose—to evaluate who is doing a good job (or not). But in reality performance appraisals are one of the most versatile tools available to managers. They can serve many purposes that benefit both the organization and the employee whose performance is being appraised.

Figure 8.1 shows the most common uses of performance appraisals. In general, these can be classified as either *administrative* or *developmental*.

Administrative Purposes

From the standpoint of administration, appraisal programs provide input that can be used for the entire range of HRM activities. For example, research has shown that performance appraisals are used most widely as a basis for compensation decisions.[5] The practice of "pay-for-performance" is found in all types of organizations. Performance appraisal is also directly related to a number of other major HR functions, such as promotion, transfer, and layoff decisions. Performance appraisal data may also be used in HR planning, in determining the relative worth of jobs under a job evaluation program, and as criteria for validating selection tests. Performance appraisals also provide a "paper trail" for documenting HRM actions that may result in legal action. Because

Figure 8.1	Purposes for Performance Appraisal

DEVELOPMENTAL	ADMINISTRATIVE
Provide performance feedback	Document personnel decisions
Identify individual strengths/weaknesses	Determine promotion candidates
Recognize individual performance	Determine transfers and assignments
Assist in goal identification	Identify poor performance
Evaluate goal achievement	Decide retention or termination
Identify individual training needs	Decide on layoffs
Determine organizational training needs	Validate selection criteria
Reinforce authority structure	Meet legal requirements
Allow employees to discuss concerns	Evaluate training programs/progress
Improve communication	Personnel planning
Provide a forum for leaders to help	Make reward/compensation decisions

of employment equity programs, employers must maintain accurate, objective records of employee performance in order to defend themselves against possible charges of discrimination in connection with such HRM actions as promotion, salary determination, and termination. Finally, it is important to recognize that the success of the entire HR program depends on knowing how the performance of employees compares with the goals established for them. This knowledge is best derived from a carefully planned and administered HR appraisal program. Appraisal systems have the capability to influence employee behaviour, thereby leading directly to improved organizational performance.[6]

Developmental Purposes

From the standpoint of individual development, appraisal provides the feedback essential for discussing strengths and weaknesses as well as improving performance. Regardless of the employee's level of performance, the appraisal process provides an opportunity to identify issues for discussion, eliminate any potential problems, and set new goals for achieving high performance. Newer approaches to performance appraisal emphasize training as well as development and growth plans for employees. A developmental approach to appraisal recognizes that the purpose of a manager is to improve job behaviour, not simply to evaluate past performance. Having a sound basis for improving performance is one of the major benefits of an appraisal program.

Companies such as Best Buy and EDS have redesigned their performance appraisal systems to focus more on employee development and learning. EDS, for example, integrated its performance appraisal system to work in concert with learning and career management objectives. The new system, called the Career Resource System, includes a detailed job description, a performance review, and a career planner to track long-term goals, as well as access to the company's automated career library. The system is ultimately linked to the company's succession policies. By creating this overall system, EDS hopes to shift the role of manager from that of "judge" to one of "coach."[7]

USING THE INTERNET

Nipissing University has eight objectives for its performance appraisal system at:

www.nipissingu.ca/hr/performance AdminEmployees.asp

Reasons Appraisal Programs Sometimes Fail

In actual practice, and for a number of reasons, formal performance appraisal programs sometimes yield disappointing results. Figure 8.2 shows that the primary culprits include lack of top-management information and support, unclear performance standards, rater bias, too many forms to complete, and use of the program for conflicting purposes. For example, if an appraisal program is used to provide a written appraisal for salary action and at the same time to motivate employees to improve their work, the administrative and developmental purposes may be in conflict. As a result, the appraisal interview may become a discussion about salary in which the manager seeks to justify the action taken. In such cases, the discussion might have little influence on the employee's future job performance.

As with all HR functions, if the support of top management is lacking, the appraisal program will not be successful. Even the best-conceived program will not work in an environment where appraisers are not encouraged by their superiors to take the program seriously. To underscore the importance of this responsibility, top management should announce that effectiveness in appraising subordinates is a standard by which the appraisers themselves will be evaluated.

Figure 8.2	Let Me Count the Ways...

There are many reasons why performance appraisal systems might not be effective. Some of the most common problems include the following:

- Inadequate preparation on the part of the manager.
- Employee is not given clear objectives at the beginning of performance period.
- Manager may not be able to observe performance or have all the information.
- Performance standards may not be clear.
- Inconsistency in ratings among supervisors or other raters.
- Rating personality rather than performance.
- The halo effect, contrast effect, or some other perceptual bias.
- Inappropriate time span (either too short or too long).
- Overemphasis on uncharacteristic performance.
- Inflated ratings because managers do not want to deal with "bad news."
- Subjective or vague language in written appraisals.
- Organizational politics or personal relationships cloud judgments.
- No thorough discussion of causes of performance problems.
- Manager may not be trained at evaluation or giving feedback.
- No follow-up and coaching after the evaluation.

Sources: Patricia Evres, "Problems to Avoid during Performance Evaluations," *Air Conditioning, Heating & Refrigeration News* 216, no. 16 (August 19, 2002): 24–26; Clinton Longnecker and Dennis Gioia, "The Politics of Executive Appraisals," *Journal of Compensation and Benefits* 10, no. 2 (1994): 5–11; "Seven Deadly Sins of Performance Appraisals," *Supervisory Management* 39, no. 1 (1994): 7–8.

Other reasons performance appraisal programs can fail to yield the desired results include the following:

1. There is little face-to-face discussion between the manager and the employee being appraised.
2. The relationship between the employee's job description and the criteria on the appraisal form isn't clear.
3. Managers feel that little or no benefit will be derived from the time and energy spent in the process, or they are concerned only with bad performances.
4. Managers dislike the face-to-face confrontation of appraisal interviews.
5. Managers are not sufficiently adept at rating employees or providing them with appraisal feedback.
6. The judgmental role of appraisal conflicts with the helping role of developing employees.
7. The appraisal is just a once-a-year event, and there is little follow-up afterward.

In many organizations, performance appraisals are conducted only once a year—but that is changing. More organizations are beginning to conduct them on a semi-annual basis, and even quarterly. An important principle of performance appraisal is that continual feedback and employee coaching must be a positive daily activity. The annual or semiannual performance review should simply be a logical extension of the day-to-day supervision process.

One of the main concerns of employees is the fairness of the performance appraisal system, as the process is central to so many HRM decisions. Employees who believe the system is unfair may consider the appraisal interview a waste of time and leave the interview with feelings of anxiety or frustration. Also, they may view compliance with the appraisal system as perfunctory and thus play only a passive role during the interview process. By addressing these employee concerns during the planning stage of the appraisal process, the organization will help the appraisal program succeed in reaching its goals.[8]

Finally, organizational politics can introduce a bias even in fairly administered employee appraisals.[9] For example, managers may inflate evaluations because they desire higher salaries for their employees or because higher subordinate ratings make them look good as managers. Alternatively, managers may want to get rid of troublesome employees, passing them off to another department by inflating their ratings.

Developing an Effective Appraisal Program

objective **2**

The HR department ordinarily has the primary responsibility for overseeing and coordinating the appraisal program. Managers from the operating departments must also be actively involved, particularly in helping to establish the objectives for the program. Furthermore, employees are more likely to accept and be satisfied with the performance appraisal program when they have the chance to participate in its development. Their concerns about fairness and accuracy in determining raises, promotions, and the like tend to be alleviated somewhat when they have been involved at the planning stage and have helped develop the performance standards themselves.

What Are the Performance Standards?

Before any appraisal is conducted, the standards by which performance is to be evaluated should be clearly defined and communicated to the employee. As discussed in Chapter 4, these standards should be based on job-related requirements derived from job analysis and reflected in an employee's job description and job specifications. When performance standards are properly established, they help translate organizational goals and objectives into job requirements that convey acceptable and unacceptable levels of performance to employees.

As shown in Figure 8.3, there are four basic considerations in establishing performance standards: strategic relevance, criterion deficiency, criterion contamination, and reliability.

Strategic Relevance

Strategic relevance refers to the extent to which standards relate to the strategic objectives of the organization. For example, if an organization has established a standard that "95 percent of all customer complaints are to be resolved in one day," then it is relevant for the customer service representatives to use such a standard for their evaluations. Companies such as 3M and Buckman Laboratories have strategic objectives that 25–30 percent of their sales are to be generated from products developed within the past five years. These objectives are translated into performance standards for their employees. General Motors and Whirlpool include other objectives such as cost, quality, and speed. They develop metrics to identify and compare their performance around the world on these measures.[10]

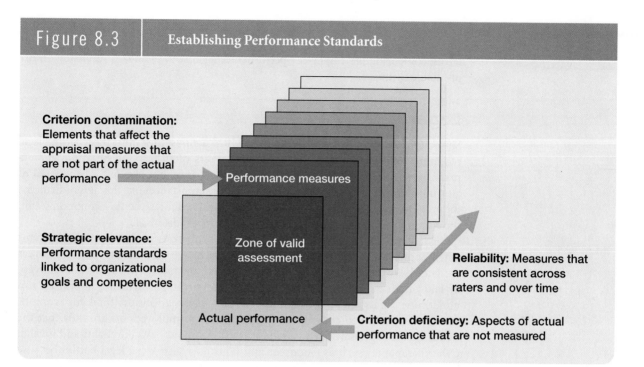

Figure 8.3   Establishing Performance Standards

Criterion contamination: Elements that affect the appraisal measures that are not part of the actual performance

Performance measures

Strategic relevance: Performance standards linked to organizational goals and competencies

Zone of valid assessment

Reliability: Measures that are consistent across raters and over time

Actual performance

Criterion deficiency: Aspects of actual performance that are not measured

Criterion Deficiency

A second consideration in establishing performance standards is the extent to which the standards capture the entire range of an employee's responsibilities. When performance standards focus on a single criterion (such as sales revenues) to the exclusion of other important but less quantifiable performance dimensions (such as customer service), then the appraisal system is said to suffer from criterion deficiency.[11]

Criterion Contamination

Just as performance criteria can be deficient, they can also be contaminated. There are factors outside an employee's control that can influence his or her performance. A comparison of performance of production workers, for example, should not be contaminated by the fact that some have newer machines than others do. A comparison of the performance of travelling salespeople should not be contaminated by the fact that territories differ in sales potential.[12]

Reliability

As discussed in Chapter 6, reliability refers to the stability or consistency of a standard, or the extent to which individuals tend to maintain a certain level of performance over time. In ratings, reliability may be measured by correlating two sets of ratings made by a single rater or by two different raters. For example, two managers may rate the same individual and estimate his or her suitability for a promotion. Their ratings could be compared to determine inter-rater reliability.

Performance standards permit managers to specify and communicate precise information to employees regarding quality and quantity of output. Therefore, when performance standards are written, they should be defined in quantifiable and measurable terms. For example, "ability and willingness to handle customer orders" is not as good a performance standard as "all customer orders will be filled in four hours with a 98-percent accuracy rate." When standards are expressed in specific, measurable terms, comparing the employee's performance against the standard results in a more justifiable appraisal.

Legal Issues

Since performance appraisals are used for HRM actions, they must meet certain legal requirements. HR professionals and their lawyers often face the situation where a manager has fired an employee for poor performance, but also left a paper trail of glowing performance reviews over the years. In circumstances like this, it is difficult for the employer to argue that the employee was dismissed for cause. As a common result, the employer must assume legal liability for wrongful dismissal.

Furthermore, employers might face legal challenges to their appraisal systems when appraisals indicate acceptable or above-average performance but employees are later passed over for promotion, disciplined for poor performance, discharged, or laid off from the organization. In these cases, the performance appraisals can undermine the legitimacy of the subsequent personnel decision. Intel, for example, was recently taken to court by a group of former employees on grounds that the performance appraisal system (used for layoff decisions) was unreliable and invalid. Other companies such as Goodyear and Ford have also faced legal battles because their performance appraisals were viewed as discriminatory against older workers.[13] In anticipation of such court cases, performance appraisals should meet the following guidelines:

- Performance ratings must be job-related, with performance standards developed through job analysis.
- Employees must be given a written copy of their job standards in advance of appraisals.

Specific, measurable job standards help remove vagueness and subjectivity from performance appraisals.

© JUPITERIMAGES

- Managers who conduct the appraisal must be able to observe the behaviour they are rating. This implies having a measurable standard with which to compare employee behaviour.
- Supervisors should be trained to use the appraisal form correctly. They should be instructed in how to apply appraisal standards when making judgments.
- Appraisals should be discussed openly with employees and counselling or corrective guidance offered to help poor performers improve their performance.
- An appeals procedure should be established to enable employees to express disagreement with the appraisal.[14]

Employers must ensure that managers and supervisors document appraisals and reasons for subsequent HRM actions. This information may prove decisive should an employee take legal action. An employer's credibility is strengthened when it can support performance appraisal ratings by documenting instances of poor performance.

Who Should Appraise Performance?

Just as there are multiple standards by which to evaluate performance, there are also multiple candidates for appraising performance. Given the complexity of today's jobs, it is often unrealistic to presume that one person can fully observe and evaluate an employee's performance. At IBM, employees with high potential are regularly reviewed by a broad cross-section of the company's leaders, not just their immediate bosses. As shown in Figure 8.4, raters may include supervisors, peers, team members, self, subordinates, customers, vendors, and suppliers. And each may be more or less useful for the administrative and developmental purposes we discussed earlier. Companies such as Cigna, Black & Decker, and Disney have used a multiple-rater approach—or 360-degree appraisal—to evaluate employee performance.[15] We will talk more about 360-degree appraisal at the end of this section.

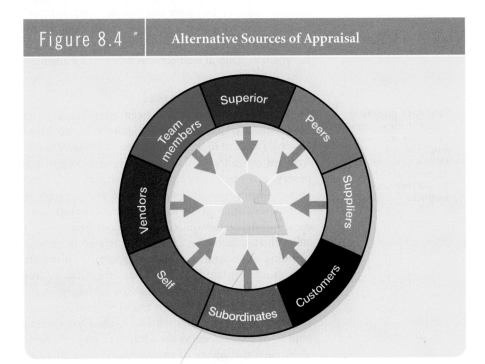

Figure 8.4   **Alternative Sources of Appraisal**

Manager/Supervisor Appraisal

manager and/or supervisor appraisal
A performance appraisal done by an employee's manager and often reviewed by a manager one level higher

Manager and/or supervisor appraisal has been the traditional approach to evaluating an employee's performance. In most instances supervisors are in the best position to perform this function, although it may not always be possible for them to do so. Managers often complain that they do not have the time to fully observe the performance of employees. These managers must then rely on performance records to evaluate an employee's performance. If reliable and valid measures are not available, the appraisal may be less than accurate. (Recall our earlier discussion of criterion deficiency and contamination.)

When a supervisor appraises employees independently, provision is often made for a review of the appraisals by the supervisor's superior. Having appraisals reviewed by a supervisor's superior reduces the chance of superficial or biased evaluations. Reviews by superiors generally are more objective and provide a broader perspective of employee performance than do appraisals by immediate supervisors.

Self-Appraisal

self-appraisal
A performance appraisal done by the employee being evaluated, generally on an appraisal form completed by the employee prior to the performance interview

Sometimes employees are asked to evaluate themselves on a self-appraisal form. The **self-appraisal** is beneficial when managers seek to increase an employee's involvement in the review process. A self-appraisal system requires an employee to complete the appraisal form prior to the performance interview. At a minimum, this gets the employee thinking about his or her strengths and weaknesses and may lead to discussions about barriers to effective performance. During the performance interview, the manager and the employee discuss job performance and agree on a final appraisal. This approach also works well when the manager and the employee jointly establish future performance goals or employee development plans. Critics of self-appraisal argue that self-raters are more lenient than managers in their assessments and tend to present themselves in a highly favourable light. There is also evidence that self-appraisals can lead employees to believe that they will have more influence over the appraisal's outcome. If that expectation isn't met, the employee can become frustrated. For this reason, self-appraisals may be best for developmental purposes rather than for administrative decisions. Used in conjunction with other methods, self-appraisals can be a valuable source of appraisal information. They at least serve as a catalyst for discussion during the appraisal.[16]

Subordinate Appraisal

subordinate appraisal
A performance appraisal of a superior by an employee, which is more appropriate for developmental than for administrative purposes

Subordinate appraisal has been used by organizations (such as Xerox and Honeywell) to give managers feedback on how their subordinates view them.[17] Subordinates are in a good position to evaluate their managers because they are in frequent contact with their superiors and occupy a unique position from which to observe many performance-related behaviours. Subordinate appraisals have also been shown to improve the performance of managers. The performance dimensions judged most appropriate for subordinate appraisals include leadership, oral communication, delegation of authority, coordination of team efforts, and interest in subordinates. However, dimensions related to managers' specific job tasks, such as planning and organizing, budgeting, creativity, and analytical ability, are not usually seen as appropriate for subordinate appraisal. Because subordinate appraisals give employees power over their bosses, managers may be hesitant to endorse such a system, particularly when it might be used as a basis for compensation decisions. However, when the information is used for developmental purposes, managers tend to be more open to the idea. And available evidence suggests that when managers heed the advice of their subordinates, their own performance can improve substantially. Nevertheless, to avoid potential problems, subordinate appraisals should be submitted anonymously and combined across several individual raters.[18]

Peer Appraisal

peer appraisal
A performance appraisal done by one's fellow employees, generally on forms that are compiled into a single profile for use in the performance interview conducted by the employee's manager

Individuals of equal rank who work together are increasingly asked to evaluate each other. A **peer appraisal** provides information that differs to some degree from ratings by a superior, since peers often see different dimensions of performance. Peers can readily identify leadership and interpersonal skills along with other strengths and weaknesses of their co-workers. A superior asked to rate a patrol officer on a dimension such as "dealing with the public" may not have had much opportunity to observe it. Fellow officers, on the other hand, have the opportunity to observe this behaviour regularly.

One advantage of peer appraisals is the belief that they furnish more accurate and valid information than appraisals by superiors. The supervisor often sees employees putting their best foot forward, while those who work with their fellow employees on a regular basis may see a more realistic picture. With peer appraisals, co-workers complete an evaluation on the employee. The forms are then usually compiled into a single profile, which is given to the supervisor for use in the final appraisal. For employees who have trouble confronting their co-workers about problems, the reviews provide a forum in which to address issues and resolve conflicts. They also provide an opportunity to hand out praise.[19]

Despite the evidence that peer appraisals are possibly the most accurate method of judging employee behaviour, there are reasons why they have not been used more frequently.[20] The reasons commonly cited include the following:

1. Peer ratings are simply a popularity contest.
2. Managers are reluctant to give up control over the appraisal process.
3. Those receiving low ratings might retaliate against their peers.
4. Peers rely on stereotypes in ratings.

When peers are in competition with one another, such as with sales associates, peer appraisals may not be advisable for administrative decisions such as salary or bonuses. Employers using peer appraisals must also be sure to safeguard confidentiality in handling the review forms. Any breach of confidentiality can create interpersonal rivalries or hurt feelings and bring about hostility among fellow employees.

Team Appraisal

team appraisal
A performance appraisal, based on TQM concepts, which recognizes team accomplishment rather than individual performance

An extension of the peer appraisal is the **team appraisal.** While peers are on equal standing with one another, they may not work closely together. In a team setting, it may be nearly impossible to separate out an individual's contribution. Advocates of team appraisal argue that, in such cases, individual appraisal can be dysfunctional because it detracts from the critical issues of the team. To address this issue, organizations such as Boeing and Texas Instruments have begun developing team appraisals to evaluate the performance of the team as a whole.[21]

A company's interest in team appraisals is frequently driven by its commitment to TQM principles and practices. At its root, TQM is a control system that involves setting standards (based on customer requirements), measuring performance against those standards, and identifying opportunities for continuous improvement. In this regard TQM and performance appraisal are perfectly complementary. However, a basic tenet of TQM is that performance is best understood at the level of the system as a whole, whereas performance appraisal traditionally has focused on individual performance.

Team appraisals represent one way to break down barriers between individuals and encourage their collective effort.[22] Frequently, the system is complemented by the use of team incentives or group variable pay. (See Chapters 10 and 16.)

Customer Appraisal

customer appraisal
A performance appraisal that, like team appraisal, is based on TQM concepts and seeks evaluation from both external and internal customers

Also driven by TQM concerns, an increasing number of organizations use internal and external **customer appraisal** as a source of performance appraisal information. External customers' evaluations, of course, have been used for some time to appraise restaurant personnel. However, companies such as Federal Express and Sears are among the companies that have utilized external customers as well. Managers establish customer service measures (CSMs) and set goals for employees (linked to company goals). Other companies survey their vendors and suppliers as part of the appraisal process. By including the firm's business partners in the performance reviews, managers hope to produce more objective evaluations, more effective employees, more satisfied customers, and better business performance.[23]

In contrast to external customers, internal customers include anyone inside the organization who depends on an employee's work output. For example, managers who rely on the HR department for selection and training services would be candidates for conducting internal customer evaluations of that department. For both developmental and administrative purposes, internal customers can provide extremely useful feedback about the value added by an employee or team of employees.

Putting It All Together: 360-Degree Appraisal

As mentioned previously, many companies are combining various sources of performance appraisal information to create multi-rater—or 360-degree—appraisal and feedback systems. Jobs are multifaceted, and different people see different things. As the name implies, 360-degree feedback is intended to provide employees with

Some managers give their teams autonomy but hold them accountable for results.

© THE IMAGE BANK/GETTY IMAGES

as accurate a view of their performance as possible by getting input from all angles: supervisors, peers, subordinates, customers, and the like. Although in the beginning 360-degree systems were purely developmental and were restricted mainly to management and career development, they have migrated to performance appraisal and other administrative applications. An estimated 90 percent of Fortune 1000 companies have implemented some form of 360-degree feedback system for career development, performance appraisal, or both. Because the system combines more information than a typical performance appraisal, it can become administratively complex. For that reason, organizations have recently begun using employee management software (EPM) to compile and aggregate the information. Approximately 20 percent use the Web or other software for their performance management systems; another 33 percent plan to do so in the near future.[24] For example, PerformancePlus and CompetencyPlus, developed by Exxceed, allow managers and employees to develop performance plans, goals, and objectives, and then track their progress over time. Managers can see all of an employee's goals and action steps on a single screen, and self-appraisals and multiple-rater reviews can be combined into a 360-degree format. After rating an employee's performance on each goal, raters can provide summary comments in three categories: victories and accomplishments, setbacks and frustrations, and general comments. To ensure security, a user ID and password are required and all the data are captured and saved in the employee's history file. Other types of EPM software can calculate and manage financial rewards based on how well employees perform as well as identify their performance gaps and manage their education, certification, and training.[25]

Although 360-degree feedback can be useful for both developmental and administrative purposes, most companies start with an exclusive focus on development. Employees may be understandably nervous about the possibility of everyone "ganging up" on them in their evaluations. In addition, organizations sometimes implement 360-feedback without clearly defining the strategic mission of the program—either the competencies on the 360-feedback form are not relevant to the firm's business objectives or they are so broad that they can't be linked to an individual employee's performance. Therefore, 360-feedback programs should be implemented only after a close scrutiny of their purposes and conducted with proper planning and evaluation. Figure 8.5 on page 360 shows a list of pros and cons of 360-degree appraisal.

When Intel established a 360-degree system, the company observed the following safeguards to ensure its maximum quality and acceptance:

- *Ensure anonymity.* Make certain that no employee ever knows how any evaluation-team member responded. (The supervisor's rating is an exception to this rule.)

- *Make respondents accountable.* Supervisors should discuss each evaluation-team member's input, letting each member know whether he or she used the rating scales appropriately, whether his or her responses were reliable, and how other participants rated the employee.

- *Prevent "gaming" of the system.* Some individuals may try to help or hurt an employee by giving either too high or too low an evaluation. Team members may try to collude with one another by agreeing to give each other uniformly high ratings. Supervisors should check for obviously invalid responses.

- *Use statistical procedures.* Use weighted averages or other quantitative approaches to combining evaluations. Supervisors should be careful about using subjective combinations of data, which could undermine the system.

- *Identify and quantify biases.* Check for prejudices or preferences related to age, gender, ethnicity, or other group factors.[26]

Figure 8.5	Pros and Cons of 360-Degree Appraisal

PROS

- The system is more comprehensive in that responses are gathered from multiple perspectives.
- Quality of information is better. (Quality of respondents is more important than quantity.)
- It complements TQM initiatives by emphasizing internal/external customers and teams.
- It may lessen bias/prejudice since feedback comes from more people, not one individual.
- Feedback from peers and others may increase employee self-development.

CONS

- The system is complex in combining all the responses.
- Feedback can be intimidating and cause resentment if employee feels the respondents have "ganged up."
- There may be conflicting opinions, though they may all be accurate from the respective standpoints.
- The system requires training to work effectively.
- Employees may collude or "game" the system by giving invalid evaluations to one another.
- Appraisers may not be accountable if their evaluations are anonymous.

Sources: Compiled from David A. Waldman, Leanne E. Atwater, and David Antonioni, "Has 360-Degree Feedback Gone Amok?" *Academy of Management Executive* 12, no. 2 (May 1998): 86–94; Bruce Pfau, Ira Kay, Kenneth Nowak, and Jai Ghorpade, "Does 360-Degree Feedback Negatively Affect Company Performance?" *HR Magazine* 47, no. 6 (June 2002): 54–59; Maury Peiperl, "Getting 360-Degree Feedback Right," *Harvard Business Review* 79, no. 1 (January 2001): 142–47; Joyce E. Bono and Amy E. Colbert, "Understanding Responses to Multi-Source Feedback: The Role of Core Self-Evaluations," *Personnel Psychology* 58, no. 1 (Spring 2005): 171–205.

Based on the experiences of companies like Canadian Tire, described in Reality Check, it appears that 360-degree feedback can provide a valuable approach to performance appraisal. Its success, as with any appraisal technique, depends on how managers use the information and how fairly employees are treated.

Training Appraisers

A weakness of many performance appraisal programs is that managers and supervisors are not adequately trained for the appraisal task and provide little meaningful feedback to subordinates. Because they lack precise standards for appraising subordinates' performance and have not developed the necessary observational and feedback skills, their appraisals often become nondirective and meaningless. Therefore, training appraisers can vastly improve the performance appraisal process. Says one HR manager: "What's not important is the (appraisal) form or the (measuring) scale. What's important is that managers can objectively observe people's performance and objectively give feedback on that performance." Notwithstanding, in a survey of 55 HR managers from medium and large companies, more than half said their companies did either little or no evaluation of how well their managers do appraisals.[27]

Reality Check

Canadian Tire 360-Degree Matrix

"Accentuate the positive; build on leadership strengths" is the principal theme of leadership performance evaluation and development conducted by the Canadian Tire Corporation as described by Janice Wismer, vice-president of human resources. Canadian Tire is a network of interrelated businesses with retail, financial, and petroleum interests. About 45 000 employees work in 1000 retail stores across Canada.

The customized 360-degree feedback process used at Canadian Tire is research-based and designed to build a cadre of great leaders. The first step in the design of the 360-degree feedback instrument was to benchmark other organizations that had effective 360-degree feedback processes. Twenty-seven key employees at Canadian Tire were interviewed to identify the attributes of their great leaders as measured by the standards of the organization. These key leadership attributes were then discussed and evaluated in workshops with important stakeholders. A total of 16 competencies were identified: seven related to "who one is"—characteristics such as trustworthy, passionate, and curious. Nine others focused on "what one can do for the team, business, and enterprise"—such as make strategic choices, motivate and celebrate, communicate authentically.

To date, about 170 managers have been assessed by an average of nine colleagues, including peers, subordinates, and bosses. Colleagues complete a self-survey, and all feedback assessment is analyzed relative to their own organization and to industry standards, which are maintained in a database. A confidential feedback report is given to each individual.

In addition to the generation of individual reports, an aggregate one-page executive summary is produced. The report, presented as a matrix, provides a visual summary colour-coded under each competency comparing aggregate feedback data for all individuals in a defined business unit. The sample 360-degree matrix shown below lists key attributes across the horizontal axis and the employee's feedback along the vertical axis. In order to maintain confidentiality, identifiers are assigned to the supervisors and managers so that they can see their relative standing but without knowing the identity of the other employees. In the colour-coding, red signifies a weak performance, yellow is an average performance, and green indicates exceptional strengths. By using this 360-degree matrix, HR can identify areas where groups of employees need professional development, thus investing training dollars where it matters most. In the example, Executives A, B, and C are perceived as generally excellent across most of the eight areas of interest, while Executives M, N, and O are experiencing considerable difficulty. In addition, most of the executive team performed well in areas 1, 2, and 3, having most difficulty in area 8. In this case, individual development plans may work well for executives having problems in areas 1, 2, and 3, while a group development solution may be best designed for area 8.

According to Ed Haltrecht, Ph.D., CHRP, who specializes in measurement and organizational leadership development, in most organizations when performance feedback is presented, both the employee and the manager focus on the reds—the weaknesses—and try to work out methods of development to improve this area. What is unique about Canadian Tire is that the focus is on the positive. It has found that improvements in weak areas (provided it is not a fundamental flaw) do not affect overall performance, while improvements in areas of

(continued on next page)

strength bring managers from good to extraordinary. The goal is to identify and strengthen attributes so employees will distinguish and present themselves as extraordinary. Individuals first address any "fundamental flaws"—either a very weak attribute of the individual or, more importantly, elements regarded as critical to the organization. In the sample 360-degree matrix, Executives I, L, N, and O have potential fundamental flaws in areas 1 and 2. If there are no fundamental flaws, then development focuses on building strengths. This combination has resulted in measurable gains in performance.

This approach is research based. A recently published book, *The Extraordinary Leader: Turning Good Managers into Great Leaders* by John Zenger and Joseph Folkman, presents

Executive	1. Treats others with respect.	2. Gives credit to others who have contributed or performed well.	3. Shows consistency between words and action.	4. Models the core values of the corporation; leads by example.	5. Treats team members as individuals based on knowledge of their strengths and development needs.	6. Takes actions that build a high level of commitment to work group goals and objectives.	7. Obtains resources so that the team has the knowledge, skills, and experience required to deliver results.	8. Where there is underlying conflict, helps parties involved bring up their issues and get to the heart of the problem.	Mean
A	5.0	4.9	4.9	4.6	4.8	4.6	4.6	4.5	4.7
B	5.0	4.8	4.9	4.9	4.9	4.8	4.3	3.7	4.7
C	5.0	4.7	4.5	4.7	4.7	4.7	4.5	4.2	4.6
D	4.8	4.6	4.2	4.7	4.3	4.3	4.6	4.1	4.4
E	4.7	5.0	4.7	4.0	3.7	4.0	4.3	4.3	4.4
F	4.8	4.3	4.3	4.5	4.4	4.3	4.1	3.2	4.2
G	4.6	4.2	4.2	4.2	4.2	4.1	4.2	3.9	4.2
H	4.5	4.4	4.1	4.2	4.3	3.9	3.9	4.1	4.2
I	4.4	3.8	4.0	4.3	4.0	4.3	4.5	3.7	4.2
J	4.4	4.3	4.5	4.2	4.1	4.2	3.9	4.0	4.2
K	4.6	4.2	4.5	4.0	4.5	4.2	3.6	4.3	4.1
L	3.8	4.4	4.3	4.3	3.7	4.1	4.5	3.9	4.1
M	4.4	4.2	4.4	4.1	4.2	4.0	4.0	4.2	4.1
N	4.3	3.8	4.1	3.9	4.0	4.0	3.5	2.9	3.9
O	3.3	4.1	4.0	3.6	3.8	3.8	3.9	3.3	3.6
Mean	4.5	4.3	4.4	4.2	4.2	4.2	4.1	3.9	4.2

several significant findings based on 225 000 evaluations of 20 000 people. Poor leaders were identified as those scoring in the bottom 10 percent; extraordinary leaders scored in the top 10 percent. Employee turnover in a call centre was 19 percent for the units managed by the poor managers, 14 percent for the middle group, and 9 percent for the extraordinary leaders. In another case that looked at a bank, net incomes for the bank generated by those groups whose managers were extraordinary, average, and poor were $7 million, $3.7 million, and $1.9 million respectively. Employee satisfaction indices were at the 80th percentile for top managers compared to the 18th percentile for the bottom-scoring managers. Likewise, Union Vulnerability indices, which measure how attractive the organization is to a union's membership drive, reflected the 91st percentile for the top-scoring managers compared to the 10th percentile for the poor managers—that is, poorer managers are more likely to attract union interest. Although the pay structure was the same across different departments, those led by the top-scoring managers had employees who were at the 65th percentile in satisfaction with company pay and job security; the employees of average managers were in the 50th percentile; and poor managers' employees scored at the 37th percentile for satisfaction with company pay and job security.

Canadian Tire's leadership development system also recognizes two other significant research findings: first, extraordinary leaders have about three competencies that they excel at and developing a few strengths to very high performance levels has a greater impact than improving several competencies from poor to average. Second, competencies travel together and improvement in one leads to significant progress in others. Identifying these companion competencies has proven to be extremely worthwhile. In a nutshell, these are the findings: start with the right set of competencies or attributes; focus on strengths; eliminate any fundamental flaws; and pay attention to companion attributes.

The assessment feedback process at Canadian Tire is seen as a tool for dialogue and for focusing on what makes a great company and what matters in leadership. Those employees who try to improve are given a developmental opportunities guidebook. Canadian Tire has discovered that the best development methods are stretch challenging assignments, coaching and mentoring, personal feedback, talks with consultants, and training programs.

Establishing an Appraisal Plan

Training programs are most effective when they follow a systematic process that begins with an explanation of the objectives of the performance appraisal system. It is important for the rater to know the purpose for which the appraisal is to be used. For example, using the appraisal for compensation decisions rather than development purposes may affect how the rater evaluates the employee, and it may change the rater's opinion of how the appraisal form should be completed. The mechanics of the rating system should also be explained, including how frequently the appraisals are to be conducted, who will conduct them, and what the standards of performance are. In addition, appraisal training should alert raters to the weaknesses and problems of appraisal systems so they can be avoided.

Eliminating Rater Error

Appraisal training should focus on eliminating the subjective errors made by managers in the rating process. Gary Latham of the University of Toronto and Kenneth

Wexley, an American industrial psychologist, stress the importance of performance appraisal training by noting that

> Regardless of whether evaluations are obtained from multiple appraisers or from only the employee's immediate superior, all appraisers should be trained to reduce errors of judgment that occur when one person evaluates another. This training is necessary because to the degree to which a performance appraisal is biased, distorted, or inaccurate, the probability of increasing the productivity of the employee is greatly decreased. Moreover, wrong decisions could be made regarding whom to promote, retain, or replace, which in turn will penalize the organization's bottom line. In addition, when a performance appraisal is affected by rating errors, the employee may be justified in filing a discrimination charge.[28]

With any rating method, certain types of errors can arise that should be considered. The "halo error" discussed in Chapter 6 is also common with respect to rating scales, especially those that do not include carefully developed descriptions of the employee behaviours being rated. Provision for comments on the rating form tends to reduce halo error. The "horn error" is the opposite of the halo effect. It occurs when a manager focuses on one negative aspect about an employee and generalizes it into an overall poor appraisal rating. A personality conflict between a manager and his or her employees increases the probability of the horn effect, which can lead to a high level of frustration on the employee's part if it's not corrected.[29]

Some types of rating errors are *distributional errors* in that they involve a group of ratings given across various employees. For example, raters who are reluctant to assign either extremely high or extremely low ratings commit the **error of central tendency.** In this case, all employees are rated about average. To such raters it is a good idea to explain that, among large numbers of employees, one should expect to find significant differences in behaviour, productivity, and other characteristics.

In contrast to central tendency errors, it is also common for some raters to give unusually high or low ratings. For example, a manager may erroneously assert, "All my employees are excellent" or "None of my people are good enough." These beliefs give rise to what is called **leniency or strictness error.** [30] One way to reduce this error is to clearly define the characteristics or dimensions of performance and to provide meaningful descriptions of behaviour, known as "anchors," on the scale. Another approach is to require ratings to conform to a *forced ranking,* a type of system initially developed by GE, purportedly with good results. Managers appraising employees under a *forced-distribution* system are required to place a certain percentage of employees into various performance categories. For example, it may be required that 10 percent of ratings be poor (or excellent). This is similar to the requirement in some schools that instructors grade on a curve. A variation of this is *peer ranking,* a system whereby employees in a work group are ranked against one another from best to worst. Although forced distribution and peer ranking may solve leniency and strictness errors, they can create other rating errors—particularly if most employees are performing above standard. Moreover, if the system has a disparate impact on a legally protected group, such as minority or older employers, it can result, and has resulted, in discrimination suits. Even so, more organizations are using forced-ranking systems. However, other companies, including Ford and Goodyear, described in The Business Case, abandoned their forced-ranking systems after lawsuits, lower morale, decreased teamwork, and destructive employee competition ensued following their use. Because of the legal issues related to forced ranking, companies that use these methods obviously need to carefully train their appraisers.[31]

error of central tendency
A performance-rating error in which all employees are rated about average

leniency or strictness error
A performance-rating error in which the appraiser tends to give employees either unusually high or unusually low ratings

The Business Case

Rank and Yank

Research shows that performance appraisals can have a positive financial impact, but there is the potential to lose money if the wrong system is chosen. Goodyear Tire & Rubber Co. abandoned a performance-rating system for salaried employees just as discrimination attorneys were planning to file a class-action lawsuit over it. Goodyear said it was dropping major parts of its program, including its so-called 10-80-10 feature, which essentially graded all salaried employees on a curve. The top 10 percent were rated A, the middle 80 percent were rated B, and the bottom 10 percent were rated C. Those falling in the bottom 10 percent weren't eligible for raises or bonuses and were warned that they might lose their jobs.

The lawsuit alleged that the workers who got C ratings were humiliated and stigmatized among their peers and managers. The legal arm of the AARP, formerly known as the American Association of Retired Persons, joined the lawsuit as co-counsel. Most of the plaintiffs who got C rankings in the case were Goodyear employees who were over 50 years old. "This case will send a clear message that performance rating schemes that target older workers for unfair treatment are illegal and will not be tolerated," said Laurie McCann of AARP.

Jack McGilvrey, a 59-year-old salaried employee, was one of those named in the suit. He claimed that he always received ratings of at least "good/effective performer" in his formal performance reviews up through the late 1990s. In 2000, he was ranked "highly effective." But in February 2001, he was transferred to a new department and shortly thereafter was given a C rating in his performance review. The suit asserted that Mr. McGilvrey didn't deserve the rating and received it as part of Goodyear's plan to discriminate against older employees. He was later dismissed.

The lawsuit against Goodyear has many parallels to one filed in 2001 against Ford Motor Co. In that case, also joined by AARP, the company modified its plans in the face of a legal challenge. The Ford case was eventually settled.

In modifying its white-collar ranking system, Goodyear said it would replace those A, B, and C rankings with the terms *exceeds expectations, meets expectations,* and *unsatisfactory.* There will be no requirement to assign those ratings to set percentages of employees. The company also said it was stepping up training for managers so they learn to do a better job of conducting performance reviews. Goodyear has about 28 000 salaried employees around the world.

Source: Timothy Aeppel, "Goodyear Ends Ratings System Ahead of Discrimination Suit," *The Wall Street Journal,* September 12, 2002: B8. Copyright © 2002 Dow Jones. Reprinted by permission of the publisher, Dow Jones, via Copyright Clearance Center.

recency error
A performance-rating error in which the appraisal is based largely on the employee's most recent behaviour rather than on behaviour throughout the appraisal period

Some rating errors are *temporal* in that the performance review is biased either favourably or unfavourably, depending on the way performance information is selected, evaluated, and organized by the rater over time. For example, when the appraisal is based largely on the employee's recent behaviour, good or bad, the rater has committed the **recency error.** Managers who give higher ratings because they believe an employee is "showing improvement" may unwittingly be committing recency error. Without work-record documentation for the entire appraisal period, the rater is forced to recall recent employee behaviour to establish the rating. Having the rater routinely document employee accomplishments and failures throughout the whole appraisal period can minimize the recency error. One way for managers to do this is by keeping a diary or a log. Rater training also will help reduce this error.

contrast error
A performance-rating error in which an employee's evaluation is biased either upward or downward because of comparison with another employee just previously evaluated

Contrast error occurs when an employee's evaluation is biased either upward or downward because of another employee's performance, evaluated just previously. For example, an average employee may appear especially productive when compared with a poor performer. However, that same employee may appear unproductive when compared with a star performer. Contrast errors are most likely when raters are required to rank employees in order from the best to the poorest. Employees are evaluated against one another, usually on the basis of some organizational standard or guideline. For example, they may be compared on the basis of their ability to meet production standards or their "overall" ability to perform their job. As with other types of rating error, contrast error can be reduced through training that focuses on using objective standards and behavioural anchors to appraise performance.[32]

similar-to-me error
A performance-rating error in which an appraiser inflates the evaluation of an employee because of a mutual personal connection

Similar-to-me error occurs when appraisers inflate the evaluations of people with whom they have something in common. For example, if both the manager and the employee are from small towns, the manager may unwittingly have a more favourable impression of the employee. The effects of a similar-to-me error can be powerful, and when the similarity is based on race, religion, gender, or some other protected category, it may result in discrimination.

Furthermore, raters should be aware of any stereotypes they may hold toward particular groups—such as male/female or white/black—because the observation and interpretation of performance can be clouded by these stereotypes. For example, one study found that men who experience conflicts between family and work received lower overall performance ratings and lower reward recommendations than men who did not experience such conflicts. Women, on the other hand, were judged no differently, whether they experienced family-work conflicts or not. A host of organizations such as Avenor, a Montreal-based pulp and paper company, have developed formal training programs to reduce the subjective errors commonly made during the rating process. This training can pay off, particularly when participants have the opportunity to (1) observe other managers making errors, (2) actively participate in discovering their own errors, and (3) practise job-related tasks to reduce the errors they tend to make.[33]

Feedback Training

Finally, a training program for raters should provide some general points to consider for planning and conducting the feedback interview. The interview not only provides employees with knowledge of results of their evaluation, but also allows the manager and employee to discuss current problems and set future goals.

Training in specific skills should cover at least three basic areas: (1) communicating effectively, (2) diagnosing the root causes of performance problems, and (3) setting goals and objectives.[34] A checklist can be used to assist supervisors in preparing for the appraisal interview. As shown in Highlights in HRM 8.1, the checklist reflects the growing tendency of organizations such as AT&T and Honeywell to have employees assess their own performance prior to the appraisal interview. The performance appraisal interview will be discussed in detail later in the chapter.

Highlights in HRM 8.1

Supervisor's Checklist for the Performance Appraisal

Scheduling
1. Schedule the review and notify the employee ten days to two weeks in advance.
2. Ask the employee to prepare for the session by reviewing his or her performance, job objectives, and development goals.
3. Clearly state that this will be the formal annual performance appraisal.

Preparing for the Review
1. Review the performance documentation collected throughout the year. Concentrate on work patterns that have developed.
2. Be prepared to give specific examples of above- or below-average performance.
3. When performance falls short of expectations, determine what changes need to be made. If performance meets or exceeds expectations, discuss this and plan how to reinforce it.
4. After the appraisal is written, set it aside for a few days and then review it again.
5. Follow whatever steps are required by your organization's performance appraisal system.

Conducting the Review
1. Select a location that is comfortable and free of distractions. The location should encourage a frank and candid conversation.
2. Discuss each topic in the appraisal one at a time, considering both strengths and shortcomings.
3. Be specific and descriptive, not general and judgmental. Report occurrences rather than evaluating them.
4. Discuss your differences and resolve them. Solicit agreement with the evaluation.
5. Jointly discuss and design plans for taking corrective action for growth and development.
6. Maintain a professional and supportive approach to the appraisal discussion.

Performance Appraisal Methods

In the discussion that follows, we will examine in some detail the methods that have found widespread use, and we will briefly touch on other methods that are used less frequently. Performance appraisal methods can be broadly classified as measuring traits, behaviours, or results. Trait approaches continue to be more popular despite their inherent subjectivity. Behavioural approaches provide more action-oriented information to employees and therefore may be best for development. The results-oriented approach is gaining popularity because it focuses on the measurable contributions that employees make to the organization.

Trait Methods

Trait approaches to performance appraisal are designed to measure the extent to which an employee possesses certain characteristics—such as dependability, creativity, initiative, and leadership—that are viewed as important for the job and the organization in general. The fact that trait methods are the most popular is due in large part to the ease with which they are developed. However, if not designed carefully on the basis of job analysis, trait appraisals can be notoriously biased and subjective.

Graphic Rating Scales

graphic rating-scale method
A trait approach to performance appraisal whereby each employee is rated according to a scale of characteristics

In the **graphic rating-scale method** each trait or characteristic to be rated is represented by a scale on which a rater indicates the degree to which an employee possesses that trait or characteristic. An example of this type of scale is shown in Highlights in HRM 8.2. There are many variations of the graphic rating scale. The differences are to be found in (1) the characteristics or dimensions on which individuals are rated, (2) the degree to which the performance dimension is defined for the rater, and (3) how clearly the points on the scale are defined. In Highlights in HRM 8.2 the dimensions are defined briefly, and some attempt is made to define the points on the scale. Subjectivity bias is reduced somewhat when the dimensions on the scale and the scale points are defined as precisely as possible. This can be achieved by training raters and by including descriptive appraisal guidelines in a performance appraisal reference packet.[35]

Also, the rating form should provide sufficient space for comments on the behaviour associated with each scale. These comments improve the accuracy of the appraisal because they require the rater to think in terms of observable employee behaviours while providing specific examples to discuss with the employee during the appraisal interview.

Mixed-Standard Scales

mixed-standard scale method
A trait approach to performance appraisal similar to other scale methods but based on comparison with (better than, equal to, or worse than) a standard

The **mixed-standard scale method** is a modification of the basic rating-scale method. Rather than evaluating traits according to a single scale, the rater is given three specific descriptions of each trait. These descriptions reflect three levels of performance: superior, average, and inferior. After the three descriptions for each trait are written, they are randomly sequenced to form the mixed-standard scale. As shown in Highlights in HRM 8.3 on page 370, supervisors evaluate employees by indicating whether their performance is better than, equal to, or worse than the standard for each behaviour.

Forced-Choice Method

forced-choice method
A trait approach to performance appraisal that requires the rater to choose from statements designed to distinguish between successful and unsuccessful performance

The **forced-choice method** requires the rater to choose from statements, often in pairs, that appear equally favourable or equally unfavourable. The statements, however, are designed to distinguish between successful and unsuccessful performance. The rater selects one statement from the pair without knowing which statement correctly describes successful job behaviour. For example, forced-choice pairs might include the following:

1. _____ a) Works hard   _____ b) Works quickly
2. _____ a) Shows initiative   _____ b) Is responsive to customers
3. _____ a) Produces poor quality   _____ b) Lacks good work habits

The forced-choice method is not without limitations, the primary one being the cost of establishing and maintaining its validity. The fact that it has been a source of frustration to many raters has sometimes caused the method to be eliminated from appraisal programs. In addition, it cannot be used as effectively as some of the other

Highlights in HRM 8.2

Graphic Rating Scale with Provision for Comments

Appraise employee's performance in PRESENT ASSIGNMENT. Check (✔) most appropriate square. Appraisers are *urged to freely use* the "Remarks" sections for significant comments descriptive of the individual.

1. KNOWLEDGE OF WORK: Understanding of all phases of his/her work and related matters

Needs instruction or guidance	Has required knowledge of own and related work	Has exceptional knowledge of own and related work
☐ ☐	☐	✔ ☐

Remarks: *Is particularly good on gas engines.*

2. INITIATIVE: Ability to originate or develop ideas and to get things started

Lacks imagination	Meets necessary requirements	Unusually resourceful
☐ ✔	☐ ☐	☐

Remarks: *Has good ideas when asked for an opinion, but otherwise will not offer them. Somewhat lacking in self-confidence.*

3. APPLICATION: Attention and application to his/her work

Wastes time Needs close supervision	Steady and willing worker	Exceptionally industrious
☐ ☐	✔ ☐	☐

Remarks: *Accepts new jobs when assigned.*

4. QUALITY OF WORK: Thoroughness, neatness, and accuracy of work

Needs improvement	Regularly meets recognized standards	Consistently maintains highest quality
☐ ☐	☐ ☐	✔

Remarks: *The work he turns out is always of the highest possible quality.*

5. VOLUME OF WORK: Quantity of acceptable work

Should be increased	Regularly meets recognized standards	Unusually high output
☐ ☐	✔	☐

Remarks: *Would be higher if he did not spend so much time checking and rechecking his work.*

methods to help achieve the commonly held objective of using appraisals as a tool for developing employees by such means as the appraisal interview.

Essay Method

essay method
A trait approach to performance appraisal that requires the rater to compose a statement describing employee behaviour

Unlike rating scales, which provide a structured form of appraisal, the **essay method** requires the appraiser to compose a statement that best describes the employee being appraised. The appraiser is usually instructed to describe the employee's strengths and

Highlights in HRM 8.3

Example of a Mixed-Standard Scale

DIRECTIONS: Please indicate whether the individual's performance is above (+), equal to (0), or lower than (–) each of the following standards.

1. _____ Employee uses good judgment when addressing problems and provides workable alternatives; however, at times does not take actions to prevent problems. *(medium PROBLEM SOLVING)*

2. _____ Employee lacks supervisory skills; frequently handles employees poorly and is at times argumentative. *(low LEADERSHIP)*

3. _____ Employee is extremely cooperative; can be expected to take the lead in developing cooperation among employees; completes job tasks with a positive attitude. *(high COOPERATION)*

4. _____ Employee has effective supervision skills; encourages productivity, quality, and employee development. *(medium LEADERSHIP)*

5. _____ Employee normally displays an argumentative or defensive attitude toward fellow employees and job assignments. *(low COOPERATION)*

6. _____ Employee is generally agreeable but becomes argumentative at times when given job assignments; cooperates with other employees as expected. *(medium COOPERATION)*

7. _____ Employee is not good at solving problems; uses poor judgment and does not anticipate potential difficulties. *(low PROBLEM SOLVING)*

8. _____ Employee anticipates potential problems and provides creative, proactive alternative solutions; has good attention to follow-up. *(high PROBLEM SOLVING)*

9. _____ Employee displays skilled direction; effectively coordinates unit activities; is generally a dynamic leader and motivates employees to high performance. *(high LEADERSHIP)*

weaknesses and to make recommendations for his or her development. Often the essay method is combined with other rating methods. Essays may provide additional descriptive information on performance that is not obtained with a structured rating scale, for example.

The essay method provides an excellent opportunity to point out the unique characteristics of the employee being appraised. This aspect of the method is heightened when a supervisor is instructed to describe specific points about the employee's promotability, special talents, skills, strengths, and weaknesses. A major limitation of the essay method is that composing an essay that attempts to cover all of an employee's essential characteristics is a very time-consuming task (though when combined with other methods, this method does not require a lengthy statement). Another disadvantage of the essay method is that the quality of the performance appraisal may be influenced by the supervisor's writing skills and composition style. Good writers may simply be able to produce more-favourable appraisals. A final drawback of this appraisal method is that it tends to be subjective and may not focus on relevant aspects of job performance.

Behavioural Methods

As mentioned previously, one of the potential drawbacks of a trait-oriented performance appraisal is that traits tend to be vague and subjective. We discussed earlier that one way to improve a rating scale is to have descriptions of behaviour along a scale, or continuum. These descriptions permit the rater to readily identify the point where a particular employee falls on the scale. Behavioural methods have been developed to specifically describe which actions should (or should not) be exhibited on the job. They are frequently more useful for providing employees with developmental feedback.

Critical Incident Method

critical incident
An unusual event that denotes superior or inferior employee performance in some part of the job

The critical incident method, described in Chapter 4 in connection with job analysis, is also used as a method of appraisal. Recall that a **critical incident** occurs when employee behaviour results in unusual success or unusual failure in some part of the job. A favourable critical incident is illustrated by the janitor who observed that a file cabinet containing classified documents had been left unlocked at the close of business. The janitor called the security officer, who took the necessary action to correct the problem. An unfavourable incident is illustrated by the mail clerk who failed to deliver an express mail package immediately, instead putting it in with regular mail to be routed two hours later. The manager keeps a log or diary for each employee throughout the appraisal period and notes specific critical incidents related to how well they perform. When completing the appraisal form, the manager refers to the critical incident log and uses this information to substantiate an employee's rating of outstanding, satisfactory, or unsatisfactory in specific performance areas and overall. This method can also help a manager counsel employees when they are having performance problems while the problem is still minor. It also increases the objectivity of the appraisal by requiring the rater to use job performance criteria to justify the ratings.[36]

Behavioural Checklist Method

One of the oldest appraisal techniques is the behavioural checklist method. It consists of having the rater check the statements on a list that the rater believes are characteristic of the employee's performance or behaviour. A checklist developed for computer salespeople might include a number of statements like the following:

_____ Is able to explain equipment clearly
_____ Keeps abreast of new developments in technology
_____ Tends to be a steady worker
_____ Reacts quickly to customer needs
_____ Processes orders correctly

Behaviourally Anchored Rating Scale (BARS)

behaviourally anchored rating scale (BARS)
A behavioural approach to performance appraisal that consists of a series of vertical scales, one for each important dimension of job performance

A **behaviourally anchored rating scale (BARS)** consists of a series of five to ten vertical scales—one for each important dimension of performance identified through job analysis. These dimensions are anchored by behaviours identified through a critical-incident job analysis. The critical incidents are placed along the scale and are assigned point values according to the opinions of experts. A BARS for the job of firefighter is shown in Highlights in HRM 8.4 on page 372. Note that this particular scale is for the dimension described as "Firefighting Strategy: Knowledge of Fire Characteristics."

A BARS is typically developed by a committee that includes both subordinates and managers. The committee's task is to identify all the relevant characteristics or dimensions of the job. Behavioural anchors in the form of statements are then

Highlights in HRM 8.4

Example of a BARS for Municipal Fire Companies

FIREFIGHTING STRATEGY: Knowledge of Fire Characteristics. This area of performance concerns the ability of a firefighter to use his or her knowledge of fire characteristics to develop the best strategy for fighting a fire. It involves the following activities: Observe fire and smoke conditions and locate source of fire. Size up fire and identify appropriate extinguishing techniques and ventilation procedures. Consult preplan reports. Apply knowledge of heat and fluid mechanics to anticipate fire behaviour. Identify and screen or saturate potential exposures using direct or fog streams or water curtains. Identify and remove or protect flammable or hazardous materials.

HIGH	7	—Finds the fire when no one else can
	6	—Correctly assesses best point of entry for fighting fire
		—Uses type of smoke as indicator of type of fire
	5	
		—Understands basic hydraulics
AVERAGE	4	
	3	—Cannot tell the type of fire by observing the colour of flame
		—Cannot identify location of the fire
	2	
		—Will not change firefighting strategy in spite of flashbacks and other signs that accelerants are present
LOW	1	

Source: Adapted from Landy, Jacobs, and Associates. Reprinted with permission.

established for each of the job dimensions. Several participants are asked to review the anchor statements and indicate which job dimension each anchor illustrates. The only anchors retained are those that at least 70 percent of the group agree belong with a particular dimension. Finally, anchors are attached to their job dimensions and placed on the appropriate scales according to values that the group assigns to them.

At present there is no strong evidence that a BARS reduces all of the rating errors mentioned previously. However, some studies have shown that scales of this type can yield more-accurate ratings. One major advantage of a BARS is that personnel outside the HR department participate with HR staff in its development. Employee participation can lead to greater acceptance of the performance appraisal process and of the performance measures that it uses.

The procedures followed in developing a BARS also result in scales that have a high degree of content validity. The main disadvantage of a BARS is that it requires considerable time and effort to develop. In addition, because the scales are specific to particular jobs, a scale designed for one job may not apply to another.

behaviour observation scale (BOS)
A behavioural approach to performance appraisal that measures the frequency of observed behaviour

Behaviour Observation Scale (BOS)

A **behaviour observation scale (BOS)** is similar to a BARS in that they are both based on critical incidents. However, Highlights in HRM 8.5 shows that rather than asking

Highlights in HRM 8.5

Sample Items from Behaviour Observation Scales

INSTRUCTIONS: Please consider the sales representative's behaviour on the job in the past rating period. Read each statement carefully, then circle the number that indicates the extent to which the employee has demonstrated this *effective* or *ineffective* behaviour.

For each behaviour observed, use the following scale:

5 represents *almost always*   95–100% of the time
4 represents *frequently*   85–94% of the time
3 represents *sometimes*   75–84% of the time
2 represents *seldom*   65–74% of the time
1 represents *almost never*   0–64% of the time

SALES PRODUCTIVITY	ALMOST NEVER				ALMOST ALWAYS
1. Reviews individual productivity results with manager	1	2	3	4	5
2. Suggests to peers ways of building sales	1	2	3	4	5
3. Formulates specific objectives for each contact	1	2	3	4	5
4. Focuses on product rather than customer problem	1	2	3	4	5
5. Keeps account plans updated	1	2	3	4	5
6. Keeps customer waiting for service	1	2	3	4	5
7. Anticipates and prepares for customer concerns	1	2	3	4	5
8. Follows up on customer leads	1	2	3	4	5

USING THE INTERNET

Forms for appraising performance can be viewed at:

www.hr.uwaterloo.ca/forms/forms.html

the evaluator to choose the most representative behavioural anchor, a BOS is designed to measure how frequently each of the behaviours has been observed.

The value of a BOS is that this approach allows the appraiser to play the role of observer rather than of judge. In this way, he or she may more easily provide constructive feedback to the employee. Research shows that users of the system frequently prefer it over the BARS or trait scales for (1) maintaining objectivity, (2) distinguishing good performers from poor performers, (3) providing feedback, and (4) identifying training needs.[37]

Results Methods

Rather than looking at the traits of employees or the behaviours they exhibit on the job, many organizations evaluate employee accomplishments—the results they achieve through their work. Advocates of results appraisals argue that they are more objective and empowering for employees. Looking at results such as sales figures and production output involves less subjectivity and therefore may be less open to bias. Furthermore, results appraisals often give employees responsibility for their outcomes, while giving them discretion over the methods they use to accomplish them (within limits). This is empowerment in action.

Productivity Measures

A number of results measures are available to evaluate performance. Salespeople are evaluated on the basis of their sales volume (both the number of units sold and the dollar amount in revenues). Production workers are evaluated on the basis of the number of units they produce and perhaps the scrap rate or number of defects that are detected. Purchasing agents at Gaines Pet Foods in Cobourg, Ontario use performance measurements such as the purchasing cycle time. Executives are frequently evaluated on the basis of company profits or growth rate. Each of these measures directly links what employees accomplish and results that benefit the organization. In this way, results appraisals can directly align employee and organizational goals.

But there are some problems with results appraisals. First, recall our earlier discussion of criteria contamination. Results appraisals may be contaminated by external factors that employees cannot influence. Sales representatives who have extremely bad markets or production employees who can't get materials will not be able to perform up to their abilities. It may be unfair to hold these employees accountable for results that are contaminated by circumstances beyond their control.

Furthermore, results appraisals may inadvertently encourage employees to "look good" on a short-term basis, while ignoring the long-term ramifications. Line supervisors, for example, may let their equipment suffer to reduce maintenance costs. If the appraisal focuses on a narrow set of results criteria to the exclusion of other important process issues, the system may suffer from criterion deficiency and may unintentionally foster the attitude that "what gets measured gets done." In fact, in any job involving interaction with others, it is not enough to simply look at production or sales figures. Factors such as cooperation, adaptability, initiative, and concern for human relations may be important to job success. If these factors are important job standards, they should be added to the appraisal review. Thus, to be realistic, both the results and the methods or processes used to achieve them should be considered.[38]

Management by Objectives

One method that attempts to overcome some of the limitations of results appraisals is **management by objectives (MBO)**. MBO is a philosophy of management first proposed by Peter Drucker in 1954 that has employees establish objectives (such as production costs, sales per product, quality standards, and profits) through consultation with their superiors and then uses these objectives as a basis for evaluation.[39] MBO is a system involving a cycle (Figure 8.6) that begins with setting the organization's common goals and objectives and ultimately returns to that step. The system acts as a goal-setting process whereby objectives are established for the organization (Step 1), departments (Step 2), and individual managers and employees (Step 3).

As Figure 8.6 illustrates, a significant feature of the cycle is the establishment of specific goals by the employee, but those goals are based on a broad statement of employee responsibilities prepared by the supervisor. Employee-established goals are discussed with the supervisor and jointly reviewed and modified until both parties are satisfied with them (Step 4). The goal statements are accompanied by a detailed account of the actions the employee proposes to take in order to reach the goals. During periodic reviews, as objective data are made available, the progress that the employee is making toward the goals is then assessed (Step 5). Goals may be changed at this time as new or additional data are received. At the conclusion of a period of time (usually six months or one year), the employee makes a self-appraisal of what he or she has accomplished, substantiating the self-appraisal with factual data wherever possible. The "interview" is an examination of the employee's self-appraisal by the

management by objectives (MBO)
A philosophy of management that rates performance on the basis of employee achievement of goals set by mutual agreement of employee and manager

Figure 8.6 | Performance Appraisal under an MBO Program

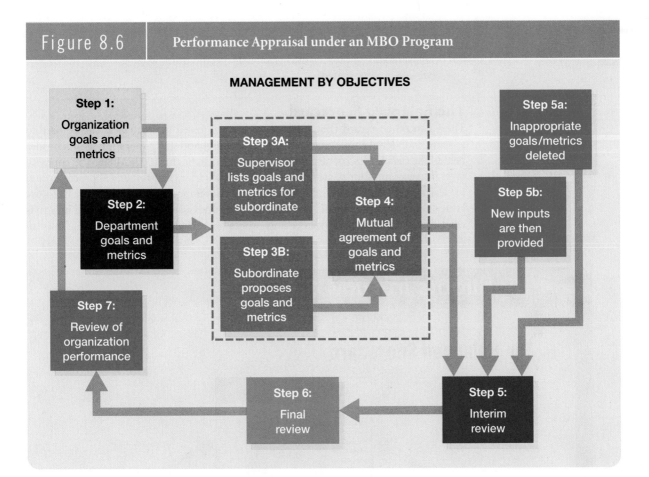

MANAGEMENT BY OBJECTIVES

supervisor and the employee together (Step 6). The final step (Step 7) is reviewing the connection between individual and organizational performance. To ensure success, MBO programs should be viewed as part of a total system for managing, not as merely an addition to the manager's job. Managers must be willing to empower employees to accomplish their objectives on their own, giving them discretion over the methods they use (but holding them accountable for outcomes). The following guidelines may be especially helpful:

1. Managers and employees must be willing to establish goals and objectives together. Goal setting has been shown to improve employee performance, typically ranging from 10 to 25 percent. Goal setting works because it helps employees focus on important tasks and makes them accountable for completing these tasks. It also establishes an automatic feedback system that aids learning, because employees can regularly evaluate their performance against their goals.[40]

2. Objectives should be quantifiable and measurable for the long and short term. However, goal statements should be accompanied by a description of how that goal will be accomplished.

3. Expected results must be under the employee's control. Recall our early discussion of criterion contamination.

4. Goals and objectives must be consistent for each level (top executive, manager, and employee).
5. Managers and employees must establish specific times when goals are to be reviewed and evaluated.

The Balanced Scorecard

The Balanced Scorecard (BSC), which we first discussed in Chapter 2, can be used to appraise individual employees, teams, business units, and the corporation itself. The idea behind the Balanced Scorecard model is shown in Highlights in HRM 8.6. The appraisal takes into account four related categories: (1) financial, (2) customer, (3) processes, and (4) learning. These internal processes—product development, service, and the like—are critical for creating customer satisfaction and loyalty. Customer value creation in turn is what drives financial performance and profitability. Highlights in HRM 8.7 shows an

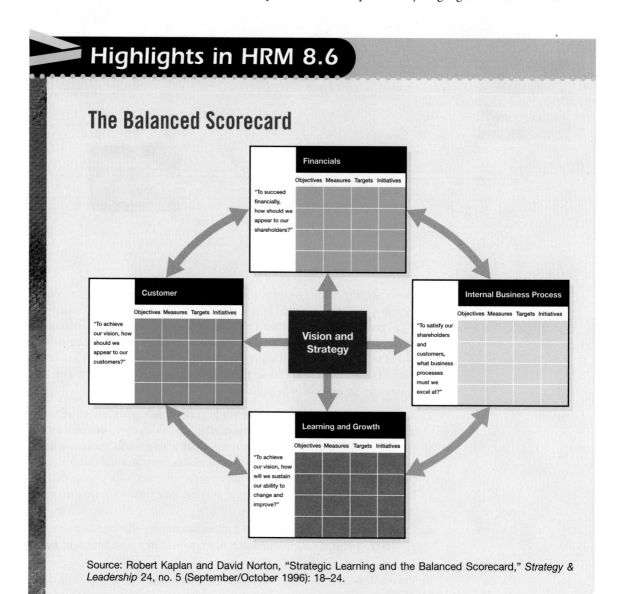

Highlights in HRM 8.6

The Balanced Scorecard

Financials

"To succeed financially, how should we appear to our shareholders?"

Objectives　Measures　Targets　Initiatives

Customer

"To achieve our vision, how should we appear to our customers?"

Objectives　Measures　Targets　Initiatives

Vision and Strategy

Internal Business Process

"To satisfy our shareholders and customers, what business processes must we excel at?"

Objectives　Measures　Targets　Initiatives

Learning and Growth

"To achieve our vision, how will we sustain our ability to change and improve?"

Objectives　Measures　Targets　Initiatives

Source: Robert Kaplan and David Norton, "Strategic Learning and the Balanced Scorecard," *Strategy & Leadership* 24, no. 5 (September/October 1996): 18–24.

Highlights in HRM 8.7

Enbridge Scorecard

KEY PERFORMANCE INDICATOR	UNIT	BASELINE	ANNUAL TARGET	MONTH OF: JANUARY 2006				YEAR-TO-DATE			
MEASURE				ACTUAL	ACTUAL TARGET	ACTUAL TARGET	VARIANCE	ACTUAL	ACTUAL TARGET	VARIANCE	VARIANCE
Financial											
Department O&M	000$	30,839	33,598								
Customer											
Int. Client Satisfaction —Quality & Value of Services	%	95	93.8								
Employee											
Company Absenteeism (Annualized)	Days	2.33	2.85								
Critical Employee Retention	%	99.8	97.5								
Attraction/Recruitment Effectiveness	%	81	86								
Career/Learning Opportunities	%	63.2	59								
Company Employee Survey—Employee Engagement	%	61.6	64								
Company Employee Survey—Supervisory Effectiveness	%	67.3	67.7								
Company Succession Readiness	%	55.1	51.3								

Source: Jane Haberbusch, VP of Human Resources, Enbridge.

example of a scorecard used for this process at Enbridge. As you can see, the corporation's objectives have already been spelled out on the scorecard. Similar in some ways to MBO, the BSC enables managers to translate broad corporate goals into divisional, departmental, and team goals in a cascading fashion. Many firms have adopted the Balanced Scorecard approach, but it is neither a flawless nor a simple performance management system. For example, in a survey conducted by the Society for Human Resource Management, 73 percent of organizations using the approach said they had clearly articulated the strategic direction of their firm. But only 44 percent of those firms said the direction was communicated well to employees.

Some recommendations for ensuring the method's success include the following:

- *Translate the strategy into a scorecard of clear objectives.* As the BSC process begins with strategic objectives, unless these are clear the rest of the system is doomed to ambiguity and potential failure. Translating a strategy into objectives provides managers and front-line employees with goals that are more understandable and attainable. Typically, having fewer goals adds clarity and focus.

- *Attach measures to each objective.* In order for managers and employees to know if and when the objectives are achieved, clear measures must be attached to each goal. Each objective should be given at least one metric that can be measured either by a pre-existing system or manually within an organization.

- *Cascade scorecards to the front line.* It is often said that the real strategic work happens at the front line. In order for all employees to understand how their roles and job duties are aligned with higher-level goals, scorecards should be cascaded to the individual level. Cascading scorecards ensures that strategy then becomes "everyone's" job.

- *Provide performance feedback based on measures.* As with other performance management systems, unless managers provide employees with solid feedback on how they are doing, the system is likely to be ineffective. As part of this process, employees must know that they are accountable for achieving their objectives and providing an explanation when they do not hit their targets.

- *Empower employees to make performance improvements.* Individuals, on their own or working in teams, may understand ways of achieving higher performance. One of the benefits of a results-based system such as the BSC is that it gives employees the latitude to continuously improve best-practices methods.

- *Reassess strategy.* One of the key benefits of the BSC is that it is a continuous-loop process. Managers should monitor performance and use this information to reassess the strategy and make continuous adjustments. Those who have had the best success with the BSC argue that the system helps improve communication and learning rather than fixing in place a mechanical set of controls.[41]

Which Performance Appraisal Method to Use?

The choice of method should be based largely on the purpose of the appraisal. Figure 8.7 lists some of the strengths and weaknesses of trait, behaviour, and results approaches to appraisal. Note that the simplest and least expensive techniques often yield the least-accurate information. However, research has not always supported a clear choice among appraisal methods. While researchers and HR managers generally believe that the more sophisticated and more time-consuming methods offer more useful information, this may not always be the case. Says Ronald Gross, an industrial psychologist and human

	ADVANTAGES	**DISADVANTAGES**
Figure 8.7	**Summary of Various Appraisal Methods**	

	ADVANTAGES	DISADVANTAGES
Trait Methods	1. Are inexpensive to develop 2. Use meaningful dimensions 3. Are easy to use	1. Have high potential for rating errors 2. Are not useful for employee counselling 3. Are not useful for allocating rewards 4. Are not useful for promotion decisions
Behavioural Methods	1. Use specific performance dimensions 2. Are acceptable to employees and superiors 3. Are useful for providing feedback 4. Are fair for reward and promotion decisions	1. Can be time-consuming to develop/use 2. Can be costly to develop 3. Have some potential for rating error
Results Methods	1. Have less subjectivity bias 2. Are acceptable to employees and superiors 3. Link individual performance to organizational performance 4. Encourage mutual goal setting 5. Are good for reward and promotion decisions	1. Are time-consuming to develop/use 2. May encourage a short-term perspective 3. May use contaminated criteria 4. May use deficient criteria

resources consultant, "I can't judge a performance-appraisal system just by looking at the paperwork. The back of an envelope can work just fine. I've seen many systems fail miserably because they're too complex, too time-consuming, and too burdensome. I've never seen a system fail because it was too simple."[42] One way to assess whether an organization's appraisal system is effective is by doing an annual, or at least periodic, audit of the process. Highlights in HRM 8.8 shows a sample survey that HR managers can ask

Highlights in HRM 8.8

Appraising the Appraisal System

Using a graphical rating scale of 1 (strongly disagree) to 5 (strongly agree), rate your performance management system in relation to the following statements:

- Our performance management system reflects our company's mission and values; it reflects our desired company culture.
- Our performance management system has the full commitment and active participation of our CEO and senior management team.
- Our business strategy is clear, including our key business drivers and the metrics used to track them (for example, financial, operational, employee engagement, customer and client).
- Our managers understand how to cascade our company goals down through the organization to ensure that they are effectively linked to individual employee goals.
- Individual goals are truly linked to our business drivers, and effective two-way communication links are clearly established.

(continued on next page)

- Our performance appraisal process distinguishes between observable behavioural dimensions and the frequency of those behaviours (for examples, appraisals based on core competencies or the mastery of certain behaviours).
- Our performance management system incorporates feedback from multiple sources (such as, 360-degree feedback and/or another form of multirater feedback).
- Our performance management system outlines clear standards of performance and rewards eligibility for high performers, solid performers, and marginal performers in the following scenarios:
  - Merit increases
  - Annual incentives
  - Long-term incentives
  - Discretionary incentives
- Our performance management system provides an ongoing comprehensive training program for:
  - Managers conducting performance appraisals
  - Individuals being appraised
- Our performance management system provides additional support services for professional and career development to managers and employees.
- We are able to accurately determine the ROI of the PMS.
- Our existing technology supports our performance management system objectives as designed (that is, in accordance with system requirements) to include:
  - The various raters and reviewers we wish to involve in the process
  - The capture of information throughout the performance cycle (including planning, forecasting, progress review, and end-of-year evaluation)
  - Sharing data across HR and other business applications (including pay, learning and development, workforce, and succession planning)
  - Providing the necessary level of data security and archiving
- Our performance management system is capable of real-time analysis of performance data to identify trends in relation to:
  - Performance differentiation
  - Pay differentiation
  - Performance gaps/developmental needs
- Our internal business partners are able to access and use the performance management system.

Source: Leslie A. Weatherly, "Performance Management: Getting It Right from the Start," *HR Magazine* 49, no. 3 (March 2004): S1–S12. Reprinted with permission of HR Magazine published by the Society for Human Resource Management, Alexandria, VA.

both managers and employees to complete on a periodic basis. This should give HR a better sense of whether the appraisal processes is improving.

Of course, having a first-rate appraisal method does no good if the manager simply "shoves it in a drawer." Even a rudimentary system, when used properly, can initiate a discussion between managers and employees that genuinely drives superior performance. These issues are discussed next under the topic of performance appraisal interviews. In addition, performance appraisals shouldn't be just for middle managers and rank-and-file employees. If the organization's goals are to cascade downward, the firm's top executives need to be involved in the appraisal process as well.

Appraisal Interviews

The appraisal interview is perhaps the most important part of the entire performance appraisal process. The appraisal interview gives a manager the opportunity to discuss a subordinate's performance record and to explore areas of possible improvement and growth. It also provides an opportunity to identify the subordinate's attitudes and feelings more thoroughly and thus to improve communication.

Unfortunately, the interviewer can become overburdened by attempting to discuss too much, such as the employee's past performance and future development goals. Dividing the appraisal interview into two sessions, one for the performance review and the other for the employee's growth plans, can alleviate time pressures. Moreover, by separating the interview into two sessions, the interviewer can give each session the proper attention it deserves. It can be difficult for a supervisor to perform the role of both evaluator and counsellor in the same review period. Dividing the sessions may also improve communication between the parties, thereby reducing stress and defensiveness.

The format for the appraisal interview will be determined in large part by the purpose of the interview, the type of appraisal system used, and the organization of the interview form. Most appraisal interviews attempt to give feedback to employees on how well they are performing their jobs and on planning for their future development. Interviews should be scheduled far enough in advance to allow the interviewee, as well as the interviewer, to prepare for the discussion. Usually ten days to two weeks is a sufficient amount of lead time.

Three Types of Appraisal Interviews

The individual who has probably studied different approaches to performance appraisal interviews most thoroughly is Norman R. F. Maier. In his classic book *The Appraisal Interview*, he analyzes the cause-and-effect relationships in three types of appraisal interviews: tell-and-sell, tell-and-listen, and problem solving.

Tell-and-Sell Interview

The skills required in the tell-and-sell interview include the ability to persuade an employee to change in a prescribed manner. This may require the development of new behaviours on the part of the employee and skillful use of motivational incentives on the part of the appraiser/supervisor.

Tell-and-Listen Interview

In the tell-and-listen interview, the skills required include the ability to communicate the strong and weak points of an employee's job performance during the first part of the interview. During the second part of the interview, the employee's feelings about the appraisal are thoroughly explored. The supervisor is still in the role of appraiser, but the method requires listening to disagreement and coping with defensive behaviour without attempting to refute any statements. The tell-and-listen method assumes that the opportunity to release frustrated feelings will help reduce or remove those feelings.

Problem-Solving Interview

The skills associated with the problem-solving interview are consistent with the nondirective procedures of the tell-and-listen method. Listening, accepting, and responding to feelings are essential elements of the problem-solving interview. However, this method goes beyond an interest in the employee's feelings. It seeks to stimulate growth and development in the employee by discussing the problems, needs, innovations, satisfactions, and dissatisfactions the employee has encountered on the job since the last appraisal interview. Maier recommends this method, because the objective of appraisal is normally to stimulate growth and development in the employee.

Managers should not assume that only one type of appraisal interview is appropriate for every review session. Rather, they should be able to use one or more of the interview types, depending on the topic being discussed or on the behaviour of the employee being appraised. The interview should be seen as requiring a flexible approach.

Conducting the Appraisal Interview

While there are probably no hard-and-fast rules for how to conduct an appraisal interview, some guidelines may increase the employee's acceptance of the feedback, satisfaction with the interview, and intention to improve in the future. Many of the principles of effective interviewing discussed in Chapter 6 apply to performance appraisal interviews as well. Here are some other guidelines that should also be considered.

Ask for a Self-Assessment

As noted earlier in the chapter, it is useful to have employees evaluate their own performance prior to the appraisal interview. Even if this information is not used formally,

There are different approaches to performance appraisal interviews. A problem-solving approach may be the best.

© RACHEL EPSTEIN/PHOTOEDIT

the self-appraisal starts the employee thinking about his or her accomplishments. Self-appraisal also ensures that the employee knows against what criteria he or she is being evaluated, thus eliminating any potential surprises.

Recent research evidence suggests that employees are more satisfied and view the appraisal system as providing more procedural justice when they have input into the process. When the employee has evaluated his or her own performance, the interview can be used to discuss areas in which the manager and the employee have reached different conclusions—not so much to resolve the "truth," but to work toward a resolution of problems.

Invite Participation

The core purpose of a performance appraisal interview is to initiate a dialogue that will help an employee improve his or her performance. To the extent that an employee is an active participant in that discussion, the more likely it is that the root causes and obstacles to performance will be uncovered, and the more likely it is that constructive ideas for improvement will be raised. In addition, research evidence suggests that participation is strongly related to an employee's satisfaction with the appraisal feedback, the extent to which the employee believes it is fair and useful, and his or her intention to improve performance. As a rule of thumb, supervisors should spend only about 30–35 percent of the time talking during the interview. The rest of the time they should be listening to employees respond to questions.

Express Appreciation

Praise is a powerful motivator, and in an appraisal interview, particularly, employees are seeking positive feedback. It is frequently beneficial to start the appraisal interview by expressing appreciation for what the employee has done well. In this way, he or she may be less defensive and more likely to talk about aspects of the job that are not going so well. However, try to avoid obvious use of the "sandwich technique" in which positive statements are followed by negative ones, which are then followed by positive statements. This approach may not work for several reasons. Praise often alerts the employee that criticism will be coming. If managers follow an appraisal form, the problem of the sandwich technique will often be avoided. Furthermore, if employees are kept informed of their behaviour on a regular basis, there will be no need to use this appraisal technique.

Minimize Criticism

Employees who have a good relationship with their managers may be able to handle criticism better than those who do not. However, even the most stoic employees can absorb only so much criticism before they start to get defensive. If an employee has many areas in need of improvement, managers should focus on those few objective issues that are most problematic or most important to the job. Some tips for using criticism constructively include the following:

- *Consider whether it is really necessary.* Frustration with performance problems sometimes leads to criticism that is little more than a manager "letting off steam." Make certain that the criticism focuses on a recurrent problem or a consistent pattern of behaviour.
- *Don't exaggerate.* Even managers who dislike criticizing may find that, once they get started, they tend to overdo it. Sometimes we overstate problems in

order to be convincing or to demonstrate our concern. Try to keep criticism simple, factual, and to the point. Avoid using terms such as *always, completely*, and *never.*

- *Watch your timing.* Properly timed criticism can often mean the difference between success and failure. Even good criticism given late in the day, for example, can touch a raw nerve if the employee is tired.

- *Make improvement your goal.* "Laying it on the line" is not likely to be useful unless it clarifies a path to improved performance. Criticism needs to be complemented with managerial support. This point is elaborated on next.[43]

Change the Behaviour, Not the Person

Managers frequently try to play psychologist, to "figure out" why an employee has acted a certain way. However, when dealing with a problem area, in particular, remember that it is not the person who is bad, but the actions exhibited on the job. Avoid suggestions about personal traits to change; instead suggest more acceptable ways of performing. For example, instead of focusing on a person's "unreliability," a manager might focus on the fact that the employee "has been late to work seven times this month." It is difficult for employees to change who they are; it is usually much easier for them to change how they act.

Focus on Solving Problems

In addressing performance issues, it is frequently tempting to get into the "blame game" in which both manager and employee enter into a potentially endless discussion of why a situation has arisen. Frequently, solving problems requires an analysis of the causes, but ultimately the appraisal interview should be directed at devising a solution to the problem.

Be Supportive

One of the better techniques for engaging an employee in the problem-solving process is for the manager to ask, "What can I do to help?" Employees frequently attribute performance problems to either real or perceived obstacles (such as bureaucratic procedures or inadequate resources). By being open and supportive, the manager conveys to the employee that he or she will try to eliminate external roadblocks and will work with the employee to achieve higher standards.

Establish Goals

Since a major purpose of the appraisal interview is to make plans for improvement, it is important to focus the interviewee's attention on the future rather than the past. In setting goals with an employee, the manager should observe the following points:

- Emphasize strengths on which the employee can build rather than weaknesses to overcome and how the employee's efforts will contribute to the organization during the coming year.

- Concentrate on opportunities for growth that exist within the framework of the employee's present position and drop unproductive tasks.

- Limit plans for growth to a few important items that can be accomplished within a reasonable period of time.

> ▶ Establish specific action plans that spell out how each goal will be achieved. These action plans may also include a list of contacts, resources, and timetables for follow-up.

Many managers are as nervous about administering appraisals as employees are about receiving them. Some supervisors may be tempted to establish difficult goals with their subordinates. The ethical issues surrounding unreasonable goals are discussed in Ethics in HRM.

Ethics in HRM

Stretch Goals

Employees are being asked to set performance goals, labelled "stretch goals," that ask them to do such things as double their sales or increase response time to customers threefold. Research has shown that the establishment of goals results in higher productivity. So if goals are good, are super goals better?

"Not necessarily," says Steve Kerr, General Electric's chief learning officer. In his opinion, most managers don't know how to manage stretch targets. Companies set ambitious goals for their employees but fail to provide them with the resources they need to achieve them. They are saying, in effect, "We aren't going to give you any more people or money, so your solution is to work smarter and be creative." The only resource left to employees is their personal time, and so North Americans are working harder than employees in any other developed country. They are working evenings and weekends, with fewer vacations. "That's immoral," says Kerr. "Companies have a moral obligation to provide the tools to meet tough goals."

How should stretch goals be managed? The goal must be seen as achievable, and not provoke a reaction of "You've got to be kidding." People must also realize that creative energy can be increased. For example, in one innovation training program, teams are given an orange and told that each person must handle the orange, but that the orange must end up in the hands of the person who started with it. All teams start by throwing the orange to team members; this takes nine seconds. They try to reduce the time to seven seconds by throwing faster or in tighter circles. When told that it is possible to do this task in one second, they get creative: they stack their hands and the first person drops the orange through the stacked but open hands and catches it at the bottom.

If the stretch goals aren't achieved, then punishment should not be used. Be careful with high achievers who are already stretching, or these winners will feel like losers if they can't meet impossible goals. Provide the tools; asking people to double their quota without ensuring backup is demoralizing. Finally, share the wealth. If the achievement results in additional funds flowing to the organization, split the incremental savings or gains.

Some employees, masters at the politics of organizations, play games with stretch goals. They negotiate hard for modest, achievable goals, while arguing that these are stretch targets. Others, with high needs for achievement, accept the stretch targets. At bonus time, the modest goal setters have met or surpassed their goals and receive merit increases. Having failed to achieve impossible targets, the less Machiavellian employees receive nothing.

Source: Adapted from S. Sherman, "Stretch Goals: The Dark Side of Asking for Miracles," *Fortune*, November 13, 1995: 231.

Follow Up Day to Day

Ideally, performance feedback should be an ongoing part of a manager's job. Feedback is most useful when it is immediate and specific to a particular situation. Unfortunately, both managers and employees are frequently happy to finish the interview and file away the appraisal form. A better approach is to have informal talks periodically, perhaps quarterly, to follow up on the issues raised in the appraisal interview. Levi Strauss, for example, offers employees informal feedback and coaching sessions on an ongoing basis. This puts managers in more of a coaching role versus that of a judge.

Improving Performance

In many instances the appraisal interview will provide the basis for noting deficiencies in employee performance and for making plans for improvement. Unless these deficiencies are brought to the employee's attention, they are likely to continue until they become quite serious. Sometimes underperformers may not understand exactly what is expected of them. However, once their responsibilities are clarified, they are in a position to take the corrective action needed to improve their performance.

Identifying Sources of Ineffective Performance

Performance is a function of several factors, but perhaps it can be boiled down to three primary concerns: ability, motivation, and environment. Each individual has a unique pattern of strengths and weaknesses that play a part. But talented employees with low motivation are not likely to succeed. In addition, other factors in the work environment—or even in the external environment, which includes personal, family, and community concerns—can affect performance either positively or negatively. Figure 8.8 may provide a better picture of how these three factors (motivation, environment, and ability) can influence performance.

It is recommended that a diagnosis of poor employee performance focus on these three interactive elements. As shown in Highlights in HRM 8.9, if an employee's performance is not up to standards, the cause could be a skill problem (knowledge, abilities, technical competencies), an effort problem (motivation to get the job done), and/or

Figure 8.8	Factors That Influence Performance

MOTIVATION	ENVIRONMENT	ABILITY
• Career ambition	• Equipment/materials	• Technical skills
• Employee conflict	• Job design	• Interpersonal skills
• Frustration	• Economic conditions	• Problem-solving skills
• Fairness/satisfaction	• Unions	• Analytical skills
• Goals/expectations	• Rules and policies	• Communication skills
	• Management support	• Physical limitations
	• Laws and regulations	

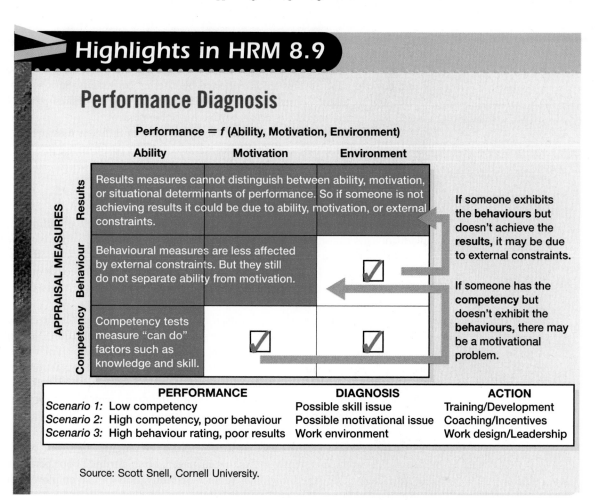

Highlights in HRM 8.9

Performance Diagnosis

Performance = *f* (Ability, Motivation, Environment)

		Ability	Motivation	Environment
APPRAISAL MEASURES	**Results**	Results measures cannot distinguish between ability, motivation, or situational determinants of performance. So if someone is not achieving results it could be due to ability, motivation, or external constraints.		
	Behaviour	Behavioural measures are less affected by external constraints. But they still do not separate ability from motivation.	☑	
	Competency	Competency tests measure "can do" factors such as knowledge and skill.	☑	☑

If someone exhibits the **behaviours** but doesn't achieve the **results**, it may be due to external constraints.

If someone has the **competency** but doesn't exhibit the **behaviours**, there may be a motivational problem.

PERFORMANCE	DIAGNOSIS	ACTION
Scenario 1: Low competency	Possible skill issue	Training/Development
Scenario 2: High competency, poor behaviour	Possible motivational issue	Coaching/Incentives
Scenario 3: High behaviour rating, poor results	Work environment	Work design/Leadership

Source: Scott Snell, Cornell University.

some problem in the external conditions of work (poor economic conditions, worker shortages due to downsizing, difficult sales territories).[44] Any one of these problem areas could cause performance to suffer.

Performance Diagnosis

Although performance appraisal systems can often tell us who is not performing well, they typically cannot reveal why. Unfortunately, research evidence suggests that managers often make wrong attributions for poor performance. They often assume that poor performance is first due to lack of ability, second to poor motivation, and then to external constraints. Ironically, research evidence also suggests that we tend to make just the opposite attributions about our own performance. We first attribute poor performance to external constraints such as bad luck or factors out of our control. If the problem is internal, then we typically attribute it to temporary factors such as motivation or energy ("I had a bad day") and only as a last resort admit that it might be due to ability.

So what can be done to diagnose the real reasons for poor performance? More specifically, how can managers identify the root causes and get to work on a solution that improves performance? By comparing different performance measures, managers can begin to get an idea of the underlying causes of performance problems. For example, as shown in Highlights in HRM 8.9, results measures cannot distinguish between ability, motivation, and situational determinants of performance. So if someone is not achieving desired results it could be due to ability, motivation, or external constraints. On the other hand, behavioural measures are less affected by external constraints. So if someone is demonstrating all the desired behaviours but is not achieving the desired results, logic suggests that it may be due to factors beyond his or her control.

Other kinds of diagnoses are possible by comparing different measures of performance. And only by correctly diagnosing the causes of performance problems can managers—and employees—hope to improve them.

Managing Ineffective Performance

Once the sources of performance problems are known, a course of action can be planned. This action may lie in providing training in areas that would increase the knowledge and/or skills needed for effective performance. A transfer to another job or department might give an employee a chance to become a more effective member of the organization. In other instances, greater attention may have to be focused on ways to motivate the individual.

If ineffective performance persists, it may be necessary to transfer the employee, take disciplinary action, or discharge the person from the organization. Not only is the ineffective behaviour likely affecting the manager and the organization as a whole, it is also probably affecting the person's co-workers. Whatever action is taken to cope with ineffective performance, however, should be done with objectivity, fairness, and a recognition of the feelings of the individual involved. A new manager may also need training in this area because it is one of the most difficult aspects of being a manager.

A final word of caution when it comes to managing performance problems: Because research consistently shows that managers often attribute poor performance to characteristics of the individuals (ability or motivation), while employees themselves typically blame external factors for their miscues, this can establish a negative cycle if not handled properly. Managers who assume that employees are not motivated or not capable may begin to treat them differently (perhaps supervising them too closely or watching for their next mistake). This can actually decrease an employee's motivation and cause him or her to withdraw. Seeing this, the manager may confirm his or her initial beliefs that the employee does not "measure up." As you can see, this "set-up-to-fail" syndrome can be self-fulfilling and self-reinforcing. It is hoped that the ideas and suggestions given in this chapter will help managers accurately identify who is performing well (and why) and give them some focus for improving employee productivity.[45]

SUMMARY

objective 1

Performance appraisal programs serve many purposes, but in general those purposes can be clustered into two categories: administrative and developmental. The administrative purposes include decisions about who will be promoted, transferred, or laid off. They can also include compensation decisions. Developmental decisions include those related to improving and enhancing an individual's capabilities. These include identifying a person's strengths and weaknesses, eliminating external performance obstacles, and establishing training needs. The combination of administrative and developmental purposes of performance appraisal reflect, in a specific way, human resources management's larger role of integrating the individual with the organization.

In many organizations, performance appraisals are seen as a necessary evil. Managers frequently avoid conducting appraisals because they dislike playing the role of judge. Further, if managers are not adequately trained, subjectivity and organizational politics can distort the reviews. This situation tends to be self-defeating in that such managers frequently do not develop good feedback skills and are often not prepared to conduct an appraisal. As a consequence, the appraisal is done begrudgingly once a year and then forgotten.

The success of an organization depends largely on the performance of its human resources. To determine the contributions of each individual, it is necessary to have a formal appraisal program with clearly stated objectives. Carefully defined performance standards that are reliable, strategically relevant, and free from either criterion deficiency or contamination are essential foundations for evaluation. Appraisals should be treated with the same concerns for validity as are selection tests. For example, ratings must be job-related, employees must understand their performance standards in advance, appraisers must be able to observe job performance, appraisers must be trained, feedback must be given, and an appeals procedure must be established.

Using multiple raters is frequently a good idea because different individuals see different facets of an employee's performance. The supervisor, for example, has legitimate authority over an employee and is in a good position to discern whether he or she is contributing to the goals of the organization. Peers and team members, on the other hand, often have an unfiltered view of an employee's work activity, particularly related to issues such as cooperation and dependability. Subordinates often provide good information about whether an employee is facilitating their work, and customers (both internal and external) can convey the extent to which an employee adds value and meets their requirements. Self-appraisal is useful, if for no other reason than it encourages employees to think about their strengths, weaknesses, and future goals. An increasing number of organizations are using multiple raters—or 360-degree appraisal—to get a more comprehensive picture of employee performance. Regardless of the source of appraisal information, appraisers should be thoroughly trained in the particular methods they will use in evaluating their subordinates. Participation in developing rating scales, such as a BARS, automatically provides such training.

Several methods can be used for performance appraisal. These include trait approaches (such as graphic rating scales, mixed-standard scales, forced-choice forms, and essays), behavioural methods (such as critical-incident ratings, checklists, BARS, and BOS), and results methods (MBO). The choice of method depends on the purpose of the appraisal. Trait appraisals are simple to develop and complete, but they have problems in subjectivity and are not useful for feedback. Behavioural methods provide more specific information for giving feedback but can be time-consuming and costly to develop. Results appraisals are more objective and can link individual performance to the organization as a whole, but they may encourage a short-term perspective (such as annual goals) and may not include subtle yet important aspects of performance.

The degree to which the performance appraisal program benefits the organization and its members is directly related to the quality of the appraisal interviews that are conducted. Interviewing skills are best developed through instruction and supervised practice. Although there are various approaches to the interview, research suggests that employee participation and goal setting lead to higher satisfaction and improved performance. Discussing problems, showing support, minimizing criticism, and rewarding effective performance are also beneficial practices. In the interview, deficiencies in employee performance can be discussed and plans for improvement can be made.

KEY TERMS

behaviour observation scale
(BOS), 372
behaviourally anchored rating
scale (BARS), 371
contrast error, 366
critical incident, 371
customer appraisal, 358
error of central tendency, 364
essay method, 369

forced-choice method, 368
graphic rating-scale method, 368
leniency or strictness error, 364
management by objectives
(MBO), 374
manager and/or supervisor
appraisal, 356
mixed-standard scale method,
368

peer appraisal, 357
performance appraisal, 348
performance management, 348
recency error, 365
self-appraisal, 356
similar-to-me error, 366
subordinate appraisal, 356
team appraisal, 357

DISCUSSION QUESTIONS

1. Eighty percent of Canadian organizations have performance appraisal systems. List some reasons why 20 percent would not choose to implement one.
2. Develop a list of the characteristics of effective service for fast food servers at places such as Tim Hortons. Over your next five visits, rate the servers against the criteria that you have developed. Did your criteria meet the performance standards of relevant and reliable, or were they subject to criterion deficiency or contamination?
3. Develop a ten-item checklist to be used to rate student behaviour. (Example: always submits assignments on time.) Rate your own behaviour against this list. Then ask friends and family members to rate your behaviour. Are there differences? If so, how would you explain them?
4. Take two of the items from question 3, and develop a behaviourally anchored rating scale for each of these items. Then rate yourself and ask others to rate you using the BARS. Did the ratings change? If so, why?
5. Think of a friend or a family member whose behaviour you wish to change (example; your friend is usually late for events that you have organized). Using the problem-solving interview, and the

suggestions for conducting an effective appraisal interview, provide appraisal feedback to your friend.
6. What sources could be used to evaluate the performance of people working in the following jobs?
   a. Sales representative
   b. TV repairer
   c. Director of nursing in a hospital
   d. HR manager
   e. Air traffic controller
7. In many organizations, evaluators submit ratings to their immediate superiors for review before discussing them with the individual employees they have rated. What advantages are there to this procedure?
8. What are the pros and cons of trait, behaviour, and results appraisals?
9. Three types of appraisal interviews are described in this chapter.
   a. What different skills are required for each type of appraisal interview? What reactions can one expect from using these different skills?
   b. How can one develop the skills needed for the problem-solving type of interview?
   c. Which method do you feel is the least desirable? Why?

INTERNET EXERCISE

Use the forms found on the University of Victoria website to appraise

1. the performance of members of your study or work groups at http:/web.uvic.ca/uvicpea

2. the performance of your instructor at http:/web.uvic.ca/uvicpea/instructor

HRM Experience

Performance Diagnosis

Managing performance is an important—yet delicate—process for managers to undertake. They need to make tough calls at times regarding who is performing well or not. Also, they need to play the role of coach to help each employee improve his or her performance. One of the toughest aspects of performance management is assessing why someone is not performing well. Although it may be easy to spot who is not performing well, it is not always easy to diagnose the underlying causes of poor performance (such as motivation, ability, and external constraints). But without a correct diagnosis, it is nearly impossible to cure the problem.

Assignment

Following are descriptions of three different employees. Describe the potential causes of poor performance in each case. For each potential cause, identify appropriate solutions to enhance performance.

1. *Carl Spackler* is the assistant greenskeeper at Bushwood Country Club. Over the past few months, members have been complaining that gophers are destroying the course and digging holes in the greens. Although Carl has been working evenings and weekends to address the situation, the problem persists. Unfortunately, his boss is interested only in results, and because the gophers are still there, he contends that Carl is not doing his job. He has accused Carl of "slacking off" and threatened his job.

2. *Clark Griswold* works in research and development for a chemical company that makes nonnutritive food additives. His most recent assignment has been the development of a nonstick aerosol cooking spray, but the project is way behind schedule and seems to be going nowhere. CEO Frank Shirley is decidedly upset and has threatened that if things don't improve, he will suspend bonuses again this year as he did last year. Clark feels dejected, because without the bonus he won't be able to take his family on vacation.

3. *Bonnie Molloy* is the host of a local television talk show called *Morning City*. Although she is a talented performer and comic, Bonnie has an unacceptable record of tardiness. The show's producer, David Bellows, is frustrated, because the problem has affected the quality of the show. On several occasions, Bonnie was unprepared when the show went on the air. Bellows has concluded that Bonnie is not a morning person and has thought about replacing her with a different host.

BIZFLIX EXERCISES

Seabiscuit: George Rides Seabiscuit

This scene will show you several aspects of appraising and improving performance. Watch for performance standards, peer appraisal, behaviour shaping, and coaching.

Combine a jockey who is blind in one eye with an undersized, ill-tempered thoroughbred and an unusual trainer. The result: the Depression-era champion racehorse

Seabiscuit. This engaging film shows the training and development of Seabiscuit by trainer "Silent" Tom Smith (Chris Cooper) and jockey Red Pollard (Tobey Maguire). The enduring commitment of owner Charles Howard (Jeff Bridges) ensures the ultimate success of Seabiscuit on the racing circuit.

The *Seabiscuit* scene is a composite edited from DVD Chapter 21 toward the end of the film. In earlier scenes, Red severely injured a leg—he cannot ride Seabiscuit in the competition against War Admiral. Samuel Riddle (Eddie Jones), War Admiral's owner, has described any new rider as immaterial to the race's result. The scene begins with Red giving George Wolff (Gary Stevens), Seabiscuit's new jockey, some tips about riding him.

What to Watch for and Ask Yourself

- Does Red set clear performance standards for George? If he does, what are they?
- Red and George are both jockeys who competed against each other in earlier races. Do these scenes show peer appraisal or appraisal by people of different rank or position? Which characteristics of the performance appraisal process does this scene show?
- An earlier section, "Performance Appraisal Methods," discussed many approaches to performance appraisal. Which method or methods most closely match(es) what occurs in these scenes? Identify examples in the scenes that match the performance appraisal method or methods you picked.

case study 1

Online Performance Management

Hospitals are assessed every few years against a set of national standards. The assessors are external experts as well as internal staff. As part of a recent assessment, Mount Sinai Hospital in Toronto, Ontario, was asked to improve its performance management system. Additionally, staff had indicated in surveys that they wanted a performance review that was regular, fair, and consistent. Mount Sinai chose an automated system that would support their Balanced Scorecard measurement system, which measures efficiency and growth, safety, patient and family-centred care, learning, and innovation.

Debbie Fischer, senior VP of organizational development and strategic projects, praises the new online system. Managers now have access to previous performance appraisals and feedback from other employees, and can make comparisons by area of competency or by work group. They can generate reports about competency gaps and training plans. The system contains reminders about appraisal and training dates. Multiple raters can provide input, and may assess anecdotally or numerically or a combination of both. Trent Dark, director of organizational developmemt at Mount Sinai, says "there are metrics and benchmarks for the different categories, and we track competencies in teamwork, leadership and change management. There are milestones for specific activities such as training."

The process starts with an employee self-evaluation. This evaluation is given to the manager who works with the employee to develop a learning plan.

QUESTIONS

1. An expert in hospital accreditation, Evelyn Dean, states "The best way to start performance management in a health care environment is with training and development. Hospital employees value learning and professional development. A focus on development helps with union support as well." Why would the union be interested in the performance management system?
2. What are the advantages of an online performance management system? Can you think of some potential problems with this system?

Source: Adapted from Susan Singh, "Mount Sinai Goes Online for Performance Management" *Canadian HR Reporter*, June 20, 2005, pp. 1–4.

case study 2

Workload Worries

A hotel's receiving department is responsible for checking deliveries of food and beverages, checking what has been received against what has been ordered, and verifying the quality of the merchandise received. In May 2000 an employee of the Westin Ottawa failed to check a case of vegetables, which had started to rot. The receiver, who had been with the hotel for 17 years, admitted that he had not checked the vegetables. As a result, his supervisor gave him a written warning. The employee grieved, stating that he was too busy because the workload was excessive.

There was an investigation, which indicated that the grievor had not worked any overtime, nor had he requested permission to work any overtime. It was also noted that during the receiver's vacation period, the replacement worker had been able to perform the job without any difficulty. There was also evidence that the receiver was taking excessive breaks.

As a result of this investigation, the grievance was denied. In addition, the employee was sent a letter reminding him of his job responsibilities and of the need to restrict himself to the scheduled breaks. As a last step he was given a procedure to follow if he believed that the work was becoming excessive.

QUESTIONS

1. Discuss how a performance appraisal system might have prevented this grievance.
2. Which performance appraisal method would you recommend for this type of job?

case study 3

Bank of Montreal's Balanced Scorecard

In 1990, the Bank of Montreal (BMO) had one major goal: to focus the entire workforce on success. It's a simple idea, but not so easy in execution. How would the company get entry-level tellers to think of their work not just as a means to a paycheque, but as a direct contribution to BMO shareholders? How would it remind corporate executives that their jobs were not just to boost the bottom line, but to charm entire communities?

The answer was BMO executives' Balanced Scorecard approach. To be competitive, executives decided, the bank had to meet the needs of four stakeholders: BMO shareholders, customers, employees, and communities. Executives translated that idea into four goals: Shareholders needed a return on equity, customers needed good service, employees needed to feel loyal and satisfied, and communities needed to feel that the bank made a difference in their neighbourhoods. Return on investment would determine satisfaction for shareholders; surveys and feedback would determine satisfaction for customers, employees, and communities.

Every single department and every employee in every department had to understand how their work contributed to the success of those four goals. So each employee's and each department's performance ratings were revised to reflect their contribution toward each goal. Employees in the customer service department, for instance, were rated by their return on equity (judged by their cost-effectiveness), their customer satisfaction (judged by customer feedback), and their community involvement (judged by any outreach programs or increase in customers).

In some cases, departments were assigned a specific stakeholder. For example, HR was put in charge of the employee piece, ensuring competent, committed workers in a cost-effective way. Similarly, the company's senior vice-president of HR was responsible for training and education aspects to ensure competency, and work/life and career-development programs to help with employee commitment. At the end of the year, the scores from everyone's performance ratings were translated into indexes, ratings from 1 to 10. The index for the employee stakeholder piece was determined by ratings for competency, commitment, and cost-effectiveness. The four indexes for BMO shareholders, customers, employees, and communities were then rolled up into one figure of merit to determine the bonus of BMO's CEO.

QUESTIONS

1. What are the strengths and weaknesses of a Balanced Scorecard approach to performance appraisal?
2. Do you think it's fair to base the bonus paid to BMO's CEO on the four indices comprising the firm's Balanced Scorecard?
3. Do you believe that a Balanced Scorecard approach would be more effective for the administrative or for the developmental purposes of appraisal discussed in this chapter?

CAREER COUNSEL

Obtain a rating of your performance by consulting www.belcourt5e.nelson.com

NOTES AND REFERENCES

1. Susan Scherreik, "Your Performance Review: Make It Perform," *Business Week*, no. 3762 (December 17, 2001): 139; Dick Grote, "Performance Evaluations: Is It Time for a Makeover?" *HRFocus* 77, no. 11 (November 2000): 6–7; Duncan Brown, "Marking the Scorecard: Performance Appraisal Models Are Changing, Shedding Their Reputation for Being Top-Down, Demotivating Influences on a Company," *Grocer* 227, no. 7 (December 4, 2004): 72; "Employers Need to Do a Better Job of Performance Management," *Managing Training & Development* (April 2003): 8.

2. David Brown, "Performance Management Elusive for Public Sector HR," *Canadian HR Reporter*, February 23, 2004, 17.

3. Matthew Boyle, "Performance Reviews: Perilous Curves Ahead," *Fortune* 143, no. 11 (May 28, 2001): 187–88; Susanne Scott and Walter Einstein, "Strategic Performance Appraisal in Team-Based Organizations: One Size Does Not Fit All," *Academy of Management Executive* 15, no. 2 (May 2001): 107–16; "Study Questions Performance Appraisal," *Australasian Business Intelligence* (May 1, 2003); Drew Robb, "Building a Better Workforce: Performance Management Software Can Help You Identify and Develop High-Performing Workers," *HRMagazine* 49, no. 10 (October 2004): 86–93.

4. Jonathan A. Segal, "86 Your Appraisal Process?" *HRMagazine* 45, no. 10 (October 2000): 199–206; Barry Witcher and Rosie

Butterworth, "Honshin Kanri: How Xerox Manages," *Long-Range Planning* 32, no. 3 (June 1999): 323–32.

5. Janet Wiscombe, "Can Pay for Performance Really Work?" *Workforce* 80, no. 8 (August 2001): 28–34; Charlotte Garvey, "Meaningful Tokens of Appreciation: Cash Awards Aren't the Only Way to Motivate Your Workforce," *HRMagazine* 49, no. 8 (August 2004): 101–106.

6. David Allen and Rodger Griffeth, "Test of a Mediated Performance-Turnover Relationship Highlighting the Moderating Roles of Visibility and Reward Contingency," *Journal of Applied Psychology* 86, no. 5 (October 2001): 1014–21; Charles Pettijohn, Linda Pettijohn, and Michael D'Amico, "Characteristics of Performance Appraisals and Their Impact on Sales Force Satisfaction," *Human Resource Development Quarterly* 12, no. 2 (Summer 2001): 127–46; Scott and Einstein, "Strategic Performance Appraisal in Team-Based Organizations," 107–16.

7. Donna Doldwasser, "Me a Trainer?" *Training* 38, no. 4 (April 2001): 60–66; Rebecca Ganzel, "Mike Carter," *Training* 38, no. 7 (July 2001): 28–30; Carla Joinson, "Making Sure Employees Measure Up," *HRMagazine* 46, no. 3 (March 2001): 36–41; Ashish Chandra and Zachary D. Frank, "Utilization of Performance Appraisal Systems in Health Care Organizations and Improvement Strategies for Supervisors," *The Health Care Manager* 23, no. 1 (January–March 2004): 25–31; Morton D. Rosenbaum, "Gratitude Adjustment: When a Pat on the Back Isn't Enough," *Meetings & Conventions* 39, no. 7 (June 2004): 20; James W. Smither, Manuel London, and Richard R. Reilly, "Does Performance Improve Following Multisource Feedback?" *Personnel Psychology* 58, no. 1 (Spring 2005): 33–67.

8. Kathryn Bartol, Cathy Durham, and June Poon, "Influence of Performance Evaluation Rating Segmentation on Motivation and Fairness Perceptions," *Journal of Applied Psychology* 86, no. 6 (December 2001): 1106–19; Elizabeth Douthitt and John Aiello, "The Role of Participation and Control in the Effects of Computer Monitoring on Fairness Perceptions, Task Satisfaction, and Performance," *Journal of Applied Psychology* 86, no. 5 (October 2001): 867–74; Anne P. Hubbell, "Motivating Factors: Perceptions of Justice and Their Relationship with Managerial and Organizational Trust," *Communication Studies* 56, no. 1 (March 2005): 47; Rebecca M. Chory-Assad, "Room for Improvement," *Training* 40, no. 11 (December 2003): 18–20.

9. John Newman, J. Mack Robinson, Larry Tyler, David Dunbar, and Joseph Zager, "CEO Performance Appraisal: Review and Recommendations/Practitioner Application," *Journal of Healthcare Management* 46, no. 1 (January/February 2001): 21–38; Bob Losyk, "How to Conduct a Performance Appraisal," *Public Management* 84, no. 3 (April 2002): 8–12.

10. Michael Arndt, "3M: A Lab for Growth?" *Business Week*, no. 3766 (January 21, 2002): 50–51; "General Motors and Whirlpool: Two Approaches for Developing Performance Benchmarks," *HRFocus* 77, no. 6 (June 2000): 7–10; Doug Cederblom, "From Performance Appraisal to Performance Management: One Agency's Experience," *Public Personnel Management* 31, no. 2 (Summer 2002): 131–40; Sean Way and James Thacker, "The Successful Implementation of Strategic

Human Resource Management Practices: A Canadian Survey," *International Journal of Management* 18, no. 1 (March 2001): 25–32; "Anonymous 360-Feedback Drives Vauxhall Strategy," *Personnel Today* (August 19, 2003): 16; Cindy Romaine, "Staying Relevant: Competencies and Employee Reviews," *Information Outlook* 8, no. 7 (April 2004): 21–25.

11. Jason D. Shaw and Nina Gupta, "Job Complexity, Performance, and Well-Being: When Does Supplies Values Fit Matter?" *Personnel Psychology* 57, no. 4 (Winter 2004): 847–80.

12. Joel Lefkowitz, "The Role of Interpersonal Affective Regard in Supervisory Performance Ratings: A Literature Review and Proposed Causal Model," *Journal of Occupational and Organizational Psychology* 73, no. 1 (March 2000): 67–85; Scott Highhouse, "Assessing the Candidate As a Whole: A Historical and Critical Analysis of Individual Psychological Assessment for Personnel Decision Making," *Personnel Psychology* 55, no. 2 (Summer 2002): 363–397.

13. Timothy Aeppel, "Goodyear Ends Ratings System ahead of Lawsuit," *The Wall Street Journal*, September 12, 2002, B8; "How to Stay 'Legal' with Performance Evaluation and Testing," *Managing Training & Development*, no. 4 (February 2004): 9.

14. Jilly Welch, "Intel Faces Fight over Termination Quotas," *People Management* 3, no. 13 (June 26, 1997): 9; David Martin, Kathryn Bartol, and Patrick Kehoe, "The Legal Ramifications of Performance Appraisal: The Growing Significance," *Public Personnel Management* 29, no. 3 (Fall 2000): 379–406; Gillian Flynn, "Getting Performance Reviews Right," *Workforce* 80, no. 5 (May 2001): 76–78. For a review of other performance appraisal court cases, see Clinton O. Longnecker and Frederick R. Post, "Effective and Legally Defensible Performance Appraisals," *Journal of Compensation and Benefits* 11, no. 6 (May/June 1996): 41–46; David C. Martin, Kathryn M. Bartol, and Patrick E. Kehoe, "The Legal Ramifications of Performance Appraisal: The Growing Significance," *Public Personnel Management* 29, no. 3 (Fall 2000): 381.

15. Joan Brett and Leanne Atwater, "360-Degree Feedback: Accuracy, Reactions, and Perceptions of Usefulness," *Journal of Applied Psychology* 86, no. 5 (October 2001): 930–42; Bruce Pfau, Ira Kay, Kenneth Nowak, and Jai Ghorpade, "Does 360-Degree Feedback Negatively Affect Company Performance?" *HRMagazine* 47, no. 6 (June 2002): 54–59; Maury Peiperl, "Getting 360-Degree Feedback Right," *Harvard Business Review* 79, no. 1 (January 2001): 142–47; Ruth Thaler-Carter, "Whither Global Leaders?" *HRMagazine* 45, no. 5 (May 2000): 82–88; Robert Gandossy and Tina Kao, "Talent Wars: Out of Mind, Out of Practice," *Human Resource Planning* 27, no. 4 (December 2004): 15–20.

16. Bob Rosner, "Squeezing More Respect out of Your Team," *Workforce* 79, no. 7 (July 2000): 80; Dick Grote, "The Secrets of Performance Appraisal: Best Practices from the Masters," *Across the Board* 37, no. 5 (May 2000): 14–20; Edward J. Inderrieden, Robert E. Allen, and Timothy J. Keaveny, "Managerial Discretion in the Use of Self-Ratings in an Appraisal System: The Antecedents and Consequences," *Journal of Managerial Issues* 16, no. 4 (Winter 2004): 460–484.

17. Jeffrey Seglin, "Reviewing Your Boss," *Fortune* 143, no. 12 (June 11, 2001): 248; Ann Harrington, "Workers of the World, Rate Your Boss!" *Fortune* 142, no. 6 (September 18, 2000): 340–42; Robert Thompson, "Management Lite: Less Control, More Innovation," *HRMagazine* 44, no. 8 (August 1999): 10.

18. Brett and Atwater, "360-Degree Feedback," 930–42; Paula Silva and Henry L. Tosi, "Determinants of the Anonymity of the CEO Evaluation Process," *Journal of Managerial Issues* 16, no. 1 (Spring 2004): 87–103.

19. Ann Pomeroy, "Great Places, Inspired Employees: The Nation's Best Employers Show That Inspiring Employee Involvement through Good HR Practices Makes Good Business Sense," *HRMagazine* 49, no. 7 (July 2004): 44–64.

20. John Drexler, Jr., Terry Beehr, and Thomas Stetz, "Peer Appraisals: Differentiation of Individual Performance on Group Tasks," *Human Resource Management* 40, no. 4 (Winter 2001): 333–45.

21. Scott and Einstein, "Strategic Performance Appraisal in Team-Based Organizations," 107–16; Debbie Kibbe and Jill Casner-Lotto, "Ralston Foods: From Greenfield to Maturity in a Team-Based Plant," *Journal of Organizational Excellence* 21, no. 3 (Summer 2002): 57–67; Simon Taggar and Mitchell Neubert, "The Impact of Poor Performers on Team Outcomes: An Empirical Examination of Attribution Theory," *Personnel Psychology* 57, no. 4 (Winter 2004): 935–69.

22. Bradley Kirkman and Benson Rosen, "Powering Up Teams," *Organizational Dynamics* 28, no. 3 (Winter 2000): 48–66; Matthew Valle and Kirk Davis, "Teams and Performance Appraisal: Using Metrics to Increase Reliability and Validity," *Team Performance Management* 5, no. 8 (1999): 238–43.

23. Michael Cohn, "Best Buy Beefs Up Customer Value at the Call Center," *Internet World* 8, no. 6 (June 2002): 42–43; Joe Kohn, "Isuzu Has IDEA for Boosting Sales," *Automotive News* 76, no. 5973 (March 4, 2002): 41; D. L. Radcliff, "A New Paradigm of Feedback," *Executive Excellence* 19, no. 4 (April 2002): 20.

24. Pfau, Kay, Nowak, and Ghorpade, "Does 360-Degree Feedback Negatively Affect Company Performance?" 54–59; Peiperl, "Getting 360-Degree Feedback Right," 142–47; Jack Kondrasuk, and Matt Graybill, "From Paper to Computer," *The Human Resource Professional* 13, no. 6 (November/December 2000): 18–19.

25. David W. Bracken, Lynn Summers, and John Fleenor, "High-Tech 360," *Training and Development* 52, no. 8 (August 1998): 42–45; Gary Meyer, "Performance Reviews Made Easy, Paperless," *HRMagazine* 45, no. 10 (October 2000): 181–84; Douglas P. Shuit, "Huddling with the Coach—Part 2," *Workforce Management* 84, no. 2 (February 1, 2005): 5; "Ceridian and Softscape Announce an Agreement to Deliver Employee Performance and Development Solutions," *Payroll Manager's Report* (May 2004): 13.

26. "Performance Appraisal," *HRMagazine* 47, no. 10 (October 2002): 146; Frank E. Kuzmits, Arthur J. Adams, Lyle Sussman, and Louis E. Raho, "360-Feedback in Health Care Management: A Field Study," *The Health Care Manager* 23, no. 321 (October–December 2004): 321–29.

27. Gary E. Roberts, "Perspectives on Enduring and Emerging Issues in Performance Appraisal," *Public Personnel Management* 27, no. 3 (Fall 1998): 301–20; William Hubbartt, "Bring Performance Appraisal Training to Life," *HRMagazine* 40, no. 5 (May 1995): 166, 168; Filip Lievens, "Assessor Training Strategies and Their Effects on Accuracy, Interrater Reliability, and Discriminant Validity," *Journal of Applied Psychology* 86, no. 2 (April 2001): 255–64; Dick Grote, "Performance Appraisals: Solving Tough Challenges," *HRMagazine* 45, no. 7 (July 2000): 145–50; Leslie A. Weatherly, "Performance Management: Getting It Right from the Start," *HRMagazine* 49, no. 3 (March 2004): S1–S12.

28. Gary P. Latham and Kenneth N. Wexley, *Increasing Productivity through Performance Appraisal*, 2nd ed. (Reading, MA: Addison-Wesley, 1994), 137.

29. Lefkowitz, "The Role of Interpersonal Affective Regard in Supervisory Performance Ratings," 67–85; Edwin Arnold and Marcia Pulich, "Personality Conflicts and Objectivity in Appraising Performance," *The Health Care Manager* 22, no. 3 (July–September 2003): 227.

30. Deidra J. Schleicher and David V. Day, "A Cognitive Evaluation of Frame-of-Reference Rater Training: Content and Process Issues," *Organizational Behaviour and Human Decision Processes* 73, no. 1 (January 1998): 76–101; Wanda Smith, K. Vernard Harrington, and Jeffery Houghton, "Predictors of Performance Appraisal Discomfort: A Preliminary Examination," *Public Personnel Management* 29, no. 1 (Spring 2000): 21–32.

31. Gail Johnson, "Forced Ranking: The Good, the Bad, and the Alternative," *Training* 41, no. 5 (May 2004): 24–31; Christine A. Amalfe and Eileen Quinn Steiner, "Forced Ranking Systems: Yesterday's Legal Target?" *New Jersey Law Journal* (March 28, 2005).

32. Lisa Keeping and Paul Levy, "Performance Appraisal Reaction: Measurement, Modeling, and Method Bias," *Journal of Applied Psychology* 85, no. 5 (October 2000): 708–23.

33. Wendy Boswell and John Boudreau, "Employee Satisfaction with Performance Appraisals and Appraisers: The Role of Perceived Appraisal Use," *Human Resource Development Quarterly* 11, no. 3 (Fall 2000): 283–99; Adam B. Butler and Amie Skattebo, "What Is Acceptable for Women May Not Be for Men: The Effect of Family Conflicts with Work on Job-Performance Ratings," *Journal of Occupational and Organizational Psychology* 77, no. 4 (December 2004): 553–64; Cheri Ostroff, Leanne E. Atwater, and Barbara J. Feinberg, "Understanding Self-Other Agreement: A Look at Rater and Ratee Characteristics, Context, and Outcomes," *Personnel Psychology* 57, no. 1 (Summer 2004): 333–37.

34. Kristina E. Chirico, M. Ronald Buckley, Anthony R. Wheeler, Jeffrey D. Facteau, H. John Bernardin, and Danielle S. Beu, "A Note on the Need for True Scores in Frame-of-Reference (FOR) Training Research," *Journal of Managerial Issues* 16, no. 3 (Fall 2004): 382–98.

35. Stephen C. Behrenbrinker, "Conducting Productive Performance Evaluations in the Assessor's Office," *Assessment Journal* 2, no. 5 (September/October 1995): 48–54; Aharon Tziner, Christine Joanis, and Kevin Murphy, "A Comparison of

Three Methods of Performance Appraisal with Regard to Goal Properties, Goal Perception, and Ratee Satisfaction," *Group & Organization Management* 25, no. 2 (June 2000): 175–90.

36. Elaine Pulakos, Sharon Arad, Michelle Donovan, and Kevin Plamondon, "Adaptability in the Workplace: Development of a Taxonomy of Adaptive Performance," *Journal of Applied Psychology* 85, no. 4 (August 2000): 612–24; Leslie A. Weatherly, "Performance Management: Getting It Right from the Start," *HRMagazine* 49, no. 3 (March 2004): S1–S12; Edwin Arnold, and Marcia Pulich, "Personality Conflicts and Objectivity in Appraising Performance," *The Health Care Manager* 22, no. 3 (July–September 2003): 227.

37. Latham and Wexley, *Increasing Productivity*; Tziner, Joanis, and Murphy, "A Comparison of Three Methods of Performance Appraisal," 175–90; Simon Taggar and Travor Brown, "Problem-Solving Team Behaviours: Development and Validation of BOS and a Hierarchical Factor Structure," *Small Group Research* 32, no. 6 (December 2001): 698–726.

38. Daniel Bachrach, Elliot Bendoly, and Philip Podsakoff, "Attributions of the 'Causes' of Group Performance as an Alternative Explanation of the Relationship between Organizational Citizenship Behaviour and Organizational Performance," *Journal of Applied Psychology* 86, no. 6 (December 2001): 1285–93; Susan Leandri, "Measures That Matter: How to Fine-Tune Your Performance Measures," *Journal for Quality and Participation* 24, no. 1 (Spring 2001): 39–41.

39. Peter F. Drucker, *The Practice of Management* (New York: Harper & Brothers, 1954), reissued by HarperCollins in 1993; Janice S. Miller, "High Tech and High Performance: Managing Appraisal in the Information Age," *Journal of Labor Research* 24, no. 3 (Summer 2003): 409–425.

40. E. Locke and G. Latham, *A Theory of Goal Setting and Task Performance* (Englewood Cliffs, NJ: Prentice Hall, 1990). See also John J. Donovan and David J. Radosevich, "The Moderating Role of Goal Commitment on the Goal Difficulty-Performance Relationship: A Meta-Analytic Review and Critical Reanalysis," *Journal of Applied Psychology* 83, no. 2 (April 1998): 308–15; Cindy Romaine, "Staying Relevant: Competencies and Employee Reviews," *Information Outlook* 8, no. 4 (April 2004): 21–25; Gail Johnson, "Room for Improvement," *Training* 40, no. 11 (December 2003): 18–20.

41. Jack Steele, "Transforming the Balanced Scorecard into Your Strategy Execution System," *Manage* 53, no. 1 (September/October 2001): 22–23. See also Robert Kaplan and David Norton, "Strategic Learning and the Balanced Scorecard," *Strategy & Leadership* 24, no. 5 (September/October 1996): 18–24; Robert Kaplan and David Norton, "Using the Balanced Scorecard as a Strategic Management System," *Harvard Business Review* (January–February 1996): 75–85; Joe Mullich, "Get in Line: People Talk about Aligning Corporate, Departmental and Employee Goals, But Not Many Actually Do It," *Workforce Management* 82, no. 13 (December 2003): 43; "Good Appraisal Is Simple, Happens Often, Experts Say," *The Orlando Sentinel* (via *Knight-Ridder/Tribune News Service*), December 3, 2003.

42. Deloris McGee Wanguri, "A Review, an Integration, and a Critique of Cross Disciplinary Research on Performance Appraisals, Evaluations, and Feedback," *Journal of Business Communications* 32, no. 3 (July 1995): 267–93; Tziner, Joanis, and Murphy, "A Comparison of Three Methods of Performance Appraisal," 175–90; "Good Appraisal Is Simple, Happens Often, Experts Say."

43. Kwok Leung, Steven Su, and Michael Morris, "When Is Criticism Not Constructive? The Roles of Fairness Perceptions and Dispositional Attributions in Employee Acceptance of Critical Supervisory Feedback," *Human Relations* 54, no. 9 (September 2001): 1155–87; Ted Pollock, "Make Your Criticism Pay Off," *Electric Light & Power* 81, no. 1 (January 2003): 31.

44. "Focus on Success," *Aftermarket Business* 115, no. 2 (February 2005): 1.

45. Helen Wilkie, "The Tricky Art of Criticism," *HRMagazine* 49, no. 12 (December 2004): 77–83.

chapter 9

Managing Compensation

After studying this chapter, you should be able to

Explain employer concerns in developing a strategic compensation program.

Define the wage curve, pay grades, and rate ranges as parts of the compensation structure.

Indicate the various factors that influence the setting of wages.

Identify the major provisions of the laws and regulations affecting compensation.

Differentiate the mechanics of each of the major job evaluation systems.

Discuss the current issues of equal pay for work of equal value and pay compression.

Explain the purpose of a wage survey.

A n extensive review of the literature indicates that important work-related variables leading to job satisfaction include challenging work, interesting job assignments, equitable rewards, competent supervision, and rewarding careers.[1] It is doubtful, however, whether many employees would continue working were it not for the money they earn. Employees desire compensation systems that they perceive as being fair and commensurate with their skills and expectations. Pay, therefore, is a major consideration in HRM because it provides employees with a tangible reward for their services, as well as a source of recognition and livelihood. Employee compensation includes all forms of pay and rewards received by employees for the performance of their jobs. *Direct compensation* encompasses employee wages and salaries, incentives, bonuses, and commissions. *Indirect compensation* comprises the many benefits supplied by employers, and *nonfinancial compensation* includes employee recognition programs, rewarding jobs, organizational support, work environment, and flexible work hours to accommodate personal needs.

Both managers and scholars agree that the way compensation is allocated among employees sends a message about what management believes is important and the types of activities it encourages.[2] Furthermore, for an employer, the payroll constitutes a sizable operating cost. In manufacturing firms compensation is seldom as low as 20 percent of total expenditures, and in service enterprises it often exceeds 80 percent. A strategic compensation program, therefore, is essential so that pay can serve to motivate employee production sufficiently to keep labour costs at an acceptable level. This chapter will be concerned with the management of a compensation program, job evaluation systems, and pay structures for determining compensation payments. Included will be a discussion of laws and regulations that affect wage and salary rates. Chapter 10 will review financial incentive plans for employees. Employee benefits that are part of the total compensation package are then discussed in Chapter 11.

Strategic Compensation Planning

objective **1**

What is strategic compensation planning? Simply stated, it is the compensation of employees in ways that enhance motivation and growth, while at the same time aligning their efforts with the objectives, philosophies, and culture of the organization. Strategic compensation planning goes beyond determining what market rates to pay employees—although market rates are one element of compensation planning—to purposefully linking compensation to the organization's mission and general business objectives.[3] Commenting on the importance of strategic compensation planning to organizational success, Gerald Ledford and Elizabeth Hawk, two compensation specialists, note, "Companies throughout the economy have begun to rethink their compensation systems in search for competitive advantage."

Additionally, strategic compensation planning serves to mesh the monetary payments made to employees with specific functions of the HR program. For example, in the recruitment of new employees, the rate of pay for jobs can increase or limit the supply of applicants. A compensation specialist speaking to one of the authors noted, "The linkage of pay levels to labour markets is a strategic policy issue because it serves to attract or retain valued employees while affecting the organization's relative payroll budget." For example, colleges and universities know that they cannot attract or retain qualified professors unless their pay strategy is linked to competitive market rates.

Many fast-food restaurants, such as Burger King and Taco Bell—traditionally low-wage employers—have needed to raise their starting wages to attract a sufficient number of job applicants to meet staffing requirements. If pay rates are high, creating a large applicant pool, then organizations may choose to raise their selection standards and hire better-qualified employees. This in turn can reduce employer training costs. When employees perform at exceptional levels, their performance appraisals may justify an increased pay rate. For these reasons and others, an organization should develop a formal HR program to manage employee compensation.

We will discuss three important aspects of strategic compensation planning: linking compensation to organizational objectives, the pay-for-performance standard, and motivating employees through compensation.

Linking Compensation to Organizational Objectives

Compensation has been revolutionized by heightened domestic competition, globalization, increased employee skill requirements, and new technology. Therefore, an outcome of today's dynamic business environment is that managers have needed to change their pay philosophies from paying for a specific position or job title to rewarding employees on the basis of their individual competencies or work contributions to organizational success. A recent study showed that 91 percent of responding organizations had a company compensation philosophy linking their pay strategy with organizational performance. As the authors of this study noted, "A written compensation philosophy indicates senior management understands and is committed to aligning their business strategy with pay, suggesting that alignment can have a positive impact on organizational effectiveness."[4]

value-added compensation
Evaluating the individual components of the compensation program to see whether they advance the needs of employees and the goals of the organization

Increasingly, compensation specialists speak of value-added compensation.[5] A **value-added compensation** program, also called value-chain compensation, is one in which the components of the compensation package (benefits, base pay, incentives, and so on), both separately and in combination, create value for the organization and its employees. Using a value-added viewpoint, managers ask questions such as "How does this compensation practice benefit the organization?" and "Does the benefit offset the administrative cost?" Payments that fail to advance either the employee or the organization are removed from the compensation program.

It is not uncommon for organizations to establish very specific goals for joining their organizational objectives to their compensation program.[6] Formalized compensation goals serve as guidelines for managers to ensure that wage and benefit policies achieve their intended purpose. The more common goals of a strategic compensation policy include the following:

1. To reward employees' past performance[7]
2. To remain competitive in the labour market
3. To maintain salary equity among employees
4. To mesh employees' future performance with organizational goals
5. To control the compensation budget
6. To attract new employees[8]
7. To reduce unnecessary turnover[9]

To achieve these goals, policies must be established to guide management in making decisions. Formal statements of compensation policies typically include the following:

1. The rate of pay within the organization and whether it is to be above, below, or at the prevailing market rate
2. The ability of the pay program to gain employee acceptance while motivating employees to perform to the best of their abilities
3. The pay level at which employees may be recruited and the pay differential between new and more senior employees
4. The intervals at which pay raises are to be granted and the extent to which merit and/or seniority will influence the raises
5. The pay levels needed to facilitate the achievement of a sound financial position in relation to the products or services offered

The Pay-for-Performance Standard

pay-for-performance standard
A standard by which managers tie compensation to employee effort and performance

This quote from compensation specialist Edward E. Lawler III illustrates the importance of pay-for-performance as a strategic pay practice: "A most dramatic pay trend is the increased adoption by *Fortune* 1000 corporations of pay-for-performance programs."[10] Why is this statement significant? A **pay-for-performance standard** serves to raise productivity and lower labour costs in today's competitive economic environment. It is agreed that managers must tie at least some reward to employee effort and performance. Without this standard, motivation to perform with greater effort will be low, resulting in higher wage costs to the organization. Additionally, most employees believe that their compensation should be directly linked to their relative performance.

The term "pay for performance" refers to a wide range of compensation options, including merit-based pay, bonuses, salary commissions, job and pay banding, team/group incentives, and various gainsharing programs.[11] (Gainsharing plans are discussed in Chapter 10.) Each of these compensation systems seeks to differentiate between the pay of average performers and that of outstanding performers. In 2002, when Plum Creek Timber Company, merged with The Timber Company, it emphasized a pay-for-performance philosophy by forming new salary ranges based on each job's impact on the business and incentive rewards linked more directly to individual and company performance.[12] Interestingly, productivity studies show that employees will increase their output by 15 to 35 percent when an organization installs a pay-for-performance program.

Unfortunately, designing a sound pay-for-performance system is not easy. Consideration must be given to how employee performance will be measured. For example, measuring an employee's output may be relatively easy and objective on an assembly line but more difficult (and subjective) when the employee works in a service environment. Other concerns include the monies to be allocated for compensation increases, which employees to cover, the payout method, and the periods when payments will be made. A critical issue concerns the size of the monetary increase and its perceived value to employees. Projected annual salary budget increases for 2006 are 3.4 percent.[13] These percentages only slightly exceed yearly increases in the cost of living. Although differences exist as to how large a wage or salary increase must be before it is perceived as meaningful, a pay-for-performance program will lack its full potential when pay increases only approximate rises in the cost of living.

Motivating Employees through Compensation

Pay constitutes a quantitative measure of an employee's relative worth. For most employees, pay has a direct bearing not only on their standard of living, but also on the status and recognition they may be able to achieve both on and off the job. Because pay represents a reward received in exchange for an employee's contributions, it is essential, according to the equity theory, that the pay be equitable in terms of those contributions. It is essential also that an employee's pay be equitable in terms of what other employees are receiving for their contributions.

Pay Equity

Simply defined, equity embraces the concept of fairness. Equity theory, also referred to as *distributive fairness*, is a motivation theory that explains how people respond to situations in which they feel they have received less (or more) than they deserve.[14] Central to the theory is the role of perception in motivation and the fact that individuals make comparisons.[15] It states that individuals form a ratio of their inputs (abilities, skills, experiences) in a situation to their outcomes (salary, benefits) in that situation. They then compare the value of that ratio with the value of the input/output ratio for other individuals in a similar class of jobs either internal or external to the organization. If the value of their ratio equals the value of another's, they perceive the situation as equitable and no tension exists. However, if they perceive their input/output ratio as inequitable relative to others', this creates tension and motivates them to eliminate or reduce the inequity. The strength of their motivation is proportional to the magnitude of the perceived inequity. Figure 9.1 illustrates pay equity and feelings of being fairly paid.

Lumber workers are often paid on a pay-for-performance basis.

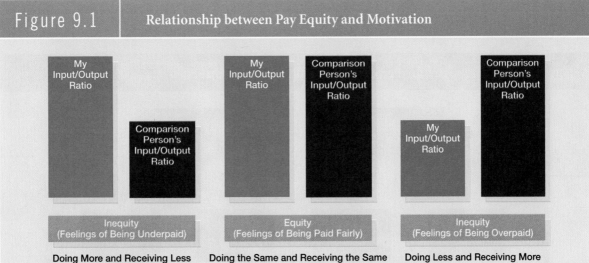

Figure 9.1	Relationship between Pay Equity and Motivation

The greater the perceived disparity between my input/output ratio and the comparison person's input/output ratio, the greater the motivation to reduce the inequity.

pay equity
An employee's perception that compensation received is equal to the value of the work performed

For employees, **pay equity** is achieved when the compensation received is equal to the value of the work performed. Research clearly demonstrates that employees' perceptions of pay equity, or inequity, can have dramatic effects on their motivation for both work behaviour and productivity. Managers must therefore develop strategic pay practices that are both internally and externally equitable. Compensation policies are *internally* equitable when employees believe that the wage rates for their jobs approximate the job's worth to the organization. Perceptions of *external* pay equity exist when the organization is paying wages that are relatively equal to what other employers are paying for similar types of work.

Expectancy Theory and Pay

The expectancy theory of motivation predicts that one's level of motivation depends on the attractiveness of the rewards sought and the probability of obtaining those rewards.[16] The theory has developed from the work of psychologists who consider humans as thinking, reasoning people who have beliefs and anticipations concerning future life events. Expectancy theory therefore holds that employees should exert greater work effort if they have reason to expect that it will result in a reward that is valued.[17] To motivate this effort, the value of any monetary reward should be attractive. Employees also must believe that good performance is valued by their employer and will result in their receiving the expected reward.

Figure 9.2 shows the relationship between pay-for-performance and the expectancy theory of motivation. The model predicts, first, that high effort will lead to high performance (expectancy). For example, if an employee believes she has the skills and abilities to perform her job, and if she works hard (effort), then her performance will improve or be high. Second, high performance should result in rewards that are appreciated (valued). Elements of the compensation package are said to have *instrumentality* when an employee's high performance leads to monetary rewards that are valued. As we previously stated that pay-for-performance leads to a feeling of pay satisfaction, this feeling should reinforce one's high level of effort.

Thus, how employees view compensation can be an important factor in determining the motivational value of compensation. Furthermore, the effective communication of pay information together with an organizational environment that elicits

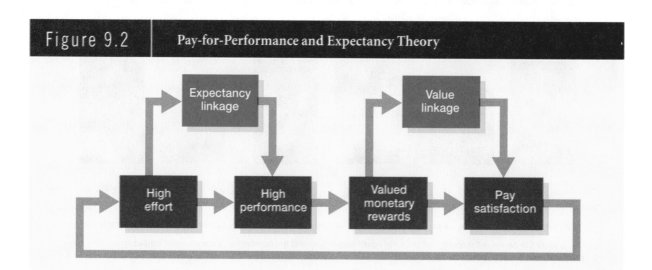

Figure 9.2   Pay-for-Performance and Expectancy Theory

employee trust in management can contribute to employees' having more accurate perceptions of their pay. The perceptions employees develop concerning their pay are influenced by the accuracy of their knowledge and understanding of the compensation program's strategic objectives.

Pay Secrecy

Misperceptions by employees concerning the equity of their pay and its relationship to performance can be created by secrecy about the pay that others receive. There is reason to believe that secrecy can generate distrust in the compensation system, reduce employee motivation, and inhibit organizational effectiveness. Yet pay secrecy seems to be an accepted practice in many organizations in both the private and the public sector.

Managers may justify secrecy on the grounds that most employees prefer to have their own pay kept secret. Probably one of the reasons for pay secrecy that managers may be unwilling to admit is that it gives them greater freedom in compensation management, because pay decisions are not disclosed and there is no need to justify or defend them. Employees who are not supposed to know what others are being paid have no objective base for pursuing complaints about their own pay. Secrecy also serves to cover up inequities existing within the internal pay structure. Furthermore, secrecy surrounding compensation decisions may lead employees to believe that there is no direct relationship between pay and performance.

Pay secrecy, however, may not promote a positive strategic pay program. In one study concerning employees' knowledge of their base pay, results showed that (1) knowledge of base pay is the strongest predictor of pay satisfaction, which is highly associated with work engagement, and (2) knowledge of base pay more strongly predicts pay satisfaction than does the actual amount of pay received by employees.[18] Expectancy theory, previously discussed, would also argue for an "open" strategic pay philosophy.

The Bases for Compensation

hourly work
Work paid on an hourly basis

piecework
Work paid according to the number of units produced

Work performed in most private, public, and not-for-profit organizations has traditionally been compensated on an hourly basis. It is referred to as **hourly work,** in contrast to **piecework,** in which employees are paid according to the number of units they produce. Hourly work, however, is far more prevalent than piecework as a basis for compensating employees.

Employees compensated on an hourly basis are classified as *hourly employees*, or wage earners. Those whose compensation is computed on the basis of weekly, biweekly, or monthly pay periods are classified as *salaried employees*. Hourly employees are normally paid only for the time they work. Salaried employees, by contrast, are generally paid the same for each pay period, even though they occasionally may work more hours or fewer than the regular number of hours in a period. They also usually receive certain benefits not provided to hourly employees.

Employment practices are a provincial jurisdiction, and each province has its own employment standards act. Each of these acts contains a provision that requires the employer to reimburse the employee at a specified rate after he or she has worked the minimum required hours. This rate is usually 1.5 times the employee's base hourly rate of pay. A number of employers offer overtime pay that is more generous than what the act specifies. Some acts provide for time in lieu of overtime; thus, four hours of overtime paid at 1.5 would be the equivalent of six hours in either pay or time off in lieu of payment. Supervisory and management personnel are not usually paid overtime; still other personnel work overtime for free (see Ethics in HRM). Each of the employment standards acts includes a list of people who are exempt from the overtime provision.

Because so many American companies are operating in Canada, the terms *exempt* (to describe employees not covered in the overtime provisions of the U.S. Fair Labor Standards Act) and *nonexempt* (to describe employees covered by the overtime provisions of the U.S. Fair Labor Standards Act) are often heard, although neither has any relevance in Canadian legislation.[19] These terms are used specifically to denote *supervisory* and *nonsupervisory* roles. U.S. legislation stipulates that only nonexempt (i.e., nonsupervisory) workers are entitled to overtime pay.

USING THE INTERNET

You can determine the salary of almost any job by using sites such as:

http://salarywizard.monster.ca

Ethics in HRM

Working for Free

Two restaurants in Ontario, one in Port Hope and the other in Belleville, were benefiting from the services of more than 20 people (called volunteers or agents) who were not being paid wages but made their money on the tips customers left for them. The province's Employment Standards Act stipulated that waiters must be paid $5.95 an hour (less than the minimum wage, due to tips), and that every employer must pay a minimum wage. The restaurants argued that they provided a location where workers could act as service agents and undertake their business, relying on tips for income. Were the waiters working for free?

Elaine Chu worked at a local fast-food restaurant to earn enough money to support herself while she attended university part-time. Her job title was night manager, and she worked the 4 p.m. to 11 p.m. shift. During this shift she was the only employee on duty, and she did all of the food preparation, serving, and cleanup. Most nights, customers arrived after the movies (around 11 p.m.), and Chu was expected to work into the next shift until the crowd dispersed. She received no overtime pay for these extra hours because employers were not required to pay overtime for managers. Did Chu's employer misuse the title "manager" in order to circumvent its obligations with respect to overtime pay? To be deemed a true manager, an individual should have staff reporting to him or her, should have responsibility for a major aspect of the business, and should provide counselling to more junior staff through performance appraisal. Was Chu working for free?

According to a Statistics Canada survey, one-fifth of all employees put in extra hours at work, and 60 percent of these are unpaid, with workers averaging nine unpaid hours per week. White-collar employees are working for free, and they know why: they are afraid of losing their jobs.

The amount of unpaid overtime varies by province and by sector. In Alberta, about 14 percent of workers work overtime for free, while only 7 percent of those in PEI do so. Teachers and professors put in the most unpaid overtime, with about 20 percent of them working more than 50 hours a week.

Sources: www.jobquality.ca/indicator Retrieved June 30, 2006; Bruce Little, "Canadians Work Overtime for Free," *The Globe and Mail*, July 14, 1997: B6; Susan Bourette, "Volunteer Waiters Work Only for Tips," *The Globe and Mail*, July 27, 1997: A7.

Determining Compensation—The Wage Mix

Employees may inquire of their managers, "How are the wages for my job determined?" In practice, a combination of *internal* and *external* factors can influence, directly or indirectly, the rates at which employees are paid. Through their interaction these factors constitute the wage mix, as shown in Figure 9.3.[20] For example, the area wage rate for administrative assistants might be $9.75 per hour. However, one employer may elect to pay its administrative assistants $11.50 per hour because of their excellent performance. The influence of government legislation on the wage mix will be discussed later in the chapter.

Internal Factors

The internal factors that influence wage rates are the employer's compensation strategy, the worth of a job, an employee's relative worth in meeting job requirements, and an employer's ability to pay.

Employer's Compensation Strategy

Highlights in HRM 9.1 on page 408 illustrates the compensation strategies of two organizations, Tri Star Performance and Preventive Health Care. The pay strategy of Preventive Health Care is to be an industry pay leader, while Tri Star Performance seeks to be wage-competitive. Both employers strive to promote a compensation policy that is internally fair.

Tri Star Performance and Preventive Health Care, like other employers, will establish numerous compensation objectives that affect the pay employees receive. As a minimum, both large and small employers should set pay policies reflecting (1) the internal wage relationship among jobs and skill levels, (2) the external competition or an employer's pay position relative to what competitors are paying, (3) a policy of rewarding employee performance, and (4) administrative decisions concerning elements of the pay system such as overtime premiums, payment periods, and short-term or long-term incentives.

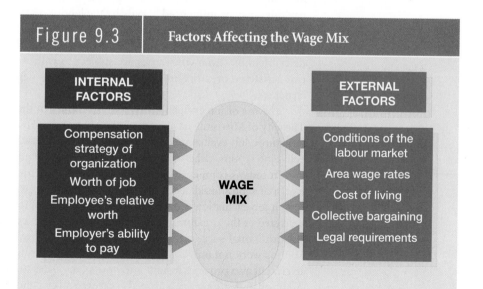

Figure 9.3   Factors Affecting the Wage Mix

INTERNAL FACTORS

Compensation strategy of organization

Worth of job

Employee's relative worth

Employer's ability to pay

WAGE MIX

EXTERNAL FACTORS

Conditions of the labour market

Area wage rates

Cost of living

Collective bargaining

Legal requirements

Highlights in HRM 9.1

Comparison of Compensation Strategies

Compensation strategies and objectives can differ widely across large and small employers as well as across employers in the private and public sectors. Here are the compensation strategies at Tri Star Performance and Preventive Health Care.

Tri Star Performance

- Promote pay-for-performance practices
- Pay market-competitive compensation
- Achieve internal and external pay equity
- Achieve simplicity in compensation programs
- Strive for employee commitment and a collaborative work environment
- Promote gender fairness in pay and benefits
- Comply with all governmental compensation regulations
- Minimize increased fixed costs

Preventive Health Care

- Be a pay leader in the healthcare industry
- Promote open and understandable pay practices
- Ensure fair employee treatment
- Offer benefits promoting individual employee needs
- Offer compensation rewarding employee creativity and achievements
- Offer compensation to foster the strategic mission of the organization
- Obtain employee input when developing compensation practices
- Emphasize performance through variable pay and stock options

Worth of a Job

Organizations without a formal compensation program generally base the worth of jobs on the subjective opinions of people familiar with the jobs. In such instances, pay rates may be influenced heavily by the labour market or, in the case of unionized employers, by collective bargaining. Organizations with formal compensation programs, however, are more likely to rely on a system of *job evaluation* to aid in rate determination. Even when rates are subject to collective bargaining, job evaluation can assist the organization in maintaining some degree of control over its wage structure.

The use of job evaluation is widespread in both the public and the private sector. The City of Mississaugua and Star Data Systems use job evaluation in establishing wage structures. Job evaluations most frequently cover clerical, technical, and various blue-collar job groups. Other jobs covered are managerial and top executive positions.

In today's competitive environment, compensation professionals believe that the worth of a job should be based on more than market prices or using only an internally driven job evaluation program. Rather, a job's value should be based on *the total value* delivered to the organization.[21] That is, some jobs may simply be more important to organizational success than others regardless of how they are internally evaluated. Valuing work not only properly enables organizations to price "important" jobs effectively, but also provides insight into how a job relates to overall organizational success. Additionally, valuing work properly serves to attract and retain the right talent to drive organizational performance.[22]

Employee's Relative Worth

In both hourly and salary jobs, employee performance can be recognized and rewarded through promotion and with various incentive systems. (The incentive systems used most often will be discussed in the next chapter.) Superior performance can also be rewarded by granting merit raises on the basis of steps within a rate range established for a job class. If merit raises are to have their intended value, however, they must be determined by an effective performance appraisal system that differentiates between employees who deserve the raises and those who do not. This system, moreover, must provide a visible and credible relationship between performance and any raises received. Unfortunately, too many so-called merit systems provide for raises to be granted automatically. As a result, employees tend to be rewarded more for merely being present than for being productive on the job.

Employer's Ability to Pay

Pay levels are limited by earned profits and other financial resources available to employers. This is clearly illustrated by financially burdened companies such as Air Canada that ask their employees for pay cuts. Furthermore, an organization's ability to pay is determined in part by the productivity of its employees. This productivity is a result not only of their performance, but also of the amount of capital the organization has invested in labour-saving equipment. Generally, increases in capital investment reduce the number of employees required to perform the work and increase an employer's ability to provide higher pay for those it employs.

Economic conditions and competition faced by employers can also significantly affect the rates they are able to pay. Competition and recessions can force prices down and reduce the income from which compensation payments are derived. In such situations, employers have little choice but to reduce wages and/or lay off employees, or, even worse, to go out of business.

Low unemployment rates in Alberta force employers to compete for labour and drive wages up.

External Factors

The major external factors that influence wage rates include labour market conditions, area wage rates, cost of living, collective bargaining if the employer is unionized, and legal requirements. The legal requirements of compensation will be discussed later in the chapter.

Labour Market Conditions

The labour market reflects the forces of supply and demand for qualified labour within an area. These forces help influence the wage rates required to recruit or retain competent employees. It must be recognized, however, that counterforces can reduce the full impact of supply and demand on the labour market. The economic power of unions, for example, may prevent employers from lowering wage rates even when unemployment is high among union members. Government regulations also may prevent an employer from paying at a market rate less than an established minimum.

Area Wage Rates

A formal wage structure should provide rates that are in line with those being paid by other employers for comparable jobs within the area. Data pertaining to area wage rates may be obtained from local wage surveys. Wage survey data also may be obtained from a variety of sources, including compensation consulting firms such as Mercer Management Consulting and free from some companies such as Monster.ca. The Conference Board of Canada also conducts an annual compensation survey. Smaller employers use government or local board of trade surveys to establish rates of pay for new and senior employees. Others engage in a cooperative exchange of wage information or rely on various professional associations for these data.

Wage surveys (discussed fully later in the chapter) serve the important function of providing external wage equity between the surveying organization and other organizations competing for labour in the surrounding labour market. Importantly, data from area wage surveys can be used to prevent the rates for jobs from drifting too far above or below those of other employers in the region. When rates rise above existing area levels, an employer's labour costs may become excessive. Conversely, if they drop too far below area levels, it may be difficult to recruit and retain competent personnel. Wage survey data must also take into account indirect wages paid in the form of benefits.

Cost of Living

consumer price index (CPI)
A measure of the average change in prices over time in a fixed "market basket" of goods and services

Because of inflation, compensation rates have had to be adjusted upward periodically to help employees maintain their purchasing power. Employers make these changes with the help of the **consumer price index (CPI).** The CPI is a measure of the average change in prices over time in a fixed "market basket" of goods and services. The consumer price index is based on prices of food, clothing, shelter, and fuels; transportation fares; charges for medical services; and prices of other goods and services that people buy for day-to-day living. Statistics Canada collects price information on a monthly basis and calculates the CPI for the nation as a whole and various Canadian cities. Employers in a number of communities monitor changes in the CPI as a basis for compensation decisions.

Changes in the CPI can have important effects on pay rates. Granting wage increases solely on the basis of the CPI helps compress pay rates within a pay structure, thereby creating inequities among those who receive the wage increase. Inequities also result from the fact that adjustments are made on a cents-per-hour basis rather than a percentage basis. For example, a cost-of-living adjustment of 50 cents represents a 7.1-percent increase for an employee earning $7 per hour, but only a 4.2-percent increase for one earning $12 per hour. Unless adjustments are made periodically in employee base rates, the desired differential between higher- and lower-paying jobs will gradually be reduced. The incentive to accept more-demanding jobs will also be reduced.

escalator clauses
Clauses in collective agreements that provide for quarterly cost-of-living adjustments in wages, basing the adjustments on changes in the consumer price index

Employees who are members of a union may receive wage increases through **escalator clauses** found in their collective agreement. These clauses provide for quarterly cost-of-living adjustments (COLA) in wages based on changes in the CPI. The most common adjustments are 1 cent per hour for each 0.3- or 0.4-point change in the CPI. COLAs are favoured by unions during particularly high periods of inflation.

Collective Bargaining

One of the primary functions of a labour union, as emphasized in Chapter 14, is to bargain collectively over conditions of employment, the most important of which is compensation.[23] The union's goal in each new agreement is to achieve increases in

real wages
Wage increases larger than rises in the consumer price index; that is, the real earning power of wages

real wages—wage increases larger than the increase in the CPI—thereby improving the purchasing power and standard of living of its members. This goal includes gaining wage settlements that equal or exceed the pattern established by other unions within the area.

The agreements negotiated by unions tend to establish rate patterns within the labour market. As a result, wages are generally higher in areas where organized labour is strong. To recruit and retain competent personnel and avoid unionization, nonunion employers must either meet or exceed these rates. The "union scale" also becomes the prevailing rate that all employers must pay for work performed under government contract. The impact of collective bargaining therefore extends beyond the segment of the labour force that is unionized.

Job Evaluation Systems

objective **3**

job evaluation
A systematic process of determining the relative worth of jobs in order to establish which jobs should be paid more than others within an organization

As we discussed earlier, one important component of the wage mix is the worth of the job. Organizations formally determine the value of jobs through the process of job evaluation. **Job evaluation** is the systematic process of determining the *relative* worth of jobs in order to establish which jobs should be paid more than others within the organization. Job evaluation helps establish internal equity between various jobs. The relative worth of a job may be determined by comparing it with others within the organization or by comparing it with a scale that has been constructed for this purpose. Each method of comparison, furthermore, may be made on the basis of the jobs as a whole or on the basis of the parts that constitute the jobs.[24]

Three traditional methods of comparison provide the basis for the principal systems of job evaluation. We will begin by discussing the simpler nonquantitative approaches and conclude by reviewing the more popular quantitative system. Also discussed is a newer method of job evaluation—work evaluation. Regardless of the methodology used, it is important to remember that all job evaluation methods require varying degrees of managerial judgment.

Job Ranking System

job ranking system
The simplest and oldest system of job evaluation by which jobs are arrayed on the basis of their relative worth

The simplest and oldest system of job evaluation is the **job ranking system,** which arrays jobs on the basis of their relative worth. One technique used to rank jobs consists of having the raters arrange cards listing the duties and responsibilities of each job in order of the importance of the jobs. Job ranking can be done by a single individual knowledgeable about all jobs or by a committee composed of management and employee representatives.

Another common approach to job ranking is the paired-comparison method. Raters compare each job with all other jobs by means of a paired-comparison ranking table that lists the jobs in both rows and columns, as shown in Figure 9.4 on page 412. To use the table, raters compare a job from a row with the jobs from each of the columns. If the row job is ranked higher than a column job, an X is placed in the appropriate cell. After all the jobs have been compared, raters total the Xs for row jobs. The total number of Xs for a row job will establish its worth relative to other jobs. Differences in rankings should then be reconciled into a single rating for all jobs. After jobs are evaluated, wage rates can be assigned to them through use of the salary survey discussed later in the chapter.

Figure 9.4	Paired-Comparison Job Ranking Table

Column Jobs / Row Jobs	Senior Administrative Secretary	Data-Entry Operator	Data-Processing Director	File Clerk	Systems Analyst	Programmer	Total
Senior Administrative Secretary	—	X		X		X	3
Data-Entry Operator		—		X			1
Data-Processing Director	X	X	—	X	X	X	5
File Clerk				—			0
Systems Analyst	X	X		X	—	X	4
Programmer		X		X		—	2

Directions: Place an X in the cell where the value of a row job is higher than that of a column job.

The basic disadvantage of the job ranking system is that it does not provide a very precise measure of each job's worth. Another weakness is that the final ranking of jobs indicates the relative importance of the job, not the differences in the degree of importance that may exist between jobs. A final limitation of the job ranking method is that it can be used only with a small number of jobs, probably no more than 15. Its simplicity, however, makes it ideal for use by smaller employers.

Job Classification System

job classification system
A system of job evaluation in which jobs are classified and grouped according to a series of predetermined wage grades

In the **job classification system,** jobs are classified and grouped according to a series of predetermined grades. Successive grades require increasing amounts of job responsibility, skill, knowledge, ability, or other factors selected to compare jobs. For example, Grade GS-1 from the federal government grade descriptions reads as follows:

> GS-1 includes those classes of positions the duties of which are to perform, under immediate supervision, with little or no latitude for the exercise of independent judgment (A) the simplest routine work in office, business, or fiscal operations; or (B) elementary work of a subordinate technical character in a professional, scientific, or technical field.

The descriptions of each of the job classes constitute the scale against which the specifications for the various jobs are compared. Managers then evaluate jobs by comparing job descriptions with the different wage grades in order to "slot" the job into the appropriate grade. While this system has the advantage of simplicity, it is less precise than the point system because the job is evaluated as a whole.

Point System

point system
A quantitative job evaluation procedure that determines the relative value of a job by the total points assigned to it

The **point system** is a quantitative job evaluation procedure that determines a job's relative value by calculating the total points assigned to it.[25] It has been successfully used by many organizations including the Province of Alberta. Although point systems are rather complicated to establish, once in place they are relatively simple to understand and use. The principal advantage of the point system is that it provides a more refined basis for making judgments than either the ranking or classification systems and thereby can produce results that are more valid and less easy to manipulate.

The point system permits jobs to be evaluated quantitatively on the basis of factors or elements—commonly called *compensable factors*—that constitute the job.[26] The skills, efforts, responsibilities, and working conditions that a job usually entails are the more common major compensable factors that serve to rank one job as more or less important than another. More contemporary factors might include fiscal accountability, leadership, teamwork, and project accountability. The number of compensable factors an organization uses depends on the nature of the organization and the jobs to be evaluated. Once selected, compensable factors will be assigned weights according to their relative importance to the organization. For example, if responsibility is considered extremely important to the organization, it could be assigned a weight of 40 percent. Next, each factor will be divided into a number of degrees. Degrees represent different levels of difficulty associated with each factor. An example of this can be found in Highlights in HRM 9.2.

Highlights in HRM 9.2

Job Evaluation Factors at McMaster University

The job evaluation system developed at McMaster University comprises the following factors. For illustration purposes, examples of the sub-factor at the low end and high end of scoring points are provided.

Factor 1 Applied Reasoning and Analytical Skills
Level 1 low The job requires applying known skills to straightforward problems.
Level 7 high In addition to the skills set out in Level 6, the job requires some of the following: conceptualization of unique hypotheses, applying the reasoning process to develop unique solutions, developing new methodologies to gather/generate new data, authoring materials that contribute to growth of a body of knowledge.

Factor 2 Breadth of Knowledge
Level 1 low The job requires knowledge of processes limited in scope or narrow in range.
Level 3 high The job requires knowledge of processes in multiple areas or fields of studies.

Factor 3: Adaptation to Change/Updating of Learning
Level 1 low The technologies or knowledge base used in this job are relatively stable. When necessary the incumbent may be required to upgrade skills and become familiar with new functions and practices. Adapting to infrequent major change may be required.

(continued on next page)

Level 4 high The technology or knowledge base is constantly changing, influenced by evolving technologies and/or the business/academic environment. There is ongoing and substantial change in the methods used and knowledge required in the job. Continuous effort is required to keep knowledge and skills up to date.

Factor 4 Interpersonal Skill

Level 1 low Interactions require common courtesy, effective listening and comprehension skills and the ability to work cooperatively with others.

Level 5 high Interactions require a regular use of highly developed and proven effective counselling, mediation, persuasion and/or negotiation skills, where the issues are complex, communication is difficult, and/or the outcome contentious.

Source: For a complete list of subfactors and level descriptions, refer to this website: www.workingatmcmaster.ca/job evaluation plan. Retrieved June 24, 2006. Used by permission of McMaster University Human Resources Services.

The Point Manual

The point system requires the use of a *point manual*. The point manual is, in effect, a handbook that contains a description of the compensable factors and the degrees to which these factors may exist within the jobs. A manual also will indicate—usually by means of a table—the number of points allocated to each factor and to each of the degrees into which these factors are divided. The point value assigned to a job represents the sum of the numerical degree values of each compensable factor that the job possesses.

For example, the job factors illustrated in Highlights in HRM 9.2 represent those covered by the job evaluation plan of McMaster University. Each of the factors listed in this manual has been divided into four to seven degrees. The number of degrees into which the factors in a manual are to be divided can vary, depending on the relative weight assigned to each factor and the ease with which the individual degrees can be defined or distinguished. A statement is provided defining each of the degrees, as well as each factor as a whole. The definitions should be concise and yet distinguish the factors and each of their degrees.

Using the Point Manual

Job evaluation under the point system is accomplished by comparing the job descriptions and job specifications, factor by factor, against the various factor-degree descriptions contained in the manual. Each factor within the job being evaluated is then assigned the number of points specified in the manual. When the points for each factor have been determined from the manual, the total point value for the job as a whole can be calculated. The relative worth of the job is then determined from the total points that have been assigned to that job. This system is described in Highlights in HRM 9.3.

Work Valuation

work valuation
A job evaluation system that seeks to measure a job's worth through its value to the organization

Work valuation is a relatively new job evaluation system championed to meet the demands of a dynamic business environment. The cornerstone for **work valuation** is that work should be valued relative to the business goals of the organization rather than by an internally applied point-factor job evaluation system.[27] As noted by one compensation specialist, "Valuing work properly enables organizations to not only price individual jobs effectively, but provides insight into how jobs relate to overall organizational goals and objectives and how roles ultimately contribute to organizational

Highlights in HRM 9.3

Proven Methods in Job Evaluation

Star Data Systems of Markham, Ontario, is a company that produces software programs and currently employs around 500 people. To facilitate Star Data's growth, the director of human resources implemented a job evaluation program as a means of "paying people fairly and equitably, complying with pay equity legislation, and being able to attract high-calibre candidates."

Following proven models, all employees were required to complete job questionnaires. The process involved having the employees answer questions that related to the compensable factors chosen for the job evaluation process. Of the ninety-two descriptions prepared, 47 were deemed benchmark positions and 45 were deemed nonbenchmark positions. Examples of benchmark positions at Star Data included marketing coordinator, network support technicians, assistant controller, and shipper/receiver. Among the nonbenchmark positions were exchange reporter, product specialist, and technical sales analyst.

To ensure fairness and equity in the evaluation process, Star Data formed a job evaluation committee made up of employees from various levels in the organization. An outside consultant was hired to train committee members to evaluate positions in an unbiased manner. Job evaluation was used to determine the relative value placed on all positions in the organization. A point-factor method was applied. The focus of the evaluations was the requirements of the job. Each job was measured against four compensable factors: skill, which included the subfactors of knowledge and experience; working conditions, which involved consideration of work environment factors; responsibility, which focused on interpersonal skills, communications, judgment, problem solving, scope of responsibility, and impact of results; and effort. All these compensable factors, along with their subfactors, were tailor-made to fit Star Data's business needs.

Weightings were determined for each of the compensable factors in the evaluation process based on the value of the particular factor to the organization, the value placed on the factors by other companies in the industry, the requirements of pay equity legislation, and input from the consulting group. Since working conditions and effort were not deemed to be deterrents for completing the work, only a 5-percent weight was assigned to that factor; in contrast, skill received a 40-percent weighting.

Having completed its evaluation of the positions, the committee assigned a point total to each position, which allowed a hierarchy to be developed. Based on the point totals, the positions were divided into groups to form 12 salary grades. Using the benchmark positions found in each salary grade, salary and pay information was collected from competitors and other organizations to arrive, via salary surveys, at an average market salary as the midpoint. This methodology ensured that the plan was competitive with the external marketplace.

Star Data, with a new salary grade format, was in a position to analyze internal salaries against the new ranges and to review any pay equity issues. All employees in the organization knew their own salary ranges, their position within the range, and whether salary adjustments would be necessary.

In the future, Star Data will ensure that the system is maintained in a bias-free manner, that the salary administration program remains competitive with the external marketplace, and that salaries are administered fairly and consistently. The company plans to remain competitive by participating in annual surveys and by making necessary salary and range adjustments as conditions warrant. The ultimate responsibility rests with the managers to provide constructive and timely performance reviews and salary increases that are tied directly to performance.

success."[28] Additionally, work valuation serves to direct compensation dollars to the type of work pivotal to organizational goals.

With work valuations, work is measured through standards that come directly from business goals. For example, jobs might be valued relative to financial, operational, or customer service objectives. All forms of work, employee roles, and ways of organizing work (such as teams) are valued. The work evaluation process ends with a work hierarchy that is an array of work by value to the organization. The work hierarchy is eventually priced through wage surveys to determine individual pay rates.

Job Evaluation for Management Positions

Because management positions are more difficult to evaluate and involve certain demands not found in jobs at the lower levels, some organizations do not attempt to include them in their job evaluation programs for hourly employees. Rather, they employ either a standardized (purchased) program or customize a point method to fit their particular jobs. However, regardless of the approach adopted, point plans for executive and managerial employees operate similarly to those for other groups of employees.

One of the better-known standardized job evaluation programs for evaluating executive, managerial, and professional positions is the **Hay profile method,** developed by Edward N. Hay. The three broad factors that constitute the evaluation in the "profile" are knowledge (or know-how), mental activity (or problem solving), and accountability.[29] The Hay method uses only three factors because it is assumed that these factors represent the most important aspects of all executive and managerial positions. The profile for each position is developed by determining the percentage value to be assigned to each of the three factors. Jobs are then ranked on the basis of each factor, and point values that make up the profile are assigned to each job on the basis of the percentage-value level at which the job is ranked.

Hay profile method
A job evaluation technique using three factors—knowledge, mental activity, and accountability—to evaluate executive and managerial positions

The Compensation Structure

Job evaluation systems provide for internal equity and serve as the basis for wage-rate determination. They do not in themselves determine the wage rate. The evaluated worth of each job in terms of its rank, class, points, or monetary worth must be converted into an hourly, daily, weekly, or monthly wage rate. The compensation tool used to help set wages is the wage and salary survey.

objective

4

wage and salary survey
A survey of the wages paid to employees of other employers in the surveying organization's relevant labour market

Wage and Salary Surveys

The **wage and salary survey** is a survey of the wages paid by employers in an organization's relevant labour market—local, regional, or national, depending on the job. The labour market is frequently defined as the area from which employers obtain certain types of workers. The labour market for office personnel would be local, whereas the labour market for engineers would be national. It is the wage and salary survey that permits an organization to maintain external equity—that is, to pay its employees wages equivalent to the wages similar employees earn in other establishments.

When job evaluation and wage-survey data are used jointly, they link the likelihood of both internal and external equity. Although surveys are conducted primarily to gather competitive wage data, they can also collect information on employee benefits or organizational pay practices (such as overtime rates or shift differentials).

Collecting Survey Data

USING THE INTERNET

Statistics Canada offers a variety of useful links to various databases that contain information on compensation at:

www.statcan.ca

While many organizations conduct their own wage and salary surveys, a variety of "preconducted" pay surveys are available to satisfy the requirements of most public and not-for-profit or private employers. Companies such as Watson Wyatt (www.watson.wyatt.com), Hewitt Associates (www.hewitt.com), Mercer Human Resources Consulting (www.mercerHR.com) Hay Management Associates (www.haygroup.com), and the Conference Board of Canada (www.conferenceboard.ca) conduct annual surveys.

Highlights in HRM 9.4 describes the results of compensation surveys for those working in human resources management.

Highlights in HRM 9.4

Compensation Surveys for HR Professionals

Salaries for HR professionals and managers are as follows:

TITLE	LOW	MEDIAN	HIGH
HR Assistant	$33,815	$37,817	$41,273
Recruiter	41,092	48,980	55,050
Manager, Compensation	54,497	63,246	78,246
Director	96,010	106,327	78,246
VP HR	104,996	123,660	141,921

A study done by the Human Resources Professionals Association of Ontario showed the value of professional certification. Those people working in HR who had achieved the CHRP (Certified Human Resources Professional) earned on average $67,000, compared to the average annual earnings of $50,000 for those without a CHRP. Clearly, the CHRP has an economic value in employers' minds.

Sources: http://salarywizard.ca. Retrieved April 12, 2006; D. Brown, "More Respect, Better Pay for HR: Toronto Study," *Canadian HR Reporter* 15, no. 20 (November 18, 2002): 2; M. Belcourt and A. Templer, "The CHRP Edge," *HR Professional*, April/May 2002: 30; M. Belcourt and A. Templer, "The CHRP Edge: Part 2," *HR Professional*, December 2002/January 2003: 36.

Many provinces and cities conduct surveys and make them available to employers. Besides these government surveys, boards of trade and professional associations conduct special surveys tailored to their members' needs. Employers with global operations can purchase international surveys through large consulting firms. While all of these third-party surveys provide certain benefits to their users, they also have various limitations. Two problems with all published surveys are that (1) they are not always compatible with the user's jobs and (2) the user cannot specify what specific data to collect. To overcome these problems, organizations may collect their own compensation data.

HRIS and Salary Surveys

Wage and benefits survey data can be found on numerous websites. The previously mentioned Conference Board of Canada survey is an example. Also readily available are commercial products such as those offered at www.salary.com: the Salary Wizard, Comp Analyst, and Survey Finder surveys. Survey Finder has a database of hundreds of compensation surveys offered by more than 50 independent vendors. Managers and compensation specialists can search for applicable surveys for either purchase or participation.[30]

Employer-Initiated Surveys

Employers wishing to conduct their own wage and salary survey must first select the jobs to be used in the survey and identify the organizations with whom they actually compete for employees. Since it is not feasible to survey all the jobs in an organization, normally only key jobs, also called benchmark jobs, are used. Characteristics of key jobs include the following:

1. They are important to employees and the organization.
2. They contain a large number of positions.
3. They have relatively stable job content.
4. They have the same job content across many organizations.
5. They are acceptable to employees, management, and unions as appropriate for pay comparisons.

The survey of key jobs will usually be sent to ten or 15 organizations that represent a valid sample of other employers likely to compete for the employees of the surveying organization. A diversity of organizations should be selected—large and small, public and private, new and established, and union and nonunion—since each classification of employer is likely to pay different wage rates for surveyed jobs.

After the key jobs and the employers to be surveyed have been identified, the surveying organization must decide what information to gather on wages, benefit types, and pay policies. For example, when requesting pay data, it is important to specify whether hourly, daily, or weekly pay figures are needed.[31] In addition, those conducting surveys must state whether the wage data are needed for new hires or for senior employees. Precisely defining the compensation data needed will greatly increase the accuracy of the information received and the number of purposes for which it can be used. Once the survey data are tabulated, the compensation structure can be completed.

The Wage Curve

The relationship between the relative worth of jobs and their wage rates can be represented by means of a **wage curve.** This curve may indicate the rates currently paid for jobs within an organization, the new rates resulting from job evaluation, or the rates for similar jobs currently being paid by other organizations within the labour market. A curve may be constructed graphically by preparing a scattergram consisting of a series of dots that represent the current wage rates. As shown in Figure 9.5, a freehand curve is then drawn through the cluster of dots in such a manner as to leave approximately an equal number of dots above and below the curve. The wage curve can be relatively straight or curved. This curve can then be used to determine the relationship between the value of a job and its wage rate at any given point on the line.

wage curve
A curve in a scattergram representing the relationship between relative worth of jobs and wage rates

Pay Grades

pay grades
Groups of jobs within a particular class that are paid the same rate

From an administrative standpoint, it is generally preferable to group jobs into **pay grades** and to pay all jobs within a particular grade the same rate or rate range. When the classification system of job evaluation is used, jobs are grouped into grades as part of the evaluation process. When the point system is used, however, pay grades must be established at selected intervals that represent either the point or the evaluated monetary value of these jobs. The graph in Figure 9.6 on page 420 illustrates a series of pay grades designated along the horizontal axis at 50-point intervals.

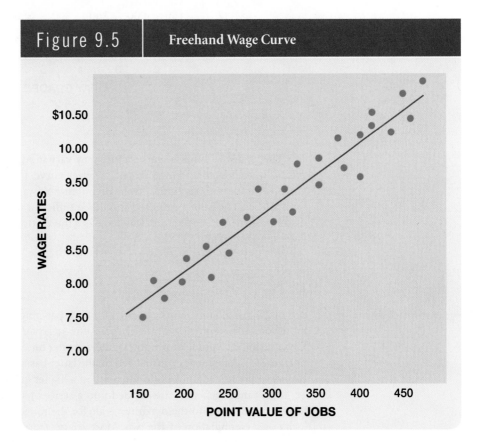

Figure 9.5 | Freehand Wage Curve

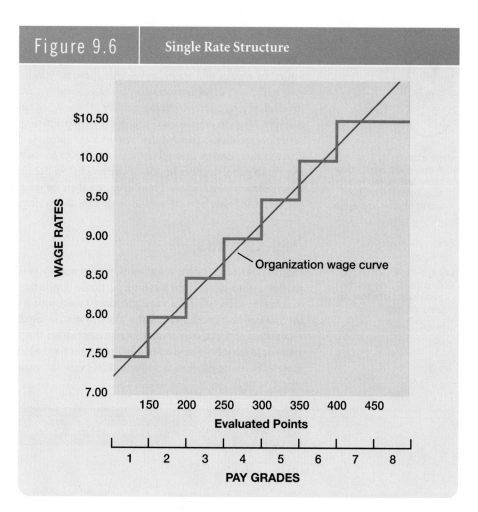

Figure 9.6 | **Single Rate Structure**

The grades within a wage structure may vary in number.[32] The number is determined by such factors as the slope of the wage curve, the number and distribution of the jobs within the structure, and the organization's wage administration and promotion policies. The number utilized should be sufficient to permit difficulty levels to be distinguished, but not so great as to make the distinction between two adjoining grades insignificant.

Rate Ranges

Although a single rate may be created for each pay grade, as shown in Figure 9.6, it is more common to provide a range of rates for each pay grade. The rate ranges may be the same for each grade or proportionately greater for each successive grade, as shown in Figure 9.7. Rate ranges constructed on the latter basis provide a greater incentive for employees to accept a promotion to a job in a higher grade.

Rate ranges generally are divided into a series of steps that permit employees to receive increases up to the maximum rate for the range on the basis of merit or seniority or a combination of the two. Most salary structures provide for the ranges of adjoining pay grades to overlap. The purpose of the overlap is to permit an employee

| Figure 9.7 | Wage Structure with Increasing Rate Ranges |

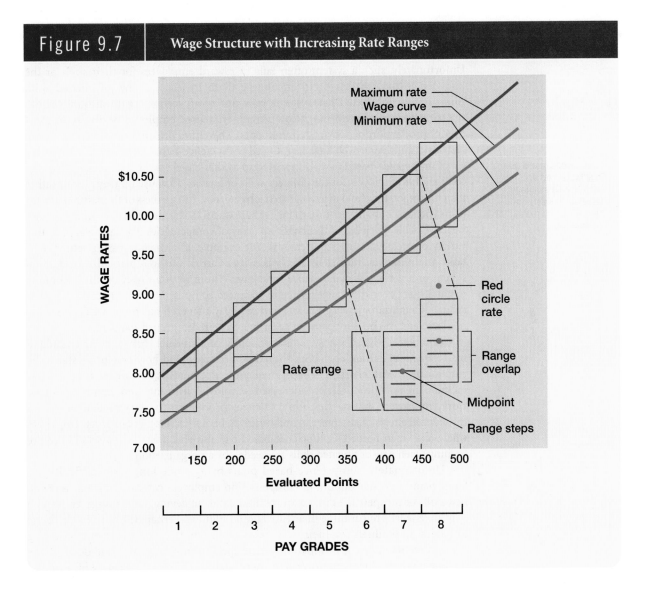

with experience to earn as much as or more than a person with less experience in the next-higher job classification.

The final step in setting up a wage structure is to determine the appropriate pay grade into which each job should be placed on the basis of its evaluated worth. Traditionally, this worth is determined on the basis of job requirements without regard to the performance of the person in that job. Under this system, the performance of those who exceed the requirements of a job may be acknowledged by merit increases within the grade range or by promotion to a job in the next-higher pay grade.

Organizations may pay individuals above the maximum of the pay range when employees have high seniority or promotional opportunities are scarce. Wages paid above the range maximum are called **red circle rates.** Because these rates are exceptions to the pay structure, employers often "freeze" these rates until all ranges are shifted upward through market wage adjustments.

red circle rates
Payment rates above the maximum of the pay range

Competence-Based Pay

The predominant approach to employee compensation is still the job-based system. Unfortunately, such a system often fails to reward employees for their skills or the knowledge they possess or to encourage them to learn a new job-related skill. Additionally, job-based pay systems may not reinforce an organizational culture stressing employee involvement or provide increased employee flexibility to meet overall production or service requirements. Therefore, organizations such as Nortel Networks and Honeywell have introduced competence-based pay plans.

competence-based pay
Pay based on an employee's skill level, variety of skills possessed, or increased job knowledge

Competence-based pay, also referred to as skill-based pay or knowledge-based pay, compensates employees for the different skills or increased knowledge they possess rather than for the job they hold in a designated job category.[33] Regardless of the name, these pay plans encourage employees to earn higher base wages by learning and performing a wider variety of skills (or jobs) or displaying an array of competencies that can be applied to a variety of organizational requirements. For example, in a manufacturing setting, new tasks might include various assembly activities carried out in a particular production system or a variety of maintenance functions. Within service organizations, employees might acquire new knowledge related to advanced computer systems or accounting procedures. Organizations will grant an increase in pay after each skill or knowledge has been mastered and can be demonstrated according to a predetermined standard.

Competence-based pay systems represent a fundamental change in the attitude of management regarding how work should be organized and how employees should be paid for their work efforts. The most frequently cited benefits of competence-based pay include greater productivity, increased employee learning and commitment to work, improved staffing flexibility to meet production or service demands, and the reduced effects of absenteeism and turnover, because managers can assign employees where and when needed. Competence-based pay also encourages employees to acquire training when new or updated skills are needed by an organization.

Unfortunately, competence-based plans bring some long-term difficulties.[34] Some plans limit the amount of compensation employees can earn, regardless of the new skills or competencies they acquire. Thus, after achieving the top wage, employees may be reluctant to continue their educational training. Perhaps the greatest challenge in paying individuals for their skills, knowledge, and competencies is developing appropriate measures. It is difficult to write specific knowledge and skill descriptions for jobs that employees perform and then establish accurate measures of acquired skills or knowledge.

Broadbanding

Organizations that adopt a competence-based or skill-based pay system frequently use *broadbanding* to structure their compensation payments to employees. Broadbanding simply collapses many traditional salary grades into a few wide salary bands.[35] Broadbands may have midpoints and quartiles or they may have extremely wide salary ranges or no ranges at all. Banding encourages lateral skill building while addressing the need to pay employees performing multiple jobs with different skill-level requirements. Additionally, broadbands help eliminate the obsession with grades and, instead, encourage employees to move to jobs in which they can develop in their careers and add value to the organization. Paying employees through broadbands enables organizations to consider job responsibilities, individual skills and competencies, and career mobility patterns in assigning employees to bands.

A competence-based pay program will encourage employees to increase their job-related knowledge and skills.

© JEFF GREENBERG/PHOTOEDIT

Government Regulation of Compensation

objective **6**

Compensation management, like the other areas of HRM, is subject to provincial and federal regulations. In each province there is an employment standards act that establishes minimum requirements with respect to wages, hours of work, and overtime. Provincial as well as federal minimum requirements can be obtained by contacting the appropriate federal or provincial office.

The Canada Labour Code

USING THE INTERNET

Canada's Labour Code can be found at:

http://laws.justice.gc.ca

Part III of the Canada Labour Code and the Canada Labour Standards Regulations set minimum labour standards for all employees and employers in works or undertakings that fall within federal jurisdiction, including interprovincial highway and rail transportation, pipelines, telecommunications, air transport, fishing, and banking. Federal Crown corporations are covered by the Canada Labour Code, but federal public service employees are not. Employees working under these classifications are subject to a 40-hour workweek. Managerial and professional employees are not covered by the hours-of-work provisions and may be required to exceed those hours. Revisions are constantly being made to these standards; HR managers must keep abreast of these changes to ensure compliance in the workplace.

Employment Standards Acts

The Employment Standards Acts of each province and territory establish minimum standards with a view to protecting both employees and employers in certain employment situations. Collective agreements are permitted to override the provisions of these acts as long as employees are not being provided with less than what the acts have stipulated, and as long as these overrides benefit the employee. Employers who operate in more than one province must become fully informed of the different requirements that exist in each province. This information is generally available on the Internet.

Each province's act contains a provision that stipulates that an overtime rate of 1.5 times the base rate must be paid for all hours worked in excess of the set minimum prescribed in the province. For example, if an employee works 45 hours in a province that legislates the minimum workweek as 40 hours, he or she is entitled to overtime for the extra five hours at 1.5 times his or her base rate. Particular groups, including lawyers, doctors, engineers, and managers, are exempt from overtime requirements.

Other Legislation

Employment equity is under federal jurisdiction for all federally regulated companies, as well as for companies not covered under the Canada Labour Code that have dealings with federally legislated companies. Pay equity is covered provincially where applicable. As we discussed in Chapter 2, legislation relating to employment equity and pay equity is designed to ensure that fair employment practices are applied to all members of designated groups.

Significant Compensation Issues

As with other HR activities, compensation management operates in a dynamic environment. For example, as managers strive to reward employees in a fair manner, they must consider controls over labour costs, legal issues regarding male and female wage payments, and internal pay equity concerns. Each of these concerns is highlighted in four important compensation issues: equal pay for comparable worth, wage-rate compression, living-wage laws, and low salary budgets.

Equal Pay for Work of Equal Value

One of the most important gender issues in compensation is equal pay for work of equal value. (In Ontario, the definition is "equal pay for work of equal or comparable value.") The issue stems from the fact that jobs performed predominantly by women are paid less than those performed by men. This practice results in what critics term *institutionalized sex discrimination*, causing women to receive lower pay for jobs that may be different from but comparable in worth to those performed by men. The issue of equal pay for work of equal value goes beyond providing equal pay for jobs that involve the same duties for women as for men. It is not concerned with whether a female secretary should receive the same pay as a male secretary. Rather, the argument for comparable worth is that jobs held by women are not compensated the same as those held by men, even though both job types may contribute equally to organizational success.

Measuring Comparability

Advocates of comparable worth argue that the difference in wage rates for predominantly male and female occupations rests in the undervaluing of traditional female occupations. To remedy this situation, they propose that wages should be equal for jobs that are "somehow" equivalent in total worth or compensation to the organization. Unfortunately, there is no consensus on a comparable worth standard by which to evaluate jobs, nor is there agreement on the ability of current job evaluation techniques to remedy the problem. Indeed, organizations may dodge the comparable worth issue by using one job evaluation system for clerical and secretarial jobs and another system for other jobs. Reality Check on page 426 outlines some of the issues that face pay equity specialists. Furthermore, the advocates of comparable worth argue that current job evaluation techniques simply serve to continue the differences in pay between the sexes. However, others believe that job evaluation systems can be designed to measure different types of jobs, in the same way that apples and oranges can be compared (see Figure 9.8 on page 427). The Business Case on page 427 describes two large settlements that have resulted from pay equity issues.

The Issue of Wage-Rate Compression

wage-rate compression
Compression of differentials between job classes, particularly the differential between hourly workers and their managers

Earlier, when we discussed the compensation structure, it was noted that the primary purpose of the pay differentials between the wage classes is to provide an incentive for employees to prepare for and accept more-demanding jobs. Unfortunately, this incentive is being significantly reduced by **wage-rate compression**—the reduction of differences between job classes. Wage-rate compression is largely an internal pay-equity concern. The problem occurs when employees perceive that there is too narrow a difference between their compensation and that of colleagues in lower-rated jobs.

There is no single cause of wage-rate compression. For example, it can occur when unions negotiate across-the-board increases for hourly employees but managerial personnel are not granted corresponding wage differentials. Such increases can result in part from COLAs provided for in collective agreements. Other inequities have resulted from the scarcity of applicants in computers, engineering, and other professional and technical fields. Job applicants in these fields frequently have been offered starting salaries not far below those paid to employees with considerable experience and seniority. Wage-rate compression often occurs when organizations grant pay adjustments for lower-rated jobs without providing commensurate adjustments for occupations at the top of the job hierarchy.

Identifying wage-rate compression and its causes is far simpler than implementing organizational policies to alleviate its effect. Organizations wishing to minimize the problem may incorporate the following ideas into their pay policies:[36]

1. Give larger compensation increases to more-senior employees.
2. Emphasize pay-for-performance and reward merit-worthy employees.
3. Limit the hiring of new applicants seeking exorbitant salaries.
4. Design the pay structure to allow a wide spread between hourly and supervisory jobs or between new hires and senior employees.
5. Provide equity adjustments for selected employees hardest hit by pay compression.

Reality Check

Pay Equity

Linda Sullivan, program specialist, Ontario Pay Equity Commission, talks about current issues in pay equity: "Most private sector employers should have implemented pay equity by now, and our role is to monitor them for compliance. However, organizations with ten to 99 employees have the highest rate of noncompliance because they do not have resources, including a dedicated HR professional, and some positions are held by family members. Last year we monitored the food services sector. A family-owned bakery, for example, would need to identify female and male jobs, compare them, and make the required pay adjustments. In these family-owned enterprises, one can find the traditional breakdown where, for example, the bakers are male, and the customer service positions (i.e., the [people] working at the counter) are female. The bakers are paid more than positions in customer service. The multitude of tasks needed in customer service, such as communication skills, organizational skills, dealing with people who are upset, dealing with customers quickly are typically overlooked in female-dominated jobs and are not credited. These tasks within each job must be carefully identified and compensated.

"Smaller organizations in the public sector have different types of problems. In the public sector, it is difficult to do pay equity in a lot of organizations, because these organizations only have jobs held by women. For example, women usually hold all jobs in a day care centre. These organizations can't compare male and female jobs because there are no male jobs. So, in 1993, when the pay equity act was amended, another method of comparing jobs for these types of organizations was added: a proxy comparison method. The proxy comparison method allowed organizations to take key jobs, such as a day care supervisor or an early childhood educator, and compare these to similar jobs in a larger public sector employer, such as a large municipal day care centre. The municipal sector had already done pay equity, comparing male and female jobs in the day care centre to male jobs in the municipality. The small day care centre could compare the early childhood educator job and borrow their pay equity results, i.e., through a proxy comparison method.

"A third issue is, without a doubt, the degree of emotion felt by those who believe that they are being paid unfairly. For example, I had an e-mail from a woman about her work situation, where she had been hired and was doing what she felt was an equivalent job to a male colleague, but was being paid less. So she went to her manager and raised the issue with her, and a change was made to her wage, which she felt was justified. Then she realized once again, while they had raised her wage, she was still being paid considerably less than her male colleague doing work of equal or less value. The employer has not done pay equity. To me, what was striking about this situation was how emotional and betrayed the woman felt. The employers don't realize that employees feel so strongly about this unfair treatment. In a lot of these situations, women end up looking for other work, leaving the organization and costing the employer thousands of dollars required to recruit and train new employees."

Figure 9.8	How Can You Compare Apples and Oranges?

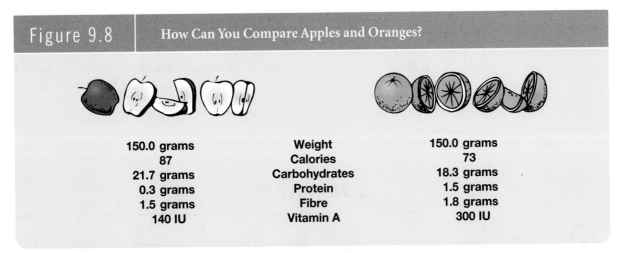

150.0 grams	Weight	150.0 grams
87	Calories	73
21.7 grams	Carbohydrates	18.3 grams
0.3 grams	Protein	1.5 grams
1.5 grams	Fibre	1.8 grams
140 IU	Vitamin A	300 IU

Source: M. Belcourt, "Human Resource Management" in *Introduction to Canadian Business*, edited by J. Plinuissen (Toronto: McGraw-Hill Ryerson and Captus Press, 1994): 410.

The Business Case

Cashing Out

Bell Canada had to pay out $100 million in cash and added pension benefits to over 4000 mostly female employees, to settle a pay equity dispute started in the early 1990s. The union argued that thousands of Bell employees, who were mostly women, were underpaid compared with those in male-dominated positions. Those working in female-dominated jobs were making, on average, two to five dollars less an hour than men in comparable jobs. The request for salary adjustments was based on a study of the work performed by telephone operators, clerical staff, sales associates, and others. Most of those employees were women. Their salaries were compared with other job functions that were dominated by men.

In July 1998, the Canadian Human Rights Tribunal ruled that there was a substantial and illegal wage gap between job categories dominated by men and those jobs dominated by women in the federal government. For example, Canada Post could not explain the wide wage gap between clerical workers, who were mostly women, and male-dominated employees in an operations group and so had to pay 6000 current and former clerical workers about $150 million in back pay. (Note that Canada Post is appealing this ruling, in a case which is approaching its twenty-third year in court!) The tribunal determined that the federal government had underpaid those mainly female workers in administrative support occupational categories. Each employee was entitled to about $30,000 in pay retroactive to March 1985. The Public Service Alliance of Canada, the union representing the workers affected by the tribunal ruling, calculates that the average annual pension of workers from these groups is only $10,000 per year. The pay equity settlement would make an important difference in the standard of living for these workers and their families now and in the future.

Sources: Colin Freeze, "Bell Settles Pay Equity Dispute," *The Globe and Mail*, May 16, 2006, A5; Neco Cockburn, "Tribunal Rules Systemic Sex Discrimination at Canada Post," *CanWest News*, October 8, 2005, 1; Uyen Vu, "22 Years and Counting," *Canadian HR Reporter*, November 7, 2005: 1.

Remember, wage-rate compression can cause low employee morale, leading to issues of reduced employee performance, higher absenteeism and turnover, and even delinquent behaviour such as employee theft.

In the next chapters, you will learn about pay for performance programs and employee benefits, all of which must be combined to ensure that compensation objectives are met.

SUMMARY

 Establishing compensation programs requires both large and small organizations to consider specific goals—employee retention, compensation distribution, and adherence to a budget, for instance. Compensation must reward employees for past efforts (pay-for-performance) while motivating employees' future performance. Internal and external equity of the pay program affects employees' concepts of fairness. Organizations must balance each of these concerns while still remaining competitive. The ability to attract qualified employees while controlling labour costs is a major factor in allowing organizations to remain viable in the domestic or international markets.

 The basis on which compensation payments are determined, and the way they are administered, can significantly affect employee productivity and the achievement of organizational goals. Internal influences include the employer's compensation policy, the worth of the job, the performance of the employee, and the employer's ability to pay. External factors influencing wage rates include labour market conditions, area wage rates, cost of living, the outcomes of collective bargaining, and legal requirements.

 Organizations use one of four basic job evaluation techniques to determine the relative worth of jobs. The job ranking system arranges jobs in numerical order on the basis of the importance of the job's duties and responsibilities to the organization. The job classification system slots jobs into pre-established grades. Higher-rated grades will require more challenging responsibilities, working conditions, and job duties. The point system of job evaluation uses a point scheme based on the compensable job factors of skill, effort, responsibility, and working conditions. The more compensable factors a job possesses, the more points are assigned to it. Jobs with higher accumulated points are considered more valuable to the organization. The work valuation system evaluates jobs based on their value relative to organizational goals—financial, customer service, and so on—and the job's contribution to organization success.

 Wage surveys determine the external equity of jobs. Data obtained from surveys will facilitate establishing the organization's wage policy while ensuring that the employer does not pay more, or less, than needed for jobs in the relevant labour market.

 The wage structure is composed of the wage curve, pay grades, and rate ranges. The wage curve depicts graphically the pay rates assigned to jobs within each pay grade. Pay grades represent the grouping of similar jobs on the basis of their relative worth. Each pay grade will include a rate range. Rate ranges will have a midpoint and minimum and maximum pay rates for all jobs in the pay grade.

 The federal and provincial governments regulate compensation through the Canada Labour Code, Employment Standards Acts, child labour provisions, and employment equity/pay equity legislation. The concept of equal pay for work of equal value seeks to overcome the fact that jobs held by women are compensated at a lower rate than those performed by men.

The concept of comparable worth seeks to overcome the fact that jobs held by women are compensated at a lower rate than those performed by men. This happens even though both types of jobs may contribute equally to organizational productivity. Wage-rate compression largely affects managerial and senior employees as the pay given to new employees or the wage increases gained through collective agreements erode the pay differences between these groups.

KEY TERMS

competence-based pay, 422
consumer price index (CPI), 410
escalator clauses, 410
Hay profile method, 416
hourly work, 405
job classification system, 412
job evaluation, 411

job ranking system, 411
pay equity, 404
pay-for-performance
 standard, 402
pay grades, 419
piecework, 405
point system, 413

real wages, 411
red circle rates, 421
value-added compensation, 401
wage and salary survey, 417
wage curve, 419
wage-rate compression, 425
work valuation, 414

DISCUSSION QUESTIONS

1. Tomax Corporation has 400 employees and wishes to develop a compensation policy to correspond to its dynamic business strategy. The company wishes to employ a high-quality workforce capable of responding to a competitive business environment. Suggest different compensation objectives to match Tomax's business goals.

2. Since employees may differ in terms of their job performance, would it not be more feasible to determine the wage rate for each employee on the basis of his or her relative worth to the organization? Explain.

3. What is job evaluation? Explain the differences between the major job evaluation systems, noting the advantages and disadvantages of each.

4. Describe the basic steps in conducting a wage and salary survey. What are some factors to consider?

5. One of the objections to granting wage increases on a percentage basis is that the lowest-paid employees, who are having the most trouble making ends meet, get the smallest increase, while the highest-paid employees get the largest increase. Is this objection a valid one? Explain.

6. Federal laws governing compensation raise important issues for both employers and employees. Discuss the following:
   a. The effect of mandatory overtime
   b. The effects of raising the minimum wage

7. The Pay Equity Commission proposes three methods to make pay equity comparisons:
   • the job-to-job comparison method
   • the proportional value comparison method
   • the proxy comparison method.
   Read about these methods on www.labour.gov .on.ca/pec/peo/english/guidelines/ge_10.html (Retrieved April 12, 2006). What are some of the problems of developing a pay system based on each of these methods?

INTERNET EXERCISE

Observe the jobs at your employer or educational institution. Find jobs that are filled mostly by women, and jobs at similar levels that are male dominated. For example, most secretarial jobs are female dominated, and most truck driver or janitor jobs are male dominated. Using the guidelines found on the website of the

Ontario Pay Equity legislation www.gov.on.ca/lab/pec/peop/english/evalu/welcome.html, follow the steps to create a gender-neutral job evaluation system to rate these jobs. You also might want to test your knowledge of pay equity provisions by taking the Pay Equity Quiz found at www.gov.on.ca/lab/peo/english/quiz/start.html.

HRM Experience

Why This Salary?

A question frequently asked is, "Why is that person paid more than I am when we both perform the same job?" The answer to this question lies in understanding the components of the wage mix as discussed in this chapter. While we may disapprove of the idea that someone is paid more or less than we are for similar work, nevertheless, factors both internal and external to the organization influence the final salary paid to a job or a specific person. Often we have little control over the wage mix factors. However, at other times, we can improve our wage by gaining additional job experience or seniority, or by obtaining increases in job knowledge or skills. This project is designed to give you experience in understanding why jobs are paid different salaries.

Assignment

The website of Monster.ca (http://salarywizard.monster.ca) provides a salary calculator for the Canadian market, giving salary ranges for jobs and a comparison tool for the national average. For example, in 2006 a HR assistant working in Winnipeg earned a median salary of $35,593. Using this site, determine the salaries paid to these occupations, *nationally*, and then answer the questions that follow as to why the differences in salaries exist. Relate these reasons to the internal and external factors of the wage mix that are discussed in the text.

Occupation	National Median Annual Salary	Low	High
• HR Assistant	$37,817	33,815	$41,273
• Librarian	$		
• Construction labourer	$		
• Computer systems administrator	$		
• Police officer	$		
• Motor coach operator	$		
• Lawyer	$		

1. What factors may account for the wide differences among salaries for different occupations?
2. Now check on compensation rates in your city and compare these to Toronto or Vancouver and Lethbridge, Alberta. What factors account for the differences among salaries for identical occupations in different cities?
3. What factors may account for the differences among salaries for the identical occupation in different organizations?

You may work individually or in teams to complete this skill-building exercise.

BIZFLIX EXERCISES

The Wedding Date: How Much Is Nick Mercer's Job Worth?

These scenes from *The Wedding Date* occur in two parts. Watch Part I, "Nick's Job," first. Apply the job evaluation concepts discussed in this chapter to decide the worth of Nick Mercer's (Dermot Mulroney) job.

Kat Ellis (Debra Messing) wants a date to accompany her to her sister Amy's (Amy Adams) wedding. She also wants to show her ex-fiancé that she can recover from him dumping her two years earlier. These requirements become part of her frantic search of the male escort classified advertisements. She hires Nick Mercer, who turns out to be much more dashing and charming than she expected. This lighthearted romantic comedy will entertain you from beginning to end.

There are two sets of scenes with a chalkboard between them. Part I comes from the "Trying Too Hard" segment that appears in the first ten minutes of the film. Kat and Nick have arrived at Heathrow Airport, London, England. Part II comes from the "A Simple Business Transaction" segment that appears a few minutes later. They have arrived at the cocktail party honouring Amy and her fiancé, Edward Fletcher-Wooten (Jack Davenport).

The Part I chalkboard reads, "Nick's Job"; the Part II chalkboard reads, "Nick's Pay." Pause the scenes at the start of Part II to consider the first question below. Kat and Nick return to the cocktail party after Kat straightens the coats in the closet.

What to Watch for and Ask Yourself

- From your viewing of Part I, how much is Nick Mercer's job as Kat's date worth? If you have seen this film, do not try to recall how much Nick received.
- The opening of this chapter includes the following observation: "Employees desire compensation systems that they perceive as being fair and commensurate with their skills and expectations." Does Nick believe he is paid fairly in Part II of the scenes? Does he place any conditions on his job and its compensation?
- Review the earlier section "Significant Compensation Issues." Do any issues raised in that section apply to these scenes? Why or why not?

case study 1

Pay Decisions at Performance Sports

Katie Perkins's career objective while attending university was to obtain a degree in small-business management and to start her own business after graduation. Her ultimate desire was to combine her love of sports and a strong interest in marketing to start a mail-order golf equipment business aimed specifically at beginning golfers.

In February 2006, after extensive development of a strategic business plan and a loan in the amount of $75,000 from the Federal Business Development Bank, Performance Sports was begun. Based on a marketing plan that stressed fast delivery, error-free customer service, and large discount pricing, Performance Sports grew rapidly. At present the company employs 16 people: eight customer service representatives earning between $9.75 and $11.25 per hour; four shipping and receiving associates paid between $8.50 and $9.50 per hour; two clerical employees each earning $8.75 per hour; an assistant manager earning $13.10 per hour; and a general manager with a wage of $15.00 per hour. Both the manager and assistant manager are former customer service representatives.

Perkins intends to create a new managerial position, purchasing agent, to handle the complex duties of purchasing golf equipment from the company's numerous equipment manufacturers. Also, the mail-order catalogue will be expanded to handle a complete line of tennis equipment. Since the position of purchasing agent is new, Perkins isn't sure how much to pay this person. She wants to employ an individual with five to eight years of experience in sports equipment purchasing.

While attending an equipment manufacturers' convention in Las Vegas, Nevada, Perkins learns that a competitor, East Valley Sports, pays its customer service representatives on a pay-for-performance basis. Intrigued by this compensation philosophy, Perkins asks her assistant manager, George Balkin, to research the pros and cons of this payment strategy. This request has become a priority because only last week two customer service representatives expressed dissatisfaction with their hourly wage. Both complained that they felt underpaid relative to the large amount of sales revenue each generates for the company.

QUESTIONS

1. What factors should Perkins and Balkin consider when setting the wage for the purchasing agent position? What resources are available for them to consult when establishing this wage?
2. Suggest advantages and disadvantages of a pay-for-performance policy for Performance Sports.
3. Suggest a new payment plan for the customer service representatives.

case study 2

Canada Post

Canada Post Corporation employs 67 000 workers, which makes it one of Canada's largest employers. In 1997 it revised its job evaluation system for postmasters and assistants. The old system, which had been in place since 1976, did not take into account changes that had arisen since 1981, when Canada Post became a Crown corporation.

A human resources consulting firm, Watson Wyatt Worldwide, was hired to assist with the entire process. According to Linda Tremblay of Organization Planning and Development, Canada Post, the job evaluation system was revised to incorporate employee input, to be responsive to federal pay equity legislation, and—most importantly—to reflect corporate culture and values.

The new job evaluation system measured the content and relative value of jobs. The system evaluated jobs according to their "typical" or "normal" components—that is, tasks that were done on a regular basis. These compensable factors were a function of the job itself, not of the performance of the person doing the job.

The four factors considered and their relative weights were as follows:

A: Responsibilities—What type of responsibilities does the job entail? 60 percent
B: Skills—What particular skills are needed to accomplish the job? 25 percent
C: Working Conditions—What working conditions apply to the job? 11 percent
D: Effort—What amount of effort does the job require? 4 percent
Total 100 percent

An example of an item under C: Working Conditions:
This factor measures the surroundings or physical conditions under which your work must be done and the extent to which they make your job disagreeable. Consider

whether elements such as those listed are present, and the relative amount and continuity of exposure:

Place a checkmark beside all those that apply:

- adverse weather conditions
- confined work space
- dirt/dust
- fumes
- inadequate lighting
- lack of privacy
- noisy conditions
- temperature extremes
- verbal abuse/public harassment
- other

Job evaluation criteria, such as in the above example, were used in each of the four areas and are summarized as below:

JOB EVALUATION CRITERIA

COMPENSABLE FACTORS	COMPONENTS
Responsibilities	Internal and external contacts
	Decision making
	Supervision of employees
	Responsibility for property maintenance
	Responsibility for rural routes, suburban services, and/or stage services
	Points of call
	Responsibility for contractor invoices
	Responsibility for a till and/or authorized allowance
Skills	Knowledge areas (such as budget process, collective agreement, contacted services in mail operations or property management, financial practices, procedures knowledge, product knowledge, primary sortation, final sortation, sales and customer service techniques, personnel management techniques)
	Job-related experience
Working conditions	Physical work environment
	Travel
Effort	Physical effort
	Multiple demands

Employees completed the job evaluation questionnaire for their own jobs. The completed questionnaires were reviewed by supervisors, managers, and human resources staff.

Total points were then allocated to each job, which corresponded to one of six job bands. Collective agreement negotiations were used to set the rates of pay for each of the six job bands.

Source: Interview and correspondence with Linda Tremblay, Canada Post Corporation.

CAREER COUNSEL

To find out what compensation you can expect to receive in your career, visit the *Managing Human Resources* website (www.belcourt5e.nelson.com)

NOTES AND REFERENCES

1. Don Hellriegel and John W. Slocum, Jr., *Organizational Behaviour*, 10th ed. (Mason, OH: South-Western, 2004): 51.

2. Edward E. Lawler III, "Pay Practices in *Fortune* 1000 Corporations," *WorldatWork* 12, no. 4 (Fourth Quarter 2003): 45–64. See also Ann Pomeroy, "Global Compensation Strategies and HR," *HRMagazine* 50, no. 5 (May 2005): 14.

3. For a frequently referenced book on strategic compensation planning, see Edward E. Lawler III, *Strategic Pay: Aligning Organizational Strategies and Pay Systems* (San Francisco: Jossey-Bass, 1990). See also Thomas J. Bergmann and Vida Gulbinas Scarpello, *Compensation Decision Making*, 4th ed. (Mason, OH: South-Western, 2002): Chapter 2.

4. John Cummings and Laurie Brannen, "The New World of Compensation," *Business Finance* 11, no. 6 (January 2005): 8. See also Dow Scott, Richard S. Sperling, Thomas D. McMullen, and Marc Wallace, "Linking Compensation Policies and Programs to Organizational Effectiveness," *WorldatWork* 12, no. 4 (Fourth Quarter 2003): 35.

5. Robyn T. Costello, "Value-Added Compensation Statements: Developing Strategic Content for a Winning Communication," *Employee Benefits Journal* 27, no. 3 (September 2002): 24–29.

6. George T. Milkovich and Jerry M. Newman, *Compensation*, 8th ed. (Boston: McGraw-Hill Irwin, 2005).

7. John A. Menefee and Ryan O. Murphy, "Rewarding and Retaining the Best: Compensation Strategies for Top Performers," *Benefits Quarterly* 20, no. 3 (Third Quarter 2004): 13–15. See also Steve Bates, Patrick Mirza, and Adrienne For, "Top Pay for Best Performance," *HRMagazine* 48, no. 1 (January 2003): 30.

8. Bronwyn Fryer, "HBR Case Study: In a World of Pay," *Harvard Business Review* 81, no. 11 (November 2003): 31–38.

9. Jude T. Rich, "Sitting on a Gold Mine: Reducing Employee Turnover at All Costs," *WorldatWork* 11, no. 2 (Second Quarter 2002): 44–51. See also Claudia Zeitz Poster, "Retaining Key People in Troubled Companies," *Compensation and Benefits Review* 34, no. 1 (January–February 2002): 7–11.

10. Lawler, "Pay Practices in *Fortune* 1000 Corporations," 45.

11. Michelle Brown and John S. Heywood, *Paying for Performance: An International Comparison* (Armonk, NY: M. E. Sharpe, 2002).

12. Barbara Crowe, Ilene Siscovick, and Marjorie Pieper, "Designing a Work Force Architecture for Merger Success," *WorldatWork* 12, no. 3 (Third Quarter 2003): 39–46.

13. Eric Beauchesne, "Tight Labour Market has Employers Willing to Pay Up," *CanWest News*, September 7, 2005, page 1.

14. For one of the classic articles on equity theory, see J. Stacey Adams, "Integrity in Social Exchange," in L. Berkowitz (ed.), *Advances in Experimental Social Psychology* (New York: Academic Press, 1965): 276–99.

15. Andrew J. DuBrin, *Fundamentals of Organizational Behaviour*, 3rd ed. (Mason, OH: South-Western, 2005): 114–16.

16. Victor H. Vroom, *Work and Motivation* (San Francisco: Jossey-Bass, 1994). This landmark book, originally published in 1964, integrates the work of hundreds of researchers seeking to explain choice of work, job satisfaction, and job performance.

17. Joseph Champoux, *Organizational Behaviour: Essential Tenets*, 2nd ed. (Mason, OH: South-Western, 2003): Chapter 8.

18. Robert L. Heneman, Paul W. Mulvey, and Peter V. LeBlanc, "Improve Base Pay ROI by Increasing Employee Knowledge," *WorldatWork* 11, no. 4 (Fourth Quarter 2002): 23–36.

19. Detailed discussion of exempt and nonexempt rules under the Fair Labor Standards Act can be found at www.dol.gov.

20. Ira Feder, "Fine-Tuning the Pay Mix for Potential Cost Savings," *WorldatWork* 12, no. 2 (Second Quarter 2003): 6.

21. James R. Bowers, "Valuing Work: An Integrated Approach," *WorldatWork* 12, no. 2 (Second Quarter 2003): 28–39.

22. Robert L. Heneman, Peter V. LeBlanc, and Tim L. Reynolds, "Using Work Valuation to Identify and Protect the Talent Pool," *WorldatWork* 11, no. 2 (Third Quarter 2002): 31–41.

23. William H. Holley, Jr., Kenneth M. Jennings, and Roger S. Wolters, *The Labor Relations Process*, 8th ed. (Mason, OH: South-Western, 2005): Chapter 6.

24. Robert L. Heneman, "Job and Work Evaluation," *Public Personnel Management* 32, no. 1 (Spring 2003): 1–25.

25. Fred Hilling, "Job Evaluation Is Here to Stay," *WorldatWork* 12, no. 3 (Third Quarter 2003): 14–21.

26. Deborah Keary, Saundra Jackson, and Vicki Neal, "Job Evaluation, Health Coverage, Discipline," *HRMagazine* 49, no. 1 (January 2004): 39–40.

27. Robert L. Heneman, Peter V. LeBlanc, and Howard Risher, "Work Valuation Addresses Shortcomings of Both Job Evaluation and Market Pricing," *Compensation and Benefits Review* 35, no. 1 (January–February 2003): 7–11.

28. James R. Bowers, "Valuing Work," *WorldatWork* 12, no. 2 (Second Quarter 2003): 28.

29. Craig Skenes and Brian H. Kleiner, "The Hay System of Compensation," *Management Research News* 26, no. 2 (2003): 109.

30. Nona Tobin, "Can Technology Ease the Pain of Salary Surveys?" *Public Personnel Management* 31, no. 1 (Spring 2002): 65–76.

31. Michael O'Malley, "What Is Base Salary?" *WorldatWork* 12, no. 3 (Third Quarter 2003): 22–28.

32. Gregory A. Stoskopf, "Choosing the Best Salary Structure for Your Organization," *WorldatWork* 11, no. 4 (Fourth Quarter 2004): 28–36.

33. R. Eugene Hughes, "Skill or Diploma? The Potential Influence of Skill-Based Pay Systems on Sources of Skills Acquisition and Degree Programs," *Work Study* 52, no. 4/5 (2003): 179–83.

34. Patricia K. Zingheim and Jay R. Schuster, "Reassessing the Value of Skill-Based Pay," *WorldatWork* 11, no. 3 (Third Quarter 2002): 72–77.

35. Andrew S. Rosen and David Turetsky, "Broadbanding: The Construction of a Career Management Framework," *WorldatWork* 11, no. 4 (Fourth Quarter 2002): 45–55.

36. Andrew L. Klein, Kimberly M. Keating, and Lisa M. Ruggiero, "The Perils of Pay Inequity: Addressing the Problems of Compression," *WorldatWork* 11, no. 4 (Fourth Quarter 2002): 56–62.

chapter 10

Pay-for-Performance: Incentive Rewards

After studying this chapter, you should be able to

objective 1

Discuss the basic requirements for successful implementation of incentive programs.

objective 2

Identify the types of, and reasons for implementing, individual incentive plans.

objective 3

Explain why merit raises may fail to motivate employees adequately and discuss ways to increase their motivational value.

objective 4

Indicate the advantage of each of the principal methods used to compensate salespeople.

objective 5

Differentiate how gains may be shared with employees under the Scanlon, Rucker, and Improshare gainsharing systems.

objective 6

Differentiate among profit-sharing plans and explain advantages and disadvantages of these programs.

objective 7

Describe the main types of ESOP plans and discuss the advantages of ESOP to employers and employees.

n the previous chapter we emphasized that the worth of a job is a significant factor in determining the pay rate for that job. However, pay based solely on this measure may fail to motivate employees to perform to their full capacity. Unmotivated employees are likely to meet only minimum performance standards. Recognizing this fact, over 80 percent of Canadian companies offer some form of incentive to workers. These organizations are attempting to get more motivational mileage out of employee compensation by tying it more closely to organizational objectives and employee performance. Jessica Smilko and Kathy Van Neck, compensation specialists, note this fact about variable pay: "Employees are embracing variable compensation as a means of aligning employee behaviour with organizational goals."[1] When incentives are linked with output, workers will increasingly apply their skills and knowledge to their jobs and will be encouraged to work together as a team. Therefore, in their attempt to raise productivity, managers are focusing on the many variables that help determine the effectiveness of pay as a motivator.

In this chapter we will discuss incentive plans in terms of the objectives they hope to achieve and the various factors that may affect their success. Because many organizations have implemented broad-based incentive programs, for discussion purposes we have grouped incentive plans into three broad categories: individual incentive plans, group incentive plans, and enterprise incentive plans, as shown in Figure 10.1.[2]

Strategic Reasons for Incentive Plans

variable pay
Tying pay to some measure of individual, group, or organizational performance

A clear trend in strategic compensation management is the growth of incentive plans, also called **variable pay** programs, for employees throughout the organization. Ken Abosch, compensation specialist with Hewitt Associates LLC, notes, "There's no question that most corporations have turned away from fixed forms of compensation in favour of variable forms. There has been an abandonment of entitlement programs."[3]

Incentive rewards are based entirely upon a pay-for-performance philosophy (see Chapter 9). Incentive pay programs establish a performance "threshold" (a baseline performance level) that an employee or group of employees must reach in order to qualify for incentive payments. According to one compensation manager, "The performance

Figure 10.1	Types of Incentive Plans

INDIVIDUAL	GROUP	ENTERPRISE
Piecework	Team compensation	Profit sharing
Standard hour plan	Scanlon Plan	Stock options
Bonuses	Rucker Plan	Employee stock ownership
Merit pay	Improshare	plans (ESOPs)
Lump-sum merit pay	Earnings-at-risk plans	
Sales incentives		
Incentives for professional employees		
Executive compensation		

threshold is the minimum level an employee must reach in order to qualify for variable pay." Additionally, incentive plans emphasize a shared focus on organizational objectives by broadening the opportunities for incentives to employees throughout the organization. Incentive plans create an operating environment that champions a philosophy of shared commitment through the belief that every individual contributes to organizational performance and success.

Incentive Plans as Links to Organizational Objectives

Contemporary arguments for incentive plans focus on linking compensation rewards, both individual and group, to organizational goals. Specific company goals or objectives might be to lower labour costs, improve customer satisfaction, expand product markets, or maintain high levels of productivity and quality, which in turn improve the market for Canadian goods and services in a global economy. By meshing compensation and organizational objectives, managers believe that employees will assume "ownership" of their jobs, thereby improving their effort and overall job performance. Incentives are designed to encourage employees to put out more effort to complete their job tasks—effort they might not be motivated to expend under hourly and/or seniority-based compensation systems. Also, incentive pay is highly valued as a compensation strategy to attract and retain top-performing employees.[4] Figure 10.2 outlines the different compensation approaches to attract and retain staff. Figure 10.3 summarizes the major advantages of incentive pay programs as noted by researchers and HR professionals.

Do incentive plans work? Various studies, along with reports from individual organizations, show a measurable relationship between incentive plans and improved organizational performance. In the area of manufacturing, productivity often improves

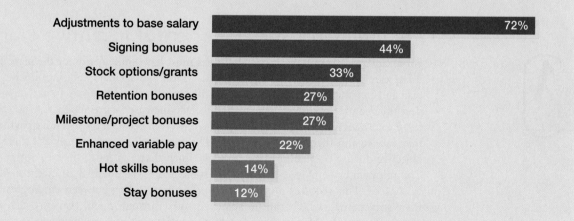

| Figure 10.2 | Compensation Approaches to Attract and Retain Staff |

Nearly 80% of Canadian firms have at least one compensation strategy designed to attract and retain key employees. Here is a look at the different methods organizations are using.

Adjustments to base salary — 72%
Signing bonuses — 44%
Stock options/grants — 33%
Retention bonuses — 27%
Milestone/project bonuses — 27%
Enhanced variable pay — 22%
Hot skills bonuses — 14%
Stay bonuses — 12%

Source: *Compensation Planning Outlook*, 2004 Conference Board of Canada, but taken from Gail Pickard, "On the Charts," Guide to Recruitment and Staffing, *Canadian HR Reporter*, December 1, 2003, G3.

Figure 10.3	Advantages of Incentive Pay Programs

- Incentives focus employee efforts on specific performance targets. They provide real motivation that produces important employee and organizational gains.
- Incentive payouts are variable costs linked to the achievement of results. Base salaries are fixed costs largely unrelated to output.
- Incentive compensation is directly related to operating performance. If performance objectives (quantity and/or quality) are met, incentives are paid. If objectives are not achieved, incentives are withheld.
- Incentives foster teamwork and unit cohesiveness when payments to individuals are based on team results.
- Incentives are a way to distribute success among those responsible for producing that success.

by as much as 20 percent after the adoption of incentive plans. Improvements, however, are not limited to goods-producing industries. Service organizations, not-for-profits, and government agencies also show productivity gains when incentives are linked to organizational goals. For example, after implementing a rating-based incentive program—based on customer satisfaction criteria—Shell Oil developed a consistent brand experience at thousands of independent stations. Bob Hull, program implementation director for Shell, notes, "When you have a good experience at a Shell station you'll come back."[5] Cadillac dealers who meet sales and customer satisfaction targets receive a cash bonus, merchandise awards, and a plaque to hang in the showroom.[6]

Unfortunately, studies also show that variable pay plans may not achieve their proposed objectives or lead to organizational improvements. First, incentive plans sometimes fail to satisfy employee expectations for pay gains. Second, management may have failed to give adequate attention to the design and implementation of the plan, leaving employees confused about how incentive payments are calculated. Third, employees may have little ability to affect performance standards. Furthermore, the success of an incentive plan will depend on the environment that exists within an organization. A plan is more likely to work in an organization where morale is high, employees believe they are being treated fairly, and there is harmony between employees and management.

Requirements for a Successful Incentive Plan

For an incentive plan to succeed, employees must have some desire for the plan. This desire can be influenced in part by how successful management is in introducing the plan and convincing employees of its benefits. Encouraging employees to participate in developing and administering the plan is likely to increase their willingness to accept it.

Employees must be able to see a clear connection between the incentive payments they receive and their job performance. This connection is more visible if there are objective quality or quantity standards by which they can judge their performance. Commitment by employees to meet these standards is also essential for incentive plans to succeed. This requires mutual trust and understanding between employees and their supervisors, which can be achieved only through open, two-way channels of communication. Management should never allow incentive payments to be seen as an *entitlement*. Instead, these payments should be viewed as a reward that must be earned through effort. This perception can be strengthened if the incentive money is distributed to employees in a separate cheque. Compensation specialists also note the following as characteristics of a successful incentive plan:

- Financial incentives are linked to valued behaviour.
- The incentive program seems fair to employees.
- Productivity/quality standards are challenging but achievable.
- Payout formulas are simple and understandable.

Furthermore, the best-managed incentive pay programs are clearly and continuously communicated to employees. This is true during both good and bad economic periods. According to Roisin Woolnough, compensation consultant, "Communicate what you are doing and why it is critical to success. Everyone needs to know what the goals are and what the rewards are for achieving those goals."[7] Proactive organizations find it advisable to evaluate the operation and administration of their variable pay programs. Highlights in HRM 10.1 provides one diagnostic tool for the periodic review and assessment of incentive programs.

Highlights in HRM 10.1

Assessing Incentive Program Effectiveness

MasterBrand Cabinets and Waterloo Industries, manufacturers of tool storage products, have spent several years broadly implementing incentive programs. With a hard-working and dedicated workforce, each company has identified broad-based incentives as a key element in achieving business goals. To ensure continued success with their incentive programs, managers at both organizations are expected to make periodic reviews and assessment of their incentive programs. Here is an example of one diagnostic assessment tool.

INCENTIVE PROGRAM ASSESSMENT TOOL

GENERAL ASSESSMENT	UNSURE	LOW	SOME	HIGH
1. To what extent do incentive program measures support business and operational objectives?	❑	❑	❑	❑
2. To what extent do employees understand how to influence program measures?	❑	❑	❑	❑
3. To what extent have employee behaviours changed as a result of the program?	❑	❑	❑	❑
4. To what extent has plant leadership actively engaged employees in improving performance?	❑	❑	❑	❑
5. To what extent is there an effective infrastructure to support the program (e.g., communications, tracking)?	❑	❑	❑	❑
6. Overall, how would you rate plant management's satisfaction with the program?	❑	❑	❑	❑
7. Overall, how would you rate employee (program participant) satisfaction with the program?	❑	❑	❑	❑

Source: Christian M. Ellis and Cynthia L. Paluso, "Blazing a Trail to Broad-Based Incentives," *WorldatWork Journal* 9, no. 4 (2000): 33–41. Used with permission, WorldatWork, Scottsdale, Arizona.

Setting Performance Measures

Measurement is key to the success of incentive plans because it communicates the importance of established organizational goals. What gets measured and rewarded gets attention.[8] For example, if the organization wants to be a leader in quality, then performance indexes may focus on customer satisfaction, timeliness, or being error-free. If being a low-priced producer is the goal, then emphasis should be on cost reduction or increased productivity with lower acceptable levels of quality. While a variety of performance options are available, most focus on quality, cost control, or productivity. Highlights in HRM 10.2 provides five proven guidelines on how to establish and maintain an effective performance measurement program.

For some organizations, linking incentive payments to formalized performance measures has not obtained positive results for either employees or the organization.[9]

Highlights in HRM 10.2

Setting Performance Measures—The Keys

Both large and small organizations have established performance measures to improve operational success while rewarding employees for their performance outcomes. Establishing meaningful performance measures is one of the important and difficult challenges facing management today. Before managers or supervisors develop and implement organizational measures, they should consider the following guidelines.

- Performance measures—at all organizational levels—must be consistent with the strategic goals of the organization. Avoid nonrelevant measures that are not closely linked to the business or what employees do in their work.
- Define the intent of performance measures and champion the cause relentlessly. Demonstrate that performance measures are, in fact, good business management, and hold managers and employees accountable for their success.
- Involve employees. A critical step in any measurement program is the development of an employee involvement strategy outlining the nature of employee participation, implementation, and ongoing management of the performance management program. Segment the workforce based on nature of work and potential for impact. Consider which measurements require customization. Acceptance of a performance measurement program is heightened when employees "buy into" the process.
- Consider the organization's culture and workforce demographics when designing performance measures. For example, organizations with a more traditional hierarchical structure may need more time to introduce performance measurements compared to flatter organizations, which are more fluid and less steeped in control and command characteristics.
- Widely communicate the importance of performance measures. Performance messages are the principles and guidelines that communicate to employees about required performance levels and why the organization needs to achieve those levels of success.

Source: Adapted from Christian M. Ellis, "Improving the Impact of Performance Management," *Workspan* 45, no. 2 (February 2002): 7–8.

Failure can often be traced to the choice of performance measures. Therefore, measures that are quantitative, simple, and structured to show a clear relationship to improved performance are best. Overly quantitative, complex measures are to be avoided. Also, when selecting a performance measure, it is necessary to evaluate the extent to which the employees involved can actually influence the measurement. Finally, employers must guard against "ratcheting up" performance goals by continually trying to exceed previous results. This eventually leads to employee frustration and employee perception that the standards are unattainable. The result will be a mistrust of management and a backlash against the entire incentive program.

Administering Incentive Plans

While incentive plans based on productivity can reduce direct labour costs, to achieve their full benefit they must be carefully thought out, implemented, and maintained. A cardinal rule is that thorough planning must be combined with a "proceed with caution" approach. Compensation managers repeatedly stress a number of points related to the effective administration of incentive plans. Three of the more important points are, by consensus, as follows:

1. Incentive systems are effective only when managers are willing to grant incentives based on differences in individual, team, or organizational performance. Allowing incentive payments to become pay guarantees defeats the motivational intent of the incentive. The primary purpose of an incentive compensation plan is not to pay off under almost all circumstances, but rather to motivate performance. Thus, if the plan is to succeed, poor performance must go unrewarded.
2. Annual salary budgets must be large enough to reward and reinforce exceptional performance. When compensation budgets are set to ensure that pay increases do not exceed certain limits (often established as a percentage of payroll or sales), these constraints may prohibit rewarding outstanding individual or group performance.
3. The overhead costs associated with plan implementation and administration must be determined. These may include the cost of establishing performance standards and the added cost of record keeping. The time consumed in communicating the plan to employees, answering questions, and resolving any complaints about it must also be included in these costs.

Individual Incentive Plans

In today's competitive world, one word, *flexibility*, describes the design of individual incentive plans.[10] For example, technology, job tasks and duties, and/or organizational goals (such as being a low-cost producer) impact the organization's choice of incentive pay programs. Incentive payments may be determined by the number of units produced, by the achievement of specific performance goals, or by productivity improvements in the organization as a whole. In addition, in highly competitive industries such as foods and retailing, low profit margins will affect the availability of monies for incentive payouts. All of these considerations suggest that tradition and philosophy, as well as economics and technology, help govern the design of individual incentive systems.

Piecework

straight piecework
An incentive plan under which employees receive a certain rate for each unit produced

differential piece rate
A compensation rate under which employees whose production exceeds the standard amount of output receive a higher rate for all of their work than the rate paid to those who do not exceed the standard amount

One of the oldest incentive plans is based on piecework. Under **straight piecework,** employees receive a certain rate for each unit produced. Their compensation is determined by the number of units they produce during a pay period. At Steelcase, an office furniture maker, employees can earn more than their base pay, often as much as 35 percent more, through piecework for each slab of metal they cut or chair they upholster. Under a **differential piece rate,** employees whose production exceeds the standard output receive a higher rate for *all* of their work than the rate paid to those who do not exceed the standard.

Employers include piecework in their compensation strategy for several reasons. The wage payment for each employee is simple to compute, and the plan permits an organization to predict its labour costs with considerable accuracy, as these costs are the same for each unit of output. The piecework system is more likely to succeed when units of output can be measured readily, when the quality of the product is less critical, when the job is fairly standardized, and when a constant flow of work can be maintained.

Computing the Piece Rate

Although time standards establish the time required to perform a given amount of work, they do not by themselves determine what the incentive rate should be. The incentive rates must be based on hourly wage rates that would otherwise be paid for the type of work being performed. Say, for example, the standard time for producing one unit of work in a job paying $11.50 per hour was set at 12 minutes. The piece rate would be $2.30 per unit, computed as follows:

$$\frac{60 \text{ (minutes per hour)}}{12 \text{ (standard time per unit)}} = 5 \text{ units per hour}$$

$$\frac{\$11.50 \text{ (hourly rate)}}{5 \text{ (units per hour)}} = \$2.30 \text{ per unit}$$

Piecework: The Drawbacks

Despite their obvious advantages—including their direct tie to a pay-for-performance philosophy—piecework systems have a number of disadvantages that offset their usefulness. One of the most significant weaknesses of piecework, as well as of other incentive plans based on individual effort, is that it may not always be an effective motivator. If employees believe that an increase in their output will provoke disapproval from fellow workers (often referred to as "rate busting"), they may avoid exerting maximum effort because their desire for peer approval outweighs their desire for more money. Also, jobs in which individual contributions are difficult to distinguish or measure, or in which the work is mechanized to the point that the employee exercises very little control over output, may be unsuited to piecework. Piecework may also be inappropriate in the following situations:

- When quality is more important than quantity
- When technology changes are frequent
- When productivity standards on which piecework must be based are difficult to develop

Importantly, piecework incentive systems can work against an organizational culture promoting workforce cooperation, creativity, or problem solving because each of these goals can infringe on an employee's time and productivity and, therefore, total incentive earned.

Standard Hour Plan

standard hour plan
An incentive plan that sets rates based on the completion of a job in a predetermined standard time

Another common incentive technique is the **standard hour plan,** which sets incentive rates on the basis of a predetermined "standard time" for completing a job. If employees finish the work in less than the expected time, their pay is still based on the standard time for the job multiplied by their hourly rate. Standard hour plans are popular in service departments in automobile dealerships. For example, if the standard time to install an engine in a truck is five hours and the mechanic completes the job in four and a half hours, the payment would be the mechanic's hourly rate times five hours. Standard hour plans are particularly suited to long-cycle operations or jobs or tasks that are nonrepetitive and require a variety of skills. However, while standard hour plans can motivate employees to produce more, employers must ensure that equipment maintenance and product quality do not suffer as employees strive to do their work faster to earn additional income.

Bonuses

bonus
An incentive payment that is supplemental to the base wage

A **bonus** is an incentive payment that is given to an employee beyond one's normal base wage. It is frequently given at the end of the year and does not become part of base pay. Bonuses have the advantage of providing employees with more pay for exerting greater effort, while at the same time the employees still have the security of a basic wage. Bonus payments are common among managerial and executive employees, but recent trends show that they are increasingly given to employees throughout the organization.

Depending on who is to receive the bonus, the incentive payment may be determined on the basis of cost reduction, quality improvement, or performance criteria

Employees in manufacturing plants often work under individual incentive plans such as piecework.

© DAVE BARTRUFF/CORBIS

established by the organization. At the executive level, for example, performance criteria might include earnings growth or enterprise-specific agreed-on objectives.

When some special employee contribution is to be rewarded, a spot bonus is used. A **spot bonus,** as the name implies, is given "on the spot," normally for some employee effort not directly tied to an established performance standard. For example, a customer service representative might receive a spot bonus for working long hours to fill a new customer's large order. Spot bonuses are championed as useful retention and motivational tools for overburdened employees, especially during lean financial times. Lauren Sejen, compensation expert with Watson Wyatt Worldwide, notes, "I think spot bonuses are one of the most underutilized forms of rewards, given how well employees respond to them. These plans make perfect sense."[11]

spot bonus
An unplanned bonus given for employee effort unrelated to an established performance measure

Merit Pay

A merit pay program (merit raise) links an increase in base pay to how successfully an employee performs his or her job. The merit increase is normally given on the basis of an employee's having achieved some objective performance standard—although a superior's subjective evaluation of subordinate performance may play a large role in the increase given. Merit raises can serve to motivate if employees perceive the raise to be related to the performance required to earn it.[12]

Theories of motivation, in addition to behavioural science research, provide justification for merit pay plans as well as other pay-for-performance programs.[13] However, research shows that a merit increase in the range of 7 to 9 percent is necessary to serve as a pay motivator. Employees may welcome lower percentage amounts, but low salary increases may not lead to significantly greater effort on the part of employees to drive business results. Consequently, with low salary budgets (see Chapter 9), organizations wishing to reward top performers will be required to distribute a large portion of the compensation budget to these individuals.[14] A meaningful merit increase will catch the attention of top performers while sending a signal to poor-performing employees. A strategic compensation policy *must differentiate* between outstanding and good or average performance. Furthermore, increases granted on the basis of merit should be distinguishable from cost-of-living or other general increases.

Problems with Merit Raises

Merit raises may not always achieve their intended purpose. Unlike a bonus, a merit raise may be perpetuated year after year even when performance declines. When this happens, employees come to expect the increase and see it as being an entitlement, unrelated to their performance. Furthermore, what are referred to as merit raises often turn out to be increases based on seniority or favouritism. These reasons probably explain why an outstanding 96 percent of the senior executives in the Federal Public Service (i.e., nearly everyone) received merit pay in 2001–2002.[15] A superior's biased evaluation of subordinate performance may play a large role in the increase given. Even when merit raises are determined by performance, the employee's gains may be offset by inflation and higher income taxes. Compensation specialists also recognize the following problems with merit pay plans:

1. Money available for merit increases may be inadequate to raise satisfactorily all employees' base pay.
2. Managers may have no guidance in how to define and measure performance; there may be vagueness regarding merit award criteria.

3. Employees may not believe that their compensation is tied to effort and performance; they may be unable to differentiate between merit pay and other types of pay increases.

4. The performance appraisal objectives of employees and their managers are often at odds.

5. There may be a lack of honesty and cooperation between management and employees.

6. It has been shown that "overall" merit pay plans do not motivate higher levels of employee performance.

merit guidelines
Guidelines for awarding merit raises that are tied to performance objectives

While there are no easy solutions to these problems, organizations using a true merit pay plan often base the percentage pay raise on **merit guidelines** tied to performance appraisals. For example, Highlights in HRM 10.3 illustrates a guideline chart for awarding merit raises. The percentages may change each year, depending on various internal or external concerns such as profit levels or national economic conditions as indicated by changes in the consumer price index. Under the illustrated merit plan, to prevent all employees from being rated outstanding or above average, managers may be required to distribute the performance rating according to some preestablished formula (such as only 10 percent can be rated outstanding). Additionally, when setting merit percentage guidelines, organizations should consider individual performance along with such factors as training, experience, and current earnings.

Lump-Sum Merit Pay

lump-sum merit program
Program under which employees receive a year-end merit payment, which is not added to their base pay

To make merit increases more flexible and visible, organizations such as Boeing, Timex, and Westinghouse have implemented a **lump-sum merit program.** Under this type of plan, employees receive a single lump-sum increase at the time of their review, an increase that is not added to their base salary. Lump-sum merit programs offer several advantages. For employees, an advantage is that receiving a single lump-sum merit payment can provide a clear link between pay and performance. For example, a 6-percent merit increase granted to an industrial engineer earning $58,000 a year translates into a weekly increase of $66.92—a figure that looks small compared with a lump-sum payment of $3,480. For employers, lump-sum payments essentially freeze base salaries, thereby maintaining annual salary and benefit costs, as the level of benefits is normally calculated from salary levels. Organizations using a lump-sum merit program will want to adjust base salaries upward after a certain period of time. These adjustments should keep pace with the rising cost of living and increases in the general market wage.

Incentive Awards and Recognition

Awards are often used to recognize productivity gains, special contributions or achievements, and service to the organization. Merchandise awards, personalized gifts, theatre tickets, vacations, gift certificates, and personalized clothing represent popular noncash incentive awards.[16] Tangible awards presented with the right message and style can make employees feel appreciated while at the same time underscoring a company's values.[17]

Research clearly shows that noncash incentive awards are most effective as motivators when the award is combined with a meaningful employee recognition program. Bob Nelson, president of Nelson Motivation, states, "Employers should take care to tie awards to performance and deliver awards in a timely, sincere and specific way."[18]

Highlights in HRM 10.3

Merit Pay Guidelines Chart

A merit pay guidelines chart is a "look-up" table for awarding merit increases on the basis of (1) employee performance, (2) position in the pay range, and, in a few cases, (3) time since the last pay increase. Design of any merit guidelines chart involves several concerns. Specifically,

- What should unsatisfactory performers be paid? Since their performance is marginal or below standard, the common response is "nothing."
- What should average performers be paid? Common practice is to grant increases commensurate with cost-of-living changes (see Chapter 9). The midpoint of the merit guidelines chart should equal the local or national percentage change in the consumer price index (CPI).
- How much should superior or outstanding performers be paid? Profit levels, compensation budgets, or psychological concerns predominate here.

The following merit pay guidelines chart shows the pay range for each pay grade as divided into five levels (quintiles), with 1 at the bottom of the pay range and 5 at the top. On the left, employee performance (as determined by the annual appraisal) is arranged in five levels from high (outstanding) to low (unsatisfactory). An employee's position in his or her salary range and performance level indicates the percentage pay increase to be awarded. For example, a person at the top of the pay range (5) who gets a performance rating of "outstanding" will be awarded a 6-percent pay increase. However, an outstanding performer at the bottom of the pay range (1) will receive a 9-percent increase.

Because the purpose of the guidelines chart is to balance conflicting pay goals, it compromises, by design, the relationship between merit increases and performance appraisal ratings. The highest-rated performers will not always be the employees with the highest percentage increase. Notice that a superior performer in quintiles 1, 2, and 3 can receive a percentage increase as much as or more than that of an outstanding performer in quintile 5. As a result, employees are likely to learn that pay increases are not determined just by performance. However, as we learned in Chapter 9, if money is to serve as a motivator, expectancy theory specifies that employees must believe there is a link between performance and pay increases if performance is to remain at a high level.

MERIT PAY GUIDE CHART

PERFORMANCE LEVEL	QUINTILE (POSITION IN RANGE), PERCENT				
	1	2	3	4	5
Outstanding (5)	9	9	8	7	6
Superior (4)	7	7	6	5	4
Competent (3)	5	5	4	3	3
Needs improvement (2)	0	0	0	0	0
Unsatisfactory (1)	0	0	0	0	0

Importantly, awards and employee recognition should highlight how employee performance contributes to specific organizational objectives. Figure 10.4 outlines the types of recognition awards being given by Canadian organizations.

Sales Incentives

The enthusiasm and drive required in most types of sales work demand that sales employees be highly motivated. This fact, as well as the competitive nature of selling, explains why financial incentives for salespeople are widely used. These incentive plans must provide a source of motivation that will elicit cooperation and trust. Motivation is particularly important for employees away from the office who cannot be supervised closely and who, as a result, must exercise a high degree of self-discipline.

Unique Needs of Sales Incentive Plans

Incentive systems for salespeople are complicated by the wide differences in the types of sales jobs.[19] These range from department store clerks who ring up customer purchases to industrial salespeople who provide consultation and other highly technical services. Salespeople's performance may be measured by the dollar volume of their sales and by their ability to establish new accounts. Other measures are the ability to promote new products or services and to provide various forms of customer service and assistance that do not produce immediate sales revenues.[20]

Performance standards for sales employees are difficult to develop, however, because their performance is often affected by external factors beyond their control.

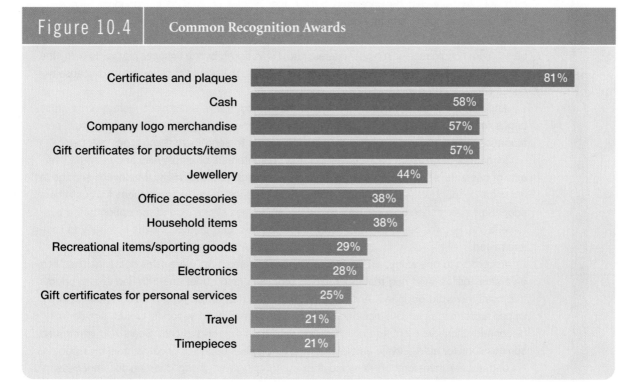

Figure 10.4 | **Common Recognition Awards**

Award	Percentage
Certificates and plaques	81%
Cash	58%
Company logo merchandise	57%
Gift certificates for products/items	57%
Jewellery	44%
Office accessories	38%
Household items	38%
Recreational items/sporting goods	29%
Electronics	28%
Gift certificates for personal services	25%
Travel	21%
Timepieces	21%

Source: WorldatWork's Trends in Employee Recognition 2005, but taken from Daphne Woolf, "On the Charts," Report on Total Rewards, *Canadian HR Reporter,* February 30, 2006.

Economic and seasonal fluctuations, sales competition, changes in demand, and the nature of the sales territory can all affect an individual's sales record.[21] Sales volume alone therefore may not be an accurate indicator of the effort salespeople have expended.

In developing incentive plans for salespeople, managers are also confronted with the problem of how to reward extra sales effort and at the same time compensate for activities that do not contribute directly or immediately to sales. Furthermore, sales employees must be able to enjoy some degree of income stability.[22] Many schemes to reward employees for reaching sales goals are threatened by instances of unethical behaviour where the needs of the employees are not aligned with the needs of the customer, as reported in Ethics in HR.

Ethics in HR

Counter-Productive Compensation

I started worrying about the corrupting influence of incentive schemes when, in a period of one month, I was asked by three employees at three different companies to help them achieve their bonuses. The first case happened after I purchased a car and was asked by the sales representative to complete an evaluation form and to give him high ratings so that he would get his bonus. The second instance took place after I had another car serviced and was told by the mechanic that I would be contacted by an agency that conducted independent ratings on employee performance, and that I had better rate him as a "10" because no other mark would get him the bonus. Then, a few days later, I wanted to move some money from one bank to another bank where I could receive a higher interest rate. I was asked by the financial adviser to delay the transfer of my money until the following month (even though it would cost me money) because her bonus was calculated at the end of the month.

Apparently my experience is not unique. At one company, employees were given a small bonus for every voluntary and spontaneous complementary letter received about their performance. Of course, employees began asking clients to send them these types of letters.

Incentives may create conflict between the best interests of employees and the best interests of customers. In order to receive commissions and bonuses, many employees engage in unethical conduct. When Alberta Government Telephones rewarded employees for customers adopting a new phone optional service, some employees simply added the option to the customer's line, and the customer would have to notice this, and then phone the company to have it removed.

According to one study, almost half of the respondents, who were sales personnel, had lied on a sales call, a third had made unrealistic promises, and about one-fifth had sold products that customers did not need. Another study reported that employees working in call centres, whose performance targets included handling a customer in ten seconds, would "accidentally" disconnect those who spoke English poorly (and thus slowed the call). Sears had introduced commissions for auto-service employees, and employees began to cheat to meet their quotas. An undercover investigation revealed that customers were being charged for unnecessary repairs.

Unions have concerns about incentive programs, and are usually not supportive of them. For example, Toronto Hydro tried to implement an incentive program that would include gift certificates, extra breaks, and prizes such as cameras. The union, Local 1 of the Canadian Union of Public Employees, was invited to participate in the committee to design the rewards program, but declined because the allocation of rewards was seen to be inherently subjective. The program was going to reward people for "going above and beyond," but this may mean different things to different people. The union argued that if going "above and beyond" means carrying a larger than normal workload, such as journalists covering an election campaign, or a group of nurses working through the SARS epidemic, then paying for overtime is how the organization should reward these workers. Also some organizations reward employees for attendance, but again the union says: "If someone is blessed with good health, why should somebody else with poor health be treated differently?" The union is particularly opposed to incentive programs linked to health and safety. If the unit is depending on a cash payout for reaching X days without an injury, the first person to be injured can be coerced into covering up the injury, so that his peers qualify for the reward. Furthermore, assessing and compensating employees outside of the performance appraisal provisions of the collective agreement is in breach of the collective agreement.

Sources: Adapted from Uyen Vu, "Morale Booster or Minefield," *The Canadian HR Reporter*, August 9, 2004, 13; M. Choquette, "Compensation That Corrupts," The Conference Board of Canada, 1999: 254–99.

Types of Sales Incentive Plans

straight salary plan
A compensation plan that permits salespeople to be paid for performing various duties that are not reflected immediately in their sales volume

Compensation plans for sales employees may consist of a straight salary plan, a straight commission plan, or a combination salary and commission plan. A **straight salary plan** permits salespeople to be paid for performing various duties not reflected immediately in their sales volume. It enables them to devote more time to providing services and building up the goodwill of customers without jeopardizing their income. The principal limitation of the straight salary plan is that it may not motivate salespeople to exert sufficient effort in maximizing their sales volume.

straight commission plan
A compensation plan based on a percentage of sales

On the other hand, the **straight commission plan,** based on a percentage of sales, provides maximum incentive and is easy to compute and understand. For example, total cash compensation might equal total sales volume times some percentage of total sales, say 2 percent. Under a straight commission plan salespeople may be allowed a salary draw. A *draw* is a cash advance that must be paid back as commissions are earned.

However, the straight commission plan is limited by the following disadvantages:

1. Emphasis is on sales volume rather than on profits.
2. Customer service after the sale is likely to be neglected.
3. Earnings tend to fluctuate widely between good and poor periods of business, and turnover of trained sales employees tends to increase in poor periods.
4. Salespeople are tempted to grant price concessions.

combined salary and commission plan
A compensation plan that includes a straight salary and a commission

The **combined salary and commission plan** is the most widely used sales incentive program. A salesperson working under a 70/30 combination plan would receive total cash compensation paid out as 70-percent base salary and 30-percent commission. The ratio of base salary to commission can be set to fit organizational objectives. The following advantages indicate why the combination salary and commission plan is so widely used:

1. The right kind of incentive compensation, if linked to salary in the right proportion, has most of the advantages of both the straight salary and the straight commission forms of compensation.
2. A salary-plus-incentive compensation plan offers greater design flexibility and can therefore be more readily set up to help maximize company profits.
3. The plan can develop the most favourable ratio of selling expense to sales.
4. The field sales force can be motivated to achieve specific company marketing objectives in addition to sales volume.

Incentives for Professional Employees

Like other salaried workers, professional employees—engineers, scientists, and lawyers, for example—may be motivated through bonuses and merit increases. In some organizations, unfortunately, professional employees cannot advance beyond a certain point in the salary structure unless they are willing to take an administrative assignment. When they are promoted, their professional talents are no longer utilized fully. In the process, the organization may lose a good professional employee and gain a poor administrator. To avoid this situation, some organizations have extended the salary range for professional positions to equal or nearly equal that for administrative positions. The extension of this range provides a double-track wage system, as illustrated in Chapter 7, whereby professionals who do not aspire to become administrators still have an opportunity to earn comparable salaries.

Professional employees can receive compensation beyond base pay. For example, scientists and engineers employed by high-tech firms are included in performance-based incentive programs such as profit sharing or stock ownership. These plans encourage greater levels of individual performance. Cash bonuses can be awarded to those who complete projects on or before deadline dates. Payments may also be given to individuals elected to professional societies, granted patents, or meeting professional licensing standards.

The Executive Pay Package

Executive compensation plans consist of five basic components: (1) base salary, (2) short-term incentives or bonuses, (3) long-term incentives or stock plans, (4) benefits, and (5) perquisites. Each of these elements may receive different emphasis in the executive's compensation package depending on various organizational goals and executive needs.[23]

Base Executive Salaries. Executive base salaries represent between 30 and 40 percent of total annual compensation.[24] An analysis of executive salaries shows that the largest portion of executive pay is received in long-term incentive rewards and bonuses. For example, in Canada, on average, a CEO would receive $600,000 in base salary, a bonus of $450,000, and long-term incentives such as stock options worth $1,000,000. The levels of competitive salaries in the job market exert perhaps the greatest influence on executive base salaries. An organization's compensation committee—normally members of the board of directors—will order a salary survey to find out what executives earn in comparable enterprises. For example, by one estimate, 96 percent of companies in the Standard & Poor's 500-stock index use a technique called *competitive benchmarking* when setting executive pay or to remain competitive for executive talent. As noted in *Business Week,* company boards reason that a CEO who doesn't earn as much as his or her peers is likely to "take a hike."[25] Comparisons may be based on organization size, sales volume, or industry groupings. Thus, by analyzing the data from published studies, along with self-generated salary surveys, the compensation committee can determine the equity of the compensation package outside the organization.[26]

Executive Short-Term Incentives. Annual bonuses represent the main element of executive short-term incentives. A bonus payment may take the form of cash or shares and may be paid immediately (which is frequently the case), deferred for a short time, or deferred until retirement. Most organizations pay their short-term incentive bonuses in cash (in the form of a supplemental cheque), in keeping with their pay-for-performance strategy. By providing a reward soon after the performance, and thus linking it to the effort on which it is based, they can use cash bonuses as a significant motivator. Deferred bonuses are used to provide a source of retirement benefits or to supplement a regular pension plan.

Incentive bonuses for executives should be based on the contribution the individual makes to the organization. A variety of formulas have been developed for this purpose. Incentive bonuses may be based on a percentage of a company's total profits or a percentage of profits in excess of a specific return on shareholders' investments. In other instances the payments may be tied to an annual profit plan whereby the amount is determined by the extent to which an agreed-on profit level is exceeded. Payments may also be based on performance ratings or the achievement of specific objectives established with the agreement of executives and the board of directors.[27]

In a continuing effort to monitor the pulse of the marketplace, more organizations are tying operational yardsticks to the traditional financial gauges when computing executive pay. Called *Balanced Scorecards,* these yardsticks may measure things such as customer satisfaction, the ability to innovate, or product or service leadership. Notes David Cates, a compensation principal with Towers Perrin, a Balanced Scorecard "allows companies to focus on building future economic value, rather than be driven solely by short-term financial results." Mobil Oil uses a Balanced Scorecard that better indicates exactly where the company is successful and where improvement is needed.

Executive Long-Term Incentives. Stock options are the primary long-term incentive offered to executives.[28] The principal reason driving executive stock ownership is the desire of both the company and outside investors for senior managers to have a significant stake in the success of the business—to have their fortunes rise and fall with the value they create for shareholders. Stock options can also be extremely lavish for executives. For example, for 2006, Hank Swartout of Precision Drilling Inc received $55 million and Hunter Harrison of CN railways received $27.2 million when they cashed out their options.[29] Not surprisingly, the creativity in designing a stock option program seems almost limitless.[30] Figure 10.5 highlights several common forms of long-term incentives.

Short-term incentive bonuses are criticized for causing top executives to focus on quarterly profit goals to the detriment of long-term survival and growth objectives. Therefore corporations such as Nova Chemicals and Canadian Tire have adopted compensation strategies that tie executive pay to long-term performance measures. Each of these organizations recognizes that compensation strategies must also take

Figure 10.5	Types of Long-Term Incentive Plans

STOCK PRICE APPRECIATION PLANS

Stock options	Rights granted to executives to purchase shares of their organization's stock at an established price for a fixed period of time. Stock price is usually set at market value at the time the option is granted.
Stock appreciation rights (SARs)	Cash or stock award determined by increase in stock price during any time chosen by the executive in the option period; does not require executive financing.
Stock purchase	Opportunities for executives to purchase shares of their organization's stock valued at full market or a discount price, often with the organization providing financial assistance.
Phantom stock	Grant of units equal in value to the fair market value or book value of a share of stock; on a specified date the executive will be paid the appreciation in the value of the units up to that time.

RESTRICTED STOCK/CASH PLANS

Restricted stock	Grant of stock or stock units at a reduced price with the condition that the stock not be transferred or sold (by risk of forfeiture) before a specified employment date.
Restricted cash	Grant of fixed-dollar amounts subject to transfer or forfeiture restrictions before a specified employment date.

PERFORMANCE-BASED PLANS

Performance units	Grants analogous to annual bonuses except that the measurement period exceeds one year. The value of the grant can be expressed as a flat dollar amount or converted to a number of "units" of equivalent aggregate value.
Performance shares	Grants of actual stock or phantom stock units. Value is contingent on both predetermined performance objectives over a specified period of time and the stock market.
Formula-value grants	Rights to receive units or the gain in value of units determined by a formula (such as book value or an earnings multiplier) rather than changes in market price.
Dividend units	Rights to receive an amount equal to the dividends paid on a specified number of shares; typically granted in conjunction with other grant types, such as performance shares.

into account the performance of the organization as a whole. Important to shareholders are such performance results as growth in earnings per share, return on shareholders' equity, and, ultimately, share price appreciation. A variety of incentive plans, therefore, have been developed to tie rewards to these performance results, particularly over the long term. Additionally, stock options can serve to retain key executive personnel when exercising the options is linked to a specified vesting period, say two to four years (this type of incentive is called "golden handcuffs").

Stock options are under attack.[31] Some object to the sheer magnitude of these incentive rewards. The link between pay and performance that options are championed to provide can also be undermined when compensation committees grant additional options to executives even when company share prices fall or performance indexes decline. Peter Clapman, chief counsel for TIAA-CREF, the world's largest pension system, notes, "It's sort of heads you win, tails let's flip again." Even worse for shareholders is the dilution problem. Every option granted to executives makes the shares of other stockholders less valuable.

Executive Benefits. The benefits package offered executives may parallel one offered to other groups of employees. Various programs for health insurance, life insurance, retirement plans, and vacations are common. However, unlike other employee groups, the benefits offered executives are likely to be broader in coverage and free of charge. Additionally, executives may be given financial assistance in the form of trusts for estate planning, payment of mortgage interest, and legal help.

perquisites
Special nonmonetary benefits given to executives; often referred to as *perks*

Executive Perquisites. **Perquisites** are nonmonetary rewards given to executives. Perquisites, or *perks,* are a means of demonstrating the executive's importance to the organization. The status that comes with perks—both inside and outside the organization—shows a pecking order and conveys authority. Corporate executives may simply consider perks a "badge of merit." Perks can also provide tax savings to executives, because some are not taxed as income.

The dark side of perks is that they are viewed as wasteful spending and overly lavish. The public was outraged when they learned that the CEO of Hydro One Inc; Eleanor Clitheroe, was a member of seven private clubs (five more than that allowed), and received a company-financed Mercedez-Benz and Dodge minivan, and over $300,000 in limousine charges for family usage.[32] A recent study, however, shows that perks can facilitate company productivity by saving executive time (for example, private planes and chauffeur service) or improve or maintain executive health (for example, spas, health clubs, and company cabins). Therefore, the cost of perks should be weighed against the added efficiency and managerial effectiveness they generate.[33] Highlights in HRM 10.4 shows the more common perks offered to executives.

Highlights in HRM 10.4

The "Sweetness" of Executive Perks

Compensation consulting firms such as Coopers and Lybrand LLP, WorldatWork, and Hewitt Associates regularly survey companies nationwide to identify the perks they provide for executives and other top managers. Below are listed popular executive perks along with some less popular perquisites.

Prevalent Perquisites

- Company car
- Company plane
- Financial consulting
- Company-paid parking
- Estate planning
- First-class air travel

- Physical exams
- Mobile phones
- Large insurance policies
- Income tax preparation
- Country club membership
- Luncheon club membership

Less Prevalent Perquisites

- Chauffeur service
- Children's education
- Spouse travel

- Personal home repairs
- Legal counselling
- Vacation cabins

Executive Compensation: Ethics and Accountability

The top executive paycheques for 2005 were, as usual, off-the-chart amazing. Consider the total annual compensation drawn in 2005 by the following executives:[34]

Hank Swartout	Precision Drilling Trust	$74.8 million
Hunter Harrison	CN Railway Co.	$56.2 million
Mike Zafirovski	Nortel Networks	$37.4 million
John Hunkin	CIBC	$29.5 million
James Buckee	Talisman Energy Inc.	$23.3 million

In 2003, the ratio between average CEO compensation and worker pay was 301:1, up from 282:1 in 2001 and 42:1 in 1982.[35] Figures show that in Japan the ratio is 15:1 and in Europe 20:1.[36] Canadian executives earn about half of their American counterparts.[37] Management expert Peter F. Drucker has warned that the growing pay gap between CEOs and employees could threaten the very credibility of leadership. He believes that no leader should earn more than 20 times the pay of the company's lowest-paid employee.[38]

Given the large amount of these compensation packages, the question asked by many is: "Are top executives worth the salaries and bonuses they receive?" The answer may depend on whom you ask. Corporate compensation committees justify big bonuses in the following ways:

1. Large financial incentives are a way to reward superior performance.
2. Business competition is pressure-filled and demanding.
3. Good executive talent is in great demand.
4. Effective executives create shareholder value.

Stock options and perks are seen as tools to attract and retain executives.

Others justify high compensation as a fact of business life, reflecting market compensation trends.

Nevertheless, in an era of massive downsizing, low wage increases, and increased workloads for layoff survivors, strong criticism is voiced regarding the high monetary awards given to senior executives.[39] Furthermore, with the large compensation packages awarded to senior managers and top-level executives, cries for performance accountability and openness abound. The 2004 annual Executive Pay Scoreboard published by *Business Week* argues that to justify the big bucks, CEOs and top executives should produce a surge in shareholder value. Yet in 2004 many top executives failed to beat the S&P 500 for total shareholder return over the past three years. In *Business Week*'s analysis, a large percentage of top-paid executives simply did not ace "our pay-for-performance analysis."[40] While some high-paid executives do improve performance measures, such as return on equity, earnings per share, and return to shareholders, clearly others do not.

A critical question with exorbitant executive pay is not always what is legal or externally equitable but what is right or ethical. Compensation committees sometimes fail to fulfill their obligations and corporate boards can be stacked with cronies willing to rubber-stamp high pay packages. Furthermore, the run of greed-inspired scandals beginning in 2001 with Enron has extended to other companies such as Hollinger International and the dot-coms, raising concerns about the ethical behaviour of executives at these organizations and others. While not all executive pay is exorbitant and not all executive behaviour is unethical, nevertheless angry employees, government officials, and shareholders argue for change.[41]

Group Incentive Plans

The emphasis on cost reduction and total quality management has led many organizations to implement a variety of group incentive plans.[42] Group plans enable employees to share in the benefits of improved efficiency realized by major organizational units or various individual work teams. These plans encourage a cooperative—rather than individualistic—spirit among all employees and reward them for their total contribution to the organization. Such features are particularly desirable when working conditions make individual performance difficult, if not impossible, to measure.

Team Compensation

team incentive plan
A compensation plan in which all team members receive an incentive bonus payment when production or service standards are met or exceeded

As production has become more automated, as teamwork and coordination among workers have become more important, and as the contributions of those engaged indirectly in production or service tasks have increased, team incentive plans have grown more popular. **Team incentive plans** reward team members with an incentive bonus when agreed-on performance standards are met or exceeded. Furthermore, the incentive will seek to establish a psychological climate that fosters team cooperation.

One catch with setting team compensation is that not all teams are alike (see Chapter 4). For example, cross-functional teams, self-directed teams, and task force teams make it impossible to develop one consistent type of team incentive plan. And, with a variety of teams, managers find it difficult to adopt uniform measurement standards or payout formulas for team pay.[43] According to Steven Gross, Hay manager, "Each type of team requires a specific pay structure to function at its peak."

In spite of this caveat, organizations typically use the three-step approach to establishing team incentive payments. First, they set performance measures on which incentive payments are based. Improvements in efficiency, product quality, or reduction in materials or labour costs are common benchmark criteria. For example, if labour costs for a team represent 30 percent of the organization's sales dollars, and the organization pays a bonus for labour cost savings, then whenever team labour costs are less than 30 percent of sales dollars, those savings are paid as an incentive bonus to team members. Information on the size of the incentive bonus is reported to employees on a weekly or monthly basis, explaining why incentive pay was or was not earned. Second, the size of the incentive bonus must be determined. Figure 10.6 presents the commonly stated advantages and disadvantages of team incentive pay.

| Figure 10.6 | The Pros and Cons of Team Incentive Plans |

PROS

- Team incentives support group planning and problem solving, thereby building a team culture.
- The contributions of individual employees depend on group cooperation.
- Unlike incentive plans based solely on output, team incentives can broaden the scope of the contribution that employees are motivated to make.
- Team bonuses tend to reduce employee jealousies and complaints over "tight" or "loose" individual standards.
- Team incentives encourage cross-training and the acquiring of new interpersonal competencies.

CONS

- Individual team members may perceive that "their" efforts contribute little to team success or to the attainment of the incentive bonus.
- Intergroup social problems—pressure to limit performance (for example, team members are afraid one individual may make the others look bad) and the "free-ride" effect (one individual puts in less effort than others but shares equally in team rewards)—may arise.
- Complex payout formulas can be difficult for team members to understand.

Gainsharing Incentive Plans

gainsharing plans
Programs under which both employees and the organization share financial gains according to a predetermined formula that reflects improved productivity and profitability

Gainsharing plans are organizational programs designed to increase productivity or decrease labour costs and share monetary gains with employees. These plans are based on a mathematical formula that compares a baseline of performance with actual productivity during a given period. When productivity exceeds the baseline, an agreed-on savings is shared with employees. Inherent in gainsharing is the idea that involved employees will improve productivity through more effective use of organizational resources.

Although productivity can be measured in various ways, it is usually calculated as a ratio of outputs to inputs. Sales, pieces produced, kilograms, total standard costs, direct labour dollars earned, and customer orders are common output measures. Inputs frequently measured include materials, labour, energy, inventory, purchased goods or services, and total costs. An increase in productivity is normally gained when:

- Greater output is obtained with less or equal input.
- Equal production output is obtained with less input.

Although gainsharing is a popular reward system for employees, experience with these techniques has pointed up a number of factors that contribute to either their success or their failure. Highlights in HRM 10.5 on page 459 discusses common considerations when establishing a gainsharing program.[44]

There are three typical gainsharing plans. Two plans, the Scanlon and Rucker Plans, emphasize participative management and encourage cost reductions by sharing with employees any savings resulting from these reductions. The third plan, Improshare, is based on the number of finished goods that the employee work teams complete in an established period.

Highlights in HRM 10.5

Lessons Learned: Designing Effective Gainsharing Programs

Will your gainsharing program be successful? While there are no exact keys to success, gainsharing proponents cite the following as important components of a meaningful gainsharing plan.

- Enlist *total* managerial support for the gainsharing effort. While top-management support is critical, without the encouragement of middle and lower-level managers (those directly involved in program implementation), gainsharing efforts invariably fail.
- When developing new programs, include representatives from all groups affected by the gainsharing effort—labour, management, employees. Inclusion, not exclusion, serves to build trust and understanding of the program's intent and operation.
- Prevent political gamesmanship whereby involved parties are more interested in preserving their self-interests than in supporting the group effort. The political manipulation of the bonus calculation to hold down payouts is a certain obstacle to all gainsharing programs.
- Bonus payout formulas must be seen as fair, must be easy for employees to calculate, must offer payouts on a frequent basis, and must be large enough to encourage future employee effort. The goal is to create a pay-for-performance environment.
- Establish effective, fair, and precise measurement standards. Standards must encourage increased effort without being unreasonable.
- Be certain that employees are predisposed to a gainsharing reward system. Is there a "cultural readiness" for gainsharing? If changes are indicated, what needs to be done? Will employees need additional skills training or training in other competencies in order to make anticipated organizational improvements?
- Launch the plan during a favourable business period. Business downturns jeopardize payments. A plan is likely to fail if it does not pay out under normal conditions in its first two or three years of operation.

objective 5

Scanlon Plan
A bonus incentive plan using employee and management committees to gain cost-reduction improvements

The Scanlon Plan

The philosophy behind the **Scanlon Plan** is that employees should offer ideas and suggestions to improve productivity and, in turn, be rewarded for their constructive efforts. According to Scanlon's proponents, effective employee participation, which includes the use of committees on which employees are represented, is the most significant feature of the Scanlon Plan. Improvement or gains largely come from "working smarter, not harder." Figure 10.7 illustrates the Scanlon Plan suggestion process, including the duties and responsibilities of two important groups—the *shop* and *screening* committees.

Financial incentives under the Scanlon Plan are ordinarily offered to all employees (a significant feature of the plan) on the basis of an established formula. This formula is based on increases in employee productivity as determined by a norm that has been established for labour costs.

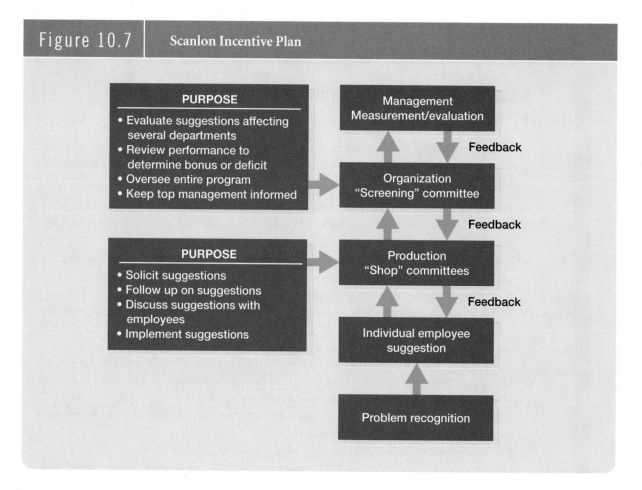

Figure 10.7 | Scanlon Incentive Plan

PURPOSE
- Evaluate suggestions affecting several departments
- Review performance to determine bonus or deficit
- Oversee entire program
- Keep top management informed

PURPOSE
- Solicit suggestions
- Follow up on suggestions
- Discuss suggestions with employees
- Implement suggestions

Management Measurement/evaluation

Feedback

Organization "Screening" committee

Feedback

Production "Shop" committees

Feedback

Individual employee suggestion

Problem recognition

Rucker Plan
A bonus incentive plan based on the historical relationship between the total earnings of hourly employees and the production value created by the employees

The Rucker Plan

The share-of-production plan (SOP), or **Rucker Plan,** normally covers just production workers but may be expanded to cover all employees. As with the Scanlon Plan, committees are formed to elicit and evaluate employee suggestions. The Rucker Plan, however, uses a far less elaborate participatory structure. The financial incentive of the Rucker Plan is based on the historical relationship between the total earnings of hourly employees and the production value that employees create. The bonus is based on any improvement in this relationship that employees are able to realize. Thus, for every 1 percent increase in production value that is achieved, workers receive a bonus of 1 percent of their total payroll costs.[45]

Lessons from the Scanlon and Rucker Plans

Perhaps the most important lesson to be learned from the Scanlon and Rucker Plans is that any management expecting to gain the cooperation of its employees in improving efficiency must permit them to become involved psychologically as well as financially in the organization. If employees are to contribute maximum effort, they must have a feeling of involvement and identification with their organization, which does not come out of the traditional manager-subordinate relationship. Consequently, it is important for organizations to realize that while employee cooperation is essential to

The Scanlon and Rucker gainsharing plans rely on employee suggestions for cost savings and productivity improvements.

© AP PHOTO/BEN MARGOT

the successful administration of the Scanlon and Rucker Plans, the plans themselves do not necessarily stimulate this cooperation. Furthermore, the attitude of management is of paramount importance to the success of either plan. For example, when managers show little confidence and trust in their employees, the plans tend to fail.

Improshare

Improshare
A gainsharing program under which bonuses are based on the overall productivity of the work team

Improshare—improved productivity through sharing—is another gainsharing program. Individual production bonuses are typically based on how much an employee produces above some standard amount, but Improshare bonuses are based on the overall productivity of the *work team*. Improshare output is measured by the number of finished products that a work team produces in a given period. Both production (direct) employees and nonproduction (indirect) employees are included in the determination of the bonus.[46]

The bonus is based on productivity gains that result from reducing the time it takes to produce a finished product. The employees and the company each receive payment for 50 percent of the improvement. Since a cooperative environment benefits all, Improshare promotes increased interaction and support between employees and management. Companies such as Hinderliter Energy Equipment pay the bonus as a separate cheque to emphasize that it is extra income.

Enterprise Incentive Plans

Enterprise incentive plans differ from individual and group incentive plans in that all organizational members participate in the plan's compensation payout. Enterprise incentive plans reward employees on the basis of the success of the organization over an extended time period—normally one year, but the period can be longer. Enterprise incentive plans seek to create a "culture of ownership" by fostering a philosophy of cooperation and teamwork among all organizational members. Common enterprise incentive plans include profit sharing, stock options, and employee stock ownership plans (ESOPs).

Profit-Sharing Plans

Profit sharing is any procedure by which an employer pays, or makes available to all regular employees, special current or deferred sums based on the organization's profits. As defined here, profit sharing represents cash payments made to eligible employees at designated time periods, as distinct from profit sharing in the form of contributions to employee pension funds.

Profit-sharing plans are intended to give employees the opportunity to increase their earnings by contributing to the growth of their organization's profits. These contributions may be directed toward improving product quality, reducing operating costs, improving work methods, and building goodwill rather than just increasing rates of production. For example, Inco Ltd. revised its longstanding profit-sharing plan from paying a bonus when the price of nickel rose above a designated threshold to pay when the company achieves profit levels. Canadian Pacific Railway Inc. bases its payouts on safety, service, and productivity, each with specific performance targets related to different business units. Over three years, $62 million was saved and $21 million was paid out to employees.[47] Profit sharing can help stimulate employees to think and feel more like partners in the enterprise and thus to concern themselves with the welfare of the organization as a whole. Its purpose therefore is to motivate a total commitment from employees rather than simply to have them contribute in specific areas.

A popular example of a highly successful profit-sharing plan is the one in use at Lincoln Electric Company, a manufacturer of arc-welding equipment and supplies. This plan was started in 1934 by J. F. Lincoln, president of the company. Each year the company distributes a large percentage of its profits to employees in accordance with their salary level and merit ratings. It is not uncommon for employees' annual bonuses to exceed 50 percent of annual wages. The success of Lincoln Electric's incentive system depends on a high level of contribution by each employee. Unquestionably there is a high degree of respect among employees and management for Lincoln's organizational goals and for the profit-sharing program.

Variations in Profit-Sharing Plans

Profit-sharing plans differ in the proportion of profits shared with employees and in the distribution and form of payment. The amount shared with employees may range from 5 to 50 percent of the net profit. In most plans, however, about 20 to 25 percent of the net profit is shared. Profit distributions may be made to all employees on an equal basis, or they may be based on regular salaries or some formula that takes into account seniority and/or merit. The payments may be disbursed in cash, deferred, or made on the basis of combining the two forms of payments.

Weaknesses of Profit-Sharing Plans

In spite of their potential advantages, profit-sharing plans are also prone to certain weaknesses. The profits shared with employees may be the result of inventory speculation, climatic factors, economic conditions, national emergencies, or other factors over which employees have no control. Conversely, losses may occur during years when employee contributions have been at a maximum. The fact that profit-sharing payments are made only once a year or deferred until retirement may reduce their

profit sharing
Any procedure by which an employer pays, or makes available to all regular employees in addition to base pay, special current or deferred sums based on the profits of the enterprise

motivational value. If a plan fails to pay off for several years in a row, this can have an adverse effect on productivity and employee morale.

Stock Options

What do the following companies—Apple Computer, Yahoo, Coca-Cola, TD Bank, Nike, Quaker Oats, and Sara Lee—have in common? The answer: Each of these diverse organizations offers a stock option program to its employees. In TD Bank's case, about 75 percent of their employees participate in the plan. According to WorldatWork, a compensation association, the use of stock options is a very prevalent method of motivating and compensating hourly employees, as well as salaried and executive personnel. This appears true regardless of the industry surveyed or the organization's size.[48]

Stock option programs are sometimes implemented as part of an employee benefit plan or as part of a corporate culture linking employee effort to share performance. However, organizations that offer stock option programs to employees do so with the belief that there is some incentive value to the systems. By allowing employees to purchase shares, the organization hopes they will increase their productivity, assume a partnership role in the organization, and thus cause the share price to rise.[49] Furthermore, stock option programs have become a popular way to boost morale of disenfranchised employees caught in mergers, acquisitions, and downsizing.

Stock option plans grant to employees the right to purchase a specific number of shares of the company's stock at a guaranteed price (the option price) during a designated time period. Although there are many types of options, most options are granted at the stock's fair market value. Not uncommon are plans for purchasing shares through payroll deductions. The stock option and other pay for performance plans are described in Reality Check on page 464.

When stock prices rise, employee stock plans can be financially rewarding to employees. In July 2004, employees in Boeing's Share Value Trust program received stock awards that paid out about $900 apiece in shares or cash to more than 200 000 current or former Boeing employees. Boeing estimated the payouts would total about $142.5 million.[50] Additionally, stock ownership plans serve as productivity incentives for employees at Motorola, and espresso servers at Starbucks.

Unfortunately, in the wake of various corporate scandals, employee stock option plans have come under criticism (see "Executive Compensation: Ethics and Accountability" earlier in this chapter). Criticism largely focuses on executive abuses and faulty accounting procedures. Fortunately, stock options continue to be a popular and effective way to pay for the performance of employees and managers.[51]

employee stock ownership plans (ESOPs)
Stock plans in which an organization contributes shares of its stock to an established trust for the purpose of purchase by its employees

Employee Stock Ownership Plans (ESOPs)

Canadian Tire and Sears Canada have established **employee stock ownership plans (ESOPs)**—stock plans in which employees can acquire shares in the firm that employs them. There are three main types of employee stock plans. An employee stock bonus plan is the simplest. An employer provides company shares to employees at no cost to the employee by just granting them or by linking the granting to some kind of performance pay plan. An employee stock purchase plan allows employers to purchase shares, but not pay full market price for these shares. Under an employee stock option plan, employees are given the option to purchase shares in the company at some future date, at a set price, which they would exercise if the market price rises to exceed this price.

Reality Check

Pay for Performance at Lombard Canada

Recently promoted to HR Director from Manager of Compensation & Benefits at Lombard Canada, Sandy Bernier is ever aware that pay policies are critical to ensuring a stable and productive workforce. Lombard's overall compensation strategy is to lead the marketplace at the 75th percentile for base pay and to have an incentive plan that is based on performance. This mixed approach to compensation allows Lombard to pay competitively and to reward high performers based on the value they add to the company. For example, an individual's bonus will depend partly on his or her own achievements and partly on corporate performance. According to Bernier, corporate performance has exceeded its target every year for the last four years, which has permitted full bonuses to be awarded to all employees.

In order to ensure all systems and processes are up-to-date, a thorough job analysis for all positions under the senior management team has been conducted using a hybrid point factor system. All jobs are then graded and employees are paid within the salary range for the position they are performing. Lombard has 11 salary ranges and regularly participates in external salary surveys to ensure that they are using the most up-to-date salary information. Furthermore, each time a new hire is recruited, the job description is reviewed to ensure its accuracy and relevance to the position and any updates needed are made immediately. For all senior-level positions, an individual ad hoc analysis is conducted annually that compares each position to the marketplace. This is an effective approach to executive compensation as it looks at each position and its uniqueness and is not trying to slot a senior position into a restrictive salary range.

According to Bernier, one of the greatest challenges facing today's compensation and benefits teams is the soaring costs of healthcare—many companies are seeing double-digit premium increases each year. There are also a lot of psychological claims being introduced; these are challenging as they are difficult to manage. To add to this challenge, with the new privacy legislation many companies find it difficult to administer their short-term disability inhouse. One way to combat rising healthcare costs is to educate employees about their benefits plan and ways to contain costs. Bernier has done these types of presentations to employees across Canada.

As a major insurance company Lombard is fairly traditional in its approach to benefits, but being an employee of this type of company provides its own unique perks. Along with a flexible health and dental plan, Lombard offers its employees a stock ownership plan where 1 to 10 percent of an employee's salary can be voluntarily deducted from payroll; the company matches this amount by 30 percent. If company ROE targets are met for the year, the company will then put an additional 20 percent to the plan for a total 50-percent match. This plan provides employees with an opportunity to invest in the company's long-term performance, and employees have a vested interest in how the company is doing. To add to this perk, the money in the fund can also be withdrawn once a year at any time, without penalty, and the employee can use it or place it in an individual RRSP for additional tax savings. Finally, employees are offered a perk that is not easily attained in today's market place: after four years of service they are eligible to apply for the mortgage subsidy program, and are also given a 40-percent discount on home and auto insurance if they have their insurance coverage with Lombard.

Advantages of ESOPs

ESOPs can increase employees' pride of ownership in the organization, providing an incentive for them to increase productivity and help the organization prosper and grow. Employees may become more interested in how the company is managed, and hold managers to higher and different performance standards, such as maximizing share value. Stock plans have the additional advantage of not requiring companies to pay out in cash, and so firms can reward employees with shares. For employees, the advantages include a form of saving for retirement, and in some cases, like Microsoft, employees could become millionaires.

Problems with ESOPs

Generally, ESOPs are more likely to serve their intended purposes in publicly held companies than in privately held ones. A major problem with the privately held company is its potential inability to pay back the shares of employees when they retire. These employees do not have the alternative of disposing of their shares on the open market. Thus, when large organizations suffer financial difficulties and the value of the companies' shares falls, so does the value of the employees' retirement plan.

Other problems with ESOPs include the following:

> ### USING THE INTERNET
>
> The ESOP Association Canada outlines four main motives for implementing stock ownership plans in Canada:
>
> www.esop-canada.com

- The more retirement income comes from these plans, the more dependent a pensioner becomes on the price of company shares. Future retirees are vulnerable to stock market fluctuations as well as to management mistakes.

- Employees may become demotivated and frustrated if the share price falls, even though they have worked productively.

- Finally, although studies show that productivity improves when ESOPs are implemented, these gains are not guaranteed. ESOPs help little unless managers are willing to involve employees in organizational decision making. Unfortunately, ESOPs are sometimes set up in ways that restrict employee decision making and expose the ESOP to risk, though providing investors with large potential gains.

Overall, do incentive plans work? The answer can be found in The Business Case.

The Business Case

Organizational Benefits of Incentive Plans

Incentive pay is a strategic tool used most often to attract and retain employees and to improve organizational outcomes. Organizations pay an average of 9 percent of total payroll dollars on variable compensation programs. Is this money well spent?

- Four out of five organizations report that incentive compensation is an effective tool for attracting and retaining employees.
- About one-third of employers reported that compensation had a positive effect on operating results. In another study, retail stores that used the Scanlon Plan had higher sales

(continued on next page)

performance, more favourable customer satisfaction scores, and lower turnover than a control group. Higher-performing companies are more likely to provide stock options and feel strongly that these options influence behaviour among professional ranks.

- The offering of stock options is associated with improved company performance. Bonuses seem to be more tightly linked to increased profits than are long-term incentives.
- Companies that had CEOs who earned above median salary increases deliver a return to shareholders of 29.4 percent compared to an 8.6-percent return for those companies that had CEOs who earned below median salary increases.

Sources: *Business BC*, "More Firms Tie Executive Pay to Performance," *The Vancouver Sun*, December 1, 2005; D. Scott, *WorldatWork*, "Survey of Compensation Policies and Practices," www.worldatwork.org/research, March 2003; D. Scott, J. Floyd, P.G. Benson, and J.W. Bishop, "The Impact of the Scanlon Plan on Retail Store Performance," *WorldatWork Journal* 11, no. 3 (Third Quarter, 2002); D.J. Gherson, "Getting the Pay Thing Right," *Workspan* 43, no. 6 (June 2000); K.H. Van Neek and J.E. Smilko, "Variable Pay Plans," *WorldatWork Journal* 11, no. 4 (Fourth Quarter 2002).

SUMMARY

The success of an incentive pay plan depends on the organizational climate in which it must operate, employee confidence in it, and its suitability to employee and organizational needs. Importantly, employees must view their incentive pay as being equitable and related to their performance. Performance measures should be quantifiable, be easily understood, and bear a demonstrated relationship to organizational performance.

Piecework plans pay employees a given rate for each unit satisfactorily completed. Employers implement these plans when output is easily measured and when the production process is fairly standardized. Bonuses are incentive payments above base wages paid on either an individual or team basis. A bonus is offered to encourage employees to exert greater effort. Standard hour plans establish a standard time for job completion. An incentive is paid for finishing the job in less than the pre-established time. These plans are popular for jobs with a fixed time for completion.

Merit raises will not serve to motivate employees when they are seen as entitlements, which occurs when these raises are given yearly without regard to changes in employee performance. Merit raises are not motivational when they are given because of seniority or favouritism or when merit budgets are inadequate to sufficiently reward employee performance. To be motivational, merit raises must be such that employees see a clear relationship between pay and performance and the salary increase must be large enough to exceed inflation and higher income taxes.

Salespeople may be compensated by a straight salary, a combination of salary and commission, or a commission only. Paying employees a straight salary allows them to focus on tasks other than sales, such as service and customer goodwill. A straight commission plan causes employees to emphasize sales goals. A combination of salary and commission provides the advantages of both the straight salary and the straight commission form of payments.

The Scanlon, Rucker, and Improshare gain-sharing plans pay bonuses to employees unrelated to profit levels. Each of these plans encourages employees to maximize their performance and cooperation through suggestions offered to improve organizational performance. The Scanlon Plan pays an employee a bonus based on saved labour cost measured against the organization's sales value of production. The bonus under the Rucker Plan is based on any improvement in the relationship between the total earnings of hourly employees and the value of production that employees create. The Improshare bonus is paid when employees increase production output above a given target level.

 Profit-sharing plans pay to employees sums of money based on the organization's profits. Cash payments are made to eligible employees at specified times, normally yearly. The primary purpose of profit sharing is to provide employees with additional income through their participation in organizational achievement. Employee commitment to improved productivity, quality, and customer service will contribute to organizational success and, in turn, to their compensation. Profit-sharing

plans may not achieve their stated gains when employee performance is unrelated to organizational success or failure. This may occur because of economic conditions, other competition, or environmental conditions. Profit-sharing plans can have a negative effect on employee morale when plans fail to consistently reward employees.

Employee stock ownership plans (ESOPs) allow employees to be granted or to purchase shares in the company. The advantages of ESOPs include increasing commitment through ownership and the possibility of increased retirement savings. The disadvantages include the risk of savings erosion if the share price falls, and the effect on employees who work hard, but see no link to company performance.

KEY TERMS

bonus, 445
combined salary and commission plan, 451
differential piece rate, 444
employee stock ownership plans (ESOPs), 463
gainsharing plans, 458

Improshare, 461
lump-sum merit program, 447
merit guidelines, 447
perquisites, 455
profit sharing, 462
Rucker Plan, 460
Scanlon Plan, 459

spot bonus, 446
standard hour plan, 445
straight commission plan, 451
straight piecework, 444
straight salary plan, 451
team incentive plan, 457
variable pay, 438

DISCUSSION QUESTIONS

1. Working individually or in groups, identify the factors necessary for a successful incentive plan.
2. List all the ways that a manager at a fast-food retail outlet can reward exceptional performance. Which ways would you prefer and why? Compare your answers to those of other students.
3. A frequently heard complaint about merit raises is that they do little to increase employee effort. What are the causes of this belief? Suggest ways in which the motivating value of merit raises may be increased.
4. Using your employee experience or an online salary locator, determine the salary of the CEO and the lowest paid employee for a public organization. What is the ratio? How does it compare with the

American ratio of 301:1 or the Japanese ratio of 15:1? How would you explain the ratio to employees who are asking questions about the reasons for their levels of compensation?
5. What are the reasons for the success of the Scanlon and Rucker Plans?
6. Because of competitive forces within your industry, you have decided to implement a profit-sharing plan for your employees. Discuss the advantages of profit sharing and identify specific characteristics that will ensure success for your plan.
7. What are some reasons for the implementation of ESOPs? Cite some of the potential problems concerning their use.

INTERNET EXERCISE

Incentives are not just for employees. Parents sometimes use them for motivating their children. Read about how one self-employed individual created an incentive plan for himself at www.inc.com/articles/1998/01/11390.html.

Now try to establish an incentive plan for yourself in one of the roles you play: student, employee, self-employed, or parent. Compare your plan to the requirements for a successful incentive plan outlined in this chapter.

HRM Experience

Awarding Salary Increases

Because pay-for-performance is an important factor governing salary increases, managers must be able to defend the compensation recommendations they make for their employees. Merit raises granted under a pay-for-performance policy must be based on objective appraisals if they are to achieve their intended purposes of rewarding outstanding employee performance. As managers know, however, other factors that can affect salary recommendations must be dealt with. These may include the opinions of the employee's peers or extenuating circumstances such as illness or family responsibilities. The purpose of this exercise is to provide you with the experience of granting salary increases to employees based on their work performance and other information.

Assignment

Following are the work records of five employees. As their supervisor, you have just completed their annual appraisal reviews and it is now time to make recommendations for their future salary. Your department budget has $7,400 allocated for salary increases. Distribute the $7,400 among your employees based on the descriptions for each subordinate.

a. Janet Jenkins currently earns $37,000. Her performance appraisal rating was very high. She is respected by her peers and is felt to be an asset to the work group. She is divorced and has three young children to support.

b. Russell Watts earns a salary of $32,000. His annual performance appraisal was average. Several members of the work group have spoken to you about the difficulty involved in Russell's job. They feel that it is a tough and demanding job and that he is doing his best.

c. Jack Perkins earns $27,250. His performance appraisal was below average and he seems to have difficulty adjusting to his co-workers. Jack has had a difficult time this past year. His wife passed away early in the year and his father has recently been diagnosed as terminally ill.

d. Rick Jacobson earns $25,000. His performance appraisal was above average. He is respected by his peers and is generally considered to be a "good guy."

e. Paula Merrill earns $25,850. Her performance appraisal was very high. Her peers are upset because they feel that she is working only to provide a second income. Moreover, her peers see her as trying to "show them up."

Share your results with other class members. Be prepared to explain your allocation of money.

BIZFLIX EXERCISES

Scent of a Woman: Freddie Bisco's Incentives

The scene from *Scent of a Woman* shows many aspects of incentive rewards and employee performance discussed in this chapter. Watch for types of incentives and the positive and negative effects of incentives as you view the scene.

Young Charlie Simms (Chris O'Donnell) wants to earn extra money over Thanksgiving weekend for airfare to go home during his Christmas break. He becomes a guide and caretaker for ill-tempered, retired, blind Lt. Col. Frank Slade (Al Pacino). Charlie, from Gresham, Oregon, is quiet and reserved and has had little experience with the opposite sex. He attends the exclusive Baird Preparatory School on a scholarship. His wild New York City weekend with Frank Slade bonds them forever. This film is a remake of *Profumo di Donna,* a 1974 Italian film.

This scene is an edited version from the end of the "Tango Lessons" segment and the beginning of "The Ferrari" segment that appear about halfway through the film. It follows the despondent hotel room scene and the tango lesson Slade gave Donna (Gabrielle Anwar) in

The Waldorf Astoria restaurant. It begins shortly after Freddie Bisco (Leonard Gaines), the Ferrari salesman, says to Charlie, "Yeah, this is a valid Oregon driver's licence, . . ." Freddie does not want to let either Charlie or Slade test-drive a Ferrari. The scene ends after Slade says, "I'm a grey ghost too." The film cuts to the Ferrari rounding a New York City street corner with Charlie driving.

What to Watch for and Ask Yourself

- Assume that Freddie Bisco receives a sales incentive for each Ferrari he sells. Does Freddie appear highly motivated by this incentive reward system? What is the evidence from the scene?
- Freddie does not work for Frank Slade. Is the $2,000 that Slade gives Freddie the same as a bonus discussed earlier in this chapter? If yes, which type of bonus is it?
- Did you perceive any negative effects of Freddie Bisco's incentives that he experienced in this scene?

case study 11

Pay-for-Performance: Lenox Hits Some Problems

Merit pay programs continue to be one of the more popular pay-for-performance compensation strategies. Yet, as compensation specialists note, these programs often fail to achieve their intended objective and can "backfire" when not administered properly. Consider the experience of Lenox Technology when it implemented a merit pay program for its managers.

There is no debate among industry analysts that the electronics industry is fiercely competitive. Therefore, strategic compensation programs tied to organization objectives are common and prized for improving employee performance. Furthermore, as one industry executive noted, "Compensation budgets are not always large and we need to get as much 'bang for our buck' as possible."

Lenox Technology, a five-year-old company, had traditionally given its managers annual increases based on the consumer price index for the company's metropolitan area plus general across-the-board salary increases. This payment philosophy allowed all managers to maintain their standard of living while guaranteeing them a yearly raise. However, the biggest complaint with the pay program—

as voiced by company officials—concerned the lack of motivation to increase employee performance, as all managers received the same annual increases regardless of individual performance.

In June 2002, Lenox, in what was described by one manager as a "shocking" announcement, implemented a merit pay incentive plan. Across-the-board increases and cost-of-living raises were eliminated. Annual salary increases were now to be based solely on individual performance. As Joe Tittle, compensation manager for Lenox, stated, "The days of entitlements are over."

While some top-performing managers welcomed the merit raise program as a way to "finally get ahead," overall the new pay plan met with general dissatisfaction. Both managers and their immediate supervisors complained about the philosophy behind the program and its administration. What was once viewed by Lenox as a strategic way to maximize the salary budget and spur managerial performance has become a headache for company officials.

QUESTIONS

1. Identify and discuss concerns managers might have with Lenox's merit pay plan. What are the advantages for starting a merit pay program?
2. Why might supervising managers resist a merit pay program?
3. Develop a program to introduce a pay-for-performance plan in an organization. Consider what should be covered, who should be involved, and so on.
4. Develop a merit pay guideline chart based on the following levels of performance evaluation: superior, above average, average, below average, and poor. Use current cost-of-living figures for your area or salary survey data available to you to guide your merit percentage increases.

case study 2

Team-Based Incentive Rewards: It's Not All Roses

Network Cable, Inc. is a service provider for cable TV and high-speed Internet connections. Network Cable operates in an area described as a "high-growth market."

In January 2003 Tara Gilbert, vice-president of human resources for Network Cable, convinced company president and CEO Jeff Lesitner that restructuring the organization workforce into teams would benefit both Network Cable and its employees. Cost savings, improved morale, and team synergy were cited as inherent benefits of teams. Based on these assessments, in June 2003 a select group of three senior managers, plus Tara Gilbert and the company's financial officer, implemented teams within the company's installation department. Here, 40 service installers were formed into eight teams of five installers each. Management set performance goals for the installation teams linked to attractive incentive rewards (cash bonuses above base salaries) when performance goals are reached. Performance measures included indexes for improved installation time, customer satisfaction scores, additional sales, equipment maintenance, and repair/callback problems. Each team could earn incentive bonuses up to a maximum of $15,000 annually with cash bonuses shared equally by each team member—a possible cash reward of $3,000 for each installer. Team bonuses after the first year were as follows: two teams, $15,000; one team, $12,500; one team, $7,300; one team, $3,150.

During August 2004 Tara Gilbert sent to all installers and their supervisors a survey requesting feedback on the satisfaction with teams and, specifically, the incentive rewards program. While survey results were generally positive, not all was rosy. Problems could be grouped into the following categories:

1. Some installers believed that various team members did not "buy into" the team concept and were simply "free riders"—average employees who benefited from the efforts of superior employees.
2. There was a general feeling that several teams were routinely assigned difficult installations that prevented them from achieving high performance goals.
3. Teams did not always display the motivation and synergy expected, as "bickering" was prevalent between average performers and super performers. Average performers complained that high performers made them look bad.
4. A high percentage of survey respondents (29 percent) felt the incentive rewards program was unfair and asked for a return to fixed across-the-board salary increases.

QUESTIONS

1. Do results from the survey illustrate typical complaints about teams and specifically about team incentive rewards? Explain.
2. If appropriate, what changes would you recommend to improve the incentive reward program? Be specific.
3. Would management have benefited from employee involvement in the initial design and implementation of the program? Explain.

CAREER COUNSEL

Take the incentive survey on the *Managing Human Resources* website to discover what types of incentives are motivating for you. www.belcourt5e.nelson.com

NOTES AND REFERENCES

1. Jessica Smilko and Kathy Van Neck, "Rewarding Excellence through Variable Pay," *Benefits Quarterly* 20, no. 3 (Third Quarter 2004): 21–25.
2. Steven E. Gross and Helen M. Friedman, "Creating an Effective Total Reward Strategy: Holistic Approach Better Supports Business Success," *Benefits Quarterly* 20, no. 3 (Third Quarter 2004): 7. See also Kathleen H. Van Neck and Jessica E. Smilko, "Variable Pay Plans: Creating a Financial Partnership with the Work Force," *WorldatWork* 11, no. 4 (Fourth Quarter 2002): 74–79.
3. Michelle Conlin and Robert Berner, "A Little Less in the Envelope This Week," *Business Week*, February 18, 2002, 64.
4. John A. Menefee and Ryan O. Murphy, "Rewarding and Retaining the Best," *Benefits Quarterly* 20, no. 3 (Third Quarter 2004): 13–21.
5. Leo Jakobson, "Shell Goes Further," *Incentive* 178, no. 5 (May 2004): 20.
6. Libby Estell, "Cadillac Standards," *Innovative* 177, no. 7 (July 2003): 22–23.

7. Roisin Woolnough, "How to Set Up an Incentive Scheme," *Personnel Today*, February 14, 2004, 22.

8. Christian M. Ellis, "Improving the Impact of Performance Management," *Workspan* 45, no. 2 (February 2002): 7–8.

9. Gregory A. Stoskopf, "Taking Performance Management to the Next Level," *Workspan* 45, no. 2 (February 2002): 26–31.

10. George T. Milkovich and Jerry M. Newman, *Compensation*, 8th ed. (Boston: McGraw-Hill Irwin, 2005).

11. Chris Taylor. "On-the-Spot Incentives," *HR Magazine* 49, no. 5 (May 2004): 80–84.

12. Don Hellriegel and John W. Slocum, Jr., *Organizational Behaviour*, 10th ed. (Mason, OH: South-Western, 2004): Chapter 6.

13. Robert Vecchio, *Organizational Behaviour*, 5th ed. (Mason, OH: South-Western, 2002).

14. Steve Bates, "Top Pay for Best Performance," *HRMagazine* 48, no. 1 (January 2003): 31–38.

15. Kathryn May, "PS Bonuses Expose Myth of Merit Pay," *The Ottawa Citizen*, July 10, 2003, A1.

16. Danine Alati, "Ring of Honor," *Inventive* 177, no. 11 (November 2003): 34.

17. Kenneth Hein, "Motivators of the Year," *Inventive* 177, no. 10 (October 2003): 40.

18. Charlotte Garvey, "Meaningful Tokens of Appreciation," *HRMagazine* 49, no, 8 (August 2004): 102.

19. Bill Gauthier, "The Sales Compensation Challenge: Meeting the Diverse Needs of Multiple Business Units," *Workspan* 45, no. 3 (March 2002): 34–38.

20. David H. Johnston, "Strategic Initiative in Sales Compensation," *WorldatWork* 12, no. 2 (Second Quarter 2003): 75–82.

21. Paul R. Dorf and Lisette F. Masur, "The Tough Economy Prompts Companies to Shift Their Approach to Sales Compensation," *Journal of Organizational Excellence* 23, no. 2 (Spring 2004): 35–42.

22. David Fiedler, "Should You Adjust Your Sales Compensation?" *HRMagazine* 47, no. 2 (February 2002): 79–82.

23. Bruce R. Ellig, "Executive Compensation 101: Considering the Many Elements," *WorldatWork* 11, no. 1 (First Quarter 2002): 11–20.

24. Total annual compensation is the sum of an executive's annual and long-term compensation. Annual compensation consists of salary, bonus, and other yearly pay. Long-term compensation consists of stock awards, the value of any stock options exercised during the year, and any other long-term compensation (such as payouts from long-term incentive plans, director's fees, and special bonuses).

25. Louis Lavelle, "The Artificial Sweetener in CEO Pay," *Business Week*, September 10, 2001, 102.

26. Blair Jones, David Leach, and Jesse Purewal, "What's Next for the Compensation Committee?" *WorldatWork* 12, no. 4 (Fourth Quarter 2003): 6–14.

27. Richard Ericson, "Addressing Structural Issues in Executive Incentive Plan Design," *WorldatWork* 11, no. 1 (First Quarter 2002): 59–69.

28. Daren Fonda and Daniel Kadlec, "The Rumble over Executive Pay," *Time*, May 31, 2004, 62–64.

29. Janet McFarland, "How Much Is Too Much? The Struggle to Keep Pay in Line with Performance," *The Globe and Mail*, May 9, 2006, B9.

30. Donna Stettler, "Restricted Stock: The Option to Options?" *WorldatWork* 13, no. 1 (First Quarter 2004): 19–28. See also Seymour Burchman and Blair Jones, "The Future of Stock Options," *WorldatWork* 13, no. 1 (First Quarter 2004): 29–38.

31. Louis Lavelle, "Are Options Headed for Extinction?" *Business Week*, May 2, 2005, 12. See also Louis Lavelle, Amy Borrus, Robert D. Hof, and Joseph Weber, "Options Grow Onerous," *Business Week*, December 1, 2003, 36–37; and Nanette Byrnes, Andrew Park, Joseph Weber, and David Welch, "Beyond Options," *Business Week*, July 28, 2003, 34–36.

32. David Olive, "Clitheroe's Notorious Perks Regular Fare in Private Sector," *Toronto Star*, July 24, 2002, E11.

33. "An Unfair Rap for CEO Perks?" *Business Week*, June 7, 2004, 32.

34. Janet McFarland, "How Much Is Too Much? The Struggle to Keep Pay in Line with Performance," *The Globe and Mail*, May 9, 2006, B9.

35. Fonda and Kadleg, "The Rumble over Executive Pay," 62–64.

36. Louis Aguilar, "Exec-Worker Pay Gap Widens to Gulf," *The Denver Post*, July 8, 2001, 16A.

37. *Report on Business Magazine*, "50 Best Paid Executives," July 13, 5–6.

38. Reported in *The Wall Street Journal*, April 11, 2002, B15.

39. Fonda and Kadleg, "The Rumble over Executive Pay," 64.

40. Lavelle, "A Payday For Performance," 78.

41. Nanette Byrnes, "Which Is Better—Stock or Options?" *Business Week*, July 21, 2003, 25.

42. Jerry McAdams and Elizabeth J. Hawk, "Making Group Incentive Plans Work," *WorldatWork* 9, no. 3 (Third Quarter 2002): 28–34.

43. Milkovich and Newman, *Compensation*.

44. Gregory K. Shives and K. Dow Scott, "Gainsharing and EVA: The U.S. Postal Service Experience," *WorldatWork* 12, no. 1 (First Quarter 2003): 21–30.

45. The Rucker Plan uses a somewhat more complex formula for determining employee bonuses. For a detailed example of the Rucker bonus, see Milkovich and Newman, *Compensation*.

46. The standard of Improshare's measurement system is the base productivity factor (BPF), which is the ratio of standard direct labour hours produced to total actual hours worked in a base period. The productivity of subsequent periods is then measured by enlarging standard direct labour hours earned by the BPF ratio to establish Improshare hours (IH). The IH is then compared with actual hours worked in the same period. If earned hours exceed actual hours, 50 percent of the gain is divided by actual hours worked to establish a bonus percentage for all employees in the plan.

47. Conference Board of Canada, "Variable Pay Offers a Bonus for Unionized Workers," www.conferenceboard.ca/press/20. Retrieved April 13, 2006.

48. Seymour Burchman and Blair Jones, "The Future of Stock Options: From Starring Role to Ensemble Player," *WorldatWork* 13, no. 1 (First Quarter 2004): 29–38.

49. "Don't Get Rid of Stock Options, Fix 'Em," *Business Week*, March 4, 2002, 120.

50. J. Lynn Lunsford, "Boeing's Workers to Get a Windfall from Stock's Rise," *The Wall Street Journal*, July 2, 2004, B2.

51. Martin J. Somelofske, Rahim Bhayani, and Sarah Levin, "Stock Options: The Reports of My Demise Are Greatly Exaggerated," *WorldatWork* 12, no. 1 (First Quarter 2003): 48–56.

NEL

Employee Benefits

After studying this chapter, you should be able to

 **objective 1** Describe the characteristics of a sound benefits program.

 objective 5 Describe benefits that involve payment for time not worked.

 objective 2 Indicate management concerns about the costs of employee benefits, and discuss ways to control those costs.

 **objective 6** Discuss recent trends in retirement policies and programs.

objective 3 Identify and explain the employee benefits required by law.

 **objective 7** Indicate the major factors involved in managing pension plans.

 objective 4 Discuss suggested ways to control the costs of healthcare programs.

 objective 8 Describe the types of work–life benefits employers can provide.

What is the best-kept secret in Canada today? According to surveys, it is the hidden payroll, i.e., employee benefits. Compensation surveys indicate that most employees are unable to name accurately the benefits they receive, and about 50 percent of employees underestimate the value of their benefits.[1] Though benefits are largely undervalued and misidentified, they are still an important issue for both employers and employees. It is clear that benefits are not a "fringe" but rather an integral part of the compensation package. Additionally, since most benefits are provided voluntarily by employers, they become a significant cost and an employment advantage for employers, while providing needed psychological and physical assistance to employees. The importance of benefits to both sides cannot be overstated.

Virtually all employers provide a variety of benefits to supplement the wages or salaries they pay their workers. These benefits, some of which are required by law, must be considered a part of total compensation. Therefore, in this chapter we look at the characteristics of employee benefits programs. We will study the types of benefits required by law, the major discretionary benefits that employers offer, the employee services they provide, and the retirement programs in use. The chapter concludes with a discussion of popular and highly important work–life benefit programs.

Employee Benefits Programs

objective 1

Employee benefits constitute an indirect form of compensation intended to improve the quality of work lives and personal lives of employees. As discussed later, benefits typically represent up to 40 percent of total payroll costs to employers.[2] In return, employers generally expect employees to be supportive of the organization and to be productive. Since employees have come to expect an increasing number of benefits, the motivational value of these benefits depends on how the benefits program is designed and communicated. Once viewed as a gift from the employer, benefits are now considered rights to which all employees are entitled.

HRIS and Employee Benefits

USING THE INTERNET

A broad view of benefits in Canada can be found at:

www.benefitscanada.ca

With the large number of benefits offered to employees today, administering an organization's benefits program can be both costly and time-consuming. Even for small employers with 30 to 40 employees, keeping track of each employee's use of a benefit or request for a change of benefits can be cumbersome. For example, even rather straightforward tasks, such as monitoring employees' sick leave, become complex as the size of the organization grows.

Fortunately, interactive employee benefit systems are becoming mainstream for most employers. Employees at TransAlta Corporation in Calgary can obtain information about their pension plans and enroll in a flexible benefits plan by logging onto the company website whenever it is convenient for them. For the third of its employees without access to computers, TransAlta has installed kiosks on company premises. The benefits of a human resources information system (HRIS) (explained in Chapter 1) are reduced costs, increased efficiencies, and accuracy.[3] Online benefits programs create a form of self-service administration. One intent of online programs is to eliminate the annual open enrollment period for various benefits, thereby providing greater flexibility in benefits selection. An important advantage to an interactive benefits program is the significant savings in administration costs. Once an online system is operational, it is easy and inexpensive to adapt to employer and employee demands. However, while the Internet can be used effectively in benefits administration, security must always be a concern when transmitting benefits information.[4]

Perhaps no part of the HR function is more technologically advanced than benefits administration. A wide variety of commercially developed software packages have been developed that serve to facilitate benefits administration in such areas as pensions, variable pay, workers' compensation, health benefits, and time-off programs. Descriptions of and advertisements for a variety of benefits software programs are regularly found in HR journals such as *Canadian HR Reporter* and *Human Resource Professional*. Software programs represent a cost-effective way to manage employee benefits programs when employers lack the resources or expertise.

Requirements for a Sound Benefits Program

The soundness of a benefits program hinges on two factors: (1) selecting benefits that target important employee needs while promoting strategic organizational objectives and (2) effective administration of benefits programs. Gone are the days of providing a particular benefit because other employers are doing it, because someone in authority believes it is a good idea, or because the benefit is "popular" at the moment. Therefore, benefit specialists recommend paying attention to certain basic considerations.

Strategic Benefits Planning

Like any other component of the HR program, an employee benefits program should be based on specific objectives. The objectives an organization establishes will depend on many factors, including the size of the firm; its location; its degree of unionization; its profitability; and industry patterns. Most important, these aims must be compatible with the organization's strategic compensation plan (see Chapter 9), including its philosophy and policies.

The chief objectives of most benefits programs are to

- Improve employee work satisfaction
- Meet employee health and security requirements
- Attract and motivate employees
- Retain top performing employees
- Maintain a favourable competitive position

In a 2004 survey of employees, about half stated that a good benefits plan would make them stay with their current employer. Another survey found that four out of ten employers use wellness programs and subsidized fitness programs as a retention strategy.[5] Furthermore, these objectives must be considered within the framework of cost containment—a major issue in today's programs.

Unless the organization plans to develop a flexible benefits plan (to be discussed later), a uniform package of benefits should be developed. This involves carefully considering the various benefits that can be offered, the relative preference shown for each benefit by management and the employees, the estimated cost of each benefit, and the total amount of money available for the entire benefits package.

Allowing for Employee Involvement

Before a new benefit is introduced, the need for it should first be established. Many organizations create committees composed of managers and employees to administer, interpret, and oversee their benefits policies. Opinion surveys are also used to obtain employee input. Having employees participate in designing benefits programs helps to ensure that management is moving in the direction of satisfying employee wants. Pan Canadian Petroleum formed 11 focus groups of randomly selected employees to provide insights and valuable feedback on their pension investments.[6]

Benefits for a Diverse Workforce

To serve their intended purpose, employee benefits programs must reflect the social changes that Canada is constantly facing. Particularly significant are changes in the diversity and lifestyles of the workforce; the changes make it necessary to develop new types of benefits to meet shifting needs. Therefore, more employers are tailoring their benefits programs to be family-friendly. (Specific family-friendly benefits are discussed later in the chapter.) For example, as we have indicated throughout this book, the number of women in the workforce is continuing to grow. Which benefits are most valuable to them (and to men) will be determined largely by whether they have dependent children and whether they have a spouse who has benefits coverage.

Unfortunately, benefits plans sometimes provide little advantage to employees, limiting the organization's ability to attract and retain quality employees. For example, many employers provide unneeded medical benefits to the young and single in the form of dependants' coverage. Likewise a well-designed—and costly—defined benefits pension program may not serve the needs of employees or the employer of a predominantly younger workforce. Similarly, the employer's contribution to the pension plan for a 30-year-old employee is roughly one-fourth the contribution for a 50-year-old employee for the same amount of pension commencing at age 65. This difference in funds spent on older workers in effect discriminates against younger workers, although in legal terms it is not regarded as discriminatory.

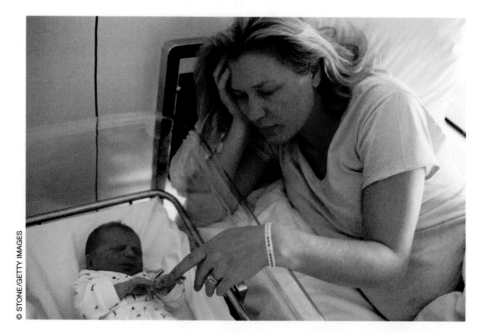

Many employers offer family-friendly benefits, such as extended maternity leave.

© STONE/GETTY IMAGES

Providing for Flexibility

flexible benefits plans (cafeteria plans)
Benefits plans that enable individual employees to choose the benefits that are best suited to their particular needs

To accommodate the individual needs of employees, many organizations are embracing **flexible benefits plans,** also known as cafeteria plans. When Zabeen Hirji, senior vice-president of human resources for RBC, surveyed 16 000 of their 65 000 employees about their benefits preferences, the number one request was for flexibility.[7] These plans enable individual employees to choose the benefits that are best suited to their particular needs. They also prevent certain benefits from being wasted on employees who have no need for them. Typically, employees are offered a basic or core benefits package of life and health insurance, sick leave, and vacation. Requiring a core set of benefits ensures that employees have a minimum level of coverage to protect against unforeseen financial hardships. Employees are then given a specified number of credits that they may use to "buy" whatever other benefits they need. Other benefits options might include prepaid legal services, financial planning, or long-term-care insurance.[8] Compensation specialists often see flexible benefits plans as ideal. Employees select the benefits of greatest value to them, while employers manage benefits costs by limiting the dollars employees have to spend.

Honeywell Canada considered three types of flexible benefits programs: cafeteria-style, whereby employees could choose any benefits they wanted; a module approach, whereby employees could select among prepackaged sets of benefits; and a core-plus-options plan, whereby employees could choose among options to augment a basic level of protection. Employees were able to select health and dental benefits that suited their life stages and that matched well with the plans their spouses had. Figure 11.1 lists the most commonly cited advantages and disadvantages of flexible benefits programs.

Because cafeteria plans increase the complexity of administering the entire benefits program, organizations may elect to outsource the handling of this function to a professional benefits vendor. About a third of Canadian firms rely on third parties to

Figure 11.1	Flexible Benefits Plans: Advantages and Disadvantages

ADVANTAGES

- Employees select benefits to match their individual needs.
- Benefit selections adapt to a constantly changing (diversified) workforce.
- Employees gain greater understanding of the benefits offered to them and the costs incurred.
- Employers maximize the psychological value of their benefits program by paying only for the highly desired benefits.
- Employers limit benefit costs by allowing employees to "buy" benefits only up to a maximum (defined) amount.
- Employers gain competitive advantage in the recruiting and retention of employees.

DISADVANTAGES

- Poor employee benefits selection results in unwanted financial costs.
- There are certain added costs to establishing and maintaining the flexible plan.
- Employees may choose benefits of high use to them that increase employer premium costs.

perform these types of transactional services for their plans.[9] Paying a service or contract fee to these firms may be particularly cost-effective for the smaller employer. Furthermore, benefits programs must be flexible enough to accommodate the constant flow of new laws and regulations that affect them. A number of consulting firms specializing in benefits can help managers track changes in all phases of the programs they oversee.

Communicating Employee Benefits Information

Many employees do not believe what their employers tell them about soaring benefits costs, and employees and employers are at loggerheads over how effectively benefits are used. Therefore, it becomes critical that organizations effectively—and frequently—communicate the benefits package to employees. Court cases in Canada have established that it is the employer's responsibility to properly inform and disclose information about benefits. In *Spinks v. Canada*, an employee was not advised of certain pension options when he started with a new employer—specifically, that he was eligible to purchase past service in connection with his prior employment. The Federal Court of Appeal ruled that the employee had been poorly advised. In other cases, such as *Schmidt v. Air Products of Canada*, the courts have ruled that employee brochures, which usually aren't considered to be legal documents, may in fact be legally binding.[10]

While it is important to communicate information about employee benefits, there is no legislation that mandates how this is to be done. Various provincial pension benefits acts and federal laws regulating pension benefits state that employers operating a pension plan must provide specific information to employees. However, there are differences among provinces about what must be communicated. The sponsor of a registered retirement plan (RPP) has until six months after the end of the plan's fiscal year to provide active plan members with statements of their pension benefits. (Quebec regulations require annual pension statements for retired and deferred vested members.) The employee's name, date of birth, and date of hire must be included in the pension statement, along with the pension plan membership date, vesting date, and normal retirement date. Most provinces also require the name of the employee's spouse and/or pension plan beneficiary.[11]

Employers use a number of methods to communicate benefits to employees such as the following:

- In-house publications (employee handbooks and organizational newsletters)
- Group meeting and training classes
- Audiocassettes/videotapes
- Bulletin boards
- Payroll inserts/pay stub messages
- Specialty brochures

The City of Regina, Saskatchewan, arranged to deliver pension presentations to all its 300 firefighters, a group of employees who are difficult to reach because of their shift work, by arranging these presentations on different days of the week at fire halls.[12] Also, the topic is usually covered in new-hire orientation programs. Managers who are conducting orientations should be allowed plenty of time to inform new employees of the benefits program and to answer any questions. Some employers summarize benefits information on a paycheque stub as a reminder to employees of their total compensation. Highlights in HRM 11.1 provides a list of recommendations for communicating benefits.

Employee self-service systems have made it possible for employees to gather information about their benefits plans, enroll in their plans of choice, change their benefits coverage, or simply inquire about the status of their various benefits accounts without ever contacting an HR representative. Coopers & Lybrand uses a benefits information line to provide its employees with instant access to a wide variety of HR and benefits information by telephone. Employees can access their individual account information by entering a personal identification number (PIN). Other organizations use networked PCs or multimedia kiosks to the same purpose. These latter approaches enable employees to click on icons to access different benefits and to type in new information to update their records. Once an update or change has been made, the new information is permanently entered into the organization's HR information system without the need for paperwork.

It is also important for each employee to have a current statement of the status of her or his benefits. The usual means is a personalized computer-generated statement, as illustrated in Figure 11.2 on page 482.

Highlights in HRM 11.1

Crafting an Effective Benefits Communication Program

A well-designed benefits communication program will greatly enhance employees' appreciation of their benefits while ensuring that employers receive the intended value of these offerings. An effective program provides information to employees frequently and in a timely and cost-effective manner. Compensation specialists recommend the following when administering a benefits communication program.

In building an identity:
- Design materials that are eye-catching and of high interest to employees.
- Develop a graphic logo for all material.
- Identify a theme for the benefits program.

In writing benefits materials:
- Avoid complex language when describing benefits. Clear, concise, and understandable language is a must.
- Provide numerous examples to illustrate benefits specifics.
- Explain all benefits in an open and honest manner. Do not attempt to conceal unpleasant news.
- Explain the purpose behind the benefit and the value of the benefit to employees.

In publicizing benefits information:
- Use all popular employee communication techniques.
- Maintain employee self-service (ESS) technology to disseminate benefits information and to update employee benefits selections.
- Use voice mail to send benefits information.
- Employ presentation software to present information to groups of employees.
- Maintain a benefits hot line to answer employee questions.

| Figure 11.2 | Communicating Benefits as Part of Total Rewards |

This statement summarizes the scope and value of your total rewards package at ABC. It was prepared with data current as of December 31, 2006, and it includes your 2007 benefit elections. We encourage you to review this statement carefully and to share it with your family.

Your 2006 Total Rewards

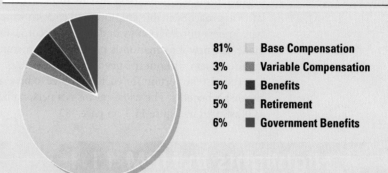

81%	Base Compensation
3%	Variable Compensation
5%	Benefits
5%	Retirement
6%	Government Benefits

	ABC Pays	You Pay
Base Compensation	$49,000	—
Variable Compensation	$ 1,500	—
• Long-term incentive plan	$ 0	—
• Other bonus/incentive plan	$ 1,500	—
Benefits	$ 2,954	$ 1,412
• Health and dental plans	$ 1,797	$ 576
• Flexible spending account	—	$ 500
• Long-term disability plan	$ 346	—
• Basic life/AD&D insurance	$ 201	—
• Optional life/AD&D insurance	—	$ 183
• Optional dependant life insurance	—	$ 153
• Other benefits	$ 610	—
Retirement	$ 2,944	$ 998
• Pension Plan	$ 2,495	—
• Savings Plan	$ 499	$ 998
Government Benefits	$ 3,808	$ 2,620
Your 2006 Total Rewards	$60,256	

Source: Made available with permission from Mercer Human Resource Consulting (www.mercer.com).

As the field of benefits becomes increasingly complex, and as employees become more sophisticated about financial planning, the need to hire and train benefits experts also grows. For those interested in specializing in this field, a good career move would be to become a certified employee benefit specialist (CEBS). In cooperation with the Wharton School at the University of Pennsylvania, Dalhousie University in Halifax sponsors a program leading to the CEBS designation. This ten-course program covers total compensation, health benefits, and strategic human resources.

Concerns of Management

objective **2**

Managing an employee benefits program requires close attention to the many forces that must be kept in balance if the program is to succeed. Management must consider union demands, the benefits other employers are offering, tax consequences, and rising costs, which are discussed in The Business Case.

The escalating cost of health care benefits is a concern to employers, who must strike an appropriate balance between offering quality benefits and keeping costs under control. The shift in benefit planning from entitlement to self-responsibility is discussed in Reality Check on page 484.

The Conference Board of Canada has published a list of cost containment strategies, which include the following:

- Contribution changes, such as increasing deductibles.
- Dollar limits, such as a dollar cap on specific benefits such as eyeglasses.
- Coverage changes (e.g., limits on hospital upgrades).
- Benefit caps (e.g., on dispensing fees).
- Use of preferred providers and flexible benefits.[13]

USING THE INTERNET

For information about the Certified Employee Benefit Specialist program at Dalhousie University, go to:

http://collegeofcontinuinged.
dal.ca/de/cebs.html

The Business Case

Managing the Costs of Benefits

Mandatory benefits cost employers a minimum of 12 percent of payroll; when voluntary benefits are included, these costs may rise to 50 percent of payroll, up from 15 percent in the 1950s. These costs continue to increase at rates higher than inflation. The main area of concern is with healthcare costs. While governments pay for about 70 percent of healthcare expenditures, employers and individuals pay for the rest, and these costs are escalating. For example, drug costs have been rising by 16 percent annually (higher than any other country) and drug costs represent as much as 70 percent of healthcare costs (excluding dental and vision care costs). These benefits represent a fixed rather than a variable cost, so management must decide whether it will be able to afford this cost in bad economic times. As managers can readily attest, if an organization is forced to discontinue a benefit, the negative effects of cutting it often outweigh any positive effects that accrued from providing it.

A current trend (and one not universally liked by employees) is for employers to require employees to pay part of the costs of certain benefits (e.g., through co-payments or higher deductibles). The Royal Bank used to pay 100 percent of benefits but now requires employees to pay a small deductible. At all times, benefit plan administrators are expected to select vendors of benefit services that have the most to offer for the cost. Furthermore, besides the actual costs of employee benefits, there are the costs of administering them, including direct labour costs, overhead charges, office space, and technology. But a big part of the escalating costs is the employee attitude of entitlement. Employees think that they are "entitled" to 12 days of sick leave so they take it, or that they since they have paid $50 for $600 of vision care they should use it.

Sources: Gloria Gonzalez, "Canadian Firms Seek to Stem Rising Costs of Benefits," *Business Insurance*, March 22, 2004, 3; D. Brown, "Runaway Drug Costs Make Benefit Upgrades Impractical," *Canadian HR Reporter*, 16, no. 12 (June 16, 2003); S. Felix, "Gimme Gimme," *Benefits Canada* 24, no. 7 (July 2000): 20–21.

Reality Check

Benefits Planning: From Entitlement to Self-Responsibility

In recent years, we have witnessed major upheavals in the area of benefits. Never before have there been such large increases in the cost of providing benefits as senior executives in companies throughout Canada try to change the "entitlement mindset" so prevalent in employees. Human resources professionals and senior executives can no longer make decisions regarding benefits plans without the assistance of benefits consultants. We met with Daphne Woolf of William H. Mercer Limited to discuss trends in benefit coverage.

Woolf specializes in the design and implementation of flexible benefits plans, strategic planning as it relates to compensation and benefits, and the design and monitoring of programs for promoting workplace health. She provides companies with extensive experience in evaluating funding, administration, and utilization for the purpose of identifying ways to contain benefit plan costs. A visionary in her own right, she leads the national and central region task forces on flexible benefits for Mercer.

"First of all, we need to look at the drivers of change. We see four things happening: our demographics are changing as people age; we have double-income families; the workplace is becoming increasingly diverse; benefits are being taxed to greater extents; and human rights legislation is changing with respect to who should be covered. Due to the high costs of providing benefit coverage, we are seeing a shift in responsibility from the provinces to third parties and individuals. The provinces are covering less, and this trend will continue to grow. The final, most important, underlying issue is increased sensitivity to the magnitude of these trends and the resulting benefit cost impacts.

"The entitlement mindset stems from the fact that, 15 years ago, benefits were considered fringe. Now they are viewed as part of total compensation, which is a change in mentality. Employers are starting to move away from this entitlement mindset to self-responsibility. Employees are not used to making their own health care decisions, and it is a challenge for employers to educate their employees sufficiently and sway them to a different way of thinking. As the population ages, employees' needs for benefits are increasing; at the same time, the quality of their benefits must decrease in response to the high costs. Based on some of our studies, what we are seeing for the first time is that employees are making employment decisions based on benefits. Employers look at dealing with these benefit trends by revisiting their philosophy and benefits objectives. For example, does an employer pay for smoking cessation, include high deductibles, offer choice, or provide coverage for dependants?

"We are seeing an increase in flexible benefit plans. Our belief is that in five years the majority of plans will be flexible, and an employer who waits may be disadvantaged. Employers are better off as flex leaders than flex followers. You want to create your own plan, not have to base your program design on what someone else has done. Now you can 'anti-select' the benefit costs of the spouse's plan, allowing your employee to 'cash out' or allocate flex credits to stock plans or an RRSP. In the future, however, employees and their dependants may not opt out of your plan, and this would potentially increase your costs. So going flex sooner than later, if it's in keeping with corporate objectives, makes sense for many employers who have employees with spouses who work elsewhere. It is going to be a much tougher sell in the future if employees don't learn what the costs are today—they'll still be thinking entitlement when they get older and their provincial medicare does not cover as much.

"Managers have to start watching the cost of illness and absenteeism and realize the lost production costs of paying for time off. These costs add to the overall cost of benefits and should be tied to compensation so that employees can appreciate those benefits. We are also moving toward managed care. We have to look at providing the same level of health care at the same cost. That means putting caps on dispensing fees where drugs are concerned and getting second opinions to ensure that unnecessary procedures are not being administered.

"Americans have moved to a two-tiered system, and Canada is not far behind. While this is not currently a problem, it will be soon. For instance, if a patient wants a second opinion for something serious such as cancer, he or she may have to wait to see another specialist. In a two-tiered system, the patient can pay to have a second opinion immediately. This would not be reimbursed by the provincial health plan. We are beginning to see the collapse of provincial medicare as we now know it.

"There is an increase in health promotion. We are talking about wellness programs, which may focus on stress reduction, fitness in the workplace, and smoking-cessation programs. Employers are seeing the value in keeping employees healthy and productive, that is, preventing the claims costs. In one of my presentations, 'Taking the Fluff Out of Health Promotion,' I specifically outline the advantages of introducing health promotion programs to target cost pressures within the organization. Employers can yield a favourable return on investment if they ensure the right steps are taken to implement health promotion to secure effective cost containment. We are also diverging from traditional medicine to naturopathy and other paramedic services.

"In essence, employers are revisiting the extension of benefits to part-timers, retirees, and dependants. There is a movement toward providing incentive-based benefits—that is, using benefits to reward performance—and, with this, bringing things back to the overall compensation strategy. Employee expectations have become unrealistic mainly because they have not been educated. Once informed, we find that employees become a valuable resource. They need to understand the numbers. Employee focus groups are fast becoming the way to heed the transition from entitlement mindset to self-responsibility.

"[Finally], the trends are moving somewhere in the middle between the American health care system and Canada's. [In the future], flexible benefit plans will be the plan of choice so that educating the employee will be paramount if we are to move from an entitlement mindset to self-responsibility. Your plan should be devised considering an overall philosophy with particular attention to the strategic plan of your organization. Benefits can no longer be taken for granted as the costs of providing this commodity are at a premium. What constitutes benefits must be expanded beyond the basic dental, life insurance, and drug plans. Benefits strategies cannot be short term, but rather must be long range, and in this regard benefit consultants can provide value-added advice. Selecting the right consultant to work with you is just as important as determining your overall benefits philosophy. This philosophy is key to the design of your program as it sets the stage for what your benefit plan will entail."

About 20 percent of employers are choosing at least one of these methods to control costs. Lafarge Canada is one of those employers trying to contain the costs of benefits for its 8000 employees, which have been rising at 6 to 10 percent per year. Their goal is to keep the escalation in costs at the annual rate of inflation. Steelco stopped reimbursing its employees for over-the-counter medicines such as cold remedies and ended coverage for private or semi-private hospital rooms. Air Canada is requiring its employees to pay 30 percent of the costs of the benefits.[14]

Employee Benefits Required by Law

objective 3

Legally required employee benefits amount to 12 percent of the benefits packages that Canadian employers provide.[15] These benefits include employer contributions to the Canada and Quebec pension plans, employment insurance, workers' compensation insurance, and (in some provinces) provincial medicare.

Canada and Quebec Pension Plans (CPP/QPP)

The Canada and Quebec pension plans cover almost all Canadian employees between the ages of 18 and 70. (Certain migratory and casual workers who earn less than the specified amount may be excluded.) To receive a retirement benefit, an individual must apply to Human Resources and Social Development Canada at least six months in advance of retirement.

Although similar in concept, the CPP and QPP differ in how much they pay out to participants. Both plans require employers to match the contributions made by employees. The revenues generated by these contributions are used to pay three main types of benefits: retirement pensions, disability benefits, and survivors' benefits. Governments do not subsidize these plans; all contributions come from employers and employees. Self-employed individuals can also contribute to the plan. With Canada's population aging, funds from the CPP will not be able to meet the needs of retirees unless those currently working, and their employers, significantly increase their contributions.

Canada has cross-border agreements with several countries to protect the acquired social security rights of people who have worked and lived in both countries and who meet the minimum qualifications for benefits from either country. A contributor's rights to benefits under CPP or QPP are not affected or impaired in any way by a change of employment or residence in Canada. All Canadian workers have "universal portability"—that is, the right to claim benefit credits wherever they are employed in Canada.

Employment Insurance (EI)

Employment Insurance (EI) benefits are payable to claimants who are unemployed and are actively seeking employment. A person who becomes unemployed is usually entitled to what most Canadians still call "Unemployment Insurance" (or "UI"), which was what this program used to be called. The new name reflects a change in focus from basic income support to active employment measures.[16]

The amount of benefit paid is determined by the number of hours of employment in the past year and the regional unemployment rate. Individuals are entitled to unemployment insurance after they have contributed enough for a qualifying period and after a waiting period. The waiting period may vary with the individual's situation. Also, employees who resign from their jobs or who are terminated for cause may be ineligible for benefits unless they can prove there was no reasonable alternative to leaving their jobs. Just causes include sexual harassment, health concerns, and moving to another town or city because of a spouse's reassignment.

Additional benefits may be extended for situations involving illness, injury, or quarantine, or for maternity, parental, or adoption leave. If an organization does not offer sick leave benefits, the employee may have to apply to EI for sick benefits. The benefit amount, which is calculated on the same basis as the regular benefit, varies across jurisdictions. Sickness or disability benefits are available for up to 15 weeks. A combination of maternity, parental, or adoptive benefits may be available up to a cumulative maximum of one year in some provinces.

Employees and employers both contribute to the EI fund. An EI premium reduction is available to employers who cover their employees under an approved wage-loss plan. The amount of the reduction depends on the supplement being given to the employee and therefore varies from company to company. Work-sharing programs have recently come into existence as a means of reducing the overall burden on EI. Under work sharing, an organization reduces the workweek of all employees in a particular group instead of laying them off. The company pays for the time worked, and the employee draws EI for the rest of the workweek.

Workers' Compensation Insurance

workers' compensation insurance
Insurance provided to workers to defray the loss of income and cost of treatment resulting from work-related injuries or illness

Workers' compensation insurance is based on the theory that compensation for work-related accidents and illnesses should be considered one of the costs of doing business and should ultimately be passed on to the consumer. Individual employees should not be required to bear the cost of their treatment or loss of income; nor should they be subjected to complicated, delaying, and expensive legal procedures.

Workers' compensation is a form of insurance. It was created by an act of Parliament to help workers injured on the job return to the workplace. Each provincial and territorial board is empowered by the relevant legislation to amend and collect assessments (i.e., insurance premiums), to determine the right to compensation, and to pay the amount due to the injured worker. This system of collective liability is compulsory. Employers' contributions are assessed as a percentage of their payroll. The percentage varies with the nature of the industry. For example, in a high-risk industry such as mining, the assessment rates are higher than in knowledge-based industries.

Workers' compensation is based on the following principles:

- Employers share collective liability, though contributions may vary among employers in the same industry (e.g., some provinces punish employers who do not maintain a safe and healthy work environment by levying additional fines).
- Injured workers are compensated regardless of the financial status of the employer, and this compensation is based on loss of earnings.
- The system is no-fault and nonadversarial, and thus offers no recourse to the courts.

Injured employees have their incomes protected through sick leave provisions.

Benefits are paid out of an employer-financed fund and include medical expenses stemming from work-related injuries, survivors' benefits (including burial expenses and pensions), and wage-loss payments for temporary, total, or partial disability. Permanent disability benefits may be disbursed as a lump-sum payment or as a permanent disability pension with rehabilitation services. The amount paid depends on the employee's earnings and provincial legislation.

Employees cannot be required either to make contributions toward a workers' compensation fund or to waive their right to receive compensation benefits. Payments made to claimants are effectively nontaxable. Premiums paid for by the employer may be deducted as expenses and are not deemed a taxable benefit for employees.

Figure 11.3 lists the steps that an HR department can take to control workers' compensation costs.

Figure 11.3	Reducing Workers' Compensation Costs: Key Areas

1. Perform an audit to assess high-risk areas in the workplace.
2. Prevent injuries by proper ergonomic design of the workplace and effective assessment of job candidates.
3. Provide quality medical care to injured employees from physicians with experience and preferably with training in occupational health.
4. Reduce litigation by ensuring effective communication between the employer and the injured worker.
5. Manage the care of the injured worker from time of injury until return to work. Keep a partially recovered employee at the worksite.
6. Provide extensive worker training in all related health and safety areas.

Provincial Hospital and Medical Services

People who have been resident in a Canadian province for three months are eligible to receive health care benefits. Applications must be made and approval given before coverage starts. Benefits include services provided by physicians, surgeons, and other qualified health professionals; hospital services such as standard ward accommodation and laboratory and diagnostic procedures; and hospital-administered drugs. Many employers offer third-party benefit coverage, which entitles their employees to additional benefits such as semi-private or private accommodation, prescription drugs, private nursing, ambulance services, out-of-country medical expenses that exceed provincial limits, vision and dental care, and paramedic services. Depending on the employer, all or just a portion of the services may be covered.

Discretionary Major Employee Benefits

Besides the mandated benefits, most employers offer other benefits such as health care and dental plan; payment for time not worked, life insurance, retirement programs, and pension plans.

Healthcare Benefits

The benefits receiving the most attention from employers today, owing to sharply rising costs and employee concerns, are healthcare benefits. In the past, health insurance plans covered only medical, surgical, and hospital expenses. Today employers are under pressure to include prescription drugs as well as dental, optical, and mental healthcare benefits in the packages they offer their workers. Drugs now represent the second largest health expenditures, second only to hospital costs.

Cost Containment

The growth in healthcare costs can be attributed to a number of factors, including the greater need for health care by an aging population, the costs associated with technological advances in medicine, the growing costs of healthcare labour, and the overuse of costly healthcare services.

With the significant rise in healthcare costs, it is understandable that employers seek relief from these expenses. The approaches used to contain the costs of healthcare benefits include reductions in coverage, increased deductibles or co-payments, and increased coordination of benefits to ensure that the same expense is not paid by more than one insurance reimbursement. A list of cost containment strategies is provided in Figure 11.4 on page 490. Some employers seek to control the costs of benefits by providing benefits only to full-time employees—see Ethics in HRM on page 490. Cost containment strategies must be subject to a cost/benefit analysis.

Employee assistance programs and wellness programs can help organizations cut the costs of health care benefits. Highlights in HRM 11.2 on page 491 focuses on a team approach to cost reduction.

Other Health Benefits

In the past two decades, more and more employees have been receiving dental care insurance as a benefit. Besides their obvious purpose, dental plans encourage

| Figure 11.4 | **Cost Containment Strategies** |

Employers can reduce the cost of benefits in the following ways:

1. Education and Motivation
   - Communicate the costs of benefits.
   - Provide incentives to employees to reduce costs.
   - Teach employees how to live healthy lifestyles, and how to plan for retirement.
2. Change Coverage
   - Introduce dollar limits on benefits.
   - Eliminate duplicate coverage for spouses.
   - Remove upgrades.
   - Introduce minimum fees to be paid by employees.
3. Change the System
   - Form partnerships with pharmacies to provide discounts.
   - Move to defined contribution plans.
   - Move to a claims management approach, and audit claims.

Ethics in HRM

The Real Value of a Full-Time Job

Full-time workers get more pay (when you calculate hours worked and rate of pay per hour) and also more benefits than part-time workers. The percentages of benefits received by full-time and part-time workers differ substantially, as the following table indicates:

BENEFIT	FULL-TIME WORKERS	PART-TIME WORKERS
Employer pension plan	58%	19%
Healthcare plan	68	18
Dental plan	63	16
Paid sick leave	66	18
Paid vacation leave	80	30

These differences have a profound impact on employees' lives: one in eight of Canada's 2.6 million part-time workers spend their spare time looking for full-time employment. If benefits are important to them, they should be looking for a large employer in a unionized environment. Unionized employees are twice as likely as their nonunionized counterparts to be covered. The probability of receiving benefits also increases if the employer is unionized, and if the job is permanent rather than temporary.

The issue of benefits for part-time workers is a concern to the government and should also concern taxpayers. Part-time workers are least able to afford their own benefits; as a result, through social transfer payments, society ends up paying for the services they need, such as health care and retirement plans. However, in a groundbreaking move, the Royal Bank of

Canada now provides full benefits and bonuses to its 7500 part-time and casual workers. Should governments pass legislation to force employers to offer the same benefits to part-timers as full-timers?

Sources: "Unionization and Fringe Benefits," *Perspectives on Labour and Income* 3, no. 8, 75-001-XIE, August 2002; Bruce Little, "The Full-Scale Advantages of Full-Time Time Work," *The Globe and Mail*, July 14, 1997; Brenda Lipsett and Mark Reesor, *Job-Related Benefits for Employees*, Human Resources Development Canada, June 1997.

employees to receive regular dental attention. Typically, the insurance pays a portion of the charges and the subscriber pays the remainder.

Another fairly new benefit that many employers are offering is optical care. Typically, the coverage includes visual examinations and a percentage of the costs of lenses and frames.

Highlights in HRM 11.2

A Team Approach to Cost Containment

The University of New Brunswick (UNB) in Fredericton has long done what so many other organizations are only starting to do: The Fringe Benefits Review Committee was established to assist it in devising strategies to combat increases in benefits costs. According to Jim O'Sullivan, the university's vice-president of finance and administration, the committee was organized in "an effort to repair relations with angry faculty representatives after the university's board of governors was perceived to have unilaterally eliminated an existing benefit."

The committee, comprising management as well as unionized and nonunionized employees, had the task of reviewing the university's group file, health, and long-term disability (LTD) plans. Although the board of governors still holds the final decision-making authority, the committee alone is responsible for making benefits recommendations and working out the details; its efforts have resulted in a $3.8-million benefits surplus.

For more than 20 years, the employees have shared the costs of the university's group insurance plan, thus allowing the university to maintain effective cost control and to plan redesigns. Because the plan costs are shared, employees are aware that increasing benefits will mean higher contributions for both sides. To keep LTD claims down, employees have allowed the university to follow up directly with workers on disability claims to help them return to work faster. Compared to other universities with similar workforces, UNB has the lowest claims. For many other organizations, the price tag for health care, drug, and dental benefits has grown annually, but UNB has managed to hold benefit costs below the general rate of inflation. O'Sullivan attributes the savings to the cost-sharing partnership.

As in many other organizations, the employee assistance program is fully paid for by the employer. However, because the development of this program was discussed with the committee, employees played a major role in selling this plan to their co-workers. O'Sullivan believes

(continued on next page)

that the plan is cost-effective in the long term. "Failure to seek treatment for personal problems," he notes, "would eventually affect job performance and lead to higher costs for health and LTD insurance."

The university has been self-insuring benefits—that is, paying for and managing its own risk, rather than contracting with an external insurance provider—with a pay-as-you-go philosophy, since the 1970s. Commercial insurance is purchased only to provide protection against catastrophic losses. For example, the LTD plan is self-insured for the first ten years of any claim, after which commercial insurance coverage comes into effect.

Employer and employee representative groups each have control over their half share of surplus funds. When there has been a surplus, consideration has been given to declaring contribution holidays or to implementing new benefits, but both sides, concerned that the good times could come to an end, have decided to act conservatively. The surplus funds are invested by the university's endowment fund investment managers; investment income is used to improve employees' benefits.

"I do believe we have developed a realistic balance between the operation of a responsive and competitive benefits package and the need to maintain effective cost controls," states O'Sullivan. "In this way, we have not only helped meet our overall financial objectives but have created positive spinoffs for labour–management relations generally."

Payment for Time Not Worked

The "payment for time not worked" category of benefits includes the following: statutory holiday pay and vacation pay; time off for bereavement, jury duty, and military duty; rest periods and coffee breaks; and maternity benefits (which usually involve some form of salary continuance).

Vacations with Pay

It is generally agreed that vacation time is essential to the well-being of employees. Eligibility for vacations varies by industry, by locale, and by size of the organization. To qualify for longer vacations of three, four, or five weeks, one may expect to work for five, ten, or 15 years. The average annual number of vacations days in Canada is 19, but about one in four employees does not take all of their vacation allotment and a surprising 10 percent never take their vacation time allotment. The reasons? They did not schedule in advance, prefer cash in lieu of time, and are too busy at work.[17]

Paid Holidays

Both hourly and salaried workers can expect to be paid for statutory holidays as designated by each province. The standard statutory holidays are New Year's Day, Good Friday, Canada Day (Memorial Day in Newfoundland), Labour Day, and Christmas Day. Other holidays commonly recognized by the various provinces are Victoria Day and Thanksgiving Day. Some provinces have their own special statutory holidays. Many employers give workers an additional one to three personal days off (i.e., personal use days).

Sick Leave

Employees who cannot work because of illness or injury are compensated in various ways. Most employers offer short-term disability and long-term disability plans.

Short-term disability plans include salary continuance programs, sick leave credits, and weekly indemnity plans. Most public employees, and many in private firms—especially in white-collar jobs—receive a set number of sick leave days each year to cover such absences. Sometimes employees are permitted to accumulate the sick leave they do not use to cover prolonged absences. Accumulated vacation leave is sometimes treated as a source of income when sick leave benefits have been exhausted. Group insurance that provides income protection during a long-term disability is also becoming more common. LTD plans normally provide a disabled employee with 50 to 70 percent of pre-disability income. Yet another alternative, depending on the situation, is workers' compensation insurance, which was discussed earlier in the chapter.

Severance Pay

severance pay
A lump-sum payment given to terminated employees by an employer at the time of an employer-initiated termination

An employee who is being terminated is sometimes given a one-time payment. Known as **severance pay,** it can amount to anywhere from a few days' wages to several months', with the exact payment depending on length of service. There are not strict rules for severance pay, but the following are guidelines based on court decisions:

- Two weeks per year of service for those working as labourers, production workers, and administrative support staff.
- Three weeks per year of service for those employed in technical, professional, supervisor, and managerial jobs.
- Four weeks per year of service for those employed as senior managers.[18]

Employers that are downsizing often use severance pay to soften the impact of unexpected termination on employees. An employee is not entitled to severance pay if a reasonable offer of alternative employment is refused.

USING THE INTERNET

Go to Benefits Canada and click on benefits finder to determine the benefits to which you may be entitled:

www.benefitscanada.gc.com

objective **6**

Life Insurance

Group life insurance is the benefit most commonly provided by an employer. The purpose is to provide financial security to the dependants of the employee, in case of his/her death.

Retirement Programs

Retirement is an important part of life and requires careful preparation.
When convincing job applicants to come work for them, employers usually emphasize the retirement benefits that can be expected after a certain number of years of employment. As we noted earlier, it is common for each employee, once a year, to receive a personalized statement of benefits that contains information about projected retirement income from pensions and employee investment plans.

Retirement Policies

Canadian employees may retire at age 55 and begin drawing a reduced pension from CPP/QPP as well as funds from other sources such as RRSPs. Alternatively, some individuals can work until 71 in some provinces, at which time they must retire. Mandatory retirement at age 65 in Canada is slowly being abolished. Statistics Canada reported that 61 is the average age of retirement, with women leaving work at 58 and men at 62. The higher the household income, the lower the age of retirement.[19] Many are retiring because they have lost their jobs and cannot find other work. However, as we have seen, there is a growing trend for individuals in their golden years to take on part-time employment as a means of supplementing their income.

To avoid making layoffs and to reduce salary and benefits costs, employers often encourage early retirement. This encouragement often takes the form of increased pension benefits or cash bonuses, sometimes referred to as the **silver handshake.** Some companies, including IBM Canada, have given generously to encourage the early retirement of workers. Ontario Hydro presented its employees with various options to retire early; these included an early retirement allowance, a voluntary separation allowance, a special retirement program, and a voluntary retirement program. The incentives succeeded; most employees with 25 years of service opted for the special retirement program.[20] An employer can offset the cost of retirement incentives by paying lower compensation to replacements and/or by reducing its workforce.

For employees, the main factors in a decision to retire early are health, personal finances, and job satisfaction. Lesser factors include an attractive pension and the possibility of future layoffs. Highlights in HRM 11.3 summarizes the reasons that employees choose to retire.

silver handshake
An early retirement incentive in the form of increased pension benefits for several years or a cash bonus

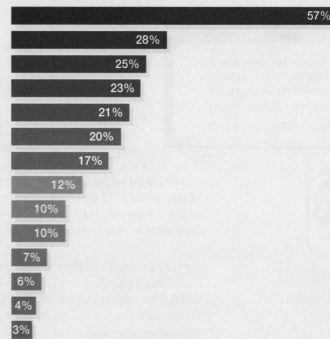

Highlights in HRM 11.3

Why Retire?

A survey asked people why they would want to retire (respondents could choose more than one category, so results add up to more than 100).

Pursue a dream/leisure interests	57%
Volunteer/contribute to society	28%
Not respected in my current job	25%
No longer want to work	23%
Spouse/colleagues retiring	21%
Retirement package	20%
Financial goals met	17%
Career change	12%
Health concerns	10%
Relocating	10%
Start own business	7%
Expect to lose job	6%
Physical tasks too demanding	4%
Dependant care responsibilities	3%

Source: U. Vu, "Wave of Retirements Coming; Few Organizations Getting Ready," *Canadian HR Reporter,* May 5, 2003: 2.

Preretirement Programs

Most people are eager to retire; some are bitterly disappointed once they do. In an attempt to lessen the disappointment, some employers offer programs to help employees prepare for retirement. These programs typically include seminars and workshops, where lectures, videos, and printed materials are offered. Usually they cover topics such as how to live on a reduced, fixed income and how to cope with lost prestige, family conflict, and idleness. Also discussed are more concrete topics such as pension plans, health insurance coverage, retirement benefits and provincial health care, and personal financial planning.

At Consumers Gas, employees between 50 and 53 can attend, with their spouses, a three-day seminar that covers six subject areas: positive outlook, leisure time, health, home, financial planning, and estate planning. At other organizations, these programs have a more individual focus. CIBC, which has over 40 000 employees at 1800 different locations, provides its employees with tools such as tapes, books, videos, and computer programs. The Retirement Council of Canada recommends that 1 percent of a company's pension program be earmarked for retirement planning programs.[21]

Some organizations now offer retirement seminars to their younger employees as well. For instance, at Siemens Canada, employees as young as 35 are being offered the same financial sessions as employees 55 and over.

To help older workers get used to the idea of retirement, some organizations are experimenting with retirement rehearsal. Polaroid offers employees an opportunity to try out retirement through an unpaid three-month leave program. The company offers another program that permits employees to cut their hours gradually before retirement. Employees are paid only for hours worked, but receive full medical insurance and prorated pension credits. Most experts agree that preretirement planning is a much-needed, cost-effective employee benefit.[22]

Pension Plans

Originally, pensions were based on a *reward philosophy*; in other words, employers viewed pensions mainly as a reward to employees who stayed with them until retirement. Employees who quit or were terminated before retirement were not seen as deserving retirement benefits. Since then, most unions have negotiated vesting requirements into their contracts, and vesting has become required by law. Put another way, pensions are now based on an *earnings philosophy;* they are seen as deferred income that employees accumulate during their working lives; in other words, the pension belongs to the employee after a specified number of years of service, whether or not she or he remains with the employer until retirement.

Since the CPP/QPP legislation was enacted in 1966, pension plans have been used to supplement the protection provided by government-sponsored programs. Most private pension plans and a significant number of public plans now integrate their benefits with CPP/QPP benefits.

It is up to the employer whether to offer a pension plan. Because these plans are so expensive, companies are always looking for the least expensive ways to provide them to their employees.

Types of Pension Plans

Pensions can be categorized in two basic ways: according to contributions made by the employer, and according to the amount of pension benefits to be paid. In a

objective **1**

contributory plan
A pension plan in which contributions are made jointly by employees and employers

noncontributory plan
A pension plan in which contributions are made solely by the employer

defined benefit plan
A pension plan in which the amount an employee is to receive on retirement is specifically set forth

defined contribution plan
A pension plan that establishes the basis on which an employer will contribute to the pension fund

contributory plan, contributions to a pension plan are made jointly by employees and employers. In a **noncontributory plan,** the contributions are made solely by the employer. Most plans in privately held organizations are contributory.

When pension plans are classified by the amount of pension benefits to be paid, there are two basic types: the defined benefit plan and the defined contribution plan. Under a **defined benefit plan,** the retirement benefit is determined according to a predefined formula. This amount is usually based on the employee's years of service, average earnings during a specific period of time, and age at time of retirement. A variety of formulas exist for determining pension benefits; the one used most often is based on the employee's average earnings (usually over a three- to five-year period immediately preceding retirement) multiplied by the number of years of service with the organization. A deduction is then made for each year the retiree is under 65. As noted earlier, pension benefits are usually integrated with CPP/QPP. Very few employers introduce this type of plan, because it places them under the legal obligation to pay benefits regardless of the performance of the pension plan.

A **defined contribution plan** establishes the basis on which an employer will contribute to the pension fund. These plans come in a variety of forms: some involve profit sharing; others involve employers matching employee contributions; still others are employer-sponsored RRSP plans. The size of the pension the employee will get is determined by the funds in his or her account at the time of retirement and what retirement benefits (usually in the form of an annuity) these funds will purchase. These plans are not as predictable (i.e., secure) as defined benefit plans. However, even under defined benefit plans, retirees may not receive the benefits promised them if the plan is not adequately funded.

Defined benefit plans, with their fixed payouts, are falling out of use and have dropped to 40 percent of companies.[23] They are less popular with employers nowadays because they cost more and because they require compliance with complicated government rules.[24] All new pension plans in Canada, such as those introduced by MacMillan Bloedel and Molson Breweries, are defined contribution plans.

Registered retirement savings plans (RRSPs) have experienced tremendous growth in recent years because the funds in these plans are allowed to accumulate tax-free until they are withdrawn. RRSPs have annual contribution limits; also, if withdrawals are made from them before retirement, tax must be paid on them. Some employers offer group RRSPs, which have some advantages over individual RRSPs: they are deducted from payroll and have mass-purchasing power.

Federal Regulation of Pension Plans

Registered pension plans (RPPs) are subject to federal and provincial regulations. The federal Income Tax Act prescribes limits and standards that affect the amount of contributions that can be deducted from income; it also mandates how pension benefits can be taxed. (It is estimated that the government loses about $5 billion a year in taxes because it does not tax private pension plans.) In the federal jurisdiction and most provincial ones, there are laws that state how pension plans must be operated. For example, the actuarial assumptions on which the funding is based must be certified by an actuary at specified intervals.

vesting
A guarantee of accrued benefits to participants at retirement age, regardless of their employment status at the time

An important issue to employees is vesting. **Vesting** is a guarantee of accrued benefits to participants at retirement age, regardless of their employment status at that time. Vested benefits that have been earned by the employee cannot be revoked by the employer. Employees with two years of service in an organization are considered, with regard to their pension plans, fully vested and locked in.

Pension Portability

For a long time, most pension plans lacked portability; in other words, employees who changed jobs were unable to maintain equity in a single pension. Unions addressed this concern by encouraging multiple-employer plans. These plans cover the employees of two or more unrelated organizations in accordance with a collective agreement. They are governed by boards of trustees on which both the employers and the union are represented. Multiple-employer plans tend to be found in industries in which few companies have enough employees to justify an individual plan. They are also found often in industries in which employment tends to be either seasonal or irregular. These plans are found in the following manufacturing sectors: apparel, printing, furniture, leather, and metalworking. They are also found in nonmanufacturing industries such as mining, construction, transport, entertainment, and private higher education.

Employees who leave an organization can leave their locked-in funds in their current pension plan, or they can transfer those funds into a locked-in RRSP or into their new employer's pension plan (if one exists).

Pension Funds

A pension fund can be administered through a trusted plan or through an insured one. In a *trusted* plan, the pension contributions are placed in a trust fund. The fund is then invested and administered by trustees. The trustees are appointed by the employer; but if there is a union, the union sometimes appoints them. Contributions to an *insured* pension plan are used to purchase insurance annuities. These funds are administered by the insurance company that is providing the annuities.

Government benefits such as CPP/QPP and Old Age Security will be stretched thin as baby boomers grow older, and some private pensions may be vulnerable to poorly performing investments. It should also be noted that the pension funds of some organizations are not adequate to cover their obligations. Here is another interesting question: "Whose money is it?" When a pension fund has generated a surplus over plan (and many of them have), management tends to see this surplus as part of the organization's portfolio of assets; not surprisingly, employees tend to view it as their own money. Highlights in HRM 11.4 describes this debate.

Highlights in HRM 11.4

Whose Money Is It?

Ray Bekeris worked 12-hour shifts as a steelworker for 30 years for Cold Metal Products, a steel manufacturing plant based in Hamilton, Ontario. Cold Metal Products went bankrupt, and Ray discovered that his pension plan was gone too. After the banks and other secured creditors got their money, there was almost none left for the employees. Canadian bankruptcy laws favour secured creditors and employees are at the bottom of the list. Actuaries view this as reasonable, because creditors would not risk their investment if they were not at the top of the list to be repaid. This is not heartless because banks are investing people's money and want some expectation of a return. But this means that employees become unwitting investors. To illustrate, a company is in trouble and the employer stops making its contributions to the

(continued on next page)

pension plan. They use this money to finance the company, perhaps prolonging the bankruptcy. The employees, who are likely unaware of this, become unintentional investors, but with no rights or no voice. And it is not just private companies using pension plan funds as if the funds were their own money. There is a case before the courts that is deemed the most important pension court case in history. Legal firms representing 670 000 public service employees and retirees are suing the federal government because it appropriated the pension surplus (of $30 billion in 1999). Employees believed that they were paying into a pension plan where the money would be held safely and then distributed to them, not to the general coffers of the government.

Bankruptcies and appropriation of pension surpluses are not the only threats to pension plans. Most pension plans can cover only 80 percent of their obligations. These facts should stimulate employees to not rely on organizational pension plans, but to save wisely for their own retirements.

Source: Diane Swain, "How Safe is Your Pension?" *CBC News online*. From *The National*, November 15, 2004. Retrieved March 10, 2006 from www.cbc.ca/news/background/pension and from "Public Service Pension Plan: Pension Grab Court Case Begins," www.pipsc.ca/english/newsletteres/c-dec05/6.html.

Employee Services: Creating a Work–Life Setting

objective 8

Employee services, like other benefits, represent a cost to the employer. But they are often well worth the cost. More and more different services are being offered by employers to make life at work more rewarding and to enhance the well-being of employees. "Wellness is good for business," says Ann Coll of Husky Injection Molding Systems. The employees at Husky's plant in Bolton, Ontario, enjoy a subsidized cafeteria with organic vegetarian meals, a $500-stipend for vitamins, and a fitness centre that is open around the clock.

Creating a Family-Friendly Setting

Eddie Bauer, an outdoor clothing and equipment supplier, offers its employees take-out dinners and one paid "balance day" off a year. The Human Resources Professionals Association of Ontario allows a half-day of paid leave for employee birthdays. These organizations, and many others, are seeking to create a family-friendly organizational environment that allows employees to balance work and personal needs. Programs like these help employees manage their time; employers benefit by attracting good workers and by reducing the various interruptions that affect workplace productivity.[25] Figure 11.5 lists some of the more popular employer-sponsored work–life benefits.

employee assistance programs (EAPs)
Services provided by employers to help workers cope with a wide variety of problems that interfere with the way they perform their jobs

Employee Assistance Programs

To help workers cope with a wide variety of problems that interfere with their work performance, organizations have developed **employee assistance programs (EAPs).** Typically, an EAP provides diagnosis, counselling, and referral services for alcohol or

Figure 11.5	Family-Friendly Benefits: Balancing Work and Home Needs

- Child care/elder care referral services
- Time off for children's school activities
- Employer-paid on-site or near-site child care facilities
- Flexible work hours scheduling
- Employee-accumulated leave days for dependant care
- Subsidized temporary or emergency dependant care
- Extended leave policies for child/elder care
- Sick child programs (caregiver on call)
- Work-at-home arrangements/telecommuting
- Partial funding of child care costs
- Customized career paths

drug problems, emotional problems, and financial or family crises. (EAPs will be discussed in more detail in Chapter 12.) It has been estimated that employees' stress adds as much as 8 percent to payroll costs. The point of EAPs is to help employees solve their personal problems, or at least to prevent those problems from turning into crises that affect their ability to work productively. To handle crises, many EAPs offer 24-hour hotlines. Between 7 and 10 percent of employees use EAPs.[26] The Public Service Commission of the Yukon Government provides a summary of employee and employer responsibilities when using the employee assistance program to deal with the personal problems of employees that affect their work performance (see Highlights in HRM 11.5 on page 500).

Counselling Services

An important part of an EAP is the counselling services it provides to employees. While most organizations expect managers to counsel subordinates, some employees will have problems that require professional counselling. Most organizations refer such individual employees to outside services such as family counselling services, marriage counsellors, and mental health clinics. Some organizations have a clinical psychologist, counsellor, or comparable specialist on staff to whom employees may be referred.

Child and Elder Care

Consider these statistics:

- About 32 percent of Canadians have elder care responsibilities.
- Employees spend an average of 23 hours each month on elder care.[27]

A recent survey indicated that nearly 60 percent of employees are reporting feeling rushed, drained, or overwhelmed by family responsibilities for child and elder care, while working. Great West Life Insurance Company, based in Winnipeg, has hired a family services coordinator to help their employees with family issues. The coordinator recommends products, such as personal alarm systems, or services, such as adult day care in the community.[28] In the past, working parents had to make their own arrangements with sitters or with nursery schools for pre-school children. Today,

Highlights in HRM 11.5

Yukon Government's Public Service Commission

Employee Assistance Program

To assist employees to deal with personal problems that are affecting or have the potential to affect their work performance.

Employee Rights and Responsibilities

- To maintain work performance at an acceptable level
- To voluntarily seek or accept confidential assistance or advice when deteriorating or impaired work performance is being caused by a personal, health, or behavioural problem.
- To cooperate in any treatment program that is established and continue the program to completion.
- An employee who accepts the referral, counseling, and rehabilitation available under EAP does so without prejudice to job security.

Supervisory Responsibilities

- Recognize that a problem exists
- Document the facts
- Confront the employee with the facts
- Try to find a solution within the work situation without diagnosing the underlying personal/ behavioural problem.
- Refer employee to EAP if the problem cannot be resolved in the workplace.
- Follow up with the EAP adviser on the employee's progress.
- Work with the EAP adviser in establishing course of action to reintegrate employee into work environment.
- Monitor the work performance of the employee against clearly established objectives and support the employee in the integration process.

Source: Government of Yukon, Public Service Commission 2006.

benefits may include financial assistance, alternative work schedules, and family leave. For many employees, on-site or near-site child care centres are the most visible, prestigious, and desired solutions.

Ontario Hydro has provided the space and is paying the occupancy costs for a program it calls Hydro Kids. This program encompasses three on-site daycare centres, which are open to company employees. These nonprofit centres are operated by the parents themselves, who hire the child care staff and manage day-to-day operations. Parents pay market rates for the child care services.[29] Ford Motor Company of Canada offers its employees as much as $2,000 a year in child care assistance.

A growing benefit offered employees with children experiencing a short illness is called mildly ill child care. Medical supervision is the primary difference between these

© SUSAN VAN ETTEN/PHOTOEDIT

Caring for one's aging parents and relatives is a growing concern for employees.

elder care
Care provided to an elderly relative by an employee who remains actively at work

facilities and traditional daycare arrangements. Mildly ill care facilities serve children recovering from colds, flu, ear infections, chicken pox, or other mild illnesses that temporarily prevent them from attending regular school or day care. See Highlights in HRM 11.6 on page 502 for the benefits of these arrangements as cited by CIBC.

Responsibility for the care of aging parents and other relatives is another fact of life for more and more employees. The term **elder care,** as used in the context of employment, refers to situations where an employee provides care to an elderly relative while remaining actively at work. Most caregivers are women.

There is no doubt that elder care responsibilities detract from work efficiency: from time lost to take a parent to the doctor, to loss of concentration due to worry, work time being spent making care arrangements, never knowing when an emergency will occur, and calls from neighbours and relatives disrupting the workday. When combined, these responsibilities lead to a situation where neither the care giver nor the employee role is filled adequately. Lost productivity due to absenteeism of those caring for elders can cost a 1000-employee company without an elder care program as much as $400,000 per year. TransAmerica Corporation, an insurance and financial services organization, reported that 1600 missed workdays per year were attributed to 22 percent of its employees who were caring for an elderly relative, for an annual loss to the corporation of $250,000. For larger companies, these costs can run into the millions.[30]

To reduce the negative effects of care giving on productivity, organizations can offer elder care counselling, educational fairs and seminars, printed resources, support groups, and special flexible schedules and leaves of absence. Schering-Plough, a pharmaceuticals manufacturer, uses an 800-line for elder care referrals. IBM has established a nationwide telephone network of more than 200 community-based referral agencies. Some employers band together to come up with better solutions to the challenge of elder care.

AT&T has given grants to community organizations to recruit, train, and manage elder care volunteers where its employees live and work. Travellers Corporation, a financial services company, is part of a consortium of employers that trains family care workers; it also shares with employees the cost of three days' in-home care for family emergencies.[31] Interest in and demand for elder care programs will increase dramatically as baby boomers move into their early 50s and find themselves managing organizations and experiencing elder care problems with their own parents.

Other Services

The variety of benefits and services that employers offer today could not have been imagined a few years ago. Some are fairly standard, and we will cover them briefly. Some are unique and obviously grew out of specific concerns, needs, and interests.

Highlights in HRM 11.6

CIBC Cares

CIBC was the first Canadian corporation to open an employer-sponsored centre dedicated to backup child care. Every parent has faced the hardship of finding emergency care, when regular child care arrangements break down due to a caretaker's illness, or when schools are closed for professional development days or snow days. The CIBC Children's Centre offers special play areas for children of different ages and is licensed under the Day Nurseries Act. The centre is operated by ChildrenFirst, which designs, develops, and operates innovative backup child care facilities in North America. Nearly 800 parents used the CIBC Children's Centre in the first six months of operation, with a resultant saving of 2528 employee days. At an average daily rate of about $200, the productivity saving was estimated to be over one-half million dollars. The intangible benefits include increased attraction and retention of employees, allowing them to achieve better work–life family balance. CIBC discovered through surveys that 90 percent of Canadians want organizations to focus on more than profits, 60 percent form an impression of a company based on its social responsibility, and 17 percent have avoided a company's products because of its lack of social responsibility.

Sources: David Brown, "CIBC Day Care Saves 2500 Absence Days," *Canadian HR Reporter,* November 17, 2003: 1; ChildrenFirst, www.childrenfirst.com; CIBC, www.cibc.com; presentation made by Joyce M. Phillips, Executive Vice-President human resources, CIBC in April 2003.

Figure 11.6 outlines emerging benefits. Some of the more creative and unusual benefits are group insurance for employee pets, free baseball tickets for families and friends, on-site barbers and car washers, and dropoffs for dry cleaning. Highlights in HRM 11.7 on page 504 describes the perks at Intuit Canada.

Legal Services

Legal service plans are generally of two types: access plans and comprehensive plans. *Access plans* provide free telephone or office consultation and document review, as well as discounts on legal fees for more complex matters. *Comprehensive plans* cover other services such as representation in divorce cases, real estate transactions, and civil and criminal trials.

Covered employees normally pay a monthly or annual fee to be enrolled in the plan. When the need for legal assistance arises, the employee may choose a lawyer from a directory of providers and incur no legal fees. Pre-paid legal programs are typically offered as part of an employer's cafeteria benefits plan.

Financial Planning

One of the newer benefits is financial planning. Primarily available to executives and middle managers, it will likely become available to more employees through flexible benefits programs. Financial planning programs cover investments, tax planning and management, estate planning, and similar.

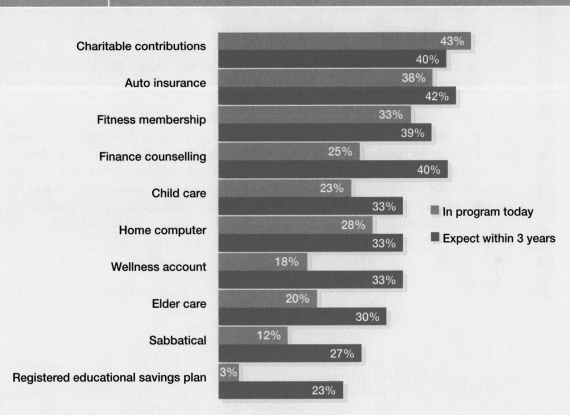

Figure 11.6 Emerging Benefits

- Charitable contributions: 43% / 40%
- Auto insurance: 38% / 42%
- Fitness membership: 33% / 39%
- Finance counselling: 25% / 40%
- Child care: 23% / 33%
- Home computer: 28% / 33%
- Wellness account: 18% / 33%
- Elder care: 20% / 30%
- Sabbatical: 12% / 27%
- Registered educational savings plan: 3% / 23%

■ In program today
■ Expect within 3 years

Source: T. Humber, "Perquisites No Longer a Perquisite?" *Canadian HR Reporter* 16, no. 3 (February 10, 2003): G7. Used with permission, Hewitt Associates, 2006.

Housing and Moving Expenses

The days of "company" houses are now past, except in some remote areas and the armed forces. However, a variety of housing services is usually provided in nearly all organizations that move employees from one office or plant because of a transfer or a relocation. These services may include helping employees find living quarters, paying for travel and moving expenses, and protecting transferred employees from loss when selling their homes.

Transportation Pooling

Daily transportation to and from work is a major concern of employees. The result may be considerable time and energy devoted to organizing car pools and scrambling for parking spaces. Employer-organized van pooling is common among private and public organizations in metropolitan areas. For example, Molson Breweries introduced transportation pooling after the company consolidated its facilities and moved to a remote location. Employees appreciated the savings on expenses and the reduced commuting stress. Many employers report that tardiness and absenteeism are reduced by van pooling.

Highlights in HRM 11.7

Perks at Intuit

Intuit Canada, which develops financial software, employs about 400 employees at its Edmonton offices and is rated one of Canada's top employers. The benefits program it offers employees is one of the reasons for its success. First, Intuit offers the standard benefits package, for which it pays 100 percent of the premiums. Then the fun stuff begins. There is a staff lounge with pool table, foozball, ping pong, and a gas fireplace. Down the hall, employees work out in the company gym, playing volleyball, basketball, and floor hockey. A complete fitness centre, with a free towel service, is greatly valued by employees. For the long hours and stress, Intuit even provides three nap rooms after listening to employees who said they just wanted a place to crash for an hour or two. Intuit pays for employees and their families to relax at the annual corporate retreat at Alberta's Jasper Park Lodge. For Intuit, the benefit of these benefits is the ability to attract and retain the best people.

Source: T. Humber, "Perquisites No Longer a Prerequisite," *Canadian HR Reporter* 16, no. 3 (February 10, 2003): G7–G9.

Credit Unions

Credit unions exist in many organizations to serve the financial needs of employees. They offer a variety of deposits as well as other banking services and make loans to their members. Although the employer may provide office space and a payroll deduction service, credit unions are operated by the employees under federal and provincial legislation and supervision.

Recreational and Social Services

Many organizations offer some type of sports programs in which personnel may participate on a voluntary basis. Bowling, softball, golf, baseball, and tennis are often provided as intramural programs. In addition to intramurals, many organizations have teams that represent them in competitions with other local organizations. Memberships at health clubs and fitness centres, or discounts on memberships, are also popular offerings (see Chapter 12).

Many social functions are organized for employees and their families. Employees should play a major role in the planning if these functions are to succeed. However, the employer should retain control of all events associated with the organization, because of possible legal liability. For example, employers can be held liable for injuries to third persons caused by an employee's actions arising from employment. "Employment" in this context can include attending a company party, if the employee was urged or obligated to attend it. Thus, an employer could be held responsible for an accident occurring while an employee is driving to or from an employer-sponsored event.

SUMMARY

Benefits are an established and integral part of the total compensation package. In order to have a sound benefits program, there are certain basic considerations. It is essential that a program be based on specific objectives that are compatible with the organization's philosophy and policies, as well as affordable. Through committees and surveys, a benefits package can be developed to meet employees' needs. Through the use of flexible benefits plans, employees are able to choose those benefits that are best suited to their individual needs. An important factor in how employees view the program is the full communication of benefits information through meetings, printed materials, and annual personalized statements of benefits.

Since many benefits represent a fixed cost, management must pay close attention in assuming more benefit expense. Increasingly, employers are requiring employees to pay part of the costs of certain benefits. Employers also shop for benefits services that are competitively priced.

Nearly one-quarter of the benefits packages provided by employers are legally required. These benefits include employer contributions to retirement plans, employment insurance, and workers' compensation insurance.

The cost of healthcare programs has become the major concern in the area of employee benefits. Several approaches can be used to contain healthcare costs, including reduction in coverage, increased coordination of benefits, and increased deductibles. Employee assistance programs (EAPs) and wellness programs can also help cut the costs of healthcare benefits.

Included in the category of benefits that involve payments for time not worked are vacations with pay, paid holidays, sick leave, and severance pay. Most Canadian workers receive 10 to 15 days' vacation leave plus statutory holidays. In addition to vacation time, most employees—especially in white-collar jobs—receive a set number of sick leave days. A one-time payment of severance pay may be given to employees who are being terminated.

Many provinces have abolished mandatory retirement, and now employees can choose when to retire. However, many employers provide incentives for early retirement in the form of increased pension benefits or cash bonuses. Some organizations now offer preretirement programs, which typically include seminars, workshops, and informational materials.

Once a pension plan has been established, it is subject to federal and provincial regulation to ensure that benefits will be available when the employee retires. While two types of plans are available—defined benefit and defined contribution—most employers now opt for the latter. The amount an employee receives on retirement is based on years of service, average earnings, and age at time of retirement. Usually, pension benefits are integrated with CPP/QPP. Pension funds are administered through either a trustee or an insurance plan.

The types of service benefits that employers typically provide include EAPs, counselling services, child care, and elder care. Other benefits are prepaid legal services, financial planning, housing and moving, transportation pooling, credit unions, and social and recreational opportunities.

KEY TERMS

contributory plan, 496
defined benefit plan, 496
defined contribution
  plan, 496
elder care, 501

employee assistance programs
  (EAPs), 498
flexible benefits plans
  (cafeteria plans), 479
noncontributory plan, 496

severance pay, 493
silver handshake, 494
vesting, 496
workers' compensation
  insurance, 487

DISCUSSION QUESTIONS

1. You are a small employer wishing to establish a benefits program for your employees. What things should you consider to ensure that the program is a success for your employees?

2. Many organizations are concerned about the rising cost of employee benefits and question their value to the organization and to the employees.
   a. In your opinion, what benefits are of greatest value to employees? To the organization? Why?
   b. What can management do to increase the value to the organization of the benefits provided to employees?

3. Benefits may total from 23 percent to 36 percent of total payroll costs. Name three ways in which you, as an employer, would try to reduce the costs of benefits.

4. This chapter leaves the impression that it is the responsibility of the government and the employer to look after an employee's health. What is the employee's responsibility? More than half of Canadians are overweight and about 15 percent are obese. The costs to Canada's healthcare system are $2 billion a year and growing. Overweight employees typically cost 140 percent more than others in health services. An emerging viewpoint is that employees who smoke or do not exercise or are obese should pay a larger percentage of health benefits. Outline the rationale for and against this perspective.

5. Do you agree with the argument that the benefits for time not worked are the ones most readily available to reduce employer costs? Explain.

6. Employers used to prescribe a mandatory retirement age—usually 65. What do you think are the advantages and disadvantages of a mandatory retirement age? What factors may affect an individual's decision to retire at a particular time, and what factors may affect his or her ability to adjust to retirement?

7. Research the court case driven by current and retired federal public servants. What are the arguments being used by the lawyers representing the employees and what is the case that the federal government is using to defend itself? You be the judge . . . how would you decide?

8. Assume your team has been hired as a benefits consultant by a small business with 50 to 60 employees. What benefits do you believe this employer should offer, given its limited resources? Explain why you would offer these benefits.

INTERNET EXERCISE

Using key search terms such as employee benefits and perks, discover what employers are offering their employees in terms of innovative or unusual benefits. Make a list of these. Try to assess their cost to the employer, and then describe the potential benefits of each perk. At the end of this analysis, decide if you think the benefit is worth the cost.

HRM Experience

Understanding Employer Benefit Programs

Compensation surveys indicate that a majority of employees are unable to accurately name the benefits they receive and employees vastly underestimate the cost of benefits paid by their employers.

This exercise will help you more fully understand the benefits discussed in this chapter. Additionally, you will explore, in detail, the benefits and services offered by your employer and other employers in your area.

Assignment

Working in teams of four to six individuals, obtain information on the benefits package offered by your employer or other employers in your area. Once the information is gathered, be able to identify (1) each benefit offered, (2) what the benefit provides the employee, (3) employee eligibility (if required), and (4) how the benefit is paid for (employer, employee, or a combination of both). Compare benefit packages. Be prepared to discuss your findings with the class.

BIZFLIX EXERCISES

Erin Brockovich: Erin Gets Benefits, with Dental

The chapter discussed the important role of employee benefits in the employment relationship. Watch this scene from *Erin Brockovich* and assess the importance of benefits to Erin.

Erin Brockovich (Julia Roberts), a single mother of three, needs a job and convinces skeptical attorney Ed Masry (Albert Finney) to hire her. She quickly discovers a potentially large case against Pacific Gas & Electric Company (PG&E) for environmental pollution. Based on a true story, the film has many dramatic and funny moments. Roberts received the 2000 Best Actress Academy Award.

The scene comes from the "Ed Comes Over" segment that appears about 45 minutes into the film. It follows Erin's discussion with her neighbour George (Aaron Eckhart) about her one-year reign as Miss Wichita. This scene ends with Ed Masry saying he is drawing the line on benefits. The film continues with Ed reviewing the limited information Erin got from the Lohantan Regional Water Board office. Erin and her

three children revisit the office to copy more information for the case.

What to Watch for and Ask Yourself

- The first section of this chapter, "Employee Benefits Programs," opened with this sentence: "Employee benefits constitute an indirect form of compensation intended to improve the quality of work lives and personal lives of employees." Does this quotation apply to Erin in this scene? If *yes,* in what way does it apply to her and her life situation?
- Erin and Ed are unclear about what benefits, except medical and dental, his firm provides. Which benefits discussed in this chapter would a typical small law firm give to its employees? See the earlier section "Discretionary Major Employee Benefits" for some ideas.
- Erin negotiates a 10-percent pay raise from Ed, suggesting that pay is important to her. Does the scene suggest that benefits are also important to Erin? Why or why not?

case study 1

Evaluate the Work–Life Climate in Your Company

What is the quality of the work–life environment in your company? The following survey provided by the Work and Family Connection will help provide a "case analysis" of the climate in your organization. Answers to the 20 questions will provide clear insights about your company's position in the work–life area.

AGREE OR DISAGREE WITH THE FOLLOWING STATEMENTS:

1. My manager/supervisor treats my work–life needs with sensitivity.
2. It is usually easy for me to manage the demands of both work and home life.
3. My career path at this company is limited because of the pressure of home life demands.
4. My job at this company keeps me from maintaining the quality of life I want.
5. My manager/supervisor is supportive when home life issues interfere with work.
6. My manager/supervisor focuses on results, rather than the time I am at my desk.
7. My manager/supervisor has a good understanding of flexible work hour practices.
8. If I requested a flexible work arrangement my manager/supervisor would support me.
9. My manager/supervisor is often inflexible or insensitive about my personal needs.
10. I believe my manager/supervisor treats me with respect.
11. My manager/supervisor allows me informal flexibility as long as I get the job done.
12. My manager/supervisor tends to treat us like children.
13. My manager/supervisor seldom gives me praise or recognition for the work I do.
14. My manager/supervisor seems to care about me as a person.
15. I would recommend this company to others.
16. The work I do is not all that important to this company's success.
17. If I could find another job with better pay, I would leave this organization.
18. If I could find another job where I would be treated with respect, I would take it.
19. If I could find another job where I could have more flexibility, I would take it.
20. I am totally committed to this company.

For a perfect score, you should answer "Disagree" to questions 3, 4, 9, 12, 13, 16, 17, 18, and 19 and "Agree" to all the rest (questions 1, 2, 5, 6, 7, 8, 10, 11, 14, 15, and 20).

To score, begin by giving yourself 20 points. Then deduct one point for every "wrong" response from the total score.

If your score is 18 to 20: Congratulations! Your organization is leading the nation in flexibility and supportiveness.

If your score is 14 to 17: Your organization is probably more supportive and flexible than most, but you have room to grow.

If your score is 11 to 13: You could be open to other job offers in the race for talent among employees.

If your score is 10 or less: Your managers will need help to manage the 21st century workforce.

Source: Used with permission of the Work and Family Connection, 5195 Beachside Drive, Minnetonka, Minnesota 55343; phone 1-800-487-7898 or www.workfamily.com.

case study **2**

True North's Family-Friendly Benefits: An Unexpected Backlash

True North Consulting Services (TNCS), a provider of HR software application systems, prides itself on the variety of benefits it offers employees. In addition to health care, pension, and vacation benefits, the company also offers an attractive family-friendly benefits package including flexible schedules, child and elder care assistance, counselling services, adoption assistance, and extended parental leave. Unfortunately, in recent months, the company's progressive work–life policy has experienced a backlash from several employees, as the following case illustrates.

In March 2004, Teresa Wheatly was hired by True North as a software accounts manager. With excellent administrative and technical skills, plus four years of experience at Adaptable Software, True North's main competitor, Teresa became a valued addition to the company's marketing team. As a single mother with two grade-school children, Teresa received permission to take Fridays off. She was also allowed to leave work early or come in late to meet the demands of her children. Teresa is one of 11 software account managers at True North.

The problem for True North, and particularly Janis Blancero, director of marketing, began in the fall of 2004. On September 15, Dorothy McShee, citing "personal reasons"—which she refused to discuss—requested a four-day workweek for which she was willing to take a 20-percent cut in pay. When Dorothy asked for the reduced work schedule, she sarcastically quipped, "I hope I don't have to have kids to get this time off." On October 3, Juan Batista, a world-class marathon runner, requested a flexible work hours arrangement in order to accommodate his morning and afternoon training schedule. Juan is registered to run the London, England, marathon. Just prior to Juan's request, Susan Woolf asked for, and was granted, an extended maternity leave to begin after the birth of her first child in December. If these unexpected requests were not enough, Blancero has heard comments from senior account managers about how some employees seem to get "special privileges," while the managers work long hours that often require them to meet around-the-clock customer demands. Janis has adequate reason to believe that there is hidden tension over the company's flexible work hours program. Currently, True North has no formal policy on flexible schedules. Furthermore, with the company's growth in business combined with the increasing workload of software account managers and the constant service demands of some customers, Blancero realizes that she simply cannot grant all the time-off requests of her employees.

Source: Adapted from Alden M. Hayashi, "Mommy-Track Backlash," *Harvard Business Review* 79, no. 3 (March 2001): 33–42.

QUESTIONS

1. Do managers like Janis Blancero face a more complicated decision when evaluating the personal requests of employees versus evaluating employees' individual work performance? Explain.
2. **a.** Should True North establish a policy for granting flexible work schedules? Explain.
   b. If you answered yes, what might that policy contain?
3. If you were Janis Blancero, how would you resolve this dilemma? Explain.

CAREER COUNSEL

Design your own benefits package by completing the Flexible Benefits exercise on the *Managing Human Resources* website (www.belcourt5e.nelson.com).

NOTES AND REFERENCES

1. J. Taggart, "Putting Flex Benefits through Their Paces," *Canadian HR Reporter* 15, no. 21 (December 2, 2002): G3.

2. The Canadian Payroll Association, "Compensation Planning 2003," *Dialogue* [online magazine] www.payroll.ca. November/December 2002: 14–17.

3. S. Felix, "Techno Benefits," *Benefits Canada* 24, no. 1 (January 2000): 27–34.

4. Jan Everett, "Internet Security," *Employee Benefits Journal* 23, no. 3 (September 1998): 14–18. See also Alan R. Parham, "Developing a Technology Policy," *Employee Benefits Journal* 23, no. 3 (September 1998): 3–5.

5. Jeff Holloway, "Recruiting On Principle: Selling A Company's Values," *Canadian HR Reporter*, November 22, 2004, 7; Jacqueline Taggart and Joy Sloane, "If the Pitch Is Total Rewards, Flex Benefits Are the Home Run," *Canadian HR Reporter*, February 23, 2004 G3.

6. Dian Cohen, "Parallel Goals," *Benefits Canada* 22, no. 6 (June 1998): 98.

7. Todd Humber, "RBC Organizes Pay, Benefits Training, Work Environment into a Single Package," *Canadian HR Reporter*, February 23, 2004, G1.

8. Ronald W. Perry and N. Joseph Cayer, "Cafeteria Style Health Plans in Municipal Govt.," *Public Personnel Management* 28, no. 1 (Spring 1999): 107–17; Jon J. Meyer, "The Future of Flexible Benefit Plans," *Employee Benefits Journal* 25, no. 2 (June 2000): 3–7. See also Carolyn Hirschman, "Kinder, Simpler Cafeteria Rule," *HRMagazine* 46, no. 1 (January 2001): 74–79.

9. L. Byron and R. Dawson, "Flex Benefits Are More Popular Than Ever with Employers and Employees," *Benefits*, Benefits Canada, www.benefitscanada.com/magazine/article.jsp?content= 20030624_134506_4312, April 2003.

10. "Communication Break Down: Employers Must Properly Inform Employees of Their Entitlement Benefits or Face Expensive and Time Consuming Court Challenges," *Benefits Canada* 21, no. 1 (January 1997): 27, 29.

11. M. Paterson, "Making a Statement: Are You Ready to Turn an Obligation into an Opportunity?" *Benefits Canada*, February 1995: 19–21.

12. "Great Communication Challenge," *Benefits Canada* 21, no. 9 (October 1997): 25–26.

13. J. MacBride-King, *Managing Corporate Health Care*, Conference Board of Canada, October 1995, Report 158–95: 10.

14. David Brown, "Employees Willing to Help Defray the Costs of Benefits," *Canadian HR Reporter*, June 14, 204, 1; Uyen Vu, "HR Responds to Cost Crunch with Workforce Cuts," *Canadian HR Reporter*, May 31, 2004, 1; Greg Keenan, "Stelco Cuts Benefits for Salaried Workers," *The Globe and Mail*, May 15, 2006, B3; Gloria Gonzalez, "Canadian Firms Seek to Stem Rising Costs of Benefits," *Business Insurance*, March 22, 2004, 3; Jacqueline Taggart, "No Easy Answer for Cost Conundrum," *Canadian HR Reporter*, April 19, 2004, 11.

15. Jacqueline Taggart, "No Easy Answer for Cost Conundrum," *Canadian HR Reporter*, April 19, 2004, 11.

16. "FTNT Employment Insurance: More Than a New Name," *Work Life Report* 10, no. 2 (1996): 1–4, 5.

17. Wallance Immen, "Working Life Blues: Can't Shake the Job," *The Globe and Mail*, May 17, 2006, C1.

18. Richard Long, *Strategic Compensation in Canada*, 3rd edition (Toronto: Nelson Thomson, 2006).

19. Dorothy Lipovenko, "Job Losses Force Early Retirement," *The Globe and Mail*, September 8, 1995: A8.

20. Doug Burn, "Wheel of Fortune: How Much Should an Organization Gamble on Early Retirement Planning?" *Human Resources Professional* 11, no. 4 (May 1994): 13–17.

21. David McCabe, "Retiring the Side: Approaches to Retirement Planning Range From the Conservative to the Revolutionary," *Human Resources Professional* 11, no. 4 (May 1994).

22. Catherine D. Fyock, "Crafting Secure Retirements," *HRMagazine* 35, no. 7 (July 1990): 30–3.

23. Ron Robins, "Moral Investing," *HR Professional*, April/May 2005, 16.

24. Larry Light, "The Power of the Pension Funds," *Business Week*, November 6, 1999: 154–58.

25. "Employers Help Workers Achieve Balance in Life," *HRFocus* 75, no. 11 (November 1998): S3.

26. T. Humber, "Stress Attack," *Canadian HR Reporter* 16, no. 3 (February 10, 2003): G1 and G10.

27. A. Tomlinson, "Trickle Down Effect of Retiring Boomers," *Canadian HR Reporter* 15, no. 11 (June 3, 2002): 1, 12.

28. Betty Healey, "Support for Employees Providing Support," *Canadian HR Reporter*, September 13, 2004, 17; Uyen Vu,

"At Great-West There's Elder Care Help on Staff," *Canadian HR Reporter*, September 13, 2004, 18.

29. Sonya Felix, "Running on Empty," *Benefits Canada* 21, no. 16 (June 1997): 109–14.

30. Elaine Davis and Mary Kay Krouse, "Elder Care Obligations Challenge the Next Generation," *HRMagazine* 41, no. 7 (July 1996): 98–103; Rodney K. Platt, "The Aging Workforce," *Workspan* 44, no. 1 (January 2001): 26.

31. Sue Shellenbarger, "Firms Try Harder, but Often Fail, to Help Workers Cope with Elder-Care Problems," *Wall Street Journal*, June 23, 1993: B1.

NEL

Safety and Health

After studying this chapter, you should be able to

objective 1 Summarize the common elements of federal and provincial occupational health and safety legislation.

objective 2 Describe what management can do to create a safe work environment.

objective 3 Identify the measures that should be taken to control and eliminate health hazards.

objective 4 Describe the organizational services and programs for building better health.

objective 5 Explain the role of employee assistance programs in HRM.

objective 6 Indicate methods for coping with stress.

Occupational safety and health accidents are both numerous and costly to employers. To prevent losses such as these, employers are concerned with providing working conditions—in all areas of employment—that provide for the safety and health of their employees.

While the laws safeguarding employees' physical and emotional well-being are certainly an incentive, many employers are motivated to provide desirable working conditions by virtue of their sensitivity to human needs and rights. The more cost-oriented employer recognizes the importance of avoiding accidents and illnesses wherever possible. Costs associated with sick leave, disability payments, replacement of employees who are injured or killed, and workers' compensation far exceed the costs of maintaining a safety and health program. A recent study conducted found that employers saved $1.95 and $3.75 for each $1 invested in workplace safety.[1] Accidents and illnesses attributable to the workplace may also have pronounced effects on employee morale and on the goodwill that the organization enjoys in the community and in the business world.

Managers at all levels are expected to know and enforce safety and health standards throughout the organization. They must ensure a work environment that protects employees from physical hazards, unhealthy conditions, and unsafe acts of other personnel. Through effective safety and health programs, the physical and emotional well-being of employees may be preserved and even enhanced.

After discussing the legal requirements for safety and health, we shall focus in the rest of the chapter on the creation of a safe and healthy work environment and on the management of stress.

Safety and Health: It's the Law

occupational injury
Any cut, fracture, sprain, or amputation resulting from a workplace accident or from an exposure involving an accident in the work environment

occupational illness
Any abnormal condition or disorder, other than one resulting from an occupational injury, caused by exposure to environmental factors associated with employment

Consider these facts:

- According to the Association of Workers' Compensation Boards of Canada statistics, in 2002 there were 900 workplace-related deaths, which means about four Canadian workers die every working day.
- There are over one million work-related injuries each year.
- There are 340 000 injuries serious enough to cause the worker to miss at least one day of work.
- Over $12 billion is paid out to injured workers and their families, annually.[2]

The burden on the nation's commerce as a result of lost productivity and wages, medical expenses, and disability compensation is staggering. And there is no way to calculate the human suffering involved.

Occupational health and safety is regulated by the federal, provincial, and territorial governments. Statutes and standards vary slightly from jurisdiction to jurisdiction, although attempts have been made to harmonize the various acts and regulations. An **occupational injury** is any cut, fracture, sprain, or amputation resulting from a workplace accident. The worker's involvement in the accident can be direct, or the worker can simply be near enough to the accident to be injured as a result of it. An **occupational illness** is any condition or disorder (other than one resulting from an occupational injury) caused by the work environment. An occupational illness can be acute or chronic; it can result from inhaling, absorbing, ingesting, or directly contacting an illness-causing agent. Those working in the field agree that occupational illnesses are under-reported because few diseases are caused solely by work-related factors, and cause and effect can be difficult to determine. Consider, for example, the case of a mine worker who has contracted a lung disease, but who also smokes heavily.

Acts and Regulations

All HR managers should become familiar with the occupational health and safety laws that apply to their organization. The various acts and government departments that enforce the legislation are listed in Figure 12.1.

Duties and Responsibilities

The fundamental duty of every employer is to take every reasonable precaution to ensure employee safety. The motivating forces behind workplace legislation were effectively articulated in the landmark case *Cory v. Wholesale Travel Group*:

Figure 12.1	Occupational Health and Safety in Canada	
JURISDICTION	**LEGISLATION**	**ENFORCEMENT**
Canada	Canada Labour Code, Regulations	Labour Canada
Alberta	Occupational Health and Safety Act	Department of Labour
British Columbia	Regulations under Workers' Compensation Act	Workers' Compensation Board
Manitoba	Workplace Safety and Health Act	Department of Environment and Workplace Health and Safety
New Brunswick	Occupational Health and Safety	Occupational Health and Safety Commission
Newfoundland and Labrador	Occupational Health and Safety Act	Department of Labour
Nova Scotia	Occupational Health and Safety Act	Department of Labour
Ontario	Workplace Safety and Insurance Act	Ministry of Labour
Prince Edward Island	Occupational Health and Safety Act	Department of Fisheries and Labour
Quebec	Act Respecting Occupational Health and Safety	Commission de la Santé et de la Sécurité du Travail
Saskatchewan	Occupational Health and Safety Act	Department of Labour
Northwest Territories	Safety Act	Commissioner NWT
Yukon	Occupational Health and Safety Act	Commissioner of the Yukon Territories; administered by the Workers' Compensation Board
Nunavut	Safety Act	For information only; not an official act

Regulatory legislation is essential to the operation of our complex industrial society; it plays a legitimate and vital role in protecting those who are most vulnerable and least able to protect themselves. The extent and importance of that role has increased continuously since the onset of the Industrial Revolution. Before effective workplace legislation was enacted, labourers—including children—worked unconscionably long hours in dangerous and unhealthy surroundings that evoke visions of Dante's inferno. It was regulatory legislation with its enforcement provisions which brought to an end the shameful situations that existed in mines, factories and workshops in the nineteenth century. The differential treatment of regulatory offences is justified by their common goal of protecting the vulnerable.

Duties of Employers

Besides providing a hazard-free workplace and complying with the applicable statutes and regulations, employers must inform their employees about safety and health requirements. Employers are also required to keep certain records, to compile an annual summary of work-related injuries and illnesses, and to ensure that supervisors are familiar with the work and its associated hazards (the supervisor, in turn, must ensure that workers are aware of those hazards). An organization with many employees may have a full-time health and safety officer.

In all jurisdictions, employers are required to report to the Workers' Compensation Board all accidents that cause injuries and diseases. Accidents resulting in death or critical injuries must be reported immediately; the accident must then be investigated and a written report submitted. In addition, employers must provide safety training and be prepared to discipline employees for failing to comply with safety rules. Employers are increasingly being required to prove due diligence. This includes establishing a comprehensive occupational health and safety management system; providing competent supervision, training, and instruction; and taking every reasonable precaution in the workplace for the health and safety of workers. Highlights in HRM 12.1 provides a list of health and safety procedures for new employees.

Duties of Workers

Employees are required to comply with all applicable acts and regulations, to report hazardous conditions or defective equipment, and to follow all employer safety and health rules and regulations, including those prescribing the use of protective equipment.

Workers have many rights that pertain to requesting and receiving information about safety and health conditions. They also have the right to refuse unsafe work without fear of reprisal. (Some professionals such as police, firefighters, teachers, and health care workers have only a limited right of refusal, the logic being that their work is inherently dangerous.) An employee who suspects that work conditions are hazardous can report this concern to his or her supervisor; this will trigger an investigation by the supervisor and a worker representative.

A work refusal investigation can result in either the employee's return to work or his or her continued refusal. In the latter case, the appropriate ministry is notified and an investigator is dispatched to the job site to provide a written decision. If a replacement worker is used, he or she must be notified of the previous employee's refusal to work.

USING THE INTERNET

All the provincial occupational health and safety programs can be found on the website of the Canadian Centre for Occupational Health and Safety at:

www.ccohs.ca

USING THE INTERNET

For a description of the best features of a health and safety program, go to the website for the Canadian Centre for Occupational Health and Safety and click on Basic OH&S Program Elements:

www.ccohs.ca/oshanswers/
hsprograms/basic.html

USING THE INTERNET

The Industrial Accident Prevention Association (IAPA) offers diploma programs for workers, supervisors, and health and safety representatives:

www.iapa.ca

Highlights in HRM 12.1

Health and Safety Checklist for New Employees

By the end of a new employee's first week, an employee should be familiar with the following health and safety procedures and issues:

1. Fire Safety
   - Identify the evacuation alarm sound.
   - Show his/her evacuation route and assembly point, and any alternative route.
   - Show where the extinguishers are in the work area.
   - Explain when water and other extinguishers can/cannot be used.
   - Show how to use extinguishers and what to do after use.
   - Show where the alarm point is and how to sound it.
   - Explain use of elevators and lifts in fire situation.

2. Housekeeping and Access
   - Explain reasons for maintaining clear access.
   - Explain hazards caused by obstructing gangways.

3. Smoking
   - State where smoking is/is not allowed, and give reasons.

4. Accidents and Abnormal Occurrence
   - Explain reporting procedure and reasons.
   - Show the way to casualty (or first aid).
   - Explain action in case of serious injury to oneself or another.
   - Give two examples of abnormal occurrence.
   - Include any hazard special to the job.

5. Lifting (manual handling)
   - Demonstrate correct manual handling methods.

6. Uniforms, Overalls
   - Explain issue, care, and cleaning arrangements.

7. Personal Clothing—Contamination
   - Explain action in the event of clothing being contaminated (give two examples).

8. Protective Equipment
   - Show how to wear equipment issued in department, and explain need for it.

9. Personal Hygiene
   - Explain reasons for attention to personal hygiene.
   - Give two examples of risk of cross-infection.
   - Explain why it is necessary to report contact with notifiable diseases, and give examples of diseases.

10. Absence
    - Know what to do in the event of sickness or other absence.
    - Know to consult Occupational Health staff.

(continued on next page)

11. Electrics
    - Demonstrate checks required before using electrical equipment.
    - Explain action if faults found.

12. Material Hazards
    - Identify any dangerous materials or objects, and explain how to handle them.
    - Supply workplace hazardous information sheets.

13. Chemical Hazards
    - Demonstrate safe handling methods for corrosive liquids, compressed gases, flammable solvents, other classes (appropriate to immediate workplace) (WHMIS).

14. Spillages
    - Explain what must be done in the event of spillages.

15. Disposal
    - Show waste/rubbish disposal system and explain hazards.

16. Machine Equipment Hazards
    - Explain correct handling of equipment.
    - Explain lock out/tagging procedures (appropriate to immediate workplace).

17. Health and Safety Management
    - Explain the role of the Occupational Health Department.
    - Identify the health and safety representatives and explain their roles.
    - Explain the correct procedure if a hazard or problem is identified.
    - Explain the functions of the safety committee.
    - Describe the responsibilities of employees in health and safety.

Source: Adapted from B. Pomfret, "Sound Employee Orientation Program Boosts Productivity and Safety," *Canadian HR Reporter,* January 25, 1999, 17.

Duties of Supervisors

A supervisor is generally defined as a person (with or without a title) who has charge of a workplace and authority over a worker. Occupational health and safety acts require supervisors to do the following: advise employees of potential workplace hazards; ensure that workers use or wear safety equipment, devices, or clothing; provide written instructions where applicable; and take every reasonable precaution to guarantee the safety of workers.

Duties of Joint Health and Safety Committees

Most jurisdictions require that health and safety committees be set up, with both union and management representation. The point of these joint committees is to establish a non-adversarial climate for creating safe and healthy workplaces. In Ontario, at least one management rep and one worker rep must be certified. The certification program provides training in the following subjects: safety laws, sanitation, general safety, rights and duties, and indoor air quality.

Read about how a world leader in H&S structures the committees to produce award-winning safety environments (see Highlights in HRM 12.2).

Highlights in HRM 12.2

A World Leader in H&S

When Novopharm merged with Teva Pharmaceuticals to become the world's largest producer of generic drugs, the company decided to pursue an aggressive growth strategy. Part of the strategy as the leader in the manufacture of pharmaceuticals was also to become the leader in environmental health and safety. The objectives were to develop a safety culture and a safety management system, to improve occupational safety compliance with internal standards, reduce the number of accidents and improve Novopharm's management rating. According to Roberto Ocon, the corporate director of environmental health, safety, and security at Novopharm, a series of high-level initiatives, processes, and procedures were developed in order to achieve this goal.

The Teva Global Group hired a new vice president of Global Environmental Health and Safety to assess the current state of programs and support Operations and EHS personnel.

At Novopharm, the Environment Health and Safety department was transitioned into the Operations department. This move ensured that environmental health and safety would become a part of the culture at Novopharm and also part of the day-to-day operations.

The Environment Health and Safety (EHS) manager position was elevated to a Director position reporting directly to the Executive VP of Operations. The new position sits on the Senior Operations Leadership Management team. This increased the visibility of the environmental health and safety resources.

H&S coordinators became managers positioned directly at the sites of each of the three manufacturing facilities in Ontario. In addition to having health and safety experience, these managers were also specialized in other disciplines (Industrial Hygiene, Ergonomics, Training).

The EHS managers within each of the site locations reported in a dotted line to the site operations directors and directly to the EHS Director. Being on-site and "walking" the floor on a regular basis allowed these new EHS managers to become an integral part of daily operations and encouraged an open dialogue with employees who were able to openly express their concerns regarding health and safety.

As a further measure to support health and safety, the occupational health nurse visited each site at least one day each week, to address and promote employee wellness programs.

Moving forward, three hierarchal levels of environmental health and safety committees were established to promote this culture throughout Novopharm. At the highest level, an environmental health and safety council was established as a champion of new initiatives and to set strategy. Meeting two to three times per year, this council includes all senior management, the President and CEO of Novopharm, the VP of human resources, the executive VP of commercial development, the Global VP of EHS and the executive VP of Operations. The next level is the Steering Committee where Roberto Ocon chairs quarterly meetings with the heads of operations, the labour relations director, Corporate Director of Engineering, Technical Services Director and the Director of Quality Assurance. At this level, a work plan is established and targets are set. Furthermore, to ingrain the new initiatives across Novopharm, health and safety targets are included in each director's Project Management Plan where they are accountable for their performance in attaining health and safety mandates. At the third level, the employee

(continued on next page)

committee meets monthly and explores methods in which to execute the directives. At this level, employees, the site manager, the site director, and the health and safety committee explore creative ideas and behaviour-based changes to promote health and safety.

As a result of implementing this new infrastructure into the culture of Novopharm, health and safety initiatives in its Ontario locations reached new levels of excellence. In a period of two years, Novopharm went from a reactive culture with poor involvement in safety activities to a very pro-active culture with employee involvement in safety activities at all levels of the organization, a 40-percent compliance improvement, a 90-percent reduction in accidents, which was the best in Teva in 2005, as well as one of the best accident rates in the industry. They also went from an average risk management rating to superior.

This won its sites the Health and Safety Award of Excellence for Teva worldwide as well as being given a prestigious Superior Risk Management Award. The award was based on performance from the work plan objectives and for the reduction in workplace accidents. An outside risk management group that rates the facilities' programs and compliance with regulations grants this last award through a yearly audit. Where Health and Safety has often been seen as an outside "policing" group, it has now become and integral part of operations and culture at Novopharm. Furthermore, instead of HR being used as a reference group in this process, it is now a contributing partner to the health and safety of its employees. In essence, it moves the department away from being reactive (after accidents) to being proactive, in protecting employees on a daily basis. To demonstrate the level of commitment across the organization to its new programs, when a site director posted his commitment to health and safety on a large white board, every employee signed it. When the Global CEO visited Canada, he signed it too and in doing so, demonstrated the level of commitment, buy-in, and dedication to the health and safety of employees at Novopharm.

Supervisors are required to advise employees of potential workplace hazards and ensure that workers wear safety equipment.

© DANA WHITE/PHOTOEDIT

Penalties for Employer Noncompliance

The penalties for violating occupational health and safety regulations vary across provinces and territories. Most health and safety acts provide for fines up to $500,000, and offenders can be sent to jail. Lear Corporation was fined $125,000 for not ensuring that a worker was wearing fall protection equipment, when working on a conveyor belt at 3.35 metres. Hershey Canada was fined $50,000 for a violation that resulted in a serious hand injury to an employee.[3] Bill C-45, also known as the corporate killing law, makes it possible for criminal charges to be brought against co-workers, supervisors, and executives when a worker is killed or injured on the job.

Workers' Compensation

Under workers' compensation, injured workers can receive benefits in the form of a cash payout (if the disability is permanent) or wage loss payments (if the worker can no longer earn the same amount of money). Unlimited medical aid is also provided, along with vocational rehabilitation, which includes physical, social, and psychological services. The goal is to return the employee to his or her job (or some modification thereof) as soon as possible. Sun Life Assurance Company of Canada has a return-to-work awards program, which will give premium credits to employers that allow injured workers to change jobs or duties to enable these employees to return to work. A person who has been off work for six months has a 50-percent chance of returning; after 12 months, a 20-percent chance; and after two years, a 10-percent chance. Weyerhaeuser Co. Ltd of Vancouver's coordinated back-to-work program resulted in a 47-percent reduction in duration of claims and a 39-percent reduction in the costs of the claims.

Compensation has become a complex issue. The definitions of accidents and injuries have recently been expanded to include industrial diseases and stress. An **industrial disease** is a disease resulting from exposure to a substance relating to a particular process, trade, or occupation in industry.

Equally problematic is compensation for stress, which is discussed in more detail later in the chapter. Stress-related disabilities are usually divided into three groups: physical injuries leading to mental disabilities (e.g., clinical depression after a serious accident); mental stress resulting in a physical disability (ulcers or migraines); and mental stress resulting in a mental condition (anxiety over work load or downsizing leading to depression). Most claims, it should be pointed out, result from accidents or injuries.

The emphasis in workers' compensation has been shifting away from simply making assessments and payments, toward creating safety-conscious environments where there will be fewer work-related accidents, disabilities, and diseases. In some industrial sectors, employers are working together to establish rules and training programs to further the cause of accident prevention.

USING THE INTERNET

The National Institute of Disability Management and Research was established by business, labour, government, insurance, and rehabilitation representatives to promote best practices in disability management:

www.nidmar.ca

---

industrial disease
A disease resulting from exposure to a substance relating to a particular process, trade, or occupation in industry

---

USING THE INTERNET

Find more information at the Ontario Workplace Safety and Insurance Board website:

www.wsib.on.ca/wsib/wsibsite.nsf/Public/Certification Training

---

Creating a Safe Work Environment

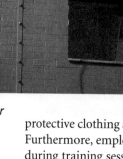

objective **2**

We have seen that employers are required by law to provide safe working conditions for their employees. To achieve this objective, the majority of employers have a formal safety program. Typically, the HR department or the industrial relations department is responsible for the safety program. While the success of a safety program depends largely on managers and supervisors of operating departments, the HR department typically coordinates the safety communication and training programs, maintains safety records required by legislation, and works closely with managers and supervisors in a cooperative effort to make the program a success. As Dennis Locking, the HR manager for Calgary-based Volker Stevin, a growing road building company with more than 1000 employees, states, "Safety is all about the way that you run your business. Wherever you see poor safety, there is always a poorly run company. If a company has a poor attitude towards safety, then it makes us wonder if that attitude is indicative of other aspects of their business."[4]

Organizations with formal safety programs generally have an employee-management safety committee that includes representatives from management, each department or manufacturing/service unit, and employee representatives. Committees are typically involved in investigating accidents and helping to publicize the importance of safety rules and their enforcement.

Safety begins with proper instruction, as these fire-fighters demonstrate in this training exercise.

Promoting Safety Awareness

Probably the most important role of a safety awareness program is motivating managers, supervisors, and subordinates to be champions of safety considerations. In one study conducted, "survey results showed a direct correlation between an increase in management's commitment to safety in the workplace and a decrease in accidents." If managers and supervisors fail to demonstrate awareness, their subordinates can hardly be expected to do so. Unfortunately, many managers and supervisors wear their "safety hats" far less often than their "production, quality control, and methods of improvement hats."

Most organizations have a safety awareness program that entails the use of several different media. Safety lectures, commercially produced films, specially developed videocassettes, and other media such as pamphlets are useful for teaching and motivating employees to follow safe work procedures.

The Key Role of the Supervisor

One of a supervisor's major responsibilities is to communicate to an employee the need to work safely. Beginning with new-employee orientation, safety should be emphasized continually. Proper work procedures, the use of protective clothing and devices, and potential hazards should be explained thoroughly. Furthermore, employees' understanding of all these considerations should be verified during training sessions, and employees should be encouraged to take some initiative in maintaining a concern for safety. Since training by itself does not ensure continual adherence to safe work practices, supervisors must observe employees at work and reinforce safe practices. Where unsafe acts are detected, supervisors should take immediate action to find the cause. Supervisors should also foster a team spirit of safety among the work group.

Proactive Safety Training Program

Safety training is not only good business; in certain occupational areas safety and health training is legally required. When training is mandated, employers must keep accurate records of all employee education. Violations can incur criminal penalties.

In companies that voluntarily undertake safety and health training, one study found the most frequent topics to be (1) first aid, (2) defensive driving, (3) accident prevention techniques, (4) hazardous materials, and (5) emergency procedures.[5] Most programs emphasize the use of emergency first-aid equipment and personal safety equipment.

HR professionals, and safety directors in particular, advocate employee involvement when designing and implementing safety programs.[6] Employees can offer valuable ideas regarding specific safety and health topics to cover, instructional methods, and proper teaching techniques.[7] Furthermore, acceptance for safety training is heightened when employees feel a sense of ownership in the instructional program.

Information Technology and Safety Awareness and Training

Several reasons are advanced for the use of the Internet and information technology in safety and health training. First, enhanced delivery modes facilitate the development of both managers and employees.[8] Videos, PowerPoint presentations, and interactive CD-ROM training are ideal methods for standardized safety, environmental, and health instruction. Second, information technology allows organizations to customize their safety and health training needs.[9] At Stanley Works, the company's Internet is the number one tool for reducing health and safety problems. According to Kevin Nelson, employee health and safety director, "The Internet functions as the organization's SWAT team to develop and implement timely and efficient health and safety programs." Third, information technology is ideally suited for regulatory instruction.[10]

Enforcing Safety Rules

Specific rules and regulations concerning safety are communicated through supervisors, bulletin board notices, employee handbooks, and signs attached to equipment. Safety rules are also emphasized in regular safety meetings, at new-employee orientations, and in manuals of standard operating procedures.[11]

Penalties for violation of safety rules are usually stated in the employee handbook. In a large percentage of organizations, the penalties imposed on violators are the same as those for violations of other rules. They include an oral or written warning for the first violation, suspension for repeated violations, and, as a last resort, dismissal. However, for serious violations—such as smoking around volatile substances—even the first offence may be cause for termination.

While discipline may force employees to work safely, safety managers understand that the most effective enforcement of safety rules occurs when employees willingly obey and "champion" safety rules and procedures. This can be achieved when management actively encourages employees to participate in all aspects of the organization's safety program. For example, opportunities for employee involvement include (1) jointly setting safety standards with management, (2) participation in safety training, (3) involvement in designing and implementing special safety training programs, (4) involvement in establishing safety incentives and rewards, and (5) inclusion in accident investigations. There are many workable incentives—for example, gift certificates, cash awards, trips, dinners, and gifts such as clothing or jewellery. Economy Carriers, a transportation company based in Edmonton, offers an employee points program. It audits 18 operational areas for safety; on the basis of that audit, employees accumulate safety points, which they can use for purchases. Two researchers looked at 24 studies where positive reinforcement and feedback were used to enhance safe behaviour. In all the studies, incentives were found to improve safety conditions or reduce accidents.[12]

The Procter & Gamble plant in Belleville, Ontario, won an award for its novel approach to incentives. The plant manager calculated that P&G would receive a refund from workers' compensation of about $200,000 a year if injuries were eliminated at the plant. He then set up a plan that would allow this refund to go to the local hospital if the target of zero injuries was achieved. With this community-based incentive, P&G employees met the target and the hospital received a large donation.[13]

Figure 12.2 provides the steps recommended for launching a successful safety incentive program.

Investigating and Recording Accidents

Every accident, even those considered minor, should be investigated by the supervisor and a member of the safety committee. Such an investigation may determine the factors contributing to the accident and reveal what corrections are needed to prevent it from happening again. Correction may require rearranging workstations, installing safety guards or controls, or, more often, giving employees additional safety training and reassessing their motivation for safety.[14]

Employers are required to keep certain records and to compile and post annual summaries of work-related injuries and illnesses. From these records, organizations

Figure 12.2	Steps in a Successful Safety Incentive Program

- Obtain the full support and involvement of management by providing cost benefits.
- Review current injury and health statistics to determine where change is needed.
- Decide on a program of action and set an appropriate budget.
- Select a realistic safety goal such as reducing accidents by a set percentage, improving safety suggestions, or achieving a length of time without a lost-time injury. Communicate your objectives to everyone involved.
- Select incentive rewards on the basis of their attractiveness to employees and their fit with your budget.
- Develop a program that is both interesting and fun. Use kickoff meetings, posters, banners, quizzes, and/or games to spark employee interest. Give all employees a chance to win.
- Communicate continually the success of your program. Provide specific examples of positive changes in behaviour.
- Reward safety gains immediately. Providing rewards shortly after improvements reinforces changed behaviour and encourages additional support for the safety program.

can compute their incidence rates (i.e., the number of injuries and illnesses per 100 full-time employees during a given year). The standard equation for computing the incidence rate is shown below; 200 000 constitutes the base for 100 full-time workers who work 40 hours a week, 50 weeks a year:

$$\text{Incidence rate} = \frac{\text{Number of injuries and illnesses} \times 200\ 000}{\text{Total hours worked by all employees during period covered}}$$

The same formula can be used to compute incidence rates for (1) the number of workdays lost because of injuries and illnesses, (2) the number of nonfatal injuries and illnesses without lost workdays, and (3) cases involving only injuries or only illnesses.

Incidence rates are useful for making comparisons between work groups, between departments, and between similar units in the same organization. They also provide a basis for making comparisons with other organizations doing similar work. The occupational health and safety departments in each province and Human Resources and

Ethics in HRM

Bury the Record

A supervisor was instructing a group of new recruits in the cleaning of metal parts in an assembly plant. She was attempting to demonstrate the cleaning technique to two employees at one workstation, while at another workstation another new employee was trying to clean the parts himself. The cleaning liquid was highly toxic. The employee felt restricted by his safety gloves and so removed them. His eyes started to water, and instinctively he rubbed them with his solution-soaked hands. The pain was overwhelming, and no water was immediately available with which he could rinse his eyes. The employee suffered some temporary vision loss.

Who is to blame? The worker who started to clean without receiving full instructions and without using the issued gloves? The supervisor who could have forbidden the worker to start work until she explained the safety aspects? Or the company that failed to post warning signs about the hazardous nature of the cleaning solvent and did not have an eye-washing facility available?

Because workplace accidents increase workers' compensation premiums and the number of inspections, the company had an interest in not reporting the accident. Furthermore, because the company had instituted a reward program that provided incentives to employees for accident-free days, even the employees did not want to report the accident. Thus the supervisor and the employees agreed to "bury the record." According to one survey of Canadian workers, 30 percent are afraid to report accidents, 29 percent know someone who reports false claims, and 27 percent know that their employers are not reporting accidents. This is illegal. Another company was fined $600,000 for misleading the Workplace Health and Safety Insurance Board after it deliberately chose not to report that injured workers had missed time at work. In a highly publicized case in 2003, a young worker fell five storeys to his death, landing just one metre from the supervisor, who was his uncle. The first thing the supervisor did was call 911, and he was overheard telling workers, "Workers' comp will be here right away, so you get that railing up right now."

Source: Adapted from Ipsos Reid, July 2003, as described in *Canadian HR Reporter*, April 19, 2004, 17.

Social Development Canada compile data that employers can use to measure their safety records against those of other organizations. As noted in Ethics in HRM, organizations that report and investigate their own accidents often face more inspections, higher insurance premiums, and possible lawsuits. Reality Check provides an overview of H&S issues in Canada today.

Reality Check

CN Centre for Occupational Health and Safety

The CN Centre for Occupational Health and Safety is a research institute founded at Saint Mary's University in Halifax, Nova Scotia, through an endowment from CN. According to Kevin Kelloway, the director of the CN Centre, the mandate of the centre is (a) to coordinate and conduct research in occupational health and safety; (b) to build capacity for occupational health and safety research in Nova Scotia; and (c) to provide mechanisms for training and education in occupational health and safety.

Professor Kelloway, as co-author of the book *Managing Occupational Health and Safety*, says, "The hottest issue in safety is the role of human resources. We have taken engineering approaches to their limit. It is no longer the case that if we provide protective wear or put guards on equipment, that workers are safe. Engineering approaches are not sufficient. Now we are looking at these issues from a people perspective: How do we get people to work safely? What does it mean to work safely?

"There is another shift in thinking about safety and it is the recognition that compliance with legislation and standards is also not enough. We know that the old motto 'If you are compliant with the law, you have a safe workplace' is not true. Let me give you an example. WHMIS training is compulsory across Canada and all employers give WHMIS training to their employees. These organizations are fully compliant. But does that mean that the employees remember what they have learned? Does this guarantee that they pay attention to all the symbols? An employer can comply and still have unsafe work practices.

"The focus now is on safety initiative. How do we keep people and companies focused on safety? There is a role for leaders. One thing we found in our research is that active leadership which is continually promoting safety is necessary. When leaders stop talking, the minute they stop promoting safety, safety declines. There is a role for HR, to create a culture in which employees feel secure talking about safety, and mechanisms for channelling safety concerns exist. For example, do employees raise safety issues about potential safety hazards? If they raise concerns, are they treated as complainers? Is there a process to identify safety hazards? Part of the role of HR is to create that environment and provide those channels.

"It is always difficult to motivate safety, because it is the absence of something (an accident, an injury). From employees' perspective, they want to get their work done, and the organization encourages this. Of course, they want to work safely, but to get work done, shortcuts are more efficient. A good analogy is that we all want to drive safely but many of us will take risks to get home quickly. Rationally, driving safely is the most important goal, but behaviourally people drive as if saving fifteen seconds was important."

Creating a Healthy Work Environment

objective 3 ▷

From the title alone, occupational health and safety legislation was clearly designed to protect the health, as well as the safety, of employees. Because of the dramatic impact of workplace accidents, however, managers and employees alike may pay more attention to these kinds of immediate safety concerns than to job conditions that are dangerous to their health. It is essential, therefore, that health hazards be identified and controlled.[15] Furthermore, pressure from the federal government and unions, as well as increased public concern, has given employers a definite incentive to provide the safest and healthiest work environment possible.

Health Hazards and Issues

At one time health hazards were associated primarily with jobs found in industrial processing operations. In recent years, however, hazards in jobs outside the plant, such as in offices, healthcare facilities, and airports, have been recognized and preventive methods adopted. Substituting materials, altering processes, enclosing or isolating a process, issuing protective equipment, and improving ventilation are some of the common preventions. This section will review several of the more important health concerns to employees and employers.

Chemical Hazards

When a boiler maker at Teck Cominco Ltd., a smelter plant in Trail, British Columbia, started to experience symptoms that resembled motion sickness, he never associated it with exposure to poisonous thallium metal. Like many workers, he had limited awareness of the chemicals in the workplace. It is estimated that more than 65 000 different chemicals are currently in use with which humans may come into contact. Many of these chemicals are harmful, lurking for years in the body with no outward symptoms until the disease they cause is well established. Increasingly, employees are complaining of physiological reactions to low-level chemical exposures in the environment, such as headaches, dry nasal passages, and nausea. These complaints have several labels, such as total allergy symptom, 20th-century disease, and multiple chemical sensitivity. (For a full discussion of chemical hazards, read Chapter 5 in *Management of Occupational Health and Safety* 3rd ed., by Kevin Kelloway, Lori Francis, and James Montgomery, 2006.)

Workplace Hazardous Materials Information Systems

In the belief that workers have the right to know about potential workplace hazards, industry, labour, and government have joined forces to develop a common information system for labelling hazardous substances. The Workplace Hazardous Materials Information System (WHMIS) is based on three elements:

1. *Labels.* Labels are designed to alert the worker that the container holds a potentially hazardous substance. The two types of labels (supplier labels and workplace labels) must contain specified and regulated information, including product identifiers and data on safe handling and material safety. WHMIS class symbols and subclass designations are shown in Figure 12.3 on page 528.

2. *Material Safety Data Sheets (MSDSs).* A **Material Safety Data Sheet** identifies the product and its potentially hazardous ingredients and suggests procedures for handling the product safely. The MSDS information must be comprehensive, current, and available in English and French.

Material Safety Data Sheets (MSDSs)
Documents that contain vital information about hazardous substances

3. *Training.* Workers must be trained to check for labels and to follow specific procedures for handling spills. Training workers is part of the due diligence required of employers; it also becomes an important factor in the event of a lawsuit. The Peel Board of Education in Ontario has developed a computer-based program to train workers in WHMIS. This program allows illiterate workers to respond to audio commands by touching the screen.

| Figure 12.3 | **Class Symbols and Subclass Designations** |

The subclass designations are shown below the class designation.

CLASS & SUBCLASS DESIGNATIONS

COMPRESSED GAS

CORROSIVE MATERIAL

OXIDIZING MATERIAL

POISONOUS AND
INFECTIOUS MATERIAL
Materials Causing
Immediate and
Serious Toxic Effects

Materials Causing
Other Toxic Effects

Biohazardous
Infectious Material

FLAMMABLE AND
COMBUSTIBLE MATERIAL
Flammable Gas
Flammable Liquid
Flammable Solid
Flammable Aerosol
Reactive Flammable Material

DANGEROUS REACTIVE
MATERIAL

Source: *Solvents in the Workplace,* Cat. no. B01230 (Toronto Industrial Accident Prevention Association, March).

Indoor Air Quality

Between 60 and 70 percent of all workers now spend their days in offices and many complain about headaches, dizziness, disorientation, fatigue, and eye, ear, and throat irritation. As a consequence of energy concerns, commercial and residential construction techniques have been changed to increase energy efficiency of heating, ventilating, and air-conditioning systems. This has included sealing windows, reducing outside air intake, and in general "buttoning up" buildings—thus resulting in the "sick building syndrome" (SBS) and "building related illnesses" (BRI) that give rise to such employee complaints. One expert estimates that between 10 and 25 percent of buildings have the characteristics of SBS.[16] Popular office equipment, including photocopying machines, computer terminals, fax machines, and laser printers, contributes to these health complaints.

Four basic ways to overcome polluted buildings are to (1) eliminate tobacco smoke, (2) provide adequate ventilation, (3) maintain the ventilating system, and (4) remove sources of pollution. It is now common practice in both office and industrial settings, as well as public facilities (airports, hotels, schools, and so on), to monitor and manage the quality of indoor air.

Tobacco Smoke. For the past ten years probably the most heated workplace health issue has been smoking. In a study published in the *Journal of the American Medical Association,* findings showed that "in businesses that permitted smoking, more than 60 percent of the office air samples contained nicotine levels above the 'significant risk' level of 6.8 micrograms per cubic metre."[17] Because of findings such as these, smokers have been banned from lighting up on airplanes, at work, and in restaurants and hotels. Furthermore, nonsmokers, fuelled by studies linking "passive smoking" (inhaling other people's smoke) with disease and death and irritated by smoke getting in their eyes, noses, and clothes, have demanded a smoke-free environment. Employers will benefit from this ban. Smokers on average miss 6.16 days of work per year, nearly double the rate of nonsmokers.[18] A Labour Canada study found that employees who smoke cost companies about $2,500 more per year (than nonsmoking employees) in increased absenteeism, lost productivity, and increased health and life insurance premiums.[19] It has been documented that healthcare costs are higher for smokers; for this reason, some employers are charging smokers more for health insurance or are reducing their benefits. Many employers, however, prefer positive reinforcement through wellness programs to encourage employees to stop smoking.

A British Columbia arbitrator has ruled that smoking is as addictive as cocaine and so constitutes a drug dependency. Under human rights legislation, employers may have to allow workers with a substance abuse problem to take a leave of absence to seek treatment. If nicotine addiction is accepted as a disability, companies may have to provide stop-smoking programs and refrain from disciplining addicted employees who smoke.

Video Display Terminals

The expanding use of computers and video display terminals (VDTs) in the workplace has generated intense debate over the possible hazards to which VDT users may be exposed. Many fears about VDT use have been shown to be unfounded, but serious health complaints remain an issue. Problems that managers have to confront in this area fall into three major groups:

1. *Visual difficulties.* VDT operators frequently complain of blurred vision, sore eyes, burning and itching eyes, and glare.
2. *Muscular aches and pains.* Pains in the back, neck, and shoulders are common complaints of VDT operators.

3. *Job stress.* Eye strain, postural problems, noise, insufficient training, excessive workloads, and monotonous work are complaints reported by three-quarters of VDT users.

To capitalize on the benefits of VDTs while safeguarding employee health, Dr. James Sheedy, a VDT and vision expert, offers these tips on how to minimize the negative effects of computer use on the eyes and body:

- Place the computer screen 10 to 25 cm (4 to 9 inches) below eye level.
- Keep the monitor directly in front of you.
- Sit in an adjustable-height chair and use a copyholder that attaches to both the desk and the monitor.
- Use a screen with adjustable brightness and contrast controls.
- Use shades or blinds to reduce the computer-screen glare created by window lighting.

Cumulative Trauma Disorders

cumulative trauma disorders
Injuries involving tendons of the fingers, hands, and arms that become inflamed from repeated stresses and strains

Meat cutters, fish filleters, cooks, dental hygienists, textile workers, violinists, flight attendants, office workers at computer terminals, and others whose jobs require repetitive motion of the fingers, hands, or arms are reporting injuries in growing percentages. Known as **cumulative trauma disorders** or repetitive motion injuries, these musculoskeletal disorders (MSDs) are injuries of the muscles, nerves, tendons, ligaments, joints, and spinal discs caused by repeated stresses and strains. One of the more common conditions is *carpal tunnel syndrome*, which is characterized by tingling or numbness in the fingers occurring when a tunnel of bones and ligaments in the wrist narrows and pinches nerves that reach the fingers and the base of the thumb. Without proper treatment, employees with carpal tunnel syndrome can lose complete feeling in their hands. Another cumulative trauma disorder prevalent among tennis players is tennis elbow.

USING THE INTERNET

A variety of ergonomic information can be found on the Cornell University ergonomics website at:

http://ergo.human.cornell.edu/

In Chapter 4, we discussed job design and ergonomics considerations as one way to accommodate the capabilities and limitations of employees. Ergonomics techniques are also successfully used to improve or correct workplace conditions that cause or aggravate cumulative trauma disorders.[20] Continuous developments in office furniture, video display terminals, tool design, computer keyboards, and adjustable workstations are all attempts to make the work setting more comfortable—and, hopefully, more productive—but also to lessen musculoskeletal disorders. Mini-breaks involving exercise and the changing of work positions have been found helpful. Importantly, these kinds of injuries often go away if they are caught early. If they are not, they may require months or years of treatment or even surgical correction. Also, when cumulative trauma disorders result from work activities, they serve to lower employee productivity, increase employer health costs, and incur workers' compensation payments.

Key elements of successful ergonomic programs are shown in Figure 12.4.[21]

Communicable Diseases

Provisions for dealing with communicable diseases such as herpes simplex (cold sores), influenza, athlete's foot, and AIDS (acquired immune deficiency syndrome) are covered in public health legislation, not occupational health and safety legislation. In recent years, no issue has received as much attention as SARS (severe

Figure 12.4	Key Elements for a Successful Ergonomics Program

Companies with award-winning ergonomics programs list the following as common elements of success:

- *Provide notice and training for employees.* Implement a well-publicized ergonomics policy or present ergonomic information in safety policies or training programs. Train employees, supervisors, and managers in basic workplace ergonomics.

- *Conduct pre-injury hazard assessment.* Survey the workplace and work processes for potential hazards and adopt measures to lessen the exposure to ergonomic risk factors. Answer the question, "Are certain work areas more prone to ergonomic hazards than others?"

- *Involve employees.* Include employees in risk assessment, recognition of MSD symptoms, design of work-specific equipment or tools, and the setting of work performance rules and guidelines.

- *Plan and execute.* Integrate ergonomic responsibilities into the performance plans for all personnel. Demand accountability for program success.

- *File injury reports.* Encourage early reporting of MSD symptoms or injuries. Refer employees to the company's medical facilities or to the employee's personal physician for treatment.

- *Evaluate and assess the ergonomics program.* Periodically review the effectiveness of the ergonomics program. If the program appears to be ineffective, determine the underlying causes for failure and propose corrective changes.

acute respiratory syndrome). SARS is a pneumonia-like and potentially fatal illness that, in 2003, infected areas such as Hong Kong, Taiwan, Singapore, and Toronto. Employers in Canada had to make decisions about travel bans, quarantines, the right to refuse work, and what constituted a safe work environment. Provincial legislation provides certain rights for employees affected by SARS, including job-protected leave, no penalties for emergency leave, payment for those not working because of quarantines, and work refusal processes. Highlights in HRM 12.3 describes how some employers cope with pandemics.

Highlights in HRM 12.3

Are You Ready?

The last decade will be remembered for the necessity to develop disaster recovery planning and business continuity planning. Events that disrupted business included ice storms, Y2K, 9/11, strikes, and blackouts. The greatest fear is a pandemic, where it is estimated that absenteeism will run at 20 percent to 60 percent for a period of two to four weeks. Companies like UPS and FedEx would be seriously affected by a pandemic, and have contingency plans in place. But a true pandemic would cross all business sectors. HR needs to own this issue.

Human resource professionals, particularly those working in hospitals, faced a crisis in the spring of 2003 that none had seen in their working lifetimes. For the first time in the memory of

(continued on next page)

most hospital employees at Sunnybrook and Women's College Health Sciences Centre in Toronto and London Health Sciences Centre in London, Ontario, there was a code orange crisis—in other words, the most serious level. People looked to the HR team to initiate action plans to deal with sick employees, quarantined employees, and scared employees. Unlike crises such as the events of September 11, 2001, where there is one dramatic event, SARS was an escalating event, with every day creating new problems. At Sunnybrook, the HR director took every decision with the thought, "What are the repercussions? Long after SARS ends, the employees and the unions will remember how they were treated." The escalating pace was difficult. HR people had to train employees to screen 12 000 people a day and had just one weekend to design the process and hire and train staff. Communication had to be objective and immediate, not only with employees but with their worried families. For the first time, health-care workers could not leave their work behind, with most having to wear masks at home and avoid contact with their families. To deal with these concerns, staff forums were held (employees had a need to talk about their concerns). The London Health Sciences Centre faced similar issues. Both vice-presidents of HR emphasized the need for visible leadership. One immediate problem that was soon evident was the folly of any absenteeism program that motivated employees to come to work sick, which of course increased the risk of communicable diseases spreading throughout the workforce. Some employees continued to come to work even when they weren't feeling well because they were worried they would lose income, so a policy that had to be developed immediately was a commitment to maintain the wages of workers in quarantine. Another unusual problem was that certain categories of workers, such as nurses, have limited rights to refuse work. When Mount Sinai Hospital in Toronto asked employees to staff screening stations, a librarian refused to do this work as she deemed it to be unsafe. A lesson learned is the importance of preparing for an emergency by stockpiling personal protective equipment and training all staff in its use.

It is not just hospitals that have to be prepared for outbreaks of communicable diseases. Hewlett-Packard has a workforce of 8000 employees, with 3200 of them at ten sites in the Greater Toronto Area. Two HP employees were hospitalized with SARS, and one site was forced to close. Fortunately, because the site had always required employees and visitors to sign in, and access was controlled with a pass card, all those known to have been at the site were easy to trace and all pass cards were revoked. Also, because HP is a high-tech company, with all employees online all the time, communication with employees was not difficult. However, the nature of the highly mobile workforce posed problems for healthcare officials. The public health department required lists of all employees who were absent, but HR does not track absences because most HP employees work from home or offsite.

Avian flu may be the next pandemic, with an estimate of up to 58 000 deaths and 138 000 hospitalizations in Canada. Experts suggest that senior management, along with HR, drive the emergency preparedness program, and that a program team be established that would create a plan to protect human life, eliminate or minimize risk and injury, protect physical assets, minimize losses, and resume operations as quickly as possible. The plan must be communicated in advance and every employee needs to know what to do. There must be a test and practice phase, with emergency drills. Are you ready?

Sources: Michael Bennet, "Are You Ready?" *HR Professional,* October/November 2005, 21–26; Phillip Quinn, "Plan for Pandemic," *The National Post,* March 29, 2006, WK 1 and 5; B. Orr, "SARS Outbreak Teaches Valuable Lessons on a New 'Normal' State for HR Management," *Canadian HR Reporter* 16, no. 11 (June 2, 2003): 5; Ministry of Labour, "Workplace Laws and SARS," www.gov.on.ca/LAB; A. Picard, "Mommy Are You Going to Die?" *The Globe and Mail,* April 5, 2003.

Workplace Violence

Many people think of workplace violence as a physical assault. But there are many forms including:

- Threatening behaviour such as shaking fists or throwing objects
- Verbal or written threats
- Harassment—any behaviour that demeans, embarrasses, or humiliates
- Verbal abuse including swearing, insults, or condescending language
- Physical attacks including hitting, shoving, pushing, or kicking[22]

Manon Blanc at Queen's University and Kevin Kelloway, director of the CN Centre for Occupational Health and Safety at Saint Mary's University, have identified the job characteristics that put workers at risk for aggression and violence in the workplace:

- Interacting with the public
- Making decisions that influence other people's lives (e.g., terminating an employee or assigning a failing grade) or denying the public a service or request
- Supervising and/or disciplining others
- Working nights, working alone
- Handling cash, handling or guarding valuables, collecting or delivering items of value
- Caring for the physical or emotional needs of others, going to clients' homes
- Serving or selling alcohol, dealing with individuals under the influence of mind-altering substances[23]

Exposure to workplace violence results in employees fearing more incidents of violence, leading to personal strains (such as stress) and organizational strains (reduced commitment, neglect of job duties).

The Canadian Centre for Occupational Health and Safety suggests that preventive measures should include:

- *Workplace design,* such as locks or physical barriers (pass-through windows or bulletproof enclosures), lighting and electronic surveillance.
- *Administrative practices,* such as keeping cash register funds to a minimum, varying the time of day that cash is emptied, and using a security firm to deliver cash.
- *Work practices* (particularly for those working alone away from an office, such as home care workers and real estate agents) that might include having a designated contact kept informed of the employee's schedule and checking the credentials of clients.[24]

Employers in all Canadian jurisdictions are bound to take all reasonable precautions to protect the safety and health of their workers. At this time, however, only British Columbia and Saskatchewan have specific laws requiring employers to protect their workers from violence. However, under common law an employer may be held liable for the actions of employees. Nurses are victims of violence at a rate that is 16 times higher than other service workers. Almost 70 percent of nurses have been physically assaulted.[25] The family of a nurse murdered by a doctor at the Hotel Dieu Grace Hospital in Windsor, Ontario, is suing the hospital. Managers and supervisors can be trained to recognize violence indicators such as those given in Figure 12.5 on page 534. Awareness of these threatening behaviours can provide an opportunity to intervene and prevent disruptive, abusive, or violent acts. Managers must effectively communicate a zero-tolerance policy

Figure 12.5	Violence Indicators: Know the Warning Signs

Most people leave a trail of indicators before they become violent. Similarly, disgruntled former employees who commit acts of violence leave warning signs of their intent before and after termination. The following behaviours should be taken seriously when assessing situations of potential violence:

- Direct or veiled threatening statements
- Recent performance declines, including concentration problems and excessive excuses
- Prominent mood or behaviour changes; despondence
- Preoccupation with guns, knives, or other weapons
- Deliberate destruction of workplace equipment; sabotage
- Fascination with stories of violence
- Reckless or antisocial behaviour; evidence of prior assaultive behaviour
- Aggressive behaviour or intimidating statements
- Written messages of violent intent; exaggerated perceptions of injustice
- Serious stress in personal life
- Obsessive desire to harm a specific group or person
- Violence against a family member
- Substance abuse

Sources: Adapted from *Violence in the Workplace: Risk Factors and Prevention Strategies,* NIOSH Bulletin #59; Gillian Flynn, "Employers Can't Look Away from Workplace Violence," *Workforce* 79, no. 7 (July 2000): 68–70; Dannie B. Fogleman, "Minimizing the Risk of Violence in the Workplace," *Employment Relations Today* 87, no. 1 (Spring 2000): 83–98.

USING THE INTERNET

The Canadian Initiative on Workplace Violence, a social research firm, offers information at:

www.workplaceviolence.ca/

for violence and encourage employees to report any possible or observed incidents of workplace violence. A meaningful reporting procedure with clear lines of responsibility can ensure that management is promptly notified of potential security risks in order to take immediate steps to resolve the issues. Finally, organizations such as Garden Fresh, a growing restaurant chain, have formalized workplace violence–prevention policies, informing employees that aggressive employee behaviour will not be tolerated (see Highlights in HRM 12.4).

Terrorism

Once largely confined to foreign countries, terrorism is now a major concern to Canadian employers, particularly those in high-target categories such as airlines, sporting facilities, energy plants and dams, high-tech companies, financial institutions,

Highlights in HRM 12.4

Garden Fresh's Workplace Violence Prevention Policy

Garden Fresh is committed to conducting its operations in a safe manner. Consistent with this policy, acts or threats (either verbal or implied) of physical violence, including intimidation, harassment, and/or coercion, which involve or affect Garden Fresh or which occur on Garden Fresh property will not be tolerated.

Acts of threats of violence include, but are not limited to, the following:

- All threats or acts of violence occurring on Garden Fresh premises, regardless of the relationship between Garden Fresh and the parties involved in the incident.
- All threats or acts of violence occurring off of Garden Fresh premises involving someone who is acting in the capacity of a representative of the company.
- All threats or acts of violence occurring off of Garden Fresh premises involving an employee of GFRC if the threats or acts affect the legitimate interest of Garden Fresh.
- Any acts or threats resulting in the conviction of an employee or agent of Garden Fresh, or of an individual performing services for Garden Fresh on a contract or temporary basis, under any criminal code provision relating to violence or threats of violence that adversely affect the legitimate interests and goals of Garden Fresh.

Specific examples of conduct that may be considered threats or acts of violence include, but are not limited to, the following:

- Hitting or shoving an individual.
- Threatening an individual or his/her family, friends, associates, or property with harm.
- The intentional destruction or threat of destruction of company property.
- Harassing or threatening phone calls.
- Harassing surveillance or stalking.
- The suggestion or intimation that violence is appropriate.
- Possession or use of firearms or weapons.

Garden Fresh's prohibition against threats and acts of violence applies to all persons involved in the company's operation, including Garden Fresh personnel, contract and temporary workers, and anyone else on Garden Fresh property.

Violations of this policy by any individual on Garden Fresh's property, by any individual acting as a representative of Garden Fresh while off of Garden Fresh property, or by an individual acting off of Garden Fresh's property when his/her actions affect the company's business interests will lead to disciplinary action (up to and including termination) and/or legal action as appropriate.

Employees should learn to recognize and respond to behaviours by potential perpetrators that may indicate a risk of violence.

Employees shall place safety as the highest concern, and shall report all acts or threats of violence immediately. Every employee and every person on Garden Fresh's property is encouraged to report incidents of threats or acts of physical violence of which he/she is aware. The report should be made to the director of human resources, the reporting individual's immediate supervisor, or another supervisory employee if the immediate supervisor is not available.

It is the responsibility of managers and supervisors to make safety their highest concern. When made aware of a real or perceived threat of violence, management shall conduct a thorough investigation and take specific actions to help prevent acts of violence.

Nothing in this policy alters any other reporting obligation established by Garden Fresh policies or in state, federal, or other applicable law.

Source: Used with permission from Garden Fresh, 17180 Bernardo Center Drive, San Diego, Calif. 92128.

and public and commercial buildings. The heightened security procedures at these facilities show the importance employers place on the prevention of terrorist attacks, including those involving conventional explosives, nuclear devices, dirty bombs, chemical weapons, and bioweapons.

Many of the points recommended to prevent workplace violence apply equally to preventing terrorism—background checks, violence prevention policy, and so on. Additionally, counterterrorism experts recommend the following to deter terrorist attacks:

- Heightened ID checks and baggage screening
- Increased video monitoring with threat-recognition software to back up human surveillance
- Blast-resistant glass to reduce casualties
- Offsite emergency offices
- Tightened garage security with stepped-up inspections
- Staggered deliveries to reduce truck traffic[26]
- Emergency evacuation procedures, including escape routes, emergency equipment, and gathering locations[27]

At a minimum, these procedures would include escape routes, emergency equipment and gathering locations, and special assistance for disabled people and individuals responsible for the movement of employees. Practice evacuation drills at unannounced times ensure that employees know how to respond to an evacuation while preventing unnecessary confusion should a real attack occur. Although Canadians have yet to encounter a colossal domestic catastrophe, Canadian workplaces should be prepared against such an eventuality.

Crisis Management Teams

Most large organizations have formal crisis management teams. These teams, composed of both hourly and managerial employees, conduct initial risk assessment surveys, develop action plans to respond to violent situations, and, importantly, perform crisis intervention during violent, or potentially violent, encounters. For example, a crisis management team would investigate a threat reported by an employee. The team's mandate would be to gather facts about the threat, decide whether the organization should intervene, and, if so, determine the most appropriate method of doing so. Occasionally, a member of the team or an individual manager will be called upon to intervene and calm an angry employee.[28] When this occurs, the steps given in Figure 12.6 will help to defuse a volatile situation.

When violent incidents, such as the death of a co-worker, happen at work, employees can experience shock, guilt, grief, apathy, resentment, cynicism, and a host of other emotions.[29] Such incidents may require the crisis management team to perform crisis intervention through positive counselling techniques.[30]

Building Better Health

Along with improving working conditions that are hazardous to employee health, many employers provide health services and have programs that encourage employees to improve their health habits. It is recognized that better health not only benefits the individual, but also pays off for the organization in reduced absenteeism, increased efficiency, better morale, and other savings. An increased

---

| Figure 12.6 | **Calming an Angry Employee** |

If you try to defuse a tense situation, remember that anger frequently results from a person's feeling of being wronged, misunderstood, or unheard. Keep the following tips in mind to guide you:

- Strive to save the employee's dignity during an angry confrontation. Don't attack a person's rash statements or continue a muddled line of thinking.
- Hold all conversations in private. Do not allow the employee to create an embarrassing public situation for himself or herself, yourself, or other employees.
- Always remain calm. Anger or aggressiveness on your part will trigger a similar response in the employee.
- Listen to the employee with an open mind and nonjudgmental behaviour. Give the employee the benefit of hearing him or her out.
- Recognize the employee's legitimate concerns or feelings. Agree that the employee has a valid point and that you will work to correct the problem.
- If the employee is very emotional or if the engagement seems out of control, schedule a delayed meeting so people can calm down.
- Keep the discussion as objective as possible. Focus on the problem at hand, not the personalities of individuals. A cornerstone of conflict resolution is to "attack the problem, not the personality."
- If the employee appears overly aggressive, withdraw immediately and seek professional help before any further discussion with the employee.
- If your efforts fail to calm the employee, report the incident to your manager, security, or human resource personnel.

Source: Adapted from professional literature on crisis management and seminars attended by the authors.

---

understanding of the close relationship between physical and emotional health and job performance has made broad health-building programs attractive to employers as well as to employees.

Ensuring Healthful Employees

The size of the organization determines the kind of health services that can be provided to employees. Small organizations are likely to have only limited facilities, such as those required to handle first aid; many larger firms offer complete diagnostic, treatment, and emergency surgical services. Since employers are required to provide medical services after an injury, larger companies usually have nurses and physicians on full-time duty. Medium-size and smaller organizations will have one or more physicians on call.

We noted in Chapter 6 that some employers give medical examinations to prospective employees after a job offer has been made. The examination should include a medical history with specific reference to previous hazardous exposures. Exposure to hazards whose effects may be cumulative, such as noise, lead, and radiation, are especially relevant. For jobs involving unusual physical demands, the applicant's muscular development, flexibility, agility, range of motion, and cardiac and respiratory functions should be evaluated. Many organizations also give periodic examinations on a required or voluntary basis. Such examinations can help determine the effects of potential hazards in the workplace, and detect any health problems to which the employee's lifestyle or health habits may contribute.

Promoting Workplace Fitness and Health

Many organizations have developed programs that emphasize regular exercise, proper nutrition, weight control, and avoidance of substances harmful to health. Xerox gives its employees a publication called *Fitbook* that includes chapters on the hazards of smoking and the effects of alcohol and drug abuse, facts on nutrition and weight control, and guidelines for managing stress and learning to relax. The City of Victoria encourages its employees to bike to work.

Importantly, wellness programs produce measurable cost savings to employers, as described in The Business Case. Figure 12.7 gives nine steps for launching a successful wellness program, even on a limited budget. The types of employee health initiatives offered by Canadian employers can be found in Figure 12.8.

Employee Assistance Programs

A broad view of health includes the emotional as well as the physical aspects of one's life. While emotional problems, personal crises, alcoholism, and drug abuse are considered personal matters, they become organizational problems when they affect behaviour at work and interfere with job performance.[31] In Canada, productivity losses from depression, anxiety, substance abuse, and stress totalled $33 billion in 2003.[32] To be able to handle such problems, organizations offer an employee assistance program (EAP). Typically, such a program refers employees in need of assistance to inhouse counsellors or outside professionals.[33] Supervisors are often given training and policy guidance in the type of help they can offer their subordinates. However, some employees are reluctant to accept help as they risk being stigmatized. At Canadian Forces Base Winnipeg, anyone taking treatment for stress is said to be taking the "Crazy Train to the North Side." Soldiers fear that they will be unjustly accused of faking post-traumatic stress disorder.

Personal Crises

The most prevalent problems among employees are personal crises involving marital, family, financial, or legal matters. Furthermore, EAPs have been directing increased

---

Figure 12.7	Tips for Starting a Successful Wellness Program

1. Conduct a health risk assessment of employees.
2. Create incentives for employees to achieve a healthy lifestyle.
3. Create opportunities for regular physical activities during the day or before or after work.
4. Provide nutritional advice from a registered dietitian.
5. Include healthy, low-fat choices among snacks and meals provided in cafeterias and through vending machines.
6. Eliminate smoking from the work setting.
7. Negotiate discounts from area health clubs.
8. Start a health and fitness newsletter.
9. Focus on reducing one or two high-risk factors among employees.

Source: Adapted from "The Surgeon General's Call to Action to Prevent and Decrease Overweight and Obesity 2001." See www .surgeongeneral.gov/topics/obesity.

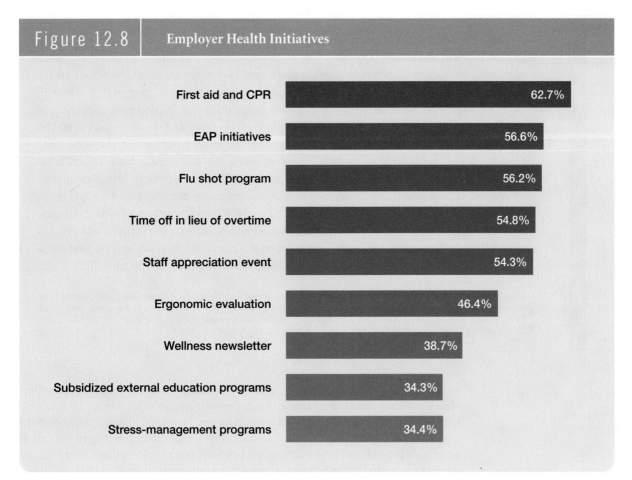

| Figure 12.8 | Employer Health Initiatives |

- First aid and CPR — 62.7%
- EAP initiatives — 56.6%
- Flu shot program — 56.2%
- Time off in lieu of overtime — 54.8%
- Staff appreciation event — 54.3%
- Ergonomic evaluation — 46.4%
- Wellness newsletter — 38.7%
- Subsidized external education programs — 34.3%
- Stress-management programs — 34.4%

Source: "Wellness Offerings," *Canadian HR Reporter*, April 5, 2004, 9.

The Business Case

Investing in Employee Health

For the 2800 employees at Husky Injection Molding Systems of Bolton, Ontario, work seems like play as they visit their children over lunch, eat fresh, healthy cafeteria food, play table tennis on their breaks, and receive an extra vacation day for staying fit. Husky spends more than $4 million a year on employee benefits, but this investment more than pays for itself in higher productivity, lower turnover, and lower absenteeism. The voluntary turnover rate is about 8 percent, which is below the industry average of 10 percent. The absenteeism rate is 3.7 days, less than half of the manufacturing industry average of 9.1 days. Injury claims are 1.5 for every 200 000 hours worked, compared with an industry average of 7.2. The annual drug benefit costs are $255 per employee compared to the industry average of $507. The estimated savings are $8.4 million a year.

(continued on next page)

Husky is not the only company seeing returns on investments in workplace well-being. Organizations in Atlantic Canada found that employees who participated in a three-month wellness program reduced the risk of heart disease and stroke, for an estimated return on the investment of $1.64 for every dollar spent. In one of the largest studies done on ROI of healthcare programs, the National Wellness program delivered wellness programs consisting of smoking cessation workshops, lifestyle and nutrition counselling, and on-site fitness to 90 000 employees in 30 locations. Those who participated had lower healthcare costs of between $5 and $16 per month. Even a one-time inexpensive program can show returns. TELUS introduced a flu immunization program and saw absences due to respiratory illness drop from 33 percent to 22 percent. Overall, studies of wellness programs document cost–benefit ratios of between $3 and $8 for every dollar spent. The benefits to organizations include decreased lost workdays, decreased workers' compensation costs, increased employee morale and productivity, reduced overtime costs, and reduced workplace injuries. Yet, only 60 percent of Canadian workplaces offer wellness programs. Why aren't more companies getting it?

Sources: Vera N. Held, "Husky's Andrée Brière on Productivity and Stress Free Employees," *HR Professional*, August/September 2005, 19–25; T. Grant, "Husky Woos Workers with Unique Perks," *The Globe and Mail*, August 20, 2001; S. Kee, "The Bottom Line on Wellness," *Canadian Health Care Manager* 9, no. 1 (Fall 2002): 23; G. Lowe, "The Dollars and Sense of Health Promotion," *Canadian HR Reporter*, September 23, 2002.

attention to the problem of domestic violence. Such problems often come to a supervisor's attention. In most instances, the supervisor can usually provide the best help simply by being understanding and supportive and by helping the individual find the type of assistance he or she needs.[34] In many cases, inhouse counselling or referral to an outside professional is recommended. In recent years, crisis hotlines have been set up in many communities to provide counselling by telephone for those too distraught to wait for an appointment with a counsellor.

Emotional Problems

While personal crises are typically fraught with emotion, most of them are resolved in a reasonable period of time and the troubled individual's equilibrium is restored. Unfortunately, when personal crises linger, stress and tension may cause or intensify a mood disorder such as depression. **Depression** is a decrease in functional activity accompanied by symptoms of low spirits, gloominess, and sadness. Highlights in HRM 12.5 lists the symptoms of depression.

About 5 percent of Canadians experience depression. With available treatment, however, 70 percent of these individuals will significantly improve, usually within a matter of weeks.

Since depression lowers individual productivity, causes morale problems, increases absenteeism, and contributes to substance abuse, it is important for managers to identify signs of depression on the job and to learn to deal with depressed employees. The more likely workplace signs of depression are decreased energy, concentration and memory problems, guilt feelings, irritability, and chronic aches and pains that don't respond to treatment. When confronted with depressed employees, managers and supervisors are encouraged to be concerned with the employee's problem, be an active listener, and—should the depression persist—suggest professional help.[35] Under no circumstances should managers attempt to play amateur psychologist and try to diagnose an employee's condition. Mood disorders such as

depression
Negative emotional state marked by feelings of low spirits, gloominess, sadness, and loss of pleasure in ordinary activities

Highlights in HRM 12.5

Depression in the Workplace

When a depressed mood persists for a few weeks, deepens, and eventually starts interfering with work and other aspects of everyday life, it has likely become an illness—or a clinical depression. In the workplace, a person with depression will exhibit many of the following signs:

Recognizing Depression
Personal Changes
- Irritability, hostility
- Hopelessness, despair
- Slowness of speech
- Chronic fatigue
- Withdrawal from or extreme dependency on others
- Alcohol or drug abuse

Workplace Changes
- Difficulty in making decisions
- Decreased productivity
- Inability to concentrate
- Decline in dependability
- Unusual increase in errors in work
- Accident proneness
- Frequent tardiness, increased "sick" days
- Lack of enthusiasm for work

Someone who has been experiencing many of these signs for a few weeks or more should seek help immediately.

Source: Reprinted by permission of Canadian Mental Health Association, Toronto.

depression are complex in nature and do not lend themselves to quick diagnoses. Furthermore, in reviewing such cases, the organization should pay particular attention to workplace safety factors, because there is general agreement that emotional disturbances are primary or secondary factors in a large portion of industrial accidents and violence.

Alcoholism

Alcoholism affects workers in every occupational category—blue-collar and white-collar. In confronting the problem, employers must recognize that alcoholism is a disease that follows a rather predictable course. Thus they can take specific actions to deal with employees showing symptoms of the disease at particular stages of its progression. Alcoholism typically begins with social drinking getting out of control. As the disease progresses, the alcoholic loses control over how much to drink and eventually cannot keep from drinking, even at inappropriate times. The person uses denial to avoid facing the problems created by the abuse of alcohol and often blames others for these problems. The first step in helping the alcoholic is to awaken the person to the reality of his or her situation.

To identify alcoholism as early as possible, it is essential that supervisors monitor the performance of all personnel regularly and systematically. A supervisor should carefully document evidence of declining performance on the job and then confront the employee with unequivocal proof that the job is suffering. The employee should be assured that help will be made available without penalty. Since the evaluations are made solely with regard to lagging job performance, a supervisor can avoid any mention of alcoholism and allow such employees to seek aid as they would for any other problem.[36]

Abuse of Illegal Drugs

The abuse of drugs by employees is one of the major employment issues today. Drug abuse is now a national problem and has spread to every industry, occupation, and employee level. Estimates of the costs of substance abuse by employees vary considerably. Besides lost productivity, there are the costs of increased numbers of accidents and injuries, and rising rates of employee theft. The costs of substance abuse can have a dramatic impact on the bottom line. Drug testing remains a controversial issue. In general, pre-employment drug or alcohol testing or random testing of current employees is prohibited by human rights laws. Furthermore, human rights legislation prohibits discrimination on the basis of disability, and drug and alcohol dependency is generally considered to be a disability.

While attention is usually focused on the abuse of illegal drugs, it should be noted that the abuse of legal drugs can also pose a problem for employees. Employees who abuse legal drugs—those prescribed by physicians—often do not realize they have become addicted or how their behaviour has changed as a result of their addiction. Also, managers should be aware that some employees may be taking legal sedatives or stimulants as part of their medical treatment and that their behaviour at work may be affected by their use of these drugs.

The Management of Stress

objective

6

HR professionals are well aware of the negative effects of workplace stress on employees' health and job performance. For example, job stress places both women and men at risk for cardiovascular problems and depression and increases employee susceptibility to infectious diseases. All of these contribute to higher healthcare costs, and can lower productivity, job satisfaction, and retention. Importantly, in a recent study on the magnitude of stress in the workplace, 54 percent of respondents indicated that they "often" or "always" come home from work in a state of fatigue, and nearly 50 percent come in to work tired.[37]

What Is Stress?

stress
Any adjustive demand caused by physical, mental, or emotional factors that require coping behaviour

Stress is any demand on the individual that requires coping behaviour. Stress comes from two basic sources: physical activity and mental or emotional activity. The physical reaction of the body to both types of stress is the same. Psychologists use two separate terms to distinguish between positive and negative forms of stress, even

eustress
  Positive stress that accompanies achievement and exhilaration

distress
  Harmful stress characterized by a loss of feelings of security and adequacy

though reactions to the two forms are the same biochemically. **Eustress** is positive stress that accompanies achievement and exhilaration. Eustress is the stress of meeting challenges such as those found in a managerial, technical, or public contact job. Eustress is regarded as a beneficial force that helps us to forge ahead against obstacles. What is harmful is **distress.** Stress becomes distress when we begin to sense a loss of our feelings of security and adequacy. Helplessness, desperation, and disappointment turn stress into distress.

The stress reaction is a coordinated chemical mobilization of the entire body to meet the requirements of fight-or-flight in a situation perceived to be stressful. The sympathetic nervous system activates the secretion of hormones from the endocrine glands that places the body on a "war footing." This response, commonly referred to as the **alarm reaction,** basically involves an elevated heart rate, increased respiration, elevated levels of adrenaline in the blood, and increased blood pressure. It persists until one's estimate of the relative threat to well-being has been re-evaluated. If distress persists long enough, it can result in fatigue, exhaustion, and even physical and/or emotional breakdown.[38] Some research has linked stress to heart disease. Other studies have shown a connection between chronic stress and hypertension (high blood pressure). High blood pressure, the most common cause of strokes, contributes to heart disease.

alarm reaction
  Response to stress that basically involves an elevated heart rate, increased respiration, elevated levels of adrenaline in the blood, and increased blood pressure

Job-Related Stress

Although the body experiences a certain degree of stress (either eustress or distress) in all situations, here we are primarily concerned with the stress related to the work setting. It is in this setting that management can use some preventive approaches.

Sources of Job-Related Stress

Causes of workplace stress are many. However, according to a study by LLuminari, a national healthcare company, four factors have a major influence on employee stress:

- *High demand:* having too much to do in too short a time.
- *High effort:* having to expend too much mental or physical energy over too long a period.
- *Low control:* having too little influence over the way a job is done on a day-to-day basis.
- *Low reward:* receiving inadequate feedback on performance and no recognition for a job well done.[39]

Other recognized job stressors include layoffs and organizational restructuring; disagreements with managers or fellow employees; prejudice because of age, gender, race, or religion; inability to voice complaints; and poor working conditions. Even minor irritations such as lack of privacy, unappealing music, and other conditions can be distressful to one person or another.

Burnout

burnout
  Most severe stage of distress, manifesting itself in depression, frustration, and loss of productivity

Burnout is a severe stage of distress. Career burnout generally occurs when a person begins questioning his or her own personal values. Quite simply, one no longer feels that what he or she is doing is important. Depression, frustration, and a loss of productivity are all symptoms of burnout. Burnout is due primarily to a lack of personal

Many Canadians report experiencing stress on the job.

fulfillment in the job or a lack of positive feedback about performance.[40] In organizations that have downsized, remaining employees can experience burnout because they must perform more work with fewer co-workers. Overachievers can experience burnout when unrealistic work goals are unattainable.[41]

Coping with Stress

Many employers have developed stress management programs to teach employees how to minimize the negative effects of job-related stress. A typical program might include instruction in relaxation techniques, coping skills, listening skills, methods of dealing with difficult people, time management, and assertiveness. All of these techniques are designed to break the pattern of tension that accompanies stress situations and to help participants achieve greater control of their lives. Organizational techniques such as clarifying the employee's work role, redesigning and enriching jobs, correcting physical factors in the environment, and effectively handling interpersonal factors should not be overlooked in the process of teaching employees how to handle stress. Stress management counsellors recommend several ways to resolve job-related stress as described in Figure 12.9.

Before concluding this discussion, we should observe that stress that is harmful to some employees may be healthy for others.[42] Most managers learn to handle distress effectively and find that it actually stimulates better performance, as it does for the CEO of Corel, as outlined in Highlights in HRM 12.6. However, there will always be those who are unable to handle stress and need assistance in learning to cope with it. The increased interest of young and old alike in developing habits that will enable them to lead happier and more productive lives will undoubtedly be beneficial to them as individuals, to the organizations where they work, and to a society where people are becoming more and more interdependent.

Figure 12.9	Tips for Reducing Job-Related Stress

- Build rewarding relationships with co-workers.
- Talk openly with managers or employees about job or personal concerns.
- Prepare for the future by keeping abreast of likely changes in job demands.
- Don't greatly exceed your skills and abilities.
- Set realistic deadlines; negotiate reasonable deadlines with managers.
- Act now on problems or concerns of importance.
- Designate dedicated work periods during which time interruptions are avoided.
- When feeling stressed, find time for detachment or relaxation.
- Don't let trivial items take on importance; handle them quickly or assign them to others.
- Take short breaks from your work area as a change of pace.

Highlights in HRM 12.6

Personal Power

Michael Cowpland, chairman, president, and CEO of software giant Corel Corp., was known for his hands-on management style—for becoming involved in every decision and having few middle managers. Virtually everyone in his company reported to him. He had no secretary and answered and returned his own mail. Cowpland regularly worked 80-hour weeks. He read 50 industry magazines in one week (he was beyond speed-reading and into hyper-reading, he said). He played tennis five times a week and squash three times, and watched a wall of 16 televisions all at the same time. He handled stress well. According to one stress researcher, the only factor that has any significant impact on a person's ability to withstand work pressure is "personal power"—having control over your time, resources, important information, work load, and so on. It is not the volume of work or work demands that makes people sick; it is the extent to which they can control it. Michael Cowpland is an example of a man who controlled his work environment.

Indeed, over 40 percent of people polled by the Canadian Mental Health Association report that the amount of stress they face in the workplace has a positive effect on their performance. Four factors trigger stress: a novel situation, an unpredictable situation, a threat to your ability, and a sense of loss of control. But some people thrive on these situations. For example, when Brian Scudmore, CEO of Vancouver based 1-800-GOTJUNK, faced competition from a former employee with whom he had shared confidential business information, he responded in this way: "It was like having a tiger behind me. It kept me sharp and it kept me moving forward. If I didn't have that competitive threat, we may not have succeeded at growing at the rate we have."

Sources: Deena Weisberg, "Running on High Octane," *National Post*, April 8, 2006, FW4; "Racquet Scientist," *Canadian Business*, June 1995; P. Froiland, "What Cures Job Stress?" *Training,* December 1993, 32–36.

SUMMARY

Occupational health and safety legislation is designed to assure, so far as possible, safe and healthful working conditions for every working person. In general, the act extends to all employers and employees. This legislation sets standards, ensures employer and employee compliance, and provides safety and health consultation and training where needed. Both employers and employees have certain responsibilities and rights under these acts. Employers not only are required to provide a hazard-free work environment, but also must keep employees informed about legislative requirements and must require their employees to use protective equipment when necessary. Employers are

required to keep employees informed of hazardous substances and instruct them in avoiding the dangers presented. Employees, in turn, are required to comply with safety standards, to report hazardous conditions, and to follow all employer safety and health regulations.

In order to provide safe working conditions for their employees, employers typically establish a formal program that, in a large percentage of organizations, is under the direction of the HR manager. The program may have many facets, including providing safety knowledge and motivating employees to use it, making employees aware of the need for safety, and rewarding them for safe behaviour. Such incentives as praise, public recognition, and awards are used to involve employees in the safety program. Maintenance of required records from accident investigations provides a basis for information that can be used to create a safer work environment.

 Job conditions that are dangerous to the health of employees are now receiving much greater attention than in the past. There is special concern for toxic chemicals that proliferate at a rapid rate and may lurk in the body for years without outward symptoms. Health hazards other than those found in industrial processing operations—such as video display terminals and cumulative trauma disorders—present special problems that must be addressed. Today tobacco smoke is not tolerated in the work environment.

 Along with providing safer and healthier work environments, many employers establish programs that encourage employees to improve their health habits. Wellness programs that emphasize exercise, nutrition, weight control, and avoidance of harmful substances serve employees at all organizational levels.

 Virtually all of the larger organizations and many of the smaller ones have found that an employee assistance program is beneficial to all concerned. While emotional problems, personal crises, alcoholism, and drug abuse are often viewed as personal matters, it is apparent that they affect behaviour at work and interfere with job performance. An employee assistance program typically provides professional assistance by inhouse counsellors or outside professionals where needed.

 An important dimension to health and safety is stress that comes from physical activity and mental or emotional activity. While stress is an integral part of being alive, when it turns into distress it becomes harmful. We have seen that many sources of stress are job-related. In recognizing the need for reducing stress, employers can develop stress-management programs to help employees learn techniques for coping with stress. In addition, organizations need to redesign and enrich jobs, clarify the employee's work role, correct physical factors in the environment, and take any other actions that will help reduce stress on the job.

KEY TERMS

alarm reaction, 543
burnout, 543
cumulative trauma
  disorders, 530
depression, 540

distress, 543
eustress, 543
industrial disease, 521
Material Safety Data Sheets
  (MSDSs), 527

occupational illness, 514
occupational injury, 514
stress, 542

DISCUSSION QUESTIONS

1. Ergonomics-related injuries now account for over 40 percent of lost-time injuries in the province of Ontario. Prepare a list of the most common types of ergonomics-related injuries, and then make suggestions about how employers could reduce these types.

2. Play a safety game that quizzes users on the dangers in the workplace at www.buildingfutures.ca. Another educational site, especially useful for summer students, can be found at the website of the Education Safety Association of Ontario: www.esao.on.ca.

3. An unhealthy work environment can lower productivity, contribute to low morale, and increase medical and workers' compensation costs. Working individually or in teams, list specific ways managers can
   a. Accommodate the desires of smokers and non-smokers
   b. Reduce the harmful affects of VDTs
   c. Address employee fears caused by AIDS

4. To live a healthier life, medical professionals say we need to identify those things we currently do that

either impair or contribute to our health. Prepare a list of those activities you do that are beneficial or harmful to your overall health. Discuss with others a way to develop a lifetime program for a healthy lifestyle.

5. Go to the website of Human Resources and Social Development Canada, and discover what the experts (including your authors!) have to say about work–life family balance, and what organizations are doing about this: www.hrsdc.gc.ca/asp/gateway.asp?hr=en/lp/spila/wlb/01home.shtml&hs=wnc. Prepare a list of the key initiatives that would make your life as an employee less stressful.

6. Both unions and management express concern for the well-being of their employees. However, union reaction to the proposed introduction of wellness initiatives is not always positive. Unions fear that information collected, for example as part of an EAP, will be kept and used against the employee experiencing performance problems. They also state that the real culprit in any employee health issue is the work context, not employee behaviour or lifestyle. So even if the employees exercise and stop smoking, work hazards still remain. They also fear reprisals for those employees unwilling to participate in programs, particularly where groups are provided with incentives for achieving program aims. (For more information on the union perspective on health and safety issues go to www.hazards.org/campaigns/index.htm.) As the HR manager responsible for the introduction of a wellness initiative, how would you deal with these union concerns?

INTERNET EXERCISE

The Canadian Labour and Business Centre (CLBC) (www.clbc.ca/Research_and_Reports/) presents 12 case studies on the health and wellness initiatives of Canadian companies such as Irving Paper, Dofasco, American Express Canada, Petro-Canada, Burrard Products Terminal, City of Regina Transit Department, and Seven Oaks Hospital in Winnipeg. In groups, prepare a summary report that outlines the motivations for introducing the initiatives, the roles of managers and employees, and the impact on employee health and workplace performance.

HRM Experience

Reducing Employee Stress

Job stress and its negative effect on both employees and the organization are a growing concern for managers and supervisors. As the text discusses, employee distress costs employers staggering amounts of money in lost productivity, absenteeism, turnover, increased workers' compensation claims, and healthcare costs. The cost of distress on the personal lives of employees is unmeasurable. Not surprisingly, stress management is an important aspect of any manager's job.

Stress-management programs typically focus on three things to reduce workplace stress: (1) They identify factors in jobs that create stress; (2) they discuss specific techniques and managerial practices that help elevate workplace stress; and (3) they help individuals identify personal characteristics that serve to increase or decrease stress for them.

Assignment

1. Working in groups of four to six individuals, identify personal experiences that caused workplace stress. Explain exactly why these incidents were stressful. Suggest ways to reduce or eliminate these stressful conditions.

2. Stress management often begins by having individuals identify their skills and abilities and jobs that will help them succeed. Assessing our preferences and skills can help us understand why some tasks or roles are more stressful than others. Identify work-related stress by answering these questions:

- What skills that I enjoy using am I currently using in my job?
- What skills that I enjoy using am I currently not using?
- What specific things about my job do I really like?
- What are things about my job that I dislike?
- Based on my personal skills and abilities, what would my perfect job be?

BIZFLIX EXERCISES

8 Mile: Working at North Detroit Stamping

When you view these scenes, watch for the safety of Jimmy's job and his work environment. Many aspects of safety and health discussed in this chapter appear in these scenes.

Jimmy "B-Rabbit" Smith, Jr. (Eminem) wants to succeed as a rapper and to prove that a white man can create moving sounds. His job at the North Detroit Stamping (NDS) plant fills his days while he pursues his music at night—and sometimes on the plant's grounds. The film's title refers to Detroit's northern city boundary, well known to local people. *8 Mile* is a gritty look at Detroit's hip-hop culture in 1995 and Jimmy's desire for acceptance by it.

The scene is an edited composite of two brief NDS plant sequences that appear in different places in the film. Part I appears early in the film in the sequence

"The Franchise." Part II appears in the last 25 minutes of the film in the "Papa Doc Payback" sequence. Jimmy arrives late for work in the first part of the scene, after riding the city bus because his car did not start. The second part occurs after his beating by Papa Doc (Anthony Mackie) and Papa Doc's gang.

What to Watch for and Ask Yourself

- What is your perception of the safety of Jimmy's job and his work environment? What has management done about job and work environment safety at North Detroit Stamping?
- Could this job and work environment create stress for Jimmy and his co-workers? Why or why not?
- How would you react to this type of work experience?

case study 11

Workplace Safety and Young Workers

Every year about 50 young Canadians are killed on the job and about 60 000 more suffer injuries serious enough to be reported to safety officials. Young workers are six times more likely to be killed or have a workplace injury than any other group. About 95 percent of those affected workers are men. This means that one in 11 young men can expect to suffer a workplace injury. Typically, these young men are employed at small manufacturing businesses, fast-food restaurants, convenience stores, and warehouses. The accidents happen within the first six months on the job. These young men lose fingers while slicing meat at the deli counter, are crushed by equipment they do not know how to operate, are electrocuted on metal ladders that touch hydro poles, or are burned handling chemicals with no protective equipment. The top five causes of injuries to young workers are slips and falls, overexertion, being struck by an object, exposure to toxic chemicals, and burns.

Less than half receive any job training. Only about 30 percent of teenagers receive instruction in first aid and CPR in their safety training, but most learn nothing about the law, their rights, hazards on the job, or safety management. Young workers are especially vulnerable because they feel invincible and lack experience. They believe the following myths:

- I can take risks; I won't die.
- I can handle anything; I am young and fit.
- Nothing will happen to me; I am safe at work.
- I must do any job my employer tells me to do.
- I am not responsible for workplace safety; this is my employer's responsibility.

Most will not ask for safety training because they are unaware of risks, are anxious to please, or are fearful of losing their jobs.

Many provinces, recognizing these risks, have added health and safety training to the high school curriculum. Most such programs discuss workplace hazards, employer rights and responsibilities, health and safety laws, and the workers' right of refusal. Alberta has the most advanced training course for young workers in Canada: Job Safety Skills, which consists of 75 hours of instruction, divided into three modules:

- Personal safety management (first aid, back care, safety and the law)
- Workplace safety practices (ergonomics, confined space entry, transportation of dangerous goods, and farm safety)
- Safety management systems (loss control, accident investigation, and a mock workshop in which students develop an entire safety program)

QUESTIONS

1. Why are there more workplace injuries among those aged 16 to 25?
2. By law, workplace safety is the responsibility of the employer and employee. Why have nearly all provinces created courses in occupational health and safety as part of the high school curriculum? Should these be mandatory courses or electives?
3. Check the website of the Industrial Accident Prevention Association (www.iapa.ca), which has excellent information on occupational health and safety (OH&S) training programs. Design a training program that an employer could provide to young workers.

Sources: Adapted from Peter Cheney, "Focus" *The Globe and* Mail, April 25, 2006, F1 and 8; S. Singh, "HR's Role in Health and Safety for Young Workers," *HR Professional* 18, no. 5 (November 2001): 17–18; L. Ramsay, "Work Can Kill You," *National Post,* September 27, 1999, C12; L. Young, "Young Workers: Changing the Face of Safety," *Occupational Health and Safety* 14, no. 4 (June–July 1998): 24–30; "Workplace Safety," *The Globe and Mail,* Friday, May 12, 2000; Government of Canada, "Youth Path, Health and Wellness," www.youth.gc.ca/healsafe.

case study 2

Safety Training at Mobile Manufacturing: It's Not Working

While a large number of organizations have successful health and safety records, unfortunately, many companies experience unacceptable health and safety incidence rates. Furthermore, simply having a safety program does not guarantee a positive safety record, as the experience of Mobile Manufacturing illustrates.

Mobile Manufacturing produces aftermarket automobile parts for cars and trucks built during the 1950s. The company's specialty area is suspension components for Ford and Chevy vehicles. Mobile Manufacturing employees work with and around a variety of machines and chemicals that have the potential to cause serious medical problems. The working environment has been described by some employees as "extremely hazardous, even life-threatening." In 2005, after an unannounced safety inspection by safety officials, the company received six citations for various health and safety violations and one proposed fine of $7,000 for a "serious" infraction. Additionally, the regulators noted that Mobile had a higher-than-average accident rate for the manufacturing industry. The company was placed on a schedule for repeat inspections.

Between January and March 2006, Mobile implemented a health and safety program specifically designed to reduce the infractions. The company purchased standardized videos, posters, and safety pamphlets for viewing by employees. Supervisors were instructed to issue "safety warnings" to careless employees. (The safety warnings are jokingly referred to as "Band-Aids" by employees.) Employees with a history of safety or health injuries or illnesses were placed on a progressive discipline schedule.

During February 2007, Mobile's safety management team compared their injury and illness incidence rates for January 2006 and January 2007. Unfortunately, there was no meaningful improvement in the company's safety and health record. Two departments, stamping and plating, experienced incidence rates for 2007 higher than those for 2006.

QUESTIONS

1. What may have contributed to the failure of the safety training program at Mobile Manufacturing? Explain.
2. What would you suggest doing to make the safety training program successful? Explain.
3. What role should supervisors play in any safety training program? Explain.

Source: Adapted from a case known to the authors. All names and locations are fictitious.

case study 3

Return to Work: What Works?

Employer costs for health-related absenteeism are rising, due mainly to rising claims for mental conditions, such as depression, anxiety, or stress. The payments for disabilities in an organization of 1000 employees are estimated to be in the range of $2 million per year. But with effective disability management and return-to-work programs, these costs can be cut by 50 percent. Two methods of managing return-to-work programs illustrate effective practices.

CIBC, in the 1990s, was dealing with increasing levels of short-term disability claims that were slowly turning into long-term disability claims. The traditional medical model was that the employee would produce a doctor's note, providing evidence of a disability, and then the manager would hear nothing for a long time. Employees on disability felt isolated and managers felt resentful. CIBC wanted to change this model and started by focusing on what the employee could do rather than what the employee couldn't do. So they started a new process. As soon as an employee is absent for six days, the file is downloaded into CIBC Health Services department, where the coordinator calls the employee's manager and then the employee. A meeting is arranged to discuss the employee's abilities, not the medical condition. Then the manager and the employee work out a return-to-work plan. Any resources needed for accommodation are provided by a central accommodation fund, not from the manager's budget. CIBC spends its money on rehabilitation, not checking on whether the person is really sick or not. Through the use of this facilitated return-to-work program CIBC has reduced its lost days by 30 percent and has won awards for its disability management program.

The traditional medical model is still prevalent, and is working well for some organizations. The disability management program at Ontario Power Generation (OPG), an employer of 11 000 in highly diverse positions from nuclear engineers to receptionists, is resource-intensive but effective. The OPG process is based on the premise that early return to work is beneficial to employees and that accommodating these employees is paramount. A team of 23 full and part-time occupational health nurses manage about 1400 major medical absences a year. The program is mandatory for any employee absent for more than five days. On day five of an absence, the supervisor notifies the nurse care coordinator that they have a major medical absence. The employee receives a medical absence form to be completed by the physician who then submits it to OPG within 14 days. The nurse care coordinator works with the employee to develop a plan for return to work. As long as the employee is cooperating, or there are valid reasons why he/she cannot cooperate with the plan, then the sick benefits continue.

QUESTIONS

1. If you were an employee with a major medical absence, which model would you prefer and why?
2. What do you think the role of the union should be under each model?

Source: Adapted from David Brown, "True Costs of Disability Make Clear Case for Return-to-Work," *Canadian HR Reporter,* May 31, 2004, 12; Andrea Davis, "DM Diagnosis," *Benefits Canada*, March 2006, 38-43; Uyen Vu, "Physical Disability Going Down; Mental Disability Going Up," *Canadian HR Reporter*, March 22, 2004, 6.

CAREER COUNSEL

The Job Stress Assessment on the *Managing Human Resources* website (www.belcourt5e.nelson.com) is designed to help you measure the amount of stress you are experiencing. Visit this site to measure your stress level and learn about strategies for managing stress.

NOTES AND REFERENCES

1. Adrian Gostick, "Delivering Timely Safety Recognition," *Occupational Safety and Health* 73, no. 9 (September 2004): 94. Anonymous, "Developing Tomorrow's Leaders," *Canadian Business* 78, 2, 59.

2. www.awcbc.org, www.iapa.ca. Retrieved July 19, 2006.

3. "Lear Corporation Canada Ltd Fined $125,000 for Health and Safety Violation," *Canada News Wire*, May 23, 2006; "Hershey Canada Fined $50,000 for Health and Safety Violation," *Canada News Wire*, August 11, 2005.

4. Rob Stewart, "The Challenge of Creating a Culture of Safety," *Canadian HR Reporter*, March 28, 2005, 11.

5. Todd Nighswonger, "Is First-Aid First in Your Workplace?" *Occupational Hazards* 64, no. 4 (April 2002): 45–47.

6. Tim W. McDaniel, "Employee Participation: A Vehicle for Safety by Design," *Occupational Hazards* 6, no. 5 (May 2002): 71–76.

7. John P. Spath, "How to Get Employees Involved in the Safety Program," *Occupational Hazards* 66, no. 9 (September 2004): 63.

8. Craig Miller, "Can the Internet Improve Safety?" *Occupational Safety and Health* 73, no. 6 (June 2004): 98.

9. G. C. Shah, "Five Steps to Digital Safety," *Occupational Safety and Health* 71, no. 3 (March 2002): 22–25.

10. Roger Brooks, "OSHA's E-Tool for Lockout/Tagout," *Occupational Safety and Health* 71, no. 4 (April 2002): 22–24.

11. Larry Hansen, "How Will They Know?" *Occupational Hazards* 66, no. 10 (October 2004): 39.

12. R. Bruce McAffee and Ashley R. Winn, "The Use of Incentives/Feedback to Enhance Work Place Safety: A Critique of the Literature," *Journal of Safety Research* 20 (1989): 7–19. See also Thomas R. Krause, John H. Hidley, and Stanley J. Hodson, "Broad-Based Changes in Behavior Key to Improving Safety Culture," *Occupational Health and Safety* 59, no. 7 (July 1990): 31–37, 50; Matthew P. Weinstock, "Rewarding Safety," *Occupational Hazards* 56, no. 3 (March 1994): 73–76; Susan J. Marks, "Incentives that Really Reward and Motivate," *Workforce* 80, no. 6 (June 2001): 108–13.

13. Tara Neal, "Tools of the Trade," *Occupational Health and Safety* 18, no. 2 (March 2002): 60–68.

14. Diana McCrohan, "Add Impact to Your Program," *Occupational Safety and Health* 73, no. 2 (February 2004): 52.

15. Terese Steinback, "Workplace Strategies for Removing Obstacles to Employee Health," *Employee Benefits Journal* 25, no. 1 (March 2000): 9–10.

16. David Brown, "Sick Buildings Lower Productivity," *Canadian HR Reporter*, March 22, 2004, 11.

17. "Smoke Gets in Your Lungs," *HRFocus* 73, no. 2 (February 1996): 17.

18. Todd Humber, "Snuffing out Smoking," *Canadian HR Reporter*, April 11, 2005, 19.

19. D. Dyck, "Wrapping Up the Wellness Package," *Benefits Canada* 23, no. 1 (January 1999): 16–20.

20. Greta Thornbory, "Dealing with MSDs," *Occupational Health* 56, no. 5 (May 2004): 18. See also Dave Heidorn, "Where Ergo Needs to Go," *Professional Safety* 49, no. 7 (July 2004): 14.

21. James M. Stewart, "Critical Elements for Effective Ergonomics," *Occupational Safety and Health* 71, no. 1 (January 2002): 43–45.

22. Canadian Centre for Occupational Health and Safety www.ccohs.ca. Retrieved July 18, 2006.

23. Kevin Kelloway, "Predictors and Outcomes of Workplace Violence," *HR Professional* 20, no. 1 (February/March 2003): 50.

24. www.ccohs.ca/. Retrieved July 19, 2006.

25. Andre Picard, "Remedy is Needed for Violence Against Nurses," *The Globe and Mail*, March 30, 2006, A17.

26. Richard S. Dunham, Rick Miller, Aren Therese Palmer, and Michael Arndt, "The War on Terror: What Companies Need to Do," *Business Week* (August 16, 2004): 26. See also Lawrence D. Mankin and Ronald W. Perry, "Terrorism Challenges for Human Resource Management," *Review of Public Personnel Management* 24, no. 1 (March 2004): 3–17.

27. Stephen V. Magyar Jr., "Do You Have an Evacuation Plan That Works?" *Occupational Safety and Health* 72, no. 12 (December 2003): 44. See also Susanne M. Bruyère and William G. Stothers, "Enabling Safe Evacuations," *HRMagazine* 47, no. 1 (January 2002): 65–67.

28. John C. DelBel, "Workplace Aggression," *Nursing Management* 34, no. 9 (July 2003): 30. See also Bruce T. Blythe and Terri Butler Stivarius, "Assessing and Defusing Workplace Threats of Violence," *Occupational Safety and Health* 73, no. 2 (February 2004): 20.

29. Claire Ginther, "A Death in the Family," *HRMagazine* 46, no. 5 (May 2001): 55–58.

30. Bruce T. Blythe, "The Human Side of Crisis Management," *Occupational Hazards* 66, no. 7 (July 2004): 37.

31. Paul Falcone, "Dealing with Employees in Crisis," *HRMagazine* 48, no. 5 (May 2003): 117.

32. Jeremy Rifkin, "Diseases of the Affluent," *The Globe and Mail*, May 16, 2006, A19.

33. Maryann Hammers, "Banking on an In-House EAP," *Workforce* 82, no. 4 (April 2003): 18.

34. Kristi D. Willbanks, "The Role of Supervisory Referral in Employee Assistance Programs," *Employee Assistance Quarterly* 15, no. 2 (1999): 13–28.

35. Zachary Meyer, "Combating Employee Depression by Integrating Behavioral, Medical, and Pharmaceutical Benefits," *Employee Benefit Plan Review* 59, no. 2 (August 2004): 13.

36. Susan K. McFarlin, William Fals-Stewart, Debra A. Major, and Elaine M. Justice, "Alcohol Use and Work-place Aggression: An Examination of Perpetration and Victimization," *Journal of Substance Abuse* 13, nos. 1–2 (2001): 303–21.

37. "Change Your Culture and Lower Your Benefit Costs," *HRFocus* 81, no. 11 (November 2004): 6.

38. Lee Ann Jackson, "Relax, Relate, Release," *Black Enterprise* 35, no. 2 (September 2004): 61.

39. "Change Your Culture and Lower Your Benefit Costs," 6.

40. Max Messmer, "Are You Burning Out Your Best Employees?" *Strategic Finance* 85, no. 11 (May 2004): 12. See also Bob Gunn, "The Antidote to Burnout," *Strategic Finance* 86, no. 3 (September 2004): 8

41. "Stop Burnout—Before It Stops Your Employees," *HRFocus* 79, no. 2 (February 2002): 3–4.

42. Sora Song, "The Price of Pressure," *Time* (July 19, 2004): 68.

Employee Rights and Discipline

After studying this chapter, you should be able to

objective 1 Explain statutory rights, contractual rights, and due process.

objective 2 Identify the job expectancy rights of employees.

objective 3 Identify and explain the privacy rights of employees.

objective 4 Explain the process of establishing disciplinary policies, including the proper implementation of organizational rules.

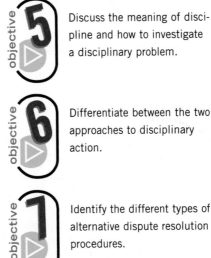

objective 5 Discuss the meaning of discipline and how to investigate a disciplinary problem.

objective 6 Differentiate between the two approaches to disciplinary action.

objective 7 Identify the different types of alternative dispute resolution procedures.

objective 8 Discuss the role of ethics in the management of human resources.

n this chapter we discuss employee rights, workplace privacy, and employee discipline. Managers note that these topics have a major influence on the activities of both employees and supervisors. For example, while drug testing, e-mail privileges, and employee monitoring are routinely debated, employers are now using location awareness technology, global positioning systems (GPSs), and company-provided cell phones to track and locate employees.[1] Furthermore, managers are discovering that the right to discipline and discharge employees—a traditional responsibility of management—is more difficult to exercise in light of the growing attention to employee rights. Disciplining employees is a difficult and unpleasant task for most managers and supervisors; many of them report that taking disciplinary action against an employee is the most stressful duty they perform. Balancing employee rights and employee discipline may not be easy, but it is a universal requirement and a critical aspect of good management.

Because the growth of employee rights issues has led to an increase in the number of lawsuits filed by employees, we include in this chapter a discussion of alternative dispute resolution as a way to foster organizational justice. Because disciplinary actions are subject to challenge and possible reversal through governmental agencies or the courts, management should make a positive effort to prevent the need for such action. When disciplinary action becomes impossible to avoid, however, that action should be taken in accordance with carefully developed HR policies and practices. Because ethics is an important element of organizational justice, the chapter concludes with a discussion of organizational ethics in employee relations.

Employee Rights and Privacy

Various employment equity laws, employment standards acts, and safety and health legislation have secured basic employee rights and brought numerous job improvements to the workplace. Employee rights litigation concerns such workplace issues as employees' rights to protest unfair disciplinary action, to have access to their personal files, to challenge employer searches and monitoring, and to be free from employer discipline for off-duty conduct.

employee rights
Guarantees of fair treatment from employers, particularly regarding an employee's right to privacy

The current emphasis on employee rights is a natural result of the evolution of societal, business, and employee interests.[2] **Employee rights** can be defined as the guarantees of fair treatment that employees expect in protection of their employment status. These expectations become rights when they are granted to employees by the courts, legislatures, or employers. Employee rights frequently involve an employer's alleged invasion of an employee's right to privacy. For example, employees may feel they have a reasonable expectation of privacy regarding their personal phone calls made from work phones, their e-mail messages made to other employees at work, or freedom from employers' random searches of their personal belongings. However, if employers tell employees that they have no right to privacy in these areas, they probably don't. One legal commentator notes, "When employers clearly state that there is no expectation of privacy, it's hard to argue that a reasonable person could have such an expectation."[3] Furthermore, the difference between an employee's legal right to privacy and the moral or personal right to privacy is not always clear. The confusion is due to the lack of a comprehensive and consistent body of privacy protection, whether from laws or from court decisions.

Employee Rights vs. Employer Responsibilities

Balanced against employee rights is the employer's responsibility to provide a safe workplace for employees while guaranteeing safe, quality goods and services to consumers. An employee who uses drugs may exercise his or her privacy right and refuse to submit to a drug test. But should that employee produce a faulty product as a result of drug impairment, the employer can be held liable for any harm caused by that product. Employers who fail to exercise reasonable care can be held negligent by outside parties or by other employees for injuries resulting from a dishonest, unfit, or incompetent employee.[4] In law, **negligence** is the failure to use a reasonable amount of care where such failure results in injury to another person.

It is here that employee rights and employer responsibilities can come most pointedly into conflict. The failure of employers to honour employee rights can result in costly lawsuits, damage the organization's reputation, and hurt employee morale. But failure to protect the safety and welfare of employees or consumer interests can invite litigation from both groups.

negligence
Failure to provide reasonable care where such failure results in injury to consumers or other employees

Employment Protection Rights

It is not surprising that employees should regard their jobs as an established right—a right that should not be taken away without just cause. Without the opportunity to hold a job, our personal well-being would be greatly curtailed. This line of reasoning has led to the emergence of three legal considerations regarding job security: statutory rights, contractual rights, and due process.

Statutory Rights

statutory rights
Rights that derive from legislation

Statutory rights are rights that derive from legislation. As we saw in Chapter 3, employment equity legislation protects employees from discrimination on the basis of grounds such as age, sex, and race. In Prince Edward Island, 314 seasonal workers received compensation from the Tory government after it was determined that they had been fired because of their political affiliation.[5] Pay equity legislation addresses inequities in how men and women are compensated; occupational health and safety legislation attempts to ensure safe and healthful working conditions; labour relations laws give employees the right to form and belong to unions, and to bargain for better working conditions (see Chapter 14).

Contractual Rights

contractual rights
Rights that derive from contracts

In contrast to statutory rights, **contractual rights** are derived from contracts. A contract is a legally binding agreement; if one party breaches the contract, a remedy can be sought through the courts. Formal contracts between employers and full-time employees are rare; however, they are standard practice for contingent workers, a growing segment of the Canadian labour force. A contract that outlines what constitutes fair notice and justification for dismissal, and that includes clauses about nonsolicitation and noncompetition, provides employers with greater flexibility but tends to limit the rights of employees and to reduce their opportunities for making a living after they have left the company. An organization should not ask an employee to sign a contract after beginning work; the courts tend to see this as unilaterally trying to change the unwritten employment contract.

Not all contracts are written. An implied contract can arise when an employer extends to an employee a promise of some form of job security. Implied contractual rights can be based on oral or written statements; those statements can be made during the pre-employment process or after the hire. Promises of job security are sometimes contained in employee handbooks, HR manuals, or employment applications. Whether promises of job security are explicit or implicit, the courts tend to rule that they are binding. In this regard, *Wallace v. United Grain Growers* was an important case. Wallace had been seduced by assurances of job security until retirement to leave his employer of 25 years and join a Winnipeg printing firm owned by United Grain Growers. Then Wallace was dismissed abruptly by his new employer. He was later awarded damages by the Supreme Court of Canada. In another case, the court found that an employer made misleading representations of a job, that the employee believed these representations, and that he suffered damages as a result of believing them. The employer was found liable. In its decision, the court stated that it is the duty of employers to ensure that the information about a job is accurate.[6]

In the following circumstances, an implied contract may become binding:

- Employees are told their jobs are secure as long as they perform satisfactorily and are loyal to the organization.
- The employee handbook states that employees will not be terminated without the right of defence or access to an appeal procedure (i.e., due process).
- An employee is persuaded to leave another organization by promises of higher wages and benefits; the hiring company then reneges after hiring that person.

To reduce their vulnerability to implied contract lawsuits, employers can do the following:

1. Train supervisors and managers not to imply contract benefits in conversations with new or current employees.

2. Include in employment offers a statement that the employee may voluntarily terminate employment with proper notice, and that the employee may be dismissed by the employer at any time and for a justified reason (just cause). The language in this statement must be appropriate, clear, and easily understood.

3. Explain the nature of the employment relationship in documents—for example, in employee handbooks, employment applications, and letters of employment.

4. Have written proof that employees have read all the documents pertaining to the employment relationship.

USING THE INTERNET

The Canadian Employment Lawyers Network provides a list of sites focusing on Canadian employment law and rights:

www.celn.org

Due Process

Management has traditionally possessed the right to direct employees and to take corrective action when needed. Nevertheless, many people also believe that a job is the property right of an employee and that the loss of employment has such serious consequences that employees should not lose their jobs without the protection of due process. Managers normally define **due process** as the employee's right to be heard through the employer's own complaint procedure. However, proactive employers will also incorporate the following principles—or rights—in their interpretation of due process:

1. The right to know job expectations and the consequences of not fulfilling those expectations.

2. The right to consistent and predictable management action for the violation of rules.

due process
Employee's right to present his or her position during a disciplinary action

3. The right to fair discipline based on facts, the right to question those facts, and the right to present a defence.

4. The right to appeal disciplinary action.

5. The right to progressive discipline.

Employment Rights Not a Guarantee

Although employees may have cause to regard their jobs as an established right, there is no legal protection affording employees a permanent or continuous job. Furthermore, in general terms, due process does not guarantee employment to workers. However, the concepts of due process and of job-as-right do obligate managers to treat their employees fairly, equitably, and consistently.

Regardless, employees have certain expectations regarding the employment relationship. This expectation is referred to as the psychological contract and includes an employee's belief about the mutual obligation between the employee and the organization.[7] For example, in exchange for their talents, energies, and technical skills, workers expect employers to provide fair compensation, meaningful work, and job training. Employees also have the right to expect sound employment practices and to be treated as individuals of dignity and substantial worth.[8] While the **psychological contract** is not a legal mandate, nevertheless, it strongly influences the employment relationship.

In Canada, in absence of a formal contract specifying the duration of employment, the employment relationship is construed as ongoing. Thus, even when employment is not necessarily considered to be permanent, the employer must provide reasonable notice as well as grounds for termination. In the United States the employment-at-will principle assumes that an employee has a right to sever the employment relationship for a better job opportunity or for other personal reasons. Likewise, an employer is free to terminate the employment relationship at any time—and without notice—for any reason, no reason, or even a bad reason. In essence, employees are said to work "at the will" of the employer. The employment-at-will relationship is created when an employee agrees to work for an employer for an unspecified period of time. Since the employment is of an indefinite duration, it can, in general, be terminated at the whim of either party. This freedom includes the right of management to unilaterally determine the conditions of employment and to make personnel decisions.

psychological contract
Expectations of a fair exchange of employment obligations between an employee and employer

Wrongful Dismissal

An employer can dismiss an employee—that is, terminate the employment relationship—for just cause. To do so, the employer must document and prove serious misconduct or incompetence on the part of the employee. Some actions that are considered serious misconduct include persistent insubordination, sexual harassment, persistent bullying, physical assault at work, sharing confidential items with third parties, competing directly against the employer, and, in certain cases, the use of drugs or alcohol in the workplace.[9] In recent years more and more employees have sued their former employers for "wrongful or unjust dismissal." One comprehensive study of wrongful dismissal suits found that employers won 40 percent of the time when the charge was dishonesty, theft, substance abuse, or abusive behaviour; 54 percent of the time when the charge was insubordination; 65 percent of the time when the charge was conflict of interest or competing with the employer; and just 25 percent of the time when the charge was poor performance.[10]

USING THE INTERNET

For additional information on wrongful dismissals, see:

http://canadaonline.about.com/cs/hremployers/

Managers, with the help of the HR department, must be able to document that the performance problems were brought to the attention of the employee and that sufficient time, training, and assistance were given to improve the weak performance. Insensitive and inappropriate behaviour by employers during a termination can be costly, as outlined in The Business Case. Also, Highlights in HRM 13.1 describes how employees can challenge a just cause case. To help avoid charges of wrongful dismissal, HR specialists recommend that employers follow the tips provided in Figure 13.1 on page 562.

Constructive Dismissal

In 1997 the Supreme Court of Canada set the standard for constructive dismissal. **Constructive dismissal** has occurred when an employer changes an employee's working conditions in such a way that compensation, status, or prestige is reduced. The changes must be substantive—that is, they must affect pay, reporting relationships, responsibilities, and location; they cannot be trivial (e.g., minor changes in working hours). Even if the employee agrees to the changed conditions (the only other option might be unemployment) or resigns, the court considers him or her to have been dismissed.[11]

Two cases illustrate the concept. One involved a Royal Trust regional manager who was earning about $150,000 in base salary and commissions when his job was eliminated.

constructive dismissal
Changing an employee's working conditions such that compensation, status, or prestige is reduced

The Business Case

Dismissal Danger

Employers must be very cautious in the way in which employee dismissals are handled. The employer must be honest and avoid making misleading statements or unfounded allegations of cause. One company had to pay a terminated employee $75,000 in punitive damages because the employer alleged the cause of the termination was insubordination, willful disobedience, and failure to achieve the expected level of performance, while the HR department was told the cause was restructuring (the punitive damages were overturned because the employee had already received a generous compensation).

The employer cannot make injurious statements or unsubstantiated allegations to potential employers, or sabotage the employee's reputation in the labour market. In one case, an employer dismissed a car sales manager after 13 years on the job and circulated a letter to other car dealers, alleging that the employee had violated company policies. The judge found the allegations unfounded and awarded an additional six months' notice for aggravated or punitive damages. In another case, the B.C. Court of Appeal awarded 18 months' damages, or salary (later reduced to 12 months), for bad faith dismissal, when the employer wrongly accused an employee of forgery, fraud, and drug abuse, making her unemployable in the labour market. The employer should try to be sensitive to the feelings and personal circumstances of the employee, and to make every effort, to the extent possible, to assist the employee in finding another job.

Sources: Peter Israel, "Cut Down on Lawsuits Just by Being Nice," *Canadian HR Reporter* 15, no. 20 (November 18, 2002): 5; J. Miller, "Highest Ever Damages for Bad Faith Dismissal Overturned," *Canadian HR Reporter* 14, no. 1 (January 15, 2001): 5.

Highlights in HRM 13.1

Firing Back!

Once you have received either verbal or written warnings about performance, a decision has usually been made to fire you. What can you do? Writing back to pick holes in the accusations is the least effective defence. Using the same weapons as management, you must prove that the just cause will not hold.

Howard Levitt, a legal expert on dismissal, offers the following advice:

- Establish in writing that you were unaware of the standards of performance or conduct. You can argue that the standards are new or were not part of the initial job offer, position description, performance evaluations, or previous warnings. The company must prove that you were grossly incompetent, so any letters of praise or good performance review should be used. Any aspects of performance that may override the weak areas should be noted. For example, if you are being dismissed for poor communication skills but your productivity figures are increasing, this should be documented. As soon as you commence employment, start a file containing all performance evaluations; letters of praise from customers, co-workers, internal clients, and supervisors; and all other examples of performance achievements. Establish a paper trail of good performance.
- Argue that the company, while complaining about poor performance, has not stated specifically what is required to improve performance.
- Assert that you were not given the time, training, assistance, or learning opportunities necessary to improve performance.
- Establish, if true, that the employer hired you knowing that you did not possess the necessary skills. Note any understanding that you would receive the appropriate training.
- State, if applicable, that the skills desired now were not part of your original job description.
- Attribute your poor performance to factors outside your control, such as a decline in sales in all regions, or poorly priced products, or a temporary illness. If possible, establish that the company contributed to the performance problem by failing to respond to your (documented) suggestions for improvement.

Leavitt further advises that letters and all other documentation be written with the assistance of a specialist. In the end, you may not get your job back, but if successful you can expect an attractive severance package.

Source: Howard Levitt, Counsel, Lang Michener, Toronto, "How Employees Can Fight Firing for Just Cause," *Toronto Star*, August 17, 1992, C1. Reprinted by permission of the author.

He was offered the position of branch manager at the company's least profitable branch, where his income would have been based solely on commissions (he had held a similar position about four promotions earlier). The court ruled that he had been constructively dismissed and awarded him damages and legal costs. In another case, Embassy Cleaners changed the working conditions of a presser, resulting in a more physically demanding job, an earlier start time (6:00 a.m. instead of 7:30 a.m.), a change in the workweek from five to six days, and a change from hourly wages to piecework. The court ruled that these changes constituted a fundamental breach of contract and hence constructive dismissal.[12]

| Figure 13.1 | Tips to Avoid Wrongful Employment Termination Lawsuits |

- *Terminate an employee only if there is an articulated reason.* An employer should have clearly articulated, easily understandable reasons for discharging an employee. The reasons should be stated as objectively as possible and should reflect company rules, policies, and practices.
- *Set and follow termination rules and schedules.* Make sure every termination follows a documented set of procedures. Procedures can be from an employee handbook, a supervisory manual, or even an intra-office memorandum. Before terminating, give employees notices of unsatisfactory performance and improvement opportunities through a system of warnings and suspensions.
- *Document all performance problems.* A lack of documented problems in an employee's personnel record may be used as circumstantial evidence of pretextual discharge if the employee is "suddenly" discharged.
- *Be consistent with employees in similar situations.* Document reasons given for all disciplinary actions, even if they do not lead to termination. Terminated employees may claim that exception-to-the-rule cases are discriminatory. Detailed documentation will help employers explain why these "exceptions" did not warrant termination.

In a nonunion context, employers can give notice of future changes in compensation, benefits, incentives, working hours, location, and so on as long as they provide actual notice equivalent to that given for dismissal. The amount of severance depends on several factors, such as age, ability to find a new job, level in the organization, and the number of years worked. For example, a 50-year-old middle manager with 25 years with the company would probably receive 17 months of severance pay. Someone who has been in the job for one to three years would probably receive two weeks of severance pay.

Whistleblowing

whistleblowing
Complaints to governmental agencies by employees about their employers' illegal or immoral acts or illegal practices

Employees engage in **whistleblowing** when they report an employer's illegal actions, immoral conduct, or illegal practices to governmental agencies charged with upholding the law.[13] As Gerard Seijts, a professor of organizational behaviour at the University of Western Ontario, states, "Whistleblowers are the catalysts of change. Because they believe in the company, they dissent. They aren't the disgruntled employees that employers say they are, but the best and the brightest." For example, an Ottawa lawyer with a background in real estate was hired by the Department of Foreign Affairs to look after a portfolio of embassies and diplomatic properties around the world, and identified excessive spending. She spent six years trying to deal with the problem internally before going public with her concerns. As she reported, "I had not even heard the term whistleblower before. I was simply doing my job to procure real estate cost effectively . . . for the Canadian taxpayer."[14]

There is almost no protection for whistleblowers in Canada, although the federal government is working on and some provinces such as Saskatchewan have enacted "whistleblower laws." (In the U.S., there is protection for all private-sector employers though the Sarbanes-Oxley Act of 2002.) These laws protect workers from retribution or retaliation by empowering the director of labour standards, for example, to deal with a complaint of wrongful dismissal or discrimination due to reporting an illegal activity.

HR professionals recommend that companies implement a whistleblowing policy that encourages employees to report illegal or immoral conduct internally rather than externally. The policy should provide for the safeguard of employee rights, a complete and unbiased investigation of the incident, a speedy report of findings, and an appeals procedure for employees who are dissatisfied with company findings.[15]

Plant Closing Notification

Thousands of jobs have been lost in Canada as a result of plant closings. These shutdowns can devastate not merely individual employees but entire communities. It has been estimated that for every 100 jobs lost from a plant closing, the local community loses 200 to 300 jobs through ripple effects. Several provincial governments have passed legislation preventing employers from unilaterally closing or relocating their facilities. For example, Ontario has passed legislation that organizations with more than 500 employees must give 16 weeks' notice. Employers can do more than just provide notice. Levi Strauss closed all of its plants in North America, including three at Edmonton, Alberta, and Stoney Creek and Brantford, Ontario, putting nearly 1000 Canadian workers out of work. However, there was no backlash, because the company assisted the employees in retraining for new careers or finding new jobs. For example, each employee was given a $2,450 allowance for retraining and made a donation $1 million to local educational institutions to provide training.[16]

Job Expectancy Rights

Once hired, employees expect certain rights associated with fair and equitable employment. Employee rights on the job relate to these issues, among others: privacy, substance abuse and drug testing, and just-cause disciplinary and discharge procedures.

Privacy Rights

Personal Information Protection and Electronic Document Act

Privacy is a fundamental human right. Privacy is our right to control information about ourselves: about who we are, what we do, where we go, what we buy, and whom we deal with. The Personal Information Protection and Electronic Documents Act (PIPEDA) came into effect on January 1, 2001, to provide Canadians with a right of privacy with respect to their personal information that is collected, used, or disclosed by an organization in the private sector. PIPEDA applies to personal information collected, used, or disclosed in the employment relationships of federally regulated works. Some provinces, including Quebec, British Columbia, Alberta, and Ontario, have enacted statutes similar to PIPEDA, often called Personal Information Protection Act (PIPA).

Some of the categories of personal information covered under PIPEDA include name, weight, age, medical records, income, purchasing and spending habits, race, blood type, fingerprints, marital status, education, and personal contact information. Controlling one's personal information means controlling the collection, use, and disclosure of that information. However, today's technology facilitates the collection and free flow of information; information can be moved and processed much more efficiently when it is in digital form. Thus, it is the ease with which digital information can be transferred that poses a threat to individual privacy.

Organizations covered by PIPEDA must obtain an individual's consent when they collect, use, or disclose the individual's personal information. The individual has a right to access personal information held by an organization

USING THE INTERNET

For further information on PIPEDA, see the federal Privacy Commissions Guide for Businesses and Organizations at:

www.privcom.gc.ca/information/ guide_e.asp

and to challenge its accuracy, if need be. Any organization that collects personal information can use that information only for the purpose for which it was collected. If an organization is going to use it for another purpose, it must obtain the individual's consent again. Individuals must also be assured by the organization that their information will be protected by adequate safeguards.

The most important legal principle with regard to data privacy law is the concept of consent. As pointed out above, organizations must get the informed, prior consent of the data subject. The data subject must be notified of the following before he or she provides any personal information:

- That he or she is about to provide personal data;
- The purposes for which the information is to be processed;
- The people or bodies to whom the data might be disclosed;
- The proposed transfer of data to other countries; and
- The security controls protecting the data.

Because privacy law obliges corporations to obtain consent from the individual whose personal information is being gathered, HR professionals should conduct an audit to determine if the organization's practice conforms to the legislation. For example, one organization collected information about the birth country of employees in order to facilitate international transfers. However, collecting this information for clerks, who will not be transferred, is unnecessary and would not meet the new standards.[17] Sources of information from selection interviews and employee evaluations may have to be made available to employees.[18]

E-Mail, Internet, and Voice Mail Privacy

The benefits of e-mail, the Internet, and voice mail are many; they provide instant delivery of messages, facilitate teamwork, increase time efficiency, offer access to global information, and promote flexible work arrangements. Unfortunately, technology also permits employees to act in unscrupulous, inappropriate, and unauthorized ways,

Monitoring employee behaviour is an important deterrent to inappropriate conduct of employees.

© DIGITAL VISION/GETTY IMAGES

creating ethical, productivity, and legal problems for employers. These illegitimate uses of technology cause employers to monitor the conduct of employees, creating significant privacy issues for both employees and managers.

Why do employers monitor their employees? The reasons are varied: to prevent intimidating behaviour of employees, to ensure effective use of company time, to prevent employee gossip, to eliminate the surfing of pornographic websites, to stop employees from doing personal business on company time, or to ensure employee safety including the prevention of sexual harassment or cyberstalking. For example, in a recent case, a sexual harassment suit cost Chevron $2.2 million because an employee sent coarse messages over the company e-mail system.[19] Additionally, employee monitoring is done to prevent personal information from becoming accessible to those with prying eyes or "hackers" who might use the information inappropriately.

Employers have a great latitude to monitor their own equipment. Court cases governing e-mail and the Internet generally grant to employers the right to monitor materials created, received, or sent for business-related reasons. Employees who erase their messages may wrongly assume their messages are gone when deleted. Although employees may assume that their right to privacy extends to e-mail, the Internet, or voice mail messages, it does not. Furthermore, employees can be disciplined or terminated for inappropriate e-mail messages or Internet use. Two recent court cases have made this very clear. In one case, the employee, with 18 years of service, was terminated for using the company Internet for personal purposes, including accessing pornography. In another case, an employee with 15 years of service was found to have been using the company Internet to manage his own unrelated travel business, for up to two hours a day on company time, using the company's computers.[20]

High technology has created tensions between employee privacy and the employer's need to know. HR experts and legal authorities strongly encourage employers to develop clear policies and guidelines that explain to employees how e-mail, the Internet, and voice mail are to be used, including when and under what conditions employees can be monitored[21] (see Figure 13.2). As with other employment policies, employees should sign a form indicating that they have read and understand the policy. This was the case when Pratt & Whitney disciplined or suspended 130 employees at its Montreal plant for violating company policy on computer use.

Figure 13.2	E-Mail and Voice Mail: Policy Guidelines

- Ensure compliance with federal and provincial legislation.
- Specify the circumstances, if any, under which the system can be used for personal business.
- Specify that confidential information not be sent on the network.
- Set forth the conditions under which monitoring will be done—by whom, how often, and with what notification to employees.
- Specify that e-mail and voice mail information be sent only to users who need it for business purposes.
- Expressly prohibit use of e-mail or voice mail to harass others or to send anonymous messages.
- Make clear that employees have no privacy rights in any material delivered or received through e-mail or voice mail.
- Specify that employees who violate the policy are subject to discipline, including dismissal.

Employee Searches and Electronic Monitoring

- General Electric employs tiny fish-eye lenses installed behind pinholes in walls and ceilings to observe employees suspected of crimes.
- DuPont uses long-distance cameras to monitor its loading docks.
- In Medicine Hat, Alberta, IDA drugstore cashiers are required to place their fingers on a pad that scans their fingerprints and allows them access to the system.

While these examples may seem a violation of privacy rights, it is not uncommon for employers to monitor employee conduct through surveillance techniques. See Figure 13.3 for how companies are using monitoring devices. Most retailers use some form of monitoring. Because employees forget passwords, Holt Renfrew, for example, uses the fingerprint scans as protection against others using passwords or cards. Indeed, the scans are now used to track time and attendance.[22] However, employees and unions worry that monitoring will be used to monitor performance. Reality Check describes the privacy issues that are facing the courts.

Why do companies search employees and monitor their activities? The answer is employee theft. Employers lose over 1 percent of annual revenues as a result of "inventory shrinkage"—that is, employee and customer theft. Thieves are like good customers: if they like what they get, they'll come back for more. The key to preventing loss through employee theft is to break up the employee dishonesty triangle—opportunity,

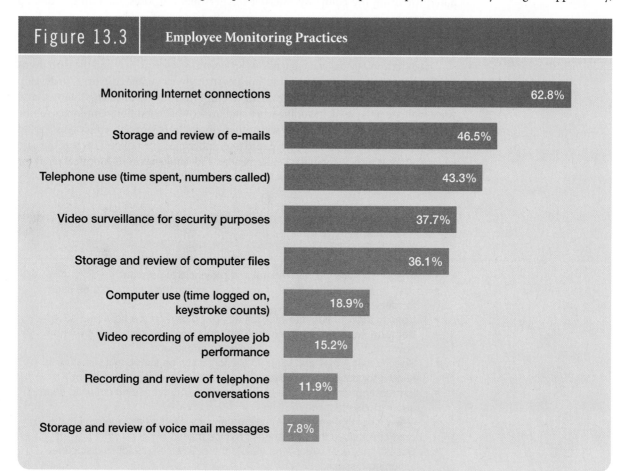

Figure 13.3   **Employee Monitoring Practices**

Practice	Percentage
Monitoring Internet connections	62.8%
Storage and review of e-mails	46.5%
Telephone use (time spent, numbers called)	43.3%
Video surveillance for security purposes	37.7%
Storage and review of computer files	36.1%
Computer use (time logged on, keystroke counts)	18.9%
Video recording of employee job performance	15.2%
Recording and review of telephone conversations	11.9%
Storage and review of voice mail messages	7.8%

Source: Uyen Vu, "Employee Resistant to Any Form of Computer Video Monitoring, Study Says," *Canadian HR Reporter,* March 8, 2004, 2.

Reality Check

Privacy Issues with New Technologies

Paul Boniferro, partner, head of the Ontario labour and employment group at McCarthy Tétrault, Canada's largest law firm with offices in Vancouver, Calgary, London, Ottawa, Montreal and Quebec City, and London UK describes a case involving the use of biometric scanning.

"We have a client in the property management industry. The security officers and building maintenance staff were being asked to no longer use access passes and punch cards, but to have their hands scanned by a biometric system.

The idea of using a biometric scanning device started with 9/11. The problem for landlords was that no one knew who was in the towers of the World Trade Center. Property managers are responsible for knowing who is in the building for security purposes and for emergency events.

Swipe cards can be exchanged or stolen and so are not reliable methods of identification. Furthermore, the employer had heard that employees were giving each other their punch cards for logging in, and effectively stealing time from the employer.

The employer wanted to install a biometric entry system for security, for emergency contact, and for tracking employee time for payroll purposes. The biometric system scans and reads handprints, which are unique to every individual, and therefore solved both the problems of employee identification and time theft.

The employees refused, saying that it was an invasion of their privacy. They felt that "Big Brother" wanted to control their whereabouts and know where they were at all times. In a similar case a grievance was launched against an employer, alleging a breach of privacy. The case went to an arbitrator.

In this case, the arbitrator agreed with the union (and the employees) and based her decision on these factors:

1. The employer has to first establish that there is an issue and a problem that needs to be controlled. In this case, the theft of time was not established as an issue that needed to be addressed.
2. The company has to establish that there is no other reasonable and less intrusive method to manage the three issues.
3. The employer has to establish that all necessary precautions have been taken to protect the privacy of the employees.
4. Furthermore, the employer must consult with the union about the implementation and the protection of employees' privacy.

The employer was not allowed to use the system. However, in another similar situation, in a manufacturing environment, the current employees were allowed to keep their passes, but all new employees were required to use the biometric system. Existing employees, on a voluntary basis, could use the system. The company also charged $25 to replace lost cards, and over time employees no longer wanted the hassle of the cards. Now, 100 percent of its employees are using the biometric system.

rationalization, and financial need. Experts recommend the following strategies for decreasing employee theft:

- Install security cameras that can tilt, scan, and zoom.
- Tag products to minimize "sweethearting"—a practice in which the cashier does not scan a product that a friend or accomplice is checking out. The tags are deactivated when they are scanned; if they aren't, an alarm sounds.
- Scrutinize job application forms. Be on the alert for lack of references, skipped portions of the form, conflicting dates of employment, lack of explanation for leaving old jobs, and long gaps between jobs.
- Check references thoroughly.
- Limit access to the cash office. Keep the door locked, and have employees store personal belongings elsewhere.[23]

Managers must be diligent when conducting employee searches. Improper searches can lead to employee lawsuits charging the employer with invasion of privacy, defamation of character, and negligent infliction of emotional distress. Employers are advised to develop an HR search policy based on the following guidelines:

1. The search policy should be widely publicized and should advocate a probable or compelling reason for the search.
2. The search policy should be applied in a reasonable, evenhanded manner.
3. When possible, searches should be conducted in private.
4. The employer should attempt to obtain the employee's consent prior to the search.
5. The search should be conducted in a humane and discreet manner to avoid infliction of emotional distress.
6. The penalty for refusing to consent to a search should be specified.

One of the most common means of electronic monitoring by employers is telephone surveillance to ensure that customer requests are handled properly or to prevent theft.[24] Employers have the right to monitor employees, provided they do it for compelling business reasons and employees have been informed that their calls will be monitored. Some collective agreements restrict the use of video surveillance. Ethics in HRM outlines some of the issues raised by monitoring employees.

Access to Personnel Files

The information kept in an employee's personnel file can have a significant impact—positive or negative—on career development. The personnel file, typically kept by the HR department, can contain performance appraisals, salary notices, investigatory reports, credit checks, criminal records, test scores, and family data. Errors and/or omissions in personnel files, or access to the files by unauthorized people, can create employment or personal hardships. As an employee you have the right to check and change the facts on your file (example, start date) but not opinions (such as your performance assessment). Employment professionals recommend that organizations develop a policy on employee files that includes, as a minimum, the points noted in Figure 13.4 on page 570.

Camera-Equipped Phones

General Motors and defence contractor Syzygy Technologies are two companies that ban employee use of camera phones, personal digital assistants, and similar digital devices. Reasons for the ban include protecting competitive proprietary information

Ethics in HRM

Supervising or Super-Spying?

Cameras monitor much of our everyday life, often without our knowledge. Surveillance systems may be monitoring you as you leave the lobby of your apartment building, as you enter the underground garage, as you drive on the highway to work, as you purchase a coffee at the variety store, and even at some workplaces. Pinhole cameras the size of a quarter can fit into a picture on the wall, a telephone, or a ceiling device that looks like a water sprinkler. They can catch an employee loading up on office supplies; they can even determine whether the employee is using chat lines or the Internet for personal reasons. Some employers keep records of the calls employees make, and their duration. A standard feature on network-management software enables the administrator to pull up the screen of any employee on the network.

Employees who work as customer representatives, handling 60 to 80 calls a day, may have their conversations monitored by supervisors or a trainer to ensure that the information given is accurate and that service standards are maintained. At one firm that raises money for charities, employees are required to make 8500 keystrokes an hour; failure to achieve this standard is noted electronically. (Distractions are minimized by covering windows, forbidding conversation unrelated to business, and facing all desks in the same direction.) Eight cameras are capable of zooming in on any desk, in case any employee is displaying materials unrelated to work.

Even babysitters and nannies are being targeted for electronic monitoring. Cameras hidden in books watch the children and the babysitter or nanny while anxious parents are at work. Parents insist that this surveillance enables them to ensure the safety and emotional security of their children; babysitters and nannies are outraged at the lack of trust and invasion of their privacy.

According to a national director with the Canadian Union of Postal Workers, "Surveillance and monitoring is really about power, and the uneven levels of power in the workplace. If it is abused by employers, then it really becomes a powerful weapon that is used to control the behaviour of workers, or as a source of discipline." A 2000 study found that people consider these electronic monitoring systems to be highly invasive and unfair. As one employee said, "I feel like when some prisoners are braceleted so that they know where they are."

Sources: David Zwieg, "The Line Between Benign and Invasive Monitoring Technologies," *HR Professional* 19, no. 4 (August/September, 2002): 36–38; J. Powell, "Keeping an Eye on the Workplace," *Financial Post,* September 6, 1997, 24; M. Gooderham, "Rise in Technology Lets Everyone Be a Spy," *The Globe and Mail,* June 7, 1995, A1; A.M. Stewart, "For a Nervous Breakdown, Please Press One," *The Globe and Mail,* June 1, 1994, A25; G. Arnaut, "Electronic Big Brother Is on the Job," *The Globe and Mail,* October 22, 1996, C1; R. Fulford, "Tolerating Electronic Sweatshops," *The Globe and Mail,* December 14, 1994, C1.

and safeguarding employee privacy. Companies routinely ban such devices from restrooms and wellness and exercise facilities because of the risk of privacy violations. John Sweeney, information specialist at SHRM, notes, "Employees using such facilities should feel safe and have no concerns that they might be photographed without their consent."[25]

Figure 13.4	**Personnel Files: Policy Guidelines**

- Ensure compliance with applicable laws.
- Develop different categories of personnel information, depending on legal requirements and organizational needs.
- Specify where, when, how, and under what circumstances employees may review or copy their files.
- Identify company individuals allowed to view personnel files.
- Prohibit the collection of information that could be viewed as discriminatory or could form the basis for an invasion-of-privacy suit.
- Audit employment records on a regular basis to remove irrelevant, outdated, or inaccurate information.

Employee Conduct Outside the Workplace

Consider the following situation. On Monday morning the owner of ABC Corporation reads in the newspaper that a company employee has been charged with robbery and assault on a local convenience store owner. The employee has been released pending trial. A phone call to the employee's supervisor reveals that the employee has reported to work. What should the owner do?

New technologies enable employers to monitor staff very closely, even on their personal time. While most courts uphold the right of the employer to monitor employees at the workplace, particularly if there is a justifiable reason to collect evidence, the monitoring of employees outside the workplace is more complex. For example, recent court cases have suggested that videotaping an employee inside his home is an unreasonable invasion of privacy. Videotaping in a public place was found reasonable in other cases. For example, an employee of the City of Toronto who worked as an arborist claimed to have injured himself at work and yet was videotaped cutting and removing branches from trees while off duty, work that he claimed he could not do.[26] Another company hired a private investigator to follow a travelling sales representative and fired her for stealing company time and money because she was using a company car to pick up her husband and drive him to work when she was supposed to be visiting clients. Another company fired its president after it discovered the reason for his absences during the day were fitness sessions at the gym.[27] But off-duty conduct can extend beyond job duties, to attitudes. The Peel Board of Education fired a teacher who met with racists and supported white supremacists. The firing was upheld even though there was no evidence that his views were expressed in the classroom. Where the public nature of the employee's job (e.g., police officer or teacher) creates an image problem for the organization, courts might uphold firing them for their off-duty behaviour. Generally, however, little of what an employee does outside the workplace bears discipline by the employer.[28]

Workplace romances pose many dilemmas for organizations. Power differentials are often a factor (as between a manager and a secretary, or a new employee and a co-worker with a lot of seniority). When a power-differentiated romance goes sour, charges of sexual harassment can easily arise. Behaviour that was acceptable in a consensual relationship between employees can quickly evolve into harassment when one party to the relationship stops welcoming the conduct. Such romances can also be sources of workplace violence (i.e., jilted lover arrives at work with a weapon).

USING THE INTERNET

Further legal resources on the topics discussed in this chapter can be found on the website of Canada Law Book at:

www.canadalawbook.ca

Furthermore, workplace romances can lead to charges of favouritism. When an employee involved in an office romance with a superior gets preferential treatment, charges of "reverse harassment" can easily arise. Workplace romances can create morale problems—jealousy, resentment, hard feelings, and so on—when other employees feel unfairly treated. Romances involving supervisors and their underlings can have profound effects on organizational operations and productivity. One study found that despite all this, only 6 percent of surveyed organizations had a policy on employee dating or fraternization.[29]

Substance Abuse and Drug Testing

The impact on employers of employee drug abuse is staggering. It is estimated that drug abuse by employees costs Canadian employers an estimated $4.1 billion a year for alcohol, $6.8 billion for tobacco, and $823.1 million for illicit drugs—a total of $11.8 billion in productivity losses. That represents 1.7 percent of the gross domestic product, or $414 per capita.[30] Most human rights commissions see drug and alcohol as dependencies; it follows that testing for these dependencies is a form of discrimination. Compared with nonabusing employees, substance abusers have been found to

- take three times as much sick leave
- file five times more workers' compensation claims;
- have four times more accidents on the job; and
- make twice as many mistakes.[31]

In these litigious times, an employer's failure to ensure a safe and drug-free workplace can result in astronomical liability claims when consumers are injured because of a negligent employee or faulty product. The Canadian government has not introduced legislation on drug testing; such legislation does exist south of the border. Canadians are generally more opposed to drug testing than Americans.[32] Companies that do use drug testing are faced with high costs, error rates as high as 40 percent, and employee resistance.[33] Even if an employee tests positive, he or she is rarely terminated. Substance abuse is considered a disability and the employer is obligated to offer treatment. At the same time, companies with drug-testing policies report reductions in absenteeism, sick days, and accidents. Highlights in HRM 13.2 on page 572 describes some issues with drug testing.

Genetic Testing

With advances being made in genetics, it is now possible to identify the genetic basis for human diseases and illnesses. Genetic findings present opportunities for individualized prevention strategies and early detection and treatment. Unfortunately, the knowledge gained through genetic testing can also be used discreetly by employers to discriminate against or stigmatize individuals who are applying for employment or are currently employed. For example, genetic testing can identify an individual's risk of developing common diseases and disorders such as cancer, heart disease, and diabetes. Diseases like these can raise employment costs (e.g., recruitment, training, and medical costs).

Employers must remember that there is no scientific evidence linking unexpressed genetic factors to an individual's ability to perform a job. There are few federal or provincial laws, or court decisions, governing employers' use of genetic information. The employer is at risk by not hiring or promoting a candidate because of knowledge about a predisposition to a disease that would cause insurance costs to rise or cause lowered job performance.[34]

Highlights in HRM 13.2

Riding High

The debate over performance-enhancing (or -diminishing) drugs reached new levels at the 1998 Winter Olympics in Japan when Ross Rebagliati found his gold medal in snowboarding in jeopardy after he tested positive for marijuana. At most companies in Canada, if Rebagliati had been an employee he would not have been tested for drugs and would not have been fired for testing positive. Drug-testing laws in Canada are very strict; testing is allowed only in jobs where safety is a critical issue, as it is at Ontario Hydro's nuclear power plants. Greyhound Canada in Calgary does random drug tests on bus drivers who are bidding for routes to the United States, where drug testing in the transportation sector is mandatory.

The Addiction Research Foundation points out that while drug tests show that drugs have been used, they do not indicate the level of impairment and therefore whether the user is "under the influence." Also, drugs such as cocaine take only three days to clear the body, whereas others such as marijuana can take three weeks. The inability to prove impaired performance, coupled with concerns about people's right to privacy, has made the courts hesitant to give companies the authority to conduct random drug tests, or to ask employees if they have a history of substance abuse.

One advertising agency tolerates the use of drugs on the grounds that "ad people tend to be creative and live on the edge." However, most companies suspecting substance abuse would take immediate action (e.g., referral to an employee assistance program) and resort to discharge or extended disability leave if the employee's performance continued to deteriorate.

Source: M. Gibb-Clark and E. Church, "Pot Policing Fails the Workplace Test," *The Globe and Mail,* February 12, 1998, B16. Reprinted with permission from *The Globe and Mail.*

Disciplinary Policies and Procedures

objective 4

The rights of managers to discipline and discharge employees are increasingly limited. There is thus a great need for managers at all levels to understand discipline procedures. Disciplinary action taken against an employee must be for justifiable reasons, and there must be effective policies and procedures to govern its use. Such policies and procedures assist those responsible for taking disciplinary action and help ensure that employees will receive fair and constructive treatment. Equally important, these guidelines help prevent disciplinary action from being voided or reversed through the appeal system.

Disciplinary policies and procedures should extend to a number of important areas to ensure thorough coverage. Figure 13.5 presents a disciplinary model that illustrates the areas where provisions should be established. The model also shows the logical sequence in which disciplinary steps must be carried out to ensure enforceable decisions.

A major responsibility of the HR department is to develop, and to have top management approve, its disciplinary policies and procedures. The HR department is also responsible for ensuring that disciplinary policies, as well as the disciplinary action taken against employees, are consistent with the collective agreement (if one exists)

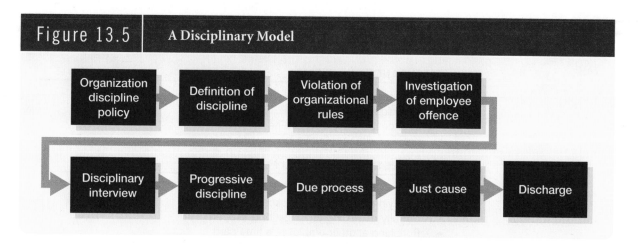

Figure 13.5 | **A Disciplinary Model**

Organization discipline policy → Definition of discipline → Violation of organizational rules → Investigation of employee offence → Disciplinary interview → Progressive discipline → Due process → Just cause → Discharge

and conform to current laws. However, the primary responsibility for preventing or correcting disciplinary problems rests with an employee's immediate supervisor. This person is best able to observe evidence of unsatisfactory behaviour or performance and to discuss the matter with the employee. Should discipline become necessary, the employee's immediate supervisor is the logical person to apply the company's disciplinary procedure and monitor employee improvement.

The Results of Inaction

Figure 13.6 on page 574 lists the more common disciplinary problems identified by managers. Failure to take disciplinary action in any of these areas only serves to aggravate a problem that eventually must be resolved. Failure to act implies that the performance of the employee concerned has been satisfactory. If disciplinary action is eventually taken, the delay will make it more difficult to justify the action if appealed. In defending against such an appeal, the employer is likely to be asked why an employee who had not been performing or behaving satisfactorily was kept on the payroll. Or an even more damaging question might be, "Why did that employee receive satisfactory performance ratings (or perhaps even merit raises)?"

Such contradictions in practice can only aid employees in successfully challenging management's corrective actions. Unfortunately, some supervisors try to build a case to justify their corrective actions only after they have decided that a particular employee should be discharged. The following are common reasons given by supervisors for their failure to impose a disciplinary penalty:[35]

1. The supervisor had failed to document earlier actions, so no record existed on which to base subsequent disciplinary action.
2. Supervisors believed they would receive little or no support from higher management for the disciplinary action.
3. The supervisor was uncertain of the facts underlying the situation requiring disciplinary action.
4. Failure by the supervisor to discipline employees in the past for a certain infraction caused the supervisor to forgo current disciplinary action in order to appear consistent.
5. The supervisor wanted to be seen as a likable person.

Figure 13.6	Common Disciplinary Problems

ATTENDANCE PROBLEMS

- Unexcused absence
- Chronic absenteeism
- Unexcused/excessive tardiness
- Leaving without permission

DISHONESTY AND RELATED PROBLEMS

- Theft
- Falsifying employment application
- Willfully damaging organizational property
- Punching another employee's time card
- Falsifying work records

WORK PERFORMANCE PROBLEMS

- Failure to complete work assignments
- Producing substandard products or services
- Failure to meet established production requirements

ON-THE-JOB BEHAVIOUR PROBLEMS

- Intoxication at work
- Insubordination
- Horseplay
- Smoking in unauthorized places
- Fighting
- Gambling
- Failure to use safety devices
- Failure to report injuries
- Carelessness
- Sleeping on the job
- Using abusive or threatening language with supervisors
- Possession of narcotics or alcohol
- Possession of firearms or other weapons
- Sexual harassment

Setting Organizational Rules

The setting of organizational rules is the foundation for an effective disciplinary system. These rules govern the type of behaviour expected of employees. Organizations as diverse as Gerber Products, Steelcase, and Pitney Bowes have written policies explaining the type of conduct required of employees. Because employee behaviour standards are established through the setting of organizational rules and regulations, the following suggestions may help reduce problems in this area:

1. Rules should be widely disseminated and known to all employees. It should not be assumed that employees know all the rules.

2. Rules should be reviewed periodically—perhaps annually—especially those rules critical to work success.

3. The reasons for a rule should always be explained. Acceptance of an organizational rule is greater when employees understand the reasons behind it.

4. Rules should always be written. Ambiguity should be avoided, as this can result in different interpretations of the rules by different supervisors.

5. Rules must be reasonable and relate to the safe and efficient operation of the organization. Rules should not be made simply because of personal likes or dislikes.

6. If management has been lax in the enforcement of a rule, the rule must be restated, along with the consequences for its violation, before disciplinary action can begin.

7. Employees should sign a document stating that they have read and understand the organizational rules.

When seeking reasons for unsatisfactory behaviour, supervisors must keep in mind that employees may not be aware of certain work rules. Before initiating any disciplinary action, therefore, it is essential that supervisors determine whether they have given their employees careful and thorough orientation in the rules and regulations relating to their jobs. In fact, the proper communication of organizational rules and regulations is so important that arbitrators cite *neglect in communicating rules* as a major reason for reversing the disciplinary action taken against an employee.[36]

The Hot-Stove Approach to Rule Enforcement

hot-stove rule
A rule of discipline that can be compared with a hot stove in that it gives warning, is effective immediately, is enforced consistently, and applies to all employees in an impersonal and unbiased way

Regardless of the reason for the disciplinary action, it should be taken as soon as possible after the infraction has occurred and a complete investigation has been conducted. HR professionals often use the **hot-stove rule** to explain the correct application of discipline. A hot stove gives warning that it should not be touched. Those who ignore the warning and touch it are assured of being burned. The punishment is an immediate and direct consequence of breaking the rule never to touch a hot stove. Likewise, a work rule should apply to all employees and should be enforced consistently and in an impersonal and unbiased way. Employees should know the consequences of violating the rule, so that it has preventive value.

objective **5**

discipline
(1) Treatment that punishes, (2) orderly behaviour in an organizational setting, or (3) training that moulds and strengthens desirable conduct—or corrects undesirable conduct—and develops self-control

Defining Discipline

In management seminars conducted by the authors of this text, when managers are asked to define the word **discipline,** their most frequent response is that discipline means punishment. Although this answer is not incorrect, it is only one of three possible meanings. As normally defined, **discipline** has these meanings:

1. Treatment that punishes
2. Orderly behaviour in an organizational setting
3. Training that moulds and strengthens desirable conduct—or corrects undesirable conduct—and develops self-control

To some managers, discipline is synonymous with force. They equate the term with the punishment of employees who violate rules or regulations. Other managers think

© PHOTODISC RED/GETTY IMAGES

Discipline should never be viewed as punishment but rather as a way to correct undesirable employee behaviour.

of discipline as a general state of affairs—a condition of orderliness in which employees conduct themselves according to standards of acceptable behaviour. Discipline viewed in this manner can be considered positive when employees willingly practise self-control and respect organizational rules.

The third definition considers discipline a management tool used to correct undesirable employee behaviour. Discipline is applied as a constructive means of getting employees to conform to acceptable standards of performance. Many organizations define *discipline* in their policy manuals as training that "corrects, moulds, or perfects knowledge, attitudes, behaviour, or conduct." Discipline is thus viewed as a way to correct poor employee performance. As these organizations emphasize, discipline should be seen as a method of training employees to perform better or to improve their job attitudes or work behaviour.

When taken against employees, disciplinary action should never be thought of as punishment. Discipline can embody a penalty as a means of obtaining a desired result; however, punishment should not be the intent of disciplinary action. Rather, discipline must have as its goal the improvement of the employee's future behaviour. To apply discipline in any other way—as punishment or as a way of getting even with employees—can only invite problems for management, including possible wrongful discharge suits.

Investigating the Disciplinary Problem

It's a rare manager who has a good, intuitive sense of how to investigate employee misconduct. Too frequently investigations are conducted in a haphazard manner; worse, they overlook one or more investigative concerns.[37] In conducting an employee investigation, it is important to be objective and to avoid the assumptions, suppositions, and biases that often surround discipline cases. Figure 13.7 on page 578 lists seven questions to consider in investigating an employee offence. Attending to each question will help ensure a full and fair investigation while providing reliable information free from personal prejudice.[38]

Documentation of Employee Misconduct

"It's too complicated." "I just didn't take time to do it." "I have more important things to do." These are some of the frequent excuses used by managers who have failed to document cases of employee misconduct. The most significant cause of inadequate documentation, however, is that managers have no idea of what constitutes good documentation. Unfortunately, the failure of managers to record employee misconduct accurately can result in the reversal of any subsequent disciplinary action. The maintenance of *accurate* and *complete* work records, therefore, is an essential part of an effective disciplinary system. For documentation to be complete, the following eight items should be included:

1. Date, time, and location of the incident(s)
2. Negative performance or behaviour exhibited by the employee—the problem

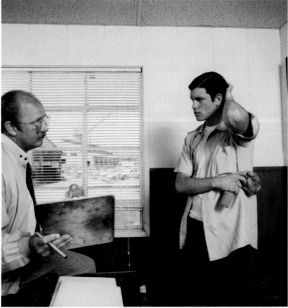

An investigative interview should always be held in private and should elicit the comments and concerns of the employee.

3. Consequences of that action or behaviour on the employee's overall work performance and/or the operation of the employee's work unit

4. Prior discussion(s) with the employee about the problem

5. Disciplinary action to be taken and specific improvement expected

6. Consequences if improvement is not made, and a follow-up date

7. The employee's reaction to the supervisor's attempt to change behaviour

8. The names of witnesses to the incident (if appropriate)

When preparing documentation, it is important for a manager to record the incident immediately after the infraction takes place, when the memory of it is still fresh, and to ensure that the record is complete and accurate. Documentation need not be lengthy, but it must include the eight points in the preceding list. Remember, a manager's records of employee misconduct are considered business documents, and as such they are admissible as evidence in arbitration hearings, administrative proceedings, and courts of law. As noted by one manager at a seminar on discipline, "When taking corrective action against an employee, the importance of compiling a complete and objective disciplinary record simply cannot be overstated."

The Investigative Interview

Before any disciplinary action is initiated, an investigative interview should be conducted to make sure employees are fully aware of the offence.[39] This interview is necessary because the supervisor's perceptions of the employee's behaviour may not be entirely accurate.[40] The interview should concentrate on how the offence violated the performance and behaviour standards of the job. It should avoid getting into personalities or areas unrelated to job performance. Most important, the employee must be given a full opportunity to explain his or her side of the issue so that any deficiencies for which the organization may be responsible are revealed.

Approaches to Disciplinary Action

objective 6

If a thorough investigation shows that an employee has violated some organization rule, disciplinary action must be imposed. Two approaches to disciplinary action are progressive discipline and positive discipline.

Progressive Discipline

progressive discipline
Application of corrective measures by increasing degrees

Generally, discipline is imposed in a progressive manner. By definition, **progressive discipline** is the application of corrective measures by increasing degrees. Progressive discipline is designed to motivate an employee to correct his or her misconduct voluntarily. The technique is aimed at nipping the problem in the bud, using only enough corrective action to remedy the shortcoming. However, the sequence and severity of the disciplinary action vary with the type of offence and the circumstances surrounding it. Because each situation is unique, a number of factors must be considered in determining how severe a disciplinary action should be. Some of the factors to consider are listed in Figure 13.7.

The typical progressive discipline procedure includes four steps. From an oral warning (or counselling) that subsequent unsatisfactory behaviour or performance will not be tolerated, the action may progress to a written warning, to a suspension without pay, and ultimately to discharge. The "capital punishment" of discharge is utilized only as a last resort. Organizations normally use lower forms of disciplinary action for less severe performance problems. It is important for managers to remember that three important things occur when progressive discipline is applied properly:

1. Employees always know where they stand regarding offences.
2. Employees know what improvement is expected of them.
3. Employees understand what will happen next if improvement is not made.

Figure 13.7	Considerations in Disciplinary Investigations

1. In very specific terms, what is the offence charged?
   - Is management sure it fully understands the charge against the employee?
   - Was the employee really terminated for insubordination, or did the employee merely refuse a request by management?
2. Did the employee know he or she was doing something wrong?
   - What rule or provision was violated?
   - How would the employee know of the existence of the rule?
   - Was the employee warned of the consequence?
3. Is the employee guilty?
   - What are the sources of facts?
   - Is there direct or only indirect evidence of guilt?
   - Has anyone talked to the employee to hear his or her side of the situation?
4. Are there extenuating circumstances?
   - Were conflicting orders given by different supervisors?
   - Does anybody have reason to want to "get" this employee?
   - Was the employee provoked by a manager or another employee?
5. Has the rule been uniformly enforced?
   - Have all managers applied this rule consistently?
   - What punishment have previous offenders received?
   - Were any other employees involved in this offence?
6. Is the offence related to the workplace?
   - Is there evidence that the offence hurt the organization?
   - Is management making a moral judgment or a business judgment?
7. What is the employee's past work record?
   - How many years of service has the employee given the organization?
   - How many years or months has the employee held the present job?
   - What is the employee's personnel record as a whole, especially his or her disciplinary record?

Positive Discipline

Some HR professionals believe that progressive discipline has certain flaws, including its intimidating and adversarial nature, that prevent it from achieving the intended purpose. For these reasons, organizations are using an approach called **positive,** or **nonpunitive, discipline.** Positive discipline is based on the concept that employees must assume responsibility for their personal conduct and job performance.[41]

positive, or nonpunitive, discipline
A system of discipline that focuses on early correction of employee misconduct, with the employee taking total responsibility for correcting the problem

Positive discipline requires a cooperative environment in which the employee and the supervisor engage in joint discussion and problem solving to resolve incidents of employee irresponsibility. The approach focuses on early correction of misconduct, with the employee taking total responsibility for resolving the problem. Nothing is imposed by management; all solutions and affirmations are jointly reached. HR managers often describe positive discipline as "nonpunitive discipline that replaces threats and punishment with encouragement."

While positive discipline appears similar to progressive discipline, its emphasis is on giving employees reminders rather than reprimands as a way to improve performance. The technique is implemented in three steps. The first is a conference between the employee and the supervisor. The purpose of this meeting is to find a solution to the problem through discussion, with oral agreement by the employee to improve his or her performance. The supervisor refrains from reprimanding the employee or threatening him or her with further disciplinary action. Supervisors may document this conference, but a written record of this meeting is not placed in the employee's file unless the misconduct occurs again.

If improvement is not made after this first step, the supervisor holds a second conference with the employee to determine why the solution agreed to in the first conference did not work. At this stage, however, a written reminder is given to the employee. This document states the new or repeated solution to the problem, with an affirmation that improvement is the responsibility of the employee and a condition of continued employment.

When both conferences fail to produce the desired results, the third step is to give the employee a one-day *decision-making leave* (a paid leave). The purpose of this paid leave is for the employee to decide whether he or she wishes to continue working for the organization. The organization pays for this leave to demonstrate its desire to retain the person. Also, paying for the leave eliminates the negative effects for the employee of losing a day's pay. Employees given a decision-making leave are instructed to return the following day with a decision either to make a total commitment to improve performance or to quit the organization. If a commitment is not made, the employee is dismissed with the assumption that he or she lacked responsibility toward the organization. The positive discipline process used by Banner Health is shown in Highlights in HRM 13.3 on page 580 and the one used by Volkswagen Canada is described in Highlights in HRM 13.4 on page 582.

Discharging Employees

When employees fail to conform to organizational rules and regulations, the final disciplinary action in many cases is discharge. Because discharge has such serious consequences for the employee—and possibly for the organization—it should be undertaken only after a deliberate and thoughtful review of the case. If an employee is fired, he or she may file a wrongful discharge suit claiming the termination was "without just or sufficient cause," implying a lack of fair treatment by management.

If an employee termination is to be upheld for good cause, what constitutes fair employee treatment? This question is not easily answered, but standards governing

Highlights in HRM 13.3

The Banner Health System Performance Recognition Policy

Recognition is the foundation of the Performance Recognition process. It is based on the belief that you have control over your own behaviour and are accountable for your actions. Your desire to exhibit the behaviours that are expected of Banner Health employees can be directly affected by the feedback you receive. Sincerely expressed appreciation affirms that you are making a difference and adding value to the organization. Recognition can also indicate to you when performance enhancement or improvement needs to occur. When you experience this recognition, your efforts can increase, as well as your satisfaction with your workplace.

Coaching

Each of us has been involved in coaching at some time. When we coach each other, within or outside of our own department, we provide feedback, guidance, and training. Our goal is always to help someone be successful.

Coaching may be formal or informal, based upon the seriousness of the performance problem. Formal coaching is a structured process requiring you to develop a mutually agreed-upon plan of action for improvement.

Supervisors generally coach for one of two reasons:

- Performance Enhancement: These discussions help us by clarifying expectations, providing feedback, identifying opportunities for development in reaching our goals, and recognizing our accomplishments. The supervisor may document these discussions as a reminder to a follow-up, or as a means of tracking progress in meeting our goals.
- Performance Improvement: These discussions occur if there is a recognized need for improvement in performance. Coaching objectives include clarification of expectations, identification of the cause for current performance not meeting those expectations, development of effective solutions, and commitment to correct the problem.

Formal Discipline

If performance does not improve after coaching, or a single incident occurs that warrants a more serious response, the supervisor may apply the Formal Discipline levels of Performance Recognition. *This Formal Discipline process does not apply to employees in their Conditional Period or to those in a Supplemental position.* At each step in the Formal Discipline process, a sincere effort will be made to encourage you to take responsibility for your problem and commit to making a change. Recognition and coaching may occur between the levels of the Formal Discipline process to provide you feedback on your progress, and to identify concerns.

Levels of Formal Discipline

1. Initial Reminder

The Initial Reminder requires a formal discussion between the supervisor and the employee. This is the first level of Formal Discipline, and should be used when a performance problem has not been corrected through coaching. It may also be used if the seriousness of the problem warrants beginning at the Initial Reminder level without previous coaching.

2. Advanced Reminder

The Advanced Reminder is the second level of the Formal Discipline process, and should be used if continued or additional performance problems have occurred following the Initial Reminder. The Advanced Reminder level of Formal Discipline may also be used if the seriousness of the problem warrants a more advanced level of Formal Discipline.

A memo summarizing the discussion and reinforcing the need for improvement will be written and discussed with you. Your supervisor will follow up to ensure the problem has been corrected and to recognize performance improvement.

3. Decision-Making Leave (DML)

The DML is the last formal level in the Performance Recognition process. This step is taken as a result of a sustained or serious performance problem. Following a discussion of the problem and your failure to live up to the agreement for correcting the problem, you will be given a day of leave with pay (*not* from your PTO hours) to seriously consider your intentions of making a total commitment to improve your performance.

Upon return from the DML, if your decision is to make an immediate and sustained improvement in your overall work performance, you will report this to your supervisor. You and your supervisor will develop an action plan. If you decide not to meet performance expectations, you may return to work under directed compliance or you may resign. You will be given a memo summarizing the DML discussion and your decision.

Deactivation

If you maintain an overall satisfactory work record after a formal level of discipline, your immediate supervisor will acknowledge improvement. If you have not received any additional Formal Discipline, the previous Formal Discipline will no longer be active after the following time periods: Initial Reminder, 6 months; Advanced Reminder, 12 months; Decision-Making Leave, 12 months.

Crisis Suspension

Certain types of incidents warrant removing you immediately from the workplace. These incidents would require the supervisor to address the problem immediately; for an example, a safety or security issue, or any offense when a DML or termination may be the appropriate level of response for the first occurrence. If termination is likely, you will be removed from the work schedule until the completion of the investigation. Crisis suspension requires consultation with Human Resources/Employee Relations.

Termination

Termination may occur when:

- Following the DML, you do not immediately improve and maintain an overall satisfactory work record, or
- You commit an offence so serious that progressing through the Formal Discipline levels of Performance Recognition is not warranted.

Termination is not a formal step in the Performance Recognition process, but is the result of your refusal or inability to meet the performance expectations.

Source: Adapted from Banner Health Performance Recognition Policy. Used with Permission of Banner Health.

Highlights in HRM 13.4

Volkswagen Canada's Positive Discipline Program

Positive discipline is a method for attempting to solve employee problems before they develop into serious situations. It treats employees as adults and emphasizes turning inappropriate behaviour around instead of punishing employees every time they do something wrong. Positive discipline relies on frontline coaching and counselling to help employees identify inappropriate behaviour; it also suggests ways of turning that behaviour around. Positive discipline allows supervisors to treat their fellow employees in a fair and consistent manner. Most employees will respond to coaching and counselling. For employees who do not correct their behaviour—or who are involved in an incident so serious that coaching or counselling is deemed inappropriate—there are steps in place to impress on every employee the seriousness of their actions and the consequences of continued poor behaviour. The following is a general outline of the program.

There are five general methods used in the Positive Discipline Program:

- Coaching and Counselling
- Step 1: Verbal Reminder
- Step 2: Written Warning
- Step 3: Decision Making
- Step 4: Termination

There are three categories of work rule violations:

- Work Performance
- Attendance
- Misconduct

There are three degrees of severity of workplace violations:

- Minor
- Major
- Grave

There are two other major ingredients of the Positive Discipline Program:

- Praise
- Goal Setting

Guidelines

- The union, if requested, may be involved in every step of the discipline process, but must be involved in Step 1 and higher.
- An employee may, under certain circumstances, be sent home with or without pay pending an investigation into the incident. The union should be involved in any investigation into serious incidents.
- Counselling should be the preferred method of correcting behaviour when a problem first appears.
- Praise should be used often, whenever an employee has corrected a potential problem, had a step deactivated, performed beyond his/her normal duties, or any other time the supervisor feels it is appropriate. This praise should be done both orally and in writing.

- Goal setting should be used at every step in the disciplinary process in order to ensure both the supervisor and the employee know exactly what is expected of them.
- This program is aimed at those very few employees who insist on conducting themselves in an inappropriate manner. The vast majority of our employees may never have to encounter the various steps of this program.

Source: Donald McQuirter, Manager of Human Resources, Volkswagen Canada Inc.

just-cause discharge do exist. These rules consist of a set of guidelines that are applied by arbitrators to dismissal cases to determine if management had just cause for the termination. These guidelines are normally set forth in the form of questions, provided in Figure 13.8. For example, before discharging an employee, did the manager forewarn the person of possible disciplinary action? A no answer to any of the seven questions in Figure 13.8 generally means that just cause was not established and that management's decision to terminate was arbitrary, capricious, or discriminatory. The significance of these guidelines is that they are being applied not only by arbitrators in discharge cases, but also by judges in wrongful discharge suits. It is critical that managers at all levels understand the just cause guidelines, including their proper application. Reality shows such as *The Apprentice,* in which Donald Trump fires someone every week, demonstrate termination procedures that would ensure employee litigation in Canada (see Highlights HRM 13.5 on page 584).

Informing the Employee

Regardless of the reasons for a discharge, it should be done with personal consideration for the employee affected. Every effort should be made to ease the trauma a discharge creates.[42] The employee must be informed honestly, yet tactfully, of the exact

Figure 13.8	"Just Cause" Discharge Guidelines

1. Did the organization forewarn the employee of the possible disciplinary consequences of his or her action?
2. Were management's requirements of the employee reasonable in relation to the orderly, efficient, and safe operation of the organization's business?
3. Did management, before discharging the employee, make a reasonable effort to establish that the employee's performance was unsatisfactory?
4. Was the organization's investigation conducted in a fair and objective manner?
5. Did the investigation produce sufficient evidence of proof of guilt as charged?
6. Has management treated this employee under its rules, orders, and penalties as it has other employees in similar circumstances?
7. Did the discharge fit the misconduct, considering the seriousness of proven offence, the employee's service record, and any mitigating circumstances?

Highlights in HRM 13.5

You're Fired!

Donald Trump's catch phrase, "you're fired," is familiar to the thousands who watched *The Apprentice,* a popular reality show where contestants compete to be Trump's apprentice, and where, each week, at least one competitor is fired. But Canadian managers should not view Trump as a role model, because he makes ten termination mistakes:

1. Each person being terminated is brought into a boardroom where he or she is terminated in front of his or her peers, not in private with Trump.
2. They are terminated not only in front of their peers, but also with two of Trump's advisers watching, thereby creating a firing squad-like atmosphere. There should only be one adviser and Trump.
3. Prior to termination, all of the team members know that one of the select group being pulled into the boardroom will be terminated. The termination should be kept secret among only senior management.
4. The person being terminated is advised of all the things that they did wrong. They are never given a warning and the chance to correct the behaviour before being fired.
5. They are terminated for cause where there is likely no legal cause for their termination.
6. They are terminated without being provided what they are entitled to under applicable employment standards legislation.
7. They are terminated without reasonable notice of termination or compensation in lieu of notice pursuant to the employer's obligation under common law.
8. They are not provided with a letter of reference, outplacement counselling, or anything that will assist them in the transition to new employment.
9. They may have been enticed to leave secure employment to be "employed" by Trump, which would increase Trump's liability when firing them.
10. An employee terminated in this manner would likely be entitled to significant "Wallace" damages. That is because they were ostracized in front of their peers and Trump's advisers, terminated with cause when there was no cause, and made to feel worthless.

Source: Adapted from Natalie MacDonald, "Great Television Does Not Translate Into Great Policy," *Canadian HR Reporter,* January 31, 2005, R 9.

reasons for the action. Such candour can help the employee face the problem and adjust to it in a constructive manner.

Managers may wish to discuss, and even rehearse, with their peers the upcoming termination meeting. This practice can ensure that all important points are covered while giving confidence to the manager. While managers agree that there is no single right way to conduct the discharge meeting, the following guidelines will help make the discussion more effective:

1. Come to the point within the first two or three minutes, and list in a logical order all reasons for the termination.
2. Be straightforward and firm, yet tactful, and remain resolute in your decision.
3. Make the discussion private, businesslike, and fairly brief.

4. Don't mix the good with the bad. Trying to sugarcoat the problem sends a mixed message to the employee.

5. Avoid making accusations against the employee and injecting personal feelings into the discussion.

6. Avoid bringing up any personality differences between you and the employee.

7. Provide any information concerning severance pay and the status of benefits and coverage.

8. Explain how you will handle employment inquiries from future employers.[43]

Termination meetings should be held in a neutral location, such as a conference room, to prevent the employee from feeling unfairly treated. When discussing the termination, management must never provoke the employee or allow the employee to become belligerent toward management. Should the employee become agitated, or show signs of hostility, the meeting should be stopped immediately with notification given to security or the HR department.

Finally, when terminated employees are escorted off the premises, the removal must not serve to defame the employee. Managers should not give peers the impression that the terminated employee was dishonest or untrustworthy. Furthermore, managers are advised never to discuss the discharge or "bad-mouth" the terminated employee with other employees, customers, or other individuals.

Due Process

Management has traditionally possessed the right to direct employees and to take corrective action when needed. Nevertheless, when employees are alleged to have violated organizational rules, many individuals also believe that employees should not be disciplined without the protection of due process. HR managers normally define due process as the employee's right to be heard—the right of the employee to tell his or her side of the story regarding the alleged infraction of organizational rules. Due process serves to ensure that a full and fair investigation of employee misconduct occurs. Normally, due process is provided employees through the employer's appeals procedure. However, proactive employers will additionally incorporate the following principles—or rights—in their interpretation of due process:

1. The right to know job expectations and the consequences of not fulfilling those expectations.

2. The right to consistent and predictable management action for the violation of rules.

3. The right to fair discipline based on facts, the right to question those facts, and the right to present a defence.

4. The right to progressive discipline.

5. The right to appeal disciplinary action.

alternative dispute resolution (ADR)
A term applied to different types of employee complaint or dispute resolution procedures

Alternative Dispute Resolution Procedures

In unionized workplaces, grievance procedures are stated in virtually all collective agreements. In nonunion organizations, however, **alternative dispute resolution (ADR)** procedures are a developing method to address employee complaints.[44] The employer's interest stems from the desire to meet employees' expectations for fair treatment in the workplace while guaranteeing them due process—in the hope of minimizing discrimination claims or wrongful discharge suits.[45]

Step-Review Systems

As Figure 13.9 illustrates, a **step-review system** is based on a pre-established set of steps—normally four—for the review of an employee complaint by successively higher levels of management. These procedures are patterned after the union grievance systems we will discuss in Chapter 14. For example, they normally require that the employee's complaint be formalized as a written statement. Managers at each step are required to provide a full response to the complaint within a specified time period, perhaps three to five working days.

An employee is sometimes allowed to bypass the meeting with his or her immediate supervisor if the employee fears reprisal from this person. Unlike appeal systems in unionized organizations, however, nonunion appeal procedures ordinarily do not provide for a neutral third party—such as an arbitrator—to serve as the judge of last resort. In most step-review systems, the president, chief executive officer, vice-president, or HR director acts as the final authority, and this person's decision is not appealable. Some organizations give employees assistance in preparing their complaint cases. For example, an employee who desires it may be able to get advice and counsel from a designated person in the HR department before discussing the issue with management.

Unfortunately, step-review systems may not yield their intended benefits. Employees may believe that management is slow in responding to complaints and that management's response often does not solve the problem. Furthermore, employees may believe that, regardless of policies forbidding reprisal, supervisors would still hold it against them if they exercised their rights as spelled out in the step-review system. These concerns should not lead to the conclusion that all step-review systems are ineffective, but rather that management must take special precautions to ensure that the systems work and provide the benefits intended.

Peer-Review Systems

A **peer-review system,** also called a complaint committee, is composed of equal numbers of employee representatives and management appointees. Employee representatives are normally elected by secret ballot by their co-workers for a rotating term, whereas management representatives are assigned, also on a rotating basis. A peer-review system functions as a jury because its members weigh evidence, consider arguments, and, after deliberation, vote independently to render a final decision.

Organizations consider one of the benefits of the peer-review system to be the sense of justice that it creates among employees. The peer-review system can be used as the sole method for resolving employee complaints, or it can be used in conjunction with a step-review system. For example, if an employee is not satisfied with management's action at step 1 or 2 in the step-review system, the employee can submit the complaint to the peer-review committee for final resolution.

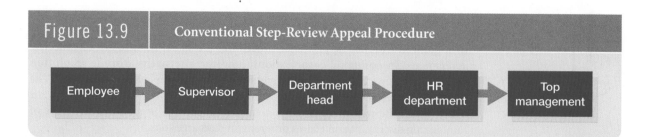

Figure 13.9   Conventional Step-Review Appeal Procedure

Employee → Supervisor → Department head → HR department → Top management

Open-Door Policy

open-door policy
A policy of settling grievances that identifies various levels of management above the immediate supervisor for employee contact

The open-door policy is an old standby for settling employee complaints. The traditional **open-door policy** identifies various levels of management above the immediate supervisor that an aggrieved employee may contact; the levels may extend as high as a vice-president, president, or chief executive officer. Typically the person who acts as "the court of last resort" is the HR director or a senior staff official.

The problems with an open-door policy are well documented. Two of its major weaknesses are the unwillingness of managers to listen honestly to employee complaints and worker reluctance to approach managers with their complaints. As an employee once told the authors of this text, "My manager has an open-door policy but the door is only open one inch." Obviously this employee felt he had little opportunity to get through to his manager. Other problems are attributed to this system as well. The open-door policy generally fails to guarantee consistent decision making because what is fair to one manager may seem unfair to another. Higher-level managers tend to support supervisors for fear of undermining authority. And, as a system of justice, open-door policies may lack credibility with employees. Still, the open-door policy is often successful when it is supported by all levels of management and when management works to maintain a reputation for being fair and open-minded.

Ombudsperson System

ombudsperson
A designated individual from whom employees may seek counsel for resolution of their complaints

An **ombudsperson** is a designated individual from whom employees may seek counsel for the resolution of their complaints. The ombudsperson listens to an employee's complaint and attempts to resolve it by seeking an equitable solution between the employee and the supervisor. This individual works cooperatively with both sides to reach a settlement, often employing a problem-solving approach to the issue. Because the ombudsperson has no authority to finalize a solution to the problem, compromises are highly possible and all concerned tend to feel satisfied with the outcome.

To function successfully, ombudspeople must be able to operate in an atmosphere of confidentiality that does not threaten the security of the managers or subordinates who are involved in a complaint. For example, complaints of sexual harassment, abuse of power, or issues that deal with circumstances that violate the law or unethical behaviour (whistleblowing) require high degrees of confidentiality to protect those involved. While ombudspeople do not have the power to decide employee complaints, it is recommended that they have access to high levels of management to ensure that employee complaints receive fair treatment.

Mediation

mediation
The use of an impartial neutral to reach a compromise decision in employment disputes

mediator
A third party in an employment dispute who meets with one party and then the other in order to suggest compromise solutions or to recommend concessions from each side that will lead to an agreement

Along with arbitration, mediation is fast becoming a popular way to resolve employee complaints. **Mediation** employs a third-party neutral (called a mediator) to help employees and managers reach voluntary agreement acceptable to both parties. The essence of mediation is compromise. The **mediator** holds a meeting with the employee and management, listens to the position of each side, gathers facts, then, through discussion, suggestions, and persuasion obtains an agreement that will satisfy the needs and requirements of both sides. A mediator serves primarily as a fact finder and to open up a channel of communication between the parties. Unlike arbitrators, mediators have no power or authority to force either side toward an agreement. They must use their communication skills and the power of persuasion to help the parties resolve their differences. A cornerstone of mediation is that the parties maintain control over the settlement outcome.

Mediation is a flexible process that can be shaped to meet the demands of the parties. Also, it can be used to resolve a wide range of employee complaints, including discrimination claims or traditional workplace disputes.[46] Employees like the process because of its informality. According to one authority, "Mediation might be described as a private discussion assisted by an impartial third party."[47] Settlements fashioned through mediation are readily acceptable by the parties, thus promoting a favourable working relationship.

Arbitration

At the 1996 Summer Olympics, the athletes were required by the International Olympic Committee (IOC) to agree to take any Olympic dispute (including those over drug testing) to a special arbitration panel for a binding decision. The point of this was to avoid costly and disruptive battles in U.S. courts.[48]

In the same vein, private employers may require employees to submit their employment disputes to binding arbitration. (Arbitration is discussed in depth in Chapter 14.) Arbitration can save litigation costs and avoid time delays and unfavourable publicity. However, to ensure that their arbitration policies are legal, employers must

- have a clear, well-defined, and widely communicated arbitration policy;
- specify those topics subject to arbitration;
- inform employees of the rights they are relinquishing by signing an arbitration agreement;
- provide a procedurally fair arbitration system; and
- allow for the nonbiased selection of an arbitrator or arbitration panel.[49]

Managerial Ethics in Employee Relations

objective **8**

ethics
A set of standards of conduct and moral judgments that help to determine right and wrong behaviour

Throughout this textbook we have emphasized the legal requirements of HRM. Laws, agency rulings, and court decisions impact all aspects of the employment process—recruitment, selection, performance appraisal, safety and health, labour relations, and testing. Managers must comply with governmental regulations to promote an environment free from litigation.

However, beyond what is required by the law is the question of organizational ethics and the ethical—or unethical—behaviour engaged in by managers. **Ethics** can be defined as a set of standards of acceptable conduct and moral judgment. Ethics provides cultural guidelines—organizational or societal—that help us decide between proper or improper conduct. Therefore, ethics, like the legal aspects of HR, permeates all aspects of the employment relationship. For example, managers may adhere to the organization's objective of hiring members from the designated groups, but how those employees are supervised and treated once employed gets to the issue of managerial ethics. We have presented Ethics in HRM boxes in each chapter of this book to illustrate the complexity of ethical dilemmas.

Compliance with laws and the behavioural treatment of employees are two completely different aspects of the manager's job. While ethical dilemmas will always occur in the supervision of employees, it is how employees are treated that largely distinguishes the ethical organization from the unethical one. Interestingly, a recent research study, *Employee Trust and Organizational Loyalty,* sponsored by the Society for Human Resource Management, showed that employee perceptions of ethical behaviour by their organizational leadership may be the most important driver of employee trust and loyalty. According to the study, of critical interest to employees is the consistent and credible communication of information about the organization's ethical standards and its values, the organization's mission, and its workplace policies.[50] We believe that managerial ethics in employee relations requires honesty in all dealings between employees and their managers, including mutual respect throughout the performance of workplace duties.

Many organizations have their own code of ethics that governs relations with employees and the public at large.[51] This written code focuses attention on ethical values and provides a basis for the organization, and individual managers, to evaluate their plans and actions. HR departments have been given a greater role in communicating the organization's values and standards, monitoring compliance with its code of ethics, and enforcing the standards throughout the organization. Organizations now have ethics committees and ethics ombudspeople to provide training in ethics to employees. The ultimate goal of ethics training is to avoid unethical behaviour and adverse publicity; to gain a strategic advantage; and, most of all, to treat employees in a fair and equitable manner, recognizing them as productive members of the organization.

SUMMARY

There are three legal considerations involving job security. Statutory rights are rights that derive from legislation. Contractual rights derive from contracts, which are legally binding agreements. Due process refers to the rights of employees to present their positions during a disciplinary action.

Both employees and employers have rights and expectations in the employment relationship. The due-process right of employees is the right for them to express their views concerning an incident; statutory and contractual rights have to do with the rights of employees and employers to terminate the employment relationship. Under the implied contract concept, an employer's oral or written statements may form a contractual obligation that can preclude the automatic termination of employees.

Once employed, employees expect certain rights regarding fair and equitable treatment on the job. These rights extend over such issues as substance abuse and drug testing, searches and surveillance, off-duty privacy, e-mail and voice mail privacy, and plant closing notification.

The HR department, in combination with other managers, should establish disciplinary policies. This will help achieve both acceptance of the policy and its consistent application. To reduce the need for discipline, organizational rules and procedures should be widely known, reviewed on a regular basis, and written and explained to employees. The rules must relate to the safe and efficient operation of the organization. When managers overlook the enforcement of rules, they must re-emphasize the rule and its enforcement before disciplining an employee.

The term *discipline* has three meanings—punishment, orderly behaviour, and training of employee conduct. When used with employees, discipline should serve to correct undesirable employee behaviour, creating within the employee a desire for self-control. This third definition of discipline can be achieved only when managers conduct a complete and unbiased investigation of employee misconduct. Investigation of employee misconduct begins with proper documentation of wrongdoing. When managers are investigating employee problems they need to know specifically the infraction of the employee, whether the employee knew of the rule violated, and any extenuating circumstances that might justify the employee's conduct. When employees are to receive discipline, the rule must be uniformly enforced and the past work record of the employee must be considered.

The two approaches to discipline are progressive discipline and positive discipline. Progressive discipline follows a series of steps based on increasing the degrees of corrective action. The corrective action applied should match the severity of the employee misconduct. Positive discipline, based on reminders, is a cooperative discipline approach in which employees accept responsibility for the desired employee improvement. The focus is on coping with the unsatisfactory performance and dissatisfactions of employees before the problems become major.

 Alternative dispute resolution procedures present ways by which employees exercise their due-process rights. The most common forms of ADR are step-review systems, peer-review systems, the open-door policy, the ombudsperson system, mediation, and arbitration.

Ethics in HRM extends beyond the legal requirements of managing employees. Managers engage in ethical behaviour when employees are treated in an objective and fair way and when an employee's personal and work-related rights are respected and valued.

KEY TERMS

alternative dispute resolution (ADR), 585
constructive dismissal, 560
contractual rights, 557
discipline, 575
due process, 558
employee rights, 556
ethics, 588

hot-stove rule, 575
mediation, 587
mediator, 587
negligence, 557
ombudsperson, 587
open-door policy, 587
peer-review system, 586

positive, or nonpunitive, discipline, 579
progressive discipline, 577
psychological contract, 559
statutory rights, 557
step-review system, 586
whistleblowing, 562

DISCUSSION QUESTIONS

1. Do you have a right to your job? What rights do you have with respect to employment?
2. Under what conditions can an employer monitor employees? Ask a group of working students the following questions:
   - Are you monitored at work?
   - What types of monitoring are used?
   - For what purposes does your employer monitor the workplace?
   - Do you object to the monitoring? If so, why? If not, why not?
3. Millions of people have created their own blogs, and many of these are employees who describe their working conditions, colleagues, and bosses. While employers should have a reasonable expectation that employees would not publicly criticize or defame the organization, do they have a right to control the "diaries" of employees?
4. If you were asked to develop a policy on discipline, what topics would you cover in the policy?
5. You have discovered that an employee has not been keeping client files updated, as is required by your company policy. Outline the steps that you would use to deal with this performance problem.
6. Discuss why documentation is so important to the disciplinary process. What constitutes correct documentation?
7. Describe progressive and positive discipline, noting the differences between these two approaches.
8. What do you think would constitute an effective alternative dispute resolution system? What benefits would you expect from such a system? If you were asked to rule on a discharge case, what facts would you analyze in deciding whether to uphold or reverse the employer's action?
9. In groups, discuss whether the following situations are fair or not fair:
   a. Zabeen was using the company Internet to locate a nursing home for her increasingly handicapped father. Her supervisor observed this and verified it with the Information Technology unit. Zabeen was given a written reprimand. Meanwhile, Sonia used the company telephone to do her personal banking and bill paying and was not reprimanded.

b. Anthony spent his lunch hour at the gym, consisting of a strenuous workout program with a personal trainer. Meanwhile, Nicholas met his friends for lunch, sharing several beers at the local pub. Both employees felt fatigued in the afternoon, and their diminished productivity was noticed by their supervisor. Nicholas was asked to meet with his supervisor to review performance standards, and received a verbal warning. Anthony was not.

INTERNET EXERCISE

Think of a situation in which two of your friends or colleagues are having a dispute. You wish to help them by resolving the conflict through meditation. As such you must possess certain characteristics and behave in certain ways. Go to the website of the Conflict Resolution Network (www.crnetwork.ca/standardsofconduct3.asp) and read about the standards of conduct and see if you are indeed the best mediator for this situation.

HRM Experience

Learning about Employee Rights

In the constantly changing field of human resources it is imperative that both HR managers and supervisors be aware of changes that affect the organization and the process of managing employees. Nowhere is this more true than in the growing field of employee rights. As employees demand more job and employment rights regarding drug testing, monitoring, unjust dismissals, off-duty conduct, and genetic testing, employers must be knowledgeable about new laws, court rulings, and the policies of other organizations that influence each area. This knowledge will enable managers to respond to these employee concerns in a positive and proactive manner. Failure to provide employees their rights could lead to costly and embarrassing lawsuits, resulting in diminished employee loyalty or morale. The purpose of this exercise, therefore, is to familiarize yourself with issues of employee rights.

Assignment

Working individually or in teams, for each of the following employee rights topics, identify and discuss the privacy concerns for both employees and employers. Answer the questions pertaining to each topic.

- Wrongful dismissal suits
- Substance abuse and drug testing
- Searches and monitoring
- Employee conduct away from the workplace
- Genetic testing
- E-mail, Internet

1. What is the issue concerned with?
2. Why is this issue of current interest to employees and managers?
3. What rights are employees demanding?
4. What, if any, laws or court cases affect this right?
5. Generally, how are employers responding to this employee right?

BIZFLIX EXERCISES

In Good Company: Firing an Employee

This scene from the film *In Good Company* shows Mark Steckle's (Clark Greg) efforts to fire Dan Foreman (Dennis Quaid) and Carter Duryea (Topher Grace). Carefully assess Mark's behaviour against the discussion of employee rights and discipline in this chapter.

A corporate takeover brings star advertising executive Dan Foreman a new boss who is half his age. Carter Duryea—Dan's new boss—wants to prove his worth as the new marketing chief at *Sports America*, Waterman Publishing's flagship magazine. Carter applies his unique approaches while dating Dan's daughter, Alex (Scarlett Johansson).

This scene comes from the "Teddy K. Is Coming" sequence near the film's end. It starts with Mark Steckle saying to Dan Foreman, "Look, we've been carrying your fat, bloated salary for way too long." This scene follows Teddy K.'s (Malcolm McDowell) synergy speech to the assembled employees of his recent acquisition, Waterman Publishing. The film continues with Carter and Dan carrying out their plan to get some new magazine advertising.

What to Watch for and Ask Yourself

- This chapter opened with the observation that managers and supervisors find it hard to discipline employees. Does this observation apply to Mark Steckle? Why or why not?
- Does Mark follow the suggestions shown in Figure 13.1 in trying to end the employment of Dan and Carter?
- The earlier section "Disciplinary Policies and Procedures" offered guidelines and observations on correct approaches to employee discipline. Does Mark follow any of those procedures? If not, which aspects of his behaviour deviate from the procedures described earlier?

case study 1

Improving Performance Through a Progressive Discipline Policy

Simon Ouellet, former president of the Human Resources Professionals Association of Ontario, was recruited by Fantom Technologies to be vice-president–Human Resources. Fantom is a manufacturer of state-of-the-art floor care products, based in southern Ontario.

One of the first issues he faced in his new job was an unacceptable absenteeism rate. There were about 250 employees on the three assembly lines, operating two shifts a day. The average employee was absent 13 or 14 days a year. The benchmark for other manufacturing sites was eight or nine days. Simon calculated that Fantom was employing between 30 and 35 extra people to cover absences. This hurt the bottom line.

A related problem was punctuality. Employees were habitually five or ten minutes late on their shifts. In a white-collar environment with flextime, this would not have been as critical. But tardiness in this situation meant that the assembly line could not operate, and that the other employees on the three lines were forced to remain idle.

The solution was to develop a system of progressive discipline. Simon prepared a simple two-page policy. Page 1 dealt with culpable absenteeism—the behaviour in the control of employees such as arriving late, leaving work without permission, calling in sick but playing golf, and so on. Page 2 dealt with legitimate or innocent absences. Simon met with the unions and notified them that this policy would come into effect as of December 1998. All employees started at zero absences at this time.

The policy assumed that all absences were innocent. However, if an employee was absent five times in a 12-month period, the supervisor met with that employee to express concern over the absences and to identify any need for counselling or assistance. The goal of the meeting was to express legitimate concerns, reinforce that the employee was needed, and ensure that the employee accepted responsibility for managing his or her own attendance. Following this meeting, if the employee had fewer than two absences in the ensuing six months, the employee was no longer part of the program. However, if the absence pattern continued, the employee was counselled a second and third time. If no improvements resulted, a level 4 employment status review was conducted. This was done on a case-by-case basis. For example, a frequently absent employee with 28 years of good service would be treated differently from another employee with the same absenteeism record but only two years of employment.

The results were impressive. About 70 employees entered the program. Of these, eight to ten advanced to step 2, two to step 3, and none to step 4. The absenteeism rate dropped to an average of less than ten days, and punctuality was no longer an issue. Labour costs were reduced, because it meant that 20 fewer employees were needed.

QUESTIONS

1. "The policy assumed that all absences were innocent." What do you think this means?
2. The policy was active as of December 1998, and all employees were treated equally from that date, regardless of their previous absenteeism records. Was this fair?
3. Could a policy of this type be developed to manage student punctuality and absenteeism?

case study 2

You Can't Fire Me! Check Your Policy

Supervisors report that discharging an employee is one of the toughest tasks they perform as managers. Furthermore, termination for absenteeism can be particularly difficult due to the causes of absenteeism, and, in some cases, the past work record of the employee. This case illustrates a typical absentee problem faced by management.

Mary Schwartz was employed by Beach Electrical Systems for nine years. For the first six years of her employment she was considered a model employee. Mary's annual performance reviews were always above average or exceptional and she was described by her managers as a loyal and dedicated employee. However, things changed rapidly in 2000 when Mary became, as her current manager stated, "an absentee problem."

According to HR department records, in 2001 and 2002 Mary was absent 12 percent and 19 percent of the time, respectively. Her worst year was 2003, when she was absent 27.2 percent of the time. However, unlike other absent employees, Mary was always absent because of genuine and verifiable illnesses or work-related accidents. Mary's supervisor had talked to her periodically about her attendance problem, but she was never given an official warning notice—oral or written—that she would be fired if her attendance record did not improve.

The incident that caused her termination occurred on Thursday, May 20, 2004. On that day her manager notified all department employees (eight in total) that they would need to work overtime on Saturday, May 22, 2004, to complete a critical order for a highly valued and important customer. All employees agreed to work Saturday, except Mary, who cited "personal reasons," which she refused to disclose, for her refusal to work.

On Monday, May 24, 2004, her supervisor, with concurrence from the department manager, terminated her employment for "unsatisfactory attendance." Mary did not dispute the attendance record; however, she filed a grievance through the company's alternative dispute resolution procedure alleging that management did not discharge her according to the organization's published disciplinary policy. She pointed to the section in the policy manual that states, "Employees will be warned for absenteeism before they are terminated." Mary maintained that she was never officially warned as required. Management replied that Mary was well aware of her absentee problem but that warning her would have served no purpose as she was unable to prevent her continued illnesses from occurring. Additionally, her refusal to work overtime on Saturday was a further indication of her lack of concern for her job or the welfare of her company.

QUESTIONS

1. What role, if any, should Mary's past work record play in this case? Explain.
2. Does management have a right to know why employees refuse to work overtime? Explain.
3. Evaluate the arguments of Mary Schwartz and management in this case.
4. If you were a member of the company's peer-review complaint committee, how would you vote in this case? What facts would cause you to vote this way?

Source: Based on an arbitration case heard by George W. Bohlander. Names have been changed.

CAREER COUNSEL

Visit the *Managing Human Resources* website (www.belcourt5e.nelson.com) for tips on negotiating a formal employment contract.

NOTES AND REFERENCES

1. John D. Canoni, "Location Awareness Technology and Employee Privacy Rights," *Employee Relations Law Journal* 30, no. 1 (Summer 2004): 26.
2. Jeffery A. Mello, "Introduction: The Evolving Nature of the Employment Relationship: Reconsidering Employee Responsibilities and Rights," *Employee Responsibility and Rights Journal* 15, no. 3 (September 2003): 99.
3. Jonathan A. Segal, "Security vs. Privacy," *HRMagazine* 47, no. 2 (February 2002): 93–96.
4. Donald H. Weiss, "How to Avoid Negligent Hiring Law Suits," *Supervisory Management* 36, no. 6 (June 1991): 6.
5. K. Cox, "PEI to Pay Damages to 314 Workers Fired by Tories," *The Globe and Mail*, November 27, 1997, A4.
6. K. Makin, "Insensitive Firings Not Tolerated: Supreme Court Decision Will Aid Future Victims of Wrongful Dismissal, Lawyers Say," *The Globe and Mail*, October 31, 1997, A4; D. Johnston, "Promises, Promises: The Case of *Queen v. Cognos*," *Law Now* 22, no. 3 (December 1997, January 1998): 16–18.
7. Luc Sels, Maddy Janssens, and Inge Van den Brande, "Assessing the Nature of Psychological Contracts: A Validation of Sex Dimensions," *Journal of Organizational Behavior* 25, no. 4 (June 2004): 461. See also Maddy Janssens, Luc Sels, and Inge Van den Brande, "Multiple Types of Psychological Contracts: A Six Cluster Solution," *Human Relations* 56, no. 11 (November 2003): 1349.
8. Jill Kickul and Mathew A. Liso-Troth, "The Meaning behind the Message: Climate Perceptions and the Psychological Contract," *Mid-American Journal of Business* 18, no. 2 (Fall 2003): 23.
9. Karl Scholz, "The Law of Employee Dismissals," *Canadian Manager* 26, no. 4 (Winter 2001): 9–10.
10. T. Wagar, "Wrongful Dismissal: Perception vs. Reality," *Human Resources Professional* 8, no. 10 (1996).
11. J. Carlisle, "Court Sets Standard for Constructive Dismissal," *Financial Post*, April 29, 1997:
12. J. Melnitizer, "Ciciretto vs Embassy Cleaners," *Workplace News* 5, no. 2 (February 1999): 1

13. Linda Goldman and Joan Lewis, "A Private Matter," *Occupational Health* 56, no. 10 (October 2004): 12.

14. Bruce Gillespie, "Don't Wait for the Whistle," *National Post*, April 26, 2004, FE 1.

15. Benisa Berry, "Organizational Culture: A Framework and Strategies for Facilitating Employee Whistleblowing," *Employee Responsibilities and Rights Journal* 16, no. 1 (March 2004): 1.

16. Virginia Galt, "Jeans Workers Helped Face Life After Levi," *The Globe and Mail*, B1 and B12.

17. S. Cohen and A.V. Campell, "It's Time to Face the Inevitable and Comply with Privacy Laws," *Canadian HR Reporter* 15, no. 2 (January 28, 2002): 9–10.

18. David Brown, "10 Months to Get Ready," *Canadian HR Reporter* 16, no. 4 (February 24, 2003): 1, 11.

19. Robin L. Wakefield, "Computer Monitoring and Surveillance," *CPA Journal* 74, no. 7 (July 2004): 52.

20. Dan J. Shields and Valerie Jepson, "When Internet Use Turns to Abuse," *HR Professional*, April, May 2006, 28.

21. Gillian Flynn, "Internet Issues at Work," *Workforce-Vendor Directory* 80, no. 10 (2002): 33–34.

22. Marina Straus, "Print Scans: Retail Tool or Invasion of Privacy," *The Globe and Mail*, December 8, 2004, B1 and 7.

23. "Security Measures: How to Arrest Shrinkage in Your Store," *Canadian Grocer* 111, no. 5 (May 1997): 19–20; "Tough Policies Minimize Shrink," *Canadian Grocer* 107, no. 12 (December 1993): 10, 37.

24. Matthew J. Camardella, "Electronic Monitoring in the Workplace," *Employment Relations Today* 30, 3 (Fall 2003): 91.

25. John Swenney, "Camera Use," *HRMagazine* 49, no. 7 (July 2004): 42.

26. P. Israel, "Spying on Employees–and It's Perfectly Legal," *Canadian HR Reporter* 16, no. 8 (April 21, 2003): 5; "What the Courts Are Saying," *Canadian HR Reporter* 16, no. 8 (April 21, 2003): 5.

27. Marjo Johne, "Is Someone Watching You?" *The Globe and Mail*, January 10, 2003, C1.

28. Asha Tomlinson, "Off Duty Racism Gets Teacher Fired," *Canadian HR Reporter* 15, no. 8 (April 22, 2002): 1, 6; Rosalyn L. Wilcots, "Employee Discipline for Off-Duty Conduct: Constitutional Challenges and the Public Policy Exception," *Labor Law Journal* 46, no. 1 (January 1995): 3–16; Steve Bergsman, "Employee Misconduct Outside the Workplace," *HRMagazine* 36, no. 3 (March 1991): 62.

29. Sharon Clinebell, Lynn Hoffman, and John Kilpatrick, "Office Romances: Rights and Liabilities," *HRFocus* 72, no. 3 (March 1995): 19.

30. Ontario Human Rights Commission, Policy on Drug and Alcohol Testing, www.ohrc.onc.ca/english/publications/drug_alcohol_testing_eng.html.

31. *Drug-Free Workplace: Back on Track* (Virginia Beach, VA: Coastal Human Resources, 1993): Edward J. Miller, "Investigating in a Drug-Free Workplace," *HRMagazine* 36, no. 5 (May 1991): 48–51.

32. G.H. Siejts, "Canadians More Opposed to Workplace Drug Testing Than U.S Counterparts," *HR Professional*, April/May 2003, 10–12; B. Butler, "Alcohol and Drug Testing in Canada: Do You Have a Right To Test? Do You Have a Right Not To?"

Occupational Health and Safety 13, no. 1 (January–February 1997): 28–31.

33. K. Hefner and S. Garland, "Testing for Drug Use: Handle With Care," *Business Week*, March 28, 1985, 65.

34. T. Humber, "Genetic Testing in the Workplace," *Canadian HR Reporter* 15, no. 21 (December 2, 2002): 1, 10.

35. One of the original studies on this topic can be found at Edward L. Harrison, "Why Supervisors Fail to Discipline," *Supervisory Management* 30, no. 4 (April 1985): 17.

36. George W. Bohlander and Donna Blancero, "A Study of Reversal Determinants in Discipline and Discharge Arbitration Awards: The Impact of Just Cause Standards," *Labor Studies Journal* 21, no. 3 (Fall 1996): 3–18.

37. "Steps to Take before Recommending Disciplinary Action," *PM Public Management* 86, no. 6 (July 2004): 43.

38. "22 Tips for Avoiding Employee Lawsuits," *HRFocus* 80, no. 12 (December 2003): 4.

39. Jathan W. Janove, "Private Eye 101," *HRMagazine* 49, no. 7 (July 2004): 127.

40. Kelly Mollica, "Perceptions of Fairness," *HRMagazine* 49, no. 6 (June 2004): 169.

41. Readers interested in the pioneering work on positive discipline should see James R. Redeker, "Discipline, Part I: Progressive Systems Work Only by Accident," *Personnel* 62, no. 10 (October 1985): 8–12; James R. Redeker, "Discipline, Part 2: The Nonpunitive Approach Works by Design," *Personnel* 62, no. 11 (November 1985): 7–14.

42. Richard Bayer, "Firing: Letting People Go with Dignity Is Good for Business," *HRFocus* 77, no. 1 (January 2000): 10. See also Paul Falcone, "Give Employees the (Gentle) Boot," *HRMagazine* 46, no. 4 (April 2001): 121–28.

43. "The New Rules of Termination," *HRFocus* 78, no. 5 (May 2001): 1, 11–15.

44. Elizabeth Hill, "AAA Employment Arbitration: A Fair Forum at Low Cost," *Dispute Resolution Journal* 58, no. 2 (May–June 2003): 8.

45. Theodore Eisenberg and Elizabeth Hill, "Arbitration and Litigation of Employment Claims," *Dispute Resolution Journal* 58, no. 4 (November 2003–January 2004): 44.

46. Margaret M. Clark, "EEOC's Effort to Expand Mediation Gains Momentum," *HRMagazine* 48, no. 5 (May 2003): 32.

47. "How Best to Avoid Mediation Mistakes," *HRFocus* 77, no. 9 (September 2000): 2. See also Nancy Kauffman and Barbara Davis, "What Type of Mediation Do You Want?" *Dispute Resolution Journal* 53, no. 2 (May 1998): 10.

48. Norm Frauenheim, "Clause Alarms Athletes," *Arizona Republic*, May 10, 1996, C1.

49. George W. Bohlander, Robert J. Deeny, and Mishka L. Marshall, "Alternative Dispute Resolution Policies: Current Procedural and Administrative Issues," *Labor Law Journal* 47, no. 9 (September 1996): 619–26; Thomas R. Kelly and Danielle L. Berke, "What's New in ADR?" *HRFocus* 73, no. 4 (April 1996): 15.

50. Jennifer Schramm, "Perception on Ethics," *HRMagazine* 49, no. 11 (November 2004): 176.

51. "Ethical Corporate Behavior Begins with a Code of Conduct," *HRFocus* 79, no. 7 (July 2002): 8–9.

The Dynamics of Labour Relations

After studying this chapter, you should be able to

objective 1

Identify and explain the federal and provincial legislation that provides the framework for labour relations.

objective 2

Explain the reasons employees join unions.

objective 3

Describe the process by which unions organize employees and gain recognition as their bargaining agent.

objective 4

Discuss the bargaining process and the bargaining goals and strategies of a union and an employer.

objective 5

Differentiate the forms of bargaining power that a union and an employer may utilize to enforce their bargaining demands.

objective 6

Describe a typical union grievance procedure and explain the basis for arbitration awards.

Mention the word *union* and most people will have some opinion, positive or negative, regarding Canadian labour organizations. To some, the word evokes images of labour–management unrest—grievances, strikes, picketing, boycotts. To others, the word represents industrial democracy, fairness, opportunity, equal representation. Many think of unions as simply creating an adversarial relationship between employees and managers.

Regardless of attitudes toward them, since the mid-1800s unions have been an important force shaping organizational practices, legislation, and political thought in Canada. Today unions remain of interest because of their influence on organizational productivity and HR policies and practices. Like business organizations themselves, unions are undergoing changes in both operation—such as mergers and coalitions—and philosophy.

In spite of the long history of unions, the intricacies of labour relations are unfamiliar to many individuals. Therefore, this chapter describes government regulation of labour relations, the labour relations process, the reasons why workers join labour organizations, and the structure and leadership of unions. Importantly, according to labour law, once the union is certified to negotiate for bargaining-unit members, it must represent everyone in the unit equally. Therefore, in the latter sections of the chapter, we discuss the important topics of contract administration, particularly the handling of employee grievances and arbitration.

About 30 percent of all employees are unionized, with rates higher in the public sector (76 percent) than the private sector (20 percent).[1] Unions and other labour organizations can affect significantly the ability of managers to direct and control the various functions of HRM. For example, union seniority provisions in the collective agreement may influence who is selected for job promotions or training programs. Pay rates may be determined through union negotiations, or unions may impose restrictions on management's employee appraisal methods. Therefore, it is essential that managers in both the union and nonunion environment understand how unions operate and be thoroughly familiar with the important body of law governing labour relations. Remember, ignorance of labour legislation is no defence when managers and supervisors violate labour law. Before reading further, test your knowledge of labour relations law by answering the questions in Highlights in HRM 14.1.

Government Regulation of Labour Relations

objective 1

Labour relations in Canada is regulated by a multiplicity of federal and provincial laws. There are specific laws, or acts, for different sectors, industries, and workers. It is a highly decentralized system. For example, interprovincial transportation and communications are under federal jurisdiction, while manufacturing and mining are provincial. However, 90 percent of workers are governed by provincial legislation.

The Industrial Relations Disputes and Investigation Act

The Industrial Relations Disputes and Investigation Act (1948) specified the right of workers to join unions, allowed unions to be certified as bargaining agents by a labour relations board, required management to recognize a certified union as the

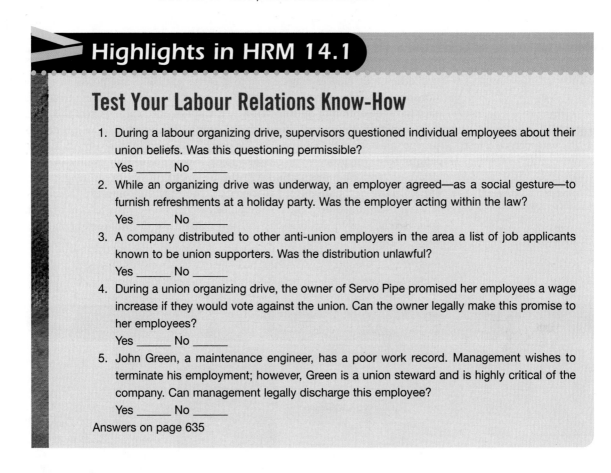

Highlights in HRM 14.1

Test Your Labour Relations Know-How

1. During a labour organizing drive, supervisors questioned individual employees about their union beliefs. Was this questioning permissible?
   Yes _____ No _____

2. While an organizing drive was underway, an employer agreed—as a social gesture—to furnish refreshments at a holiday party. Was the employer acting within the law?
   Yes _____ No _____

3. A company distributed to other anti-union employers in the area a list of job applicants known to be union supporters. Was the distribution unlawful?
   Yes _____ No _____

4. During a union organizing drive, the owner of Servo Pipe promised her employees a wage increase if they would vote against the union. Can the owner legally make this promise to her employees?
   Yes _____ No _____

5. John Green, a maintenance engineer, has a poor work record. Management wishes to terminate his employment; however, Green is a union steward and is highly critical of the company. Can management legally discharge this employee?
   Yes _____ No _____

Answers on page 635

USING THE INTERNET

For a history of labour, read the article "The Cradle of Collective Bargaining: History of Labour" at

www.humanities.mcmaster.ca/~cradle/

exclusive bargaining agent for a group of employees, required both unions and management to negotiate in good faith, outlined unfair labour practices by both unions and management, and created a two-stage compulsory conciliation process that was mandatory before strikes or lockouts became legal.[2]

The federal government later incorporated these rights into a more comprehensive piece of legislation known as the Canada Labour Code. At the same time, the Canada Labour Relations Board (LRB) was established to administer and enforce the code. Similarly, each province has a labour relations board that administers labour law. (The exception is Quebec, which has a labour court and commissioners.) The members of these boards are government appointees. The LRB is generally autonomous from the federal government and has representatives from both labour and management. The duties of the LRB include

- administrating the statutory procedures for the acquisition, transfer, and termination of bargaining rights;
- hearing complaints related to unfair labour practices;
- supervising strikes and lockout votes;
- determining whether bargaining was done in good faith; and
- remedying violations of collective bargaining legislation.[3]

The Labour Relations Process

labour relations process
Logical sequence of four events: (1) workers desire collective representation, (2) union begins its organizing campaign, (3) collective negotiations lead to a contract, and (4) the contract is administered

Individually, employees may be able to exercise relatively little power in their relationship with employers. Of course, if they believe they are not being treated fairly, they have the option of quitting. However, employees can also correct this situation by organizing and bargaining with the employer collectively. When employees pursue this option, the labour relations process begins. As Figure 14.1 illustrates, the **labour relations process** consists of a logical sequence of four events: (1) workers desire collective representation, (2) the union begins its organizing campaign, (3) collective negotiations lead to a contract, and (4) the contract is administered. Laws and administrative rulings influence each of the separate events by granting special privileges to, or imposing defined constraints on, workers, managers, and union officials.[4]

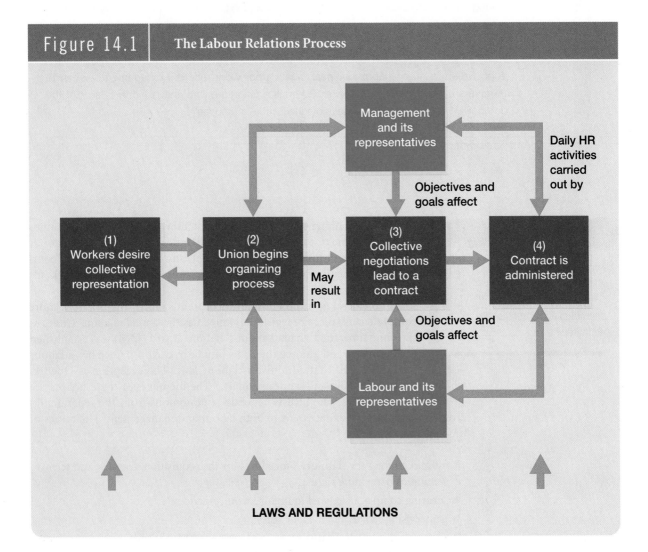

Figure 14.1 | **The Labour Relations Process**

Why Employees Unionize

objective 2

The majority of research on why employees unionize comes from the study of blue-collar employees in the private sector. These studies generally conclude that employees unionize as a result of economic need, because of a general dissatisfaction with managerial practices, and/or as a way to fulfill social and status needs. In short, employees see unionism as a way to achieve results they cannot achieve acting individually. As Highlights in HRM 14.2 illustrates, some segments of the labour force are very difficult to unionize. It should be pointed out that some employees join unions because of the union-shop provisions. A **union shop** is a provision of the collective agreement that requires employees to join as a condition of employment.

union shop
Provision of the collective agreement that requires employees to join the union as a condition of their employment

Economic Needs

Whether employees select unionization will greatly depend on whether the employees perceive the union as likely to be effective in improving various economic conditions of employment—often referred to as the union's instrumentality. Dissatisfaction with wages, benefits, and working conditions appears to provide the strongest reason to join a union. This point is continually supported by research studies that find that both union members and nonmembers have their highest expectations of union performance regarding the "bread and butter" issues of collective bargaining.[5] Hourly earnings

Highlights in HRM 14.2

Homeworkers: Canada's Invisible Labour Force

Rosanna Gonzalez (not her real name) works in the basement of her home in a small room crowded with industrial sewing machines. Rosanna is in the process of making 410 sweatshirts. To meet her deadline she will have to put in 40 hours of work in two days. There is no natural light in the airless basement room, no way to escape the flying dust and thread particles. Last week the assignment was T-shirts. Rosanna received 38 cents per shirt. She can churn one out in five minutes, but even at that speed, she still earns only about $4.50 per hour—the minimum wage a decade ago.

In most provinces the law requires that homeworkers be paid at least one dollar above minimum wage to compensate them for the use of space and equipment in their homes. But enforcement of the law is rare. Canadians are quick to condemn working conditions in Third-World countries, yet they are notably silent about abuses in their own country. Joining a union is a traditional response to abysmal working conditions. For homeworkers, unionization is a remote possibility at best. These individuals (most of whom speak no English) work in scattered and unlicensed locations and are usually unaware of their rights. Those who are aware are afraid that if they complain, they will suffer retribution at the hands of the retailers, contractors, and subcontractors with whom they do business. These women have few employment options and are often the sole providers for their children. For them the choice is clear: put up with the exploitation or don't work at all.

© GETTY IMAGES

Involving employees in decision making may reduce the desire to seek representation through unionization.

were $22 for those in unions and $18.50 for those not in a union.[6] It is these traditional issues of wages, benefits, and working conditions on which unions are built.

Dissatisfaction with Management

Employees may seek unionization when they perceive that managerial practices regarding promotion, transfer, shift assignment, or other job-related policies are administered in an unfair or biased manner. Employees cite favouritism shown by managers as a major reason for joining unions. This is particularly true when the favouritism concerns the HR areas of discipline, promotion, job assignments, and training opportunities.

We have noted throughout this book that today's employees are better educated than those of the past, and they often express a desire to be more involved in decisions affecting their jobs. Chapter 4 discussed the concept of employee empowerment and highlighted various employee involvement techniques. The failure of employers to give employees an opportunity to participate in decisions affecting their welfare may encourage union membership. It is widely believed that one reason managers begin employee involvement programs and seek to empower their employees is to avoid collective action by employees. For example, employers in the auto, semiconductor, and financial industries involve employees in collaborative programs as a means to stifle unionization. In one organizing effort by the United Auto Workers at a Nissan plant, the union lost the election because workers were satisfied with the voice in decision making that Nissan's participatory style of management gave them.

Social and Leadership Concerns

Employees whose needs for recognition and social affiliation are being frustrated may join unions as a means of satisfying these needs. Through their union, they have an opportunity to fraternize with other employees who have similar desires, interests, problems, and gripes. Simply, employees may join unions for the same reason they would join a civic organization, club, or sports team, namely to enjoy the companionship of others and to benefit in the prestige and value that organization may provide. Additionally, the union also enables them to put leadership talents to use as officers of the union and representatives of fellow employees. One study found that employees became union stewards so that they could be seen as "a fellow your buddies look to" and as a person who "stands up to the boss."[7]

Organizing Campaigns

Once employees desire to unionize, a formal organizing campaign may be started either by a union organizer or by employees acting on their own behalf.[8] Contrary to popular belief, most organizing campaigns are begun by employees rather than by union organizers. Large national unions like the United Auto Workers, the United Brotherhood of Carpenters, the United Steelworkers, and the Teamsters, however, have

objective 3

formal organizing departments whose purpose is to identify organizing opportunities and launch organizing campaigns.

Organizing Steps

The organizing process normally includes the following steps:

1. Employee/union contact
2. Initial organizational meeting
3. Formation of inhouse organizing committee
4. Application to labour relations board
5. Issuance of certificate by labour relations board
6. Election of bargaining committee and contract negotiations.

Step 1. The first step begins when employees and union officials make contact to explore the possibility of unionization. During these discussions, employees investigate the advantages of representation, and union officials begin to gather information on employee needs, problems, and grievances. Union organizers also seek specific information about the employer's financial health, supervisory styles, and organizational policies and practices. To win employee support, labour organizers must build a case *against* the employer and *for* the union. Typically there are signs, reported in Highlights in HRM 14.3, that an organizing drive is occurring.

Note also that most organizing drives take place inside the company.

Step 2. As an organizing campaign gathers momentum, the organizer schedules an initial union meeting to attract more supporters. The organizer uses the information gathered in Step 1 to address employee needs and explain how the union can secure these goals. Two additional purposes of organizational meetings are (1) to identify employees who can help the organizer direct the campaign and (2) to establish communication chains that reach all employees.

Step 3. The third important step in the organizing drive is to form an inhouse organizing committee composed of employees willing to provide leadership to the

Highlights in HRM 14.3

Is a Union Being Organized?

Senior management is sometimes the last to know that a union has targeted the company. Often the process starts after employees call a union with complaints, and want to understand their legal rights and responsibilities. Listed below are a few common signs that an organization drive is happening:

- Unusual employee behaviour of any kind
- An increase in the number of complaints about working conditions
- Demands for detailed information about employment policies
- Gatherings of employees that appear larger in number than usual, or that involve employees whose jobs are unrelated, or who would usually have no common interests
- Changes in how employees interact with their supervisors
- The presence of union leaflets or other union material

campaign. The committee's role is to interest other employees in joining the union and in supporting its campaign. An important task of the committee is to have employees sign an **authorization card** indicating their willingness to be represented by a union in collective bargaining with their employer. The number of signed authorization cards demonstrates the potential strength of the labour union.[9] Legislation across Canada states that a union must have a majority of employees as members in a bargaining unit before it can apply for a certification election. Most jurisdictions now interpret this to mean that at least 50 percent of those voting constitute a majority. In other words, those who do not cast ballots are not assumed to be voting against the certification of the union. Union membership cards, once signed, are confidential, and only the labour relations board has access to them.

Step 4. Application is made to the appropriate labour relations board. In Canada, most unions are certified without a vote if the labour relations board finds that the union has the support of the majority of the employees, based on the number of signed cards.

Step 5. The labour relations board reviews the application and initially informs both the employer and the employees about the application, which is posted so that either employees or the employer have an opportunity to challenge.

Step 6. Once the labour relations board determines that the union is certified, the bargaining committee is put in place to start negotiating a collective agreement. If the union is a national union, such as the Canadian Auto Workers, usually a national representative works with the bargaining committee to negotiate a collective agreement with the company.

Employer Tactics

Employers must not interfere with the labour relations process of certification. They are prohibited by law from dismissing, disciplining, or threatening employees for exercising their right to form a union. Employers cannot promise better conditions, such as increased vacation days, if the employees vote for no union or choose one union over another. Nor can they threaten to close the business, as one company did as workers were voting.[10] They cannot unilaterally change wages and working conditions during certification proceedings or during collective bargaining. Like unions, they must bargain in good faith, meaning that they must demonstrate a commitment to bargain seriously and fairly. In addition, they cannot participate in the formation, selection, or support of unions representing employees (see Figure 14.2).

None of these prohibitions prevents an employer from making the case that the employees have the right not to join a union and that they can deal directly with the employer on any issue. Employer resistance to unionization is the norm in Canada and opposition has been found to decrease the probability of successfully organizing.[11] When Wal-Mart consolidated its entry into Canada by buying 122 nonunionized Woolco stores, the company was widely viewed as anti-union. However, Wal-Mart spokespeople insist that they are not anti-union, but rather "pro-associate" (the Wal-Mart term for the retail salesclerk). During an organizing drive by the United Food and Commercial Workers Union, Wal-Mart's managers stated that they believed strongly in their people, would take care of them, and were ready to listen to and discuss any issue.[12]

Employers' attempts to influence employees are scrutinized closely by officials of the organizing union and by the labour relations board. In one case, an employer interfered with the organizing process and the union was automatically recognized by the labour board, even though only 5 percent of the employees had signed authorization cards.[13]

authorization card
A statement signed by an employee authorizing a union to act as his or her representative for the purposes of collective bargaining

unfair labour practices (ULPs)
Specific employer and union illegal practices that operate to deny employees their rights and benefits under federal and provincial labour law

Figure 14.2	Employer "Don'ts" During Union Organizing Campaigns

Union organizing drives are emotionally charged events. Furthermore, labour law, LRB rulings, and court decisions greatly affect the behaviour and actions of management and union representatives. During the drive, managers and supervisors should avoid the following:

- Attending union meetings, spying on employee–union gatherings, and questioning employees about the content of union meetings.
- Questioning current employees about their union sentiments—especially about how they might vote in a union election.
- Threatening or terminating employees for their union support or beliefs.
- Changing the working conditions of employees because they actively work for the union or simply support its ideals.
- Supplying the names, addresses, and phone numbers of employees to union representatives or other employees sympathetic to the union.
- Promising employees improvements in working conditions (e.g., wage increases, benefit improvements, etc.) if they vote against the union.
- Accepting or reviewing union authorization cards or pro-union petitions, since employees' names are listed on these documents.

Union Tactics

Unions also have a duty to act in accordance with labour legislation. Unions are prohibited from interfering with the formation of an employer's organization. They cannot intimidate or coerce employees to become or remain members of a union. Nor can they force employers to dismiss, discipline, or discriminate against nonunion employees. They must provide fair representation for all employees in the **bargaining unit,** whether in collective bargaining or in grievance procedure cases. Unions cannot engage in activities such as strikes before the expiration of the union contract.

Any of the prohibited activities noted above for both employers and unions are considered unfair labour practices (ULPs). Charges of ULPs are registered with the labour relations board, whose duty it is to enforce the Canada labour code. A summary of ULPs is presented in Highlights in HRM 14.4 on page 606.

Highlights in HRM 14.5 on page 606 lists the key strategies identified by HR specialists to reduce workers' motivation to join unions. Since these strategies are under the direct control of management, they can be used to help discourage or prevent unionization.

How Employees Become Unionized

The procedures for union certification vary across Canadian jurisdictions. About two-thirds of unions that attempt to organize employees in Ontario, for example, are successful.[14] As mentioned earlier, the common practice is for unions to present documentation to the appropriate labour relations board for certification. The labour relations board must certify a union before it can act as a bargaining unit for a group of employees. In order to acquire certification, the union must demonstrate that it has obtained the minimum level of membership support required by the labour relations board. Usually, the union provides evidence by submitting signed authorization cards and proof that initiation dues or fees have been paid.[15] Recognition of a union can be obtained through voluntary recognition, or regular certification, or a prehearing vote.

bargaining unit
Group of two or more employees who share common employment interests and conditions and may reasonably be grouped together for purposes of collective bargaining

Highlights in HRM 14.4

Unfair Labour Practices

Unfair labour practices by employers include

- Helping to establish or administer a union.
- Altering the working conditions of the employees while a union is applying for certification without the union's consent.
- Using intimidation, coercion, threats, promises, or exercising undue influence while a union is being organized.
- Failing to recognize or bargain with the certified union.
- Hiring professional strike breakers.

Unfair labour practices by unions include

- Contributing financial or other support to an employees' organization.
- Not representing fairly the employees in the bargaining unit.
- Bargaining or negotiating a collective agreement with an employer while another union represents the employees in the bargaining unit.
- Calling or authorizing an unlawful strike, or threatening to do so.

Highlights in HRM 14.5

Strategies to Remain Union-Free

- Offer competitive wages and benefits based on labour market comparisons and salary and benefit surveys.
- Train supervisors in progressive human relations skills, including employee motivation, job design, and employment law.
- Institute formal procedures to resolve employee complaints and grievances; these may include peer review committees, step-review complaint systems, or open-door policies.
- Involve employees in work decisions affecting job performance or the quality or quantity of the product or service provided.
- Give attention to employee growth and development needs; recognize that the workforce is growing older, more female, more vocal, better educated, less patient, and more demanding.
- Draft HR policies that reflect legal safeguards and that are fair and equitable in employment conditions such as discipline, promotions, training, and layoffs.

The best work environment, and the least receptive to unionization, is one that treats the individual with respect, dignity, and fairness, while encouraging participation in decision making.

Voluntary Recognition

All employers, except those in Quebec, may voluntarily recognize and accept a union. This rarely happens, except in the construction industry, where there is a great reliance on union hiring halls.

Regular Certification

The regular certification process begins with the union submitting the required evidence of minimum membership to the labour relations board. Generally, if an applicant union can demonstrate that it has sufficient support in the proposed bargaining unit labour boards may grant certification on that basis. (However, with changes in government, labour relations legislation is often reformed. Therefore, requirements for granting certification may change.) The labour relations board can order a representative vote if a sizable minority of workers have indicated either support or opposition to the unionization.

Prehearing Votes

If there is evidence of irregularities, such as unfair labour practices during the organizing drive, a prehearing vote may be taken. The purpose of this vote is to establish the level of support among the workers. Generally (depending on particular labour relations legislation) votes can be called if less than 50 percent of the employees indicate support for a union. Once a union is certified, employees become part of a collective and can no longer make individual arrangements for pay, hours of work, vacation, etc.

Contract Negotiation

Once a bargaining unit has been certified by the labour relations board, the employer and the union are legally obligated to bargain in good faith over the terms and conditions of a collective agreement. Usually the terms of a collective agreement apply for a minimum of one year and a maximum of three years. As the contract expiry date approaches, either party must notify the other of its intention to bargain for a renewal collective agreement or contract negotiation.

Decertification

All legislation allows for the decertification of unions under certain conditions. If the majority of employees indicate that they do not want to be represented by the union, or that they want to be represented by another union, or if the union has failed to bargain, an application for decertification can be made to the labour relations board. If a collective agreement has been reached with the employer, this application can be made only at specified times, such as a few months before the agreement expires. Either the employees or the employer can initiate the application for decertification if the union fails to bargain.

Impact of Unionization on Managers

Why would employers oppose the unionization of their employees? First, studies from the field of labour economics routinely show that wages and benefits are higher in union organizations compared to similar nonunion organizations. Second, unions can have a significant effect on the rights exercised by management in making decisions about employees. Third, unionization restricts the freedom of management to formulate HR policy unilaterally and can challenge the authority of supervisors.

Challenges to Management Decisions

Unions typically attempt to achieve greater participation in management decisions that affect their members. Specifically, these decisions may involve such issues as the subcontracting of work, productivity standards, and job content. Employers quite naturally seek to claim many of these decisions as their exclusive **management rights**—decisions over which management claims exclusive rights. However, these prerogatives are subject to challenge and erosion by the union. They may be challenged at the bargaining table, through the grievance procedure, and through strikes.

management rights
Decisions regarding organizational operations over which management claims exclusive rights

Loss of Supervisory Authority

At a recent labour-management conference a union official commented, "Contract terms covering wages, benefits, job security, and working hours are of major importance to our membership." However, for managers and supervisors, the focal point of the union's impact is at the operating level (the shop floor or office facility), where the terms of the collective agreement are implemented on a daily basis. For example, these terms can determine what corrective action is to be taken in directing and in disciplining employees. When disciplining employees, supervisors must be certain they can demonstrate *just cause* (see Chapter 13) for their actions, because these actions can be challenged by the union and the supervisor called as defendant during a grievance hearing. If the challenge is upheld, the supervisor's effectiveness in coping with subsequent disciplinary problems may be impaired. Specific contract language can also reduce the supervisor's ability to manage in such areas as scheduling, training, transfers, performance evaluation, and promotions. Under provisions of the collective agreement, supervisors may have to promote employees by seniority rather than by individual merit.

Structures, Functions, and Leadership of Labour Unions

Unions that represent skilled craft workers, such as carpenters or masons, are called **craft unions.** Craft unions include the International Association of Iron Workers, the United Brotherhood of Carpenters, and the United Association of Plumbers and Pipefitters. Unions that represent unskilled and semiskilled workers employed along industry lines are known as **industrial unions.** The Canadian Union of Postal Workers is an industrial union, as are the United Auto Workers; the United Steelworkers; the Ontario Secondary School Teachers Federation; and the Office and Professional Employees International Union. While this distinction still exists, technological changes, union mergers, and competition among unions for members have helped reduce it. Today skilled and unskilled workers, white-collar and blue-collar workers, and professional groups are being represented by both types of unions.

craft unions
Unions that represent skilled craft workers

industrial unions
Unions that represent all workers—skilled, semiskilled, unskilled—employed along industry lines

Besides unions, **employee associations** represent various groups of professional and white-collar employees. Examples of employee associations include the Federation of Quebec Nurses and the Alberta Teachers Association. In competing with unions, these associations, for all purposes, may function as unions and become just as aggressive as unions in representing members.

employee associations
Labour organizations that represent various groups of professional and white-collar employees in labour–management relations

Regardless of their type, labour organizations are diverse organizations. Each will have its own structure, objectives, and methods of governance. Most researchers when describing labour organizations divide them into three levels: (1) central labour congresses, (2) international and national unions, and (3) local unions belonging to a parent national or international union. Each level has its own reason for existence and its own operating policies and procedures.

The Canadian Labour Congress

The Canadian Labour Congress (CLC) is a central federation of unions. In 2006, the total membership of the CLC was over 3 million Canadians and represented the majority of all unions in Canada.[16] Because of its size and resources, the CLC is considered the most influential labour federation in Canada. It is mainly a service organization representing over 90 international and national unions; these finance the CLC through dues based on membership size. Like the AFL-CIO, the CLC attempts to influence legislation and promote programs that are of interest to labour. It does this by lobbying, resolving jurisdictional disputes, maintaining ethical standards, providing education and training to its members, conducting research, and representing Canadian interests in the international labour movement.

International and National Unions

International unions tend to be affiliates of American unions, with headquarters in the United States. In Canada, there are 46 international unions (with membership of nearly 2 million workers) and 221 national unions (with membership of 2.8 million). The large membership base offers a good deal of leverage to local unions engaged in strike action. The merger of three international unions—the United Steelworkers of America, the United Auto Workers, and the International Association of Machinists—into the largest industrial union in North America resulted in a strike fund of $1 billion.[17]

Both international and national unions are made up of local unions. The objectives of these "umbrella" unions are to help organize local unions, to provide strike support, and to assist local unions with negotiations, grievance procedures, and the like. These unions also represent their members' interests with internal and external constituents. By ensuring that all employers pay similar wages to their unionized workers, they also remove higher wages as a competitive disadvantage.

In Canada, most of the decision-making authority in national unions is vested in the local unions or at the bargaining unit level. This is often referred to as bottom-up unionism. Many international unions, especially craft unions, are more likely to retain a greater degree of control over the affairs of local unions. This is often referred to as top-down unionism. The officers of both types of union typically include a president, a secretary-treasurer, and several vice-presidents, all officially elected. These officers make up the executive board, which is the top policy-making body. A typical national structure is depicted in Figure 14.3 on page 610. Other positions at the national level include lawyer, economist, statistician, and public relations officer. An economics director gathers, analyzes, and disseminates economic and other information of value in collective bargaining. Many national unions also have an education director, whose job is to provide training for local union officers and stewards.

International and national unions often have social and political objectives outside their traditional goal of representing member interests. This contentious issue is discussed in Ethics in HRM on page 611.

Figure 14.3 | The Organization of a Union Local

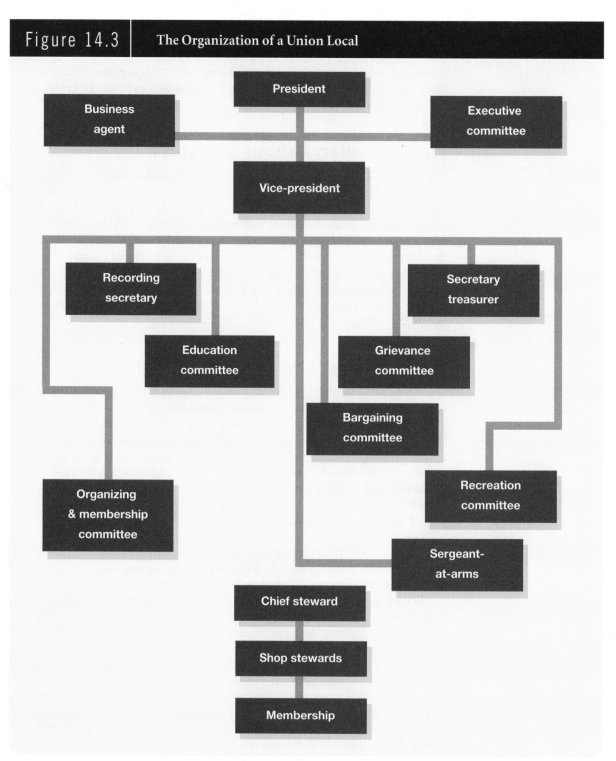

Source: F. Kehoe and M. Archer, *Canadian Industrial Relations*, 10th ed. (Oakville, ON: Century Labour Publications, 2002): 49. Reproduced by permission.

Ethics in HRM

Inflation

Members of unions and associations pay dues to support union activities. Most of this money is used to fund traditional union activities such as labour and economic research, contract negotiation, and the handling of grievances. However, sometimes the union, especially at the international and national levels, dedicates some of these funds to causes such as opposing human rights violations in China or supporting gun control in Canada. For example, the CLC is actively involved with social justice groups such as the women's movement, anti-poverty activities, churches, peace activists, and environmentalists. CUPE lobbies for safe clean water, and its Water Watch campaign to fight the privatization of water is a national priority for this union.

Union members have challenged, under the Canadian Charter of Rights and Freedoms, their obligation to contribute part of their union dues to political causes with which they disagree. The Supreme Court ruled that (1) trade unions are not in violation of the Charter if they use union dues for purposes other than collective bargaining in the narrow sense, and (2) unionized workers who object to the use of their dues have to try to get the money back themselves.

Sources: Canadian Labour Congress, www.clc-ctc.ca; Canadian Union of Public Employees, www.cupe.ca/www/WaterWatch; P.E. Larson, "Fighting for Labour," *Canadian Business Review* 13, no. 4 (1986): 8–12; P. Poiter, "Court Dashes Labour's Hopes of More Rights," *The Globe and Mail*, June 25, 1991, A5.

USING THE INTERNET

The Canada Industrial Relations Board website is a valuable source of information about unions:

www.cirb-ccri.gc.ca

Local Unions

Employees of any organization can form their own union, with no affiliation to a national or international union. In situations like this, the local is the union. There are about 270 independent local unions in Canada. Most local unions are members of national or international unions or the Canadian Labour Congress, which make available to them financial resources and advice.

Unionized employees pay union dues that finance the operation of the local union. Local unions tend to make their own decisions, but turn to the national union for collective bargaining help, research, and assistance when handling certain types of grievances. Many national unions also provide training for local unions on the roles and responsibilities of union officers. The officers of a local union are usually responsible for negotiating the local collective agreement, for ensuring the agreement is adhered to, and for investigating and processing member grievances. Most important, they help prevent their members from being treated by their employers in ways that run counter to management-established HR policies.[18] They also keep members informed through meetings and newsletters.

union steward
Employee who as a nonpaid union official represents the interests of members in their relations with management

Role of the Union (Shop) Steward

The **union (shop) steward** represents the interests of union members in their relations with immediate supervisors and other members of management. Stewards are usually elected by the union members in their own department and serve without union pay. Since stewards are full-time employees of the organization, they often spend considerable time after working hours investigating and handling members' problems. When stewards represent members during grievance meetings on organizational time, their lost earnings are paid by the local union.

A union steward can be viewed as a "person in the middle," caught between conflicting interests and groups. It cannot be assumed that stewards will always champion union members and routinely oppose managerial objectives. Union stewards are often insightful people working for the betterment of employees and the organization. So supervisors and managers at all levels are strongly encouraged to develop a professional working relationship with stewards and all union officials. This relationship can have a major bearing on union–management cooperation and on the efficiency and morale of the workforce.

Role of the Business Agent

business agent
Normally a paid labour official responsible for negotiating and administering the collective agreement and working to resolve union members' problems

Negotiating and administering the collective agreement and working to resolve problems arising in connection with it are major responsibilities of the **business agent**. In performing these duties, business agents must be all things to all people in their unions. They are often required to assume the role of counsellor in helping union members with both personal and job-related problems. They are also expected to satisfactorily resolve grievances that cannot be settled by the union stewards. Administering the daily affairs of the local union is another significant part of the business agent's job.

USING THE INTERNET

A description of a union steward's job can be found on the website of the Canadian Union of Public Employees:

www.cupe.ca/www/351/volunteers

Union Leadership Commitment and Philosophies

To evaluate the role of union leaders accurately, one must understand the nature of their backgrounds and ambitions and recognize the political nature of the offices they occupy. Union leaders—at all levels—often possess enthusiasm and a commitment to the ideals of unionism and employee welfare that is difficult for managers to understand and accept. To some managers, union officials have a "religious" zeal toward the labour movement and the advancement of member bargaining rights. Additionally, it is important for managers to understand that union officials are elected to office and, like any political officials, must be responsive to the views of their constituency. The union leader who ignores the demands of union members may risk being voted out of office or having members vote the union out as their bargaining agent.

To be effective leaders, union officials must pay constant attention to the philosophy and general goals of the labour movement. Unions have historically been very politically active, backing such parties as the NDP. The goals of many labour organizations include increased pay and benefits, job security, and improved working conditions. However, union leaders also know that unions must address the broader social, economic, and legislative issues of concern to members. The CAW continually lobbies for protective legislation favourable to the auto industry. The CLC has been an active promoter of women's issues and policies favouring job creation over deficit reduction. Finally, as part of Canada's adjustment to global competition, union leaders have been active in working with managers to make their respective industries more competitive, as described in Reality Check.

Reality Check

CAW Local 222 President

As the president of the largest local Canadian Auto Workers union (CAW, Local 222), Chris Buckley faces enormous challenges ensuring that 15 000 CAW members working mainly for General Motors in Oshawa, Ontario, have their jobs in a few years. With the announcement that GM plans to close Plant 2 by 2008 and by 2009 Plant 1 will have no product line, thousands of jobs are on the line.

Mr. Buckley emphasizes that for every CAW job in the Durham Region, seven more are created indirectly in every area from hospitality and finance to home renovations. It is for this reason that he asserts that everyone should be concerned with the declining sales of domestic cars and the impending closures of plants. Mr. Buckley states that "for too long, corporations and people haven't taken a serious look at the erosion and negative impact that the loss of union jobs has on our economy." When asked about the jobs created by foreign car manufacturers, Chris Buckley urges Canadians to take caution. The problem he asserts is from the imports that cause a trade imbalance and affect the Big Three's (GM, Ford, and Chrysler) market share. For example, in the Free Trade Agreement with South Korea, 130 000 vehicles were imported into Canada and only 400 of our vehicles were exported. "We are in effect exporting our ability to maintain our way of life by creating jobs elsewhere in the world."

In response, the CAW is therefore committed to educating Canadians about the importance of unionization in order to keep jobs secure and wages high. Accordingly, it is in the best interest of the union to negotiate high paying wages that are fair and equate to the tough work carried out by an autoworker on a day-to-day basis. "Auto workers work whistle to whistle and each task has a time line for its completion that must be attained." Also stressed is the fact the GM workers in the Oshawa plants have consistently won industry awards from J.D. Power for quality and from Habour and Associates for efficiency and productivity. In this respect, it is unimaginable to the CAW that GM would choose to close the doors on these particular plants. In response, Local 222 has submitted a business case to General Motors in order to re-invest in the Oshawa plants.

For the time being, Chris Buckley remains optimistic about the future of his union and the Canadian auto industry. While many people tend to think of auto workers as overpaid and benefits-rich, Chris Buckley reminds us that it is the hard-fought battles of unions that has resulted in benefits, such as health and safety laws, for all jobs (many of which are nonunionized).

Labour Relations in the Public Sector

Collective bargaining among federal, provincial, and municipal government employees, and among employees in parapublic agencies (private agencies or branches of government acting as extensions of government programs) has been an area of important activity for the union movement since the early 1960s. More than 75 percent of public employee are now unionized.

The three largest unions in Canada represent public-sector employees. The Canadian Union of Public Employees (CUPE) is the largest union in Canada, with

540 000 members. The second-largest union, with 337 000 members, is the National Union of Public and General Employees (NUPGE). The largest union representing employees at the federal level is the Public Service Alliance of Canada (PSAC), with 156 000 members. PSAC comprises 17 different unions representing various groups such as the Professional Institute of the Public Service of Canada (PIPS), the Social Science Employees Association (SSEA), and the Air Traffic Controllers. Growth in these unions is threatened by increased cost-cutting efforts of governments at all levels, resulting in employee reductions.

While public-sector collective bargaining is quite similar to bargaining in the private sector, a number of differences are worth noting. Below, we explore these differences in two contexts: (1) the political nature of the labour–management relationship, and (2) public-sector strikes.

USING THE INTERNET

The Public Service Staff Relations Board oversees employer–employee relations in the federal public service:

www.pslrb-crtfp.gc.ca

Political Nature of the Labour–Management Relationship

Government employees are not able to negotiate with their employers on the same basis as their counterparts in private organizations. It is doubtful that they will ever be able to do so because of inherent differences between the public and private sectors.

One of the significant differences is that labour relations in the private sector has an economic foundation, whereas in government its foundation tends to be political. Since private employers must stay in business in order to sell their goods or services, their employees are not likely to make demands that could bankrupt them. A strike in the private sector is a test of the employer's economic staying power, and usually the employer's customers have alternative sources of supply. Governments, on the other hand, must stay in business because alternative services are usually not available.

Another difference between the public and private sectors relates to the source of management authority. In a private organization, authority flows downward from the board of directors and, ultimately, from the shareholders. In contrast, authority in the public sector flows upward from the public at large to their elected representatives and to the appointed or elected managers. It follows that public employees can exert influence not only as union members but also as pressure groups and voting citizens.

Strikes in the Public Sector

Strikes by government employees create a problem for lawmakers and for the general public. Because many of the services that government employees provide, such as policing and firefighting, are considered essential to the well-being of the public, public policy is opposed to strikes by these people. However, various provincial legislatures have granted public employees the right to strike. Where striking is permitted, the right is limited to specific groups of employees—those performing nonessential services—and the strike cannot endanger the public's health, safety, or welfare. Public-sector unions contend, however, that denying them the same right to strike as employees in the private sector greatly reduces their power during collective bargaining.

Public employees who perform essential services do in fact strike. Teachers, sanitation employees, police, transit employees, firefighters, and postal employees have all engaged in strike action. To avoid potentially critical situations, various arbitration methods are used for resolving collective bargaining deadlocks in the public sector. One is **compulsory binding arbitration** for employees such as police officers,

compulsory binding arbitration
Binding method of resolving collective bargaining deadlocks by a neutral third party

final offer arbitration
Method of resolving collective bargaining deadlocks whereby the arbitrator has no power to compromise but must select one or another of the final offers submitted by the two parties

firefighters, and others in jobs where strikes cannot be tolerated; in this case, a neutral third party is appointed to resolve the deadlock. Another method is **final offer arbitration,** under which the arbitrator must select one or the other of the final offers submitted by the disputing parties. With this method, the arbitrator's award is more likely to go to the party whose final bargaining offer has moved the closest to a reasonable settlement. The government can also enact back-to-work legislation, an option being used with increasing frequency.

The Bargaining Process

objective 4

collective bargaining process
Process of negotiating a collective agreement, including the use of economic pressures by both parties

Those unfamiliar with contract negotiations often view the process as an emotional conflict between labour and management, complete with marathon sessions, fist pounding, and smoke-filled rooms. In reality, negotiating a collective agreement entails long hours of extensive preparation combined with diplomatic maneuvering and the development of bargaining strategies. Furthermore, negotiation is only one part of the **collective bargaining process.** (See Figure 14.4.) Collective bargaining also may include the use of economic pressures in the form of strikes and boycotts by a union. Lockouts, plant closures, and the replacement of strikers are similar pressures used by an employer. In addition, either or both parties may seek support from the general public or from the courts as a means of pressuring the opposing side.

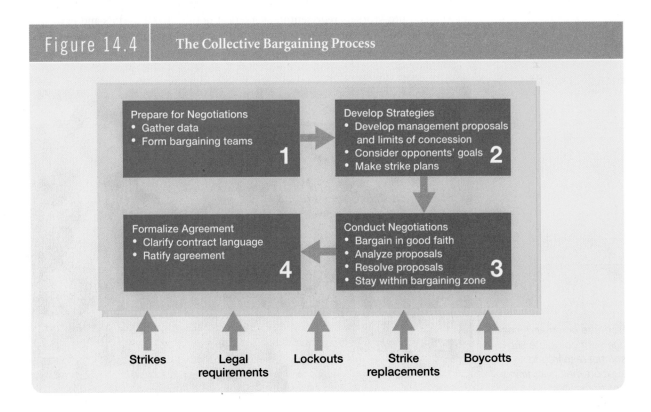

Figure 14.4 | **The Collective Bargaining Process**

Prepare for Negotiations
- Gather data
- Form bargaining teams

1

Develop Strategies
- Develop management proposals and limits of concession
- Consider opponents' goals
- Make strike plans

2

Formalize Agreement
- Clarify contract language
- Ratify agreement

4

Conduct Negotiations
- Bargain in good faith
- Analyze proposals
- Resolve proposals
- Stay within bargaining zone

3

Strikes   Legal requirements   Lockouts   Strike replacements   Boycotts

Preparing for Negotiations

Preparing for negotiations includes assembling data to support bargaining proposals and forming the bargaining team. This permits collective bargaining to be conducted on an orderly, factual, and positive basis with a greater likelihood of achieving desired goals. Negotiators often develop a bargaining book that serves as a cross-reference file to determine which contract clauses would be affected by a demand. The bargaining book also contains a general history of contract terms and their relative importance to management.[19] Assuming that the collective agreement is not the first to be negotiated by the parties, preparation for negotiations ideally start soon after the current agreement has been signed. This practice allows negotiators to review and diagnose weaknesses and mistakes made during the previous negotiations while the experience is still current in their minds.

Gathering Bargaining Data

Employers gather economic data primarily in the areas of wages and benefits. However, internal data relating to grievances, disciplinary actions, transfers, promotions, overtime, and former arbitration awards are useful in formulating and supporting the employer's bargaining position. The supervisors and managers who must live with and administer the collective agreement can be very important sources of ideas and suggestions concerning changes that are needed in the *next* agreement. Their contact with union members and representatives provides them with a firsthand knowledge of the changes that union negotiators are likely to propose.

When negotiating contracts, union bargainers talk about "taking wages out of competition." This term refers to having similar contract provisions—particularly concerning wages and benefits—between different companies in order to prevent one employer from having a favourable labour cost advantage over another. For example, the United Auto Workers representing workers at both General Motors and Ford will seek similar contract provisions. Furthermore, this allows unions to show their

Both the union and management complete substantial research to support their bargaining positions.

members that they are receiving wages and benefits comparable to those of other employees doing like work. Other negotiated collective agreements, particularly at the local and regional levels, play a significant part in settling the terms of the collective agreement.

Bargaining Teams

Normally, each side has four to six representatives at the negotiating table. The chief negotiator for management is the vice-president or manager for labour relations; the chief negotiator for the union is the local union president or national union representative. Others making up management's team may include representatives from accounting or finance, operations, employment, legal, or training. The local union president is likely to be supported by the chief steward, various local union vice-presidents, and a representative from the national union.

The initial meeting of the bargaining teams is a particularly important one because it establishes the climate that will prevail during the negotiations that follow. According to one experienced negotiator, "The conduct of negotiations largely depends on the relationship and attitude of negotiators toward one another. If you want conflict in your bargaining sessions just start off attacking the other side." This *attitudinal structuring* is done to change the attitudes of the parties toward each other, often with the objective of persuading one side to accept the other side's demands.[20]

Developing Bargaining Strategies and Tactics

Both management and union negotiators approach bargaining with a defined strategy. In tough economic periods, the employer's strategy might be cost containment or specific reductions in wages or benefits. Conversely, in times of economic growth—when a union strike would harm sales—the employer will be more willing to meet union demands. The employer's strategy should also consider proposals the union is likely to submit, goals the union is striving to achieve, and the extent to which it may be willing to make concessions or to resort to strike action in order to achieve these goals.

At a minimum, the employer's bargaining strategy must address these points:

- Likely union proposals and management responses to them
- A listing of management demands, limits of concessions, and anticipated union responses
- Development of a database to support management bargaining proposals and to counteract union demands
- A contingency operating plan should employees strike

Certain elements of strategy are common to both the employer and the union. Generally, the initial demands presented by each side are greater than those it actually may hope to achieve.[21] This is done in order to provide room for concessions. Moreover, each party usually avoids giving up the maximum it is capable of conceding in order to allow for further concessions that may be needed to break a bargaining deadlock.

The negotiation of a collective agreement can have some of the characteristics of a poker game, with each side attempting to determine its opponent's position while not revealing its own.[22] Each party normally tries to avoid disclosing the relative importance that it attaches to a proposal so that it will not be forced to pay a higher price than is necessary to have the proposal accepted. As in buying a new car, the buyer and seller employ a lot of strategy in order to obtain the best outcome possible.

Negotiating the Collective Agreement

While there is no "exact" way to negotiate a collective agreement, typically each side focuses on one issue or several related issues until agreement is reached. For each bargaining issue to be resolved satisfactorily, the point at which agreement is reached must be within limits that the union and the employer are willing to accept. In a frequently cited bargaining model, Ross Stagner and Hjalmar Rosen call the area within these two limits the **bargaining zone.** In some bargaining situations, such as the one illustrated in Figure 14.5, the solution desired by one party may exceed the limits of the other party. Thus that solution is outside the bargaining zone. If that party refuses to modify its demands sufficiently to bring them within the bargaining zone or if the opposing party refuses to extend its limit to accommodate the demands of the other party, a bargaining deadlock results.[23] For example, when bargaining a wage increase for employees, if the union's lowest limit is a 4-percent increase and management's top limit is 6 percent, an acceptable range—the bargaining zone—is available to both parties. If management's top limit is only 3 percent, however, a bargaining zone is not available to either side and a deadlock is likely to occur. Figure 14.5, which is based on the original model by Stagner

bargaining zone
Area within which the union and the employer are willing to concede when bargaining

---

Figure 14.5 | The Bargaining Zone and Negotiation Influences

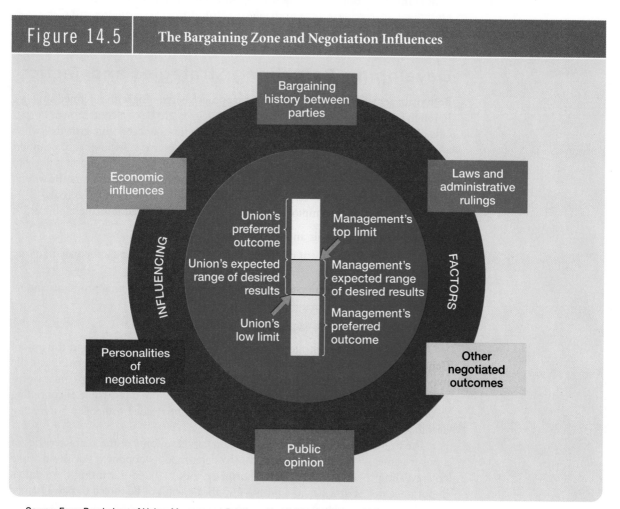

Source: From *Psychology of Union–Management Relations*, First Edition by Stagner/Rosen, 1996. Reprinted with permission of Wadsworth, a division of Thomson Learning: www.thomsonrights.com. Fax 800 731-2215.

and Rosen, shows that as bargaining takes place, several important variables influence the negotiators and their ability to reach agreement within the bargaining zone.

An employer is obligated to negotiate in good faith with the union's representatives over conditions of employment (the same obligation applies to the union representatives). Good faith requires meetings to be held at reasonable times and places to discuss employment conditions. It requires also that the proposals submitted by each party be realistic. In discussing the other party's proposals, each side must offer reasonable counterproposals for those it is unwilling to accept. Finally, both parties must sign the written document containing the agreement reached through negotiations.

Interest-Based Bargaining

Sometimes, labour–management negotiations are characterized as adversarial. With adversarial bargaining, negotiators start with defined positions and, through deferral, persuasion, trade, or power, the parties work toward the resolution of individual bargaining demands. With traditional bargaining—and its give-and-take philosophy—the results may or may not be to the complete satisfaction of one or both parties.[24] In fact, when one side feels it received "the short end of the stick," bitter feelings may persist throughout the life of the agreement. As noted by one labour negotiator, "adversarial bargaining does little to establish a long-term positive relationship based on open communications and trust. By its nature, it leads to suspicion and compromise."[25] To overcome these negative feelings, labour and management practitioners may use a nonadversarial approach to negotiating.

interest-based bargaining (IBB)
Problem-solving bargaining based on a win–win philosophy and the development of a positive long-term relationship

Interest-based bargaining (IBB) is based on the identification and resolution of mutual interests rather than the resolve of specific bargaining demands.[26] Interest-based bargaining is "a problem-solving process conducted in a principled way that creates effective solutions while improving the bargaining relationship."[27] The focus of bargaining strategy is to discover mutual bargaining interests with the intent of formulating options and solutions for mutual gain.

Interest-based bargaining is novel in both its philosophy and its bargaining process. Also distinct are the bargaining tools used to expedite a successful nonadversarial negotiating experience. Rather than using proposals and counterproposals as a means of reaching agreement (as with adversarial negotiations), participants use brainstorming, consensus decision making, active listening, process checking, and matrix building to facilitate the settlement of issues. An underlying goal of interest-based bargaining is to create a relationship for the future based on trust, understanding, and mutual respect, a process described in Highlights in HRM 14.6. The Business Case on page 621 outlines how IBB can save money.

Highlights in HRM 14.6

Building Trust Through IBB

The *Ottawa Citizen*, a newspaper with a circulation of 145 000 newspapers, is the largest daily newspaper in Ottawa, and the eighth largest in Canada. Approximately 65 percent of its 595 full-time employees are unionized and belong to one of three unions: the Communication Energy & Paperworkers (CEP), the Graphic Communications Union (GCU), and the Newspaper Guild. These bargaining units are also called chapels (and the shop steward is called chapel chairman)

(continued on next page)

in recognition of the time when it was illegal to hold union meetings so groups of employees wishing to meet collectively would say they were going to a "chapel [or church] meeting."

The *Ottawa Citizen* won a Vision award, a recognition by the Ottawa chapter of the Human Resources Professionals Association of Ontario for outstanding HR practices for the innovative design and implementation of an HR program based on its successful implementation of IBB. Debbie Bennett, vice-president of human resources and finance for the newspaper, describes the process: "In my opinion, IBB works when you have a good relationship that you want to improve upon, or when things are so bad that something has to change. I approached the [Newspaper] Guild, the largest union, with whom we already had a good relationship, about IBB. At the time, it had about 325 members. I started by buying them some IBB books (*Getting to Yes* and *Getting Together*) to determine if there was interest. There was. Union and management advertised for, jointly selected, and paid for a facilitator, who took us through a three-day training and relationship-building session. The entire bargaining team from both parties took part in the workshop to make sure we all understood the differences between IBB and traditional bargaining.

"For example, one difference was the ways in which we communicated, both internally to build trust and externally to our stakeholders. In IBB, we brainstormed, with the rule that no repercussions would follow if an idea was presented that everyone liked but subsequently was not found workable. In traditional bargaining, if an idea is placed on the table and then removed, it could be seen as reneging or bargaining in bad faith. The agreement to brainstorm led to very little caucus time, and a much faster bargaining pace, because the respective teams did not have to ask for a break to discuss new ideas in the hallway before presenting it to the other party.

"The tone of communications was also different. The objective at the table is to discuss issues in an open and honest manner. This objective would be hard to achieve if some of the more direct comments were quoted in public communiqués. Therefore, the parties agreed that communications to both management and union members were for the purpose of keeping everyone informed, not for the purpose of embarrassing the other party or belittling their position. The tone of communications was respectful.

"We started bargaining, with the facilitator at table, to ensure that we practised what we learned. After the third day, we no longer needed the facilitator. Usually our bargaining sessions took four to five months; this time, we finished in four to five days. Usually the changes to the collective agreement were mainly monetary; this time there were a lot of language changes. For example, like most organizations, when an employee is disciplined, a disciplinary letter is placed on file. The union wanted a sunset clause requiring automatic removal of the discipline letter after a period of time. The union's view was that a transgression should not be held against an employee forever. However, management felt a record of a serious infraction, like hitting another employee, should never be removed from the file nor should records of a repetitive problem. Through IBB, the teams came up with a clause, which said that a disciplinary letter will not automatically be removed, but will be taken to the VP who will decide on its removal based on clear criteria, such as the seriousness of the act and the repetitiveness of the behaviour.

"Overall, the effect of IBB on the labour relations climate, although always good, was to improve it."

The Business Case

The Benefits of IBB

Eleanor Gallant, manager of HR for the City of Charlottetown, Prince Edward Island, worked closely with PANS (Police Association of Nova Scotia—PEI local 301) and CUPE to establish a process of interest-based bargaining. The goal was not to repeat the past when negotiations dragged on for four years, ending in strikes and arbitration (for those without the right to strike). The process began before the contract opened again in 2002. In preparation, to encourage the interest of the parties, the director of HR for the city of Saint John, New Brunswick, was invited to speak about the success of IBB in that city. Some basic rules for the process of negotiating the collective agreement were put into place, including no lawyers would be present, there would be no discussion about the bargaining mandate with outsiders, and union and management officials would sit next to each other at the table, not on opposing sides.

The issue of time off in lieu of overtime serves as an example of how IBB worked in the City of Charlottetown. When the police officers were required to work overtime, they wanted to be compensated with time off instead of overtime pay. Management had refused this request due to bookkeeping complexities. However, the IBB process demonstrated the value of this arrangement to both parties. The two parties reached an agreement to hire part-time officers when extra hours were needed. The police officers were less stressed with less overtime, and the city saved money, because part-time police officers were less costly than full-time police officers being paid overtime rates.

Here are the savings produced by IBB for negotiations with PANS:

	Traditional bargaining	IBB
Time to reach agreement	4 years	8 days
Number of grievances	0	0
Amount that would have been spent on arbitration	$30,000	0

Here are the savings produced by IBB for negotiations with CUPE:

	Traditional bargaining	IBB
Time to reach agreement	4 years	8 days
Number of grievances	275	1
Amount that would have been spent on arbitration	$180,000	0

Management and Union Power in Collective Bargaining

Fortunately, the great majority of labour–management negotiations are settled peacefully. However, should negotiations become deadlocked, bargaining can become highly adversarial as each side will now employ its bargaining power to achieve its desired ends. The party's **bargaining power** consists of its economic, political, and social influence to achieve its demands at the expense of the other side.

bargaining power
The power of labour and management to achieve their goals through economic, social, or political influence

Union Bargaining Power

The bargaining power of the union may be exercised by striking, picketing, or boycotting the employer's products or services. A strike is the refusal of a group of employees to perform their jobs. Unions usually seek strike authorization from their members to use as a bargaining ploy to gain concessions that will make a strike unnecessary.[28] A strike vote by the members does not mean they actually want or expect to go out on strike. Rather, it is intended as a vote of confidence to strengthen the position of their leaders at the bargaining table.

Of critical importance to the union is the extent, if any, to which the employer will be able to continue operating through the use of supervisory and nonstriking personnel and employees hired to replace the strikers. In some jurisdictions, employers face restrictions to their right to hire replacement workers. In the 1990s the use of "scabs" at the Royal Oak Mine in Yellowknife so infuriated a striking miner that he blew up the mine killing nine workers. (Employers have the right to dismiss workers who engage in sabotage or violence during a strike.) The violence and strife associated with the use of replacement workers has caused Quebec and British Columbia to forbid their use. However studies have shown that the use of replacement workers shortens the duration of the strike.[29]

In organizations with high levels of technology and automation, and consequently fewer employees, continuing service with supervisors and managers is more likely. Among the highly automated telephone companies, most services can be maintained by supervisors during a strike. According to one authority, "Because of technological change, striking in many industries no longer has the effect of curtailing the employer's operations significantly."[30] Consequently, the greater the ability of the employer to continue operating, the less the union's chances of gaining its demands through a strike.

When a union goes on strike, it pickets the employer by placing people at business entrances to advertise the dispute and to discourage others from entering the premises. Because unions often refuse to cross another union's picket line, the pickets may serve to prevent the delivery and pickup of goods or performance of other services. For example, a Teamster truck driver may refuse to deliver produce to a food store whose employees are out on strike with the United Food and Commercial Workers Union. Once a strike has been settled, the workers are entitled to return to their jobs, though not necessarily their previous positions. The right to return to work is often an issue to be negotiated. Although laws vary, employees are often required to submit in writing their intention to return to their jobs once a strike is finalized.

Another economic weapon of the union is the *boycott*, which is a refusal to patronize the employer. For example, production employees on strike against a hand tool manufacturer might picket a retail store that sells the tools made by the struck employer. Unions will also use handbills, radio announcements, e-mail campaigns, and newspaper ads to discourage the purchase of the employer's product or service.

Picketing is used by unions to publicize their disputes and discourage people from entering the premises.

Management Bargaining Power

When negotiations become deadlocked, the employer's bargaining power largely rests on being able to continue operations in the face of a strike *or* to shut down operations entirely.

Another prevalent bargaining strategy is for the employer to continue operations by using managers and supervisors to staff employee jobs. In one case, nearly 30 000 managers left their offices to serve as operators, technicians, and customer service representatives during a strike between Verizon and the Communications Workers of America. As noted previously, technological advances enhance the employer's ability to operate during a strike.

In extreme situations, the employer may elect to lock out its employees. The lockout is a bargaining strategy by which the employer denies employees the opportunity to work by closing its operations. In a highly publicized case, during the 2004–2005 National Hockey League season, management locked out players represented by the National Hockey League Players Association. Besides being used in bargaining impasses, lockouts may be used by employers to combat union slowdowns, damage to their property, or violence within the organization that may occur in connection with a labour dispute.[31] Employers may still be reluctant to resort to a lockout, however, because of their concern that denying work to regular employees might hurt the organization's image.

Resolving Bargaining Deadlocks

Unions and employers in all types of industries—sports, transportation, entertainment, manufacturing, communication, and healthcare—have used mediation and arbitration to help resolve their bargaining deadlocks. As discussed in Chapter 13, mediation is a voluntary process that relies on the communication and persuasive skills of a mediator to help the parties resolve their differences. In many jurisdictions, conciliation is compulsory before a legal strike or lockout. The conciliator, appointed by the provincial ministry of labour, attempts to reach a workable agreement.

arbitrator
Third-party neutral who resolves labour dispute by issuing a final decision in the disagreement

Unlike a mediator, an **arbitrator** assumes the role of a decision maker and determines what the settlement between the two parties should be. In other words, arbitrators write a final contract that the parties *must* accept. Compared with mediation, arbitration is not often used to settle private-sector bargaining disputes. In the public sector, where strikes are largely prohibited, the use of *interest arbitration* is a common method to resolve bargaining deadlocks. Generally, one or both parties are reluctant to give a third party the power to make the settlement for them. Consequently, a mediator typically is used to break a deadlock and assist the parties in reaching an agreement. An arbitrator generally is called on to resolve disputes arising in connection with the administration of the agreement, called *rights arbitration* or *grievance arbitration*, which will be discussed shortly.

USING THE INTERNET

One of the newer forms of mediation is online mediation. Check out how experts can be used by visiting these sites:

www.mediate.com/odr/

www.adrr.com

The Collective Agreement

When negotiations are concluded, the collective agreement becomes a formal *binding* document listing the terms, conditions, and rules under which employees and managers agree to operate. Highlights in HRM 14.7 on page 624 shows some of the major articles in a collective agreement and also provides examples of some new and

Highlights in HRM 14.7

Items in a Collective Agreement

Typical clauses will cover

- Wages
- Grievance procedures
- Vacations
- No strike/no lockout clause
- Holidays
- Overtime
- Work schedules
- Safety procedures

- Management rights
- Severance pay
- Union security
- Seniority
- Transfers
- Pensions and benefits
- Discipline
- Outsourcing

Progressive clauses will cover

- Employee access to records
- Limitations on use of performance evaluation
- Elder care leave, child care, work–family balance provisions
- Flexible medical spending accounts
- Protection against hazards of technology equipment
- Limitations against electronic monitoring
- Bilingual stipends
- Domestic partnership benefits

progressive contract clauses. Two important items in any collective agreement pertain to the issue of management rights and the forms of security afforded the union.

The Issue of Management Rights

Management rights have to do with the conditions of employment over which management is able to exercise exclusive control. Almost without exception, the collective agreement contains a *management rights* clause. This clause states that "management's authority is supreme in all matters except those it has expressly conceded in the collective agreement, or in those areas where its authority is restricted by law." Management rights might include the right of management to determine the products to produce, to determine the location of production or service facilities, or to select production equipment and procedures. The following is an example of a clause defining management rights in one collective agreement:

> It is agreed that the company possesses all of the rights, powers, privileges, and authority it had prior to the execution of this agreement; and nothing in this agreement shall be construed to limit the company in any way in the exercise of the regular and customary functions of management and the operation of its business, except as it may be specifically relinquished or modified herein by an express provision of this agreement.[32]

Union Security Agreements

As we noted at the beginning of this chapter, unions must represent all bargaining-unit members equally regardless of whether employees join the union or not. In exchange for this obligation, union officials will seek to negotiate some form of compulsory membership as a condition of employment. Union officials argue that compulsory membership precludes the possibility that some employees will receive the benefits of unionization without paying their fair share of the costs. A standard union security provision is dues checkoff, which gives the employer the responsibility of withholding union dues from the paycheques of union members who agree to such a deduction.

Other common forms of union security found in collective agreements are different types of "shop" agreements. These agreements—in varying degrees—attempt to require employees to join the union. For example, the *union shop* provides that any employee who is not a union member upon employment must join the union within 30 days or be terminated. Another, the *agency shop*, provides for voluntary membership. However, all bargaining-unit members must pay union dues and fees.

Administration of the Collective Agreement

Negotiation of the collective agreement, as mentioned earlier, is usually the most publicized and critical aspect of labour relations. Strike deadlines, press conferences, and employee picketing help create this image. Nevertheless, as managers in unionized organizations know, the bulk of labour relations activity comes from the day-to-day administration of the agreement, because no agreement could possibly anticipate all the forms that disputes may take. In addition, once the agreement is signed, each side will naturally interpret ambiguous clauses to its own advantage.[33] These differences are traditionally resolved through the grievance procedure.

Negotiated Grievance Procedures

objective **6**

grievance procedure
Formal procedure that provides for the union to represent members and nonmembers in processing a grievance

The **grievance procedure** typically provides for the union to represent the interests of its members (and nonmembers as well) in processing a grievance. It is considered by some authorities to be the heart of the bargaining agreement, or the safety valve that gives flexibility to the whole system of collective bargaining.[34]

The grievance procedure is normally initiated by the union—or an individual employee—when it feels management has violated some article of the collective agreement. In one case, the union filed a grievance against a supervisor when it believed the supervisor promoted an employee out of seniority order—called a bypass grievance. A significant benefit of the grievance procedure is that it provides a formal and orderly procedure for the union to challenge the actions of management without resort to force. One authority has noted, "The grievance procedure fosters cooperation, not conflict, between the employer and the union."[35]

The operation of a grievance procedure is unique to each individual collective bargaining relationship, but it is required under Canadian labour relations codes. For example, grievance procedures normally specify how the grievance is to be initiated, the number and timing of steps that are to compose the procedure, and the identity of representatives from each side who are to be involved in the hearings at each step.

When a grievance cannot be resolved at one of the specified steps, most agreements provide for the grievance to be submitted to a third party—usually an arbitrator—whose decision is final. Some collective agreements provide for mediation as a way to resolve employee grievances. When used, *grievance mediation* will be listed as a formal step in the grievance procedure preceding arbitration.[36]

The Grievance Procedure in Action

In order for an employee's grievance to be considered formally, it must be expressed orally and/or in writing, ideally to the employee's immediate supervisor. Because grievances are often the result of an oversight or a misunderstanding, many of them can be resolved at this point. Whether it is possible to resolve a grievance at the initial step will depend on the supervisor's ability and willingness to discuss the problem with the employee and the steward. Additionally, HR professionals acknowledge that grievance handling is more successful when supervisors are trained formally in resolving grievances, including familiarization with the terms of the collective agreement and the discussion of the problem in a rational and objective manner. A grievance should not be viewed as something to be won or lost. Rather, both sides must view the situation as an attempt to solve a human relations problem.

In some instances a satisfactory solution may not be possible at the first step because there are legitimate differences of opinion between the employee and the supervisor or because the supervisor does not have the authority to take the action required to satisfy the grievant. Personality conflicts, prejudices, emotionalism, stubbornness, or other factors may also be barriers to a satisfactory solution at this step.

Rights Arbitration

rights arbitration
Arbitration over interpretation of the meaning of contract terms or employee work grievances

The function of **rights arbitration** is to provide the solution to a grievance that a union and an employer have been unable to resolve by themselves. As mentioned earlier, arbitration is performed by a neutral third party (an arbitrator or impartial umpire). This third party's decision dictates how the grievance is to be settled.[37] Both parties are obligated to comply with the decision.

The Decision to Arbitrate

In deciding whether to use arbitration, each party must weigh the costs involved against the importance of the case and the prospects of gaining a favourable award. It would seem logical that neither party would allow a weak case to go to arbitration if there were little possibility of gaining a favourable award. Logic, however, does not always prevail. For example, it is not unusual for a union to take a weak case to arbitration in order to demonstrate to the members that the union is willing to exhaust every remedy in looking out for their interests. Union officers also are not likely to refuse to take to arbitration the grievances of members who are popular or politically powerful in the union, even though their cases are weak. Moreover, unions have a legal obligation to provide assistance to members who are pursuing grievances. Because members can bring suit against their unions for failing to process their grievances adequately, many union officers are reluctant to refuse taking even weak grievances to arbitration.

Management, on the other hand, may allow a weak case to go to arbitration to demonstrate to the union officers that management "cannot be pushed around." Also, managers at lower levels may be reluctant to risk the displeasure of top management by stating that a certain HR policy is unworkable or unsound. Stubbornness and mutual antagonism also may force many grievances into arbitration because neither party is willing to make concessions to reach an agreement, even when it may recognize that it is in the wrong.

The Arbitration Process

In our experience, employees unfamiliar with arbitration find the process confusing and often stressful. This is true for employees in the nonunion, as well as the union, setting. Arbitration hearings have the appearance of a court hearing but without many of the formalities of a court proceeding.

submission to arbitrate
Statement that describes the issues to be resolved through arbitration

The process begins with the swearing-in of witnesses and the introduction of a formal statement known as the **submission to arbitrate,** which is a statement of the problem to be resolved. Such a statement might read: "Was the three-day suspension of Alex Hayden for just cause? If not, what is the appropriate remedy?" The parties will then make opening statements, followed by the presentation of facts and evidence, and the oral presentation of witnesses. The hearing will conclude with each side making summary statements that are arguments in support of its position.

In arbitrating a dispute, it is the responsibility of the arbitrator to ensure that each side receives a fair hearing during which it may present all of the facts it considers pertinent to the case. The primary purpose of the hearing is to assist the arbitrator in obtaining the facts necessary to resolve a human relations problem rather than a legal one. The arbitrator, therefore, has a right to question witnesses or to request additional facts from either party. After conducting the hearing and receiving post-hearing briefs (should the parties choose to submit them), the arbitrator customarily has 30 days in which to consider the evidence and render an award. In the majority of cases, the costs of arbitration are shared equally by the parties.

The Arbitration Award

arbitration award
Final and binding award issued by an arbitrator in a labour–management dispute

The **arbitration award** is a formal written document given to both sides. As in grievance procedures, there is no specific format to an arbitration award but typically the award contains five parts: (1) the submission to arbitrate, (2) the facts of the case, (3) the positions of the parties, (4) the opinion of the arbitrator, and (5) the decision rendered. As might be expected, the decision of the arbitrator is of major importance to the parties. However, the reasoning behind the decision—the opinion—is equally important as it can provide guidance concerning the interpretation of the collective agreement and the resolution of future disputes arising from its administration. In pointing out the merits of each party's position, the reasoning that underlies the award can help lessen the disappointment and protect the self-esteem of those representing the unsuccessful party. The opinion will also evaluate the evidence presented by each side in support of its position and, in discipline cases, whether management had just cause for the action taken against an employee. (See Chapter 13 for a discussion of just cause in arbitration.) Importantly, in deciding a case, the arbitrator has the power to modify the outcome requested by both sides. It is not uncommon, for example, for an arbitrator to reduce a discharge to a suspension without pay for a specific time period.

Because of the importance and magnitude of arbitration in both the union and nonunion setting, the process by which arbitrators make decisions and the factors that influence those decisions are of continuing interest to managers. Typically, arbitrators use four factors when deciding cases:

1. The wording of the collective agreement (or employment policy in nonunion organizations)
2. The submission agreement as presented to the arbitrator
3. Testimony and evidence offered during the hearing
4. Arbitration criteria or standards (similar to standards of common law) against which cases are judged

When deciding the case of an employee discharged for absenteeism, for example, the arbitrator would consider these factors separately and/or jointly. Arbitrators are essentially constrained to decide cases on the basis of the wording of the collective agreement, or employment policy, and the facts, testimony, and evidence presented at the hearing.

In practice, arbitration decision making is not an exact science. In fact, the decisions of arbitrators can be rather subjective. Arbitrators can, and do, interpret contract language differently (for example, What does "just-cause discharge" actually mean?), they assign varying degrees of importance to testimony and evidence, they judge the truthfulness of witnesses differently, and they give arbitration standards greater or lesser weight as they apply to facts of the case. Each of these influences introduces subjectivity into the decision-making process.

SUMMARY

Labour relations legislation in Canada recognizes the right of employees to form and join unions, and prohibits both unions and employers from engaging in unfair labour practices. Provincial labour relations laws are administered and enforced by labour relations boards.

Studies show that workers unionize for different economic, psychological, and social reasons. While some employees may join unions because they are required to do so, most belong to unions because they are convinced that unions help them improve their wages, benefits, and various working conditions. Employee unionization is largely caused by dissatisfaction with managerial practices and procedures.

A formal organizing campaign is used to solicit employee support for the union. Once employees demonstrate their desire to unionize, the union will file an application with the labour relations board for approval of the union as the certified bargaining agent. If the labour relations board feels that there were irregularities in the application process, it has the power to call for a vote.

Negotiating a collective agreement is a detailed process. Each side prepares a list of proposals it wishes to achieve while additionally trying to anticipate proposals desired by the other side. Bargaining teams must be selected and all proposals must be analyzed to determine their impact on and cost to the organization. Both employer and union negotiators are sensitive to current bargaining patterns within the industry, general cost-of-living trends, and geographical wage differentials. Managers establish goals that seek to retain control over operations and to minimize costs. Union negotiators focus their demands around improved wages, hours, and working conditions. An agreement is reached when both sides compromise their original positions and final terms fall within the limits of the parties' bargaining zone.

Currently, there is an increased interest in nonadversarial negotiations—negotiations based on mutual gains and a heightened respect between the parties. Interest-based bargaining is one form of nonadversarial negotiations.

The collective bargaining process includes not only the actual negotiations but also the power tactics used to support negotiating demands. When negotiations become deadlocked, bargaining becomes a power struggle to force from either side the concessions needed to break the deadlock. The union's power in collective bargaining comes from its ability to picket, strike, or boycott the employer. The employer's power during negotiations comes from its ability to lock out employees or to operate during a strike by using managerial or replacement employees.

When differences arise between labour and management they are normally resolved through the grievance procedure. Grievance procedures are negotiated and thus reflect the needs and desires of the parties. The typical grievance procedure consists of three, four, or five steps—each step having specific filing and reply times. Higher-level managers and union officials become involved in disputes at the higher steps of the grievance procedure. The final step of the grievance procedure may be arbitration. Arbitrators render a final decision to problems not resolved at lower grievance steps.

The submission to arbitrate is a statement of the issue to be solved through arbitration. It is simply the problem the parties wish to have settled. The arbitrator must answer the issue by basing the arbitration award on four factors: the contents of the collective agreement (or employment policy), the submission agreement as written, testimony and evidence obtained at the hearing, and various arbitration standards developed over time to assist in the resolution of different types of labour–management disputes. Arbitration is not an exact science, because arbitrators give varying degrees of importance to the evidence and criteria by which disputes are resolved.

KEY TERMS

arbitration award, 627
arbitrator, 623
authorization card, 604
bargaining power, 622
bargaining unit, 605
bargaining zone, 618
business agent, 612
collective bargaining
    process, 615

compulsory binding
    arbitration, 614
craft unions, 608
employee associations, 608
final offer arbitration, 615
grievance procedure, 625
industrial unions, 608
interest-based bargaining
    (IBB), 619

labour relations process, 600
management rights, 608
rights arbitration, 626
submission to arbitrate, 627
unfair labour practices
    (ULPs), 604
union shop, 601
union steward, 611

DISCUSSION QUESTIONS

1. There has been a substantial increase (some estimate 40 percent) in the number of individuals who are self-employed. Some see this as a positive sign (i.e., of an increase in entrepreneurial activity); others see it as a response to the lack of permanent employment opportunities. The labour laws in each province effectively ignore independent workers. For many of them, wages (i.e., contract rates) are low, working conditions are difficult, and income security does not exist. Prepare to debate solutions to this issue, taking one of two sides: "Governments should change labour laws to recognize and protect self-employed workers," or, "Unions should organize these independent contractors and fight for better treatment."

2. *Fast Food High* is a film produced by CTV and inspired by the real story about how a group of teenage workers tried to organize a union at

McDonald's in Orangeville, Ontario. Watch the film, and discuss in groups the reasons why these workers want to form a union, and the effectiveness of their efforts.

3. Contrast the arguments concerning union membership that are likely to be presented by a union with those likely to be presented by an employer. What are your reasons for joining a student union, and how do they compare with the reasons for joining a labour union?

4. Describe the steps in the traditional organizing drive. What "nontraditional" organizing tactics are unions using to increase their membership ranks?

5. A group of students wants a Burger King fast-food franchise on their university campus. University administrators want a health-food restaurant. Resources allow for only one food outlet. Divide the class into bargaining teams, with one team representing the students, and the other team representing the university administrators. (If there is another issue on your campus use the real and current issue instead.) After the groups have started bargaining, consult the Career Counsel website to assess the negotiating styles employed by each team.

6. The negotiations between Data Services International and its union have become deadlocked. What form of bargaining power does each side possess to enforce its bargaining demands? What are the advantages and disadvantages of each form of bargaining power for both the employer and union?

7. Indira Singh has decided to file a grievance with her union steward. The grievance alleges that she was "bypassed" by a junior employee for a promotion to senior technician.
   a. Explain the steps her grievance will follow in a formal union–management grievance procedure.
   b. Should her grievance go to arbitration, explain the process of an arbitration hearing and identify the criteria used by the arbitrator to resolve her claim.

INTERNET EXERCISE

Wilfrid Laurier University, based in Waterloo, Ontario, experienced a labour dispute with the Wilfrid Laurier Staff Association in 2002. During the negotiations the university provided regular updates on the issues and impact on operations on this site: http://info.wlu.ca/~wwwpa/campus_update/work-stoppage/index.shtml.

Using the information provided, identify the issues that led to the dispute. What was the impact on university operations? How was the dispute settled?

HRM Experience

Learn about Unions

Unions, like business organizations, are dynamic and varied organizations. Some unions are very large, such as the Canadian Auto Workers (CAW) and represent workers nationally. Others are smaller in size—and represent only specific groups of employees or organize only in a designated geographic area. This exercise will help you learn more about unions.

Assignment

Working individually or in teams, select four or five different unions or employee associations and report on the following. Vary your selections (large/small, public/private, and so on) to widen your understanding of labour organizations.

- History of the union
- Membership size and type of employees represented
- Mission of the union
- Structure of the union, including its major departments
- National officers
- Names of employers with whom they have an agreement
- Special benefits they offer members
- Other interesting or pertinent information

National unions and their locals along with library research can also provide information. Be prepared to present your findings during a class discussion.

BIZFLIX EXERCISES

Bread & Roses: Join the Union; Get Bread and Roses

Make sure you have read this chapter before watching this scene from *Bread & Roses.* Before viewing the scene, note your perceptions of unions. Do the same after watching the scene. It strongly relates to discussions of why employees unionize and of union-organizing campaigns.

"Justice for Janitors" is the union-organizing slogan that drives Sam Shapiro's (Adrien Brody) efforts to organize the janitors who work for Angel Services in Los Angeles. Unionized janitors earn over $8.00 an hour plus benefits; nonunionized janitors earn $5.75 an hour with no benefits. These nonunionized janitors are mainly immigrants from different countries. Maya (Pilar Padilla) becomes an early supporter of the cause, although she risks losing her job and getting deported. Director Ken Loach launches a political polemic that grippingly tells the story of workers calling for fair wages and fair treatment by their employers.

This scene comes from the "Standing Strong" segment near the end of the film. Sam has worked untiringly to organize the Angel Services workers who work in a building with a prominent law firm as a major tenant. A large group of janitors, both union and nonunion, have marched to the building's lobby. Sam rallies them to continue their fight for fair wages,

benefits, and reinstatement of the workers fired by Perez (George Lopez) at Angel Services. The film continues after this scene to show that the workers won. Angel Services agrees to reinstate all fired workers plus higher wages and benefits.

What to Watch for and Ask Yourself

- What was your perception of unions and union organizers before you watched this scene? What was your perception after you watched this scene? If your perception changed, why do you think it changed?
- An earlier chapter section, "Why Employees Unionize," describes several factors that motivate people to become union members. Based on this scene, which factors do you think drive these janitors to want to join a union? You also can refer to Figure 14.1, "The Labour Relations Process," for guidance with this question.
- An earlier section, "Organizing Campaigns," describes many parts of a union-organizing campaign. Sam Shapiro is the union organizer. Compare the chapter section to this scene, and infer which steps occurred. Also, assess Sam Shapiro's effectiveness as a union organizer.

Wal-Mart Stores in Canada

In 2006, Wal-Mart was operating more than 6500 stores with 1.8 million employees around the world. In the early 1990s Wal-Mart Stores Inc. expanded into Canada, with the purchase of 122 stores from the failing Woolco chain. Wal-Mart had refused to purchase nine Woolco stores, which were unionized.

Wal-Mart tries to distinguish itself from other retailers by its culture. For example, it calls its workers "associates," not employees. Every day at 8:45 a.m., a compulsory meeting is held at each store during which company managers share financial information and performance targets and respond to questions. The meeting ends with the Wal-Mart cheer. The company operates an open-door policy, whereby any employee can talk to any member of management about issues, and receive answers, without being threatened with reprisal. The sundown rule ensures that management responds to the questions before sundown the same day.

The first Wal-Mart store ever to be unionized was in Windsor, Ontario, where the United Steelworkers (Retail and Wholesale Division) was certified by the Ontario Labour Relations Board. On April 14, 1997, the United Steelworkers began its organizing drive. On April 26, the store manager became aware that associates were being approached to sign unionization cards. The district manager was told of the organizing drive and the next morning attended the morning meeting. The district manager asked the associates why they would want to join a union and spent the day circulating through the store to discuss their problems or concerns. By April 27, 84 associates had signed cards. On April 29, an associate asked to speak at the morning meeting, and there expressed her opposition to the union, ending with the statement, "A union will only cause discontentment in our store, and I assure you as I am standing here, Wal-Mart will not put up with it." (Management did not ask, nor did the associate reveal, why she wanted to speak.) An inside organizer was prevented from responding because it was 9 a.m. and customers were waiting to enter the store.

Between May 4 and May 9, Wal-Mart managers—including managers from outside the store—responded to questions placed in a question-and-answer box, and to those raised while they wandered about the store. Most of the questions focused on compensation and hours of work. However, one associate testified that one manager said that things would change if the employees were unionized—for example, the profit-sharing plan would be revoked. During one meeting, the managers were asked if the store would close; they replied, "It would be inappropriate for your company to comment on what it will or will not do if the store is unionized." On May 9, the union lost the vote, with 151 employees voting against it, and 43 voting for it.

The Ontario Labour Relations Board nonetheless certified the union, because the employer violated the Labour Relations Act by not disassociating itself from the remarks made by the associate at the meeting; by not allowing the inside organizer to respond; by subtly threatening job security; and by allowing outside managers in the store from May 4 to 9. The OLRB stated that the union had 84 cards signed before the managers' visits, and a week later, this support had dropped. A second vote would not change the outcome, because the threat to job security could not be erased from employees' minds. The legislation that allows the OLRB to overturn a certification board has now been changed.

Despite numerous organizing drives, Wal-Mart has successfully prevented unionization, and most of their 278 Canadian stores with 70 000 employees remain union-free.

The United Food and Commercial Workers Union (UFCW) charged Wal-Mart with unfair labour practices in thwarting a union organizing drive in British Columbia by discrediting the key organizer and by advising employees that if he turned up at their homes, they could call the police. The B.C. Labour Board said, "Wal-Mart has an anti-union history . . . and simply cannot resist the temptation to get involved in certification campaigns. While Wal-Mart has tended not to repeat its mistakes, there is no shortage of new ones that it finds ways to make." In the company's view, not being able to answer employee concerns about unionization is not part of their culture of open communication. But two labour relations boards believe that the company has gone too far in communication, by, for example, distributing anti-union literature at a store in Quesnel, B.C. Wal-Mart is seeking to change labour laws to allow it to address employee concerns.

QUESTIONS

1. What were the rights of Wal-Mart, the employer, during these two organizing drives?
2. The certification of the first Wal-Mart was hailed by labour as a milestone event. Why?
3. In your opinion, can Wal-Mart remain union-free indefinitely? Why or why not?

Sources: Adapted from Uyen Vu, "Wal-Mart Seeks to Change Labour Laws," *Canadian HR Reporter*, September 13, 2004, 1; V. Galt, "Wal-Mart Must Give Union Access," *The Globe and Mail*, May 13, 2003, B5; J. Hobel, "Allegation of Union Vote Rigging Investigated at Wal-Mart," *Canadian HR Reporter*, September 20, 1999, 1, 19; "Employer Interference: The Wal-Mart Case," *Worklife Report* 11, no. 2, 1–4.

case study 2

The Union Drive at Apollo Corporation: ULPs and Organizing Tactics

Bob Thomas was discharged after 19 years as a plant maintenance engineer with Apollo Corporation. During that time he had received average, and sometimes below-average, annual performance appraisals. Thomas was known as something of a complainer and troublemaker, and he was highly critical of management. Prior to his termination, his attendance record for the previous five years had been very poor. However, Apollo Corporation had never enforced its attendance policy, and Thomas had never been disciplined for his attendance problems. In fact, until recently, Apollo management had been rather laid-back in its dealings with employees.

Apollo Corporation produces general component parts for the communications industry—an industry known for intense competitive pressures. To meet this competitive challenge, Jean Lipski, HR director, held a series of meetings with managers in which she instructed them to tighten up their supervisory relationship with employees. They were told to enforce HR policies strictly and to begin disciplinary action against employees not conforming to company policy. These changes did not sit well with employees, particularly Bob Thomas. On hearing of the new management approach, Thomas became irate and announced, "They can't get away with this. I wrote the book around here." But secretly Thomas believed his past conduct was catching up with him, and he became concerned about protecting his job.

One night after work, Thomas called a union organizer of the Brotherhood of Machine Engineers and asked that a union drive begin at Apollo. Within a week employees began handing out flyers announcing a union meeting. When Lipski heard of the organizing campaign and Thomas's leadership in it, she decided to terminate his employment. Thomas's termination paper read: "Discharged for poor work performance and unsatisfactory attendance." Thomas was called into Lipski's office and told of the discharge. After leaving her office, Thomas called the union organizer, and they both went to the regional office of the LRB to file an unfair labour practice charge on Thomas's behalf. The ULP alleged that he was fired for his support of the union and the organizing drive.

Jean Lipski had little experience with unions in general and no specific experience with union-organizing campaigns. Unfortunately for Lipski, the Brotherhood of Machine Engineers, Local 1463, began an organizing drive against Apollo on June 1. Although the union's initial efforts were confined to passing out flyers about an organizational meeting, by June 10 it was obvious that employee support for the union had grown and union campaigning had greatly intensified. The question faced by Lipski was no longer, "Should Apollo do something?" but rather, "What should Apollo do?" It was obvious to Lipski that the union was committed to a full-fledged effort to unionize the company's employees. Supervisors reported to her that union supporters were passing out authorization cards in order to petition the LRB for a certification election.

QUESTIONS

1. What, if any, violation of the law did Apollo Corporation commit?
2. What arguments will Jean Lipski and Bob Thomas use to support their cases?
3. List things that managers should *not* do lest they commit unfair labour practices.

CAREER COUNSEL

For feedback on how you handle conflict, complete the Managing Conflict Questionnaire on the *Managing Human Resources* website (www.belcourt5e.nelson.com).

You can also learn about six negotiating strategies and how they can be used in salary negotiations.

NOTES AND REFERENCES

1. "Union Membership in Canada," Workplace Information Directorate, Labour Program, Human Resources and Skills Development Canada, January 1, 2006.
2. Bruce E. Kaufman, "Reflections on Six Decades in Industrial Relations: An Interview with John Dunlop," *Industrial and Labor Relations Review* 55, no. 2 (January 2002): 324–48; C. Heron, *The Canadian Labour Movement: A Short History* (Toronto: James Lorimer & Company, 1989); M. Gunderson, A. Ponak, and D. Gottlieb Taras, *Union Management Relations in Canada*, 4th ed. (Toronto: Addison Wesley Longman, 2001).
3. M. Gunderson, A. Ponak, and D. Gottlieb Taras, *Union Management Relations in Canada*, 4th ed. (Toronto: Addison Wesley Longman, 2001).
4. Readers interested in reading more about the labour relations process can consult Gunderson, et al., *Union Management*

Relations in Canada, 4th ed.; J. Godard, *Industrial Relations: The Economy and Society* (Toronto: McGraw-Hill Ryerson, 1994).
5. Maureen Hannay, "The Unionization of Professionals," *Journal of Labor Research* 23, no. 3 (Summer 2002): 487–98. See also John A. McClendon, Hoyt N. Wheeler, and Roger D. Weikle, "The Individual Decision to Unionize," *Labor Studies Journal* 23, no. 3 (Fall 1998): 34–54.
6. Juliet O'Neill, "Commission Wrestles with Outdated Labour Laws and Workforce They are Meant to Cover: The Challenges Facing Canada's Workforce," *CanWest News*, November 8, 2005, 1.
7. For a pioneering study on why workers unionize, see E. Wight Bakke, "Why Workers Join Unions," *Personnel* 22, no. 7 (July 1947): 3.
8. Kate Bronfenbrenner and Robert Hickey, "Successful Union Organizing in the United States—Clear Lessons, Too Few Examples," *Multinational Monitor* 24, no. 6 (June 2003): 9.

9. William H. Holley, Kenneth M. Jennings, and Roger S. Wolters, *The Labor Relations Process*, 8th ed. (Mason, OH: South-Western, 2005).

10. Lorna Harris, "Labour Board Punishes Employer for Heavy Handed Efforts to Block Union," *Canadian HR Reporter* 15, no. 9 (May 6, 2002): 6.

11. K.J. Bentham, "Employer Resistance to Union Certification: A Study of Canadian Jurisdictions," *Relations Industrielles*, Winter 2002: 159–87.

12. J. Heinz, "Union Attempts to Organize Wal-Mart Stores in Ontario," *The Globe and Mail*, June 3, 1995, B3.

13. Discussion with CAW business representative, July 1995.

14. S.D. Smith, "Rising Union Certification Trends in Ontario," HROI White Paper, #020, 2001, July 24, 2001.

15. Canada Labour Relations Board regulations and Ontario Labour Relations Act.

16. "Union Membership in Canada," Workplace Information Directorate, Labour Program, Human Resources and Skills Development Canada, January 1, 2006.

17. Ibid.

18. E. Kevin Kelloway and Julian Barling, "Members' Participation in Local Union Activities: Measurement, Prediction, and Replication," *Journal of Applied Psychology* 78, no. 2 (April 1993): 262–78.

19. John A. Fossum, *Labor Relations: Development, Structure, Process*, 6th ed. (Homewood, IL: BPI-Irwin, 1995): 312.

20. For the original description of attitudinal structuring, see Richard E. Walton and Robert B. McKersie, *A Behavioral Theory of Labor Negotiations* (New York: McGraw-Hill, 1965). This book is considered a classic in the labour relations field.

21. Leigh Thompson, *The Mind and Heart of the Negotiator*, 3rd ed. (Upper Saddle River, NJ: Prentice Hall, 2004).

22. Thomas R. Colosi, "The Principles of Negotiation," *Dispute Resolution Journal* 57, no. 1 (February–April 2002): 28–31.

23. Ross Stagner and Hjalmar Rosen, *Psychology of Union-Management Relations* (Belmont, CA: Wadsworth, 1965): 95–97. This is another classic in the field of labour–management relations.

24. Nils O. Fonstad, Robert B. McKersie, and Susan C. Eaton, "Interest-Based Negotiations in a Transformed Labor–Management Setting," *Negotiation Journal* 20, no. 1 (January 2004): 5. See also Robert B.

25. McKersie, Susan E. Eaton, and Thomas A. Kochan, "Kaiser Permanente: Using Interest-Based Negotiations to Craft a New Collective Bargaining Agreement," *Negotiation Journal* 20, no. 1 (January 2004): 13.

25. Joe Stanley, interview by author, Phoenix, Arizona, January 5, 2005.

26. The FMCS has a complete and comprehensive program to train labour and management negotiators in the art and techniques of interest-based bargaining (IBB). Information on the IBB program can be obtained from the FMCS national headquarters at 2100 K Street, N.W., Washington, DC 20427, or from FMCS district offices.

27. *Interest-Based Negotiations: Participants' Guidebook* (Washington, DC: Federal Mediation and Conciliation Service, 1998): 11.

28. "US Airways Group Inc.: Flight Attendants Union Mails Strike-Authorization Ballots," *The Wall Street Journal* (Eastern Edition), November 20, 2004, 1.

29. Shannon Klie, "Replacement Workers Put Pressure on the Union . . . But At What Cost?" *Canadian HR Reporter*, October 24, 2005, 11, 12.

30. Bill McDonough, president of United Food and Commercial Workers Union Local 99, interview by author, January 12, 2005, Phoenix, Arizona.

31. Bill Coffin, "Labor Lockout Hurts More Than Shipping," *Risk Management* 49, no. 12 (December 2002): 8.

32. Labor agreement, Wabash Fibre Box Company and Paperworkers.

33. John B. Larocco, "Ambiguities in Labor Union Contracts: Where Do They Come From?" *Dispute Resolution Journal* 59, no. 1 (February–April 2004): 38.

34. *Grievance Guide*, 11th ed. (Washington, DC: BNA Books, 2003).

35. Vera Riggs, Labor-Management Relations Conference, August 11, 2004, Phoenix, Arizona.

36. Peter J. Conodeca, "Ready . . . Set . . . Mediate," *Dispute Resolution Journal* 56, no. 4 (November 2001–January 2002): 32–38.

37. Arbitration awards are not final in all cases. Arbitration awards may be overturned through the judicial process if it can be shown that the arbitrator was prejudiced or failed to render an award based on the essence of the agreement.

ANSWERS TO HIGHLIGHTS IN HRM 14.1

1. No. Individual questioning of employees about their union membership or activities is unlawful.

2. Yes. However, this must be part of normal conduct and cannot be interpreted as a gesture to buy votes.

3. Yes. Blacklisting of job applications or employees is against labour law.

4. No. During an organizing drive, an employer cannot promise improvements in wages or benefits as a means of defeating the union.

5. Yes. Employees can be disciplined or discharged for work-related misconduct but not solely because of their union affiliations or union sentiments.

International Human Resources Management

After studying this chapter, you should be able to

objective **1**

Identify the types of organizational forms used for competing internationally.

objective **2**

Explain the economic, political-legal, and cultural factors in different countries that HR managers need to consider.

objective **3**

Explain how domestic and international HRM differ.

objective **4**

Discuss the staffing process for individuals working internationally.

objective **5**

Identify the unique training needs for international assignees and their employees.

objective **6**

Identify the characteristics of a good international compensation plan.

objective **7**

Reconcile the difficulties of home- and host-country performance appraisals.

objective **8**

Explain how labour relations differ around the world.

When you pick up a newspaper or turn on the TV, you'll notice that stories are constantly being told about companies competing globally. These stories might include mergers of North American and international companies, such as Daimler-Benz and Chrysler a few years ago. Or they might highlight companies expanding into other markets, such as Research In Motion in Asia or Scotiabank in the Dominican Republic. Or the stories might focus on international companies gaining dominance here in Canada, such as ING or Wal-Mart. "No matter what kind of business you run, no matter what size you are, you're suddenly competing against companies you've never heard of all around the world that make a very similar widget or provide a very similar service," as one global manager put it. In fact, nearly three-quarters of HR professionals from companies large and small in a wide range of industries and countries say they expect their company's international business to grow in the coming years.[1] Some of these companies are handling the challenge well. Others are failing miserably as they try to manage across borders. More often than not, the difference boils down to how people are managed, the adaptability of cultures, and the flexibility of organizations.

Up until this point in the book, we have emphasized HRM practices and systems as they exist in Canada. This is not so much an oversight on our part as it is a deliberate decision to explain the HR practice in the most fundamental manner possible. Nonetheless, the topic of international HRM is so important that we wanted to dedicate an entire chapter to its discussion. In this chapter we will observe that much of what has been discussed throughout this text can be applied to international operations, provided one is sensitive to the requirements of a particular international setting.

The first part of this chapter presents a brief introduction to international business firms. In many important respects, the way a company organizes its international operations influences the type of managerial and human resources issues it faces. In addition, we briefly describe some of the environmental factors that also affect the work of managers in a global setting. Just as with domestic operations, the dimensions of the environment form a context in which HRM decisions are made. A major portion of this chapter deals with the various HR activities involved in the recruitment, selection, development, and compensation of employees who work in an international setting.

Managing Across Borders

objective **1**

international corporation
A domestic firm that uses its existing capabilities to move into overseas markets

International business operations can take several different forms. A large percentage carry on their international business with only limited facilities and minimal representation in foreign countries. Others, particularly Fortune 500 corporations, have extensive facilities and personnel in various countries of the world. Dell, for example, actually employs more people outside the United States than within it. Managing these resources effectively and integrating their activities to achieve global advantage is a challenge to the leadership of these companies.

Figure 15.1 shows four basic types of organizations and how they differ in the degree to which international activities are separated to respond to the local regions and integrated to achieve global efficiencies. The **international corporation**

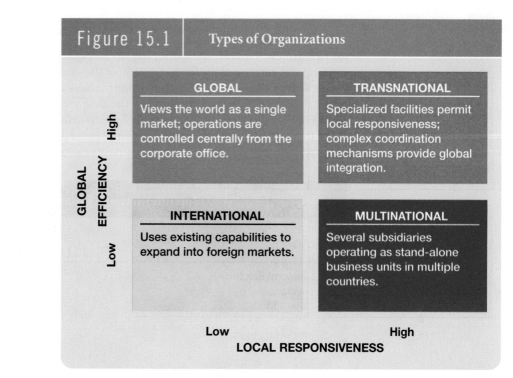

Figure 15.1 | Types of Organizations

GLOBAL
Views the world as a single market; operations are controlled centrally from the corporate office.

TRANSNATIONAL
Specialized facilities permit local responsiveness; complex coordination mechanisms provide global integration.

INTERNATIONAL
Uses existing capabilities to expand into foreign markets.

MULTINATIONAL
Several subsidiaries operating as stand-alone business units in multiple countries.

GLOBAL EFFICIENCY — High / Low

LOCAL RESPONSIVENESS — Low / High

is essentially a domestic firm that builds on its existing capabilities to penetrate overseas markets. Companies such as Honda, General Electric, and Procter & Gamble used this approach to gain access to Europe—they essentially adapted existing products for overseas markets without changing much else about their normal operations. (One such adaptation, for example, was P&G's extremely successful introduction of a detergent brick used on washboards in India.)

A **multinational corporation (MNC)** is a more complex form that usually has fully autonomous units operating in multiple countries. Shell, Philips, and ITT are three typical MNCs. These companies have traditionally given their foreign subsidiaries a great deal of latitude to address local issues such as consumer preferences, political pressures, and economic trends in different regions of the world. Frequently these subsidiaries are run as independent companies, without much integration. The **global corporation,** on the other hand, can be viewed as a multinational firm that maintains control of operations back in the home office. Japanese companies, such as Matsushita and NEC, tend to treat the world market as a unified whole and try to combine activities in each country to maximize efficiency on a global scale. These companies operate much like a domestic firm, except that they view the whole world as their marketplace.

Finally, a **transnational corporation** attempts to achieve the local responsiveness of an MNC while also achieving the efficiencies of a global firm. To balance this "global/local" dilemma, a transnational uses a network structure that coordinates specialized facilities positioned around the world. By using this flexible structure, a transnational provides autonomy to independent country operations but brings these separate activities together into an integrated whole. For most companies, the transnational form represents an ideal, rather than a reality. However, companies such as Ford, Unilever, and Shell have made good progress in restructuring operations to function more transnationally.[2]

multinational corporation (MNC)
A firm with independent business units operating in multiple countries

global corporation
A firm that has integrated worldwide operations through a centralized home office

transnational corporation
A firm that attempts to balance local responsiveness and global scale via a network of specialized operating units

Although various forms of organization exist, in this chapter we will generally refer to any company that conducts business outside its home country as an international business. Canada, of course, has no monopoly on international business. International enterprises are found throughout the world. A number of European and Pacific Rim companies have been conducting business on an international basis much longer than their Canadian counterparts. The close proximity of European countries, for example, makes them likely candidates for international trade. Figure 15.2 shows a list of some of the top international companies.[3]

Figure 15.2	Top International Companies

	MARKET VALUE (BILLIONS OF U.S. DOLLARS)
1. General Electric	$286.10
2. Microsoft	263.99
3. ExxonMobil	244.93
4. Pfizer	244.89
5. Wal-Mart Stores	232.22
6. Citigroup	210.86
7. Johnson & Johnson	161.36
8. Royal Dutch/Shell Group	158.48
9. BP	153.24
10. AIG	150.97
	SALES (BILLIONS OF U.S. DOLLARS)
1. Wal-Mart Stores	$244.52
2. ExxonMobil	204.51
3. General Motors	184.21
4. Royal Dutch/Shell	179.43
5. BP	178.72
6. Ford Motor	162.59
7. DaimlerChrysler	156.84
8. Toyota Motor	134.23
9. General Electric	131.70
10. Allianz	126.80
	PROFITS (BILLIONS OF U.S. DOLLARS)
1. Citigroup	$15.32
2. General Electric	15.13
3. Altria Group	11.10
4. ExxonMobil	11.01
5. Royal Dutch/Shell	9.42
6. Bank of America	9.25
7. Pfizer	9.18
8. Wal-Mart Stores	8.04
9. Toyota Motor	7.90
10. Microsoft	7.83

Source: Chester Dawson, "The Global 1000," *Business Week*, July 14, 2003, 34.

These companies are in a strong position to affect the world economy in the following ways:

1. Their production and distribution extend beyond national boundaries, making it easier to transfer technology.
2. They have direct investments in many countries.
3. They have a political impact that leads to cooperation among countries and to the breaking down of barriers of nationalism.

How Does the Global Environment Influence Management?

In Chapter 1, we highlighted some of the global trends affecting human resources management. One of the major economic issues we discussed was the creation of free-trade zones within Europe, North America, and the Pacific Rim. Twenty-five member countries now comprise the European Union (EU), whose goal is to facilitate the flow of goods, services, capital, and human resources across national borders in Europe in a manner similar to the way they cross provincial borders in Canada.[4] A similar transition occurred within North America with the passage of the North American Free Trade Agreement (NAFTA) in 1994. NAFTA created the world's largest free market. Since its passage, commerce between Canada, the United States, and Mexico has nearly tripled. There has been a great deal of debate about whether NAFTA has cost Canadian jobs. However, a report has shown that jobs have increased in all three countries, with 7 percent in the U.S., 10 percent in Canada, and 22 percent in Mexico.[5]

Like NAFTA, numerous trade agreements, including the Association of Southeast Asian Nations (ASEAN), East Asia Economic Group, Asia-Pacific Economic Cooperation (APEC), and South Asian Association for Regional Cooperation (SAARC), have significantly facilitated trade among Asian countries, making Asia the fastest-growing region in the world. China—its fastest-growing country—has emerged as a dominant trade leader since instituting trade reforms in the late 1970s. In the last decade and a half, China's economy has grown fourfold, drastically altering political and trading relations among nations. Some industry analysts estimate that the country now produces 50 percent of the world's cameras, 30 percent of air conditioners and televisions, 25 percent of washing machines, and 20 percent of refrigerators worldwide. In addition, China's 1.3 billion people represent a massive, largely untapped consumer market for global companies. Today more cars are sold in China than in Europe, for example. Driving this trend are big multinational corporations such as General Electric, Toyota, and Intel, which are building or expanding their manufacturing units in the country. But many smaller firms are heading to China as well. "It's not so much that [companies] want to go East: They feel that they have no choice," said one international HR staffing consultant. "They must be in China. It's not a question of if, but a question of how." In addition to China, India's economy is also growing very quickly.[6]

The fact that international corporations can choose the countries in which they do business or relocate operations generally results in the selection of countries that have the most to offer. In addition to economic factors, political-legal factors are a huge consideration. In many countries, particularly those in Africa, property rights are poorly protected by governments. Whoever has the political power or authority can seize others' property with few or no repercussions. Civil unrest can also lead to the poor enforcement of property rights. This gives companies less incentive to locate factories or invest there. Another issue relates to intellectual property rights—rights related to patents, trademarks, and so forth. Despite the fact that private property

objective

rights are now generally enforced in China, intellectual property rights have seen little protection. For example, when General Motors formed a joint venture with a Chinese company to produce and sell a new automobile in the country, a knockoff version of the car could be seen on China's streets even before GM and its partner were able to manufacture their first car. Environmental restrictions also make some countries more attractive to do business in than others.

Beyond the economic and political-legal issues just mentioned, a country's **cultural environment** (communications, religion, values and ideologies, education, and social structure) also has important implications when it comes to a company's decision about when and how to do business there. Because of language and culture similarities, many Canadian companies are finding the United States, Ireland, and the United Kingdom attractive places to locate their facilities, particularly call centres. Eastern Europe has also begun to attract interest because citizens there are well educated and largely possess English-speaking skills.

Figure 15.3 summarizes the complexity of the cultural environment in which HR must be managed. Culture is an integrated phenomenon. By recognizing and

cultural environment
The communications, religion, values and ideologies, education, and social structure of a country

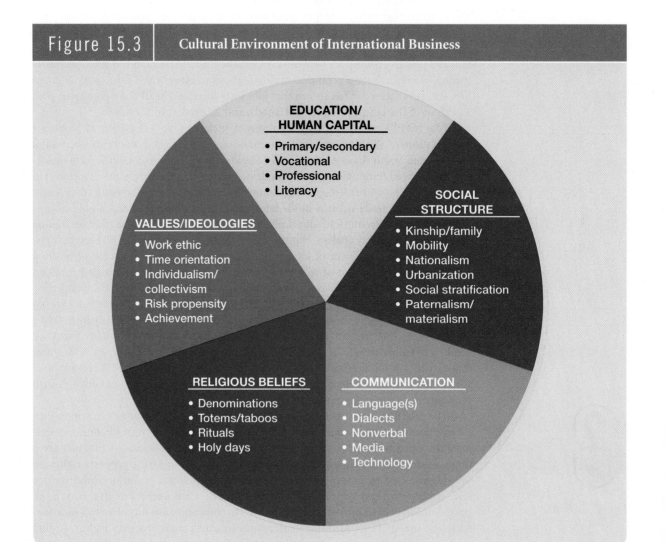

Figure 15.3   Cultural Environment of International Business

EDUCATION/
HUMAN CAPITAL
• Primary/secondary
• Vocational
• Professional
• Literacy

SOCIAL
STRUCTURE
• Kinship/family
• Mobility
• Nationalism
• Urbanization
• Social stratification
• Paternalism/
  materialism

VALUES/IDEOLOGIES
• Work ethic
• Time orientation
• Individualism/
  collectivism
• Risk propensity
• Achievement

RELIGIOUS BELIEFS
• Denominations
• Totems/taboos
• Rituals
• Holy days

COMMUNICATION
• Language(s)
• Dialects
• Nonverbal
• Media
• Technology

host country
A country in which an international corporation operates

accommodating taboos, rituals, attitudes toward time, social stratification, kinship systems, and the many other components listed in Figure 15.3, managers stand a better chance of understanding the culture of a **host country**—a country in which an international business operates. Different cultural environments require different approaches to human resources management. Highlights in HRM 15.1 describes some of these cultural differences. Strategies, structures, and management styles that are appropriate in one cultural setting may lead to failure in another. Even in countries that have close language or cultural links, HR practices can be dramatically different. In some countries night shifts are taboo. In other countries employers are expected to provide employees with meals and transportation between home and work. In India, workers generally receive cash bonuses on their wedding anniversaries with which to buy their spouses gifts, and dating allowances are provided to unmarried employees. These are practices that would never occur to Canadian managers and HR practitioners.[7] Throughout this chapter we will discuss several HR issues related to adapting to different cultural environments.

objective **3**

Domestic vs. International HRM

International HRM differs from domestic HRM in several ways. In the first place, it necessarily places a greater emphasis on functions and activities such as relocation, orientation, and translation services to help employees adapt to new and different

Highlights in HRM 15.1

Understanding the Importance of Cultural Differences

A North American company decided to open an office in Paris and sent the future manager to find office space and hire employees. The manager found a great location at a good price on the outskirts of Paris. Then she advertised the vacant positions in French business magazines. When she interviewed her first candidate, an alumnus of the École Polytechnique de Paris, she asked the candidate for a copy of his transcript and his grade point average. At first, he evaded the request. Then he refused, saying that he was a graduate of the most prestigious Grande École, and added, as he left the office, "Besides, your company's offices are not exactly in the best part of town." That same day, all other alumni of the École Polytechnique who were scheduled for interviews cancelled their appointments.

The manager, from the home country, had failed to understand cultural differences between North Americans and the French. In France, the location of the office is important, and the most desirable locations are the city centres. Only second-rate companies locate offices in the suburbs of Paris. Secondly, the French educational system is hierarchical and highly selective, and those attending the École Polytechnique de Paris are considered to be the very best graduates. These graduates are in high demand and a North American company would be very fortunate to hire one. Networking in France is done through alumni associations, and so word would spread quickly about this failed interview. The lesson to be learned is that hiring local talent requires sensitivity to local culture and customs.

Source: Adapted from Lionel Laroche, "Hiring Abroad," *CMA Management*, 76, 1, March 2002, 57.

environments outside their own countries and to help newly hired employees in foreign countries adapt to working for companies headquartered outside their borders. In years past, the internationalization has grown at a faster pace than the internationalization of the HRM profession, causing executives in the very best of companies to lament that their HR policies have not kept pace with the demands of global competition. But this is changing. Today, global HR management has become a front-and-centre issue for a wide variety of firms. Many larger corporations, and even smaller ones doing business in key international markets, now have full-time HR managers devoted solely to assisting with the globalization process. British Airways, for example, has a team of HR directors who travel around the world to help country managers stay updated on international concerns, policies, and programs. Coca-Cola provides support to its army of HR professionals working around the world. A core HR group in the company's Atlanta headquarters holds a two-week HR orientation twice a year for the international HR staff. This program helps international HR practitioners share information about HR philosophies, programs, and policies established either in Coca-Cola's headquarters or in another part of the world that can be successfully adopted by others.[8] Because doing business internationally can be extremely complex, many companies also hire international staffing firms such as Boston Global Consulting. These firms have expertise when it comes to relocating employees, establishing operations abroad, and helping with import/export and foreign tax issues.

HR information systems (HRIS) have also come a long way in terms of helping firms improve their international coordination. A good HR information system can facilitate communication, record keeping, and a host of other activities worldwide. Some HRISs are designed to track the whereabouts of employees travelling or on assignment. This can be important in the event of a transportation accident, a natural disaster such as a tsunami, a terrorist attack, or civil strife if evacuation plans must be implemented. Occasionally, however, even the seemingly simplest of cultural differences can be difficult to overcome when a company attempts to set up a global HRIS: When Lucent first rolled out a PeopleSoft system to more than 90 countries, the company's managers found that the order of employees' names was so important—and so varied—that it took two months to settle on a name format allowing employees to be entered into the system. As you can see, even seemingly small cultural differences can create major headaches for the international HR manager.[9]

International Staffing

When a company expands globally, HR managers are generally responsible for ensuring that operations are staffed. There are three main ways a company can staff a new international operation. First, the company can send people from its home country. These employees are often referred to as **expatriates,** or **home-country nationals.** Second, it can hire **host-country nationals,** natives of the host country, to do the managing. Third, it can hire **third-country nationals,** natives of a country other than the home country or the host country.

Each of these three sources of overseas workers provides certain advantages and certain disadvantages. Most corporations, such as the Four Seasons Hotel (described in Reality Check), use all three sources for staffing their multinational operations, although some companies exhibit a distinct bias for one or another of the three sources.[10]

expatriates, or home-country nationals
Employees from the home country who are on international assignment

host-country nationals
Employees who are natives of the host country

third-country nationals
Employees who are natives of a country other than the home country or the host country

© JEREMY HORNER/CORBIS

Global companies have the challenge of managing operations—and people— in many different countries.

Reality Check

Selecting for Service

Four Seasons Hotels, with a staff of over 25 000, manages 50 hotels and luxury resorts around the world, from Bali to Boston. The Four Seasons brand is synonymous with luxury and first-class service standards. The execution of the strategy of being the best in the world starts with leaders who are passionate about the corporation's customer service and employee relations values. These leaders can take a concept such as "We will deliver exceptional personal service" and paint a picture for employees that is clear and motivational and that results in the delivery of that exceptional personal service.

Does the perception of service excellence depend on the country or culture in which Four Seasons operates? John Young, executive vice-president of human resources, states that the Four Seasons guest is typically a sophisticated global traveller who has acquired a sensitivity to differences in culture without negative preconceptions. Nevertheless, Four Seasons trains service staff to be sensitive to guests' needs and to minimize or avoid culture and language problems. For example, in Asia, when an English-speaking guest gives a food or beverage order, the service staff are trained to repeat the order. This is done not only to prevent a potential service error, but also to avoid loss of face for the employee. In North America, a repetition of the order would be seen as redundant.

So that employees can meet these high performance expectations, Four Seasons selects employees based on their service attitudes. Candidates for employment must undergo four behaviourally based interviews (including one with the general manager) to determine their service attitudes and current skills and knowledge. As Young says: "Customer service is the

(continued on next page)

heart and soul of our business, and we need to assess if a candidate has sensitivity to the needs and wants of others. Of course, we also look at high levels of knowledge, skill, and experience, but these can be trained. We continuously adapt our service to match guest needs. For example, many years ago, in our Seattle hotel, one of the valet parking attendants noted that on weekends our guests were disproportionately families with children. On his own initiative, he put chocolate chip cookies and milk in cars that he was returning to these departing guests. They loved it. This practice has now become one of Four Seasons' standards."

Four Seasons does not have a rigid formula for selecting home country nationals or expatriates for any given country. The ratios depend on three factors: regulations, economics, and corporate management development needs. Young continues: "For example, Indonesia used to have a rule that no more than three expatriates could be employed per hotel. So we set expatriate reduction targets to meet this regulation. Economically it made sense for us, since an expatriate general manager could cost us as much as 75 or 80 local employees. And finally, we will choose candidates based on their need for global exposure and professional development, to match our targeted needs for international expansion.

"Our biggest challenge in international HR now is management development in the context of our growth plans. We need to develop culturally appropriate leadership in preparation for specific new locations on a defined time line. If we cannot find managers who can speak the language, and understand the culture, then our ability to grow is limited. Recently we opened a hotel in Puerto Vallarta. We found a Spanish-speaking general manager from Colombia who, over time, was able to integrate the Four Seasons way of doing business with the Mexican culture. Business culture in Mexico tends to be very rule and policy driven. Employees continuously asked, 'What is the policy. . .' in HR, sales, everything." Over time, the general manager learned to deal with the questions by no longer looking to home office for all the rules, but by asking himself and his team, "What should the rule be in our situation?"

"We cannot just hire the management talent we want from other sectors or hotel chains on short lead time, because of differences in operating standards and corporate culture. For example, we were opening a hotel with a general manager recruited from Hilton International. As he toured the new facility with Issy Sharp, our founder and CEO, the general manager said that the lounge facilities ought to be larger. He explained that this would make guests more comfortable while waiting for their dinner reservations. Issy replied, 'At Four Seasons our guests do not wait for their reservations.' These cultural differences, across countries, across sectors, and across competitors, underline the importance of our investing the time and effort in developing our own management talent, which is culturally and linguistically fluent, mobile, and imbued with our service culture."

This attention to the selection and development of high-performance employees has resulted in Four Seasons being named by *Fortune* magazine one of the 100 best employers for three consecutive years. Consequently, Four Seasons is now able to attract more and better applicants. Four Seasons is also widely recognized as the best luxury hotel chain in the world. Furthermore, the turnover rate at Four Seasons is one of the lowest in the hospitality sector. Even those employees who have left are often recaptured as they elect to return to the kind of culture that treats them as they treat the guests.

As shown in Figure 15.4, at early stages of international expansion, organizations often send home-country expatriates to establish activities (particularly in less-developed countries) and to work with local governments. This is generally very costly. Expatriate assignments cost companies, on average, $1 million over a three-year period. This can be three to five times what a domestic assignment costs. As a result, many companies are taking greater pains to more clearly outline the overall goal of the foreign assignment and its timetable for completion. Ingersoll-Rand, an international equipment maker, now carefully documents in detail what should be accomplished during an assignment abroad—whether the assignment is designed to enhance an assignee's leadership skills, improve productivity and sales targets abroad, transfer specific technology to a foreign operation, or staff it with local, expatriate, or third-country nationals.

Nearly 70 000 Canadians are working abroad, mainly in the U.S. (44 percent), followed by Europe (33 percent), then Asia/Pacific (15 percent), and Central and South America (8 percent). Most employees now consider foreign work credentials essential or extremely useful.[11] Figure 15.5 on page 648 lists the reasons that Canadians are sent on global assignments.

In recent years, there has also been a trend to send expatriates on shorter, project-based assignments (two to 12 months versus one to three years) and to shift more quickly toward hiring host-country nationals. This has three main advantages:

1. Hiring local citizens is generally less costly than relocating expatriates.
2. Since local governments usually want good jobs for their citizens, foreign employers may be required to hire locally.
3. Most customers want to do business with companies (and people) they perceive to be local versus foreign.

Because Canadian companies want to be viewed as true international citizens, there has also been a trend away from hiring expatriates to head up operations in

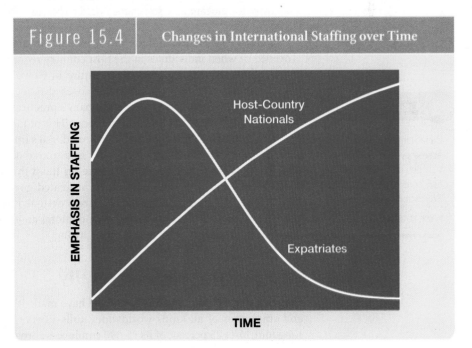

Figure 15.4 | Changes in International Staffing over Time

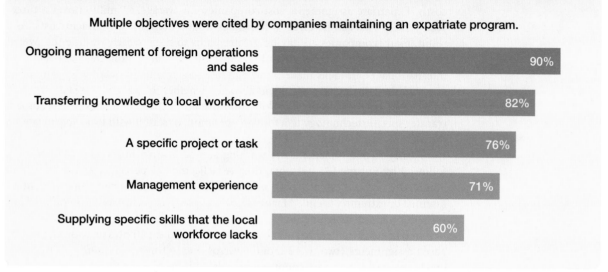

Figure 15.5 | **Why Canadians Are Sent on Global Assignments**

Multiple objectives were cited by companies maintaining an expatriate program.

Ongoing management of foreign operations and sales	90%
Transferring knowledge to local workforce	82%
A specific project or task	76%
Management experience	71%
Supplying specific skills that the local workforce lacks	60%

Source: "Why Canadians are Sent on Global Assignments," *Canadian HR Reporter*, December 1, 2003, 22.

foreign countries, especially European countries. Bombardier and Four Seasons, which have strong regional organizations, tend to replace their expatriate managers with local managers as quickly as possible. Highlights in HRM 15.2 describes some of the issues in checking references of locals. In addition to hiring local managers to head their foreign divisions and plants, more companies are using third-country nationals. Third-country nationals are often multilingual and already acclimated to the host country's culture—perhaps because they live in a nearby region. Thus, they are also less costly to relocate and sometimes better able to cope culturally with the foreign environment.

Companies tend to continue to use expatriates only when a specific set of skills is needed or when individuals in the host country require development. For example, after embarking on a joint venture in China with a formerly state-owned enterprise, Ingersoll-Rand discovered that it had to educate its Chinese employees not only on the company's practices and culture, but also on free-market, Western business practices. This required the company's expatriates to stay in China longer than planned.[12] It's important to note, however, that while top managers may prefer one source of employees over another, the host country may place pressure on them that restricts their choices. Such pressure takes the form of sophisticated government persuasion through administrative or legislative decrees designed to employ host-country individuals. Tax incentives, tariffs, and quotas are frequently implemented by the host country to encourage local hiring.

USING THE INTERNET

Canadian employers wishing to assess over 15 000 academic credentials of foreign-born employees can consult the not-for-profit World Education Services at:

www.wes.org/ca/

Recruiting Internationally

Improved telecommunications and travel have made it easier to match up employers and employees of all kinds worldwide. Rolls-Royce, headquartered in the United Kingdom, hires 25 percent of its 25 000 employees abroad. Because its customers come

Highlights in HRM 15.2

Reference Checking

An American company was very impressed with the 20-page résumé of a candidate for a management position for its new Japanese office. The promising candidate had worked on a wide variety of deals. However, upon checking his references, the company learned that indeed he had been involved in all these deals—as the interpreter!

Those checking references in foreign countries have to be aware of privacy regulations. For example, in Canada and the United States, there are privacy laws that govern what data is and is not allowed to be accessed and used by potential employers. An employee working in the Indian office of a Canadian company is covered by the laws of India, not Canada.

There are also cultural differences in the ways references are checked. If you wanted to know if a candidate had a criminal history in Latin America, you would need to know the name of the applicant's mother. It is also helpful to understand the political context in which reference checking is done. One candidate who had worked in a country that had just recently become a democracy supplied the name of his former supervisor as a reference. However, when the supervisor was contacted, he claimed to have never known the candidate. After the call, the supervisor phoned the applicant and said, "A company called asking about you, but don't worry. I told them that I don't know you and that you never worked for us." Based on the practices of the former government, the supervisor was sensitive to any kinds of investigative questions.

Source: Adapted from Traci Canning, "Hiring Global," *HR Professional,* June/July 2006, 34.

from around the globe, Rolls-Royce figures its workforce should as well. Airbus, the European commercial jet maker, recruits engineers from universities and colleges all over Europe. American-based Boeing's need for engineers is so great that it also recruits internationally and has even opened a design centre in Moscow. The trend is likely to continue as the populations in developed countries age and HR managers search for talent elsewhere. Even China, despite its massive population, faces labour shortages because laws there prohibit couples from having more than one child.

HR departments must be particularly responsive to the cultural, political, and legal environments both domestically and abroad when recruiting internationally. Companies such as Starbucks, Levi Strauss, and Honeywell have made a special effort to create codes of conduct for employees throughout the world to ensure that standards of ethical and legal behaviour are known and understood. PepsiCo has taken a similar approach to ensuring that company values are reinforced (even while recognizing the need for adapting to local cultures). The company has four core criteria that are viewed as essential in worldwide recruiting efforts: (1) personal integrity, (2) a drive for results, (3) respect for others, and (4) capability. Zurich, a Swiss financial and insurance company with operations in North America and Europe, makes sure its inbound North American assignees take diversity and sexual harassment courses. This training is rarely provided in other parts of the world.[13]

In general, however, employee recruitment in other countries is subject to more government regulation than it is in Canada. Regulations range from those that cover procedures for recruiting employees to those that govern the employment of foreign labour or require the employment of the physically disabled, war veterans, or displaced people. Many Central American countries, for example, have stringent regulations about the number of foreigners that can be employed as a percentage of the total workforce. Virtually all countries have work permit or visa restrictions that apply to foreigners. A **work permit** or **visa** is a document issued by a government granting authority to a foreign individual to seek employment in that government's country. Whatever the employee's destination, HR managers need to ensure that work permits and visas are applied for early in the relocation process.[14]

work permit or visa
A government document granting a foreign individual the right to seek employment

Multinational companies (MNCs) tend to use the same kinds of internal and external recruitment sources as in their home countries. At the executive level, companies use search firms such as Korn/Ferry in North America or Spencer Stuart in the U.K. At lower levels more informal approaches tend to be useful. While unskilled labour may be readily available in a developing country, recruitment of skilled workers may be more difficult. Many employers have learned that the best way to find workers in these countries is through referrals and radio announcements because many people lack sufficient reading or writing skills. Other firms use international recruiting firms to find skilled labour abroad. Some countries, in fact, require the employment of locals if adequate numbers of skilled people are available. Specific exceptions are sometimes granted (officially or unofficially) for contrary cases, as for Mexican farm workers in Canada and for Italian, Spanish, Greek, and Turkish workers in Germany and the Benelux countries (Belgium, the Netherlands, and Luxembourg). Read Highlights in HRM 15.3 to learn why the hospitality industry in Canada employs foreign workers. Foreign workers invited to perform needed labour are usually referred to as **guest workers.** Although hiring nonnationals may result in lower direct labour costs for a company, the indirect costs—those related to housing, language training, health services, recruitment, transportation, and so on—can be substantial. Some companies competing in industries with acute talent shortages are nonetheless finding the expenditures worthwhile. Nursing is one such industry.[15]

guest workers
Foreign workers invited to perform needed labour

Apprenticeships

A major source of trained labour in European nations is apprenticeship training programs (described in Chapter 7). On the whole, apprenticeship training in Europe is superior to that in Canada. In Europe, a dual-track system of education directs a large number of youths into vocational training. The German system of apprenticeship training, one of the best in Europe, provides training for office and shop jobs under a three-way responsibility contract between the apprentice, his or her parents, and the organization. At the conclusion of their training, apprentices can work for any employer but generally receive seniority credit with the training firm if they remain in it. France has been able to draw on its "Grandes Écoles" for centuries. Created during the Renaissance to fulfill a need that universities weren't meeting at the time, the Grandes Écoles educate prospective engineers up to the equivalent level of Master of Engineering. Snecma, an international equipment supplier headquartered in Paris, hires about 80 percent of its employees from the Grandes Écoles.[16]

Staffing Transnational Teams

In addition to focusing on individuals, it is also important to note that companies are increasingly using transnational teams to conduct international business. **Transnational teams** are composed of members of multiple nationalities working on projects that span multiple countries. General Electric's LightSpeed VCT, a state-of-the-art medical scanner, was designed with input from cardiologists around the world. The

transnational teams
Teams composed of members of multiple nationalities working on projects that span multiple countries

Highlights in HRM 15.3

Importing Culture

The Inn at Manitou in Ontario's Muskoka District has a staff of about 70, half of whom are not Canadian. The decision to recruit outside Canada for this Relais et Chateux luxury hotel and spa was made after years of trying to find Canadian workers and train them to offer the type of service that a luxury inn must offer.

Ben Wise, the inn's owner, gives several reasons for employing non-Canadians. The first is culture: "We hire Europeans, who have a culture of hospitality. To serve people is not perceived by Europeans to be denigrating. Canadians berate the job of a waiter, saying that they are not waiters, but on their way to be stockbrokers. Being a waiter is a profession in Europe. Chefs are celebrities in Europe."

In Europe, jobs in the hospitality sector are seen as professions for which extensive training is necessary. Europeans arrive at Wise's inn with four to five years of training and experience at some of the best hotels. Canadian candidates cannot compete. Wise tried to train Canadians, but four weeks of on-the-job training could not match the extensive training Europeans receive. Besides, he didn't think it was fair to ask the inn's clients to put up with the mistakes and deficiencies of workers in training.

Another reason was the seasonal nature of the hospitality industry in Muskoka District: "Canadians have a summer job mentality to these positions. Consequently, a report on their performance is of no value to them. There is little we can do to motivate them to meet our service expectations. Europeans are serious. Their future employment depends on our performance evaluations and our references."

So each year The Inn at Manitou places ads in trade magazines, screens hundreds of applicants, interviews and selects those with training and experience at the best resorts and hotels, and finally arranges work permits for the lucky 30. Why lucky? "Canada has a fascinating appeal for Europeans, especially the French, who must have all read books about a charming little cabin in the woods, with mountains, space, and fresh water."

machine's innards were designed by GE engineers in four different countries, and the software to run it written by multiple teams working together from India, Israel, France, and the U.S.[17] Teams such as these are especially useful for performing tasks that the firm as a whole is not yet structured to accomplish. For example, they may be used to transcend the existing organizational structure to customize a strategy for different geographic regions, transfer technology from one part of the world to another, and communicate between headquarters and subsidiaries in different countries. In GE's case, the company realized its competitors were developing their own medical scanning technology more quickly. GE decided it could no longer afford to duplicate its efforts in different divisions around the world—that these groups would have to work together as a team.

Sometimes companies send employees on temporary assignments abroad as part of transnational teams lasting, say, a few months. This might be done to break down cultural barriers between international divisions or disseminate new ideas and technologies to other regions. In other instances, employees are transferred for extended periods of time. Years ago, Fuji sent 15 of its most experienced engineers from Tokyo to a Xerox facility in Webster, New York. Over a five-year period, the engineers worked with a team of American engineers to develop the "world" copier. The effort led to a joint venture that has lasted for decades. Fuji-Xerox now employs approximately 34 000 people globally at 60 member companies around the world.[18]

The fundamental task in forming a transnational team is assembling the right group of people who can work together effectively to accomplish the goals of the team. For GE's LightSpeed team, this frequently meant holding eight-hour global conference calls encompassing numerous time zones. (The call times were rotated so that no single team had to stay up all night for every call.) Many companies try to build variety into their teams in order to maximize responsiveness to the special needs of different countries. For example, when Heineken formed a transnational team to consolidate its production facilities, it ensured that team members were drawn from each major region within Europe. Team members tended to have specialized skills, and members were added only if they offered some unique skill that added value to the team.

Selecting Employees Internationally

As you might imagine, selection practices vary around the world. In Canada managers tend to emphasize merit, with the best-qualified person getting the job. In other countries, however, firms tend to hire on the basis of family ties, social status, language, and common origin. The candidate who satisfies these criteria may get the job even if otherwise unqualified. Much of this is changing—there has been a growing realization among organizations in other nations that greater attention must be given to hiring those most qualified. In addition to a person's qualifications, various other hiring laws, particularly those related to discrimination, are enforced around the world. Labour union restrictions, which we will discuss later in the chapter, can also have an impact on hiring.

Expatriate employees receive intensive training on their host countries, the cultural differences, negotiation tactics, business practices, everyday living, and other aspects of working and living successfully in a foreign country.

© THE IMAGE BANK/GETTY IMAGES

Selecting Global Managers

Selecting a global manager depends on a variety of different employment factors, including the extent of contact the manager will have with local citizens and the government and the degree to which the foreign environment differs from the home environment. For example, if the job involves extensive contacts with the community, as with a chief executive officer, this factor should be given appropriate weight. The magnitude of differences between the political, legal, socioeconomic, and cultural systems of the host country and those of the home country should also be assessed.[19]

global manager
A manager equipped to run an international business

Levi Strauss has identified the following six skill categories for the **global manager,** or manager equipped to run an international business:

- Ability to seize strategic opportunities
- Ability to manage highly decentralized organizations
- Awareness of global issues
- Sensitivity to issues of diversity
- Competence in interpersonal relations
- Skill in building community[20]

If a candidate for expatriation is willing to live and work in a foreign environment, an indication of his or her tolerance of cultural differences should be obtained. On the other hand, if local nationals have the technical competence to carry out the job successfully, they should be carefully considered for the job before the firm launches a search (at home) for a candidate to fill the job. As stated previously, most corporations realize the advantages to be gained by staffing international operations with host-country nationals wherever possible.

Selecting home-country and third-country nationals requires that more factors be considered than in selecting host-country nationals. While the latter must of course possess managerial abilities and the necessary technical skills, they have the advantage of familiarity with the physical and cultural environment and the language of the host country. Figure 15.6 compares the advantages and disadvantages of hiring global managers from these three different groups. The discussion that follows, however, will focus on the selection of expatriate managers from the home country, along with their compensation and performance appraisals.

core skills
Skills considered critical to an employee's success abroad

augmented skills
Skills helpful in facilitating the efforts of expatriate managers

Colgate-Palmolive, Whirlpool, and Dow Chemical have further identified a set of **core skills** that they view as critical for success abroad and a set of **augmented skills**

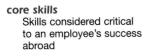

Figure 15.6	Comparison of Advantages in Sources of Overseas Managers	
HOST-COUNTRY NATIONALS	**HOME-COUNTRY NATIONALS (EXPATRIATES)**	**THIRD-COUNTRY NATIONALS**
Less costly	Talent available within company	Broad experience
Preferred by host-country governments	Greater control	International outlook
Intimate knowledge of environment and culture	Company experience	Multilingualism
Language facility	Mobility	
	Experience provided to corporate executives	

that help facilitate the efforts of expatriate managers. These two types of skills are shown in Highlights in HRM 15.4. Many of these skills are not significantly different from those required for managerial success at home. Although in years past the average expatriate manager was a North American-born Caucasian, more companies today are seeing the advantages of assigning expatriates depending on their ethnicity. But such a decision needs to be considered carefully. For example, an Indian-Canadian candidate applying for a position in India may never have actually visited the country or may not relate well to the culture. Ultimately, the candidate best qualified for the job should be sent. Unfortunately, talented women are frequently overlooked for global managerial positions—perhaps because companies believe they will fare poorly in foreign, male-dominated societies or because they believe women have less desire to go abroad. However, many women who have been given international assignments have performed quite well. Because locals know how unusual it is for a woman to be given a foreign assignment, they frequently assume that the company would not have sent a woman unless she was the very best. In addition, because women expatriates are novel (particularly in managerial positions), they are very visible and distinctive and may even receive special treatment not given to their male colleagues.[21]

Several steps are involved in selecting individuals for an international assignment, and the sequencing of these activities can make a big difference:

Step 1: Begin with self-selection. Employees should begin the process years in advance by thinking about their career goals and interest in international work. By beginning with self-selection, companies can more easily avoid the problems of forcing otherwise promising employees into international assignments where they would be unhappy and unsuccessful. For individuals with families, decisions about relocation are more complicated. Employees should seek information to help them predict their chances of success living abroad. Companies such as EDS and Deloitte & Touche give their employees self-selection instruments to help them consider the pros and cons of international assignments. Other companies give these tools to candidates' spouses as well. At Solar Turbines, a San Diego-based manufacturer of industrial gas turbines, a candidate's spouse and sometimes his or her children undergo a day of assessment to see how well they are likely to respond to an international assignment.[22]

Step 2: Create a candidate pool. After employees have self-selected, organizations can build a database of candidates for international assignments. Information in the

Highlights in HRM 15.4

Skills of Expatriate Managers

CORE SKILLS	AUGMENTED SKILLS
Experience	Technical skills
Decision making	Negotiation skills
Resourcefulness	Strategic thinking
Adaptability	Delegation skills
Cultural sensitivity	Change management
Team building	
Maturity	

For many reasons, women often make very successful expatriates.

failure rate
The percentage of expatriates who do not perform satisfactorily

database might include availability, languages, country preferences, and skills.

Step 3: Assess core skills. From the short list of potential candidates, managers can assess each candidate on technical and managerial readiness relative to the needs of the assignment. Although many factors determine success abroad, the initial focus should be on the requirements of the job.

Step 4: Assess augmented skills and attributes. As shown in Figure 15.7, expatriate selection decisions are driven typically by technical competence as well as professional and international experience. In addition, however, an increasing number of organizations have also begun considering an individual's ability to adapt to different environments. Satisfactory adjustment depends on flexibility, emotional maturity and stability, empathy for the culture, language and communication skills, resourcefulness and initiative, and diplomatic skills.[23]

Even companies that believe they have selected the best candidates frequently experience high expatriate **failure rates.** Figure 15.8 on page 656 shows the major causes of assignment failure. By far, the biggest factor tends to be a spouse's inability to adjust to his or her new surroundings.[24] There are a number of ways to improve the success of expatriate assignments. One important step is to involve spouses early on in the process. In addition, training and development for both expatriates and their spouses can have a big impact. We discuss this next.

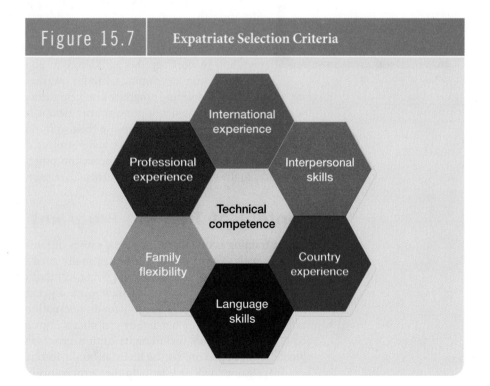

| Figure 15.7 | **Expatriate Selection Criteria** |

Figure 15.8	Causes of Expatriate Assignment Failure

- Family adjustment
- Poor performance
- Lifestyle issues
- Other opportunities arise
- Work adjustment
- Business reasons
- Bad selection
- Repatriation issues

Training and Development

objective **5**

USING THE INTERNET

The Outpost Expatriate Network is an online information centre for Shell expatriates and their families:

www.outpostexpat.nl/

Although companies try to recruit and select the very best people to send abroad, once they are selected it is often necessary to provide them with some type of training. Not only is this type of training important for expatriate managers, it is also important for the foreign employees they will ultimately supervise. To know and understand how the Japanese or Chinese negotiate contracts or how businesspeople from Latin America view the enforcement of meeting times, for example, can help expatriate managers and their employees deal with each other more successfully. The biggest mistake managers can make is to assume that people are the same everywhere. Corporations that are serious about succeeding in global business are tackling these problems head-on by providing intensive training. At Motorola this type of training is conducted at divisions worldwide by Motorola University, the company's educational arm. All employees, including division heads, receive 40 hours of training each year to learn, in part, how to work together as "Motorola People."[25]

Apart from developing talent for overseas assignments, most companies have found that good training programs also help them attract needed employees from the host countries. In less-developed countries especially, individuals are quite eager to receive the training they need to improve their work skills. Increasingly, organizations such as the World Bank, ExxonMobil, and Petroleos de Venezuela are entering into partnerships with university executive education programs to customize the training experiences to the specific needs of expatriate managers and foreign nationals.

Content of Training Programs

Lack of training is one of the principal causes of failure among employees working internationally. Those working internationally need to know as much as possible about (1) the country where they are going, (2) that country's culture, and (3) the history, values, and dynamics of their own organizations. Figure 15.9 gives an overview of what one needs to study for an international assignment. In many cases, the employee and his or her family can obtain a great deal of general information about the host country, including its culture, geography, social and political history, climate, food, and so on, via the Internet, books, lectures, videotapes, and DVDs. The knowledge gained will at least help the participants have a better understanding of

| Figure 15.9 | Preparing for an International Assignment |

To prepare for an international assignment, one should become acquainted with the following aspects of the host country:

1. Social and business etiquette
2. History and folklore
3. Current affairs, including relations between the host country and Canada
4. Cultural values and priorities
5. Geography, especially its major cities
6. Sources of pride and great achievements of the culture
7. Religion and the role of religion in daily life
8. Political structure and current players
9. Practical matters such as currency, transportation, time zones, hours of business
10. The language

USING THE INTERNET

Visit a great resource for information on living, relocating, and working overseas:

www.escapeartist.com

their assignments. Sensitivity training can also help expatriates overcome ethnic prejudices they might harbour. Expatriates can simulate a field experience in sensitivity training by visiting a nearby subculture in their native countries or by actually visiting a foreign country prior to relocating there.

However, at least five essential elements of training and development programs prepare employees for working internationally: (1) language training, (2) cultural training, (3) assessing and tracking career development, (4) managing personal and family life, and (5) repatriation—a final, but critical, step.[26]

Language Training

Communication with individuals who have a different language and a different cultural orientation is extremely difficult. Most executives agree that it is among the biggest problems for the foreign business traveller. Students who plan careers in international business should start instruction in one or more foreign languages as early as possible. The top-ranked China Europe International Business School (CEIBS), jointly founded by the Chinese government and the European Union in 1994, also offers language training. Some companies do their own language training. Multinational companies as well as businesses that outsource work abroad stand to benefit from this type of training.

Fortunately for most Canadians, English is almost universally accepted as the primary language for international business. Particularly when many people from different countries are working together, English is usually the designated language for meetings and formal discourse. Many companies provide instruction in English for those who are required to use English in their jobs. Dow Chemical requires that all employees across the globe be fluent in English so they can communicate more easily with one another. At Volkswagen's Shanghai operation, only after workers pass German-language examinations do they become eligible for further training in Germany. Learning the language is only part of communicating in another culture, though. Even with an interpreter, much is missed. The following list illustrates the complexities of the communication process in international business.

1. In England, to "table" a subject means to put it on the table for present discussion. In North America, it means to postpone discussion of a subject, perhaps indefinitely.

2. In Canada, information flows to a manager. In cultures in which authority is centralized (such as Europe and South America), the manager must take the initiative to seek out the information.

3. Getting straight to the point is uniquely North American. Many Europeans, Arabs, and others resent directness in communication.

4. In Japan, there are 16 ways to avoid saying "no."

5. When something is "inconvenient" to the Chinese, it is most likely downright impossible.

6. In most foreign countries, expressions of anger are unacceptable; in some places, public display of anger is taboo.

7. The typical North American must learn to treat silences as "communication spaces" and not interrupt them.

8. In general, North Americans must learn to avoid gesturing with the hand. For example, a college sports-related hand signal made by George W. Bush and his family members during his second inauguration shocked Norwegians around the world; in Norway, the gesture is a satanic symbol. Nonverbal communication training can help businesspeople avoid some of these communication pitfalls.[27]

Cultural Training

Cross-cultural differences represent one of the most elusive aspects of international business. Brazilians tend to perceive North Americans as always in a hurry, serious, reserved, and methodical, whereas the Japanese view North Americans as relaxed, friendly, and impulsive. Why do these different perceptions exist and how do they affect the way we do business across borders?

Managerial attitudes and behaviours are influenced, in large part, by the society in which managers have received their education and training. Similarly, reactions of employees are the result of cultural conditioning. Each culture has its expectations for the roles of managers and employees. On her first day on the job abroad, one expatriate manager recalls her boss ordering a bottle of wine to split between the two of them at lunch. Although this is a common practice in Britain, the expatriate manager was initially taken aback. Likewise, what one culture encourages as participative management another might see as managerial incompetence: An American manager in Asia once complained that meetings held in his foreign place of employment accomplished nothing. He was used to arriving at a final decision during meetings. But to his Asian co-workers, meetings were solely a place in which to share ideas. Decisions were to be made only later.[28] Being successful depends on one's ability to understand the way things are normally done and to recognize that changes cannot be made abruptly without considerable resistance, and possibly antagonism, on the part of local nationals.

A wealth of data from cross-cultural studies reveals that nations tend to cluster according to similarities in certain cultural dimensions such as work goals, values, needs, and job attitudes. Using data from eight comprehensive studies of cultural differences, Simcha Ronen and Oded Shenkar have grouped countries into the clusters shown in Figure 15.10.

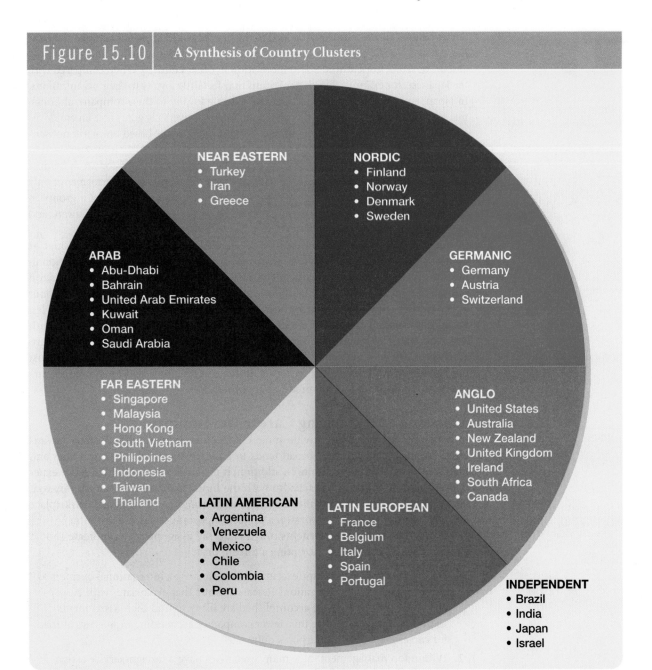

Figure 15.10 | A Synthesis of Country Clusters

NEAR EASTERN
- Turkey
- Iran
- Greece

NORDIC
- Finland
- Norway
- Denmark
- Sweden

ARAB
- Abu-Dhabi
- Bahrain
- United Arab Emirates
- Kuwait
- Oman
- Saudi Arabia

GERMANIC
- Germany
- Austria
- Switzerland

FAR EASTERN
- Singapore
- Malaysia
- Hong Kong
- South Vietnam
- Philippines
- Indonesia
- Taiwan
- Thailand

ANGLO
- United States
- Australia
- New Zealand
- United Kingdom
- Ireland
- South Africa
- Canada

LATIN AMERICAN
- Argentina
- Venezuela
- Mexico
- Chile
- Colombia
- Peru

LATIN EUROPEAN
- France
- Belgium
- Italy
- Spain
- Portugal

INDEPENDENT
- Brazil
- India
- Japan
- Israel

Source: Simcha Ronen and Oded Shenkar, "Clustering Countries on Attitudinal Dimensions: A Review and Synthesis," *Academy of Management Review* 10, no. 3 (July 1985): 435–54. Copyright © 1985 by *Academy of Management Review*. Reprinted with permission of the *Academy of Management Review* via Copyright Clearance Center.

Ronen and Shenkar point out that while evidence for the grouping of countries into Anglo, Germanic, Nordic, Latin European, and Latin American clusters appears to be quite strong, clusters encompassing the Far Eastern and Arab countries are ill defined and require further research, as do clusters of countries classified as independent. Many areas, such as Africa, have not been studied much at all. It should also be noted that the clusters presented in Figure 15.10 do not include Russia and the former satellites of the

Soviet Union. Those countries, if added to the figure, would likely fall between the Near Eastern and Nordic categories. Studying cultural differences can help managers identify and understand work attitudes and motivation in other cultures. When compared with the Japanese, for example, North Americans may feel little loyalty to their organizations. In Japan, employees are more likely to feel a strong loyalty to their company, although this may be changing. Japanese companies no longer universally guarantee an employee a job for life, and layoff decisions are increasingly being made based on merit, not seniority—a practice unthinkable in the country in the past. Latin Americans tend to view themselves as working not only for a particular company but also for an individual manager. Thus managers in Latin American countries can encourage performance only by using personal influence and working through individual members of a group. In North America, competition has been the name of the game; in Japan, Taiwan, and other Asian countries, cooperation is more the underlying philosophy.[29]

One of the important dimensions of leadership, whether in international or domestic situations, is the degree to which managers invite employee participation in decision making. While it is difficult to find hard data on employee participation across different countries, careful observers report that Canadian managers are about in the middle on a continuum of autocratic to democratic decision-making styles. Scandinavian and Australian managers also appear to be in the middle. South American and European managers, especially those from France, Germany, and Italy, are toward the autocratic end of the continuum; Japanese managers are at the most participatory end. Because Far Eastern cultures and religions tend to emphasize harmony, group decision making predominates there.[30]

Assessing and Tracking Career Development

International assignments provide some definite developmental and career advantages. For example, working abroad tends to increase a person's responsibilities and influence within the corporation. In addition, it provides a person with a set of experiences that are uniquely beneficial to both the individual and the firm. In this way, international assignments enhance a person's understanding of the global marketplace and offer the opportunity to work on a project important to the organization.[31]

To maximize the career benefits of a managerial assignment, a candidate should ask two key questions before accepting a foreign post:

1. Do the organization's senior executives view the firm's international business as a critical part of their operation? Research shows that expatriates with clear goals that truly need to be accomplished are likely to find their assignments more rewarding. Realizing this, fewer companies are sending expatriates abroad for career development purposes only.

2. Within top management, how many executives have a foreign-service assignment in their background, and do they feel it important for one to have overseas experience? Colgate-Palmolive sees a foreign assignment as part of an extended career track rather than as a one-off assignment. A successful foreign assignment tends to lead to another and another. "Our top priority is to identify, develop, and retain the next two to three generations of leaders," said one Colgate-Palmolive manager. Part of that strategy includes directly using the knowledge of the company's current and former expatriates.

culture shock
Perpetual stress experienced by people who settle overseas

Managing Personal and Family Life

As noted previously, one of the most frequent causes of an employee's failure to complete an international assignment is personal and family stress. **Culture shock**—a disorientation that causes perpetual stress—is experienced by people who settle overseas for extended periods. The stress is caused by hundreds of jarring and disorienting incidents such as being unable to communicate, having trouble getting the telephone to work, being unable to read the street signs, and a myriad of other everyday matters that are no problem at home. Soon minor frustrations become catastrophic events, and one feels helpless and drained, emotionally and physically. Highlights in HRM 15.5 shows some of the primary sources of stress at different stages of an international assignment, as well as some of the responses that individuals and organizations use to cope with these types of stress.

Highlights in HRM 15.5

Stressors and Coping Responses in the Developmental Stages of Expatriate Executives

	PRIMARY RESPONSE	EXECUTIVE COPING RESPONSE	EMPLOYER COPING RESPONSE
Expatriate selection	Cross-cultural unreadiness	Engage in self-evaluation	Encourage expatriate's self- and family evaluation. Perform an assessment of potential and interests.
Assignment	Unrealistic evaluation of stressors to come. Hurried time frame.	Think of assignment as a growth opportunity rather than an instrument to vertical promotion	Do not make hard-to-keep promises. Clarify expectations.
Pre- and post-arrival training	Ignorance of cultural differences	Do not make unwarranted assumptions of cultural competence and cultural rules	Provide pre-, during, and, and post-assignment training support-seeking behaviour.
Arrival	Cultural shock. Stressor reevaluation. Feelings of lack of fit and differential treatment.	Do not construe identification with the host and parent cultures as mutually exclusive. Seek social support.	Provide post-arrival training. Facilitate integration in expatriate network.
Novice	Cultural blunders or inadequacy of coping responses. Ambiguity owing to inability to decipher meaning of situations.	Observe and study functional value of coping responses among locals. Do not simply replicate responses that worked at home.	Provide follow-up training. Seek advice from locals and expatriate network.

(continued on next page)

Transitional	Rejection of host or parent culture	Form and maintain attachments with both cultures	Promote culturally sensitive policies at host country. Provide Internet access to family and friends at home. Maintain constant communication and periodic visits to parent organization.
Mastery	Frustration with inability to perform boundary spanning role. Bothered by living with a cultural paradox.	Internalize and enjoy identification with both cultures and walking between two cultures.	Reinforce rather than punish dual identification by defining common goals.
Repatriation	Disappointment with unfulfilled expectations. Sense of isolation. Loss of autonomy.	Realistically reevaluate assignment as a personal and professional growth opportunity	Arrange pre-repatriation briefings and interviews. Schedule post-repatriation support meetings.

Source: J. Sanchez, P. Spector, and C. Cooper, "Adapting to a Boundaryless World: A Developmental Expatriate Model," *Academy of Management Executive* 14, no. 2 (May 2000): 96–106.

In Chapter 5, we observed that more and more employers are assisting two-career couples in finding suitable employment in the same location. To accommodate dual-career partnerships, some employers are providing informal help finding jobs for the spouses of international transferees. However, other companies are establishing more formal programs to assist expatriate couples. These include career- and life-planning counselling, continuing education, intercompany networks to identify job openings in other companies, and job-hunting/fact-finding trips. In some cases, a company may even create a job for the spouse—though this is not widely practised. The available evidence suggests that while a spouse's career may create some problems initially, in the long run it actually may help ease an expatriate's adjustment process.[32]

Repatriation

repatriation
The process of employee transition home from an international assignment

An increasing number of companies such as Enbridge are developing programs specifically designed to facilitate **repatriation**—that is, helping employees make the transition back home. Coming back is often difficult. An employee recently repatriated from Colombia walked outside his Edmonton office and waited for his driver, not remembering that he had driven his own car to work. Another family, repatriated from Kazakhstan, had to be restrained from purchasing all the fresh vegetables at the supermarket, because over there, if there was fresh produce, you hoarded it because it might not be there next week. Repatriation programs are designed to prepare employees for adjusting to life at home (which at times can be more difficult than adjusting to a foreign assignment). ExxonMobil employees are given a general idea of what they can expect following a foreign assignment even before they leave home. Unfortunately, not all companies have career development programs designed for repatriating employees.

Several studies have found that the majority of companies do not do an effective job of repatriation. Here are some general findings:

1. About 36 percent of Canadian companies have a repatriation plan.
2. Another third have programs to facilitate appropriate career positions upon repatriation.
3. Over two-thirds provide career planning assistance toward the end of assignment, while 8 percent provide this assistance after repatriation.
4. About one-fifth of companies start planning for repatriation even before the candidate leaves.[33]

Employees often lament that their organizations are vague about repatriation, their new roles within the company, and their career progression. In many cases, employees abroad have learned how to run an entire international operation—or at least significant parts of it. When they return home, however, their responsibilities are often significantly diminished. In fact, the evidence suggests that only a fraction of them are actually promoted. It is also not at all uncommon for employees to return home after a few years to find that there is *no* position for them in the firm and that they no longer know anyone who can help them—their longtime colleagues have moved to different departments or even different companies. This frequently leaves the repatriated employee feeling alienated.

Even when employees are successfully repatriated, their companies often do not fully utilize the knowledge, understanding, and skills developed on their assignments. This hurts the employee, of course, but it also hurts the firm's chances of utilizing the employee's expertise to gain a competitive advantage. Not surprisingly, expatriates frequently leave their companies within a year or two of coming home. Some experts say the number of expatriates who do so is as high as 50 percent.

At companies with good repatriation processes, employees are given guidance about how much the expatriate experience may have changed them and their families. Some firms introduce former expatriates and their spouses to other former expatriates at special social events. And more companies are making an effort to keep in touch with expatriates while they are abroad, which has been made easier by e-mail, instant messaging, and videoconferencing. Colgate's division executives and other corporate staff members frequently visit international transferees. Dow appoints a high-level manager who serves as a home-country contact for information about organizational changes, job opportunities, and anything related to salary and compensation. Monsanto's repatriation program is designed not only to smooth the employee's return to the home organization but also to ensure that the expatriate's knowledge and experience are fully utilized. To do so, returning expatriates get the chance to showcase their new knowledge in debriefing sessions. Some companies also create databases of expatriates to help other employees who go abroad later.[34] A repatriation checklist is shown in Highlights in HRM 15.6 on page 664.

Compensation

objective 6

One of the most complex areas of international HRM is compensation. Different countries have different norms for employee compensation. For North Americans, while nonfinancial incentives such as prestige, independence, and influence may be motivators, money is likely to be the driving force. Other cultures are more likely to emphasize respect, family, job security, a satisfying personal life, social acceptance,

Highlights in HRM 15.6

Repatriation Checklist

Before they go:

- Make sure there is a clear need for the international assignment. Don't send someone abroad unnecessarily. Develop a clear set of objectives and expectations and timeframes in which they should be met.
- Make sure that your selection procedures are valid. Select the employee and also look at and involve the employee's family.
- Provide (or fund) language and cultural training for the employee and the employee's family.
- Offer counselling and career assistance for the spouse.
- Establish career-planning systems that reward international assignments and lead to promotion and knowledge sharing.

While they are away:

- Jointly establish a developmental plan that focuses on the goal to be achieved.
- Tie performance objectives to the achievement of the goal.
- Identify mentors who can be a liaison and support person from home.
- Keep communications open so that the expatriate is aware of job openings and opportunities.
- Arrange for frequent visits back home (for the employee and the family). Make certain they do not lose touch with friends and relatives.

When they come back home:

- Throw a "welcome home" party and arrange for a meeting with other former expatriates.
- Offer counselling to ease the transition.
- Arrange conferences and presentations to make certain that knowledge and skills acquired away from home are identified and disseminated.
- Set up an expatriate database to help other employees who go abroad later.
- Get feedback from the employee and the family about how well the organization handled the repatriation process.

Sources: Adapted from Bennet & Associates, Price Waterhouse, and Charlene Marmer Solomon, "Repatriation Planning Checklist," *Personnel Journal* 14, no. 1 (January 1995): 32; Charlene Marmer Solomon, "Global HR: Repatriation Planning," *Workforce* 2001, special supplement, 22–23.

advancement, or power. Since there are many alternatives to money, the rule is to match the reward with the values of the culture. In individualistic cultures, such as Canada, pay plans often focus on individual performance and achievement. However, in collectively oriented cultures such as Japan and Taiwan, pay plans focus more on internal equity and personal needs.[35]

Figure 15.11 shows some of the primary forces shaping global pay strategies. In general, a guiding philosophy for designing pay systems might be "think globally and act locally." That is, executives should normally try to create a pay plan that supports the overall strategic intent of the organization but provides enough flexibility to customize particular policies and programs to meet the needs of employees in specific

Figure 15.11	Forces Driving Global Pay

CULTURAL PREFERENCES	PERSONAL PREFERENCES
Importance of status	Attitudes toward risk
Role of individual vs. organization vs. government	Quality of life vs. work Short- vs. long-term
Equality vs. disparity Achievement vs. relationships	Competitiveness vs. solidarity

ECONOMIC CONDITIONS	SOCIAL CONSTRAINTS
Size of economy	Income tax rates, social costs
Types of industries, natural resources	Laws and regulations
Inflation, unemployment Protectionism vs. open market	Collective bargaining, worker participation
Skills, education of workforce	

Source: Steven Gross and Per Wingerup, "Global Pay? Maybe Not Yet!" *Compensation and Benefits Review* 31, no. 4 (July/August 1999): 25–34.

USING THE INTERNET

What salary would you receive if you worked in a foreign city? See the international salary calculator at:

www.salaryexpert.com

locations. After a brief discussion of compensation practices for host-country employees and managers, we will focus on the problems of compensating expatriates.

Compensation of Host-Country Employees

As shown in Figure 15.12 on page 666, hourly wages vary dramatically from country to country, from more than $30 on average in Norway and Germany to just $5–$10 in Taiwan and Portugal and less than a dollar in developing countries. Host-country employees are generally paid on the basis of productivity, time spent on the job, or a combination of these factors. In industrialized countries, pay is generally by the hour; in developing countries, by the day. The piece-rate method is quite common. In some countries, including Japan, seniority is an important element in determining employees' pay rates. When companies commence operations in a foreign country, they usually set their wage rates at or slightly higher than the prevailing wage for local companies. Eventually, though, they are urged to conform to local practices to avoid "upsetting" local compensation practices. In Italy, Japan, and some other countries, it is customary to add semiannual or annual lump-sum payments equal to one or two months' pay. These payments are not considered profit sharing but an integral part of the basic pay package. Profit sharing is legally required for certain categories of industry in Mexico, Peru, Pakistan, India, and Egypt among the developing countries and in France among the industrialized countries. Compensation patterns in Eastern Europe are in flux as these countries make the adjustment to more-capitalistic systems.

Employee benefits can range dramatically from country to country as well. In France, for example, benefits are about 70 percent, compared with around 30 percent in Canada. Whereas in North America most benefits are awarded to employees by

Figure 15.12 | Hourly Wages in Different Countries*

COUNTRY	$/HOUR
Norway	31.55
Germany (former West)	31.25
Switzerland	27.87
Belgium	27.73
Sweden	25.18
United States	21.97
France	21.13
Britain	20.37
Japan	20.09
Australia	20.05
Canada	19.28
Italy	18.35
Spain	14.96
Israel	11.73
Korea	10.28
Portugal	6.23
Taiwan	5.84
Brazil	2.67
Mexico	2.48
China	0.63
Sri Lanka	0.49

*Hourly compensation costs in U.S. dollars for production workers in manufacturing.

Source: U.S. Department of Labor, Bureau of Labor Statistics, November 2004.

employers, in other industrialized countries most of them are legislated or ordered by governments. Some of these plans are changing. Defined contribution plans are on the rise, sex equality is becoming important, and stock ownership is being tried.[36]

Because the largest cost for most companies is labour, it plays a prime role in international HR decision making. However, some people believe that companies are overcapitalizing on worldwide compensation differences. Many firms (Nike included) have generated bad press for charging hundreds of dollars for their individual products while the people who make them—sometimes children in developing countries working under terrible conditions—earn only a few cents on the dollar. This has led to international political protests, as discussed in Ethics in HRM, and pressure on firms to exercise greater global social responsibility. As Nike discovered, it's pressure they can't afford not to take seriously. Starbucks clearly takes good corporate citizenship seriously. Among Starbucks' many initiatives is its association with Fair Trade and Conservation International to help farmers in Third-World countries get a premium for the coffee they grow. We will discuss more on the fair treatment of workers in Third-World countries toward the end of the chapter.

Compensation of Host-Country Managers

In the past, remuneration of host-country managers has been ruled by local salary levels. However, increased competition among different companies with subsidiaries in the same country has led to a gradual upgrading of host-country managers' salaries.

Ethics in HRM

Canadian vs. Third-World Attitudes Toward Child Labour

About 250 million children, one in every six in the world, performs work that is involuntary, hazardous, or illegal. Although the largest number (70 percent) work in farming, fishing, hunting, and forestry, about 10 percent work as soldiers or prostitutes. Canadians are among the first to deplore the use of child labour. We are noted for our media campaigns against it, and our child impact assessments affect our choice of suppliers. Because we don't use child labourers ourselves, we are quick to condemn countries that do. Foreigners resent it when Westerners preach about the issue. In developing countries, child workers are the norm. The family is seen as the labour unit, with children contributing, according to their abilities, to the production of food and goods or services for sale. In these countries, there is no social welfare or insurance: children's earnings often make the difference between starvation and survival. Furthermore, school is not an alternative for many child labourers. Schools for those who can afford them are often crowded, ill-equipped, and harsh in their treatment of children.

Programs designed to stop the use of child labourers, such as the child impact assessment, result in cosmetic changes. These changes in turn encourage corruption among fixers, brokers, and consultants, which results in child labourers being driven into the underground economy where they are at the mercy of labour contractors. Until Westerners can understand the culture of Third-World countries, and the deeply embedded roots of child labour, their interventions and sanctions will only cause more problems.

Ikea has a commercial interest in minimizing child labour because bad publicity harms business. Ikea takes a unique approach to this issue. The company helps the mothers of these children to develop small business through a cooperative lending program. Once the mothers achieve financial independence they send their children to school.

Sources: Edward Luce, "Ikea Leads the Way in Trying to End Child Labour in India," *The Financial Post*, September 15, 2004; Mohammad Qadeer, "Why the Third World Needs Child Labour," *The Globe and Mail*, November 7, 1997, A8; Bill Varner, "Child Labour Remains Huge Problem: ILO," *The Globe and Mail*, May 7, 2002, B12.

Overall, international firms are moving toward a narrowing of the salary gap between the host-country manager and the expatriate. Unilever, for example, used to leave the compensation arrangements largely to the boss of a region or a big country. Now brand managers in different countries increasingly compare notes, so they see potential discrepancies based on market differences and expatriate assignments. So the company moved from a narrow grading structure to five global work levels. Managers' pay is still based on the country they work in, but there will be regional convergence so that in time there will be a pan-European rate.[37]

Compensation of Expatriate Managers

If the assignment is going to be successful, the expatriate's compensation plan must be competitive, cost-effective, motivating, fair, easy to understand, consistent with international financial management, relatively easy to administer, and simple to communicate. To be effective, an international compensation program must:

1. Provide an incentive to leave Canada
2. Allow for maintaining a North American standard of living
3. Provide for security in countries that are politically unstable or present personal dangers
4. Include provisions for good healthcare
5. Take into account the foreign taxes the employee is likely to have to pay (in addition to domestic taxes) and help him or her with tax forms and filing
6. Provide for the education of the employee's children abroad, if necessary
7. Allow for maintaining relationships with family, friends, and business associates via trips home and other communication technologies
8. Facilitate re-entry home
9. Be in writing[38]

For short-term assignments, usually those that are project-based, expatriates are frequently given per-diem (per-day) compensation. These managers might reside in hotels and service apartments instead of leasing houses. They are also less likely to bring their family members with them. The assignment becomes more like a commuting assignment in which the expatriate spends the week in the host country and returns home on the weekend.

For longer-term assignments, there are two basic types of compensation systems. The first is **home-based pay,** based on the **balance-sheet approach,** a system designed to equalize the purchasing power of employees at comparable positions living overseas and in the home country and to provide incentives to offset qualitative differences between assignment locations.[39] The balance-sheet approach generally comprises the following steps:

Step 1: Calculate base pay. Begin with the home-based gross income, including bonuses. Deduct taxes and pension contributions.

Step 2: Figure cost-of-living adjustment (COLA). Add a cost-of-living adjustment to the base pay. Typically, companies don't subtract when the international assignment has a lower cost of living. Instead, they allow the expatriate to benefit from the negative differential. Often a housing allowance is added in here as well.

Step 3: Add incentive premiums. General mobility premiums and hardship premiums compensate expatriates for separation from family, friends, and domestic support systems, usually 15 percent of base salary, although in recent years, some companies have reduced this amount. Sometimes incentive premiums are paid for hazardous duty or harsh conditions the expatriate might experience while abroad.

Step 4: Add assistance programs. These additions are often used to cover added costs such as moving and storage, automobile, and education expenses.

The differentials element is intended to correct for the higher costs of overseas goods and services so that in relation to their domestic peers expatriates neither gain purchasing power nor lose it. It involves a myriad of calculations to arrive at a total differential figure, but in general, as we have said, the cost typically runs between three and five times the home-country salary. Fortunately, employers do not have to do extensive research to find comparative data. They typically rely on data published quarterly by federal government departments, such as External Affairs, for use in establishing allowances to compensate civilian employees for costs and hardships related to assignments abroad. Alternately, they consult international relocation

home-based pay
Pay based on an expatriate's home country's compensation practices

balance-sheet approach
A compensation system designed to match the purchasing power in a person's home country

experts to make sure all of the relocation bases are covered. For example, in some countries expatriates are mandated by local law to participate in host-country programs—whether or not their pay packages are home- or host-based.[40]

host-based pay
Expatriate pay comparable to that earned by employees in a host country

localization
Adapting pay and other compensation benefits to match that of a particular country

The second type of compensation system is **host-based pay.** Companies are under pressure to move expatriates to host-based pay because it is generally less costly. Host-based pay is compensation that is equivalent to that earned by employees in the country where the expatriate is assigned. This process is called **localization.** When an employee is localized, his or her compensation is set on par with local standards and practices. Incentive premiums are generally phased out, and the employee pays only local taxes and falls under the social benefit programs established by the government of the host country. Some companies localize only certain aspects of the pay package or do so gradually over a course of three to five years.

Usually the decision to localize an employee depends on whether he or she will ultimately remain abroad or return home. In many companies the decision depends on whether the employee or the employer is the driving force behind the localization. An expatriate employee with a strong desire to remain in the host country beyond the planned length of assignment (perhaps because he or she married a local or has simply fallen in love with the country), is likely to be more amenable to localization. Localization shouldn't be viewed as a cost-saving panacea, however. There are many countries in which expatriates would refuse to "go local." Forcing an employee to do so can ultimately result in a failed assignment costing the company much more money than it would have saved by localizing him or her.

Another serious issue related to expatriate compensation is medical care. Employees are unlikely to consent to going abroad if they cannot get healthcare comparable to what's available in their home countries. Often Canadian-based plans can't cover expatriate employees or efficiently deal with claims that need to be reimbursed in foreign currency. One solution is to transfer the employee to a global employment company that can provide these types of benefits. Basically, the employee is transferred to the global employment company, which administers all of his or her benefits as well as those of numerous employees working for other companies. Still another issue is the need to provide expatriates and employees who travel abroad with security. Citigroup hires private drivers for employees doing business in countries such as Mexico—even for employees on extended stays. Companies can also purchase travel-related insurance covering a range of services such as evacuation and disability or travel-related injuries.[41] HR managers are generally responsible for evaluating and implementing these different types of programs.

Performance Appraisal

objective 7

As we noted earlier, individuals frequently accept international assignments because they know that they can acquire skills and experiences that will make them more valuable to their companies. Frequently, however, it can be difficult for the home office to evaluate the performance of employees working abroad. Even the notion of performance evaluation is indicative of a North American management style that focuses on the individual, which can cause problems in Asian countries such as China, Japan, and Korea and Eastern European countries such as Hungary and the Czech Republic. Performance appraisal problems can contribute to failure rates among expatriates and actually derail an individual's career rather than enhance it.[42]

Who Should Appraise Performance?

In many cases, an individual working internationally has at least two allegiances: one to his or her home country (the office that made the assignment) and the other to the host country in which the employee is currently working. Superiors in each location frequently have different information about the employee's performance and may also have very different expectations about what constitutes good performance. For these reasons, the multirater (360-degree) appraisal discussed in Chapter 8 is gaining favour among global firms. There are exceptions, however. Thai workers do not see it as their business to evaluate their bosses, and Thai managers do not think subordinates are in any way qualified to assess them. Before implementing a different appraisal process, HR managers need to understand how the process is likely to be received in the host country.[43]

Home- vs. Host-Country Evaluations

Domestic managers are frequently unable to understand expatriate experiences, value them, or accurately measure their contribution to the organization. Geographical distances create communication problems for expatriates and home-country managers, although e-mail, instant messaging, and other HR information systems technologies have begun to help close the gap.[44] Still, local managers with daily contact with the expatriate are more likely to have an accurate picture of his or her performance. Host-country evaluations can sometimes be problematic, though. First, local cultures may influence one's perception of how well an individual is performing. As noted earlier in the chapter, participative decision making may be viewed either positively or negatively, depending on the culture. Such cultural biases may not have any bearing on an individual's true level of effectiveness. In addition, local managers sometimes do not have enough of a perspective on the entire organization to know how well an individual is truly contributing to the firm as a whole.

Given the pros and cons of home-country and host-country evaluations, most observers agree that performance evaluations should try to balance the two sources of appraisal information. Although host-country employees are in a good position to view day-to-day activities, in many cases the individual is still formally tied to the home office. Promotions, pay, and other administrative decisions are connected there, and as a consequence, the written evaluation is usually handled by the home-country manager. Nevertheless, the appraisal should be completed only after vital input has been gained from the host-country manager. As discussed in Chapter 8, multiple sources of appraisal information can be extremely valuable for providing independent points of view—especially if someone is working as part of a team. If there is much concern about cultural bias, it may be possible to have people of the same nationality as the expatriate conduct the appraisal.

Performance Criteria

Because expatriate assignments are so costly, many HR managers are increasingly under pressure to calculate the return on investment of these assignments. What did the firm get for the million dollars it spent to send an expatriate abroad? Has the expatriate achieved the goals set forth in the assignment in the appropriate time frame? Obviously, the goals and responsibilities inherent in the job assignment are among the most important criteria used to evaluate an individual's performance, and different goals necessitate measuring different criteria. The Expatriate Technology Forum (ETF), comprising multinational companies such as Philips, Shell, and Heineken, has developed benchmarks and other standards HR professionals can use to calculate ROI. The criteria are tied to the various reasons employees were sent abroad in the first place—whether the goal was to transfer technical skills or best practices, improve a division's financial performance, or develop managerial talent.[45] The Business Case outlines the costs of employee expatriates and initiatives companies can undertake to improve ROI.

The danger with ROI calculations, however, is that there is a temptation to resort to using "easy" criteria such as productivity, profits, and market share to measure an expatriate's performance. These criteria may be valid—but they are still deficient if they do not capture the full range of an expatriate's responsibility. Other, more subtle factors should be considered as well. Leadership development, for example, involves a

The Business Case

The Costs of Employing Expatriates

Organizations typically make selection decisions on the basis of a match between job requirements and the candidates' skills and abilities. But selection decisions in international assignments must always compare the costs of employing locals versus expatriates. The chart below compares the cost of employing a Canadian manager in the United Kingdom to employing a U.K. manager. The case involves a manager, based in Ontario, who earns about $85 000 a year, with a $17 000 bonus, who is to be sent on a three-and-a-half-year assignment to London, England. He is married with one school-age child who attends private school. This manager receives an automobile allowance as well as a trip home per year. The company pays for the relocation, household goods storage, and tax return preparations.

Total cost of assignment for 3.5 years:

Cost Element	$
Base salary	297,500
Bonus	59,500
Gross income	357,000
Cost of living allowance	92,800
Housing allowance	135,000
Education allowance	61,500
Automobile allowance	55,300
Home leaves	32,400
Relocation, storage, and tax return	76,300
Additional tax expenses	175,500
Total Cost	**$985,800**

The costs of sending this manager on an international assignment are nearly a million dollars, compared to the approximately $300,000 it would cost to employ a U.K.–based manager.

(continued on next page)

Below is a list of initiatives that would improve return on investment (ROI) of expatriates:

Better candidate selection	32%
Career-planning skills	26
Communicating objectives	24
Assignment preparation	20
Monitoring program	17
Cross-cultural training	10
Developing or expanding intranet	7
Communication/recognition	6
Web-based cultural training	5
Mandating destination support	4
Other	17

Sources: Andrea Poe, "Selection Savvy," *HRMagazine* 47, no. 4 (April 2002): 77–83; Jeff Bitten, "Compensation Strategies for International Assignments," *Canadian HR Professional* 18, no. 2 (April/May 2001): 29–31.

much longer-term value proposition. In many cases, an expatriate is an ambassador for the company, and a significant part of the job is cultivating relationships with citizens of the host country. As we discussed at the beginning of this chapter, an individual's success or failure is affected by a host of technical and personal factors. For example, as one might guess, it is much easier to adjust to similar cultures than to dissimilar ones. A Canadian can usually travel to the United Kingdom or Australia and work with locals almost immediately. Send that same individual to Hungary or Malaysia, and the learning curve is more steep. And the expatriate's adjustment period may be even longer if the company has not yet established a good base of operations in the region. The first individuals transferred to a country have no one to show them the ropes or to explain local customs. Even relatively simple activities such as navigating the rapid-transit system can prove to be problematic. The U.S. State Department has developed rating systems that attempt to distinguish the different degrees of difficulty associated with different regional assignments. These difficulty factors need to be considered and built into the appraisal system.[46]

Providing Feedback

Performance feedback in an international setting is clearly a two-way street. Although the home-country and host-country superiors may tell an expatriate how well he or she is doing, it is also important for expatriates to provide feedback regarding the support they are receiving, the obstacles they face, and the suggestions they have about the assignment. More than in almost any other job situation, expatriates are in the very best position to evaluate their own performance.

In addition to ongoing feedback, an expatriate should have a debriefing interview immediately on returning home from an international assignment. These repatriation interviews serve several purposes:

1. They help expatriates reestablish old ties with the home organization and may prove to be important for setting new career paths.
2. The interview can address technical issues related to the job assignment itself.

3. The interview may address general issues regarding the company's overseas commitments, such as how relationships between the home and host countries should be handled.

4. The interview can be very useful for documenting insights an individual has about the region. These insights can then be incorporated into training programs for future expatriates. However, if the learning is not shared, then each new expatriate to a region may have to go through the same cycle of adjustment.[47]

The Labour Environment Worldwide

objective **8**

A country's labour environment plays a large role in international business and HR decisions. As we have said, wages and benefits vary dramatically across the world as do safety, child, and other legal regulations. In many countries, the state's regulation of labour contracts is profound and extensive. Labour unions around the world differ significantly as well. Differences exist not only in the collective bargaining process but also in the political-legal conditions. For example, the EU prohibits discrimination against workers in unions, but in many other countries, including countries in Central America and Asia, labour unions are illegal. China has only one union, the All-China Federation of Trade Unions, an 80-year-old Communist Party institution that for decades has aligned itself more closely with management than workers. In some countries, only workers at larger firms are allowed to organize.[48]

Union strength depends on many factors, such as the level of employee participation, per capita labour income, mobility between management and labour, homogeneity of labour (racial, religious, social class), and unemployment levels. These and other factors determine how well a union will be able to represent labour effectively. Nearly all of Sweden's workers are organized, giving the unions in this country considerable strength and autonomy. By contrast, in countries with relatively high unemployment, low pay levels, and no union funds with which to support social welfare systems, unions are driven into alliance with other organizations: political party, church, or government. This is in marked contrast to Canada, where the union selected by the majority of employees bargains only with the employer, not with other institutions. By contrast, the unions in many European countries (such as Sweden) have a great deal of political power and are often allied with a particular political party. When employers in these countries deal with unions, they are, in effect, dealing indirectly with governments.

In a number of countries, however, including Japan, Germany, New Zealand, and the United Kingdom, unions have been losing some of their power. Ironically, the power of the unions to gain high wages and enforce rigid labour rules has been blamed for hurting competitiveness, particularly in European countries. Laws make it difficult to fire European employees, so workers are hired only sparingly. Unemployment benefits are very generous, so people tend to remain unemployed for longer rather than seek work. But because companies are increasingly tempted to offshore jobs to lower-labour-cost countries, unionized workers are beginning to make more concessions. For example, at Bosch in France, union bosses opposed management's plan to lengthen the workweek. But fearful workers overruled the union bosses, voting instead for the longer workweek.[49] As the power of unions declines a bit, the trend has been to demand compensation in other ways—through benefits or through greater participation in company decision making. Various approaches to participation will be discussed later.

Collective Bargaining in Other Countries

We saw in Chapter 14 how the collective bargaining process is typically carried out in companies operating in Canada. When we look at other countries, we find that the process can vary widely, especially with regard to the role of government. Collective bargaining can take place at the firm, local, or national level. In Australia and New Zealand, for most of the 20th century labour courts had the authority to impose wages and other employment conditions on a broad range of firms (many of which were not even privy to the suits brought before the courts). In the United Kingdom and France, the government intervenes in all aspects of collective bargaining. Government involvement is only natural where parts of industry are nationalized. Also, in countries with heavy nationalization government involvement is more likely to be accepted, even in the nonnationalized companies. At Renault, the French government–owned automobile manufacturer, unions use political pressures in their bargaining with managers, who are essentially government employees. The resulting agreements then set the standards for other firms. This is true in spite of the fact that union membership rates in France have declined dramatically since the 1970s. In developing countries the governments commonly have representatives present during bargaining sessions to ensure that unions with relatively uneducated leaders are not disadvantaged in bargaining with skilled management representatives. Still, in these countries a union may do little more than attempt to increase wages and leave the rest of the employment contract unchanged. In more-developed countries, goals related to other aspects of the employment relationship, such as workweek lengths, safety requirements, and grievance procedures, are more likely to be pursued.

International Labour Organizations

The most active of the international union organizations has been the International Confederation of Free Trade Unions (ICFTU), which has its headquarters in Brussels. The ICFTU is a confederation of 215 national trade union centres, representing 125 million trade union members in 145 countries and territories. Cooperating with the ICFTU are numerous International Trade Secretariats (ITSs), which are really international federations of national trade unions operating in the same or related industries. In addition to the ITSs, the ICFTU also cooperates with the European Trade Union Confederation (ETUC). The ETUC represents 60 million trade unionists from 76 organizations and 11 industry federations in 34 Western, Central, and Eastern Europe countries. Another active and influential organization is the International Labour Organization (ILO), a specialized agency of the United Nations created in 1919. The ILO perhaps has had the greatest impact on the rights of workers throughout the world. It promotes the rights of workers to organize, the eradication of forced and child labour, and the elimination of discrimination. Over the decades, 178 countries have voluntarily committed to nearly 200 international conventions proposed by the ILO. The organization has been effective because it involves nation-states as well as workers and their employers. In recent years, the ILO has redefined its mission based on the "Decent Work Agenda." The Decent Work Agenda promotes the idea that there is an ethical dimension of work. This ethical dimension includes decent homes, food, education, the right to organize, and social programs to protect workers when they are elderly, disabled, or unemployed. Moreover, the agenda pertains to workers worldwide, including the self-employed—a situation common in agricultural-based, developing countries. Given the fact that half of the world's population lives on $2 a day or less, that 250 million children around the world are forced to work, and only 20 percent of people globally are covered by any sort of social insurance programs, these are worthy goals. Some companies, however, oppose the decent pay initiative, believing it promotes unionization.[50]

Labour Participation in Management

In many European countries, provisions for employee representation are established by law. An employer may be legally required to provide for employee representation on safety and hygiene committees, worker councils, or even boards of directors. While their responsibilities vary from country to country, worker councils basically provide a communication channel between employers and workers. The legal codes that set forth the functions of worker councils in France are very detailed. Councils are generally concerned with grievances, problems of individual employees, internal regulations, and matters affecting employee welfare.

A higher form of worker participation in management is found in Germany, where representation of labour on the board of directors of a company is required by law. This arrangement is known as **codetermination** and often by its German word, *Mitbestimmung*. While sometimes puzzling to outsiders, the system is fairly simple: Company shareholders and employees are required to be represented in equal numbers on the supervisory boards of large corporations. Power is generally left with the shareholders, and shareholders are generally assured the chairmanship. Other European countries and Japan either have or are considering minority board participation.[51]

Each of these differences makes managing human resources in an international context more challenging. But the crux of the issue in designing HR systems is not choosing one approach that will meet all the demands of international business. Instead, organizations facing global competition must balance multiple approaches and make their policies flexible enough to accommodate differences across national borders. Throughout this book we have noted that different situations call for different approaches to managing people, and nowhere is this point more clearly evident than in international HRM.

codetermination
Representation of labour on the board of directors of a company

SUMMARY

 objective 1
There are four basic ways to organize for global competition: (1) The international corporation is essentially a domestic firm that has leveraged its existing capabilities to penetrate overseas markets; (2) the multinational corporation has fully autonomous units operating in multiple countries in order to address local issues; (3) the global corporation has a world view but controls all international operations from its home office; and (4) the transnational corporation uses a network structure to balance global and local concerns.

 objective 2
In addition to economic considerations, political-legal and cultural factors in different parts of the world make some countries more desirable to do business in than others.

International HRM places greater emphasis on a number of responsibilities and functions such as relocation, orientation, and translation services to help employees adapt to a new and different environment outside their own country.

 Many factors must be considered in the selection and development of employees. Though hiring host-country nationals or third-country nationals automatically avoids many potential problems, expatriates are preferable, but more costly, in some circumstances. When expatriates are hired, most companies try to minimize their stay. Operations are handed off to host-country nationals as soon as possible.

 Once an expatriate is selected, an intensive training and development program is essential to qualify that person and his or her spouse for the assignment. Wherever possible, development should extend beyond information and orientation training to include sensitivity training and field experiences that will enable the manager to understand cultural differences better. Those in charge of the international program should provide the help needed to protect managers from career development risks, re-entry problems, and culture shock.

 Compensation systems should support the overall strategic intent of the organization but be customized for local conditions. Compensation plans must give expatriates an incentive to leave Canada; meet their standard-of-living, healthcare, and safety needs; provide for the education of their children, if necessary; and facilitate repatriation.

Although home-country managers frequently have formal responsibility for appraising individuals on foreign assignments, they may not be able to fully understand expatriate experiences because geographical distances pose communication problems. Host-country managers may be in the best position to observe day-to-day performance but may be biased by cultural factors and may not have a view of the organization as a whole. To balance the pros and cons of home-country and host-country evaluations, performance evaluations that combine the two sources of appraisal information is one option.

In many European countries—Germany, for one—employee representation is established by law. Organizations typically negotiate the agreement with the union at a national level, frequently with government intervention. In other countries union activity is prohibited or limited to only large companies. European unions have much more political power than many other unions around the world, although their power has declined somewhat, due to globalization forces. The International Confederation of Free Trade Unions (ICFTU), the European Trade Union Confederation (ETUC), and the International Labour Organization (ILO) are among the major worldwide organizations endeavouring to improve the conditions of workers.

KEY TERMS

augmented skills, 653
balance-sheet approach, 668
codetermination, 675
core skills, 653
cultural environment, 642
culture shock, 660
expatriates, or home-country nationals, 644
failure rate, 655

global corporation, 639
global manager, 653
guest workers, 650
home-based pay, 668
host-based pay, 669
host country, 643
host-country nationals, 644
international corporation, 638

localization, 669
multinational corporation (MNC), 639
repatriation, 662
third-country nationals, 644
transnational corporation, 639
transnational teams, 650
work permit or visa, 650

DISCUSSION QUESTIONS

1. Identify a Canadian company attempting to open offices in Asia. Interview one of the decision-making managers to determine the kinds of problems that they will face, and the preparations they are undergoing to deal with these.

2. If you were starting now to plan for a career in international HRM, what steps would you take to prepare?

3. What cultural differences exist between North Americans, Asians, and South Americans that would affect HR policies?

4. Scotiabank operates in 50 countries and employs Canadians such as Ajay Mundkur to staff its New Delhi office. What are the advantages of employing Canadians with roots in the host country?

5. In what ways are North American managers likely to experience difficulties in their relationships with employees in foreign operations? How can these difficulties be minimized?

6. Talk with a foreign student on your campus; ask about his or her experience with culture shock on first arriving in Canada. What did you learn from your discussion?

7. If the cost of living is lower in a foreign country than in Canada, should expatriates be paid less than they would be at home? Explain your position. Who should ultimately decide whether an employee should be localized or not?

8. The most common reason for failure of an expatriate assignment is the spouse. Go to www.expat.or.id/info/mythsofexpatlife.html and summarize the problems faced by spouses. What HR policies and practices would help reduce the magnitude of these problems?

9. What are the major differences between labour-management relations in Europe and those in Canada?

INTERNET EXERCISE

About 25 000 young Canadians (18 to 30 years of age) found overseas work through the Department of Foreign Affairs youth program last year. Having international experience is a very useful credential. Think about a country in which you would like to acquire work or educational experiences.

Using the Foreign Affairs website, www.voyage.gc.ca, determine what documentation you would need to work or study in your country of choice. Click on Country Profiles and prepare a list of cultural differences between Canada and your chosen country.

HRM Experience

A Canadian (Expatriate) in Paris

There is often a great deal of work involved in setting up expatriate assignments. The administrative requirements can be far ranging and extend beyond the employee to also include family issues. Suppose you were faced with the following scenario. What would be the most pressing considerations that you would need to address?

The Scenario
You are the head of HR for Sarip International, a consulting firm specializing in hotel and restaurant management. Your firm is opening an office in Paris, France, and Jim Verioti, director

of sales and marketing, has been asked to assume responsibilities for the expansion. Jim understands that the expatriate assignment will last two to three years, and although he has travelled to Europe for work on several occasions, this is his first long-term assignment overseas. He has a lot of questions about what he can expect and also some personal constraints.

Jim and his wife Betty have just moved into their new home (their mortgage is around $1,500 per month). In addition, Betty is an elementary school teacher and doesn't really know how the move will affect her job security. Their three children, Veronica (14), Reggie (12), and Archie (10), are of ages at which school considerations are very important. A friend told them about the American School in Paris, and this is a consideration. None of the Veriotis speak French.

Assignment

Working in teams of four to six individuals, put together the package that would allow Jim to move his family to Paris while still maintaining his present lifestyle (his current annual salary is $140,000 plus incentives). Address at least the following issues:

1. Visas and permits
2. Relocation allowance and housing
3. Language and culture training
4. Spousal employment concerns
5. Health/medical/insurance issues
6. Compensation and incentives
7. Education for the children

The following websites may be helpful to you, but other resources may prove valuable as well.

- Canadian Embassy in Paris (www.dfait-maeci.gc.c/canadaeurope/france)
- French Embassy in Canada (www.ambafrance-ca.org)
- Expatica.com (www.expatica.com/france.asp)
- The Paris France Guide (www.parisfranceguide.com/)
- Easy Expat (www.easyexpat.com/en/pa/index_city.htm)
- Centers for Disease Control (www.cdc.gov/travel/)
- Travlang (currency calculator) (www.travlang.com/money/)

BIZFLIX EXERCISES

Mr. Baseball: Tolerance of Cultural Differences

This chapter emphasized the importance of tolerance of cultural differences for success as an expatriate. Watch this *Mr. Baseball* scene carefully while considering the questions below.

The New York Yankees trade aging baseball player Jack Elliot (Tom Selleck) to the Chunichi Dragons, a Japanese team. This lighthearted comedy traces Elliot's bungling entry into Japanese culture. It exposes his cultural misconceptions, which almost cost him everything—including his new girlfriend, Hiroko Uchiyama (Aya Takanashi). After Elliot slowly begins to understand Japanese culture and Japanese baseball, his teammates finally accept him. This film shows many examples of Japanese culture, especially its love for baseball.

This scene is an edited version of the "Welcome to Japan" sequence that appears early in the film. Jack Elliot arrives at Nogoya International Airport, Tokyo, Japan. Yoji Nishimura (Toshi Shioya) meets him and acts as Jack's interpreter and guide. The film continues after this scene with the unfolding adventure of Jack Elliot playing for the Chunichi Dragons.

What to Watch for and Ask Yourself
- Is Jack Elliot culturally sensitive or culturally insensitive?
- Does he make any cross-cultural errors on his arrival in Japan? If yes, what are they?
- Review the earlier chapter section "Training and Development." What type of training would you recommend for Jack Elliot?

case study 1

Cultural Conundrum

Anna has enjoyed great success in the Toronto office of a global company. When she was offered an assignment in Tokyo, she approached the job with the full confidence of her employer that she could oversee the reorganization of the subsidiary. By asking her extensive network of colleagues about Japan, she learned a few tips. For example, she learned that when a Japanese businessman hands you his business card, it is proper to read the card before taking it, and to never throw it on the desk. Even with tips like these, however, Anna's assignment was heading toward failure.

After six months, she was very discouraged and when she returned home for the holidays, she reported the following problems:

- Although everyone spoke English, there were communication problems.
- Everything took too long to complete, with deadlines missed and employees not following schedules.
- Although she asked her employees for feedback and information, and received promises that these would be forthcoming, no data arrived.

The company's response was to give her cross-cultural training, in which Anna learned the following:

- In Japanese culture, group identity supersedes individual identity. Loyalty is to the group, and criticisms of performance are taboo. Group meetings are the norm, and one-on-one meetings designed to facilitate feedback make employees very uncomfortable.
- Japanese culture is based on hierarchy and is organized to recognize the power differentials between superiors and subordinates. Japanese workers do not expect to have input into decisions; their only expectation is to be told what to do. If forced to participate in decision making, the typical Japanese will avoid uncertainty by accumulating every possible item of information to support the decision.
- Japan is a masculine society and women are employed in low-status positions. Anna's credibility as a decision maker would be questioned, and male employees would be uncomfortable working for her.

The communication problems only compounded the difficulty of the situation. Yes, the employees spoke English. But there were cultural differences. To a direct request to meet a deadline that they perceived as impossible, employees would save face (for themselves and the person making the request) by saying that they would do their best. Saying no is not part of Japanese culture.

Anna made the mistake of transferring her management style, which was successful in Toronto, to Tokyo, without understanding the cultural differences.

QUESTIONS

1. Exactly what preparation should Anna's company have given her before she started her assignment?
2. In general, what should a candidate for an international assignment do to prepare for a job, in the absence of company orientation and training?
3. Many believe that women on international assignments prove to be very effective, because they are both task oriented (a North American cultural imperative) and relationship oriented (an important attribute in Asian and other cultures). Why did these two sets of skills not help Anna?

Source: Adapted from Z. Fedder, "Same Language, Different Meanings," *Canadian HR Reporter* 13, no. 11 (June 5, 2000): 9, 13; S. McKay, "Women Going Global," *Financial Post Magazine,* December 1998, 38–54.

case study 2

Recruiting and Retaining International Employees

Cambior, based in Longueil, Quebec, is one of Canada's largest gold producers, employing 2700 people at mines in Quebec, Peru, French Guyana, and Surinam. Of these, over 1000 are based outside of Canada. Their HR policies for managing these international employees are described below:

Staffing

Cambior has had no problems recruiting employees for its operations. They find that candidates who are attracted to international assignments tend to apply to organizations where these are possible.

Cambior uses three types of postings in order to staff its mines:

- Short-term assignments that are used for special projects or during construction of the mine.
- Home-based assignments where employees will spend periods of time at the mine and then return home for rest and recuperation. The longest period that an employee is on-site is 30 days, followed by 26 days of recuperation.
- Long-term assignments, usually for executives, who move with their families close to the mine. The biggest problem with these assignments are the education of the children and working spouses.

Compensation

Cambior uses a tax equalization policy that guarantees an employee on assignment will be no better or worse off as a result of taxes. If the taxes are higher in the host country, then the company absorbs the costs of these extra payments. If they are lower, the excess reverts to the company. Employees are also given hardship allowances. Cambior has established an Employee Leasing Company that hires the employees for these international secondments, which allows the employee to retain home-based benefits such as pension plans and employment insurance.

Health and Safety

Cambior has found that safety standards are consistent across their international operations, but health issues are more complex. For example, employees need to be educated about malaria, and special provisions are made for other diseases not normally found in Canada. Employees have to feel assured that if there is a serious health issue, that they will receive rapid medical treatment. Each site has a complete medical facility. Medical evacuations are done when the condition is life threatening.

Violence is an issue in developing countries. Special sessions on topics such as kidnap training and emergency evacuation are provided.

QUESTIONS

1. Describe the advantages and limitations of Cambior's staffing policies. How would you compare these to the advantages and limitations of employing host country nationals?
2. What kinds of hardships would Cambior employees face? What would be appropriate compensation for these conditions?
3. What benefits required by law in Canada would be unlikely to be provided in developing countries?

Sources: Adapted from N. Bedard, "Human Resources for A Global Company," *CIM Bulletin*, 97, 1978, 2004, 99–100, www.cambio.com.

CAREER COUNSEL

Take the culture quiz on the *Managing Human Resources* website (www.belcourt5e.nelson.com) to assess your sensitivity to other cultures.

NOTES AND REFERENCES

1. Peter Dowling, Denice E. Welch, and Randall S. Schuler, *International Human Resource Management: Managing People in a Multinational Context*, 3rd ed. (Cincinnati, OH: South-Western, 1999); Nancy J. Adler, *International Dimensions of Organizational Behaviour* (Cincinnati, OH: South-Western, 1997); J. Michael Geringer, Colette Frayne, and John Milliman, "In Search of 'Best Practices' in International Human Resource Management: Research Design and Methodology," *Human Resource Management* 41, no. 1 (Spring 2002): 5–30; "Cendant Mobility Survey Shows Continued Challenges around Repatriation Management; Focus on Cost Control Also Driving New Approaches to Global Assignments, Say Global Mobility Practitioners," *PR Newswire* (April 28, 2004).

2. Abagail McWilliams, David Van Fleet, and Patrick Wright, "Strategic Management of Human Resources for Global Competitive Advantage," *Journal of Business Strategies* 18, no. 1 (Spring 2001): 1–24.

3. Charles Dawson, "The Global 1000," *Business Week*, no. 3841 (July 14, 2003): 34; Cristina Lindblad, "The Global 1000: The World's Most Valuable Companies," *Business Week*, no. 3791 (July 15, 2002): 58–80.

4. M. F. Wolff, "Innovation and Competitiveness among EU Goals for Knowledge Economy," *Research Technology Management* 44, no. 6 (November/December 2001): 2–6; Tony Emerson, "The Great Walls: The United States and Europe Are Leading the Race to Carve Up the Trading World," *Newsweek*, April 23, 2001, 40. For more information about the European Union online, see the Europa website at http://europa.eu.int.

5. William Thorbecke and Christina Eigen-Zucchi, "Did NAFTA Cause a Giant Sucking Sound?" *Journal of Labour Research* 23, 4, Fall 2002, 647–58.

6. Sadanand Dhume, "Just Quit It," *Far Eastern Economic Review* 165, no. 36 (September 12, 2002): 46–50; George Koo, "Fast Lane to China: Companies That Never Thought of Doing Business

Overseas Are Now Looking to the Thriving Chinese Economy," *Computer Technology Review* 24, no. 4 (April 2004): 42.

7. Interested readers can access this journal online at www.tandf .co.uk/journals/online/0958-5192.html; Beth McConnell, "Global Forum Speakers to Share Insights on International HR," *HRMagazine* 48, no. 3 (March 2003): 115–17.

8. DeeDee Doke, "Perfect Strangers: Cultural and Linguistic Differences between U.S. and U.K. Workers Necessitate Training for Expatriates," *HRMagazine* 49, no. 12 (December 2004): 62.

9. Readers interested in codes of conduct and other ethical issues pertaining to international business might read the following: Bill Roberts, "Going Global," *HRMagazine* 45, no. 8 (August 2000): 123–28.

10. Carla Joinson, "No Returns," *HRMagazine* 47, no. 11 (November 2002): 70–77; Frank Jossi, "Successful Handoff," *HRMagazine* 47, no. 10 (October 2002): 48–52; Steve Bates, "Study Discovers Patterns in Global Executive Mobility," *HRMagazine* 47, no. 10 (October 2002): 14; Morgan McCall and George Hollenbeck, "Global Fatalities: When International Executives Derail," *Ivey Business Journal* 66, no. 5 (May/June 2002): 74–78; Leslie Gross Klass, "Fed Up with High Costs, Companies Thin the Ranks of Career Expats," *Workforce Management* 83, no. 10 (October 1, 2004): 84.

11. Wallace Immen, "Going Abroad to Get Ahead," *The Globe and Mail,* February 22, 2006, C1.

12. David Lipschultz, "Bosses from Abroad," *Chief Executive* 174 (January 2002): 18–21.

13. Readers interested in codes of conduct and other ethical issues pertaining to international business might read Nadar Asgary and Mark Mitschow, "Toward a Model for International Business Ethics," *Journal of Business Ethics* 36, no. 3 (March 2002): 238–46; Diana Winstanley and Jean Woodall, "The Adolescence of Ethics in Human Resource Management," *Human Resource Management Journal* 10, no. 4 (2000): 45; J. Brooke Hamilton and Stephen Knouse, "Multinational Enterprise Decision Principles for Dealing with Cross-Cultural Ethical Conflicts," *Journal of Business Ethics* 31, no. 1 (May 2001): 77–94; Michael Maynard, "Policing Transnational Commerce: Global Awareness in the Margins of Morality," *Journal of Business Ethics* 30, no. 1 (March 2001): 17–27.

14. "Keeping Out the Wrong People: Tightened Visa Rules Are Slowing the Vital Flow of Professionals into the U.S.," *Business Week,* no. 3902 (October 4, 2004): 90; "Security Delays Hurt U.S. Business," *Legal Times,* August 23, 2004.

15. Anne E. Kornblut, "Bush Cites Political Hurdles in Plan for 'Guest Workers,'" *The New York Times,* March 24, 2005, A6.

16. "Society: Affirmative Action? Oui! At Long Last, France Takes a Page from America in Order to Manage Diversity—and Bring Minorities into Elite Schools," *Newsweek International,* April 12, 2004, 30.

17. Snell et al., "Designing and Supporting Transnational Teams: The Human Resource Agenda," *Human Resource Management* 37, no. 2: 147–58; Debra Shapiro, Stacie Furst, Gretchen Spreitzer, and Mary Ann Von Glinow, "Transnational Teams in the Electronic Age: Are Team Identity and High Performance at

Risk?" *Journal of Organizational Behaviour,* 23 (June 2002): 455–67; Claude Philipps, Harold Sirkin, Duane Filtz, and Scott Kirsner, "Time [Zone] Travelers: They Bounce from Beijing to Bangalore at a Moment's Notice," *Fast Company,* no. 85 (August 2004): 60–67.

18. Snell et al., "Designing and Supporting Transnational Teams," 147–58; Leslie Gross Klass, "Fed Up with High Costs, Companies Thin the Ranks of Career Expats," *Workforce Management* 83, no. 10 (October 1, 2004): 84.

19. Andrea Poe, "Selection Savvy," *HRMagazine* 47, no. 4 (April 2002): 77–83; "Exploiting Opportunity: Executives Trade Stories on Challenges of Doing Business in Global Economy," *Business Mexico* 15, no. 2 (February 2005): 54–58.

20. Yehuda Baruch, "No Such Thing as a Global Manager," *Business Horizons* 45, no. 1 (January/February 2002): 36–42.

21. Sheree R. Curry, "Offshoring Swells Ranks of 'Returnees' Working Back in Their Native Countries," *Workforce Management* 84, no. 2 (February 1, 2005): 59; Margaret Linehan and Hugh Scullion, "Selection, Training, and Development for Female International Executives," *Career Development International* 6, no. 6 (2001): 318–23; Nancy Lockwood, "The Glass Ceiling: Domestic and International Perspectives," *HRMagazine* 49, no. 6 (June 2004): S1–11.

22. Nancy Wong, "Mark Your Calendar! Important Tasks for International HR," *Workforce* 79, no. 4 (April 2000): 72–74; Robert O'Connor, "Plug the Expat Knowledge Drain," *HRMagazine* 47, no. 10 (October 2002): 101–107; Andrea Graf and Lynn K. Harland, "Expatriate Selection: Evaluating the Discriminant, Convergent, and Predictive Validity of Five Measures of Interpersonal and Intercultural Competence," *Journal of Leadership & Organizational Studies* 11, no. 2 (Winter 2005): 46–63.

23. McCall and Hollenbeck, "Global Fatalities: When International Executives Derail," 74–78; Poe, "Selection Savvy," 77–83; Juan Sanchez, Paul Spector, and Cary Cooper, "Adapting to a Boundaryless World: A Developmental Expatriate Model," *Academy of Management Executive* 14, no. 2 (May 2000): 96–106; Eric Krell, "Evaluating Returns on Expatriates: Though Difficult to Ascertain, Measuring the Return on the Cost of Expatriate Assignments Is Necessary to Justify the Expensive Investment," *HRMagazine* (March 2005): 12.

24. Riki Takeuchi, Seokhwa Yun, and Paul Tesluk, "An Examination of Crossover and Spillover Effects of Spousal and Expatriate Cross-Cultural Adjustment on Expatriate Outcomes," *Journal of Applied Psychology* 87, no. 4 (August 2002): 655–66; Poe, "Selection Savvy," 77–83; Talya Bauer and Sully Taylor, "When Managing Expatriate Adjustment, Don't Forget the Spouse," *Academy of Management Executive* 15, no. 4 (November 2001): 135–37; Iris I. Varner and Teresa M. Palmer, "Role of Cultural Self-Knowledge in Successful Expatriation," *Singapore Management Review* 27, no. 1 (January–June 2005): 1–25.

25. "Motorola to Increase Operations in China," *The New York Times,* November 8, 2001, C4; Peter J. Buckley, Jeremy Clegg, and Hui Tan, "Knowledge Transfer to China: Policy Lessons from Foreign Affiliates," *Transnational Corporations* 13, no. 1 (April 2004): 31–73.

26. Lionel Laroche, John Bing, and Catherine Mercer Bing, "Beyond Translation," *Training & Development* 54, no. 12 (December 2000): 72–73; Sabrina Hicks, "Successful Global Training," *Training & Development* 54, no. 5 (May 2000): 95.

27. Managers who are interested in setting up a language-training program or who wish to evaluate commercially available language-training programs should consult the "Standard Guide for Use-Oriented Foreign Language Instruction." The seven-page guide is put out by the American Society for Testing and Materials (ASTM), (610) 832-9585, www. astm.org. See also "Why Top Executives Are Participating in CEIBS and IESE's Joint Global Management Programme," *PR Newswire*, July 19, 2004.

28. Jared Wade, "The Pitfalls of Cross-Cultural Business," *Risk Management* 51, no. 3 (March 2004): 38–43.

29. Vipin Gupta, Paul Hanges, and Peter Dorman, "Cultural Clusters: Methodology and Findings," *Journal of World Business* 37, no. 1 (Spring 2002): 11–15; Jane Terpstra-Yong and David Ralston, "Moving toward a Global Understanding of Upward Influence Strategies: An Asian Perspective with Directions for Cross-Cultural Research," *Asia Pacific Journal of Management* 19, no. 2 (August 2002): 373–404.

30. Ping Ping Fu et al., "The Impact of Societal Cultural Values and Individual Social Beliefs on the Perceived Effectiveness of Managerial Influence Strategies: A Meso Approach," *Journal of International Business Studies* 35, no. 4 (July 2004): 33; Geert Hofstede, *Culture's Consequences: Comparing Values, Behaviors, Institutions, and Organizations across Nations* (Thousand Oaks, CA: Sage, 2001).

31. Lisa Bohannon, "Going Global," *Career World* 29, no. 6 (April/May 2001): 28–30; Aimin Yan, Guorgong Zhu, and Douglas T. Hall, "International Assignments for Career Building: A Model of Agency Relationships and Psychological Contracts," *Academy of Management Review* 27, no. 3 (July 2002): 373–91; Justin Martin, "The Global CEO: Overseas Experience Is Becoming a Must on Top Executives' Resumes, According to This Year's Route to the Top," *Chief Executive* no. 195 (January–February 2004): 24–31.

32. "Prudential Relocation Survey Finds Spouses' Experiences a Key Factor in the Success of International Work Assignments," *Canadian Corporate News*, December 7, 2004.

33. Virginia Galt, "It's Not Easy to Come Home Again," *The Globe and Mail*, February 22, 2006, C6.

34. Mila Lazarova and Paula Caligiuri, "Retaining Repatriates: The Role of Organizational Support Practices," *Journal of World Business* 36, no. 4 (Winter 2001): 389–401; "Expatriate Administration: New Realities and HR Challenges," *Employee Benefit News* (March 1, 2005) pITEM05090007; "For Those Working Abroad, Moving Home Can Be Jarring," *The Kansas City (Missouri) Star* (via Knight-Ridder/Tribune Business News), February 22, 2005.

35. Calvin Reynolds, *Guide to Global Compensation and Benefits* (New York: Harcourt, 2001); Gary Parker, "Establishing Remuneration Practices across Culturally Diverse Environments," *Compensation & Benefits Management* 17, no. 2 (Spring 2001): 23–27; Timothy Dwyer, "Localization's Hidden Costs," *HRMagazine* 49, no. 6 (June 2004): 135–141.

36. Caroline Fisher, "Reward Strategy Linked to Financial Success: Europe," *Benefits & Compensation International* 32, no. 2 (September 2002): 34–35; "Comparative Analysis of Remuneration: Europe," *Benefits & Compensation International* 31, no. 10 (June 2002): 27–28; Fay Hansen, "Currents in Compensation and Benefits: International Trends," *Compensation and Benefits Review* 34, no. 2 (March/April 2002): 20–21.

37. Chao Chen, Jaepil Choi, and Shu-Cheng Chi, "Making Justice Sense of Local-Expatriate Compensation Disparity: Mitigation by Local Referents, Ideological Explanations, and Interpersonal Sensitivity in China-Foreign Joint Ventures," *Academy of Management Journal* 45, no. 4 (August 2002): 807–17.

38. Patricia Zingheim and Jay Schuster, "How You Pay Is What You Get," *Across the Board* 38, no. 5 (September/October 2001): 41–44; "Benefits for Expatriate Employees: International," *Benefits & Compensation International* 31, no. 10 (June 2002): 26–27; Steven P. Nurney, "The Long and Short of It: When Transitioning from a Short-Term to a Long-Term Expatriate Assignment, Consider the Financial Implications," *HRMagazine* 50, no. 3 (March 2005): 91–95.

39. Stephan Kolbe, "Putting Together an Expat Package: As More and More Companies Adopt an International Outlook, They Are Increasingly Sending Staff on Overseas Assignments—Usually Involving a Complex Relocation Package," *International Money Marketing* (September 2004): 33.

40. The U.S. State Department Index of Living Costs Abroad can be found at www.state.gov/travel/.

41. Barbara Hanrehan and Donald R. Bentivoglio. "Safe Haven: Accommodating the Needs of Employees and Families in Hostile Environments Can Increase Expenses and Alter Tax Liability," *HRMagazine* 47, no. 2 (February 2002): 52–54.

42. Paul Hempel, "Differences between Chinese and Western Managerial Views of Performance," *Personnel Review* 30, no. 2 (2001): 203–15.

43. "Cross-Cultural Lessons in Leadership: Data from a Decade-Long Research Project Puts Advice to Managers in Context, Country by Country," *MIT Sloan Management Review* 45, no. 1 (Fall 2003): 5–7.

44. Paula Caligiuri, "The Big Five Personality Characteristics as Predictors of Expatriate's Desire to Terminate the Assignment and Supervisor-Rated Performance," *Personnel Psychology* 53, no. 1 (Spring 2000): 67–88; Calvin Reynolds, "Global Compensation and Benefits in Transition," *Compensation and Benefits Review* 32, no. 1 (January/February 2000): 28–38; Charlene Marmer Solomon, "The World Stops Shrinking," *Workforce* 79, no. 1 (January 2000): 48–51; Stephenie Overman, "Mentors without Borders: Global Mentors Can Give Employees a Different Perspective on Business Matters," *HRMagazine* 49, no. 3 (March 2004): 83–87.

45. Frank Jossi, "Successful Handoff," *HRMagazine* 47, no. 10 (October 2002): 48–52; Paula Caligiuri and David Day, "Effects of Self-Monitoring on Technical, Contextual, and Assignment-Specific Performance," *Group & Organization Management* 25, no. 2 (June 2000): 154–74.

46. Mark Mendenhall and Gary Oddou, eds., *Readings and Cases in International Human Resource Management* (Cincinnati, OH: South-Western, 1999).

47. Ariane Berthoin, "Expatriates' Contributions to Organizational Learning," *Journal of General Management* 26, no. 4 (Summer 2001): 62–84; Peter J. Buckley, Jeremy Clegg, and Hui Tan, "Knowledge Transfer to China: Policy Lessons from Foreign Affiliates," *Transnational Corporations* 13, no. 1 (April 2004): 31–73.

48. Bernhard Ebbinghaus and Jelle Visser, *The Societies of Europe: Trade Unions in Western Europe since 1945* (London, England: Palgrave Macmillan, 2000); John Pencavel, "Unionism Viewed Internationally," *Journal of Labor Research* 26, no. 1 (Winter 2005): 65–98.

49. Christopher Rhoads, "Germany Faces Storm over Tech Staffing—Labor Groups Are Enraged by Proposal to Import Badly Needed Workers," *The Wall Street Journal,* March 7, 2000, A23; "European Workplaces Tighten Policies as Countries Struggle to Compete Worldwide," *Pittsburgh (Pennsylvania) Post-Gazette* (via Knight-Ridder/Tribune Business News), November 28, 2004.

50. Dharam Gahi, "Decent Work: Universality and Diversity" (discussion paper, International Institute for Labour Studies 2005), 1–22; Jean-Michael Servais, "Globalization and Decent Work Policy: Reflections upon a New Legal Approach," *International Labour Review* 143, no. 1–2 (Spring–Summer 2004): 104–108; "Philosophical and Spiritual Perspectives on Decent Work," *International Labour Review* 143, no. 3 (Autumn 2004): 290–292. Interested readers can find more information about international trade unions by checking out the websites of the ICFTU (www.icftu.org) and the ILO (www.ilo.org).

51. Dirk Kolvenbach and Ute Spiegel, "The Reform of the Works Council Constitution Act in Germany and Its Effects on the Co-Determination Rights of the Works Council," *International Financial Law Review* (2001): 59–65; Pencavel, "Unionism Viewed Internationally," 65–98.

Creating High-Performance Work Systems

After studying this chapter, you should be able to

objective **1** Discuss the underlying principles of high-performance work systems.

objective **4** Recommend processes for implementing high-performance work systems.

objective **2** Identify the components that make up a high-performance work system.

objective **5** Discuss the outcomes for both employees and the organization.

objective **3** Describe how the components fit together and support strategy.

objective **6** Explain how the principles of high-performance work systems apply to small and medium-sized and large organizations.

This chapter is available on the Managing Human Resources website (www.belcourt5e.nelson.com)

Excalibur Cases

INTRODUCTION

Excalibur, the Canadian University Tournament in Human Resources, is held annually in March in Montreal, Québec. This case competition attracts entrants from universities across Canada. Teams of three students, coached by their professors, are asked to demonstrate their knowledge of human resources management to a jury of practitioners and professors. The teams analyze the HR issues facing real Canadian companies and are given ninety minutes to prepare their cases, and another twenty minutes to present their recommendations to the jury. The top three winning teams receive cash awards. The tournament is managed by the Québec HR Association L'Ordre des CRHA et CRIA du Québec, supported by the Canadian Council of Human Resources Association. The following cases have been used in previous Excalibur Tournaments.

Source: Cases from Excalibur, the Canadian University Tournament in Human Resources (from 2000 to 2005) Lafarge Corporation: Managing the Challenges of Internationalization (2000); Le Cirque du Soleil: How to Manage Growth (2001); BCE Emergis: Searching for Concrete Solutions (2002); Labatt Breweries: A Hot Summer in Store (2003); Telus Sourcing Solutions: Instilling a New Culture (2004); Transcontinental: A Challenging Integration Process Ahead (2005).

Le Cirque du Soleil: How to Manage Growth

Case 1

Founded in 1984 by a group of young street performers, Cirque du Soleil has been in constant evolution since its creation. The company enjoys excellent international recognition and is said to have reinvented circus arts. In 1984 Cirque du Soleil had sales of $1.7 million, 50 employees, and 23 performers; in 2000, sales were expected to reach $407 million and it would employ 1370 people and 445 performers. It planned to present seven shows in 2000 on three continents: North America, Europe, and Asia. Also, in order to adequately manage all its personnel, it had four separate headquarters. Besides international headquarters in Montreal, it has four other head offices: Montreal (called Headquarters—America), Amsterdam (Headquarters—Europe), Las Vegas (Headquarters—Las Vegas), and Singapore (Headquarters—Asia-Pacific).

While Cirque du Soleil wanted to find and exploit new niches related to presenting shows, the majority of its revenues came from ticket sales. Thus the vital nucleus of the Cirque remained presenting shows. The Cirque had four fixed shows, two touring shows in Asia, one in North America, and another in Europe. A touring show comprised 150 to 200 people, including 50 to 70 performers, and it had to relocate on average every six weeks, which demanded very skilled logistics and effective planning of the entry authorizations for the different countries on the tour. Relocating meant moving personnel, their baggage, and the Cirque's equipment from town to town. It also meant lodging all these people and ensuring they obtained the required visas and work permits in order to be able to practise their art in the countries the tour was visiting.

To attain the level of excellence set by Cirque du Soleil, talent scouts and recruiters travelled the globe in search of artists, creators, coaches, musicians, etc. Consequently, the Cirque's performers and personnel came from more than thirty countries and spoke many languages. Also, while the average age of employees was relatively young at thirty-two, the age of the performers and employees ranged from three to sixty-two.

In short, Cirque du Soleil was an international company that reflected the level of excellence it had achieved in the past and its constant desire to push the limits.

Development Project

As well as continuing to create and produce new shows, Cirque du Soleil wanted to diversify its commercial activities. Indeed, it wanted to see itself develop the production of audiovisual works such as the soundtracks of the different shows, explore the field of publishing, and continue to promote some strategic agreements with partners in the hotel business. Cirque du Soleil had also set itself the objective of adding two or three tours within five years, which would have the effect of bringing the number of employees required to achieve such an objective to about 2000.

Management

Cirque du Soleil had adopted a management style in its own image, that is, dynamic, vibrant, and imaginative. The organic nature of how it operated put each employee in a position that allowed him or her to contribute to a common work. Cirque du Soleil firmly believed that, by appealing to everyone's intelligence, all objectives are achievable. Also, communications were extremely open and the authority that certain hierarchical titles could impose was practically nonexistent. And a Cirque du Soleil core value was respect for cultural diversity.

In spite of the continuous growth the company had experienced, it had always known how to ensure cohesion among employees and maintain a strong sense of belonging.

Challenges to Be Met

Given its growth plans, in relation to both the number of shows presented and the establishment of new commercial activities, Cirque du Soleil needed to apply itself to adapting its structure and, above all, to ensuring that its managers have the ability to support such development. In this respect, several managers who had grown up with Cirque du Soleil and who had thus acquired broad operating experience were having some difficulty moving to a strategic management mode. Given their extensive knowledge of how the Cirque operated, they too often remained occupied or preoccupied with operating questions, rather than investing their energy more in strategic planning.

Also, given the increased number of tours planned, another problem that already existed was likely to get bigger. Due to the difficult touring conditions, such as the frequent relocations, the increased number of shows per week, and challenging working conditions in general, the turnover rate among employees was very high. On average, they worked for the Cirque between nineteen and twenty-four months, which created a turnover rate of 18 to 22 percent. In spite of the efforts made to reduce the inconveniences inherent in touring, problems still remained. For example, the Cirque offered the services of a tutor to child performers and to the children of performers.

However, because of the costs this would have entailed, this service could not be offered to all the children of its personnel. Despite the attractive salaries, Cirque du Soleil was experiencing some difficulties in retaining its touring personnel.

Finally, it is important to note that, both in the touring shows and in International Headquarters in Montreal, the presence of many people of different nationalities, speaking different languages, was a challenge. Indeed, while the presence of Quebec and Canadian performers at International Headquarters and on tours was often secondary, dealing with several nationalities greatly influenced the quality of communications. And, depending on the cultural baggage of each person, the perception of the message communicated could differ greatly. Since cultural references are very divergent, what are innocuous gestures to some have unexpected implications for others. However, despite these difficulties in perception, Cirque du Soleil had always greatly valued cultural diversity and had always emphasized the richness it brought, rather than the differences it created. Nonetheless, the Cirque du Soleil had to constantly manage stereotypes and prejudices. This situation was even more palpable at International Headquarters in Montreal since the performers who worked there were, for the most part, passing through, either with the aim of learning a new number or to take up training again following an injury. Also, people of the same nationality often grouped together without mixing too much with other performers of different nationalities.

QUESTIONS

You have been given a mandate by Cirque du Soleil to propose solutions to the problems raised by the facts described above.

To do so, you must

1. State your understanding of the situation at Cirque du Soleil;
2. Precisely determine the needs of Cirque du Soleil in the short and medium term;
3. In the light of those needs, make provisions for the obstacles envisaged;
4. Finally, establish a plan of action by formulating possible solutions to the problems you have identified. You must then justify the proposed solutions, taking into account the values transmitted by Cirque du Soleil.

Labatt Breweries: A Hot Summer in Store

Case 2

In 1847, John Kinder Labatt laid the foundations of a brewing company in London, Ontario, that would later become Labatt Breweries. The company quickly branched out. In 1878, it established an agency in Montreal to distribute its products. Twenty years later, the company took steps to satisfy growing demand in the Toronto area and opened a sales office and a small warehouse. When Prohibition was introduced in the United States in 1900, the company's expansion was temporarily delayed. It survived, however, and in 1946 began a series of acquisitions that made it one of the largest breweries in Canada. The launch of Labatt Blue in 1951 helped cement the company's status as Canadian industry leader. In 1995 the world-renowned company was sold to Belgium's Interbrew SA, the third-largest brewing consortium in the world.

Today Labatt produces over sixty beers, employs 3800 employees, and operates eight breweries from coast to coast, in St. John's, Halifax, Montreal, Toronto, London, Edmonton, Creston, and New Westminster. Its most popular brands are Labatt Blue, Budweiser, Keith's, Labatt Wildcat, and Kokanee. In Quebec alone, 893 million 341-mL bottles are produced each year, an amount equal to 3.1 million hL, or 23 percent of the total Canadian production of 13.64 million hL. Labatt's products are distributed to over 22 000 outlets, and 20 percent of the production is exported. The Montreal brewery is the largest in Canada, closely followed by the London, Ontario, plant, which produces 2.97 million hL. Worldwide, Interbrew produces 180 beers that are distributed in more than 110 countries in Europe, North America, and the Asia-Pacific region. Interbrew's most popular brands are Stella Artois, Bass, and Beck's.

Innovation has set Labatt apart from other breweries. In fact, it was Labatt that marketed the first twist-off cap, the first light beer, and the first non-alcoholic beer in Canada. More recently, the company made history by creating the first lemonade-flavoured malt beer. Shortly after, in 1997, to address ever-growing demand for and popularity of specialty beers and imported beers, Labatt created the Oland Specialty Beer Company (OSBC).

The quest for innovation that has characterized the company since its early days is entirely consistent with its mission statement to deliver superior quality products made from the finest ingredients using proven methods. The company's stated goal is to become Canada's leading brewer, a goal that plays out in market share points, given the intense competition in national and world markets. From 1997 to 2001, the brewing industry was characterized by a wave of mergers. Since then, the number of players on the market has fallen considerably and the remaining companies have gotten larger. To remain competitive and make further inroads, Interbrew has been using a strategy called "The World's Local Brewer" to become a larger presence in mature and emerging markets through strategic acquisitions and internal growth.

Culture Shock

With its background of family tradition, Labatt had managed through the years to foster a strong sense of belonging among its employees. Staff members were genuine ambassadors for the company's products, always eager to represent the company during community events, for example. The culture of excellence, performance, and quality that built the company's reputation was widely shared by a vast majority of employees—managers, representatives, and shop workers alike.

When Interbrew bought the company in the mid-1990s, harsher market conditions had chipped away at the relationship between the employees and their company. To function in an ultra-competitive world market, the organization has worked very hard over the last few years to optimize productivity. To achieve this, it reduced its workforce and increased the work load. The new operating methods have caused much discontent among unionized employees in the plants and fostered a feeling of nostalgia for the way things were.

In Quebec, the last round of labour negotiations in 1996 intensified the culture shock that accompanied the acquisition. When the collective agreement was reopened, management proposed retirement incentives in an effort to reduce production manpower and increase the company's competitiveness. Although the older workers hailed the proposal, it caused deep dissatisfaction among younger employees, whose main goal was access to permanent positions. This was a very controversial issue, as indicated by the fact that the proposal passed by a mere 52 percent. The collective agreement was to be in effect for six years.

It is important to note that 90 percent of Labatt's Quebec employees are unionized, and the company's 150 managers are not. In all, there were nine bargaining units belonging to the Teamsters Union, a number that had remained unchanged since the beginning of unionization within the company. So far the company has had no strikes and only one lockout. The current HR managers agree that labour relations on the whole are still very good.

But the discontent caused by the last agreement has turned things upside down. Over the last three years there has been an increase in the number of grievances filed. Most of the grievances were about tighter management and fewer workers.

Negotiation on the Horizon

Given that the collective agreement was expiring in December of 2002, Labatt started negotiating with its various bargaining units in Quebec in the fall. The Montreal-area plant and delivery workers—traditionally the strongest unit—had always been the first unit to start the round of negotiations. This time around, however, the scenario has changed. Following a period of union raiding in July of 2002, the Montreal unit left the Teamsters Union and joined the ranks of the Confederation of National Trade Unions (CNTU) on February 28, 2003. The CNTU, it should be noted, is based primarily in Quebec and has always adopted a more confrontational and left-leaning stance than other labour unions. The Teamsters, for their part, prefer using a business approach.

The switch raised many question marks. Not only does the employer have to face a brand-new union, it also has to learn to work with a labour union whose philosophy is entirely different from that of its predecessor. In fact, this will be the very first collective agreement the CNTU negotiates with the brewing industry. Representation on the employer's side remains unchanged. Only one negotiator is appointed to conclude an agreement with all the unions, including the new one.

It is already understood that worker status (regular, temporary, casual) will be at the heart of the upcoming debates. Worker expectation on the issue is running very high, because many workers are still considered temporary despite having logged ten or so years of continuous service with the company. The aging of the worker population is a fact that will put the issue of early retirement back on the table.

Meanwhile, the employer has entered into an agreement with another large bargaining unit that could possibly pave the way for upcoming discussions. The agreement was conducted with the other union and was satisfactory for most of the distribution workers in the province. In fact, the final proposal received 93 percent approval. This new collective agreement has already come into effect and expires only in seven years. Under the agreement, many employees will retire over the next few months owing to improvements to the pension plan; consequently, the same number of temporary employees will receive permanent employee status.

Despite this happy ending, there are many unanswered questions. In particular, the company is unsure about the impact of the new situation over the near, medium, and long term. Will other units join the ranks of the CNTU? Will negotiations lead to a conflict during the summer season, which is somewhat of a peak season for the company? Will the agreement concluded with the first unit create a domino effect during upcoming negotiations? Given the atmosphere of uncertainty, management decides to send a memo to all employees to advise them of the new CNTU unit. The letter also describes the agreement with the unit belonging to the Teamsters Union and the main gains the employees made. The company also states its intention to step up production to increase inventory and thus avoid a shortage if a conflict should occur over the summer.

QUESTIONS

It is in this context that your consulting team is to conduct an analysis and issue recommendations on an appropriate communications and negotiation strategy to adopt in the near and long term.

To do this, you must

1. Briefly explain your understanding of Labatt's overall situation;

2. Establish a diagnosis of the challenges that Labatt is facing in the area of labour relations;

3. In light of the main challenges, formulate two to four possible strategies and the main obstacles to implementing them over the near term (2003), the medium term (four years), and the long term (seven years);

4. Propose and justify your action plan by presenting tangible solutions that are viable and consistent with Labatt's values.

Lafarge Corporation: Managing the Challenges of Internationalization

Case 3

Founded in 1956, Lafarge Corporation is one of the main North American suppliers of building materials such as cement, concrete, and gypsum boards, and it is one of five divisions of Groupe Lafarge SA, a worldwide leader in the field of building products, whose head office is in Paris, France. Groupe Lafarge SA employs more than 66 000 people in sixty-five countries and its revenues reached 9.8 billion euros (about $15 billion Cdn) in 1998. Lafarge Corporation alone employs more than 10 000 people in more than 700 plants throughout North America. Its American head office is located in Virginia, while the Canadian head office is in Montreal.

Lafarge Corporation must apply the human resources policies and programs issued by Groupe Lafarge SA's head office. In fact, Groupe Lafarge SA has a vision of operational excellence that implies the setup of recognized human resources practices and the harmonization of operations methods among all its divisions; it considers that this standardization represents the key to its success. The management orientations are dictated to all divisions, resulting in management styles and standardized operations that operate in spite of the cultural differences. Groupe Lafarge SA reinforces its competitive position via acquisitions as well as internal development of its human resources according to standardized management models.

Employees of Groupe Lafarge SA are at the core of the corporate strategy, and their commitment is the basis of the company's success. Group Lafarge SA has a participative management style that prevails in all companies operating on the five continents. However, the group's rapid and recent growth, mainly achieved through acquisitions, particularly in newly industrialized countries, entails some standardization challenges. The company was therefore forced to redefine this management style to include key words such as involvement, efficiency, and example.

All division administrators must have strong leadership skills and guide their team members toward the enhanced profitability that allows them to further contribute to the synergy that is essential to the global success of the group. Ten years ago, almost half of the employees of Groupe Lafarge SA were French; today, French employees represent only 19 percent of its total manpower. The group's international human resources recruitment policy has three principles: expatriation, short-term postings in foreign countries, and recruitment of local residents. In fact, its international exchanges aim to increase the international representation of its teams. Currently, 12 percent of the administrators have accumulated international experience in order to establish stability and standardization among the companies. The group must double this number over the next five years in order to comply with its major development orientations. These international postings generally last between two and five years and are currently assigned to employees who volunteer.

The company needs to attract employees with strong development potential and proven leadership skills. It must then offer them interesting careers; geographical mobility as much as internal transfers to new challenges is strongly encouraged. Hiring personnel who demonstrate willingness to move at the international level represents one of the main objectives of the group.

The Problem

In the case of Lafarge Corporation, most exchanges occur between the American and Canadian subsidiaries and sometimes between North American and European plants. However, exchanges between plants located in newly developed countries and those in European and North American plants are almost nonexistent, although these must increase considerably. Furthermore, although several Canadians have volunteered for postings in the United States, the opposite is not as frequent. Indeed, remuneration as well as American fiscal laws makes it difficult to arrange or facilitate transfers from the United States to Canada. This situation applies also to Canadians who have accepted a posting in the United States. Finally, few among them volunteer for transfers to plants located in newly industrialized countries.

Lafarge Corporation, in cooperation with Groupe Lafarge SA's head office, is responsible for fulfilling its own personnel needs. Even with the support of Groupe Lafarge SA, and in spite of the access to a pool of volunteer employees working in other plants, it is especially challenging for Lafarge Corporation to find specialized employees, notably for its cement division. In fact, most of the positions to be filled demand a university degree (diploma is the French word) in engineering, and many potential candidates with this degree are also actively sought by oil and chemical companies. The objective of the international exchange program is to transfer knowledge among the various groups as well as implementing, standardizing, and optimizing operations. Therefore, it is essential to have a critical mass of qualified employees before participating in the international exchange program.

QUESTIONS

Your mandate is to propose solutions to problems pertaining to recruitment, international mobility, career management, and succession planning, keeping in mind the notion of cultural integration in the case of employees taking part in the international mobility program.

1. *Analyzing the Situation.* Explain your understanding of the situation. What are the corporate objectives and the short-term and mid-term requirements?

2. *Action Plan.* Further to the analysis of the situation, list the potential solutions to the challenges of recruitment, international mobility, and personnel retention as well as standardizing management styles. You must justify the proposed solutions. These solutions must be developed and proposed while taking into account the process of career management and succession planning.

TELUS Sourcing Solutions: Instilling a New Culture

Case 4

Background

The health care institutions in the Calgary area are grouped together under a single entity known as the Calgary Health Region (CHR), a regional board that oversees 33 institutions, 22 000 employees, and 55 collective agreements. In 2002, CHR executives identified a need to implement a human resources information system, having so far relied on hard copies for managing the bulk of their HR files and transactions. In the fall of the same year, a call for tenders was issued and TELUS Canada was awarded a contract on the strength of its outsourcing bid, which included the development of solutions using PeopleSoft software. Over the years TELUS Canada had acquired several companies, some of which had expertise in HR outsourcing.

The outsourcing proposal involved the creation of a new branch of TELUS Canada called TELUS Sourcing Solutions (TSS). The negotiations between Calgary Health Region and TELUS took approximately 11 months, ending in a 15-year agreement to begin on September 16, 2003. The agreement stipulates that TSS is to supply CHR with the systems they need to manage human resources, benefits, pensions, compensation, recruitment, workforce planning, occupational health and safety, payroll, and some of the CHR's strategic planning, particularly in the area of recruitment. In fact, TSS would take over 95 percent of CHR's HR administrative and transactional functions (see Appendix A).

On December 1, 2003, 165 employees from CHR's Human Resources Operations were officially transferred to the new company. Some of the employees were already

APPENDIX A
The objective of the partnership between TSS and CHR is for TSS to be the expert in the Administrative quadrant allowing CHR to focus on being the expert in the other three quadrants.

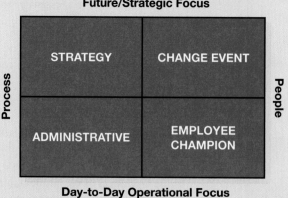

Source: Human Resources Champions, David Ulrich, Harvard Business School Press, 1997.

unionized, and some bargaining units were merged. The 55 or so employees who remained with the CHR's Human Resources Operations were generalists who would oversee strategic HR management within the various CHR units. During the transition process special care was devoted to communications. For example, individual meetings were held with each employee to explain the coming changes and their potential impact on jobs and working conditions, including salary, benefits, and so forth. Each employee's tasks and responsibilities in the new organization were confirmed in writing. Furthermore, employees were invited to attend group meetings organized every two weeks to discuss questions related to the transition. Union representatives also attended the meetings. The atmosphere was positive despite the scope of the changes that were taking place.

Challenges and Culture Change

Although much has been achieved so far, most of TSS's objectives have yet to be reached. Senior managers are hoping that all the data available on Calgary Health Region's 22 000 employees will be transferred to the new human resources management system within six to twelve months. By then the company also hopes that most of the paper files so widely in use will be eliminated. Above all it wants to fully honour its main client's requests and needs and ultimately receive market recognition as a credible and reliable source of human resources management services.

A sizeable challenge is in store for employees in the way of exposure. As employees of the Calgary Health Region, they worked behind the scenes for an organization whose main vocation was to offer excellence in health care and accessibility for the entire community. Now the same employees are working for a firm whose primary mandate is to offer quality human resources management services in a credible and efficient manner. Moreover, it may take some time to achieve credibility in the company's data because currently there are only manual data to work with.

Within the CHR, employees worked in a bureaucratic environment where there was little room for innovation and improvement. In their new work environment, however, they will be appraised for their performance and customer service abilities, which will be measured against the customer service expectations stipulated in the contract between TSS and CHR. From now on, management's expectations of their employees, and the client's expectations of TSS, will include organizational efficiency, the satisfaction of HR clients and employees, and the integrity of HR data. TSS employees will henceforth be working in a totally results-oriented environment.

An Operations Committee has been established for the period of the transition to address difficulties experienced by employees in the face of the many changes unfolding. Some technical tools will soon be made available to workers to support the migration of the company's technology. Despite the changes in the environment, employee morale is good and the work climate is extremely positive. Senior managers are open to suggestions in the hope that the excellent atmosphere the company has enjoyed so far will be preserved.

The executive is currently made up of five directors who spent several years at CHR, and a CEO recruited from the outside who is newly arrived from the U.K. (see Appendix B).

QUESTIONS

Under these conditions your consulting firm is asked to analyze the situation and issue recommendations on the strategies and methods to adopt to help bring about the needed culture change and allow TSS to position itself as a competitive player in

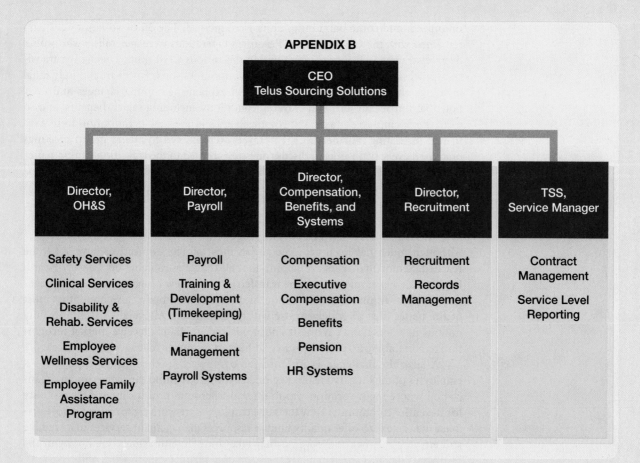

APPENDIX B

human resources outsourcing. To that end, you must achieve the following while keeping in mind the goal of establishing a new high-performance culture:

1. Make a proposal to TSS executives concerning the human resources management tools that would help TSS reach the new organizational goals.
2. Identify potential challenges to implementing the solutions you are proposing.
3. Identify ways to prevent and/or overcome these challenges.

Transcontinental: A Challenging Integration Process Ahead

Case 5

Background

Founded in 1976, Transcontinental Inc. is a major player in the printing and publishing field, not only in Quebec, but also in the rest of Canada and across North America as a whole. Initially involved in printing operations, the company is now active in the following three market segments: media, information products printing, and marketing products printing. Through its media arm, it produces a number of business magazines such as *Commerce, Investment Executive,* and *Affaires Plus.* It is also behind the success of *Canadian Living* and *Elle Québec.* Lastly, thanks to its venture into the marketing sector, Transcontinental prints hundreds of millions of advertising flyers each year. Listed on the Toronto Stock Exchange, the company reported revenues of over CDN$2 billion in 2004, making it the seventh largest printer in North America, the fourth largest print media group in Canada, the leading Canadian publisher of consumer magazines, the second largest publisher of local and regional newspapers (including *La Presse* and *The Globe and Mail*), and a leader in the door-to-door distribution of advertising material. Each of these three sectors has grown at their own pace, through new contracts and through acquisitions. The developing Newspaper Group has to compete in a saturated market in Quebec. In addition, although Transcontinental was originally a Quebec organization, in the last few years it has expanded into the other provinces. The Group is particularly active in Ontario and Quebec, where it prints a number of daily and weekly papers as well as advertising flyers for major organizations.

Recent Developments

Transcontinental also recently took on the Atlantic market, acquiring several newspapers and printing plants in the four Atlantic provinces from the CanWest Group. More specifically, in Prince Edward Island, the company acquired two dailies that are printed on their own presses, *The Charlottetown Guardian* and Summerside's *The Journal-Pioneer.* To optimize the use of its printing presses, the Summerside plant also handles the printing of business documents, such as business cards, posters, etc. Unfortunately, the equipment in both plants is obsolete and substantial investments are needed to maintain product quality and accelerate production. After the acquisition, Transcontinental had three options open to it. It could maintain the *status quo* and invest in modernizing both plants, limit its investments by concentrating its activities in just one of the two plants, or start from scratch with new state-of-the-art facilities.

For strategic and market positioning reasons, the company decided to build a completely new plant in another city. Located in Borden, near the Confederation Bridge linking PEI to New Brunswick, the new facility will allow Transcontinental to serve New Brunswick as well and thus significantly boost its overall profitability. The company also hopes to obtain the contract to print the *National Post* on the Island. This decision means a major professional change for the 132 Charlottetown and 40 Summerside employees.

Challenges

The average age of employees in both plants is 40 and many have worked at the company for a number of years. In fact, some of them have never even had to look for a job. The announcement of a possible move, followed by the posting of upcoming jobs, created considerable anxiety and stress for most employees.

Given their small size, the two plants have always applied traditional management procedures, whereby each employee was assigned a specific task according to his or her technical and occupational skills. Because the employees in both facilities have been in competition with each other nearly all their working lives, they are on their guard and somewhat reluctant to collaborate. Each group is convinced that it is the one that has done the best work over the years. These employees are also worried that the almost family-like atmosphere they have enjoyed up to now will change. In addition, because their companies have been bought and sold several times in recent years, they have trouble trusting the representatives of another new buyer, i.e., Transcontinental.

Since the equipment in the new plant will be highly computerized, modernizing its workstations will lead to a reduction in the workforce. Each of the two plants has its own management team; each plant also employs a person to handle payroll and a number of other administrative tasks. About half of the 172 Charlottetown and Summerside workers will lose their jobs. In accordance with its values, the company's job selection process will focus on soft skills rather than expertise, something these employees are not used to. Transcontinental values teamwork, employee commitment, individual professional development, continuous improvement, and entrepreneurship. In fact, according to François Olivier, senior vice president in charge of the transition, the company still cultivates the same values of sharing, commitment, and mobilization as it did when it was founded in 1976. Transcontinental also wants to be able to rely on mobile and versatile workers who are able to multi-task and easily move from printing to newspaper distribution, for instance. The new plant's equipment moreover will need to be operated by workers who have the required technological skills or at least an aptitude for acquiring such skills.

Several significant outside variables play a role as well. Because Transcontinental also owns dailies that are produced and printed on their own premises, the company has to take public opinion into account to make sure its papers will not be boycotted by local advertisers and readers.

In this context, your team of consultants is required to analyze the situation and make recommendations as to the strategies and measures to put in place over the next three months to help build a harmonious team and enable the company to continue its operations in the region.

QUESTIONS

You are required to:

1. Briefly outline your understanding of Transcontinental's overall position;
2. Make a diagnosis of the challenges facing the company's management in Prince Edward Island;
3. Recommend strategies and actions Transcontinental can put in place to consolidate these activities.

BCE Emergis: Searching for Concrete Solutions

Case 6

BCE Emergis is a service provider that offers its customers integrated electronic business (e-business) solutions. The company as we know it today was created following a merger between MPACT Immedia and a unit of Bell Emergis in 1998. Since that time, it has continued to grow by acquiring various companies that market integrated e-business solutions or by merging with them.

More specifically, BCE Emergis provides other businesses with electronic solutions for supply, sales, customer service, invoicing, security, on-site support, and payment functions. In line with the company's mission, these services target business-to-business rather than business-to-consumer e-commerce. Although it is not limited to specific market segments, BCE Emergis has acquired expertise in the health insurance and financial services sectors. For example, thanks to the online technology it has developed, 80 percent of Canadian group insurance holders pay only the amount deductible under their coverage when their prescription is filled by a pharmacist. With this system, using the insured's card and an electronic database, the pharmacist can immediately obtain any relevant information directly from the insurer and is automatically electronically reimbursed by the insurer for each transaction.

Although 65 percent of BCE Emergis is held by Bell Canada Enterprises (BCE), it is a separate entity with its own distinct organizational culture. When the company was founded, it had a workforce of 350 and posted earnings of $75 million. Despite the ups and downs of the economy and the dramatic stock market slide in the new economy sector, BCE Emergis has continued to grow. Today it has 2600 employees who generate more than $650 million in business income. As mentioned above, the company's growth is partly due to the mergers and acquisitions it has carried out since its inception, which also explains why its employees work in a number of cities across Canada and the United States (half in Canada and half in the United States).

Thanks to its ingenious business model, BCE Emergis came through the economic crisis in the new economy with flying colours, realizing recurring revenue generated by fees paid by its customers each time they use the product purchased. In fact, not only did the company survive during this financially troubled period, but it also continued to increase its business income. This business model, unique to BCE Emergis, has earned it the nickname "new economy blue chip."

As for its objectives, the company wants to continue to grow and to expand its activities in e-commerce solutions for the financial service, primarily in the United States. Although in Canada the BCE name has already secured the company widespread recognition and is a guarantee of quality service and professionalism, the situation is somewhat different in the United States. In that country, Emergis still has to make itself known through its quality products and services and groundbreaking approach. In the next few years, it therefore intends to continue its efforts in the United States and, once it has established its reputation, consolidate its position.

Dynamic Human Capital

Because of its continued growth through mergers and acquisitions, BCE Emergis is in some ways a melting pot of different cultures and subcultures. Recognizing the importance of the entrepreneurial spirit in all the companies it has acquired, it makes an effort to retain and integrate their senior managers. To sustain their motivation and fuel their entrepreneurial spirit, BCE Emergis involves them in strategic planning, particularly in the development of its own management philosophy. However, keeping these executives can raise certain challenges when it comes to integrating the acquired companies and their employees into the Emergis culture.

In the several years the company has been in operation, its dynamic has been unique, to say the least, as it deals with the arrival of large numbers of competitive, imaginative, and entrepreneurially oriented employees, numerous and very diverse management programs, as well as the mix of cultures belonging to each of the companies acquired. As a result, it became a priority to set up a bona fide human resources department in order to steer all these employees and cultures in the same direction. The human resources department (which had a minimal staff in 1999) was thus reorganized and now employs more than twenty-five people. Members of this team are assigned to a number of subgroups (recruitment, support, customers, compensation, organizational development and training, and internal communications) where they meet the needs of various BCE Emergis organizations in both Canada and the United

States. In addition, it has also proven important to create a variety of management models to respond to senior management's requirements and strategic vision.

However, its "new economy blue chip" had to determine exactly what its values were in order to institute its own organizational culture. Eleven core competencies were therefore identified to prepare a competency profile for potential BCE Emergis employees. These competencies are set out below:

1. Technical skills
2. Energy
3. Professional ethics
4. Initiative, proactive and entrepreneurial approach
5. Teamwork skills
6. Flexibility
7. Alertness
8. Leadership
9. Action oriented
10. Customer service oriented
11. Business acumen

Without establishing policies and based on the competency profile, the human resources team developed the following programs exemplifying the "Emergis Way":

I. **Compensation program**
   - Base pay + performance bonus.
   - Stock option plan.
   - Flexible group insurance.

II. **"Best and brightest" recognition program**
   - Hiring of industry "stars."
   - Acknowledgment of exceptional achievements via a contest for outstanding employees, "BCE Competence: outstanding employees."

III. **Strategic talent development program**
   - Development of tools for identifying the potentially most effective employees to give them the opportunity to access strategic positions within the organization.

VI. **Training environment program**
   - Promotion of a resources training environment that will ensure growth within the company and in strategic positions in Canada and the United States, whatever future acquisitions the company makes.

V. **Development of executive management skills program**

VI. **Online recruitment program**

VII. **Internal referral for recruitment program**

Structure and Development

Although BCE Emergis is experiencing tremendous growth, it now has to focus on managing the influx of new employees and their integration. To achieve this end, the company needs to retain and motivate its current employees as well as those it continues to attract. In fact, BCE Emergis has maintained its spectacular development in an extremely difficult economic context; each day it receives up to 300 résumés and job applications, which it manages with its efficient database. However, with the recovery of the new economy, the company will have to compete with all other employers to retain the employees it has recruited and trained. Even though BCE Emergis compares favourably with other companies in the same sector, its employee turnover should be monitored.

Furthermore, integrating new companies, their managers, and their employees remains a challenge. Since most of the acquisitions are made in the United States, and given the general and organizational cultural differences, integrating all these resources the "Emergis way" is no easy task. While attempting to implement common human resources management programs, BCE Emergis certainly does not want to smother or, even worse, destroy its employees' entrepreneurial spirit, which is of such value to its mission. The challenge for the human resources team is to strike a balance between precision and structure on the one hand, and innovation and entrepreneurship on the other.

The stock option plan that is an integral part of the compensation program, and which was set up as an incentive to retain employees, could eventually become less attractive. The low prices of some options that could be exercised in the near future could propel some employees into the "young millionaires" category. However, those options granted at prices that are now much higher than the market price will be less of an incentive for employees to stay with the company.

QUESTIONS

With respect to integrating new Canadian and American human resources, your team of consultants should analyze the company's growth and work with the human resources team to ensure it continues.

You are required to:

1. Outline your understanding of the overall situation at BCE Emergis;
2. Prepare a diagnosis of the company's human resources management challenges;
3. Considering the main challenges, determine two to four strategies and the major obstacles to their implementation;
4. Propose and support your action plan by presenting concrete, viable solutions consistent with the values inherent to BCE Emergis.

A

Achievement tests
Measures of what a person knows or can do right now

Alarm reaction
Response to stress that basically involves an elevated heart rate, increased respiration, elevated levels of adrenaline in the blood, and increased blood pressure

Alternative dispute resolution (ADR)
Term applied to different types of employee complaint or dispute resolution procedures

Apprenticeship training
System of training in which a worker entering the skilled trades is given thorough instruction and experience, both on and off the job, in the practical and theoretical aspects of the work

Aptitude tests
Measures of a person's capacity to learn or acquire skills

Arbitration award
Final and binding award issued by an arbitrator in a labour–management dispute

Arbitrator
Third-party neutral who resolves labour dispute by issuing a final decision in the disagreement

Assessment centre
Process by which individuals are evaluated as they participate in a series of situations that resemble what they might be called upon to handle on the job

Attrition
Natural departure of employees from organizations through quits, retirements, and deaths

Augmented skills
Skills helpful in facilitating the efforts of expatriate managers

Authorization card
Statement signed by an employee authorizing a union to act as his or her representative for the purposes of collective bargaining

B

Balanced Scorecard (BSC)
Measurement framework that helps managers translate strategic goals into operational objectives

Balance-sheet approach
Compensation system designed to match the purchasing power in a person's home country

Bargaining power
Power of labour and management to achieve their goals though economic, social, or political influence

Bargaining unit
Group of two or more employees who share common employment interests and conditions and may reasonably be grouped together for purposes of collective bargaining

Bargaining zone
Area within which the union and the employer are willing to concede when bargaining

Behaviour modelling
Approach that demonstrates desired behaviour and gives trainees the chance to practise and role-play those behaviours and receive feedback

Behaviour modification
Technique that operates on the principle that behaviour that is rewarded, or positively reinforced, will be exhibited more frequently in the future, whereas behaviour that is penalized or unrewarded will decrease in frequency

Behaviour observation scale (BOS)
Behavioural approach to performance appraisal that measures the frequency of observed behaviour

Behavioural description interview (BDI)
Interview in which an applicant is asked questions about what he or she actually did in a given situation

Behaviourally anchored rating scale (BARS)
Behavioural approach to performance appraisal that consists of a series of vertical scales, one for each important dimension of job performance

Benchmarking
Process of comparing the organization's processes and practices with those of other companies

Bona fide occupational qualification (BFOQ)
A justifiable reason for discrimination based on business reasons of safety or effectiveness

Bonus
Incentive payment that is supplemental to the base wage

Burnout
Most severe stage of distress, manifesting itself in depression, frustration, and loss of productivity

Business agent
Normally a paid labour official responsible for negotiating and administering the collective agreement and working to resolve union members' problems

C

Career counselling
Process of discussing with employees their current job activities and performance, their personal and career interests and goals, their personal skills, and suitable career development objectives

Career networking
Process of establishing mutually beneficial relationships with other business people, including potential clients and customers

Career paths
Lines of advancement in an occupational field within an organization

Career plateau
Situation in which for either organizational or personal reasons the probability of moving up the career ladder is low

Codetermination
Representation of labour on the board of directors of a company

Collective bargaining process
Process of negotiating a collective agreement, including the use of economic pressures by both parties

Combined salary and commission plan
Compensation plan that includes a straight salary and a commission

Compensatory model
Selection decision model in which a high score in one area can make up for a low score in another area

Competence-based pay
Pay based on an employee's skill level, the variety of skills possessed, or increased job knowledge

Competency assessment
Analysis of the sets of skills and knowledge needed for decision-oriented and knowledge-intensive jobs

Compulsory binding arbitration
Binding method of resolving collective bargaining deadlocks by a neutral third party

Concentration
Term applied to designated groups whose numbers in a particular occupation or level are high relative to their numbers in the labour market

Concurrent validity
Extent to which test scores (or other predictor information) match criterion data obtained at about the same time from current employees

Construct validity
Extent to which a selection tool measures a theoretical construct or trait

Constructive dismissal
Changing an employee's working emotions such that compensation, status, or prestige is reduced

Consumer price index (CPI)
Measure of the average change in prices over time in a fixed "market basket" of goods and services

Content validity
Extent to which a selection instrument, such as a test, adequately samples the knowledge and skills needed to perform a particular job

Contractual rights
Rights that derive from contracts

Contrast error
Performance rating error in which an employee's evaluation is biased either upward or downward because of comparison with another employer just recently evaluated

Contributory plan
Pension plan in which contributions are made jointly by employees and employers

Cooperative training
Training program that combines practical on-the-job experience with formal educational classes

Core competencies
Integrated knowledge sets within an organization that distinguish it from its competitors and deliver value to customers

Core skills
Skills considered critical to an employee's success abroad

Core values
Strong and enduring beliefs and principles that the company uses as a foundation for its decisions

Corporate social responsibility
Responsibility of the firm to act in the best interests of the people and communities affected by its activities

Craft unions
Unions that represent skilled craft workers

Criterion-related validity
Extent to which a selection tool predicts, or significantly correlates with, important elements of work behaviour

Critical incident
Unusual event that denotes superior or inferior employee performance in some part of the job

Critical incident method
Job analysis method by which important job tasks are identified for job success

Cross-training
Process of training employees to do multiple jobs within an organization

Cross-validation
Verifying the results obtained from a validation study by administering a test or test battery to a different sample (drawn from the same population)

Cultural audits
Audits of the culture and quality of work life in an organization

Cultural environment
Communications, religion, values and ideologies, education, and social structure of a country

Culture shock
Perpetual stress experienced by people who settle overseas

Cumulative trauma disorders
Injuries involving tendons of the fingers, hands, and arms that become inflamed from repeated stresses and strains

Customer appraisal
Performance appraisal, which, like team appraisal, is based on TQM concepts and seeks evaluation from both internal and external customers

D

Defined benefit plan
Pension plan in which the amount an employee is to receive on retirement is specifically set forth

Defined contribution plan
Pension plan that establishes the basis on which an employer will contribute to the pension fund

Depression
Negative emotional state marked by feelings of low spirits, gloominess, sadness, and loss of pleasure in ordinary activities

Designated groups
Women, visible minorities, aboriginal peoples, and persons with disabilities who have been disadvantaged in employment

Differential piece rate
Compensation rate under which employees whose production exceeds the standard amount of output receive a higher rate for all of their work than the rate paid to those who do not exceed the standard amount

Discipline
(1) Treatment that punishes; (2) orderly behaviour in an organizational setting; or (3) training that moulds and strengthens desirable conduct—or corrects undesirable conduct—and develops self-control

Distress
Harmful stress characterized by a loss of feelings of security and adequacy

Diversity management
Optimization of an organization's multicultural workforce in order to reach business objectives

Downsizing
Planned elimination of jobs

Dual-career partnerships
Couples in which both members follow their own careers and actively support each other's career development

Due process
Employee's right to present his or her position during a disciplinary action

E

Elder care
Care provided to an elderly relative by an employee who remains actively at work

E-learning
Learning that takes place via electronic media

Employee assistance programs (EAPs)
Services provided by employers to help workers cope with a wide variety of problems that interfere with the way they perform their jobs

Employee associations
Labour organizations that represent various groups of professional and white-collar employees in labour–management relations

Employee empowerment
Granting employees power to initiate change, thereby encouraging them to take charge of what they do

Employee involvement groups (EIs)
Groups of employees who meet to resolve problems or offer suggestions for organizational improvement

Employee leasing
Process of dismissing employees who are then hired by a leasing company (which handles all HR-related activities) and contracting with that company to lease back the employees

Employee rights
Guarantees of fair treatment from employers, especially regarding an employee's right to privacy

Employee stock ownership plans (ESOPs)
Stock plans in which an organization contributes shares of its stock to an established trust for the purpose of purchase by its employees

Employee teams
Employee contributions technique whereby work functions are structured for groups rather than for individuals and team members are given discretion in matters traditionally considered management prerogatives, such as process improvements, product or service development, and individual work assignments

Employment equity
Employment of individuals in a fair and nonbiased manner

Entrepreneur
One who starts, organizes, manages, and assumes responsibility for a business or other enterprise

Environmental scanning
Systematic monitoring of the major external forces influencing the organization

Ergonomics
Interdisciplinary approach to designing equipment and systems that can be easily and efficiently used by human beings

Error of central tendency
Performance rating error in which all employees are rated about average

Escalator clauses
Clauses in collective agreements that provide for quarterly cost-of-living adjustments in wages, basing the adjustments on changes in the consumer price index

Essay method
Trait approach to performance appraisal that requires the rater to compose a statement describing employee behaviour

Ethics
Set of standards of conduct and moral judgments that help determine right and wrong behaviour

Eustress
Positive stress that accompanies achievement and exhilaration

Expatriates, or home-country nationals
Employees from the home country who are on international assignment

External fit
Situation in which the work system supports the organization's goals and strategies

F

Failure rate
Percentage of expatriates who do not perform satisfactorily

Fast-track program
Program that encourages young managers with high potential to remain with an organization by enabling them to advance more rapidly than those with less potential

Final offer arbitration
Method of resolving collective bargaining deadlocks whereby the arbitrator has no power to compromise but must select one or another of the final offers submitted by the two parties

Flexible benefits plans (cafeteria plans)
Benefits plans that enable individual employees to choose the benefits that are best suited to their particular needs

Flextime
Flexible working hours that permit employees the option of choosing daily starting and quitting times, provided that they work a set number of hours per day or week

Flow data
Data that provide a profile of the employment decisions affecting designated groups

Forced-choice method
Trait approach to performance appraisal that requires the rater to choose from statements designed to distinguish between successful and unsuccessful performance

Functional job analysis (FJA)
Quantitative approach to job analysis that utilizes a compiled inventory of the various functions or work activities that can make up any job and that assumes that each job involves three broad worker functions: (1) data, (2) people, and (3) things

G

Gainsharing plans
Programs under which both employees and the organization share financial gains according to a predetermined formula that reflects improved productivity and profitability

Global corporation
Firm that has integrated worldwide operations through a centralized home office

Global manager
Manager equipped to run an international business

Globalization
Trend toward opening up foreign markets to international trade and investment

Graphic-rating scale method
Trait approach to performance appraisal whereby each employee is rated according to a scale of characteristics

Grievance procedure
Formal procedure that provides for the union to represent members and nonmembers in processing a grievance

Guest workers
Foreign workers invited to perform needed labour

H

Hay profile method
Job evaluation technique using three factors—knowledge, mental activity, and accountability—to evaluate executive and managerial positions

High-performance work system (HPWS)
Specific combination of HR practices, work structures, and processes that maximizes employee knowledge, skill, commitment, and flexibility

Hiring freeze
Practice whereby new workers are not hired as planned, or workers who have left the organization are not replaced

Home-based pay
Pay based on an expatriate's home country's compensation practices

Host-based pay
Expatriate pay comparable to that earned by employees in a host country

Host country
Country in which an international corporation operates

Host-country nationals
Employees who are natives of the host country

Hot-stove rule
Rule of discipline that can be compared with a hot stove in that it gives warning, is effective immediately, is enforced consistently, and applies to all employees in an impersonal and unbiased way

Hourly work
Work paid on an hourly basis

Human capital
Knowledge, skills, and capabilities of individuals that have economic value to an organization

Human resources information system (HRIS)
Computerized system that provides current and accurate data for purposes of control and decision making

Human resources management (HRM)
Process of managing human talent to achieve an organization's objectives.

Human resources planning (HRP)
Process of anticipating and making provision for the movement of people into, within, and out of an organization.

I

Improshare
Gainsharing program under which bonuses are based on the overall productivity of the work team

Industrial disease
Disease resulting from exposure to a substance relating to a particular process, trade, or occupation in industry

Industrial engineering
Field of study concerned with analyzing work methods and establishing time standards

Industrial unions
Unions that represent all workers—skilled, semiskilled, unskilled—employed along industry lines

Instructional objectives
Desired outcomes of a training program

Interest-based bargaining (IBB)
Problem-solving bargaining based on a win–win philosophy and the development of a positive long-term relationship

Internal fit
Situation in which all the internal elements of the work system complement and reinforce one another

International corporation
Domestic firm that uses its existing capabilities to move into overseas markets

Internship programs
Programs jointly sponsored by colleges, universities, and other organizations that offer students the opportunity to gain real-life experience while allowing them to find out how they will perform in work organizations

J

Job
Group of related activities and duties

Job analysis
Process of obtaining information about jobs by determining the duties, tasks, or activities those jobs

Job characteristics model
Job design theory that purports that three psychological states (experiencing meaningfulness of the work performed, responsibility for work outcomes, and knowledge of the results of the work performed) of a jobholder result in improved work performance, internal motivation, and lower absenteeism and turnover

Job classification system
System of job evaluation in which jobs are classified and grouped according to a series of predetermined wage grades

Job description
Statement of the tasks, duties, and responsibilities of a job to be performed

Job design
Outgrowth of job analysis that improves jobs through technological and human considerations in order to enhance organization efficiency and employee job satisfaction

Job enrichment
Enhancing a job by adding more meaningful tasks and duties to make the work more rewarding or satisfying

Job evaluation
Systematic process of determining the relative worth of jobs in order to establish which jobs should be paid more than others within an organization

Job family
Group of individual jobs with similar characteristics

Job posting and bidding
Posting vacancy notices and maintaining lists of employees for upgraded positions

Job progressions
Hierarchy of jobs a new employee might experience, ranging from a starting job to jobs that successively require more knowledge and/or skill

Job ranking system
Simplest and oldest system of job evaluation by which jobs are arrayed on the basis of their relative worth

Job specification
Statement of the knowledge, skills, and abilities required of the person who is to perform the job

K

Knowledge workers
Workers whose responsibilities extend beyond the physical execution of work to include planning, decision making, and problem solving

L

Labour relations process
Logical sequence of four events: (1) workers desire collective representation, (2) union begins its organizing campaign, (3) collective negotiations lead to a contract, and (4) the contract is administered

Leniency or strictness error
Performance rating error in which the appraiser tends to give employees either unusually high or unusually low ratings

Localization
Adapting pay and other compensation benefits to match that of a particular country

Lump-sum merit program
Program under which employees receive a year-end merit payment, which is not added to their base pay

M

Management by objectives (MBO)
Philosophy of management that rates performance on the basis of employee achievement of goals set by mutual agreement of employee and manager

Management forecasts
Opinions (judgments) of supervisors, department managers, experts, and others knowledgeable about the organization's future employment needs

Management rights
Decisions regarding organizational operations over which management claims exclusive rights

Manager and/or supervisor appraisal
Performance appraisal done by an employee's manager and often reviewed by a manager one level higher

Managing diversity
Being aware of characteristics common to employees, while also managing employees as individuals

Markov analysis
Method for tracking the pattern of employee movements through various jobs

Material Safety Data Sheets (MSDSs)
Documents that contain vital information about hazardous substances

Mediation
The use of an impartial neutral to reach a compromise decision in employment disputes

Mediator
Third party in an employment dispute who meets with one party and then the other in order to suggest compromise solutions or to recommend concessions from each side that will lead to an agreement

Mentors
Executives who coach, advise, and encourage individuals of lesser rank

Merit guidelines
Guidelines for awarding merit raises that are tied to performance objectives

Mission
Basic purpose of the organization as well as its scope of operations

Mixed-standard scale method
Trait approach to performance appraisal similar to other scale methods but based on comparison with (better than, equal to, or worse than) a standard

Multinational corporation (MNC)
Firm with independent business units operating in multiple countries

Multiple cutoff model
Selection decision model that requires an applicant to achieve some minimum level of proficiency on all selection dimensions

Multiple hurdle model
Sequential strategy in which only the applicants with the highest scores at an initial test stage go on to subsequent stages

N

Negligence
Failure to provide reasonable care where such failure results in injury to consumers or other employees

Nepotism
Preference for hiring relatives of current employees

Noncontributory plan
Pension plan in which contributions are made solely by the employer

Nondirective interview
Interview in which the applicant is allowed the maximum amount of freedom in determining the course of the discussion, while the interviewer carefully refrains from influencing the applicant's remarks

O

Occupational illness
Abnormal condition or disorder, other than one resulting from an occupational injury, caused by exposure to environmental factors associated with employment

Occupational injury
Cut, fracture, sprain, or amputation resulting from a workplace accident or from an exposure involving an accident in the work environment

Offshoring
Business practice of sending jobs to other countries

Ombudsperson
Designated individual from whom employees may seek counsel for the resolution of their complaints

On-the-job training (OJT)
Method by which employees are given hands-on experience with instructions from their supervisor or other trainer

Open-door policy
Policy of settling grievances that identifies various levels of management above the immediate supervisor for employee contact

Organization analysis
Examination of the environment, strategies, and resources of the organization to determine where training emphasis should be placed

Organizational capability
Capacity to act and change in pursuit of sustainable competitive advantage

Orientation
Formal process of familiarizing a new employee with the organization, the new job, and the work unit

Outplacement services
Services provided by organizations to help terminated employees find a new job

Outsourcing
Contracting outside the organization to have work done that formerly was done by internal employees

P

Panel interview
Interview in which a board of interviewers questions and observes a single candidate

Pay equity
Employee's perception that compensation received is equal to the value of the work performed

Pay-for-performance standard
Standard by which managers tie compensation to employee effort and performance

Pay grades
Groups of jobs within a particular class that are paid the same rate

Peer appraisal
Performance appraisal done by one's fellow employees, generally on forms that are compiled into a single profile for use in the performance interview conducted by the employee's manager

Peer-review system
System for reviewing employee complaints that utilizes a group composed of equal numbers of employee representatives and management appointees, which functions as a jury because its members weigh evidence, consider arguments, and, after deliberation, vote independently to render a final decision

Performance appraisal
Process, typically performed annually by a supervisor for a subordinate, designed to help employees understand their roles, objectives, expectations, and performance success

Performance management
Process of creating a work environment in which people can perform to the best of their abilities

Perquisites
Special nonmonetary benefits given to executives; often referred to as *perks*

Person analysis
Determination of the specific individuals who need training

Piecework
Work paid according to the number of units produced

Point system
Quantitative job evaluation procedure that determines the relative value of a job by the total points assigned to it

Position
Different duties and responsibilities performed by only one employee

Position analysis questionnaire (PAQ)
Questionnaire covering 194 different tasks that, by means of a five-point scale, seeks to determine the degree to which different tasks are involved in performing a particular job

Positive, or nonpunitive, discipline
System of discipline that focuses on the early correction of employee misconduct, with the employee taking total responsibility for correcting the problem

Predictive validity
Extent to which applicants' test scores match criterion data obtained from those applicants/employees after they have been on the job for some indefinite period

Proactive change
Change initiated to take advantage of targeted opportunities

Process audit
Determining whether the high-performance work system has been implemented as designed

Profit sharing
Procedure by which an employer pays, or makes available to all regular employees in addition to base pay, special current or deferred sums based on the profits of the enterprise

Progressive discipline
Application of corrective measures by increasing degrees

Promotion
Change of assignment to a job at a higher level in the organization

Psychological contract
Expectations of a fair exchange of employment obligations between an employee and employer

R

Reactive change
Change that occurs after external forces have already affected performance

Real wages
Wage increases larger than rises in the consumer price index; that is, the real earning power of wages

Realistic job preview (RJP)
Informing applicants about all aspects of the job, both desirable and undesirable facets

Reasonable accommodation
Attempt by employers to adjust the working conditions or schedules of employees with disabilities or religious preferences

Recency error
Performance rating error in which the appraisal is based largely on the employee's most recent behaviour rather than on the behaviour throughout the appraisal period

Red circle rates
Payment rates above the maximum of the pay range

Reengineering
Fundamental rethinking and radical redesign of business processes to achieve dramatic improvements in cost, quality, service, and speed

Reliability
Degree to which interviews, tests, and other selection procedures yield comparable data over time and alternative measures

Relocation services
Services provided to an employee who is transferred to a new location, which might include help in moving, in selling a home, in orienting to a new culture, and/or in learning a new language

Repatriation
Process of employee transition home from an international assignment

Replacement charts
Listings of current jobholders and persons who are potential replacements if an opening occurs

Rights arbitration
Arbitration over interpretation of the meaning of contract terms or employee work grievances

Rucker Plan
Bonus incentive plan based on the historic relationship between the total earnings of hourly employees and the production value created by the employees

S

Scanlon Plan
Bonus incentive plan using employee and management committees to gain cost-reduction improvements

Selection
Process of choosing individuals who have relevant qualifications to fill existing or projected job openings

Selection ratio
Number of applicants compared with the number of people to be hired

Self-appraisal
Performance appraisal done by the employee being evaluated, generally on an appraisal form completed by the employee to the performance review

Severance pay
Lump-sum payment given to terminated employees

Sexual harassment
Unwelcome advances, requests for sexual favours, and other verbal or physical conduct of a sexual nature in the working environment

Silver handshake
Early retirement incentive in the form of increased pension benefits for several years or a cash bonus

Similar-to-me error
Performance rating error in which an appraiser inflates the evaluation of an employee because of a mutual personal connection

Situational interview
Interview in which an applicant is given a hypothetical incident and asked how he or she would respond to it

Six Sigma
Process used to translate customer needs into a set of optimal tasks that are performed in concert with one another

Skill inventories
Files of employee education, experience, interests, skills, etc., that allow managers to quickly match job openings with employee backgrounds

Spot bonus
Unplanned bonus given for employee effort unrelated to an established performance measure

Staffing tables
Graphic representations of all organizational jobs, along with the numbers of employees currently occupying those jobs and future (monthly or yearly) employment requirements

Standard hour plan
Incentive plan that sets rates based on the completion of a job in a predetermined standard time

Statutory rights
Rights that derive from legislation

Step-review system
System for reviewing employee complaints and disputes by successively higher levels of management

Stock data
Data showing the status of designated groups in occupational categories and compensation level

Straight commission plan
Compensation plan based on a percentage of sales

Straight piecework
Incentive plan under which employees receive a certain rate for each unit produced

Straight salary plan
Compensation plan that permits salespeople to be paid for performing various duties that are not reflected immediately in their sales volume

Strategic human resources management (SHRM)
Pattern of human resources deployments and activities that enable an organization to achieve its strategic goals

Strategic planning
Procedures for making decisions about the organization's long-term goals and strategies

Strategic vision
Statement about where the company is going and what it can become in the future; clarifies the long-term direction of the company and its strategic intent

Stress
Adjustive demand caused by physical, mental, or emotional factors that require coping behaviour

Structured interview
Interview in which a set of standardized questions having an established set of answers is used

Submission to arbitrate
Statement that describes the issues to be resolved through arbitration

Subordinate appraisal
Performance appraisal of a superior by an employee, which is more appropriate for developmental than for administrative purposes

Succession planning
Process of identifying, developing, and tracking key individuals for executive positions

SWOT analysis
Comparison of strengths, weaknesses, opportunities, and threats for strategy formulation purposes

Systemic discrimination
Exclusion of members of certain groups through the application of employment policies or practices based on criteria that are not job-related

T

Task analysis
Process of determining what the content of a training program should be on the basis of a study of the tasks and duties involved in the job

Task inventory analysis
Organization-specific list of tasks and their descriptions used as a basis to indentify components of jobs

Team appraisal
Performance appraisal, based on TQM concepts, that recognizes team accomplishment rather than individual performance

Team incentive plan
Compensation plan in which all team members receive an incentive bonus payment when production or service standards are met or exceeded

Telecommuting
Use of personal computers, networks, and other communications technology such as fax machines to do work in the home that is traditionally done in the workplace

Termination
Practice initiated by an employer to separate an employee from the organization permanently

Third-country nationals
Employees who are natives of a country other than the home country or the host country

Total quality management (TQM)
Set of principles and practices whose core ideas include understanding customer needs, doing things right the first time, and striving for continuous improvement

Transfer
Placement of an individual in another job for which the duties, responsibilities, status, and remuneration are approximately equal to those of the previous job

Transfer of training
Effective application of principles learned to what is required on the job

Transnational corporation
Firm that attempts to balance local responsiveness and global scale via a network of specialized operating units

Transnational teams
Teams composed of members of multiple nationalities working on projects that span multiple countries

Trend analysis
Quantitative approach to forecasting labour demand based on an organizational index such as sales

U

Underutilization
Term applied to designated groups that are not utilized or represented in the employer's workforce proportional to their numbers in the labour market

Unfair labour practices (ULPs)
Specific employer and union illegal practices that operate to deny employees their rights and benefits under federal and provincial labour laws

Union shop
Provision of the collective agreement that requires employees to join the union as a condition of their employment

Union steward
Employee who as a nonpaid union official represents the interests of members in their relations with management

V

Validity
Degree to which a test or selection procedure measures a person's attributes

Validity generalization
Extent to which validity coefficients can be generalized across situations

Value-added compensation
Evaluating the individual components of the compensation program to see if they advance the needs of employees and the goals of the organization

Value creation
What the firm adds to a product or service by virtue of making it; the amount of benefits provided by the product or service once the costs of making it are subtracted

Variable pay
Tying pay to some measure of individual, group, or organizational performance

Vesting
Guarantee of accrued benefits to participants at retirement age, regardless of their employment status at the time

Virtual team
Team with widely dispersed members linked together through computer and telecommunications technology

W

Wage and salary survey
Survey of the wages paid to employees of other employers in the surveying organization's relevant labour market

Wage curve
Curve in a scattergram representing the relationship between relative worth of jobs and wage rates

Wage-rate compression
Compression of differentials between job classes, particularly the differential between hourly workers and their managers

Whistleblowing
Complaints to governmental agencies by employees about their employers' illegal or immoral acts or illegal practices

Work permit or visa
Government document granting a foreign individual the right to seek employment

Work valuation
Job evaluation system that seeks to measure a job's worth through its value to the organization

Workers' compensation insurance
Insurance provided to workers to defray the loss of income and cost of treatment resulting from work-related injuries or illness

Y

Yield ratio
Percentage of applicants from a recruitment source that make it to the next stage of the selection process

name index

organization index